REVISED EDITION

The Federal Income Taxation of Mortgage-Backed Securities

Completely Updated and Expanded

■ James M. Peaslee

■ David Z. Nirenberg

PROBUS PUBLISHING COMPANY
Chicago, Illinois
Cambridge, England

ISBN 1-55738-483-5

Printed in the United States of America

BB

1 2 3 4 5 6 7 8 9 0

For

Rickie, Lauren and Alexandra

Elaine, Paul and Sarah

Contents

Preface

The five years that have passed since the publication of the first edition have borne witness to a number of significant changes in the tax law and in market practices relating to mortgage-backed securities. These changes warranted (much to the authors' regret) a comprehensive revision and expansion of the book. Some of the more important developments covered in the Revised Edition are as follows:

- The IRS has taken a number of steps to implement pertinent changes in the law brought about by the Tax Reform Act of 1986 and earlier legislation affecting debt instruments. These steps include the adoption of regulations governing REMICs and regulations dealing with original issue discount (OID).

- The effective date of the taxable mortgage pool (TMP) rules (January 1, 1992), which as of the publication date of the first edition seemed far in the future, has arrived.

- A change in the tax law in 1988 allowed the creation of interest only and other high coupon REMIC regular interests.

- The issuance of interest only and other high coupon REMIC regular interests combined with greater than expected mortgage prepayments has brought to the fore a question concerning the proper treatment of negative accruals of OID.

- A number of new deal structures have been created, including so-called "kitchen sink" transactions, structures that combine mortgage-backed securities with interest rate swaps and other financial derivatives, and structures in which subordinated securities are divided into mezzanine, senior subordinated and junior subordinated classes.

- In response to the downturn in the real estate markets, there has been an increase in the securitization of financially distressed mortgages.

- A number of developments relate to negative or nominal value residual interests. A market has developed in which transferors pay transferees a fee to induce them to "purchase" negative value residual interests. Under the

REMIC regulations, certain transfers of noneconomic residual interests that have a significant tax avoidance purpose are disregarded for tax purposes. The Revenue Reconciliation Act of 1993 adopted a new mark to market regime for securities dealers. Under recently adopted regulations, that regime does not apply to certain negative value residual interests.

- In 1989, the IRS overhauled its rules governing information reporting for mortgage-backed securities.
- The IRS has clarified the treatment of excess servicing.

New material is included in most chapters of the book. The overview of the different types of mortgage-backed securities in Chapter 2 includes a new Part F dealing with financially distressed mortgages. In addition, the discussion of pass-through debt certificates in Part G comments briefly on kitchen sink transactions.

The new and improved Chapter 3 covers more comprehensively than before the classification of non-REMIC trusts and other unincorporated entities. The chapter addresses, among other new topics, the effect on the classification of an investment trust of incurring liabilities and entering into swaps and other financial derivatives. Part D discusses proposed regulations that have been issued defining a TMP.

Chapter 4, dealing with the qualification and taxation of REMICs, has grown considerably, mostly because of the adoption of the REMIC regulations. The chapter also addresses multiple-tier REMICs, combinations of REMIC interests with other financial instruments, and financially distressed mortgages.

The task of describing the types of permitted REMIC regular interests has been shifted from Chapter 4 to a new Chapter 5. Chapter 5 includes many examples illustrating some of the more exotic types of regular interests that can be created under the REMIC rules. Chapter 5 also addresses the effect of contingencies (such as basis risk).

Chapter 6, which discusses the taxation of REMIC regular interests and other mortgage-backed securities taxable as debt, includes a new Part G, which comments on the deductibility of economic losses attributable to the prepayment of interest only and other high coupon regular interests, and the treatment of losses (or reductions in income) stemming from mortgage defaults and delinquencies. Chapter 6 also discusses changes in the treatment of excess servicing and bond stripping transactions.

The discussion in Chapter 7 of the taxation of REMICs has been revised and expanded to reflect the REMIC regulations. The chapter also describes new rules limiting tax motivated transfers of residual interests and analyzes certain substantive tax issues raised by the existence of negative value residual interests.

A new Chapter 8 discusses the taxation of TMPs and holders of equity interests in TMPs. Chapter 9, which is concerned with special rules for institutional investors, has a new Part E devoted to securities dealers. Part E discusses the mark-to-market regime adopted in 1993. Chapter 10, dealing with foreign investors, has been expanded to cover investments in trusts that hold some real estate (as contrasted with mortgages) and trusts that enter into swaps and other derivative transactions. Chapter 11 has been substantially rewritten to reflect the new information reporting requirements for REMIC regular interests and pay-through bonds.

The glossary has been revised to encompass new terms used in the book. The appendices include a new Appendix B, listing state tax exemptions for REMICs. The primary source materials in Appendix C have been updated to reflect developments in the last five years. The REMIC regulations and the proposed TMP regulations are reproduced in Appendix C. Appendix D reprints the most current versions of the IRS forms relating to REMICs.

Chapter 5 in the first edition discussing mortgage conduit programs has been deleted. The note/bond programs described in that chapter seem to have fallen out of fashion. Readers interested in a description of note/bond programs are referred to the first edition. The discussion of bond defeasance transactions in Chapter 6 also has been removed, because defeasance techniques have not been used widely by issuers of mortgage-backed securities.

Many people contributed to the revised edition. The authors with to acknowledge the efforts of their colleagues at Cleary, Gottlieb, Steen & Hamilton and Weil, Gotshal & Manges, including particularly Douglas Borisky, Sherri Druckman, Carolyn DuPuy, Larry Gelbfish, Daniel Kolb, Jeffrey Koppele, Lisa Levy, Elizabeth Mannette, Belinda Williams-Monroe, Erika Nijenhuis and Kirk Van Brunt. We also wish to acknowledge the contribution of Martin J. Rosenblatt, who commented on financial accounting matters, and the substantial efforts of Carol Barnstable and the other people of Probus Publishing Company.

Since publication of the first edition, the authors have had, between them, three daughters and one son.

James M. Peaslee
David Z. Nirenberg

New York City
February 1994

Preface to First Edition

Every so often, there is a contest between a concrete sidewalk and a germinating plant. Mortar to form the sidewalk is poured over the habitat of the plant. The plant grows, pushing upward against the hard surface. Eventually, cracks form and the plant breaks through. Reflecting on the events of the early 1980s (in particular the period before enactment of the Tax Reform Act of 1986), it would not be wrong to suggest that the public mortgage markets were the plant and the Internal Revenue Code the slab of concrete.

Stating the point differently, tension developed in the early 1980s between tax policy objectives and the needs of the developing mortgage-backed securities markets. for the most part, reasonable accommodations between the two have been reached. However, this harmony was achieved only after a struggle and at the cost of creating an unusually complex and difficult body of law.

This book describes and analyzes the federal income tax law governing mortgage-backed securities from the perspective of issuers, investors and sponsors. Although mortgage-backed securities receive principal attention, the tax principles governing those securities (other than the REMIC rules) will often apply to securities backed by other types of financial assets.

The time is ripe for a book on the present subject, for two reasons. The first is the Tax Reform Act of 1986. A persistent problem in applying the Internal Revenue Code to mortgage-backed securities has been that the law was not framed with the unusual characteristics of those securities in mind. In that regard the 1986 legislation was a watershed, making a number of important law changes directed specifically at the mortgage markets. Although much remains to be done in implementing these changes, the general course of future tax law developments can be foreseen much more clearly than before.

The second reason is that the mortgage markets appear to have matured to the point where the pace at which fundamentally new securities are being introduced has slowed significantly. Thus, from the perspective of an observer attempting to identify and analyze transaction patterns, the target is moving a little less quickly than in prior years.

Given its subject matter, this book is unlikely to be viewed by many as light reading. Nonetheless, it has been written for the interested general reader as well as tax professionals. The book is self-contained and does not assume that the reader has any detailed prior knowledge of tax law. Moreover, many of the more arcane points that would engage only tax specialists are addressed in footnotes. Thus, the book can be used as either a general guide or a reference work.

The book is divided into five general topics: Chapter 1 identifies the distinguishing characteristics of mortgage-backed securities. Chapters 2 through 5 describe the different types of mortgage-backed securities and the vehicles used to create them (for example, grantor trusts, owner trusts and REMICs). The topics addressed include the tax classification of non-REMIC issuers, the organization and taxation of REMICs and mortgage conduit programs. Chapters 6 through 9 describe the tax treatment of investors, including investors subject to special rules, such as real estate investment trusts, mutual funds, banks, thrift institutions, pension plans and foreign investors. Chapter 10 discusses legending and information reporting. Finally, the tax treatment of sponsors is dealt with in Chapter 11.

One subject that has been much discussed but perhaps not well understood is the "phantom income" that is associated with certain investments in mortgage residuals. In addition to an extensive treatment of the subject in the text (Chapter 7, Part E), we have included (as Appendix A) a very thoughtful article by Thomas B. Lupo of Salomon Brothers Inc which analyzes the sources and measurement of phantom income. The article illustrates with tables and graphs the phantom income present in typical fixed and floating rate collateralized mortgage obligation and interest only/principal only structures.

We have also included a glossary of tax terms and reprints of some of the principal source materials in the area. A table of citations and a detailed index will facilitate use of the book as a reference work.

An earlier version of this work was included as Chapter 46 in *The Handbook of Mortgage-Backed Securities* (F. Fabozzi, Ed., revised ed., Probus Publishing, 1988). In transforming that chapter into a book, additions have been made throughout. The discussion of REMICs has been significantly expanded. Furthermore, there are completely new sections addressing entity classification, mortgage conduit programs, pass-through debt certificates, defeasance, the TEFRA registration requirements and legending and information reporting.

There is scant legal authority on many of the issues addressed in this book, and we anticipate that the views will not receive universal approval. Moreover, some topics may warrant further examination, particularly in light of changing market conditions. We would be pleased to receive comments or suggestions.

We are grateful to our colleagues at Cleary, Gottlieb, Steen & Hamilton for the help and encouragement they have given to this project. We wish to acknowledge particularly the contributions of Amanda E. Allen, S. Douglas Borisky, Jeffrey L.

Dodson, Sherri Druckman, Miriam L. Greenberg, Suzanne F. Greenberg, Nicholas Gunther, Betty Johnson and Lawrence Silverstein. We also wish to acknowledge the substantial efforts of Midge Stocker and the people of Probus Publishing Company.

James M. Peaslee
David Z. Nirenberg

New York City
July 1988

Chapter 1

Distinguishing Characteristics of Mortgage-Backed Securities

The subject of this book is the U.S. federal income taxation of mortgage-backed securities.[1] The enactment of the Tax Reform Act of 1986 (TRA 1986) was a watershed event in this area.[2] TRA 1986 gave birth to a new scheme for taxing pools of mortgages that qualify as *real estate mortgage investment conduits* or *REMICs* and the holders of REMIC securities. The legislation also changed the treatment of discount on non-REMIC mortgage-backed securities to take account of the unusual payment characteristics of those securities. The REMIC rules have had the effect of increasing greatly the variety of mortgage-backed securities that are routinely issued to include many that would have been considered fanciful in 1986.

This book is concerned primarily with mortgage-backed securities that are supported exclusively (or almost so) by (1) payments made on a fixed pool of mortgages, or (2) payments made on a fixed pool of mortgages together with earnings from the reinvestment of those payments over a short period (generally not more than six months).[3] Typically, these securities have two payment features that distinguish them economically from conventional publicly held debt obligations: their principal amount (if any) is payable in installments and they are subject to mandatory calls to the extent the mortgages that fund them are prepaid.

Some mortgage-backed securities are further distinguishable from conventional, callable bonds by the fact that their value is attributable largely or entirely to rights to a fixed or variable share of the interest on mortgages and/or reinvestment earnings. These securities are issued at a very high premium over their principal

---

1   The discussion in this book is current through February 1, 1994 and is, of course, subject to change through subsequent legislation, administrative actions, or judicial decisions.

2   Relevant portions of TRA 1986 were clarified and changed by the Technical and Miscellaneous Revenue Act of 1988 (TAMRA). Citations are made throughout this book to the legislative history of TRA 1986 and TAMRA, specifically to the conference committee report on TRA 1986, H.R. Rep. No. 841, 99th Cong., 2d Sess. (September 18, 1986) (the Conference Report); the *General Explanation of the Tax Reform Act of 1986* (JCS-10-87), published (with a blue cover) by the Joint Committee on Taxation (May 4, 1987) (the Blue Book); and House Ways and Means Committee Report on TAMRA, H.R. Rep. No. 795, 100th Cong., 2d Sess. (July 26, 1988) (the TAMRA House Report).

3   Thus, debt obligations that are secured by mortgages, but have payment terms unrelated to those of the mortgage collateral, are not addressed.

1

amount (which may be zero). Because the unamortized premium is forfeited if the securities are prepaid, holders of such securities may experience a zero or negative rate of return, even in the absence of defaults. The highly contingent nature of these securities poses a problem for any system that seeks to measure periodic income and loss.

In terms of tax attributes, mortgage-backed securities may differ from conventional debt instruments in two other respects. First, in the hands of institutional investors, mortgage-backed securities may qualify for certain tax benefits associated with investments in real property mortgages. Second, certain types of mortgage-backed securities are treated for tax purposes as ownership interests in the underlying mortgages rather than as equity or debt of the issuing entity. This "look-through" feature raises a host of tax issues.

The federal income tax questions peculiar to mortgage-backed securities relate primarily to the features described above, the legal structures that are used in transforming whole mortgages into non-REMIC mortgage-backed securities and the REMIC rules.

This book addresses only federal tax issues. Readers are cautioned that while the state or local income or franchise tax consequences of issuing, investing in, or sponsoring mortgage-backed securities often mirror the federal consequences, there can be material differences. Many states have adopted whole or partial tax exemptions for entities that qualify as REMICs under federal law. A list of these exemptions may be found in Appendix B.

Chapter 2

Types of Mortgage-Backed Securities

A. Introduction

The principal types of mortgage-backed securities currently available are pass-through certificates, pay-through bonds, equity interests in issuers of pay-through bonds, and REMIC interests. REMIC interests are either *regular interests* (which from a tax perspective resemble pay-through bonds) or *residual interests* (which from a tax perspective resemble equity interests in issuers of pay-through bonds that are taxed as partnerships).

These securities have two common features: first, they can be used, alone or in combination, to repackage whole mortgages in a manner that increases their attractiveness as investments, and second, the issuers of the securities generally are not subject to tax on the income from the underlying mortgages as it passes through their hands to investors.

It would not be economical to issue a mortgage-backed security unless it were possible to eliminate all material incremental taxes on the issuer. Thus, it is not ordinarily feasible to issue mortgage-backed securities in the form of stock of a corporation. The income from mortgages held by the corporation would bear the full weight of the corporate income tax because no offsetting deductions would be allowed in computing the corporation's taxable income for dividends paid on the stock.

The various types of mortgage-backed securities that are currently available address the problem of the issuer level taxes in different ways. Pass-through certificates are generally issued by a *grantor trust*, which is not considered to be a taxable entity; indeed, for almost all federal income tax purposes, the trust is simply ignored. Issuers of pay-through bonds, or the owners of such issuers, are generally subject to income tax on the taxable income from the mortgages supporting the bonds (which is gross income less deductions), but the burden of that tax typically is small because of the interest deductions allowed for interest on the bonds. A REMIC is exempt from tax by statute (except for certain penalty taxes).

The ability of a non-REMIC issuer of pay-through bonds to avoid an issuer-level income tax changed dramatically at the beginning of 1992, when special tax rules governing *taxable mortgage pools* or *TMPs* became effective. These rules automatically classify as a corporation any trust, partnership, or other entity if at least 80 percent of its assets are debt obligations, more than half of those obligations are real estate mortgages, and the entity issues two or more classes of pay-through bonds with different maturities. A TMP is, with limited exceptions, subject to corporate tax on its taxable income and cannot join in a consolidated return with other corporations. In most although not all cases, it would be economically infeasible for an entity to issue pay-through bonds if it would as a result become a TMP. The TMP rules were enacted as an adjunct to the 1986 REMIC legislation to ensure that, after a five-year transition period, REMICs (which are subject to certain tax avoidance rules) would be the exclusive means of issuing multiple class mortgage-backed securities without an issuer level tax. The definition of a TMP is discussed in detail in Part D of Chapter 3.

The paradigm example of a TMP is an *owner trust* [1] that is formed to hold mortgage collateral and issue pay-through bonds. Without regard to the TMP rules, such a trust would be classified as a partnership or grantor trust, and its income would be taxable only to its equity owners. At the time of enactment of TRA 1986, owner trusts were widely used as issuers of pay-through bonds because they allowed the equity of the issuer to be spread among multiple owners without incremental tax costs. Trusts issuing pass-through certificates are not TMPs.

Parts B through E of this chapter describe more fully pass-through certificates, pay-through bonds, equity interests in issuers of pay-through bonds, and REMIC interests. Although REMIC interests may take the form of pass-through certificates, pay-through bonds, or equity interests, except where otherwise indicated, these terms will be used in this book to refer only to securities not subject to the REMIC rules.

Ordinarily, the mortgages underlying mortgage-backed securities are not in default when the securities are issued, and either are expected to produce only modest default losses or are guaranteed or insured against loss by third parties. Unless otherwise stated, the discussion in Parts B through E below relates only to securities of this type. Special considerations applicable to securities supported from the beginning by pools of financially distressed loans are discussed in Part F.

Most of the mortgage-backed securities that are issued today take the form of pass-through certificates or REMIC interests. Nonetheless, a discussion of pay-through bonds, and equity interests in issuers of such bonds, continues to be relevant for three principal reasons. First, REMICs were patterned after (and designed to improve on) pre-1992 owner trusts that issued pay-through bonds. Some knowledge of these predecessor securities is helpful in understanding the REMIC rules. Second, entities holding mortgages and issuing pay-through bonds may not be

---

1   The term "owner trust" is used to distinguish the trust from the indenture trust for the pay-through bonds.

TMPs, either because they issue only a single class of debt, or because the mortgages are financially troubled. (The TMP rules contain an exception for entities formed to liquidate distressed loans.) Last, techniques developed in the mortgage area are being used to finance automobile loans and other nonmortgage receivables. While issuers without real property mortgages cannot take advantage of the REMIC rules, they also are not TMPs.[2]

Part G of this chapter considers another type of trust security that takes the form of a pass-through certificate but has the economic characteristics of debt of the issuing trust. These securities will be referred to as *pass-through debt certificates*. They have been issued almost exclusively by trusts holding automobile loans or credit card or other nonmortgage receivables, but in special cases the structure could have applications for mortgages. Moreover, the tax analysis of the certificates provides an interesting contrast to the analysis of more conventional types of asset-backed securities.

This chapter is intended to provide only an overview of the different types of mortgage-backed securities. The substantive tax rules governing each are discussed in detail in later chapters.

B. Pass-Through Certificates

1. General Description

In their most common form, pass-through certificates are issued by a trust[3] that holds a fixed pool of mortgages. The mortgages may bear interest at a fixed or adjustable rate. The arrangement is created by a sponsor who transfers the mortgages to the trust against receipt of the certificates and then, typically, sells all or a portion of the certificates to investors. The certificates evidence ownership by the holders of specified interests in the assets of the trust.

To avoid an entity level tax, the trust must be classified as a trust for tax purposes and not as an association taxable as a corporation. Trust classification can be achieved only if the trust has, with a limited exception, a single class of ownership interests, and the power under the trust agreement to change the composition of the mortgage pool or otherwise to reinvest mortgage payments is severely restricted.[4] (The exception to the single-class-of-ownership requirement allows

---

2   A bill was introduced in Congress in 1993 that would create a new vehicle for issuing securities backed by nonmortgage receivables. See H.R. 2065 (introduced May 11, 1993) (providing for the creation of Financial Asset Securitization Investment Trusts, or FASITs). See also American Bar Association, Tax Section, Committee on Financial Transactions, "Legislative Proposal to Expand the REMIC Provisions of the Code to Include Nonmortgage Assets," 46 *Tax Law Review* 299 (Spring 1991). Further, certain municipal bond dealers have proposed the establishment of a new vehicle, a *Tax Exempt Municipal Investment Conduit (TEMIC)*. See "Draft of TEMIC Legislation Available," 94 *Tax Notes Today* 4-64 (January 6, 1994).

3   In some cases, the trust is replaced with a custodial arrangement. Whether the difference in name has any consequences depends on the functional characteristics of the arrangement. See Chapter 3, footnote 10.

4   The classification of non-REMIC issuers is discussed in Chapter 3. A trust would also avoid an

stripped certificates and senior and subordinated certificates, as described in the following two sections.)

Given these tax constraints, pass-through certificates are generally issued in a single class, with each holder having a pro rata interest in the mortgage pool. Thus, if 1000 such certificates are issued, each would represent a right to 1/1000 of each payment of principal and interest on each mortgage in the pool. Mortgage payments received by the trustee are passed through to certificate holders, generally monthly in parallel with the receipt of mortgage payments by the trust. The distributions are reduced by fees for mortgage servicing, pool administration, and any applicable guarantees or pool insurance. These fees generally are fixed in advance over the life of the pool so that certificate holders can be guaranteed a specified "pass-through rate" of interest on the principal balance of the certificates, representing the earnings on the mortgages after deduction of such fees. Depending on the mortgages in the pool and the fees charged, the pass-through rate may be fixed or variable.[5]

A trust that issues pass-through certificates and is classified as a trust is taxed under the grantor trust rules set forth in section 671.[6] Consequently, for federal income tax purposes, the trust is effectively ignored and certificate holders are recognized as the owners of the mortgages held by the trust.[7]

---

entity-level tax if it is classified as a partnership, rather than a trust or corporation. However, a typical trust issuing pass-through certificates would be treated as a corporation if it failed to be a trust. See Chapter 3, Part C.2.

5   The pass-through rate will always represent economically a weighted average of the interest rates (net of fees) on the mortgages. Thus, the pass-through rate will be a fixed number only if the interest rate on each mortgage, net of the fees payable out of such interest, is the same for all mortgages held by the trust and constant over time. ·

6   Except as otherwise noted, all section references in this book are to the Internal Revenue Code of 1986 (Code). For federal income tax purposes, a trust is usually recognized to be a taxpayer and is subject to tax at the rates applicable to individuals on the portion of its income that it does not distribute currently to beneficiaries. Certain trusts, however, are ignored for most federal income tax purposes under the so-called *grantor trust rules* found in sections 671 through 679. These rules originally were created to prevent the separate tax identity of a trust from being used to shift income to lower bracket taxpayers (such as from wealthy parents to a family trust or to its beneficiaries) in cases where the grantor (the person creating the trust) retains an economic interest in, or significant rights of control over, the trust. The rules provide that if the grantor of a trust retains specified interests in the trust, including a right to income, then the grantor is treated for tax purposes as the owner of the assets of the trust and the income from those assets is included in the grantor's own tax return. To that extent, the trust is ignored for tax purposes. While the owner of a pass-through certificate issued by a trust holding mortgages is not, strictly speaking, the grantor of the trust, the grantor trust rules have been seized upon by the Internal Revenue Service (sometimes referred to herein as the *Service* or *IRS*) as a basis for disregarding the issuing trust and treating certificate holders as tax owners of the mortgages, according to their interests. Certificate holders, viewed as grantors, are subject to the grantor trust rules because they have a right to all distributions of income and corpus from the trust. See section 677; G.C.M. 34347 (September 14, 1970) (discusses whether purchasers of GNMA pass-through certificates can be treated as grantors). It views the initial purchasers as grantors on the ground that the sponsor of the certificates is creating them for sale and is acting as a broker on behalf of initial purchasers. Although subsequent transferees are not discussed, the many rulings that have been issued treating certificate holders as trust owners under the grantor trust rules (see footnotes 11 through 14 below) do not distinguish between initial and subsequent holders.

7   The Service has reached this conclusion in a number of settings. See, e.g., Revenue Ruling 90-55,

One consequence of disregarding the separate existence of a pass-through trust is that certificate holders who report taxable income under a cash method of accounting (which is true of virtually all holders who are individuals) must report income for tax purposes based on the timing of receipts of mortgage payments by the trust, *not* on the timing of distributions made to them by the trust.[8] The trustee is viewed as an agent collecting mortgage payments on the certificate holders' behalf. While certificate holders are obliged to include in income the gross amount of interest on the mortgages, they are allowed deductions (subject to special limitations in the case of individuals) for mortgage servicing and other expenses paid out of such interest, again on the theory that those amounts are paid on their behalf. An individual certificate holder's deductions for servicing and other expenses may be limited under section 67, which provides that an individual is allowed certain miscellaneous itemized deductions (including deductions for investment expenses) only to the extent that the aggregate amount of such deductions exceeds 2 percent of the individual's adjusted gross income.[9] In addition, an individual is subject to an alternative minimum tax (AMT) at graduated rates up to 28 percent of alternative minimum taxable income (AMTI) if such tax exceeds the individual's regular fed-

---

1990-2 C.B. 161 (a grantor trust has no taxable year because "the grantor must report the gross income from the trust property as if the trust does not exist"), Revenue Ruling 90-7, 1990-1 C.B. 153 (exchange of trust certificates for a pro rata share of trust assets not a taxable event; reverses earlier revenue ruling which relied on case law treating such an exchange as a taxable event), Revenue Ruling 88-103, 1988-2 C.B. 304 (grantor may avoid gain on involuntary conversion of property under section 1033(a)(2) if a trust of which he is the grantor purchases suitable replacement property), Revenue Ruling 87-61, 1987-2 C.B. 219 (grantor's transfer of appreciated property to a foreign grantor trust ignored for purposes of section 1491, which imposes an excise tax on transfers of appreciated property to a foreign trust), Revenue Ruling 85-45, 1985-1 C.B. 183 (sale to third party of home held by grantor trust deemed direct sale by grantor entitling her to elect to defer gain under section 121), Revenue Ruling 85-13, 1985-1 C.B. 184 (transfer of grantor trust assets to grantor in exchange for a promissory note is not a sale or exchange and the grantor takes a carryover basis in the trust assets; case to the contrary not followed), and Revenue Ruling 81-98, 1981-1 C.B. 40 (grantor's transfer of an installment note to a grantor trust does not result in a disposition of the note). Note that a grantor trust generally is required to file an income tax information return. See Chapter 11, footnote 44 and accompanying text. For a general discussion of the status of grantor trusts as entities for tax purposes, see M. Ascher, "When to Ignore Grantor Trusts: The Precedents, a Proposal and a Prediction," 41 *Tax Law Review* 253 (1986).

8   Similarly, accrual method holders would report income as it accrues on the mortgages, as distinguished from the certificates. This practice is sometimes not followed by REMICs holding pass-through certificates. See Chapter 6, footnote 2.

9   Treasury Regulation § 1.67-2T requires any "affected investor" who is treated as the owner of an interest in a grantor trust to take into account his proportionate share of the trust's expenses as if he had incurred such expenses and earned the related income directly. For this purpose, an "affected investor" is an individual (excluding a nonresident alien whose income is not connected effectively with a U.S. trade or business), any entity (including a trust or estate) that computes its income in the same manner as an individual, and certain pass-through entities. This regulation does not indicate how expenses of a grantor trust that has more than one class of ownership interest should be allocated among the classes. Possibly, the rules for single-class REMICs described in Chapter 7, Part D, or the more flexible rules for nonpublicly offered regulated investment companies (RICs) found in Treasury Regulation § 1.67-2T(k), will be used as a model. In addition, although REMICs and certain nonpublicly offered RICs are required to report allocations of expenses to affected investors (see Chapter 11 (REMICs) and Treasury Regulation § 1.67-2T(n) (RICs)), there is at present no comparable reporting requirement for grantor trusts.

eral income tax liability. No deduction is allowed for investment expenses in computing an individual's AMTI.[10] The Service has issued public rulings that confirm these tax consequences for pass-through certificates guaranteed by the Government National Mortgage Association (GNMA),[11] the Federal Home Loan Mortgage Corporation (FHLMC)[12] and the Federal National Mortgage Association (FNMA)[13] and for certificates representing interests in pools of conventional mortgages that are supported by private mortgage insurance.[14]

Because pass-through certificate holders are treated as the owners of the assets of the issuing trust, to the extent those assets include mortgages on personal residences that are loans to individuals, the holders are subject to special rules regarding premium and discount on obligations of individuals.[15] For the same reason, institutional investors that derive tax advantages from directly owning real property loans benefit equally from owning pass-through certificates evidencing interests in those loans.[16] Pass-through certificates are not considered governmental obligations for these and most other tax purposes even if there is Federal Housing Administration insurance on, or a Veterans' Administration guarantee of, the mortgages underlying the certificates, or there is a guarantee of the certificates by the United States or a U.S. sponsored agency.[17] A pass-through certificate backed by residential mort-

---

10   See section 56(b)(1)(A)(i).

11   Revenue Ruling 70-544, 1970-2 C.B. 6, and Revenue Ruling 70-545, 1970-2 C.B. 7, both modified by Revenue Ruling 74-169, 1974-1 C.B. 147 (GNMA certificates are "qualifying real property loans" under section 593(d), as well as "loans secured by an interest in [residential] real property" under section 7701(a)(19)(C)(v), in each case, to the extent the property underlying the mortgages is the type of real property interest described in the relevant Code section) and clarified by Revenue Ruling 84-10, 1984-1 C.B. 155 (certificate holders must take account of their proportionate shares of prepayment penalties, assumption fees, and late charges consistent with their method of accounting); G.C.M. 34347 (September 14, 1970).

12   Revenue Ruling 71-399, 1971-2 C.B. 433, amplified by Revenue Ruling 81-203, 1981-2 C.B. 137 (a *pledged account mortgage*, a residential mortgage loan for which the obligor's savings account is pledged as additional collateral, constitutes a "loan secured by an interest in [residential] real property" under section 7701(a)(19)(C)(v) and, within certain limits, the full amount of such loans that underlie a FHLMC participation certificate will be treated as "qualifying real property loans" under section 593(d)). See also Revenue Ruling 80-96, 1980-1 C.B. 317 (Revenue Ruling 71-399 applies to pools with respect to which (1) FHLMC makes regular payments each month on an estimated basis, with adjustments in the following month, and (2) FHLMC retains any interest for the month of prepayment on mortgages that prepay on or before the twentieth day of the month and remits a full 30 days of interest on mortgages that prepay after the twentieth day of the month, in each case, as an adjustment to FHLMC's servicing and guarantee fee), Revenue Ruling 74-300, 1974-1 C.B. 169 (a REIT that owns FHLMC participation certificates is considered to own "real estate assets" under section 856(c)(5)(A) and interest income on such a certificate is considered "interest on obligations secured by mortgages on real property or on interests in real property" under section 856(c)(3)(B)), Revenue Ruling 74-221, 1974-1 C.B. 365, and Revenue Ruling 72-376, 1972-2 C.B. 647.

13   Revenue Ruling 84-10, 1984-1 C.B. 155; G.C.M. 39113 (January 12, 1984).

14   Revenue Ruling 77-349, 1977-2 C.B. 20. See also P.L.R. 9018053 (February 6, 1990).

15   See generally Chapter 6).

16   See Chapter 9, Part A.

17   See Chapter 6, footnotes 115 and 147. Pass-through certificates guaranteed by GNMA are not considered obligations of the United States for purposes of 31 U.S.C. § 3701, which exempts such

gages is not a "security" within the meaning of section 165(g)(2) for which ordinary bad debt deductions may not be claimed.[18]

Pass-through certificates that are readily marketable may, however, be considered to be securities or other obligations that are distinct from the underlying mortgages for some tax purposes. These purposes include the TEFRA registration requirements,[19] information reporting,[20] the recently adopted section 475, which requires dealers in securities to account for them on a mark-to-market basis,[21] section 1236, which requires a dealer in securities to identify securities as investments in order to obtain capital gain treatment,[22] the straddle rules of section 1092,[23] a special rule in the Netherlands Antilles tax treaty,[24] and possibly the wash sale rules of section 1091.[25]

---

obligations from certain state taxes, nor are they obligations of the United States for purposes of the constitutional immunity of federal obligations from state taxation. *Rockford Life Ins. Co. v. Ill. Dep't of Rev.*, 482 U.S. 182 (1987). However, pass-through certificates guaranteed by the United States or a U.S. sponsored agency are treated as "Government securities" for purposes of the diversification test for RICs found in section 851(b). The definition of that term, for purposes of section 851, is borrowed from the Investment Company Act of 1940, 15 U.S.C. § 80a-1 et seq. (ICA 1940). Pass-through certificates issued by the Federal Agricultural Mortgage Corporation are specifically excluded from the definition of "Government securities" for purposes of ICA 1940 and thus are not Government securities for purposes of section 851(b)(4). See section 12 U.S.C.A. § 2279aa-12 (1993). In Revenue Ruling 92-89, 1992-2 C.B. 154, the Service provided a nonexclusive list of securities that it determined were Government securities for purposes of section 851(b)(4). For an analysis of the treatment of pass-through certificates in the hands of RICs, see G.C.M. 39626 (April 29, 1987).

18 This definition is limited to obligations issued by a corporation or government, and thus would not include a trust certificate backed by residential mortgages. See Chapter 6, text accompanying footnote 147.

19 Pass-through certificates backed by residential mortgages may be "registration-required obligations" within the meaning of section 163(f)(2) even though obligations issued by natural persons are not within that term. See Chapter 10, Part A.2.

20 See Chapter 11, Part B.2.

21 Section 475(c)(2) includes within the definition of "securities" interests in widely held or publicly traded trusts, and evidences of an interest in debt instruments (whether or not widely held or publicly traded). Section 475 was added to the Code by the Revenue Reconciliation Act of 1993 (RRA 1993).

22 G.C.M. 39551 (June 30, 1986) (discusses section 1236 as one of a number of sections using the term "security").

23 The straddle rules apply to offsetting positions in "personal property" which is generally defined in section 1092(c) as "personal property of a type which is actively traded". A pass-through certificate can meet this definition if the certificate is actively traded, even though the underlying mortgages themselves are not traded.

24 See Revenue Ruling 79-251, 1979-2 C.B. 271 (under the U.S.-Netherlands Antilles treaty, where bonds received more favorable treatment, GNMA pass-through certificates are not "mortgage notes (not including bonds) secured by real property" on the ground that, because the certificates are marketable, highly liquid, and issued in registered serial form, they more closely resemble "bonds"). With a minor exception, the treaty was terminated by the United States effective January 1, 1988.

25 See G.C.M. 39551 (June 30, 1986). Section 1091 applies only if the securities sold and acquired are substantially identical, which in the case of pass-through certificates requires that they be backed by the same mortgages. *FNMA v. Comm'r.* 90 T.C. 405, 425 (1988), *aff'd,* 896 F.2d 580 (D.C. Cir. 1990), *cert. denied,* 499 U.S. 974 (1991). The *Cottage Savings* case, discussed in

2. Stripped Pass-Through Certificates

Pass-through certificates may also represent, instead of a pro rata share of all payments on the underlying mortgages, a right to a fixed percentage of the principal
payments and a different fixed percentage of the interest payments.[26] Such pass-
through certificates are often referred to as *stripped mortgage-backed securities* or
stripped pass-through certificates. They are generally sold when there is a divergence of views regarding anticipated prepayment rates. The principal component of
a mortgage, viewed in isolation without interest, is more valuable the earlier it is
repaid. On the other hand, interest ceases when principal is repaid, so that the
interest component of a mortgage, standing alone without principal, is more valuable the later the date on which principal is repaid. Thus, by varying the mix
between principal and interest, the effect of prepayments on a class of pass-through
certificates can be changed.

The earliest stripped pass-through certificates that were publicly available *reduced* the effect on investors of changes in prepayment speeds by transforming
discount or premium mortgages into par securities. To illustrate this type of transaction, suppose that a thrift institution holds a pool of mortgages bearing interest at a
rate of 10 percent (net of servicing) at a time when the current market rate of
interest for pass-through certificates is 8 percent. If the thrift believes that investors
will assume a higher prepayment rate, and thus would be willing to pay a smaller
premium for a pro rata interest in the mortgages, than the thrift thinks is appropriate,
the thrift could keep the premium, and insulate investors from the risk of a reduction in yield resulting from prepayments, by retaining a right to 1/5 of each interest
payment on the mortgages and selling pass-through certificates at par with an 8
percent pass-through rate.[27] Similarly, if the thrift held discount mortgages and
wished to sell pass-through certificates at par based on those mortgages, it could
accomplish its objective by allocating to the certificates all of the interest payments
but only a fraction of the principal payments.[28]

Chapter 12 footnote 15, while not addressing the wash sale point, looked to the individual mortgages underlying a participation interest in a pool of mortgages in deciding if two participation
interests differed materially in kind or extent, so that an exchange produced a realized loss under
section 1001.

26   In general, these percentages must be set at the time of issuance of the certificates and may not be
changed subsequently. Otherwise, the trust issuing the certificates would be considered an association taxable as a corporation under the Sears regulations and would be subject to an entity-level
tax. See Chapter 3, Part C.1.d. The percentages need not, however, be the same for all mortgage
loans held by a trust or, with respect to any particular mortgage loan, for all interest payments or
all principal payments.

27   Alternatively, if the thrift can find a different group of investors who anticipate slow prepayment
rates, it could sell to those investors the strip of interest payments. The sale could be effected
mechanically by transferring the mortgages to a trust in return for two classes of certificates that
would be sold to the two investor groups. One class of certificates would be entitled to 100% of
the principal payments and 80% of the interest payments on the mortgages; the other class would
be entitled to 20% of the interest payments.

28   Another example of a common pass-through arrangement that may be viewed as a sale of rights to
different percentages of principal payments and interest payments is one in which the underlying

Stripped pass-through certificates have also been created that *increase* the effect on *all* investors of variations in prepayment speeds by creating greater discounts and premiums than are inherent in the underlying mortgages. At the extreme, there is a complete separation in the ownership of rights to interest and principal. In a typical transaction, mortgages are transferred to a trust in exchange for two classes of certificates. One class (referred to as *PO Strips*) represents the right to receive 100 percent of each principal payment on the mortgages. The other class (*IO Strips*) represents the right to receive 100 percent of each interest payment. PO Strips, which are similar to zero coupon bonds payable in installments, are issued at a substantial discount and are purchased by investors who expect a high rate of prepayments compared with the market as a whole, or who wish to hedge against a risk of loss from declining interest rates. (Declining interest rates generally increase prepayments and thus increase the value of PO Strips.) IO Strips, which are issued with what amounts to an infinite premium, are purchased by investors who expect a low rate of prepayments or who wish to hedge against a risk of loss from rising interest rates.

3. Senior/Subordinated Pass-Through Certificates

Pass-through certificates typically provide for some type of credit support that protects investors from defaults or delinquencies in payments on the underlying mortgages. The credit support may take the form of a guarantee, insurance policy, or other agreement by the sponsor or a third party to replace defaulted or delinquent payments or purchase defaulted or delinquent loans. Credit support can also be provided in whole or in part by creating senior and subordinated classes of pass-through certificates. Mortgage defaults or delinquencies are charged first against distributions that otherwise would be made on the subordinated class until they are exhausted, thereby protecting the senior class. Additional credit support may be provided through a reserve fund that is funded initially either with cash provided by the sponsor or with monies diverted from the subordinated class during the early years of the pool. It is common practice to require that any reserve fund be held outside of the trust as security for a limited recourse guarantee of the mortgages, to avoid possible classification of the trust as an association taxable as a corporation.[29] For the same reason, it was also common practice before 1992 to restrict the transfer of subordinated certificates by the trust sponsor. This concern was eliminated by an IRS ruling.[30]

---

mortgages have a range of stated interest rates and an "excess servicing" fee is charged to reduce the interest that is passed through on the higher coupon mortgages. Such arrangements are discussed in Chapter 3, footnotes 99–101 and accompanying text, Chapter 6, text following footnote 54, and Chapter 12, footnotes 2–5.

29   See Chapter 3, Parts C.1.c.(vii) (inside reserve funds) and 2.c.(iv) (outside reserve funds).

30   The restriction on transfers stemmed from the Sears regulations which are discussed in Chapter 3, Part C.1. The ruling, Revenue Ruling 92-32, 1992-1 C.B. 434, is described in Chapter 3 at footnote 75.

Holders of senior or subordinated pass-through certificates generally are taxed in the same manner as if the subordination feature did not exist. It is not entirely clear, however, how the subordination feature should be taken into account. One approach would be to treat the feature as a guarantee of the underlying mortgages written by the holder of the subordinated certificates in favor of the holders of the senior certificates that is secured solely by the subordinated certificates.[31] Under that view, payments received by the senior certificate holders as a result of the subordination feature would be treated in the same manner as other payments under a guarantee, namely, as if they were the corresponding payments of principal or interest on the defaulted or delinquent mortgages.[32] Subordinated certificate holders would be required to report income from the mortgages as if they were entitled to receive their full share of the mortgage payments, even if some or all of those payments are diverted to the holders of the senior certificates. Subordinated certificate holders would be treated as if they had purchased the senior certificate holders' share of the payments on the delinquent or defaulted mortgages and generally would be allowed a bad debt deduction, subject to the rules of section 166, when the rights to those payments become wholly or partially worthless.[33]

One question raised by the guarantee approach is whether it is necessary to impute a guarantee fee payable by the senior to the subordinated certificate holders. Such a fee would raise a host of tax issues.[34] While the guarantee analysis may be

---

31 This analysis is supported by Example 2 in the Sears regulations, discussed in Chapter 3, Part C.1.d. The example justifies the treatment of a trust with senior and subordinated classes as one in which the existence of multiple classes is "incidental" to the purpose of investing in trust assets, on the ground that the arrangement is substantially equivalent to a single class trust coupled with a limited recourse guarantee running from the holders of the subordinated class to the senior certificate holders.

32 Cf. Revenue Ruling 76-78, 1976-1 C.B. 25 ("proceeds of insurance…representing maturing interest on defaulted obligations of a state or political subdivision thereof are excludable from…gross income" as if they were interest payments by the obligor); Treasury Regulation §§ 1.861-2(a)(5), 1.862-2(a)(5) (the source of interest paid under a guarantee is the same as the source of the guaranteed interest).

33 See Treasury Regulation § 1.166-9 (treatment of payments under a guarantee as a bad debt). Bad debt deductions are discussed in Chapter 6, Part G.2.

34 One issue is whether the fee would be considered to be charged up front or over time. If the fee were charged up front, it might be necessary for a senior certificate holder to allocate some portion of the cost of its certificate to the guarantee. Cf. P.L.R. 7821008 (February 15, 1978) (one-time guarantee fee must be amortized over the life of the loan). In practice, however, separate allocations to guaranties are rarely made, regardless of the fee structure. Other issues would include (1) whether the fee is subject, in the hands of a subordinated certificate holder, to U.S. withholding tax if the holder is a foreign investor (the U.S. withholding tax is discussed in Chapter 10), or to the tax on unrelated business taxable income (described in Chapter 9) if the holder is a pension plan or other tax-exempt investor subject to tax only on such income; (2) whether the fee is qualifying income for purposes of the REIT income tests (described in Chapter 9); (3) whether payment of the fee causes a trust to become subject to the bond stripping rules described in Chapter 6 (on the ground that part of the "interest" payable to the subordinated certificate holders represents a fee payable out of interest owned by the senior certificate holders so that the senior certificate holders have a greater than pro rata right to interest); and (4) whether, in the case of senior certificate holders who are individuals, the fee paid is deductible only as a miscellaneous itemized deduction (see footnotes 9 and 10 above). The imputation of a guarantee fee may also affect the tax treatment

helpful in accounting for income or losses of investors, hopefully, the Service would not carry it to this extreme.

An alternative approach would be to make a special allocation of income of the trust between the classes in a way that reflects actual cash distributions. Thus, the senior certificate holders would be allocated the interest payments they receive and the subordinated investors would be allocated the interest they receive, plus the interest that accrues but is not paid to them on account of mortgage delinquencies or defaults.[35] Under this view, holders of subordinated certificates would not be considered to receive their pro rata shares of mortgage interest that is actually distributed to holders of senior certificates. Thus, the fairly rare breed of subordinated certificate holder that reports income under a cash method of accounting could enjoy an income deferral advantage.[36] One benefit of the allocation theory is that it clearly would not require the imputation of a guarantee fee.

C. Pay-Through Bonds

Unlike pass-through certificates, which represent an ownership interest in mortgages, a pay-through bond is a debt obligation of a legal entity that is collateralized by mortgages (or interests in mortgages). A holder is considered to own the bond, but not an interest in the underlying mortgages, in the same way that the holder of a public utility bond, for example, would be considered the owner of the bond but not of the power generating station that secures it. Although the payment terms of a pay-through bond and of the underlying mortgage collateral are not identical, the relationship between them may be quite close. In most cases, the mortgages, and earnings from the reinvestment of mortgage payments over a short period, are expected to be the sole funding source for payments on the bonds, and mortgage prepayments are "paid through," in whole or in part, to bondholders in the form of mandatory calls on the bonds.[37] Steps required to ensure that pay-through bonds will be recognized to be the issuer's debt for tax purposes are discussed in Part D.

---

of a sale of certificates by the sponsor of a trust. See Chapter 12, footnotes 18 and 19.

35 Accrued interest allocated to subordinated investors that are accrual method taxpayers would be included in income until it is shown to be uncollectible as discussed in Chapter 6, Part G.2. The allocation approach was followed in G.C.M. 38311 (March 18, 1980). G.C.M. 38311 was revoked by G.C.M. 39040 (September 27, 1983) in anticipation of the issuance of the Sears regulations. As discussed in Chapter 3, Part C.1.e, one goal of these regulations was to ensure that holders of interests in grantor trusts could be taxed as owners of the underlying assets without the need to adopt complex income allocation rules similar to those applicable to partnerships. The allocation approach outlined in the text could arguably raise this concern, although the allocations in the typical senior/subordinated trust would in fact be fairly straightforward.

36 Under section 448, most C corporations (corporations that are not S corporations) are prohibited from using a cash method of accounting.

37 To protect bondholders from the effects of changes in prepayment rates, an issuer could guarantee bondholders a specified minimum or maximum prepayment rate. To support the guarantee, the issuer might purchase a minimum or maximum prepayment guarantee written by a third party. A minimum prepayment guarantee is a contract that requires the guarantor to lend, and the issuer to borrow, an amount, or requires them to buy and sell mortgage collateral in an amount, equal to the

A *collateralized mortgage obligation (CMO)* is a type of pay-through bond which is divided into classes. As described further below, these classes typically have different maturities and payment priorities. Most often, CMOs are issued by a special purpose entity organized by a sponsor. The entity is typically an owner trust or corporation, although a partnership or possibly even a limited liability company could be used.[38] As described in the introduction to this chapter and further in Chapter 3, Part D, owner trusts and other noncorporate issuers of pay-through bonds may be classified as corporations for tax purposes under the TMP rules if they issue bonds after 1991.

Where the issuer is an owner trust, the trust is established pursuant to a trust agreement between the sponsor and an independent trustee, acting as *owner trustee.* The owner trustee is usually a commercial bank. In most transactions, the sponsor initially transfers a nominal amount of cash to the owner trustee against the receipt of certificates representing the equity or ownership interest in the owner trust. When the CMOs are issued, the mortgage collateral is transferred to the owner trustee in exchange for the net proceeds of the CMOs plus any additional cash equity contribution that may be made to the owner trust, either by the sponsor or by other investors in exchange for new ownership certificates. The sponsor may retain its certificates or sell all or a portion of them to others. The owner trustee pledges the mortgage collateral to another commercial bank acting as *bond trustee* on behalf of the holders of the CMOs under a bond indenture.[39] Over the life of the CMOs, the bond trustee collects payments on the collateral, reinvests those payments over a short period, makes payments on the CMOs, pays expenses, and remits any excess to the owner trustee, which distributes such excess (after paying or providing for expenses) to the owners of the equity of the owner trust. Equity interests in issuers of pay-through bonds are discussed further in Part D below.

---

excess (if any) from time to time of the actual principal balance of the mortgage collateral over its scheduled principal balance. A maximum prepayment guarantee is a contract that requires the guarantor to borrow, and the issuer to lend, an amount equal to the excess (if any) from time to time of the scheduled mortgage principal balance over the actual principal balance. In either case, the scheduled principal balance of the mortgages would be calculated assuming prepayments at the guaranteed rate.

38   There are a number of reasons why an owner trust may be preferred over a partnership as an issuer of CMOs. First, unlike a partnership, a trust does not typically dissolve upon a bankruptcy of an equity owner. Second, an owner trust that is not classified as a corporation under the TMP rules could potentially take the position that it is a grantor trust, and not a partnership, for tax purposes and thereby avoid various tax complexities that arise from partnership treatment (see Chapter 7). Third, it may be easier to market "trust" interests than "partnership" interests. The desire to avoid unlimited liability has not traditionally been a reason favoring use of an owner trust over a partnership, because the owners of trust equity are typically made liable for claims against the trust (other than liability to repay the CMOs, which are nonrecourse obligations) in order to establish that the trust lacks the "corporate characteristic" of limited liability. See Chapter 3, Part C.2.c.(i).

39   The collateral backing CMOs often takes the form of pass-through certificates guaranteed by the United States or a U.S. sponsored agency, although when the sponsor is a nongovernmental person, the CMOs themselves are not obligations of, or guaranteed by, the United States or such an agency.

If the issuer of CMOs is not an owner trust, the structure is substantially the same, with the issuer and the owners of its equity replacing the owner trustee and the beneficiaries of the trust. If the issuer (whatever its state-law form) is classified as a corporation for federal income tax purposes, it will be necessary to provide for the payment of corporate income tax before distributions are made to equity owners. If the issuer is a member of a group of corporations filing consolidated tax returns, there may be a tax sharing agreement spelling out, as among group members, the issuer's obligation to pay tax.[40] The federal income tax treatment of the holders of CMOs is not generally affected by whether the issuer is classified as a corporation, trust, or partnership.

CMOs are a more recent innovation than pass-through certificates. They are similar to pass-through certificates in that they are funded primarily out of payments received on a fixed pool of mortgages or interests in mortgages and, as a group, closely resemble those mortgages or interests in terms of the timing and amounts of payments. Unlike pass-through certificates, however, CMOs are typically divided into classes that have different maturities and different priorities for the receipt of principal, and in some cases interest. Most often, there are "fast-pay" and "slow-pay" classes. Thus, all principal payments (including prepayments) may be made first to the class having the earliest stated maturity date until it is retired, then to the class with the next earliest maturity date until it is retired, and so on. Alternatively, principal payments may be allocated among classes to ensure to the extent possible that designated classes receive principal payments according to a fixed schedule. Under that arrangement, the greater stability in the timing of payments on the designated classes (often called *planned amortization class* or *PAC bonds*) would be balanced by greater variability in the timing of payments on the remaining classes (often called *support classes*). Payment priorities may also change (either temporarily or permanently) based on the occurrence of some triggering event (such as interest rates reaching a certain level). Classes of this type are known colloquially as *nonsticky jump classes* (where changes in priorities are temporary) and *sticky jump classes* (where changes are permanent). Another common feature of CMOs is an *interest accrual* or *compound interest class* that receives no interest or principal payments until all prior classes have been fully retired. Until that time, the interest that accrues on an interest accrual class is added to its principal balance and a corresponding amount is paid as additional principal on prior classes. When CMOs were first issued, there was typically only one interest accrual class which was the class with the latest stated maturity date. It supported all prior classes. Because the different classes of CMOs were typically denominated by letters indicating payment priority, accrual bonds became known as *Z bonds*. More recently, issues of CMOs have included classes of Z bonds that are inserted between other classes of bonds

---

40   As a matter of tax law, each group member would be severally liable to the Service for the group's entire tax, regardless of what a tax-sharing agreement may provide. See Treasury Regulation § 1.1502-6(a). A TMP is not permitted to join in a consolidated return. See Chapter 8.

with shorter and longer terms, and accrual classes that support (colloquially, are local to) only certain designated prior classes.

Three other differences between CMOs and pass-through certificates are worth noting. First, CMOs may bear interest at a floating rate (a rate that varies directly, or in some cases inversely, with an index of market rates of interest, such as LIBOR), even though interest is paid on the mortgage collateral at a fixed rate. Second, CMOs generally provide for quarterly payments, with the issuer being responsible for reinvesting monthly receipts on the mortgages until the next CMO payment date. Finally, CMOs are usually callable at the option of the issuer at a time when a material amount of CMOs remain outstanding, so that the issuer can potentially benefit from increases in the value of the collateral by selling the collateral and retiring the CMOs.[41]

Tax considerations dictated the original choice of pay-through bonds over pass-through certificates as the vehicle for creating mortgage-backed securities with different maturities or a floating interest rate not related to the mortgage collateral. If a typical non-REMIC pass-through trust issued multiple classes of pass-through certificates (that is, ownership interests in the trust) having either of these features, then it is likely that the trust would be classified as an association taxable as a corporation and the certificates would be treated as stock.[42] As a result, the trust would be subject to corporate income tax on the gross income from the mortgages it holds with no deduction for "dividends" paid to certificate holders. An issuer of pay-through bonds, or its owners, may also be subject to corporate income tax on the taxable income of the issuer. However, because pay-through bonds are recognized for tax purposes to be debt of the issuer, deductions are allowed for interest on the bonds.

The status of pay-through bonds as debt obligations of the issuer rather than ownership interests in the underlying mortgages has other tax consequences. One is that holders are taxed based on the payments they are entitled to receive on the bonds rather than on the payments received by the issuer on the underlying mortgages. A second consequence is that pay-through bonds are not taxed as obligations of individuals or real property loans.[43]

D. Equity Interests in Issuers of Pay-Through Bonds

It will be helpful to consider separately the economic and tax-related features of equity interests in issuers of pay-through bonds. As an economic matter, such an equity interest represents a right to all surplus cash derived from the mortgage

---

41 As discussed in footnote 44, below, and accompanying text, the reinvestment of mortgage payments and call rights may be needed to conclude that the CMOs will be recognized to be debt of the issuer for federal income tax purposes.

42 Whether a trust would in fact be classified as an association if it issued multiple classes of ownership interests would depend on the particular characteristics of the trust. The classification of non-REMIC issuers is discussed in detail in Chapter 3.

43 See Chapters 6 and 9.

collateral that is not needed to pay debt service or other issuer expenses. The sources of surplus cash are discussed further below. From a tax perspective, equity interests represent a potential liability to pay tax on any taxable income derived from the collateral and pay-through bonds. Such taxable income is generally the entire income from the mortgage collateral plus reinvestment income minus the deductions allowed for interest paid on the bonds and expenses. Because of mismatches in the timing of income on mortgages and deductions for interest on bonds, issuers of pay-through bonds can generate substantial "phantom income" that would result in significant additional present value tax costs if tax were required to be paid on such income.

The economic and tax features of an equity interest in an issuer of pay-through bonds are discussed in the next two sections. Because an issuer of pay-through bonds is highly leveraged, the treatment of the issuer and its owners under U.S. generally accepted accounting principles (GAAP) (specifically, whether the issuer's assets and liabilities must be reported on an owner's balance sheet) is significant in evaluating those interests. The current GAAP standards are also briefly described.

1. Economic Features

Where an issuer of debt has assets that produce uncertain cash flows and debt with a fixed payment schedule, substantial equity is needed to fill in the gap and provide assurance to creditors that they will be paid. By contrast, virtually no equity would be needed by an issuer of pay-through bonds to protect bond holders if the bonds provided for payments matching in the aggregate the payments (including prepayments) to be made on the underlying mortgages, and that collateral was essentially risk free from a credit standpoint (for example, because it benefits from a GNMA, FNMA, or FHLMC guarantee). A dollar-for-dollar matching of payments on assets and liabilities could be achieved without giving the bonds "equity features" since the underlying assets are themselves debt instruments.

Unfortunately, the most efficient economic result is not generally achievable for tax reasons. An issuer that was a pure conduit would run a material risk of losing deductions for interest it pays on its bonds, on the ground that the bonds should be recharacterized for tax purposes as disguised ownership interests in the issuer or in a separate entity holding the collateral.[44] Typically, debt of an entity is recharacter-

---

44   See Statement of Dennis E. Ross, Acting Tax Legislative Counsel, U.S. Treasury, before the Subcommittee on Taxation and Debt Management of the Senate Finance Committee, relating to S. 1959 and S. 1978, early versions of the REMIC legislation, January 31, 1986 at 3:

Ideally, [a] corporate issuer [of CMOs] would have no residual economic or tax consequences from its holding of the underlying mortgages, which is consistent with the intention that beneficial ownership of the mortgages be transferred to secondary investors. Although this economic result might be accomplished by leaving the issuer without significant capital and issuing obligations that, in the aggregate, exactly mirrored the characteristics of the underlying mortgages, this would in turn threaten the issuer's status for tax purposes as the owner of the mortgages and the issuer of corporate debt. Thus, if the issuer had no significant equity and the CMOs were designed to match exactly the cash flow from the underlying mortgages, the CMOs could be deemed to

ized as an ownership interest on the ground that it bears the risks of the business and therefore has the economic features of equity, regardless of its stated terms.[45] Such recharacterization arguments are particularly persuasive where the purported debt is held by the acknowledged equity owners. Here, the pay-through bonds would, in general, be highly rated and held by independent investors. The concern, then, with a pure conduit issuer is not that the bonds would be equity under traditional tax principles, but instead that the arrangement would be found to represent, in substance, a disguised multiple class trust.[46]

This line of argument has never been tested in court. Nonetheless, it has sufficient plausibility that most tax counsel have been unwilling to opine that pay-through bonds will be recognized to be debt for tax purposes unless there is some significant mismatch between the terms of the bonds and the underlying collateral. Ideally, the mismatch should result in an equity interest that has a variable cash return that reflects the performance of the issuer. The equity should be integrally related to the borrowing and not have characteristics that might allow it to be viewed as a separate ownership interest in the collateral.[47]

Although there are no hard and fast rules and opinions differ, most tax counsel would consider the following combination of factors sufficient to conclude that a typical issue of CMOs backed by GNMA, FNMA, or FHLMC pass-through certificates will be recognized to be debt for tax purposes: (1) the regular interval between payments on the bonds is not less than three months and monthly mortgage payments are reinvested until needed to make payments on the bonds in money market instruments earning interest at a current market rate at the time they are purchased,[48]

---

constitute equity interests in the issuer or to represent instead direct interests in the underlying mortgages. Either characterization could leave the issuer with a tax liability on the mortgage income that would more than offset the economic advantages of the multiple class structure.

See also Joint Committee on Taxation, *Description of Bills Relating to the Tax Treatment of Mortgage Related and Other Asset-Backed Securities (S. 1959 and S. 1978) and Environmental Zones (S. 1839)* (JCS-3-86), January 30, 1986, at 13.

45   For a general discussion, see B. Bittker & J. Eustice, *Federal Income Taxation of Corporations and Shareholders,* 6th Ed. (1994), Chapter 4, Part A. Section 385 gives the Service authority to issue regulations determining whether an interest in a corporation is to be treated as stock or debt (or in part stock and in part debt). Regulations were issued under this section in the early 1980s, but they were criticized on a number of grounds and withdrawn.

46   See footnote 42, above, for the treatment of multiple class trusts.

47   To illustrate, suppose that an 8% pass-through certificate with a principal amount of $100 is held by an entity that issues bonds with a principal amount of $98, bearing interest at 7%. If the issuer were entitled to receive, as a return on equity, 2% of each distribution on the certificate plus all interest in excess of 7%, the equity arguably could be viewed as a separate ownership interest in the collateral, consisting of a 2% pro rata interest in the collateral and a one percentage point interest strip. Under this view, the collateral for the bonds would be limited to the remaining interest in the certificate, which would exactly match the bonds.

48   The existence of a "special redemption right" (a right to call bonds between regular payment dates if reinvesting mortgage payments until the next regular payment date could result in a bond default because of low reinvestment rates) should not be considered to convert the bonds to monthly-pay obligations if, as is normally the case, the call would be exercised only in very unusual circumstances. Where most or all of the CMOs bear interest at a floating rate, monthly payments on the

(2) the issuer has a right to call the bonds at a price of 100% of their principal amount when the total outstanding principal amount of bonds has been reduced to approximately 20% of the original aggregate principal amount of all bonds,[49] and (3) the cash payments available to be distributed to the equity owners, determined based on reasonable assumptions as to reinvestment rates, expenses, and mortgage prepayments, have a present value at the time of issuance of the bonds, calculated using as the discount rate the highest initial yield of any class of bonds, of between one and two percent of the aggregate issue price of all of the bonds. If these tests are met, tax counsel typically would not insist on any minimum initial balance sheet equity or rights to substitute mortgage collateral.

An issuer that has these features will produce some surplus cash that is available for distribution on the equity interests. The cash would be attributable to the spreads between the rates of interest on the mortgages and on one or more classes of bonds, reinvestment income that exceeds the amounts assumed in sizing the issue of bonds, gain resulting from the exercise of rights to call the bonds, and any excess of budgeted over actual administrative expenses.

It should be emphasized that the discussion above relates to issuers that hold collateral with minimal credit risk. Where credit risk is a factor, material amounts of equity would ordinarily be required for nontax reasons, and the economic performance of an equity interest would reflect actual default experience. Different considerations would then apply in evaluating the risk of recharacterization of pay-through bonds as equity interests.[50]

2. Tax Features

The taxes imposed with respect to an equity interest in an issuer of pay-through bonds will depend on the amount and timing of the issuer's taxable income, the tax classification of the issuer (whether it is a corporation, partnership or trust) and the circumstances of the equity owners.

Any equity interest can be expected to generate taxable income equaling the economic income from the investment based on the actual or anticipated cash

---

CMOs are not uncommon.

49   The significance of this factor would be reduced if the stated rate of interest on the classes of bonds that will be outstanding when the call right becomes exercisable is so low that it is very unlikely that the call right will be exercised when the 20% threshold is reached. The likelihood of exercise could be increased by lowering the call price to below par.

50   Where, because of overcollateralization, a class of pay-through bonds has significantly better credit quality than the collateral, the difference in credit ranking would itself be an important factor in resisting the recharacterization of the bonds. On the other hand, if a class of bonds is subordinate and quite risky from a credit standpoint, that class could be viewed as equity under the more traditional standards that apply in evaluating debt instruments. See footnote 45 above. Where the issuer is taxable as a corporation and issues subordinated debt, consideration should be given to the special rules for high yield discount obligations in sections 163(e)(5) and (i), which may defer or disallow deductions for interest on debt instruments that have a term exceeding five years, a yield to maturity of at least 500 basis points over the applicable Federal rate, and significant original issue discount.

distributions thereon. Issuers of pay-through bonds may also produce taxable income that is noneconomic in the sense that it will always be reversed through subsequent losses. Such income, which is commonly referred to as *phantom income,* generally arises when pay-though bonds are divided into different classes with staggered maturities, and the longer-term classes have higher yields than the shorter-term classes. A more thorough discussion of phantom income may be found in Chapter 7, Part E, and in Appendix A.

If the issuer of an equity interest is classified for tax purposes as a partnership or trust, then it is not itself subject to tax; instead, its taxable income is allocated among the equity owners in accordance with their respective interests. Such income is taxable to them regardless of the cash distributions they receive. The ultimate tax burden depends on the circumstances of the owners (e.g., whether they have offsetting losses or tax credits).

The result is quite different where an issuer is a corporation (or classified as a corporation). A corporation is subject to the corporate income tax on its taxable income. Unless a corporation is a member of an affiliated group of corporations filing a consolidated return, losses or credits of shareholders cannot be used to reduce the corporation's tax bill. A corporation can join in a federal consolidated return with other corporations only if other group members own at least 80 percent of its stock, measured by voting power and value (but disregarding certain nonvoting, nonparticipating preferred stock).[51] However, TMPs must file separate returns. In the absence of tax consolidation, earnings of a corporation are potentially subject to a second layer of taxation when they are distributed to shareholders. The additional shareholder taxes would be reduced by the dividends received deduction in the case of distributions made to corporations.[52] They may also be reduced by tax losses or credits available to the shareholders.

3. GAAP Treatment

A significant issue to consider in evaluating an equity interest in an issuer of pay-through bonds is whether the owner will be required under GAAP to show all or any portion of the assets of the issuer in its own financial statements. The traditional answer to this question is that assets and liabilities are required to be included in an equity owner's financial statements if (1) the pay-through bonds are shown as liabilities on the issuer's own financial statements (i.e., they cannot be offset against the related collateral), and (2) the issuer is consolidated with the

---

51 Different standards may apply in determining if corporations can join in a combined or consolidated return for purposes of state or local income or franchise taxes.

52 Under current law, the dividends received deduction would be 80% if the shareholder owns at least 20% (but less than 80%) of the issuer's stock in terms of vote and value and 70% for smaller investments. A corporation that owns at least 80% of the issuer's stock and does not file a consolidated return with the issuer may qualify for a 100% dividends received deduction. Sections 243(a) and (c). For further discussion of the tax burdens on the income of TMPs, see Chapter 8.

owner because the owner "controls" the issuer (which generally means that it owns more than 50 percent of the issuer's equity securities, measured by voting power).

Current GAAP standards do not allow pay-through bonds to be removed from the issuer's balance sheet unless, among other things, "all but a nominal portion of the future economic benefits inherent in the associated collateral have been irrevocably passed to the [bond holders]."[53] This test requires nominal equity. It is virtually impossible to have an equity interest that is sufficiently small to remove bonds from the issuer's balance sheet and still conclude that bonds will be recognized to be debt for tax purposes. Accordingly, the traditional approach to avoiding GAAP reporting of liabilities has been to limit an equity owner's interest to 50 percent or less.

As indicated in the last section, tax consolidation of the issuer with an equity owner (which, unlike financial accounting consolidation, is generally desirable) requires an 80 percent ownership link if the issuer is a corporation, but can be achieved effectively with any level of ownership if the issuer is taxed as a partnership or trust. Prior to enactment of the REMIC rules, a very common transaction pattern was to issue pay-through bonds through an owner trust that was taxed as a partnership or trust and was owned by multiple owners, no one of which owned as much as 50 percent.

The GAAP standards were relaxed somewhat in 1989, through a consensus of the Emerging Issues Task Force allowing an equity interest in a special-purpose issuer of pay-through bonds to be treated as a nonequity investment if certain conditions are met.[54] The ownership of a nonequity instrument does not result in GAAP consolidation regardless of how much of the instrument is owned. Under the consensus, nonequity treatment generally can be achieved by any investor that is not a sponsor of the issuer if the collateral consists solely of a fixed pool of high credit quality mortgages or mortgage-backed securities for which prepayments are probable and can be reasonably estimated, and the owner is not personally liable for claims against the issuer (other than a remote claim for administrative claims or costs).

---

53   Financial Accounting Standards Board, FASB Technical Bulletin No. 85-2, "Accounting for Collateralized Mortgage Obligations (CMOs)," March 18, 1985, at 2 (footnotes omitted). The Technical Bulletin states that the necessary future economic benefits inherent in the collateral associated with an issue of pay-through bonds will be considered to be irrevocably passed to bond holders only if two tests are met: "(1) Neither the issuer nor its affiliates have the right or obligation to substitute collateral or obtain it by calling the [pay-through bonds, with an exception for clean-up calls]. (2) The expected residual interest, if any, in the collateral is nominal." Id. (footnotes omitted). Although pay-through bonds that are considered debt obligations of the issuer for federal income tax purposes likely will be considered liabilities of the issuer under the Technical Bulletin, recognition of pay-through bonds as debt of the issuer under the Technical Bulletin would not necessarily result in similar treatment for federal income tax purposes.

54   See Emerging Issues Task Force, EITF Issue No. 89-4, "Accounting for a Purchased Investment in a Collateralized Mortgage Obligation Instrument or in a Mortgage-Backed Interest-Only Certificate," Issue 1.

E. REMICs

As the prior discussion indicates, a grantor trust cannot issue pass-through certificates that are divided into multiple classes with staggered maturities. Also, pay-through bonds cannot be created that provide for payments, in the aggregate, that precisely mirror the payments on a fixed pool of mortgage collateral. Thus, certain securities that are attractive economically cannot be issued as either pass-through certificates or pay-through bonds, because they have a class structure inconsistent with the grantor trust rules and match the underlying mortgages too closely to be recognized for tax purposes as debt. Moreover, even if a security could be issued as a pay-through bond, compared with an ownership interest in mortgages, debt often has financial accounting disadvantages (the need to show the debt on someone's balance sheet) and tax disadvantages for certain institutional investors (the debt is not considered a real property loan). Finally, holders of equity interests in issuers of pay-through bonds may realize phantom income.

To address some of these concerns, TRA 1986 enacted the REMIC rules (sections 860A through 860G). These rules treat a pool of mortgages that meets certain requirements as a REMIC if an appropriate election is made, and state how the REMIC and the holders of interests therein will be taxed. The Service has issued extensive REMIC regulations under the REMIC sections of the Code.[55] The discussion below provides only a brief overview of the REMIC rules, which are described in detail in other chapters.

The REMIC rules are applied to a pool of mortgages and related securities based on their functional characteristics, without regard to legal form. Thus, a REMIC may be a state law trust, corporation, or partnership, or simply a segregated pool of mortgages that is not a separate legal entity. Similarly, REMIC interests may be evidenced by ownership certificates, debt instruments, stock, partnership interests, or a contractual right to receive payments. The functional approach of the REMIC rules allows the state law legal form of a REMIC and the interests therein to be structured to best achieve financial accounting and other nontax objectives.

By statute, a REMIC is not subject to an entity level tax (except for certain penalty taxes). Instead, the income from its assets is allocated among the holders of REMIC interests. All of the interests in a REMIC must be either *regular interests* or *residual interests*, as those terms are defined in the REMIC rules. There is no required number of classes of regular interests. By contrast, a REMIC must have one (and only one) class of residual interests. In general, regular interests resemble conventional debt in that they must have a specified principal amount, and interest thereon (if any) must be based on a fixed or floating rate. A regular interest may also entitle the holder to a nonvarying "specified portion" of the interest payments on underlying mortgages, with or without some additional claim to principal. There

---

55   These regulations were proposed on September 27, 1991 (FI-88-86, 1991-2 C.B. 926) and adopted on December 23, 1992 (T.D. 8458, I.R.B. 1993-8, 20). Each set of regulations was accompanied by a preamble that describes the regulations and some of the underlying reasoning. The regulations are generally effective for REMICs having a startup day after November 11, 1991.

are no similar limitations on the economic characteristics of residual interests. Credit losses may be allocated in any way that is desired among different classes of REMIC interests. Further, a REMIC can hold assets in a credit or expense reserve fund.

The income of a REMIC is allocated among the different classes of interests as follows: The income of holders of each class of regular interests is determined as if those interests were debt of the REMIC. The holders of the residual interest are allocated all income of the REMIC, determined as if it were a taxable entity but reduced by the interest deductions that would be allowed to the REMIC if the regular interests were debt.

The allocation of income among REMIC interests is similar to the allocation that would be made if the REMIC were an owner trust taxed as a partnership and the regular interests and residual interests were pay-through bonds and equity interests in the trust, respectively. However, there are important differences between REMICs and owner trusts. First, as previously noted, there is no requirement that a REMIC or REMIC interests take any particular legal form. Second, the characterization of regular interests as debt of a REMIC follows directly from the statute, and there is no requirement that a REMIC have any minimum equity value or that the payments on regular interests and the underlying mortgages be mismatched. In addition, for purposes of determining the taxation of the sponsor of a REMIC and the status of regular interests as real property loans in the hands of institutional holders, regular interests are treated as ownership interests in the underlying mortgages rather than as debt.

While the REMIC rules represent a significant step forward in the tax law governing mortgage-backed securities, they are not the answer to every prayer. The REMIC rules were created primarily to permit the issuance of multiple class pass-through certificates. They achieve that goal, but do little more. The REMIC rules do not, for example, offer much relief from the restrictions on management powers that apply to grantor trusts. The permitted activities of a REMIC are limited, in much the same manner as a grantor trust, to holding a fixed pool of mortgages and distributing payments currently to investors. Indeed, in some respects (particularly in disposing of assets), a REMIC has even less freedom of action than a grantor trust. Another significant problem with the taxation of non-REMIC mortgage-backed securities—the phantom income that is recognized by issuers, or the owners of issuers, of certain pay-through bonds—also is not resolved by the REMIC rules. Indeed, they make it *worse*. Where a REMIC issues multiple classes of regular interests with staggered maturities, phantom income is realized by residual interest holders in much the same manner as if they held equity interests in an owner trust and the regular interests were pay-through bonds. However, the REMIC residual holders must contend with certain anti-tax avoidance rules that do not apply to owner trusts. As explained in the introduction to this chapter, the TMP rules were adopted largely to prevent taxpayers from choosing owner trusts over REMICs in order to achieve more favorable treatment of holders of equity interests.

F. Securities Backed by Financially Distressed Mortgages

Traditionally, the mortgages supporting mortgage-backed securities have an overall high credit quality at the time the securities are issued, either on their own merit or because of third party credit support. The plight of the real estate market in recent years has led to the issuance of securities supported by loans that either are nonperforming, or are performing but not expected to be repaid according to their terms. Another category of problem loan is one that has been modified in a workout and has some equity features (such as contingent interest based on the borrower's cash flow or the value of collateral).

The presence of financially distressed mortgages raises a number of tax issues, which are addressed in various contexts in this book. A grantor trust can generally hold defaulted loans, but extensive workout activities could potentially jeopardize the tax status of the trust.[56] A partnership or other noncorporate issuer of pay-through bonds that holds distressed loans may be able to avoid qualifying as a TMP, and thus avoid classification as a corporation, by relying on special rules for "seriously impaired" loans and liquidating entities.[57] A REMIC may hold defaulted or delinquent loans, but property acquired by a REMIC on foreclosure of such a loan may not qualify as the type of "foreclosure property" that a REMIC can hold.[58] Finally, special considerations apply in measuring the income of holders of REMIC regular interests, pay-through bonds, or pass-through certificates that are affected by credit losses.[59]

G. Pass-Through Certificates Taxable as Debt

1. Description of Structure

Ordinarily, non-REMIC trusts issue one of two types of interests: pass-through certificates that are treated for tax purposes as ownership interests in the assets of the trust, or debt instruments that are recognized for those purposes to be debt of the trust. (See Parts B and C of this chapter.) Trusts formed to hold automobile, credit card, and other nonmortgage receivables have issued to investors a third type of interest that takes the *form* of a pass-through certificate but represents *economically* debt of the issuing trust. These certificates are referred to here as *pass-through debt certificates*. Pass-through debt certificates are cast as ownership interests notwithstanding their economic similarity to debt so the sponsor can characterize the sale of the certificates as a sale of trust assets rather than a borrowing for financial accounting or other nontax purposes.

In a typical transaction, the payments due on pass-through debt certificates are not tied directly to payments made on any identified fixed pool of receivables,[60] and

---

56   See Chapter 3, Part C.1.b.

57   See Chapter 3, Part D.2.e.

58   See Chapter 4, Part C.6.b.

59   See Chapter 6, Part G.2.

the trust is not fully protected against the risk of delinquencies and defaults on the receivables it holds. Sometimes, floating rate pass-through certificates are issued that are backed by fixed rate receivables. The trust is able to make required payments on the certificates despite the mismatching of receipts and payments and delinquency or default losses because the amount of certificates it issues is significantly smaller than the amount of trust assets. In other words, there is, to use a debt term, substantial overcollateralization. The residual interest in the trust (that is, the right to all assets remaining after making payments on the certificates) is retained by the trust sponsor.

2. Tax Analysis

a. Overview. The federal income tax analysis of pass-through debt certificates is somewhat complex. In most transactions, it is very clear that the certificates are debt (either of the issuing trust or of the sponsor) except in name. Where that is true, the certificates should be taxed as debt (and not as ownership interests in the trust), at least if the certificates are consistently treated as debt for tax purposes by the trust and the holders of interests in the trust. Nonetheless, as discussed further below, this conclusion is open to potential challenge by the Service on the ground that the parties to a transaction should be bound by their choice of form.

If in a particular case pass-through debt certificates were characterized for tax purposes as ownership interests in the issuing trust, the trust would not be classified as a trust (because it would have multiple ownership classes).[61] Instead, it would be classified either as an association taxable as a corporation or as a partnership, depending on the terms of the trust and its interests. In the transactions where issuers are not able to conclude with a high degree of confidence that the debt characterization of the pass-through debt certificates will withstand challenge, steps are taken to ensure that if the debt argument fails, the trust will be classified as a partnership so that the trust itself will not be subject to tax. The classification of trusts that issue pass-through debt certificates is discussed further in Chapter 3, Part C.2.c.(iii).

Two aspects of the taxation of pass-through debt certificates warrant further discussion: the question of whether the issuing trust and the holders of interests therein are bound by the form of the certificates as ownership interests notwithstanding their economic similarity to debt, and the consequences to investors of treating pass-through debt certificates as partnership interests if the debt argument fails.

b. Overcoming Form. Although the form taken by a transaction is one factor used in determining how it will be taxed, it is a basic (if sometimes disregarded) tenet of tax

---

60   To bridge gaps between the timing of receipts and payments, the trust may have a right to reinvest payments until they are needed to make payments on the certificates. In addition, the trust sponsor may have the right to add new receivables to the trust or to substitute new receivables for old ones.

61   The trust would not be classified as a trust because it would have multiple classes of ownership interests and almost certainly would not fall within the exception in the Sears regulations for "incidental" multiple ownership classes. Furthermore, in many cases, the trust would be considered to have a power to vary the investment of certificate holders. See Chapter 3, Part C.

law that economic substance controls. Thus, if pass-through debt certificates are economically debt of the issuing trust or sponsor, they should be treated accordingly for federal income tax purposes.

It is not difficult to find examples of sale transactions that have been recharacterized as borrowings. One such transaction is a sale–repurchase agreement or "repo," which is universally acknowledged to be taxable as a secured loan.[62] Also, courts have allowed taxpayers to treat sales of receivables as borrowings for tax purposes when the terms clearly indicated a financing.[63] A number of authorities have treated trusts issuing certificates to investors as mere security devices.[64]

Nevertheless, private parties to a transaction face a higher burden of proof than the Service in establishing that the form of a transaction should not control. Unlike the IRS, the parties were responsible for the choice of form. Moreover, if the parties to a transaction are not held to its form, there is a risk of inconsistent treatment by different parties, and also a concern that if the form was chosen with a view to achieving particular tax results that were the subject of bargaining between the parties, then the bargain will not be carried out. Thus, it is likely that pass-through debt certificates will be treated as debt for tax purposes only if in a particular case (1) it is clear that the certificates represent debt economically,[65] and (2) the risk of inconsistent treatment and frustrated expectations is small.[66] One argument that could be made to lessen the required showing by taxpayers is that a pass-through debt certificate is not in form unambiguously equity, but instead is a hybrid that has some formal characteristics of both equity and debt.[67] With a view to eliminating

---

62 See, for example, Revenue Ruling 77-59, 1977-1 C.B. 196; Revenue Ruling 74-27, 1974-1 C.B. 24.

63 See, e.g., *Stein v. Director of Internal Revenue*, 135 F. Supp. 356 (E.D.N.Y. 1955); *Gatlin v. Comm'r*, 34 B.T.A. 50 (1936). See generally W. Cliff & P. Levine, "Reflections on Ownership— Sales and Pledges of Installment Obligations," 39 *Tax Lawyer* (1985) at 37.

64 See Chapter 3, footnote 69. The sponsors of these trusts generally are liable, through a lease of trust property or other arrangement, to make required payments on trust certificates, which supports treatment of the trust as a security device.

65 Compare Chapter 12, footnotes 9 and 11.

66 See *Illinois Power Co. v. Comm'r*, 87 T.C. 1417 (1986), *acq.* ("strong proof" and consistent treatment required to overcome form); *Comm'r v. Danielson*, 378 F.2d 771 (3rd Cir.), *cert. denied*, 389 U.S. 858 (1967) (in a situation where there was a risk of inconsistent treatment and frustrated expectations, the form of a contract could be overcome only if there was fraud in concluding the contract that would be sufficient to void it in a suit between the parties). See also *Estate of Durkin v. Comm'r*, 99 T.C. 561, 571 (1992) (extensive discussion of taxpayer's ability to disregard form; finds against taxpayers who were seeking treatment different from tax return characterization of transaction after that characterization had been successfully challenged by IRS). For a general discussion of this topic, see W. Blatt, "Lost in a One-Way Street: The Taxpayer's ability to Disavow Form," 70 *Oregon L. Rev.* 381 (1991), R. Smith, "Substance and Form: A Taxpayer's Right to Assert the Priority of Substance," 44 *Tax Lawyer* 137 (1990), V. Rosen, "Substance and Form—A Taxpayer's Weapon," 1970 *S. Calif. Inst.* 689.

67 For a discussion of the effect of ambiguous terms, see *Coulter Electronics, Inc. v. Comm'r*, T.C.M. 1990-186, 59 T.C.M. (CCH) Dec. 46, 518, *affd. without opinion*, 943 F.2d 1318 (11th Cir. 1991). The legal differences between the claims of a holder a of pass-through debt certificate and the claims of a trust creditor are not that great. In each case the trust promises to make certain scheduled payments to investors out of trust assets and the investor can sue the trust for a failure

the problem of inconsistent treatment and frustrated expectations, pooling and servicing agreements under which pass-through debt certificates are issued generally require the sponsor, the trust (for purposes of filing tax returns and information reporting), and the certificate holders to treat the certificates as debt of the issuing trust for federal income tax purposes. The intended tax treatment is also clearly spelled out in the offering documents.

c. Taxation of Certificates as Partnership Interests. As noted earlier, steps may be taken to ensure that if pass-through debt certificates are not recognized as debt, the issuing trust will be classified as a partnership. As a partnership, the trust itself would not be subject to tax. Instead, the sponsor and certificate holders would be treated as partners and would be required to include in income their distributive shares of the income of the trust. It is likely that each certificate holder's share would approximately equal the interest income such holder would have reported had the certificates been classified as debt.[68] As a result, most U.S. investors would not be significantly affected if pass-through debt certificates were characterized as partnership interests.[69] However, as explained in the next three paragraphs, certificate holders that are non-U.S. persons, pension plans, or other tax-exempt organizations, and possibly certain financial institutions, may have a strong desire to avoid such a characterization.

First, if pass-through debt certificates are characterized as debt of the issuing trust, then certificates held by non-U.S. investors would ordinarily be free of U.S. withholding tax under the portfolio interest exemption (described in Chapter 10, Part B.2.). On the other hand, if the certificates were characterized as partnership interests, the tax treatment of a foreign certificate holder would depend on whether, based on an examination of the scope and nature of the trust's activities, the trust is considered to be engaged in a trade or business (as contrasted with mere investment

---

to perform. There is no statute comparable to a corporation law that limits the claims of equity holders in order to protect trust creditors. Also, the claim against a trust represented by a pass-through debt certificate typically is described as a right to a share of trust assets that varies with the assets so as to remain at a specified dollar level. Traditional equity interests entitle the holder to a fixed share of assets, not a fixed dollar amount. Although pass-through debt certificates typically are treated as ownership interests in determining the GAAP treatment of the sponsor, they may not be so treated for other nontax purposes (such as bank regulatory or bankruptcy purposes).

68 Distributions of interest that must be made without regard to the income of the trust would likely be treated as "guaranteed payments" subject to section 707(c). As such, they would be includible in income by certificate holders without regard to the income of the partnership, and would be deductible by the partnership in a manner similar to a partnership expense. Guaranteed payments that are deductible by the partnership under the partnership's method of accounting in any partnership taxable year would be includible in income by partners in their taxable years ending within or with such partnership taxable year. See section 706(a) and Treasury Regulation § 1.707-1(c). Almost certainly, the partnership would use the accrual method of accounting and would have a taxable year which is the calendar year. See sections 448(a)(2) (method of accounting) and 706(b) (taxable year).

69 The tax treatment would not, of course, be identical. For example, there would be differences in accounting for discount and premium. Some of the tax consequences for trust beneficiaries of classifying a trust as a partnership are discussed in the context of owner trusts in Chapter 7, Part C.

activities) within the United States. If the trust is considered to be engaged in a trade or business within the United States,[70] then the income of a foreign holder from the certificates would be considered to be effectively connected with a U.S. trade or business and would be taxed in substantially the same manner as if the investor were a U.S. person.[71] Furthermore, the trust would be subject to a withholding tax (which would be creditable against the foreign investor's tax obligation) equal to the foreign holder's allocable share of the trust's income that is effectively connected with the U.S. trade or business multiplied by the highest marginal income tax rate for individuals or corporations, as the case may be,[72] and if the holder is a corporation, income from the certificates that is withdrawn from the United States would be subject to a 30 percent branch profits tax (unless such tax is reduced or eliminated under a treaty).[73] Alternatively, if the trust is not considered to be engaged in a U.S. trade or business, the foreign holder might be subject to a 30 percent withholding tax (unless such tax is reduced or eliminated under a treaty) on its allocated share of the interest from the receivables held by the trust.[74] The exemption for portfolio interest would not generally apply to such interest because consumer receivables are not typically in "registered form."[75]

Pension plans, charitable organizations, individual retirement accounts, and certain other entities that are generally tax exempt are subject to tax under section 511 on their *unrelated business taxable income (UBTI)*.[76] Income from pass-through debt certificates would not be included in UBTI if the certificates were treated as debt of the issuing trust.[77] On the other hand, if income on pass-through debt certificates issued by a trust were characterized as a share of partnership income, then the status of such income as UBTI would depend on the character of the trust income allocated to the certificates.[78] Under a special rule enacted in 1987 that was

---

70   A trust that issues pass-through debt certificates is more likely to be considered to be engaged in a trade or business than an owner trust that issues pay-through bonds because the trustee for such a trust (including servicers acting on behalf of the trustee) typically has more power to manage trust assets than is granted to an owner trustee. See the discussion of owner trusts in Chapter 10, footnote 46.

71   See section 875 (foreign member of a partnership is considered to be engaged in a U.S. trade or business if the partnership is so engaged) and sections 871(b) and 882 (taxation of income effectively connected with a U.S. trade or business).

72   Section 1446; Revenue Procedure 89-31, 1989-1 C.B. 895 (provides guidance in applying section 1446, including procedures for establishing whether a partner is a non-U.S. person).

73   See section 884.

74   The statement in the text assumes that guaranteed payments (see footnote 68) would be treated as a share of partnership income for purposes of the withholding tax rules, although this result is not clear. See Treasury Regulation § 1.707–1(c). See Sheldon I. Banoff, "Guaranteed Payments for the Use of Capital: Schizophrenia In Subchapter K," *Taxes* (December 1992), 820 (discusses possible treatment of such payments as interest paid by the partnership, a share of partnership income, or a special category of ordinary income).

75   The rule discussed in Chapter 10, Part B.2., that allows pass-through certificates to be analyzed, in effect, as debt of the issuing trust for purposes of applying the portfolio interest definition would not literally apply because it is limited to interests in grantor trusts.

76   The tax on UBTI is discussed further in Chapter 9, Part B.

77   See sections 512(b)(1) and (5) (which exclude from UBTI interest and capital gains).

repealed in 1993, income from pass-through debt certificates was automatically includible in UBTI if the issuing trust was considered a publicly traded partnership.[79]

Finally, characterization of pass-through debt certificates as partnership interests could affect holders that are banks, or thrifts, or other financial institutions to which section 582(c) applies. That section provides that income from the sale of a "bond, debenture, note, or certificate or other evidence of indebtedness" by such an institution is always ordinary in character. It is not clear that the rule would apply to the certificates if they were partnership interests.[80] As a result of TRA 1986, long-term capital gains realized by corporations are no longer taxed at preferential rates, but capital losses continue to be deductible only as an offset to capital gains.

3. Application to Mortgages

Except as described in the next paragraph, the tax structure described in this Part G has not been widely used by trusts that hold real property mortgages (as opposed to automobile or credit card receivables), for several reasons. First, since the beginning of 1987, such a trust potentially could qualify as a REMIC. If the REMIC rules applied, the pass-through debt certificates would be considered regular interests in the REMIC. Thus, the principal tax objectives of sponsors of pass-through debt certificates (avoidance of a tax on the issuing trust and treatment of the certificates as debt) would be achieved with certainty under the REMIC rules. Second, if the REMIC rules did not apply, the risks that a sponsor would be required to assume (in terms of a mismatching between payments on the mortgages and on the certificates) in order to establish that pass-through debt certificates are economically debt of the issuing trust are likely to be more significant for mortgages than for other consumer receivables, because mortgages have longer maturities and, ordinarily, less predictable payment patterns. Third, the steps required to make available a partnership backup argument could represent an additional economic cost.[81] Finally, the availability of a partnership backup argument would be constrained by the TMP rules, which can be applied under an anti-avoidance rule to an entity that does not borrow but has outstanding equity classes resembling debt.[82]

---

78 See section 512(c)(1). To the extent the trust earns interest income, and the trust does not borrow, such income should not be includible in UBTI. See section 512(b)(1). The effect of the possible characterization of income as a guaranteed payment should be considered. See footnotes 68 and 74 above.

79 See section 512(c)(2), enacted by the Revenue Act of 1987 *(RA 1987)*, effective for partnership interests acquired after December 17, 1987. This rule was repealed by the RRA 1993, effective for partnership years beginning on or after January 1, 1994. A *publicly traded partnership* is defined in section 469(k)(2) as any partnership, if interests in such partnership are traded on an established securities market, or are readily tradable on a secondary market (or the substantial equivalent thereof). For guidance in determining if a partnership is publicly traded, see Notice 88-75, 1988-2 C.B. 386.

80 See Chapter 7, footnote 15 and Chapter 9, Part D. Further, while debt instruments are always securities for purposes of section 475 (mark-to-market rules for dealers in securities), interests in partnerships are treated as securities only if they are widely held or publicly traded, or can be characterized as evidences of an interest in debt instruments.

81 These steps are discussed in Chapter 3, Part C.2.c.(iii).

Despite these considerations, mortgage-backed securities resembling pass-through debt certificates have been issued recently in so-called "kitchen sink" transactions.[83] These transactions are unusual in that neither the REMIC rules nor the TMP rules apply. Typically, a trust acquires existing agency-backed interest-only and principal-only pass-through certificates or REMIC regular interests.[84] The trust issues two classes of beneficial ownership certificates, a senior floating rate class (F) that bears interest at a spread over an interest rate index (generally LIBOR), and a residual class (R). All cash is distributed on the F class until it is retired, after which distributions are made on the R class. Because of contingencies affecting payments of principal, the F class may not meet the definition of a REMIC regular interest.[85] For that reason, the trust does not make a REMIC election. The trust is structured, in much the same way as a trust issuing pass-through debt certificates, so that it is classified as a partnership rather than an association taxable as a corporation.[86] The trust is not a TMP because it does not have debt classes with multiple maturities.[87]

From an economic standpoint, the F class bears a strong resemblance to debt of the trust.[88] Nonetheless, the argument for overcoming the form of the F class as an ownership interest is somewhat weaker here than in typical transaction where pass-through debt certificates are issued, because the trust assets consist of a fixed pool of mortgage-backed securities, the timing of payments on the F class is tied to the timing of receipts on those assets, and the F class is subject to some risk of nonpayment because of factors other than mortgagor defaults. For that reason, the F certificates are typically sold on the basis that they will be characterized as partnership interests for tax purposes, but with disclosure that they may be recharacterized as debt.

---

82   See Chapter 3, Part D.2.g.

83   The term refers to the fact that the underlying mortgage-backed securities consist of "everything but the kitchen sink."

84   Because the assets are typically guaranteed by FHLMC or FNMA, there is virtually no risk of nonpayment because of mortgagor defaults.

85   The aggregate principal amount of the mortgage-backed securities held by the trust is ordinarily less than the principal amount of the F class, with the result that part of the F principal must be paid out of interest on those securities. The amount of interest available to pay F principal depends on the rate of mortgage prepayments and, in cases where interest on the securities held by the trust is based on an interest index, the value of the index. The REMIC regulations generally prohibit contingencies affecting the principal amount of a regular interest, subject to certain exceptions. The exceptions do not cover variations in an interest index or prepayment speeds (unless it can be demonstrated that the risk of nonpayment attributable to these factors is remote). See Chapter 5, Part D.1.

86   See Chapter 3, Part C.2.c.(iii).

87   This would be true even if the F class were treated as a debt class for purposes of applying the TMP definition. For a discussion of the possible recharacterization of an equity class under the TMP rules, see Chapter 3, Part D.2.g.

88   Debt treatment is suggested by the following: the floating rate of interest on the F class does not generally match the rate of interest on the assets, there is no correspondence between the principal and interest components of the F class and of the assets, and the F class has a right to receive all cash flow before any amount is paid to the R class.

Chapter 3

Classification of Non-REMIC Issuers

A. Introduction

A non-REMIC issuer of mortgage-backed securities may be classified for federal income tax purposes as a corporation, partnership, or trust, or as an agency or co-ownership arrangement. The choice can affect dramatically the taxation of the issuer and its owners. Indeed, perhaps the greatest tax-related fear in the mortgage-backed securities area is that an arrangement that is expected to qualify as a trust will instead be classified as a corporation and fall victim to the corporate income tax.

Apart from the TMP rules and rules governing publicly traded partnerships that are engaged in an active business (not including the holding of mortgages for investment),[1] the Code offers scant guidance in classifying entities.[2] Instead, the classification of an entity is determined primarily under the Treasury's entity classification regulations. These regulations are described generally in Part B of this chapter, and then applied to investment trusts (which are the most common type of non-REMIC issuer of mortgage-backed securities) in Part C. The TMP rules treat as corporations certain entities that hold mortgages and issue two or more classes of debt with different maturities, regardless of how they would be classified under the Treasury regulations. TMPs are discussed in Part D.

---

1   Section 7704, which was enacted by RA 1987, generally classifies publicly traded partnerships as corporations for tax purposes. (For the definition of *publicly traded partnership*, see Chapter 2, footnote 79.) However, section 7704 does not apply to a partnership if (1) more than 90% of its gross income is derived from passive sources, including interest and gain from the sale or disposition of debt instruments held as capital assets (other than interest or gain derived in a financial business) and (2) it is not registered under the Investment Company Act of 1940. The legislative history indicates that the exception for financial businesses was intended to apply to banks, insurance companies, and securities dealers and, by extension, to other similarly active businesses.

2   For corporations, section 7701(a)(3) states only that "[t]he term 'corporation' includes associations, joint-stock companies, and insurance companies," without defining *association* or *company*. A partnership is defined in section 7701(a)(2): "The term 'partnership' includes a syndicate, group, pool, joint venture, or other unincorporated organization, through or by means of which any business, financial operation, or venture is carried on, and which is not, within the meaning of this title, a trust or estate or a corporation. . . ."

B. Overview of Entity Classification Regulations

The entity classification regulations (Treasury Regulation §§ 301.7701–2 through 301.7701–4) classify entities based on their activities and the rights and obligations of their owners. Although local law will determine for an entity the nature of its permitted activities and the rights and obligations of its equity holders—thereby influencing the entity's classification under the regulations—the status of an entity under local law (such as the fact that it is called a trust and is governed by the state law relating to fiduciaries) is not generally controlling.[3]

The regulations identify six major characteristics of a "pure corporation" that, taken together, distinguish it from other organizations. These are:

- Associates,
- An objective to carry on business and divide the gains therefrom,
- Continuity of life,
- Centralization of management,
- Liability for corporate debts limited to corporate property, and
- Free transferability of interests.

An unincorporated organization is treated as a corporation if, taking account of these factors, it more closely resembles a corporation than a partnership or trust.[4] An unincorporated organization that is classified as a corporation for federal income tax purposes is referred to as an *association taxable as a corporation*, or *association* for short.

---

3   See Treasury Regulation § 301.7701–1(c). However, an organization formed as a domestic corporation may be automatically classified as a corporation, on the ground that the functional tests in the regulations apply only to "unincorporated organizations". See Treasury Regulation § 301.7701–2(a)(3); *O'Neill v. United States*, 410 F.2d 888 (6th Cir. 1969); *United States v. Empey*, 406 F.2d 157 (10th Cir. 1969); Revenue Ruling 70-101, 1970-1 C.B. 278; G.C.M. 37953 (May 14, 1979) and G.C.M. 37127 (May 18, 1977). This question would be relevant if, for example, the transferability of corporate shares were restricted and the shareholders assumed personal liability for corporate debts, as is allowed under some state corporation statutes. At present, an entity organized under foreign law is always considered an unincorporated organization for this purpose. See Revenue Ruling 88-8, 1988-1 C.B. 403. The earlier view was to the contrary. See G.C.M. 34376 (November 13, 1970); P.L.R. 8426031 (March 26, 1984). It is not clear why a distinction should be drawn between domestic and foreign organizations. The recent decision of the Service to classify domestic limited liability companies under the regulations (see footnote 4 below) may signal a loss of faith in *per se* classification approaches, although a limited liability company differs in some respects from a corporation (e.g., because it generally lacks continuity of life).

4   The regulations state that, in addition to the six major characteristics, in some cases, other factors may be found that are significant in classifying an organization. Nonetheless, most authorities applying the regulations focus primarily, if not exclusively, on the six major corporate characteristics. Cf. Revenue Ruling 79-106, 1979-1 C.B. 448 (lists a number of "minor" factors not given significance in classifying limited partnerships except insofar as they bear on the six major characteristics). At one point, the Service generally would not rule that an entity was a partnership if it had the corporate characteristic of limited liability. See Revenue Procedure 72-13, 1972-1 C.B. 735. This is no longer the case. See Announcement 88-118, I.R.B. 1988-37, 26, and Revenue Ruling 88-76, 1988-2 C.B. 360 (Wyoming limited liability company classified as a partnership).

Typically, the last four corporate characteristics just listed are also present in state law trusts, and thus are not relevant in distinguishing trusts from associations. A typical state law trust is classified as an association if and only if it has the two remaining corporate characteristics: associates and an objective to carry on business and divide the gains therefrom.[5] For convenience, these two characteristics will be referred to here collectively as a *business objective*. A trust that engages in an active business would be considered to have a business objective. Special standards apply in determining whether an investment trust (generally a trust holding investment assets on behalf of a group of investors) has a business objective.

A business objective is common to corporations and partnerships. Thus, it is not a factor in distinguishing between them. An organization that has a business objective is classified as an association if it has three or four of the remaining four corporate characteristics; otherwise, it is classified as a partnership (assuming it has more than one owner).[6]

The Service has issued guidelines for obtaining private letter rulings that an entity is a partnership. No similar guidelines have been issued for investment trusts.[7]

Although issuers of mortgage-backed securities generally have more than one owner, a state law trust may be used to hold mortgages even where there is only a single investor. The trust could be formed for various reasons: to make the investment more liquid by issuing to the investor transferable trust certificates; to protect the investor from personal liability for claims against the trust; or, where the trust issues debt or other nonequity securities to third parties, to protect them from a bankruptcy of the investor. The requirement of "associates" would not prevent a single-owner trust from being classified as an association if it carries on a business and has at least three of the last four corporate characteristics.[8] A single-owner trust that conducts business and has two or fewer of those characteristics cannot be a partnership (because a partnership requires two or more partners). Instead, the trust

---

5 See Treasury Regulation § 301.7701–2(a).

6 See Treasury Regulation § 301.7701–2(a).

7 The current partnership ruling guidelines are contained in Revenue Procedure 89-12, 1989-1 C.B. 798; Revenue Procedure 91-13, 1991-1 C.B. 477 (checklist for ruling requests); Revenue Procedure 92-33, 1992-1 C.B. 782 (transfers of "substantially all" interests); Revenue Procedure 92-35, 1992-1 C.B. 790 (continuity of life does not exist if remaining general partners or a majority in interest of limited partners can continue partnership after bankruptcy or retirement of general partner); Revenue Procedure 92-87, 1992-2 C.B. 496 (rulings not issued for limited partnerships formed under Uniform Limited Partnership Act (ULPA) that meet standards of Revenue Procedure 92-88); and Revenue Procedure 92-88, 1992-2 C.B. 496 (ruling guidelines for ULPA partnerships). Revenue Procedure 82-58, 1982-2 C.B. 847, amplified by Revenue Procedure 91-15, 1991-1 C.B. 484 (checklist for ruling requests), contains ruling guidelines for liquidating trusts (see Treasury Regulation § 301.7701-4(d)).

8 See *Hynes v. Comm'r*, 74 T.C. 1266 (1980); G.C.M. 38707 (May 1, 1981) (agreeing with result in *Hynes*, but indicating that "a one beneficiary trust should be classified as an association only when the facts of the case clearly warrant such treatment"). See also P.L.R. 8552010 (September 25, 1985) (trust with a single beneficiary was classified as an association because it possessed centralized management, continuity of life, and limited liability).

would be ignored (i.e., it would not be recognized to be an entity and its activities would be attributed to the owner).[9]

C. Classification of Investment Trusts

Most unincorporated issuers of mortgage-backed securities are either state law trusts, or similar contractual arrangements under which one person holds property on behalf of another, or property is owned jointly by more than one person. Because the analysis of such a contractual arrangement under the regulations would be substantially the same as the analysis of a state law trust, the term *trust* or *state law trust* will sometimes be used here to refer to both types of issuers.[10]

---

9   See G.C.M. 39395 (June 24, 1983); P.L.R. 8533003 (May 7, 1985). In P.L.R. 8852017 (September 27, 1988), the Service held that a single-beneficiary trust would be a partnership or corporation depending on whether the trust had the requisite number of corporate characteristics; apparently, the Service assumed that there would in the future be more than one beneficiary. See also footnote 10 below (discussing when a contractual arrangement is a state law trust).

10   If a contractual arrangement is not a state law trust, then one may ask whether it is any kind of organization at all. Not all contracts relating to the ownership of property create entities that have an independent status for tax purposes. For example, if a person holds property as a nominee or agent for one other person, and the arrangement is terminable at will by the principal, ordinarily no recognized organization would be considered to exist. On the other hand, contractual arrangements for issuing mortgage-backed securities typically are not terminable at will by any one person and have greater independence from the parties than a nominee or agency relationship. Cf. G.C.M. 34347 (September 14, 1970) ("The separation of control from beneficial ownership which is present in the instant case makes characterization of the mortgage pool as mere coownership by the certificate holders untenable.") Cf. Revenue Ruling 92-105, 1992-2 C.B. 204 (Illinois land trust created by one individual was not a trust or any other type of entity for federal income tax purposes, so that interests in the trust were not "trust certificates" that could not qualify for like kind exchange treatment under section 1031, where the beneficiary had the right to direct the trustee in dealing with the property, was entitled to all income or proceeds from the property, and was liable to pay any taxes and liabilities relating to the property); *Lewis & Co. v. Comm'r*, 301 U.S. 385 (1937) (trustee holding real property held to be an agent); Revenue Ruling 73-100, 1973-1 C.B. 613 (arrangement whereby taxpayer deposited securities with a security holder did not create a trust because taxpayer was recognized as the owner of the securities and retained the right to control the securities and receive the income thereon, although such rights could be forfeited); Revenue Ruling 70-567, 1970-2 C.B. 133 (custodian without ordinary fiduciary duties not a trust); Revenue Ruling 69-300, 1969-1 C.B. 167 (custodian of stock had sufficient fiduciary duties to be a trustee); and Treasury Regulation § 301.7701-7 (fiduciary distinguished from agent). The importance of determining whether an organization exists depends on how the organization would be classified if it did exist. In terms of substantive tax results, finding an organization to be present would matter in most cases not at all, some, or a great deal if the organization would be taxed as a grantor trust, partnership, or association, respectively. Moreover, if a contractual arrangement has characteristics that would cause it to be classified as a partnership or association if it were tested under the regulations, then it is very likely that an organization would be found to exist. For these reasons, whether an organization exists for tax purposes is normally subsumed in the question of how the organization would be classified under the regulations if it was assumed to exist. One circumstance where it may be important to know whether a grantor trust exists is where the trust is being used to convert mortgages into debt obligations in registered form that may qualify for the portfolio interest exemption in the hands of a foreign investor. See Chapter 10, footnotes 19 and 53. Also, trustees must file tax returns that mere agents need not file. See Chapter 11, footnote 44 and accompanying text.

As the foregoing discussion indicates, two questions must be asked in classifying a state law trust. The first is whether the trust has a business objective. If it does not, it will be recognized to be a trust. If the trust has such an objective, the next question is how many (if any) of the last four corporate characteristics it possesses. The discussion in the next two sections follows this approach, beginning with the business objective test.

1. Presence of a Business Objective

a. Family Trusts, Business Trusts, and Investment Trusts. In deciding whether a trust has a business objective, it will be helpful to distinguish between family trusts, business trusts, and investment trusts. As described below, a business trust always has a business objective, a family trust (as we are using the term) does not, and an investment trust may or may not have a business purpose depending on its activities and ownership structure. Virtually all trusts that issue mortgage-backed securities are investment trusts.

(i) Family trusts. In a typical family trust, one person (the grantor or settlor) transfers title to property to a trustee for the purpose of protecting or conserving it on behalf of beneficiaries other than the grantor. The beneficiaries receive their interest in the trust as a gift or as a result of a personal relationship with the grantor. They do not play any role in the formation or management of the trust.

A typical family trust that holds and manages property for investment does not have a business objective. Its beneficiaries are not "associates."[11] In addition, such a trust does not have "an objective to carry on business and divide the gains therefrom," provided that its permitted activities are confined to the protection and conservation of property, or, stated negatively, the trust is not used as a vehicle to conduct a profit-making business. In determining whether a family trust has a business objective, it makes no difference whether the interests of the beneficiaries are the same. Indeed, multiple interests (for example, income to one individual for life, with the remainder to another) are common.

(ii) Business trusts. A business trust is a trust that is not simply an arrangement to protect and conserve property but is instead a device to conduct a profit-making business that would ordinarily be carried on through a corporation or partnership.[12] A business trust may be organized by its beneficiaries or by a third party and have one or many ownership classes. As indicated above, a business trust always has a business objective, and thus is not classified as a trust. The mere fact that a trust is

---

11   Treasury Regulation § 301.7701–4(a). See also *Elm Street Realty Trust v. Comm'r*, 76 T.C. 803, 813 (1981) (extended discussion of whether trust beneficiaries are "associates"); see also *Estate of Bedell v. Comm'r*, 86 T.C. 1207 (1986).

12   Treasury Regulation § 301.7701-4(b).

organized under a business trust statute does not result in its treatment as a business trust for tax purposes if it is not used to carry on a business.[13] The possible treatment of trusts holding mortgages as business trusts is discussed in Part C.1.b, below.

(iii) Investment trusts. An investment trust is a trust that is formed to hold or manage investments on behalf of beneficiaries who contributed property to the trust, either directly or by purchasing interests in the trust from prior owners. An investment trust is similar to a family trust in that it simply protects and conserves property on behalf of its beneficiaries and does not conduct a business. The major difference is that the beneficiaries of an investment trust are not chosen by the grantor as the objects of his bounty, but are brought together as investors acting in their own interest for profit.

At one time, the Service took the extreme position that virtually all investment trusts should be classified as associations, apparently because they are organized for profit. However, this position was rejected by the courts, which generally held that investment trusts could qualify to be trusts if their assets were fixed.[14] The regulations now concede the basic point and permit an investment trust to be classified as a trust if it meets requirements relating to (1) the activities of the trust and (2) the nature of its ownership interests.[15] These requirements are described in Parts C.1.d–f, below. Although the standards for classifying investment trusts based on their activities have been established for years, the limitations on the structure of ownership interests were created partly in response to developments in the public mortgage markets and date only from 1984.

b. Trusts Holding Mortgages as Business Trusts. In virtually all cases, a trust holding a portfolio of mortgages need not fear classification as a business trust, because it is a passive vehicle for holding investment assets and does not conduct a business. A question could arise concerning the status of a trust as a business trust, however, where a trust acquires the real property underlying a mortgage, particularly where the property is commercial property that requires active management.

Any holder of a real estate mortgage that is not guaranteed by a third party must contemplate the possibility that it will end up acquiring the underlying collateral through a foreclosure proceeding (or voluntary conveyance) if the mortgagor

---

13 The Delaware Business Trust Act (Del. Code Ann., Title 12, Chap. 38) was amended in 1992 to make it clear that a "business trust" organized thereunder could be a passive vehicle that is not conducting any business. Section 3801(a) of the Act, as amended, includes the following: "A business trust may be organized to carry on any lawful business or activity . . . (including, without limitation, for the purpose of holding or otherwise taking title to property, whether in an active or custodial capacity)." Also, section 3809 recognizes that a business trust may be classified as a trust for federal income tax purposes.

14 The two principal cases are *Comm'r v. Chase Nat'l Bank,* 122 F.2d 540 (2d Cir. 1941) (fixed investment trust was not an association) and *Comm'r v. North American Bond Trust,* 122 F.2d 545 (2d Cir. 1941), *cert. denied,* 314 U.S. 701 (1942) (investment trust was an association where there was a power to vary the investment of certificate holders).

15 Treasury Regulation § 301.7701–4(c).

defaults. Although this result could be avoided by selling a defaulted loan or by allowing a third party to buy the collateral in a foreclosure proceeding, the mortgagee may be able to realize significantly more proceeds by acquiring the property and selling it after some reasonable period. A trust holding mortgages faces the same choices as other mortgagees, and thus will have a strong commercial desire to be able to acquire the mortgaged property following a default. Although the management of real property may in some circumstances be considered a business activity, in the normal case where a mortgagor default was not expected when a mortgage was acquired, the acquisition of real property by a trust following a default, and the holding and management of the property for a reasonable time pending sale, clearly would be consistent with the protection and conservation of the mortgage portfolio and would not be considered a business activity.[16] On the other hand, there could be some risk of finding a business activity if the trust held foreclosure property beyond a reasonable liquidation period, particularly if the trust actively managed or developed the property.[17] The length of that period would depend on the nature of the property and market conditions. The REMIC foreclosure property rules may provide a useful analogy, although they do not, of course, apply directly to non-REMIC trusts.[18]

Where mortgages are already in default (or default is likely) when they are transferred to a trust, and it is expected that the underlying property will be acquired by the trust, then it could be argued that the purpose of the trust is to manage and sell the underlying real estate and not to hold the mortgages for investment.[19]

---

16   See P.L.R. 8146064 (August 21, 1981) (trust recognized to be a trust where the trustee had the power to take title to property securing an obligation held by the trust and was required to sell such property in a commercially reasonable manner). The ability to hold property acquired on foreclosure is a typical feature of an investment trust holding secured loans, and it is interesting that it is not mentioned more often in the rulings addressing the classification of those trusts. Presumably the reason is that it is considered a normal incident of ownership of secured loans. A trust that holds and disposes of real property acquired on foreclosure of a mortgage is in somewhat the same position as a liquidating trust, which is treated as a trust for tax purposes because it is formed to liquidate particular assets and not to conduct an ongoing business. See Treasury Regulation § 301.7701-4(d). This regulation cautions that if a liquidation is unreasonably prolonged or the liquidation purpose becomes so obscured by business activities that the declared purpose of liquidation can be said to be abandoned, the trust will lose its status as a liquidating trust.

17   Although an owner of rental real estate is not ordinarily considered to be engaged in a business, the owner may be so engaged if, on a regular and continuous basis, he does anything more than collect rents and maintain and repair the property. See, e.g., Revenue Ruling 73-522, 1973-2 C.B. 226, and cases cited therein (dealing with when a non-U.S. investor holding real estate is engaged in a U.S. trade or business). See also Revenue Ruling 78-371, 1978-2 C.B. 344 (trust with broad powers to deal with real property is an association) and Revenue Ruling 79-77, 1979-1 C.B. 449 (trust holding a single piece of property subject to net lease classified as a trust).

18   These rules, which are described in Chapter 4, Part A.2.b.(iii), generally limit the period foreclosure property can be held to two years, although an extension of up to a total of six years can be granted by the Service. Another possible analogy is a liquidating trust which, under the current Service ruling guidelines, can have a term not exceeding three years. See footnote 7 above.

19   Compare the special REIT rule that excludes property acquired upon foreclosure of a mortgage from the definition of foreclosure property where the mortgage was in default when acquired by the REIT. See Chapter 4, text following footnote 255.

Whether this characterization is accurate, and whether the trust would have a business objective as a result, would depend on the facts of the particular case. The mere existence of a mortgage default does not necessarily mean that the trust will acquire the underlying property, because the intent may be to modify or sell the loan if the default is not cured and not to acquire the property.[20] If the defaulted mortgages represent only a minor portion of the entire loan portfolio (for example, because the trust acquires a seller's entire loan portfolio, including both nondefaulted and defaulted loans), then the possibility of acquiring real estate upon foreclosure of the defaulted loans should be regarded as incidental to the conservation of the whole portfolio rather than an independent business activity. Apart from the general tax authorities distinguishing business and investment activity, there is no guidance on these points.

c. Permitted Activities of Investment Trusts. A trust that is sufficiently passive to qualify as an investment trust may nonetheless be considered to have a business objective because its investments are not fixed. Specifically, section 301.7701-4(c)(1) of the Treasury regulations states that an investment trust will not be classified as a trust "if there is a power under the trust agreement to vary the investment of the certificate holders." This language has been applied in numerous authorities. It has been interpreted to preclude *any* power to reinvest trust assets that may be used to take advantage of market variations to improve the investment of certificate holders. On the other hand, a discretionary power to sell trust assets is allowed if the proceeds of such a sale may not be reinvested.[21] It makes no difference whether the power is exercisable by the trustee or by a third party, such as an investment advisor or trust sponsor.

---

20   If it is expected that a trust acquiring defaulted loans will modify a substantial number of loans and actively market them, an issue could also arise as to whether it is a dealer in mortgage loans. For the definition of a dealer, see Chapter 9, Part E.

21   Revenue Ruling 78-149, 1978-1 C.B. 448 ("The existence of a power to sell trust assets does not give rise to a power to vary the investment. Rather, it is the ability to substitute new investments, the power to reinvest, that requires an investment trust to be classified as an association."); Revenue Ruling 73-460, 1973-2 C.B. 424 (investment trust qualifies as a trust even though the trustee has the power to sell assets to redeem certificates). Apparently, a trustee's power to sell for profit is not a prohibited power. In P.L.R. 8137121 (June 19, 1981), the trust had the power to sell four different groups of investment grade diamonds in a specified order during four designated liquidation periods lasting one year, and was required to distribute the sales proceeds to the certificate holders or use them to pay expenses. Upon notice from the transaction agent that a different group could be sold for more than the group scheduled to be sold, however, the trustee could sell that group in place of the scheduled group. In addition, although the trustee was obligated to sell the group for the highest bid in excess of a determined minimum price, if it did not receive such a bid, it could postpone the sale until the next liquidation period. See also P.L.R. 8331065 (May 2, 1983) (upon a vote of certificate holders representing a majority of units, trustee could sell royalties in such manner as it deemed in the best interest of the unit holders); T.A.M. 8412003 (May 19, 1982) (trustee had power "to sell at any time and from time to time all or any part of royalties for cash in such a manner as it deems in the best interests of the unit holders"); T.A.M. 8223015 (February 26, 1982) (same).

The power-to-vary test focuses on the ultimate investment of certificate holders in the trust. A power to vary investments held by a trust would also presumably be a power to vary an investment in the trust. The investment of certificate holders could also be altered by contributing new investment assets to the trust that are not identical to the existing assets. Any action that affects one group of certificate holders at the expense of another might also be viewed as a power to vary.[22] The effect of liabilities on the power-to-vary test is discussed in Parts C.1.c.(x) and (xi), below, dealing with borrowings and financial derivatives.

The no-power-to-vary requirement does not, of course, mean that the returns on investments must be fixed. For example, an investment trust can hold a debt instrument that pays interest at a floating rate. This conclusion can be justified on the ground that the relevant investment incorporates the floating rate feature, so that the investment is not changed, or on the ground that any changes occur automatically and not through the exercise of investment discretion.

The balance of this discussion of the power-to-vary test is divided into 11 parts, dealing with (1) the existence of a "power," (2) the requirement that the power be under the "trust agreement," (3) the ability to acquire assets after formation of a trust, (4) temporary reinvestments, (5) modifications of, and distributions on, trust investments, (6) partnership interests and loan participations, (7) reserve funds inside the trust, (8) nondiscretionary reinvestments, (9) the effect of certificate holder approval of a reinvestment, (10) the incurrence of liabilities, and (11) participation in swaps and other financial derivatives.

(i) Existence of a "power." In determining whether a power to vary investments is present, a sharp distinction must be drawn between the existence of such a power and its actual use. All powers granted under the relevant trust agreement are taken into account, whether or not they are actually used or expected to be used, and whether or not their use is contingent on the occurrence of events outside of the trust's control.[23] This principle clearly does not mean that ambiguous or unclear language in a trust agreement must be interpreted in favor of finding a power to vary, but only that a power to vary that does in fact exist under the relevant contracts, properly construed, cannot be ignored because it will or may not be used.

The need to take account of all powers that are granted regardless of their practical significance places a premium on careful drafting. Many trust agreements for investment trusts that are intended to be classified as trusts for tax purposes include a statement expressing that intent and providing that the agreement should be construed to further that intent. Such a provision could provide a basis, under the contract, for negating the effect of a provision that would create a power to vary and

---

22   The ability to discriminate among classes of certificate holders is limited by the Sears regulations discussed in Part C.1.d. below.

23   *Helvering v. Coleman-Gilbert Associates*, 296 U.S. 369 (1935). See also Revenue Ruling 78-149, 1978-1 C.B. 448 (a right to replace bonds called by the issuer prior to maturity with other similar bonds is a power to vary); G.C.M. 37067 (March 28, 1977) (same).

is not significant in the administration of the trust. Obviously, it would be better not to be the first to put this argument to the test.

(ii) Power under "trust agreement." The regulations refer to a power to vary investments "under the trust agreement". While there seems to be no authority construing this phrase, it can safely be assumed that the "trust agreement" would extend to any document under which a person may act as agent of, or for the benefit of, the trust or certificate holders, regardless of how it is labelled. For example, a management agreement relating to trust investments, an asset purchase and sale agreement, or a subscription agreement for trust certificates, are all potential candidates.

On the other hand, the trust agreement language may be useful in limiting the powers affecting trust investments that need to be taken into account in classifying a trust. For example, if a trust holds a security, and under the terms of the security the issuer has a right to alter its economic terms, one reason (among others) for concluding that the right is not a power to vary is that it does not arise under the trust agreement. For further discussion of issuer or other third party rights to modify investments, see Parts C.1.b(v) and (vi) below.

(iii) Assets acquired after formation. In a case where a trust beneficiary is entitled to a pro rata share of each trust asset, the investment of the beneficiaries can be varied not only by reinvesting trust assets, but also by contributing new assets to the trust that are not identical to those it already has. Indeed, in the seminal case that articulated the power-to-vary standard, such a power existed because the sponsor of the trust reserved the right to make such contributions.[24] On the other hand, a power to contribute additional assets that are identical to those already held is not a power to vary.[25]

In recognition of the fact that it may take time to fund an investment trust, the Service has allowed some latitude in identifying or changing investments during a startup period. Thus, proceeds of the issuance of pass-through certificates by a trust can be used by the trustee to acquire mortgages not specifically identified on the issue date;[26] for a short period following the creation of a trust, the trust sponsor can

---

24   *Comm'r v. North American Bond Trust,* 122 F.2d 545 (2d Cir. 1941), *cert. denied,* 314 U.S. 701 (1942).

25   *Comm'r v. Chase National Bank of City of New York,* 122 F. 2d 540 (2d Cir. 1941) (no power to vary the investments found where depositor could make up additional units of the same number and type of stock as originally deposited); P.L.R. 9329014 (April 23, 1993) (same); P.L.R. 8940067 (July 12, 1989) (sponsor permitted from time to time to deposit additional gold bullion and coins in return for additional trust units; intention was that a portfolio's gold per unit or net asset value per unit would not change by reason of the additional deposit); P.L.R. 8907045 (November 23, 1988), supplemented by P.L.R. 8915035 (January 13, 1989) (established trust permitted, apparently without time limit, to sell new certificates to investors if the money raised is used to purchase stock identical in mix to the stock held by the trust); and P.L.R. 8105055 (November 14, 1980) (no power to vary the investments found where trustee had power to subdivide each trust unit into three units without diluting the holders' beneficial interest in the trust property).

transfer additional securities (similar, but not identical, to those originally deposited) in exchange for additional certificates to sell to new investors, even though, as discussed above, such transfers would alter the investment of prior certificate holders;[27] and a trust that receives upon formation a contract to purchase bonds "when issued" within 90 days of formation of the trust can substitute within a short period new bonds of a similar type for bonds not delivered under the contract.[28]

(iv) Temporary reinvestments. Although the power-to-vary test generally prohibits reinvestments, a trust can temporarily reinvest payments received on investments pending distribution as long as the temporary investments are in high-quality debt instruments that mature no later than the anticipated distribution date and are held to maturity.[29] Although there are no certain guidelines in the area, an investment should be considered temporary if the period is needed to bridge the gap between the timing of distributions on investments and on trust certificates (i.e., addresses an administrative timing problem) and is not longer than seven months.[30] In any event, barring unusual circumstances, a period longer than thirteen months is unlikely to be considered temporary.[31] The types of high-quality instruments in which funds may be invested should include U.S. government securities, bank

---

26   Revenue Ruling 75-192, 1975-1 C.B. 384 (no specific time given by which mortgages must be purchased, although the period was probably short). See also G.C.M. 38456 (July 25, 1980) which discusses whether an investment trust can originate loans (rather than purchase existing loans) with monies deposited in trust: "[W]e see no basis for imposing an absolute limit on the amount of activity that the trustee of a fixed investment trust may undertake in initially placing the funds held in trust. The regulations and the case law restrict the ability of the trustee to vary the investments of the trust, but do not focus on the initial investment activity."

27   Revenue Ruling 89-124, 1989-2 C.B. 262; P.L.R. 8918026 (February 2, 1989) (additional investors permitted for four months); P.L.R. 8931056 (May 10, 1989) (during 90-day period following creation of trust, if securities necessary to maintain the same mix of securities originally deposited are unavailable, sponsor could deposit cash or a letter of credit to be used to acquire such securities when they become available, securities identical to other securities originally deposited or replacement securities (i.e., securities of the same type as securities originally deposited); a replacement security must have, among other characteristics, a maturity or disposition date substantially the same as, a yield and current return equivalent to, and a rating at least equal to, the security of original issue that it replaces).

28   Revenue Ruling 86-92, 1986-2 C.B. 214; P.L.R. 9329014 (April 23, 1993); P.L.R. 8707007 (October 31, 1986).

29   Revenue Ruling 75-192, 1975-1 C.B. 384 (monthly mortgage payments could be invested until quarterly distribution dates in obligations of or guaranteed by the United States, or any agency or instrumentality thereof, and certificates of deposit of any bank or trust company having a minimum stated surplus and capital, and held to maturity); G.C.M. 36132 (January 8, 1975) (temporary investments allowed if purpose is to prevent funds from being nonproductive and not to take advantage of market fluctuations). The ability to invest funds temporarily should extend to any monies received by a trust that are available to be distributed (including, for example, the proceeds of sale of trust assets). See, e.g., P.L.R. 9319028 (February 11, 1993) (refers to the temporary investment of proceeds of sale of stock).

30   See P.L.R. 8311007 (September 9, 1982) (Revenue Ruling 75-192 applied to fixed investment trust that provided for semiannual distributions); P.L.R. 8905011 (October 28, 1988) (same).

31   In an analogous setting, temporary investments are allowed by REMICs for a period not exceeding 13 months. See Chapter 4, Part A.2.b.(i) (definition of cash flow investment).

deposits, bankers' acceptances, highly-rated commercial paper, repurchase agreements relating to high-quality debt instruments, and money market funds.[32] The purpose of the requirement that debt instruments be held to maturity is to prevent a trust from earning trading gains. Thus, it should not prevent a trust from holding interests in money market funds that have no maturity date but maintain a constant per share value.[33] Some trusts allow a mortgage servicer with a high credit rating to keep payments received on mortgages, and to invest those payments for its own account, until the funds are needed to make distributions. Such an arrangement could be viewed as a temporary reinvestment of funds in a short-term note of the servicer. Since the note would be of high quality and would mature before the next trust distribution date, the arrangement should fall within the authorities governing temporary reinvestments.

(v) Modifications of and distributions on trust investments. If the trustee of a trust uses the cash proceeds from one investment to acquire another in lieu of distributing the cash to certificate holders, it is easy to see that trust assets have been reinvested. The line between reinvestment and conservation and protection of assets is not so easily drawn where an investment is modified, or otherwise transformed into different property (or arguably different property), without the receipt of cash (or the right to receive cash) by the trust.

For purposes of discussion, it will be helpful to distinguish five cases: (1) the trust has no discretion to approve or disapprove of a modification; (2) the trust has discretion to approve or disapprove of a modification, but no discretion to set the terms of the modified investment, and the investment will be impaired if the modification is not approved; (3) same as (2) except that the trust can participate in setting the terms of the modified investment; (4) the trust has discretion to approve or disapprove of a modified investment but does not participate in setting its terms, and there would be no impairment if the modification is not approved; and finally (5) the trust has discretion to approve or disapprove of the modification and to set its terms and there would be no impairment of the investment if the modification is not made. As discussed below, it seems that no power to vary would be involved in cases (1) through (3), such a power would exist in case (5), and case (4) is in between. Needless to say, many factual variations are possible, and it will not always be easy to determine into which of these categories a transaction will fall. For example, whether an investment will be impaired if it is not modified will not always be obvious.

---

32   See T.A.M. 8412003 (May 19, 1982) (government securities, certificates of deposit, and sale-repurchase agreements); P.L.R. 8907045 (November 23, 1988), supplemented by P.L.R. 8915035 (January 13, 1989) (government securities); P.L.R. 8321033 (February 17, 1983) (investment in "money-market funds with total assets of $50,000,000 or more" allowed). In a case where a trust holds investments denominated in a foreign currency, debt instruments denominated in that currency that are the highest quality available should qualify as permitted temporary investments even though they are not as highly rated as U.S. government debt.

33   See G.C.M. 36132 (January 8, 1975) (discusses purpose of maturity limitation); footnote 32.

A modification of an investment may or may not be treated as a taxable exchange of a new investment for an old one. The substantive tax consequences of a change in the terms of an investment would not seem to have much significance in resolving the trust classification issue, because those consequences do not hinge on the existence of a discretionary power to vary investments.[34]

No discretion. The easiest case to address is one where an investment is changed according to its terms without the exercise of any discretionary rights by the trust. Involuntary changes of this type would occur, for example, if the issuer of a debt obligation exercises a right to exchange it for another security, if a debt obligation is exchanged for another security by operation of law (e.g., debt issued by company A is exchanged for debt of company B following a merger of A into B), or if an in-kind distribution is made on an investment (for example, interest is paid on a bond in the form of other bonds). Because there is no discretionary reinvestment in these circumstances, the trust should have no obligation to dispose of any new property it is considered to receive.[35]

Discretion to approve or disapprove and impairment. A second case is one where the trust can approve or disapprove of a change in an investment but any action taken by the trust is intended to preserve the value of an existing investment that may otherwise be impaired. The most obvious example is foreclosing on a mortgage and acquiring the underlying collateral. Although this action changes the trust's economic position, the action is taken to preserve the value of the original investment.[36] The Service has ruled that a trust can accept an offer by a debtor to

---

34 As discussed in Chapter 4, Part C.2., a change in the economic terms of a debt instrument is generally treated under section 1001 as an exchange of a new instrument for an old one if the change is (1) a modification (i.e., is not made in accordance with the terms of the instrument) and (2) is significant. Despite the difference in standards, a modification that is not a taxable event under section 1001 on the ground that it is not significant is unlikely to be treated as a "variation" in an investment for purposes of the power-to-vary test.

35 See *Comm'r v. Chase National Bank of City of New York*, 41 B.T.A. 430 (1940), *aff'd*, 122 F.2d 540 (2d Cir. 1941). In *Chase*, no power to vary investments was found, although the trustee was required (1) to retain shares of stock received as stock dividends or as distributions in the course of a change in the corporate structure of the issuer, a merger, consolidation, or action taken by a protective committee for the shareholders' interests, to surrender shares of stock pursuant to a plan for change in the corporate structure of an issuer, its merger, or reorganization, and (2) to follow the majority of common shareholders with respect to action proposed by any such protective committee. See also P.L.R. 9329014 (April 23, 1993) (no power to vary found where trustee had power, unless instructed otherwise by depositor, to retain securities received as a result of an exchange or substitution of securities, or a merger, spin-off, split-up, or other reorganization, where the trustee was required to reject offers to issue new securities or to exchange securities for securities held by the trust and must vote securities in the same proportion as other holders); P.L.R. 8221142 (March 1, 1982) (no power to vary found where trustee had the power (1) on the instructions of the depositor, to accept an offer by the issuer of any security to accept a new security in exchange and substitution for the security held by the trust or to accept a tender offer for a security and (2) in the absence of instructions from the depositor, in the case of stock dividends or stock splits, to accept new securities; the powers allowed in (1) are surprisingly broad).

36 P.L.R. 8146064 (August 21, 1981) (no power to vary found where trust holding pool of real estate contracts and mortgages could acquire title to property securing a contract or mortgage and was required to dispose of the property in a commercially reasonable manner). Although it is also true

exchange old debt for new debt of the debtor (or more generally, to modify the terms of outstanding debt) where the debtor is in default or default will probably occur in the foreseeable future.[37] Similarly, a trustee can consent to a substitution of new mortgages for defective mortgages that did not conform to representations and warranties made upon transfer of the mortgages in trust during an initial period following the date of the transfer.[38] The Service has also ruled that a trustee may consent to changes in the credit support of a bond if necessary to preserve the credit rating of the bond.[39]

Outside of the default setting, it may not always be easy to apply an impairment standard. For example, suppose that a trust holds 10 percent of an issue of widely held mortgage bonds. The issuer of the bonds asks the holders for their consent (which requires a 2/3 approval) to a change in financial covenants and offers to pay a fee to those who consent (but not to other holders). If the trust were certain that consent would not be granted without its affirmative vote, then the bonds would not be impaired (through the waiver) if the trust refuses the offer. On the other hand, if the trust believes that the consent would be given regardless of its vote, then the bonds would be impaired with no compensation if it votes no. To complicate the question further, suppose that the waiver of the covenant would allow the issuer to build a new building next to the one that secures the bonds and that that project would potentially increase the value of the collateral for the bonds.

Discretion to modify with impairment. If an investment is impaired, the trust should be allowed to take any action needed to preserve its value, even if that includes not simply approving or disapproving of a modification, but also negotiating the terms of any workout or exchange.[40]

Discretion to approve or disapprove without impairment. A trust could be given a power to approve or disapprove of a change in an investment in circum-

---

that a default would be an event that is outside of the control of the trust, that fact alone would not be enough to prevent the existence of a power to vary. See footnote 23 above.

37   Revenue Ruling 73-460, 1973-2 C.B. 424. Although this ruling refers to an offer by an obligor of obligations to issue new obligations in exchange therefor pursuant to a plan for the refunding or refinancing of such obligations, the same result should be reached where the obligor offers to exchange obligations of other issuers (or other investment property) in satisfaction of its debt. Such an exchange would seem to be analogous to accepting a voluntary transfer of collateral securing a mortgage. The mere fact that the property transferred was not collateral for the extinguished debt should be irrelevant. In each case, the trust's motive for accepting the property would be a desire to maximize the value of property received in satisfaction of a defaulted loan.

38   Revenue Ruling 71-399, 1971-2 C.B. 433 (substitution permitted for a period of two years).

39   Revenue Ruling 90-63, 1990-2 C.B. 270 (any increase in value of the bonds would be incidental to maintaining the value of trust property; thus, the increase would not be the result of trading in securities and thereby profiting from market fluctuations); P.L.R. 8707007 (October 31, 1986).

40   Revenue Ruling 73-460, discussed above in footnote 37, does not state whether the trust negotiated the terms of the debt exchange, and should not be limited to cases where the trust is a passive participant. Similarly, a trust that acquires mortgaged property following a mortgage default (see footnote 36 above) would in almost all cases need to exercise some discretion managing the property for the period it is held by the trust. A factual question would arise as to when the activities of the trust extend beyond preservation of assets to the conduct of an independent, profit-making activity. Cf. footnote 16 above.

stances where the trust has no ability to negotiate the terms of the modified investment and the original investment would not be impaired if the change is not made. For example, a trust might hold a security that is convertible at the holder's option into another security, or might hold a debt instrument that allows the holder to choose among alternative mechanisms for setting interest rates.[41] Another example would be an offer made to a class of security holders, including the trust, to exchange securities for other securities.[42] It is not clear whether a power to vary would exist in these circumstances. One argument against finding a power is that the trust's choices are sufficiently confined so that it cannot take advantage of variations in the market. Also, where the trustee's power exists under the terms of an investment, it can be said that the "investment" has not changed even though its economic features have been varied.[43]

A recent ruling outside of the mortgage area held that a trust did not have a power to vary because it was able to vote stock that it held in a corporation for or against a plan to merge that corporation with a second corporation and could accept stock or securities of the second corporation (with or without cash) in exchange for the shares already owned if the plan was consummated. The ruling noted that the trust had no power to determine the consideration to be received in the merger because the terms of the exchange were negotiated by the parties without the input of the trustee.[44] One difference between the merger case and an offer to exchange securities is that the merger either will or will not happen based on the vote of all stockholders, whereas an exchange by the trust pursuant to an offer will only occur if the trust consents.

In a case where a trust holds investments that allow the holder to change their economic terms, a concern over the effect of such a term on the power-to-vary test might be allayed by requiring the trust to change or not change the economic terms based on a formula. See *Nondiscretionary reinvestments* below.

Discretion to modify and no impairment. A power of the trust to modify the material terms of an investment, or to exchange it for other property, where the trustee negotiates the terms of the modification or exchange, and the investment is

---

41 An argument could be made that a convertible security will be impaired if a conversion option is not exercised when it makes clear economic sense to do so, on the ground that part of the cost of a convertible security is allocable to the conversion feature and that amount will be effectively forfeited if the option cannot be exercised. There appear to be no authorities applying the power-to-vary test to convertible securities. In P.L.R. 8221142 (March 1, 1982), the trust agreement for a trust holding convertible securities prohibited exercise of the conversion rights.

42 In P.L.R. 8221142 (March 1, 1982) an investment trust was classified as a trust where the depositor had the right to direct the trust to accept an offer by the issuer of any security to accept a new security in exchange and substitution for the security or to accept a tender offer for a security held by the trust. This ruling is more liberal than other authorities. See footnote 35 above.

43 A change in a debt instrument made in accordance with its terms generally is not treated as a modification of the instrument for purposes of section 1001. See Chapter 4, Part C.2. There seems to be no authority discussing whether the same principle would be applied to the power-to-vary test.

44 P.L.R. 9319028 (February 11, 1993).

not impaired, should be treated as a power to vary. Such an exchange or modification is practically equivalent to a sale for cash and a reinvestment.

(vi) Partnership interests and loan participations. A trust may hold a partnership interest. Ordinarily, a member of a partnership (including a limited partner) is treated as engaging in any trade or business in which the partnership is engaged.[45] Does a parallel rule apply to attribute to a trust the business purpose, or power to vary investments, of any partnership in which it invests?

The answer should be "no" in a case where the trust is a limited partner and has no right to manage partnership affairs, and the Service has so held.[46] This conclusion is supported by the arguments that (1) the trust's "investment" is the limited partnership interest itself which is not varied, and (2) any powers to vary investments or engage in business at the partnership level do not arise under the trust agreement. On the other hand, partnership activities are likely to be attributed to a trust that is a general partner, because of the management role played by a general partner. Whether attributing partnership activities to a trust would actually affect the tax status of the trust would depend, of course, on the permitted activities of the partnership.[47]

Somewhat similar issues arise where a trust invests in a participation interest in a loan and the terms of the loan can be varied by the other participants without the consent of the trust.[48] Since the other participants would be acting in their own interests and not on behalf of the trust, a strong argument can be made that any power to alter the loan in this fashion would not be attributed to the trust.

(vii) Inside reserve funds. An investment trust may wish to hold, and invest, trust assets in a reserve fund. Such a fund could be used to pay expenses, or to

---

45   See, e.g., sections 512(c)(1) and 875.

46   In G.C.M. 38201 (December 14, 1979), the Service held that where a trust holds a limited partnership interest as a passive investment, analogous to an investment in corporate stock, and the trustee's activities are limited to protecting and conserving the trust's investment in the limited partnership, then there is no basis for attributing the partnership's activities to the trust. In P.L.R. 8210049 (December 9, 1981), the Service followed the rationale of G.C.M. 38201 in classifying a trust, all of the assets of which consisted of limited partnership interests in a partnership formed for the purpose of investing in oil and gas operations, as a trust. Cf. P.L.R. 9041014 (July 11, 1990) (trust holding limited partnership interests for beneficiaries in separate revocable accounts classified as a trust because it did not have an objective to carry on business and divide the gains therefrom).

47   In several private letter rulings, the Service has attributed the activities of a partnership to a trust that was the general partner of the partnership and owned close to 100% of the total interests in the partnership. The trusts were not found to have a power to vary, however, because of the limitations imposed on the activities of the partnerships. See P.L.R. 8632025 (May 12, 1986); P.L.R. 8626030 (March 26, 1986); and P.L.R. 8113068 (December 31, 1980).

48   For example, suppose that a trust owns a 10% interest in a loan and that the participants have the right, with a two-thirds vote, to approve any change in the loan that does not involve a decrease or delay in the payments that are due. In these circumstances, the other participants could agree, for example, to waive a financial covenant in exchange for a material increase in the rate of interest payable on the loan.

guarantee the performance of trust assets by, for example, making up for cash flow shortfalls attributable to mortgage defaults or delinquencies. A number of rulings classify investment trusts holding reserves of the first type as trusts.[49] The authorities on credit reserves are more limited.[50]

Although the law in this area is not a shining beacon, it should be possible for an investment trust to invest and reinvest assets held in either type of reserve fund without creating a power to vary if the investments are subject to the same constraints that apply to temporary investments (see Part C.1.c.(iv) above) and if the reserve fund is not excessive.[51] Two grounds supporting this view are that (1) the purpose of the reserve would be not to earn a return on investment but instead to protect the remaining investments, and (2) the permitted fund investments would not give the trust berth to take advantage of market variations. A limited power to reinvest assets held in a credit reserve fund would be consistent with the policy allowing trustees greater freedom to manage trust assets to present credit losses.[52]

Where the unused balance of a reserve fund is not distributed pro rata to all certificate holders, but is instead paid to the sponsor, to fewer than all certificate holders or to a third party, an additional issue arises as to whether the existence of a claim to reserve fund assets may cause the trust to run afoul of the Sears regulations (discussed below) governing multiple class trusts.[53]

To avoid the power-to-vary and multiple class trust issues, credit reserve funds that benefit investment trusts are often held outside of the trust and are used to

---

49   See, e.g., Revenue Ruling 90-7, 1990-1 C.B. 153 (reserve for administrative expenses); Revenue Ruling 73-460, 1973-2 C.B. 424 (reserve for any applicable taxes or other governmental charges). Neither ruling describes the reserve fund assets. See also P.L.R. 8636052 (June 10, 1986) (trust classified as a trust where trustee had power to invest cash reserve for payment of liabilities in interest-bearing accounts or certificates of deposit with a maturity date prior to the next distribution date); P.L.R. 8331065 (May 2, 1983) (same).

50   G.C.M. 38311 (March 18, 1980) held that an investment trust that had senior and subordinated interests did not have a power to vary the investment of certificate holders by reason of its power to invest reserve fund monies in short-term, high-quality debt instruments. The G.C.M. cites *Royalty Participation Trust v. Comm'r*, 20 T.C. 464 (1953), *acq.* 1953-2 C.B. 6, which allowed an investment trust holding oil and gas royalty interests to set aside 5% of the income of the trust to acquire new properties on the ground that the reinvestment feature was a limited power to offset the effects of depletion. G.C.M. 38311 was revoked by G.C.M. 39040 (September 27, 1983), but the revocation appears to have been based primarily on concern over the multiple class nature of the trust in G.C.M. 38311. See footnote 67 below.

51   In this regard, the size of a credit reserve fund should reflect the size and credit quality of the mortgage pool, and should decline as the size of the pool declines. Although not, of course, directly relevant, REMICs, which in terms of their permitted activities were modeled after grantor trusts, can maintain reserve funds to protect against credit defaults or delinquencies or to pay expenses, provided the reserve fund assets are not actively traded and the fund is reasonable in size. See Chapter 4, Part A.2.b.(ii).

52   See Revenue Ruling 73-460, 1973-2 C.B. 424 (power to accept new debt instrument in workout setting) and Revenue Ruling 90-63, 1990-2 C.B. 270 (power to consent to changes in credit support of bonds to preserve their credit rating), discussed above in the text at footnotes 37 and 39, respectively.

53   See footnote 84 below.

support a limited recourse guarantee. The entity classification issues raised by out-side reserve funds are discussed in more detail below.[54]

(viii) Nondiscretionary reinvestments. Suppose that trust assets can be openly reinvested, but the reinvestments are specified in advance. For example, imagine that a trust holds mortgages that are subject to prepayment. In order to insulate investors from the effects of prepayments, on the closing date of the trust, the trust enters into a guaranteed investment contract with an insurance company that re-quires all prepayments to be reinvested with the insurance company at a predeter-mined rate for the remaining term of the prepaid mortgages. Are such reinvestments prohibited by the power-to-vary test?

Although there is no clear authority on point, the answer should be "no". A power to vary investments, as it is described in Service rulings, is "one whereby the trustee, or some other person, has some kind of managerial power over the trusteed funds that enables him to take advantage of variations in the market to improve the investment of all the beneficiaries."[55] An automatic reinvestment plan of this type involves no managerial power and is unaffected by market variations. Indeed, the reinvestment may impair the investment of certificate holders if the reinvestment rate turns out to be less than a current market rate.

The example above should be contrasted with the facts of a 1978 ruling where a trustee for an investment trust holding a portfolio of municipal bonds rated "me-dium grade" had a right to reinvest prepayments received on bonds that were prepaid, within 20 days after receiving such funds, in other newly issued municipal bonds of the same grade, maturing no later than the last maturity date of the bonds originally deposited in the trust.[56] The ruling concluded that the reinvestment power was a managerial power that allowed the trust to take advantage of variations in the market, because the trustee could take advantage of differences in the prices and credit quality of the bonds that met the reinvestment criteria.[57] In the example just discussed, there is no discretion of any kind to choose new investments.

(ix) Certificateholder approval. If a trust has a power to reinvest cash rather than distributing it to investors, but each reinvestment requires the specific approval of certificate holders, does the approval requirement prevent the trust from having a power to vary?

The approval requirement should allay any concerns over the reinvestment if each and every investor that has an interest in the new investment has approved the investment and thereby waived its right to the cash distribution. Under those cir-cumstances, the arrangement is equivalent to the making of a cash distribution to all investors and the use of that cash by those approving the reinvestment to make a

---

54   See Part C.2.c.(iv).

55   Revenue Ruling 75-192, 1975-1 C.B. 384; Revenue Ruling 78-149, 1978-1 C.B. 448.

56   Revenue Ruling 78-149, 1978-1 C.B. 448.

57   See G.C.M. 37067 (March 28, 1977), which relates to Revenue Ruling 78-149.

new investment.[58] On the other hand, if fewer than all of the certificate holders can approve of the reinvestment and bind those that object, the Service could argue that a power to vary exists, because some investors can exercise managerial discretion on the part of others.[59]

(x) Incurrence of debt. It may be desirable to use an investment trust to create a leveraged investment by having the trust issue debt instruments that are recognized to be debt for tax purposes.[60] There appears to be no authority analyzing directly the effect of debt issuances of this type on the status of an investment trust.[61]

The incurrence of debt should not be considered a business activity that prevents a trust from qualifying as an "investment trust." Borrowing is a common adjunct of investment.[62]

---

58   Cf. Revenue Ruling 81-238, 1981-2 C.B. 248 (no power to vary exists when certificate holders may elect to have their trust distributions reinvested in a new fixed investment trust pursuant to an automatic reinvestment plan); G.C.M. 38652 (March 6, 1981) (discusses Revenue Ruling 81-238).

59   A requirement of less than unanimous approval by certificate holders of reinvestments by an investment trust may be relevant in determining whether the trust will be classified as an association if it is found to have a business purpose, because the requirement could defeat the corporate characteristic of centralized management. There seems to be no direct link, however, between the power-to-vary test and the existence of centralized management. The centralized management factor is discussed below in Part C.2.a.(ii).

60   If the debt were treated as an ownership interest in the trust or in trust assets, then an issue would arise as to whether the trust has multiple classes of ownership interests and thus must contend with the Sears regulations discussed below. The discussion in this section assumes that the debt is recognized to be debt for tax purposes.

61   Owner trusts that issue debt and are considered to have a business objective are discussed in Part C.2.c.(i) below. In addition to the types of trust borrowings discussed in the text, investment trusts often borrow for liquidity reasons. For example, a mortgage servicer may be obligated to advance payments that are due and not yet received from mortgagors. While such advances could be viewed as purchases of interests in the defaulted loans rather than as loans to the trust, the loan characterization is more accurate in a case where the advance is payable out of all trust assets, particularly if the advance is interest bearing. Cf. P.L.R. 9018053 (February 6, 1990) (surety's right to be reimbursed by a trustee after a claim is made under a policy guaranteeing receipt by the certificate holders of principal and interest did not create a power to vary because the policy could not change; surety's reimbursement right would not constitute an interest in the trust). Advances in a default setting could be distinguished from other borrowings on the ground that they relate directly to the preservation of assets. One ruling involving a leveraged trust investment is P.L.R. 8747084 (August 31, 1987). In this ruling, a trust that issued two classes of certificates of beneficial interest and one or two classes of bonds was classified as an association because the multiple classes of beneficial interest violated the Sears regulations. The authors understand that the two classes of certificates were created deliberately to achieve association status. The ruling makes no mention of the possible effect of the bonds on trust classification. At one time, the Service had a policy against issuing rulings on the tax status of owner trusts in leveraged lease transactions, but the issues troubling the Service most likely related to the leasing activity and not the mere incurrence of debt. See Revenue Procedure 89-3, 1989-1 C.B. 761, section 5.27. In Revenue Ruling 78-371, 1978-2 C.B. 344, a trust having broad powers to deal with real property, including a power to borrow, was classified as an association, but the right to borrow was only one of a number of powers taken into account.

62   See, e.g., *Continental Trading, Inc. v. Comm'r*, 265 F.2d 40 (9th Cir. 1959) (borrowing activities within the U.S. by a foreign corporation did not give rise to a U.S. trade or business); section 163(d) (denies a deduction for investment interest expense in excess of investment income); P.L.R. 7601220630A (January 22, 1976) recognizes that a family trust may borrow funds or mortgage

Where a trust is the obligor under a loan, the power of the trustee to modify the terms of that loan or to refinance it with another lender may have as great an effect on the distributions made to certificate holders as modifying the terms of an investment or selling one investment and reinvesting the proceeds. A question arises whether such a power is a power to vary the investment of the certificate holders. Phrased differently, is the investment of the certificate holders that cannot be varied only their indirect ownership of investment assets, or instead, their right to distributions on the certificates they hold? The authorities discussing the power-to-vary test uniformly focus on the power to vary the certificate holders' indirect ownership of assets. The explanation, however, may be simply that borrowings have not been at issue. Until the point is resolved, caution should be exercised in granting a trust discretion to alter the terms of debt if it is critical that the trust lack a business objective.

If the power-to-vary test does take account of borrowings, then the principles governing investment assets, described above, should be relevant in determining if such a power exists in a particular case. For example, the right of a trust borrower to switch between different interest rate modes would seem to create a power to vary if and to the extent a similar right to switch the rates payable on debt instruments held by a trust would create such a power.[63] On the other hand, if debt is in place when a trust is formed and there is no discretionary power to change the terms of the debt to take advantage of market variations, then the debt should not give rise to a prohibited power. Where a trust has a power to sell trust assets, and is required under the terms of a borrowing to use all or a portion of the proceeds to repay debt, the early repayment would seem to be incidental to the sale. The economic life of the trust is shorter because of the sale and repayment, but no new investment is involved.

Hopefully, as interest in leveraged investment trusts grows, authorities addressing these points will arise.

(xi) Swaps and other derivatives. It may be possible to improve investment returns by using an investment trust to combine a pool of fixed investments with a notional principal contract or other derivative financial instrument. For example, a portfolio of floating rate mortgages could be paired with an interest rate swap that requires payment of a series of payments at a floating rate in exchange for a series of fixed payments. The swap would effectively convert the interest payments on the mortgages to a fixed rate.

The discussion in the last section of trusts incurring debt would be relevent for trusts entering into derivative financial instruments to the extent they represent liabilities of the trust. However, many derivative instruments may change their status as assets or liabilities over time as market conditions change. It seems unlikely that contracts of this type would receive better treatment than investment

---

trust property and qualify as a trust.
63   See Part C.1.c.(v).

assets in applying the power-to-vary test. At any rate, entering into a derivative instrument should not convert a trust into a business trust, and should create a power to vary only if there is a discretionary power to alter the terms of the instrument.[64]

Two special aspects of swaps are worth mentioning. First, although swaps typically provide for the exchange of two streams of level periodic payments, a swap can be structured with significant non-periodic payments. For substantive tax purposes, swaps of this type are likely to be treated as a notional principal contract combined with an embedded loan.[65] For example, the making of a significant non-periodic payment by a trust in exchange for future payments from the counterparty would be viewed as a loan to the counterparty. It would seem that the same analysis should apply in determining if there is a power to vary. However, as discussed in Part C.1.c.(viii) above, a reinvestment that is contractually required and does not involve any element of discretion should not result in a power to vary, so the existence of an embedded loan or borrowing in that context should not matter.

Notional principal contracts may have "option" components. An option as typically understood involves a choice whether or not to exercise the option, so it may be asked whether such features imply the existence of a power to vary. The answer is that it depends on the specific terms of the agreement. If the option feature means that the trustee can make choices between alternatives that affect the return of investors, then a power to vary most likely would exist if a similar right relating to an investment asset would create such a power. On the other hand, if the option feature does not involve any choices but means only that the returns under the agreement are one-sided (i.e., the trust makes money if the market moves in one direction but is not exposed to a corresponding loss if the market moves in the other direction), then the option feature should not be troublesome.

Lastly, if a swap terminates prematurely, a trust could receive a termination payment from the counterparty. A power to use such a payment to pay a premium on a replacement swap entered into with another counterparty on market terms would seem to involve a power to vary.[66]

d. Multiple Ownership Classes—Overview. The entity classification regulations were amended in the mid-1980s to prohibit, with a limited exception, the issuance by investment trusts of more than one class of ownership interests. The amendments were proposed by the Service in 1984 and finalized in 1986.[67] Because the amendments

---

64   An example in the REMIC regulations assumes that an investment trust can hold REMIC regular interests and an interest rate cap agreement, but the cap in the example is a pure asset requiring no future payments by the trust. See Treasury Regulation § 1.860G-2(i)(2), Example.

65   See Treasury Regulation § 1.446-3(g)(4).

66   Cf. Revenue Ruling 78-149, 1978-1 C.B. 448 (a right to replace bonds called by the issuer prior to maturity with other similar bonds is a power to vary). If the termination results from a default of the counterparty, then greater flexibility might be allowed. Cf. footnote 37 above (which refers to a ruling approving a default related modification of a debt obligation, without a change in obligors).

67   See T.D. 8080, 1986–1 C.B. 371, and LR–68–84, 1984–1 C.B. 777. The amendments apply to arrangements, any interest in which is initially issued after April 27, 1984. The proposed regula-

were directed in part at a trust sponsored by Sears Mortgage Securities Corporation that issued "fast-pay" and "slow-pay" certificates, they are universally, if unofficially, known as the *Sears regulations.*

The Sears regulations state that if an investment trust that otherwise would be classified as a trust (based on its activities) has multiple classes of ownership interests, then it will ordinarily be classified as a partnership or association, not as a trust. However, this general rule does not apply if "the trust is formed to facilitate direct investment in the assets of the trust and the existence of multiple classes of ownership interests is incidental to that purpose." The exception for "incidental" multiple classes is applied in three examples in the regulations, which are discussed below.

Two general comments on the effect and reach of the regulations are in order. First, a multiple class trust that does not benefit from the "incidental" exception is not necessarily classified as an association. Instead, such a trust is treated, in effect, as if it had a business objective. Accordingly, it is actually classified as an association only if it has at least three of the last four major corporate characteristics listed in Part B of this chapter. This refinement is small comfort for conventional pass-through trusts, because they typically possess a majority of those remaining characteristics, but for certain other trusts (described below in Part C.2.), it is the reason for their deliverance from the corporate tax. Second, the Sears regulations apply only when a trust has two or more classes of *ownership* interests. Thus, a trust that has a single class of equity and one or more classes of debt would not come within their reach.[68] The treatment of claims against a trust as ownership interests is discussed further below in Part C.1.g.

The Sears regulations do not apply to lease financing transactions in which a trust owns and leases property and issues different classes of certificates backed by lease payments that are treated as different classes of debt of the lessee for tax

---

tions applied to "arrangements" and not merely to "trusts." The change in wording does not appear to be significant. See footnote 10, above. The first shot fired in the battle against multiple class trusts was the announcement in Revenue Procedure 83–52, 1983–2 C.B. 569, of a policy of not ruling on the classification of multiple class fixed investment trusts. Previously such rulings had been issued. See P.L.R.s 8223085 (March 12, 1982), 8208102 (November 20, 1981) and 8110142 (December 12, 1980). See also G.C.M. 38311 (March 18, 1980), which approved the classification as a trust of an investment trust with senior and subordinated ownership interests. G.C.M. 38311 was revoked by G.C.M. 39040 (September 27, 1983) on the ground that the status of multiple class trusts was under study by the Service.

68   Although the regulations do not define the phrase *multiple classes of ownership interests,* any difference in the terms of ownership interests would potentially create multiple classes. However, differences that are not economically significant are perhaps more likely to fall within the exception for "incidental" multiple classes. The existence of a right of individual holders of pass-through certificates to require redemption of those certificates by the issuing trust should not be considered to create multiple ownership classes, even though the right is exercised by some holders but not others, provided the right extends to all holders. Cf. Revenue Ruling 90–7, 1990–1 C.B. 153 (trust with redeemable certificates treated as a trust) and Revenue Ruling 73–460, 1973–2 C.B. 424 (same). Compare the discussion in Part D.2.b, below, of whether an entity has debt with two or more maturities for purposes of the TMP definition.

purposes (and should not apply, more broadly, to any trust arrangement that is viewed as a security device for issuing debt).[69]

The dimensions of the exception for "incidental" multiple classes are far from clear. The explanation of the exception in the Treasury Decision that adopted the final Sears regulations,[70] while helpful, is too vague to be definitive in applying the exception in concrete cases:

> Whether the existence of multiple classes of ownership interests is incidental to the use of an investment trust as a vehicle to facilitate direct investment, or instead reflects a purpose to provide investors with diverse interests in the trust assets, generally depends on the extent to which the investment attributes of interests in the trust diverge from direct ownership of the trust assets. The extent of such divergence may, in turn, be reflected by the extent to which the interests of the investors in a multiple class trust could be reproduced without resort to multiple classes of ownership. For example, the creation of a subordinated and preferred class of interests in a trust holding real estate mortgages may be incidental to the purpose of the trust to facilitate direct investment in the mortgages, where the subordinated interest is retained as a security device by the originator of the mortgages, and is in lieu of a direct guarantee to investors. The final regulations provide additional examples of the classification of investment trusts with multiple classes of ownership interests. Further guidance as to the application of the new standard will be provided through the administrative rulings process.

Three examples in the regulations[71] apply the "incidental" standard to trusts that hold debt securities.

Example 1 is based on the original Sears transaction. In the example, a trust holds a pool of residential mortgages and issues two classes of certificates. Mortgage principal payments, both scheduled and prepaid, are made entirely on one class until that class has been retired and then entirely on the second class. The purpose of the arrangement is to provide the holders of the later maturing class with "call protection." Thus, according to the example, the trust creates interests in the mortgages that differ significantly from direct investments in the mortgages. As a consequence, the existence of multiple classes is not incidental to any purpose of the trust to facilitate direct investment.

In Example 2, a trust issues two classes of certificates to the sponsor of the trust in exchange for a pool of residential mortgages originated by the sponsor. The two classes are identical, except that one class is subordinated to the other in the event of a default on the underlying mortgages. The sponsor of the trust sells the senior class and retains the subordinated class. The trust has multiple classes of ownership interests. However, the interests of the certificate holders are substantially equivalent to (1) undivided interests in the pool of mortgages, coupled with (2) a limited recourse guarantee running from the sponsor, as holder of the subordinated class, to

---

69   See T.D. 8080, 1986-1 C.B. 371 (preamble to final Sears Regulations), *citing* I.R.-84-63, 1984-24 I.R.B. 29 (May 17, 1984). For examples of trusts treated as security devices, see Revenue Ruling 76-265, 1976-2 C.B. 448, and Revenue Ruling 61-181, 1961-2 C.B. 21. Cf. Revenue Ruling 85-42, 1985-1 C.B. 36 (in substance defeasance a nontaxable pledge of collateral).

70   T.D. 8080, 1986–1 C.B. 371.

71   See Treasury Regulation § 301.7701–4(c)(2).

the holders of the senior class. In such circumstances, the existence of multiple classes is considered incidental to the trust purpose of facilitating direct investment in the mortgages.

Finally, in Example 4, a trust holds a portfolio of bonds and issues certificates evidencing interests in the bonds. Each certificate represents the right to receive a particular payment on a specific bond. The example states that under section 1286 of the Code (discussed in detail in Chapter 6), stripped coupons and stripped bonds are treated as separate bonds for federal income tax purposes.[72] Although the trust has multiple classes, the multiple classes simply provide each certificate holder with a direct interest in what is treated under section 1286 as a separate bond. Given the similarity of the interests acquired by the certificate holders to the interests that could be acquired by direct investment, the multiple classes of trust interests merely facilitate direct investment in the assets held by the trust.[73]

Example 2 is the authority supporting the trust classification of a non-REMIC trust that has senior and subordinated classes of pass-through certificates. (See Chapter 2, Part B.3 for a discussion of these types of certificates.) The example states that the sponsor of the trust retains the subordinated certificates, but this fact is not critical. After initially adopting a contrary view,[74] the Service has ruled that subordinated certificates created under the authority of Example 2 can be freely transferred.[75] The holding of the example is based partly on the similarity of the arrangement to a single class trust coupled with a guarantee. The example does not describe the terms for repaying to the subordinated class amounts that are diverted to the senior class because of mortgagor defaults, but any repayment schedule that does not accelerate payments on the senior class or subordinated class beyond what they would be if no default had occurred should be allowed.[76]

---

72   In fact, section 1286(a) treats stripped coupons and stripped bonds as separate bonds for purposes of the original issue discount and market discount rules of the Code (part V of subchapter P, sections 1271 through 1288), but not for purposes of other Code provisions, including the entity classification rules under section 7701. As suggested below, the true relevance of section 1286 appears to be that it supplies a body of substantive tax rules that make it easy to tax investors as owners of trust property under the grantor trust rules.

73   The last example in the regulations, Example 3, deals with a trust that holds stock and issues two classes of certificates. One class of certificates represents the right to dividends on the underlying stock and the right to the value of such stock up to a specific amount. The other class represents the right to appreciation in the stock above that amount. The example states that the multiple classes of interest are intended to fulfill varying investment objectives by allowing a separation of dividend income from capital appreciation, and that the trust is not formed to facilitate direct investment in the stock. It should be noted that there is no counterpart to section 1286 that applies generally to partial ownership interests in stock (although RRA 1993 added a new section 305(e) dealing with the principal components of stripped preferred stock).

74   See P.L.R. 8929030 (April 21, 1989) (sale of a subordinated interest in a trust holding motor vehicle installment sales contracts would take the trust outside of Example 2).

75   Revenue Ruling 92-32, 1992-1 C.B. 776; P.L.R. 9244036 (August 30, 1992) (same, except that transfers were limited and rights and obligations under an outside reserve fund were transferred along with the subordinated trust interest).

76   Compare the rule described in Chapter 4, text following footnote 190, for the reimbursement of amounts paid to a REMIC under a credit enhancement contract.

Example 4 in the regulations is the authority for allowing the creation of multiple ownership classes that qualify as stripped bonds or stripped coupons within the meaning of section 1286. Because Example 4 specifically references section 1286, interpretations of that section that enlarge its scope should cause a corresponding expansion of the exception for "incidental" ownership classes.

It should be possible to combine the principles of Examples 2 and 4 to create non-pro rata senior and subordinated ownership interests in a trust. One example of such an arrangement would be a trust that holds mortgages bearing interest at a 12 percent rate and that issues (1) a subordinated class of certificates representing the right to 10 percent of mortgage principal and 10/12 of the interest thereon, and (2) two senior parity classes representing the right to 2/12 of all interest, and 90 percent of the principal and 10/12 of the interest thereon, respectively.

e. Reasons for Sears Regulations. The description of the Sears regulations in the preceding section leaves two related questions unanswered: why were the regulations adopted and what is the purpose of the exception for "incidental" multiple ownership classes? While it is difficult to answer these questions confidently based on the regulations and their accompanying official explanation, the regulations appear to be concerned more with the practical issue of taxation of investors than with the abstract question of whether a multiple class trust more closely resembles a traditional business organization (corporation or partnership) or a trust.

If a multiple class trust were classified as a trust, then the beneficiaries would be taxable under the grantor trust rules. Those rules essentially ignore the trust and treat beneficiaries as if they were owners of partial interests in trust assets. The purpose of the regulations and the exception appears to be to ensure that holders of interests in a multiple class trust are taxed under the grantor trust rules only where their interests in the trust are similar to direct interests in property for which there are established tax rules.[77] Obviously, this condition is more likely to be met when each investor has a specified interest in each item of trust property that does not change over time.

The importance of certainty in taxing investors is suggested by comparing Example 1 in the regulations, in which a trust did not qualify under the "incidental" exception, with Examples 2 and 4, in which the exception was held to apply. As

---

77   Concern over the proper taxation of investors was expressed in the Treasury Decision that adopted the final Sears regulations (T.D. 8080, 1986-1 C.B. 371):

Multiple class trusts depart from the traditional form of fixed investment trust in that the interests of the beneficiaries are not undivided, but diverse. The existence of varied beneficial interests may indicate that the trust is not employed simply to hold investment assets, but serves a significant additional purpose of providing investors with economic and legal interests that could not be acquired through direct investment in the trust assets. Such use of an investment trust introduces the potential for complex allocations of trust income among investors, with correspondingly difficult issues of how such income is to be allocated for tax purposes. These issues are properly foreign to the taxation of trust income, where rules have not developed to accommodate the varied forms of commercial investment, and no comprehensive economic substance requirement governs the allocation of income for tax purposes.

discussed below, the first example poses difficult issues in measuring the income tax effects of shifting interests in trust assets that are not present in the other two.

These examples also establish that the "incidental" exception is not limited to multiple class trusts in which the differences between classes are "incidental" (that is, of secondary importance) to the economic objectives of the trust. If the exception were so limited, Examples 2 and 4 would have the same outcomes as Example 1. Thus, some other framework for analysis of the exception—we suggest certainty in taxing investors under the grantor trust rules—must be found.

In Example 1, a trust holds residential mortgages that are subject to prepayment at any time and issues "fast-pay" and "slow-pay" classes of certificates. Because of the possibility of prepayments and the payment priorities of the classes, it is not possible to identify either class with particular payments of principal or interest on the mortgages held by the trust. To see why, suppose first that none of the mortgages prepays. Under that assumption, the class with the earlier maturity would receive the first principal payments on *each* of the mortgages held by the trust until that class is fully retired, and the later maturing class would be entitled to all subsequent principal payments. (Interest on the mortgages would be allocated with the related principal.) On the other hand, if mortgages are in fact prepaid, the prepaid principal would be directed exclusively to the earlier maturing class until it is retired. Thus, by comparison with the allocation of principal that would be made if the mortgages did not prepay, the earlier maturing class would receive a greater interest in the mortgages that prepay and, in return, the later maturing class would receive a greater interest in the mortgages that remain.

Because the certificates in Example 1 do not evidence fixed interests in any specified property of the trust, it is unclear how the grantor trust rules would be applied to the certificate holders if the trust were classified as a trust. Presumably, it would be necessary to apply those rules in steps. The first step would be to identify rights to payments on each mortgage with each of the two classes of certificates, assuming no mortgage prepayments.[78] Then, when prepayments occur, the holder of each certificate would be treated as if that holder exchanged the rights to payments initially identified with that certificate for rights to payments on other mortgages.[79] These exchanges would occur in each month in which more than one class is outstanding and mortgage principal is prepaid. Moreover, each monthly exchange would have to take into account all prior exchanges in determining the payment rights that are relinquished by each certificate holder. Devising a system of rules to

---

78   Although it often would be more realistic to assume some positive level of prepayments, such an assumption would be valid only for a pool of mortgages, not for purposes of identifying each certificate with interests in any individual mortgage.

79   One analogy is the treatment of a single class trust that issues redeemable certificates. If the trust sells an item of property to redeem certificates of any holder, the remaining holders are treated as if they had sold their shares of such property and used their shares of the proceeds to purchase from the holder of the redeemed certificates that holder's preredemption interest in each of the remaining assets of the trust. However, giving effect to an exchange of interests in trust property would be far more complex in a trust that has multiple classes.

account for a succession of mortgage payment swaps may be thought to stretch the grantor trust rules beyond recognition.[80]

Example 2 is similar to Example 1 in that the payments on the underlying mortgages that are identified with the senior and subordinated classes of certificates may shift over time. In particular, if a mortgage defaults or becomes delinquent, the senior holders exchange their interest in the defaulted or delinquent payments for a corresponding interest in nondefaulted mortgages or mortgage payments previously allocated to the subordinated holders. However, Example 2 avoids the need for a new system of tax rules to account for these shifts by analyzing the arrangement as (1) a single class trust in which all certificate holders have pro rata interests, coupled with (2) a guarantee written outside of the trust by the subordinated holders in favor of the senior holders. The ability to account for shifts in interest under rules governing guarantees made it easier to apply the grantor trust rules. That being said, the Service has not spelled out the substantive tax rules governing senior/subordinated arrangements, and the guarantee approach is itself somewhat complex.[81]

In Example 4, each class of certificates is at all times identified with the same, specific payments on the underlying bonds. Thus, unlike Examples 1 and 2, the interest of certificate holders in trust assets does not shift over time, and the certificates represent more conventional, partial ownership interests in trust assets. Nonetheless, in concluding that the "incidental" exception applies, the example relies on the fact that section 1286 applies to certificate holders. Thus, the example places some weight on the existence of a body of established rules for taxing partial ownership interests in debt instruments.[82]

---

80 One way to tax investors that is mechanically straightforward would be to ignore individual payments on the underlying mortgages and treat each class of certificates as if it were a class of pay-through bonds issued by the trust. However, such an approach, by treating certificates as a debt security of the trust rather than an ownership interest in trust assets, would be fundamentally at odds with grantor trust principles. Moreover, the approach might be objectionable to the Service because it would allow phantom income to disappear. Phantom income is discussed in Chapter 7, Part E, and in Appendix A. To state the point differently, taxing pass-through certificates as debt of the trust would be tantamount to taxing the trust as a REMIC in which all pass-through certificates qualify as regular interests, the residual interest has no economic value, and the tax on the income allocated to the residual interest is waived.

81 See Chapter 2, Part B.3. Another factor that may have contributed to the difference in outcomes in Examples 1 and 2 is that the event that causes the shifting of interests between different classes in Example 2 is a mortgagor default. While the analogy is far from perfect, trustees have been allowed greater latitude in managing assets of a trust to prevent credit losses. See footnotes 37 and 39 and accompanying text above.

82 This line of reasoning was even more apparent in the proposed Sears regulations, which included an exception for "mere custodial arrangements formed to allow investors to own specifically identifiable stripped coupons or stripped bonds within the meaning of section 1232B [the predecessor of section 1286]." The preamble to the proposed regulations (LR-68–84, 1984–1 C.B. 777, 779) offers the following explanation of the exception:

In section 1232B of the Code, Congress has provided a method for taxing transactions involving..."stripped bonds" and "stripped coupons." Thus, it would be inconsistent with section 1232B to treat typical "coupon stripping" arrangements in which bonds are held by a custodian and interests in specifically identifiable stripped coupons or bonds are sold as either associations or partnerships.

The importance of section 1286 to the outcome in Example 4 is also suggested by comparing it

The logic of Example 4 should extend to any case in which a trust owns multiple properties and issues different classes of certificates, each representing an interest in discrete items of property. Functionally, such an arrangement would be equivalent to a series of separate, single class trusts.[83] The principles of Example 2 and 4 can be combined, by creating classes of ownership interests in a trust that represent interests in separate items of trust property, and then subordinating one class to another in the event of delinquencies or defaults.[84] The subordination feature would be tantamount to a nonrecourse guarantee and should be allowed on that basis. Indeed, the guarantee analysis is more compelling than in Example 2, because unlike Example 2, the different classes relate to distinct properties.

f. Further Applications of "Incidental" Exception. Although the examples in the Sears regulations are helpful, it is not difficult to imagine multiple class ownership arrangements that do not fall squarely within any of them. How does one decide whether the "incidental" exception will apply to such an arrangement?

In view of Example 4, the existence of multiple ownership interests in one or more loans will pose a problem only if the allocation between classes of the right to each payment of principal or interest on each loan can change at some time over the life of the arrangement. Two types of varying ownership interests can be imagined: first, arrangements in which shifts in interests in different loans in a pool are made between classes based on the performance of the pool (illustrated by Examples 1 and 2 in the regulations), and second, arrangements in which changes in interests are confined to reallocations of rights to payments on individual loans.[85] The "incidental" exception is far more likely to apply to the second type of arrangement than the first, for two related reasons.

---

with Example 3. In general terms, Example 3 involves an allocation between different classes of investors of rights to identified payments (including rights to appreciation) on stock. The unfavorable outcome in Example 3 could be explained by the fact that, with the exception of the limited rule in section 305(e) for the principal component of stripped preferred stock (which was added to the Code by RRA 1993), there is no section comparable to section 1286 governing the tax treatment of holders of partial non-pro rata interests in stock.

83   By way of analogy, there is considerable law in the mutual fund area addressing whether a single legal entity that is divided into separate funds should be treated for tax purposes as a single corporation or a series of separate corporations. Prior to the enactment of section 851(h) by TRA 1986, which generally recognizes the separate existence of series funds, the answer depended on whether the legal entity was a corporation or a trust. Individual funds within a trust were recognized; funds within a corporation were not. For the treatment of trusts, see G.C.M. 39211 (January 13, 1984); *National Securities Series v. Comm'r*, 13 T.C. 884 (1949). Corporations are addressed in Revenue Ruling 56-246, 1956-1 C.B. 316; *Union Trusteed Funds, Inc. v. Comm'r*, 8 T.C. 1133 (1947). Compare also the TMP portion rule described in Part D.2.d, below.

84   One example of such an arrangement would be a trust that has an inside reserve fund that is owned by the sponsor and is used to provide credit support for mortgages held by the trust, where the sponsor's only ownership interest in the trust is its subordinated interest in the reserve fund. The use of reserve funds in investment trusts is discussed further in Part C.1.c.(vii).

85   This second type of arrangement may exist even if many loans are held together in a pool. The key distinction from the first type of arrangement is that the interests of different classes in one loan are not affected by the performance of other loans.

One reason is that it is unlikely that interests that can shift between different loans in a pool of loans can be duplicated without resort to multiple classes.[86] By contrast, it would always be possible, in theory at least, to duplicate changing partial interests in a single debt obligation by having the borrower exchange the obligation for a bundle of separate securities that mimic those interests. Thus, each partial interest in the debt obligation can be viewed conceptually as one class of ownership interests in a single item of property (the related separate security), in the same manner that the rights to each payment of interest and principal in Example 4 in the regulations were considered interests in a separate bond.[87]

A second reason why shifting multiple ownership interests are more likely to be considered "incidental" if the shifts are limited to reallocations of rights to payments on individual loans is that the practical opportunities for constructing interests that depart significantly from recognized direct ownership interests in property are much fewer if the shifts are so confined.

With this background, we now consider three specific examples of multiple classes of ownership interests in individual loans that differ in some respects from conventional stripped bonds or coupons of the type described in Example 4. The examples involve synthetic floating rate interests, payments of principal and interest on a noncallable bond that are reallocated between investors following a default, and serialized sinking fund payments on a term bond. Although the last two transaction patterns are not likely to be directly relevant to mortgage-backed securities, they are discussed here because of the light they may shed on the scope of the "incidental" exception.

(i) Synthetic floating rate interests. Consider a trust that holds a pool of adjustable rate mortgages. The "incidental" exception would clearly apply if the trust issued one class of certificates representing the right to all principal payments and another class representing the right to all interest payments. Such a separation of payments would represent a classic stripping transaction, and would fall within Example 4. Further, it does not require much of a leap to extend Example 4 to an arrangement in which interest payments on a floating rate loan are divided between (1) a right to all interest due on the loan up to a fixed number of basis points, plus a right to a fixed percentage of all remaining interest due on the loan,[88] and (2) a right to all interest due in excess of the interest described in (1).[89]

---

86 The excerpt from the preamble to the Sears regulations quoted in footnote 77 states that the ability to reproduce investor interests without resort to multiple classes is relevant in determining whether the "incidental" exception applies.

87 Compare the treatment of a trust that issues certificates treated as separate classes of debt discussed above at footnote 69.

88 One (but not both) of the fixed number of basis points, or the fixed percentage, referred to in clause (1) could of course be zero.

89 Interests of the type described in the text (an allocation of a fixed number of basis points of interest to one person with the remainder to another) are often created in practice as a result of the reclassification of "excess servicing" as an ownership interest in the mortgages. The excess servicing would almost always be less than the minimum amount of interest payable on the mortgages,

Floating rate interests in a loan can also be created *synthetically* by changing the allocation of fixed interest payments between investors. For example, suppose that two ownership interests are created in a fixed rate loan. One represents the right to all principal on the loan, plus interest thereon, based on an index of market interest rates but capped at the fixed rate of interest on the loan. The second ownership interest represents the right to all remaining interest. Such an arrangement is factually quite different from the transactions described in the preceding paragraph because the changes in the amounts of interest received by the two investors are attributable entirely to the allocation formula and not to fluctuations in the interest paid on the loan.

A less extreme but more common example of a synthetic floating rate strip may arise where an allocation of interest payments on a floating rate loan is capped at an artificially high level. To illustrate, suppose that an adjustable rate mortgage pays interest at an indexed rate, subject to a cap of 11 percent. All principal on the mortgage, plus interest at the indexed rate minus 100 basis points, subject to a cap of 11 percent, is allocated to one investor (call him A). The remaining interest is allocated to a second investor B. Under this arrangement, B is entitled to a constant 100 basis points of interest, provided the indexed rate does not exceed 11 percent. However, as that rate increases above 11 percent, interest on the loan is shifted from B to A, notwithstanding that interest on the underlying loan is fixed at 11 percent. Interest allocated to B would be eliminated when the indexed rate reaches 12 percent.[90]

Substantial arguments can be made in favor of extending the "incidental" exception to synthetic floating rate interests of the type described in the two preceding paragraphs. Under current law, "authentic" floating rate strips can be created by stripping floating rate loans. Thus, it is not implausible to view a synthetic floating rate strip as a single interest in a separate item of property (in terms of the discussion at the beginning of this section, a separate security that might have been issued by an issuer on its own). More significantly, if authentic floating rate strips are taxable under the stripped bond rules, and they have the same economic features as synthetic floating rate strips, then the same substantive tax rules could be applied to holders of the synthetic strips. If synthetic strips were treated as stripped bonds or

---

so that the same percentage of principal would be paid monthly as excess servicing regardless of the floating rate of interest on the loans. However, once it is accepted that interest on a floating rate loan can qualify as "stripped coupons" even though the interest can vary in amount based on changes in the amounts due on the loan, there should be no bar to allocating a fixed number of basis points of interest to one person, with the remainder to another, where that fixed number is higher than the minimum interest payable on the loan. The effect on trust classification of recharacterizing excess servicing as an ownership interest is discussed below in footnotes 99–101 and accompanying text.

90   It may be possible to avoid the problem of varying ownership interests in this example, without changing A's economic position, by giving B's interest to the servicer as a fee, provided that the total fee received by the servicer represents reasonable compensation for the services performed and is not in part a disguised ownership interest. See footnotes 99–101 and accompanying text. The additional servicing fee would have to be paid to the servicer in its capacity as servicer, and therefore should be assigned in connection with any transfer of servicing.

stripped coupons under section 1286, they would benefit directly from Example 4 in the regulations.

This line of reasoning has some merit, but is subject to two qualifications. First, if a floating rate interest in a loan is created synthetically, then it is necessary to consider not only that interest but also the remaining interest in the loan. The remnant is less likely to resemble an authentic strip. However, this argument is losing its force as inverse floating rate debt instruments become commonplace, as they have in the REMIC and municipal bond areas. Those instruments can, of course, be used to create authentic inverse floating rate strips.[91] Second, by definition a synthetic strip has terms that do not reflect the actual terms of a loan. To the extent that the argument for bringing synthetic strips within the "incidental" exception rests on their similarity to authentic strips, how much similarity is required and how in practical terms is the line between permitted and forbidden interests to be drawn and policed? Obviously, no comparable line drawing process is needed for authentic strips because by definition they track the terms of an actual loan. The "specified portion" rules in the REMIC regulations could serve as a model in defining permitted synthetic strips, but as of this writing, the Service has yet to take this step.[92] It would require an intrepid captain to sail on these uncharted waters without the benefit of further regulations or other authoritative guidance.[93]

The possible use of swaps (as an alternative to additional ownership classes) to carve up interest payments on mortgages is discussed in Part C.1.g, below.

(ii) Reallocation of payments on a single bond following a default. The earliest types of stripping transactions involved U.S. Treasury obligations that were thought to be risk free from a credit standpoint and provided no right to accelerate principal following a default. Suppose, however, that the object of a stripping transaction is a noncallable corporate bond that does not enjoy the same protection against adversity and has an acceleration right. Suppose further that all rights to interest on the bond are purchased by one investor (the "interest investor") and all rights to principal are purchased by a second investor (the "principal investor"). Each investor purchases its right to receive payments on the bond at a price substantially below the aggregate amount of those payments. If the bond defaults and is accelerated, principal may be paid, in whole or in part, prior to maturity, in which event rights to interest would be prematurely terminated. If the prepaid principal were allocated entirely to the principal investor, the interest investor would suffer an unanticipated loss (the forfeiture of future interest payments) and the principal investor would realize a corresponding unanticipated benefit (increase in the present value of noninterest bearing principal payments attributable to their prepayment).

---

91 See Chapter 5, Part C.3 (discussing variable rate regular interests) and Part E.4 (stripping of regular interests).

92 The specified portion rules are discussed in Chapter 5, Part C.4. Section 1286(f) grants the Service unusually broad authority to issue regulations under the stripped bond rules.

93 For further discussion of this topic, see G. Howell and C. Cosby, "Exotic Coupon Stripping: A Voyage to the Frontier Between Debt and Option," 12 *Virginia Tax Review* (1993), 531.

Assuming that the economic purpose of the transaction is to carve up the bond into smaller bonds with different maturities, but not to reallocate credit risk, it would make more sense to divide all payments that are received following a default between the two investors in proportion to the present values, at the time of the default, of the payments they would have received in the absence of the default. However, such an arrangement departs from a conventional stripping transaction in that the allocation of rights to payments of principal and interest on the bond would shift, in favor of the interest investor, in the event of a default.

There are strong arguments in favor of applying section 1286 and the "incidental" exception to such an arrangement, particularly if the likelihood of a default is remote. First, the arrangement resembles Example 2 in that the principal investor is partially ceding its interest in the bond in favor of the interest investor in the event of a default. The two transactions are technically distinguishable because the principal investor is not guaranteeing a payment that the interest investor is entitled to receive as the owner of rights to interest on the bond, but is instead supplementing the interest investors' payment rights. On the other hand, credit support agreements often take the form of a right to sell defaulted claims, and the shifting interests in the example could be seen, by analogy to Example 2, as separate ownership by the two investors of rights to principal and interest payments, coupled with a default-related put on the interest payments written by the principal investor in favor of the interest investor. If the likelihood of default is small, the put would have nominal value and could perhaps be ignored unless and until a default occurs. The shift of payments in the present example should be easier to contend with than the shift in Example 2, because only one debt instrument is involved, and the purpose of the shift is to equalize credit risk rather than to favor one investor over another.

A second argument is that the two partial ownership interests in the bond would be economically identical to conventional serial zero coupon bonds that are redeemable upon acceleration at their accreted value (issue price plus accrued discount). Thus, it is easy to view those interests as separate securities that might have been issued directly by the issuer. Finally, while it is difficult to know how much, if any, weight to place on the common understanding of the word *incidental* in applying the exception in the Sears regulations,[94] where the likelihood of a default is remote, a shift in the allocation of payments in the event of a default should in fact be of secondary importance to investors.

(iii) Serialization of sinking fund bonds. Often, term bonds are retired in part prior to maturity through operation of a sinking fund. In modern practice, a sinking fund is not a pot of money but a requirement that bonds be retired by the issuer according to a schedule over time through market purchases or, failing that, mandatory redemptions. Bonds selected for redemption to satisfy a sinking fund requirement are ordinarily chosen through a lottery. If an investor acquires a large portion of the outstanding term bonds, the uncertainty of the lottery is reduced. Suppose

---

94   See the second full paragraph following footnote 77.

that with a view to reducing such uncertainty and taking advantage of a rising yield curve, all or substantially all of the term bonds of a single class are deposited in a trust, and the rights to identified sinking fund principal payments, and the related interest, are allocated to different investors.[95]

Although the authors understand that the Service at one point refused to issue a private letter ruling approving an arrangement of this type, there are substantial arguments that the "incidental" exception should apply.

Section 1286 does not seem to apply in the present case because rights to interest on the term bonds would be allocated ratably in proportion to principal.[96] Nonetheless, the investors could be taxed in a straightforward manner using the rules that would apply if they had purchased the term bonds outside of the trust. The different interests in the term bond would resemble conventional serial bonds that might have been issued as separate securities. Although the arrangement involves the division of the term bonds into interests with shorter and longer maturities, and in that respect is similar to Example 1, carving up bonds into interests with different maturities is also a feature of the stripping transaction described in Example 4. Indeed, it is the principal motivation for most stripping transactions involving non-callable bonds. Example 1 is distinguishable on the ground that it involves shifting interests in *different* mortgages, whereas the term bonds held by the trust would be identical. Another point of distinction is that the uncertainty in the timing of payments received by investors in the term bond trust would be reduced because of the accumulation of bonds, not because of the multiple class nature of the trust. The same reduction in uncertainty would be achieved if the trust had only a single class.[97]

g. Definition of "Ownership Interest." The Sears regulations apply to an investment trust only if it has two or more classes of "ownership interests". Although this phrase is not defined in the regulations, it presumably refers to an interest in a trust that, absent the Sears regulations, would be taxed as an ownership interest in trust assets (and not as a debt instrument or other type of financial instrument issued by the trust, or as a right to payment for property or services provided to the trust).[98] Thus, a trust that has a single class of beneficial interests and issues debt, enters into an interest rate swap

---

95   If the trust held less than all of the term bonds, it might issue two types of certificates: first, a number of classes of "serial bond" certificates representing rights to the *minimum* sinking fund payments of principal that the trust was unconditionally entitled to receive together with all related interest, and, second, a single class of "term bond" certificates representing the right to all remaining principal and interest payments to be received by the trust.

96   See New York State Bar Association, Tax Section, "Preliminary Report of Ad Hoc Committee on Original Issue Discount and Coupon Stripping," reprinted in *Tax Notes,* March 5, 1984 (NYSBA 1984 Report) at 1022.

97   However, if the trust held less than all of the term bonds and issued both serial bond certificates and term bond certificates as described in footnote 95, then the creation of those two classes of certificates would affect to some degree the certainty of timing of payments received by individual investors.

98   Compare the discussion of the definition of a REMIC "interest" in Chapter 4, Part A.1.a.

or other form of notional principal contract, and contracts with a servicer to service trust assets, would not be considered to have more than one class of ownership interests, assuming that these nonequity claims against the trust are not recharacterized as ownership interests under general tax principles.

The area where the risk of recharacterization has received the most attention relates to the retention by the sponsor/servicer of a trust holding mortgages of a right to "excess servicing" (servicing compensation in excess of reasonable compensation for the services provided). Ordinarily, servicing fees consist of a right to a fixed number of basis points of interest, plus the right to various fees collected from mortgagors, and the right to earnings on mortgage payments before they are transferred to the trust. Also, servicing fees may be varied deliberately to smooth out distributions to certificate holders.[99] If a portion of servicing compensation is considered excessive and is recharacterized as an ownership interest in the trust, then the effect of the recharacterization on the tax status of the trust could depend on how the excess servicing is defined. Specifically, if the recharacterized amount with respect to any mortgage is considered to represent a fixed number of basis points of interest on the mortgage (calculated so that all remaining servicing compensation is reasonable), then the recharacterized servicing would represent a right to a series of stripped coupons and, although the trust would have multiple ownership classes, it would fall within the stripping exception based on Example 4 in the Sears regulations. On the other hand, if the recharacterized servicing could not be expressed as a fixed number of basis points, arguably the stripping exception would not apply, and the trust might lose its trust status under those regulations.[100]

In a 1991 ruling, the Service held that excess servicing should be viewed as an ownership interest in the related mortgages. However, the ruling took pains to cast the recharacterized servicing in the form of a fixed number of basis points of interest, and concluded that the recharacterization did not affect the tax status of the trust.[101] At the least, this ruling evidences a laudable desire on the part of the Service to limit as much as possible the adverse entity classification consequences of recharacterizing transactions with a trust, where the recharacterization is thought to be needed for other reasons.[102]

---

99 For example, adjustments may be made to offset the effects of simple interest on loans, prepayment interest shortfalls, or differences between the cap rates on individual loans. These adjustments could potentially reduce as well as increase servicer compensation, and in any event are generally speculative and not likely to be material in assessing the reasonableness of a servicer's compensation.

100 Variable strips are discussed in Part C.1.e.(i).

101 Revenue Ruling 91-46, 1991-2 C.B. 358 (normal servicing of 25 basis points recharacterized as ownership interest in the related mortgages and not in any entity to the extent value of normal servicing plus other incidental fees and income exceeds reasonable compensation). Compare Chapter 4, Part A.1.a.(ii) (excess servicing not treated as a REMIC interest).

102 The principal goal of the recharacterization of excess servicing was to increase the taxable income of sponsors from mortgage sales by requiring them to allocate a portion of their basis to the retained excess servicing.

Turning from excess servicing to swaps, suppose that a trust holding fixed rate mortgages enters into an interest rate swap that has a notional principal amount equal to the mortgage loan balance and requires the trust to pay the counterparty periodic amounts equal to the interest payments on the mortgages in exchange for payments calculated at a rate equal to a margin above LIBOR. What is the risk of recharacterization of the swap as an ownership interest in the mortgages? The risk should be negligible. It would be difficult to characterize the contract as any kind of ownership interest in the mortgages or trust, because it may represent either an asset or a liability of the counterparty depending on the value of LIBOR. Further, the contract is cast in the form of a notional principal contract and has the common economic characteristics of such contracts. Since notional principal contracts are now a recognized category of financial instrument for which a body of substantive tax law has been developed by the Service, what reason could there be for imposing on the contract a different tax regime? The close matching of the swap payments and mortgage payments, while perhaps suggestive of an ownership interest, is also a common feature of swaps, which are often used as custom-tailored hedges of identified assets or liabilities.

In some cases, divisions of cash flows that could take the form of multiple ownership classes may instead be created using swaps. For example, suppose that fixed rate mortgages are placed in a trust and there is a desire to create (1) a class A interest entitled to 50 percent of each principal payment and interest thereon at a rate equal to the lesser of LIBOR plus a spread or twice the weighted average coupon rate of interest on the mortgages, and (2) a class B interest which receives all remaining principal and interest on the mortgages. This arrangement would most likely fail to be a trust under the Sears regulations.[103] What if instead the mortgages are first divided under a participation agreement into two 50 percent pro rata interests, which are conveyed to two trusts (A and B)? Each trust issues a single class of ownership certificates. The trusts enter into a notional principal contract with each other under which A pays B amounts corresponding to interest on a principal amount equal to the principal amount of the trust A mortgage pool at a rate equal to the weighted average rate of interest on the mortgages, and B pays A interest on the same principal amount at a rate equal to the lesser of LIBOR plus a spread, or twice that mortgage rate. Although this arrangement is economically equivalent to the two-class trust described before, there is nothing artificial about the transactions as they actually occur, so why should the form be set aside? Recognizing the form has the considerable advantage that all of the parties can be taxed without dealing with the complexities of shifting ownership interests in property, and there would seem to be no reason for the Service to mount an attack. Whether the Service would agree with this assessment remains to be seen.[104]

---

103   See Part C.1.f.(i) (synthetic floating rate interests) above.

104   The recently adopted REMIC regulations recognize the separate existence of non-REMIC invest-
        ment trusts if the parties properly account for the activities of each trust. See Chapter 4, Part C.7.c.
        While it could be argued that these rules are relevant only in the REMIC context because of the

2. Classification of Trusts with a Business Objective

As explained above, if an investment trust has a business objective, it will be classified as a corporation only if has at least three of the following four corporate characteristics: continuity of life, centralized management, limited liability and free transferability of interests. A typical pass-through trust would possess all of these characteristics except possibly centralized management, and would therefore be classified as an association if it had a business objective.

The balance of this discussion of trusts with business objectives begins by reviewing some aspects of the four corporate factors that are particularly relevant to investment trusts. The discussion is not intended to be comprehensive.[105] The next section outlines an election that can sometimes be made under section 761 to avoid certain of the complexities of partnership taxation for investment trusts that are classified as partnerships. The discussion concludes by describing how the four-factor test is typically applied to owner trusts, whole loan participation arrangements, trusts with outside reserve funds, and issuers of pass-through debt certificates.

a. General. Two points should be kept in mind in applying the four-factor test to investment trusts. First, whether the factors are present in a particular trust depends on the specific terms of the trust documents and the effect of those terms under local law. Thus, the ability to manipulate the factors depends on the body of law governing the trust. It is important to check that provisions in a trust agreement designed to achieve a particular tax result will be given effect as desired under local law.[106]

Second, the entity classification tests are based on the rights and obligations of "members" of an organization. For example, an organization will lack limited liability only if a "member" is personally liable for debts of the organization. Care should be taken to identify those persons whose status as a member is significant and to ensure that they have a sufficient equity stake to be recognized as members.[107]

---

formal nature of the REMIC rules, they could also signal the standards the Service would apply in related areas.

105 For further discussion of these factors, see W. Brannan, "Lingering Partnership Classification Issues (Just When You Thought it Was Safe to Go Back into the Water)," *1 Florida Tax Review* 197 (1993).

106 Trusts used in structured finance transactions may be common law trusts or may be organized under a statute, such as the Delaware Business Trust Act (Del. Code Ann., Title 12, Chap. 38). The Delaware Business Trust Act was written with the entity classification regulations in mind and is quite flexible.

107 Following the Service's ruling guidelines for partnerships, it is common practice to require any entity that must qualify as a member to own 1% of each class of ownership interests in the entity (and to be prudent, of each class of debt or other nonequity interests that could be recharacterized as ownership interests). See Revenue Procedure 89-12, 1989-1 C.B. 798, §§ 4.01-03 (general partners of limited partnership, taken together, are required to maintain throughout the life of a partnership at least a 1% interest in the partnership's profits and losses (or, if the total investment in the partnership exceeds $50 million, a smaller percentage interest equal to 1% divided by the ratio of the total investment to $50 million, but in any event no less than a .2% interest), as well as a minimum investment at all times of at least the lesser of 1% of the total partnership capital and $500,000).

(i) Continuity of life. An entity lacks continuity of life if the death, insanity, bankruptcy, retirement, resignation, or expulsion of any member will cause a "dissolution" of the organization under local law.[108] Continuity of life is not the same as an indefinite life. It focuses not on how long an organization is expected to last (for example, whether it has a fixed term) but instead on whether its continuing life may be disrupted by changes in the status of any member. Under the regulations, partnerships formed under the Uniform Limited Partnership Act (ULPA) automatically lack continuity of life. There is no *per se* rule favoring trusts.

Investment trusts typically possess continuity of life because, as a commercial matter, it is undesirable to link the fortunes of an issuer to the status of beneficiaries, particularly if interests in the trusts are freely transferable. Where continuity of life is defeated, it is typically accomplished by having a "bankruptcy-remote" entity hold an interest in the trust and tying dissolution to the bankruptcy or dissolution of that entity. These arrangements raise two issues. Does continuity exist if (1) a dissolution can be triggered by only one of the events listed in the regulations, and (2) the triggering event is unlikely to happen (and even contractually prohibited)? Limiting the triggering event to a bankruptcy of a member should suffice.[109] As to the second point, the relevant standard is whether the member or a third party has the *power* to cause a triggering event and not whether the event is likely to occur.[110]

---

108 Treasury Regulation § 301.7701-2(b).

109 See *Larson v. Comm'r*, 66 T.C. 159, 174-5 (1976), *acq.*, 1979-1 C.B. 1 (limited partnership lacked continuity of life where only the bankruptcy of its general partner would cause a dissolution of the partnership under local law); P.L.R. 9306008 (November 10, 1992) (limited liability company lacked continuity of life when its dissolution under local law would occur only upon the bankruptcy of a member); P.L.R. 9121025 (February 22, 1991) (foreign joint venture lacked continuity of life where it would be liquidated only on the bankruptcy of a partner); and P.L.R. 9031016 (May 7, 1990) (trust that would terminate only on the bankruptcy of a grantor lacked continuity of life).

110 Treasury Regulation § 301.7701-2(b)(3) includes the following: "If the agreement provides that the organization is to continue for a stated period or until the completion of a stated transaction, the organization has continuity of life if the effect of the agreement is that no member has the power to dissolve the organization in contravention of the agreement. Nevertheless, if, notwithstanding such agreement, any member has the power under local law to dissolve the organization, the organization lacks continuity of life." Cf. Treasury Regulation § 301.7701-2(c)(4) (centralized management does not exist where general partners agree among themselves to vest management authority in a few general partners because ordinarily all partners retain the power to bind the partnership in dealings with third parties who have no notice of the management agreement). *Zuckman v. U.S.*, 524 F.2d 729 (Ct. Cl. 1975), held that a partnership lacked continuity of life where the bankruptcy or dissolution of the corporate general partner triggered a dissolution even though the corporation was contractually bound not to enter into bankruptcy or to dissolve. The court stressed the fact that the corporation had the power, under the relevant partnership law, to act in violation of its contracts to cause a dissolution of the partnership. The court also had held that the partnership automatically lacked continuity of life under the regulations because it was formed under a statute corresponding to the ULPA. Typically, the ability of a bankruptcy-remote corporation to commence a voluntary bankruptcy case is limited by requiring the action to be approved by an independent director, but there is no agreement by the corporation not to take such action because such an agreement would be unenforceable. Such a corporation also could become involved in an involuntary bankruptcy proceeding and trigger a dissolution that way. Even if a corporation is prohibited from incurring debt, it may nonetheless have the power to do so, or may be subject to noncontractual liabilities (e.g., for taxes or securities law claims).

Continuity of life could also be defeated by giving one or more beneficiaries a right to revoke the trust and trigger a dissolution, perhaps coupled with an agreement (that can be enforced only through a claim for money damages) not to exercise the right.[111]

In a case where an investment trust has some feature that benefits a particular investor and that could cause the trust not to be classified as a trust under the Sears regulations, it is arguable, although by no means certain, that continuity of life can be defeated by eliminating the offending feature upon the occurrence of a bankruptcy or dissolution of that investor. From a tax standpoint at least, the bankruptcy/dissolution would then result in a liquidation of the old entity and its transformation into a trust.[112]

Some investment trusts allow trust beneficiaries to redeem their trust units (in which case the trust generally sells trust assets as necessary and distributes cash equal to the value of the redeemed unit).[113] Although such a right allows individual investors to liquidate their interest in the trust, it does not affect continuity of life, because the withdrawal by one investor does not terminate the trust for the remaining investors. Continuity of life is also not defeated by a right of investors to amend a trust document or to terminate a trust by vote, which would be similar to a right of corporate shareholders to liquidate a corporation or amend its charter.[114]

Once the triggering event has been identified, the trust must then "dissolve". In the context of a state law partnership, this term has a technical meaning (i.e., a termination of the mutual agency which is the partnership). Also, it is fairly easy to

---

111 See Treasury Regulation § 301.7701-2(b)(3): "[I]f the agreement expressly provides that the organization can be terminated by the will of any member, it is clear that the organization lacks continuity of life."

112 To illustrate, consider the trust described in Part C.1.f.(ii) that holds a corporate bond, allocates rights to interest and principal payments to an interest investor and principal investor, and would clearly be classified as a trust but for the effect of a reallocation of payments from the principal investor to the interest investor in the event of a default on the bond. Suppose that the terms of the trust provide that upon a bankruptcy or dissolution of the interest investor, the trust will be "dissolved" and automatically reconstituted without the offending reallocation feature. It could be argued that if the trust is considered to have a business purpose, and cannot be classified as a trust, solely because of the existence of the reallocation feature, it would lack continuity of life because, for tax purposes, the trust would be liquidated as a business organization, and reconstituted as a trust, upon the bankruptcy of a member. It is not clear, however, whether the change in the tax status of an entity can be considered a "dissolution" within the meaning of the classification regulations, which ordinarily look to local law in applying the classification standards. Further, the enforceability of a term that conditions forfeiture of a valuable right upon a bankruptcy or dissolution of an investor would need to be considered.

113 See footnote 68 above. In the case of a trust characterized as a partnership, a redemption right could affect whether the trust is a publicly traded partnership under section 7704. See Notice 88-75, 1988-2 C.B. 386.

114 See Revenue Ruling 71-277, 1971- C.B. 422; Revenue Ruling 71-434, 1971-2 C.B. 430; G.C.M. 34407 (January 22, 1971); and G.C.M. 34449 (March 8, 1971). In P.L.R. 9002056 (October 18, 1989), a limited liability company was held to lack continuity of life where its articles of association required that all shareholders vote to dissolve the company upon the dissolution, bankruptcy or insolvency of a member. Recently, the holding in this ruling has been questioned by IRS officials.

know when a dissolution has occurred, because the relevant state law refers to "dissolution" events. For organizations formed solely by contract or under statutes that do not have a dissolution concept, it would seem to be necessary for a "dissolution" to be followed (subject to the discussion of reconstitution below) by a winding up and termination in order to give content to the term. In the case of a passive vehicle such as an investment trust, a dissolution cannot lead to a cessation of business activities, because there are none; but at least the trust can be required to change course by selling and disposing of its assets in a commercially reasonable manner.[115]

A limited partnership will lack continuity of life if an event affecting a general partner causes a dissolution even though there is a power in all remaining general partners, or in a majority in interest of all remaining partners (both limited and general) to continue the partnership.[116] A right to reconstitute a trust that requires the consent of all beneficiaries (other than the one that caused the dissolution) would clearly defeat continuity of life.[117] The same result should hold true if only a majority in interest of the remaining beneficiaries can continue a trust following a dissolution event.[118]

---

115 Suppose that a trust has pledged all of its assets to secure a borrowing and that the indenture prohibits the sale of assets until the debt is repaid. If the debt is expected to be outstanding over the entire life of the trust, then a dissolution that triggers a requirement to sell assets (subject to the terms of the indenture) may have no practical significance. Query whether a "dissolution" would be considered to occur under these circumstances. If it makes a difference, a technical dissolution can be achieved for a trust organized under the Delaware Business Trust Act by providing that, in a case where a trust is continued following a "dissolution," the old trust is terminated and a new successor trust (that is considered a different trust under the Act) is formed. See Del. Code Ann. Title 12, §§ 3808 (events affecting beneficial owners do not cause a dissolution unless otherwise provided in the governing instrument), and 3806(b)(6) (transfer of trust assets to a new trust).

116 Treasury Regulation § 301.7701-2(b)(1).

117 See Revenue Ruling 88-79, 1988-2 C.B. 361 (Missouri business trust having both managers and passive participants as beneficiaries lacked continuity of life when the trust agreement provided that the trust would dissolve upon the death, insanity, bankruptcy, retirement, or resignation of any manager, unless all remaining managers and a majority of participants agreed to continue the trust, where these trust provisions were effective under local law). A fortiori, a trust reconstitution provision that required the consent of all beneficiaries would defeat continuity of life. See also P.L.R. 9147012 (December 7, 1990) (trust lacked continuity of life where it could be continued with unanimous consent; P.L.R. 9107028 (November 20, 1990) (same; trust was apparently formed under the Delaware Business Trust Act).

118 The rule in Treasury Regulation § 301.7701-2(b)(1) that treats a partnership as lacking continuity of life notwithstanding that it can be continued with partner consent stems from Glensder Textile Co. v. Comm'r, 46 B.T.A. 176 (1942), acq., 1942-1 C.B. 8, which is cited in the regulation. This case held that the need for partner consent made continuation of a partnership following the bankruptcy, withdrawal, etc. of a partner uncertain, which was sufficient to defeat continuity of life. If the need for a majority vote creates sufficient doubt as to the longevity of a partnership, the same should hold true for trusts or other state law entities. The trust in Revenue Ruling 88-79 (see footnote 117 above) cites Glensder Textile as relevant authority. The trust in the ruling could have been continued based on a majority vote if there had been only a single remaining manager. After expressing some reservations on the point, in Revenue Ruling 93-91, I.R.B. 1993-41, 21, the Service held that the partnership majority-in-interest standard applies to limited liability companies, and by extension should apply to a trust. For an earlier contrary view, see P.L.R. 9010027 (December 7, 1989) (limited liability company possesses continuity of life when the members

(ii) Centralized management. A trust has centralized management if the trustee, or any other person (or group of persons which does not include all of the beneficiaries) has continuing exclusive authority to make the "management decisions necessary to the conduct of the business for which the organization was formed." Centralized management means a concentration of continuing exclusive authority to make "independent business decisions on behalf of the organization which do not require ratification by members of such organization. Thus, there is no centralized management when the centralized authority is merely to perform ministerial acts as an agent at the direction of a principal."[119]

Centralized management would exist in an investment trust that has a business objective if the trustee has the exclusive power to make investment decisions. The trustee would not have such a power if its actions are subject to the direction of, or ratification by, all or a majority in interest of the beneficiaries.[120] In order for a trust to lack centralized management, it is not essential that all beneficiaries participate (or have a right to participate) in management. By analogy to a limited partnership, however, centralized management is likely to exist where the managers own an interest in the trust of 20 percent or less.[121]

An organization with a business objective ordinarily has the power to make business decisions (including, in the case of an investment trust with a power to vary investments, the power to manage investments). However, an investment trust that is entirely passive may be deemed to have a business objective solely by application of the Sears regulations. In that event, there would be no person (including the trustee and the beneficiaries) who has the authority to make nonministerial, management decisions for the trust, so that the trust should be considered to lack

---

could avoid a dissolution under state law by a vote of a majority of its members to continue the company).

119   Treasury Regulation § 301.7701-2(c).

120   See Treasury Regulation § 301.7701-2(c)(4); Revenue Ruling 64-220, 1964-2 C.B. 335; P.L.R. 8510001 (September 28, 1984); P.L.R. 8119056 (February 13, 1981); P.L.R. 8113078 (December 31, 1980); and P.L.R. 8104157 (October 31, 1980). It is not necessary that the beneficiaries actually exercise the power to direct or ratify actions of a trustee, but only that they have the right to do so. Under many state laws, beneficiaries who participate in the management of a trust become liable for obligations of the trust. See G.C.M. 39395 (May 7, 1985), describing New York law. The beneficiaries of a Delaware Business Trust, however, can manage it without being exposed to personal liability for trust debts. See sections 3803 (liability) and 3806 (management).

121   See Treasury Regulation § 301.7701-2(c)(4) (centralized management exists in a limited partnership if substantially all of the interests in the partnership are owned by the limited partners; ability of limited partners to remove a general partner will be taken into account); *Glensder Textile Co. v. Comm'r*, 46 B.T.A. 176 (1942), *acq.*, 1942-1 C.B. 8 (limited partnership lacked centralized management because general partners holding a 42% interest in the partnership "were acting in their own interest . . . and not merely in a representative capacity for a body of persons having a limited investment and a limited liability. . . . Nor were the limited partners here able to remove the general partners and control them as agents, as stockholders may control directors."). The Service generally will not rule that centralized management is lacking in a limited partnership if the general partners have an interest of 20% or less, although factors demonstrating direct or indirect limited partner control over the general partners also will be considered. Revenue Procedure 89-12, 1989-1 C.B. 798, § 4.06. See also G.C.M. 36292 (May 29, 1975) (earlier statement of 20% test).

centralized management.[122] No authorities have been found specifically addressing this point.

(iii) Limited liability. An organization has the corporate characteristic of limited liability if under local law there is no member who is personally liable for the debts of or claims against the organization (i.e., who may be liable to a creditor to the extent the organization's assets are insufficient to pay claims).[123]

Although general partners are jointly and severally liable for partnership debts, the corporate characteristic of limited liability is defeated if each member is liable for only its proportionate share of the organization's debts.[124] A member who is personally liable for debts of an organization does not lose personal liability because another person agrees to indemnify the member against such liability,[125] and liability of any person can be limited to claims that arise during the period in which that person is a member.[126] Thus, for example, an investment trust that benefits from a guarantee by a federally sponsored agency would lack limited liability if each certificate holder is personally liable for its proportionate share of the claims against the trust arising while it is an owner, even though the agency indemnifies the certificate holders against any such liability.

Limited liability is defeated if members are personally liable for claims against an organization even if it is very unlikely that there will be any such claims.[127]

---

122   A trust with no management powers would resemble neither a corporation (which is centrally managed) nor a partnership (which is managed by its members). However, the four-factor test looks to whether an organization resembles a corporation, not whether it is similar to other unincorporated business organizations. The four characteristics are described in Treasury Regulation § 301.7701-2(a)(1) as "major characteristics ordinarily found in a pure corporation". Also, an organization with a business objective that has two, and lacks two, of the four characteristics is classified as a partnership (assuming it has at least two members), even though it may resemble neither a corporation nor a conventional partnership. The view that resemblance to a corporation is the relevant test is borne out by the fact that the corporate characteristic of limited liability does not exist in an organization if its members are severally liable for claims against the organization, even though a partner would have joint and several liability. See footnote 124, below.

123   See Treasury Regulation § 301.7701-2(d).

124   See *Bush #1 c/o Stonestreet Lands Co. v. Comm'r*, 48 T.C. 218, 233-4 (1967), *acq.*, 1968-2 C.B. 2; P.L.R. 7951006 (August 21, 1979); P.L.R. 7903084 (October 20, 1978); P.L.R. 7404300620A (April 30, 1974); and G.C.M. 38025 (July 20, 1979).

125   Treasury Regulation § 301.7701-2(d)(1). Similarly, if under local law no member of an organization is personally liable for the debts of the organization, then the organization will possess limited liability, notwithstanding the members' endorsement or guarantee of the organization's liabilities. See *Richlands Medical Association v. Comm'r*, 60 T.C.M. 1572 (1990). On the other hand, Revenue Ruling 88-79, 1988-2 C.B. 361, confirms that where a trust is formed by contract, unlimited liability may be created contractually under the trust agreement. Cf. *Zuckman v. U.S.*, 524 F.2d 729 (Ct. Cl. 1975) (an organization will lack continuity of life if any member has the power under local law to dissolve the organization, notwithstanding that such member contractually surrenders the right to cause the organization's dissolution); P.L.R. 9002056 (October 18, 1989), described in footnote 114, above.

126   The regulations state that personal liability exists for each general partner in a general partnership subject to a statute corresponding to the Uniform Partnership Act, and under the UPA, a general partner is liable only for claims that arise while he is a partner. See UPA (1914) § 17 (incoming partner not personally liable for obligations arising before admission).

Further, there is no prohibition against having particular classes of creditors agree contractually to waive claims against members. Partnerships regularly incur nonrecourse debt without losing limited liability.

Limited liability will not exist if some (but not all) of the beneficiaries of a trust are personally liable for trust claims. It would be prudent in such a case to follow the principles that apply in determining whether personal liability exists for general partners of a limited partnership. Thus, the trust beneficiaries that are liable should have substantial assets that can be reached by partnership creditors, or should not be under the control of the other beneficiaries.[128]

(iv) Free transferability of interests. An organization has the corporate characteristic of free transferability of interests if each of its members, or those members owning substantially all of the interests in the organization, have the power, without the consent of other members, to substitute for themselves in the same organization a person who is not a member.[129] Such a right of substitution exists only if the transferor can confer all of the attributes of his interest in the organization on the transferee. Thus, a power to assign a right to distributions, but not a right to participate in management, is not enough to create free transferability.[130] An organization lacks free transferability if under local law a transfer of a member's interest results in a dissolution of the old organization and the formation of a new one.

A few comments on the free transferability test are in order. Free transferability can be defeated by limiting the transfer of enough interests so that less than "substantially all" of the interests are freely transferable. A Service ruling guideline

---

127 The regulations do not require that there be actual liabilities. A test based on the existence of actual liabilities would be very difficult to apply.

128 Treasury Regulation § 301.7701-2(d)(2) states that a limited partnership has limited liability if the general partner has no substantial assets (other than his interest in the partnership) which could be reached by a partnership creditor and it is merely a "dummy" acting as the agent of the limited partners. The regulation states that if an organization is engaged in financial transactions which involve large sums of money, and if the general partners have substantial assets (other than their interests in the partnership), there exists personal liability although the assets of such general partners would be insufficient to satisfy any substantial portion of the obligations of the organization. The Service generally will rule that a general partner meets the substantial assets test if its net worth (excluding its partnership interest) is at least 10% of the total contributions to the partnership (or in the case of an individual general partner, the lesser of that 10% amount or $1 million). See Revenue Procedure 89-12, 1989-1 C.B. 798, § 4.07; Revenue Procedure 92-88, 1992-2 C.B. 496, § 4.03 (adds rule for individual general partners). If a general partner does not meet the net worth test, then a favorable ruling may still be given if it can be demonstrated that the general partner will act independently of the limited partners. See G.C.M. 39798 (October 24, 1989) for a discussion of the showing that must be made.

129 Treasury Regulation § 301.7701-2(e).

130 An assignment of a right to distributions could nonetheless affect entity classification. For example, where a trust certificate provides the holder with management rights that are necessary to defeat centralized management, the separation of those rights from the right to distributions arguably could cause the certificate holder to not be "acting in [its] own interest" and thus affect whether the entity has centralized management. See footnote 121, above. More generally, consideration should be given to whether an assignment of a right to distributions affects the status of the transferor as a "member". See the text at footnote 107, above.

requires, in order for an entity to lack free transferability, that the transferability of more than 20 percent of the interests be restricted.[131] An interest is not freely transferable if its transfer is conditioned on obtaining the consent of other members. Clearly, the reference to "other members" does not mean that *all* other members must consent. In the context of a limited partnership, a general partner, who may hold only a small interest in the partnership, is generally given the power to consent to transfers of limited partnership interests. With respect to a trust that does not allocate management rights to fewer than all beneficiaries, requiring the consent of the holders of a majority of the interests in the trust will almost certainly defeat free transferability.[132] Requiring the consent of any member or members owning a smaller, but still significant, interest should also do the job, although the authorities are not as clear on this point.[133] Where consent is required, the party giving it should have the power to withhold it for any reason (i.e., consents should not be subject to a reasonableness standard).[134] Provisions allowing transfers in certain limited circumstances should be approached with caution. Depending on the circumstances,

---

131 See Revenue Procedure 92-33, 1992-1 C.B. 782 (although what constitutes "substantially all" of the interests in an organization generally depends upon the facts and circumstances, the Service generally will rule that a partnership lacks free transferability of interests if, throughout the life of the partnership, the partnership agreement expressly restricts the transferability of partnership interests representing more than 20% of all interests in partnership capital, income and losses). See also *Zuckman v. U.S.*, 524 F.2d 729 (Ct. Cl. 1975) (61% not substantially all); P.L.R. 7830135 (April 28, 1978) (67.76% not substantially all).

132 See Revenue Ruling 88-79, 1988-2 C.B. 361 (trust lacked free transferability where the trust had manager and nonmanager participants, the managers owned an aggregate interest of 10%, a manager could not transfer or assign its interest without the consent of the other managers, and assignees of the participants could become substitute participants only with the consent of a majority of managers). Where a trust has only a single class of interests, consent by a majority of trust interests would seem to be at least as restrictive as consent by a majority of managers. See also Revenue Ruling 93-91, I.R.B. 1993-41, 22 (limited liability company lacked free transferability where consent of holders of interests entitled to a majority of non-transferred profits required to effect transfer); P.L.R. 8450082 (September 13, 1984) (trust lacked free transferability of interests where admission of a new settlor or assignment of a trust interest required the consent of not less than 75% of the settlors); and P.L.R. 7830135 (April 28, 1978) (owner trust lacked free transferability of interests where consent of equity owners holding at least 60% of the aggregate interests of all equity owners was required to transfer or assign an interest in the trust).

133 By analogy to a limited partnership, it should be possible to eliminate free transferability by conditioning transfers on obtaining the consent of a designated certificate holder owning at least a 1% interest in the trust. In effect, the designated party would act as the trust manager for purposes of giving such consents. Transfers could also be conditioned on obtaining consent from any other certificate holder or holders who own some minimum interest (e.g., 5%), are not affiliated with the transferor or transferee, and are not a party to the transfer. A consent mechanism of this type would allow a transferor to "shop" to some extent for consents among certificate holders. On the other hand, if the person(s) who can give the required consent must have a meaningful interest in the trust and must be independent of the parties to the transfer, the consent requirement has some teeth. Further, stock in a corporation typically can be transferred without any consents, so that a trust subject to such a mechanism would not resemble a corporation, which should be all that is required. See footnote 122, above.

134 Cf. *Larson v. Comm'r*, 66 T.C. 159, 183 (1976) (limited partnership interests that could be transferred with the consent of the general partner which could not be unreasonably withheld were considered to be freely transferable where no grounds for refusing such consent were suggested).

they could result in at least a modified form of free transferability.[135] The rule that distinguishes transfers of rights to receive distributions from transfers that effect a full substitution of one member for another has been applied to interests in trusts held by passive investors where the other rights of ownership seemed quite limited.[136]

(v) Entities owned by related parties. At one time, the Service took the position that an entity owned by two subsidiaries of a common parent corporation could not lack continuity of life, because the parent would be free to continue the entity following its dissolution without securing the consent of any outside interests. Further, even though each subsidiary's right to transfer its equity interest was conditioned on obtaining consent of the other subsidiary owner, the entity possessed free transferability of interests, because the parent effectively could make all transfer decisions.[137] In a 1993 ruling, the Service reversed itself on the continuity of life point and clarified its views on free transferability.[138] At least in a case where an entity dissolves automatically under local law, without any action being taken by the owners, upon the occurrence of a bankruptcy or other event relating to an owner, the fact that a common owner can revive the entity without the consent of outside interests will no longer be considered to create continuity of life. The ruling

---

135   For example, a member may wish to be able to transfer an interest to an affiliate without the consent of other owners. Two private letter rulings imply that such a transfer right could create free transferability. See P.L.R. 8117024 (January 27, 1981) (limited liability company lacked free transferability where one of the shareholders had the power to transfer its interest to a wholly owned affiliate without the consent of the other shareholders, because the shareholder with the power did not own substantially all of the interests in the company); P.L.R. 8012080 (December 28, 1979) (same). Where an owner anticipates that it may want to transfer a trust interest to an identified affiliate, one way to do this is to have that affiliate own some interest in the trust from the beginning. The consent requirement applies only to transfers to a nonmember. An owner's power to transfer its interest to an owner's successor in interest may not create free transferability. See P.L.R. 9210019 (December 6, 1991) (limited liability company lacked free transferability although no consent was required for transfers of interests by reason of the death, dissolution, divorce, liquidation, merger, or termination of a transferor member); but see G.C.M. 38012 (July 13, 1979) (trust possessed a modified form of free transferability because a corporate participant could transfer, without the consent of the other participants, its ownership interest in connection with a merger or consolidation with another corporation).

136   See Revenue Ruling 88-79, 1988-2 C.B. 361 (business trust lacked free transferability where all of the rights of a nonmanager participant could be freely transferred except for the right to vote on amendments to the trust agreement and the right to vote on whether to continue the trust upon the death, resignation, etc., of a manager).

137   See Revenue Ruling 77-214, 1977-1 C.B. 408; G.C.M. 37013 (February 25, 1977). See also *MCA, Inc. v. U.S.*, 685 F.2d 1099 (9th Cir. 1982) (holding that foreign entities owned by a controlled foreign corporation (CFC) and an employee trust for the benefit of the CFC's directors lacked free transferability and continuity of life, although the same two individuals controlled the CFC's board of directors and trust's board of trustees and they were the chief executive officers of the CFC's two corporate shareholders); P.L.R. 9239014 (June 25, 1992) (limited partnership lacked free transferability where the two 49.5% limited partners, who were husband and wife, could not transfer their interests without the consent of the corporate general partner, all of whose outstanding stock was owned by the husband). For a discussion of entities with a single owner, see footnote 9, above, and accompanying text.

138   Revenue Ruling 93-4, I.R.B. 1993-3, 5.

states more broadly that "the presence or absence of separate interests is not relevant to the determination of whether an entity possesses continuity of life." Regarding free transferability, the Service reaffirmed its earlier view that requiring consent from an affiliate was not a meaningful transfer restriction, but clarified that an interest in an entity owned by related parties will not be considered freely transferable if the entity's governing documents either prohibit transfer or provide for the dissolution of the entity upon the transfer of an interest, assuming these provisions are effective under local law.

b. Election Out of Partnership Rules. An investment trust that has a business objective, more than one owner and two or fewer corporate characteristics is classified as a partnership. There are a number of potentially significant differences between the tax treatment of trusts beneficiaries and partners. As detailed elsewhere, the holder of an interest in a grantor trust is treated as if it owned directly an interest in trust assets (with the trust being ignored). By contrast, a partnership is recognized to be an entity (and a partnership interest is treated as an interest in an entity) for various tax purposes.[139]

In a case where an investment trust will be (or at least might be) classified as a partnership and not as a trust, the parties may seek to "elect out" of the complex partnership rules of subchapter K of the Code. Section 761(a)(1) authorizes the Service to adopt regulations excluding from all or a part of subchapter K any unincorporated organization that is availed of for investment purposes only, and not for the active conduct of a business. Regulations under this section allow co-owners of investment property to make such an election, but only if, among other requirements, income of the owners may be adequately determined without computing partnership taxable income, and the owners reserve the right separately to take or dispose of their interests in the property.[140] A right to dispose of interests in property separately will not exist if there are substantial restrictions on the transfer of trust interests.[141] Whether the income of the co-owners can be adequately determined without computing partnership income is a less clear cut standard and will depend on the particular terms of the investment.[142] The mechanics for making the election are spelled out in the regulations.[143]

---

139 Some of these differences are outlined in Chapter 7, Part C, which discusses the tax treatment of equity interests in non-REMIC owner trusts.

140 Treasury Regulation § 1.761-2(a).

141 G.C.M. 37016 (February 25, 1977).

142 If an investment trust has a business objective because it has more than one class of ownership interests and the Sears regulations apply, the Service might be expected to argue as a general matter that the income measurement and allocation rules of subchapter K are needed to determine the income of individual investors. The preamble to the final Sears regulations (quoted above in the text following footnote 70) includes the following: "[The existence of multiple classes] introduces the potential for complex allocations of trust income among investors, with correspondingly difficult issues of how such income is to be allocated for tax purposes. These issues are properly foreign to the taxation of trust income, where rules have not developed to accommodate the varied forms of commercial investment, and no comprehensive economic substance requirement governs

c. Applications of Entity Classification Tests. This section discusses briefly how the entity classification tests are often applied to four types of arrangements: owner trusts that are not subject to the TMP rules, whole loan participation arrangements, issuers of pass-through debt certificates, and outside reserve funds providing credit support for an investment trust. Combinations of classification factors differing from those described below are, of course, possible.

(i) Owner trusts that are not TMPs. As described in Chapter 2, Parts C and D, a typical owner trust issues pay-through bonds and has equity interests that can be held by a number of different owners. An owner trust that issues debt after December 31, 1991 and qualifies as a TMP automatically will be classified as a corporation under the TMP rules (discussed in Part D below). Thus, this discussion is relevant only for owner trusts not affected by the TMP rules.

To protect bond holders from events affecting the equity owners, owner trusts ordinarily continue in existence notwithstanding the bankruptcy, dissolution, or withdrawal of those owners. Accordingly, owner trusts possess the corporate characteristic of continuity of life.

On the other hand, owner trusts typically lack the three remaining corporate characteristics referred to above. They lack centralized management, because the equity owners have the power to direct or veto the actions of the owner trustee.[144] In addition, they lack limited liability, because the equity owners are personally liable

---

the allocation of income for tax purposes." An economic substance requirement does apply in making allocations of partnership income under subchapter K (section 704), and those rules would be avoided through a complete election out of subchapter K. On the other hand, at least in some cases, the income allocation issues raised by the existence of multiple classes seem to be fairly straightforward. For example, if the event that may cause a shift in the interests of investors is unlikely to happen (as is true in the example discussed above in Part C.1.f.(ii) involving a reallocation of payments on a bond following a default), the potential shift probably could be ignored unless and until it occurs, at which point income would be based on the allocation of cash. Also, a number of trusts have been formed (particularly in the municipal bond area) that hold a class of fixed rate bonds purchased at par and issue at par two classes of certificates that are entitled to a fixed percentage of the principal payments on the bonds and variable portions of the interest on the bonds, determined under a formula. The trusts are expected to be taxed as partnerships and often provide for an election under section 761. In this setting, a number of tax practitioners have taken the position that the election is available because the interest received by the trust can be allocated based on what each class is entitled to receive.

143   See Treasury Regulation § 1.761-2(b). The election can be made by including a statement in the trust documents expressing the intent not to be subject to subchapter K without making any filing with the Service.

144   Where the assets of the owner trust are all pledged to the indenture trustee for the bonds, certain rights to manage the assets of the owner trust may be exercisable by the indenture trustee or a third party acting on its behalf. It is uncertain whether rights to control assets that are incidental to a pledge of assets would be taken into account in determining whether the owner trust has centralized management. The fact that the indenture trustee is representing the bond holders and not the trust beneficiaries suggests that it should not be treated as a manager of the owner trust. In any event, the powers granted to the indenture trustee would typically be ministerial in the absence of a default. See footnote 122, above and accompanying text. Also, the indenture trustee would not generally have the "exclusive" power to manage the owner trust. For example, it would not have the power to exercise any rights to call bonds.

for claims against the owner trust, other than the obligation to make payments on the pay-through bonds. Finally, interests in the trust are not freely transferable, because the ability of an equity owner to substitute a new owner in its place is subject to the consent of at least one other unrelated equity owner owning a minimum percentage interest in the trust, which may be withheld for any reason.

Under most owner trust agreements, all equity owners are treated the same. However, it would be possible under the regulations to exclude some equity owners from management, to limit the liability of some equity owners, and to permit some equity owners to freely transfer their interests without affecting the classification of the owner trust, provided, in general, that the equity owners that remain liable have at least a 1 percent interest in the trust and that the equity owners who do not participate in management, and those entitled to freely transfer their interests, own less than "substantially all" (generally 80 percent) of the equity interests.

(ii) Whole loan participations. It is not uncommon for the legal owner of mortgages to grant some interest in the mortgages to another person under a participation agreement or some other form of contract that does not create a state law trust. The contract typically lasts over the entire life of the mortgages. The legal owner generally would retain a substantial beneficial interest in the mortgages. Although a participation arrangement would not ordinarily provide any power to vary the investment of the participants, a business objective could be considered to exist under the Sears regulations because of the creation of diverse ownership interests that do not fall within the "incidental" exception.

While the particular terms of a participation arrangement must be examined in each case, a participation arrangement would normally be classified as a partnership if a business objective is present, because it would lack centralized management and limited liability. Either the legal owner would be the principal beneficial owner of the mortgages and would have all rights to manage them (directly or through agents), or all participants would share in management. In addition, if the participation arrangement is not a state law trust, there would be no basis for limiting the liability of the participants (or at least of the legal owner of the mortgages) to third parties for claims arising out of the arrangement. If in a particular case the participants wanted to have additional protection against the possible existence of an association, the participation agreement could be written so that it would terminate upon the bankruptcy of the legal owner, or the assignment of participation interests could be restricted.

(iii) Issuers of pass-through debt certificates. As described in Chapter 2, Part G, issuers of pass-through debt certificates take the position that the certificates are debt for federal income tax purposes. If the certificates are characterized as debt, then they should be treated as limited recourse obligations of the sponsor, and the issuing trust should be viewed simply as a device to hold collateral for the debt, not as a separate entity for tax purposes.[145] However, because of the form of the certifi-

cates, it may not always be possible to conclude with certainty that the debt characterization of the certificates will be upheld. If the certificates were treated as ownership interests rather than as debt, the trust would be recognized to be an entity for tax purposes and would almost certainly be considered to have a business objective under the Sears regulations. Thus, as a precaution, in transactions where there is uncertainty as to the status of the certificates, the trust would have features ensuring its classification as a partnership if the debt argument were to fail.[146]

If the pass-through debt certificates were treated as ownership interests, the trust would resemble a limited partnership, with the sponsor being the general partner and the certificate holders the limited partners. Centralized management ordinarily does not exist in a limited partnership (and thus by analogy would not exist in the trust for any period in which the sponsor manages the trust) if the general partner (sponsor) has a greater than 20 percent interest in the partnership (trust).[147] On the other hand, centralized management may exist for any period in which a third party who does not own any interest in the trust assumes management responsibilities (such as following a default by the sponsor in carrying out those responsibilities).

The corporate characteristic of free transferability of interests exists only if members owning "substantially all" of the interests in an organization can freely transfer those interests. Thus, the trust would lack this characteristic if the sponsor owns an interest in the trust greater than 20 percent and is prohibited from assigning that interest (whether or not the sponsor is also managing the trust). An organization lacks limited liability if *any* member has personal liability for claims against the organization. Thus, limited liability would be defeated if the sponsor has such personal liability.[148] Finally, the trust may or may not lack continuity of life. If the trust agreement provides that upon a bankruptcy of the sponsor, there is an "event of acceleration" that does not result in a prompt sale of trust assets but nonetheless shortens the life of the trust, then it may be possible to conclude that the trust lacks continuity of life. Greater certainty would be gained if a bankruptcy of the sponsor triggered an obligation to sell trust assets as soon as is commercially reasonable. If such a term were included in a trust, perhaps the risk of an early collapse would be

---

145   For authorities treating trusts as mere security devices, see footnote 69, above.

146   In cases where the certificates are divided into classes, concern over possible equity treatment may be confined to certain classes. For example, if there are senior and junior classes of certificates, the risk of equity treatment may exist primarily for the junior classes. In that event, the references to certificate holders below in the text should be read to mean holders of classes of certificates for which equity treatment is considered to be a material risk.

147   The sponsor's interest in the trust would generally be a residual interest, whereas the certificate holders would receive a fixed return or a variable return based on an interest rate index. Under these circumstances, it may not be an easy task to determine whether the sponsor's interest exceeds 20%.

148   The statement in the text assumes that the sponsor has a sufficient interest in the trust to be recognized to be a member and that the sponsor either has substantial assets or is not a "dummy" of the certificate holders. The sponsor would not need to be liable for the claims of other certificate holders against the trust.

mitigated by having the sponsor hold its interest through a bankruptcy-remote entity.

(iv) Outside reserve funds. An investment trust may benefit from credit support in the form of a guarantee payable out of monies in a reserve fund held outside of the trust.[149] The fund may be owned by the trust sponsor, its successor, or a third party. The owner typically has the right to direct the investment of the reserve (which is limited to high-quality debt instruments), receives any monies released unused from the reserve, and is required to pay certain related expenses. Such reserve funds are often found in trusts having senior and subordinated interests, and in that case may be funded through a combination of initial contributions and distributions received on the subordinated interests. The subordinated interests may be transferable together with the rights and obligations of the reserve fund.

An outside reserve fund can be viewed most simply as an asset of the owner that is pledged to secure a nonrecourse guarantee. Under that view, the owner would be treated for tax purposes as earning all income on the fund, and as receiving and paying amounts paid into and out of the fund. The pledge would not create a separate entity for tax purposes, and no classification issues would arise. This analysis is compelling in most cases, particularly where the owner of the reserve owns no interest in the related trust, the reserve is not transferable, and the owner can at its option replace the reserve with other forms of credit support such as a letter of credit. On the other hand, if a reserve fund is to be funded out of distributions on a class of trust interests and must be transferred to any successor holder of that interest, then a question could arise as to whether the fund is truly outside of the trust or alternatively whether the arrangements establishing the reserve could be viewed as a separate investment trust.

Barring unusual circumstances, there is little reason to think that an outside reserve would be folded into the related trust. The rights of the reserve fund owner and of the investors are quite distinct. The fund owner holds liquid assets which are exposed to the risk of credit losses, and the investors hold an interest in the guaranteed assets. Moreover, from a tax policy perspective, as long as the documents are clear in spelling out ownership of the fund and the existence of the guarantee, and the parties report the transaction accordingly, it is difficult to imagine a reason for challenging the arrangement. The treatment of outside reserves in the REMIC regulations supports the view that the taxpayer's form will not be upset.[150]

Where there is a concern that a reserve fund arrangement might be evaluated as a separate entity, classification as an association generally can be avoided by ensuring that the arrangement lacks centralized management and limited liability.

---

149   For a discussion of trust classification issues raised by an inside reserve, see Part C.1.c.(vii) and footnote 84, above. See also Chapter 4, Parts A.2.b.(ii) and C.7.b, discussing inside and outside reserve funds for REMICs.

150   See Chapter 4, Part C.7.b. A recent ruling assumes that a trust with an outside reserve fund can be classified as a trust, but the effect of the reserve is not at issue in the ruling. See P.L.R. 9202011 (October 8, 1991).

D. Taxable Mortgage Pools

The complex scheme for classifying unincorporated non-REMIC issuers of mort-gage-backed securities detailed above is essentially irrelevant for any entity that is a *taxable mortgage pool*, or *TMP*, and, in general, issues debt after December 31, 1991. Under section 7701(i), such an entity is automatically classified as a corpora-tion (but nonetheless is not eligible to join in the filing of a consolidated return with other corporations). The goal of Congress in adopting the TMP rules was to ensure that the net income of a TMP was subject to income tax. That end was achieved by subjecting TMPs to the corporate income tax. This Part D discusses the definition of a TMP and effective date issues. The tax treatment of TMPs and their owners is considered in Chapter 8.

The paradigm example of a TMP is an owner trust that owns real estate mort-gages, or interests therein, and issues pay-through bonds. More technically, an entity[151] is a TMP if it is not a REMIC and (1) substantially all of its assets are debt obligations, and more than 50 percent of those obligations are real estate mortgages (the *asset test*), (2) the entity is the obligor under debt obligations with two or more maturities (the *maturities test*) and (3) payments on those debt obligations bear a relationship to payments on the debt obligations the obligor holds as assets (the *relationship test*).[152] The Service has issued proposed regulations that, while not yet effective as of this writing, provide substantial assistance in understanding these tests.[153] The TMP definition is applied not only to legal entities but also to "por-tions" of entities (specifically, segregated pools of assets that are expected to be used to service debt). A domestic building and loan association, and portions thereof, are excluded from the TMP definition.[154] The proposed TMP regulations would also provide relief for certain state or local government issuers of mortgage revenue bonds.[155]

The TMP rules are unforgiving in that there is no escape based on a reasonable good faith belief that an entity is not a TMP, and no express authority has been granted to the Service to waive TMP status where a taxpayer "inadvertently" quali-

---

151   Use of the term "entity" does not mean that only legal entities can be TMPs. As discussed below, a portion of an entity may also be a TMP.

152   Section 7701(i)(2)(A).

153   See Proposed Regulation § 301.7701(i) (FI-55-91, December 23, 1992) (the proposed TMP regu-lations). The proposed TMP regulations would be effective 30 days after they are published in final form. Although the discussion below reflects the proposed TMP regulations, readers are cautioned that they could be changed significantly before being adopted as final regulations.

154   See section 7701(i)(2)(C). A domestic building and loan association is defined in section 7701(a)(19)(C). If an organization were to lose its qualification under section 7701(a)(19)(C) and become a TMP, presumably TMP status would cease upon requalification, although the issue is not clear. Cf. Proposed Regulation § 301.7701(i)-3(c)(2) (TMP status terminates only when the last related debt obligation is retired).

155   Proposed Regulation § 301.7701(i)-4(a). Further, a governmental issuer could argue in some in-stances that any corporation created under the TMP rules is exempt from taxation under section 115 (or otherwise). See, e.g., Revenue Ruling 59-41, 1959-1 C.B. 13 (corporation formed by a local government to issue bonds and buy a water system is nontaxable).

fies as a TMP. On the other hand, the proposed TMP regulations contain a broadly worded anti-avoidance rule that will allow the Service to convert into TMPs transactions entered into with a view to achieving the same economic effects as a TMP while avoiding the TMP rules. Given the reach of the TMP definition, the prospects for accidental TMPs are good.

Some of the most difficult issues that arise in applying the TMP rules concern entities that acquire financially troubled real estate mortgages. The TMP rules do not extend to entities formed to acquire direct equity investments in real estate, and a distressed mortgage, although in form a debt instrument, may resemble such an investment more than a secured loan. This topic is discussed in more detail in Part D.2.e below.

The balance of this Part D will consider the relationship of the TMP rules to the REMIC rules, the TMP definition, and effective date issues.

1. Relationship to REMIC Rules

According to the legislative history of TRA 1986, the purpose of the TMP rules is to make REMICs "the exclusive means of issuing multiple class real estate mortgage-backed securities without the imposition of two levels of taxation."[156] While it is understandable that Congress, having taken the trouble to create REMICs, would want them to be used, why go so far as to penalize alternative vehicles? The answer is that the REMIC legislation contains safeguards to ensure that "phantom income" earned by holders of residual interests is subject to tax in all events, and Congress did not want those safeguards to be evaded through the use of other types of issuers.[157]

Given this purpose, it is not surprising that the TMP rules extend to entities that cannot meet the technical requirement of the REMIC definition. To illustrate some

---

156 Conference Report at II-239; Blue Book at 427.

157 The preamble to the proposed TMP regulations confirms this point: "[Section 7701(i)] is directed at the type of real estate mortgage pool that is used to collateralize and service multiple class securities. For tax purposes, the income accruing on the mortgages in this type of pool may initially exceed the deductions accruing on the securities, resulting in what is often referred to as 'phantom income.' Section 7701(i) was enacted to prevent this phantom income from being diverted to persons that can offset the income or otherwise avoid the tax attributable to the income." This purpose is borne out by the treatment of REITs that are also TMPs. Such a REIT can avoid corporate tax in the normal way by claiming a deduction for dividends it pays, but the income of its shareholders is subject to the same excess inclusion rules (which ensure taxation of phantom income) as apply to REMIC residual interests. See section 7701(i)(3), discussed in Chapter 8, Part D. In private letter rulings, the Service has described the legislative purpose somewhat differently: "The REMIC rules and the TMP provisions were meant to regulate self-liquidating pools of amortizing mortgages. . . . Any arrangement that functions like a REMIC but fails to qualify under Section 860D is classified as a TMP." P.L.R. 9326009 (March 25, 1993); P.L.R. 9302024 (October 20, 1992). The problem of diverting phantom income to tax-exempt parties is in fact less significant for non-REMIC issuers than for REMICs, because the equity interests in non-REMIC issuers (unlike REMIC residual interests) must have some value in order for their borrowings to be recognized to be debt for tax purposes. See Chapter 2, Part D.1. Thus, phantom income cannot be transferred to a tax-exempt entity by giving such an entity an economically insignificant equity interest.

of the differences, all but a *de minimis* amount of the assets of a REMIC must be qualified mortgages or certain permitted investments. By contrast, under the proposed TMP regulations, an entity could be a TMP if as little as 41 percent of its assets, measured by tax basis, consist of real property mortgages (and the percentage could be well below this number measured by fair market value).[158] Certain real estate related instruments that are not qualified mortgages for REMICs are nonetheless treated as real estate mortgages in the hands of a TMP. These include pay-through bonds issued after December 31, 1991, equity interests in various pass-through arrangements that are not grantor trusts, and REMIC residual interests.[159] Further, a TMP can engage in activities that would disqualify a REMIC, such as issuing additional interests or acquiring additional property after formation, or issuing types of interests (for example, multiple equity classes, guarantees, or options) that would violate the REMIC interests test.

A TMP that does not or cannot elect REMIC status may be subject to a higher tax burden than a REMIC because of the second layer of tax that generally applies to shareholders of a corporation.[160] This additional tax applies to net income attributable to the equity of a TMP and, unlike a REMIC, a TMP must have a material amount of equity in order for its debt obligations to be recognized to be debt for tax purposes.[161] Given the choice, an issuer of multiple classes of mortgage-backed securities generally will prefer to be a REMIC and not a TMP.

2. Definition of TMP

As indicated above, an entity is a TMP if it meets an asset test, a maturities test and a relationship test. These tests may be applied to only a portion of an entity. Special rules apply to financially troubled loans and liquidating arrangements. The proposed TMP regulations test whether an entity is a TMP generally only as of a "testing date" (generally the date on which it issues debt). Finally, the Service may expand the TMP definition under an anti-avoidance rule. The next seven sections discuss the three tests, the portion rule, the treatment of troubled loans, testing dates, and the anti-avoidance rule.

a. Asset Test. An entity meets the asset test if "substantially all" of its assets consist of debt obligations (or interests therein) and over 50 percent of those debt obligations are real estate mortgages (or interests therein). Under the proposed TMP regulations, an entity must use the tax basis of its assets in applying both parts of the test.[162]

---

158 An entity would qualify as a TMP if substantially all (which could potentially be as low as 80%) of its assets consist of debt obligations, and more than 50% of those obligations are real property mortgages. The tax basis of assets is used in applying these tests. See Part D.2.a below.

159 See Part D.2.a below.

160 Where equity in a TMP is owned by a domestic corporation, the tax imposed directly on distributions to that corporation generally will be reduced or, if the distributee owns at least 80% of the equity in the TMP, eliminated, by the dividends received deduction. See Chapter 8, footnote 11.

161 For a discussion of this requirement, see Chapter 2, footnote 44.

The proposed TMP regulations state that whether "substantially all" of an entity's assets are debt obligations is determined based on all the facts and circumstances, without stating what facts or circumstances might be relevant.[163] However, under a safe harbor rule, an entity will fail the substantially all test if less than 80 percent of its assets are debt obligations.[164]

The proposed TMP regulations do not define the term "debt obligation" but presumably any instrument that is treated as debt for tax purposes would fall within the definition.[165] However, as discussed in section f below, the term does not include a real estate mortgage that is "seriously impaired."

Two special rules apply in measuring assets. First, equity interests held by an entity in a REIT, S corporation, partnership, or "other pass-through arrangement" are deemed to have the same composition as the entity's share of the assets of the pass-through arrangement.[166] Second, "credit enhancement contracts," defined gen-

---

162 Proposed Regulation § 301.7701(i)-1(c)(1). The use of tax basis, rather than fair market value, has the advantage of greater certainty, but can produce distortions where tax basis departs significantly from fair market value. The safe harbor *de minimis* rule in Treasury Regulation § 1.860D-1(b)(3) that is used in applying the REMIC assets test also measures assets by their tax basis, but under section 860F(b)(2), a REMIC's initial basis in contributed property equals the property's fair market value. One technical question is whether basis is tested before or after giving effect to the classification of an entity as a corporation under the TMP rules. To illustrate, suppose that A and B each make equity contributions to a partnership consisting of mortgages (with a basis of 40 and a fair market value of 100) and unsecured debt (with a basis and fair market value of 50). The partnership pledges the assets to secure debt and pays to each of A and B cash proceeds of the borrowing of 120. If the partnership is recognized to be partnership, then the contribution would be tax free under section 721 and the partnership would have the same tax basis in the assets as A and B, so that the tax basis of the mortgages would be less than half of the tax basis of all of the debt obligations it holds. On the other hand, if the partnership were classified as a corporation under the TMP rules, section 351(b)(1) would require A and B to recognize the unrealized gain in the contributed mortgages (because A and B would receive cash "boot" exceeding the amount of gain). As a result, the tax basis of the mortgages would increase to their fair market value, and the asset test would be met. It would seem to be appropriate to assume that an entity is not a TMP in applying the asset test to determine if it is a TMP, but the point is not entirely clear.

163 Conceivably, the facts and circumstances test would prevent an entity from being a TMP where the mechanical tests in the regulations appear to be distortive (e.g., where an entity has substantial assets other than debt obligations that have a low tax basis, or where the debt obligations are expected to be sold and used to buy operating assets). In the area of reorganizations, a substantially all test has been applied giving more weight to core operating assets than to incidental assets such as passive investments. See, e.g., Revenue Ruling 57-518, 1957-2 C.B. 253. Such a distinction would not make sense for TMPs.

164 Proposed Regulation § 301.7701(i)-1(c)(2)(ii).

165 By contrast, the REMIC regulations have a special definition of "obligation" that is intended to broaden the term to allow credit impaired loans to be qualified mortgages. See Chapter 4, Parts A.2.a.(i) and C.6.

166 Proposed Regulation § 301.7701(i)-1(c)(3). Thus, if a REIT has assets consisting of 100 of real estate and 100 of real estate mortgages, and liabilities of 50, and an entity owns 50% of the stock of the REIT which it purchased for 70, the stock would be considered to represent 35 of real estate and 35 of real estate mortgages. It is not clear whether the tax basis or fair market value of the REIT's assets would be used in determining the composition of its assets, although most likely tax basis would be used. In cases where an entity does not own a substantial (or even controlling) interest in a pass-through arrangement, its ability to obtain information as to the composition of the assets of the pass-through of a type that would be useful in applying the TMP tests may be limited.

erally in the same manner as in the REMIC regulations, are not treated as separate assets, but rather are part of the asset to which they relate.[167]

The second part of the assets test asks whether more than 50 percent of the debt obligations held by an entity are real estate mortgages (or interests therein). The proposed TMP regulations define a "real estate mortgage" to include an obligation (including a participation or certificate of beneficial ownership therein) that is principally secured by an interest in real property, a REMIC regular or residual interest, or a stripped bond or coupon representing a right to a payment on a real estate mortgage.[168] The definitions of "principally secured" and "interests in real property" are generally the same as the definitions of those terms in the REMIC regulations.[169] As discussed above, the TMP term "real estate mortgage" includes certain instruments that could not be qualified mortgages in the hands of a REMIC.[170] One way in which the TMP term is narrower is that it excludes "seriously impaired" loans.[171]

If a pass-through arrangement has multiple classes of economic interests having different rights to share in the profits or losses from designated assets, then presumably the economic terms of the classes would determine how the assets are allocated among those classes.

167   Further, assets supporting such a contract are not, solely because they support the guarantee represented by the contract, considered to be assets of an entity. See Proposed Regulation § 301.7701(i)-1(c)(4). The REMIC definition of credit enhancement contract, found at Treasury Regulation § 1.860G-2(c), is discussed at length in Chapter 4, Part C.1. In applying the portion rule described in section d below, the assets of a portion exclude not only credit enhancement contracts, but also any assets that "serve primarily the same function as credit enhancement contracts".

168   Proposed Regulation § 301.7701(i)-1(d). The word "includes" implies that other obligations not listed could fall within the definition, but there is no indication of what those other obligations might be.

169   See Chapter 4, Part A.2.a.(ii). Thus, in general, an obligation is principally secured by real estate if the value of the real estate collateral is at least 80% of the adjusted issue price of the obligation, or if substantially all of the proceeds of the obligation were used to acquire, improve or protect real estate which at the date of origination is the only property pledged to secure the obligation. The 80% collateral test is applied in the proposed TMP regulations only when a loan is originated (and, unlike the rule for REMICs, not also when it is contributed to an entity).

170   See footnote 159, above. One way in which the definition is broader is that it includes an obligation that is secured by a second obligation that is principally secured by real property. See Proposed Regulation § 301.7701(i)-1(d)(3)(ii). This rule is oddly written in two respects. First, read literally, it would seem to apply regardless of the relationship of the collateral to the obligation that is secured. Thus, it could be read to treat an obligation as a real estate mortgage if it is 20% secured by a pay-through bond, even though 80% security would be required if the pay-through bond were a direct interest in real estate. Almost certainly, the intent was to treat collateral consisting of an obligation that is principally secured by real property the same as a direct interest in real property in applying the principally secured definition. A second quirk in the rule is that it only applies to a debt obligation secured by a second debt obligation that is a real estate mortgage under the "principally secured" portion of the definition. Thus, for example, a debt obligation secured by a REMIC residual interest would not seem to be a real estate mortgage (unless in the particular case, the residual interest also met the definition of an obligation principally secured by an interest in real property).

171   The TMP term is also narrower because it excludes obligations that meet the 80% collateral test when they are contributed to an entity but not at origination. See footnote 169, above. The rule for seriously impaired obligations, which is discussed in section e below, provides that "real estate mortgages" that are seriously impaired will not be treated as "debt obligations". Since the real estate mortgage portion of the TMP asset test looks to the portion of the "debt obligations" of an

b. Maturities Test. An entity meets the maturities test if it is the obligor under "debt obligations with 2 or more maturities". The term "debt obligation" is discussed at the end of this section. It may be assumed (and the proposed TMP regulations confirm) that the maturities test would be met if two debt obligations have different stated maturity dates. A more difficult question is when to treat two obligations with the same stated maturity date as having different maturities because of differences in the timing of payments before maturity.

Following the TRA 1986 legislative history, the proposed TMP regulations state that obligations have two or more maturities if "the holders of the obligations possess different rights concerning the acceleration of or delay in the maturities of the obligations."[172] The regulations confirm that holders of a class of obligations do not have different rights to receive payments simply because a portion of an issue may be selected at random for redemption if all obligations are equally likely to be redeemed.[173]

The only case identified in the regulations where differences in rights to principal payments do not produce two or more maturities is where the differences are attributable solely to an unequal allocation of credit risk (i.e., the risk that payments of principal or interest on an obligation will be reduced or delayed because of a default on an asset that supports the obligation).[174] An example shows that this measure of grace would allow the maturity of a senior class that suffers a payment default to be accelerated without accelerating a junior class, and would allow a junior class to bear interest at a higher rate to compensate for its subordinated ranking.[175]

Although the proposed TMP regulations do not address the point, it would be very surprising if a difference in interest rates that is not attributable to credit risk would result in multiple maturities.[176] This conclusion is supported by the normal meaning of "maturity," which looks to the timing of principal payments. More fundamentally, differences in interest rates, without more, should not produce the

---

entity that are real estate mortgages, a real estate mortgage that is not treated as a debt obligation because it is seriously impaired is excluded from both the numerator and denominator in applying the more-than-50% real estate mortgages test.

172   Proposed Regulation § 301.7701(i)-1(e)(1). The TRA 1986 legislative history has a similar statement (but refers to different rights relating to the acceleration of maturities, rather than to different rights of holders concerning the acceleration of or delay in maturities). See Conference Report at II-240, n. 24; Blue Book at 427, n. 95. It is unlikely that the reference in the proposed TMP regulations to the rights of *holders* is significant. While it could be read to mean that certain rights of an issuer, such as a right to prepay obligations, would be disregarded, any right of an issuer could be said to affect the rights of holders.

173   Proposed Regulation § 301.7701(i)-1(e)(3), Example 1. See also P.L.R. 9214017 (January 3, 1992) to the same effect.

174   Proposed Regulation § 301.7701(i)-1(e)(2).

175   Proposed Regulation § 301.7701(i)-1(e)(3), Example 2.

176   To take a simple case, suppose that two classes have identical rights to principal but one bears interest at a fixed rate and one at a floating rate. Assuming that interest is paid at least annually on both classes (whether or not on the same dates), the two classes should be considered to have the same maturity.

pattern of expected increases in weighted average interest rates that creates phantom income.[177] On the other hand, if two classes are identical except that interest on one is deferred and paid as "deferred interest" only after a significant delay, the effect could be the same as if principal were deferred, and there would be a substantial argument in favor of finding two maturities.[178]

In other areas, the weighted average maturity of a debt obligation is sometimes calculated taking account of interest payments. While these rules might be looked to by the Service as an analogy in applying the TMP maturities test, the value of the analogy should be examined in light of the policy objectives in each area.[179]

The maturities test requires that there be "debt obligations" with two or more maturities. The proposed TMP regulations do not define this term. Although any claim against an entity that is treated as indebtedness for tax purposes could potentially be a debt instrument, it is unlikely that the drafters of section 7701(i) intended to go so far. The legislative history indicates that the TMP rules were aimed at issuers of multiple classes of "mortgage-backed securities,"[180] and it can be argued that obligations must bear some resemblance to investment securities to be counted toward the maturities test. The line between a "security" and other debt obligations is blurry at best. One way to draw it would be to piggyback on the REMIC rules, and disregard, in applying the maturities test, any debt instrument that would not be an "interest" for purposes of the REMIC interests test.[181] In any event, working

---

177   For a description of the sources of phantom income, see Chapter 7, Part E, and Appendix A.

178   One case where it would seem to be appropriate not to find different maturities is where interest on one or more but not all debt classes may be deferred to reflect negative amortization on underlying floating rate mortgages that arises when the interest accrual rate on those mortgages exceeds the maximum payment rate.

179   The REMIC regulations use the term "anticipated weighted average life." See Treasury Regulation § 1.860E-1(a)(3)(iv). The weighted average life of a regular interest is generally calculated taking only principal payments into account. However, all payments are included in the calculation for residual interests and for regular interests that have no specified principal amount or disproportionately high interest. The proposed OID regulations also have a definition of weighted average maturity. The average takes account of all payments on a debt instrument other than payments of qualified stated interest. See Treasury Regulation § 1.1273-1(e)(3). Qualified stated interest is discussed in Chapter 6, Part C.1. Interest is generally qualified stated interest if it is paid evenly over the life of an instrument, but not if it is accelerated or deferred. While the Service could take the position that interest that is not qualified stated interest should be treated as principal in applying the TMP maturities test, such an approach may not give sufficient weight to the differences between the OID and TMP regimes. The purpose of the OID rules is to spread interest income evenly over the life of a debt instrument. Finding that an interest payment is not qualified stated interest, and therefore is included in OID, affects only the timing of interest income and deductions. By contrast, the purpose of the TMP rules is to prevent the avoidance of tax on phantom income, and characterizing interest as principal for purposes of the TMP maturities test could change the tax status of an issuer and have serious tax consequences. It might be appropriate to develop an alternative standard for TMPs that is more tolerant of differences in the timing of interest payments, particularly where those differences were not adopted intentionally to evade the TMP rules.

180   The Conference Report at II-239 includes the following: "The conferees intend that REMICs are to be the exclusive means of issuing multiple class real estate mortgage-backed securities without the imposition of two levels of taxation. Thus, the conference agreement provides that a [TMP] is treated as a taxable corporation. . . ."

capital loans, servicer advances, or other obligations arising in the ordinary course of business (e.g., accounts payable) should not be considered debt obligations.[182] A ruling or regulation addressing these points would be most welcome.

c. Relationship Test. The last element of the TMP definition is the relationship test. The purpose of this test is to distinguish pay-through bonds from conventional debt by requiring that payments on bonds be linked (or to use the statutory phrase, "bear a relationship") to the payments on the underlying mortgages or other debt collateral. Under the proposed TMP regulations, this test is met if, under the terms of the debt obligations issued by an entity (referred to in the regulations as "liability obligations") or an "underlying arrangement", the timing and amounts of payments on the liability obligations are in large part determined by the timing and amount of payments (or projected payments) on the obligations held by the entity (referred to as "asset obligations"). There is a special rule for applying the relationship test to liquidating entities, which is considered in section e below.

Applying the test requires identifying the "payments" on asset obligations, determining if there is the requisite relationship between those payments and the payments on the liability obligations, and determining if that relationship exists under the terms of the liability obligations or an underlying arrangement.

(i) Payments on asset obligations. The TMP rules are aimed at borrowings that are expected to be repaid using payments on debt obligations collected from bor-rowers (as contrasted with proceeds of sales). The definition of "payments" on asset obligations in the proposed TMP regulations is consistent with this view. The regu-lations would include in the term payments of principal and interest, including prepayments and payments under credit enhancement contracts, but would exclude the proceeds of settlements at a substantial discount, or of foreclosures or sales, unless the settlement, foreclosure, or sale was arranged, whether in writing or other-wise, prior to the issuance of the liability obligations.[183] It is unclear what it means to "pre-arrange" one of these events. The most significant factor should be whether the proceeds to be realized from the event have been fixed in amount. The proposed regulations shed no light on this point.

181　See Chapter 4, Part A.1. The TMP definition of debt obligation would, of course, be narrower than the REMIC definition of interest since it would be limited to instruments that are treated as debt for tax purposes.

182　Obligations of this type would not produce phantom income, which is a good reason for disregard-ing them. See footnote 157 above. Proposed Regulation § 301.7701(i)-1(c)(4) treats credit en-hancement contracts, including an advance to make up for defaults or protect collateral, as part of the related assets for purposes of the TMP assets test. This rule strongly implies that rights to reimbursement under such contracts would not be treated as debt obligations in applying the maturities test, although the proposed TMP regulations do not address the point specifically. Compare Treasury Regulation § 1.860D-1(b)(2)(iii), which provides that a right of reimbursement under a credit enhancement contract is not an "interest" in a REMIC.

183　Proposed Regulation § 301.7701(i)-1(f)(2). Literally read, the regulation purports to define only what amounts are "included" in payments on asset obligations, but the clear implication of the regulation is also to exclude the items mentioned in the text.

The proposed TMP regulations do not define the "payments" on liability obligations. Presumably, all payments are included.

(ii) Terms of debt obligations or underlying arrangement. The required relationship must arise "under the terms of the liability obligations (or underlying arrangement)." It might be argued, based on this language, that a liability obligation must somehow specify that payments thereon are measured by payments on asset obligations of the issuer (that is, a mere *de facto* relationship does not suffice). However, the reference to an "underlying arrangement" makes it risky to rely on this view. It could be argued that an underlying arrangement exists in any case where the payment terms of a liability obligation are structured based on cash flows available from specified asset obligations, even if the payments on the liability obligations are not expected to be affected by any advance or delay in the timing of payments on the asset obligations. Such an interpretation, however, would take the TMP definition well beyond a traditional issuer of pay-through bonds.[184] The only example of an underlying arrangement given in the proposed TMP regulations is a case where the timing and amount of payments on liability obligations are determined by the performance of a group of assets or an index or model that has an expected payment experience similar to that of the asset obligations.[185] This result makes sense, since the net effect of the arrangement is that the timing and amount of payments on the liability obligations are not fixed and are correlated with variations in the timing and amount of payments on the asset obligations.

(iii) Required relationship. The most critical element of the relationship test is the nature of the relationship that must exist between payments on assets and liabilities. According to the legislative history, the relationship between the assets of a TMP and its debt obligations typically would be such that payments of its obligations must be made within a period of time from when payments on the assets are received.[186]

Under the proposed TMP regulations, the required link would exist if the "timing and amount of payments on the liability obligations are in large part determined by the timing and amount of payments or projected payments on the asset obligations."[187] Thus, both the timing *and* amount of payments must be linked. The

---

184 In such a case, the required relationship between the payments on asset obligations and liability obligations, discussed in the next section in the text, may well not exist. Proposed Regulation § 301.7701(i)-1(f) states that "[f]or purposes of the relationship test, any payment arrangement that achieves a substantially similar result is treated as satisfying the test." This language suggests that the focus of the underlying arrangement rule is not to change the basic reach of the TMP definition, but rather to get at attempts to avoid the definition through clever drafting.

185 See Proposed Regulation § 301.7701(i)-1(f)(i). See also Proposed Regulation § 301.7701(i)-1(g)(3), Example 2 (example applies anti-avoidance rule where payments on bonds issued by one corporation are based on payments received on mortgages owned beneficially by an affiliated corporation).

186 Conference Report at II-240. Curiously, the corresponding passage in the Blue Book at 427 omits this statement.

"large part" language is masterfully vague. At a minimum, it indicates that a dollar-for-dollar matching is not needed, but whether the required correlation is 70 percent, or only 30 percent will do, is not obvious.[188]

The reference to "projected payments" presumably means payments that will be projected from time to time over the life of an issue, and not payments projected solely at the start. If the latter interpretation were adopted, then the relationship test would be met where payments on liability obligations are scheduled taking account of the expected performance of a pool of mortgages, even though the payments on the liability obligations are fixed and actual mortgage payments are likely to differ materially from the projections. It seems very unlikely that such an interpretation was intended.[189]

d. Portion Rule. The reason for the portion rule can best be explained with examples. Suppose that a partnership holds a pool of mortgages and also substantial other assets. If the partnership transferred the mortgages to a trust that issued multiple classes of pay-through bonds, the trust would be a TMP. Can the partnership avoid the TMP rules by issuing the same debt itself and arguing that, because of its non-mortgage assets, the asset test is not met?

Alternatively, suppose that a partnership owning several pools of mortgages and no other assets transfers each pool to a separate trust that issues a single class of debt that is expected to be repaid in full from the related mortgage pool. None of these trusts, viewed separately, is a TMP because each trust has only one class of debt. If the partnership chose instead to hold the mortgages and issue the debt directly, would the TMP definition be met by the partnership, since it would be the obligor on more than one class of debt?

The starting point in answering these questions is section 7701(i)(2)(B), which treats any "portion" of an entity that meets the TMP definition as a TMP.[190] According-ing to the TRA 1986 legislative history, the portion rule may be applied to treat as a TMP any arrangement under which mortgages are segregated for the benefit of creditors holding debt of varying maturities which depends on the timing of payments on the mortgages.[191] Thus, in the first example above, where the partnership

---

187   See Proposed Regulation § 301.7701(i)-1(f)(1).

188   Compare the phrase "substantial part" that was contained in the pre-1984 definition of a collaps-ible corporation found in section 341(b)(1). This phrase was the source of considerable litigation, and was replaced in 1984 with "2/3."

189   The discussion in the TRA 1986 legislative history of the portion rule (described in the next section of the text) suggests that Congress thought that the timing of payments on debt of a TMP would be tied (presumably on an ongoing basis) to the timing of payments on assets: "Under the conference agreement, any portion of an entity that meets the definition of a TMP is treated as a TMP. For example, if an entity segregates mortgages in some fashion and issues debt obligations in two or more maturities, which maturities depend upon the timing of payments on the mortgages, then the mortgages and the debt would be treated as a TMP, and hence as a separate corporation." Conference Report at II-240.

190   The portion rule is analogous to the rule allowing a REMIC election to be made for a segregated pool of assets. See Chapter 4, footnote 3.

issues debt against mortgages it holds directly, the mortgage pool and related obligations would be a TMP.

The outcome in the second example, in which a partnership issues only one class of debt payable out of each mortgage pool it holds, is less clear under the statute. The Code states that a portion of an entity that meets the TMP definition will be treated as a TMP, but does not say that an entity may be divided into portions to avoid TMP status. As discussed below, however, the proposed TMP regulations would reach this result.

The proposed TMP regulations attack the portion problem in an interesting way. They define a portion through "reverse engineering" using the relationship test. Specifically, a portion is defined as all assets that "support" one or more issues of debt obligations.[192] Obligations are supported by assets for this purpose if, under the terms of the debt obligations (or underlying arrangement), the timing and amount of payments thereon are in large part determined, either directly or indirectly, by payments or projected payments on the assets (or a group of assets that includes the assets).[193] In this context, all proceeds and receipts from an asset are treated as payments on the asset.

The gist of this definition is that an asset, to be included in a portion, must be expected to contribute to the payment of debt service. The proposed regulations amplify this point by stating that a portion does not include assets that primarily serve the same function as credit enhancement contracts (i.e., that would be called upon to pay debt service if the expected revenue source is impaired through defaults or other unexpected events),[194] and more broadly does not include assets that are "unlikely" to produce any "significant" cash flows for the holders of the debt obligations.[195] To hammer the point home, the regulations state that an asset is not included in a portion solely because the holders of the debt obligations have recourse to the holder of that asset.[196]

A second feature of the portion rule is that, for purposes of the maturities test, a portion is treated as the obligor (and apparently the only obligor) of all debt

---

191   See Conference Report at II-240; Blue Book at 427.

192   Proposed Regulation § 301.7701(i)-2(a).

193   Proposed Regulation § 301.7701(i)-2(a).

194   Proposed Regulation § 301.7701(i)-2(b)(1). An asset must "primarily" serve the same function as a credit enhancement contract to be excluded from a portion. Thus, in a case where debt obligations are secured by a pool of mortgages and the mortgages exceed in size the debt to take account of credit risk, but there is no separate identification of the mortgages that serve as credit support, it seems unlikely that any of the mortgages would be considered to serve "primarily" a credit support function. This conclusion is bolstered by the language that includes within a portion an asset that is part of a group of assets that support a debt obligation.

195   Proposed Regulation § 301.7701(i)-2(b)(2). It is not clear when cash flows would be considered to be "significant" for this purpose. The regulation states that the rule may apply to exclude assets from a portion even though the holders of the related debt obligations are legally entitled to cash flows from the assets. Thus, even if a sale of a building causes a series of debt obligations to be redeemed out of proceeds of the sale, the building is not included in a portion if it is not likely to be sold.

196   Proposed Regulation § 301.7701(i)-2(b)(3).

obligations it supports.[197] Thus, the maturities test would not be met in the second partnership example above with respect to any pool of mortgages that supports only a single class of debt obligations. The regulations do not explain why the maturities test is singled out, and whether a portion can be treated as a separate entity to avoid TMP status in any other circumstances.[198]

The proposed regulations illustrate the portion rule with an example.[199] In the example, a corporation with substantial nonmortgage assets holds three pools of mortgages that support three different issues of obligations. Two of the issues have multiple maturities and one consists of a single class. Each class of debt is secured by a separate letter of credit and a lien on an office complex. It is anticipated that the cash flow from each mortgage pool will service its related bonds. Each of the three mortgage pools is treated as a separate portion. Those portions do not include the office complex (which primarily provides credit support). The letters of credit are not separate assets but are considered to be incidental to the related mortgages. For purposes of the maturities test, each portion is treated as a separate obligor. Apparently, this means that the two pools supported by multiple classes of debt are TMPs and the one supported by a single class is not, although this conclusion is not stated in the example.

e. Arrangements Involving Financially Distressed Mortgages. Partnerships have often been formed in recent years for the purpose of acquiring financially distressed mortgage loans. The purchase price is typically provided through a combination of equity contributions and debt. The debt may include senior debt and subordinated debt with a later maturity date. The partnership's business plan is to attempt to bring the loans current (based on their original terms or modified terms) and then sell them, or to realize proceeds through foreclosures and sales of real property. Generally, the issued obligations are expected to be retired primarily from sources other than scheduled payments of principal and interest on the loans.

It can be argued that liquidating arrangements of this type are not TMPs under the statute, either because the defaulted mortgages are in substance equity interests in real property and not "real estate mortgages," or on the ground that the relation-

---

197   Proposed Regulation § 301.7701(i)-2(c).

198   To illustrate one case where the issue would arise, suppose that an entity holds two pools of debt obligations, A and B, and uses each to support an identified separate issue of debt obligations (the A and B issues) with multiple maturities. Suppose further that pool A consists of 100 of mortgages and pool B consists of 50 of unsecured loans. The A and B pools would be treated as separate portions for purposes of applying the maturities test, and that test would be met because the A and B issues each include two or more maturities of debt. The A pool would, and the B pool would not, qualify as TMPs if they were separately tested. Further, the entity as a whole (consisting of both pools) would seem to qualify as a TMP, given that the mortgages in the A pool represent more than half of the assets of the entity. It is not entirely clear whether the TMP is the entity or simply the A pool. If the entity holding the A and B pools is already a corporation, it may prefer to have the TMP definition apply to the entity as a whole, because the corporate tax would apply in any event and there then would be no need to deal with the tax consequences of establishing a separate nonconsolidated corporation.

199   Proposed Regulation § 301.7701(i)-2(d).

ship test is not met because the debts of the entity will be paid primarily from proceeds of the loans and not "payments" thereon.[200] The Service has issued a number of rulings holding, without much discussion, that liquidating arrangements are not TMPs.[201]

The proposed TMP regulations provide relief to liquidating entities in three ways. First, real estate mortgages that are "seriously impaired" are excluded from the definition of "debt obligation."[202] Since a seriously impaired mortgage is not a debt obligation, it also is not a real estate mortgage for purposes of applying the more-than-50 percent-mortgages branch of the TMP assets test.[203]

Second, the definition of "payments" on debt obligations excludes proceeds from a disposition of a loan or the underlying collateral if the disposition is not pre-arranged.[204] As a result, an entity that expects to receive only such proceeds could not be a TMP. On the other hand, an entity that will receive some payments, and some proceeds that are not payments, will need to determine whether the amounts treated as payments determine in large part the payments on the entity's debt, which is not an easy test to apply.

Lastly, the proposed TMP regulations provide a special rule that treats a liquidating entity meeting certain criteria as failing to meet the relationship test.[205] The

---

200   There are also policy arguments against applying the TMP rules to a liquidating entity. First, such an entity is less likely to produce phantom income for its equity owners than a traditional owner trust, because the yield structure of its debt will reflect considerations other than the yield curve, and because interest on the loans it holds may be uncollectible and therefore not subject to accrual. See Chapter 6, Part G.2. Second, the term of the investment generally will be shorter than the life of a typical mortgage pool, so that any phantom income that does exist will be reversed over a shorter period. Third, the equity in a liquidating entity is likely to be both substantial and highly speculative, and therefore less likely to be transferred to non-taxpaying entities for tax avoidance reasons. Finally, REMICs are not well suited to such arrangements, so that the policy of using the TMP club to force a REMIC election does not make sense. See Chapter 4, Part C.6.

201   See, e.g., P.L.R. 9339022 (October 1, 1993); P.L.R. 9326009 (March 25, 1993); P.L.R. 9302024 (October 20, 1992).

202   See Proposed Regulation § 301.7701(i)-1(c)(5). Whether a real estate mortgage is seriously impaired depends on all facts and circumstances. However, an entity may always treat a single family residential mortgage that is more than 89 days delinquent, or a multi-family residential or commercial real estate mortgage that is more than 59 days delinquent, as seriously impaired, unless the entity is receiving, or anticipates receiving, principal and interest payments on the loan that are substantial and relatively certain as to amount, or other proceeds from a pre-arranged disposition or workout of the loan.

203   See footnote 171 above. Real estate mortgages for this purpose presumably would be defined in accordance with Proposed Regulation § 301.7701(i)-1(d) and thus would include other mortgaged-backed securities (REMIC regular and residual interests, pass-through certificates and pay-through bonds). It is not clear how the "seriously impaired" test would be applied to such securities. One issue is whether to look through to the underlying assets or to examine the terms of the security itself. Another question is how the impairment test would be applied, if necessary, to such a security. In most cases, the holder of a mortgage-backed security is entitled to payments only to the extent of available funds, so that credit losses on the underlying assets would not trigger a default on the security. Nonetheless, delays or losses on a security attributable to defaults on the underlying mortgages should be taken into account in determining if it is seriously impaired.

204   See Part D.2.c.(i) above.

205   Proposed Regulation § 301.7701(i)-1(f)(3). An entity can benefit from the rule if: (1) the entity's organizational documents manifest clearly that the entity is formed for the primary purpose of

rule may have the effect of requiring the liquidation to be completed within three years, which is not always possible.

f. Testing Dates. One of the most troublesome features of the TMP definition in the Code is that it can be read to apply continuously over the life of an entity. Under a continuous testing approach, it might be necessary, to avoid TMP status, to monitor the composition of an entity's assets over the life of a debt issue to ensure that the percentage of debt obligations consisting of real estate mortgages never exceeds 50 percent. The proposed TMP regulations would provide relief in this area by treating an entity as a TMP only if it meets the definition on a "testing day." A testing day is any day on which an entity issues a debt obligation that meets the relationship test and is significant in amount.[206]

An issuer could attempt to abuse the testing date rule by avoiding the TMP definition on the date when debt is issued and then changing the facts (e.g., by exchanging mortgages for nonmortgage collateral). The anti-avoidance rule discussed in the next section was adopted with just such planning in mind.

Under the proposed TMP regulations, once an entity is classified as a TMP, it remains a TMP until the last debt obligation satisfying the relationship test is retired.[207]

g. Anti-Avoidance Rule. The proposed TMP regulations include an "anti-avoidance rule" that allows the Service to disregard or make other adjustments to a transaction (or series of transactions) if the transaction (or series) is entered into with a view to achieving the same economic effect as a TMP while avoiding the TMP rules.[208] The authority includes treating equity interests issued by a non-REMIC entity as debt "if the entity issues equity interests that correspond to maturity classes of debt."[209]

---

liquidating its assets and distributing proceeds of liquidation; (2) the entity's activities are all reasonably necessary to and consistent with the accomplishment of liquidating assets; (3) the entity plans to satisfy at least 50% of the total issue price of each of its liability obligations having a different maturity with proceeds from liquidation and not with scheduled payments on its asset obligations; and (4) either the entity liquidates within three years of the time it first acquires assets to be liquidated or, if it does not so liquidate, the payments the entity receives on its asset obligations after that time are paid through to the holders of its liability obligations in proportion to their adjusted issue prices. If the last requirement is read to mean that an entity that issues senior and subordinated debt and fails to liquidate within three years must place debt classes that remain outstanding after three years on a parity, then the requirement would seem to be impractical as a commercial matter.

206 Proposed Regulation § 301.7701(i)-3(c)(1). The regulation also requires that the testing day be on or after 30 days after final regulations are published. It is not clear what the rule is supposed to be for entities that issue debt after December 31, 1991 and before this effective date. Effective date issues are discussed further in Part D.3. below.

207 Proposed Regulation § 301.7701(1)-3(c)(2).

208 Proposed Regulation § 301.7701(i)-1(g)(1).

209 This part of the regulation is based on section 7701(i)(2)(D), which states that "to the extent provided in regulations, equity interests of varying classes which correspond to maturity classes of debt shall be treated as debt for purposes of [the TMP definition]." This rule is probably not self-executing in the absence of regulations, and thus would seem to be ineffective for entities that

However, an ownership interest in an investment trust that is classified as a trust will not be treated as a debt obligation of the trust under this authority.[210]

Three examples in the regulations indicate that the anti-avoidance rule may be used to treat an arrangement as a TMP where TMP status is sought to be avoided by separating the steps required to create the TMP, or by dividing assets and liabilities among affiliated entities.[211] There are no examples illustrating the rule recharacterizing equity as debt.

The equity recharacterization rule requires that equity classes correspond to maturity classes of debt.[212] The purpose of the TMP rules should play a significant role in deciding if this correspondence exists. As noted above, that purpose is to prevent the avoidance of tax on "phantom income," which is noneconomic income taxed to an equity class based on the method of allocation of deductions among two or more other classes having different maturities and yields. Given this purpose, it would be reasonable to test whether an equity class corresponds to a maturity class of debt by asking whether the substantive tax rules applicable to that class, when combined with the rules applicable to a true debt class or another equity class, have the effect of creating phantom income for any class of equity that is not treated as debt.[213] It is easy to imagine a class of partnership interests that receives an allocation of income corresponding to the interest that would be earned by a class of debt, and that could therefore meet this test.[214] Hopefully, the authority to treat equity classes as debt will be exercised only in fairly clear cases where equity classes bear a close resemblance (both economically and for tax purposes) to debt.

---

      are not subject to any final TMP regulations that may be adopted. See generally R. Crnkovich & K. Heller, "'To the Extent' Provisions: When Do They Operate Without Regulations," 76 *J. Tax'n* 176 (1992).

210   Proposed Regulation § 301.7701(i)-1(g). This rule would protect senior/subordinated trusts and other multiple class trusts that fall within the "incidental to" exception to the Sears regulations, and may also apply to single class owner trusts that issue pay-through bonds. See Part C above.

211   Proposed Regulation § 301.7701(i)-1(g)(3). The examples involve: (1) creating an entity with two classes of bonds by transferring assets to a trust with a single class of bonds and, with a view to avoiding the TMP rules, subsequently transferring the equity of the first trust to a second trust that issues another class of bonds; (2) with a view to avoiding the TMP definition, having one corporation issue multiple classes of bonds which are indirectly collateralized with certificates of interest in a trust holding mortgages previously organized by a second affiliated corporation, where the payments on those mortgages "bear a relationship" to the payments on the bonds; and (3) issuing multiple classes of bonds collateralized with nonmortgage collateral and, with a view to avoiding the TMP rules, reserving a right (which is later exercised) to substitute mortgage collateral.

212   Although the rule refers to equity classes (plural), it is likely that it would apply to an equity class that, together with an actual debt class, resembles maturity classes of debt.

213   Under this formulation, the recharacterization rule could never be applied to an arrangement with a single class of equity, which makes sense.

214   For example, suppose that a partnership would qualify as a TMP if it issued Class A debt maturing in 2 years and bearing interest of 4% and Class B debt maturing in 5 years and bearing interest of 6%. If the partnership replaced the Class B debt with an economically identical class of partnership interests, that class could receive an allocation of partnership income (or guaranteed payments under section 707(c)) matching in timing and amount the interest that would have been earned on Class B.

3. Effective Date Issues

Although the TMP rules were enacted in 1986, at the same time as the REMIC rules, their effective date was generally delayed until January 1, 1992 to allow a transition period in which to test the viability of the REMIC regime.[215] Despite the 1992 effective date, an entity in existence on December 31, 1991 does not become subject to the TMP rules unless and until the first day after 1991 on which there is a "substantial transfer" of cash or property to such entity (other than, the legislative history states, in payment of debt obligations held by the entity).[216]

The "substantial transfer" test could raise troublesome issues. For example, suppose that an entity meets the TMP definition as a result of a debt issuance before 1991, and has substantial activities other than financing mortgages. Would a post-1991 capital contribution to the entity to expand its business bring the TMP rules into play? Also, what if an equity owner wishes to contribute funds to an entity to pay down debt or to meet expenses. Again, would the contribution, if substantial, end the protection of the grandfather rule?

The proposed TMP regulations would clarify that the protection of the transition rule is jeopardized only by a transfer to an entity that is both significant in amount and, most importantly, connected to the entity's issuance of debt obligations that meet the maturities and relationship tests.[217] An example illustrates that the receipt by an entity of $10 million of proceeds from the issuance of such debt would meet these tests.[218]

The proposed TMP regulations generally would be effective only 30 days after they are published as final regulations. They do not address how the TMP rules are to be applied before that time. For the most part the regulations apply section 7701(i) in a reasonable way, and it may be expected that they will be looked to as a source of guidance in construing the statute even where they do not technically apply.

---

215 See section 675(c)(1) of TRA 1986. However, under section 675(c)(3) of TRA 1986, for purposes of applying the special wash sale rule for REMIC residual interests in section 860F(d) (which, among other things, can defer losses where residual interests are sold and replaced with an interest in a TMP), section 7701(i) applies to taxable years beginning after 1986.

216 Section 675(c)(3) of TRA 1986; Conference Agreement at II-241; Blue Book at 427. The Service indicated in a ruling that a workout of troubled mortgage loans held by an entity would not be viewed as a transfer for this purpose, even though apparently the changes could rise to the level of an exchange under section 1001. See P.L.R. 9138026 (June 19, 1991).

217 Proposed Regulation § 301.7701(i)-3(b).

218 Proposed Regulation § 301.7701(i)-3(b)(4).

Chapter 4

Qualification and Taxation of REMICs

As indicated in Chapters 1 and 2, TRA 1986 brought to life a new scheme for taxing pools of mortgages that qualify as REMICs. Chapter 2, Part E briefly describes the circumstances that led to enactment of the REMIC rules, the overall operation of those rules, and the different types of REMIC interests. This chapter considers in greater detail the qualification and taxation of REMICs. The tax treatment of REMIC interests in the hands of investors is addressed in Chapters 6 (regular interests) and 7 (residual interests). The definition of a REMIC regular interest is the topic of Chapter 5.

Part A of this chapter describes the tests that must be met in order for an entity to qualify as a REMIC. Although a REMIC is generally exempt from federal income taxes, it may be subject to certain penalty taxes on prohibited transactions and contributions, and to taxes at corporate rates on income from foreclosure property. These taxes are discussed in Part B. Part C considers a number of special topics: credit enhancement contracts, modifications and assumptions of mortgages, convertible mortgages, prepayment premiums, prepayment interest shortfalls, financially distressed mortgages, and integration. The integration topic embraces multiple-tier REMICs, outside reserve funds, and the packaging of REMIC securities with non-REMIC securities such as options and swaps. This chapter concludes by reviewing, in Part D, the mechanics for making a REMIC election and other procedural matters.

A. REMIC Qualification Tests

To qualify as a REMIC, an entity must elect to be a REMIC and must (1) meet a test relating to the interests in the entity (*interests test*), (2) meet a test relating to the assets of the entity (*assets test,*) and (3) adopt arrangements designed to ensure that "disqualified organizations" will not hold residual interests and that information needed to calculate the tax on transfers of residual interests to such organizations (described in Chapter 7) will be made available by the entity (*arrangements test*).[1] These tests are described in this Part A. Part C addresses a number of features of mortgage pools and mortgage-backed securities that raise questions under both the interests and assets tests. Certain issues relating to the REMIC election are examined in Part D.

An entity that meets the interests test, assets test, and arrangements test, and properly makes a REMIC election, will qualify as a REMIC regardless of its legal form. A REMIC can be organized, for example, as a state law trust, a corporation, or a partnership. Correspondingly, REMIC interests may be cast as beneficial interests in a trust, stock or partnership interests.[2] A segregated pool of assets may be a REMIC even if it has no separate existence under local law, provided all interests in the REMIC are based solely on assets of the REMIC.[3] Allowing an entity to qualify as a REMIC without regard to its legal form is consistent with the intent of Congress that the REMIC rules deal comprehensively and exclusively with the arrangements for issuing multiple class mortgage-backed securities.[4]

A REMIC is not considered to be formed until (1) the sponsor identifies the assets of the REMIC, such as through execution of an indenture with respect to the assets, and (2) the REMIC issues its regular and residual interests.[5] The day on

---

1   The REMIC qualification tests are set forth in section 860D. In addition to the requirements mentioned in the text, section 860D(a)(5) states that a REMIC must have a taxable year which is the calendar year. The calendar year requirement should be viewed more as a rule governing the taxation of REMICs than part of the definition because a REMIC as such would not have a taxable year unless the election was made and was effective.

2   Conference Report at II-226 (form of entity), II-228 (form of interests); Blue Book at 413, 415.

3   Treasury Regulation § 1.860D-1(c)(1). This regulation also requires that the assets identified as part of the segregated pool be treated for all federal income tax purposes as assets of the REMIC. This requirement would prevent assets within an entity from being "segregated" by creating contractual claims against those assets in favor of a purported REMIC that do not amount to whole or partial ownership interests in those assets for tax purposes.

4   See the Senate Report on TRA 1986, S. Rep. No. 99-313, 99th Cong., 2d Sess., at 791:
     The committee recognizes the increasing extent to which real estate mortgages are traded on secondary markets and the increasing extent to which multiple-class arrangements are used in the "packaging" of mortgages. The committee understands that considerable uncertainty exists concerning several aspects of the Federal income tax treatment of these types of securities. Accordingly, the committee wishes to provide rules to clarify the treatment of such securities. The committee believes that the best method for doing so is to provide a new type of vehicle for the issuance of such multiple class securities, and to provide rules that are as comprehensive as possible for the taxation of all transactions relating to the use of such vehicles.
     See also the Conference Report at II-230, discussing the fact that the state law form of a REMIC is irrelevant:
     The conferees intend that where the requirements for REMIC status are met, that the exclusive set of rules for the treatment of all transactions relating to the REMIC and of holders of interests therein are to be those set forth in the provisions of the conference agreements.

5   Treasury Regulation § 1.860D-1(c)(2). Although the assets of a REMIC must be identified on

which the REMIC issues all of its regular and residual interests is referred to as the "startup day." However, a REMIC sponsor may contribute property to a REMIC in exchange for regular and residual interests over any period of 10 consecutive days and the REMIC may designate any one of those 10 days as the startup day. In that event, the day so designated is treated as the startup day, and all interests issued by, and all property transferred to, the REMIC within the 10-day period are considered to be issued or transferred on that day.[6] There is no requirement that a REMIC be organized in the United States or under U.S. law.[7]

Except with respect to foreclosure property, where a REMIC is required in some circumstances to manage property through an independent contractor in order to avoid REMIC-level taxes, there are no tax-related restrictions on who may manage or operate a REMIC or its assets. For example, the servicer of the mortgages held by a REMIC can be (and often is) related to the REMIC's sponsor and can hold all or any portion of the residual interest in the REMIC.

1. Interests Test

A REMIC meets the interests test if all of the interests in the REMIC are either regular interests or residual interests, and there is one (and only one) class of residual interests (and all distributions, if any, with respect to such interests are made pro rata).[8] There is no limit on the number of classes of regular interests and, apparently, no requirement that there be even one.[9]

---

formation, as discussed in the text at footnote 63 below, qualified mortgages may be acquired under a fixed-price contract after the REMIC is formed. The definition of "sponsor" is discussed in Chapter 12.

6   See section 860G(a)(9) and Treasury Regulation § 1.860G-2(k). Prior to the enactment of TAMRA, section 860G(a)(9) defined the startup day as "any day selected by a REMIC which is on or before the 1st day on which interests in such REMIC are issued." This language required a REMIC to "select" a startup day, and as a result the practice developed of including a designation of the startup day in REMIC documentation. Strictly speaking, no such designation is required under current law if all REMIC interests are issued on the same day. A REMIC must be considered to issue all of its interests on the startup day in order to meet the REMIC interests test. See Part A.1.d below.

7   By contrast, section 851(a) requires that a regulated investment company be a domestic corporation. Section 856(a)(3) has the same effect for real estate investment trusts (see Revenue Ruling 89-130, 1989-2 C.B. 117). It may be desirable for a foreign entity that would otherwise not be subject to U.S. taxation to make a REMIC election in order to prevent U.S. holders of its securities from being subject to certain special rules that apply to foreign corporations holding passive investments. See Chapter 8, footnote 5. Footnote 103 below and Chapter 5, Part E.7, discuss the status as qualified mortgages of mortgages secured by foreign property, and regular interests denominated in a foreign currency, respectively. Chapter 10 considers other international aspects of REMICs.

8   Sections 860D(a)(2) and (a)(3).

9   The explicit requirement in section 860D(a)(3) that there be "1 (and only 1)" class of residual interests and the absence of similar language applicable to regular interests strongly implies that there is no need to have any classes of regular interests. The preamble to the final REMIC regulations also supports this view: "The REMIC *must* issue one, and only one, class of residual interests. A REMIC *may* issue one or more classes of regular interests." (emphasis added) But see Conference Report at II-228; Blue Book at 415 ("[a]ll of the interests in the REMIC must consist

The interests test serves at least two purposes: First, it ensures that there is a clear set of rules governing the tax treatment of all types of REMIC interests by limiting those interests to regular and residual interests. Second, the test plays a significant role in shaping the permitted activities of a REMIC by preventing a REMIC from entering into transactions that create nonqualifying interests. For example, the test would generally stand in the way of a REMIC that wishes to write an option (with the exceptions discussed below for options on qualified mortgages) or a guarantee of third party obligations.[10] The requirement that regular and residual interests be issued on the startup day prevents a REMIC from refinancing existing liabilities or raising new capital to expand.[11]

The balance of this discussion of the interests test will address the definition of an interest in a REMIC, the definitions of regular and residual interests (a more detailed description of regular interests may be found in Chapter 5), the requirement that REMIC interests be issued on the startup day, and other miscellaneous requirements.

a. Definition of Interest. In order to apply the interests test, it is necessary to know what an *interest* is. The Code does not define the term, and there is no guidance in the legislative history, other than a statement that the right to receive payment from a REMIC for goods or services rendered in the ordinary operation of the REMIC is not an interest.[12]

One possible definition of a REMIC interest is: any right to receive one or more payments from a REMIC that would be recognized to be indebtedness, or an equity interest in an entity, in the absence of the REMIC rules. This definition captures most of the obvious types of interests, but is both overly broad and overly narrow in some respects. It is too broad because it would treat as an interest rights to payments on loans that are made to a REMIC in the ordinary course of its operations, including, for example, certain servicer advances that are made in respect of defaulted or delinquent mortgage payments.[13]

---

of one or more classes of 'regular interests' and a single class of 'residual interests'.") While the REMIC rules could not function unless a REMIC has at all times a class of residual interests to which the taxable income of the REMIC can be allocated, there is no similar reason that compels the presence of any classes of regular interests. Thus, an entity does not lose its status as a REMIC merely because all of its regular interests are retired. Similarly, an entity should be able to qualify as a REMIC even if no regular interests are ever issued.

10   A regular interest can, however, in some cases have the economic features of an option (see Chapter 5), and an option of this type is clearly allowed.

11   Similarly, the assets test inhibits the growth of a REMIC by limiting its ability to acquire new assets after the startup day.

12   Conference Report at II-229; Blue Book at 416.

13   If an advance is recoverable out of all of the assets of the REMIC, or even out of future mortgage payments generally, without regard to recoveries of the particular defaulted or delinquent payments that caused the advance, then the advance could be viewed as a loan to the REMIC. Hence, the advance would create a REMIC interest if the term encompassed all debt of the REMIC. On the other hand, if the advance was repayable only out of such recoveries, it might be viewed as a purchase from the REMIC of the rights to the defaulted or delinquent payments and not as a loan.

One way in which the definition is too narrow is that residual interests (which must be *interests*) may take forms that would not be, in the absence of the REMIC rules, either debt or equity interests in an entity. For example, if a REMIC is a segregated pool of assets within a legal entity, the residual interest could consist of (1) the rights of ownership of the REMIC's assets, subject to the claims of regular interest holders, or (2) if the regular interests take the form of debt secured under an indenture, a contractual right to receive distributions released from the lien of the indenture.[14] Neither of these interests is debt or an equity interest in an entity. Furthermore, it is not necessary that a residual interest entitle the holder to any payments or otherwise have any value,[15] and, presumably, a right to nothing would be neither debt nor an equity interest.[16] A definition of interest limited to traditional debt or equity interests would also be too narrow because it would exclude claims under other types of financial instruments, such as options or notional principal contracts.

The foregoing discussion suggests that an interest in a REMIC should be defined as either (1) any right to receive money or other property from the REMIC that arises from an investment in the REMIC or under a financial instrument to which the REMIC is a party, or (2) any type of property interest in, or contract with, a REMIC that is designated as a residual interest. Although the first part of the definition is admittedly vague, the intent is that a servicer's right to repayment of an advance, and other claims arising in the ordinary administration of the REMIC, would not be interests thereunder because they would not relate to an investment in a REMIC or a financial instrument. In addition, recognized ownership interests in identified property would not be considered interests in any REMIC that happens to own interests in the same property; instead, they would be interests in the property. While the suggested definition appears to be reasonable, it should be emphasized that it does not have authoritative support.

Perhaps acknowledging the difficulty of formulating a test that is clear enough to be useful and properly carries out the special policies of the REMIC rules when applied in a broad range of factual settings, the REMIC regulations do not offer a general definition of interest. Instead, they add content to the term by removing from its scope a list of specific claims against a REMIC that includes most of the categories of claims that arise in the ordinary operation of a REMIC and cannot qualify as regular interests. The list is expressly stated to be not exclusive.[17] Thus,

---

14   Although the right to receive distributions released from the lien of the indenture typically would be designated a residual interest, the right to those distributions could also potentially be structured as a regular interest, provided that one of the debt instruments is designated as the residual interest.

15   See footnote 45, below, and accompanying text.

16   If it were necessary for a residual interest holder to have some rights against an entity in order to be recognized to be an interest holder, perhaps the requirement could be satisfied by granting the holder rights to vote on certain limited matters affecting the entity (e.g., amendments to its governing documents), or a right to all residual assets of the entity even though the possibility that there will be any such assets is remote or nonexistent. It would make little sense, however, to hang the qualification of a REMIC on such niceties once it is acknowledged that no real economic stake, in the form of a meaningful right to money or other property, is required.

there is room to argue that other "administrative" claims are not REMIC "interests." Obviously, the argument will have the most force for items resembling those on the list.

As detailed below, the excluded claims are: payments for servicing, stripped interests, rights of reimbursement arising from guarantees of REMIC assets or other credit enhancement contracts, certain rights to acquire mortgages or other REMIC assets, and certain *de minimis* interests.

(i) Servicing. The right to receive from a REMIC payments that represent reasonable compensation for services provided to the REMIC in the ordinary course of its operation, including the servicing of mortgages owned by the REMIC, is not an interest in the REMIC.[18] The treatment of servicing compensation that exceeds reasonable levels is considered immediately below under "stripped interests."

(ii) Stripped interests. A REMIC may hold rights to identified payments on qualified mortgages that are stripped bonds or stripped coupons under section 1286.[19] In that event, other interests in the same mortgages would be held by someone else. Those remaining interests are considered interests in the mortgages and not in the REMIC. For this purpose, it makes no difference whether the stripped bonds or coupons are created contemporaneously with the formation of the REMIC or in an independent transaction.[20] Although not stated expressly in the regulations, if a REMIC owns a subordinated interest in a grantor trust holding qualified mortgages, the implicit guarantee by the REMIC (as holder of the subordinated class) in favor of the senior class also should not be treated as a REMIC interest.[21]

Rights to compensation for the servicing of mortgages may be recharacterized for tax purposes as an ownership interest in the mortgages if the compensation exceeds a reasonable charge for the services performed.[22] Based on the discussion in the preceding paragraph, recasting excess servicing as an ownership interest in mortgages would not give rise to an additional REMIC interest to the extent such interest represents rights to identified interest payments that are stripped coupons

---

17   See Treasury Regulation § 1.860D-1(b)(2).

18   Treasury Regulation § 1.860D-1(b)(2)(i). The regulation states that payments for services may be expressed as a specified percentage of interest payments due on qualified mortgages or as a specified percentage of earnings from permitted investments. This language should not be read to exclude other measures of compensation.

19   Section 1286 is discussed in Chapter 6, Part D.1.

20   Treasury Regulation § 1.860D-1(b)(2)(ii).

21   For purposes of applying the Sears regulations and, possibly, determining the income of holders, subordinated grantor trust interests are viewed as pro rata interests in the underlying mortgages combined with the writing of a nonrecourse guarantee by the subordinated interest holders. See Chapter 2, Part B.3. However, a REMIC is clearly allowed to own subordinated interests in grantor trusts, which must mean that the implicit guarantee is not treated as a REMIC interest. See Conference Report at II-227, footnote 5; Blue Book at 413, footnote 67; Treasury Regulation § 1.860G-2(a)(5).

22   The possible recharacterization of excess servicing is discussed in Chapter 3, footnotes 99–101 and accompanying text.

under section 1286.[23] The REMIC regulations confirm this result.[24] They also state that the right to contingent payments on a mortgage contributed to a REMIC, such as a right to share in appreciation of property or mortgagor profits, is not an interest in a REMIC if that right is retained outside of the REMIC.

(iii) Claims under credit enhancement contracts. A right of reimbursement against a REMIC arising under a credit enhancement contract is not a REMIC interest.[25] Credit enhancement contracts are discussed in Part C.1, below. The term encompasses a broad range of guarantees of timely payments on mortgages or REMIC interests, and servicer advances.[26] For this purpose, a right of reimbursement includes a right to receive interest on an advance, presumably without regard to whether it is payable at the net mortgage rate charged by the REMIC, if the advance relates to a payment on a qualified mortgage, or at a separately negotiated rate.[27]

(iv) Rights to acquire mortgages or other assets. A right to purchase REMIC assets could potentially be viewed as an interest in the REMIC, at least if the purchase price is (or may be) less than the assets' fair market value at the time of purchase. However, the REMIC regulations exclude from the definition of interest the right or obligation[28] of a third party to purchase mortgages and other assets from a REMIC pursuant to a clean-up call or qualified liquidation (as defined in the next paragraph) or on conversion of a convertible mortgage.[29] Convertible mortgages are discussed in Part C.3 below. Ordinarily, a contract to buy assets from a REMIC in connection with a clean-up call or qualified liquidation would serve only to facili-

---

23   See also Revenue Ruling 91-46, 1991-2 C.B. 358 (excess servicing representing a fixed number of basis points of interest treated as stripped coupons and not an interest in the REMIC or other entity that owns the mortgages). For further discussion of this ruling, see Chapter 3, text at footnote 101.

24   Treasury Regulation § 1.860D-1(b)(2)(ii). After stating the general rules for stripped bonds or coupons, the regulations include the following: "For example, the right of a mortgage servicer to retain a servicing fee in excess of reasonable compensation from payments it receives on mortgages held by a REMIC is not an interest in the REMIC." This statement is not expressly limited to excess servicing that is treated as stripped coupons rather than some other type of ownership interest in mortgages, although the words "for example" suggest this interpretation. Those words were not in the predecessor section in the REMIC regulations proposed in 1991.

25   Treasury Regulation § 1.860D-1(b)(2)(iii).

26   If a contract guarantees mortgages held by a REMIC, and some of those mortgages are not qualified mortgages, then the contract would literally fall outside of the definition of credit enhancement contract. See Part C.1.a, below. However, it would be perverse, to say the least, for the Service to try to undermine a REMIC's right to own a *de minimis* amount of nonqualifying assets by arguing that a guarantee relating to nonqualifying mortgages automatically violates the REMIC interests test.

27   Certain categories of credit enhancement contracts, such as bank letters of credit, typically would provide for an interest charge at market rates on amounts advanced.

28   Although the exclusion of third-party obligations (as well as rights) from the definition of interest is helpful to ensure that bilateral agreements to buy and sell, and puts held by a REMIC, are allowed as well as options to buy from a REMIC, an obligation of a third party in favor of a REMIC would be more problematic under the assets test than under the interests test. See generally Part A.2, below.

29   Treasury Regulation § 1.860D-1(b)(2)(iv).

tate the retirement of classes of REMIC interests when loan or class balances are reduced to a low level, or the winding up of a REMIC, and would not have significant economic consequences. Under the regulations, however, a REMIC apparently could be organized with a fixed term shorter than the anticipated term of the qualified mortgages, and rely on a contractual right to sell the mortgages upon expiration of the REMIC's term in a qualified liquidation at a price sufficient to ensure the repayment at that time of REMIC interests.

The terms *clean-up call* and *qualified liquidation* have special meanings. A clean-up call is a redemption of a class of regular interests that occurs when, by reason of prior payments with respect to those interests, the administrative costs associated with servicing that class outweigh the benefits of maintaining the class.[30] A qualified liquidation is defined in section 860F(a)(4) as a transaction in which a REMIC adopts a plan of complete liquidation and, within a 90-day period beginning on the date of adoption of the plan, sells its noncash assets, and distributes or credits the sales proceeds and other cash, less assets retained to meet claims, to holders of REMIC interests.[31]

The regulations do not require that the purchase price paid to acquire assets in connection with a clean-up call or a qualified liquidation equal the fair market value of the purchased assets at the time of the purchase, an amount representing a reasonable estimate of such fair market value, or any other amount.[32] If a REMIC enters into a contract to resell qualified mortgages to the person from which it acquired the mortgages at a price other than their fair market value at the time of sale, consideration should be given to the possible recharacterization of the arrangement as a loan to the buyer secured by the qualified mortgages.[33] Such a loan would not be a qualified mortgage.[34]

---

30   See Treasury Regulation § 1.860G-2(f). The regulation lists a number of factors to be taken into account in the weighing process. The redemption of a class in order to profit from a change in interest rates is generally not a clean-up call. Under a safe harbor rule, however, a redemption of a class of regular interests with an outstanding principal balance of no more than 10% of its original principal balance is always a clean-up call. Dispositions of assets and capital contributions that are made to facilitate a clean-up call are exempted from the 100% taxes generally applicable to dispositions of assets by, and contributions to, a REMIC. See sections 860F(a)(5)(B) and 860G(d)(2)(A). These taxes are discussed in Part B, below.

31   Treasury Regulation § 1.860F-1 states that a qualified liquidation need not be in any special form, and that a REMIC will be considered to have adopted a plan of liquidation on any date specified as the first day in the 90-day liquidation period in a statement attached to its final return. Dispositions of assets and capital contributions that are made to facilitate a qualified liquidation are exempted from the 100% taxes generally applicable to dispositions of assets by, and contributions to, a REMIC. See sections 860F(a)(2)(A)(iv) and 860G(d)(2)(A). These taxes are discussed in Part B, below. Read literally, the definition of qualified liquidation would not permit an in-kind distribution of property other than cash. It is very unlikely, however, that such a limitation was intended, particularly since under section 860F(c) a distribution of property by a REMIC is treated as a sale for purposes of gain recognition. See Chapter 7, text accompanying footnote 30.

32   By contrast, convertible mortgages must be purchased upon conversion at their unpaid principal amount. See Part C.3, below.

33   For a discussion of this issue, see Chapter 12, Part A.1.

34   See footnotes 95–96 and 255, below.

Where a third party has not only a right, but also an obligation, to purchase mortgages in connection with a clean-up call or qualified liquidation, the REMIC will have a corresponding right to require such purchase. The REMIC regulations do not state whether such a right would be a qualifying REMIC asset,[35] although it would be nonsensical to exclude a third-party purchase obligation from the definition of interest and then disqualify a REMIC on the ground that a REMIC's right to sell is an impermissible REMIC asset. This problem may be solved technically in most cases by the fact that, under a safe-harbor rule, assets of a REMIC with no positive tax basis may be disregarded in applying the assets test.[36] A REMIC would have no positive tax basis in a right to sell under an executory contract, assuming that the only consideration paid for the contract is the REMIC's obligation to sell.

(v) De minimis interests. Trusts that are intended to qualify as REMICs are sometimes formed by contributing a nominal amount to the trust that is returned, generally without interest, either on the startup day or upon termination of the REMIC. The REMIC regulations contain a *de minimis* rule that excludes from the definition of interest for purposes of the interests test an interest issued to facilitate the creation of a REMIC if, as of the startup day, the fair market value of that interest is less than the lesser of $1,000, or 1/1,000 of 1 percent (i.e., $1,000 per $100 million) of the aggregate fair market value of all of the regular and residual interests in the REMIC.[37] Thus, an interest valued at exactly $1,000 is not *de minimis*. The exclusion does not apply to interests that are specifically designated as REMIC interests; otherwise, many nominal value residual interests would fall within the rule.

Even without the special *de minimis* rule, it may be possible in many cases to disregard contributions made to facilitate the organization of a REMIC. For example, if the contributed funds are returned to the contributor on or before the startup day, the right to the funds would not be a REMIC interest. Alternatively, if contributed funds are not returned until the REMIC is terminated, they could potentially be excluded from the REMIC by holding the funds in a separate account and defining the REMIC as all assets of the entity other than that account. The right to the account should not then be treated as a REMIC interest.

b. Definition of Regular Interest. A *regular interest* is defined in section 860G(a)(1) as any interest that

- is issued on the startup day[38]

---

35   As discussed in Part C.3, below, the right of a REMIC to sell convertible mortgages on conversion is treated as an incident of the converted mortgages for purposes of the assets test.

36   See text accompanying footnote 56 below. Also, a REMIC should not have any gain attributable to the contract (as distinguished from gain realized on the sale of assets under the contract) that would be subject to the 100% prohibited transactions tax discussed in Part B below.

37   Treasury Regulation § 1.860D-1(b)(1)(ii). The fair market value of an interest created by contributing money to an entity would generally be less than the contributed amount if that amount does not bear interest for the period it is held by the entity.

38   This requirement is discussed in Part A.1.d below.

- is designated as a regular interest
- has fixed terms
- provides that interest payments (or similar amounts), if any, at or before maturity either are payable based on a fixed rate (or to the extent provided in regulations, at a variable rate), or consist of a specified portion of the interest payments on qualified mortgages and such portion does not vary during the period such interest is outstanding, and
- unconditionally entitles the holder to receive a specified principal amount (or, if the interest is not in the form of debt, a similar amount).

These requirements are discussed in detail in Chapter 5.

c. Definition of Residual Interest. A *residual interest* is defined in section 860G(a)(2) as any interest in a REMIC that is

- issued on the startup day[39]
- designated as a residual interest, and
- not a regular interest.

In most cases, these requirements are easily met. A residual interest is designated as such by providing a description of the terms and conditions of the residual interest in the REMIC's first, timely filed tax return.[40] An interest that is designated a residual interest will automatically fail to qualify as a regular interest because an interest can be a regular interest only if it is designated as such.

In order for a REMIC to meet the interests test, there must be only one class of residual interests and all distributions (if any) on that class must be made pro rata to all holders of that class. Thus, a REMIC may not redeem all or a portion of the residual interests held by one owner without redeeming a corresponding portion of the residual interests held by each other owner. Thus, sinking fund and "retail" residual interests (in which payments are made to investors chosen by lot or to investors that are estates or otherwise have special liquidity needs) are not permitted.[41] If a REMIC agrees to pay taxes or other expenses attributable to holders of residual interests, or contracts with one but not all of those holders, care should be taken to ensure that the REMIC's obligation will not result in non-pro rata distributions on the residual interest.[42] There is no comparable requirement that contributions to a REMIC by residual interest holders be made pro rata by all holders.[43]

---

39   This requirement is discussed in Part A.1.d below.

40 . See Treasury Regulation § 1.860G-1(c).

41   Compare Chapter 5, Part E.2.

42   It is not uncommon for a REMIC to agree to bear any expenses incurred by a holder of a residual interest in carrying out its responsibilities as the tax matters person for the REMIC. (The tax matters person is described in Part D.2 below.) However, those expenses should be considered expenses of the REMIC and not personal expenses of the holder the payment of which may give rise to a deemed distribution. Cf. Revenue Ruling 76-365, 1976-2 C.B. 110 (corporation's payment of expenses relating to reorganization not treated as payment to shareholders).

The requirement that distributions be made pro rata will ensure in most cases that a purported single class of residual interests will not be treated as more than one class (which could result in disqualification of the REMIC). In light of the ban on multiple residual classes, terms (including voting rights) that favor one holder or groups of holders of a class of residual interests over another holder or group should be avoided.[44]

As described in Part A.3, in order to meet the REMIC arrangements test, a residual interest must be issued in registered (i.e., not bearer) form and generally will bear a legend advising holders of restrictions on transfers to disqualified organizations. Special considerations apply to transfers of noneconomic residuals and transfers of residuals to non-U.S. persons (see Chapter 7).

There is no requirement that a residual interest have any minimum value or entitle the holder to any distributions.[45] Correspondingly, any purported interest in a REMIC that is designated as a residual interest should be considered an "interest" in the REMIC even though the holder is not entitled to any distributions.[46]

d. Timing of Issuance of REMIC Interests—Pre-Existing Entities. As indicated above, regular and residual interests must be issued on the startup day. In order to meet this test, regular or residual interests must be issued on the same day, or within a 10-consecutive-day period if the REMIC designates a day within that period as the startup day.[47]

In most cases, the requirements for the timing of issuance of REMIC interests are easily met. A REMIC is typically organized as a state law trust. The trust is newly organized with no assets (or only *de minimis* assets),[48] and on a single day the sponsor contributes the mortgages and other assets comprising the REMIC to the trust in exchange for certificates representing all of the beneficial interests in the trust. Under these circumstances, the interests in the REMIC are clearly issued on one day, which is the startup day.

Although not certain, the requirement that REMIC interests be issued on the startup day would seem to preclude the making of a REMIC election by an entity

---

43   Contributions to a REMIC are discussed in Part B.2 below.

44   The REMIC rules specifically contemplate the designation of one holder of the residual interest as the "tax matters person" so that designation (and any associated allocation of rights and responsibilities) must be allowed. One analogy to the requirement of a single class of residual interests is section 1361(b)(1)(D), which requires that an S corporation have only one class of stock. Under section 1361(c)(4), a corporation is not treated as having more than one class of stock because of differences in voting rights among shares of common stock, but there is no counterpart to this rule for REMICs. Extensive regulations have been issued construing the one-class-of-stock requirement under section 1361. See Treasury Regulation § 1.1361-1(l).

45   See Treasury Regulation § 1.860G-1(c). Section 860D(a)(3) refers to the distributions, "if any," with respect to a residual interest.

46   See discussion above at footnote 16.

47   See text accompanying footnote 6 above.

48   A nominal contribution made to the trust to organize it before the startup day may be disregarded under the *de minimis* rule discussed above at footnote 37.

with a pre-REMIC history. For example, suppose that a sponsor owns an existing pool of mortgages through a trust or other entity and wishes to borrow against those assets by having the entity make a REMIC election and issue regular interests. The entity would likely not qualify as a REMIC because the equity interest in the entity was issued before the REMIC's earliest possible startup day.[49] The problem can be addressed readily (1) by transferring the entity's assets to a trust, or otherwise segregating assets of the entity, and making the REMIC election with respect to the trust or segregated assets and not the pre-existing entity,[50] (2) if the entity is a grantor trust, by transferring interests in the trust to a new trust, and making the election for the new trust, or (3) by liquidating the old entity and transferring its assets to a new entity.[51]

e. Other Requirements. There are no requirements concerning the number of holders or concentration of ownership of either regular or residual interests. There are no tax-related restrictions on the transfer of regular interests, and no such restrictions on transfers of residual interests other than those that may be imposed by a REMIC to meet the arrangements tests (see Part A.3 below). A REMIC's organizational documents may restrict the transfer of non-economic residual interests, and transfers to non-U.S. persons, in circumstances where such transfers would not be effective for tax purposes, although contractual restrictions of this type are not required.[52] If, for

---

49   A REMIC election might be permitted for a pre-existing entity on the ground that the election causes, for tax purposes, a deemed liquidation of the old entity and the deemed creation of a new entity to which the REMIC rules apply. Such a deemed liquidation could have significant tax consequences. For example, if the entity is a corporation, such a liquidation could result in taxable gain for the liquidated entity and for the equity holders. Because of these consequences, the Service might be reluctant to adopt the deemed liquidation approach without having in place a statutory mechanism for obtaining consents of all affected equity holders to the REMIC election. Compare section 1362(a)(2) (all shareholders must consent to an election to treat a corporation as an S corporation). Further, there seems to be little to gain in working out the mechanics for allowing an existing entity to make a REMIC election when in almost all cases taxpayers can avoid the problem by forming a new entity or segregating assets.

50   There is no reason why the segregated assets comprising the REMIC could not be all of the assets held by the entity at the time when the REMIC is formed. Compare the discussion of two-tier REMICs in Part C.7.a below.

51   While the issue would need to be evaluated in light of the particular facts of the transaction, in general a purported liquidation followed by a transfer of the liquidated entity's assets to a REMIC should not be challenged on the ground that the new entity is a successor to the old. The "liquidation-reincorporation" doctrine that applies to corporations is based on the reorganization rules of the Code which apply only to corporations, and there is no REMIC counterpart to the successor partnership rules in section 708(b). Under section 860A(a), with an exception that is not relevant here, a REMIC is not treated as a corporation or partnership for purposes of the income tax subtitle of the Code. Further, the development of a successor entity theory would conflict with the Congressional intention that the REMIC rules were intended to operate mechanically and to override general principles of tax law. See footnote 4. For discussion of the liquidation-reincorporation doctrine for corporations, see B. Bittker & J. Eustice, *Federal Income Taxation of Corporations and Shareholders,* 6th Ed., ¶ 12.64 (1994).

52   The restrictions serve the purpose of ensuring that the party responsible for reporting tax information to residual interest holders, and for withholding on distributions to non-U.S. persons or backup withholding, will know who the "tax owners" of the residual interest are. See Chapters 10

some non-tax reason, it is desirable for a REMIC interest *not* to be transferable, transfer restrictions could be imposed without running afoul of the REMIC rules.[53]

2. Assets Test

The assets test is met by an entity if at all times, except during an initial and final period, substantially all of its assets are *qualified mortgages* or *permitted investments*.[54] There are three types of permitted investments: *cash flow investments, qualified reserve assets,* and *foreclosure property.*

The assets test plays a major role in determining the activities in which a REMIC may be engaged. The definition of qualified mortgage allows a REMIC to acquire and hold a fixed pool of mortgages, and to replace those mortgages during an initial period (three months, or in the case of defective mortgages, two years). A REMIC can also receive and invest (in cash flow investments) proceeds of mortgages pending distribution of such proceeds to REMIC interest holders, maintain (in qualified reserve assets) a reserve to pay expenses and make up for mortgage defaults and delinquencies, and hold (as foreclosure property) real property acquired upon foreclosure of a mortgage.

The requirement that *substantially all* of a REMIC's assets consist of qualified mortgages or permitted investments is satisfied only if a REMIC owns no more than a *de minimis* amount of other assets.[55] The REMIC regulations contain a safe-harbor rule under which the *de minimis* test is considered to be met if the aggregate tax basis of those other assets is less than one percent of the aggregate tax basis of all of the REMIC's assets.[56] If a REMIC holds a *de minimis* amount of assets that are not qualified mortgages or permitted investments, the REMIC election is not terminated; however, as described in Part B below, any net income attributable to those other assets is confiscated through a 100 percent tax.

The assets test applies continuously over the entire life of a REMIC except during an initial period and final period. Thus, in theory, if a REMIC holds more than a *de minimis* amount of nonqualifying assets for an instant in time, it would cease to be a REMIC, effective as of the beginning of the calendar year in which the event occurs.[57] The initial grace period extends from the startup day to the end of

---

(foreign withholding) and 11 (information reporting).

53 Compare section 856(a)(2) (beneficial ownership of a REIT must be evidenced by transferable shares or transferable certificates of beneficial ownership).

54 See section 860D(a)(4).

55 Treasury Regulation § 1.860D-1(b)(3)(i); Conference Report at II-226; Blue Book at 413.

56 Treasury Regulation § 1.860D-1(b)(3)(ii). A REMIC that does not meet the safe harbor may still demonstrate that it owns no more than a *de minimis* amount of other assets. Two factors that could influence whether other assets are *de minimis* are whether the REMIC had a reasonable belief that the assets were qualified mortgages or permitted investments, and whether the assets are held for only a short period after discovery that they are not such assets.

57 The rule which allows the Service to disregard inadvertent terminations of a REMIC may be useful in such a case. See Part D.1 below. Prior to the enactment of TAMRA, the assets test applied only at the close of the initial grace period and each quarter ending thereafter (rather than continuously).

the "3rd month" (which presumably means third calendar month) beginning after the startup day. The final period begins with the adoption of a plan of liquidation in connection with a qualified liquidation and ends, not more than 90 days later, with the liquidation of the REMIC.[58]

The two grace periods are less important than might be supposed. The initial grace period does not allow a REMIC to raise funds and use them over time to acquire mortgages in market transactions. As discussed below, a "qualified mortgage" generally may be purchased after the startup day only under a fixed-price contract in effect on the startup day.[59] The initial grace period would ensure that an entity qualifies as a REMIC if it receives a contribution of cash on the startup day that is used during the initial period to pay expenses or to make distributions on REMIC securities. However, those amounts may well be qualified reserve assets (if they are used to pay expenses) or cash flow investments (if they can be characterized as payments received on the REMIC's qualified mortgages and are used to make distributions on REMIC interests).[60] Similarly, the final grace period is not generally needed to ensure that a REMIC is not disqualified during the liquidation period. Following adoption of a plan of liquidation, a REMIC typically sells its assets and distributes the proceeds to holders of interests in the REMIC. The proceeds of sale of qualified mortgages would be cash flow investments while held pending distribution, and, in general, other permitted investments held by the REMIC on the date of adoption of the plan should retain their status as permitted investments until the REMIC terminates. All this being said, the two grace periods obviate the need to examine with care the composition of a REMIC's assets during the startup and liquidation phases of its existence, and avoid the harsh consequences that might otherwise result from applying the assets test on a continuous basis during those periods.

A REMIC can meet the assets test even if it holds only a single qualified mortgage. Thus, the REMIC rules can be used to create partial ownership interests in a single loan as an alternative to relying on the stripped bond rules of section 1286.

We turn now to a more detailed discussion of qualified mortgages and permitted investments.

---

58   Qualified liquidations are discussed above at footnote 31. As discussed in footnote 130, below, sales of qualified reserve fund assets during the final period could arguably affect the status of a qualified reserve fund prior to the beginning of the period.

59   See footnote 63, below. The ability of a REMIC to purchase mortgages pursuant to a fixed-price contract is often helpful if a mortgage that the sponsor purchased for forward delivery and intended to contribute to the REMIC is not, in fact, delivered to the sponsor in time to include it in the REMIC on the startup day. Income earned on funds held pending their use to purchase mortgages would potentially be subject to the 100% prohibited transactions tax. The tax applies to "net income" from prohibited transactions, so that the amount of the tax on such funds depends significantly on whether interest paid on regular interests is taken into account in calculating net income. See text accompanying footnote 171 below.

60   For a discussion of the possible treatment as cash flow investments of payments received on qualified mortgages before they are contributed to the REMIC, see Part A.2.b.(i) below.

a. Qualified Mortgages. A *qualified mortgage* is defined[61] as (1) any obligation (including any participation or certificate of beneficial ownership therein) which is principally secured by an interest in real property, and is either transferred to the REMIC on the startup day in exchange for regular or residual interests,[62] or purchased within three months after the startup day pursuant to a fixed-price contract in effect on the startup day,[63] (2) any regular interest in another REMIC which is transferred to the REMIC on the startup day in exchange for regular or residual interests in the REMIC,[64] or (3) any qualified replacement mortgage. A REMIC residual interest is never considered a qualified mortgage regardless of its state law form.[65]

Under the first part of the definition, a qualified mortgage must be (1) an obligation (including any participation or certificate of beneficial ownership therein), which is (2) principally secured by (3) an interest in real property. Each part of the definition warrants some discussion.

(i) Obligations (and interests in obligations). The word *obligation* is not defined in the Code. It could be read broadly to include any contractual claim, or might be limited to instruments that are considered "debt obligations" for federal income tax purposes.[66] Such a limitation could raise questions in at least two cir-

---

61   See section 860G(a)(3).

62   Under the REMIC regulations, a sponsor may contribute property to a REMIC in exchange for REMIC interests over any period of 10 consecutive days and designate any one of those days as the startup day, in which case all REMIC interests are treated as issued on that day. Treasury Regulation § 1.860G-2(k). While not expressly stated in the regulations, any assets that are transferred within the 10-day period should also be considered to be transferred to the REMIC on the startup day. See section 860G(a)(9) (to the extent provided in regulations, issuances of interests in, *and* transfers to, a REMIC within a period not exceeding 10 days shall be treated as occurring on the day within that period selected by the REMIC).

63   There are no authorities applying the fixed-price contract rule, and it raises a number of questions. It is not clear whether the requirement of a "fixed" price could be stretched to include a price determined under a fixed formula. It would require courage to test the proposition without further authoritative guidance on the point, particularly if the formula is intended to track changes in market values. The TAMRA House Report at 81, footnote 42, contains an oblique sentence discussing the fixed-price requirement that implies that price adjustments to reflect fluctuations in market value are not allowed. Another question is whether an option to purchase could be regarded as a "contract." The term would normally imply an obligation both to buy and sell. In any event, a contract term that, in accordance with market practice, allows some variation in the quantity of mortgages to be purchased, and the presence of other normal closing conditions, should not prevent the contract from qualifying under the rule. Caution should be exercised in modifying a contract after the startup day. A material modification (particularly one relating to price or the mortgages to be purchased) may be regarded as a termination of the old contract and formation of a new one.

64   Note that REMIC regular interests cannot be purchased within the three months following the startup day but must be transferred on the startup day.

65   Treasury Regulation § 1.860G-2(a)(6).

66   An instrument that is characterized as debt for tax purposes but does not take the form of debt should be considered an obligation. Two examples of such an instrument are installment land contracts and rights to excess servicing that are treated as a stripped coupon. See Treasury Regulation § 1.860G-2(a)(5) (installment sale contracts) and the text at footnote 76 below.

cumstances: (1) where the mortgage under consideration is a nonrecourse obligation that is secured by property having, at the time of origination of the mortgage, a fair market value less than its principal amount, and (2) where the mortgage has contingent payment features. Excessive nonrecourse debt may be disregarded altogether for tax purposes.[67] A mortgage with contingent features tied to the fortunes of the issuer or the value of the collateral could in some circumstances be treated, in whole or in part, as an equity interest in a joint venture operating the property or in the underlying property (and to that extent not as an obligation).[68] Loans with both excessive principal and contingent interest sometimes arise in a workout setting, where defaulted debt may be exchanged for new debt having a reduced rate of noncontingent interest, some contingent interest, and a principal amount that exceeds the current value of the underlying real property.[69]

The REMIC regulations provide relief in these circumstances by stating that, for purposes of the definition of qualified mortgage and qualified replacement mortgage, the term "obligation" includes any "instrument" that provides for total noncontingent principal payments that at least equal the instrument's issue price, even if that instrument also provides for contingent payments.[70] There is nothing in this definition that requires an instrument to be characterized in whole or in part as debt for tax purposes.

A few comments on the special definition are in order. First, it is inclusive rather than exclusive. Thus, it does not prevent a conventional debt instrument from qualifying as an "obligation" merely because it was issued at a premium (i.e., does not have noncontingent principal payments at least equal to its issue price). Second, it is not limited to cases in which a debt instrument provides for some contingent payments.[71] Thus, a nonrecourse debt instrument that has no stated payment contin-

---

67   There is a body of authority (aimed principally at tax shelters) that ignores nonrecourse debt for tax purposes in its entirety if it substantially exceeds, at the time of origination, the fair market value of the related collateral. See, e.g., *Estate of Franklin v. Comm'r.*, 544 F.2d 1045 (9th Cir. 1976). See also *Pleasant Summit Land Corp. v. Comm'r*, 863 F.2d 263 (3rd Cir. 1988) (nonrecourse debt ignored to the extent it exceeds fair market value of collateral).

68   Cf. *Farley Realty Corp. v. Comm'r*, 279 F.2d 701 (2d Cir. 1960); Revenue Ruling 83-51, 1983-1 C.B. 48 (under certain circumstances, contingent interest on a shared appreciation mortgage constitutes interest under section 163); Revenue Ruling 76-413, 1976-2 C.B. 213 (contingent interest on a mortgage loan based in part on proceeds of sale of land acquired and developed with proceeds of the loan considered "interest on obligations secured by mortgages on real property" under section 856(c)); and section 856(j)(income from shared appreciation features treated as gain from underlying real property).

69   For a more complete discussion of the treatment of financially troubled mortgages, see Part C.6 below.

70   Treasury Regulation § 1.860G-2(a)(7). The regulation illustrates the rule by stating that an instrument that was issued for $100x and provides for noncontingent principal payments of $100x, interest payments at a fixed rate, and contingent payments based on a percentage of the mortgagor's gross receipts is an obligation.

71   Despite the heading of the section ("Certain instruments that call for contingent payments are obligations"), the text does not require any contingency, but instead applies "even if" a contingency is present. Further, it would be paradoxical if instruments with contingencies received better treatment than those without.

gencies but is secured by property valued at less than its principal amount can benefit from the rule. Third, although the word "instrument" could encompass state law equity securities, the requirement that an instrument provide noncontingent "principal" payments at least equal to its issue price implies that the instrument must take the form of a debt instrument or an interest in a debt instrument.[72] Fourth, principal payments should be considered "noncontingent" even though they are subject to a material risk of default.[73] Fifth, although not stated, the "issue price" of an instrument is presumably its issue price as measured for purposes of calculating original issue discount.[74] Finally, in order to come within the rule, the same "instrument" that provides for contingent payments must also provide the required principal payments. Although a mortgage that has contingent interest based on the performance of the underlying property was clearly intended to be a single "instrument" for this purpose,[75] there may be circumstances where different rights could be considered distinct "instruments" even though they are packaged together. This result is particularly likely where the rights are by their terms separately assignable, or one of the rights is an option that can be exercised only by making an additional cash payment.

The special definition of "obligation" does not limit the size of an obligation by comparison with the value of the underlying collateral. The drafters may have thought, quite reasonably, that such a limitation was not needed in light of the independent requirement, discussed in the next section, that a qualified mortgage be "principally secured" by an interest in real property.

---

72   Compare the regular interest definition in section 860G(a)(1)(A) which requires that an interest unconditionally entitle the holder to receive a specified principal amount "(or other similar amount)". This language was intended to accommodate instruments that do not take the form of debt. See footnote 2 above. The need for an instrument to take the form of debt in order to be a "qualified mortgage" is also implied by the requirement that it be "secured" by an interest in real property. For a discussion of the treatment of pass-through certificates as qualified mortgages, see footnote 76 below.

73   Compare Proposed Regulation § 1.1275-4(b)(1) (a payment is not considered contingent merely because the amount of or the liability for the payment may be impaired by insolvency or default). Note also that the holder of a regular interest is considered to be "unconditionally" entitled to principal payments despite the existence of a default risk. See Chapter 5, Part D.1.

74   See section 1273(b) (definition of issue price under OID rules), section 860G(a)(10) ("issue price" of REMIC interests based generally on OID definition), and Treasury Regulation § 1.860G-2(a)(1)(i) (refers to the "adjusted issue price" of an obligation held by a REMIC, which is clearly a term borrowed from the OID area; see footnote 79 below). For a discussion of the definition of issue price, see Chapter 6, Part C.1; and Chapter 7, footnote 31. If an instrument were not considered a "debt instrument" within the meaning of section 1275(a)(1), then technically the OID rules, and the OID related definition of "issue price", would not apply. However, given the purpose of the regulation, to eliminate questions raised by the possibility that an instrument may not qualify as a debt for tax purposes, it would be sensible to apply the OID definition as if the instrument were debt. In any event, the technical issue of whether the OID definition applies will often not be significant, because the most plausible alternate definition of issue price is the fair market value of an instrument on issuance, and in most cases this amount will not exceed the issue price as determined for purposes of the OID rules.

75   See the example described in footnote 70 above.

The statutory definition of a qualified mortgage refers not only to an obligation, but also to "any participation or certificate of beneficial interest" in an obligation. This added language ensures that non-REMIC pass-through certificates (including senior and subordinated pass-through certificates and IO and PO Strips) can be qualified mortgages, at least to the extent the underlying assets are qualified mortgages or other related assets that would be considered permitted investments if held by a REMIC.[76] It is not clear whether an interest in a fixed pool of mortgages that is classified for tax purposes as a partnership could be a qualified mortgage (either generally, or under some set of circumstances).[77]

(ii) Principally secured. Under the REMIC regulations,[78] an obligation is considered to be "principally secured" by an interest in real property only if

- the fair market value of the interest in real property securing the obligation (1) was at least 80 percent of the adjusted issue price[79] of the obligation at

---

76   See Conference Report at II-227, footnote 5; Blue Book at 413, footnote 67. The treatment of stripped bonds and coupons is discussed further in Part A.1.a.(ii) above. Treasury Regulation § 1.860G-2(a)(5) states that "[o]bligations secured by interests in real property include the following: . . . mortgage pass-thru certificates guaranteed by GNMA, FNMA, FHLMC, or CMHC (Canada Mortgage and Housing Corporation); other investment trust interests that represent undivided beneficial ownership in a pool of obligations principally secured by interests in real property and related assets that would be considered to be permitted investments if the investment trust were a REMIC, and provided the investment trust is classified as a trust under [Treasury Regulation § 301.7701-4(c)—i.e., is a grantor trust]." The tax classification of trusts is discussed at length in Chapter 3. The reference to "assets that would be considered permitted investments" should be read to refer to broad categories of assets and not to require strict compliance with the REMIC definitions. Thus, for example, interests in a trust that is not formed to avoid the REMIC rules should not be precluded from being a qualified mortgage because it holds foreclosure property for more than two years. A pass-through trust that is not a REMIC would have no reason to adhere to the REMIC rules, and a trust formed before enactment of TRA 1986 could not have anticipated them. Similarly, pass-through certificates formed outside of the U.S., such as the CMHC guaranteed certificates referred to above, would not be subject to any U.S. tax rules. Note that the test of whether an asset held by a pass-through trust would be a permitted investment if the trust were a REMIC does not necessarily require that the assets of the trust would be permitted investments of the REMIC acquiring interests in the trust if they were acquired directly. For example, a pass-through certificate issued by a trust should not fail to be a qualified mortgage merely because on the date of its acquisition by the REMIC, the trust already owns real estate acquired in a foreclosure. Compare Treasury Regulation § 1.860G-2(b)(6), discussed below at footnote 174.

77   The regulation cited in footnote 76, which refers to interests in grantor trusts, is inclusive rather than exclusive. Cf. Treasury Regulation § 1.856-3(g) (partnership interest treated as real property mortgages under REIT rules to the extent the partnership holds real property mortgages). One concern with extending the definition of qualified mortgage to interests in trusts or partnerships is whether activities of the trust or partnership would be attributed to the REMIC. See footnote 172 below. A substantial argument could be made that a pass-through certificate that is classified as a partnership interest is an "obligation" under the special definition in the REMIC regulations described in the text at footnote 70 (because it is an "instrument" that provides for principal payments), although that rule does not address whether the "obligation" is considered to be "secured" by an interest in real property.

78   Treasury Regulation § 1.860G-2(a)(1).

79   The adjusted issue price of an obligation is a term used in applying the original issue discount rules of the Code and is discussed in Chapter 6, text following footnote 40. The adjusted issue price of a mortgage at the time of its origination would generally equal the amount loaned by the originator

the time the obligation was originated, or (2) is at least 80 percent of the adjusted issue price of the obligation at the time the sponsor contributes the obligation to the REMIC;[80] or

- substantially all of the proceeds of the obligation were used to acquire or to improve or protect an interest in real property that, at the origination date, is the only security for the obligation.[81]

The second part of this definition covers real estate construction or acquisition loans. Although the point is not clear, it would be reasonable to consider the "substantially all" portion of the test to be met if proceeds of an obligation equal to at least 80 percent of the issue price of the obligation are used for the stated purpose.[82] It seems likely that proceeds of an obligation that are used to refund a prior obligation would be considered used for the same purposes for which the proceeds of the refunded obligation were used, but again there is no authority covering the point.[83]

The first part of the definition, which compares the value of real property collateral with the amount of a loan, deserves more attention. The value-at-*origination* part of the test generally avoids the need to revalue real property collateral at any time after the initial underwriting of a loan. However, the rule is not limited to cases where the post-origination value of real estate collateral is unknown. For example, the test would appear to be met even if the mortgaged property burned to the ground the day before a mortgage loan was transferred to the REMIC and that fact was known to the REMIC's sponsor.[84]

---

to the mortgagor. See Chapter 6, footnote 27.

80   In a double-tier REMIC structure (see Part C.7.a below), the qualified mortgages held by the upper-tier REMIC consist of regular interests issued by the lower-tier REMIC, which are treated as qualified mortgages without regard to whether they are principally secured by real property. See section 860G(a)(3)(C).

81   For purposes of this test, third party guarantees or other credit enhancements are not viewed as additional security for an obligation, and an obligation is not considered to be secured by property other than real property because the borrower is personally liable on the obligation. See Treasury Regulation § 1.860G-2(a)(1)(ii).

82   In other contexts, "substantially all" sometimes means more than 80% and sometimes means less. The argument for using the 80% test described in the text would be based on the first part of the definition of "principally secured".

83   Cf. Treasury Regulation § 1.103-7(d) (for purposes of applying rules that allow interest on municipal bonds to be tax-exempt only if the proceeds are used for prescribed purposes, the proceeds of a refunding issue are considered to be used for the purposes for which the proceeds of the refunded issue were used). The case for treating proceeds of a refunding loan as used for the purposes for which the refunded loan was used is particularly strong where the refunded loan is a bridge loan. Cf. *Huntsman v. Comm'r*, 905 F.2d 1182 (8th Cir. 1990) (debt used to refinance a bridge loan is considered to be incurred in connection with the purchase or improvement of the property financed with the bridge loan for purposes of section 461(g)(2), relating to the deductibility of points).

84   In such a case, the loan would most likely not be held for long by the REMIC because the loan would fail to meet a representation that typically is made by the sponsor to the effect that, at closing, the property securing each loan is in good repair. If it were known with certainty to all the parties on the startup day that the sponsor will be required to repurchase a loan at a fixed price, an issue could arise as to whether the REMIC should be viewed as making a loan to the sponsor. Compare the text accompanying footnotes 33 and 34, above. At least in the case of a commercial mortgage, a significant decline in the value of real property securing a loan may also signal that

Under the regulations, a mortgage loan is considered to be "originated" not only when the loan is made, but also when there is a "significant modification" of the loan (with an exception for modifications occasioned by defaults or reasonably foreseeable defaults). Modifications of qualified mortgages are discussed in Part C.2 below.

The 80 percent test in the regulations compares the value of real estate collateral with the amount of the secured loan. Thus, the ratio of real estate collateral to other collateral is irrelevant. A loan that on origination is secured by real property valued at 80 percent of the loan balance and personal property valued at 100 percent of the loan balance would be considered "principally" secured by an interest in real property despite the fact that less than half of the collateral consists of real property. Similarly, the inclusion in the collateral for a loan of a "buy-down" fund that is used to subsidize mortgage payments will not prevent the entire loan from being principally secured by real property if the real estate collateral (disregarding the fund) meets the 80 percent test.[85]

The 80 percent test requires a comparison of the value of real estate collateral with the adjusted issue price of a loan on the same date (either the date of origination or the date of contribution). Thus, the original value of real property may not be compared with the date-of-contribution loan balance. To illustrate, suppose that upon origination, a loan has an adjusted issue price of 100 and real estate collateral valued at 70. Several years later, when the loan has been paid down to 50, it is contributed to a REMIC. The loan does not automatically meet the 80 percent test because the original value of the collateral (70) is more than 80 percent of the current loan balance (80 percent of 50, or 40). Instead, it is necessary to test whether the value of the real estate at the time of the contribution is at least 40.

In the mortgage industry, the adequacy of the collateral securing a loan is often measured by looking at the ratio of the amount of the loan to the value of the collateral. Many residential loans are originated with loan-to-value ratios of approximately 80 percent. This 80 percent figure should not be confused with the 80

---

the loan is likely to default. For a discussion of the problems that may arise when financially troubled mortgages are transferred to a REMIC, see Part C.6. Consider also the special rule for releases of collateral discussed in the text accompanying footnote 99, below.

85   The right to receive payments from a buy-down fund would not be treated as a separate asset of the REMIC in addition to the related mortgage if either the fund was considered to be owned by the mortgagor and was additional collateral for the mortgagor's payment obligations, or the fund was considered to be owned by a third party other than the REMIC or the mortgagor and served only to guarantee payments due from the mortgagor. In the latter case, the right to payments from the fund would be a credit enhancement contract that is treated as part of the related mortgage. Credit enhancement contracts are discussed in Part C.1 below. On the other hand, a buy-down fund could pose a problem if the fund were considered to be owned by the REMIC holding the related mortgage, because such a fund would not be a qualified mortgage or permitted investment. Two terms of a buy-down arrangement that are particularly important in determining who owns the fund are whether the mortgagor is liable for all mortgage payments, including those that are to be made out of the buy-down fund, and whether the mortgagor is credited with the fund balance in the event of a prepayment or assumption. For further discussion of buy-down funds, see Chapter 6, footnotes 74 and 75.

percent test in the REMIC regulations, which requires a loan-to-value ratio not exceeding 125 percent.[86]

In measuring the value of the real property securing a loan, the property must be allocated among the various obligations it secures if there is more than one. The value of real property securing an obligation is reduced by the amount of any lien on the property that is senior to the obligation being tested, and by a proportionate amount of any lien that is on a parity with the tested obligation.[87] The REMIC regulations do not provide for any specific "marshalling of the assets" of a debtor in determining whether a particular loan is principally secured. Thus, for example, if mortgage 1 in the amount of 100 is secured by both property A with a value of 300 and property B with a value of 100, a 75 principal amount loan secured solely by a mortgage on property B which is *pari passu* with mortgage 1 would appear not to meet the 80 percent test, notwithstanding the substantial overcollateralization of mortgage 1 by property A.

The regulations do not state how contingent obligations such as guarantees are to be measured for purposes of the calculation, although in the absence of guidance to the contrary, it would seem to be prudent to take such obligations into account at their face amount (if that can be determined). Similarly, the regulations do not address the effect on the status of a mortgage loan of parity or senior liens that do not exist on the date the 80 percent test is applied but are contemplated or permitted under the terms of the loan. The Service might contend that the adequacy of the real property collateral needs to be retested as of each date on which a new senior or parity loan comes into existence. At least where the later liens arise in commercially reasonable circumstances and are not designed as an end run around the 80 percent test, however, it would be difficult for the Service to disregard the language of the regulations requiring collateral to be tested only on origination or the date of contribution to a REMIC. The analysis would be quite different if the creation of senior or parity liens were considered a loan modification that caused a deemed exchange of the affected mortgage for tax purposes under section 1001, but no such exchange should occur if the new lien is permitted under the terms of the mortgage.[88]

---

86   Note that the REMIC rules count only real property collateral and not other security interests.

87   Treasury Regulation § 1.860G-2(a)(2). The reference to "lien" would presumably include tax liens or other liens securing nondebt obligations. To illustrate the treatment of liens, suppose that property valued at 100 secures debt of 110, consisting of a first mortgage of 80 and two parity second mortgages of 15 each. In that case, the value of the real property securing the first mortgage and each second mortgage would be 100 and 10 (15/30 times 100–80) respectively. Thus, the first mortgage would meet the 80% test, but the second mortgages would not. Note that the second mortgages in this example could be transformed into qualified mortgages by making an appropriate REMIC election. In particular, if the mortgages were combined into a single mortgage of 110, that mortgage would meet the 80% test (100 is more than 80% of 110) and could therefore be transferred to a REMIC. The REMIC would then issue regular interests corresponding to the desired first and second mortgages. Those regular interests, like all regular interests, would be qualified mortgages in the hands of another REMIC.

88   The Service could argue that the creation of a new parity or senior lien should be considered a "release" of an existing lien on real property, although such an argument would appear to distort the normal meaning of the term. Loan modifications and releases are discussed in Part C.2.

Under a safe-harbor rule, an obligation is treated as principally secured by real property if, at the time when the sponsor contributes the obligation to the REMIC, the sponsor reasonably believes that either of the two prongs of the 80 percent test is met.[89] A sponsor does not have such a reasonable belief if it actually knows or has reason to know that the obligation fails both tests. If the safe harbor applies to an obligation and the REMIC later discovers that the obligation did not in fact meet either part of the test, then the obligation becomes a "defective obligation" on the date of discovery and is subject to certain rules governing defective mortgages.[90]

The regulations state that, for purposes of the safe harbor, a sponsor's reasonable belief may be based on representations and warranties made by the originator of the obligations, or evidence that loans originated in accordance with the originator's underwriting criteria would meet one of the tests.[91] Presumably, such a belief might also be founded on appraisals, representations from a source other than the originator, or possibly even statistical information,[92] depending on what is in fact reasonable under the circumstances.

The regulations do not have a general definition of "secured." The regulations imply that property will be considered to "secure" an obligation regardless of the state law mechanics involved, as long as the effect is to make the property specific security for the obligation with the same priority as a mortgage or deed of trust.[93] Although there is no direct authority in the REMIC area, it should not be necessary to record (or otherwise perfect) a mortgage or other security interest in order for it to count as a qualifying security interest, at least if the mortgagee has the right to record and there is a good business reason for not recording (e.g., avoiding a mortgage recording tax).[94] An obligation is not considered to be secured by real

---

89 Treasury Regulation § 1.860G-2(a)(3). Note that the reasonable belief must exist when an obligation is contributed to a REMIC and not on the startup day. Thus, if a qualified replacement mortgage is transferred to a REMIC after the startup day, the sponsor's belief with respect to that mortgage would be tested on the date of transfer.

90 Defective mortgages are discussed in the text beginning at footnote 111 below.

91 Treasury Regulation § 1.860-2(a)(3)(ii). Although Treasury Regulation § 1.860G-2(a)(3)(ii)(B) refers to both tests, it is not clear how underwriting criteria could ever assure that a loan meets the 80% test on the date of contribution to a REMIC if the test was not also met at origination.

92 Statistical techniques might perhaps be used to adjust the values of real property determined under relatively recent appraisals for changes in prices between the date of the appraisals and the valuation date that is relevant for REMIC purposes.

93 The regulations include in the list of obligations that may be considered secured by real property "mortgages, deeds of trust, and installment land contracts". See Treasury Regulation § 1.860G-2(a)(5). Compare the definitions of "secured" in Treasury Regulation §§ 1.163-10T(o), 1.593-11(b)(2) and 301.7701-13(j)(2), which track the definition given in the text.

94 In the case of a REIT, there is authority holding that the failure to record a lien will not prevent a loan from qualifying as a "mortgage". See G.C.M. 39484 (March 5, 1986); Private Letter Ruling 8611044 (December 16, 1985). Although Treasury Regulation § 1.163-10T(o) treats a loan as being "secured by" real property only if the security interest is recorded or otherwise perfected, the purpose of this regulation is presumably to create a bright line test to prevent individuals from converting nondeductible "personal interest" into "qualified residence interest" where there was no intent to secure the indebtedness by the borrower's residence. It seems much less likely that unrecorded mortgages would be created to allow REMIC financing.

   If a REMIC holds an unrecorded mortgage, and another mortgage that would otherwise be on

property if it is secured by another obligation that is itself directly secured by real property. As a result, non-REMIC pay-through bonds are not qualified mortgages.[95]

It is not clear whether an unsecured loan that is supported by a guarantee or other credit enhancement contract that is in turn secured by real property would be considered secured by an interest in real property, although there are substantial arguments in favor of this result.[96]

The collateral securing a loan could change while the loan is held by the REMIC. Such a change could affect the status of the loan as a qualified mortgage either under the general rule in the regulations governing loan modifications (discussed in Part C.2 below), or under a special rule governing releases of collateral. In general terms, a modification of a mortgage is treated as an exchange of the old mortgage for a new one if (1) the modification is a "significant modification" that would be treated as such an exchange under general tax principles, and (2) the modification is not one that is disregarded under the REMIC regulations. Modifications occasioned by, among other things, a default or reasonably foreseeable default are disregarded under the REMIC regulations. A change in the collateral underlying a loan not occasioned by a default may or may not be treated as an exchange under

---

a parity or subordinate to the unrecorded mortgage becomes senior to the unrecorded mortgage because it is perfected first, the Service might contend that the REMIC's mortgage needs to be retested to determine if it remains "principally secured" by real property on the theory that the lien on the real estate in favor of the first mortgage loan was partially released. Such an argument would be a stretch. Compare the discussion of after-arising liens in footnote 88. There is clearly no need to record the assignment of a mortgage to a REMIC in order for the REMIC to be recognized to be the owner of the mortgage for tax purposes, and this point should not be confused with the recording of the mortgage lien.

95   Treasury Regulation § 1.860G-2(a)(6). This regulation carves out REMIC regular interests from the rule requiring obligations to be directly secured by real property in order to be considered principally secured by interests in real property. However, as indicated in footnote 80 above, there is no requirement that regular interests be principally secured by real property in order to be treated as qualified mortgages. In order to ensure that obligations secured by other obligations are not considered qualified mortgages, TAMRA deleted the words "directly or indirectly" from the phrase "principally secured, directly or indirectly, by an interest in real property" in the first part of the definition of a qualified mortgage in section 860G(a)(3)(A). See also the Blue Book at 413, footnote 67. Contrast the REMIC rule with Revenue Ruling 80-280, 1980-2 C.B. 207 ("hypothecation loans" secured by notes secured by real property are "real property mortgages" for purposes of the REIT rules).

96   The principal argument in favor of treating a secured guarantee as equivalent to a direct security interest is that it places the REMIC in the same legal and economic position as a direct security interest, by giving it a right to collect from the real property collateral if the REMIC is not paid amounts due on the guaranteed loan when they are due. As indicated in the text accompanying footnote 93, above, the state law form of a security interest should not be critical. The arrangement is distinguishable from a loan secured by a second loan that is secured by real estate because, in the case of a secured guarantee, a default on the guaranteed loan will always trigger a right to collect from the collateral; where the security is a second loan, the right to collect from the collateral will depend on the existence of a default on the second loan. Compare the discussion in footnote 255 below of the treatment as a qualified mortgage of a guaranteed loan that is recharacterized as a loan to the guarantor. An argument for treating security for a guarantee as equivalent to security for the guaranteed loan could also be made based on the rule in Treasury Regulation § 1.860G-2(c)(1) that treats a credit enhancement contract as part of the mortgage to which it relates for purposes of the REMIC assets test.

the REMIC regulations depending on, among other factors, whether the change is made in accordance with the terms of the loan and whether the loan is recourse or nonrecourse.[97] A modification of a loan that causes a deemed exchange of a new loan for the old one would automatically terminate the status of a loan as a qualified mortgage unless the new loan meets the definition of a qualified replacement mortgage. That definition generally would be met only if the value of the real estate collateral is at least 80 percent of the loan balance at the time of the modification,[98] and could not in any event be met if the exchange occurs more than two years after the startup day.

In addition to the general provisions governing loan modifications, the REMIC regulations contain a special rule (release rule) that in all cases treats a loan held by a REMIC as ceasing to be a qualified mortgage if the REMIC "releases its lien on real property" securing the loan.[99] Given the discussion above, it appears that the release rule was aimed at cases in which the release of collateral would not otherwise result in the creation of a new loan (e.g., because it is permitted without consent under the terms of the loan). The only exception to the release rule is a limited one for a loan that is, according to its terms and for commercial reasons, "defeased" using government securities as the new collateral at least two years after the startup day.

The release rule appears to contemplate a *complete* release of real property collateral, although this conclusion is not certain. One can imagine at least four different ways in which a partial release of real estate collateral could be handled. First, the release rule described above could be applied, thereby causing the mortgage to lose its status as a qualified mortgage. This result is not compelled by the language of the release rule ("release" could mean "complete release") and would be difficult to justify if the loan continued to meet the 80 percent test after giving effect to the release. Second, the loan could be retested to see if it in fact continues to meet the 80 percent test, by comparing the current fair market value of the real estate collateral with the loan balance immediately following the release. Third, the loan could be retested using the value of the real property and the loan balance originally assumed in applying the qualified mortgage definition, but excluding the assumed value of the collateral that has been released.[100] Finally, the release could be ignored on the ground that if it does not give rise to an exchange of one loan for another under general tax principles, it also should be disregarded in applying the qualified mortgage definition. It might be necessary to temper this last approach with an anti-abuse rule that allows a release to be ignored only if the release was not planned on the REMIC's startup day.

---

97   See Part C.2.c below.

98   Consideration should also be given to the possibility that the modified loan would meet the "principally secured" test as a refinancing of a construction or acquisition loan. See footnote 83 above.

99   Treasury Regulation § 1.860G-2(a)(8).

100   This approach could be difficult to apply in a case where the collateral that is released was not separately valued for purposes of the original 80% test.

While there are no hard and fast rules, it would seem to be most reasonable as a general rule to apply the second of the four approaches described above. In practice, the third approach is often used in a case where a loan is secured by multiple properties and the documents contemplate releases of individual properties conditioned on the prepayment of a specified portion of the loan. In any event, a partial release in a default setting should be ignored. As discussed in Part C.2 below, the REMIC regulations generally allow loan modifications of any type in a workout setting, and it is not evident why releases of collateral should be treated differently from other loan modifications.[101]

(iii) Real property. Under the general statutory definition, a qualified mortgage must be principally secured by an *interest* in *real property.* The REMIC regulations define these terms the same way they are defined for purposes of the REIT rules. Thus, *real property* generally means land or improvements thereon such as buildings and other inherently permanent structures (including items that are structural components of the buildings or structure).[102] Local law definitions are not controlling. The real property can be residential or commercial. There is no requirement that the property be located within the United States.[103] An *interest* in real property includes a fee ownership or co-ownership interest, leaseholds, options to acquire real property or leaseholds thereon, timeshare interests and stock in a cooperative housing corporation,[104] but does not include mineral, oil, or gas royalty interests.[105]

---

101   One problem with this argument is that it would seem to apply equally to partial releases of collateral and to full releases, and at least in the case of a full release, the release rule unambiguously requires that a loan lose its status as a qualified mortgage. The tension between the two rules in this case should not pose much of a practical problem. A workout in which a REMIC agrees to a complete release of real estate collateral without a full satisfaction of the secured obligation should be a rarity. See also the text following footnote 190 (payments under a credit enhancement contract can continue to be made after real property has been sold).

102   Treasury Regulation § 1.860G-2(a)(4), which refers to § 1.856-3(d). This last regulation elaborates on the basic definition as follows: "The term [real property] includes, for example, the wiring in a building, plumbing systems, central heating or central air-conditioning machinery, pipes or ducts, elevators or escalators installed in the building, or other items which are structural components of a building or other permanent structure. The term does not include assets accessory to the operation of a business, such as machinery, printing press, transportation equipment which is not a structural component of the building, office equipment, refrigerators, individual air-conditioning units, grocery counters, furnishings of a motel, hotel, or office building, etc. even though such items may be termed fixtures under local law." See also Treasury Regulation § 1.48-1(c) (definition of "tangible personal property" which excludes buildings and structural components). By contrast, the definitions of real property in Treasury Regulation §§ 1.593-11(b)(1) and 301.7701-13(j)(4) (defining, in general terms, a real estate loan for purposes of sections 593(d) and 7701(a)(19)(C)) look to local law.

103   Cf. Revenue Ruling 74-191, 1974-1 C.B. 170 (for purposes of the REIT rules, real estate assets include foreign real estate and obligations secured by such real estate). The examples of obligations secured by interests in real property given in Treasury Regulation § 1.860G-2(a)(5) include mortgage pass-through certificates guaranteed by CMHC (Canada Mortgage and Housing Corporation).

104   The rule treating loans secured by stock in a residential co-op as obligations secured by real property for purposes of the REMIC rules is also found in the statute. See section 860G(a)(3), flush language. This rule only applies to stock in a cooperative housing corporation as defined in

Loans are also considered to be secured by real property to the extent they are secured by manufactured housing or mobile homes that meet certain minimum size and other requirements (but not loans secured by recreational vehicles, campers, or similar vehicles).[106]

Credit enhancement contracts are considered to be part of the pool of mortgages to which they relate and not a separate asset. Thus, to the extent those contracts are considered assets of a REMIC, they are qualified mortgages if the related mortgages are qualified mortgages. Credit enhancement contracts are discussed in Part C.1 below.

(iv) Qualified replacement mortgages. Qualified mortgages also include *qualified replacement mortgages*, which are defined in section 860G(a)(4). A qualified replacement mortgage is any obligation[107] that would be a qualified mortgage if it were transferred to the REMIC on the startup day, and that is received for (1) another obligation within the three-month period beginning on the startup day,[108] or (2) a "defective" obligation within the two-year period beginning on the startup day.

---

section 216, so that the failure of a co-op to meet the requirements of that section could potentially affect the status as a qualified mortgage of a loan secured by stock in the corporation. However, such a corporation has a substantial incentive to meet the requirements of section 216 because otherwise interest and real estate taxes paid by the corporation would not be deductible by the tenant-shareholders. A loan needs to be secured by real estate only upon origination or contribution to a REMIC, so it would seem that the status of a co-op at those times is the critical issue. Also, the safe-harbor based on the reasonable belief of the sponsor (see footnote 89 above) should, where applicable, protect against the failure of a co-op to qualify under section 216. Debt incurred to purchase a co-op that cannot be secured by the co-op shares because of financing limitations imposed by the co-op would not appear to be a qualified mortgage; there is no REMIC counterpart to section 163(h)(4)(B) which treats such loans as secured for purposes of the definition of qualified residence interest.

105   Treasury Regulation § 1.860G-2(a)(4) which refers to § 1.856-3(c). There appears to be no rule requiring that a leasehold interest have any minimum term, although the term of a leasehold could, of course, affect its market value, and hence the ability to meet the "principally secured" test. Section 856(c)(6)(C) (on which the REMIC definition is based) defines an interest in real property to include "leaseholds" without further embellishment. Compare Treasury Regulation §§ 1.593-11(b)(3) and 301.7701-13(j)(3), which require a leasehold term extending or automatically renewable for a period of 30 years, or for a period of 10 years beyond the scheduled final maturity date of a mortgage, in order for a loan to be, in general terms, a real estate loan for purposes of sections 593(d) and 7701(a)(19)(C).

106   The manufactured housing or mobile homes must be "single family residences" under section 25(e)(10). See Treasury Regulation § 1.860G-2(a)(5); Notice 87-41, 1987-1 C.B. 500.

107   Section 860G(a)(4) refers to a qualified replacement mortgage as an *obligation*. This language should not be read to exclude from the term regular interests that are not in the form of obligations. The Conference Report at II-227 and the Blue Book at 413 use the broader term *property* in lieu of *obligation* in describing qualified replacement mortgages. Also, TAMRA amended section 860G(a)(4)(A) to broaden the categories of qualified mortgages that could be replacement mortgages from "any obligation . . . which would be described in paragraph (3)(A) [of section 860G(a)]" to "any obligation . . . which would be a qualified mortgage". The amended reference clearly encompasses regular interests referred to in paragraph (3)(C) of section 860G(a).

108   Note that this is not the same period as the initial period during which the assets test is not applied (which extends through the end of the third month beginning after the startup day). See the text following footnote 57 above.

Section 860G(e)(5) authorizes regulations "providing that a mortgage will be treated as a qualified replacement mortgage only if it is part of a bona fide replacement (and not part of a swap of mortgages)." To date, no such regulations have been issued.[109]

Subject to the "anti-swap" rule just mentioned, a qualified mortgage can be replaced for any reason within three months after the startup day, but a mortgage can be replaced thereafter (until the second anniversary of the startup day) only if it is defective.[110] The regulations[111] define a *defective mortgage* as a qualified mortgage that

- is in default or with respect to which a default is reasonably foreseeable[112]
- was fraudulently procured by the mortgagor
- was not in fact principally secured by an interest in real property, or
- does not conform to a customary representation or warranty given by the sponsor or prior owner of the mortgage regarding the characteristics of the mortgage, or the characteristics of the pool of mortgages of which the mortgage is a part.[113]

When a defect results from a misrepresentation as to the characteristics of a *pool* of mortgages (e.g., percentage of loans located in one state), it should be possible to treat any individual loans as defective if those loans are removed from the REMIC in order to cure the misrepresentation.

The treatment of defaulted loans as defective means that a guarantor of qualified mortgages can be given the right to replace a defaulted loan within two years after the startup day in lieu of paying under the guarantee.

A defect may prevent a loan from being a qualified mortgage. Most typically, this will occur when the defect relates to the existence or adequacy of real property

---

109   For further discussion of this provision, see Chapter 12, footnote 39 and accompanying text.

110   Also, a defective mortgage can be sold by a REMIC at any time at a gain without incurring a prohibited transactions tax, as described further in Part B below.

111   Treasury Regulation § 1.860G-2(f)(1).

112   Although the regulations do not define the term default, presumably a default is any event treated as a default under the terms of the mortgage.

113   The regulations state that a representation that payments on a qualified mortgage will be received at a rate no less than a specified minimum or no greater than a specified maximum is not considered a customary representation. A representation as to the rate of actual prepayments of a pool of mortgages at or immediately prior to the transfer to the REMIC is, however, customary for many types of REMIC transactions. A number of pooling and servicing agreements relating to REMICs have included a representation that the mortgages to be transferred to the REMIC are qualified mortgages as defined in section 860G(a)(3). Although it is not clear when a novelty becomes a custom, a good argument can be made that such a representation has become "customary" with the result that a failure of a loan to be a qualified mortgage for any reason would cause the loan to be defective. The principal reason why a loan would fail to be a qualified mortgage is that it is not principally secured by real property, and the failure to meet this test is an independent ground for being "defective". One case where a loan might fail to be a qualified mortgage for reasons unrelated to its security is where the loan purports to be, but in fact is not, a REMIC regular interest or qualifying pass-through certificate.

collateral. The regulations state that a loan suffering from a defect that would prevent the loan from being a qualified mortgage if the defect had been discovered before the startup day will be treated as if it were a qualified mortgage until 90 days after the REMIC discovers the defect.[114] Thus, if the loan is removed from the REMIC before expiration of the 90-day period, the REMIC will suffer no adverse consequences as a result of the failure of the loan to be a qualified mortgage. If the loan is held after 90 days, it may still be exchanged for a qualified replacement mortgage if the exchange takes place within two years after the startup day (although the exchange may be a prohibited transaction).[115]

A modification of a qualified mortgage may be considered, for tax purposes generally, to result in a deemed exchange of the original loan for the modified loan. In that event, the modified loan would be a qualified mortgage only if it meets the definition of a qualified replacement mortgage or a special savings rule for REMICs applies. Loan modifications are discussed in Part C.2 below.

If a sponsor has breached a customary representation or warranty with respect to a mortgage and the breach cannot be cured, the typical remedy is to require the repurchase of the defective loan or, if two years have not yet passed since the startup day, an exchange of the loan for a qualified replacement mortgage. Provided the defect does not affect the loan's status as a qualified mortgage, a sponsor could

---

114   Treasury Regulation § 1.860G-2(f)(2). The regulations do not discuss whose discovery of a defect is considered a discovery by a REMIC. In the case of a REMIC organized as a trust, a discovery of the defect by the trustee would presumably be attributed to the REMIC, and the same may be true for a discovery by a loan servicer or a person regularly providing administrative services to the trust. A discovery of the defect by a sponsor or originator should not be attributed to the REMIC unless it is otherwise acting on behalf of the REMIC. It is not entirely clear how the 90-day rule for defective loans relates to the rule, described above at footnote 89, that treats a loan as being principally secured by real property if the sponsor reasonably believes that it is so secured until 90 days after discovery that it is not so secured. As currently written, the protection of the 90-day rule for defective loans in Treasury Regulation § 1.860G-2(f)(2) is not conditioned on any one having reasonably believed that a defective loan was a qualified mortgage when it was contributed to the REMIC. If no such reasonable belief is required to take advantage of the 90-day rule for defective loans, then what is the point of the safe harbor based on the sponsor's reasonable belief? The answer may be that if a mortgage is transferred to a REMIC and there is not a reasonable belief at that time that the mortgage is a qualified mortgage, then the date on which it is "discovered" that the mortgage is not a qualified mortgage (which starts the 90-day clock running) will be no later than the startup day.

115   In addition, if the loan represents more than a *de minimis* amount of the REMIC's assets, its presence would cause the REMIC to fail the assets test. See text accompanying footnote 55, above. Treasury Regulation § 1.860G-2(f)(2) states that "even if the REMIC holds the defective obligation beyond the 90-day period, the REMIC may, nevertheless, exchange the defective obligation for a qualified replacement mortgage so long as the requirements of section 860G(a)(4)(B) [which sets out the time periods in which obligations may be exchanged for qualified replacement mortgages] are satisfied." It is not clear what this language accomplishes, since the definition of a qualified replacement mortgage does not require that the replacement mortgage be exchanged for a "qualified mortgage" but only for an "obligation." By contrast, the definition of prohibited transaction in section 860F(a)(2)(A) carves out "the substitution of a qualified replacement mortgage for a *qualified mortgage*" (emphasis added). Query whether an exchange of a loan that has a defect preventing it from being a qualified mortgage, occurring more than 90 days after discovery of the defect, is a prohibited transaction? The language quoted in the third sentence of this footnote may have been intended to provide a negative answer to this question.

also remedy the defect by making a payment to the REMIC equal to the diminution in value of the loan caused by the defect. A temporary investment of such a payment would be a permitted investment, and it does not appear that the receipt of such a payment would have adverse consequences under the REMIC rules.[116]

b. Permitted Investments. In addition to qualified mortgages, a REMIC may hold *permitted investments*. There are three types of permitted investments: *cash flow investments, qualified reserve assets,* and *foreclosure property.*[117]

(i) Cash flow investments. A *cash flow investment* is an investment of payments received under qualified mortgages for a temporary period between receipt of those payments and the regularly scheduled date for distribution of those payments to REMIC interest holders. These investments must be passive assets (including, for example, guaranteed investment contracts) earning a return in the nature of interest.[118] The regulations[119] define the term "payments received on qualified mortgages" broadly to include:

- payments of principal (including prepayments) or interest on a mortgage
- payments under credit enhancement contracts
- proceeds from the disposition of a mortgage
- cash flows from foreclosure property and proceeds from the disposition of such property
- payments by a sponsor or prior owner of a mortgage for breach of a customary warranty relating to a mortgage, and
- prepayment penalties required to be paid under the terms of a qualified mortgage when the mortgagor prepays the obligation.

A payment received on a mortgage is invested for a "temporary period" if it is invested from the time of receipt until the REMIC distributes the payment to REMIC interest holders, provided the period does not exceed 13 months.[120] Payments need not be distributed to holders on the next scheduled payment date either

---

116   See Treasury Regulation § 1.860G-2(g)(1)(ii)(D) ("payments received on qualified mortgages" that may be invested in cash flow investments include payments by a sponsor or prior owner of a defective obligation in lieu of the repurchase of the obligation where the obligation was transferred to the REMIC in breach of a customary warranty). One issue is whether any income realized as a result of the receipt of such a payment would be subject to the prohibited transactions tax. However, any such income should be considered to be "attributable to" the defective mortgage and therefore free of the tax. The prohibited transactions tax is discussed in Part B.1 below.

117   Section 860G(a)(5).

118   Treasury Regulation § 1.860G-2(g)(1)(i); Conference Report at II-227; Blue Book at 414. Income from so-called money market funds that are taxed as regulated investment companies should be treated as a return in the nature of interest for this purpose, even though such income is technically a dividend.

119   Treasury Regulation § 1.860G-2(g)(1)(ii).

120   Treasury Regulation § 1.860G-2(g)(1)(iii).

for the class of interests on which the payments ultimately will be made, or for other classes. For example, if a REMIC makes monthly distributions on regular interests and annual distributions on the residual interest, amounts to be distributed on the residual interest can be invested until the next distribution date for that class. Also, payments to be made on the regular interests in this example could be held until the second following payment date. The regulations state that in determining the length of time that a REMIC has held an investment in a commingled fund or account, the REMIC may use any reasonable accounting method (such as first-in-first-out). Some payments on qualified mortgages are never distributed on REMIC interests, but are instead used to pay expenses or are added to a qualified reserve fund. Presumably, payments of that type either would qualify as a cash flow investment, for a period not exceeding 13 months, until used for the intended purpose, or once identified as a payment to be used to pay expenses or to be added to a qualified reserve fund, would be a qualified reserve asset.

Typically, qualified mortgages are transferred to a REMIC effective as of a cut-off date which precedes the startup day. In that event, the REMIC is entitled to payments received on the qualified mortgages during the period between the cut-off date and the startup day. Although there is no specific authority addressing the point, those payments should be considered payments on qualified mortgages (so that they can be cash flow investments).

Cash flow investments are "investments of" payments received on qualified mortgages. That term should be broad enough to cover income earned on those investments (and on the reinvestment of such income). The REMIC rules clearly contemplate that cash flow investments will produce income.[121]

The definition of cash flow investment does not prohibit the trading of such investments, but any gain from the disposition of a cash flow investment (except in connection with a qualified liquidation) is subject to a 100 percent prohibited transactions tax.[122] Typically, cash flow investments mature on or prior to the date when the invested funds are needed to make distributions, and are held to maturity.[123]

Income from cash flow investments may be paid to a mortgage servicer as part of its servicing compensation, either directly, or by permitting the servicer to make mortgage payments to the REMIC (without interest) only when they are needed to make distributions to investors. In a case where earnings on cash flow investments are not paid to the servicer, they would generally be allocated economically to the

---

121 Treasury Regulation § 1.860G-2(g)(1)(i) states that cash flow investments must be passive investments earning a return in the nature of interest. Also, the REMIC rules contemplate that earnings on cash flow investments may be kept by a REMIC and used to pay down REMIC interests (rather than being paid to a third party as a fee). See, e.g., section 860G(a)(1), flush language (a REMIC interest does not fail to be a regular interest because the timing of principal payments may be contingent on income from permitted investments); section 860G(a)(7)(B) (qualified reserve fund may be used to pay amounts due on regular interests in the event of lower than expected returns on cash flow investments).

122 This tax is discussed below in Part B.1.

123 Compare the rule for grantor trusts described in Chapter 3, Part C.1.c.(iv).

residual interest. A regular interest is not generally permitted to receive interest at a variable rate equal to the earnings received from cash flow investments.[124]

(ii) Qualified reserve assets. A *qualified reserve asset* is any intangible property (other than a REMIC residual interest) held for investment and as part of a qualified reserve fund. An asset need not generate any income to be a qualified reserve asset.[125]

A *qualified reserve fund* is any reasonably required reserve to provide for full payment of

- expenses of the REMIC, or
- amounts due on regular or residual interests in the event of
  - defaults (including delinquencies)[126] on qualified mortgages
  - lower than expected returns on cash flow investments
  - prepayment interest shortfalls, or
  - any other contingency that could be provided for under a credit enhancement contract.[127]

To the extent a reserve exceeds a reasonably required amount, the reserve must be promptly and appropriately reduced.[128] It may also be increased, through the retention of payments on qualified mortgages or contributions of money from residual interest holders, if the reserve is less than reasonably required.[129] A special rule limits the trading of reserve fund assets.[130]

---

124 A regular interest is permitted to bear losses resulting from lower than reasonably expected returns on permitted investments (including cash flow investments). See Chapter 5, footnote 110 and text following footnote 116. However, if a REMIC is structured so that permitted investments are invested at current market rates (and not, for example, in a guaranteed investment contract at a fixed rate), a "reasonably expected" rate might be quite low.

125 Treasury Regulation § 1.860G-2(g)(3). The exclusion of REMIC residual interests from the definition of qualified reserve asset is not found in the statute (section 860G(a)(7)(A)), but is of little moment. For nontax reasons, most residual interests would not be suitable reserve fund assets.

126 See Conference Report at II-227 and Blue Book at 414 (defaults include delinquencies).

127 Treasury Regulation § 1.860G-2(g)(2). Credit enhancement contracts and prepayment interest shortfalls are discussed below in Parts C.1 and C.5, respectively. The regulation goes beyond section 860G(a)(7)(B)(i) by allowing a qualified reserve fund to be used to provide protection (1) for residual interests as well as regular interests against risks other than expenses, and (2) against prepayment interest shortfalls.

128 Treasury Regulation § 1.860G-2(g)(3)(ii)(A). The statute (section 860G(a)(7)(B)) states more precisely that a qualified reserve fund must be "promptly and appropriately reduced as payments of qualified mortgages are received." It is clear that the "appropriate" size of a reserve is not necessarily proportionate to the amount of qualified mortgages. See the text following footnote 133 below.

129 Treasury Regulation § 1.860G-2(g)(3)(ii). The Service has authority under section 860G(e)(1) to adopt regulations to prevent unreasonable accumulations of assets in a REMIC. No regulations have been issued under this authority. Residual interest holders can contribute cash to a qualified reserve fund over the life of the REMIC without subjecting the REMIC to the 100% tax on certain contributions. See Part B.2 below.

130 Under section 860G(a)(7)(C), a reserve fund is not treated as a qualified reserve fund for any year (and all subsequent years) if more than 30% of the gross income from the assets in such fund for

The regulations make the somewhat obvious point that in determining whether a reserve is reasonable, consideration should be given to the credit quality of the qualified mortgages (taking account of related guarantees), the expected amount of expenses and the availability of proceeds from qualified mortgages to pay those expenses.[131] The amount of a reserve is presumed to be reasonable, and to have been promptly and appropriately reduced, if it does not exceed the amount required by a nationally recognized independent rating agency to give the rating for REMIC interests desired by the sponsor, or the amount required by a third-party insurer or guarantor (who does not own directly or indirectly an interest in the REMIC) as a requirement of providing credit enhancement.[132] However, the Service may overcome the presumption if, in light of all relevant factors, the amounts required by the rating agency or the third-party insurer are not commercially reasonable.[133]

The fact that the regulations permit a number of factors to be taken into account in sizing a reserve confirms that a reserve need not be reduced strictly in proportion to reductions in the principal amount of qualified mortgages in order to be "promptly and appropriately reduced" as payments on qualified mortgages are received. For example, reserves may be allowed to build up over time to reflect the lower risk of default losses in early years. As a further illustration, a reserve might equal 5 percent of the aggregate principal amount of the mortgages, but no less than the principal amount of the three largest loans.

A reserve fund can be combined with the creation of senior and junior classes of regular interests. Most often, the reserve is used to provide additional credit

---

the year is derived from the sale or disposition of property held for less than three months (disregarding gain on the disposition of an asset if the disposition is required to prevent default on a regular interest where the threatened default results from a default on one or more qualified mortgages). Presumably the holding period of assets would be measured under section 1223 and other Code provisions governing holding periods. Curiously, there is no exception from the rule for dispositions of assets required to meet reserve fund obligations unrelated to mortgage defaults, or made in connection with a qualified liquidation. The purpose of the special rule for qualified liquidations is to allow a REMIC to liquidate without concern that it will violate the REMIC assets test. See the text at footnote 58 above. In that light, it would be odd if sales of reserve fund assets after adoption of a plan of liquidation were counted in applying the 30% limitation to periods in the same year prior to the adoption of the plan.

131   Treasury Regulation § 1.860G-2(g)(3)(ii)(A); see also Conference Report at II-227 and Blue Book at 414.

132   Treasury Regulation § 1.860G-2(g)(3)(ii)(B). One problem with applying this presumption is that a rating agency or third-party insurer may be unwilling to confirm (at least in writing) that a reserve of a certain size is needed to obtain a rating or credit enhancement. Note that the regulations allow the sponsor to control the size of the reserve by determining the desired rating for REMIC interests, which is clearly appropriate. The presumption does not apply to reserves required by a third-party insurer or guarantor who owns an interest in a REMIC "directly or indirectly (within the meaning of section 267(c) of the Code)". This section provides ownership attribution rules for the ownership of corporate stock. Presumably, it should be applied substituting "REMIC interest" for "stock." Section 267(c) would treat a REMIC interest owned by an entity as being owned by the entity's owners, but would not attribute to an entity a REMIC interest owned by the owners of the entity. Thus, if the insurer were, for example, a corporate subsidiary of the owner of the REMIC interest, the presumption could apply.

133   Treasury Regulation § 1.860G-2(g)(3)(ii)(C).

support for the senior class, but that is not always the case. A better overall economic result might be achieved by using a junior class to provide credit support for the senior securities and establishing a reserve fund to upgrade the credit quality of the junior class. In such a structure, the reserve established to protect the junior class may need to be quite large by comparison with the size of the junior class (and may even grow to equal the amount of that class) in order to achieve the desired credit quality for that class given its subordinated ranking. That fact alone should not signify that the reserve is unreasonably large, particularly if it can be established that the two-class structure permits the use of a smaller reserve fund than would be needed if the REMIC had only parity classes.

As a practical matter, it is unlikely that a sponsor would ever deliberately overfund a reserve. Reserve assets are typically invested in short-term, high-quality debt instruments that produce a low yield, and there is likely to be a strong economic incentive to keep the reserve at the lowest levels possible consistent with achieving the desired credit quality for the REMIC interests.

A few additional comments on the definition of qualified reserve asset are in order. First, a qualified reserve fund cannot be used to protect REMIC interest holders against risks other than the specific ones listed above. For example, a qualified reserve fund could not be used to prevent a default caused by basis risk[134] or a flaw in the bond structure. If it is desirable to establish a reserve for these purposes, consideration should be given to the use of an outside reserve.[135]

Second, the requirement that a qualified reserve asset be *held for investment* could be read to imply that a reserve fund must be funded and cannot consist of letters of credit or other guarantee type contracts. Apparently this was not the intent; the "held for investment" phrase was meant only to prevent the holding of active business assets. At any rate, this question has become largely moot in light of the rules in the REMIC regulations treating credit enhancement contracts as incidental to qualified mortgages.[136]

Third, the *expenses* that may be paid with qualified reserve assets are not defined. They should include any expenses incurred in the ordinary course of managing the REMIC or its assets, whether or not the expenses must be capitalized for income tax purposes. For example, if a REMIC holds foreclosure property and makes an expenditure to preserve the value of the property, it should be possible to use a reserve fund to pay that item, even though it is added to the REMIC's basis in the property. The other REMIC tests ensure that a REMIC's activities are appropriately circumscribed. Thus, there is no need to transform the word "expenses" into a term of art to police those activities.

There is no express requirement that the expenses funded by a reserve be unexpected. Thus, it should be possible to establish a reserve to fund the trustee or

---

134   Basis risk is a risk created by a mismatch between the rates of interest on the mortgages and on the regular interests. See Chapter 5, Part D.

135   Outside reserve funds are discussed in Part C.7.b, below.

136   Credit enhancement contracts are discussed in Part C.1, below.

servicing fees that are expected to be incurred over the life of a REMIC, provided it can be demonstrated that such a reserve is reasonably required.[137]

Finally, a qualified reserve fund can be used to fund protective advances (advances made to protect the value of mortgaged property) because such advances can be provided for under a credit enhancement contract.[138]

Reserve funds that are outside a REMIC are discussed in Part C.7.b below.

(iii) Foreclosure property. Foreclosure property is real property (including interests in real property, and personal property incident to such real property) that is acquired by a REMIC in connection with the default or imminent default of a qualified mortgage held by the REMIC, and is not held longer than a specified grace period.[139] The grace period is generally two years from the date on which the property is considered to be acquired,[140] but is subject to extension for up to an additional four years if it is established to the satisfaction of the Service that an extension is necessary for the orderly liquidation of the REMIC's interest in the property.[141] Where a REMIC holds a pass-through certificate that was not created to avoid the REMIC rules, the retention by the trust of foreclosure property for more than two years should not prevent the certificate from continuing to be a qualified mortgage.[142] A rule that may prevent property from qualifying as foreclosure property if the related loan was financially troubled when it was acquired by the REMIC is discussed in Part C.6.b below.[143] There is no requirement that foreclosure prop-

---

137   As indicated above, Treasury Regulation § 1.860G-2(g)(3)(ii)(A) states that the expected amount of expenses of the REMIC, and the expected availability of proceeds from qualified mortgages to pay the expenses, are factors that should be taken into account in sizing a reserve. This language should not be read to imply that a reserve can never be used to fund expected expenses. For example, in a case where the qualified mortgages are risky investments, it may be reasonable to ensure performance of the basic servicing and administrative functions of a REMIC by depositing amounts required to pay those amounts in a reserve and investing the reserve in high quality securities.

138   The treatment of rights to receive protective advances from third parties as credit enhancement contracts is discussed below at footnote 192. If a qualified reserve fund is used to fund a protective advance, then presumably the right to repayment of the advance would itself be viewed as a qualified reserve asset.

139   Section 860G(a)(8). Foreclosure property is generally defined by reference to the definition that applies to REITs under section 856(e), but without regard to the requirement in section 856(e)(5) that an election be made to treat property as foreclosure property. Eliminating the election requirement for REMICs is sensible because there are no circumstances other than error in which the election would not be made by a REMIC.

140   For this purpose, property is considered to be acquired when the REMIC becomes the owner of the property for federal income tax purposes. See Treasury Regulation § 1.856-6(b).

141   See section 856(e)(3) and Treasury Regulation § 1.856-6(g), which gives detailed guidance on the procedures and standards to be applied in obtaining an extension. A request for extension must be filed more than 60 days before the date on which the grace period otherwise would expire. Subject to some limitations, the grace period is automatically extended while the application is pending.

142   See footnote 76, above (treatment of pass-through certificates as qualified mortgages) and the text accompanying footnote 172, below (activities of pass-through trust not attributed to REMIC for purposes of prohibited transactions rules).

143   See text following footnote 255, below.

erty be acquired in a foreclosure proceeding. All that is needed is for the REMIC to reduce the property to ownership or possession, by agreement or process of law, after there was default (or default was imminent) on a qualified mortgage which such property secured.[144]

Although typically REMIC regular interests are not secured directly by real property, if a regular interest is so secured and is held as a qualified mortgage by another REMIC, the collateral acquired upon default of the regular interest could be foreclosure property in the hands of the owning REMIC.

Property will cease to be foreclosure property, for purposes of applying the REMIC rules *other* than the assets test, if one of the events listed in section 856(e)(4) occurs. (These events are described in the next paragraph.) Although the occurrence of such an event will not in and of itself disqualify a REMIC, it will cause any net income from the affected property to become subject to the 100 percent prohibited transactions tax, because the property will no longer be considered a permitted investment for purposes of applying the tax.[145]

In general terms, the events causing property to cease to be foreclosure property (except for purposes of the assets test) are: entering into a lease that provides for, or results in, certain types of nonqualifying rents;[146] performing construction work on the property (unless the construction was in progress when the property was acquired by the REMIC); or using the property in a trade or business[147] more than 90 days after it was acquired by the REMIC unless that trade or business is conducted through an independent contractor.[148]

---

144   See sections 860G(a)(8) and 856(e)(1).

145   Whether foreclosure property will generate any net income may depend critically on whether net income is reduced by deductions for interest on regular interests. See text accompanying footnote 171, below. The prohibited transactions tax would apply not only to operating income but also to gain on disposition of the property. However, there is unlikely to be much, if any, gain on resale. Under Treasury Regulation § 1.166-6, the tax basis of property acquired by bidding in a defaulted loan in a foreclosure sale is the fair market value of the property, but such fair market value is, in the absence of clear and convincing evidence to the contrary, presumed to be the bid price. Note that loss from a sale of property in a prohibited transaction is not taken into account in determining the taxable income of a REMIC (and hence, the income of residual interest holders).

146   This rule will not apply if the property is acquired subject to a lease that produces nonqualifying rental income. However, in that event, nonqualifying net income from the property earned by the REMIC would be subject to a regular corporate tax. See Part B.3 below.

147   The phrase "trade or business" is a tax term of art that is not defined in the Code but has been fleshed out through numerous rulings and cases. In general, the mere ownership of real estate, and the collection of rental income therefrom and the payment of expenses, is not a trade or business, but a trade or business may exist if the management or use of the property goes beyond this point. See, e.g., Revenue Ruling 73-522, 1973-2 C.B. 226.

148   An independent contractor is defined in section 856(d)(3), and excludes a person who owns, directly or indirectly, and applying certain attribution rules, more than 35% of the "shares, or certificates of beneficial interest" in the REMIC. Query whether only residual interests would be counted, and if not, how different classes of interests would be weighted, in applying this test.

3. Arrangements Test

The arrangements test is met by an entity if it adopts reasonable arrangements designed to ensure that (1) residual interests in the entity are not held by disqualified organizations, and (2) the entity will make available information necessary for the application of section 860E(e), which imposes a tax on transfers of residual interests to disqualified organizations and on pass-through entities holding residual interests in which interests are owned by disqualified organizations. These taxes are described in Chapter 7, Part E.4.e. A disqualified organization is defined below; generally, it is any governmental entity that is not subject to tax under the Code. The required arrangements must remain in place throughout the life of the REMIC. They may not be limited to transfers made in connection with the original distribution of residual interests.

The REMIC regulations[149] state that an entity is considered to meet the first part of the arrangements test if

- its residual interests are in registered (i.e., not bearer) form[150]

- the entity's organizational documents clearly and expressly prohibit a disqualified organization from acquiring *beneficial* ownership[151] of a residual interest,[152] and

---

149 Treasury Regulation § 1.860D-1(b)(5)(i). The regulations state that a REMIC is "considered to have adopted" reasonable arrangements to ensure that a disqualified organization will not hold a residual interest if it meets the requirements set forth in the text. This language suggests that the test can be met in other ways, although the tests in the regulations are not very onerous. The organizational documents for a REMIC sometimes provide elaborate mechanisms for unwinding a prohibited transfer, which may include a right on the part of the REMIC to sell residual interests held by a disqualified organization. These additional safeguards are not mandated by the regulations. The fact that the Code provides a tax on transfers to disqualified organizations in addition to transfer restrictions shows that the drafters understood that a REMIC might be unable to police transfers of residual interests, particularly where residual interests are held through nominees. Requiring that residual interests be issued in registered form does not ensure that the identity of the beneficial owner will be known to the REMIC. For a discussion of required reporting by nominee owners of residual interests of the names and addresses of their principals, see Chapter 11, Part E.

150 The regulations cross-reference Treasury Regulation § 5f.103–1(c) for the definition of registered form. The so-called TEFRA registration requirements applicable to debt instruments are discussed in Chapter 10, Part A.

151 It is somewhat curious that the regulation refers to beneficial ownership. Although the statutory language (residual interests "held by disqualified organizations") would support the regulation in the absence of any other guidance on the treatment of nominees, the REMIC rules deal directly with residual interests held by nominees. Under section 860E(e)(6), a nominee holding a residual interest on behalf of a disqualified organization is treated as a pass-thru entity that is taxed on excess inclusion income attributable to that interest. Thus, tax on excess inclusion income cannot be avoided by transferring a beneficial (but not record) interest in a residual interest to a disqualified organization.

152 The regulations do not require that these restrictions be enforceable as a state law matter or that they in fact be enforced, but clearly a REMIC should not be launched with the intention that the transfer restrictions will be ignored. See text at footnote 153 below. Even a well intentioned REMIC may not in fact be able to police transfers of beneficial interests in residual interests, either because it does not know who the beneficial owners are (see footnote 149 above) or possibly because of state law restrictions on the ability to limit transfers of beneficial interests in property.

- notice of the prohibition is provided through a legend on the document that evidences ownership of the residual interest, or through a conspicuous statement in a prospectus or private offering document used to offer the residual interest for sale.

Even if these measures are taken, the arrangements test might not be met if it is contemplated when the REMIC is formed that disqualified organizations will in fact own residual interests.[153]

As a small concession to practical needs, a disqualified organization can own a residual interest in connection with the original formation of a REMIC if it has a binding contract to sell the interest and the sale occurs within seven days after the startup day.[154] Allowing a brief period of ownership is essential if the sponsor of the REMIC is a disqualified organization.

Under the regulations, an entity is considered to meet the second part of the arrangements test if its organizational documents require it to provide to the Service, and to persons liable for the taxes imposed under 860E(e) on transfers of residual interests to disqualified organizations, a computation showing the present value of the total anticipated excess inclusions with respect to the residual interest for periods after the transfer. It is not clear what this documentation requirement achieves since the regulations independently obligate a REMIC to provide such information on request. The entity may charge the person liable for the tax (although unfortunately not the Service) a reasonable fee for providing such information. In any event, a REMIC has no obligation to determine if its residual interests have been transferred to a disqualified organization.[155]

A *disqualified organization* is defined (in section 860E(e)(5)) as the United States, any state or political subdivision thereof, any foreign government, any international organization, or, generally, any agency or instrumentality of any of the foregoing (not including FNMA or FHLMC);[156] any tax-exempt entity (other than a farmers' cooperative described in section 521) that is not subject to tax on excess inclusions;[157] and any rural electrical or telephone cooperative described in section 1381(a)(2)(C). The definition does not include REITs, RICs, or other pass-thru entities. Accordingly, they can freely purchase residual interests without jeopardizing the REMIC status of the issuer. However, a pass-thru entity may itself be subject to tax if interests in the entity are owned by disqualified organizations.[158]

---

153   See TAMRA House Report at 80.

154   Treasury Regulation § 1.860E-2(a)(2); TAMRA House Report at 80. The sponsor of a REMIC is always considered to exchange mortgages for regular and residual interests in the REMIC even if the mortgages are in fact sold for cash. See Chapter 12, Part C.

155   See Treasury Regulation §§ 1.860D-1(b)(4)(ii) and (5)(ii), and 1.860E-2(a)(5). The requested information must be provided within 60 days of the request.

156   FNMA and FHLMC are removed from the definition by the last sentence of section 860E(e)(5). Both organizations are taxable and a majority of the board of directors of FNMA is selected by its shareholders. See 12 U.S.C.A. § 1723(b).

157   Excess inclusions are described in Chapter 7, Part E.4.

158   The tax on pass-thru entities is described in Chapter 7, Part E.4.e.(ii).

B. REMIC Taxes

Under section 860A(a), a REMIC is not subject to any income taxes (technically any tax imposed under subtitle A of the Code) except for the taxes imposed under the REMIC rules of the Code. Those rules subject a REMIC to three taxes: a 100 percent tax on net income from prohibited transactions, a 100 percent tax on certain contributions to a REMIC after the startup day, and a tax at the highest corporate rate on certain income from foreclosure property. Clearly, the purpose of the two 100 percent taxes is to regulate the activities of a REMIC (and in that way to supplement the assets and interests tests). The tax on income from foreclosure property eliminates the benefit of the REMIC's tax exemption in a case where it is forced to acquire property but the income from that property is thought to be "active income" of a type that should not enjoy pass-through treatment.

We will consider first the two 100 percent taxes, beginning with the prohibited transactions tax, and then turn to the tax on income from foreclosure property.

1. Prohibited Transactions Tax

Despite the name, a *prohibited transaction* is not in fact prohibited. Instead, such transactions are subject to tax penalties. Most significantly, a tax is imposed on REMICs by section 860F(a)(1) equal to 100 percent of the net income derived from prohibited transactions. In addition, under section 860C(b)(1)(C), losses and deductions, as well as income or gain, allocable to prohibited transactions are not taken into account in determining the taxable income of a REMIC (and thus the income of residual interest holders).[159]

As defined in sections 860F(a)(2) and (a)(5), prohibited transactions include the receipt of any fee or other compensation for the performance of services[160] and the receipt of income attributable to any asset which is neither a qualified mortgage nor a permitted investment. As noted earlier in Part A.2, a REMIC can hold any amount of these non-permitted assets until the end of the third month beginning after the startup day, and thereafter may hold a *de minimis* amount, without failing the assets test.

Prohibited transactions also include any disposition of a qualified mortgage, other than a disposition:

- pursuant to the substitution of a qualified replacement mortgage for a qualified mortgage (or the repurchase in lieu of substitution of a defective obligation)[161]

---

159 The basis of a residual interest is not reduced by the amount of lost deductions, so that they will eventually be reflected in the income of a residual interest holder, although possibly as a capital loss.

160 However, a reasonable fee charged for information relating to the tax on transfers of residual interests to disqualified organizations is not income from a prohibited transaction. Treasury Regulation § 1.860E-2(a)(5).

161 The word "repurchase" should not be read to require a purchase only by the original seller. Although typically a mortgage is "defective" because it violates a customary representation or

- pursuant to the foreclosure, default, or imminent default of the qualified mortgage
- pursuant to the bankruptcy or insolvency of the REMIC[162]
- pursuant to a qualified liquidation[163]
- required to prevent default on a regular interest where the threatened default resulted from a default on one or more qualified mortgages, or
- to facilitate a clean-up call.[164]

A prohibited transaction also includes the realization of gain from the disposition of a cash flow investment other than pursuant to a qualified liquidation. Gains from the disposition of qualified reserve assets are not prohibited transactions, but trading in such assets is otherwise restricted.[165]

In applying the prohibited transaction rules, the term *disposition* does not include the repayment by the obligor of an obligation held by a REMIC.[166] The sale of a convertible mortgage pursuant to a purchase agreement following a conversion is treated as a prepayment of the loan for this purpose.[167] An argument can be made that the same treatment would be appropriate for a sale of a mortgage at par to a

---

warranty given by the original seller and the mortgage is in fact "repurchased" by the original seller as a remedy for the breach, there seems to be no tax policy reason why the identity of the purchaser should matter. A mortgage may also be considered defective simply because it is in default, but there is a separate prohibited transactions tax exemption for sales of defaulted mortgages. The definition of a "defective obligation" is discussed above in the text at footnote 111. Although a defective obligation cannot be exchanged for a qualified replacement mortgage more than two years after the startup day, a repurchase "in lieu of substitution" of a defective obligation can occur at any time.

162 It is not clear how it would be determined that a REMIC is insolvent for this purpose. If a REMIC were considered insolvent to the extent its liabilities exceed the fair market value of its assets (cf. section 108(d)(3)), and REMIC regular interests were considered liabilities for this purpose equal in amount to their adjusted issue prices, then many REMICs would be insolvent from time to time, even in the absence of any default, as a result of declines in the market value of qualified mortgages attributable to increases in market interest rates. If a REMIC consists of a segregated pool of assets, it might be reasonable to treat the REMIC as bankrupt or insolvent if the asset owner is bankrupt or insolvent, even if the REMIC viewed in isolation is not.

163 For the definition of "qualified liquidation", see the text accompanying footnote 31 above.

164 A "clean-up call" is defined in the text accompanying footnote 30 above.

165 See footnote 130 above.

166 See the Conference Report at II-231, footnote 11; Blue Book at 418, footnote 77; Treasury Regulation § 1.860G-2(d)(2) (which assumes that prepayments are not dispositions). If a loan is significantly modified and the modification is treated as an exchange of the old loan for a new modified loan, then any gain should be treated as gain from the repayment of the old loan (by delivery of the new loan) rather than from a disposition of the loan.

167 Treasury Regulation § 1.860G-2(d)(2). Moreover, there typically would be no gain from such a disposition. Under the same regulation, the disposition is treated as a prepayment for purposes of applying the PAC method, with the result that all remaining original issue discount or, generally, market discount on the loan (other than *de minimis* discount) is accrued (and treated as interest on the mortgage rather than gain from sale) in the accrual period in which the conversion occurs. For a description of the PAC method, see Chapter 6, Part C.2. Convertible mortgages are discussed in Part C.3 below.

servicer in lieu of requiring enforcement by the servicer of a due on sale clause, but there is no specific authority supporting this view.

In contrast to a REMIC, a grantor trust can dispose of assets without limitation as long as the sales proceeds are not reinvested.[168]

The 100 percent tax applies to the *net* income from prohibited transactions. Such net income is defined, in section 860F(a)(3), as the excess of the gross income from prohibited transactions over the deductions allowed which are directly connected with such transactions, except that losses from any prohibited transactions may not be taken into account as offsets to gains.[169] The REIT rules include two similar definitions of net income.[170] Thus, practices in the REIT area may be relevant in applying the REMIC definition. The REIT rules treat deductions for interest paid on debt of a REIT as deductions "directly connected with" the production of income from foreclosure property to the extent the debt (whether or not secured by the property) is attributable to the carrying of the property,[171] which gives reason to hope that, at least in determining net income derived by a REMIC from the holding of property, an allocated portion of the interest deductions allowed to the REMIC with respect to its regular interests may be taken into account.

If a REMIC holds a pass-through certificate representing an interest in a grantor trust that was purchased in the market, or created under a program operated by one of the U.S. sponsored agencies, then the REMIC would have no control over the actions of the issuing trust. In these circumstances, the actions of the trust should not be attributed to the REMIC for purposes of applying the prohibited transaction rules.[172] The limitations on the powers of the trustee that must exist in order for the trust to qualify as a grantor trust ensure that the REMIC cannot frustrate the purposes of the REMIC rules by engaging in an active business indirectly through the trust.[173]

---

168   See Chapter 3, footnote 21.

169   In some circumstances, the tax on prohibited transactions might be avoided by entering into transactions (with, for example, the servicer of the REMIC) on other than arm's length terms (ensuring that the REMIC has no gain from such a transaction). Such a transaction would of course risk being recharacterized as a transaction made on arm's length terms (thus, potentially giving rise to the tax) and a payment by the REMIC to the counterparty. Cf. section 7872. However, such a recharacterization would not result in a prohibited transactions tax if in a particular case the deemed payment would be deductible in calculating net income.

170   They are the definition of "net income from foreclosure property" in section 857(b)(4)(B) and the definition of "net income derived from prohibited transactions" in section 857(b)(6)(B).

171   See Treasury Regulation § 1.857-3(e).

172   A technical argument supporting this view is that the definition of qualified mortgage includes "any certificate of beneficial ownership" in real property mortgages. Thus, from the REMIC's perspective, the qualified mortgage is the certificate and not the underlying loans. Although the matter is less clear, the rule described in the text should apply as well to privately packaged pass-through certificates created in connection with the formation of the REMIC, at least if those certificates have the same terms as other pass-through certificates that have been sold directly to investors. Cf. Treasury Regulation § 1.860G-2(a)(5) (GNMA, FNMA, and FHLMC mortgage pass-through certificates are automatically treated as obligations secured by interests in real property; private label certificates are so treated only if assets of the issuing trust are REMIC eligible assets).

The REMIC regulations take a stab in the right direction by stating that the modification of a mortgage loan that backs a non-REMIC pass-through certificate will not be treated as a modification of the pass-through certificate so long as the investment trust structure was not created to avoid the prohibited transaction rules of section 860F(a).[174] While it could be argued that this regulation implies that relief will not be granted for actions taken by grantor trust trustees other than loan modifications, such a reading almost certainly is not correct. For example, the drafters could not have intended that a sale of mortgages by a grantor trust pursuant to a clean-up call affecting the trust would result in a prohibited transactions tax for a REMIC holding an interest in the trust where the sale is not pursuant to a clean-up call or qualified liquidation of the REMIC.

2. Tax on Contributions

Under section 860G(d), a REMIC is subject to a 100 percent tax on any contribution made to the REMIC after the startup day, with exceptions for *cash* contributions that are:

- made within three months after the startup day[175]
- made to facilitate a clean-up call or qualified liquidation
- payments in the nature of a guarantee
- made to a qualified reserve fund by a residual interest holder, or
- allowed in regulations.

No regulations permitting additional contributions have been issued. The tax effectively prohibits all contributions to a REMIC after the startup day of property other than money, thereby eliminating the need to develop special tax rules for such transfers.

Apart from the minor point of avoiding post-startup day contributions in kind, it is not clear why the contributions tax is needed in addition to the REMIC interests test and assets test. The interests test already prevents the issuance of REMIC interests after the startup day and thus prevents transfers to a REMIC in exchange for new REMIC interests. Further, the assets test generally does not allow a REMIC to hold assets contributed to a REMIC (in more than a *de minimis* amount) after the close of the third month beginning after the startup day, except as part of a qualified reserve fund. The tax was not aimed at contributions to such a fund, since they are exempted from the tax, at least if the transferor is a residual interest holder. Prior to the enactment of TAMRA, the assets test applied only every three months and not

---

173   These restrictions are discussed in Chapter 3, Part C.1.c.

174   Treasury Regulation § 1.860G-2(b)(6). Modifications of mortgages are discussed in Part C.2 below.

175   It is not clear why the initial period is defined as described in the text and not, as it is for purposes of the assets test, as the period ending with the close of the third month beginning after the startup day. See the text following footnote 57, above.

continuously (as it does now except during an initial and final period), so that a contribution would not have violated the assets test if the contributed assets were distributed on REMIC interests before the end of the quarter. Perhaps the contributions tax, which was also added by TAMRA, was devised to address this possibility under old law, and was not reevaluated in light of the change in the assets test.

The 100 percent tax applies to any *contribution* to a REMIC but the term is left undefined. The word suggests that the drafters had in mind something akin to an equity contribution.[176] The residual interest in a REMIC could be viewed for this purpose as analogous to the equity interest in other entities. For that reason, a transfer of property to a REMIC by a residual interest holder, for no consideration other than an increase in the value of the residual interest, is particularly likely to be considered a contribution.[177]

Under general tax principles, contributions should include disguised contributions resulting from transactions with a REMIC that are not on arm's length terms. However, a sale of mortgages to a REMIC pursuant to a fixed-price contract[178] should not be considered a contribution merely because the market value of the mortgages increases between the date the contract is entered into and the date of sale. A discrepancy between the contract price and current market value does not indicate that the agreement was not on arm's length terms. Moreover, if the contract price was excessive, the contribution might be considered to have been made when the contract was entered into, on or before the startup day.

A payment to a REMIC that is required under a credit enhancement contract should never be viewed as a contribution. The payment seems to be more in the nature of an insurance payment than a capital infusion. More technically, the rule in the REMIC regulations that treats payments made under a credit enhancement contract as a payment under the related mortgages[179] would seem to preclude treating those payments as a contribution.

As noted above, the Code exempts from the 100 percent tax payments "in the nature of a guarantee." Thus, even if payments under a credit support agreement were considered a contribution, they would be exempted from tax under this rule. The exemption should also cover some types of payments that are not contractually required but serve to make up for REMIC losses and in that way "guarantee" REMIC assets or securities. Consider the following two examples:

---

176 Outside of the REMIC context, it is recognized that a corporation may receive capital contributions from persons not acting as shareholders. See section 362(c), which has special basis rules for such contributions.

177 If a person not holding a residual interest made a transfer to a REMIC to benefit the residual interest holders, then the transaction should probably be viewed as a payment to, and contribution by, them.

178 For a discussion of the treatment as qualified mortgages of loans purchased under such contract within the three-month period beginning on the startup day, see text accompanying footnote 63, above. The contributions tax was not intended to prevent the making of contributions to fund the purchase of mortgages under such a contract because the tax does not apply to cash contributions within three months after the startup day.

179 See text at footnote 208, below.

Suppose that a REMIC owns a defaulted commercial mortgage, or foreclosure property, and does not have the resources to continue to hold and properly manage the property. Suppose further that an immediate sale could be made only at a severely depressed price, and that the class of REMIC interests that will bear the loss is a class of regular interests. The holders of those regular interests may wish to make contributions to the REMIC to allow it to pay expenses relating to the property for some period. Alternatively, they may be willing to purchase the property at a greater than market price (representing a disguised contribution), in order to gain control over the property. Such contributions should be viewed as contributions "in the nature of a guarantee" that benefit the REMIC classes that would bear the loss if the contributions were not made.[180]

A second case where a contribution might be made to a REMIC that is not contractually required is where an error was made in structuring the REMIC that will result in a cash deficiency. The parties responsible for the error and other participants in the transaction might wish to make up for the deficiency whether or not they are contractually or otherwise legally obligated to do so, to avoid being associated with a transaction that is flawed. Again, such contributions plausibly could be characterized as payments in the nature of a guarantee.

3. Tax on Income from Foreclosure Property

Under section 860G(c), REMICs are subject to tax, at the highest marginal federal corporate income tax rate, on "net income from foreclosure property." The income that is subject to tax is the income that would be taxable to the REMIC "if the REMIC were a real estate investment trust."[181] The most likely source of income

---

180   The definition of credit enhancement contract includes the right of a servicer or other third party to make *optional* advances to a REMIC to make up for delinquent payments on qualified mortgages or to pay expenses to protect collateral securing a mortgage. See footnote 194 below. Because of the optional feature, such advances presumably would be made only for the purpose of benefiting the party making the advances because that party would otherwise bear all or a portion of any credit losses with respect to the mortgages. As a payment made under a credit enhancement contract, such an advance should not be subject to the contributions tax, even though it is clear that the advance will not be repaid. From a tax policy perspective, it is difficult to see why it should make a difference in applying the contributions tax whether a payment to a REMIC takes the form of an advance that likely will not be repaid or an unconditional contribution of funds, if in each case the contribution is made to offset a default loss.

181   The tax on REITs is imposed under section 857(b)(4). If the REMIC were a REIT then, under Treasury Regulation § 1.857-3(e), the REIT would be allowed to take an allocable portion of its interest expense into account in computing the tax. If this means in the REMIC context that net income from foreclosure property is computed net of deductions for interest on regular interests allocable to foreclosure property, then for the typical REMIC, where substantially all the capital is provided through regular interests, there should not be material amounts of such income. Although the statutory language could be clearer, it is very likely that the rule measuring net income as if the REMIC were a REIT was not intended to affect any of the substantive tax rules that apply to REMICs but not to REITs. Thus, for example, the calculation should not require a determination of whether REMIC regular interests, which are automatically treated as debt under the REMIC rules, would be debt or equity if issued by a REIT. A different conclusion would introduce a large measure of uncertainty into the calculation. Other issues raised by the treatment of a REMIC as a hypothetical REIT are discussed in footnotes 182 and 183.

subject to tax is rental income that is not treated as "rents from real property" under section 856(d), because the rents are contingent on net profits received from a party related to the REMIC,[182] or received with respect to property if the REMIC provides services to the lessee of the property that are not customarily provided in connection with the rental of space for occupancy only, and those services are not provided through an independent contractor.[183] The tax at corporate rates also applies to gains from the sale of foreclosure property that is held by a REMIC as a dealer (e.g., because the REMIC is seeking to liquidate the property by subdividing it and selling individual units rather than selling the property to a single buyer). If a REMIC does not simply receive income from foreclosure property but enters into a lease that gives rise to rents that are not "rents from real property," performs certain construction work, or engages in any business activity more than 90 days after the property is acquired other than through an independent contractor, then the property will cease to be foreclosure property and net income from the property will become subject to the 100 percent prohibited transactions tax.[184]

C. Special Topics

This Part C addresses seven special topics:

- credit enhancement contracts
- modifications and assumptions of mortgages
- convertible mortgages
- prepayment premiums

---

182   See section 856(d)(2). It is not clear whether a REMIC could be considered to be related to a lessor. The relevant REIT test in section 856(d)(2)(B) requires that a REIT own a direct or indirect interest of 10% or more in the lessor, and ownership of such an interest by a REMIC would run afoul of the assets test. There are constructive ownership rules in section 856(d)(5) that would treat a corporation as owning any interest in a lessor that is owned by any person owning 10% or more by value of the stock of a corporation, and this rule would apply to a REIT because a REIT must be classified as a corporation for tax purposes. These rules would not ordinarily apply to a REMIC (and other rules for trusts and partnerships would not apply) because, under section 860A(a), a REMIC is not, except as provided in the REMIC rules, treated as a corporation, partnership, or trust for tax purposes. However, the rule measuring the REMIC's tax as if it were a REIT could have the effect of requiring a REMIC to be treated as a REIT in applying the constructive ownership rules described above, because it would necessarily be a corporation if it were a REIT. A practical problem with this approach is that it could require a determination to be made as to whether the various REMIC classes would be stock or debt of the REMIC if the REMIC were a corporation (and not a REMIC). Compare the discussion in footnote 181.

183   Section 856(d)(2)(C) appears to create a rule that automatically excludes income from the definition of "rents from real property" if the property is not managed through an independent contractor from whom the REIT does not derive any income. However, the last sentence of section 856(d)(2) limits the scope of the rule to allow services customarily provided in connection with the rental of space for occupancy only. See Treasury Regulation § 1.512(b)-1(c)(5). For the definition of independent contractor, see footnote 148 above. In applying that definition, consideration should be given to whether a REMIC would be subject to the constructive ownership rules applicable to corporations under section 856(d)(5). Cf. footnote 182 above.

184   See text at footnote 146 above.

- prepayment interest shortfalls
- financially troubled mortgages, and
- integration.

The integration topic refers to the possible treatment of assets or liabilities that are in form outside a REMIC as REMIC assets or liabilities. Bringing assets and liabilities inside a purported REMIC could prevent the entity from meeting one of the REMIC qualification tests. The transaction patterns considered under the integration heading are: multiple-tier REMICs, outside reserve funds, and the combination of REMIC interests with other financial instruments in a single investment unit.

1. Credit Enhancement Contracts

Although the drafters of the REMIC rules clearly understood that qualified mortgages might benefit from guarantees or other forms of contractual credit support, the Code makes no express provision for any type of credit support benefiting a REMIC other than inside reserve funds. The legislative history is equally silent on the matter.[185] Fortunately, the REMIC regulations fill in the gap.[186] They define a new term *credit enhancement contract* and allow a REMIC to enter into, and require performance under, such a contract without running afoul of the assets or interests tests.[187] The next two sections discuss the definition of credit enhancement contract and consider the consequences for a REMIC of entering into a credit enhancement contract (or a similar agreement that does not benefit from the special rules for credit enhancement contracts).

a. Definition of Credit Enhancement Contract. A credit enhancement contract is defined as any arrangement whereby a person agrees to guarantee

- full or partial payment of the principal or interest payable on a qualified mortgage or on a pool of such mortgages, or
- full or partial payment on one or more classes of regular interests or on the class of residual interests

in the event of

- defaults or delinquencies on qualified mortgages
- unanticipated losses or expenses incurred by the REMIC, or
- lower than expected returns on cash flow investments.

---

185 In discussing the permitted size of a qualified reserve fund, the legislative history states that the size of the fund would depend on the extent and nature of any guarantees relating to the mortgages, but does not explain how guarantees should be analyzed under the REMIC rules. See Conference Report at II-227 and Blue Book at 414.

186 See Treasury Regulation §§ 1.860G-2(c) and -2(g)(1)(ii)(A).

187 A similar result was reached in Private Letter Ruling 8918045 (February 6, 1989), which predated issuance of the REMIC regulations.

The regulations give as examples of credit enhancement contracts pool insurance contracts, certificate guarantee insurance contracts, letters of credit, guarantees, and agreements whereby the REMIC sponsor, a mortgage servicer, or another third party agrees to make certain advances (advances are discussed further below).

The definition allows for considerable flexibility. A credit enhancement contract may relate to all or only a portion of the mortgages held by the REMIC, or to all or only a portion of the interests in the REMIC. Similarly, the contract may provide for liquidity advances to cover delinquencies as well as, or instead of, protection against losses attributable to the failure ever to collect amounts that are due. The protection may be limited to a dollar figure or formula amount, or be unlimited. The reference to "any arrangement . . . to guarantee" mortgage payments should encompass puts on, or contracts to sell, defaulted mortgages in addition to conventional guarantees. Further, contracts entered into before the occurrence of a mortgage default to purchase foreclosure property acquired by a REMIC following the default should be credit enhancement contracts. Foreclosure property simply replaces the defaulted mortgage.[188] As discussed in the next paragraph, delaying the timing of a sale until after a foreclosure has occurred should not be problematic.[189]

The broad flexibility in the definition of credit enhancement contract extends to the timing of payment of guaranteed amounts.[190] A guarantee arrangement does not fail to be a credit enhancement contract solely because the guarantor, in the event of a mortgage default, has the option of paying immediately the full principal amount due on acceleration of the loan, or paying principal or interest according to the original payment schedule for the loan, or according to some other payment schedule (presumably including one that is slower than the original payment schedule). Indeed, a guarantor can continue to make payments on a deferred basis even if the defaulted mortgage has been foreclosed and it has collected the proceeds of the foreclosure under its subrogation rights. Similarly, there are no explicit limits on the timing of payment and ranking of claims for reimbursement of amounts paid under a credit enhancement contract.

The definition of credit enhancement contract includes three types of advances:[191] (1) an advance to make up for delinquent payments on qualified mortgages; (2) an advance to pay taxes, hazard insurance premiums on, and other expenses incurred to protect the REMIC's security interest in property securing a qualified mortgage[192] in the event that such items are not paid by the mortgagor

---

188   Compare the discussion in footnote 192 below.

189   However, such a contract should require the property to be purchased no later than the time when it would otherwise cease to qualify as foreclosure property under the REMIC rules. The definition of foreclosure property is discussed in Part A.2.b.(iii).

190   See Treasury Regulation § 1.860G-2(c)(4).

191   See Treasury Regulation § 1.860G-2(c)(3). Such advances may be made by the REMIC sponsor, a mortgage servicer, or any third party. An advance may be a credit enhancement contract under the general definition of the term in Treasury Regulation § 1.860G-2(c)(2), even if it is not an advance described in § 1.860G-2(c)(3). The general definition states that credit enhancement contracts "may include, but are not limited to, . . . advances described in paragraph (c)(3)." An advance to pay unexpected REMIC expenses should fall within the general definition.

(this second type of advance is generally known as a "protective advance"); and (3) a *temporary* advance to pay amounts on qualified mortgages before they come due to level out the stream of cash flows to the REMIC or to provide for orderly administration of the REMIC. This last type of advance would allow a mortgage servicer to agree to pay routine bills on behalf of a REMIC that come due during a month, and then to seek reimbursement on the next date on which distributions are made on REMIC interests, or even to distribute mortgage payments a few days before they come due in respect of a small number of mortgages in a pool.[193]

An advance may be a credit enhancement contract even if it is made at the option of the advancing party (i.e., is not required). An optional advance generally would be made by a party to protect its interest as a holder of REMIC interests (particularly subordinated interests).[194]

The REMIC regulations do not restrict the sources out of which a REMIC advance may be repaid. Thus, an advance may be repayable out of all assets of a REMIC, or only out of specified assets. If the only source of repayment is the defaulted or delinquent amounts due from the mortgagor(s) whose failure to pay triggered the advance, then the advance would be functionally equivalent to a mortgage guarantee (where the guarantor is subrogated to the REMIC's claims against the defaulting party). If an advance is repayable out of all REMIC assets, then the advance may serve to provide only liquidity to the REMIC and not loss protection. It is common for a liquidity advance to be required only if the advancing party believes it will be repaid. An advance may be noninterest bearing, or may bear interest at the rate of interest on the related mortgage or at another negotiated rate.[195]

---

192 Although the phrasing is awkward, presumably expenses incurred to protect a REMIC's security interest in collateral would include not only expenses to continue the existence of a valid security interest in the collateral, but also expenses to preserve the collateral (e.g., payments for repairs) and to ensure it is not subjected to competing liens. A mortgagor typically is required to keep property in good condition, as well as to pay taxes and insurance, and it is difficult to see why an advance to pay one type of expense would be allowed and not the others. Also, it should be possible to make protective advances to pay costs relating to mortgage collateral after it is acquired by the REMIC and is held as foreclosure property. While the language of the regulations could be clearer on this point, there is no apparent reason why the payment of taxes on collateral, for example, should be allowed while the property is held as collateral but not after it is acquired in fee. The property would be acquired in order to be sold to pay back the loan to the mortgagor, so the property continues in that way to function as collateral for the loan after foreclosure. Compare the rule described in the text at footnote 119, above, treating cash flow from foreclosure property as "payments received on qualified mortgages" for purposes of the definition of cash flow investment. In any event, an advance to pay unexpected REMIC expenses should qualify as a credit enhancement contract under the general definition, even if it is not an advance described in Treasury Regulation § 1.860G-2(c)(3). See footnote 191.

193 The regulations give as an example of a temporary advance to ease REMIC administration an agreement by a servicer to advance to the REMIC on the 15th day of the month payments due on two mortgages on the 20th day of the month when all other mortgages in the pool have payment due dates on the first of the month. Treasury Regulation § 1.860G-2(c)(3)(iii).

194 For a further discussion of optional advances, see footnote 180 above (application of 100% contributions tax).

195 Cf. text accompanying footnote 27, above (rights of reimbursement under a credit enhancement contract, including rights to interest on amounts advanced, are not REMIC "interests").

Although the definition of credit enhancement contract is broad, it is not limitless. Such a contract must protect only against the specified risks listed in the definition. Two arrangements that would not make the grade are a contract that guarantees a minimum or maximum rate of prepayment of qualified mortgages[196] and a contract in the nature of a swap, cap, or floor that alters the interest flows on the qualified mortgages held by a REMIC.[197]

Determining whether the risks assumed by a third party in an agreement are appropriately circumscribed so that the arrangement is a credit enhancement contract should be an easy task if the agreement relates directly to a REMIC's qualified mortgages. On the other hand, if the agreement guarantees payments due on one or more classes of REMIC interests, evaluating the agreement would in most cases require a close examination of the economic structure of the REMIC to ensure that there are no risks that could trigger a payment obligation under the agreement but are not of a type that can be covered by a credit enhancement contract. Stating the point differently, qualification of one or more agreements as credit enhancement contracts may require that the cumulative amount of payments to the REMIC required under the agreement not at any time exceed the cumulative cash shortfall attributable to permitted risks.[198]

Where mortgages are transferred to a REMIC and the risk of substantial credit losses is high, the retention of credit risk by the transferor might result in the recharacterization of the transfer, under general tax principles, as a secured loan to the transferor. The consequences of such a recharacterization are discussed in Part C.6 below (financially distressed mortgages).[199] The special rules for credit enhancement contracts do not eliminate the need to determine if the REMIC is the tax owner of the enhanced assets.

b. Treatment of Credit Enhancement Contracts and Similar Arrangements. This section discusses how the REMIC assets and interests tests (described in Part A above) are applied (1) to credit support arrangements that do not benefit from any special rules in the REMIC regulations, and (2) to credit enhancement contracts as defined in the regulations. The first part of the discussion is relevant not only for arrangements

---

196   A minimum prepayment guarantee could take the form of a contract to sell qualified mortgages at a fixed price at a specified time without regard to the existence of defaults. It could be argued that such a contract would serve to protect a REMIC against losses attributable to reductions in the market value of the qualified mortgages below the sale price, but any such losses could hardly be characterized as "unanticipated."

197   Combinations of REMIC interests with other financial instruments are discussed in Part C.7.c.

198   In applying this test, it should not be necessary to take account of sources of funds other than credit enhancement contracts that might have been used to make up for the deficiency but cannot be so used under the REMICs' organizational documents. There is no requirement that a credit enhancement contract be the *last* line of defense against mortgage defaults or unanticipated expenses. Contrast the definition of qualified reserve fund discussed above at footnote 131. The treatment of a guarantee of REMIC interests that does not qualify as a credit enhancement contract is discussed in section b.(i) below.

199   See the text accompanying footnote 254, below.

that do not, or possibly might not, fall within the definition of credit enhancement contract, but also for REMICs with a startup day before November 12, 1991 (to which the REMIC regulations do not, by their terms, apply).

(i) Other arrangements. In evaluating guarantee arrangements that do not benefit from the special rules for credit enhancement contracts, a distinction might be drawn between guarantees of REMIC interests and guarantees of REMIC assets. The former type of guarantee could be considered to be entirely "outside" of the REMIC (i.e., to be an arrangement involving holders of REMIC interests but not the REMIC itself).[200] Under this view, the guarantee would not violate the assets or interests test or give rise to prohibited transactions taxes.[201]

On the other hand, a direct guarantee of assets held by the REMIC would be a REMIC asset, and payments thereunder would be made by or to the REMIC. Unless the guarantee were considered to be incidental to, and part of, the REMIC's qualified mortgages, or a qualified reserve asset,[202] its presence could, depending on the circumstances, violate the assets test.[203] In the absence of a special rule, a concern would also arise as to whether the guarantor's claim for reimbursement of amounts paid under such a guarantee would be a REMIC interest that is not allowed under the interests test.[204]

---

200   For further discussion of the treatment of contracts that are "outside" of a REMIC, see Part C.7 below. If a guarantee were considered a direct guarantee of REMIC interests rather than a guarantee of REMIC assets, then it would be necessary to consider whether any portion of the investors' cost for the REMIC interests should be allocated to the guarantee.

201   An "outside" guarantee would be an asset of the holders of the guaranteed REMIC interests, and not of the REMIC; payments thereunder by the guarantor would be made directly to those holders and not through the REMIC; and any payments made by the REMIC to reimburse the guarantor would represent payments on the guaranteed REMIC interests held by the guarantor as a successor to the original holders, and not payments on a separate REMIC "interest" held by the guarantor.

202   The definition of qualified reserve asset is discussed in Part A.2.b.(ii) above. The principal question regarding qualification of a guarantee as a qualified reserve asset is whether it would be considered to be "held for investment" by the REMIC. See text accompanying footnote 136, above. Also, for a REMIC with a startup day before November 12, 1991, to which the REMIC regulations do not by their terms apply, a guarantee may not be a qualified reserve asset to the extent it protects the REMIC's residual interest as well as regular interests. See footnote 127 above.

203   In applying the assets test, a distinction should be drawn between the guarantee and the payments thereunder. The guarantee itself, if it is not a qualifying asset, might be considered a *de minimis* asset. See the text at footnote 55 above. However, payments under the guarantee could exceed *de minimis* amounts. If those payments were not treated as payments under the guaranteed mortgages, then, depending on the circumstances, they still might be viewed as cash flow investments. Specifically, a payment under a guarantee of a mortgage generally gives the guarantor a right to receive from the mortgagor the defaulted or delinquent payment that is guaranteed. The payment under the guarantee might be viewed as proceeds from the disposition by the REMIC of the right to that mortgage payment (and thus a cash flow investment). See Part A.2.b.(i) above for the definition of cash flow investment.

204   The interests test is discussed in Part A.1 above. If a guarantor can look only to the defaulting mortgagor for reimbursement of a payment under a guarantee, then the guarantor should be considered to acquire an interest in the mortgage, but not in the REMIC, in exchange for its payment.

Under general tax principles, payments under a guarantee are often considered to have the same character as the payments they replace, which is at least a step toward integrating a guarantee of a REMIC's qualified mortgages with the mortgages.[205] Further, an integration approach was applied to a REMIC by the Service in a private letter ruling that predated issuance of the REMIC regulations.[206] The argument for disregarding a credit support agreement might be weaker for a liquidity facility that is repayable out of all REMIC assets than for a conventional guarantee, because the connection between the liquidity facility and the REMIC's assets would be more attenuated.

(ii) Credit enhancement contracts. The REMIC regulations remove all doubt as to the treatment under the REMIC assets and interests tests of arrangements that qualify as credit enhancement contracts. The regulations state that such a contract is not treated as a separate asset of the REMIC for purposes of the assets test but, instead, is treated as part of the mortgages or mortgage pool to which the contract relates.[207] This characterization applies to all types of credit enhancement contracts, including those taking the form of guarantees of REMIC interests rather than direct guarantees of mortgages, and those protecting against unexpected losses or expenses, or lower-than-expected returns on cash flow investments. The reasoning may be that because all REMICs are securitization vehicles for mortgages, any agreement protecting REMIC interests, or compensating for unexpected shortfalls, can be viewed as incidental to the REMIC's mortgages. Similarly, payments on credit enhancement contracts received by a REMIC are treated as "payments received on qualified mortgages" for purposes of the definition of "cash flow investment," with the result that those payments, and investments made with those payments, are permitted investments if held for a temporary period by the REMIC.[208] Although not explicitly stated in the regulations, the same analysis should shield income attributable to such payments from the prohibited transactions tax.[209]

The REMIC regulations also provide that any collateral supporting a credit enhancement contract is not treated as an asset of the REMIC solely because it supports the guarantee represented by the contract.[210] This result is consistent with the treatment of outside reserve funds. See Part C.7.b, below.

---

205 See, e.g., Treasury Regulation §§ 1.861-2(a)(5) and 1.862-1(a)(5) (payments under a guarantee have same source as the guaranteed payments); Revenue Ruling 76-78, 1976-1 C.B. 25, Revenue Ruling 72-575, 1972-2 C.B. 74, and Revenue Ruling 72-134, 1972-1 C.B. 29 (payments of defaulted interest under municipal bond insurance policy is tax-exempt).

206 P.L.R. 8918045 (February 6, 1989).

207 Treasury Regulation § 1.860G-2(c)(1).

208 Treasury Regulation § 1.860G-2(g)(1)(ii)(A).

209 The prohibited transactions tax would apply to a payment that is considered to be "attributable to any asset that is neither a qualified mortgage nor permitted investment." Section 860F(a)(2)(B). A payment that is "received on" a qualified mortgage for purposes of the definition of cash flow investment should be considered "attributable to" a mortgage in applying the prohibited transactions tax, given the similar purposes of the assets test and prohibited transactions tax. The prohibited transactions tax is discussed in Part B.1 above.

Turning to the interests test, as already mentioned in Part A.1 above, the regulations exclude from the definition of "interest" for purposes of this test all rights to reimbursement from a REMIC for advances made under credit enhancement contracts, even if the credit enhancer is entitled to interest on the amounts advanced.

2. Modifications and Assumptions of Mortgages

a. General. Under section 1001, a change in the terms of a debt obligation is treated as a deemed exchange of the original obligation for the one with modified terms, if the modified obligation differs "materially either in kind or in extent" from the original.[211] If the modification of a mortgage held by a REMIC were viewed, for purposes of the REMIC assets test, as a deemed exchange by the REMIC of the original mortgage for a new loan, the consequences could be severe. The "new" mortgage would not be a qualified mortgage unless it is a qualified replacement mortgage, which would be impossible if the date of the exchange is more than two years after the startup day. If the new mortgage is not a qualified mortgage, then all income from the new mortgage would be subject to the prohibited transactions tax (described in Part B.1), and the REMIC election would terminate unless the new mortgage, together with other nonpermitted assets, is considered *de minimis* in amount. Also, if a mortgage contributed to a REMIC was modified before the contribution and the modification caused a deemed exchange of loans, then, in the absence of a special rule to the contrary, the value of the real property collateral at the time of the modification (rather than at the time the loan was originated) would be relevant in determining whether the loan is "principally secured by an interest in real property" and is therefore a qualified mortgage.[212]

The REMIC regulations contain special rules governing loan modifications that alleviate some of these concerns.[213] As background to a discussion of these rules, it will be helpful to consider first the types of modifications that are likely to be significant for REMICs and the standards that would be applied in determining if those modifications are "material" within the meaning of section 1001.

b. Likely Modifications. A mortgage held by a REMIC generally can be modified only with the consent of the mortgagor and the mortgage servicer, and the servicer's ability to give such consent is limited by the applicable servicing agreement.

Mortgage servicing agreements typically allow the servicer to modify the payment terms of mortgages only in connection with a default or reasonably foreseeable default. Particularly in the case of commercial loans, a servicer might also be given the right to waive financial covenants, to release collateral, to waive a due-on-encumbrance clause, or to accept prepayments (with or without a premium) not

---

210   Treasury Regulation § 1.860G-2(c)(1).

211   Treasury Regulation § 1.1001-1(a); Proposed Regulation § 1.1001-3(a).

212   For a discussion of the "principally secured" test, see Part 2.a.(ii) above.

213   For a ruling issued prior to issuance of the regulations that allowed certain modifications to be disregarded, see P.L.R. 8803008 (September 24, 1987).

otherwise allowed. Further, a mortgage may be assumed by a buyer of the mort-gaged property, or the property taken subject to such mortgage. Such a buyer may be able to assume the mortgage because it has no effective due-on-sale clause that accelerates the loan upon transfer of the property, or because such a clause is waived. An assumption generally does not affect the terms of a mortgage other than the identity of the obligor (e.g., the interest rate and payment schedule).

Wholly apart from the servicing agreement, mortgages may by their terms allow for various changes in payment terms, such as the resetting of a variable interest rate, or the conversion of a floating rate to a fixed rate, and related changes in amortization schedules. Convertible mortgages are discussed further in Part C.3 below.

c. Material Modifications. Until recently, the question of whether a loan modification causes a deemed exchange under section 1001 has been resolved on an *ad hoc* basis. A number of authorities address the issue in particular factual settings.[214] Under these authorities, virtually any nontrivial change in payment terms (with the exception in some circumstances of a deferral of principal) is considered a material change. Although there are fewer authorities applying section 1001 to changes in financial covenants or other nonpayment terms, a change in nonpayment terms can cause a deemed exchange if the change is in fact material. The payment of a waiver fee by the party seeking the change would be a factor indicating that the change is material.

In the 1991 *Cottage Savings* case,[215] the U.S. Supreme Court applied the stand-ards of section 1001 to a swap of mortgage pools that were similar economically but involved different mortgagors and properties. The taxpayer had claimed a tax loss on the exchange. The court held that the exchange was taxable. The two pools differed materially for purposes of section 1001 since they involved "legally distinct entitlements" (namely, claims against different borrowers). This decision created some controversy as to the proper interpretation of section 1001, and spurred the IRS to act. At the end of 1992, the Service issue proposed regulations that for the first time set forth a comprehensive series of tests for determining if a loan modifi-cation will be treated as a deemed exchange.[216] These tests will apply technically only to modifications made at least 30 days after the regulations are finalized (assuming they are eventually finalized), although the principles of the regulations are likely to be applied in practice to modifications before then, at least in cases where the outcome is uncertain under prior authorities. The rules will almost cer-tainly be changed in some significant respects prior to adoption.

---

214   For a discussion of these authorities, see G. Henderson & S. Goldring, *Failing and Failed Busi-nesses* (CCH Tax Transaction Library, 1993 Ed.), Ch. 4; P. Winterer, "'Reissuance' and Deemed Exchanges Generally," 37 *Tax Lawyer* 509 (1984); New York State Bar Association, Tax Section, "Report of Ad Hoc Committee on Provisions of the Revenue Reconciliation Act of 1990 Affecting Debt-for-debt Exchanges," 51 *Tax Notes* 79 (April 8, 1992).

215   *Cottage Savings Ass'n v. Comm'r.,* 499 U.S. 554 (1991).

216   See Proposed Regulation § 1.1001-3 (December 2, 1992).

A comprehensive summary of the proposed regulations is beyond the scope of this work, but a few points are worth mentioning. Under the proposed regulations, a change in a mortgage will be treated as a deemed exchange only if the change represents a "modification" of the mortgage and the modification is "significant." In general terms, any formal or informal alteration in any legal right or obligation of the mortgagor or mortgagee will be a modification unless it occurs by operation of the original terms of the instrument. An exercise or waiver of a right under the instrument will be by operation of the original terms if the exercise or waiver is "unilateral" (i.e., generally does not require the consent of the other party, and does not require the payment of a waiver fee by the other party unless the amount was fixed when the loan was originated). An assumption of a residential mortgage is considered to be made according to the mortgage's terms if under those terms an assumption is allowed with the mortgagor's consent but such consent cannot be unreasonably withheld. Also, the conversion of an adjustable rate mortgage to a fixed rate mortgage is not a modification if the mortgagor has the right to effect the conversion upon payment of a fixed fee that is not dependent on market interest rates. Although an agreement to forebear temporarily the pursuit of remedies upon default is not considered a change in terms, there is no general rule that allows modifications in a workout setting to be disregarded.

Modifications that are considered significant under the proposed regulations include a more than 25-basis-point change in yield, a material deferral of payments, a change in the borrower under a recourse obligation, or a release or substitution of a substantial portion of the collateral supporting a nonrecourse loan. A partial prepayment of a loan is not a significant modification if the terms of the remaining portion of the loan are not significantly modified, even if the prepayment is accompanied by a commercially reasonable prepayment penalty.[217] A change in the collateral securing a recourse obligation will not be a significant modification.

If these proposals are incorporated in final regulations, they will supplant the existing body of law governing loan modifications and make it much easier to determine if a change in loan terms will trigger a deemed exchange.

d. REMIC Regulations. The REMIC regulations erect a fairly complex structure for evaluating mortgage modifications.[218] The rules may be summarized as follows:

1. A modification of a mortgage does not create a new loan if the modification is not a "significant modification" that is treated as a deemed exchange under the general standards of section 1001 and the regulations thereunder *and* does not involve a release of real estate collateral.[219]

---

217 Proposed Regulation § 1.1001-3(e)(2)(ii). By contrast, Proposed Regulation § 1.1274-1(c)(1) (withdrawn December 21, 1992) treated the making of any payment on an obligation not provided in the terms of the obligation as a modification.

218 Treasury Regulation § 1.860G-2(b). For the treatment of modifications of loans held by REMICs to which the REMIC regulations do not apply, see P.L.R. 8803008 (September 18, 1987)

219 Although the phrase "significant modification" is also used in the proposed section 1001 regulations discussed above in the text, the modification rules in the REMIC regulations are independent

2. Subject to the four exceptions described in the next paragraph, a significant modification of a mortgage is treated as the issuance of a new mortgage in exchange for the original mortgage on the date the modification occurs. If the significant modification occurs *after* the obligation is contributed to a REMIC, then unless the new mortgage is a qualified replacement mortgage, the new mortgage will not be a qualified mortgage and the deemed exchange will be a prohibited transaction.[220] As discussed in Part A.2, the new mortgage will be a qualified replacement mortgage if the exchange occurs within the three-month period beginning on the startup day, or occurs thereafter on or before the second anniversary of the startup day if the modified mortgage is in default or otherwise "defective," and will not be a qualified replacement mortgage if the exchange is after the second anniversary of the startup day. If the significant modification occurs *before* the mortgage is contributed to the REMIC, the modified loan will be viewed as having been originated on the date the modification occurs for purposes of determining if it is "principally secured by an interest in real property."

3. The following modifications are never treated as significant modifications even if they would be so treated under the general standards of section 1001:[221]
   - changes in the terms of the mortgage occasioned by default or a reasonably foreseeable default[222]
   - an assumption of the mortgage[223]
   - a waiver of a due-on-sale clause or a due-on-encumbrance clause, and
   - the conversion of a "convertible adjustable rate mortgage."

---

of those proposed regulations and will apply whether or not those regulations are finalized or apply to the mortgages held by a REMIC.

220 Treasury Regulation § 1.860G-2(b)(1)(i) states flatly that such a deemed exchange will be a prohibited transaction. As discussed in Part B.1, however, not all dispositions of qualified mortgages that are not made in exchange for a qualified replacement mortgage are prohibited transactions. On the other hand, earning income from a mortgage that is not a qualified mortgage is a prohibited transaction.

221 It is not entirely clear whether these exceptions apply only for purposes of the REMIC qualification tests, or also in computing taxable income of the REMIC. The language of the regulations can reasonably be construed to support the broader reading, although this result may be unintended. Specifically, Treasury Regulation § 1.860G-2(b)(3) states that the excepted changes are not treated as significant modifications "for purposes of paragraph (b)(1)." That paragraph spells out the specific consequences of the new issuance of a loan under the REMIC qualification tests but also contains the general statement that if there is a significant modification, the modified loan is treated as one that was newly issued in exchange for the unmodified loan.

222 The phrase "occasioned by" should allow modifications to be made in a workout setting that are not required by the circumstances giving rise to the workout, as long as a default or foreseeable default is the factor that precipitates the workout. For example, a default could be used to change payment terms to reflect current market conditions.

223 A mortgage is considered to be assumed for this purpose if the buyer of the mortgaged property acquires the property subject to the mortgage without assuming personal liability, the buyer becomes liable but the seller also remains liable, or the buyer becomes liable and the seller is released. Treasury Regulation § 1.860G-2(b)(5).

Convertible mortgages and financially troubled mortgages are discussed in Parts C.3 and C.6 below. Although the exception for defaulted loans would seem to accommodate almost any change in terms that does not cause the mortgage to cease to be an obligation,[224] the other three are quite narrow. For example, the exception for assumptions probably would not sanction any modification beyond the substitution or addition of obligors.

4. Although not entirely clear, any release of the lien on real property securing a mortgage may require that the status of the mortgage as "an obligation secured primarily by real property" be retested. The release of a small amount of collateral could have disproportionately large consequences if the release requires the adequacy of the real estate collateral to be retested based on current market values. This t opic, including the special rule allowing the defeasance of a mortgage with government securities in limited circumstances, is discussed in connection with the definition of qualified mortgage in Part A.2.a.(ii) above.[225]

Modifications of mortgage loans held by grantor trusts are discussed in Chapter 3.[226]

3. Convertible Mortgages

Residential mortgages are typically subject to prepayment at any time without premium at the option of the borrower. Consequently, a borrower under an adjustable rate mortgage can effectively convert the mortgage to a fixed-rate loan (or vice versa) by refinancing. However, a refinancing involves substantial closing costs.

Recognizing the reality of the borrowers' position, some originators have offered convertible mortgages that typically start out bearing interest at an adjustable rate but permit the borrower to convert to a fixed rate. The fixed rate is a market rate at the time of conversion, measured by the rates being offered on fixed rate loans by the originator or perhaps an index of current market rates. The borrower is generally required to undergo a credit review as a condition to conversion, but the process is still cheaper and more streamlined than if the loan were refinanced. Convertible mortgages could provide for conversion from fixed to adjustable rates or from one adjustable rate to another, although the pattern described above is the most common.

---

224 For example, if a defaulted mortgage actually is exchanged for stock of the borrower, it is unlikely that the exchange would be viewed as a mere modification of the mortgage that falls within the rule. The fact that a modified loan would be considered, under general tax principles, to be transformed into an equity interest in the underlying real estate (or in the mortgagor) on account of the addition of contingent payments or the decline in value of the real estate at the time of the modification would not prevent application of the rule for modifications of defaulted loans. Compare the special definition of obligation in Treasury Regulation § 1.860G-2(a)(7) discussed above in Part A.2.a.(i).

225 See text at footnote 99.

226 See Chapter 3, Part C.1.c.(v).

A REMIC that holds convertible mortgages faces three tax questions. First, if the REMIC does not wish to hold loans that have been converted, can the REMIC ensure a market for such loans at a predetermined price by entering into a "liquidity contract" with a third party? Second, what is the effect of a conversion on the REMIC's taxable income if the REMIC acquired the convertible mortgages at a discount or premium? Finally, if the REMIC wishes to continue to hold a mortgage following conversion, is the conversion treated as a deemed exchange of the old loan for a new one, with the result that the mortgage may cease to be a qualified mortgage, and does the change in interest rates affect the status of REMIC interests as regular interests? As discussed in Part C.2 above, the REMIC regulations resolve the deemed exchange question favorably for mortgages that are "convertible mortgages" as defined below.[227] The qualification of REMIC interests as regular interests is discussed in Chapter 5.[228]

The REMIC regulations use the term "purchase agreement" to refer to the most common type of liquidity contract relating to convertible mortgages, and then resolve in a straightforward way the technical issues that a REMIC would face in entering into and selling mortgages under such an agreement.[229]

Under the regulations, a purchase agreement is treated as incidental to the convertible mortgage to which it relates, and not as a separate REMIC asset for purposes of the assets test. Also, the sale of a convertible loan under a purchase agreement is treated under the REMIC rules and in determining the REMIC's income as a prepayment of the mortgage, which is a sensible result.[230] Concerns over the treatment of a purchase agreement as a prohibited REMIC interest are allayed by carving out from the definition of "interest" the right to acquire, or obligation to purchase, mortgages on conversion of a convertible mortgage.[231] If the

---

227 The same result might be reached under general tax law principles. A conversion can be viewed simply as a change in interest rate provided by the terms of the debt obligation, which would not ordinarily be considered a section 1001 exchange. Under the proposed section 1001 regulations (discussed in the text beginning at footnote 216 above), the conversion of a mortgage will not be considered a loan modification if the conversion occurs under the original terms of the mortgage and the mortgagor is not charged a fee to effect the conversion other than one that was fixed in amount when the loan was originated. See Proposed Regulation § 1.1001-3(d), Example 5.

228 As discussed in Chapter 5, a regular interest can pay interest at a rate that conforms to the rate on qualified mortgages, either as a specified portion rate, or as a weighted average variable rate.

229 The rules governing purchase agreements are found in Treasury Regulation § 1.860G-2(d). A purchase agreement is defined in Treasury Regulation § 1.860G-2(d)(3) as "a contract between the holder of a convertible mortgage and a third party under which the holder agrees to sell and the third party agrees to buy the mortgage for an amount equal to its current principal balance plus accrued but unpaid interest if and when the mortgagor elects to convert the terms of the mortgage." Note that the definition requires an agreement binding on both sides; an option by the REMIC to sell would not be a purchase agreement as defined.

230 Apparently, the conversion itself is not treated as a prepayment for purposes of computing the REMIC's income. See Treasury Regulation § 1.860G-2(b)(3)(iv) (conversion of convertible mortgage does not result in deemed exchange, and thus a retirement of the old loan). This regulation is discussed in Part C.2.d above.

231 Treasury Regulation § 1.860D-1(b)(2)(iv). Note that the exception is not limited to "purchase agreements".

purchaser under a purchase agreement defaults on its obligation to purchase a converted mortgage, the REMIC may sell the mortgage in a market transaction and treat the proceeds of sale as amounts paid pursuant to the purchase agreement.[232]

For purposes of the REMIC rules, a convertible mortgage is defined as follows:

> [a] mortgage that gives the obligor the right at one or more times during the term of the mortgage to elect to convert from one interest rate to another. The new rate of interest must be determined pursuant to the terms of the instrument and must be intended to approximate a market rate of interest for newly originated mortgages at the time of the conversion.[233]

The definition is not limited to mortgages that convert from an adjustable to a fixed rate, but covers any case where the new rate is intended to be a market rate. Although the definition refers only to the conversion "from one interest rate to another," it should be read to cover any change in the terms of the mortgage that would normally accompany the new choice of rate.

4. Prepayment Premiums

This section considers two types of prepayment premiums: those paid on qualified mortgages held by a REMIC, and those paid on REMIC regular interests. As discussed further below, premiums on regular interests are not allowed unless they represent a pass-through of prepayment premiums received by the REMIC.

a. Mortgage Prepayments. Residential mortgages are typically subject to prepayment at any time by the mortgagor without the payment of any penalty or premium in addition to principal plus accrued and unpaid interest. By contrast, fixed rate commercial loans often provide for optional rights to prepay with a penalty. The penalty may be a fixed amount which declines over time or an amount determined under a "yield-maintenance" formula that is based on market interest rates at the time of the prepayment and is intended to preserve the economic position of the lender in cases where rates have gone down.

A REMIC that holds a qualified mortgage can receive a prepayment premium in connection with the prepayment of the mortgage and pass it through to REMIC interest holders without adverse tax consequences. The REMIC would recognize gross income equal to the premium received, but that income would be offset with a deduction to the extent the premium is paid to holders of regular interests as discussed below. The prohibited transactions tax that applies to income from certain dispositions of mortgages would not apply to the premium because a prepayment is not considered a "disposition" for this purpose.[234] The prepayment premium would be treated as a cash flow investment and, thus, may be held and invested temporarily pending distribution to holders of REMIC interests.[235]

---

232   Treasury Regulation § 1.860G-2(d)(4).
233   Treasury Regulation § 1.860G-2(d)(5).
234   See text accompanying footnote 166, above.

A REMIC that receives a prepayment premium could, of course, distribute the premium to holders of its residual interests without violating the REMIC interests test, because there are no limitations on the payments that may be made on residual interests. The payment of premiums on a purported regular interest raises more complex questions: Are those premiums a variable amount of interest that can be paid on regular interests only as provided in regulations, additional principal that violates the requirement that the amount of principal paid on a regular interest not be contingent, or perhaps a third category of payment that is neither principal nor interest?[236] The REMIC regulations resolve these issues indirectly by stating that an interest in a REMIC will not fail to qualify as a regular interest solely because "customary prepayment penalties" received with respect to qualified mortgages are allocated among and paid to regular interest holders.[237] This language would countenance the pass-through of yield-maintenance as well as fixed premiums. The regulation allows the premiums to be allocated among classes of regular interests in any way that is desired. In many cases, the premium would be paid to the classes of investors that are affected most adversely by the prepayment.[238]

In the case of REMICs holding commercial loans, it may be desirable to allow the servicer to negotiate a full or partial waiver of a no-call period or a prepayment premium. The principal tax issue raised by such a waiver is whether, in the case of a partial prepayment of a mortgage, the waiver could be considered to result in a significant modification of the portion of the mortgage remaining after the prepayment, with the consequences described in Part C.2 above. However, such a waiver should not be considered a significant modification of the remaining portion of the mortgage if its terms are unchanged.[239]

b. Premiums on Regular Interests. Except in the case just discussed where prepayment premiums received by a REMIC on its qualified mortgages are passed through, the REMIC regulations prohibit the payment on a regular interest of any premium determined with reference to the length of time that the regular interest is outstanding.[240] The IRS has not explained the reason for this ban; presumably, it reflects the view that a REMIC should not be used to protect investors against prepayment risks except by allocating the payments it receives. In any event, a REMIC would not ordinarily be able to fund a prepayment premium paid on a regular interest that is not matched by a premium payment received. If the premium were funded by selling qualified mortgages that had appreciated in value due to a drop in market interest rates,

---

235   Treasury Regulation § 1.860G-2(g)(1)(ii)(E).

236   The definition of regular interest is discussed in Chapter 5. It is not clear whether prepayment premiums are properly characterized for tax purposes as additional interest or gain from disposition of the prepaid loans. See Chapter 6, footnote 39.

237   Treasury Regulation § 1.860G-1(b)(2).

238   The regulations give as an example of a permitted allocation an allocation of all or substantially all premiums to holders of a class of interest-only regular interests.

239   See footnote 217, above, and accompanying text.

240   Treasury Regulation § 1.860G-1(b)(1).

the net income from those sales would generally be subject to a 100 percent prohibited transactions tax.[241]

5. Prepayment Interest Shortfalls

When a residential mortgage held by a REMIC is prepaid by the borrower in the middle of the month, the terms of the mortgage typically provide that interest is due only through the date of the prepayment and not for the entire month. Unless the prepaid amounts can be reinvested for the balance of the month at a rate at least equal to the rate of interest on the prepaid mortgages (net of applicable fees), the prepayment will cause a shortfall in the interest available for distribution to investors on the next monthly distribution date.

The REMIC regulations offer three mechanisms for dealing with *prepayment interest shortfalls* (as defined in the regulations).[242] The shortfall can be made up by reducing the interest paid on regular or residual interests,[243] by drawing on an inside reserve fund,[244] or through a payment by a third party required by agreement. Such an agreement is not treated as a separate REMIC asset and payments thereon are treated as payments on qualified mortgages.[245]

6. Financially Distressed Mortgages

A REMIC may hold financially distressd real estate mortgages in one of two circumstances: where the impairment in credit quality arose only after the loan was acquired by the REMIC and where it existed before. The REMIC rules work well for loans of the first type. Additional issues are raised when a REMIC acquires

---

241 One issue is whether the deduction allowed for premiums paid could be taken into account in calculating net income from the prohibited transaction. The tax would not apply in the case of a clean-up call or qualified liquidation. The prohibited transactions tax is discussed in Part B.1 above.

242 A "prepayment interest shortfall" is defined in Treasury Regulation § 1.860G-2(e) as an amount with respect to a prepaid mortgage equal to the excess of the interest that would have accrued on the mortgage during the accrual period if it had not prepaid over the interest that actually accrued up to the date of the prepayment. The term, as defined, is not reduced by any amount earned from the reinvestment of the prepayment.

243 See Treasury Regulation § 1.860G-1(b)(3)(v) (an interest does not fail to qualify as a regular interest solely because interest is contingent on prepayments made on the underlying mortgages). By contrast, the amount of principal payable on a regular interest may not be contingent on such prepayments. There is no need for a rule allowing prepayment interest shortfalls to reduce distributions on residual interests because payments on those interests need not meet any special requirements.

244 Treasury Regulation § 1.860G-2(g)(2) (qualified reserve funds can be used to provide for the full payment of prepayment interest shortfalls). The regulations are more liberal than the statute, which makes no mention of prepayment interest shortfalls in defining qualified reserve funds. See section 860G(a)(7).

245 Treasury Regulation § 1.860G-2(e). One way in which a third party could protect against prepayment interest shortfalls is by writing a guaranteed investment contract allowing a REMIC to earn a minimum return on prepaid amounts. However, a third party can also agree to make up a shortfall even if prepaid amounts are not reinvested.

loans that are already distressed. The importance of these additional issues increased at the beginning of 1992 when the TMP rules became effective. As discussed in Chapter 3, those rules are intended to force a REMIC election for multiple-class entities that hold real estate mortgages. They have led taxpayers to look closely at REMICs as securitization vehicles for low-grade loans.

The next two sections outline the tax treatment of mortgages that default after they are acquired by a REMIC, and of loans that are troubled when acquired.

a. Post-Acquisition Defaults. The REMIC rules do a good job accomodating qualified mortgages that become financially troubled during the period they are held by the REMIC. Often, qualified mortgages benefit from some type of third-party credit support. In that event, the third party makes up for defaults or delinquencies and, if the default is not cured, generally purchases the defaulted loan from the REMIC before foreclosure proceedings or a workout begin. As detailed elsewhere, REMICs can enter into credit enhancement contracts and dispose of (including, until the second anniversary of the startup day, replace) defaulted loans.[246]

If a qualified mortgage is in default, and does not benefit from third-party credit support (or the credit support is exhausted), then there are four basic courses of action the REMIC may pursue: First, the REMIC could sell the loan at a loss. Second, the REMIC could hold the loan, collect whatever payments it can thereon and, if they are not sufficient to repay the loan, eventually write off the loan balance. In this connection, the REMIC could foreclose on the mortgage, force sale of the collateral to a third party, and apply the sale proceeds to the repayment of the loan. Third, the REMIC and the borrower could amend the terms of the loan, with the REMIC then holding or selling the modified loan. Finally, the REMIC could foreclose on the loan, bid in the loan in the foreclosure sale, and acquire ownership of the collateral. The REMIC would then hold and sell the real estate. A bankruptcy of the borrower could intervene, but the menu of end results would be basically the same.

The REMIC rules deal with these possibilities in an appropriate way. If the REMIC sells the loan at a loss, the loss would be allowed as an ordinary deduction in computing the REMIC's taxable income.[247] However, to the extent the loss prevents a class of regular interests from receiving its full principal amount plus any interest thereon that has accrued and been deducted by the REMIC, the REMIC would have discharge of indebtedness income offsetting the loss.[248] The proceeds of

---

246 Credit enhancement contracts are discussed in Part C.1. As discussed in Part B.1, the prohibited transactions tax does not apply to dispositions of defaulted mortgages. A qualified replacement mortgage includes a mortgage that is exchanged for a "defective" mortgage in the first two years following the startup day, and a mortgage in default or for which default is reasonably foreseeable, is considered defective. See text accompanying footnote 112 above, and Treasury Regulation § 1.860G-2(f)(1)(i).

247 See Treasury Regulation § 1.860C-2(a) (treating all gains or losses from the disposition of any asset by a REMIC as ordinary). This regulation is discussed in Chapter 7, text accompanying footnote 27.

248 See Chapter 7, text accompanying footnote 37.

the sale would be a cash flow investment that can be held temporarily pending distribution to REMIC interest holders. Similarly, if a loan is wholly or partly worthless, the REMIC would be allowed a bad debt deduction.[249] A modification of a qualified mortgage occasioned by a default or reasonably foreseeable default would not prevent the loan from continuing to be a qualified mortgage.[250] Finally, property acquired on foreclosure is generally "foreclosure property" (at least for purposes of the assets test) if it is disposed of within two years.[251]

b. Pre-Acquisition Defaults. Where a mortgage that is transferred to a REMIC is or has been financially troubled, a number of additional issues need to be addressed. They relate to the status of the mortgage as a qualified mortgage, the status of any property acquired on foreclosure as foreclosure property, and the calculation of income from the loan. The REMIC regulations contain a number of favorable rules in this area.

In order for a mortgage to be a qualified mortgage, it must be an "obligation" that is "principally secured" by real property. Although the financial condition of a debtor could raise a question as to whether a loan is an "obligation" under general tax principles, in the REMIC setting, these issues are largely put to rest by a special rule that treats any instrument as an obligation if it provides for total noncontingent principal payments at least equal to the instrument's issue price, even if it also provides for contingent payments.[252]

Once it is determined that a REMIC holds an obligation, it must still be "principally secured" by real property in order to meet the definition of a qualified mortgage. Because the value of property may be tested for this purpose at the date of origination of the loan, the 80 percent test would not ordinarily be affected by any decline in value of the mortgaged property. If a loan has been modified in a workout after origination but before contribution to the REMIC, however, it could be considered to be newly "originated" with the result that the presumably depressed value of the collateral on the date of the modification would be relevant. The REMIC regulations address this point by allowing a default-related modification to be ignored in testing the status of a loan as a qualified mortgage, even if the modification occurs before the loan is acquired by a REMIC.[253]

If in connection with the transfer of a troubled real estate mortgage to a REMIC, the sponsor guaranteed the loan, then the REMIC could conceivably be viewed for federal income tax purposes as holding an obligation of the guarantor rather than a direct interest in the real estate mortgage.[254] Such a recharacterization

---

249 See Chapter 7, footnote 27.
250 Loan modifications are discussed above in Part C.2.
251 Foreclosure property is discussed in Part A.2.b.(iii).
252 See Treasury Regulation § 1.860G-2(a)(7), which is discussed in Part A.2.a.(i) above.
253 See Treasury Regulation § 1.860G-2(b)(3)(i), which is discussed in Part C.2.d above.
254 The possible recharacterization of a sale as a financing is discussed in Chapter 12, Part A.1. Although a guarantee alone is not ordinarily enough to cause a sale to be recharacterized as a financing, such treatment could result, under a benefits and burdens of ownership test, if the guarantee significantly upgraded the quality of the guaranteed loan. A REMIC sponsor could

would raise two concerns: first, that the obligation held by the REMIC was originated when the guarantee was created, so that the adequacy of the real estate collateral needs to be retested at that time, and second, that the loan to the guarantor would not be considered to be "secured" by real estate to any extent. Although obligations secured by real estate mortgages (as contrasted with interests in real estate) are not considered to be principally secured by real property, it is at least arguable that this rule would not apply where a guarantee is recharacterized as a loan to the guarantor.[255]

The financial condition of a debtor at the time when a real estate loan is transferred to a REMIC may also affect whether property acquired upon foreclosure of the loan is treated as foreclosure property. As discussed in Part A.2.b.(iii), foreclosure property is generally defined as property acquired in connection with a default of a qualified mortgage held by a REMIC that would be foreclosure property under section 856(e) if acquired by a REIT. The regulations under section 856(e) exclude from the definition of foreclosure property property acquired upon foreclosure of a loan where the REIT trustee has "improper knowledge" with respect to such loan.[256] Improper knowledge exists if the loan was made, or was acquired by the REIT, with an intention to foreclose the loan, or if the loan was acquired when the REIT knew, or had reason to know, that default would occur.

In order to understand this regulation, it is necessary to review briefly the purpose of the foreclosure property rules in the REIT setting. REITs, unlike REMICs, are allowed to hold for investment direct interests in real property. They are also allowed to buy new properties after formation of the REIT and to finance the acquisition by incurring debt or issuing new equity. There are no restrictions on the terms or number of classes of interest in a REIT. Thus, in many respects, a REIT resembles a conventional business corporation.

---

retain substantial credit risk without raising the recharacterization issue discussed in the text by taking back a sizeable subordinated interest in the REMIC.

255   For a description of this rule, which is found in Treasury Regulation § 1.860G-2(a)(6), see footnote 95, above. The rule was aimed at non-REMIC collateralized mortgage obligations, which are specifically referenced in the regulation. In order to be recognized as debt for tax purposes, CMOs have payment terms that differ from the underlying real property mortgages. See Chapter 2, Part D.1. Thus, a default could occur on the mortgages securing a CMO without a default occurring on the CMOs and vice versa, and it is appropriate to view the CMOs as obligations separate from the underlying mortgages. By contrast, in a case where a guaranteed real property mortgage is recharacterized as a loan to the guarantor, the guarantee generally would be triggered only if there was a default on the mortgage. Further, in that event, if the guarantor did not perform, the REMIC would typically have the right, as the legal owner of the loan, to enforce the mortgage and foreclose on the collateral. Thus, it could easily be said that the obligation held by the REMIC is secured by real property, despite the recharacterization of the arrangement. Cf. Revenue Ruling 80-280, 1980-2 C.B. 207 (nonrecourse "hypothecation" loan that was secured by real estate mortgages considered a real estate mortgage under the REIT rules where the REIT had the right to enforce payments due on the loans). This ruling presents a harder case than a guarantee because the loan in the ruling was in the form of a loan secured by other loans and defaults on the secured loan could occur independently of defaults on the underlying loans.

256   Treasury Regulation § 1.856-6(b)(3).

Despite the greater freedom allowed to a REIT to buy and finance property, REITs are intended to be investment vehicles rather than active traders or developers of real property. Thus, a minimum percentage of a REIT's income must be derived from passive sources. Passive income includes gains from sales of real property if the property is not held in a dealer capacity. Passive income also includes rent, with certain exceptions for contingent rents based on net income. Also, not more than 30 percent of the income of a REIT may be derived from gains from the sale of real estate held for less than four years (certain other categories of income also count toward the 30 percent limit).

Until 1974, there were no special provisions in the REIT rules for foreclosure property. As a result, any real property acquired by a REIT upon foreclosure of a loan was subject to the same limitations as real property acquired directly. This treatment produced some unfairness. A REIT might be forced involuntarily to acquire a real estate project that was more active than one it would have acquired as an investment. Also, a REIT might find that in order to realize value from a project, it was required to market the project actively in pieces, which could result in its acting as a dealer. To address these concerns, a number of special rules for foreclosure property were added in 1974. They generally allow a REIT to receive nonqualifying income from foreclosure property without losing its status as a REIT. Any such nonqualifying income is, however, subject to a corporate tax. Property ceases to be foreclosure property if it is used in a way that is inconsistent with its being held for liquidation or if it is held too long. In that event, the REIT does not automatically lose its status as a REIT, but the rules generally applicable to real estate held by a REIT apply. A REIT must elect, on a property by property basis, to treat property as foreclosure property. The election is provided because of the corporate tax that applies to certain categories of income from foreclosure property that would not otherwise apply.

The purpose of the "improper knowledge" regulation cited above (which is based on the legislative history of the 1974 legislation)[257] is to prevent a REIT that wants to acquire real property from taking advantage of the special foreclosure property rules by acquiring a defaulted mortgage secured by that real property and then acquiring the property through foreclosure. The foreclosure property rules were meant to apply only where property was acquired inadvertently.

In the REMIC setting, the issues are quite different. It is true, of course, that a REMIC cannot acquire real estate directly, so that there might be said to be an interest similar to the one found in the REIT area in preventing the indirect transfer to a REMIC of real estate though the transfer of defaulted loans. However, why would anyone ever want to use an indirect means to allow a REMIC to hold a real estate investment? The limitations on the capital structure of a REMIC would be very confining. A REMIC could not issue new debt to finance capital improvements or other expenditures, or even to refinance a borrowing to take advantage of lower

---

257   See Sen. Rep. No. 93-1357, relating to P.L. 93-625, 93d Cong. 2d Sess., reproduced at 1975-1 C.B. 517, 524–525.

rates. A REMIC can have only a single, true equity class, and income on that class is subject to the excess inclusion rules. Among other things, those rules could prevent the use of losses from other real estate activities to offset income from a REMIC. If real property held by a REMIC appreciates, it cannot be withdrawn from the REMIC without triggering recognition of the gain. A REMIC cannot earn any services income or acquire property after the startup day. An investor who bought the real estate by purchasing the REMIC's residual interest would not be able to adjust the REMIC's "inside basis" in calculating taxable income.

All this would be true if the REMIC assets test freely permitted real property to be held by a REMIC. In fact, such property could be held at best subject to the limitations imposed with respect to foreclosure property. Those limitations would require the foreclosure property to be disposed of within two years unless a ruling from the Service extending the period was obtained. If that period was exceeded, either the REMIC would lose its status as a REMIC or all net income from the property, as well as any gain on sale, would be subject to a 100 percent tax.

Perhaps most significantly, what benefit would a REMIC achieve over a partnership, which is the more traditional vehicle for real estate development? The inefficiencies associated with providing artificial equity in non-REMIC CMO structures[258] would not exist in a traditional real estate investment because true equity would be required for economic reasons. The TMP rules do not, of course, apply to entities that hold real estate, as contrasted with mortgages.

The foregoing discussion suggests that the likelihood that a sponsor would transfer a real estate mortgage to a REMIC with the expectation that it will be converted into real estate through foreclosure are exceedingly small. But if that is true, what is wrong with applying the rule in the REIT regulations to REMICs?

The problem arises from the part of the regulation that applies where there is knowledge that a "default" will occur. It is very common for at least some of the loans transferred to a REMIC to be delinquent to some extent at the time of transfer. Under the loan documents, such delinquencies are usually characterized as defaults, although in practice they are not regarded as serious defaults until the period of delinquency extends to several months.[259] Further, a REMIC sponsor might wish to transfer a loan to a REMIC that was seriously delinquent if it believed the default would be cured without resulting in foreclosure (either through a payment in full of amounts due by the borrower or a loan modification). In this circumstance, any acquisition of real property by the REMIC would be the product of an unanticipated event, which is the case the foreclosure property rules were designed to address.

There is no authority applying the "improper knowledge" test in the REMIC area.[260] Because the Code extends the REIT definition of foreclosure property to

---

258   See Chapter 2, Part D.1.

259   Compare the guidelines for determining when loans are "seriously impaired," and therefore not considered real estate mortgages for purposes of the definition of a TMP, discussed in Chapter 3, Part D.2.e.

260   The preamble to the final REMIC regulations states that the Service "may" provide future guidance on this point.

REMICs, the Service or a court may be unwilling to disregard the "improper knowledge" regulation unless the regulation (as it applies to REMICs) is changed. It could, however, reasonably be applied to a REMIC by construing the references to "default" to mean a default that is expected to result in the ownership of real property by the REMIC. Under this reading, the regulation would almost never apply to REMICs, which is an appropriate outcome for the reasons given above.

7. Integration

The flexibility of the REMIC vehicle can be enhanced by combining a REMIC either with other REMICs or with assets or liabilities held or incurred outside of the REMIC. Three examples of such arrangements are: multiple-tier REMICs, outside reserve funds, and investment units consisting of REMIC regular interests and other financial instruments, such as swaps or options. In each of these cases, it is critical that the "outside" assets or liabilities not be brought "inside" and be treated as assets or liabilities of the REMIC.

Substantial arguments can be made in favor of recognizing form (and against integration) in these settings. Consider the following:

- The REMIC rules were intended to provide an *exclusive* set of tax rules governing mortgage-backed securities that apply if certain mechanical tests are met.[261] It would be at odds with the goal of the legislation to rely on "integrated transaction" arguments developed in other areas to bring within a REMIC assets or liabilities that the parties expressly excluded.

- A REMIC need not be a legal entity but can consist of a segregated pool of assets within a larger entity that has its own assets and liabilities.[262] This rule strongly implies that a REMIC will not be expanded beyond its designated assets.

- Combining a REMIC with other securities or structures does not involve tax abuse that requires the form to be disregarded (assuming that the economics of the arrangement are consistent with the form chosen by the parties, and that the REMIC assets and interests are clearly identified so that there is no doubt regarding the proper calculation of income of the REMIC and of holders of REMIC interests). To the extent the parties exclude assets or liabilities from a REMIC, they are not relying on the REMIC rules to avoid an entity level tax on the arrangement holding or establishing those assets or liabilities. Thus, combining other assets or liabilities with a REMIC does not extend the effect of the REMIC rules beyond their intended limits.

As discussed in the next three sections below, the Code or REMIC regulations specifically sanction multiple-tier REMICs, outside reserve funds and REMICs formed together with investment trusts that hold other financial instruments. While

---

261   See footnote 4, above.
262   See footnote 3, above.

these rules cover much ground, in light of the arguments given above, there is little reason to think that these arrangements should be treated more favorably than others that raise similar issues but have not been specifically sanctioned.

a. Multiple-Tier REMICs. The definition of qualified mortgage includes a regular interest in another REMIC. This rule permits the creation of multiple-tier REMIC structures in which all or some of the regular interests issued by one "lower-tier" REMIC are owned by a second "upper-tier" REMIC. If desired, the stacking of REMICs potentially could be carried through many tiers, although two is the most typical pattern.[263] By far the most common reason for tiering REMICs is tax driven, to create REMIC regular interests that cannot be created with one REMIC. This technique is illustrated in Chapter 5. A second reason for tiering REMICs might be to allow the aggregation into a single REMIC of pools of mortgages originated by different parties, where each originator wishes to retain an economic residual interest in its own pool of mortgages that for some reason cannot qualify as a regular interest and must, therefore, be a residual interest class.

If a REMIC were formed to hold regular interests that had been issued by a second REMIC in a prior, unrelated transaction, there would be no argument for integrating the two REMICs. By contrast, where the two REMICs are formed at the same time, the regular interests in the lower-tier REMIC are all issued to the upper-tier REMIC, the upper-tier REMIC has no substantial assets other than those regular interests, and the upper-tier REMIC is not permitted to dispose of the regular interests in the lower-tier REMIC (except perhaps in circumstances that cannot be foreseen), a substantial argument could be made that the two REMICs should be integrated and viewed as a single entity under general tax principles, if those principles applied. The combined entity would then fail to qualify as a REMIC either because it has two residual interests or, if the upper-tier REMIC is created to permit the issuance of regular interests that cannot be created through a single REMIC, because the purported regular interests are not regular interests in fact.

It is abundantly clear that general tax principles are overridden in this setting, and that two REMICs formed as described above will not be integrated. A number of authorities support this view. First, in determining the extent to which regular or residual interests qualify as real property loans under various Code sections, special rules apply to interests in REMICs that are part of a "tiered structure." The definition is broad enough to encompass virtually any multiple-REMIC arrangement that would raise an integration issue.[264] These special rules obviously assume that

---

263   The grouping of REMICs raises a question about how to refer to them collectively. For example, there is a gaggle of geese, a pride of lions, a school of fish, and now a [fill in term] of REMICs. Among the words that might be chosen are: *rabble, race, ragout, rain, rally, rampage, rash, repast, retinue, revue, rhapsody, richness, repetition,* and *reunion.* If in a particular case there is some structural mishap, the right word might be *recission.*

264   For this purpose, two REMICs are considered to be "tiered" if it was contemplated when both REMICs were formed that some or all of the regular interests of one REMIC would be held by the

"tiered" entities are not integrated into a single entity. Second, the REMIC regulations state that two or more REMICs may be created pursuant to a single set of organizational documents even if, for state law or federal securities law purposes, those documents create only one organization.[265] The only limitation is that the documents must clearly and expressly identify the assets of, and the interests in, each REMIC, and each REMIC must independently meet the REMIC qualification tests.[266] Although this rule is not limited to multiple-tier REMICs, it was undoubtedly fashioned with them in mind. Finally, the regulations governing information reporting by REMICs acknowledge the existence of tiering by exempting from certain requirements "a REMIC all of whose regular interests are owned by one other REMIC".[267] Similarly, recently proposed regulations under the OID rules of the Code contain an example involving a two-tier REMIC.[268]

b. Outside Reserve Funds. As discussed in Part A above, one of the types of permitted investments of a REMIC is a qualified reserve asset. In at least two cases, however, it may be desirable to hold reserve fund assets outside of a REMIC: where the economic owners of the reserve fund (i.e., the persons entitled to receive fund assets remaining on termination of the REMIC) cannot hold their interest in the fund in the form of a residual interest,[269] and where a reserve is used for purposes for which an inside reserve cannot be used.[270]

The REMIC regulations broadly sanction the use of outside reserves. The regulations state[271] that a reserve fund maintained to pay expenses of a REMIC, or to make payments to REMIC interest holders, is an outside reserve fund and not a REMIC asset, only if[272] the REMIC's organizational documents clearly and expressly

---

other. The rules for tiered structures are described in Chapter 9, text accompanying footnote 25.

265   Treasury Regulation § 1.860F-2(a)(2)(i).

266   In practice, the regular interests in a lower-tier REMIC are often defined by describing in a chart or table the upper-tier regular interests that correspond to each class of lower-tier interests.

267   These REMICs are exempted from the requirement of filing a Form 8811. See Treasury Regulation § 1.6049-7(b)(1)(i).

268   Proposed Regulation § 1.1275-2(c)(4), Example 2.

269   The reserve might be supplied, for example, by a governmental organization that, as a disqualified organization, cannot hold a residual interest. See the discussion of the arrangements test in Part A.3. In addition, distributions on a residual interest must be pro rata, so that non-pro rata interests in a reserve cannot be created through a REMIC. Another barrier to the use of inside reserves is that only residual interest holders can make contributions to an inside reserve fund after the startup day. See the text following footnote 175.

270   For example, an outside reserve might protect against basis risk. See Chapter 5, text accompanying footnote 65. Prior to issuance of the REMIC regulations, outside reserves were sometimes used to make up for prepayment interest shortfalls (which were not specifically listed in the Code as a permitted function of an inside reserve). Prepayment interest shortfalls are discussed in Part C.5, above.

271   Treasury Regulation § 1.860G-2(h).

272   Presumably, the phrase "only if" should be read to mean "if and only if."

- provide that the reserve fund is an outside reserve fund and not an asset of the REMIC

- identify the owner(s) of the reserve fund, either by name, or by description of the class (e.g., subordinated regular interest holders) whose membership comprises the owners of the fund, and

- provide that, for all federal tax purposes, amounts transferred by the REMIC to the fund are treated as amounts distributed by the REMIC to the designated owner(s) or transferees of the designated owner(s).

Concluding that reserve fund assets are outside of a REMIC does not complete the analysis of the effect of the fund on the REMIC qualification tests. In order to serve its purpose, there must exist contractual rights to draw on the fund. If those rights were considered REMIC assets, then they must run the gauntlet of the REMIC assets test. Also, if an outside fund can be reimbursed from REMIC assets, the reimbursement claim must not be a prohibited REMIC interest.

The treatment of claims against an outside reserve fund is not specifically addressed in the REMIC regulations, although the special rules for outside reserve funds obviously assume that such claims can in some way be reconciled with the REMIC qualification tests. If a REMIC were considered to hold a claim against an outside reserve fund, such a claim could, depending on the circumstances, potentially be a qualified reserve asset or a credit enhancement contract. A technical obstacle to viewing such a claim as a qualified reserve asset is the requirement that such an asset be "held for investment."[273] In order to qualify as a credit enhancement contract, claims against a reserve would, of course, need to be limited to the purposes for which such a contract may be used (principally, protection against defaults, unexpected expenses or losses, and prepayment interest shortfalls). The definition would cover the most common uses of reserves.[274]

As an alternative to viewing claims against an outside reserve as qualifying REMIC assets, payments from an outside reserve could in some cases be considered to bypass the related REMIC and be made directly to holders of REMIC interests, or to third parties to pay expenses. This analysis would be plausible only where the reserve is not used to discharge an obligation of the REMIC.[275] If REMIC interest

---

273   See text following footnote 135 above. Also, there is no explicit rule that would allow a claim against a REMIC for reimbursement of amounts paid in respect of a qualified reserve asset to be disregarded as a REMIC interest. Compare the rule for reimbursements under credit enhancement contracts discussed in text accompanying footnote 25 above. This problem would not, of course, arise to the extent the reserve is used to pay REMIC expenses without a right of reimbursement.

274   One use of a reserve that would not qualify is providing protection against basis risk. Basis risk is discussed in Chapter 5, text accompanying footnote 65. The REMIC regulations appear to contemplate the possibility that reserve funds may be used to collateralize a credit enhancement contract by providing that the collateral supporting such a contract is not treated as a REMIC asset solely because it supports the guarantee represented by that contract. Treasury Regulation § 1.860G-2(c)(1).

275   Compare the discussion of other credit support arrangements in Part C.1.b.(i). A payment that discharges an obligation is considered under general tax principles to be a payment to the obligor.

holders were considered to have direct rights against a reserve, then those rights would need to be taken into account, as property separate from the protected REMIC interests, in determining the holders' income tax treatment. To the extent the reserve protects against defaults or delinquencies on REMIC interests, rights against the reserve would be equivalent to a third-party guarantee.[276] If the reserve supplements the payments due by the REMIC on REMIC interests, then the claim against the reserve will represent an additional financial instrument that is packaged together with those REMIC interests. Where a reserve is a single account that is used for more than one purpose (e.g., credit support and protection against basis risk), it may be difficult to characterize the claim against the reserve. Units consisting of REMIC interests and other financial instruments are discussed in the next section.

One further tax issue raised by the use of an outside reserve fund is whether the arrangement for holding and investing the reserve could be characterized as an association for federal income tax purposes. This topic is discussed in Chapter 3.[277]

c. Packaging REMIC Interests with Other Financial Instruments. The REMIC rules permit mortgage cash flows to be allocated in many different ways among multiple classes of interests but otherwise do not allow those flows to be changed. For example, a REMIC cannot enter into an interest rate swap to convert fixed rate loans into floating rate investments or vice versa.[278] Similarly, it cannot protect against excessive mortgage prepayments by entering into a guaranteed investment contract to reinvest prepayments for more than a temporary period, or against prepayments that are too slow by entering into a contract to sell mortgages at a fixed price. These financial instruments or contracts would violate the assets or interest test or give rise to income subject to the 100 percent prohibited transactions tax.

A REMIC sponsor that wishes to alter the cash flows on mortgages in a way that cannot be accomplished solely by making allocations among REMIC interests

---

See, e.g., *Old Colony Trust Co. v. Comm'r*, 279 U.S. 716 (1929) (payment of corporate officer's income taxes was additional compensation to the officer). A reserve fund payment made to a holder of a REMIC interest to make up for a defaulted or delinquent amount due on the REMIC interest would not discharge the REMIC's obligation if the defaulted or delinquent amount continues to be owed by the REMIC to the reserve fund.

276 The possible need to allocate a portion of the cost of a debt instrument to a guarantee is discussed in Chapter 2, footnote 34. To avoid violating the REMIC interests test, the reserve fund should not be given a claim against a REMIC in exchange for making a payment to a REMIC interest holder except by succeeding to claims which the holder already had against the REMIC.

277 See Chapter 3, Part C.2.c.(iv).

278 This statement assumes that the swap cannot be integrated with the related mortgages for purposes of applying the REMIC rules. At present, there is no general tax rule allowing notional principal contracts (the tax term used to describe swaps) to be integrated with related debt obligations. Section 988(d) and Treasury Regulation § 1.988-5 allow debt instruments and related hedges involving foreign currency transactions to be integrated for various federal tax purposes, although there is no specific authority addressing whether these rules, if they applied in a particular case, would permit a swap to be treated as incidental to a qualified mortgage (and not as a separate asset or liability) for purposes of the REMIC assets and interests tests.

may seek to achieve the desired results by creating REMIC regular interests and packaging those interests with other financial instruments for sale as a unit to investors. For example, a regular interest could be placed in a trust with an interest rate swap or other notional principal contract, a contract providing for the sale of interests at a predetermined price to the extent needed to bring their unsold principal balances down to scheduled amounts, or possibly even a contract providing for the reinvestment of prepayments to the extent prepayments cause the principal balances to drop below specified levels. Certificates evidencing beneficial interests in the trust would then be sold to investors.

Packaging arrangements of this type raise three principal tax issues: How will the vehicle used to hold the regular interests and other financial instrument be classified for tax purposes? Will the additional financial instrument affect the tax status of the REMIC? How will investors be taxed? The entity classification question is discussed in Chapter 3. The other two issues are addressed here, first in general terms and second by examining a concrete example involving a REMIC regular interest combined with an interest rate swap.

The REMIC regulations contain a rule, parallel to the rule for multiple-tier REMICs described above, allowing one or more REMICs and one or more "investment trusts" that are created in a single document to be respected as separate entities if their assets and income are accounted for in a manner that respects their separate existence.[279] The principal significance of this rule seems to be to eliminate any concern that the use of a single set of documents would automatically require integration for tax purposes. It does not go further and eliminate the need to consider whether any rights or obligations that exist between the REMIC and investment trust (once they are viewed as separate entities) are consistent with the REMIC rules.

A separate regulation fills in part of the gap by providing that "contractual rights" held by an investment trust that also holds regular interests in a REMIC will not be treated as a REMIC *asset* (even if the REMIC and the trust are created contemporaneously pursuant to the same set of organizational documents) as long as those rights are accounted for as trust property separate and apart from the regular interests.[280] The treatment of such contractual rights is illustrated by an example involving a floating rate regular interest that is paired with an interest rate cap.[281] Although there is no corresponding safe-harbor rule that prevents investment trust *liabilities* from being REMIC interests, there is no apparent reason why different principles would apply to liabilities. The regulations do not define the term "investment trust," although presumably any trust that is classified as a grantor trust under the Sears regulations (described in Chapter 3) would qualify.[282]

---

279   Treasury Regulation § 1.860F-2(a)(2)(ii). The rule applies even if for state law or federal securities law purposes the documents create only one organization.

280   Treasury Regulation § 1.860G-2(i)(1).

281   Treasury Regulation § 1.860G-2(i)(2). The example shows how an interest rate cap can be used to protect against "basis risk." Basis risk is considered further in Chapter 5, footnote 120 and accompanying text.

The anti-integration rules in the regulations require a separate "accounting" for two entities or assets without explaining the meaning of the term. While the word could connote only a requirement of separate bookkeeping, it could also be read to imply some requirement that the separate terms of the REMIC and other financial instrument properly reflect the economics of the transaction. At any rate, the anti-integration rules should not insulate taxpayers from a possible recasting of a transaction (or the individual elements of a transaction) by the Service to reflect arm's length pricing, if the transaction is not based on market terms.

Another issue to tackle where non-REMIC financial instruments are married to REMIC regular interests is how investors will be taxed. The guiding principle here is that if the non-REMIC instrument is viewed as outside of the REMIC for purposes of applying the REMIC qualification tests, then, under current law, it must also be treated as a distinct financial instrument in the hands of investors.[283] Thus, where the other financial instrument is an asset, each investor must allocate its basis between that instrument and the regular interests in proportion to their fair market values at the time of purchase.[284] A similar allocation is required to determine the "issue price" of the REMIC's regular interests.[285] The timing and character of income from the financial instrument will generally be the same as if it had been issued separately from the regular interests and, thus, will depend on the type of instrument involved.[286] In addition, the financial instrument generally will not be a real property mortgage where that is relevant to the tax treatment of investors.[287]

Since investment units consisting of regular interests and other financial instruments are sold to investors based on the economic characteristics of the whole unit, it is somewhat frustrating that the tax law requires each component to be separately tracked. This approach also poses practical problems. For example, how do inves-

---

282 An example illustrating the rule allowing combinations of regular interests and contractual rights involves a REMIC and a "pass-through trust that is intended to be classified as a trust under section 301.7701-4(c) of this chapter [the Sears regulations]." See Treasury Regulation § 1.860G-2(i)(2). See also Treasury Regulation § 1.860G-2(a)(5) (refers to "investment trusts" that are classified as grantor trusts). Although less clear, the term investment trust should also include any trust that is an investment trust within the meaning of the Sears regulations but is classified as a partnership because it has multiple ownership classes and less than three corporate characteristics.

283 See, however, the rule described in footnote 278, above, allowing certain debt instruments to be integrated with currency hedges.

284 Treasury Regulation §§ 1.860G-2(i)(2)(iii) and 1.1012-1(d). Where the instrument is a liability, the amount of the liability should be added to the purchase price for the unit to determine the basis in the regular interests. For an illustration, see the discussion of regular interests combined with interest rate swaps immediately below.

285 Where a debt instrument (including a REMIC regular interest) is issued together with other property as an investment unit, then under section 1273(c), the issue price of the debt instrument is determined, for purposes of applying the OID rules of the Code, by first determining the issue price of the unit as if it were a debt instrument and then by allocating the issue price of the unit to each element of the unit based on relative fair market values.

286 However, the fact that the instrument is held together with the regular interest could result in application of the "straddle" rules of the Code. See sections 263(g) and 1092.

287 See Chapter 9, Part A.

tors determine the separate values of the regular interests and other financial instrument comprising a unit when they are not separately traded?

The principal issues raised by pairing regular interests with another financial instrument can be illustrated with a simple example. Suppose that a REMIC that is organized as a trust issues a class of fixed rate regular interests (the "Class A interests") to a trustee for a second trust (the "investment trust"). The investment trust enters into an interest rate swap agreement with a third party that (as described below) effectively converts the Class A interests into floating rate instruments. The investment trust is formed under the same trust agreement as the REMIC and the trustees of the two trusts are the same. The trust agreement states that the swap is not included in the REMIC and separately identifies the payments to be made on all REMIC interests. The terms of the swap are, of course, set forth in the swap agreement. The investment trust issues a single class of certificates evidencing pro rata beneficial interests in the trust. The trust agreement states that the investment trust is intended to be treated for federal income tax purposes as a grantor trust that holds the swap and Class A interests and is owned by the certificate holders.

Under the swap agreement, the investment trust is required to make fixed monthly payments to the counterparty corresponding to the interest payments due on the Class A interests, in exchange for payments, on the same date in each month, equal to LIBOR applied to the notional principal amount of the contract (which equals the principal amount of the Class A interests). Fixed and floating payments due on the same day are netted. The swap has market terms when entered into, so that no initial payment is made between the counterparty and the investment trust. Over time, however, the contract may represent economically a net liability or net asset of the trust depending on the current fixed market rate for a comparable fixed/LIBOR swap. The trust's obligation to make swap payments is a nonrecourse obligation of the trust that is secured only by the Class A interests. That obligation does not depend, however, on the receipt of payments on the Class A interests. In the event of a default by the investment trust under the swap, the counterparty has the right to terminate the swap. If at that time the swap represents a net liability of the trust, the counterparty may force the sale of the Class A interests and collect out of the sales proceeds a termination payment representing the value of the swap. Similarly, if the counterparty defaults, the investment trust may terminate the swap and, if it has positive value to the trust, collect a termination payment from the counterparty. Any such payment would be distributed immediately to investors. It is assumed that the investment trust (viewed separately) would be classified as a grantor trust for federal income tax purposes.[288]

The first tax issue is whether the rights and obligations of the investment trust under the swap will be considered to be assets and liabilities of the REMIC. Under the standard in the REMIC regulations, the swap should be considered outside the REMIC if it is "accounted for" in a way that reflects its existence outside of the REMIC.[289] The test should be met. The swap and REMIC are clearly identified as

---

288   See Chapter 3, Part C.3.c.(xi).

separate arrangements. More substantively, the REMIC has no claim to amounts due under the swap and no obligation to the swap counterparty (other than its obligation to make payments on the Class A interests).[290] It is helpful that the payment obligations of the investment trust under the swap are not dependent on receiving payments on the Class A interests, and that the swap can be separated from the Class A interests in the event of a default under the swap by either the investment trust or the counterparty.[291]

Assuming that the investment trust is classified as a grantor trust,[292] an investor purchasing a trust certificate would be treated as if it had directly acquired the Class A interests and entered into the swap. As a result, certificate holders would face tax consequences quite different from, and more complex than, the consequences of an investment in a single debt instrument having the payment characteristics of the trust certificate. If at the time of purchase of a certificate by an investor, the swap has a zero or positive value, then the premium (if any) deemed paid by the investor to enter into the swap, and the price paid to acquire the Class A interests, would be determined by allocating the investor's cost for the certificate between the swap and the regular interests in proportion to their fair market values. If the swap has a negative value to the investor, then the investor should be considered to acquire the regular interests at a price equal to their fair market value and to receive a swap premium equal to the difference between that value and the cost of the certificate. Any swap premium would be spread over the life of the swap under the normal rules governing notional principal contracts.[293] If the swap premium is considered to be significant, then the swap may be considered to involve an embedded loan to the recipient of the premium.[294] Net swap payments (adjusted for the amortization of

---

289 Note that the swap could at some point represent a net liability of the investment trust. As indicated above in the text following footnote 281, there is no safe-harbor nonintegration rule in the REMIC regulations specifically covering the liability case.

290 Needless to say, it would severely damage the argument for separate treatment of the swap in this example if the REMIC had any obligation to make floating rate interest payments in respect of the Class A interests.

291 This example is only an illustration of one, fairly straightforward fact pattern, and is not meant to suggest that the factors in the example supporting separate treatment need be present in all cases.

292 Some of the additional issues that would arise if the trust were classified as a partnership are discussed in Chapter 2, Part G.2.c (consequences of possible partnership classification of trusts issuing debt certificates) and Chapter 7, Part C (treatment of owner trusts classified as partnerships). One issue that is unique to notional principal contracts is that income earned by a foreign investor from such a contract held through a U.S. partnership would arguably be sourced in the U.S. and thus would potentially be subject to the U.S. 30% withholding tax. See Chapter 10, at footnote 66.

293 See Treasury Regulation § 1.446-3. These regulations do not specifically address the treatment of premiums paid on notional principal contracts having principal balances that may vary based on mortgage prepayments. Where a notional principal contract is not hedged (except by holding a debt instrument), the regulations allow a swap premium to be spread over the life of a contract in generally the same manner as if it were premium on a debt instrument. See Treasury Regulation § 1.446-3(f)(2)(iii).

294 See Treasury Regulation § 1.446-3(g)(4). Among other possible consequences, the existence of a borrowing could affect the tax treatment of investors that are generally tax-exempt because of the debt-financed property rules in section 514. See Chapter 9, Part B.

swap premium) would be ordinary income or deductions and would be accounted for under an accrual method. The timing of inclusion or deduction of a swap premium that is deemed received or paid by a certificate holder would not necessarily be the same as the timing of deduction or inclusion of any corresponding amount of premium or discount at which the investor is considered to acquire the Class A interests. Swap payments appear to be deductible by individual investors only as miscellaneous itemized deductions subject to the 2 percent of adjusted gross income floor.[295] The swap, to the extent it represents an asset, and income from the swap, would not qualify as income from a real property mortgage for purposes of the various Code provisions governing such loans. The swap and Class A interest may be a straddle that is subject to the loss deferral, holding period tolling, and interest capitalization rules of sections 1092 and 263(g). Finally, income from the receipt of payments under the swap realized by an investor that generally is tax exempt but is subject to tax on unrelated business taxable income would not be subject to that tax, provided the investment is not considered to be debt financed.[296]

D. REMIC Elections and Other Procedural Matters

1. Elections

In order to qualify as a REMIC, an entity must elect to be a REMIC.[297] REMICs are required to file annual tax returns (on Form 1066).[298] The return for any calendar year is due on April 15 of the following year but that date may be extended in the same manner as a partnership return.[299] A REMIC election is made by timely filing a duly executed return for the year that includes the startup day. The requirement that the return be timely filed is in the regulations but not in the statute.[300] As a result, the Service can, in its discretion, validate an election made through the late filing of a return.[301] To obtain an extension in the time for making an election, a taxpayer must generally show good cause, submit the request for relief before the due date of the REMIC return, or within such period thereafter as the Service may consider reasonable under the circumstances, and show that the granting of the extension will not jeopardize the interests of the government. A number of rulings have been issued granting such requests.[302] They make for good reading in an area that spawns few human interest stories.

---

295   In addition, those payments appear not to be deductible for purposes of the alternative minimum tax. See Chapter 2, footnotes 9 and 10 and accompanying text.

296   Treasury Regulation § 1.512(b)-1(a).

297   See section 860D(a)(1).

298   REMIC tax returns are discussed in detail in Chapter 11, Part C.

299   Treasury Regulation § 1.860F-4(b)(1).

300   See section 860D(b)(1) (election made on first return) and Treasury Regulation § 1.860D-1(d)(1) (requires timely filing).

301   The standards for granting such requests are set forth in Treasury Regulation § 301.9100-1 and Revenue Procedure 92-85, 1992-2 C.B. 490. See Treasury Regulation § 1.860D-1(d)(1) (in discussing REMIC return, refers to section 1.9100-1 for rules regarding extensions of time for making elections).

Because the REMIC election is made on a return that is due several months after the end of the year that includes the startup day, a question arises whether the decision to make the election for a mortgage pool needs to be made when the pool is formed or can be postponed until the return's filing date. Although the issue does not often arise in practice, it is possible to imagine circumstances in which such a postponement could be desirable. Suppose a sponsor transfers mortgages that have a substantial built-in gain or loss to a trust which issues pay-through bonds secured by the mortgages. Assume the bonds would be recognized to be debt in the absence of the REMIC rules. The sponsor may wish to look at the results for the entire year before deciding whether to recognize the gain or loss currently (by making a REMIC election). Alternatively, suppose that after formation of a purported grantor trust but before April 15 of the following year the parties become aware of some feature of the trust that could result in its classification as an association if a REMIC election is not made. Can the trust be spared an entity-level tax simply by filing Form 1066?

There is no explicit requirement in the Code that the intention to form a REMIC be present on the date of its birth. Regular and residual interests must be "designated" as such, but the REMIC regulations make it clear that the designation can be made simply by describing the classes on the first, timely filed Form 1066.[303] Also, a REMIC is required to file a Form 8811 containing information needed for information reporting within 30 days after the startup day, but the filing of this form does not amount to the filing of a REMIC election.[304] Thus, it appears the decision whether or not to make the election can be delayed. However, because REMIC elections are typically made in circumstances where REMIC status is essential to avoid an entity level tax and interests are sold based on an agreement to make the election, the circumstances where the decision to elect is delayed should be rare (and most likely limited to private transactions).

Once a valid REMIC election is made for an entity, it cannot be revoked.[305] It continues in effect until an event occurs that causes the entity to cease to qualify as a REMIC. If such an event occurs, the REMIC terminates, effective as of the *beginning* of the year in which the event occurs.[306] The Service has authority to overlook an inadvertent termination of a REMIC if the circumstance that caused the termination is corrected, but it is not clear how useful this authority will prove to be. One significant issue is whether consents of all REMIC interest holders will be

---

302   See, e.g., P.L.R.s 9309043 (December 9, 1992), 9239007 and 9239010 (June 24, 1992) (companion rulings), 9144014 (July 30, 1991), 9139007 (June 26, 1991), 9111057 (December 19, 1990).

303   See footnote 40 above, and Chapter 5, footnote 2.

304   See Treasury Regulation § 1.6049-7(b)(1)(i): "The submission of Form 8811 to the Internal Revenue Service does not satisfy the election requirement specified in section 1.860D-1T(d) [now 1.860D-1(d)] and does not require election of REMIC status." The reason for stating that the submission of the form does not require a REMIC election is that the form is also required to be filed by issuers of non-REMIC CMOs. Form 8811 is discussed in Chapter 11, Part A.3.

305   Treasury Regulation § 1.860D-1(d)(1).

306   See section 860D(b)(2)(A).

required to prevent the termination.[307] Further, the inadvertent termination rule may not provide relief to entities that failed to qualify as REMICs from the start.[308]

The rule that terminates the REMIC election for an entity for the entire year in which the entity ceases to be a REMIC should not apply if the entity is liquidated during the year but qualifies as a REMIC for all periods in which it exists. Otherwise, a REMIC could not liquidate and remain a REMIC throughout its life, except in a case where the liquidation happens to take place on January 1.

If the REMIC election for an entity terminates before it is liquidated at a time when it holds mortgages and has interests outstanding, what are the tax consequences? While the statute and legislative history do not address the point, presumably the REMIC is considered to distribute its assets to the holders of its regular and residual interests, in proportion to the fair market values of their respective interests, on the date when the termination becomes effective. They, in turn, would be deemed to exchange the distributed assets for the equity or debt interests that they would be treated as holding in the absence of the REMIC rules. For example, if the REMIC would be classified as an association taxable as a corporation in the absence of the REMIC rules, holders of regular interests would be considered to receive either debt or stock of the association, and holders of residual interests would presumably be considered to receive stock.[309] In any event, the REMIC

---

307   The authority to disregard inadvertent terminations is found in section 860D(b)(2)(B), which reads
       as follows:
       INADVERTENT TERMINATIONS. —If—
       (i) an entity ceases to be a REMIC,
       (ii) the [Service] determines that such cessation was inadvertent,
       (iii) no later than a reasonable time after the discovery of the event resulting in such
       cessation, steps are taken so that such entity is once more a REMIC, and
       (iv) such entity, *and each person holding an interest in such entity at any time during
       the period specified pursuant to this subsection* [presumably, the period during which
       the cessation would otherwise be effective], agrees to make such adjustments (consis-
       tent with the treatment of such entity as a REMIC or a C corporation [a taxable
       corporation]) as may be required by the [Service] with respect to such period,
       then, notwithstanding such terminating event, such entity shall be treated as continuing
       to be a REMIC (or such cessation shall be disregarded for purposes of subparagraph
       (A) [which prevents a REMIC from becoming a REMIC again following a termina-
       tion]) whichever the [Service] determines to be appropriate. (emphasis added)
       The practical significance of this grant of authority depends on whether REMIC interest holders
       will always be required to consent to an agreement between the REMIC and the Service, or if not,
       the circumstances in which such consent will be required. Obtaining consents from interest holders
       could be very difficult if the interests are widely held. It is not clear why such consents should be
       required if the REMIC election is continued. Although the language of section 860D(b)(2)(B) does
       not refer to implementing regulations, the legislative history suggests that the section was intended
       only to authorize the issuance of regulations dealing with inadvertent terminations. Conference
       Report at II-229; Blue Book at 416.
308   Section 860D(b)(2)(B) (quoted in footnote 307) applies when "an entity *ceases* to be a REMIC"
       [emphasis added]. Section 1362(f) has a similar inadvertent termination rule for S corporations.
       Section 601 of H.R. 13, the proposed Tax Simplification Act of 1993 introduced in the U.S. House
       of Representatives on January 5, 1993, would amend this section to allow the Service to validate
       an invalid S election where the failure properly to elect S status was inadvertent.
309   If the termination occurs after 1991, an unincorporated entity may be classified as an association
       under the TMP rules described in Chapter 3, Part D.

would recognize gain upon the distribution in the same manner as if it had sold the distributed property, and the net income (if any) from such deemed sale arguably would be subject to the 100 percent prohibited transactions tax unless the liquidation was a qualified liquidation.[310] The REMIC interest holders would be taxed in the same manner as if they had received from the REMIC cash equal to the fair market value of the property they are deemed to receive.[311]

2. Other Procedural Matters

a. General. In general, a REMIC is treated as a partnership, and holders of residual interests are treated as partners, for purposes of subtitle F of the Code (sections 6001 through 7872).[312] Subtitle F is concerned mostly with tax procedure and administration. It addresses, among other topics, the filing of tax returns, information reporting, the payment, collection, and refund of taxes, statutes of limitation, penalties and interest, tax shelter registration, and judicial proceedings.[313]

Subtitle F provides special rules for the treatment of partnership items which, with two exceptions, apply to all REMICs.[314] The exceptions apply to a REMIC for

---

310 For the definition of qualified liquidation, see footnote 31 and accompanying text. The rule allowing a plan of liquidation to be adopted merely by stating a date on Form 1066 is particularly helpful in cases where the event terminating a REMIC is not planned (but would be less helpful if the terminating act is discovered only upon audit after the return was filed).

311 Section 860F(c) states that if a REMIC makes a distribution of property with respect to any regular or residual interest, then (1) gain shall be recognized to the REMIC on the distribution in the same manner as if it had sold such property to the distributee at its fair market value, and (2) the basis of the distributee in such property shall be its fair market value. The Conference Report at II-234 states that distributions are treated as actual sales for purposes of the prohibited transactions rules. See also the Blue Book at 421. However, if the liquidation is a qualified liquidation, then gain recognized upon the distribution of assets generally would not be subject to a prohibited transactions tax. Note that it might be possible to characterize the liquidation not as a distribution by the REMIC of the assets it holds immediately prior to the liquidation but instead as a transfer by the REMIC of those assets to the new entity that is considered to come into existence upon termination of the REMIC, followed by a distribution of the interests in the new entity to holders of interests in the REMIC. Under that analysis, net income recognized by the REMIC upon distribution of the interests in the new entity might be subject to the prohibited transactions tax, whether or not there is a qualified liquidation, as income from a nonpermitted asset. Cf. Revenue Ruling 84-111, 1984-2 C.B. 88 (formal steps control whether the incorporation of a partnership should be treated as a distribution of partnership assets followed by a transfer of those assets by partners to a corporation, a transfer of assets by the partnership to the corporation followed by a distribution of stock, or a transfer of partnership interests to the corporation followed by a liquidation of the partnership).

If a REMIC distributes to holders of regular interests in retirement of those interests property having a fair market value greater than the adjusted issue price of those interests, then the REMIC will ordinarily be allowed a deduction for the difference between the two amounts as a retirement premium. If the REMIC is subject to a prohibited transactions tax with respect to net income recognized upon such a distribution of assets, it will be an important question whether any gain with respect to the assets may be offset by the premium deduction in calculating such net income. It would be quite unfair not to allow the deduction.

312 See section 860F(e). As discussed in Chapter 11, footnotes 56 and 57, there is an exception to this rule relating to the authority to sign tax returns.

313 REMIC tax returns and information reporting are discussed in Chapter 11.

any taxable year if for that year the REMIC's residual interest is held by one holder,[315] or (unless the REMIC elects otherwise) 10 or fewer holders each of which is an individual (other than a nonresident alien) or an estate.[316] Three of the more important of these provisions warrant a brief mention here.

First, the tax treatment of a REMIC and of particular REMIC items is generally determined at the REMIC level. Thus, if there is a controversy with the Service over such matters, the dispute would ordinarily be resolved through a single consolidated REMIC proceeding, rather than through separate proceedings involving each holder of a residual interest. In general, the REMIC would be represented in the consolidated proceeding by a "tax matters person" designated by the REMIC, although certain holders of residual interests would also have a right to participate.[317] Second, each holder of a residual interest is required to report income from such interest on its own tax return in a manner consistent with the information reported to it by the REMIC on Schedule Q, or to include with its return a statement identifying the discrepancy.[318] Finally, the statute of limitations for the assessment of tax on a residual interest holder with respect to any REMIC item may be affected by actions taken by the REMIC. In particular, the statute for any taxable year of the REMIC will not expire before the date which is three years after the date on which the REMIC filed its tax return for that year (or if later the date on which the return was originally due), and the expiration date may be extended by an agreement between the Service and the tax matters person.[319]

b. Payment of REMIC Taxes. The procedural issues discussed in the immediately preceding section relate primarily to the payment of taxes by holders of REMIC residual interests on their shares of the taxable income of the REMIC. However, as

---

314   These rules are set forth in sections 6221 through 6233. Subject to the exceptions described in the text, the rules apparently apply to any entity that files a REMIC tax return, even if it is later determined that the entity did not qualify as a REMIC (section 6233 and Treasury Regulation § 301.6233-1T).

315   The transitory ownership of the residual interest by the REMIC sponsor should be ignored for purposes of applying this rule if the sponsor transfers the residual interest to an investor on the startup day and does not report any income from the residual interest.

316   See Treasury Regulation § 1.860F-4(a) and section 6231(a)(1)(B). Pending legislation dealing with large partnerships would extend the ten-holder exception to holders that are C corporations. See section 314 of H.R. 13, the Tax Simplification Act of 1993, introduced in the U.S. House of Representatives on January 5, 1993.

317   The tax matters person must be the holder of a residual interest either at the time the designation is made or at some time during the taxable year of the REMIC for which the designation is made. See Treasury Regulation §§ 1.860F-4(d) and 301.6231(a)(7)-1T. Form 1066 includes a space for designating a tax matters person. The organizational documents for a REMIC typically authorize the party performing administrative services for the REMIC to carry out the responsibilities of the tax matters person on behalf of the tax matters person if that party would not otherwise be the tax matters person. The preamble to the final REMIC regulations states that the Service is considering providing future guidance that would expand the class of persons that may be designated as the tax matters person.

318   Section 6222.

319   Section 6229.

discussed in Part B above, a REMIC may itself be subject to tax. Further, if an entity that makes a REMIC election does not qualify to be a REMIC, and would be classified as a corporation in the absence of a valid REMIC election, the electing entity would be liable for a corporate income tax.

The amount of any tax imposed on a REMIC for a taxable year is payable upon filing the tax return for the year (or if that date is extended or no return is filed, on the last due date for filing the return without extension).[320] There is no requirement that estimated amounts of such taxes be paid during the year.[321] The general procedural rules applicable to income taxes (e.g., statutes of limitations, limitations on assessment, rights to contest deficiencies in the United States Tax Court, and refunds) apply.[322] The special procedures for handling "partnership items" described in Part D.2.a above appear to apply to REMIC taxes.[323]

An entity that elects to be a REMIC but fails to qualify as a REMIC would ordinarily be subject to the procedures that would apply to the type of entity that it is (e.g., a corporation). However, if the purported REMIC files a return as a REMIC and would, if the REMIC election were valid, be subject to the special procedures just mentioned for handling partnership items, then those procedures would apply, and the issue of the appropriate tax status of the REMIC would be a partnership item.[324]

c. Recordkeeping. Presumably to assist the Service in its policing function, every REMIC is required to keep sufficient records concerning its investments to show that it has complied with the assets test and other REMIC requirements for each taxable year of its existence.[325]

---

320 Section 6151 (except where otherwise provided, when a return of tax is required, the person required to make the return shall pay such tax with the return at the time and place fixed for filing the return, determined without regard to any extension of time for filing the return). Form 1066 (the REMIC tax return) includes a Schedule J that is used in calculating any taxes due.

321 Under section 860F(e), a REMIC is treated as a partnership for purposes of subtitle F of the Code, which includes the sections relating to estimated taxes. However, there is no section requiring the payment of estimated taxes by partnerships. Compare sections 6654 and 6655, relating to estimated tax payments by individuals (including estates and trusts) and corporations, respectively. Form 1066 (the REMIC tax return) does not contemplate estimated tax payments because it makes no provision for crediting such payments against taxes due with the return.

322 Income taxes are generally referred to in the Code as "taxes imposed by subtitle A" which would include taxes imposed under sections 860A through 860G.

323 A "partnership item" is defined in section 6231(a)(3) as any item required to be taken into account for the partnership's taxable year under any provision of subtitle A (which would include items entering into the calculation of REMIC taxes—see footnote 322) to the extent regulations provide that such item is more appropriately determined at the partnership level than at the partner level. Treasury Regulation § 301.6231(a)(3)-1(a) includes in the list of those items, items of partnership income, and in some circumstances items relating to contributions to a partnership. The REMIC taxes apply to certain items of REMIC income or to contributions.

324 See section 6233 and Treasury Regulation § 301.6233-1T.

325 Treasury Regulation § 1.860D-1(d)(3).

Chapter 5

Definition of Regular Interest

A. Overview

As noted in Chapter 4, all interests in a REMIC must consist of one or more classes of regular interests and a single class of residual interests. This chapter discusses the definition of regular interest, one of the most complex aspects of the REMIC rules.

A *regular interest* is defined in section 860G(a)(1) as any interest that

- is issued on the startup day
- is designated as a regular interest
- has fixed terms
- provides that interest payments (or, if the regular interest is not in the form of debt, similar amounts), if any, at or before maturity either are payable based on a fixed rate (or to the extent provided in regulations, at a variable rate), or consist of a specified portion of the interest payments on qualified mortgages and such portion does not vary during the period such interest is outstanding, and
- unconditionally entitles the holder to receive a specified principal amount (or a similar amount).

The first two parts of the definition are straightforward. A regular interest will be considered to be issued on the startup day if it is issued on (or within 10 days of) the date of issuance of all other REMIC interests.[1] An interest may be designated as a regular interest by providing a description of the terms and conditions of the regular interest in the REMIC's first, timely filed tax return.[2]

The remaining elements of the definition cannot be dealt with so quickly. Parts B, C, and D below address, respectively, the fixed-terms requirement, permitted interest payments, and contingencies affecting the timing or amount of payments of principal and interest. Part E comments on a number of special topics pertaining to regular interests (the timing of principal payments, non-pro rata payments, modifications, the stripping of interest payments, the stapling of regular interests, registra-

---

1   See Chapter 4, footnote 6 (discussing the definition of startup day).
2   Treasury Regulation § 1.860G-1(a)(1). The description can be provided by attaching a copy of the offering circular or prospectus to the return. See Treasury Regulation § 1.860D-1(d)(2)(ii).

tion under the so-called TEFRA rules, and foreign currency denominated interests). Finally, Part F gives examples of different types of regular interests, created using both single- and double-tier REMIC structures.

Instruments having economic characteristics that are inconsistent with their qualification as regular interests can be created synthetically in some cases by combining a regular interest with an interest rate swap or other financial instrument in an investment unit. This technique is discussed in Chapter 4, Part C.7.

B. Fixed Terms

A regular interest must have fixed terms. The reason for this requirement is not given in the legislative history of the REMIC provisions, but it may have been intended to prevent taxpayers from avoiding the requirements relating to interest and principal on a regular interest by varying the terms of an existing interest.[3] Obviously, an interest can have fixed terms even though the amount and timing of the payments thereon are not fixed in advance. The normal meaning of "terms" would easily accommodate formulae for calculating payments that may vary in timing or amount.

The demands of the fixed-terms test as it is applied in the REMIC regulations are slight.[4] The test is met with respect to a regular interest if, on the startup day, the REMIC's organizational documents "irrevocably specify" (1) the principal amount (or other similar amount), (2) the interest rate or rates used to compute any interest payments (or other similar amounts), and (3) the latest possible maturity date of the interest. No mention is made of the way in which principal is to be distributed prior to maturity, although obviously as a commercial matter securities could not be issued without addressing the point.

Under the regulations, the specification of terms must be "irrevocable". However, there is very little that is done in an agreement that cannot be undone through some means. Virtually all REMIC organizational documents contain an amendment section that allows changes to the documents (and to the regular interests) in some circumstances. Generally, all holders of a class of regular interests must consent to an amendment that would delay or reduce payments on the class. Whatever the irrevocability requirement was intended to accomplish, surely it cannot call into question amendment provisions of this type.

A REMIC interest does not fail to meet the fixed-terms test solely because it is subject to default or certain other contingencies. See Part D below.

---

3   A significant modification in the terms of a regular interest would ordinarily be treated under section 1001 as the issuance of a new REMIC interest in exchange for the old one, which would violate the REMIC interests test. See Part E.3 below. Section 1001 does not generally apply, however, to alterations occurring by operation of the original terms of an instrument. See Proposed Regulation § 1.1001-3(c)(2)(i).

4   See Treasury Regulation § 1.860G-1(a)(4).

C. Permitted Interest Rates

An interest in a REMIC cannot be a regular interest unless interest payments, if any, with respect to such interest, at or prior to maturity, are payable based on a fixed rate (or to the extent provided in regulations, a variable rate), or consist of a specified portion of the interest payments on qualified mortgages (which portion does not vary during the period the interest remains outstanding). A fixed or variable rate regular interest may not bear interest at a rate that is "disproportionately high" compared with its principal amount. No such limitation applies to specified portion regular interests. Indeed, they may consist solely of rights to interest.

The next four sections consider the disproportionately high interest rule and the three categories of permitted rates (fixed, variable, and specified portion). Part F below contains examples illustrating permitted and impermissible rates.

Apart from the stated rate of interest, there are a number of factors affecting payments of interest (or other amounts in addition to principal) on a REMIC interest that may bear on its qualification as a regular interest. Two such factors—prepayment premiums and prepayment interest shortfalls—are discussed in Chapter 4, Parts C.4 and C.5. Contingencies affecting interest payments are considered in Part D.2 below.

1. Disproportionately High Interest

The definition of regular interest added to the Code in 1986 allowed only fixed or (to the extent provided in regulations) variable rate interest payments. The TRA 1986 legislative history stated that a REMIC interest would not be a regular interest if the amount of interest thereon was "disproportionately high" compared with its principal amount.[5] Thus, under the original REMIC legislation, interest-only, or other high-coupon, regular interests were not allowed. The ban on high-coupon regular interests apparently arose from doubts as to whether the tax rules governing debt instruments (which apply automatically to regular interests) should be extended to instruments having a yield that is extremely sensitive to mortgage prepayment rates and may even be negative.

The REMIC regulations treat a REMIC interest as having disproportionately high interest if it is issued with a premium of more than 25 percent (or, more technically, if the issue price of the interest exceeds 125 percent of its specified principal amount).[6] Under this test, interest on a fixed or variable rate regular interest can be very high in some periods during the life of the instrument if lower rates in other periods reduce the total premium at issuance to no more than 25 percent.[7] Stated interest rates can also be high if other factors depress value. For

---

5   Conference Report at II-229; Blue Book at 415.

6   Treasury Regulation § 1.860G-1(b)(5)(i). Note that the 125% test relates to the principal amount of the interest, not its stated redemption price at maturity as determined under the OID rules. A notional principal amount that is used in calculating interest payments but is not actually payable would, of course, not count as a principal amount for this purpose. The issue price of a REMIC regular interest is discussed in Chapter 7, footnote 31.

example, regular interests that are subordinated, have high expected prepayment rates, or bear interest at a rate that varies inversely with market interest rates, may have little or no issue premium despite a high initial interest rate.

In TAMRA, Congress relented in part. The proscription against high-premium instruments was retained for fixed or variable rate regular interests, but a new category of regular interest—one with interest payments consisting of a nonvarying specified portion of interest payments on qualified mortgages—was created that can bear interest at a disproportionately high rate. Apparently, the theory of the amendment was that strips of interest payments off of mortgages (or other regular interests) meeting the specified portion definition could exist in the form of grantor trust interests, so there was little to lose by allowing similar securities to be created under the REMIC rules.[8] The amendment may also have been founded on the realization that high-coupon REMIC securities can in fact be taxed properly as debt instruments by applying the PAC method set forth in section 1272(a)(6). This method allows actual and anticipated prepayments to be taken into account in accruing discount (or, under similar rules, premium).[9]

The discussion so far suggests that an important distinction exists under current law between fixed and variable rate regular interests, which cannot have disproportionately high interest, and specified portion regular interests, which can. As explained in Part C.4, however, a double REMIC structure can be used to create the equivalent of high-coupon fixed or variable rate regular interests. Thus, under current practice, the disproportionately high interest rule has little practical significance for the well informed, other than as a progenitor of multiple-tier REMICs.

Although fixed or variable rate regular interests may not have disproportionately high interest, there has never been a prohibition against rates that are disproportionately low or even zero.[10] Similarly, specified portion regular interests may have at or below market interest rates.

2. Fixed Rates

A regular interest may provide for interest payments based on a fixed rate. It is not clear what the phrase *based on* was intended to mean, but it should be construed to allow at least a limited degree of variability in rates.[11] Before issuance of the

---

7   For an illustration, see Part F, Example 8.

8   See Chapter 2, Part B.2. The REMIC regulations treat as specified portion regular interests certain partial interests in interest payments on a qualified mortgage that cannot clearly be created under the grantor trust rules. For example, a right to interest payments on a fixed rate mortgage in excess of LIBOR would represent a specified portion but apparently not a permitted grantor trust interest. See Chapter 3, Part C.1.f.

9   The PAC method is discussed in Chapter 6, Part C.2.

10   Section 860G(a)(1)(B) refers to interest payments "if any". See also Conference Report at II-229; Blue Book at 415.

11   For variable rates, the phrase *based on* has been used to allow a rate to be derived from an index by multiplying by a fixed factor and adding or subtracting a fixed number of basis or percentage points. See Notice 87-41, discussed in footnote 19, below; cf. Treasury Regulation §§ 1.1275-

REMIC regulations, the phrase was relied upon to justify prepayment interest short-falls and the lag periods found in typical pass-through certificates during which no interest is paid. These particular deviations from a "pure" fixed rate are now ad-dressed directly in the REMIC regulations, but other cases where some leniency is desirable surely will arise.[12]

The requirement that interest payments be payable based on a fixed rate is broad enough to accommodate both simple and compound interest.[13] Stating the point more technically, it should be possible to apply the fixed rate either to out-standing principal or to outstanding principal plus any deferred and unpaid inter-est.[14] Moreover, any reasonable convention for counting days (e.g., 30/360) should be allowed in computing interest payments.[15]

The statutory phrase "based on *a* fixed rate" [emphasis added] suggests that the fixed rate cannot be stepped up or down over time according to a schedule.[16] For REMICs that are subject to the REMIC regulations, however, the point is moot, because a rate consisting of one fixed rate during one or more accrual or payment periods and a different fixed rate or rates during other accrual or payment periods is a permitted variable rate.[17]

3. Variable Rates

Variable interest rates are allowed only to the extent provided in regulations. The REMIC regulations permit three types of variable rates: rates based on current values of an index, rates based on a weighted average of the rates on qualified mortgages, and a combination of otherwise permitted rates.[18] The regulations largely follow two notices issued by the Service in 1987, although they clarify and liberalize the notices in some respects.[19] The term "variable rate" is used herein to

---

5(b)(2) and (c)(1). If these operations are performed on a fixed rate, however, the result is another fixed rate; thus, in the context of a fixed rate the *based on* language would be superfluous if it allowed nothing more than these operations.

12   Prepayment interest shortfalls are discussed in Part C.5 of Chapter 4. A payment lag can be viewed as a positive fixed rate combined with a zero interest rate for the lag period, and combinations of fixed rates are allowed as variable rates under the regulations. See Part C.3.e below.

13   The Service has ruled privately that regular interests can pay simple interest. See P.L.R. 9046016 (August 17, 1990).

14   The ability to defer interest on a regular interest is discussed in Part D.2 below at footnote 118.

15   Compare Treasury Regulation § 1.1272-1(b)(1)(ii).

16   See, however, New York State Bar Association, Tax Section, "Report on the Federal Income Tax Treatment of Real Estate Mortgage Investment Conduits," December 30, 1989, at footnote 25 and accompanying text (a stepped rate may arguably qualify as a fixed rate).

17   See Treasury Regulation § 1.860G-1(a)(3)(vi)(A), which is discussed in Part C.3.e below. If stepped coupons are allowed only as a type of variable interest rate, then they would not be allowed except to the extent permitted in regulations, and thus could not be used for REMICs with a startup day before November 12, 1991 (the effective date of the REMIC regulations).

18   See Treasury Regulation § 1.860G-1(a)(3).

19   Notices 87-41, 1987-1 C.B. 500, and 87-67, 1987-2 C.B. 377, permitted objective interest index and weighted average rate regular interests, respectively. An "objective interest index" was de-fined for this purpose, through a cross-reference to the then-existing proposed OID regulations, as

refer to any indexed, weighted average or combination rate that is a "variable rate" (as contrasted with a specified portion or fixed rate) allowed under the REMIC regulations.

Determining a variable rate involves as many as four steps:

- First, the index value or weighted average rate must be calculated using an appropriate index or average. Certain adjustments can be made to rates on individual mortgages before an average is computed.

- Second, the index or average can be adjusted by multiplying the rate by a fixed multiple and/or adding or subtracting a fixed number of basis points.

- Third, the rate resulting from the first two steps can be limited by a cap or floor.

- Fourth, a rate derived from steps one through three can be combined with other such rates or one or more fixed rates (but not with a specified portion rate), with each individual rate applying in specified periods over the life of the regular interest.

We turn now to a more detailed discussion of the four steps outlined above, beginning with the definitions of a qualifying index rate and a weighted average rate.

a. Qualifying Index. The REMIC regulations treat as a variable rate a "qualifying variable rate for purposes of section 1271 through 1275 [dealing with OID] and the related regulations." Although the history is somewhat convoluted, as of this writing, the only type of rate that meets this definition is one based on "current values" of a "qualified floating rate" as those terms are used in certain OID regulations that were proposed at the end of 1992. These regulations were finalized in January of 1994, effective for obligations issued on or after April 4, 1994, but the REMIC rules have not yet been revised to take the final regulations into account.[20] Under both the 1992

---

a rate made known publicly and offered currently to unrelated borrowers in private lending transactions by a financial institution, or a rate reflecting an average of current yields on a class of publicly traded debt instruments. See Proposed Regulation § 1.1275-5(b) (withdrawn December 21, 1992). Notice 87-41 also stated that a rate reflecting the average cost of funds of one or more financial institutions was an objective interest index. (For the same rule under current law, see footnote 21 below.) Although Notice 87-41 did not deal expressly with combinations of rates, it was generally understood that an objective interest index included sequences of fixed and objective interest index rates, and of different objective interest index rates. See Proposed Regulation § 1.1275-5(d)(4) (withdrawn December 21, 1992).

20   The OID sections of the Code do not define any type of "qualifying variable rate". On December 21, 1992, a set of proposed OID regulations was issued that largely superseded another set of proposed regulations issued in 1986. The new proposed regulations were not immediately effective and also did not use the term "qualifying variable rate" found in the REMIC regulations. Instead, they defined two distinct categories of variable rates: a "qualified floating rate" (which has the meaning given in the next sentence in the text), and an "objective rate", which is a rate based on the price of actively traded property, including not only debt instruments but also, for example, commodities and equities (see Proposed Regulation § 1.1275-5(c)(1)). The Service clarified the cross-reference in Notice 93-11, I.R.B. 1993-6, 42. This notice states that a "qualified floating

proposed regulations and the final rules, a rate is a qualified floating rate if variations in the rate "can reasonably be expected to measure contemporaneous variations in the cost of newly borrowed funds."[21] This definition would include all of the common interest rate indices (e.g., LIBOR, a prime rate, an average of yields on Treasuries, and a rate such as COFI reflecting the average cost of funds of one or more financial institutions).[22] It may also include some indices that do not directly measure interest rates but are correlated with such rates, such as changes in a general inflation index, although this conclusion is uncertain.[23] A rate that is not based on an index but is instead determined by an auction or remarketing agent so as to allow a REMIC interest to be sold at its principal amount should be a qualified floating rate. On the other hand, an index that reflects the total return during a period on a medium or long term fixed rate debt instrument (the current yield adjusted for changes in market value) would not likely be a qualified floating rate because of the adjustment for changes in market prices. A rate is considered to be based on a "current value" of a qualified floating rate if the relevant value is determined no earlier than three months before, and no later than one year after, the date on which the rate first becomes effective.[24]

The REMIC regulations treat as a variable rate not only a single qualifying variable rate (as determined under the OID rules), but also a rate equal to the highest, lowest, or average[25] of two or more such qualifying variable rates.[26] The

---

rate" (as defined in Proposed Regulation § 1.1275-5(b)(1)) set at a current value (as defined in Proposed Regulation § 1.1275-5(a)(4)) is a "qualifying variable rate" for purposes of Treasury Regulation § 1.860G-1(a)(3)(i). The notice states further that it may be relied upon until final OID regulations are issued, at which point the REMIC regulations will be amended to conform to the language of the final OID regulations. Final OID regulations were issued on January 27, 1994, effective for obligations issued on or after April 4, 1994. See T.D. 8517, 59 Fed. Reg. 4,799 (February 2, 1994). The final regulations generally follow the proposed regulations in defining a qualified floating rate and objective rate, although there are some differences. For further discussion of the final regulations, see Chapter 6, Part C.4. As of this writing, the promised amendments to the REMIC regulations have not been issued. It seems very unlikely, however, that these amendments will restrict the types of variable rates allowed under Notice 93-11.

21 See Proposed Regulation § 1.1275-5(b)(1) and Treasury Regulation § 1.1275-5(b)(1).

22 COFI is the weighted average cost of funds index for member savings institutions of a Federal Home Loan Bank District (typically, the Eleventh). See Treasury Regulation § 1.860G-1(a)(3)(i), second sentence.

23 Proposed Regulation § 1.1275-5(d), Example 4, treated an inflation index as a qualified floating rate. The final OID regulations (see footnote 20, above) deleted the example without any explanation, even though the relevant definitions were not changed.

24 See Proposed Regulation § 1.1275-5(a)(4) and Notice 93-11, described in footnote 20, above. The same definition is in the final OID regulations.

25 The word "average" should include a weighted average as well as a simple average. It would make no sense to allow a rate based on the highest or lowest of two or more rates and not to allow an average giving more weight to one or more indices. Moreover, the weighting of rates can be accomplished by including in a simple average two or more slightly varying rates (e.g., LIBOR plus 10 basis points, LIBOR minus 10 basis points, and COFI).

26 Treasury Regulation § 1.860G-1(a)(3)(i), third sentence. This sentence refers to the highest, lowest, or average of two or more "objective interest indices" rather than "qualifying variable rates" as stated in the text, but this appears to be a mistake. The term "objective interest index" was used in the proposed OID regulations issued in 1986 that have been withdrawn. See footnote 20, above, and Proposed Regulation § 1.860G-1(a)(3)(i) (September 21, 1991). Cf. Treasury Regulation

possible use of one variable rate as a cap or floor for another variable rate (which has the effect of setting the rate at the lower or higher of the two rates) is considered in Part C.3.e below dealing with combination rates. The difference between two qualifying variable rates apparently is not a qualifying variable rate, but a regular interest paying interest at a rate based on a spread between two rates can be created using two tiers of REMICs or as a specified portion rate.[27]

As indicated above, the REMIC rules have not yet been revised to take account of the final OID regulations. It is possible (but by no means certain) that when the revisions are made, the types of variable rates that are allowed for REMIC regular interests will be expanded to include rates based on the yield or changes in the price of one or more items of actively traded personal property.[28]

b. Weighted Average Rates. It may be desirable as a commercial matter to determine interest payments on a REMIC regular interest simply by passing through the net interest received on the underlying (fixed or adjustable rate) mortgages held by the issuing REMIC. In that event, the interest rate on the REMIC interest would depend on the rates on individual mortgages, servicing fees and other expenses, and the composition of the mortgage pool from time to time. The REMIC regulations allow regular interests of this type in that they treat as a variable rate a rate based on a weighted average of the rates on some or all of the qualified mortgages held by a REMIC.[29] One constraint is that each of the qualified mortgages taken into account must itself bear interest at a fixed or variable rate.[30]

There is considerable overlap between the rules for weighted average and specified portion rates since both are based on the interest paid on qualified mortgages. The principal differences are summarized in Part C.5 below, after the discussion of specified portion rates.

The regulations contemplate a three-step process in determining a weighted average rate. First, the qualified mortgages taken into account in the calculation are identified. Second, the interest rates on those mortgages must be determined (and if necessary adjusted). Finally, a weighted average of those rates is calculated.

(i) Identification of mortgages. The mortgages taken into account in the average may be any or all of the "qualified mortgages" held by the REMIC. The term

---

§ 1.1275-5(b)(1) (if a debt instrument provides for two qualified floating rates that can reasonably be expected to have approximately the same values throughout the term of the instrument; the two rates together are considered a single qualified floating rate, two rates that are within 25 basis points of each other on the issue date meet this test).

27   See Part F, Example 26 (two-tier REMIC) and Part C.4.a (specified portion).

28   This result would occur if an "objective rate" as defined in the current proposed OID regulations (see footnote 20) is considered a qualifying variable rate for purposes of the regular interest definition.

29   See Treasury Regulation § 1.860G-1(a)(3)(ii).

30   The text beginning at footnote 41 discusses whether a qualified mortgage that has disproportionately high interest may be taken into account in a weighted average rate calculation.

has the same meaning here as for purposes of the REMIC assets test.[31] Thus, it may include regular interests in other REMICs.[32] It does not include permitted investments (as defined for purposes of the REMIC assets test), such as reserve fund assets. If a REMIC holds partial ownership interests in mortgages representing stripped bonds or stripped coupons, then rights to interest held outside the REMIC should be disregarded in any weighted average rate calculation.[33]

In the case of a REMIC that acquires foreclosure property following a mortgage default, it is common practice to account for the foreclosure property until it is finally liquidated as if it continued to represent the defaulted loan for which it was exchanged. Although the regulations do not address this point, it would make sense to follow the accounting convention adopted by the REMIC in determining whether the qualified mortgage continues to exist for purposes of calculating a weighted average rate.[34]

The qualified mortgages taken into account can be all mortgages held by the REMIC or any group of mortgages specified by the REMIC.[35] Thus, for example, it is possible to divide the mortgages held by a REMIC into subpools and to issue different classes of regular interests, with each bearing interest based on the average rate for the related subpool. While the regulations do not address the point expressly, it should be possible to include in a weighted average rate calculation only a pro rata portion of a qualified mortgage. In many cases, the effect of including only a pro rata portion of a mortgage in the calculation also can be achieved simply by reducing by a fixed percentage the interest on the mortgage that is taken into account in calculating the average.[36]

The test requires only that the *rate* of interest on a regular interest be based on a weighted average of the rates of interest on a reference pool of mortgage; there is

---

31 That test is discussed in Chapter 4, Part A.2. A REMIC can hold a *de minimis* amount of mortgages that are not qualified mortgages and still meet the assets test. See Chapter 4, text accompanying footnote 55. Under a literal reading of the regulations, interest on nonqualified mortgages could not be counted in determining a weighted average rate. However, it would be inconsistent with the purpose of the *de minimis* rule not to allow those mortgages to be counted.

32 This rule is helpful in a two-tier REMIC structure where an upper-tier REMIC holds regular interests issued by a lower-tier REMIC bearing interest at a fixed or variable rate. For illustrations of the use of weighted average rates in such an arrangement, see the examples in Part F.2.b below.

33 Although interest payments on a stripped mortgage often lose their character as interest for tax purposes under section 1286 (see Chapter 6, Part D.1), it would be reasonable to continue to treat such payments as interest for purposes of a weighted average rate computation. See footnote 46 below. For a discussion of whether qualified mortgages with disproportionately high interest may be taken into account in a weighted average rate calculation, see the text at footnote 41 below.

34 Cf. Treasury Regulation § 1.860G-2(g)(1)(ii)(C) (definition of "payments received on qualified mortgages" for purposes of the definition of cash flow investment includes cash flow and proceeds from foreclosure property); Treasury Regulation § 301.7701-13(l)(2)(viii) (for purposes of section 7701(a)(19)(C), foreclosed property is treated as having the same character as the loan for which it was given as security); section 595 (thrifts must account for losses and income on foreclosure property as adjustments to bad debts)

35 The ability to base an average on less than all qualified mortgages held by a REMIC was not clear under Notice 87-67, described in footnote 19 above.

36 See the text below at footnote 50.

no need for the *amount* of interest payments on the regular interest to bear any relationship to the amount of interest payments on those reference mortgages.[37] There is also no need for principal payments on the regular interest to be derived from, or bear any particular relationship to, principal payments on the reference mortgages.[38]

In order to be taken into account in a weighted average rate calculation, a qualified mortgage must bear interest at a fixed rate or a variable rate. This requirement would prevent the inclusion in a weighted average rate computation of contingent interest on a commercial loan the amount of which is based on revenues or profits from the project financed with the loan. Nonetheless, it should be possible to take noncontingent interest on such a loan into account in a weighted average rate, either by stripping off the right to contingent interest from the loan before it is conveyed to the REMIC,[39] or by including the entire mortgage in the REMIC, allocating contingent interest to the residual interest and taking the position that the contingent interest that is so allocated can be ignored in determining if the mortgage bears interest at a fixed or variable rate.[40]

While the regulations could be clearer on the point, it appears that a qualified mortgage can be taken into account in a weighted average rate calculation if it provides for interest at a fixed or variable rate applied to an actual principal balance, even if it has disproportionately high interest (and for that reason could not qualify as a fixed or variable rate regular interest). Although less certain, the same conclusion may also hold true for qualified mortgages that have only notional principal

---

37 Treasury Regulation § 1.860G-1(a)(3)(ii)(A) describes a weighted average interest rate as generally a rate that, if applied to the aggregate outstanding principal balance of a pool of mortgage loans for an accrual period, produces an amount of interest that equals the sum of the interest payable on the pooled loans for that accrual period. This statement simply indicates how rates should be weighted in calculating an average and should not be read to require that there be any relationship between the amount of payments on regular interests bearing interest at a weighted average rate and the amount of payments on the reference pool of mortgages.

38 A REMIC's constituent documents should be able to provide for an alternate interest rate in cases where all of the reference mortgages have been repaid or written off prior to the retirement of the related regular interest. See Treasury Regulation § 1.860G-1(a)(3)(vi) (combination rates).

39 See Chapter 4, footnote 20, the text at footnote 33 above, and footnote 40 below.

40 The preamble to the final REMIC regulations states expressly that contingent interest loans may be contributed to a REMIC with the right to contingent interest being allocated to the residual interest: "The final regulations also make it clear that certain obligations that contain contingent payment provisions can be stripped of the contingent payment rights and the holder of those rights will not be considered to hold an interest in the REMIC. . . . Of course, the owner could have contributed the entire loan to the REMIC and taken back a residual interest that consisted of the right to the contingent payments." Contingent interest can generally be excluded from a weighted average rate calculation by imposing a ceiling on the rate before the average is calculated (see the text below at footnote 50). Although the regulations do not address the point expressly, it would make sense in such a case to disregard the contingent payment feature in determining whether the loan bears interest at a fixed or variable rate. The technical problem could also be addressed using a two-tier REMIC structure. The lower-tier REMIC would issue a separate class of regular interests mirroring each qualified mortgage held by the lower-tier REMIC but excluding contingent interest, and the upper-tier REMIC would issue regular interests bearing interest at a rate equal to a weighted average of the rates on the regular interests it holds. It may also be possible to strip off contingent interest using a specified portion rate. See Part C.4.a below.

balances.[41] To illustrate the second case, suppose that the assets of REMIC A consist of (1) REMIC regular interests issued by REMIC B that are entitled to 100 percent of the interest payments on fixed rate qualified mortgages held by REMIC B and no actual principal, and (2) regular interests issued by REMIC C that are entitled to principal payments and no interest.[42] REMIC A issues a single class of regular interests (Class A) that is entitled to all of the payments received by REMIC A. Assuming that the issue price of Class A does not exceed 125 percent of its principal amount, can Class A qualify as a regular interest on the ground that interest thereon represents a weighted average of the interest on the qualified mortgages held by REMIC A? Specifically, does the fact that the interest-paying qualified mortgages held by REMIC A have disproportionately high interest prevent those mortgages from being considered to "bear interest at a fixed rate"?

A number of arguments support the view that the disproportionately high interest limitation should be applied only to the Class A interest issued by REMIC A and not separately to each of the underlying qualified mortgages. First, as a technical matter, the REMIC regulations treat the disproportionately high interest test as a separate requirement and not as part of the definition of "fixed" or "variable" rate.[43] Second, the purpose of the fixed or variable rate requirement appears to be to ensure that rates on weighted average rate securities stay within the bounds of the types of rates that have been approved for REMICs. Without the limitation, a regular interest could bear interest at any rate that might be agreed to by a mortgagor and mortgagee (including, for example, one based on mortgagor profits or the price of stock). This purpose would not be frustrated by taking high-coupon qualified mortgages into account. Finally, if the disproportionately high interest test were read into the definition of a fixed or variable rate, it would seem to be necessary to follow the same approach in interpreting the same language in the definition of a specified portion, where the result makes no sense.[44]

---

41   The proposed REMIC regulations allowed qualified mortgages with specified portion interest rates (as well as those with fixed or variable rates) to be taken into account in a weighted average rate calculation. See Proposed Regulation § 1.860G-1(a)(3)(ii) (September 21, 1991) (refers to interest at a rate described in paragraph (a)(2), which is a specified portion rate). The preamble to the final regulations does not explain why the change was made (and indeed does not mention it at all). It could be argued that the change was intended to signal that disproportionately high rate qualified mortgages can never be taken into account in a weighted average rate calculation. The authors understand from the author of the regulation that the reason for the deletion was in fact to avoid the mechanical question of how a weighted average rate is calculated for instruments with only notional principal amounts. This point potentially could be addressed by using notional principal amounts in the calculation as if they were actual principal amounts (both in calculating the average rate and in determining the principal amount of the related regular interest to which the rate is applied).

42   The issue illustrated by the example would be the same if REMIC A held IO Strips and PO Strips that are not created under the REMIC rules and are taken from different mortgages.

43   Treasury Regulation § 1.860G-1(a)(ii)(A) states that qualified mortgages taken into account in a weighted average rate calculation must "bear interest at a fixed rate or at a [variable] rate described in this paragraph (a)(3)." The ban on disproportionately high interest regular interests is found in § 1.860G-1(b)(5).

44   See text at footnote 82 below.

One possible objection to allowing interest-only and principal-only securities to be combined in a weighted average rate regular interest is that such a regular interest would not bear interest at a rate that is tied to any normal measure of interest rates because the actual principal and interest payments would be derived from different underlying mortgages. That bridge has already been crossed, however, since securities with wholly independent principal and interest components clearly can be created using the specified portion rules. Why should securities of this type be any more or less objectionable because they are created under a different set of rules?

(ii) Determination of rate. Once the qualified mortgages to be used in the calculation have been identified, it is necessary to determine the "interest rates" on those mortgages that are to be averaged. An initial question is whether the rate of interest on a mortgage should be based on the designation of payments as interest or principal under the terms of the mortgage, or should instead be based on the tax characterization of the payments. In some cases, payments of stated interest are effectively recharacterized as principal under the OID rules of the Code (technically, they are included in the stated redemption price at maturity).[45] Such a recharacterization should be ignored in calculating the interest rates on qualified mortgages.[46]

If a qualified mortgage provides for prepayment premiums, it is not clear whether those premiums would be considered additional "interest" that could potentially be taken into account in a weighted average rate calculation.[47] Regardless of how this technical question is resolved, however, otherwise qualifying classes of regular interests are not disqualified as regular interests solely because the underlying mortgages provide for prepayment premiums that are passed through to the holders of REMIC interests.[48]

The regulations permit the gross interest on mortgages to be reduced by any servicing spread, credit enhancement fees, or other REMIC expenses.[49] This result

---

45   For example, if a qualified mortgage consists of stripped bonds or stripped coupons (see footnote 33 above), the interest payments on the mortgage often would be included in its stated redemption price at maturity.

46   The conclusion in the text is supported by the fact that stated interest payable on a regular interest may be included in the stated redemption price at maturity of the regular interest without losing its status as an "interest payment" for purposes of the definition of regular interest in section 860G(a)(1)(B). This would occur, for example, if interest payments are deferred. See text at footnote 118 below. Moreover, the purpose of the weighted average rate rule is to allow interest payments received by a REMIC to be passed through as interest payments on regular interests. That purpose is best served by following the designation of payments as interest both on the mortgages and on the regular interests and ignoring the possible recharacterization of those payments under the OID rules.

47   See Chapter 6, footnote 39.

48   See Treasury Regulation § 1.860G-1(b)(2). Prepayment premiums are discussed in Chapter 4, Part C.4.

49   Treasury Regulation § 1.860G-1(a)(3)(ii)(B). The regulations do not state how the REMIC's expenses should be allocated among mortgages in a case where a weighted average rate is based on less than all mortgages. However, any reasonable method that is consistent with the economics of

is sensible since only the net amount would be available to pay interest on regular interests. Gross interest also may be reduced by a number of basis points or a fixed percentage, or a cap or floor may be applied, before the average is computed.[50] The foregoing reductions (and the caps or floors) may vary from mortgage to mortgage. This rule would allow the margins at which adjustable rate loans pay interest above an index to be adjusted to eliminate differences among loans.

(iii) Calculation of average. The next step in calculating a weighted average rate is simply to compute the average. The regulations address the mechanics of the calculation only by stating that "[g]enerally, a weighted average interest rate is a rate that, if applied to the aggregate outstanding principal balance of a pool of mortgage loans for an accrual period, produces an amount of interest that equals the sum of the interest payable on the pooled loans for that accrual period."[51] This standard will be met if the interest rates on qualified mortgages are weighted by their principal amounts (or the amount by which the interest rates on the qualified mortgages are multiplied to compute interest payments, if those amounts differ from the principal amounts).[52] If a qualified mortgage held by a REMIC is a specified portion regular interest in a second REMIC that has no actual principal amount, then interest on that qualified mortgage should be weighted based on the notional principal amount that is used in calculating interest payments thereon.[53]

The effective weight assigned to any qualified mortgage can be reduced arbitrarily by including in the interest rate on the mortgage only a fixed percentage of such interest.[54]

c. Rate Adjustments. Once the steps described in the two preceding sections have been applied to produce a variable or weighted average rate, that rate may be further adjusted by (1) multiplying the rate by a fixed multiplier, and/or (2) adding or subtracting a constant number of basis points.[55] The permitted multiplier is not limited

---

the transaction (i.e., reflects the allocation of net interest among classes of REMIC interests) should be allowed.

50   A cap generally would allow contingent interest on a mortgage to be disregarded in calculating an average rate (assuming that such a mortgage would be eligible to be included to any extent in an average rate calculation). See footnote 40 above and accompanying text. It should be possible to adjust a rate by *both* a fixed amount and a fixed percentage. See footnote 85 below ("or" generally read to mean "and/or"). The effect of percentage increases in the rates on some loans can be achieved by reducing the rates on other loans by fixed percentages and then multiplying the resulting weighted average rate by a multiple greater than one.

51   Treasury Regulation § 1.860G-1(a)(3)(ii)(A). The regulations give an example of a mortgage pool with $300,000 of 7% loans and $700,000 of 9.5% loans, which has a weighted average rate of 8.75% (0.3×7 plus 0.7×9.5).

52   For example, if interest on a mortgage is deferred and compounded, then interest on that mortgage should be weighted based on its principal balance plus deferred interest (even if the deferred interest is not added to principal under the terms of the mortgage).

53   This statement assumes that disproportionately high interest rate regular interests can be taken into account in a weighted average rate calculation. See the text beginning at footnote 41, above.

54   See text accompanying footnote 50, above.

to positive numbers or a number between zero and one. Thus, it is possible to create "super floaters" by multiplying an index by a number greater than one, and "inverse floaters" bearing interest at a rate equal to a constant number of basis points plus a negative multiple of an index.[56]

Combining the two foregoing rate adjustments with caps and floors can produce some unusual securities. For example, a regular interest may be created that effectively oscillates between two rates based on whether an index is above or below a narrow range of values.[57] Also, variable rate interests may be created that have an option flavor, in that they pay interest only if the value of an index exceeds or is less than some positive amount.[58] Although the regulations refer to adjustments based on a "fixed multiplier" and a "constant" number of basis points, adjustments can be varied over the life of a regular interest under the rule described in Part C.3.e allowing combinations of permitted rates.

d. Caps and Floors. A rate determined by applying the steps set forth above may be further adjusted by applying a cap (or floor) that establishes either (1) a maximum (minimum) rate, or (2) a maximum number of basis points by which the rate may increase (decrease) from one accrual or payment period to another or over the term of the interest.[59] It is not entirely clear how the two types of caps or floors are related. One reading would be that the maximum or minimum rate is intended to be an absolute lifetime ceiling or floor, as contrasted with the second type of limit which applies to increases or decreases from one period to another. The periodic cap or floor can limit adjustments "over the term of the instrument," however, and a limit on adjustments over the term of an instrument from an initial value would seem to be the same as a lifetime cap or floor.

The reference to a maximum or minimum "rate" could be read to mean a fixed number. However, the omission of the word "fixed" before "rate" suggests that the term may also include a variable rate. Under this interpretation, a variable rate could be established equal to the higher or lower of two variable rates by establishing one rate as a floor or cap for the other. Prior to adoption of the final REMIC regulations, which, as discussed below, allow a "funds-available" cap, the Service indicated informally that it accepted this reading of the same language in the proposed RE-MIC regulations, at least for the limited purpose of allowing an indexed rate to be

---

55   See Treasury Regulation § 1.860G-1(a)(3)(iii).

56   Cf. Proposed Regulation § 1.1275-5(d) (December 21, 1992), Example 7 (multiple of LIBOR) and Example 8 (inverse LIBOR floater is based on LIBOR under rule that treats a multiple of an index as based on the index).

57   See Part F, Example 4.

58   Id.

59   Treasury Regulations § 1.860G-1(a)(3)(iv). The "(1)" and "(2)" in the text are not found in the regulations. Although not entirely clear, it appears that, as shown in the text, the phrase "by which the rate may increase (decrease) from one accrual or payment period to another or over the term of the interest" modifies only the reference to a maximum or minimum number of basis points, and not the maximum or minimum rate.

subject to a cap equal to a weighted average rate. Such a cap served to limit interest payments to the REMIC's available funds as measured by the rate of interest on the underlying mortgages. An example in the final regulations indicates that a rate equal to the higher or lower of two variable rates can qualify as a combination rate (where the rate in effect in any period depends on which is the higher or lower rate).[60]

A similar question arises as to whether the maximum number of basis points by which a rate may increase or decrease from one period to another may be determined under a formula and not be a fixed amount. For example, a cap or floor might be set limiting the maximum increase or decrease from one period to another to 10% of the rate in effect in the prior period. Although the language is vague, the fact that the regulations do not limit the adjustments to a "fixed" number of basis points suggests that there is some flexibility in using variable periodic caps and floors.

It may be desirable to establish a cap or floor for a period that prevents the yield on the instrument from the issue date through the end of that period (calculated assuming an issue price of 100 percent of the instrument's initial principal amount) from exceeding, or being less than, some amount. Although the language of the regulations could be clearer, such a cap or floor should be allowed, on the ground that the word "rate" encompasses a permitted "fixed rate" for a regular interest which would include interest payments producing such a fixed yield.[61]

There is no requirement that caps and floors be symmetrical.[62] It is possible, therefore, to create a "ratchet bond" that pays interest at a rate that goes up with increases in a rate index but never goes down because the maximum periodic decrease is zero.

The regulations allow a cap to be placed on the number of basis points by which a rate may change "from one accrual or payment period to another or over the term of the interest." If the periods over which changes in rates may be limited can be from one accrual period to the next, or over the entire life of the instrument, it would make little sense not to allow caps on changes measured over periods between these extremes. Two examples of such rates would be (1) a regular interest that pays interest monthly at a rate based on LIBOR, with a cap that allows a maximum increase of 100 basis points in the rate of interest paid in any month during a year over the interest paid in the last month of the preceding year, or (2) a similar instrument where the cap for any month is 100 basis points over the average rate in the preceding 24 calendar months.

---

60   See footnote 71 below.

61   A regular interest that has a fixed interest rate but allows deferrals of interest or prepayments of principal (and hence has uncertain payments but a fixed yield, calculated assuming an issue price equal to its initial principal amount) would clearly be a permitted fixed rate regular interest. See footnote 118 (deferral of interest) and Part E.1 (timing of prepayments) below.

62   The rules for caps and floors are set forth in separate paragraphs in the regulations and, thus, are wholly independent.

If different caps or floors are to be used on a regular interest in different periods, consideration should be given to the possible treatment of the security as one involving a combination of rates. See Part C.3.e.

The REMIC regulations treat a rate as a variable rate if it would so qualify except that it is subject to a "funds-available" cap.[63] As the name suggests, such a cap is a limit on the amount of interest (but not principal) to be paid on an instrument in any accrual or payment period that is based on the total amount available for distribution.[64] However, it does not include a cap used as a "device" to avoid the definition of a variable rate. Whether a cap is used as such a device depends on all facts and circumstances, including (1) whether on the startup day the rate of interest payable to regular interest holders is below the rate payable on the REMIC's qualified mortgages, and (2) whether, historically, the rate of interest payable to the regular interest holders has been consistently below that payable on the qualified mortgages.

The principal function of the funds-available cap rule is to allow a REMIC to shift to regular interest holders "basis risk," which is the risk of nonpayment of interest that results from a mismatch between the rates of interest on REMIC assets and REMIC interests. An example in the regulations indicates that a funds-available cap is permitted (i.e., does not involve a "device") in the case of a REMIC that holds mortgages bearing interest at a spread of 200 basis points over COFI and issues a class of regular interests having the same principal amount as those mortgages and bearing interest (payable only out of available funds) at a rate of 100 basis points over LIBOR, where (1) there is an initial positive spread between the interest rates on the mortgages and regular interests of approximately 250 basis points, (2) the sponsor, based on historical data, does not expect the rate paid on the regular interests to exceed the weighted average rate on the mortgage pool, and (3) the positive spread is used to pay down regular interests (thereby decreasing the outstanding regular interests by comparison with the pool size).[65] A second example illustrates the use of a device. In the example, a REMIC holds commercial mortgages paying contingent interest based on the gross profits of the mortgagors. The REMIC issues regular interests bearing interest at a LIBOR-based rate, payable out of available funds, that initially exceeds the weighted average rate of interest on the mortgages. Also, based on historical data, there is a significant possibility that the LIBOR-based rate will exceed such weighted average rate in the future. The cap is

---

63   See Treasury Regulation § 1.860G-1(a)(3)(v).

64   The regulations describe a funds-available cap as one that limits interest based on total amounts "available for distribution, including both principal and interest received by an issuing entity on some or all of its qualified mortgages as well as amounts held in a reserve fund." Although this language might be read to require that reserves be depleted to make funds "available" to meet an interest payment, most likely the regulations are simply listing possible sources of available funds. Whether funds are "available" is an issue that should be left to the parties, subject to the "device" test described below in the text.

65   Treasury Regulation § 1.860G-1(a)(3)(v)(C), Example 1. Although the use of spread to pay down regular interests is a helpful factor, the example should not be read to require this feature in all cases. The device test is based on all facts and circumstances.

considered a device to create a regular interest with an impermissible rate based on the contingent interest received on the mortgages.[66]

Shortfalls arising from a difference between the interest rate on qualified mortgages and the rate on the regular interests can of course arise from factors other than basis risk (as we have used the term).[67] For a general discussion of contingencies affecting interest payments, see Part D.2 below.

The funds-available cap rule is limited to variable rate regular interests. Thus, it would not literally apply to a regular interest bearing interest at a single fixed rate.[68] In any event, a fixed-rate regular interest could potentially be allocated some degree of basis risk under the general rule allowing remote contingencies to be ignored in testing whether an interest qualifies as a regular interest.[69]

e. Combinations of Rates. Once the preceding steps have been applied to create a variable rate, that rate may be combined with other rates. Specifically, the regulations treat as a variable rate a rate based on (1) one fixed rate, or variable rate, during one or more accrual or payment periods and (2) other fixed or variable rates during other accrual or payment periods.[70] This rule does not allow a specified portion rate to be combined with other rates. One simple example of a combination rate is a rate that is fixed for five years, and at the end of year five, becomes a LIBOR-based rate. Another example is interest at a fixed multiple of LIBOR where the multiple changes according to a fixed schedule from one year to the next.

The REMIC regulations do not state clearly whether the fixed or variable rate that will apply in each future period must be fixed on the startup day or may instead be determined some time thereafter based on a formula or some other test. In at least some circumstances, however, a formula is allowed. An example in the regulations treats as a combination rate interest payable on a REMIC regular interest at a rate based on LIBOR, subject to a lifetime cap equal to the weighted average rate of interest on the REMIC's qualified mortgages (where the mortgages bear interest at fixed rates). The theory appears to be that the rate shifts between two variable rates (the LIBOR-based rate and weighted average rate) depending on which is the greater in a particular period.[71] Similarly, an interest rate on a regular interest that

---

66 Treasury Regulation § 1.860G-1(a)(3)(v)(C), Example 2.

67 A shortfall could arise, for example, where a REMIC has two pools of mortgages, one with fixed rate mortgages supporting a class of subordinate fixed rate regular interests and another with floating rate mortgages supporting an indexed based (or weighted average rate) senior variable rate class. If the allocation of losses requires a write down of the principal amount of the fixed rate class in the event of a loss on the floating rate collateral, then a shortfall could arise from the fact that the variable rate regular interests are supported, in part, by fixed rate collateral. Because that type of shortfall is an incident of the allocation of default losses, it is permitted under Treasury Regulation § 1.806G-1(b)(3)(ii).

68 Technically, a regular interest that pays interest at different fixed rates in different accrual periods is a variable rate (see text accompanying footnote 70, below), so that the funds-available cap rule would potentially apply to regular interests of this type.

69 See Part D.

70 Treasury Regulation § 1.860G-1(a)(3)(vi).

changes from one fixed or variable rate to another when the outstanding principal balance of the regular interest (or the related mortgage pool) is reduced to a specific number should be permitted.[72] In the world of mortgage-backed securities, time is often measured by outstanding principal balances. Other arrangements involving rates determined based on events occurring after the startup day should be approached with caution.[73]

4. Specified Portions

Under section 860G(a)(1)(B)(ii), a regular interest may provide for interest payments consisting of a specified portion of the interest payments on qualified mortgages if such portion does not vary during the period such interest is outstanding. Each of the three elements of the definition (specified portion, interest payments, and no variation) is considered in more detail below. As indicated in Part C.1 above, a specified portion regular interest can bear interest at a rate that is "disproportionately high" when compared to its principal amount. Indeed, the principal amount may be zero.[74] The effective rate of interest (interest divided by principal) is irrelevant in determining whether the instrument meets the definition of a regular interest.

a. Definition of Specified Portion. Under the REMIC regulations, interest is considered to represent a "specified portion" of the interest payments on one or more qualified mortgages only if the portion can be expressed as

- a fixed number of basis points of the interest payable on some or all of the qualified mortgages
- a fixed percentage of the interest that is payable, at either a fixed rate or a variable rate, on some or all of the qualified mortgages, or
- interest payable at a fixed rate or a variable rate on some or all of the qualified mortgages in excess of a fixed number of basis points or a variable rate.

The discussion of this three-part definition considers first the requirement, in the last two parts of the definition, that interest on qualified mortgages be payable at a fixed or variable rate, and then other topics.

---

71 Treasury Regulation § 1.860G-1(a)(2)(v), Example 1(ii) (describes rate on Class A as a "variable rate described in paragraph (a)(3)(vi)" which is a combination rate).

72 For an example, see footnote 38, above.

73 One concern with allowing rates to be selected after the startup day is that such a rate-setting mechanism would potentially allow interest rates to be based on factors wholly unrelated to interest on conventional debt. To take one extreme example, interest on a regular interest that is set at the beginning of each accrual period at a fixed amount based on the current value of General Motors stock arguably could be characterized as a series of fixed rates.

74 Treasury Regulation § 1.860G-1(a)(2)(iv). A specified portion regular interest can, of course, have a specified principal amount of zero and still have a *notional* principal amount that is used solely in measuring interest payments.

(i) Fixed or variable rate. The language in the second and third parts of the definition referring to interest payable at a fixed or variable rate is ambiguous. One narrow reading is that it requires *all* interest on a qualified mortgage to be taken into account in a specified portion (so that, for example, the reference to a fixed percentage of interest payable means a fixed percentage of all interest), and limits the qualified mortgages from which a specified portion of interest may be taken to mortgages that bear interest at a fixed or variable rate. An alternative, less restrictive, interpretation of the language is that it allows a specified portion of interest to be carved out of the interest on any mortgage, if the interest payments that are taken into account are first adjusted by limiting them to interest at a fixed or variable rate.[75] Phrased differently, under this view, if interest on a mortgage that is taken into account in the specified portion meets the fixed or variable rate requirement, the nature of any remaining interest on the mortgage is irrelevant.

To illustrate the difference between the two approaches, suppose that a REMIC holds a mortgage that pays interest at the prime rate of a reference bank and also has an equity kicker. The REMIC issues a class of interests that pays interest equal to 50 percent of all interest on the mortgage exclusive of the equity kicker. Such a right to interest payments can be expressed as a fixed percentage of a variable rate, but it is not a fixed percentage of interest on a variable rate mortgage.

To illustrate another case in which the issue may arise, consider a REMIC that holds a mortgage bearing interest at a rate equal to the prime rate of a bank. The REMIC issues two classes of interests, A and B. Class A pays interest equal to all interest on the mortgage in excess of LIBOR. Interest on Class B equals LIBOR times the principal amount of the mortgage, capped by all interest payable on the mortgage. Interest on Class A would qualify as a specified portion under either interpretation. Class B clearly would be a specified portion regular interest under the less restrictive approach. Although it should also be possible to reach the same conclusion under the more restrictive interpretation, opinions may differ on this point.[76]

---

75   Such a rule was requested in comments on the proposed REMIC regulations. See New York State Bar Association, Tax Section, "Report on the Proposed Real Estate Mortgage Investment Conduit Regulations" (March 19, 1992), at 53. The preamble to the final regulations includes the following description of the third part of the definition of specified portion: "The final regulations expand the definition of 'specified portion' to include a portion that can be expressed as the interest payable on some or all of the qualified mortgages in excess of a fixed number of basis points or in excess of a variable rate." While this statement arguably supports the narrower reading of the regulations, it does not address the point expressly, and may simply describe the types of strips that are most likely to be created under the expanded definition. That the drafters were not focused on this point is evidenced by the fact that the preamble makes no mention of the requirement that a specified portion be taken from interest at a fixed or variable rate, even though that requirement was added only in the final regulations. The proposed regulations allowed a fixed percentage of interest payments on a qualified mortgage to be a specified portion without regard to the nature of those payments. See Proposed Regulation § 1.860G-1(a)(2)(ii) (September 21, 1991).

76   Class B represents the excess of (1) all interest on the mortgage over (2) the excess of the prime rate over LIBOR. That excess, as such, is not a variable rate. The excess of one rate over another rate can qualify, however, as a weighted average rate, as illustrated in Part F, Example 26. On that basis, the excess of the prime rate over LIBOR should be considered a type of variable rate. This

While the language of the regulations could be clearer, the authors believe that the better interpretation is the less restrictive one, so that a rate may be first adjusted to equal a fixed or variable rate. A number of reasons support this view:

- If it were intended that specified portion interests (other than those representing a fixed number of basis points) could only be carved out of mortgages with a fixed or variable rate, it would have been a simple matter to say so directly. Compare the language in the regulations relating to weighted average rates.[77]

- The preamble to the final REMIC regulations clearly contemplates that contingent payment mortgages can be contributed to a REMIC, with the contingent payment features being allocated to the residual interest.[78] It would be natural, then, to allow noncontingent interest payments to be stripped off from other rights to interest (which would be possible under the specified portion rules if a rate can first be adjusted to equal a fixed or variable rate).[79]

- The policy reason for limiting specified portions to rates that are based on fixed or variable rates is presumably to ensure that the rates on regular interests stay within the family of permitted rates. This policy would not be frustrated by adopting the less restrictive construction of the regulations.

- It would be odd for the regulations to operate in such a manner that interest payments on a fixed or variable rate mortgage may be divided into two portions, one of which is a specified portion and the other of which is not. This may be the result under the more restrictive reading of the regulations.[80]

- The first part of the definition of specified portion allows a portion equal to a fixed number of basis points, without regard to the nature of the remaining interest paid on the mortgage. This approach is consistent with the less restrictive interpretation of the regulations in that it tests whether a right to interest is a specified portion by looking only at the four corners of the interest being created.

---

argument would be particularly persuasive if a class of regular interests bearing interest at such a rate were being created as a variable rate class in the transaction in which Classes A and B are issued.

77   See Treasury Regulation § 1.860G-1(a)(3)(ii): "A rate based on a weighted average of the interest rates on some or all of the qualified mortgages held by a REMIC is a variable rate. The qualified mortgages taken into account must, however, bear interest at a fixed rate or at a rate described in this paragraph (a)(3) [a variable rate]." Even this language is not as restrictive as it appears because interest on a mortgage can be reduced through various adjustments before an average rate is calculated. See the text accompanying footnotes 49–50, above.

78   See footnote 40 above.

79   Although it should be possible to use a weighted average rate to carve out the noncontingent payments on a pool of loans, the regulations do not address the point expressly. See footnote 40 above.

80   See footnote 76, above, and accompanying text.

Another question raised by the language requiring a specified portion to be taken from interest at a fixed or variable rate is whether a qualified mortgage can meet the test if interest on the mortgage is disproportionately high.[81] Although not certain, the fact that a qualified mortgage has disproportionately high interest should not prevent it from being considered to bear interest at a fixed or variable rate for this purpose.[82] The reasons for reaching this conclusion given above in the discussion of weighted average rates are equally applicable here.[83] In addition, it would be bizarre to introduce a disproportionately high interest test into the definition of a specified portion rate since one of the key features of such a rate is that it can be disproportionately high.[84] Lastly, because the first part of the specified portion definition refers to a "fixed number of basis points" of interest, and not to interest at a "fixed rate," there is no apparent basis for applying a disproportionately high interest test to specified portion interests of this type. What would be the policy reason for applying the disproportionately high interest limitation differently to the three parts of the definition of specified portion?

(ii) Other topics. A few other aspects of the definition of specified portion are worth noting.

The specified portion test is applied separately to each qualified mortgage from which any interest payments are taken, and the formula used in calculating the relevant portion need not be the same for all mortgages. For example, it is possible to combine in a single regular interest a fixed number of basis points of interest from some qualified mortgages and a fixed percentage (or a different number of basis points) from others.[85] On the other hand, it does not seem to be possible to

---

81 Disproportionately high interest is discussed in Part C.1 above.

82 Thus, it should be possible in a two-tier REMIC structure for the upper-tier REMIC to issue regular interests that pay interest representing a specified portion of the interest payments on specified portion regular interests issued by the lower-tier REMIC, provided the interest on those lower-tier regular interests can be expressed as a fixed rate or variable rate when applied to its actual or notional principal amount.

83 See the text at footnote 43, above.

84 See Part C.1 above.

85 Treasury Regulation § 1.860G-1(a)(2)(i) allows a specified portion that can be expressed as a fixed percentage of the interest on some or all of the qualified mortgages, a fixed number of basis points of interest on some or all of the qualified mortgages, or the excess of interest on some or all of the qualified mortgages over interest at a fixed or variable rate. In order to allow combinations of two or three of the three types of specified portions in a single regular interest (e.g., to take a fixed percentage of interest on a variable rate mortgage held by a REMIC and a fixed number of basis points from a different variable rate mortgage held by the REMIC), it is necessary only to read the word "or" to mean "and/or" which is the way it is normally used in the tax law. Cf. Treasury Regulation § 1.368-2(h). The ability to use different formulae with respect to different mortgages (e.g., to take 50% of the interest from one variable rate mortgage and 80% from another) is indicated by Treasury Regulation § 1.860G-1(a)(2)(v), Example 3, which treats as a specified portion all interest payable in excess of 7% on a pool of fixed rate mortgages bearing interest ranging from 8% to 10%. The example states that the interest strip represents a specified portion of interest because the interest payable can be expressed as a fixed percentage of the interest payable on each particular mortgage. Although the same result could be achieved by defining the specified portion as all interest in excess of 7%, that is not the way the example is written.

combine elements of the three parts of the definition of specified portion in calculating a share of interest on a single qualified mortgage. For example, it may not be possible to rely on a combination approach to take 50 percent of the excess of interest payable at a fixed or variable rate on a qualified mortgage above interest at a second variable rate.[86]

To illustrate a simple specified portion regular interest, suppose that a REMIC holds 10 mortgages that bear interest at fixed rates ranging from 8 percent to 10 percent. The REMIC could issue a class of regular interests representing the right to all interest above 8 percent. The interest payable on that regular interest would represent a fixed number of basis points of the interest on each mortgage (and also would be a fixed percentage of the interest and the excess of all interest above a fixed number). Similarly, if the mortgage pool contained adjustable rate mortgages having margins ranging from 200 to 275 basis points above some index, the specified portion could equal a fixed number of basis points with respect to each mortgage representing the excess of the margin above 200 basis points.

The rule treating as a specified portion the excess of interest on qualified mortgages above interest at a fixed or variable rate permits a wide range of different types of regular interests to be created.[87] As illustrated in Part F, these include interest payments that are similar to an interest rate cap (representing the excess of a variable rate of interest over a fixed rate)[88] and payments representing all interest payable on a pool of mortgages over floating interest based on an index (technically, the excess of all interest over interest at a variable rate).[89]

The ability to select different specified portions of interest with respect to different qualified mortgages allows the creation of classes of regular interests that represent an aggregation of strips taken off of different qualified mortgages (generally, regular interests in a lower-tier REMIC created as part of a double-tier REMIC). In some cases, the principal component of such interests is structured so that the interest rate thereon can be expressed as a (high) fixed rate, although this is not required by the specified portion rules.

---

86   The same practical effect could potentially be achieved, however, by treating as the relevant qualified mortgage only a pro rata portion of a loan. See text accompanying footnote 36, above. Further, if the regulations are interpreted to allow the rate on a qualified mortgage to be adjusted to equal a fixed or variable rate before a specified portion is taken (as discussed in the immediately preceding section), then this result could be achieved simply by including in the relevant rates only the desired percentage of a fixed or variable rate (because a fixed percentage of a fixed or variable rate is itself a fixed or variable rate). For example, if a mortgage bears interest at the prime rate, a portion of such interest equal to half the prime rate over half of LIBOR would represent the difference between two variable rates. This result can also be achieved using two tiers of REMICs. See Part F, Example 22.

87   This rule was added only in the final REMIC regulations. The preamble to the proposed REMIC regulations stated that interest-only strips representing a right to variable interest in excess of a fixed amount resemble options and might not appropriately be taxed as debt. Obviously, doubts on this score were resolved.

88   See Part F, Example 11.

89   See Part F, Example 10.

b. Interest Payments. In order to apply the specified portion rules, it is necessary to determine the "interest payable" on a qualified mortgage.[90] It would be consistent with the overall definition of regular interest to treat as "interest payable" amounts that are denominated as interest even if they are included in the stated redemption price at maturity of a mortgage under the OID rules of the Code.[91] In any event, in a two-tier REMIC structure, where an upper-tier REMIC holds regular interests issued by a lower-tier REMIC (which are treated as qualified mortgages in the hands of the upper-tier REMIC), amounts that are treated as "interest payments" on those regular interests for purposes of the definition of regular interest must be considered "interest payments" on a qualified mortgage in testing whether regular interests issued by the upper-tier REMIC meet the specified portion test. Any other result would require inconsistent readings of the phrase "interest payments" in two places in the same sentence in the statutory definition of regular interest.

A qualified mortgage may provide for some interest that is paid currently and some interest that is deferred. For example, interest payments on a residential mortgage could be graduated, resulting in some negative amortization of principal in early years. Also, a REMIC regular interest that is a qualified mortgage in the hands of another REMIC could bear interest at a fixed rate (for example 8 percent) and provide that two percentage points of the interest is paid currently and the rest is deferred. Before issuance of the REMIC regulations, a question arose as to whether it was possible to create a specified portion regular interest that is entitled to a fixed number of basis points of the interest payable currently on such a qualified mortgage. The concern was that although such a strip of interest represents a fixed fraction of the interest that accrues in each period, it would not be a fixed fraction of the interest paid (or payable), at least if the interest that accrues in one period and is paid in a later period is treated as an interest payment when paid.[92] The REMIC regulations treat a fixed number of basis points of interest payable as a specified portion whether or not it represents a fixed percentage of the interest payable. Thus, under the regulations, interest strips of this type are clearly allowed.[93]

---

90 Section 860G(a)(1)(B)(ii) refers to "interest payments" whereas the regulations use the term "interest payable". It is not clear why the regulations depart from the statute. In any event, in the absence of defaults, the amounts paid would correspond to amounts payable, and default contingencies are generally ignored. See footnotes 98 and 99 below.

91 See footnote 46 above.

92 Although deferred interest on a debt instrument is included in its stated redemption price at maturity, and therefore effectively loses its character as interest under the OID rules of the Code, it may nonetheless retain its character as an interest payment for purposes of applying the definition of regular interest. See text following footnote 119 below.

93 Cf. P.L.R. 9148040 (August 29, 1991), which treated as a specified portion of the interest payable on a qualified mortgage a right to one percentage of the interest currently payable on the mortgage and a different percentage of the interest that accrued on the mortgage but was deferred. The ruling states that this right to interest can be expressed as a fixed percentage of the total interest payable on the qualified mortgage in every period. In reaching this result, the ruling seems to equate interest accruing in a period with interest payable in the period. This reasoning, if correct, would allow a specified portion rate equal to a fixed portion of the interest accruing on a negative amortizaton mortgage, even where the specified portion cannot be expressed as a fixed number of

c. Specified Portions Cannot Vary. The specified portion must be established as of the startup day and cannot vary over the period that begins on the startup day and ends on the day that the holder of the regular interest is no longer entitled to receive payments.[94] The no variation requirement applies to the *portion* of interest paid on a qualified mortgage and not to the amount. Thus, decreases in interest payments on a regular interest that are attributable to reductions in the principal balance of qualified mortgages (and not to changes in the portion of the interest on those mortgages allocated to the regular interest) are clearly permitted. Similarly, changes in amounts that merely reflect adjustable rate features of the qualified mortgages from which the specified portion is taken are permissible. Because the no variation requirement is tied to the life of the regular interest and not of the qualified mortgages, a specified portion regular interest can have a life shorter than the life of the related qualified mortgages.[95]

The no variation rule is less significant than it appears, for two reasons. First, as discussed above, a specified portion of interest includes interest on a qualified mortgage in excess of interest at a variable rate. Because a variable rate includes a combination rate that steps up or down over time, a specified portion rate can be created that steps down or up, respectively, with changes in the combination rate. For example, if a REMIC holds an 8 percent qualified mortgage, a right to no interest for some period and 6 percent thereafter can be described as the excess of 100 percent of the interest on the qualified mortgage over a variable rate that is 8 percent for some period and 2 percent thereafter.[96]

Second, flexibility in creating the economic equivalent of varying specified portions can be gained through the use of two tiers of REMICs. In this structure, one or more fixed or variable rate classes of regular interests are issued by the lower-tier REMIC (at an issue price not exceeding 125 percent of their principal amount) with the desired pattern of interest payments. The interest payments on those lower-tier regular interests are then "stripped" by creating a class of upper-tier regular interests that is entitled to a fixed percentage (or other specified portion) of the interest on the lower-tier regular interests. Although the amount of interest paid on the upper-tier class may change to reflect changes in the interest paid on the underlying qualified mortgages (the lower-tier regular interests), such changes would not stem from any variation in the portion of interest on the qualified mortgages that is allocated to the upper-tier regular interest.[97]

The regulations state that a specified portion will not be considered to vary over time because an interest holder's entitlement to a portion of interest on some or all of the qualified mortgages depends on the absence of defaults or delinquencies on those mortgages.[98] This rule does not seem to add much, if anything, to the general

---

basis points of interest.

94   Treasury Regulation § 1.860G-1(a)(2)(ii).

95   Thus, a class of specified portion regular interests that has a small principal balance may be retired at any time by allocating principal payments preferentially to that class.

96   See Part F, Example 13.

97   For examples applying the specified portion rules to two-tier REMICs, see Part F.2.a.

rule in the regulations allowing default contingencies to be disregarded in evaluating regular interests.[99]

5. Comparison of Specified Portion and Weighted Average Rates

Weighted average and specified portion rates are both based on the interest paid on a designated pool of qualified mortgages. As a result, there is considerable overlap between the two types of rates. At the same time, there are also material differences, so that it may be desirable or necessary in some circumstances to rely on one rule rather than the other. Each of the two types of rates has been discussed in detail above. For convenience, the major differences are summarized here (the first two represent advantages of a specified portion rate; the last three are advantages of a weighted average rate):

- Only a specified portion regular interest can pay interest at a disproportionately high rate.

- A specified portion can represent the excess of interest on a mortgage over interest calculated at a fixed or variable rate. Interest taken into account in a weighted average rate calculation cannot be adjusted by subtracting out a variable rate.

- A weighted average rate (or more precisely, combinations of different weighted average rates) can represent a varying portion of the interest on the related mortgages over the life of a regular interest. A specified portion cannot.[100]

- A weighted average rate is based on the rates of interest on a reference pool of mortgages, but there is no requirement that the *amounts* of interest payments correspond. A specified portion of interest must represent a portion of the amount of mortgage interest payments.

- Once a weighted average rate is computed, it can be further adjusted by applying a cap or floor, multiplying by a factor or adding or subtracting a fixed number. A specified portion rate cannot be so adjusted.

D. Contingencies

Suppose that a REMIC regular interest provides for a schedule of interest and principal payments that, if taken at face value, meets the regular interest definition, but for some reason there is a risk that payments will not be made when scheduled (or at all). How are contingencies of this type taken into account in evaluating a regular interest?

---

98   See Treasury Regulation §§ 1.860G-1(a)(2)(iii), and -1(a)(2)(v), Example 1.

99   See Treasury Regulation § 1.860G-1(b)(3)(ii), discussed in footnotes 109 and 111 below.

100 See, however, the text following footnote 95 above.

As a first step, a distinction needs to be drawn between contingencies that are remote and those that are not. Under the REMIC regulations, an interest will not fail to qualify as a regular interest solely because of a contingency affecting the timing or amount of payments if there is only a remote likelihood that the contingency will occur.[101] Thus, the contingencies that are potentially troublesome (and receive further consideration here) are those that are at least somewhat likely to occur.

It should be noted that payment contingencies affecting REMIC regular interests generally do not result from events that represent "defaults" under the governing instrument for the REMIC. Most often, REMIC regular interests take the form of certificates of beneficial interest in a trust. Those certificates typically entitle holders to payments only to the extent of available funds. Thus, a failure to make scheduled payments that is not attributable to an unexcused failure by the REMIC or a servicer to collect and pass-through funds would not typically be a default.[102]

We consider first contingencies affecting principal and then those affecting interest payments.

1. Contingencies Affecting Principal

As indicated in Part A above, the Code defines a regular interest as an interest that "unconditionally entitles the holder to receive a specified principal amount." No rationale for this requirement is given in the legislative history of the REMIC rules. Presumably, its purpose was to ensure that regular interests have the economic features of conventional debt.[103] The functional resemblance to debt is important because regular interests are taxed as debt but need not take the form of debt for nontax purposes. At any rate, the requirement was clearly not intended to prevent instruments that are subject to the same contingencies as pass-through certificates from qualifying as regular interests.[104]

Section 860G(a)(1)(A) requires only that a holder of a regular interest be unconditionally "entitled" to principal, not that the principal in fact be paid. The

---

101   Treasury Regulation § 1.860G-1(b)(3)(vi). Although the heading to this paragraph is "Remote and Incidental Contingencies," the text does not require a contingency to be "incidental," only remote. The sole example given of a remote contingency is a failure to receive mortgage payments due to the Soldiers and Sailors Civil Relief Act (which reduces interest payments for active servicemen). Presumably, it can be inferred from this that the Treasury is not anticipating the outbreak of war (or at least one affecting significant numbers of mortgagors).

102   Similarly, if a regular interest took the form of stock of a corporation or a partnership interest, a failure to make scheduled payments would not ordinarily result in a default. It may be hoped that the risk of nonpayment because of fraud, or other material failure of a mortgage servicer or trustee to act in accordance with the REMIC's governing documents, would be disregarded under the rule for remote contingencies discussed above in the text. For a discussion of the effect on regular interests of default-related modifications, see Part E.3 below.

103   The presence of a substantial principal component can no longer be said to be an essential feature of debt, however, given that strips of interest payments are taxed as debt instruments. See the discussion of the disproportionately high interest test in Part C.1 above.

104   In contrast with a conventional debt instrument, the failure of a trust to make scheduled distributions on a pass-through certificate would not typically result in a contractual default by the trust. See the text at footnote 102 above.

entitlement language suggests that, at a minimum, a failure to pay resulting from contractual defaults will not affect the status of an interest as a regular interest, because the holder would have a legal right (be entitled) to be paid. The most obvious type of contractual default affecting a REMIC is a payment default by mortgagors with respect to the qualified mortgages the REMIC holds.

Perhaps out of an excess of caution, the Code states that an interest will not fail to meet the requirement of an unconditional principal amount merely because the timing (but not the amount) of the principal payments may be contingent on prepayments of qualified mortgages and the amount of income from permitted investments.[105]

The REMIC regulations implement the "unconditional entitlement" requirement by providing that the principal amount, and latest possible maturity date, of a regular interest must not be contingent, except for certain contingencies listed in the regulations.[106] The word "contingent" is not defined. Under the regulations,[107] a regular interest will not fail to qualify as a regular interest solely because the amount and timing[108] of principal payments are contingent on the absence of

- defaults or delinquencies on qualified mortgages or permitted investments[109]
- lower than reasonably expected returns on permitted investments, or
- unanticipated expenses incurred by the REMIC.[110]

Moreover, a class of regular interests can bear all or a disproportionate share of the losses attributable to these contingencies before they are borne by another class of regular interests or the residual interest (or, stated differently, can be subordinated to those other classes of REMIC interests with respect to these losses).[111]

---

105 Section 860G(a)(1), last sentence. The timing of principal payments on a regular interest is discussed further in Part E.1 below.

106 Treasury Regulation § 1.860G-1(a)(5).

107 Treasury Regulation § 1.860G-1(b)(3). In addition to the permitted contingencies listed in the text, this regulation repeats the rule relating to the timing of principal payments described in the preceding paragraph in the text.

108 Although the regulations specifically sanction certain timing contingencies affecting principal, there is no general rule suggesting that timing contingencies otherwise are not allowed. See Part E.1 below.

109 Treasury Regulation § 1.860G-1(b)(3)(ii) refers only to defaults, but it is inconceivable that defaults would be covered and not delinquencies. Compare the language in Treasury Regulation § 1.860G-1(b)(3)(iii) (refers to defaults and delinquencies) and Chapter 4, footnote 126 (statutory rule allowing reserve funds to cover mortgage defaults construed to cover delinquencies). A principal payment that is funded out of mortgage interest and will not be paid if mortgages prepay according to their terms would not be "unconditional." On the other hand, if a mortgage is not subject to prepayment so that a future interest payment would be required in the absence of a mortgagor default, then under the default rule, it should be possible to use the interest payment to support a principal payment on a REMIC regular interest.

110 Treasury Regulation § 1.860G-1(b)(3)(ii).

111 Treasury Regulation § 1.860G-1(b)(3)(iii). The legislative history of TRA 1986 states that a regular interest will not fail to be a regular interest because it is subordinated to other regular interests in the event of defaults or delinquencies on the underlying mortgages. Conference Report at II-228; Blue Book at 415. Because the legislative history did not refer to the subordination of

The requirement that regular interest holders be unconditionally entitled to principal could prevent a REMIC from having a term that requires the REMIC to liquidate at a time when it holds mortgages or other noncash assets, unless the REMIC has a contractual right to sell its assets at that time at a predetermined price sufficient to pay the principal balance of the regular interests plus accrued and unpaid interest thereon.[112] It could be argued that regular interests should be considered to receive their full entitlement to principal if they receive in liquidation an amount equal to the fair market value the regular interests would have if the REMIC were not liquidated. Placing reliance on this theory would seem to be quite risky.[113]

On the other hand, suppose that a REMIC is formed that does not have a scheduled early termination date, but all of the holders of REMIC interests agree to liquidate the REMIC prematurely. Even if the value of the REMIC's qualified mortgages is not sufficient to permit liquidating distributions on the regular interests equal to their full principal amounts, the early liquidation should not disqualify the REMIC. The regular interest holders were unconditionally entitled to receive the principal amount of their regular interests, but elected to take another amount in satisfaction of their claim.[114]

Similarly, a regular interest should not be disqualified because a REMIC uses cash that would otherwise be used to make distributions on REMIC interests to repurchase that regular interest at a negotiated price that is less than its face amount. A regular interest holder that sold its interest would be choosing voluntarily to forego its right to receive eventually the full principal amount of the regular interest.[115]

---

regular interests to residual interests, it was argued by some that "senior residuals" were not allowed. This issue was put to rest by the REMIC regulations.

112   Contracts to buy qualified mortgages in connection with a qualified liquidation of a REMIC are discussed in Chapter 4, in the text accompanying footnote 29. If a REMIC has a contract to sell its qualified mortgages upon liquidation at a price sufficient to make a full distribution on regular interests, then the possibility that the REMIC would not make such a distribution because of a default by the other party to the contract should not cause interests in the REMIC to fail to be regular interests. It would not require much strain to assimilate a default under such a contract to a default on the related mortgages for purposes of applying the rules on contingencies in the regulations. Cf. Treasury Regulation § 1.860G-2(g)(1)(ii)(B) (proceeds from the disposition of qualified mortgages are treated as payments received on qualified mortgages for purposes of the definition of cash flow investment). Moreover, as suggested above (text following footnote 104), a regular interest holder should be considered to be "entitled" to a payment that would be made in the absence of a contractual default.

113   It could also be argued that a failure to abide by the definition of regular interest only in connection with the liquidation of a REMIC should not affect the qualification of the REMIC. However, if a purported regular interest is subject to a contingency that prevents it from being unconditionally entitled to principal, that defect should prevent the REMIC interests test from being met as of the startup day.

114   As discussed in Part E.3 below, a modification of a regular interest could result in a violation of the REMIC interests test if the modified interest remains outstanding. However, a modification that effects the full retirement of a regular interest should not raise this issue. Also, a partial retirement that leaves unchanged the unpaid portion of an instrument would generally not be considered a modification. See Proposed Regulation § 1.1001-3(e)(2)(iii).

115   For further discussion of such a repurchase, see Chapter 7, text accompanying footnote 37. In

2. Contingencies Affecting Interest

The statutory definition of a regular interest does not require that holders be "unconditionally entitled" to receive interest. Following the lead of the statute, there is no statement in the REMIC regulations, similar to the one applicable to principal described above, prohibiting interest payments from being subject to contingencies. On the other hand, interest payments must be based on a fixed rate, be variable as provided in regulations, or consist of a specified portion of the interest on qualified mortgages. Contingencies affecting interest payments could be taken into account in determining whether interest falls into one of these categories.

Presumably to address this concern, the regulations include a list of contingencies affecting interest that will not disqualify a regular interest.[116] The list includes the approved contingencies affecting principal discussed in the preceding section. It also covers mortgage prepayments and deferrals of interest. The regulations state that an interest does not fail to be a regular interest solely because the amount of interest payments is affected by prepayments of the underlying mortgages,[117] or solely because the terms of that interest provide for the deferral of interest payments (apparently for any reason).[118] Prepayments of high-coupon regular interests can cause a significant economic loss, which may explain why the point is covered. Although deferred interest is often compounded, the regulations do not require compounding. Even without the regulation, the ability to defer interest on a regular interest is strongly implied by the reference in section 860G(a)(1)(B) to "interest payments . . . at or before maturity." Regular interest classes that provide for deferred interest payments—thereby extending the life of that class and permitting a more rapid pay down of other classes—are commonplace.[119]

Interest that is deferred is often compounded and added to principal under the terms of a regular interest. Nonetheless, it appears that deferred interest retains its character as interest for purposes of the regular interest definition. This result is necessary because of the requirement that a regular interest unconditionally entitle a holder to a specified principal amount. If accrued but unpaid interest were treated as "principal" and the timing of payments on the regular interest (and, thus, the amount of accrued interest) were dependent on the timing of mortgage prepayments (as is invariably true to some degree), then an interest deferral class would have a varying

---

evaluating such a repurchase under the REMIC rules, consideration would also need to be given to the sources of cash used by the REMIC to effect the repurchase (e.g., whether it requires a sale of mortgages) and to the effect of the repurchase on other classes of REMIC interests.

116   Treasury Regulation § 1.860G-1(b)(3).

117   Treasury Regulation § 1.860G-1(b)(3)(v). This section is entitled "prepayment interest shortfalls" but it extends to all types of prepayments and not just those in the middle of an interest accrual period. Prepayment interest shortfalls are discussed in Chapter 4, Part C.5.

118   Treasury Regulation § 1.860G-1(b)(3)(iv). The rule is not limited by its terms to regular interests that bear interest at a fixed or variable rate. Thus, although perhaps odd, it appears that interest could be deferred on a specified portion regular interest even if the mortgage interest from which the specified portion is taken is paid currently.

119   Compound interest classes are described further in Chapter 2, Part C.

principal amount. Although a varying principal amount could be squared with the statute by reading the word "specified" to mean "determined by a fixed formula" or "minimum" rather than "fixed," it seems easier simply to conclude that deferred interest remains interest for this purpose.

The list of permitted contingencies affecting interest payments does not include "basis risk" (the possibility of shortfalls attributable to a difference between rates of interest on qualified mortgages and regular interests). Such a risk can potentially be taken into account, however, in defining a variable rate.[120]

E. Special Topics

This Part E comments on a number of special topics pertaining to regular interests: the timing of principal payments, non-pro rata payments, modifications, stripping of interest payments, stapling of regular interests, registration under the so-called TEFRA rules, and foreign currency denominated interests.

1. Timing of Principal Payments

A regular interest must be unconditionally entitled to receive a specified amount of principal. There are no restrictions on the timing of principal payments, however, or, more precisely, on the way in which principal distributions may be allocated among classes of regular interests, or between regular interests and residual interests.[121] For example, principal can be allocated among classes in sequence (with all principal distributions being made on one class until it is retired, then on another class until it is retired, and so on) to create fast-pay and slow-pay classes; preferentially to a "stabilized" class until principal distributions reach a scheduled amount, with the balance going to "support" classes; or based on an interest index or some other formula. If principal is allocated between classes based on a formula, allocations may shift back and forth from period to period depending on current values of the formula (these classes are sometimes known as "jump classes"), or the allocation may be shifted permanently if at any time the formula achieves a threshold value (sometimes, "sticky jump" classes).[122]

---

120   See the text at footnotes 60, 63, and 71 above (discussing caps limiting interest payments to available funds). Where the risk of a shortfall due to basis risk is remote, it could be ignored under the general rule in the regulations disregarding remote contingencies. See footnote 101 above.

121   Section 860G(a)(1), last sentence, states that an interest will not fail to be a regular interest merely because the timing of principal payments may be contingent on mortgage prepayments or income from permitted investments. (Treasury Regulation § 1.860G-1(b)(3)(i)(A) is to the same effect.) This statutory language should not be read to mean that other timing contingencies would not be allowed. The general prohibition against contingencies affecting principal in Treasury Regulation § 1.860G-1(a)(5) (discussed in the text at footnote 106 above) states only that the principal amount and latest possible maturity date of a regular interest must not be contingent; contingencies affecting the timing of principal payments before maturity are not mentioned.

122   For an illustration, see Part F, Example 17. Jump classes are discussed further in Chapter 2, Part C.

Allocations of principal on a REMIC interest could potentially be based on factors that are not related to interest rates or mortgages (e.g., the value of a basket of stocks). The existence of an allocation based on such factors raises a question as to whether the REMIC interest would, under general tax principles, be "bifurcated" into a debt instrument and some other type of financial instrument. However, where the contingency affects the timing, but not the amount, of principal payments on an instrument, the risk of bifurcation under general tax principles seems quite low.[123] At any rate, a REMIC interest that qualifies as a regular interest is automatically treated as a debt instrument under the Code.[124] This rule should override any other-wise applicable Code principles requiring bifurcation.

There is no requirement that principal payments made on a class of regular interests be funded solely out of principal payments received on the mortgages held by the REMIC. Any monies available to the REMIC can be used to accelerate principal payments. Mortgage interest received by a REMIC may be available to make principal distributions on regular interests either because the rate of interest earned by the REMIC (net of expenses) exceeds the rate of interest accruing on the regular interests and, where applicable, residual interests, or because interest that accrues on a class of REMIC interests is not currently paid. Although sources other than mortgage principal may be used to affect the timing of principal payments on a regular interest, if the amount of mortgage principal payments does not at least equal the principal amount of the regular interests, consideration should be given to whether the regular interests unconditionally entitle the holders to a specified principal amount.[125]

The duration of a regular interest may be affected not only by the timing of principal payments, but also by the timing of interest payments.[126] The flexibility that exists to determine the timing of principal payments should apply equally to the timing of payments of deferred interest.

---

123 Proposed Regulation § 1.1275-4(g) (February 20, 1991) provides for the bifurcation for tax purposes of a contingent payment debt instrument into a noncontingent debt instrument and some
other type of financial instrument, where the instrument provides for both noncontingent payments
equal to or greater than the instrument's issue price, and one or more contingent payments determined, in whole or in part, by reference to the value of publicly traded stock, securities, commodities, or other publicly traded property. This regulation appears to be concerned with instruments
that provide for some payments that are, and other payments that are not, contingent in amount,
and, thus, should not apply where a contingency affects only the timing of principal payments. It
is not clear how a bifurcation approach could be applied to contingencies affecting only the timing
of payments. In any event, it is doubtful that Proposed Regulation § 1.1275-4(g) will be finalized
in its current form. See Chapter 6, text accompanying footnote 51.

124 See Treasury Regulation § 1.860G-1(b)(6): "In determining the tax under Chapter 1 of the Internal
Revenue Code, a REMIC regular interest (as defined in section 860G(a)(1)) is treated as a debt
instrument that is an obligation of the REMIC."

125 Contingencies affecting the amount of principal payments are discussed in Part D.1 above.

126 The deferral of interest payments is discussed above in footnote 118 and accompanying text.

2. Non-Pro Rata Payments

As indicated in Chapter 4, Part A.1, the REMIC interests test requires that all distributions, if any, made with respect to a class of residual interests be made pro rata. No similar restriction applies to regular interests. Although pro rata distributions within a class are the norm, classes of regular interests aimed at retail investors often provide for principal to be allocated within the class by lot (to avoid small distributions to individual holders), except that principal may be distributed preferentially to estates or certain other holders with special liquidity needs.[127]

3. Modifications

Regular interests are generally treated as debt instruments for federal income tax purposes. As a result, they are subject to the tax law principle that treats certain modifications of the terms of a debt instrument as a deemed exchange of the old debt instrument for a new instrument with modified terms.[128] A deemed exchange of a regular interest would generally cause the issuing REMIC to violate the REMIC interests test as of the date of the exchange.[129] The new instrument could not be a regular interest because it would be issued after the startup day. There are no special rules, comparable to those that apply to qualified mortgages, that would allow certain deemed exchanges (including those arising from a default) to be disregarded in applying the REMIC interests test.[130]

As a practical matter, most REMIC regular interests will never need to be modified. Perhaps the most common reason why debt instruments are modified is to take account of payment defaults or changes in the business of the issuer. However, regular interests are typically written as "pass-through" securities that are entitled to receive distributions, in specified priorities, only from available funds held by the issuing REMIC. Thus, if the REMIC does not receive amounts due from mortgagors or other third parties, the funds available for distribution, and hence the required distributions, will be correspondingly reduced. Also, the relative rights of different classes to receive delayed payments should already be spelled out in the documentation for the REMIC. Under these circumstances, there would be no default by the REMIC that requires a negotiated change in terms.[131] Moreover, be-

---

127   Retail bonds are similar to corporate sinking fund bonds where the issuer is required to redeem bonds periodically chosen by lot. A sinking fund that accumulates funds prior to a fixed "bullet" maturity date would generally not be permitted in a REMIC. Such a fund would not be a qualified reserve fund, and cash generated on the REMIC's qualified mortgages must generally be distributed within 13 months of receipt in order to qualify as a cash flow investment. See Treasury Regulation § 1.860G-2(g)(1)(iii).

128   These rules are discussed in Part C.2 of Chapter 4, in the context of modifications of qualified mortgages.

129   The REMIC interests test is discussed in Part A.1 of Chapter 4.

130   See Part C.2.d of Chapter 4.

131   Cf. footnotes 102 and 104 above.

cause REMICs must live their lives as passive conduits, modifications to accommodate business developments rarely arise.

4. Stripping of Regular Interests

One consequence of the treatment of regular interests as debt for tax purposes is that it should be possible to separate the ownership of rights to principal and interest on such interests in secondary market "stripping" transactions, just as is done with other types of debt instruments.[132] If such a transaction were undertaken in connection with the original issuance of the regular interests, however, a question would arise as to whether the transaction should be integrated with the issuance of the whole interests by the REMIC, with the result that the status of the interests as regular interests is tested as if the stripped interests had been issued directly by the REMIC. The special rule in the REMIC regulations that recognizes the separate existence of a grantor trust and REMIC should be helpful here, but does not expressly address the issue.[133] Since the enactment of TAMRA in 1988, most economically desirable stripped interests can be created directly by the REMIC, taking advantage of the rules for specified portion regular interests.[134] Thus, most transactions in which regular interests are stripped are likely to result from events not foreseen when the regular interests were priced. The risk of integration in these circumstances would be small.

5. Stapling of Regular Interests

In some cases, it may be desirable to sell an investment unit consisting of two or more regular interests issued by the same REMIC. The "stapling" of regular interests together in this fashion should not affect their status under the REMIC rules. It could be argued under general tax principles that two interests issued by a single entity that cannot be separately assigned should be analyzed as a single, integrated security. An integration approach is clearly not followed, however, in applying the REMIC rules to multiple classes of regular interests issued by a lower-tier REMIC to an upper-tier REMIC.[135] There is no apparent reason why the analysis should be different for regular interests issued directly to investors.

---

132 See Chapter 6, Part D.1 for a discussion of the stripped bond rules.

133 See Treasury Regulation § 1.860F-2(a)(2)(ii), which is discussed in Chapter 4, Part C.7.c.

134 These rules are described in Part C.4 above. Although most types of desired interest strips can be created with appropriate planning, it does not follow that every type of regular interest could be divided into separate rights to principal and interest without creating instruments that would fail to qualify as regular interests if issued directly. In some cases, specified portion interests can be created only by using a double REMIC structure. See the text following footnote 96 above.

135 The separate existence of different classes of lower-tier regular interests is recognized even though they are integrated into a single debt instrument for purposes of applying the OID rules of the Code. Treasury Regulation § 1.1275-2(c)(4), Example 2.

6. TEFRA Registration

Under the TEFRA registration rules, regular interests generally must be issued in registered form unless the Eurobond exception—allowing them to be issued in bearer form if they are targeted to non-U.S. investors—applies. See Chapter 10, Part A.

7. Denomination in Foreign Currency

There is no express requirement that a regular interest be denominated in U.S. dollars. If a REMIC interest is denominated in a foreign currency, however, a question arises as to whether the status of the interest as a regular interest would be tested in terms of foreign currency units as if those units were dollars, or instead would be tested in U.S. dollars after first translating foreign currency units into U.S. dollars under the normal rules of the Code governing foreign currency transactions, based on exchange rates at the time of accrual or payment.[136] If the latter approach were followed, the REMIC interest would be considered to provide a stream of unpredictable payments dependent on prevailing foreign exchange rates and would not qualify as a regular interest, even if it provided for a fixed principal amount, and a fixed rate of interest, in foreign currency units.

It is likely that the regular interest test would be applied to a REMIC interest based on the units of currency in which the interest is denominated, at least in the case of a regular interest bearing interest at a fixed or qualifying variable rate. The definitions of those types of rates are based on definitions found in the OID rules of the Code,[137] and the OID rules are applied to a foreign currency denominated instrument as if the foreign currency units were U.S. dollars. The amounts of accrued discount calculated in foreign currency units are translated into U.S. dollars at the average exchange rate in effect for the relevant accrual period.[138] Thus, the possibility of variations in the U.S. dollar value of payments on the instrument will not, in itself, cause it to be treated as a contingent payment obligation in applying the OID rules.[139]

In the case of a weighted average rate or specified portion regular interest, the permitted interest rate is defined by reference to the rates of interest, or amounts of interest payments, on the underlying qualified mortgages. Accordingly, it would seem that the currency in which interest payments on these types of regular interests

---

136 The tax rules governing income or deductions from a foreign currency denominated debt instrument are found in section 988 and the regulations thereunder. The discussion in the text assumes that the "functional currency" of the REMIC as defined in section 985 is the U.S. dollar.

137 The definition of a qualifying variable rate in Treasury Regulation § 1.860G-1(a)(3)(i) refers directly to the corresponding definition in the OID regulations. The definition of stated redemption price at maturity in section 1273(a)(2), which is used in calculating OID, refers to interest "based on a fixed rate" which is the same phrase found in the definition of regular interest in section 860G(a)(1)(B)(i)

138 Treasury Regulation § 1.988-2(b)(2)(ii).

139 Treasury Regulation § 1.988-2(b)(2)(i)(B)(2).

are denominated should conform to the currency in which the qualified mortgages are denominated.

Ordinarily, a swap or other contract that would permit a REMIC to exchange U.S. dollars for foreign currency at predetermined rates would not be a "permitted investment" under the REMIC rules and could not be entered into by a REMIC. The Service has issued regulations that in certain circumstances allow foreign currency denominated debt instruments that are obligations or assets of a taxpayer to be integrated with a hedging contract entered into by the taxpayer.[140] A REMIC that wishes to own assets denominated in one currency, issue regular interests denominated in a different currency, and hedge the currency risk should consider if this result could be achieved by relying on these regulations to integrate the hedge contract with the REMIC's assets or regular interests.[141]

Alternatively, if a REMIC issues foreign currency denominated regular interests, those interests could be converted into a U.S. dollar denominated security in the hands of investors by holding them together with a currency swap in a grantor trust. Assuming that the swap is a "perfect hedge" and the trustee meets certain procedural requirements, the certificates of beneficial interest in the trust would be treated, for most tax purposes, as U.S. dollar denominated debt under the integration rule.[142]

F. Examples

This Part F illustrates with examples the rules governing interest payments on regular interests.[143] The first set of examples involves a single REMIC. The remaining examples illustrate the use of a two-tier REMIC structure. Except where otherwise noted, it is assumed in each example that (1) the qualified mortgages held by the REMIC (or, in the case of a two-tier structure, the lower-tier REMIC) have an

---

140 See Treasury Regulation § 1.988-5, issued under the authority of section 988(d).

141 In addition to considering whether the particular hedging transaction meets the technical requirements of the hedging rule, it is necessary to examine two other questions. The first is whether the claim of the counterparty to the hedging contract against the REMIC could be considered an interest in the REMIC that violates the REMIC interest test, since the integrated transaction rules in the regulations would not apply to the counterparty. (The interests test is discussed in Part A.1 of Chapter 4; compare the discussion in Chapter 3, Part C.1.g of the possible treatment of claims under notional principal contracts as ownership interests in grantor trusts.) The second issue is whether the rules in the regulations integrating a debt instrument with a hedge, which are effective for most but not necessarily all tax purposes, are effective in applying the REMIC rules. Treasury Regulation § 1.988-5(a)(9) states that the effect of integration is to create a "synthetic debt instrument" for income tax purposes, having certain terms. The regulation does not state expressly that the synthetic debt instrument is treated in all cases, except as otherwise provided in the regulation, the same as a single debt instrument.

142 See Treasury Regulation §§ 1.988-5(a)(9)(ii) and (a)(9). It may not be easy to find a counterparty that is willing to write a swap that matches uncertain cash flows on a mortgage-backed security. Investment units consisting of regular interests and other financial instruments are discussed in Part C.7.c of Chapter 4.

143 These examples do not address whether any interest is qualified stated interest under the OID rules of the Code. See generally, Chapter 6, Part C.1.

initial principal amount of 100 and bear interest at a fixed rate, net of servicing, of
8 percent, (2) each REMIC has a residual interest that is not entitled to any distributions, and (3) the issue price of each class of fixed or variable rate regular interests
does not exceed 125 percent of its principal amount.[144]

1. Single REMIC

a. Qualifying Variable Rates.

Example 1. The REMIC issues two classes of regular interests, each of which
is entitled to 50% of all principal payments on the REMIC's qualified mortgages.
Class A bears interest at a rate of LIBOR plus 50 basis points, with a floor of .5%
and a cap of 16% Class B bears interest at 16% minus the rate on Class A.

Both classes bear interest at a rate based on a qualifying variable rate (a fixed
multiple of LIBOR plus a constant number of basis points, subject to fixed floors
and caps). The multiple is 1 for Class A and –1 for Class B.

Example 2. Same facts as Example 1, except that interest is based on changes
in the consumer price index (CPI) instead of LIBOR.

It is not clear if the rate of change in the CPI is a qualifying variable rate.[145]

Example 3. Same facts as Example 1, except that the rate of interest on Class
A equals the higher of (1) the current yield on six-month Treasury obligations plus
150 basis points, or (2) the prime rate of a reference bank plus 25 basis points
(subject to a floor of 1.5% and a ceiling of 16%).

A qualifying variable rate can be based on the higher of two interest indices.

Example 4. Same facts as Example 1, except that the rate on Class A is
10×(LIBOR-4), subject to a floor of 0% and a cap of 16%. The value of LIBOR on
the pricing date for the regular interests is 3.5%.

The rates on Classes A and B in Example 4 will generally oscillate between
their floors and caps. If LIBOR is equal to or less than 4%, the rates of interest will
be 0 percent on Class A and 16% on Class B. If LIBOR is equal to or greater than
5.6%, the rates will reverse (with Class A bearing interest at 16% and Class B at
0%). The rates on Classes A and B will vary directly and inversely, respectively,
with a multiple of LIBOR if LIBOR is between 4% and 5.6%. Each rate can be
expressed as a fixed multiple of a qualifying variable rate, plus or minus a constant
number of basis points, subject to a cap or floor.[146] That Class A will receive no
interest, and Class B will pay interest at its cap, based on initial values of LIBOR,
will not disqualify either class as a regular interest.

---

144   In any case where the issue price of a fixed or variable rate regular interest is too high, the problem
      generally can be addressed by allocating additional principal to the high-coupon class and adjust-
      ing interest rates. In a double-REMIC structure, the allocation of principal on upper-tier REMIC
      regular interests need not follow the allocation on lower-tier regular interests, so there is flexibility
      to allocate principal on lower-tier interests to avoid disproportionately high interest without affect-
      ing the terms of the REMIC interests that are sold to investors.

145   See footnote 23, above.

146   In the case of Class B, the formula would be 56%-10×LIBOR.

b. Weighted Average Rates.

Example 5. The mortgages held by the REMIC are adjustable rate mortgages with "teaser" rates (i.e., artificially low fixed rates for an initial period). The fully indexed interest rate is based on current Treasury yields. The dates on which the teaser rates expire, and the dates on which the indexed rates are reset, are not the same for all of the mortgages. The REMIC issues two classes of regular interests, A and B, which have initial principal amounts of 50. Both classes receive interest currently at a rate equal to a weighted average of the rates on the underlying mortgages. Class A receives all principal first until it is retired, after which principal is paid to Class B.

The rate of interest on the two classes is a weighted average of the rates on the underlying mortgages. Each of the qualified mortgages provides for interest at a variable rate (a combination rate, consisting of an initial fixed rate followed by interest based on a qualifying variable rate). Thus, the requirement that the qualified mortgages that are included in the weighted average rate calculation pay interest at a fixed or variable rate is met.

Example 6. Same as Example 5, except that the REMIC has a qualified reserve fund. The Class A and B interests bear interest at a rate equal to a weighted average of the rates of interest on *all* REMIC assets.

The Class A and B interests do not qualify as regular interests. Interest on reserve funds and cash flow investments may not be taken into account in calculating a weighted average rate.

Example 7. A REMIC holds two pools of residential mortgages, 1 and 2, which bear interest at a range of fixed rates. It issues Class A and B regular interests which pay interest based on a weighted average of the interest rates, and receive principal based on the principal, paid on the mortgages in pools 1 and 2, respectively. Class B is subordinated to Class A as to principal and interest in the event of a default on the mortgages in pool 1.

The rates on Classes A and B qualify as weighted average rates. Such a rate can be based on the rates of interest on any one or more of the qualified mortgages held by a REMIC. The same result would be obtained even if pool 2 consisted of floating rate commercial mortgages. There is no requirement that a subordinated class be identical, apart from its ranking, to the senior class it supports.

c. Combination Rates.

Example 8. The REMIC issues two classes of regular interests, A and B, each of which is entitled to 50% of all principal payments on the mortgages. Class A bears interest at a rate of 16% for five years, 8% for the next two years, and 0% thereafter. Class B bears interest at a rate of 0% for five years, 8% for the next two years and 16% thereafter.

Rates payable at different fixed (or variable) rates in different periods are allowed.

Example 9. Same facts as Example 8, except that the rates on Class A will switch from 16% to 8% to 0% (and Class B will switch from 0% to 8% to 16%), when, alternatively, (1) the principal amounts of Class A and B are reduced to a certain amount through principal payments, (2) the total amount of interest paid on Class A reaches a fixed amount, or (3) the price of General Motors stock reaches a certain level.

Although the REMIC regulations do not address the point explicitly, the first two methods for switching rates should be allowed, since the event that triggers a change in rates is directly tied to the performance of the mortgage pool. A rate setting mechanism based on factors wholly unrelated to mortgages (such as a stock price) is less likely to be allowed.

d. Specified Portion Rates.

Example 10. The REMIC's mortgages bear interest at a rate equal to an index of yields on one-year Treasury obligations plus 200 basis points up to a cap of 12%. The REMIC issues two classes of regular interests. Class A is entitled to all principal payments on the mortgages plus interest at a rate equal to the same Treasury index plus 100 basis points subject to a cap of 12%. Class B receives no principal and all interest on the mortgages not paid to Class A (i.e., 100 basis points, declining to zero as the index increases from 11% to 12%).

Class B is entitled to a specified portion of the interest on the qualified mortgages because the interest payable on that class represents all interest payable on each mortgage in excess of a qualifying variable rate. The fact that interest on Class B is a variable amount that may be "squeezed" and eliminated as the rate on Class A approaches 12% does not prevent it from being a specified portion of mortgage interest.

Example 11. Same facts as Example 10, except that Class A bears interest at a rate equal to the weighted average of the interest rates on the mortgages but subject to a cap of 9%, so that Class B is entitled to all mortgage interest in excess of 9%.

Class B is equivalent to an interest rate cap with a limited range, that receives up to 300 basis points of interest as mortgage rates increase from 9% to 12%. Interest on Class B is a specified portion representing all interest on each mortgage in excess of a fixed amount.

Example 12. The REMIC issues three classes of regular interests, A, B, and C. Classes A and B each have initial principal amounts of 50. Class C has no principal component. Class A is entitled to all principal payments until its principal amount of 50 is paid. All remaining principal is paid on Class B. Class A bears interest at a rate of 7%, Class B bears interest at a rate of 8%, and Class C is entitled to interest equal to 1% of the Class A principal amount.

Prior to the issuance of the final REMIC Regulations it was thought that Class C would not be entitled to a specified portion of the interest on the REMIC's mortgages because 100 basis points times the Class A principal balance represents a changing number of basis points of interest on the underlying mortgages (initially

50 basis points decreasing to zero when Class A is retired). The extension of the specified portion rule to rates that represent the difference between two interest rates arguably would allow Class C to be treated as a specified portion of the interest on all qualified mortgages, equal to the excess of 8% over a combination rate that starts at 7.5% and increases to 8% proportionately as the aggregate principal amount of the qualified mortgages is reduced from 100 to 50. It is more conventional, however, and under the present state of the law safer, to create regular interests of this type using a two-tier structure.[147] Compare Example 19 below.

Example 13. The REMIC issues three classes of regular interests, A, B, and C, which have initial principal balances of 80, 20, and 0, respectively. Principal is allocated pro rata between Classes A and B. Class A receives no interest. Class C receives interest on a notional principal amount equal to the Class A principal balance, at a rate of 10% for the first three years after the startup day, 5% for the next three years, and 0% thereafter. Class B is entitled to no interest for the first three years after the startup day, interest at a rate of 20% for the next three years, and thereafter interest at a rate of 40%.

Although the interest on Class C steps up over time, it represents a nonvarying specified portion of the interest on the REMIC's qualified mortgages (100% minus the interest on Class B, which is a variable combination rate).

Additional flexibility in creating specified portion regular interests can be gained by using two tiers of REMICs, as illustrated in Part F.2.a below.

e. Variable Caps.

Example 14. The REMIC issues two classes of regular interests, A and B. Class A has an initial principal amount of 80, is entitled in the absence of mortgage defaults to 80% of each principal payment on the REMIC's qualified mortgages until retired, and bears interest at a rate of LIBOR plus 100 basis points, subject to a cap equal to the weighted average interest rate on the mortgages. Class B has an initial principal amount of 20, is entitled in the absence of mortgage defaults to 20% of each principal payment on the qualified mortgages until retired, and receives all interest on the mortgages not paid to Class A. Class B is subordinated to Class A in the event of defaults or delinquencies on the mortgages.

Class A bears interest at a variable rate (a combination rate equal to the lower of a qualifying variable rate and a weighted average rate).[148] The interest on Class B represents a specified portion of the interest on the mortgages (all interest, less interest at a variable rate).[149]

---

147   Although it should be possible to create a combination rate that selects the fixed or variable rates to apply in a period based on principal balances at the beginning of the period (see the text accompanying footnote 72 above; cf Example 9 above), it is not clear if a rate can be tied directly to an outstanding principal balance through a formula.

148   See Treasury Regulation § 1.860G-1(a)(2)(v), Example 1, discussed in the text accompanying footnote 71.

149   The interest on Class B represents a combination of (1) the excess interest on the principal allocated to Class A, that is, the weighted average interest rate on the pool minus LIBOR+100,

Example 15. Same as Example 14, except that Class A is entitled to all principal payments until it is retired, at which point all principal will be paid on Class B, and the interest rate cap on Class A is a cap equal to all available interest.

Class A will qualify as a regular interest provided its cap is a permitted "funds-available cap," which depends on various factors.[150] Interest on Class B equals all interest on the mortgages less a percentage of a variable rate that decreases over time as Class A is retired. Such a rate would qualify as a specified portion rate only if a variable rate that changes under a formula based on mortgage principal balances is a permitted combination rate. Compare Example 12 above.

f. Deferral of Interest.

Example 16. The REMIC issues two classes of regular interests, A and B. Each class bears interest at a rate of 8% and has an initial principal amount of 50. The interest on Class B is deferred and compounded. All payments received on the mortgages are used to make payments of interest and then principal on Class A until it is fully retired. Thereafter, all payments are made on Class B until it is retired.

The rate of interest on each class is a fixed rate. Interest may be deferred without disqualifying a class of regular interests.

Example 17. Same as Example 16, except that all cash distributions are made on Class B (until it is retired) and not on Class A for periods in which the price of gold exceeds a specified amount.

Payments may be allocated between classes of regular interests in any way that is desired, as long as each class is unconditionally entitled to receive at some point its full principal amount and interest accrues at a permitted rate.

g. Prepayment Premiums.

Example 18. The mortgages held by the REMIC are commercial loans that are subject to prepayment at the borrower's option only upon payment of a prepayment penalty. The REMIC issues two classes of regular interests, A and B. Class A receives all mortgage principal and no interest. Class B entitles the holder to all interest paid on the mortgages and all prepayment premiums.

Class A bears interest at a fixed rate of zero. In the absence of prepayment premiums, Class B would provide for interest payments equal to a nonvarying specified portion (100%) of the interest payments on the mortgages. Class B is not disqualified as a regular interest because prepayment premiums on the mortgages

---

applied to 80% of the pool principal balance and (2) all interest on the 20% of the pool principal that is allocated to Class B. The combined interest rate can be expressed as a rate, applied to the entire pool principal balance, equal to a weighted average of the rates of interest on the entire pool minus .8×(LIBOR+100).

150   See discussion in the text beginning at footnote 63 above. Alternatively, it could be argued that a rate that switches between a LIBOR-based rate and a multiple of a weighted average rate, where the multiple depends on the ratio of mortgage principal to Class A principal, is a permitted combination rate, although at present this result is not clear. See text accompanying footnote 146, above.

are passed through to Class B holders. This conclusion would also hold true if Class B received different percentages of mortgage interest and prepayment premiums.

2. Two-Tier REMICs

The examples which follow illustrate the use of a two-tier REMIC structure in which a lower-tier REMIC issues two or more classes of regular interests to an upper-tier REMIC. Examples 19 through 22 involve regular interests that receive a specified portion of the interest payments on lower-tier REMIC regular interests. The remaining examples show how double-tier REMICs can be used to expand the categories of permitted variable rate regular interests.

a. Specified Portion Rates.

Example 19. The lower-tier REMIC issues two classes of regular interests, AL and BL, each having an initial principal amount of 50 and bearing interest of 8%. Interest is paid currently on both classes. Class AL is a fast-pay class that is entitled to all principal payments on the mortgages until it is fully retired, after which principal is paid on Class BL. The upper-tier REMIC issues three classes, A, B, and C. Class C is entitled to 1 percentage point of the interest on Class AL, Class B is identical to Class BL, and Class A is entitled to all payments on Class AL other than the interest allocated to Class C.

Class C represents a specified portion of interest paid on Class AL, which is a qualified mortgage held by the upper-tier REMIC. For a similar example involving a single REMIC, see Example 12 above.

Example 20. The lower-tier REMIC is the same as in Example 19, except that all but 1 percentage point of interest payable on Class BL is deferred and paid only after Class AL is retired (with the additional cash being used to pay principal on Class AL). The upper-tier REMIC issues Class A, which is identical to Class AL, Class C, which represents a right to 1 percentage point of interest taken off of Class BL, payable currently in each period, and Class B, which receives all payments on Class BL not allocable to Class C.

Interest on Class C can be expressed as a fixed number of basis points of interest on Class BL and, thus, meets the specified portion test.

Example 21. The lower-tier REMIC issues Classes AL and BL, each having an initial principal amount of 50 and receiving a pro rata share of mortgage principal payments. Class AL bears interest at LIBOR, subject to a floor of zero and a cap of 16%. Class BL bears interest at 16% minus LIBOR. Interest is paid currently on the two classes. The upper-tier REMIC issues two classes of interests, A and B, which have initial principal amounts of 50. Principal is allocated between the two classes based on values of LIBOR. Specifically, while both classes remain outstanding, the percentage of each principal payment that is allocated to Class A equals 10×LIBOR (between 0 and 100%), with all remaining principal being allocated to Class B. Class A is entitled to all interest on Class AL and Class B is entitled to all interest on Class BL.

Changes in interest rates affect Classes A and B in two ways: by changing the rate of interest and by changing the priority for receiving principal. For example, if interest rates increase, Class A is benefited not only because of an increase in coupon but also because it receives principal more quickly. The interest on each of Classes A and B represents a specified portion (100%) of the interest on a qualified mortgage (the Class AL and BL regular interests, respectively).

Example 22. The lower-tier REMIC issues two classes of regular interests, AL and BL, which have principal amounts of 60 and 40, respectively, and receive pro rata distributions of principal. Class AL bears interest at a rate equal to a weighted average of the interest rates on the qualified mortgages held by the lower-tier REMIC plus 4 basis points. Class BL bears interest at 6 basis points under the same weighted average rate. The upper-tier REMIC issues three classes of interests, A, B, and C. Class A corresponds to Class AL. Class B receives all principal on Class BL and interest at the lesser of LIBOR and the rate payable on Class BL. Class C is entitled to all interest on Class BL not allocated to Class B.

The interest on Class C is a specified portion of the interest on Class BL, and represents a percentage of all interest on the qualified mortgages held by the lower-tier REMIC above interest at a variable rate.[151]

b. Variable Rates. The REMIC regulations allow the creation of regular interests bearing interest equal to a fixed multiple of an interest index subject to a cap or floor. Different multiples over ranges can be created, as shown in Examples 23 through 25, by combining in an upper-tier REMIC interest payment on lower-tier classes having the appropriate ranges of rates.[152] Example 26 involves a weighted average rate equal to the difference between two variable rates.

In the first example, the goal is to create a class that increases with LIBOR for values of LIBOR between 0% and 4%, and increases 2 percentage points for each 1 percentage point increase in LIBOR above 4%, subject to a cap of 16%.

Example 23. The lower-tier REMIC issues four classes of regular interests, AL, BL, CL, and DL. Each class has an initial principal amount of 25. Principal is allocated pro rata among the four classes. Interest on Class AL equals 2×LIBOR with a floor of zero and a cap of 8%. Interest on Class BL is 4×(LIBOR-4), with a floor of zero and a cap of 24%. Interest on Class CL is the inverse of AL (8%– 2×LIBOR, subject to a floor of 0% and cap of 8%), and Class DL is the inverse of BL (24–4×(LIBOR–4)). The upper-tier REMIC issues two classes, AB and CD. Class AB represents the sum of Classes AL and BL (i.e., it has an initial principal amount of 50 and is entitled to all principal and interest received on Classes AL and BL). Class CD is the sum of Classes CL and DL.

---

151 It may be possible to achieve this result using a single REMIC. See footnote 86 above and accompanying text.

152 Such rates could arguably also be created as a combination rate (where the rate applicable in any period is determined by values of an index).

Class AB has the desired characteristics. Interest on that class can be viewed as a specified portion (100%) of the interest on Classes AL and BL, or as a weighted average of the interest on those classes.

In the next example, the desired class has the same characteristics as Class AB in Example 23, except that interest remains constant for values of LIBOR between 4% and 6%.

Example 24. Same facts as Example 23, except that Class BL bears interest of 4x(LIBOR–6), with a floor of 0% and a cap of 24% (and a corresponding adjustment is made to Class D). Class AB would then have the desired characteristics.

Regular interests can also be created with interest rate "mountains" and "valleys." Specifically, interest can be made to increase (or decrease) with increases in interest rates and then to reverse course and decrease (or increase) with further increases in rates. For example, a class that bears interest at a rate that is 16% when LIBOR is 7%, and then decreases by four times the change (positive or negative) in LIBOR from 7%, with a floor of 0% when LIBOR is equal to or less than 3% or equal to or greater than 11%, and an inverse of that class that bears interest at a rate that is 0% when LIBOR is 7% and increases to 16% when LIBOR is equal to or less than 3% or equal to or greater than 11%, can be created as follows:

Example 25. Same facts as Example 23, except that interest on Class AL equals 4x(LIBOR-3%), interest on Class BL equals 32%-4x(LIBOR-3%), interest on Class CL is the inverse of Class AL (16%-4x(LIBOR-3%)), and interest on Class DL is the inverse of Class BL (4x(LIBOR-3%)-16%). Each class has a floor of 0% and a ceiling of 16%. The upper-tier REMIC issues two classes of regular interests, AB and CD. Class AB is entitled to all of the principal distributions on Classes AL and BL, and bears interest at a rate equal to twice the weighted average of the rates on Classes AL and BL, less 16 percentage points. Class CD is entitled to all principal on Classes CL and DL, and bears interest at a rate equal to twice the weighted average of the rates on Classes CL and DL.

Class AB is the desired "mountain" regular interest and Class CD is the corresponding "valley" interest.

A two-tier structure can be used to create weighted average rate regular interests bearing interest at a rate based on a difference between two variable rates.[153]

Example 26. The facts are the same as Example 23, except that interest on Class AL equals COFI, interest on Class BL is 16%-LIBOR, interest on Class CL is 16%-COFI, and interest on Class DL equals LIBOR. Each class has a floor of 0% and a cap of 16%. Class AB is entitled to all principal payments on Classes AL and BL and bears interest at a rate of 8%+(COFI-LIBOR). Class CD receives all principal on Classes CL and DL and bears interest at the rate of 8%-(COFI-LIBOR).

---

153 The definition of specified portion in the REMIC regulations includes the excess of interest on a qualified mortgage at a variable rate above interest at a variable rate. This rule can also be used to create regular interests bearing interest at a rate equal to the difference between two variable rates.

The interest rate on Class AB (CD) can be expressed as twice the weighted average of the interest rates on Classes AL and BL (CL and DL) minus 8 percentage points.[154]

---

154   There are two possible problems with Example 26. First, the desired result will be achieved in the example only if COFI and LIBOR stay within the range of 0-16%. Outside of this range, the rates on the lower-tier classes will reflect the caps or floors and not the indexed rate. Second, if prevailing rates are low, the inverse floating rate classes (BL and CL) could conceivably have issue prices exceeding 125% of their principal amounts. Both of these problems can be resolved by multiplying the indices used in calculating interest on the lower-tier classes by a number less than one, shifting interest from Classes BL and CL to Classes AL and DL, and then making adjustments reversing these changes in computing rates on Classes AB and CD. To take one example, interest on Class AL would equal 6%+.25×COFI (subject to a cap of 14%), interest on Class BL would be 10%-.25×LIBOR subject to a floor of 2%, interest on Class CL would equal 10%-.25×COFI subject to a floor of 2%, and interest on Class DL would be 6%+.25×LIBOR (subject to a cap of 14%). The floors and caps on these interests would not be reached unless COFI or LIBOR, as the case may be, reached 32%. Also, the inverse floaters (Classes BL and CL) are less likely to be valued at more than 125% of their principal amounts because the fixed amount used in calculating the rate is reduced from 16% to 10%. The rate of interest on Class AB (CD) would equal eight times the weighted average rate on Classes AL and BL (CL and DL), minus 56 percentage points, producing the same rates as in Example 26.

Chapter 6

Taxation of Holders of Mortgage-Backed Securities Taxable as Debt

A. Introduction

As Chapter 2 indicates, from the perspective of investors, mortgage-backed securities can be divided into three groups: those taxable as debt; REMIC residual interests and equity interests in owner trusts that are not TMPs, which generally are taxed based on the net income of the REMIC or trust, respectively; and equity interests in TMPs which are treated as stock in a corporation. This chapter discusses the taxation of holders of mortgage-backed securities taxable as debt. Residual interests and equity interests in non-TMP owner trusts are the subject of Chapter 7. Chapter 8 addresses equity interests in TMPs. Special rules that apply to certain institutional and foreign investors are considered in Chapters 9 and 10, respectively.

The following categories of mortgage-backed securities are taxable as debt:

- REMIC regular interests, which the Code deems to be debt obligations of the issuing REMIC, regardless of their legal form
- pass-through certificates, which are considered ownership interests in the underlying mortgages, and
- CMOs and other pay-through bonds, which are debt obligations of the entity that issues them.[1]

References in this chapter to mortgage-backed securities should be understood to be references to one of these three types of securities. Also, except where otherwise indicated, references to debt instruments or obligations, or bonds, include REMIC regular interests.

In applying the tax rules for debt instruments to a pass-through certificate, it should be kept in mind that such a certificate is not generally considered a single security for tax purposes, but instead represents an ownership interest in each of the mortgages held by the issuing trust.[2] Technically, the holder of a pass-through

---

1   The list also includes pass-through debt certificates, assuming they are recognized to be debt of the issuing trust. See Chapter 2, Part G.

certificate should calculate income or loss for each mortgage separately by allocating among the mortgages, in proportion to their respective fair market values, the price paid for the certificate and the price received on resale. Such an allocation is rarely necessary in practice, however, because in most instances the tax results obtained by viewing the mortgages alternatively in isolation as a single aggregated debt instrument would be the same.[3] For convenience, and except where otherwise noted, the discussion in this chapter of mortgage-backed securities assumes the security is in all cases a debt obligation of one debtor (either an interest in a single mortgage or a single pay-through bond).[4]

The mortgage-backed securities considered in this chapter generally are subject to the Code rules governing conventional debt instruments. Thus, for example, stated interest on such a security generally is taxable as ordinary income as such interest accrues, for an accrual method taxpayer, or when it is received, for a cash method taxpayer.[5] Assuming the security is purchased at its principal amount, principal payments represent a nontaxable return of the investor's capital regardless of when principal is paid. Upon sale of the security, gain or loss is recognized in an amount equal to the difference between the net proceeds of such sale and the seller's *adjusted basis* in the security (generally, the seller's cost for the security, increased by amounts included in income and reduced by losses and payments received).[6] With limited exceptions, any such gains or losses are treated as capital

---

2 See Chapter 2, Part B. A pass-through certificate is not viewed as a single security in determining whether losses from the exchange of one certificate for another are allowed as a deduction. See the discussion of the *Cottage Savings* decision in Chapter 12, footnote 15. Where a REMIC holds a pass-through certificate as a qualified mortgage, it is required to compute income from the certificate under the PAC method using a Prepayment Assumption. See footnote 32 below. Although the PAC method would generally produce the same result for a pool of loans regardless of whether it is applied to the pool as a whole or to individual mortgages, the use of a Prepayment Assumption makes more sense for a large group of loans than for a small sampling, where the individual circumstances of a few mortgagors can have an unpredictable effect on prepayments. In practice, many REMICs apply the PAC method to a pass-through certificate in the same way as if it were a bond (based on the timing of distributions on the certificates, rather than on the mortgages). This treatment, if proper, would eliminate one, fairly minor, source of phantom income. See Chapter 7, the end of Part E.1.

3 This statement assumes that all of the mortgages underlying a single pass-through certificate have identical terms. Although this is rarely true in fact, because all such mortgages are generally similar to one another, and information is not reported to investors on a mortgage-by-mortgage basis, an assumption of pool-wide uniformity of mortgages is usually made in practice. Cf. P.L.R. 8052046 (September 30, 1980) (pool-wide uniformity assumed in calculating discount component of principal payments received on GNMA guaranteed pass-through certificates).

4 Although the tax principles applicable to pass-through certificates will generally achieve similar results regardless of whether they are applied at the pool or individual loan level, there are significant differences between the tax treatment of pass-through certificates, on the one hand, and REMIC regular interests or pay-through bonds, on the other hand. One difference is that the PAC method for accruing discount and premium described in Part C.2 below does not by its terms apply to pass-through certificates (other than those held as qualified mortgages by REMICs), but does apply to regular interests and pay-through bonds.

5 The description of the tax treatment of stated interest in this Part A assumes that such interest is not recharacterized as original issue discount. See Part C.1. A special accrual rule for REMIC regular interests is described in footnote 10, below.

gains or losses if the security is held as a *capital asset,* which generally would be the case unless the holder is a dealer in securities.[7] Capital gain is long term if the security has been held at the time of sale for more than one year. A preferential tax rate applies to long-term capital gain income earned by high-income individuals (although not to capital gains of corporations).[8] An amount paid as accrued interest upon sale of a mortgage-backed security between interest payment dates is treated by the seller as an interest payment and may be used by the purchaser to offset the interest received on the next interest payment date.[9]

Two exceptions to these rules apply to REMIC regular interests, but they are likely to have little, if any, practical significance for most investors.[10] Another

---

6   Under section 1044, which was added to the Code by RRA 1993, individuals and corporations (not including S corporations) may elect to defer capital gain realized on the sale of publicly traded securities (including mortgage-backed securities) to the extent the sale proceeds are reinvested in equity in a "specialized small business investment company." The amount of gain that may be rolled over is subject to annual and lifetime dollar caps (for an individual, $50,000 and $500,000, and for a corporation, $250,000 and $1,000,000).

7   Securities dealers recognize ordinary income on the sale of mortgage-backed securities (other than those not held in connection with dealer activities) and are subject to certain mark-to-market rules. See Chapter 9, Part E. Holders that are banks or thrift institutions always recognize ordinary income or loss from sales of debt obligations under section 582(c). See also *Burbank Liquidating Corporation v. Comm'r,* 39 T.C. 999 (1963), modified as to other issues, 335 F.2d 125 (9th Cir. 1964), which indicates that a mortgage may be excluded from the definition of capital asset in the hands of the originator under section 1221(4), as "accounts or notes receivable acquired in the ordinary course of trade or business for services rendered. . . . " *Federal National Mortgage Association v. Comm'r,* 100 T.C. No. 36 (June 17, 1993), extended the reach of section 1221(4) to mortgages acquired (but not originated) by FNMA. The court reasoned that because FNMA was established to enhance the efficiency of the secondary mortgage market, its purchase of mortgages was a service, so that it acquired the mortgages for services rendered. Despite its origins, FNMA is (and was in the years before the court) a privately owned, profit-making organization. Although unlikely, it will be interesting to see if this theory will be stretched to apply to other active market participants. Under section 1258, all or a portion of the gain arising from a "conversion transaction" that otherwise would be capital gain is treated as ordinary income.

8   Under section 1(h), long-term capital gains of individuals are subject to a maximum tax rate of 28%. For all taxpayers, it may be necessary to know whether gain or loss is capital or ordinary, because capital losses generally can be deducted only to the extent of capital gains.

9   Treasury Regulation § 1.61-7(d) (seller); *L.A. Thompson Scenic Ry. Co. v. Comm'r,* 9 B.T.A. 1203 (1928) (purchaser). In the case of a pass-through certificate, the amount of accrued interest at the time of a sale depends on the time that has elapsed since the last payment on the underlying mortgages, not the time since the last distribution on the certificate. See Chapter 2, footnote 8 and accompanying text. Accrued interest with which a debt instrument is issued is discussed below at footnote 28.

10   The exceptions are as follows: First, income from REMIC regular interests must always be reported under an accrual method even if the holder is otherwise a cash method taxpayer. Second, gain recognized by an investor under sale of a REMIC regular interest that otherwise would be capital gain will be treated as ordinary income to the extent such gain does not exceed the excess of (1) the income that would have been reported by the investor if it had reported income as it accrued based on a yield to the investor equal to 110% of the "applicable Federal rate" (generally, an average yield of U.S. Treasury obligations of different ranges of maturities published monthly by the Service) in effect for the month in which the interest was acquired by the investor, over (2) the ordinary income previously reported by the investor. The legislative history of the 110% rule indicates that it was intended to prevent the underaccrual of original issue discount because of the failure to take account of mortgage prepayments. Conference Report at II-232; Blue Book at 420.

special rule of minor significance relates to regular interests in "single-class RE-MICs" (a defined term which includes certain multiple-class REMICs) held by individuals and certain pass-through entities. Such holders are required to include in income, and are treated as paying, an allocable share of the REMIC's investment expenses.[11]

The tax treatment of a mortgage-backed security is more complex if the security was purchased at a price different from its principal amount, that is, at a discount or a premium. If a mortgage-backed security is purchased at a discount and the full principal amount is eventually paid, the excess of the principal amount over the cost of the security represents additional income. A question then arises as to the proper timing of recognition of that income and its character as ordinary income or capital gain. The purchase of a security at a premium raises similar concerns. These questions are addressed in the remainder of this chapter.

B. Overview of Taxation of Discount and Premium

The traditional approach to the tax treatment of a debt instrument deals separately with three sources of income—stated or coupon interest, original issue discount and market discount—and one item of expense (or offset to interest)—bond premium. Stated interest was discussed above; discount and premium are considered here.

In general, *original issue discount* or *(OID)* is discount at which a debt obligation was sold to investors in connection with its original issuance, and *market discount* is discount that arises from decreases in the market value of a debt obligation following its issuance.[12] The technical definition of OID is somewhat complicated, and includes not only discount at which an obligation is issued below its principal amount but also stated interest that is not paid currently over the life of the obligation. The most important difference, in terms of tax consequences, between OID and market discount is that, in general, OID is includible in income by the holder of a discount obligation as the discount accrues under a constant yield method, whereas (absent certain taxpayer elections) market discount is taxable only when principal payments are received or the obligation sold. In January of 1994, the

---

However, the rule is not limited to gain arising from the underaccrual of original issue discount. Moreover, prepayments are now taken into consideration in accruing original issue discount under the PAC method (described below in Part C.2) enacted by TRA 1986.

The two special rules for REMIC regular interests should not have much practical significance. Section 448, enacted by TRA 1986, requires most investors other than individuals and small businesses (annual gross receipts of not more than $5 million) to report all income under an accrual method. Moreover, stated interest on many common mortgage-backed securities must be reported by all investors under an accrual method because such interest is treated as original issue discount (see Part C.1). The rate advantage for long-term capital gains is at present limited to certain high-income individuals. See footnote 8 above.

11   See Chapter 7, text accompanying footnote 42.

12   Different OID rules apply to obligations issued for cash and those issued in exchange for property. The discussion of discount in this chapter is limited to obligations issued for cash. For a brief discussion of how the issue price is determined for a debt instrument issued in exchange for property (specifically, another debt instrument of the same issuer), see Chapter 7, footnote 8.

Service issued extensive final regulations interpreting the OID rules of the Code, which will sometimes be referred to as the *OID regulations*.[13]

There is a fundamental difference between REMIC regular interests and pay-through bonds, on the one hand, and pass-through certificates, on the other hand, which affects the status of discount as OID. Regular interests and pay-through bonds are considered obligations in their own right for tax purposes, so that any discount at which they are issued is generally OID (even if such discount can be traced to market discount on underlying mortgages). By contrast, pass-through certificates are treated as ownership interests in, rather than debt of, the issuing trust. As a result, OID will exist for those certificates only if the mortgages held by the trust have OID (which is rare for residential mortgages) or the bond stripping rules discussed below apply.

Although the Code does not require market discount on a debt instrument to be included in income by the holder as it accrues absent a holder election to accrue, it nonetheless provides a number of special rules governing market discount. Gain on the sale of a debt instrument is treated as ordinary income (which is interest income for most purposes) to the extent it does not exceed the market discount that has accrued thereon and not yet been included in income. In the case of debt instruments that have some OID, accruals of market discount are generally proportionate to accruals of OID. A principal payment on a debt instrument generally must be included in income by the holder, as a payment of accrued market discount, to the extent it does not exceed the portion of the market discount on the entire instrument that has accrued during the period the holder owned the instrument and not yet been included in income. As a result, where the holder of a debt instrument receives principal payments at least annually that equal or exceed accruals of market discount, such discount effectively will be included effectively in income as it accrues. Deductions for interest on debt incurred (or continued) to finance market discount bonds are deferred to prevent the generation of losses attributable to the current deductibility of interest and the deferral of market discount income.

Prior to 1986, there was considerable uncertainty as to how mortgage prepayments should be taken into account in accruing OID. TRA 1986 addressed the point by enacting section 1272(a)(6). This section requires OID to be accrued on REMIC regular interests and pay-through bonds based on changes in the present value of the

---

13   See Treasury Regulation §§ 1.1271-1 through 1.1275-5, which were issued on January 27, 1994 and generally are effective for obligations issued on or after April 4, 1994. See T.D. 8517, 56 Fed. Reg. 4,799 (February 2, 1994). These regulations were issued in proposed form on December 21, 1992. The 1992 proposed regulations generally superseded proposed OID regulations issued in 1986 and 1991. Taxpayers may rely on the final regulations (except for the election described in footnote 18, below) with respect to obligations issued after December 21, 1992 and before April 4, 1994. In addition, taxpayers may rely on the December 1992 proposed regulations as authority for purposes of the accuracy-related penalty under section 6662 with respect to obligations issued after December 21, 1992 and before April 4, 1994, and may rely on the earlier version of the proposed regulations as such authority for obligations issued on or prior to December 21, 1992. The final regulations were accompanied by a new temporary regulation (Treasury Regulation § 1.1275-2T(g)) which gives the Service the right to override the OID regulations to avoid unreasonable results that have a substantial effect on the present value of a taxpayer's tax liability.

instrument. Present values are calculated (1) by taking account of actual mortgage prepayments that have already occurred and projecting the rate at which future prepayments will occur using an assumed prepayment rate, and (2) using the original yield to maturity as the discount rate. This accrual method (which we refer to as the PAC method for reasons explained in Part C.2) does not by its terms apply to pass-through certificates except when they are held by a REMIC.

The special Code rules governing OID and market discount do not apply to *de minimis* amounts of discount on a debt instrument. In general, such discount is recognized by the holder ratably as principal payments are received, and is characterized as gain from the retirement of the instrument.[14]

The distinction between OID and market discount is blurred by the "bond stripping" rules of section 1286. These rules apply when rights to principal and interest on a debt obligation are held separately or in different proportions and play a significant role in the taxation of certain pass-through certificates. If rights to payments on a debt obligation qualify as stripped bonds, then, with certain exceptions, all income from the holding of those rights (both stated interest and discount) is subject to taxation under the OID rules.

With respect to *de minimis* discount, or discount on a pass-through certificate or other obligation that is not subject to the PAC method, a further distinction in determining the tax treatment of discount is whether the debtor is an individual, corporation, or other legal entity. Gain realized upon the receipt of a payment of principal on the obligation of an individual that is treated as gain from retirement of the obligation (and not as OID or accrued market discount) is *always* ordinary income, whereas gain from the retirement of an obligation of a corporation or other legal entity may be capital gain if the obligation is held as a capital asset.[15]

---

14   See Treasury Regulation § 1.1273-1(d)(5) (ratable recovery rule for *de minimis* OID). For the definition of *de minimis* discount, see footnote 21, below. A taxpayer may elect to report *de minimis* discount as if it were OID. See footnote 18, below.

15   This distinction is based on a technical quirk in the Code. In order for gain to be capital gain, it must result from a "sale or exchange" of a capital asset (see the definitions in section 1222). Under case law dating back to the early days of the tax law, gain from the extinguishment of a contractual claim, including gain realized upon retirement of a debt obligation, is not considered to result from a sale or exchange unless there is a Code provision which so states. Section 1271(a)(1) treats amounts received by the holder on retirement of a debt instrument as amounts received in exchange therefor, but this section does not apply to obligations of individuals (see section 1271(b)(1)). Because amounts received in retirement of an obligation of an individual are not received in a sale or exchange of the obligation, any resulting gain is ordinary income. On the other hand, if such an obligation is actually sold to a new holder, the sale or exchange requirement is satisfied and income from the sale can be capital gain. Section 1271(a) does not apply to obligations issued before July 2, 1982 by an issuer other than a corporation or government or political subdivision thereof (see section 1271(b)(2)). Thus, retirements of obligations issued by partnerships or trusts before this date are treated in the same manner as retirements of obligations of individuals. Apparently, the status of the original issuer applies for this purpose even if the obligation is later assumed. Section 1234A treats the termination of a right with respect to actively traded personal property as a "sale or exchange" but it does not apply to the retirement of debt instruments (whether or not through a trust or other participation arrangement). See section 1234A, last sentence.

Unlike discount, all premium on a given debt instrument is treated alike.[16] Premium on a debt instrument that is held for investment can be amortized if an election is made by the holder under section 171. Amortized premium will offset interest income to the extent thereof and otherwise will be allowed as a deduction. Premium is amortized under a constant yield method that is similar to the method used in calculating accruals of OID.[17]

To understand fully the tax treatment of mortgage-backed securities, it continues to be necessary to distinguish between stated interest, OID, market discount, and premium and to take account of the rules applicable to each. Nonetheless, the law is moving in the direction of taxing all income from holding mortgage-backed securities as it accrues, with accruals being calculated under a constant yield method, and more particularly the PAC method. A number of factors evidence this trend:

First, with respect to many common types of regular interests or pay-through bond, stated interest is treated as OID. Also, stated interest on regular interests is taxed under an accrual method even if it is not OID.

Second, the rules treating principal payments or gain on sale of an obligation as interest income to the extent of accrued market discount has reduced the significance of the distinction between market discount and OID.

Third, the TRA 1986 legislative history indicates that the PAC method can be used in accruing both market discount and premium.

Fourth, pass-through certificates that are IO or PO Strips (and others that have disproportionate rights to interest and principal) are generally subject to the bond stripping rules, which have the effect of converting income into OID.

Finally, the OID regulations include an elective rule that allows taxpayers to report all income on a debt instrument (including stated interest and all types of discount, and with adjustments for premium) under OID principles.[18]

---

16 But see P.L.R. 8724035 (March 16, 1987) which distinguished between premium on a GNMA guaranteed pass-through certificate that was attributable to the GNMA guarantee and premium that arose because of changes in interest rates. This distinction is of questionable merit, given that no separate allocation is made to the guarantee for other tax purposes.

17 Before TRA 1986, the section 171 election applied only to debt obligations of corporations or governments, and thus was not available for obligations of individuals, such as residential mortgages, or obligations of owner trusts. However, TRA 1986 extended the election to obligations of all types of issuers, effective for obligations issued after September 27, 1985. TRA 1986 is also responsible for requiring the use of a constant yield method of amortization.

18 See Treasury Regulation § 1.1272-3, which is effective for debt instruments acquired on or after April 4, 1994. The election is made for individual debt instruments, or a class of debt instruments acquired in a taxable year, by attaching a statement to the tax return for the year. The election once made cannot be revoked without IRS consent. If the election applies to a debt instrument, interest is included in income as if the instrument were newly issued on the holder's acquisition date at a price equal to the holder's adjusted basis (limited in some cases to fair market value) and all stated interest were includible in OID. The election can be made for a debt instrument with market' discount or premium only if the holder could have made the election to include such market discount in income as it accrues under section 1278(b), or to amortize premium under section 171, respectively. See Parts E and F. A taxpayer making an election under this regulation may be considered to have made an election under section 1278(b) or 171 that can affect other debt

In light of these factors, it would be reasonable, if perhaps somewhat premature, to view the rules governing OID as the basic model for taxing all income from
mortgage-backed securities, while recognizing, as the later discussion indicates, that
deviations from that model are required or permitted under current law. For that
reason, the discussion in the next four parts starts with OID, and then turns to
market discount and premium. Part C addresses the basic OID rules as they apply to
REMIC regular interests and pay-through bonds. Part D explains the effect of those
rules on pass-through certificates. Pass-through certificates have OID primarily
where they are stripped bonds or coupons subject to section 1286. Market discount
and premium are addressed in Parts E and F. The chapter concludes with a disscus-
sion in Part G of two special topics. The first is the ability of a holder of high-coupon regular interests to deduct currently negative amounts calculated under the PAC
method. Negative amounts often arise where mortgage prepayments are greater than
expected. The second topic concerns the tax consequences for investors of mortgagor defaults.

The discussion of discount in this chapter assumes that the mortgage-backed
securities in question have an original term to maturity of more than one year. A
different tax regime, which is of little relevance in the mortgage area, applies to
discount on short-term obligations.[19]

C. Original Issue Discount

This Part C explains how the OID rules apply to REMIC regular interests and
pay-through bonds. Specifically, the discussion will define OID, describe how accruals of OID are calculated under the PAC method, illustrate the method with an
example, and describe special rules for debt instruments with variable or contingent
interest. Unless otherwise stated, it is assumed that interest on a debt obligation
accrues at a fixed rate. Pass-through certificates are addressed in Part D.

1. OID Defined

Original issue discount is defined as the excess of the stated redemption price at
maturity of an obligation over its issue price.[20] However, if the amount of discount
as so defined is less than a *de minimis* amount (generally 1/4 of one percent of the

instruments the taxpayer owns.

19   In brief, the holder of a debt obligation that has a maximum term of one year or less (short-term
     obligation) is not required to include the OID, if any, relating to the obligation in income as it
     accrues unless such holder is an accrual basis taxpayer, a bank, a dealer holding the obligation in
     inventory, or another class of holder specified in section 1281. Holders not described in section
     1281 include accrued OID on a short-term obligation in income only when the obligation is sold
     or matures, but may be required under section 1282 to defer deductions for interest paid on any
     related borrowings under rules similar to those that apply to leveraged investments in long-term
     market discount obligations (See Part E.2.) In *Security Bank of Minnesota v. Comm'r*, 994 F.2d
     432 (8th Cir. 1993), the court held that sections 1281 through 1283 did not apply to short-term
     loans made by a bank in the ordinary course of its business.

20   Section 1273(a)(1).

stated redemption price at maturity times the number of complete years to maturity), then the amount of OID is considered to be zero.[21] The *stated redemption price at maturity* is not limited to the principal amount, but also includes all payments of stated interest other than *qualified stated interest payments*. A qualified stated interest payment is any one of a series of payments equal to the product of the outstanding principal balance and a single fixed rate (appropriately adjusted for the length of time between payments) that is payable unconditionally[22] at least annually during the entire term of the obligation (variable rates are discussed in section 4 below).[23]

---

21   See section 1273(a)(3). The OID regulations have a number of special rules for testing whether discount is *de minimis*. One such rule, regarding interest holidays, teaser rates and other interest shortfalls, is described in footnote 23 below. Under Treasury Regulation §§ 1.1273-1(d)(3) and (e)(3), the *de minimis* rule is applied to an installment obligation (an obligation that provides for more than one payment includible in its stated redemption price at maturity) based on the weighted average maturity of the obligation, which is calculated by dividing (1) the sum of the products of the amount of each payment includible in the obligation's stated redemption price at maturity and the number of full years (rounding down for partial years) from the issue date to the date on which each such payment is due by (2) the sum of all such payments. If accruals of OID on a debt obligation are calculated under the PAC method, described below in the text, taking account of a reasonable prepayment assumption, then the same assumption should be applied in determining the weighted average maturity of the obligation. The OID regulations provide a simpler, elective *de minimis* rule for installment obligations that call for principal payments to be made at a rate no faster than principal payments on a self-amortizing installment obligation. A holder of such an obligation is permitted to compute the *de minimis* amount as the product of 1/6 (rounded to .167) of 1% of the obligation's stated redemption price at maturity and the number of full years (rounding down for a partial year) from the issue date to the final maturity date of the obligation. A self-amortizing installment obligation is generally an installment obligation that calls for equal payments of principal and interest at fixed periodic intervals of one year or less with no significant additional payments at maturity. See Treasury Regulation § 1.1273-1(e)(2). A typical residential mortgage is a self-amortizing installment obligation.

22   Interest is payable "unconditionally" only if late payment (other than a late payment that occurs within a reasonable grace period) or nonpayment is expected to be penalized or reasonable remedies exist to compel payment (but in any event interest is not unconditionally payable if the lending transaction does not reflect arm's length dealings and the holder does not expect to enforce remedies). Treasury Regulation § 1.1273-1(c)(1)(ii). In the case of a REMIC regular interest that takes the form of a beneficial interest in a trust, payments are typically made only out of available funds, and there are no remedies if those funds are not sufficient to make current distributions of interest. Because a REMIC is merely a conduit, however, such payments should be considered unconditionally due if they would be required to be made in the absence of a default on the underlying mortgages. Compare the discussion in Chapter 5, Part D.1 of the requirement in the REMIC rules that the holder of a regular interest be "unconditionally entitled" to a specified principal amount. Where a debt instrument provides for alternative payment schedules based on a contingency, interest is qualified stated interest only to the extent of the lowest fixed rate payable under any payment schedule. See Treasury Regulation § 1.1273-1(c)(2).

23   See section 1273(a)(2) (includes in stated redemption price at maturity all interest not paid at a fixed rate at *fixed* periodic intervals of one year or less over the entire term of an instrument), and Treasury Regulation § 1.1273-1(c) (defines qualified stated interest more flexibly as outlined in the text). If a debt instrument would not have OID except for the fact that the interest rate in one or more accrual periods (as defined in section 2 below) is less than the rate applicable for the remainder of the instrument's term, then a special *de minimis* rule applies. Under that rule, for purposes of determining whether there is *de minimis* OID, the stated redemption price at maturity is treated as the sum of the issue price and the greater of the forgone interest or the amount of any true discount. See Treasury Regulation §§ 1.1273-1(d)(4), and -1(f), Examples 5 and 6. A debt instrument is considered to have *de minimis* OID under this formula where the amount of foregone interest does not exceed the true discount. To illustrate the case when the foregone interest exceeds

Thus, interest is not qualified stated interest (and is includible in OID) to the extent it is payable during any year at a rate higher than the lowest rate at which interest is payable during any year over the life of the instrument. For example, all interest on an interest accrual or compound interest bond (which provides for the complete deferral of interest for at least one year) is includible in OID. A portion of the interest on a bond with a payment lag (that is, a lag between the end of the period over which interest accrues and the date on which such interest is paid) may be includible in OID if the bond has more than *de minimis* OID.[24]

Under section 1273(b)(1), the *issue price* of a debt obligation that is part of an issue[25] of publicly offered obligations is the initial offering price to the public (excluding bond houses and brokers) at which a substantial amount of the obligations is sold;[26] thus, neither the price at which the obligations are sold to the underwriters by the issuer nor the price at which any particular obligation is sold to an investor determines the issue price. Under section 1273(b)(2), the issue price of any obligation that is not part of an issue of publicly offered obligations is the price paid for that particular obligation by the first buyer. The OID regulations combine these two definitions into one applicable to both public offerings and private placements. Under the regulations, the issue price of each debt instrument in an issue issued for money is the first price at which a substantial amount of the debt instruments is sold to investors.[27]

---

the true discount, suppose that a debt instrument with a principal amount of $1,000 and a term of 20 years is issued at a price of $990 and pays interest semi-annually at a rate of 2% for the first six months after issuance and 8% thereafter. The instrument has *de minimis* OID, because the amount of OID is conidered to be $30 (the excess of the issue price of $990 plus the forgone interest of $30, over the issue price of $990), which is less than $51 (1/4 of 1% of $1,020 times 20).

24   If to reflect the payment lag the period until the first payment date on such bond is longer than the interval between payment dates, then interest would be paid at a lower effective rate for the first year. For a special *de minimis* rule for interest holidays, see footnote 23, above. For the treatment of accrued interest, see footnote 28, below.

25   Under Treasury Regulation § 1.1275-1(f), two or more obligations are part of a single "issue" if they have the same credit and payment terms and are sold reasonably close in time either pursuant to a common plan or as part of a single transaction or a series of related transactions.

26   Ten percent is generally considered a substantial amount for this purpose. Cf. Treasury Regulation § 1.148-1(b) (definition of issue price).

27   See Treasury Regulation § 1.1273-2(a)(1). Treasury Regulation § 1.1273-2(e) states that in determining the issue price and issue date, sales to bond houses, brokers or similar persons acting in the capacity of underwriters, placement agents, or wholesalers are ignored. The price at which a mortgage is originated is traditionally thought to be its issue price. In a case where a mortgage originator regularly originates residential mortgages for resale, the originator might arguably be considered a "wholesaler". Cf. Revenue Ruling 72-523, 1972-2 C.B. 242 (mortgage originator treated as dealer in mortgages). In that event, the price paid for a mortgage by the first buyer from the originator would determine its issue price. However, a mortgage originator typically is exposed to market risk for a significantly longer period than an underwriter. Also, if the originator resells loans in the form of pass-through certificates, it would not be selling the same security it purchased, and ordinarily, a purchase price would not be stated separately for individual mortgages in a pool. Treasury Regulation § 1.1273-2(a)(1) states that the issue price of a debt instrument evidencing a loan to a natural person is the amount loaned. This language suggests that the drafters did not intend to upset the traditional rule treating the price paid for a residential mortgage by the

Accrued interest with which a debt instrument is issued is generally included in both the issue price and stated redemption price at maturity of the instrument. However, if the first interest payment is made within one year of the issue date and at least equals the amount of pre-issuance accrued interest, then such interest may be directly offset against such accrued interest (with the result that both amounts may be disregarded in OID calculations).[28]

2. OID Accruals under the PAC Method

An investor who purchases a pay-through bond having OID at a yield to maturity not less than the yield to maturity at which it was initially offered must include in income, for each taxable year in which the investor holds the bond, the portion of the OID that is considered to accrue in such year (regardless of whether the investor otherwise reports income under a cash or accrual method of tax accounting).[29] As explained in more detail below, the portion of the OID on a bond that is considered to accrue in any period generally equals the amount by which the value of the bond would increase during such period if it continued at all times to have a yield to maturity equal to its yield to maturity at the time of issuance calculated based on its issue price. This method of accruing OID is known as the *constant yield, compound interest*, or *scientific* method.[30] It gives effect to the compounding of interest by including accrued but unpaid OID in the base to which the yield to maturity of the bond is applied in calculating future accruals of such discount.

The yield to an investor of a debt obligation purchased at a discount below its principal amount is greater the shorter the life of the obligation. In the case of most

---

originator as the issue price. It is not clear why sales to wholesalers are disregarded in determining an obligation's issue *date*. The obligation would be considered to be outstanding for tax purposes beginning with the date on when it is sold by the issuer, regardless of the purchaser's identity.

28   Treasury Regulation § 1.1273-2(m). The effect of the second approach is to treat the payment and repayment of accrued interest as a separate debt instrument that has a yield of zero, rather than as part of the overall debt instrument. Pre-issuance accrued interest is the interest that accrues economically prior to the issue date, and is not determined by the periods used in calculating accruals under the terms of the instrument. To illustrate, suppose that a bond pays on the 20th day of each month one month's worth of interest and that, according to the terms of the bond, such interest accrues during the preceding calendar month. The bond is issued on October 1 with one month's worth of accrued interest. The first interest payment date is October 20, 19 days after the issue date. The pre-issuance accrued interest is 11 days worth of interest, not 30. If the purchase price is quoted with 30 days of accrued interest, then the issue price should in all events include the 19 days worth of "extra" accrued interest (with the remaining 11 days of true pre-issuance accrued interest being handled as discussed in the text).

29   The rule requiring the current inclusion in income of OID has applied to corporate obligations since 1969. It was extended to obligations of other legal entities (governments, partnerships, and trusts) effective for obligations issued after July 1, 1982. The current inclusion rule was then further broadened to encompass obligations of individuals, including residential mortgages and other consumer loans, by the Tax Reform Act of 1984 (TRA 1984), effective for obligations issued—which in the case of mortgages means closed—after March 1, 1984.

30   The constant yield method was introduced into the tax law by the Tax Equity and Fiscal Responsibility Act of 1982 (TEFRA) and first applied to corporate and government obligations issued after July 1, 1982. For corporate obligations issued on or prior to that date, OID was accrued under a straight-line method, which allocated the same portion of the discount to each year.

pay-through bonds, it is highly probable that principal will be prepaid to some degree. The possibility of prepayments raises two related issues: first, whether OID should be accrued based on a yield that is calculated assuming that prepayments will occur at some reasonable rate; and second, how income is to be adjusted to account for differences between the assumed prepayment rate (a zero rate or a reasonable estimate) and the actual prepayment rate. Prior to the enactment of TRA 1986, there were no certain answers to these questions.[31] TRA 1986 clarified that, in the case of a pay-through bond issued after December 31, 1986, (1) the yield that is used in calculating accruals of OID will be determined based on a reasonable assumption (*Prepayment Assumption*) as to the rate at which the underlying mortgages will be prepaid, and, if earnings on temporary investments would affect the timing of payments on the bond, the rate of those earnings; (2) income will be adjusted in each taxable year (whether or not principal payments are made on the bond in that year) to reflect the economic gain or loss for that year (calculated based on changes in present values assuming a constant yield) resulting from past and present differences between actual prepayment experience and the Prepayment Assumption, but assuming that future prepayments on remaining mortgages will conform to the Prepayment Assumption; and (3) in general, those adjustments will increase or decrease interest income and not be treated as capital gain or loss.[32] The method for calculating accruals of OID introduced by TRA 1986 will be referred to as the *prepayment assumption catch-up method,* or *PAC method* for short.

In general, the Prepayment Assumption for any issue of bonds corresponds to the prepayment rate assumed in pricing the initial offering of the bonds and is stated

---

31   In brief, under pre-TRA 1986 law, most tax advisors assumed that accruals of OID should be calculated as though no prepayments would be made. If a bond was fully prepaid, the holder of the bond recognized gain equal to the amount of OID that would have been included in such holder's income after the date of the prepayment if the bond had not been prepaid and the holder had held it to maturity. It was not certain how gain from a partial prepayment would be calculated for a pay-through bond that provided for more than one scheduled payment of principal, but one reasonable way to calculate such gain was to compare the amount of the prepayment with the present value of the future scheduled payments that would not be made because of the prepayment, calculated using the original yield to maturity of the bond as the discount rate. Stated differently, the gain from the prepayment equaled the increase in the present value of the obligation attributable to the prepayment. It was not clear whether any adjustment to income or to the rate of accrual of OID was required or permitted when it became clear that principal payments on a bond would be prepaid in future periods. It is unclear whether, or to what extent, the TRA 1986 amendments will influence the development of the law applicable to debt instruments issued before 1987. For a more detailed discussion of the treatment of prepayments prior to the enactment of TRA 1986, see J. Peaslee, "Federal Income Tax Treatment of Mortgage-Backed Securities" in *The Handbook of Mortgage-Backed Securities,* Frank Fabozzi, ed. (Chicago: Probus, 1985), at 591-598.

32   The new method is found in section 1272(a)(6), and applies, according to section 1272(a)(6)(C), to any regular interest in a REMIC, any qualified mortgage held by a REMIC, and "any other debt instrument if payments under such debt instrument may be accelerated by reason of prepayments of other obligations securing such debt instrument (or, to the extent provided in regulations, by reason of other events)." No regulations have been issued under this section. Section 1271(a)(2) treats gain from the sale or exchange of a debt instrument as ordinary income to the extent it does not exceed the amount of unaccrued OID thereon, if there was at the time of issuance an intention to call the instrument before maturity. This rule does not apply to obligations subject to section 1272(a)(6). See Treasury Regulation § 1.1271-1(a)(2)(ii).

in the offering materials for the bonds.[33] Once determined, the Prepayment Assumption will not change to reflect changes in prepayment rates occurring after the issuance of the bonds. The Prepayment Assumption relates to a pool of mortgages and not to classes of bonds. Accordingly, for any pool of mortgages, the same assumption must be used with respect to each class of bonds that is affected by the performance of that pool.[34] Once determined, the Prepayment Assumption will not change to reflect changes in expectations of future prepayment rates. However, the PAC method does take actual prepayment experience into account. Typically, the Prepayment Assumption with respect to a mortgage pool is expressed as an assumption that a specified percentage of the pool principal balance at the beginning of a period will be prepaid in that period, and thus automatically adjusts for differences between actual past prepayments and assumed prepayments. The specified percentage may change over the life of the mortgages in the pool (for example, be lower in earlier periods).[35] Somewhat more lenient standards apply in setting a Prepayment Assumption for commercial loans than for residential loans.[36]

---

33 The method for determining the Prepayment Assumption will eventually be set forth in Treasury regulations (see section 1272(a)(6)(B)(iii)). However, the Conference Report at II-238-II-239 and Blue Book at 426 state that Congress intended that the regulations will provide that the Prepayment Assumption for any pay-through bonds will be the assumption used in pricing the bonds, provided that assumption is not unreasonable based on comparable transactions, if any exist. For publicly offered instruments, a prepayment assumption will be treated as unreasonable only in the presence of clear and convincing evidence. Unless regulations otherwise provide, the use of a mortgage prepayment assumption based on a recognized industry standard (such as the Public Securities Association, or PSA, standard described in footnote 35 below) would be permitted. A REMIC is required to describe the Prepayment Assumption relating to its regular interests in its first tax return, and to attach to the return a statement supporting the selection of the Prepayment Assumption. See Treasury Regulation § 1.860D-1(d)(2)(iii). A description of the Prepayment Assumption must also be included in OID legends. See Treasury Regulation § 1.6049-7(g)(iv), discussed in Chapter 11, Part A.2.

34 On the other hand, where a class of bonds is backed by different mortgage pools having different interest rates or other characteristics, different prepayment speeds may be assumed for the different pools. The need to use a single Prepayment Assumption for all classes of bonds can produce some odd results in cases where prepayment risks are magnified by dividing cash flows into interest-only and principal-only securities. These securities are created to accommodate different perceptions as to likely prepayment speeds. Purchasers of interest-only, and principal-only, securities generally expect, or at least hope, that prepayments will be slower, or faster, respectively, than the market generally assumes. As a result, yields calculated for interest-only or principal-only securities using a market Prepayment Assumption are generally lower than the yields expected by investors. Of course, differences between the Prepayment Assumption and actual experience are taken into account through the catch-up feature of the section 1272(a)(6) method.

35 For example, the PSA assumption that is often used for residential mortgages assumes prepayments at an annual rate equal to a percentage that increases by .2 percentage points per month over the first 30 months after origination of a mortgage, from .2% in the first month to 6% after 30 months, and remains constant at 6% thereafter. A PSA based assumption is generally expressed as a percentage of PSA, where the assumption just described is 100% PSA, as assumption of prepayments at twice that rate is 200% PSA, etc.

36 The Conference Report at II-239, footnote 23, and the Blue Book at 426, footnote 94, acknowledge that prepayments are more difficult to predict for commercial than for residential mortgages (for example, because of smaller numbers of loans, significant differences in the terms of individual mortgages and in the circumstances of borrowers, and the wider availability of mortgage assumptions where mortgaged properties are sold), and indicate that more leeway will be allowed

A bondholder is required to include in gross income in each taxable year the sum of the *daily portions* of OID for each day during the taxable year on which it holds the bond.[37] For an investor who purchased the bond in the initial offering at the issue price, two steps are needed to determine the daily portions of OID. First, a calculation is made of the portion of the OID that is allocable to each *accrual period* during the term of the bond. For a bond that provides for payments at fixed intervals over its life except for a short initial or final period, the accrual periods are generally the periods that end on each payment date and begin on the day after the immediate preceding payment date (or in the case of the first such period, begin on the issue date).[38] Second, the portion of the OID attributed to each accrual period is allocated ratably to each day during the period to determine the daily portion of OID for that day.

Under the PAC method, the amount of OID on a bond that is attributed to each accrual period is the *excess* of:

• the sum of the present value, as of the end of the accrual period, of all of the payments, if any, to be made on the bond in future periods[39] and the amount

---

in determining a Prepayment Assumption for commercial loans. Where commercial loans provide for bullet maturities, it is common to assume in pricing securities backed by those loans that the maturity dates will be extended for some period because of the inability of borrowers to pay the mortgages when due. In practice, these extensions are often taken into account in determining a Prepayment Assumption, although strictly speaking an extension is not a prepayment. This practice may be justified on the grounds that it provides a more accurate measure of income by reflecting the actual pricing assumption (and is therefore consistent with the premises of the PAC method), and that the stated terms of a particular mortgage no longer reflect the actual terms, because of the expectation, based on the characteristics of the mortgaged property or perhaps a tacit understanding of the parties, that the borrower will be unable to pay and the holder will not immediately take any action to foreclose on the mortgage. There are as yet no authorities either approving or disapproving of this practice. Compare the discussion of the effect of default losses on the Prepayment Assumption at the end of Part G.2.

37   Section 1272(a).

38   Section 1272(a)(5) defines *accrual period* as a six-month period (or shorter period from the issue date of the bond) that ends on a day in the calendar year corresponding to the maturity date of the bond or the date six months before such maturity date. This definition is subject to change through regulations. Treasury Regulation § 1.1272-1(b)(1)(ii) provides that accrual periods may be of any length and may vary in length over the term of the debt instrument, provided that each accrual period is no longer than one year and each scheduled payment of principal or interest occurs on the first or last day of an accrual period. The regulation states further that the computation of OID is simplest if accrual periods correspond to the intervals between payment dates provided by the terms of the debt instrument, and that in computing the length of accrual periods, any reasonable counting convention may be used (e.g., 30 days per month/360 days per year). Technically, Treasury Regulation § 1.1272-1(b)(1) does not apply to debt instruments to which the PAC method applies. See Treasury Regulation § 1.1272-1(b)(2)(i) (paragraph (b)(1) does not apply to a debt instrument to which section 1272(a)(6) applies). There are no other regulations currently in effect or proposed that would alter the Code definition of accrual period for those instruments. However, while different rules may some day be adopted in determining the accrual periods for PAC method securities, it is highly likely that accrual periods based on the actual period between payment dates (with a short initial or final period) will be allowed, and this result is universally assumed in practice.

39   The present value of all future payments on a bond presumably would *not* include the value of a forthcoming payment of a call premium, for periods after the issuer has given notice to the holders

of any payments made on the bond during the accrual period that are includible in its stated redemption price at maturity, *over*

* the adjusted issue price of the bond at the beginning of such period.

The present value of the future payments on the bond would be calculated for this purpose (1) assuming that the mortgages underlying the bond will be prepaid in future periods in accordance with the Prepayment Assumption (but taking account of the actual prepayments that have occurred to date) and (2) using a discount rate equal to the yield to maturity of the bond.

The *yield to maturity* of the bond is the discount rate, assuming compounding at the end of each accrual period, that causes the present value of all future payments on the bond to equal its issue price on the issue date, calculated assuming that the bond will be prepaid in all periods in accordance with the Prepayment Assumption.[40] The *adjusted issue price* of a bond at the beginning of an accrual period equals its issue price, increased by the aggregate amount of OID on the bond attributed to all prior accrual periods, if any, and decreased by the amount of any payments made on the bond in prior periods that were includible in its stated redemption price at maturity. Thus, the adjusted issue price represents an initial purchaser's remaining capital investment in the bond, adjusted for the amount of

---

of its intention of calling the bond, assuming that the notice was given in the ordinary course, in connection with, and just prior to, the call. Otherwise, the call premium would be converted into additional interest. In general, call premium is treated as an additional payment made to retire a debt instrument and as such may be treated by holders as capital gain. See Revenue Ruling 72-587, 1972-2 C.B. 74, modified on other grounds by Revenue Ruling 80-143, 1980-1 C.B. 19; G.C.M. 39543 (August 9, 1986); G.C.M. 39309 (May 31, 1984); *Prudential Insurance Co. of America v. Comm'r*, 882 F.2d 832 (3rd Cir. 1989). In the case of a debt obligation of an individual, call premium is treated as ordinary income in the hands of the holder because of the lack of a sale or exchange. See footnote 15. Contrary to the rulings cited above, the Service takes the position that such income is interest income (Revenue Ruling 86-42, 1986-1 C.B. 82). See also Treasury Regulation § 1.163-7(c) (retirement premium is interest deductible by issuer).

40   Treasury Regulation § 1.1272-1(c)(5) provides a special rule for computing the yield to maturity of a bond that is subject to an unconditional optional call by the issuer (or put by the holder). Under that rule, in determining the bond's yield to maturity, if, as of the issue date, the amounts payable upon exercise of the option (or put) are fixed, the call (or put) is to be treated as being exercised only if the exercise would reduce (or, in the case of a put, increase) such yield. An optional call at a price not less than par of a bond that was issued at a discount below its principal amount would ordinarily increase the yield of the bond, and thus would be ignored under this rule. Subsequent adjustments are made if a call or put that is assumed to be exercised is not in fact exercised. See Treasury Regulation § 1.1272-1(c)(6). The OID regulations also provide that a timing contingency other than an unconditional issuer or holder option is not taken into account for purposes of determining a debt instrument's yield unless, as of the issue date, based on all the facts and circumstances, it is more likely than not that the instrument will not pay according to its stated payment schedule, in which case, it is assumed that payments will be made according to the most likely alternative schedule. The payment schedule determined by the issuer under these rules is binding on a holder unless the holder discloses in its tax return that it is taking a contrary position. See Treasury Regulation §§ 1.1272-1(c)(2) through (4). There is no explicit carve out from these rules for instruments subject to the PAC method, although the drafters clearly did not intend to override the PAC method where it applies. Treasury Regulation § 1.1272-1(b)(2)(i) excludes PAC method securities from the rules of "paragraph (b)(1)" but not from paragraph (c).

OID that has been earned and included in income for tax purposes but not yet paid. Special rules apply to initial short accrual periods.[41]

The method of calculating daily accruals of OID outlined above applies to any investor that purchases a pay-through bond at a price equal to or less than its adjusted issue price at the time of purchase. Where the purchase price exceeds the adjusted issue price, the holder is allowed to offset that excess amount *(acquisition premium)* against the daily portions of OID.[42] In particular, each daily portion is reduced by a fixed fraction. The numerator of the fraction is the acquisition premium and the denominator is the sum of the daily portions (determined without regard to any acquisition premium adjustment) for all days on or after the purchase date through the maturity date of the bond. Thus, if the acquisition premium for any bondholder represents 25 percent of the aggregate amount of OID that remains to be accrued after the purchase date, the amount of OID that would otherwise be required to be included in the holder's income for any day would be reduced by 25 percent.[43] An investor that buys an OID bond at a premium (i.e., a price exceeding its remaining stated redemption price at maturity) is not required to include any OID in income.[44]

---

41   Treasury Regulation § 1.1272-1(b)(4)(iii) provides that if all accrual periods are of equal length except for an initial shorter accrual period, then the OID allocable to the initial accrual period may be computed using any reasonable method. Treasury Regulation § 1.1272-1(j), Example 3, illustrates two methods, which (based on the terminology in the 1986 version of the proposed OID regulations) are generally known as the "exact" and "approximate" methods. Under the exact method, the yield used in calculating OID for the initial short period is $(1 + Y)^F - 1$, where Y is the yield for a whole accrual period and F is a fraction whose numerator is the number of days in the short period and whose denominator is the number of days in a full accrual period. Under the approximate method, the yield would be Y×F. These methods are not directly relevant in applying the PAC method, because the calculation for the initial period under that method would not involve multiplication by a yield, but instead a comparison of the issue price (which is not affected by yield) with payments received during the short accrual period and the present value of future payments as of the end of the first accrual period (the calculation of which does not involve short periods, assuming the only short period is the initial one). The short period enters into the calculation only by affecting the overall yield to maturity of the instrument that is used as the discount rate. Presumably, either the exact method or an approximate method could be used to take account of the short period in calculating the discount rate. The exact method is by far the more common choice. The OID legend that must be attached to pay-through bonds requires a calculation of OID for any short initial period based on the Prepayment Assumption, and a description of the method used to determine the yield for that period. See Treasury Regulation §§ 1.6049-7(g)(1)(v) and (vi), discussed in Chapter 11, Part A.2. The actual amount of OID allocated to the initial period will of course depend on the actual prepayments received in the first period.

42   See section 1272(a)(7).

43   See Treasury Regulation §§ 1.1272-1(b)(3)(i) and 1.1272-2(a). The formula for accounting for acquisition premium described in the text would not always produce proper results in a case where stated interest on a bond is included in its stated redemption price at maturity, because the aggregate amount of daily portions to which the fraction described in the text would be applied would then vary depending on prepayments. The aggregate adjustment would vary correspondingly, even though the acquisition premium is a fixed amount. Although there is no direct authority supporting such an approach, one simple solution that appears to be reasonable would be to exclude stated interest from OID solely for purposes of accounting for acquisition premium.

44   Section 1272(c). For the definition of premium that applies for this purpose, see Treasury Regulation § 1.1272-2(b)(2).

If prepayments on mortgages backing a discount bond are slower than assumed, it may be possible for the PAC formula to produce an amount for an accrual period that is negative. The TRA 1986 legislative history states that in such an event the amount of OID allocable to the period would be treated as zero, and the computation of OID for the next accrual period (and presumably for successive periods until the formula produced a positive amount of OID) would be made by treating the first accrual period and the later ones as a single accrual period.[45] If this approach were literally applied, it might not be possible to determine the income of one taxable year until several years later. An accrual period could span a number of years, and any positive amount of OID that eventually resulted under the formula would, under the normal rules for calculating daily portions of OID, be allocated ratably over the entire period. Hopefully, the language in the legislative history will be interpreted to mean only that no deduction for negative amounts of OID will be allowed, and the adjusted issue price at the beginning of each accrual period (determined under normal rules) will be increased by any negative amounts of OID for prior periods for which no deduction was allowed.

The prohibition against negative amounts of OID could potentially produce significantly different tax results for two bonds that are issued at the same discount below their principal amounts and that are otherwise substantially identical except that the stated interest on one bond is treated as OID whereas the stated interest on the other bond is not treated as OID. It is much less likely that a given slowdown in prepayments would produce a net negative amount of OID for the first bond than for the second.

The prohibition against deducting negative amounts determined with respect to a bond under the PAC method should be limited to cases where allowing the deduction would reduce the holder's tax basis in the bond to below its remaining principal amount. This point is discussed in Part G.1 below.

3. Example

It will help in explaining the PAC method to apply it to a concrete example. For the sake of simplicity, the example assumes an obligation that pays interest currently at a fixed rate and provides for a single payment of principal. The extension of the method to obligations that provide for payments of principal in installments is straightforward, although the computations can rapidly become burdensome. We will begin by assuming no anticipated or actual prepayments.

Consider a pay-through bond having a principal amount of $1,000 that was issued at a price of $770.60 on April 1, 1994, bears interest at an annual rate of 8 percent, payable on April 1 and October 1, and matures on April 1, 2004. Principal is required to be paid prior to maturity out of principal prepayments on the mortgage collateral. The bond has OID of $229.40. Suppose initially that the Prepayment Assumption is that no mortgage will be prepaid, and that under that assump-

---

45   See Conference Report at II-239; Blue Book at 426.

tion, the entire $1,000 will be paid at maturity. Given that assumption, the semiannual yield to maturity of the bond, based on compounding at the end of each accrual period, is 6 percent.[46] The OID allocable to the first accrual period ending October 1, 1994 is $6.24. This represents the *excess* of:

- the sum of (1) the present value as of October 1, 1994 of the future payments to be made on the bond, calculated using a discount rate equal to the yield to maturity of the bond and assuming, in accordance with the Prepayment Assumption, no future prepayments ($776.84), and (2) the principal payments made on the bond in the accrual period, which are the only payments includible in its stated redemption price at maturity ($0), *over*

- the adjusted issue price at the beginning of the accrual period, which for the first accrual period equals the issue price of $770.60.

The corresponding amount for the second accrual period ending April 1, 1995 is $6.61 [($783.45 + $0) – $776.84]. If the initial holder of the bond reports income based on the calendar year, the holder would include in income for 1994 the sum of all daily portions for the first accrual period ending October 1, 1994 ($6.24) and the sum of the daily portions for the days in the second accrual period which are on or prior to December 31, 1994. Using a 30-days-per-month/360-days-per-year convention, the second accrual period consists of 180 days, of which 90 are on or prior to December 31, 1994. Thus, the sum of the daily portions of OID for the days in the second accrual period that are on or prior to December 31, 1994 is 90/180 times $6.61, or (rounding up) $3.31. The total amount of OID includible in income by such holder in 1994 is therefore $9.55 ($6.24 + $3.31). The adjusted issue prices for the bond are plotted as line *a* in Figure 6-1.

It has been assumed so far that the pay-through bond is not expected to be, and is not in fact, prepaid. However, the PAC method accommodates both expected and actual prepayments. Expected prepayments are taken into account by assuming that the mortgages underlying the bond will prepay according to the Prepayment Assumption, both initially in calculating the yield to maturity and over time in determining the present value of future payments. Actual prepayment experience affects the amount and timing of the current payments and expected future payments that enter into the PAC formula.

To illustrate the consequences of different prepayment expectations, suppose that the Prepayment Assumption is changed and that under the new assumption the entire $1,000 principal amount of the bond will be paid four years prior to maturity on April 1, 2000. Given that assumption, the semiannual yield of the bond would increase from 6 percent to 6.87 percent. Using that yield in the formula set forth earlier,[47] and assuming that prepayments occur in accordance with the Prepayment

---

46   In other words, the present value of all interest and principal payments on the bond, calculated using a discount rate for each semiannual period of 6%, equals the $770.60 purchase price.

47   Treasury Regulation § 1.1272-1(b)(1)(i) requires yield, when expressed as a percentage, to be calculated with at least two decimal place accuracy. A greater number of significant digits was

Figure 6-1
Adjusted Issue Prices of Bond
Under Different Prepayment Assumptions

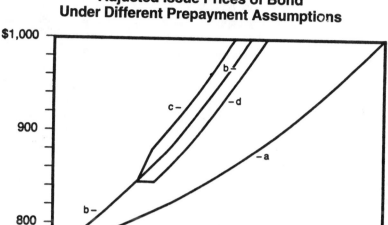

* The adjusted issue price plotted above each year is the adjusted issue price for April 1 of that year.

Assumption, the amounts of OID allocable to the first two accrual periods would increase from $6.24 and $6.61, calculated above, to $12.92 [($783.52 + $0) – $770.60] and $13.82 [($797.34 + $0) – $783.52]. The adjusted issue prices of the bond based on the new Prepayment Assumption are shown as line *b* in Figure 6-1.

To illustrate the case where prepayments are received at a faster than expected pace, suppose that prepayments on the bond described in the immediately preceding paragraph conform to the Prepayment Assumption until October 1, 1997, but because of greater than expected prepayments between October 2, 1997 and April 1, 1998, the bond is fully retired on April 1, 1998. In that event, the adjusted issue price on October 1, 1997 would equal $881.99, the present value at that time of all future payments on the bond, calculated assuming a $1,000 payment of principal on April 1, 2000. Under the PAC formula, the amount of OID allocable to the accrual period ending April 1, 1998 would equal $118.01, which is the excess of the payments received during the accrual period that are includible in the stated redemption price at maturity, or $1,000, plus the present value of all future payments ($0, because the bond is fully retired at the end of the period) over $881.99. Thus, the OID that otherwise would be included in income over two years and six months

used in the example, with the results being rounded to nearest cent.

(October 1, 1997 through April 1, 2000) is allocated instead to the accrual period ending April 1, 1998 because of the earlier than expected prepayments.

The PAC method also takes account of changes in the expected timing of future payments determined by applying the Prepayment Assumption to actual mortgage principal balances. Return once more to the bond described in the second preceding paragraph. If prepayments follow the Prepayment Assumption until October 1, 1996, the adjusted issue price of the bond at that time would be $844.73, the present value of the future payments on the bond based on a $1,000 payment of principal on April 1, 2000. If mortgage prepayments continued to track the Prepayment Assumption throughout the next accrual period ending April 1, 1997, the amount of OID that would be allocated to that period would be $18.01. However, suppose instead that during that accrual period, mortgage prepayments are, alternatively, faster or slower than anticipated. As a result, it is determined (by applying the Prepayment Assumption to the mortgages held by the issuer at the end of the accrual period) that the $1,000 principal amount will be paid six months earlier, in the case of the faster prepayments, or six months later, in the case of the slower prepayments, than originally anticipated. Moving the expected retirement date forward (or back) increases (or decreases) the present value of the future payments on the bond as of April 1, 1997 from $862.74 to $881.99 (or $844.73), and thus increases (or decreases) the amount of OID allocated under the PAC method to the accrual period ending April 1, 1997 to $37.26 (or $0), respectively.

The effect of the two six-month changes in expected retirement dates on the adjusted issue prices for the bond is shown graphically in Figure 6-1. Lines *c* and *d* show adjusted issue prices giving effect to the faster or slower prepayments, respectively, during the accrual period ending April 1, 1997 (assuming that there are no deviations from the Prepayment Assumption in subsequent periods). The effect of the difference in prepayments on the amount of OID allocated to the accrual period ending April 1, 1997 is represented by the vertical distance between line *b* and line *c* or *d*, as the case may be, on that date.

The examples just discussed involve a bond that provides for only a single payment of principal. In most cases, however, pay-through bonds provide for payments of principal in installments. The only difference that this change would cause in applying the PAC method is that the amount included in the formula for payments that are included in the stated redemption price at maturity would be positive for each accrual period during which some principal amount is paid.

4. Variable Rates

REMIC regular interests are allowed to pay interest at a variable rate, to the extent provided in regulations. As detailed in Chapter 5, the REMIC regulations allow a wide range of variable rates based on interest rate indices or a weighted average of the rates on the underlying mortgages. Combinations of different indexed, weighted average, or fixed rates are also allowed. Further, a REMIC regular interest can pay interest equal to a specified portion of the interest payments on one or more qualified mortgages bearing interest at a variable rate.

The OID regulations divide variable rate debt instruments into two groups: *variable rate debt instruments* or *VRDIs* and *contingent payment debt instruments*. Different substantive rules apply to each type of obligation. The definition of VRDI is tailored to the needs of the OID rules and is not the same as the definition of permitted variable rate regular interests. The VRDI definition is both narrower and broader in some respects.[48] Under current law, many variable rate regular interests would fall into the contingent payment category.

The OID rules are applied to a VRDI by converting the variable interest payments into equivalent fixed interest payments, and then applying the general OID rules to the resulting fixed rate instrument.[49] Qualified stated interest or OID alloc-

---

48 A VRDI is defined in Treasury Regulation § 1.1275-5(a). In general terms, a VRDI is limited to an instrument that (1) is not issued at a premium (expressed as a percentage of its noncontingent principal amount) exceeding 15% (or if the instrument has a weighted average maturity, determined as described in footnote 21 above, less than 10 years, 1.5% times such weighted average maturity); (2) pays or compounds stated interest at least annually; and (3) provides for stated interest at a rate that consists of one or more *qualified floating rates*, a single fixed rate and one or more qualified floating rates, a single *objective rate*, or a single fixed rate and a single objective rate that is a *qualified inverse floating rate*. A rate is a qualified floating rate if variations in the rate can reasonably be expected to measure contemporaneous variations in the cost of newly borrowed funds (for the particular issuer or issuers in general) in the currency in which the debt instrument is denominated (or is a positive multiple of such a rate not exceeding 1.35), and the rate is not subject to overall or periodic caps or floors, unless those caps or floors either are fixed over the life of the instrument, or are not reasonably expected as of the issue date to change significantly the yield of the debt instrument. An objective rate is a rate (other than a qualified floating rate) that is determined using a single fixed formula and is based on (1) one or more qualified floating rates (e.g., a multiple of such a rate that is negative or exceeds 1.35), (2) one or more rates that would be qualified floating rates for debt instruments denominated in another currency, (3) the yield or changes in the price of one or more items of actively traded personal property (including debt instruments, commodities and equities, but not including stock or debt of the issuer or a related party), or (4) any combination of (1) through (3). However, a variable rate is not an objective rate if it is reasonably expected that the average value of the rate during the first half of the instrument's term will differ significantly from its average value during the second half. A rate is considered to be a qualified floating rate or objective rate even though the initial rate is fixed for a period less than one year in an amount that is intended to approximate the value of the variable rate. A rate is a qualified inverse floating rate if it equals a fixed rate minus a qualified floating rate and variations in the rate can reasonably be expected to inversely reflect contemporaneous variations in the cost of newly borrowed funds. It is not clear whether this language limits an inverse floater to one based on a multiple of minus one. Apparently, the fixed rate used in calculating a qualified inverse floating rate must be set so that the initial value of the rate is not close to the floor rate. See Treasury Regulation § 1.1275-5(d), Example 9. By contrast with a VRDI, REMIC regular interests can be issued at a premium exceeding 15%, need not pay or compound interest at least annually (although they typically do), can switch between different fixed or variable rates without limitation, can be based on any positive or negative multiple of an interest rate index, can be based on a weighted average of different fixed rates (which would not be either a qualified floating rate or an objective rate), and cannot generally be based on the prices of publicly traded property (except to the extent those prices are reflected in interest rate indices). See generally Chapter 5, Part C.3.

49 See Treasury Regulation § 1.1275-5(e). The fixed rate substitute for any qualified floating rate or qualified inverse floating rate is calculated based on the value of the underlying index as of the issue date. The fixed rate substitute for an objective rate (other than a qualified inverse floating

able to an accrual period is adjusted if the actual interest for the period differs from the assumed fixed interest amount. The adjustment increases or decreases qualified stated interest if the fixed interest for the period is qualified stated interest and the adjustment is reflected in the amount actually paid during the period. Otherwise, the adjustment increases or decreases OID for the accrual period.[50]

As of this writing, the tax rules governing contingent payment debt instruments are in a state of flux. Although a set of proposed tax rules exist, they are flawed, are widely expected never to be adopted as final regulations, and to a growing extent are given little weight as a source of guidance on the tax treatment of contingent debt securities.[51] In practice, the principles of the VRDI rules are applied to all types of variable rate REMIC regular interests, and also generally to variable rate non-REMIC pay-through bonds if the variation in rates is based on changes in market interest rates, even where those rules do not technically apply.

One major payment contingency affecting most mortgage-backed securities is, of course, uncertainty as to the timing of mortgage prepayments. The PAC method takes a direct aim at this problem, and accordingly will most likely be considered to preempt any more general contingent payment rules that may be adopted as a means of dealing with prepayments. The PAC method can easily be combined with the principles of the VRDI rules. Those rules account for OID as if it were earned with respect to a hypothetical fixed rate debt instrument, and income on that instrument can be calculated under the PAC method in the normal way.

A REMIC regular interest can bear interest at a rate equal to a weighted average of the interest rates on qualified mortgages held by the REMIC (provided those mortgages themselves bear interest at a fixed or variable rate permitted under

---

rate) is a fixed rate that "reflects the yield that is reasonably expected for the debt instrument." Treasury Regulation §§ 1.1275-5(e)(2)(ii) and (e)(3)(i). Where rates are reset at different intervals over the life of a debt instrument, adjustments are made to ensure that the equivalent fixed rates all are based on the same interval. Treasury Regulation §§ 1.1275-5(e)(3)(i) (variable rates with different reset intervals) and (e)(4) (variable rate instrument with a single fixed rate). A special rule applies to a varible rate obligation that provides for interest at a rate that is fixed for an initial interval, and then is reset (e.g., through an auction) so that the fair market value of the obligation equals a fixed amount. Solely for purposes of calculating accruals of OID, the instrument is treated as if it were retired and reissued when the reset rate goes into effect. Treasury Regulation § 1.1275-5(f).

50   Treasury Regulation § 1.1275-5(e)(3)(iv).

51   The existing rules are in Proposed Regulation § 1.1275-4. One reason for the decline in the stature of these proposed rules is that a substantially different set of regulations on the same subject was released to the public in January of 1993 at the end of the Bush administration, but was then not officially issued because of a general moratorium on the issuance of Bush-era regulations adopted at the beginning of the Clinton administration. The current state of play is described in a recent report by two bar groups. See New York State Bar Association and American Bar Association, Tax Sections, Committee on Financial Transactions, "Report and Recommendation for the Treatment of Contingent Debt Instruments under Proposed Regulation Section 1.1275-4," 61 *Tax Notes* 1241 (December 6, 1993). This report recommends a new approach to the treatment of contingent payment debt instruments that would expand significantly the VRDI definition—and correspondingly shrink the role of any separate rules for contingent payment instruments —to cover virtually all current pay fixed principal instruments that do not provide for a front- or back-loading of interest. For earlier criticism of Proposed Regulation § 1.1275-4, see NYSBA 1987 Report at 388.

the REMIC rules). In a case where mortgages bear interest at different fixed rates, then the rate payable in each period will depend on the relative principal balances of the mortgages taken into account in the average. The Prepayment Assumption can be used to predict the relative balances of individual mortgages in future periods and hence the average rate. Once uncertainty as to future payments has been eliminated, the PAC method can be applied.[52] If the loans included in the weighted average include one or more variable rate loans, then the principles of the VRDI rules could be applied to address the variable rate contingency.[53]

D. Pass-Through Certificates

The degree to which the OID rules will influence the taxation of a pass-through certificate depends primarily on whether the stripped bond rules of section 1286 apply. If they do, then the OID rules will play a central role. On the other hand, OID is unlikely to be present in pass-through certificates that do not fall within that section, except in cases in which the underlying mortgages provide for negative amortization, or have teaser rates (initial below market rates) that reflect unusually

---

52   One issue that will arise in applying the PAC method is how to take account of events that occur after the issue date of a debt instrument that will cause the weighted average rate in future periods to differ from the weighted average rate that was originally assumed in determining the yield to maturity of the instrument. Consistent with the VRDI rules, changes in stated interest payments in future periods that are not scheduled to occur under the terms of the instrument should be taken into account only in those periods. To illustrate, suppose that a regular interest bears interest, payable monthly, at a rate equal to a weighted average of the rates on mortgages A, B, and C, the rates taken into account in the average (giving effect to any adjustment to those rates that are made) are 6, 7, and 8%, and each loan is subject to prepayment (so that any of the mortgages could be prepaid, leaving the remaining mortgage or mortgages behind). If the mortgages have equal scheduled principal amounts and are included in a single pool of mortgages that has a single Prepayment Assumption, then the expected rate of stated interest would be 7%. If mortgages A and B, or B and C were prepaid, the rate on the regular interest in all future periods would be 8% or 6%, respectively. If the PAC method were applied giving effect to the actual composition of the pool, then the full present value of the difference between the initial yield to maturity based on stated interest of 7% and the actual yield of the pool would be taken into account as the composition of the pool changes, producing potentially significant swings in income. This result is not appropriate. The basic thrust of the VRDI rules is to tax stated interest in the period in which it accrues under the terms of the instrument, except in cases where at the time of issuance of the instrument periods of lower and higher interest rates (in value terms) can be identified. In this example, the increase or decrease in rates that occurs was not predicted and should be taken into account only in the periods in which interest accrues at the higher or lower rates. This result can be accomplished mechanically by assuming, in applying the PAC method, that the rate of interest in future periods remains at the initially assumed rate of 7% regardless of what the actual composition of the pool may be. All interest on the regular interest should be treated as qualified stated interest, notwithstanding that interest may dip as low as 6%. The variation in rates would be no more significant here than in the case of a typical VRDI bearing interest at an indexed rate that may go up or down over its term.

53   One fairly straightforward way to achieve this result is to apply the PAC method and (1) determine the composition of the underlying mortgage pool in future periods using the Prepayment Assumption and (2) determine future interest payments on the regular interest by treating each qualified mortgage as if it paid fixed interest based on a value for the underlying rate index equal to its value on the issue date of the regular interest. Differences between assumed and actual interest payments would be accounted for in the usual way. See footnote 50, above, and accompanying text.

large discounts below market rates. The two types of pass-through certificates are considered next, beginning with those subject to the stripped bond rules.

1. Pass-Through Certificates Subject to the Stripped Bond Rules

a. Definition of Stripped Bond or Coupon. Section 1286 contains special rules governing the taxation of stripped bonds and stripped coupons. A *stripped bond* is a bond issued with coupons (which, for this purpose, include any rights to receive stated interest), where there is a separation in ownership between the bond and any coupons that have not yet come due. A *stripped coupon* is a coupon relating to a stripped bond. The tax treatment of stripped bonds and stripped coupons is generally the same, and the term *stripped bond* will be used in this discussion to refer to both.

The classic example of a bond stripping transaction is a sale by the owner of a whole bond of unmatured interest coupons to one investor and rights to principal to a second investor. (Alternatively, the seller could sell only the coupons or the rights to principal and retain the remaining interests in the bond.) IO and PO Strips represent the extension of this transaction pattern to mortgage-backed securities. Because of the extreme sensitivity of the yields of these types of securities to changes in the rate of prepayment of the underlying mortgages, they may be thought to resemble options, futures contracts or other derivative financial instruments more than debt. Nonetheless, there is little doubt that IO and PO Strips fall within section 1286. The underlying mortgages are debt obligations, and the complete separation of rights to interest and principal on a debt obligation is the clearest possible example of bond stripping.

Subject to two important exceptions described in the next paragraph, the bond stripping rules also extend to situations in which there is some but not complete separation in the ownership of rights to principal and interest. One common example is the transaction described in Chapter 2[54] in which a mortgage originator holding discount or premium mortgages creates pass-through certificates that can be sold at par by retaining a share of interest payments (in the case of the premium mortgages) or a share of principal payments (in the case of the discount mortgages).[55] Where mortgages have a range of interest rates, rights to interest payments exceeding the lowest common rate may also be retained in order to provide a single pass-through rate for investors. The retention of a partial ownership interest in mortgage interest payments is often achieved mechanically by charging excess servicing. The IRS has ruled that excess servicing (defined as a right to payments for servicing that exceed compensation at a market rate) is treated for tax purposes as an ownership interest in mortgage interest payments.[56]

---

54   See Chapter 2, Part B.2.

55   Revenue Ruling 71-399, 1971-2 C.B. 433, analyzes the tax treatment of non-pro rata interests in principal and interest payments on mortgages in a pool under the law in effect before the enactment of the bond stripping rules. See also P.L.R. 8827002 (March 30, 1988).

56   See Revenue Ruling 91-46, 1991-2 C.B. 358, discussed in Chapter 3 at footnote 101 (effect of

Section 1286 does not apply to investors purchasing an interest in a stripped mortgage (one from which some interest coupons have been removed) in two cases:[57] (1) where the stripped mortgage would be considered to have no OID under the general OID *de minimis* rule if, *immediately after* the separation in ownership of the interest strip, the stripped mortgage was newly issued at an issue price equal to the price at which it is sold to investors, and (2) where the amount of interest that has been stripped from the mortgage (including excess servicing but not including reasonable servicing compensation) does not exceed 100 basis points per annum (without regard to whether the stripped mortgage would have OID if it were newly issued).[58] Whether these exceptions apply to a stripped mortgage in the hands of any investor depends on the nature of the original stripping transaction and not on the price paid for the stripped mortgage by the investor. The first of the two rules has the practical effect of nullifying section 1286 for investors purchasing pass-through certificates from which some interest has been stripped, if those certificates were not sold immediately following the stripping transaction at a discount below their principal amount that exceeded 1/6 of 1 percent of the aggregate principal amount of the mortgages multiplied by their remaining weighted average life (calculated assuming no prepayments and by rounding partial years to zero).[59]

---

recharacterization on classification of trusts) and Chapter 12 at footnotes 2–5 and 17, and accompanying text (effect on sponsors). The recharacterization of excess servicing as an ownership interest has the effect of increasing the gain or reducing the loss recognized by the seller/servicer on sale of a mortgage pool, because of the need to allocate some amount of basis to the retained interest.

57   Technically, these exceptions do not alter the definition of a stripped bond but instead nullify the effect of section 1286 for investors by requiring them to treat discount that otherwise would be OID under section 1286 (as described in the next section) into discount that is not OID. In other words, the discount is either market discount, as defined in section 1278, or if it is *de minimis* as to any investor under the market discount *de minimis* rule, discount other than market discount or OID. Market discount is discussed in Part E below. It is not clear how these exceptions apply to a stripped mortgage in cases where the whole mortgage had OID because it was originated at a discount, although this case will rarely arise. See Part D.2 below. The rules do not affect the gain or loss recognized by the party stripping the mortgage.

58   Treasury Regulation § 1.1286-1(b) authorizes the Service to issue a statement implementing these two exceptions. Such authority was exercised in Revenue Procedure 91-49, 1991-2 C.B. 777. This revenue procedure is effective August 8, 1991. It provides rules for changing from a different method of accounting for stripped bonds to the one set forth in the revenue procedure. The general OID *de minimis* rule is described above in the text at footnote 21. The general rule is applied to a stripped mortgage by treating all payments remaining after the strip as if they were payments on a single, newly originated mortgage. In other words, the mortgage is not viewed as a collection of individual payments, each of which would be a zero coupon bond having more than *de minimis* OID. The preamble to the section 1286 regulations, T.D. 8463, I.R.B. 1993-9, 21-22, acknowledges that this aggregation approach is implicit in the *de minimis* rule for stripped mortgages, and requests comments as to whether a similar aggregation approach should be applied more generally under section 1286. Although all payments on a single mortgage are aggregated in applying the *de minimis* rule, it does not necessarily follow that all mortgages in a pool are also aggregated for this purpose. If all mortgages in a pool are not aggregated, then, in the unusual case where the net mortgage coupon (after the strip) is not the same on all mortgages in the pool, it is possible that some lower-net-coupon mortgages would have greater than *de minimis* OID and some would not. Also, under a loan by loan approach, the 100 basis point threshold could be exceeded for some mortgages and not others.

The consequences of recombining all of the stripped interests in a single debt instrument are not clear. It appears, however, that section 1286 would continue to apply to those interests in the hands of any person who has held any of them as a stripped bond, but would not apply to a new investor who purchases all of the stripped interests together.[60]

b. Treatment of Stripped Bonds. Subject to the exceptions described in the last section, section 1286 generally transforms the discount at which a stripped bond is purchased into OID. Specifically, section 1286(a) provides that if a person purchases a stripped bond, then, for purposes of applying the OID rules of the Code,[61] the stripped bond will be treated, while held by that person, as a bond originally issued on the purchase date having OID equal to the excess of the stated redemption price at maturity of the stripped bond over its purchase price.[62] However, no amount is treated as OID if that excess amount is less than a *de minimis* amount (determined by applying the general OID definition as if the stripped bond were a newly issued debt obligation with an issue price equal to the purchase price).[63] Where a stripped bond is considered to be purchased with more than a *de minimis* amount of OID, then under the OID rules of

---

59   The statement in the text assumes either that all mortgages underlying the certificates are aggregated in applying the general OID *de minimis* rule (see footnote 58 above), or that the mortgages have substantially the same remaining maturities and net mortgage coupons (after giving effect to the strip). It also assumes that all interest on the mortgages is qualified stated interest. The 1/6 of 1% formula reflects a special rule for self-amortizing loans, described in footnote 21 above. Ordinarily, the issue price of newly issued debt instruments is determined based on the price at which a portion of the issue is purchased by initial buyers. See the text at footnote 26 above. Under a literal reading of the section 1286 regulations, the issue price for an issue of pass-through certificates might be based on the price paid for each certificate by its first buyer, although it seems very unlikely that this reading was intended. To explain, the special stripped bond exception in Treasury Regulation § 1.1286-1(b)(2)(i) applies if OID is considered to be zero under section 1.1286(a). The latter section states that OID is considered to be zero if the OID determined under section 1286(a) with respect to "the purchase of a stripped bond or stripped coupon" is less than a *de minimis* amount under the general OID rule.

60   Because section 1286 applies to any person who *purchases* a stripped bond, the status of an interest in a debt instrument as a stripped bond in the hands of any particular investor should be determined when that interest is acquired by that investor. See New York State Bar Association, Ad Hoc Committee on Original Issue Discount and Coupon Stripping, "Preliminary Report on Issues to be Addressed in Regulations and Corrective Legislation," reprinted in *Tax Notes*, March 5, 1984 (NYSBA 1984 Report) at 993, 1022.

61   The stripped bond is treated as a newly issued bond for purposes of part V of subchapter P, chapter 1 of the Code (sections 1271 through 1288). The treatment of the stripped bond as a newly issued bond should apply for purpose of the effective date rules relevant to these sections. See, for example, footnotes 62, 66 and 70.

62   The stripped bond rules also affect the tax treatment of the seller. See Chapter 12, footnotes 17 and 20 and accompanying text. The OID rules of the Code were first extended to obligations of individuals by TRA 1984, effective for obligations issued after March 1, 1984 (see section 1272(a)(2)(D)). However, because section 1286 treats a stripped bond as being newly issued on each date on which it is purchased for purposes of applying the OID rules of the Code (including section 1272), the date of origination of the whole debt obligation to which the stripped bond relates is not relevant in determining whether the OID rules apply.

63   This *de minimis* rule is found in Treasury Regulation § 1.1286-1(a). For further discussion of this rule, see footnote 58, above.

the Code, the holder will be required to include such OID in income in each taxable year as it accrues. In calculating accruals of OID, all payments on a debt instrument of a single borrower should be aggregated and treated as a single stripped bond with a single yield to maturity.[64] It is not clear if rights to stated interest payments included in a stripped bond would be treated as qualified stated interest where they would be so treated if the stripped bond were a newly issued bond, or whether they would, instead, be included automatically in OID, but this issue does not have much practical significance.[65]

A significant issue that arises in calculating accruals of OID with respect to pass-through certificates that are stripped bonds is whether the PAC method applies (and, if so, what Prepayment Assumption is used). As a technical matter, the PAC method does not apply, because a pass-through certificate (other than one held by a REMIC) is not the type of security to which the method applies.[66] Nevertheless, many issuers for purposes of information reporting, and many investors, calculate income as if that method did apply, generally based on a Prepayment Assumption determined at the time of issuance of the certificates.[67] Alternatively, an investor

---

64   This aggregation approach clearly applies in testing if a stripped bond has *de minimis* OID (see footnote 58, above) and, for several reasons, should also apply in calculating accruals of OID in cases where the *de minimis* rule does not apply. First, it would be impractical to attempt to identify a separate yield for each payment on a debt instrument. Second, aggregate treatment is consistent with the general tax principle that treats a debt instrument (and all payments thereon) as having a single yield. Finally, even if individual payments would otherwise be treated separately, the OID regulations contain a rule that aggregates all debt instruments of a single issuer that are issued to a single holder. See Treasury Regulation § 1.1275-2(c). The deemed issuance that arises under section 1286 should be adequate to invoke this rule. The Service has authority under this regulation to aggregate obligations of different issuers that are issued in an arrangement designed to avoid the aggregation rule. For discussion of the effect of application of the PAC method on the aggregation of rights to payments on different loans, see the text following footnote 68, below.

65   Stated interest retains its character as such for purposes of applying the *de minimis* rule (see footnote 58, above), but it is not clear if the same holds true in applying the OID rules once it has been determined that there is greater than *de minimis* OID. This point is not very significant in practice because interest is never treated as qualified stated interest if it is paid in a way that would allow significant deferrals of income if it were not subject to the OID rules. Further, most pass-through certificates that are affected by the stripped bond rules are IO Strips and PO Strips, and all payments on those securities would be included in the stated redemption price at maturity regardless of how this technical question is resolved.

66   Except as provided in regulations, the PAC method applies under section 1272(a)(6)(C) only to REMIC regular interests, qualified mortgages held by a REMIC, and "any other debt instrument if payments under such debt instrument may be accelerated by reason of prepayments of other obligations securing such debt instrument . . ." A pass-through certificate does not literally meet this definition because the certificate itself is not a debt instrument and the underlying mortgages are not secured by other obligations. No regulations have been issued under this section. Although the PAC method applies only to debt instruments issued after December 31, 1986, a stripped bond would be treated as being issued for this purpose at the time it is purchased by each investor.

67   Issuer reporting generally would be based on the income that would be reported by an investor that purchased certificates in the initial offering at the initial offering price. Information reporting is discussed in Chapter 11. See also a Treasury Department new release dated January 15, 1985 (85 *Tax Notes Today* 12-4) announcing the Treasury STRIPS program, which states that information reporting for CATS and TIGRS (private label stripped Treasury obligations) is based on original issue prices.

might be able to use a Prepayment Assumption based on expectations as of the date on which it purchased its certificates.[68] Because the PAC method is based on the prepayment experience of a pool of mortgages, it would make sense if that method is applied to treat all mortgages underlying a pass-through certificate as a single debt instrument with a single yield. One possible disadvantage of applying the PAC method is that deductions for negative amounts determined under the method could be limited. However, negative amounts would arise primarily with respect to IO Strips and other high-coupon stripped bonds and the limitation should not apply to instruments of this type.[69]

If the PAC method does not apply to pass-through certificates that are stripped bonds, then income should be computed under a method that is similar to the PAC method except that the Prepayment Assumption used in calculating the yield to maturity and present values would be an assumption that no future mortgage prepayments will occur, and income or loss that results when a mortgage is prepaid (calculated, generally, in a manner similar to the PAC method by comparing the amount received, if any, as a result of the prepayment with the present value of the payments that would have been received if the mortgage loan had not prepaid) would be income or loss from retirement of the mortgage loan and not an adjustment to OID. Any such income or loss would be ordinary income or loss if the mortgage loans are obligations of individuals, and generally would be capital gain or loss if they are obligations of corporations, partnerships, or other legal entities and the pass-through certificates are held as capital assets.[70] Deductions for losses would not be curbed by the PAC method limitation on deductions for negative OID.

---

68   As discussed in footnote 33, above, in the case of a pay-through bond that is not subject to the stripped bond rules, the Prepayment Assumption generally is the assumption used in pricing the initial offering of the bonds. Because each purchase of a stripped bond is treated as a new issuance of a debt instrument, it is possible (although not certain) that the Prepayment Assumption for any holder of a stripped bond would be determined based on conditions at the time the holder purchased the stripped bond. Redetermining the Prepayment Assumption at the time of each purchase might produce more accurate measures of income, but it is not clear that the benefits would be substantial given the "catch-up" feature of the PAC method that takes account of differences between actual and assumed prepayment rates. Further, it is not clear how new Prepayment Assumptions would be determined. One reason for requiring the use of a single Prepayment Assumption in the case of a pay-through bond is to ensure consistency between the periodic amounts of OID included in income by investors and deducted by the issuer. That reason does not apply to a stripped bond because there is no general correspondence between OID income calculated under the stripped bond rules and deductions allowed to the issuers of the bonds that have been stripped.

69   See text following footnote 44, above, and Part G.1. Further, allowing a deduction for negative amounts attributable to prepaid loans would be consistent with the general tax principle that treats the holder of a pass-through certificate as an owner of an interest in the underlying loans.

70   The formula given in the text for calculating gain from the prepayment of a mortgage is valid for partial prepayments only if the prepayment is treated as a retirement of a portion of the mortgage determined by assuming that the retired and remaining portions of the mortgage have the same yield. For further discussion of the treatment of partial prepayments of debt instruments that are not subject to the PAC method, see the text following footnote 104, below. Gain or loss from a prepayment would be capital gain or loss only if it resulted from a "sale or exchange." As explained in footnote 15, the retirement of an obligation of an individual never results in a sale or exchange, but the retirement of an obligation of any other type of issuer generally does result in a

2. Pass-Through Certificates That Are Not Stripped Bonds

OID is not likely to be encountered in a pass-through certificate to which the stripped bond rules do not apply unless, as discussed below, interest payments on the underlying mortgages are scheduled to increase over time. The exchange of such pass-through certificates for mortgages is not treated as the creation of a new debt security for tax purposes. Accordingly, the existence or lack of OID is not affected by the price at which the certificates were originally sold. Rather, it is necessary to apply the OID definition to the original loan between the mortgagor and the mortgage originator, giving effect to the price at which the loan was originated.[71]

It is common for a mortgage lender to charge the borrower "points" in connection with the origination of a residential mortgage. From the lender's perspective, points represent discount that reduces a mortgage's issue price (rather than prepaid interest).[72] However, in most cases, points are not OID because they are de minimis in amount.[73] Where money is deposited in a "buy-down" or similar fund relating to a mortgage to make a portion of the interest payments in the early years of the loan,

---

sale or exchange. Although the rule treating retirements as a sale or exchange does not apply under section 1271(b)(2) to obligations of partnerships or trusts issued before July 2, 1982, a stripped bond should be considered for this purpose to be issued on the date of purchase by an investor.

71   As discussed in footnote 27 above, the issue price should be based on the price at which a loan is originated even if the originator intends to resell the loan.

72   See Treasury Regulation § 1.1273-2(g)(2) (payment from borrower to lender, other than a payment for services provided by the lender such as commitment fees or loan processing costs, reduces the issue price; however, the rule does not apply to a borrower with respect to points that are deductible by the borrower as prepaid interest under section 461(g)(2), described below). Before the issuance of this regulation, the Service had taken the position that the mortgagee was required to include points in income upon receipt if the points represented prepaid interest that was currently deductible by the mortgagor rather than "true discount" payable out of loan proceeds. See Revenue Ruling 70-540, 1970-2 C.B. 101, amplified by Revenue Ruling 74-607, 1974-2 C.B. 149, and clarified by Revenue Ruling 83-84, 1983-1 C.B. 97. Section 461(g)(1) generally requires a cash method taxpayer to capitalize prepaid interest. Section 461(g)(2) grants an exception to this rule for points paid in respect of any indebtedness incurred in connection with the purchase or improvement of, and secured by, the taxpayer's principal residence if the points do not exceed the points generally charged in the area in which the mortgage is originated. This exception does not apply to a mortgage refinancing, except in unusual cases where the refinanced loan represents only interim financing. See Revenue Ruling 87-22, 1987-1 C.B. 146 (refinancings are outside of section 461(g)(2)); Proposed Regulation § 1.6050H-1(f)(2)(iii) (distinguishes refinancings from acquisition loans); Revenue Procedure 92-12, 1992-1 C.B. 663 at § 4.04 (same); but see Huntsman v. Comm'r, 905 F.2d 1182 (8th Cir. 1990) (section 461(g)(2) applies to refinancing of a three-year mortgage loan on a principal residence). For purposes of information reporting under section 6050H, a recipient of points is allowed to assume that a mortgagor's funds provided at a loan closing are used first to pay points before loan proceeds are used for any other purpose. See Proposed Regulation § 1.6050H-1(f)(3)(ii), Example (1); Revenue Procedure 92-12, 1992-1 C.B. 663.

73   The de miminis rule is described above at footnote 21. Under the special 1/6 of 1% de minimis rule for self-amortizing installment obligations, discount on a typical residential mortgage would be considered de minimis if it was less than 5% of the stated redemption price at maturity in the case of a 30-year mortgage, or less than 2.5% in the case of a 15-year mortgage. A lender would generally include points representing de minimis discount in income ratably as principal payments are received. See footnote 14, above.

the fund would be treated as additional discount if it were considered the property of the mortgagee.[74] Typically, however, the fund would be viewed as an asset of the mortgagor that is pledged as collateral for the loan.[75] In any event, the OID rules of the Code would not apply to whole or pro rata interests in mortgages that are obligations of individuals if those mortgages were originated before March 2, 1984.[76] TRA 1984 extended those rules to obligations of individuals for the first time, effective for obligations issued on or after that date. A pass-through certificate would not fail to qualify as an interest in obligations of individuals because the mortgages or the certificates are guaranteed by the United States or a U.S. sponsored agency.[77]

In the case of a fixed rate residential mortgage originated after March 1, 1984, some portion of the stated interest payments may be includible in OID if the amount unconditionally payable as interest in each year, expressed as a percentage of the outstanding principal balance of the loan, is stepped up or down over the term of the loan. For example, such a mortgage generally will be considered to have OID, even if it was originated at par, if it provides for negative amortization of principal or, subject to a special *de minimis* rule for interest holidays and teaser rates, bears interest payable at fixed rates that are scheduled to increase over the life of the loan.[78] The general effect of applying the OID rules to loans with these features will

---

74   Buy-down funds are often established by sellers of property to subsidize mortgage payments by the buyer/mortgagor. As between the seller and buyer, such a fund represents economically, and for tax purposes, an offset to the purchase price. See T.A.M. 8942001 (April 28, 1989). Treasury Regulation § 1.1273-2(g)(4) treats payments made, as part of a lending transaction, by a third party to a lender, as a payment by the third party to the borrower and by the borrower to the lender (as an offset to the issue price) in "appropriate circumstances". This characterization would make sense for a seller buy-down fund only if the fund is properly viewed as an asset of the lender. Cf. Treasury Regulation § 1.1273-2(g)(5), Example 3 (cash payment by seller to lender treated as reduction in issue price).

75   Under the terms of most buy-down arrangements, the mortgagor is liable for all payments on the mortgage, including those actually made out of the buy-down fund, and is credited with the balance in the fund in the event of a prepayment or assumption. These features of the arrangement support the view that the fund is an asset of the mortgagor. See P.L.R.s 8452021 (September 20, 1984) and 8430112 (April 27, 1984) discussed in Chapter 9, Part A, which for purposes of testing the qualification of pass-through certificates backed by loans secured in part with buy-down funds as "qualifying real property loans" and "loans secured by an interest in [residential] real property" for thrift institutions, and "real estate assets" for REITs, determine that the buy-down funds are mortgagor assets. Although it would seem that a mortgagor would be allowed to deduct interest paid out of buy-down fund if the fund is considered an asset of the mortgagor, Treasury Regulation § 1.6050H-1(e)(3) appears to treat payments made from buy-down funds established by a seller of property in all cases as "not received on a mortgage" for purposes of mortgagee interest reporting under section 6050H. For further discussion of points and buy-down funds, see NYSBA 1987 Report at 413-414.

76   See section 1272(a)(2)(D).

77   See Chapter 2, Part B.1; footnote 115, below.

78   A negative amortization mortgage may bear interest at a fixed rate over its entire term, but interest is actually payable at a rate below the stated rate during the negative amortization period. During that period, the accrued and unpaid interest is added to principal. If a "rate of interest payable" was calculated for each year of the mortgage by dividing the interest payable during that year by the average outstanding principal amount of the mortgage during the year, and the lowest rate of

be to require holders (1) of a negative amortization loan to include stated interest in income as it accrues, and (2) of a loan that bears interest at increasing rates to include interest in income as it accrues based on the yield to maturity of the loan (that is, a yield representing a blend of the stated interest rates).[79]

An adjustable rate residential mortgage typically would be a VRDI. Accordingly, the OID rules generally should be applied by treating the mortgage as if it provided for fixed interest payments equal to the interest that would be paid if the applicable interest rate index were frozen at its value on the date of origination of the mortgage, with adjustments then being made in each month for differences between the assumed and actual interest rates.[80] Under that approach, subject to the special *de minimis* rule for interest holidays and teaser rates,[81] stated interest would be included in whole or in part in OID if the mortgage provides for a scheduled increase in interest payments not dependent on a change in the index. Also, if over the life of an adjustable rate mortgage, the index increases and accrued interest is not paid currently because of a payment cap, the unpaid interest would be includible in income as it accrues under the VRDI rules.[82]

If a mortgage is considered to have been issued with OID, an investor's interest therein most likely would be taxable under a method similar to the PAC method, except that the Prepayment Assumption used in calculating yield and present values would be an assumption that no prepayments will occur, and any gain from a prepayment would be treated as gain from retirement of the mortgage loan, not as an adjustment to OID.[83]

---

interest payable in any year was then determined, the amounts payable as interest in each year would be included in the stated redemption price at maturity (and hence in OID) to the extent they were payable at a rate greater than that lowest rate. See text accompanying footnote 23, above. Similarly, if a mortgage provided for payments of interest currently as the interest accrues but the stated rate of interest increased over the life of the loan, interest paid in any year at a rate greater than the lowest rate for any year would be included in OID. For a description of a special *de minimis* rule for interest holidays, teaser rates, and other interest shortfalls, see footnote 23, above.

79   Note that if all or a portion of the stated interest payments on a mortgage are included in OID, that OID would be taken into account in determining whether any discount below par at which the mortgage was issued is *de minimis*. For a special rule for calculating accruals of OID on callable loans, see footnote 40, above.

80   The VRDI rules are discussed in Part C.4 above.

81   See footnote 23, above.

82   As discussed in the text following footnote 49, above, under the VRDI rules, any increase in the variable interest for an accrual period above the assumed fixed amount is included in OID for the period if it is not paid during the period.

83   For a special rule for calculating gain from partial prepayments of a mortgage, see text following footnote 104, below. While regulations could be adopted extending the PAC method (including the use of a realistic Prepayment Assumption) to individual mortgage loans that are used to back pass-through certificates, such a development is less likely in the case of certificates that are not subject to the stripped bond rules than in the case of certificates subject to those rules. In any event, if the stripped bond rules do not apply, any such regulations would apply at the earliest only to mortgage loans that were originated after December 31, 1986. If a pass-through certificate is held by a REMIC, the PAC method would always apply to the certificate, based on the Prepayment Assumption that is used in applying the PAC method to the REMIC's regular interests. See footnote 32, above, and Chapter 7, text accompanying footnote 33.

In the unusual case where a residential mortgage has OID, the OID rules have limited significance for the borrower, because, under a special rule for consumer loans, OID can be deducted only when it is paid.[84]

E. Market Discount

1. Overview

Any discount at which an obligation is purchased below its principal amount (if the obligation has no OID), or below its adjusted issue price (if the instrument does have OID), is considered to be market discount.[85] The treatment of market discount was significantly altered by TRA 1984 and TRA 1986.

Prior to the enactment of TRA 1984, market discount on a mortgage-backed security was generally allocated among all principal payments in proportion to their amounts, regardless of when they were due.[86] The discount was included in income as principal payments were received or when the security was sold. Thus, if an obligation having an outstanding principal amount of $1,000 was purchased by an investor for $750, the investor would report 25 percent of each principal payment as income when the payment was received while it held the obligation. Such income was ordinary income (although not interest income) if the obligation was the debt of an individual; otherwise, it was generally capital gain, assuming the obligation was held as a capital asset.[87] Given the same assumption, gain realized upon sale of the obligation was always capital gain.[88] Such gain would reflect any market discount allocated to the principal of the obligation that remained unpaid at the time of the sale, because the seller's adjusted basis for purposes of computing gain would equal the portion of the initial purchase price, reflecting the market discount, that was allocated to such unpaid principal.

TRA 1984 and TRA 1986 did not change the rule of prior law that permits market discount on an obligation to be deferred until the obligation is disposed of or principal thereon is paid. However, TRA 1986 introduced a rule for allocating discount among principal payments that can significantly increase the amount of market discount income that is recognized when a principal payment is made. For

---

84   See section 1275(b)(2), which applies to debt incurred by a cash method taxpayer to acquire or carry property not used for profit or in a business. For a rule treating certain payments of principal and other amounts included in the stated redemption price at maturity as a payment first of accrued OID, see Treasury Regulation § 1.1275-2(a).

85   The term *revised* issue price is sometimes used in the market discount sections of the Code instead of adjusted issue price, but it has the same meaning. To avoid confusion, the latter term will be used in this discussion.

86   See *Morton Liftin v. Comm'r*, 36 T.C. 909 (1961), *aff'd*, 317 F.2d 234 (4th Cir. 1963); *Shafpa Realty Co. v. Comm'r*, 8 B.T.A. 283 (1927). However, in one ruling, the Service permitted a taxpayer to allocate market discount among principal payments on a pass-through certificate in a manner that took account of the timing of those principal payments. See P.L.R. 8052046 (September 30, 1980).

87   See footnote 15, above, and accompanying text.

88   But see footnote 7, above, for a special rule for banks and thrifts.

an obligation that provides for partial principal payments in each accrual period, which describes many mortgage-backed securities, this change can have the effect of substantially eliminating the difference between OID and market discount in terms of the timing of the inclusion of such discount in income.

As a result of TRA 1984, market discount income reported by the holder of an obligation is treated as ordinary interest income for most tax purposes to the extent of the portion of the discount that accrued while the holder held the obligation. TRA 1984 also provided rules to ensure that accrued market discount will not be exempted from tax under certain nonrecognition provisions in the Code. Finally, another TRA 1984 amendment defers deductions for all or a portion of the tax losses that otherwise might be generated by borrowing at market rates to finance low-coupon market discount obligations, claiming current deductions for interest expense on the borrowing and deferring the inclusion in income of the market discount until the obligation is disposed of or repaid. These special market discount rules do not apply to an obligation that has a fixed maturity date not exceeding one year from issuance.[89]

2. Detailed Discussion

TRA 1984 added to the Code section 1276, which provides that gain from a sale or other disposition of an obligation acquired with *market discount*[90] will be treated as ordinary income (generally as interest income)[91] to the extent the gain does not exceed the portion of the market discount that is considered to have accrued from the acquisition date to the time of the sale or other disposition. Subject to certain exceptions,[92] such income is recognized notwithstanding other nonrecognition rules

---

89   TRA 1984 also offers investors an election, in section 1278(b), to treat market discount as OID. Market discount obligations affected by the election are not subject to the income conversion and loss deferral rules described in the text. The election applies to all obligations acquired after the first day of the first taxable year to which the election applies, and continues in effect unless permission to terminate the election is obtained from the Service. Barring unusual circumstances, such as an expiring net operating loss carryover, this election is unlikely to be made, because it could accelerate income and in some cases convert capital gain into ordinary interest income. REMICs are treated, in effect, as if they had made the election with respect to qualified mortgages they hold. See Chapter 7, text at footnote 25. The method of making a section 1278(b) election is set forth in Revenue Procedure 92-67, 1992-2 C.B. 429. Treasury Regulation § 1.1272-3 provides taxpayers with another, largely overlapping election to treat market discount in the same manner as OID. See footnote 18, above.

90   *Market discount* is defined in section 1278(a)(2) as the excess of the stated redemption price at maturity of an obligation over its basis immediately after its acquisition by the taxpayer. However, for an obligation having OID, the stated redemption price at maturity is replaced by the adjusted issue price. (The Code actually uses the term revised issue price; see footnote 85 above.) This rule has the effect of excluding unaccrued OID from the definition of market discount.

91   However, such ordinary income is not treated as interest income for purposes of sections 871(a), 881, 1441, and 1442 (relating to the 30% withholding tax imposed on income realized by foreign investors), section 6049 (interest information reporting), or other provisions as may be specified in regulations. No such regulations have been issued.

92   See section 1276(d). These exceptions allow, among other things, transfers of obligations to a parent corporation upon liquidation of an 80% owned corporate subsidiary, by a partner to a

in the Code. Thus, for example, a holder who makes a donative transfer of a market discount obligation would recognize income up to the amount of accrued market discount even though gifts do not ordinarily trigger the recognition of gain. Similarly, under a TRA 1986 amendment to section 1286, the stripping of a market discount obligation is considered a disposition that triggers the recognition of accrued market discount.[93]

Discount that otherwise would be market discount is not treated as market discount for purposes of sections 1276 through 1278 if it is less than a *de minimis* amount.[94] Any such *de minimis* discount is included in income ratably as principal payments are received, and is characterized as gain from retirement of the debt instrument.[95]

TRA 1986 introduced a new rule for determining the amount of market discount income that is recognized when a partial principal payment is made.[96] The rule, found in section 1276(a)(3), states that a partial principal payment on an obligation will be included in gross income as ordinary income to the extent of the accrued market discount on the obligation. In other words, the market discount that must be included in income when a principal payment is received is not, as under prior law, simply the portion of the remaining market discount that is allocable to the principal paid (for example, half of such discount if half of the principal balance is paid), but instead is generally the lesser of the amount of the payment and the amount of market discount that has accrued (but not yet been included in income) on the obligation as a whole. As discussed below, special rules govern the treatment of prepayments.[97] If principal payments are made in each year at least equal to the

---

partnership or to a partner from a partnership, or in connection with a corporate reorganization, without triggering recognition of accrued market discount income. As a result of TRA 1986, accrued market discount is recognized upon a transfer of market discount bonds to a corporation in a transaction that is otherwise tax-free under section 351. See Chapter 12, footnote 30 (describes section 351). Apparently, a similar rule would apply to a transfer to a REMIC. See Chapter 12, footnote 33.

93 See Chapter 12, text accompanying footnote 20.

94 Under the *de minimis* rule, market discount is considered to be zero if it is less than 1/4 of 1% of the remaining stated redemption price at maturity multiplied by the number of complete years to maturity (after the taxpayer acquired the obligation). In the case of an obligation that provides for more than one payment that is includible in the stated redemption price at maturity, this *de minimis* rule would presumably be applied in the manner described in footnote 21, above.

95 A similar rule applies to *de minimis* amounts of OID. See footnote 14, above.

96 The rule applies to obligations subject to section 1276 that were acquired by the holder after October 22, 1986 (the date of enactment of TRA 1986).

97 Prepayments are discussed in the text following footnote 104, below. For an obligation having OID and market discount, a principal payment presumably would not be treated as a payment of accrued market discount under the new rules to the extent it is considered a payment of accrued OID. This point is not addressed in the statute or legislative history. Treasury Regulation § 1.1275-2(a) provides that any payment under a debt instrument, other than a payment of qualified stated interest, deductible points, certain pro rata prepayments, or late fees, is treated "first as a payment of OID to the extent of the OID that has accrued as of the date the payment is due and has not been allocated to prior payments, and second as a payment of principal." This rule provides an argument for treating payments of amounts includible in the stated redemption price at maturity first as payments of accrued OID to the exclusion of market discount. Another open question is whether

market discount that accrues in that year, then the new rule effectively requires market discount to be included in income as it accrues.

For a non-REMIC pass-through certificate, it appears that the rule for partial principal payments would be applied separately to each of the underlying mortgages rather than to the certificates as a whole, so that principal payments received on one mortgage would not result in the recognition of accrued market discount on other mortgages. On the other hand, a REMIC regular interest would be treated as a single obligation for this purpose, even if it takes the form of a pass-through certificate.

Subject to the discussion in the next paragraph, market discount is considered to accrue on an obligation under a straight-line method[98] unless the holder elects, on an obligation-by-obligation basis, to use a constant yield method.[99] If the election is made, accrued market discount for any period equals the portion of such discount that would have been included in the holder's income during that period as accrued OID if the obligation had been issued on the date on which it was purchased by the holder and the market discount had been OID. Sophisticated investors are likely to make a constant yield election for all of their market discount bonds, because the election slows the rate at which market discount accrues.

TRA 1986 authorized the Treasury to issue regulations to determine the amount of accrued market discount with respect to an obligation on which principal is payable in installments. The legislative history[100] states that until these regulations are issued, holders of such obligations may elect to accrue market discount either in the same manner as OID or (1) in the case of debt obligations that have OID, in proportion to the accrual of OID,[101] or (2) for debt obligations that have no OID, in proportion to payments of stated interest.[102] For an obligation that would be subject

---

payments of stated interest on an obligation that are includible in its stated redemption price at maturity will be treated to any extent as payments of accrued market discount. Section 1276(a)(3)(A) refers to a "partial principal payment" but the Conference Report at II-842 describes the rule as applying to amounts includible in the stated redemption price at maturity of a debt instrument. This question may not be very important if payments of amounts includible in the stated redemption price at maturity are treated first as a payment of accrued OID (including as OID stated interest included in the stated redemption price at maturity), with only the balance being available to be treated as a payment of accrued market discount.

98   Under this method, accrued market discount is calculated by multiplying the market discount by a fraction, the numerator of which is the number of days the holder has held the obligation and the denominator of which is the total number of days after the holder acquired the obligation to and including the maturity date. See section 1276(b)(1).

99   See section 1276(b)(2).

100   See Conference Report at II-842.

101   In other words, the amount of market discount that accrues in any period would be the product of (1) the total remaining market discount and (2) a fraction, the numerator of which is the OID for the period and the denominator of which is the total remaining OID at the beginning of the period. This method would produce uncertain results when applied to an interest-only REMIC regular interest if (1) that regular interest were considered to have OID, (2) the interest suffered losses because of high prepayments, and (3) deductions were not allowed for "negative OID." In that case, the OID accruals in the current and all future periods would be zero, so that the fraction referred to above would be 0/0. See Part G.1.

to the PAC method for accruing OID if the instrument had such discount (which would include any pay-through bond issued after December 31, 1986), the same Prepayment Assumption that would be used in accruing OID will be used in accruing market discount, regardless of which of the foregoing methods is used. Issuers of obligations subject to the PAC method are required to report information necessary to calculate accruals of market discount.[103]

If accruals of market discount are calculated under a method similar to the PAC method, then actual prepayments would be reflected automatically in the calculation of accrued discount.[104] The treatment of prepayments on a debt instrument is less clear where the PAC method does not apply (for example, in the case of pass-through certificates that are not stripped bonds). In such a case, the rate of accrual of market discount should be calculated disregarding the possibility of optional prepayments. If and when a loan is prepaid *in full*, the holder would recognize gain from retirement of the instrument. That gain would be treated as ordinary income to the extent it does not exceed the accrued market discount on the instrument that has not previously been included in income. Any remaining gain would have the same character as if the special market discount rules did not apply (see Part E.1).

Where a debt instrument is prepaid *in part*, it is necessary to address three questions: First, is the amount of prepaid principal that is treated as a payment of accrued market discount limited to the accrued market discount attributable to the portion of the instrument that is prepaid? Second, is the holder required to recognize any portion of the unaccrued market discount on the obligation? Finally, if accrued and unaccrued market discount are included in income only to the extent they are allocated to the portion of the instrument that is prepaid, how is that allocation to be made?

The treatment of partial prepayments in the OID regulations gives some indication of the current views of the Service on these points. The OID regulations contain a payment ordering rule that generally treats a payment on a debt instrument first, as a payment of accrued OID and, second, as a payment of principal. This rule

---

102   Thus, the amount of market discount in any period would be the product of (1) the total remaining amount of market discount and (2) a fraction, the numerator of which is the amount of stated interest paid in the period and the denominator of which is the total amount of stated interest remaining to be paid on the debt instrument as of the beginning of the period. Presumably, if the instrument bears interest at a floating rate based on an index, a constant value for the index in the present period and future periods would be assumed. Although the legislative history refers to stated interest "paid" in any period in calculating the fraction referred to above, it would have made more sense to refer to interest accrued, at least where stated interest is being reported under an accrual method.

103   See Chapter 11, text accompanying footnote 23.

104   Under the PAC method, the discount accruing in any accrual period may be increased as a result of prepayments received during the period if they exceed those computed under the Prepayment Assumption. Presumably, any such increase in the amount of accrued market discount in an accrual period would be taken into account in determining the amount of prepayments in that period that are treated as a payment of accrued market discount under the special rule for partial principal payments described above in the text accompanying footnote 96. Under the PAC method, economic gains attributable to prepayments are always treated as accrued discount, so there is never a need to account separately for unaccrued discount.

does not apply, however, to a *pro rata prepayment* (defined as a prepayment that results in a substantially pro rata reduction of each payment remaining to be paid on the instrument).[105] A pro rata prepayment is treated instead as a payment in retirement of a portion of the instrument, resulting in the same amount of gain or loss as if the retired portion of the instrument were a separate instrument that was retired in full. All tax attributes of the instrument (adjusted issue price, the holder's basis, and accrued but unpaid OID), determined immediately before the prepayment, are allocated between the retired and remaining portions of the instrument based on their principal amounts.

While the OID regulations make no mention of section 1276, presumably the same principles would apply in determining the effect of a prepayment on market discount. Thus, in the case of a pro rata prepayment of a market discount bond, the holder would allocate its tax basis, adjusted issue price and accrued market discount pro rata between the retired and remaining portions of the bond, and treat the prepayment as if it were a prepayment in full of the retired portion of the bond. Any other prepayment would be treated in the same manner as a scheduled payment (first, as a payment of accrued OID and, second, as a payment of accrued market discount, in each case on the obligation as a whole, third, as a return of basis that reduces the adjusted issue price dollar-for-dollar but not below zero, and, fourth, as gain from retirement of the debt instrument). Thus, the prepayment would not trigger the recognition of any unaccrued market discount except to the extent basis has been reduced to zero. Although a non-pro rata prepayment would increase the instrument's yield (calculated based on the adjusted issue price and future payments), there is no rule that adjusts the yield used in calculating future accruals of market discount under the constant yield method (where it applies).[106] In general, holders of residential mortgages would prefer the rule for non-pro rata prepayments over the rule for pro rata prepayments. Remaining market discount on those mortgages is more likely to be unaccrued than accrued because accrued market discount must be included in income as scheduled principal payments are received.

The preamble to the OID regulations states that partial retirement treatment is restricted to pro rata prepayments because that type of prepayment is common and the extension of the rule to non-pro rata prepayments would be unduly complex. These statements were apparently made without the mortgage markets in mind. Almost invariably, partial prepayments on residential mortgages are not pro rata prepayments but are credited against the last payments due. As a result, under the principles of the OID regulations, full and partial prepayment in the same amount will have different consequences for investors. Information necessary to distinguish the two types of prepayments is not ordinarily reported to holders of pass-through certificates, however, so that even a well meaning investor would be unable to treat

---

105   See Treasury Regulation §§ 1.1275-2(a) (payment ordering rule) and 1.1275-2(f) (pro rata prepayments). See also footnote 97, above. Treasury Regulation § 1.1272-1(j), Example 6, illustrates the pro rata prepayment rule.

106   See Proposed Regulation § 1.1272-1(j), Example 6 (December 21, 1992).

the two differently. Under these circumstances, holders are likely to make the simplifying assumption that all prepayments are prepayments in full.

TRA 1984 also added section 1277 to the Code, which requires the deferral of tax losses that otherwise would result from financing an investment in market discount obligations with debt that bears interest at a current market rate.

Section 1277 states that "net direct interest expense" with respect to a market discount obligation shall be allowed as a deduction in any taxable year only to the extent such expense exceeds the market discount that accrues during the days in such year on which the taxpayer held the obligation. The rate of accrual of market discount is determined under the rules of section 1276 described earlier (including the election to use a constant yield method). Net direct interest expense is the excess of the interest paid or accrued during the taxable year on debt incurred, or contin- ued, to purchase, or carry, the market discount obligation over the aggregate amount of interest on the obligation (including OID) includible in gross income for the taxable year by the holder. The "incurred or continued to purchase or carry" stand- ard used to link a borrowing with an investment in market discount obligations is amorphous and yet familiar, having been used for many years under section 265 in determining whether investments in tax-exempt bonds are debt financed.[107] A spe- cial interest expense allocation rule applies to banks and thrifts.[108]

The deductions for net direct interest expense on a market discount obligation that are disallowed under section 1277 are allowed (subject to other limitations that may apply to deductions for interest expense) (1) when the market discount obliga- tion is disposed of in a taxable transaction,[109] or (2) if the taxpayer so elects,[110] prior to such a disposition to the extent necessary to offset any net interest income on the obligation (the excess of the interest income over interest expense on related bor- rowings) recognized in years subsequent to a year in which the deductions were disallowed.

---

107   It is likely that the guidelines set forth in Revenue Procedure 72-18, 1972-1 C.B. 740, for deter- mining whether a tax-exempt bond is debt financed also will be followed in applying section 1277.

108   In calculating net direct interest expense, a bank or thrift is required to allocate to each market discount obligation that it holds a portion of its interest expense on all outstanding borrowings, including deposits, determined by multiplying such expense by a fraction, the numerator of which is the tax basis of the market discount obligation and the denominator of which is the tax basis of all of its assets. While this rule will ensure an allocation by such an institution of some interest expense against any holdings of market discount obligations, the institution's average cost of funds may be significantly lower than the rate of interest payable on any specific borrowing that other- wise might be matched against the market discount obligations under a facts and circumstances test.

109   If a market discount obligation is disposed of in a transaction in which gain or loss is not fully recognized, a deduction for the previously disallowed interest expense is allowed up to the amount of gain recognized in the transaction. The balance is preserved as a future deduction by the new holder of the obligation if its basis in the obligation is calculated by reference to its basis in the hands of the former holder, and otherwise will be allowed to the prior holder upon disposition of the property received in exchange for the market discount obligation.

110   See section 1277(b)(1).

The policy underlying section 1277 is that deductions for apparent losses resulting from a leveraged investment in a market discount obligation should be deferred, if and to the extent the losses are offset economically by the accrual of market discount, until the accrued market discount is included in income. Thus, if an investor borrows at 12 percent to finance the purchase of an 8 percent mortgage that has a yield, taking account of market discount, of 11 percent, the investor's economic loss is only 1 percent, the amount by which the rate of interest paid on the borrowing exceeds the yield on the mortgage. Obviously, income and expense would be mismatched if a deduction were allowed for the apparent additional 3 percentage point loss before the corresponding amount of accrued market discount income is recognized.

It is not entirely clear whether section 1277 would be applied to an issuer of pay-through bonds, or if such an issuer is an owner trust, to the holders of equity interests therein, on an aggregate basis treating the mortgage collateral as a single debt instrument, or whether instead the issuer or such holders would be required to allocate interest expense among individual mortgages and to compare the net direct interest expense for each mortgage with the market discount that accrues on that mortgage.[111] An aggregate approach would seem to address adequately the problem at which section 1277 is directed, and the alternative could be quite complex. Nonetheless, there is a substantial argument that a mortgage-by-mortgage calculation is required under current law.

F. Premium

Section 171 generally allows the holder of a debt instrument purchased at a premium (unless the holder is a dealer in securities) to elect to amortize such premium over the period from the date of purchase to the maturity date of the instrument (or, if it results in less rapid amortization of the premium, over the period to an earlier call date). For this purpose, premium is determined with reference to the basis of a debt instrument and the "amount payable on maturity" or, if it results in smaller amortizable bond premium for the period to an earlier call date, the "amount payable on earlier call date".[112] Amortized premium is allocated among the interest payments on a debt instrument and, to the extent so allocated, is applied against and reduces those payments. Any amount not so allocated is allowed as a deduction.[113]

---

111 As further discussed in Chapter 7, footnote 25 and accompanying text, market discount on the mortgages held by a REMIC is included in the REMIC's income as it accrues as if it were OID and neither section 1276 nor section 1277 applies. Similarly, neither section would apply if the mortgage collateral consisted entirely of mortgages to which the stripped bonds rules apply because all of the market discount then would be transformed into OID under section 1286.

112 See section 171(b)(1). For a comparison of this definition with the definition of premium that applies under the OID rules, see Part G.1 below.

113 See sections 171(a)(1) and (e). Section 171(e) was added to the Code by TRA 1986. In its original form, it treated premium amortization deductions as interest deductions. TAMRA changed the section to provide the interest offset rule described in the text. The reason for the change was apparently to benefit individuals, who can deduct interest only subject to certain limitations. See

Section 171 was significantly amended by TRA 1986, effective for debt instruments issued after September 27, 1985. Under the amended section, premium is amortized under a constant yield method. In applying that method, prepayments should be accounted for under a method similar to the PAC method, at least in the case of a debt instrument issued after December 31, 1986 to which the PAC method would apply if such instrument had been issued at a discount.[114]

For a debt instrument issued on or before September 27, 1985, an investor may elect to amortize premium under section 171 only if the instrument was issued by a corporation or a government or political subdivision thereof.[115] If the election is made, premium is amortized under the method of amortizing bond premium that the holder regularly employs, provided such method is reasonable, and otherwise under a straight-line method.

In determining whether premium may be amortized on a pass-through certificate evidencing an interest in mortgages, the date of origination of the mortgages would determine whether the new or old version of section 171 applies. Thus, an election could be made under section 171 to amortize premium on a pass-through

---

TAMRA House Report at 72.

114   For a description of these instruments, see footnote 32, above. The discussion of bond premium in the legislative history of TRA 1986 is somewhat confusing. The Conference Report at II-842 states, in explaining the amendments to the sections of the Code dealing with market discount, that until Treasury regulations are issued, in the case of a debt instrument on which principal is paid in more than one installment and that has no OID, the amount of market discount that is considered to accrue in any accrual period will be, at the holder's election, either the amount that would accrue under a constant yield method or

> the amount of discount that bears the same ratio to the total amount of remaining market discount that the amount of stated interest paid in the accrual period bears to the total amount of stated interest remaining to be paid on the debt instrument as of the beginning of the accrual period.

The method described in the quotation is essentially a straight-line method. The Conference Report then continues:

> In the case of debt instruments that would be subject to the OID rules contained in new Code sec. 1272(a)(6) (without regard to whether the debt instrument has original issue discount), the same prepayment assumption that would be made in computing OID would be made in computing the accrual of market discount. ... In addition, the conferees intend that the same rules that apply to the accrual of market discount on debt instruments whose principal is paid in more than one installment, also is [sic] applied in amortizing amortizable bond premium (within the meaning of sec. 171).

The last sentence in the quotation refers to the rules for accruing market discount on debt instruments whose principal is paid in more than one installment and not to the rules for accruing OID under section 1272(a)(6) (the PAC method). One possible implication of the reference is that, pending regulations, investors may amortize bond premium on substantially all mortgage-backed securities under a straight-line method. However, as this result is squarely contrary to the language of the section, it is uncertain whether investors may rely on the legislative history. On the other hand, because the Prepayment Assumption that would be used under the PAC method is also to be used in accruing market discount in the case of debt instruments to which the PAC method applies, the reliance on the market discount rules as a model in amortizing bond premium should be read to authorize the use of the same Prepayment Assumption, and the other mechanics of the PAC method, in applying section 171 to such instruments.

115   Nongovernmental obligations that are merely guaranteed by the United States or a U.S. sponsored agency are not considered obligations of a government for this purpose. See Revenue Ruling 258, 1953-2 C.B. 143; P.L.R. 8724035 (March 16, 1987).

certificate backed by residential mortgages that are obligations of individuals only to the extent the mortgages were originated after September 27, 1985.

Premium on a debt instrument that is not amortized under section 171 is allocated among the principal payments to be made on the instrument and is allowed as a loss deduction when those payments are made.[116] Such a loss would be an ordinary loss for an obligation of an individual (or a partnership or trust if the obligation was issued prior to July 2, 1982) and otherwise would be a capital loss, provided the obligation is held as a capital asset.[117]

G. Special Topics

This section discusses two special topics relating to the tax treatment of investors holding mortgage-backed securities taxed as debt: the deductibility by the holder of a REMIC regular interest that consists primarily of a right to receive interest payments on the underlying mortgages (an *IO Interest*) of losses from faster than expected prepayments, and accounting for mortgagor defaults.

1. Prepayment Losses Attributable to IO Interests

a. Overview. The REMIC rules as enacted in 1986 prohibited IO Interests. Specifically, the TRA 1986 legislative history did not allow REMIC regular interests to pay interest that was disproportionately high compared with its principal amount.[118] The ban on high-coupon instruments was lifted in 1988 by TAMRA in cases where interest payments can be expressed as a nonvarying specified portion of the interest payments on the underlying mortgages. The change was justified in part on the ground that similar interest strips may be created in the form of pass-through certificates. Since 1988, vast quantities of IO Interests have been issued. Because the payments on IO Interests are derived from mortgage interest payments, IO Interests drop in value as mortgages are prepaid, cutting off (irretrievably) future interest payment streams. Declines in mortgage interest rates in recent years have resulted in large prepayment losses.

This section discusses whether prepayment losses on IO Interests can be deducted before the instruments are disposed of by the holder.[119] While the issue is

---

116 The allocation would probably be made in proportion to the amounts of the principal payments, regardless of when those payments are due. See P.L.R. 8724035 (March 16, 1987); cf. Revenue Ruling 258, 1953-2 C.B. 143.

117 For a discussion of when income or loss from the retirement of a debt instrument is capital gain or loss, see footnote 15, above.

118 See Chapter 5, footnote 5 and accompanying text.

119 A more complete discussion of this topic may be found in "Memorandum for the Internal Revenue Service re: Federal Income Tax Deductions for Economic Losses Arising from Prepayments of Mortgages Underlying IO REMIC Regular Interests—The Interaction of Sections 1272(a)(6) and 171" by James M. Peaslee, December 23, 1993, reprinted in *Highlights and Documents*, January 7, 1994. The discussion assumes that the IO Interest is not held by a dealer that is subject to the mark to market rules described in Chapter 9, Part E.

clouded by the legislative history of TRA 1986, a deduction should be allowed for losses reflected in negative amounts calculated under the PAC method, on the ground that those amounts represent amortizable bond premium that is deductible under section 171.

In economic terms, an IO Interest is simply a debt instrument that is sold at a premium above its principal amount because it bears interest at a greater-than-market rate. As is true of any premium bond, the holder bears the risk of loss of the unamortized premium if the bond prepays (or in the language of section 171, is called). Given the resemblance to a conventional premium bond, it is not surprising that the best place to look to find a deduction for such negative amounts is section 171.

b. Effect of Prepayments on Bond Premium Amortization. The basic operation of section 171 is described in Part F. In evaluating the consequences of the section for IO Interests, it will be helpful to begin by considering how the prepayment of a conventional callable bond affects bond premium amortization. This can best be done through an example.

Suppose that an investor purchased for $1,200 a bond with a principal amount of $1,000 that bears interest at an annual rate of 8 percent and matures in ten years but is callable after five years at a price of $1,030.[120] Under section 171(b)(1)(B)(ii), the investor would be required to amortize the premium to the call date or maturity date, depending on which produces the smaller amortizable bond premium. In this case, amortizing premium to the maturity date would result in amortization of $20 a year (200/10),[121] and amortizing premium to the call date would result in the amortization of $34 a year (170/5). Therefore, premium would be amortized to the maturity date and the investor would be allowed to offset against coupon interest $20 in each year prior to the year in which the bond is called. As a result, the investor would have a tax basis (original cost less amortized premium) of $1,100 in the bond after five years. Suppose that the bond is actually called after five years (at the beginning of year six). In that event, the holder would be entitled to an additional bond premium deduction of $70 in year six under section 171(b)(2), equal to the excess of the basis of the bond at the beginning of the year ($1,100) over the amount received on redemption of the bond ($1,030).[122] This additional bond premium deduction would exceed the interest income reported for year six.

---

120   For the sake of simplicity, assume that the bond years referred to in the example coincide with the investor's taxable years.

121   For ease of illustration, it is assumed that the premium is amortized ratably, although, in fact, the premium would be amortized under a constant yield method.

122   For a similar example in the regulations showing the effect of a call, see Treasury Regulation § 1.171-2(a)(2)(iii). Section 171(b)(2) treats as bond premium attributable to the taxable year in which a bond is called an amount equal to the excess of the adjusted basis of such bond as of the beginning of the taxable year over the amount received on redemption of the bond or (if greater) the amount payable on maturity. In the example, the amount payable on maturity would be less than the call price.

The facts of the example are not unusual for premium bonds. The rule requiring premium to be amortized to the maturity date of a callable bond if that amortization schedule results in smaller amortization deductions often will have the result that the amortizable bond premium exceeds interest income for the year in which a callable bond is called. The regulations under section 171 clearly contemplate that bond premium deductions may exceed gross interest income.[123]

Suppose that an investor owns an IO Interest instead of a conventional bond. Assuming that premium is measured based on the principal amount (a point discussed further below), the IO Interest would be subject to section 171 and premium should be amortized under the PAC method. Under that method, faster than expected mortgage prepayments would increase the rate of recovery of bond premium by decreasing the present value of the remaining payments. Even if prepayments were sufficiently high so that amortizable bond premium in any accrual period exceeded the amount of interest income (before premium amortization), thereby producing an ordinary loss from the regular interest for the year, that result would be fully consistent with the normal operation of section 171.

c. Obstacles to Applying Section 171. There are two principal issues that must be resolved in order to apply section 171 to IO Interests. These are whether an IO interest has premium for purposes of section 171 (more technically, whether interest payments are included in the amount payable at maturity), and whether a deduction under section 171 for negative amounts calculated under the PAC method is implicitly denied by the discussion of "negative OID" in the legislative history of TRA 1986.[124] The next two sections address these points.

(i) Existence of premium. Bond premium is calculated under section 171 by comparing the holder's basis in the bond with "the amount payable at maturity (or if it results in a smaller amortizable bond premium attributable to the period to earlier call date, with reference to the amount payable on earlier call date)". Although there is very little authority interpreting this language, the reason for using the phrase "amount payable" rather than "principal payable" may have been to include premiums payable in addition to principal. At any rate, if an IO Interest provided for some actual principal payments, and interest thereon was calculated at a fixed rate applied to such principal, it should be an easy matter to conclude that the instrument has bond premium equal to the excess of its purchase price over its

---

123　See Treasury Regulation § 1.171-2(e).

124　A third issue is whether section 171(e), which as amended by TAMRA generally treats bond premium allocable to interest as an offset to such interest rather than as a separate deduction, was intended to limit bond premium amortization to interest income. The section should not be read to have this effect. As described in footnote 113, above, its purpose was to avoid subjecting premium amortization to limitations on interest deductions. The legislative history gives no hint that Congress intended to alter the basic scope of section 171, which as explained above, clearly was read prior to the enactment of TAMRA to allow deductions in excess of interest income. Section 171(a)(1), which allows such deductions, was left unchanged by TAMRA. See also sections 67(b)(12) and 1016(a)(5) (which refer to deductions under section 171).

principal amount. Although the instrument would bear interest at a very high rate, a greater-than-market coupon is a feature of all premium bonds and should not be a basis for denying application of section 171.

If the IO Interest does not provide for any actual principal payments, or has principal that does not bear a fixed relationship to interest, then an issue arises as to whether the instrument still can be considered a premium bond, or, more technically, whether the interest payments should be included in the "amount payable at maturity." The concern arises from the fact that, as explained in Part C.1, OID is measured by reference to the "stated redemption price at maturity" of a debt instrument. Stated interest is included in the stated redemption price at maturity if it is not qualified stated interest, and stated interest on an IO Interest would not be qualified stated interest if it has no actual principal amount, or a principal amount that is not related in a consistent way to the interest payments thereon.

Even if an IO Interest is considered to have OID, it does not follow that section 171 would not also apply to allow deductions for negative amounts produced under the PAC method. At least three reasons support this view:

First, the term "stated redemption price at maturity" in section 1273 is not directly applicable in determining the amount of bond premium that is subject to amortization under section 171.[125] The "amount payable at maturity" language in section 171 came into the law long before the special definition of stated redemption price at maturity in the OID rules,[126] and has not been changed, even though section 171 has been amended in other respects. Although there seems to be no authority addressing whether the term "amount payable at maturity" can include stated interest payments, it is significant that the OID definitions are not controlling.[127]

Second, a more fundamental reason why OID principles should not be applied to deny a deduction under section 171 for negative amounts calculated under the PAC method is that the tax policy reason for the special definition of stated redemption price at maturity is unrelated to the policy reasons for allowing or denying the

---

125   The stated redemption price at maturity is defined in section 1273(a)(2). Section 1273(a) states that it applies for purposes of "this subpart," which consists of sections 1271 through 1275 dealing with OID. Under section 1272(c)(1), the OID inclusion rules do not apply to any holder that has purchased a debt instrument at a "premium". This term is defined in Treasury Regulation § 1.1272-2(b)(2) by reference to the stated redemption price at maturity rather than principal amount. There is, however, nothing tying this definition to the one that applies under section 171.

126   The language in section 171 derives from section 125(b)(1) of the Internal Revenue Code of 1939, as amended, which was enacted as part of the Revenue Act of 1942. The rule in section 1273(a)(2) including interest payments in the stated redemption price at maturity was added by TRA 1984. It seems to have been taken from Treasury Regulation § 1.1232-3(b)(1)(iii)(a), adopted under the old OID rules found in section 1232. The regulation was issued in 1971 (see T.D. 7154, December 28, 1971, 1972-1 C.B. 236, 244) in response to a 1969 change in section 1232 that for the first time required holders of certain OID obligations to include OID in income as it accrues.

127   The language in section 171(e) that provides for premium to be offset against "interest payments" suggests that the drafters understood that interest payments would not be taken into account in measuring premium. That the OID rules are not all encompassing is illustrated by the fact that interest payments on an IO Interest retain their character as "interest payments" for purposes of the definition of regular interest in section 860G(a)(1) regardless of whether they are included in OID.

deduction under section 171. The OID definition was adopted to ensure that interest on a debt instrument is taxed evenly over the term of the instrument. By contrast, section 171 was intended to allow an ordinary deduction when a premium bond is prepaid at a rate faster than the rate assumed, to reflect the loss of the premium. In light of this purpose, it makes sense to measure premium based on the holder's potential economic loss. Under this standard, interest payments on an IO Interest should be disregarded in measuring premium, regardless of their relationship to principal, because unlike principal, future interest payments will never come into existence if mortgages are prepaid.

Finally, even if interest payments on an IO Interest are includible in its stated redemption price at maturity, so that the IO Interest is considered initially to have OID, it does not necessarily follow that the IO Interest will have OID throughout its life. Prepayments will eliminate future payments and thereby reduce the instrument's stated redemption price at maturity. Therefore, there is a need to coordinate sections 1272 and 171. One simple solution would be to apply section 1272 if the PAC method produces a positive amount and section 171 if it produces a negative amount (assuming, of course, that allowing a deduction for the negative amount would not reduce the holder's tax basis in the instrument to below its principal amount).

(ii) TRA 1986 legislative history. The legislative history of TRA 1986 clearly states that the method of accruing OID under section 1272(a)(6) does not allow a negative amount of OID to be attributed to any period.[128] One reading of this legislative history is that it simply restates the language of the section: the amount of OID allocated to a period under section 1272(a)(6)(A) is "the excess (if any)" of one positive number over another, and thus cannot be negative. Putting the point differently, section 1272 deals with inclusions in income, and not deductions. While it is likely that the drafters of the legislative history were merely confirming the limited scope of section 1272, given that another portion of the TRA 1986 legislative history indicates, as discussed in Part F, that premium amortization deductions are to be calculated under section 171 using the same PAC method that applies in calculating OID, a legitimate question exists as to whether the statement regarding "negative OID" was intended more broadly to deny deductions under other sections of the Code for negative amounts calculated under the PAC method.

Even if the legislative history was intended to have this effect in some cases, for the reasons given below, it is likely that the drafters intended only to deny

---

128   The Conference Report at II-239 includes the following:
The conferees intend that in no circumstances, would the method of accruing OID prescribed by the conference agreement allow for negative amounts of OID to be attributed to any accrual period. If the use of the present value computations prescribed by the conference agreement produce such a result for an accrual period, the conferees intend that the amount of OID attributable to such accrual period would be treated as zero, and the computation of OID for the following accrual period would be made as if such following accrual period and the preceding accrual period were a single accrual period.

deductions for "negative OID" in cases where the deduction would reduce the tax basis of a debt instrument to less than its principal balance.[129] In such a situation, the deduction would be artificial, in the sense that, barring a default, the apparent loss giving rise to the deduction would inevitably be reversed through the collection of principal payments. Allowing deductions for negative amounts calculated with respect to IO Interests would not reduce their tax basis to below their remaining principal balances.

A number of factors suggest that the drafters of the legislative history did not have premium instruments in mind. First, high-coupon regular interests were not allowed by TRA 1986. Second, section 1272(a)(6) is entitled "Determination of daily portions where principal subject to acceleration", and, under section 1272(a)(6)(C)(ii), applies to a debt instrument where "payments under such debt instrument may be accelerated by reason of prepayments of other obligations securing such debt instrument". In the case of a high-coupon debt instrument, the effect of a prepayment is not primarily to accelerate principal, but instead to eliminate a portion of the value of the investment. Third, applying the PAC method to a conventional premium bond will generally produce a negative amount. Thus, reading the ban on "negative OID" to apply to premium would be tantamount to saying that the PAC method cannot be applied to premium, which is contrary to the discussion of premium in the TRA 1986 legislative history.[130] Finally, the proposed treatment of negative amounts in the TRA 1986 legislative history (combining them with OID in future periods) probably reflects the understanding that the negative amounts will in fact be offset with positive amounts. This would be true for discount instruments but not for premium securities.

d. Other Considerations. Three other arguments support the view that deductions should be allowed for negative amounts calculated under the PAC method with respect to IO Interests:

(i) Comparison with IO Strips. IO Interests were allowed to be created as regular interests in 1988 based on their similarity to strips of interest taken off of pools of mortgages, and it would seem to be desirable to apply similar principles to the two to the extent possible. The owner of a pass-through certificate representing a strip of interest payments taken off of a pool of mortgages is required to allocate

---

129   Both the American and New York State Bar Associations have recommended that the legislative history of TRA 1986 not be read to prevent deductions for "negative OID" with respect to high-coupon REMIC regular interests. American Bar Association Section of Taxation, *Report Regarding Reporting Issues Relating to Tax Accounting for Discount and Premium on Investments in Mortgage Pass-Through Certificates* (September 16, 1992); New York State Bar Association Tax Section, *Report on the Proposed Real Estate Mortgage Investment Conduit Regulations* (March 19, 1992); New York State Bar Association Tax Section, *Report on the Federal Income Tax Treatment of Real Estate Mortgage Investment Conduits* (December 30, 1988).

130   Payments of qualified stated interest are not taken into account in the PAC formula. Thus, as applied to a conventional bond, the formula would produce the gross amount of amortizable bond premium and not the net amount of income from the bond (interest less premium).

its basis among the mortgages and is allowed to deduct the basis allocated to any mortgage when the mortgage is repaid.[131] The prepayment is an identifiable event that fixes the loss and makes it available under section 165 standards.[132] Allowing losses for negative amounts calculated under the PAC method achieves a similar result.

(ii) Clear reflection of income. If deductions are not allowed for negative amounts determined under the PAC method, then it is not clear when losses would be allowed prior to a sale. One possibility is that losses would be allowed under section 165 at the point when those losses are inevitable because the holder's basis exceeds the maximum aggregate amount of future payments. Computing losses on this basis would be equivalent to applying the PAC method, but using a Prepayment Assumption that there will be no future prepayments (rather than a realistic assumption) and a discount rate of zero (rather than the original yield to maturity). Congress adopted the PAC method to clear up the tax treatment of debt instruments that provide uncertain payments due to the difficulty of predicting mortgage payments. A policy decision was made that a rough approximation of future prepayments was better than no assumption at all.[133] What sense does it make to use one set of assumptions in calculating income (or even in reducing interest income to zero) and a wholly different set in calculating losses?[134] Denying a deduction for negative amounts calculated under the PAC method also can have the effect of causing uncertainty in calculating accruals of market discount.[135]

(iii) Effect on residual interests. If the holder of an IO Interest is not allowed any deductions for negative amounts calculated under the PAC method, then the issuing REMIC should not be required to include those amounts in income. Requiring the REMIC to include those amounts in income, however, would produce a

---

131   See the text accompanying footnote 2 and following footnote 69, above.

132   Section 165 allows a deduction for losses sustained during the taxable year. The regulations under section 165 state that for a loss to be deductible under that section, it must be a bona fide loss (1) evidenced by a closed and completed transaction, (2) fixed by an identifiable event, and (3) with certain exceptions, sustained in the year claimed. See Treasury Regulation § 1.165-1(b).

133   See the Senate Finance Committee report on TRA 1986 (Sen. Rep. 99-313, 99th Cong. 2d Sess.) at 792:

> The committee recognizes that, in order to measure income as accurately as possible, an essential feature of providing satisfactory rules for the taxation of the multiple classes of interests is the clarification of the application of the OID rules and related issues as applied to mortgages and mortgage-backed securities. Given the uncertainty created by the unknown timing of prepayments on mortgages, the committee believes that the OID rules adopted by the bill provide a reasonable approximation of the economic accrual of income, recognizing that the amount of OID accrued in a particular accrual period under the bill, may be either greater or less than an amount that would be accrued if there were perfect advance knowledge of the timing of prepayments.

134   As discussed earlier, different considerations apply where a loss would reduce basis to below the remaining principal amount. In that case, it can be demonstrated that the loss will be reversed.

135   See footnote 101, above.

better match with the income earned by the REMIC on the underlying whole mortgages. The holder's loss on IO Interests generally is matched economically by a gain to holders of other low-coupon REMIC regular interests that is deductible by the REMIC. Allowing the deduction, but not requiring inclusion of the offsetting income item, is distortive.

2. Delinquencies and Defaults

With most mortgage-backed securities, other than those guaranteed by (or backed by mortgages guaranteed by) the United States, there is a possibility that some portion of the interest accruing on the security will not be paid when due, and that some portion of the principal ultimately will not be collected, as a result of defaults on the underlying mortgages.[136] The significance of defaults may be magnified through the creation of subordinated classes of securities. The prospect of payment defaults or delinquencies raises three questions: (1) at what point can the holder of a security reporting income under an accrual method stop accruing interest or OID on the ground that the income ultimately will not be paid,[137] (2) when can the holder recognize a loss in respect of uncollectible principal and accrued interest, and (3) what is the character of such a loss? These issues are of greatest concern in the case of securities backed by commercial loans, where individual loans can be quite sizable and substantial periods of time may elapse following the occurrence of a default until the amount ultimately collectible becomes known.

In general, under an accrual method, taxpayers must include interest in income as it accrues even though it is not paid (or is not expected to be paid) when due. Only at the point in time when it can be demonstrated that a right to accrued interest is worthless (because the accrued amount is uncollectible) are accruals no longer required.[138] When that point is reached, prior accruals of interest are not reversed, but as discussed below, a bad debt deduction may be allowed under section 166 for the accrued amounts.[139] Although there seems to be no authority addressing the point, the principles that apply to stated interest also should apply to OID.

---

136   Although payment defaults on mortgage-backed securities also could result from defaults by the issuer of those securities, or errors in structuring the securities, given the conduit nature of these issuers and the fact that payments are typically channeled through highly rated commercial banks, defaults of this type should be very rare.

137   A taxpayer reporting interest income under a cash method would not include interest in income until it is paid. Under section 860B(b), however, all taxpayers must report income on a REMIC regular interest under an accrual method. Similarly, section 1272 requires all taxpayers to include OID in income as it accrues.

138   See, e.g., *Jones Lumber Co. v. Comm'r*, 404 F.2d 764 (6th Cir. 1968); *Atlantic Coast Line Railroad Co. v. Comm'r*, 31 B.T.A. 730 (1934), *aff'd* on other issues, 81 F.2d 309 (4th Cir. 1936); Revenue Ruling 80-361, 1980-2 C.B. 164 (accrual required during the portion of taxable year before debtor becomes insolvent and claim is worthless).

139   See Revenue Ruling 80-361, 1980-2 C.B. 164; Revenue Ruling 81-18, 1981-1 C.B 295. For the character of the deduction for uncollectible accrued interest, see footnotes 148 and 150, and accompanying text. In the case of securities held by securities dealers, interest accruals may be offset by losses from marking the securities to market. See Chapter 9, Part E.

Whether interest is uncollectible is a question of fact. The Supreme Court has not yet announced a standard for determining when an amount becomes uncollectible, and the Tax Court and the various circuit courts have phrased the standard in different ways. The Second Circuit described a debt as uncollectible when "in all probability the income will not be received."[140] The Tax Court has echoed the probability standard of the Second Circuit in one case[141] but in another announced that the test is whether there are "reasonable grounds for believing ... that such income will never be received. ..."[142] The Court of Claims explained the test as being that "substantial evidence must be presented to establish there was no reasonable expectancy of payment."[143] For an unsecured debt, demonstrating that the debtor is insolvent generally is adequate to stop accruals, but insolvency or even bankruptcy would not be enough to stop accruals for a collateralized loan if the security is adequate to cover the interest and bankruptcy or other similar laws do not prevent its ultimate collection.[144] In the case of a mortgage-backed security, the existence of credit support (including the subordination of different classes) obviously would need to be taken into account.

Because the collectibility test always depends on the facts and circumstances surrounding each loan, it is difficult to apply in practice. This is particularly so for holders of mortgage-backed securities, who generally have no direct dealings with mortgagors, and may have only limited information about their financial condition. Although in theory the collectibility test is applied based on the facts as they exist during the relevant accrual period, in practice, whether or not interest has been collected by the time the tax contest is joined is an important factor. As a result, many taxpayers stop accruing interest at the point when they think it probably will not be collected, even if it would be difficult to show that the claim is really worthless. Some taxpayers stop accruing interest automatically when a loan is more than a certain number of days delinquent. There is, however, no specific authority permitting such a blanket approach.[145]

The terms of many mortgage-backed securities permit the issuer to stop accruing interest in part, and to write down the principal balance of the security, when the

---

140 *Corn Exchange Bank v. Comm'r*, 37 F.2d 34 (2d Cir. 1945).

141 See *Georgia School-Book Depository, Inc. v. Comm'r*, 1 T.C. 463 (1943).

142 *Union Pacific Railroad Co. v. Comm'r*, 14 T.C. 401 (1950), *rev'd on other grounds*, 188 F.2d 950 (2d Cir. 1951).

143 *European American Bank and Trust Co. v. Comm'r*, 90-2 U.S.T.C. ¶ 50,333 (Cls. Ct.) *aff'd*, 92-1 U.S.T.C. ¶ 50,026 (Fed. Cir.).

144 See Revenue Ruling 80-361, 1980-2 C.B. 164 (interest stopped accruing when debtor became insolvent and as a consequence debt became uncollectible). Cf. Treasury Regulation § 1.166-2(c) (bankruptcy is generally an indication of the worthlessness of at least a part of an unsecured and unpreferred debt). Insolvency is not essential to stop accruals of interest if the uncollectibility test otherwise is met.

145 Revenue Ruling 81-18, 1981-1 C.B. 295, allowed a bank to stop accruing uncollected interest 90 days after it was due based on conformity with a bank regulatory rule. However, that rule has since been repealed so that the ruling is obsolete. See U.S. Treasury, "Report to the Congress on the Tax Treatment of Bad Debts by Financial Institutions," September 1991, 91 *Tax Notes Today* 195-28, footnote 83.

issuer determines that interest or principal on the underlying mortgages will not support the related payments on the security. These actions obviously are helpful in establishing that the unaccrued or written-down amounts are uncollectible.[146] Nonetheless, the issuer's determination would not be binding for tax purposes with respect to any investor if the investor continues to have the right to the written off amounts in the event they are collected.

Section 166 allows an ordinary deduction for certain bad debts. The deduction does not apply to "securities" as defined in section 165(g)(2), but this exception generally is relevant for mortgage-backed securities only in the case of pay-through bonds issued by entities treated as corporations for tax purposes, or by governmental entities.[147] Corporations, and noncorporate taxpayers that acquire debt instruments in the course of a trade or business, are allowed an ordinary deduction under section 166(a) when a debt instrument becomes wholly or partially worthless (except that a deduction is allowed for a partially worthless debt only to the extent it is charged off on the holder's books).[148] Nonbusiness bad debts of noncorporate taxpayers are allowed only when they become wholly worthless and only as a short-term capital loss.[149] Bad debts may include rights to unpaid interest that has accrued and been included in income.[150] Whether a debt is wholly or partially worthless

---

146   The opposite, of course, is also true. If a security allows the issuer to stop accruing interest or to write down principal, it may be quite difficult for a holder to demonstrate that amounts that continue to be shown as due on the books of the issuer are in fact uncollectible, unless the lack of action by the issuer is attributable to specific tests of worthlessness that are stricter than those that would apply for tax purposes (e.g., a requirement that amounts be written off only when a loan is finally liquidated).

147   A "security" is defined in section 165(g)(2)(C) as a "bond, debenture, note or certificate, or other evidence of indebtedness, issued by a corporation or by a government or political subdivision thereof, with interest coupons or in registered form." Virtually all mortgage-backed securities are issued in registered form, in part because of the TEFRA registration requirements described in Chapter 10, Part A. However, with the exception of pay-through bonds issued by an entity that is classified as a corporation (including a TMP that issues debt after 1991), mortgage-backed securities are not generally issued by corporations, and they are only occasionally issued by governmental entities. A REMIC is not considered a corporation for tax purposes, even if it is organized as a state-law corporation. See section 860A(a). Pass-through certificates are not themselves issued by a corporation or governmental agency, and thus would be considered "securities" for this purpose only to the extent the underlying mortgages were securities. See, e.g., Revenue Ruling 84-10, 1984-1 C.B. 155 (FNMA pass-through certificates may be qualifying real property loans within the meaning of section 593(d), even though under section 593(d)(1)(A) loans evidenced by a section 165(g)(2)(C) security cannot be such a loan). Under section 165(g)(1), a taxpayer holding a "security" that is a capital asset is allowed a capital loss if the security becomes wholly worthless.

148   At one time, section 166 allowed taxpayers to use a reserve method for bad debts, but this feature was eliminated by TRA 1986. Unlike other taxpayers, certain thrifts and small banks are entitled to use a reserve method. See Chapter 9, Part A.

149   See section 166(d).

150   See Treasury Regulation § 1.166-6(a)(2) (previously accrued interest may be included in the bad debt deduction allowable where the amount realized in the sale of property pledged to secure a loan is less than the amount of the debt and the shortfall is uncollectible). See also Revenue Ruling 80-361, 1980-2 C.B. 164; G.C.M. 38385 (May 23, 1980). The legislative history of the Bankruptcy Tax Act of 1980 can be read to provide that previously accrued interest that is lost in connection with a corporate reorganization is allowed as an ordinary distribution. See G. Henderson and S.

generally is determined based on the uncollectibility standard described above, taking account of all relevant facts and circumstances.[151] Subject to certain requirements, banks and thrifts may treat debt instruments as worthless for tax purposes in the same year they are charged off for regulatory purposes.[152]

As discussed in Part C.2 above, the PAC method allows the use of a Prepayment Assumption in calculating accruals of OID. That assumption is generally the prepayment assumption used in pricing securities. Where some level of default losses is taken into account in pricing a class of securities, it might be reasonable on economic grounds to take the loss assumption into account in calculating accruals of OID. However, there appears to be no basis for doing so.[153] A harder question is how to account for interest and principal payments under the PAC method once they are in fact determined to be uncollectible. Should they be treated as if they will be, and are, paid when due, with nonpayments being accounted for as bad debts under section 166, or should they instead be ignored in determining current and remaining payments due on the instrument? A sensible middle ground would be to disregard future payments that are uncollectible until income is reduced to zero. Additional losses then would be allowed only subject to section 166.

Goldring, *Failing and Failed Businesses* (CCH Transactions Library 1993) at ¶ 403.016, fn. 71 and accompanying text; W. Plumb, Jr., "The Bankruptcy Tax Act," 1981 *S. Cal. Instit.* 8-1, 8-66 through 8-77. See also P.L.R. 9137041 (June 18, 1991), rulings 14 and 18. In the case of a REMIC, the write-off of previously accrued income does not fit neatly into either fact pattern— pledged property is not sold and, because a REMIC is not a corporation, there cannot be a reorganization.

151   Treasury Regulation § 1.166-2. Treasury Regulation § 1.166-2(b) states that "[w]here the surrounding circumstances indicate that a debt is worthless and uncollectible and that legal action to enforce payment would in all probability not result in the satisfaction of execution on a judgment," a showing of these facts is sufficient to demonstrate worthlessness.

152   See Treasury Regulation § 1.166-2(d).

153   As indicated in footnote 36, above, a number of taxpayers have incorporated into the Prepayment Assumption an assumption that the maturity date of loans will be extended because of defaults. While it is not clear that an extension assumption will be allowed, it is more defensible than a loss assumption, because it involves only the timing of principal payments, which is the focus of the PAC method.

Chapter 7

Taxation of Holders of Equity Interests in Owner Trusts and REMIC Residual Interests

A. Introduction

This chapter discusses the federal income taxation of holders of equity interests in owner trusts that are not TMPs and REMIC residual interests. The tax characteristics that are common to both types of securities are considered first, followed by a review of special considerations applicable to owner trusts and special considerations applicable to REMIC residual interests. The chapter concludes with a discussion of phantom income. Except as otherwise indicated, in this chapter, the term "owner trust" means an owner trust that is not a TMP, the term "conduit issuer" means an owner trust or a REMIC, the term "equity interest" means an equity interest in a conduit issuer, and the terms "bond" and "CMO" include REMIC regular interests. The taxation of TMPs, and holders of equity interests in TMPs, is addressed in Chapter 8.

B. Common Tax Characteristics

Conduit issuers are generally not subject to tax.[1] Instead, each holder of an equity interest is required to include in income its share of the taxable income (or loss) of the related conduit issuer allocable to that holder without regard to the distributions made by the issuer. In computing taxable income, the conduit issuer would have income from the mortgage collateral, the reinvestment of mortgage payments, and any reserve fund investments, and would be allowed deductions for interest (includ-

---

1 A REMIC is subject to certain penalty taxes. See Chapter 4, Part B.

ing OID) and retirement premiums on the bonds it issues, and operating expenses.[2] In any period, the deductions allowed for bond interest (net of any premium received by the issuer)[3] generally would equal the income that would be reported by original holders of the bonds if they bought the bonds on the issue date at the issue price (for bond issues having more than one class, computed on a class-by-class basis), except that the OID *de minimis* rule would be ignored.[4] A conduit issuer that retires a bond for an amount less than its adjusted issue price generally would have ordinary cancellation of indebtedness income equal to the difference. It may be possible to offset that income against the basis of assets or other tax attributes if the issuer is insolvent.[5]

If a conduit issuer that acquires mortgages at a discount below their principal amount modifies a mortgage in connection with a default, the entity may recognize non-cash income equal to the excess of the issue price of the modified mortgage over the entity's tax basis in the mortgage.[6] Although REMICs benefit from a

---

2   Payments of retirement premium on the bonds would give rise to an ordinary deduction even if the premium is taxable as capital gain to bondholders. See Treasury Regulation § 1.163-7(c) (issuer); Chapter 6, footnote 39 (holders). If holders of equity interests are individuals, the deductibility of the conduit issuer's operating expenses may be limited for regular income tax purposes under section 67 and denied entirely for alternative minimum tax purposes. See the text following footnote 40, below, and Chapter 2, text accompanying footnotes 9 and 10. As a general rule, issuers of bonds are allowed deductions for underwriters' discount and other issuance expenses. Those expenses are allocated among the different classes of bonds (if there is more than one class) in proportion to their issue prices, without regard to maturities. The expenses allocated to each class are then deducted ratably over the life of that class. Revenue Ruling 70-359, 1970-2 C.B. 103. There appears to be no authority requiring amortization of noninterest expenses under a constant yield method, although the law may someday be changed to impose such a requirement. See NYSBA 1987 Report at 423. Also, it is not clear whether a prepayment assumption may be used in amortizing issuance expenses, although it would appear to be reasonable to use such an assumption. Any unamortized expenses relating to a class of bonds are deducted when that class of bonds is retired. Special rules for the treatment of issuance expenses by owner trusts are discussed in footnotes 9 and 11, below. As discussed in footnote 31, below, a REMIC is not allowed deductions for the costs of issuance of regular interests. Instead, those costs are capitalized and included in the basis of the REMIC's assets.

3   If a bond is issued at a premium, the premium would be included in income and thus effectively would offset the deduction for interest expense. Under the current version of Treasury Regulation § 1.61-12(c), such premium generally must be included in income under a straight-line method. It is expected, however, that the regulation will be amended at some point to require the use of a constant yield method. See Joint Committee on Taxation, *Explanation of Technical Corrections to the Tax Reform Act of 1984 and Other Recent Tax Legislation* (JCS-11-87) (May 13, 1987) at 14. The treatment of premium by holders of debt instruments is discussed in Chapter 6, Part F.

4   Section 163(e); Treasury Regulation §§ 1.163-7(a) and (b). The *de minimis* rule is described in Chapter 6, footnote 21. Under Treasury Regulation § 1.163-7(b)(2), an issuer may elect to deduct *de minimis* OID on a bond (attributable to an issue price less than the principal amount) not under a constant yield method but instead on a straight-line basis over the term of the bond, in proportion to stated interest payments, or at maturity. This regulation has the same effective date as the OID regulations. See Chapter 6, footnote 13. It is not clear how the term of a debt instrument that is subject to the PAC method would be determined in applying the first two of the three alternative approaches, although presumably the Prepayment Assumption used in applying that method would be taken into account.

5   See generally section 108, discussed further in footnotes 19 and 37, below, and accompanying text.

special rule that disregards such a modification in determining if the modified mortgage is a qualified mortgage, it is not clear if that rule applies in determining the REMIC's taxable income.[7] A modified debt instrument that provides for interest at a rate at least equal to the applicable Federal rate generally will have an issue price (used in measuring income from the modification) equal to its principal amount.[8]

C. Special Considerations Applicable to Owner Trusts

As discussed in Chapter 3, an owner trust may be classified either as a grantor trust or as a partnership. A major difference between grantor trusts and partnerships is that a grantor trust is essentially ignored for federal income tax purposes, whereas a partnership is recognized as an entity for some tax purposes. Thus, if an owner trust

---

6   Technically, the modification would be a taxable exchange if it is a "significant modification" within the meaning of section 1001. The standards for determining whether there has been a deemed exchange of debt instruments under section 1001 are described in Chapter 4, Part C.2. For the rule measuring gain from the exchange of property for a debt instrument by reference to the issue price of the debt instrument, see Treasury Regulation § 1.1001-1(g). The gain from modification of a mortgage should have the same character as gain from a prepayment of the mortgage. For a special rule that may treat income realized by a REMIC from the prepayment of a discount mortgage as interest income, see text accompanying footnote 33, below. In the case of an owner trust that recognizes gain from a loan modification, consideration should be given to the possible application of the installment sale rules in sections 453 and 453A and, where the mortgagor is a corporation, to the possible treatment of the modification as a tax-free recapitalization under sections 354 and 368(a)(1)(E).

7   The special REMIC rule, which is at Treasury Regulation § 1.860G-2(b), is discussed in Chapter 4, Part C.2.d. The regulation clearly applies to loan modifications that are made before a loan is transferred to a REMIC. In that context at least, it is obvious that the rule was not intended to affect the income tax treatment of the exchange.

8   The issue price of a modified mortgage would be determined under the complex rules governing debt instruments issued in exchange for property. In general, the issue price of the modified mortgage would differ from its principal amount if (1) the mortgage is traded on an established securities market before or after the modification (in which case under section 1273(b)(3) the issue price would be the fair market value of the mortgage), (2) section 1274 applies to the modification, the modification does not involve a "potentially abusive situation" as described below, and the rate of interest on the modified mortgage is less than the applicable Federal rate (in which case the issue price would be the present value of the payments on the modified mortgage, calculated using the applicable Federal rate as the discount rate), or (3) section 1274 applies and the modification involves a potentially abusive situation (in which case the issue price would be the fair market value of the mortgage). Section 1274 does not apply to debt instruments that provide for aggregate debt service payments not exceeding $250,000 or to certain mortgage assumptions. See sections 1274(c)(3)(C) and (c)(4). Under Treasury Regulation § 1.1274-3(a), a potentially abusive situation includes a "recent sales transaction." A recent sale of a mortgage to the sponsor of a conduit issuer might be considered a recent sales transaction if it allows the fair market value of the mortgage to be determined. Where the sponsor buys a mortgage as part of a portfolio of financially troubled loans, however, it may not be possible to value individual loans based on the aggregate purchase price. More complex issues that are beyond the scope of this work would arise in determining the issue price of a modified mortgage where the instrument provides for contingent payments, or is issued together with other consideration in exchange for the original mortgage. Under Treasury Regulation § 1.1274-3(d), the issuer's determination that a debt instrument is or is not issued in a potentially abusive situation is binding on a holder unless the holder discloses the fact that it is taking a contrary position on its tax return.

is classified as a grantor trust, each holder of an equity interest therein would be treated as if the holder purchased and owned directly a share of the assets of the trust, subject to its share of the indebtedness of the trust. Accordingly, each holder would have an initial tax basis in its share of the trust's assets equal to the cost of its equity interest plus its share of the aggregate adjusted issue price of the bonds at the time of purchase of the equity interest.[9] In addition, the holder's income would be computed under its own method of accounting, and the holder would make any applicable tax elections, for example, to amortize bond premium on the mortgage collateral. If the holder sold an interest in the owner trust, it would be considered to sell an interest in the underlying mortgages. Accordingly, as discussed further in Chapter 9, if the holder was a thrift institution or bank, any resulting gain or loss would be ordinary income or loss. Cash distributions from a grantor trust are not taxable.

By contrast, if an owner trust is classified as a partnership, taxable income would be computed, and in general elections made, at the partnership (or owner trust) level, using the partnership's accounting method (which almost always would be an accrual method).[10] Each holder of an equity interest would report its share of the partnership's taxable income in the holder's taxable year in which the taxable year of the partnership ends.[11] In most cases, the taxable year of the partnership would be the calendar year.[12] Each partner would be considered to own an interest in the partnership (as contrasted with a direct interest in partnership assets). The partnership interest would have an initial basis in the hands of the partner equal to its original cost (the cash purchase price, or the basis of property exchanged for such interest in a tax-free exchange), plus the partner's share of partnership liabili-

---

9   However, the adjusted issue price would be calculated without regard to the OID *de minimis* rule. See footnote 4, above, and accompanying text. A holder would not be permitted to amortize underwriters' spread or other costs of issuing bonds unless it was a holder at the time those expenses were incurred. Instead, a subsequent holder effectively would include those expenses in its basis in the mortgages because that basis would include the adjusted issue price of the portion of the bonds that was used to pay issuance costs. There is very old case law to the effect that the purchaser of property subject to debt issued at a discount is not allowed deductions for any portion of such discount but instead must treat the liability as if it had been issued at its principal amount (although the basis of the acquired property would then include the full face amount of the debt rather than its revised issue price). See, for example, *American Gas & Electric Co. v. Comm'r*, 33 B.T.A. 471 (1935), *aff'd in part and rev'd in part*, 85 F.2d 527 (2d Cir. 1936) and cases cited therein. See also *Helvering v. Metropolitan Edison Co.*, 306 U.S. 522 (1939). These authorities are overruled by Treasury Regulation § 1.163-7(a) (interpreting section 163(e)), which states that OID deductions are allowed to "an issuer (including a transferee)."

10   Section 448 generally requires a partnership to use an accrual method if it has any partner that is a corporation not taxable under subchapter S. The partnership's taxable income would reflect the amortization of bond issuance expenses paid by the partnership. However, those expenses would not be treated as paid by the partnership if the partnership was formed, or terminated and re-formed, after the issuance of the bonds. If there is only a single owner of an equity interest in the owner trust at the time the bonds are issued, and equity interests are sold to investors at a later date, the partnership would not be considered to be formed until there is more than one equity owner. Partnership terminations are discussed in footnote 13, below, and the accompanying text.

11   See section 706(a).

12   See section 706(b).

ties. Over time, such basis would be increased by the partner's share of partnership income and contributions, and decreased by the partner's share of losses and distributions (treating as distributions any reductions in the partnership's liabilities). The amount of the partnership's liabilities in respect of the bonds would equal the bonds' aggregate adjusted issue price, as described above.

Unlike a grantor trust, a partnership is considered to have its own basis in its assets (inside basis). While initially the inside basis of an owner trust that is classified as a partnership would equal the sum of the holders' bases in their equity interests (outside basis), a discrepancy could develop if (1) equity interests were sold at a gain or loss and (2) the sale did not result in (and is not followed by) a termination of the partnership under section 708.[13] Under section 708, a partnership is considered to be terminated and reformed if 50 percent or more of the total interest in partnership income and capital is sold or exchanged within a 12-month period. Any discrepancy between inside and outside bases following a sale of a partnership interest at a gain (or loss) could result in overtaxation (or undertaxation) of the purchasing partner. The partnership could eliminate or mitigate the problem by making an election under section 754 to adjust the basis of its assets for purposes of computing the taxable income of the purchasing partner.[14]

If an owner trust is classified as a partnership, then gain or loss from the sale of an equity interest may be capital gain or loss, even though, in the case of a thrift institution or bank, a sale of a direct ownership interest in the mortgages held by the trust automatically would be ordinary income or loss.[15] Such gain or loss would be computed by comparing the seller's adjusted basis in its partnership interest with the amount realized in the sale (which would include the seller's share of the trust's liabilities). Distributions of cash by a partnership to a partner are not taxable unless they exceed the partner's basis in its partnership interest, in which case the excess is treated as gain from sale of that interest. Gain from this source would be rare in the case of an owner trust because an equity owner's basis in its equity interest would include its share of the trust's liability for the bonds.

A pension plan, charity, individual retirement account, or other tax-exempt organization that is subject to tax on its unrelated business taxable income (UBTI)

---

13 If a partnership terminates, it is considered to distribute its assets to its partners, including any new partners whose purchase of partnership interests caused the termination, and the distributee partners are then considered to contribute those assets to a new partnership. See Treasury Regulation § 1.708-1(b)(1)(iv). Under the partnership tax rules, one effect of a termination is to bring the new partnership's inside basis in its assets into conformity with the partners' bases in their partnership interests.

14 If a trust, and the holders of the equity interest therein, otherwise file tax returns on the basis that the trust is a grantor trust, a "protective" section 754 election could be made. The disclosure documents for the sale of an equity interest often indicate whether the trust intends to make an election under section 754.

15 See section 741. It is not clear whether the sale of an interest in a passive partnership whose sole assets are debt instruments would be viewed as a sale of debt instruments for purposes of section 582(c). This section is discussed in Chapter 9, Part D. Gain from the sale of a partnership interest may be ordinary income to the extent attributable to accrued market discount on a market discount bond. See section 751(a). Market discount is discussed generally in Chapter 6, Part E.

under section 512 will be taxable on substantially all of its income from an equity interest in an owner trust, regardless of whether the trust is classified as a grantor trust or partnership.[16]

Where an entity classified as a partnership holds financially troubled mortgages for purposes of liquidation, an issue may arise as to whether the partnership is considered a dealer in mortgages, or in the real property acquired from mortgagors. Dealer status generally will be found to exist principally where the partnership engages in substantial merchandising efforts.[17] Income or loss from sales or exchanges of dealer property is ordinary, and in the case of mortgages and other securities (but not real estate) is calculated under a mark to market system (as if, at the end of each taxable year, mortgages held by the partnership were sold at fair market value and then repurchased).[18]

An owner trust (whether a grantor trust or partnership) may retire bonds at a price less than their adjusted issue price and thereby realize income from the discharge of indebtedness. Under section 108, such income may be deferred (or in some cases eliminated) by excluding it from gross income and offsetting the excluded amount, subject to certain limits, against the basis of assets or other tax attributes. This beneficial rule applies, however, only if the debtor is bankrupt or to the extent it is insolvent (has assets with a fair market value less than the adjusted issue price of its liabilities). The relevance of section 108 to owner trusts is limited, however, because the insolvency and bankruptcy tests are applied to equity owners rather than to the owner trust as a separate taxpayer.[19]

An investor in an owner trust that claims credits for foreign income taxes unrelated to the owner trust should consider the possible effect of its investment on

---

16 Such organizations are taxable on income from property that is "debt-financed" within the meaning of section 514. Because substantially all of the cost of the assets of an owner trust is financed with debt, substantially all of the income of an owner trust is debt-financed income. Moreover, if an owner trust is classified as a partnership and its equity interests are readily marketable, then for partnership taxable years beginning before January 1, 1994 all of the income from the partnership would be considered UBTI. The exemption for debt-financed investments in real estate in section 514(c)(9) does not apply to investments in mortgages. For a general discussion of UBTI, see Chapter 9, Part B.

17 For authorities applying the dealer definition to securities, see Chapter 9, Part E. For a good summary of the factors used in determining whether a person is a dealer in real property, see U.S. v. Winthrop, 417 F.2d 905 (5th Cir. 1969). The fact that real property was acquired in a foreclosure does not prevent it from being dealer property. See Revenue Ruling 74-159, 1974-1 C.B. 232.

18 See Chapter 9, Part E. Section 475 does not apply to real estate (as distinguished from mortgages) and real estate cannot be accounted for under an inventory system. See Revenue Ruling 69-536, 1969-2 C.B. 109. An entity that reports income from mortgages under a mark to market system would not be concerned about potential "phantom" gains from loan modifications (see text accompanying footnote 6, above) because those gains would be offset with mark to market losses from valuing a modified loan at less than its issue price.

19 See section 108(d)(6) (tests applied to partnerships at partner level). The same rule would apply automatically to a grantor trust because such a trust is generally disregarded for tax purposes. RRA 1993 adopted a generous rule allowing individuals and S corporations to defer income from the discharge of "qualified real property business indebtedness" by using it to reduce the basis of depreciable real property. This rule benefits mortgagors but not taxpayers that borrow to finance the purchase of mortgage loans.

those credits. The credit for foreign income taxes is limited under section 904 to (broadly speaking) the U.S. taxes imposed with respect to foreign source taxable income. Surprisingly, an equity owner's share of interest expense of an owner trust may be charged in part against foreign source income notwithstanding that the trust assets are wholly domestic.[20]

D. Special Considerations Applicable to REMICs

From a tax perspective, a REMIC resembles a partnership more than a grantor trust. Income or loss is computed at the level of the REMIC and is then allocated among the holders of residual interests as ordinary income or loss.[21] Specifically, taxable income or loss of the REMIC is computed for each calendar quarter, and each holder of a residual interest is considered to earn, on each day it holds such interest, that day's ratable share of the REMIC's taxable income or loss for the quarter.[22] Neither the Code nor the legislative history indicates how a REMIC should allocate its taxable income for a year among different calendar quarters. Hopefully, some flexibility will be allowed in choosing an allocation method.[23]

---

20 With limited exceptions, interest expense is allocated against foreign source income based on the portion of all assets of a taxpayer that are assets producing foreign source income. For purposes of allocating interest expense, an investor in an owner trust would be treated as if it had paid directly its share of the interest expense of the trust if either the trust is classified as a grantor trust, or it is classified as a partnership and the investor owns an interest of at least 10%. See generally section 864(e) and Treasury Regulation §§ 1.861-9T through -13T. The look-through rule for partnerships is in Treasury Regulation § 1.861-9T(e). Although interest expense incurred in an "integrated financial transaction" can be offset directly against income from the transaction, a typical owner trust would not meet the requirements of the rule (in particular, the requirement that the owner trust assets and debt mature within ten business days of each other). See Treasury Regulation § 1.861-10T(c).

21 See section 860C(e)(1); Treasury Regulation § 1.860C-1(a). There is no general rule that treats such income as interest, or as income having the same character as income of the REMIC. Such income is, however, treated as interest income for purposes of the U.S. withholding tax on non-U.S. investors. See Chapter 10, text accompanying footnote 33. Income from residual interests is portfolio income for purposes of the passive loss rules of section 469. Treasury Regulation § 1.469-2T(c)(i)(3)(A).

22 By contrast with the treatment of partners, a holder must report income as it is earned, and not in the holder's taxable year in which the REMIC's taxable year ends. In determining each day's ratable share of the REMIC's income or loss during a quarter, any reasonable counting convention may be used. Treasury Regulation § 1.860C-1(c). Limitations on the deductibility of losses are discussed below in the text accompanying footnote 49.

23 For many REMICs, it would make sense to calculate taxable income for each calendar quarter by first determining taxable income for periods corresponding to the accrual periods for their regular interests and then allocating the taxable income for each accrual period to the days within that period on a ratable basis. In determining income for a portion of a taxable year, partnerships can choose whether to pro rate results for the year or have an interim closing of the books. Treasury Regulation § 1.706-1(c)(2). The need to report taxable income to holders of residual interests quarterly rather than annually (see Chapter 11, Part C) together with the fact that income inclusions by holders are not deferred until the year in which the REMIC taxable year ends (see footnote 22, above) makes it impractical for a REMIC to determine quarterly income by pro rating the income for the year. On the other hand, Treasury Regulation § 1.860C-1(c) gives as an example of a reasonable counting convention "30 days per month/ 90 days per quarter/ 360 days

In general, the taxable income of a REMIC is determined in the same manner as in the case of an individual. However, there are five statutory exceptions to this rule.[24] First, a REMIC must use an accrual method of accounting. Second, regular interests, if not otherwise debt instruments, are treated as indebtedness of the REMIC, so that, among other consequences, interest thereon is deductible. Third, market discount on any qualified mortgage or other debt instrument held by the REMIC is includible in income as if such discount were OID (and the obligation were issued on the date on which it is acquired by the REMIC).[25] Fourth, items of income, gain, loss or deduction allocable to a prohibited transaction are disregarded. Finally, deductions for net operating loss carryovers or carrybacks are not allowed.[26] Other adjustments are found in the REMIC regulations. They treat all gain or loss from the disposition of an asset as ordinary, and allow deductions for ordinary and necessary operating expenses, interest and bad debts without regard to certain limitations that apply to individual taxpayers.[27]

The deductions allowed to a REMIC for interest or other income on a regular interest should match inclusions in income by an original holder who acquires the interest at its issue price. Thus, the discussion in Chapter 6 of the timing of income recognition by holders of regular interests is also relevant in determining the taxable

---

per year" which implies that annual pro ration is an acceptable method.

24   The general rule and the exceptions are in section 860C(b); see also Treasury Regulation § 1.860C-2(b).

25   See sections 860C(b)(1)(B) and 1276(b)(2). This rule applies only to market discount on a *market discount bond* as defined in section 1278(a)(1), and thus does not apply to an obligation having a *de minimis* amount of discount or a fixed maturity date not exceeding one year from the date of issue. For a discussion of the *de minimis* rule, see Chapter 6, footnote 94 and accompanying text.

26   Section 860C(b)(1)(D) provides that in determining a REMIC's taxable income, the deductions referred to in section 703(a)(2) (other than any deduction under section 212) shall not be allowed. Section 703(a)(2) lists items for which deductions are not allowed in computing the taxable income of a partnership. Instead, the listed items are accounted for separately in the partners' own returns. The only deductions referred to in section 703(a)(2) of possible relevance to REMICs are the deduction for personal exemptions, the deduction in section 164(a) for taxes paid or accrued to foreign countries or to possessions of the United States, and the net operating loss deduction. There is no obvious reason why a REMIC should be denied a deduction for foreign and possession taxes. In contrast to a partnership, a REMIC cannot pass those taxes through to residual interest holders so that they may be allowed as credits or deductions in the holders' returns.

27   See Treasury Regulation § 1.860C-2. This regulation provides that (1) ordinary and necessary operating expenses are deductible under section 212 (although not under section 162 because a REMIC is not considered to be engaged in a trade or business for purposes of section 162) without regard to the 2% of adjusted gross income floor on miscellaneous itemized deductions in section 67, (2) interest is deductible without regard to the section 163(d) limitation on deductions for investment interest, and (3) debts owed to a REMIC are not treated as nonbusiness debts under section 166(d) (so that ordinary deductions can be claimed under section 166(a) for debts that are wholly worthless, or are partially worthless and charged off). Notwithstanding these rules, in the highly unusual case where a REMIC owns a debt instrument that pays tax-exempt interest, a portion of the REMIC's deductions for interest and other expenses are disallowed based on the portion of the REMIC's assets that are tax-exempt obligations. Although the regulations make no mention of the overall limitation on itemized deductions (including section 212 deductions) in section 68, it is inconceivable that it was intended to apply. The flat statement in Treasury Regulation § 1.860C-2(b)(4) allowing a deduction for operating expenses should be broad enough to cover the point.

income of a REMIC. Indeed, these issues may be more significant for the REMIC than for regular interest holders because of the special anti-tax avoidance rules (discussed in Part E) applicable to residual interests. There is no counterpart to these rules for regular interests. One timing issue that is particularly significant in determining a REMIC's taxable income is whether deductions are allowed to holders (and there is a corresponding inclusion in income by the REMIC) for negative amounts determined under the PAC method with respect to high-coupon regular interests.[28]

A REMIC does not recognize gain or loss on the issuance of regular or residual interests in exchange for cash or other property.[29] If a REMIC distributes property in kind with respect to a regular or residual interest, *gain* is recognized by the REMIC in the same manner as if it had sold such property to the distributee at its fair market value, and the basis of the property to the distributee is that same amount.[30]

In order to calculate the taxable income of a REMIC, it is necessary to determine the REMIC's basis in its assets. In general terms, the REMIC's aggregate basis in its assets at the time it is formed equals the aggregate issue price of all REMIC interests (both regular interests and residual interests).[31] Although there is no clear guidance on the point, that aggregate basis presumably would be allocated first to cash and cash equivalents held by the REMIC, and then among the other assets of the REMIC in proportion to their fair market values.[32]

The most significant assets of a REMIC are the qualified mortgages that it holds. Income from holding those mortgages is determined under the rules dis-

---

28 See Chapter 6, Part G.1.

29 Conference Report at II-234, footnote 16; Blue Book at 421, footnote 82. Contributions to a REMIC after the startup day may be subject to a 100% tax. See Chapter 4, Part B.2.

30 Section 860F(c). Apparently, if property having a basis higher than its fair market value were distributed by a REMIC on a *regular* interest, the REMIC would recognize loss in accordance with the normal tax rules governing distributions of property on debt instruments (although as discussed below in the text preceeding footnote 37, the REMIC would have discharge of indebtedness income to the extent the property is considered to be disposed of at a price less than the adjusted issue price of the regular interest that is discharged in exchange for the property). It is not clear whether a loss deduction is ever allowed to a REMIC upon the distribution of loss property to residual interest holders. Distributions of property by REMICs are treated as actual sales of property for purposes of the prohibited transaction rules and the rules relating to qualified reserve funds. Conference Report at II-234; Blue Book at 421.

31 Treasury Regulation § 1.860F-2(c). The issue prices of REMIC interests would be determined under the OID rules (see Chapter 6, footnote 27 and accompanying text) as if the REMIC interests were newly issued debt, except that if an interest is issued in exchange for property, the issue price would always equal fair market value. See section 860G(a)(10) (definition of issue price); Treasury Regulation § 1.860G-1(d). Because the issue price of a REMIC interest is based on the price paid by investors (rather than the net proceeds to the issuer), organizational and syndication expenses would be included indirectly in the issue price and thus in the REMIC's basis in its assets. Apparently, no other deduction for these expenses would be allowed in calculating the taxable income of the REMIC. The treatment of organizational and syndication expenses by the sponsor of the REMIC is discussed in Chapter 12, Part C.

32 In practice, no separate allocation is made to guarantees or other credit enhancement contracts, which is consistent with their treatment as incidents of a REMIC's qualified mortgages in applying the REMIC assets test. See Chapter 4, text accompanying footnote 207.

cussed in Chapter 6, except that a REMIC must include discount in income as it accrues under the PAC method, in the same manner as if the mortgages had been issued on the date on which they were acquired by the REMIC with an issue price equal to their initial basis to the REMIC.[33] A REMIC that sells or disposes of qualified mortgages recognizes gain or loss determined under general tax principles.[34] There is no special REMIC rule that prevents the recognition of gain or loss upon an exchange of qualified mortgages for qualified replacement mortgages. Sections 267(a)(1) and 707(b), which prevent the current recognition of loss from a sale of property between certain related persons, do not seem to apply to sales or exchanges by or to a REMIC because a REMIC is not one of the types of entities listed in those sections.[35]

No Code provision permits or requires adjustments to be made to a REMIC's basis in its assets to reflect subsequent purchases of residual interests at a price greater or less than the seller's adjusted basis. The legislative history of TRA 1986 indicates that it "may be appropriate" to make such adjustments, but leaves the issue unresolved.[36] The REMIC regulations do not address the point.

A REMIC that retires a regular interest for an amount less than its adjusted issue price (e.g., as a result of a cash tender), or discharges its obligation to pay a portion of the principal and accrued interest on a regular interest as a result of a mortgage credit loss, would realize discharge of indebtedness income. The REMIC may be able to defer such income under section 108 to the extent it does not exceed the amount by which the REMIC is "insolvent" immediately prior to the discharge.[37] A REMIC is insolvent if the fair market value of its assets is less than the adjusted issue price of its regular interests (and any other obligations).[38] The amount

---

33 There is no similar rule that treats premium mortgages as if they were newly issued, thus allowing the REMIC to amortize such premium under section 171 even if the mortgages were originated before September 28, 1985. See the discussion of premium in Chapter 6, Part F.

34 One exception to this rule is found in Treasury Regulation § 1.860G-2(d)(2). It generally treats the purchase of a convertible mortgage under a liquidity agreement as a prepayment of the mortgage rather than a sale for purposes of determining the tax treatment of the REMIC. For a discussion of convertible mortgages, see Chapter 4, Part C.3. The effect of loan modifications on a REMIC's income is discussed in footnotes 6–8, above, and the accompanying text.

35 For special rules limiting the ability of a REMIC sponsor to use a REMIC to engage in mortgage swaps, see Chapter 12, footnote 39 and accompanying text.

36 Conference Report at II-233, footnote 15; Blue Book at 421, footnote 81.

37 Section 108 applies to individual debtors, and thus would apply in determining the tax treatment of a REMIC in the absence of a contrary rule. In the unusual circumstance where a REMIC transfers property in retirement of a regular interest, the amount of discharge of indebtedness income would depend on whether the regular interest is considered a "recourse" or "nonrecourse" obligation of the REMIC. In the first case, the REMIC would be considered to sell the property for a price equal to its fair market value and would realize discharge of indebtedness income to the extent the adjusted issue price of the retired regular interest exceeds such fair market value. By contrast, if the retired debt is nonrecourse, the REMIC would be considered to sell the property for a price equal to the adjusted issue price of the retired debt and no discharge of indebtedness income would be recognized. See Treasury Regulation § 1.1001-2 and section 7701(g). It may not be clear whether a regular interest is recourse or nonrecourse. Although regular interests are generally payable only out of designated assets, those assets represent all of the assets of the REMIC.

excluded from income reduces the basis of the REMIC's assets (but not below fair market value) as of the beginning of the taxable year following the discharge.[39] The special insolvency rule can be quite generous, given that many REMICs are 100 percent debt financed and the fair market value of assets can decline due to changes in market interest rates or other factors unrelated to the likelihood of payment.

Although debtors typically recognize discharge of indebtedness income when a person related to them acquires debt at a discount, apparently, this rule does not apply to REMICs.[40]

Under section 67, an individual is allowed to deduct investment expenses (other than interest) only to the extent they exceed two percent of his adjusted gross income. Also, investment expenses are not deductible in calculating AMTI, the tax base for the alternative minimum tax. In the case of investment expenses of a REMIC, these rules are applied at the investor rather than REMIC level. Specifically, a REMIC must allocate its investment expenses among certain holders of REMIC interests (referred to as "pass-through interest holders"). Pass-through interest holders are required to include the amount of allocated expenses in income and are allowed an offsetting deduction if and only if the deduction would have been allowed had they incurred the expenses directly (in other words, for individuals, the two percent limitation applies and the expenses are not deductible in calculating AMTI). A pass-through interest holder is defined generally as an individual (other than certain nonresident aliens), trust or estate, or certain pass-thru entities, including another REMIC, but not including a REIT or pension plan. Beneficial rather than record ownership is taken into account in determining whether an interest is held by a pass-through interest holder.[41]

Ordinarily, a REMIC's investment expenses are allocated pro rata among all residual interests (although only pass-through interest holders are required to take the allocated amount into account in determining their tax liability).[42] However, in the case of a *single-class REMIC*, a portion of the REMIC's investment expenses must also be allocated to each class of regular interests. In particular, a single-class REMIC must allocate its investment expenses for any calendar quarter ratably to the days in the quarter and then among the regular and residual interests outstanding on any day in proportion to the income accruing on those interests for that day.[43] A

---

38   Section 108(d)(3).

39   See sections 108(b) and 1017. In the case of a discharge of debt attributable to a loss relating to a particular REMIC asset, there is no mechanism for allocating the reduction in basis to that particular asset. Any reduction under section 1017 in the basis of a debt obligation held by a REMIC that increases market discount should be included in income as it accrues under the normal REMIC rule governing market discount income (see footnote 25, above).

40   See section 108(e)(4). It does not seem to be possible for anyone to be a person related to a REMIC within the meaning of this section. Cf. text accompanying footnote 35, above.

41   For the definition of pass-through interest holder, see Treasury Regulation § 1.67-3T(a)(2).

42   The method of allocation of investment expenses is described in Treasury Regulation §§ 1.67-3T(a) through (d).

43   As a practical matter, it would be necessary to assume, in calculating income on regular interests, that each holder is an original holder, although the regulations might be read to require the actual

single-class REMIC is defined as any REMIC that would be classified as a grantor trust in the absence of a REMIC election, including any multiple class trust that falls within the exceptions in the Sears regulations for trusts with stripped, or senior and subordinated, pass-through certificates.[44] Because of the requirement to allocate investment expenses, it will be necessary for a REMIC to determine whether any "excess servicing" with respect to the mortgages it holds (or in which it owns an interest) is truly servicing (and thus an investment expense of the REMIC) or is instead an ownership interest in the mortgages retained by the servicer (and thus not such an investment expense).[45] Similarly, where a REMIC's qualified mortgages are pass-through certificates, the REMIC will need to determine whether any excess servicing charged with respect to the mortgages underlying the certificates is truly servicing or an ownership interest in the mortgages.[46]

In the case of a REMIC that is not a single-class REMIC, as indicated above, all investment expenses are allocated pro rata among individual holders of the residual interest. Because the value of the residual typically is small compared with the REMIC's assets and expenses, the requirement to include those expenses in income without a full offsetting deduction (or any deduction in calculating AMTI) can produce seriously adverse consequences for individual holders that are out of all proportion to the value of their investments.

Special rules apply to the portion of the income from a residual interest that is an *excess inclusion.* With limited exceptions, excess inclusions are *always* subject to tax, even in the hands of tax-exempt investors. The excess inclusion rules were adopted primarily to ensure taxation of phantom income and are discussed further in that context in the next part of this chapter. Income from residual interests that is not an excess inclusion should be exempt from tax in the hands of pension plans and other tax-exempt entities that are taxable only on UBTI to the same extent as, for example, income from a partial ownership interest in mortgages (that is, residual interests should not be considered debt-financed merely because the regular interests are considered debt obligations of the REMIC for some tax purposes).[47]

---

income of each holder to be taken into account. The amount of expenses allocated to a regular interest owned by a pass-through interest holder is considered additional interest income. Such interest is generally treated the same as other interest earned on a regular interest except that it is not subject to backup withholding under section 3406. Treasury Regulation §§ 1.67-3T(b)(4) and (e).

44   The definition of single-class REMIC also includes REMICs that are "substantially similar" to multiple-class grantor trusts that have been structured with the principal purpose of avoiding the allocation of a portion of the REMIC's investment expenses to regular interest holders. In applying the definition, interests in a REMIC that take the form of debt are treated as if they were additional ownership interests in the REMIC. See Treasury Regulation § 1.67-3T(a)(2)(ii)(B). The classification of non-REMIC trusts is discussed in Chapter 3.

45   The possible recharacterization of excess servicing is discussed in Chapter 6, footnote 56 and accompanying text.

46   The amount of servicing on mortgages in a grantor trust is often reported to investors under the terms of the trust documents, although such information need not be included in IRS Form 1099s. See Chapter 11, Part B.2.

47   REMICs differ from owner trusts in this respect. Compare footnote 16 and accompanying text. It

A REMIC will have a net loss for any calendar quarter in which its deductions exceed its gross income. Such a loss may not be carried over or back to other periods by the REMIC, but instead is allocated among the current holders of the residual interest in the same manner as taxable income.[48] However, the portion of a net loss that is allocable to the holder of a residual interest will not be deductible by the holder to the extent it exceeds the holder's adjusted basis in such interest at the end of the quarter (or at the time of disposition of such interest, if earlier), determined before taking account of such loss.[49] Such adjusted basis would generally equal the cost of the interest to the holder, increased by any amount the holder has previously reported as income from such interest, and decreased (but not below zero) by any losses it has deducted and any distributions it has received.[50] The holder's basis does not include any amount on account of the REMIC's liabilities. Any loss that is not currently deductible by reason of the basis limitation may be carried forward indefinitely and deducted from the holder's share of the REMIC's taxable income in later periods, but otherwise cannot be used.[51]

---

would be very odd to create a special regime for characterizing a portion of the income from a REMIC residual interest as UBTI if the portion of such income attributable to the regular interests was intended to be treated as UBTI under the debt-financed property rules. In addition, the owner of a residual interest is not considered for other tax purposes to be an owner of an interest in the REMIC's gross assets subject to a liability represented by the regular interests. For example, a holder's adjusted basis in a residual interest does not include its share of any REMIC liabilities. Similarly, a residual interest counts as a real property loan in the hands of certain institutional investors only to the extent of their adjusted basis in the interest (see Chapter 9, Part A), and the withholding tax on a residual interest held by a non-U.S. person generally is calculated by reference to distributions by the REMIC to the holder, not payments on mortgages received by the REMIC (see Chapter 10, text accompanying footnote 36).

48   See the first paragraph of this Part D.

49   Section 860C(e).

50   If the holder of a REMIC interest received the interest upon its initial issuance in exchange for property transferred to the REMIC, then the holder's initial basis in such interest would not be cost but instead would depend on the basis of the transferred property. See Chapter 12, Part C. In any event, the basis of a REMIC interest would be increased by properly allocable organizational expenses and the amount of contributions made to the REMIC after the startup day. Treasury Regulation §§ 1.860C-1(b)(1)(ii) and 1.860F-2(b)(3). If a holder disposes of a residual interest, the basis adjustment for any allocated portion of the taxable income or net loss of the REMIC that has not previously been reflected in basis is deemed to occur immediately before the disposition. See Treasury Regulation § 1.860C-1(b)(3); Conference Report at II-234; Blue Book at 422.

51   Although residual interests typically produce income followed by losses, it is also possible to see a pattern of losses followed by income. This is likely to happen particularly where a REMIC has issued high-coupon regular interests and does not report income corresponding to negative amounts calculated under the PAC method. See Chapter 6, Part G.1.d.(iii). Prior to the adoption of the restriction on transfers of noneconomic residual interests to non-U.S. persons, residual interests often were transferred to foreign investors. An issue arose as to whether such an investor had a right to carry losses from a residual interest forward to future periods. Section 860C(e)(2)(B) allows a carryover of losses not allowed by reason of section 860C(e)(2)(A) (the basis limitation). It was not certain if a loss allocated to a non-U.S. person would be considered to be denied by reason of this limitation given that no deduction would be allowed in any event. See sections 873 and 882(c) (deductions allowed to non-U.S. persons only to the extent effectively connected with a U.S. trade or business). Cf. *Lenz v. Comm'r*, 101 T.C. No. 17 (September 30, 1993) (investment interest that is not allowed as a deduction under section 163(d)(1) because it exceeds net investment income may be carried over under section 163(d)(2) (which treats excess investment interest

If a residual interest is sold, the seller will recognize gain or (except as described below) loss equal to the difference between its adjusted basis in such interest and the amount realized in the sale.[52] Such gain or loss generally will be capital gain or loss if the residual interest is held as a capital asset, except that if the holder is a bank or thrift, the gain or loss will always be ordinary.[53] If the seller acquires (or enters into a contract or option to acquire) any residual interest in a REMIC, any equity interest in an owner trust or any interest in a taxable mortgage pool[54] that is comparable to a residual interest in a REMIC, during the period beginning six months before, and ending six months after, the date of the sale, then the sale will be treated as a "wash sale" subject to section 1091.[55] Any loss realized in a wash sale is not currently deductible, but instead increases the seller's adjusted basis in the newly acquired interest.[56]

Distributions on a REMIC residual interest are treated as a nontaxable return of capital to the extent of the holder's basis in its interest.[57] Distributions in excess of basis are treated as gain from the sale of the residual interest.[58]

---

as paid in the succeeding year) notwithstanding that the taxpayer did not have sufficient taxable income to benefit from the deduction, and could not have carried it to later years, if it had been allowed in the earlier year; loss carryovers are allowed under section 172 only for business losses).

52   In the case of a sponsor, the amount realized on the sale of an interest is reduced by the amount of syndication expenses allocable to the interest. See Chapter 12, text accompanying footnote 36.

53   See Chapter 9, Part D.

54   For this purpose, "taxable mortgage pool" has the meaning given in Chapter 3, Part D, but the January 1, 1992 effective date generally applicable to TMPs is disregarded. See Chapter 3, footnote 215.

55   See section 860F(d). Under section 1091 (without regard to section 860F(d)), a loss arising from the sale of a security may be deferred if "substantially identical . . . securities" are purchased (or an option or contract to purchase substantially identical securities is entered into) within the period beginning 30 days before and ending 30 days after the date of the sale. Apart from section 860F(d), it is unlikely that two securities backed by different mortgages would be considered substantially identical. See Chapter 12, footnote 14.

56   As discussed in the text accompanying footnotes 36 and 13–14, the taxable income allocable to the holder of a REMIC residual interest (and in certain circumstances the holder of an equity interest in an owner trust that is classified as a partnership) is not necessarily adjusted to reflect the holder's adjusted basis in the interest. Thus, the deferred loss would not necessarily be recovered over the life of the acquired interest but may instead be recognized only upon the disposition of that interest (subject to further application of the special wash sale rule if that interest is a REMIC residual interest).

57   Section 860C(c)(1); Treasury Regulation § 1.860C-1(b)(2).

58   Section 860C(c)(2). As noted in the text accompanying footnote 50, above, the holder's basis in a residual interest is increased by the amount of the REMIC's taxable income allocated to it. It is not clear whether a holder can take account of income for the calendar quarter or year in which a distribution is made in determining the portion of the distribution that is subject to tax. An argument can be made, by analogy to similar rules elsewhere in the Code, that the basis adjustment for taxable income should be made before giving effect to the distribution. Treasury Regulation § 1.1368-1(e) includes such a rule for S corporations. Treasury Regulation § 1.731-1(a)(1)(ii) allows "advances or drawings" against a partner's share of income for a year to be treated as distributions on the last day of the year. Revenue Ruling 94-4, I.R.B. 1994-2, 20, extends this rule to deemed cash distributions attributable to a reduction in a partner's share of partnership liabilities. Cf. section 316(a)(2) which treats distributions made by a corporation at any time during a year as dividends to the extent they do not exceed the earnings and profits of the year. The REMIC

E. Phantom Income[59]

1. Overview

If a conduit issuer purchased a pool of mortgages and financed the purchase entirely with borrowed funds, and the debt service on the borrowings exactly matched the payments received on the mortgages, then the issuer would have no economic gain or loss from the transaction (assuming the mortgages are held to maturity and all payments are used to repay the borrowings). Given the lack of *economic* profit or loss, it might be expected that the interest or discount income on the assets and deductions in respect of the borrowings would exactly match for tax purposes as well, resulting in no *taxable* income or loss for the issuer. While that result would hold true over the entire life of the transaction, it may not be true in any particular year. The issuer may be required to report positive amounts of taxable income in some taxable years that are offset by matching losses in other periods. Noneconomic taxable income and losses of this type are generally referred to as *phantom income* and *phantom losses*.[60]

In a typical offering of multiple class sequential-pay bonds by a conduit issuer, some phantom income will be realized in the early years after the issuance of the bonds, followed by a corresponding amount of phantom losses in subsequent years. The cause is a difference in the distribution over time of the yields that are used in calculating mortgage income and bond deductions.[61] In particular, interest deduc-

---

rule in section 860C(a)(2) that requires income from a residual interest to be accrued on a daily basis could be read to limit the increase in a holder's basis to the income accrued to the date of the distribution. It is likely, however, that the drafters of that provision were concerned with allocations between subsequent owners where ownership is transferred within a quarter. Further, if it is possible to allocate income among quarters by pro rating income for a year (see footnote 23, above), then the per day amounts could not in any event be determined until year end.

59   For a more extensive discussion of phantom income with additional numerical examples, see Appendix A.

60   Outside of the context of mortgage-backed securities, the term "phantom income" is sometimes used more broadly to refer to any type of taxable income that currently is not payable in cash, including income that reflects real economic income and eventually will yield cash.

61   It is assumed in the discussion of phantom income in the text that income from the mortgages held by the conduit issuer is determined under a constant yield method similar to the PAC method. It is also assumed that such method is applied as if the mortgages were newly issued at the time they were purchased by the conduit issuer and had an issue price equal to their cost to the conduit issuer. Similarly, it is assumed that deductions on the bonds are determined under the PAC method. In the case of a conduit issuer that issued bonds prior to January 1, 1987, it was not certain whether the PAC method, or a similar method using present value concepts to adjust for prepayments, could be used in calculating deductions on the bonds. See Chapter 6, footnote 31 and accompanying text. If such an issuer held mortgages acquired at a discount and issued sequential-pay bonds with an aggregate corresponding discount, phantom income could arise if, in contrast with the PAC method, the deduction allowed to the issuer as a result of the retirement of bonds with the proceeds of mortgage prepayments was limited to the discount allocable to the retired bonds (and thus did not include any amount on account of any increase in the present value of outstanding bonds resulting from the prepayments). The income arose from the different allocation of discount among mortgages and bonds. Assuming the mortgages were identical, the discount on the mortgages would be allocated among them in proportion to their principal amounts. When a mortgage prepaid, the entire remaining discount on that mortgage would be included in income.

tions are calculated separately for each class of bonds, based on the yield to maturity of that class. Thus, the aggregate deductions allowed in any year will be determined by reference to the weighted average yield to maturity of all classes of bonds outstanding in that year. With a rising yield curve, the yield to maturity is lower for shorter maturity classes of bonds than for longer dated classes.[62] As a result, the weighted average yield to maturity of outstanding bonds increases over time as bonds are retired. By contrast, the yield to maturity of the mortgages remains constant, because they are not divided into sequential-pay classes. The combination of income based on a fixed yield and deductions based on an escalating yield produces the pattern of phantom income and losses previously described.

Where REMIC securities are issued using two tiers of REMICs, phantom income resulting from yield curve effects is realized only by the upper-tier REMIC (and is allocated to the residual interest in that REMIC).[63] The reason is that, in determining the taxable income of the two REMICs, the lower-tier regular interests held by the upper-tier REMIC are aggregated and treated as a single class of debt obligations with a single yield.[64]

The discussion above has assumed a transaction in which a conduit issuer borrows all of the cost of purchasing a pool of mortgages. This description fits a REMIC that has only a nominal residual interest, but all other conduit issuers would have some economic equity interest. In such a case, it will be helpful in identifying phantom income and losses to divide the mortgage assets into two groups: the *bond related assets* consisting of the mortgage payments that will be used to make corresponding payments on the bonds, and the *equity related assets* consisting of the mortgage payments that will be used to make equity distributions.

The equity owners will be taxed based on the taxable income of the conduit issuer, calculated by subtracting deductions for interest on the bonds from the issuer's income from *all* of its assets. Thus, it would be possible to express the income reported in any taxable year by the equity owners as the sum of (1) the income of the conduit issuer attributable to the equity related assets and (2) a net amount of income equal to the income of the conduit issuer attributable to the bond related assets, less the deductions allowed for the bonds. The net amount of income

---

By contrast, the discount at which early maturing classes of bonds were issued typically would be disproportionately small compared with the discount at which later maturing classes were issued. Thus, if the deduction allowed to the issuer upon the retirement of bonds with the proceeds of the mortgage prepayments was limited to the remaining discount on the retired bonds, when mortgages prepaid and their proceeds were used to retire bonds, the discount deductions allowed to the issuer would be less than the discount income from the prepaid mortgages in early years and correspondingly greater in later years. The mismatching of discount income and deductions produced phantom income followed by phantom losses. Phantom income of this type could arise under prior law even if each bond class had the same yield to maturity.

62   Although many issues of bonds have complex formulas for allocating payments among bond classes, most structures have identifiable shorter and longer term classes that, as a group, have lower and higher yields reflecting the yield curve.

63   Two-tier REMICs are discussed in Chapter 4, Part C.7.a.

64   See Treasury Regulation §§ 1.1275-2(c)(1) and (c)(4) (Example 2).

(positive or negative) from the bond related assets will be referred to herein as *bond related income*.

If the yield to maturity of the bond related assets exceeds the initial weighted average yield to maturity of all of the bonds, then one component of bond related income will be a net positive amount representing the economic profit resulting from the financing of the bond related assets with the bonds. However, for the reasons given above, the bond related income also may include phantom income or losses attributable to the mismatch between the pattern of yields on the mortgages and bonds.

Phantom income can be illustrated with a simplified example. Consider a conduit issuer that purchases at par a mortgage that bears interest at a rate of 10 percent, payable annually, and provides for two principal payments of $500 each, due one year and two years after the date of purchase, respectively. At the time of such purchase, the conduit issuer issues two bonds, each of which provides for a single principal payment of $500 at maturity. The first bond is issued at par, matures at the end of one year, and bears 8 percent interest, payable at maturity. The second bond bears 10 percent interest, payable annually, matures at the end of two years, and is issued at a price of $491.44 to yield 11 percent. For simplicity, bond issuance and administrative costs are ignored. The conduit issuer is required to invest $8.56 of equity to finance the purchase of the mortgage and in exchange receives a cash distribution of $10 at the end of the first year and nothing thereafter, as shown in Table 7-1.

The taxable income, economic income, and phantom income and loss realized by the conduit issuer in each of the two years that the bonds are outstanding are shown in Table 7-2. The equity has received its entire economic return at the end of the first year. The loss of $4.50 in the second year is a phantom loss that offsets the same amount of phantom income in the first year.

Another way to describe the phantom income problem is that the owner of an equity interest is not permitted to amortize the cost of its interest directly against the cash distributions the owner expects to receive, as would be possible, for example, if the right to those distributions were treated for tax purposes as a debt obligation of the conduit issuer. Instead, the owner must recover its investment over the life of the underlying mortgages. Thus, as shown in Table 7-2, although the equity interest in the conduit issuer becomes worthless following the distribution of the $10 payment at the end of the first year, the equity investor is permitted to treat as a return of capital in that year only $4.06 (the excess of the $10 distribution over taxable income of $5.94) rather than the full $8.56 cost of the equity interest.[65]

---

65   A mismatch between the economic life of cash distributions and the period of cost recovery for tax purposes also may arise when the value of an equity interest is attributable in part to a right to receive earnings of the conduit issuer from the reinvestment of mortgage payments. Although the right to receive distributions of such earnings may be viewed as an asset from the perspective of the equity investor, future reinvestment earnings would not be recognized to be a separate asset of the conduit issuer for tax purposes. Accordingly, the portion of the cost of the equity interest that is attributable to reinvestment earnings generally would be treated as an additional amount paid for

Another less significant source of phantom income for non-REMIC issuers that does not relate to the sequential-pay nature of bonds, arises from the rule that requires holders of pass-through certificates to report income based on the timing of receipt of payments on the underlying mortgages rather than the timing of distributions on the certificates (which lags the receipt of mortgage payments). Even where there is a close matching between the payments and aggregate income on pass-through certificates and the payments and deductions on bonds, there can be an acceleration of income and subsequent loss because the period over which income is reported on the certificates (from the date of acquisition of the certificates until mortgage principal is received) is shorter than the period for accruing deductions on the bonds.

It is not clear whether the same result arises when a REMIC holds a pass-through certificate. A REMIC is required to report market discount income on qualified mortgages (including pass-through certificates) under the PAC method as such discount accrues.[66] Under the PAC method, discount accrues based on a pre-payment assumption that is applied to the entire underlying pool. Because individual mortgages lose their tax identity under this approach, many REMICs calculate income from pass-through certificates based on the distributions made on the certificates, as if they were pay-through bonds.

2. Technical Description

The discussion of phantom income given in the last section will suffice for most purposes. This section provides a more quantitative description of the relationship between yields and phantom income based on present value concepts that may be helpful to some readers.

At any point in time, the aggregate amount of future income that will be realized from any asset of the conduit issuer equals the excess of the aggregate cash payments to be received from that asset over its adjusted basis. Similarly, at any time, the aggregate amount of future deductions that will be allowed on any bond equals the excess of the aggregate payments remaining to be made on the bond over the amount at which the bond is then currently recorded as a liability for tax purposes (that is, the adjusted issue price of the bond). In addition, at any time, the adjusted basis of any mortgage equals the present value of the remaining future payments thereon, calculated using the yield to maturity of the mortgage as the discount rate, and the adjusted issue price of each class of bonds equals the present value of all future payments on that class, calculated using the yield to maturity of that class as the discount rate.

---

the mortgages held by the conduit issuer and would be recovered over the life of the mortgages (rather than over the life of the reinvestment earnings stream).

66   See footnote 25 above, and the accompanying text.

Table 7–1. Mortgage and Bond Payments

	Years from Bond Issuance		
	0	1	2
Mortgage Payments	($1,000.00)	$600	$550
Bond 1 Payments	500.00	(540)	—
Bond 2 Payments	491.44	(50)	(550)
Funds Available to Conduit Issuer	(8.56)	10	—

Table 7–2. Income and Loss of the Conduit Issuer

	First Bond Year	Second Bond Year
Mortgage Income (10% of principal balance)	$100.00	$50.00
Deduction on Bond 1 (8% of principal balance)	(40.00)	—
Deduction on Bond 2 ($50 plus original issue discount of $4.06 in first year and $4.50 in second year)	(54.06)	(54.50)
Taxable Income (Loss) (mortgage income minus bond deductions)	5.94	(4.50)
Economic Income ($10 minus $8.56)	1.44	—
Phantom Income (Loss) (taxable income minus economic income)	4.50	(4.50)

To isolate phantom income or loss from economic income attributable to the financing of the bond related assets[67] with the bonds, assume that such economic

---

[67] The terms "bond related assets" and "bond related income" are defined in the last section (Part E.1).

income is zero. Stated differently, assume that the yield to maturity of the bond related assets equals the initial weighted average yield to maturity of all of the bonds. Under that assumption, all bond related income, if any, would be phantom income. Thus, at any time, the *net* amount of phantom income (or loss) that remains to be reported in all future periods (that is, the amount of phantom income, or loss, that will not be matched by corresponding future phantom loss, or income, respectively) would equal the future income from the bond related assets minus the future deductions on the bonds, or (1) the excess of the future cash payments to be received on the bond related assets over the adjusted basis of those assets minus (2) the excess of the future cash payments on the bonds over the adjusted issue price of the bonds. Because phantom income and phantom losses must sum to zero, the same absolute number also represents the aggregate net amount of phantom loss (or income) that has been realized to date. By hypothesis, the future cash payments on the bonds and on the bond related assets will be the same. Therefore, the future cash payments in the formula cancel out, leaving as the measure of future net phantom income (or loss) at any time (and thus the amount of net phantom loss, or income, realized prior to that time), the adjusted issue price of the bonds minus the adjusted basis of the bond related assets.

Each of these two amounts is calculated as the present value of the same payment stream (the remaining payments on the bonds or the remaining payments on the bond related assets), so it is apparent that there will be a difference between the two amounts (and thus, phantom income or loss) only if there is at some time a difference in the yields to maturity used in calculating income and deductions. In particular, at any time, there will be remaining net phantom loss, and thus net phantom income for prior periods, if the adjusted basis of the remaining bond related assets exceeds the then-current adjusted issue price of the outstanding bonds. This will be the case when the weighted average yield to maturity of the bonds exceeds the yield to maturity of the bond related assets. The yield of the bond related assets remains constant over their life. We have assumed that the *initial* weighted average yield to maturity of all of the bonds equals the yield to maturity of the bond related assets. Nevertheless, if the bonds are divided into sequential-pay classes and the earlier maturing classes have lower yields than the later maturing classes, then the weighted average yield to maturity of all outstanding bonds will increase as the lower yielding classes of bonds are retired and necessarily become greater than the yield to maturity of the bond related assets.

The present value approach to measuring phantom income or losses may be illustrated by returning to the example discussed in the last section (which is summarized in Table 7-2). By the end of the first year, the equity has received its entire economic return, so that the loss of $4.50 that remains to be reported in the second year is a phantom loss. That loss equals the excess of the remaining payments on the mortgage, calculated using as the discount rate the mortgage yield of 10 percent ($500), over the present value of the remaining payments on the bonds, calculated using as the discount rate the bond yield of 11 percent ($495.50).

3. Acceleration of Net Remaining Phantom Losses through Sales of Equity Interests

When an equity interest is sold, the seller generally recognizes gain or loss equal to the difference between the amount realized in the sale and its adjusted basis in the interest. If the seller has recognized a net amount of phantom income, that amount would have increased the adjusted basis of the interest but not its value. As a result, the gain that otherwise would be realized from the sale would be decreased, or the loss would be increased, by the net amount of phantom income. Stated differently, the corresponding amount of future phantom losses that otherwise would be recognized over time generally would be accelerated into the taxable year of the sale. However, if the sale produces a net loss, this tax advantage may not be achieved for two reasons. First, for most investors other than banks, thrifts, and securities dealers, loss from the sale of an equity interest would be a capital loss that can be offset only against capital gain.[68] Second, loss from the sale of a REMIC residual interest may be deferred under the special REMIC "wash sale" rule discussed in Part D.

The effect of the timing of recognition of phantom losses on the after-tax return from an equity interest in a conduit issuer is discussed further in Appendix A.

4. Special Rules for REMICs; Excess Inclusions and Negative Value Residual Interests

a. Overview. Phantom income realized by a REMIC is taxable to the holders of the residual interest. However, unlike equity interests in owner trusts, there is no tax requirement that a REMIC residual interest have any minimum economic value.[69] In addition, because phantom income is not economic income, a residual interest could produce substantial phantom income without having any economic value. Accordingly, absent special rules, the tax on phantom income associated with residual interests could be avoided easily by reducing the economic value of those interests to a nominal sum and transferring them (and the related tax liability) to investors that are tax-exempt, or are not currently paying federal income tax (for example, because they have unrelated losses).

To frustrate such tax avoidance, a portion of the income from a residual interest, referred to as an *excess inclusion*, is, with an exception discussed below for certain thrift institutions, subject to federal income taxation in all events. Thus, an excess inclusion with respect to a residual interest (1) may not, except as described below, be offset by any unrelated losses or loss carryovers of the owner of such interest;[70] (2) will be treated as UBTI if the owner is a pension plan or other

---

68 A loss may be a capital loss even for banks and thrifts if the conduit issuer is an owner trust that is classified as a partnership or a TMP. See footnote 15, above. For taxpayers other than corporations, capital losses may be used to offset up to $3,000 of ordinary income.

69 See Chapter 4, footnote 45 and accompanying text.

70 This result is accomplished by providing in section 860E(a)(1) that the taxable income of the holder of a residual interest for any taxable year shall not be less than the excess inclusion for such year. See also Treasury Regulation § 1.860E-1(a)(1). To prevent double taxation of excess inclu-

organization that is subject to tax only on its UBTI;[71] (3) is not eligible for any exemption from, or reduction in the rate of, withholding tax if the owner is a foreign investor, as further discussed in Chapter 10;[72] and (4) may not be offset with an increased deduction for variable contract reserves if the owner is a life insurance company.[73] Any tax resulting from these rules can, however, be offset with otherwise available credits.[74]

The rule that prevents the use of unrelated losses to offset excess inclusion income does not prevent the holder of a residual interest from using losses from a disposition of the residual interest to offset excess inclusion income, provided the holder's taxable income from other sources is at least as great as its excess inclusion income. For example, if in a given taxable year, the holder has excess inclusion income of $100 and also realizes a loss of $100 from sale of the residual interest which (apart from the excess inclusion rules) is currently deductible, then the holder's taxable income would not increase because of ownership of the residual interest, provided the holder's taxable income, disregarding the residual interest, is at least $100.[75] In a case where a residual interest is held by a partnership or S corporation, the prohibition on offsetting losses might apply at both the entity and owner level, although there seems to be no authority addressing the point.[76]

If the holder of a residual interest is a corporation that is part of a group of corporations that files a consolidated federal income tax return, the entire group is ordinarily treated as one taxpayer in applying the excess inclusion rules.[77] However, thrifts are subject to a special regime (discussed below).[78]

---

sion income, such income is disregarded in calculating (and thus does not reduce) net operating losses and net operating loss carryovers and carrybacks under section 172. Section 860E(a)(5); Treasury Regulation § 1.860E-1(a)(1). The alternative minimum tax is applied to AMTI, which is taxable income with certain adjustments. Section 1003(i) of the proposed Tax Simplification and Technical Corrections Act of 1993 (H.R. 3419, as reported by the Ways and Means Committee to the full House of Representatives on November 10, 1993) would clarify retroactively that the excess inclusion floor applies to AMTI (and not to taxable income before adjustment). As a result, adjustments that ordinarily would cause AMTI to exceed taxable income will have no effect unless they increase AMTI to an amount that exceeds the amount of excess inclusion income.

71   Section 860E(b). A $1,000 deduction is allowed under section 512(b)(12) in computing UBTI. This deduction cannot be used to eliminate the tax on excess inclusion income in cases where such income is less than $1,000, because the UBTI floor operates after giving effect to all deductions allowed in calculating UBTI.

72   Section 860G(b)(2).

73   Section 860E(f).

74   The effect of the alternative minimum tax should be considered in determining the extent to which credits may be used. The foreign tax credit is the only nonrefundable credit allowed in calculating AMT liability. For a discussion of the effect of excess inclusions on the AMT, see footnote 70, above.

75   The loss on sale could be deferred under the special wash sale rule discussed in footnote 55, above, and the accompanying text. Further, the loss may be a capital loss.

76   Where a partnership or S corporation realizes excess inclusion income, the character of such income should flow through to partners or shareholders under the general conduit principles that apply to those entities. See sections 702(b) and 1366(b). Taxable income also is calculated separately by partnerships and S corporations, however, so that the loss limitation might be applied at the entity level as well. See sections 703 and 1363(b).

The tax on excess inclusion income could potentially be avoided by transferring residual interests to holders that do not pay taxes because they are governmental entities, have no assets, or are located outside of the United States. Special measures exist to prevent the avoidance of tax through transfers of this type.

The next six sections address various topics relating to excess inclusions: the definition of the term; the exemption for thrifts from the limitation on the use of losses; special rules for REITs, RICs, and other pass-thru entities; surrogate taxes that are imposed in lieu of taxes on governmental holders of residual interests; rules disregarding tax motivated transfers of residual interests; and flaws in the existing excess inclusion rules (which have the effect of overstating phantom income).

The effectiveness of the battery of rules aimed at ensuring taxation of excess inclusion income is evidenced by the fact that residual interests are often economic liabilities (i.e., have negative value), because the tax burden on the holder exceeds the value of any right to receive distributions. Certain issues raised by the existence of negative value residuals are addressed in the concluding section of this chapter.

b. Definition of Excess Inclusion. In general terms, the excess inclusion with respect to a residual interest equals the excess of the income from the holding of the interest over the income that would have accrued on the interest if it had earned income at all times from its issuance at a constant, compounded rate equal to 120 percent of a long-term U.S. Treasury borrowing rate. More precisely, in any calendar quarter, the excess inclusion is the excess, if any, of (1) the taxable income of the REMIC allocated to the holder,[79] over (2) the sum of the *daily accruals* for all days during the quarter on which the holder owns the residual interest.[80] The daily accruals are determined by allocating to each day in the calendar quarter its ratable portion of the product of the *adjusted issue price* (defined below) of the residual interest at the beginning of the calendar quarter and 120 percent of the *Federal long-term rate* (defined below) in effect at the time the residual interest was issued. The adjusted issue price at the beginning of any calendar quarter equals the issue price of the residual interest, increased by the sum of the daily accruals for all prior quarters and the amount of any contributions made to the REMIC with respect to the residual interest after the startup day, and decreased (but not below zero) by the aggregate amount of payments made on the residual interest in all prior quarters.[81] The Federal long-term rate is an average of current yields on Treasury obligations with a remaining term greater than nine years, computed and published monthly by the Service.

---

77 Section 860E(a)(3); Treasury Regulation § 1.860E-1(a)(2).
78 See Part E.4.c.
79 Thus, gains from the disposition of a residual interest during the quarter (as opposed to income earned on the residual interest during the quarter) are not taken into account.
80 A REMIC is required to report daily accruals on Form 1066, Schedule Q. See Section 860F(e). REMIC information reporting is discussed in Chapter 11.
81 Section 860E(c)(2)(B).

As an exception to the general rule just described, the Treasury has authority to issue regulations treating *all* income from the holding of a REMIC residual interest as an excess inclusion if the interest does not have *significant value*. The legislative history of TRA 1986 indicates that these regulations may be retroactive in "appropriate cases," but in any event will not apply where the value of the residual interest is at least two percent of the combined value of all REMIC interests.[82] The current REMIC regulations do not implement the significant value rule.[83] Whether it is ever implemented is likely to be of limited importance because the formula for calculating excess inclusions already is linked (through the definition of daily accruals) to the issue price of a residual interest. Thus, if a residual interest has a nominal value, the daily accruals would be close to zero, and virtually all of the income from the interest would be an excess inclusion without regard to the significant value rule.

c. Thrift Exception. Certain thrift institutions are exempt from the rule (discussed above) prohibiting excess inclusions from being offset with unrelated losses.[84] The exemption applies, however, only to residual interests that have significant value.[85] A residual interest meets this test if (1) the aggregate issue price of the residual interests in the REMIC is at least two percent of the aggregate issue price of all regular and residual interests in the REMIC, and (2) the anticipated weighted average life of the residual interest is at least 20 percent of the anticipated weighted average life of the REMIC.[86] The second part of the test prevents the two percent test from being met

---

82   Conference Report at II-235; Blue Book at 423.

83   The special thrift exception to the excess inclusion rules does, however, contain a significant value test. See the next section below.

84   See section 860E(a)(2). The relief measures are limited to thrift institutions that are eligible to calculate deductions for additions to bad debt reserves under section 593.

85   Treasury Regulation § 1.860E-1(a)(3). Section 860E(a)(2) gives the Service authority to issue regulations limiting the thrift exemption where necessary or appropriate to prevent the avoidance of tax. Although the statutory language gives no indication that a residual interest must have significant value for the thrift exemption to apply, the Blue Book (at 423, footnote 83) suggested this result. The significant value rule is, with a limited exception, effective only for residual interests acquired after September 26, 1991. See Treasury Regulation § 860A-1(b)(2)(iii).

86   Treasury Regulation § 1.860E-1(a)(3)(iii). The anticipated weighted average life of the REMIC is the weighted average of the anticipated weighted average lives of all regular and residual interests in the REMIC. The weighted average life calculation takes account of all anticipated payments (however denominated) in the case of residual interests and regular interests with disproportionately high interest (generally, an issue price greater than 125% of the principal amount). For all other regular interests, only anticipated principal payments are included in the calculation. Anticipated payments are based on the prepayment and reinvestment assumptions used in applying the PAC method (or that would have been used if regular interests with OID had been issued), and required or permitted clean-up calls or any required qualified liquidation provided for in the REMIC's organizational documents. It appears that anticipated defaults or delinquencies are not taken into account in determining anticipated payments. Where interest payments that are taken into account in a weighted average life calculation are variable, then it would be sensible to fix the rates for purposes of the calculation using the same principles that apply in accruing OID (see Chapter 6, Part C.4). Apparently, the weighted average life test is applied to a residual interest only as of the startup day for the REMIC, and not as of the date on which a thrift acquires the interest. This approach is consistent with the 2% value component of the significant value test, which clearly is based on initial values.

during only a short initial period, after which capital invested in the residual interest is withdrawn.

As indicated above, if a group of corporations files a consolidated return, the group generally is treated as one taxpayer for purposes of applying the excess inclusion rules. However, the thrift exception is applied separately to each thrift that is a member of such a group.[87] As a result, losses of a thrift generally cannot be offset against excess inclusions realized by other group members (including other thrifts) in a consolidated return. Similarly, losses of other group members generally cannot offset any excess inclusions of a thrift that exceed the losses of that thrift (determined without regard to the excess inclusions). The only exception to this rule is that a thrift and a *qualified subsidiary* are combined and treated as a single thrift (so that losses of one can offset excess inclusions of the other).[88] A corporation is a qualified subsidiary for this purpose if (1) all of its stock, and substantially all of its indebtedness, is held directly by the thrift, and (2) it is organized and operated exclusively in connection with the organization and operation of one or more REMICs.[89] Thus, a qualified subsidiary apparently cannot issue non-REMIC pay-through bonds or purchase interests in REMICs in the secondary market.

d. Pass-Thru Entities.[90] Normally, the taxable income of an entity that holds residual interests cannot be less than the excess inclusions that it realizes from those interests. How does this rule apply to REITs and RICs? These two types of entities are generally subject to a corporate tax on their taxable income, but they are allowed deductions in determining such income for dividends paid to shareholders. Can excess inclusion income be offset with a dividends paid deduction?

The answer is "yes." REITs and RICs are taxable on "real estate investment trust taxable income" (defined in section 857(b)(2)) and "investment company taxable income" (defined in section 852(b)(2)), respectively. These special brands of income are calculated by making adjustments to the "taxable income" of the REIT or RIC. One of these adjustments is the dividends paid deduction. Thus, a requirement that "taxable income" not be less than the amount of excess inclusions would not prevent the use of that deduction to eliminate the tax base of a REIT or RIC.

On the other hand, the fact that a REIT or RIC can avoid tax on its excess inclusion income does not import that the tainted character of such income disappears. Instead, the taint is shifted to the shareholders of the REIT or RIC. In the case of REITs, section 860E(d) authorizes regulations to be issued that would (1) allocate among the shareholders of a REIT the excess of the REIT's aggregate excess inclusions over REIT taxable income (as defined in section 857(b)(2), excluding

---

87   See section 860E(a)(3), and Treasury Regulation §§ 1.860E-1(a)(3)(i) and (ii).

88   Section 860E(a)(4)(A).

89   Section 860E(a)(4)(B). Presumably, in determining whether substantially all of the indebtedness of a subsidiary is owned by the thrift, regular interests in REMICs sponsored by the subsidiary would be disregarded even if they took the legal form of debt of the subsidiary. For tax purposes, those interests would be interests in the REMIC, not subsidiary debt.

90   The spelling should be blamed on Congress. See section 860E(e)(6).

any net capital gain), and (2) treat any amount so allocated to a shareholder as if it were an excess inclusion from a residual interest held by such shareholder. Similar rules apply to RICs, bank common trust funds, and certain cooperative organizations that are taxed under part 1 of subchapter T of the Code. No regulations have been issued under this grant of authority.[91] Although pass-thru entities generally can escape tax on excess inclusion income allocated to investors, as described in the next section, a pass-thru entity in which interests are owned by certain governmental entities may be taxed on excess inclusions allocated to those entities.

e. Surrogate Taxes on Excess Inclusions Allocable to Certain Governmental Entities. Although every effort has been made to ensure that excess inclusions will be subject to tax under the Code, certain organizations that are exempt from all taxes under the Code could potentially hold residual interests without paying tax on excess inclusions. The REMIC rules refer to such a holder as a "disqualified organization." The principal example of a disqualified organization is a governmental entity.[92]

A number of measures have been adopted to prevent tax on excess inclusions from being avoided through the ownership of residual interests by disqualified organizations. As described in Chapter 4, an entity cannot qualify as a REMIC unless it adopts reasonable arrangements designed to ensure that residual interests are not held by such organizations. In addition, if a disqualified organization (1) holds a residual interest despite such arrangements, or (2) becomes an indirect owner of such an interest through a pass-thru entity, then a tax is imposed on someone else as a substitute for the tax on excess inclusions that would have been paid by the disqualified organization if it had been a taxpayer. In the first of these two situations, the "surrogate tax" is imposed on the person that transferred the residual interest to the disqualified organization. In the second, the pass-thru entity is taxed. The sections which follow describe in more detail the operation of the surrogate taxes on transfers and pass-thru entities.

(i) Transfer tax. A tax is imposed on transfers of REMIC residual interests to disqualified organizations.[93] The tax is generally imposed on the transferor. However, if the transfer is made through an agent for a disqualified organization (for example, a securities firm buying as a broker for a disqualified organization), then

---

91   See Treasury Regulation § 1.860E-1(b) (regulation reserved on treatment of residual interests held by REITs, RICs, common trust funds, and subchapter T cooperatives).

92   A more complete definition of the term "disqualified organization" may be found in Chapter 4, Part A.3.

93   Section 860E(e)(1); Treasury Regulation § 1.860E-2(a). The tax applies to transfers after March 31, 1988 (other than transfers pursuant to a binding written contract in effect on such date), regardless of the date of organization of the REMIC. The tax is payable to the Service by the later of March 24, 1993, or April 15th of the year following the calendar year in which the taxable transfer occurs. In order to permit a disqualified organization to act as a sponsor of a REMIC, a transfer of a residual interest to a disqualified organization in connection with the formation of a REMIC is disregarded if the disqualified organization has a binding contract to sell the interest and the sale occurs within seven days of the startup day. Treasury Regulation § 1.860E-2(a)(2).

the tax is imposed on the agent rather than on the transferor, apparently even if the transferor is aware of the transferee's identity.[94]

A transferor or agent can protect itself from any possible liability for the tax by obtaining a statement from the transferee stating under penalties of perjury that the transferee is not a disqualified organization. Although section 860E(c)(4) refers to an "affidavit," a formal, notarized document is not required; a statement indicating that it is made under penalties of perjury will suffice. Further, because disqualified organizations do not have social security numbers (as distinguished from employer identification numbers), in the case of a transfer to an individual, the transferee's statement may simply provide a social security number and recite under penalties of perjury that the number is that of the transferee. See Treasury Regulation § 1.860E-2(a)(7). The affidavit will not be effective, however, if the transferor or agent, as the case may be, has actual knowledge, as of the time of the transfer, that the affidavit is false. Transferors of residual interests and persons buying such interests on behalf of others often obtain such affidavits as a matter of course.

If the tax applies to a transfer of a residual interest, it is calculated by multiplying the highest marginal federal corporate income tax rate by an amount equal to the present value of the total anticipated excess inclusions on such interest for periods after the transfer. Anticipated excess inclusions are determined using the same Prepayment Assumption that applies in accruing OID under the PAC method, and present values are computed using the applicable Federal rate as the discount rate.[95] Where a tax is imposed on a transfer of a residual interest to a disqualified organization, the issuing REMIC is required, within 60 days after request, to provide the information necessary for computing the tax to the person required to pay the tax and to the Service. The REMIC may charge the taxpayer (but not the Service) a reasonable fee for providing the information.[96]

The Service has authority to waive the tax on any transfer of a residual interest if, within a reasonable time after discovery that the transfer was subject to tax, steps are taken so that the interest is no longer held by the disqualified organization, and the Service is paid a surrogate tax equal to the product of the highest marginal corporate tax rate and the amount of excess inclusions that accrued on the residual interest while it was held by the disqualified organization.[97]

---

94 Treasury Regulation § 1.860E-2(a)(6) defines an "agent" to include any middleman or nominee. In a case where a residual interest is transferred to a custodian or other nominee for a disqualified organization which then continues to hold the interest on behalf of the organization, the transfer tax should not apply, on the ground that the residual interest has not been transferred "through an agent" to the organization. This result is suggested by the fact that nominees holding residual interests on behalf of a disqualified organization are liable for an ongoing surrogate tax on excess inclusions allocable to the organization (see text accompanying footnote 102, below); imposing both taxes would be overkill.

95 Treasury Regulation §§ 1.860E-2(a)(3) and (4).

96 Treasury Regulation § 1.860E-2(a)(5).

97 Section 860E(e)(7); Treasury Regulation § 1.860E-2(a)(7)(ii).

(ii) Tax on pass-thru entities. A tax is imposed on any pass-thru entity (as defined below) if a disqualified organization is the *record* holder of an interest in the entity.[98] A pass-thru entity may rely on a statement from a record holder made under penalties of perjury to establish that it is not a disqualified organization if the entity does not know that the statement is false.[99] The tax equals the highest marginal federal corporate income tax rate multiplied by the amount of excess inclusions allocable to the interest in the entity held of record by the disqualified organization.[100] No tax is imposed on a pass-thru entity if interests in the entity are owned beneficially by a disqualified organization, provided the disqualified organization is not the record holder. In these circumstances, the nominee is treated as the pass-thru entity (as described in the next paragraph) and is subject to the tax.

A *pass-thru entity* is defined as any RIC, REIT, bank common trust fund, partnership, trust or estate.[101] The term also includes cooperative organizations taxed under part 1 of subchapter T of the Code. The definition does not include corporations taxed under subchapter S, presumably because the definition of an S corporation would not allow a disqualified organization to be a stockholder. Except as provided in regulations, a person holding an interest in a pass-thru entity as a nominee for another person is treated with respect to that interest as a pass-thru entity (and the other person is treated as a record holder of an interest in the deemed pass-thru entity represented by the nominee arrangement).[102]

To illustrate how the tax operates, suppose that a REIT holds a REMIC residual interest and a broker holds stock in the REIT as a nominee for a disqualified person. In that event, the broker and not the REIT would be subject to tax on the portion of

---

98 The tax is imposed by section 860E(e)(6). It is payable to the Service by the later of March 24, 1993 or the 15th day of the fourth month following the close of the taxable year of the pass-thru entity that is subject to the tax. Treasury Regulation § 1.860E-2(b)(1). The tax generally applies to excess inclusions earned by a pass-thru entity after March 31, 1988, but only to the extent those excess inclusions are allocable to (1) an interest in the entity acquired after March 31, 1988 or (2) a residual interest acquired by the entity after that date. Certain other special effective date rules apply. See sections 1006(t)(16)(D)(iii) and (iv) of TAMRA.

99 Although the statute refers to an "affidavit, a statement under penalties of perjury of the type described in the last section discussing the transfer tax will suffice. See section 860E(e)(6)(D); Treasury Regulation § 1.860E-2(b)(2).

100 For example, if a pass-thru entity held a REMIC residual interest and realized $1,000 of excess inclusions in a taxable year, and 5% of the interests in such entity were held throughout the year by a disqualified organization, then the entity would be subject to a tax on those excess inclusions (based on the current tax rate of 35%) of $17.50 (.35 × .05 × $1,000).

101 Section 860E(e)(6)(B). Section 301 of the proposed Tax Simplification and Technical Corrections Act of 1993 (H.R. 3419, as reported by the Ways and Means Committee to the full House of Representatives on November 10, 1993), would treat any "large partnership" (generally, a partnership having at least 250 partners, or having at least 100 partners and electing large partnership status) as if it were owned entirely by disqualified organizations, and thus would subject the partnership to a tax on all of its excess inclusions. To avoid double taxation, the amount subject to tax would be excluded from the partnership's taxable income.

102 A nominee should also consider the possible effect of the transfer tax described above. See footnote 94.

the excess inclusions of the REIT that is allocable to the interests in the REIT held for the disqualified organization through the broker.

Any tax imposed on a pass-thru entity is deductible from the entity's ordinary gross income.[103] Further, a REIT or a RIC is permitted to charge against dividends paid to a disqualified organization the tax expense arising out of its ownership of stock without causing dividends paid by the REIT or RIC to be preferential within the meaning of section 562(c) (which disallows the dividends paid deduction for preferential dividends).[104] A REIT should be able to prohibit record ownership of its stock by a disqualified organization without running afoul of the tax requirement that it have transferable shares.[105]

f. Certain Tax-Motivated Transfers Disregarded. The panoply of measures described above for ensuring the payment of tax on excess inclusion income has two potential gaps: First, a residual interest could be transferred to a U.S. person that is subject to U.S. taxes but has no assets or otherwise does not intend to pay taxes that are due. Second, a residual interest could be transferred to a foreign person that, as a practical matter, will not pay U.S. taxes unless the taxes are withheld, in circumstances where the distributions on the residual interest from which tax may be withheld are less than the current tax liability.

The REMIC regulations fill in these gaps by disregarding certain transfers of residual interests where the collection of tax from the transferee is doubtful. The effect of disregarding a transfer of a residual interest is that the transferor continues to be liable for the tax on income, including excess inclusions, from the interest. Where a residual interest is newly issued to a person other than the REMIC sponsor, the REMIC sponsor is treated as the transferor.[106]

As described in the next two sections, different standards apply in disregarding transfers depending on whether the transferee is a U.S. or non-U.S. person.

(i) Transfers to U.S. persons. The regulations disregard the transfer of any "noneconomic" residual interest (described below) to a U.S. person if a significant purpose of the transfer is to impede the assessment or collection of tax.[107] Such a purpose exists if the transferor either knew or should have known (had "improper

---

103   Treasury Regulation § 1.860E-2(b)(3).

104   Treasury Regulation § 1.860E-2(b)(4).

105   Cf. Treasury Regulation § 1.856-1(d)(2) (REIT's power to redeem or to refuse to transfer shares to avoid loss of REIT status does not render shares nontransferable).

106   See Treasury Regulation §§ 1.860F-2(a)(1) and 1.860G-3(a)(1). The approach of disregarding transfers is effective, of course, only if the appropriate taxes can be collected from the transferor. A REMIC sponsor is the party that transfers mortgages directly or indirectly to the REMIC. It is implausible to think that a sponsor would be selected to form a REMIC because it is judgment proof.

107   Treasury Regulation § 1.860E-1(c)(1). The rule applies to transfers of residual interests after September 26, 1991, without regard to the REMIC's startup day. See Treasury Regulation § 1.860A-1(b)(2)(i).

knowledge") that the transferee would be unwilling or unable to pay the taxes due on its share of the taxable income of the REMIC.[108]

Under a safe harbor rule, a taxpayer is presumed not to have improper knowledge if:

- the transferor conducts *at the time of the transfer* a reasonable investigation of the financial condition of the transferee and, as a result of the investigation, finds that the transferee historically paid its debts as they came due and found no significant evidence to indicate that the transferee will not continue to do so, and

- the transferee represents to the transferor that it understands that as a holder of the residual interest, it may incur tax liabilities in excess of any cash flows on the residual interest and that the transferee intends to pay taxes associated with holding the residual interest as they become due.[109]

It is not clear why the rule is only a presumption. If there are factors indicating that the transferee will not pay taxes that become due, those factors should be taken into account in determining whether the transferor made a reasonable investigation and the proper findings, and not prevent the safe harbor from applying if its terms are met. Otherwise, the rule would be worthless.

The regulations do not explain how extensive an investigation must be in order to be reasonable. Only a fairly cursory investigation should be required where the transferee is known to conduct substantial activities other than holding residual interests, and there are no obvious signs of financial distress. Needless to say, conducting an investigation will be more difficult for transferees that are privately held companies than for an SEC reporting company.

A residual interest is considered to be noneconomic for this purpose unless *at the time of the transfer*:

- the present value of the expected future distributions thereon at least equals the product of the present value of anticipated excess inclusions and the highest marginal corporate income tax rate for the year of the transfer, and

- the transferor reasonably expects that, for each anticipated excess inclusion, the transferee will receive distributions from the REMIC at or after the time taxes accrue on the anticipated excess inclusion in an amount sufficient to satisfy the accrued taxes.[110]

---

108 The test looks to the payment of taxes that are due. Thus, the test would not fail to be met because the transferee can legally avoid taxes (e.g., because it has credits or is a thrift that can offset losses against income from the residual interest).

109 Treasury Regulation § 1.860E-1(c)(4).

110 Treasury Regulation § 1.860E-1(c)(2). The present values of anticipated distributions and anticipated excess inclusions are computed as described in the text accompanying footnote 95, above, relating to the tax on transfers of a residual interest to a disqualified organization. Treasury Regulation § 1.860E-1(c)(3).

A noneconomic residual interest includes not only interests that have a nominal fair market value at the time of the transfer, but also interests that have substantial values but may receive distributions in advance of realizing excess inclusion income. There is no requirement that distributions sufficient to pay taxes on excess inclusions be made within any particular period following the accrual of such income,[111] although delays in the timing of distributions will reduce their present value. Because the determination of whether a residual interest is noneconomic is made at the time of transfer, a residual interest that is economic for part of its life can become noneconomic (and thus have restricted transferability) at a later time.

(ii) Transfers to foreign investors. As further discussed in Chapter 10, a foreign investor holding a residual interest generally is subject to a 30 percent withholding tax on excess inclusion income. Under current law, the tax is imposed on excess inclusions not as the income accrues, but only when distributions are made on the residual interests. The REMIC regulations prevent this rule from being abused by disregarding any transfer to a foreign person of a residual interest that has "tax avoidance potential."[112] A "foreign person" should include anyone who may be subject to U.S. withholding tax.[113] A residual interest has tax avoidance potential unless, *at the time of the transfer,* the transferor reasonably expects that, for each excess inclusion, the REMIC will distribute to the transferee residual interest holder an amount that will equal at least 30 percent of the excess inclusion, and such amount will be distributed at or after the time at which the excess inclusion accrues and not later than the close of the calendar year following the calendar year of accrual.[114]

If a residual interest is transferred to a foreign person, a transfer of the residual interest by that person to a U.S. person will be disregarded (so that taxes will continue to be withheld on distributions) if the effect of the transfer would be to allow the transferor to avoid the withholding taxes on excess inclusions.[115] Thus, it

---

111   Such a requirement does apply to residual interests transferred to foreign persons, as described in the next section.

112   See Treasury Regulation § 1.860G-3, which generally is effective for transfers after April 20, 1992. See Treasury Regulation § 1.860A-1(b)(2)(ii). A less stringent version of the rule was included in the proposed REMIC regulations issued on September 27, 1991. The current version was proposed on April 20, 1992.

113   The regulations use the term "foreign person" without defining it. Presumably, it means any person that is not a "United States person" as defined in section 7701(a)(30) (see also sections 7701(a)(5) and (31)). The rule disregarding transfers to foreign persons does not apply if the income on the residual interest is subject to tax at regular tax rates as income effectively connected with a United States trade or business of the transferee. See Treasury Regulation § 1.860G-3(a)(3).

114   As discussed in Chapter 10 at footnote 35, excess inclusion income derived from sources outside of the U.S. should not be subject to U.S. withholding tax. Nonetheless, a residual interest producing income of this type could have "tax avoidance potential" under the regulations.

115   See Treasury Regulation § 1.860G-3(a)(4). The foreign person would in fact become liable for tax on the accrued excess inclusions as a result of the transfer (see Chapter 10, text accompanying footnote 36), so the concern must be that taxes due would not be paid. The rule applies not only to transfers to U.S. persons, but also to transfers to foreign persons in whose hands income from

is not possible to avoid the taxes on excess inclusions by having a foreign person hold a residual interest while excess inclusions accrue and then transferring it to a U.S. person before the related cash distributions are made.

g. Flaws in Excess Inclusion Rules. The purpose of the excess inclusion rules is to ensure that phantom income is always taxed. However, the rules are more burdensome than is necessary to achieve this goal, for three reasons. First, the calculation of excess inclusions is not cumulative; instead, each quarter stands on its own. Thus, if in one quarter the daily accruals exceed the income from a residual interest, the surplus may not be carried over and used to reduce excess inclusions in subsequent quarters. Income from a residual interest can vary significantly from one quarter to another because of uneven mortgage prepayments, among other factors.

Second, phantom income is by definition always offset eventually by phantom losses. However, there is no mechanism under current law to ensure that a holder who pays tax on excess inclusions in some periods will receive a corresponding tax benefit in later periods when phantom losses are recognized. For example, there is no rule that allows phantom losses as a deduction in calculating UBTI, allows a refund of withholding tax paid by a foreign investor, or characterizes phantom loss realized upon sale of a residual interest as an ordinary loss.

Finally, the excess inclusion definition treats economic income as an excess inclusion to the extent it is earned at a rate greater than 120 percent of the Federal long-term rate. To illustrate, suppose that the Federal long-term rate is 10 percent, the yield on a residual interest is 20 percent, and cash is distributed each year on that interest equal to the economic income accruing in the year. Even if phantom income were virtually nonexistent (for example, because there is only one class of regular interests), income earned in excess of 12 percent of the adjusted issue price would be treated as an excess inclusion and, when distributed, would reduce the adjusted issue price for purposes of calculating excess inclusions in later periods.[116]

---

the residual interest will be effectively connected with a U.S. trade or business.

116   It is not difficult to imagine how the statute could be amended to remedy these deficiencies. One approach would be to (1) redefine excess inclusions so that they more accurately measure phantom income, and (2) replace the special rules taxing otherwise tax-exempt holders of residual interests with a system of tax accounts. The change in the definition would be worthwhile even if the account system was not adopted.

Excess inclusions could be defined as the difference (positive or negative) between (1) the income reported by the holder under section 860C(a) and (2) the income the holder would have reported under that section if deductions for regular interests were calculated in all periods as if each class of regular interests had the same yield to maturity. More particularly, deductions would be calculated under (2) as if each class of regular interests had been issued at the issue price that would have produced a yield to maturity for that class equal to the combined yield to maturity for all classes (determined as if they represented a single debt instrument). Treating the regular interests as if they had a single yield would eliminate the principal source of phantom income.

The account system would work as follows: Each residual interest holder would maintain an excess inclusions tax account. The balance in the account would equal the sum of the products of the positive and negative amounts of excess inclusions that the holder has realized and a tax rate or rates. The holder would pay interest to the Treasury on the account balance. The tax rate could be a current tax rate for the year of payment or the historical rates in effect from time to time in

h. Negative Value Residual Interests. Residual interests often have negative fair market values, because the tax cost of the associated phantom income exceeds the value of any right to receive distributions. In such a case, an owner would need to pay another party to take over its ownership position.

Negative value residual interests raise at least three special tax issues: How are conventional tax ownership principles applied to identify the owner? What is the tax treatment of a payment made to a transferee to induce it to accept ownership? Can the issue price or tax basis of a residual interest be negative?

(i) Ownership. Ordinarily, the legal owner of property is also recognized to be the owner for tax purposes, provided that person also has the substantial burdens and benefits of ownership (or at least more of them than anyone else).[117] In a case where a residual interest provides for no distributions, the only significant burden or benefit of ownership would be the tax on phantom income. However, if tax consequences had to be taken into account in applying the tax ownership test, the test would be circular: a purported transfer that was effective for tax purposes would shift the burdens of ownership to the transferee; an ineffective transfer would not.

The only sensible response to this problem is to disregard tax consequences in identifying the tax owner of a residual interest. Residual interests typically entitle their holders to *some* rights vis-a-vis the issuing REMIC even where they are not expected to produce distributions (e.g., a right to prevent amendments to documents, to vote on certain matters, or to receive information). An assignment that transfers all of those rights, and is recorded on the books of the REMIC, almost certainly will be effective to shift tax ownership to the assignee (assuming the special anti-tax avoidance rules in the REMIC regulations, discussed above in Part E.4.f, do not apply). Any other conclusion would mean in practice that the ownership of negative value residual interests, once established, could never change. There is no reason to believe such a result was ever contemplated for interests of this type. The official explanation of TRA 1986 recognizes the existence of negative value residual interests without ever suggesting they are frozen in place.[118] The inclusion in the REMIC regulations of special rules disregarding tax-motivated transfers of noneconomic residuals strongly implies that transfers will be recognized in all other cases.[119]

---

the periods in which the excess inclusions were realized. The account would be eliminated when the residual interest was liquidated or sold.

117 For a discussion of the tax ownership of property in the context of sales of mortgages, see Chapter 12, Part A.1.

118 See Blue Book at 416: "The Congress intended that an interest in a REMIC could qualify as a residual interest regardless of its value. Thus, for example, an interest need not entitle the holder to any distributions in order to qualify as a residual interest." Although this language does not refer expressly to negative values, it is obvious that a residual interest that has no right to distributions and carries with it tax liabilities would be an economic liability.

119 The preamble to the proposed REMIC regulations refers specifically to negative value residuals in explaining the need for restricting tax-motivated transfers of noneconomic residual interests:
    If a sponsor creates a REMIC in which the residual interest is not entitled to any

(ii) Payments to transferees. A transferee that receives a payment to accept ownership of a residual interest (an "assumption payment") must face the question of how the payment is taxed.[120] The REMIC regulations do not address the point, and no other guidance from the Service has been forthcoming.[121]

Where a residual interest is expected to produce phantom income followed by phantom losses, the holder will be required to pay taxes to the Service on the income and then will be entitled to receive those payments back, as an offset to tax liability, as the losses are realized.[122] The assumption payment compensates the transferee for assuming the burden of making an interest-free loan to the government by replacing the earnings on that loan. The payment generally would include some risk premium, to account for the possibility that the transferee will not be able to realize value from tax losses at least equal to the original tax paid, and for uncertainty as to the term of the interest-free loan (which would depend on mortgage prepayments).[123]

---

distributions, and if it is expected that the REMIC will have taxable income over the course of its life, then that residual interest represents only a future tax liability to the residual interest holder. This is true because the residual interest holder must include in gross income the REMIC's taxable income, and the excess inclusion portion of that taxable income cannot be offset with deductions.

It has been suggested that such interests have a negative basis and a negative issue price. Existing tax rules do not accommodate such concepts. Although the proposed regulations do not address these issues, the Service is interested in comments concerning noneconomic residual interests.

Proposed section 1.860E-1(c)(1) sets forth a rule that is intended to discourage transfers of noneconomic residual interests for the purpose of avoiding the tax on excess inclusions. Under this rule, which does not apply to transfers to foreign persons, the transfer of a noneconomic residual interest is disregarded unless no significant purpose of the transfer was to impede the assessment and collection of tax.

120 The transferor, for its part, would recognize a loss equal to the sum of its tax basis in the residual interest and the amount of the assumption payment. That loss should have the same character (as capital or ordinary) as a loss recognized on the sale or exchange of a positive value residual interest. Moreover, capital loss treatment for a sponsor would be appropriate to the extent the loss is matched economically by a capital gain on the sale of regular interests. For an illustration, see the text following footnote 132, below. A seller that otherwise would recognize a capital loss might seek to argue that the loss is ordinary, because there is no "sale or exchange." Transfers of property burdened with liabilities are treated as sales or exchanges for tax purposes. An income tax liability relating to such residual interest might be distinguished on the ground that the liability is personal to the holders and does not burden the property.

121 The preamble to the proposed REMIC regulations asked for comments on the tax treatment of negative value residuals, and a number were submitted. See, e.g., the New York State Bar Association Tax Section, Committee on Pass-Through Entities, *Report on the Proposed Real Estate Mortgage Investment Conduit Regulations* (March 19, 1992) ("NYSBA 1992 REMIC Report"), 3–14. The preamble to the final REMIC regulations states that the Service "may" provide future guidance on the "proper tax treatment of a payment made by a transferor of a noneconomic residual interest to induce the transferee to acquire the interest."

122 Certain holders of residual interests would not be entitled to deduct later losses, either because they have no income to offset with losses or because of their special status as taxpayers (see the discussion of flaws in the excess inclusion rules in Part E.4.g above). As a practical matter, however, negative value residuals would always be transferred to persons who would at least expect to be able to benefit from phantom losses.

123 For additional discussion of the quantification of tax costs of phantom income, see Appendix A.

Ordinarily, a taxpayer that receives a cash payment (not representing proceeds of the sale of property or a gift) must include it in gross income unless (1) it has an obligation to return the payment (for example, because the payment represents loan proceeds or a refundable deposit),[124] or (2) the income component of the payment cannot be calculated until the occurrence of future events. One example of the second type of payment is an option premium. Under current law, such a premium is not taxed until the option lapses or is exercised, because the amount of gain or loss to be realized from the sale or purchase of property on exercise generally is unknown until the sale occurs. An assumption payment would not seem to fall into either of these two categories. It is more akin to a pure income item (replacing income on an interest-free loan).[125]

It could be argued that the assumption payment should be included in income over the period during which the interest-free loan is expected to be made by the transferee to the Service, on the ground that this treatment better reflects the economics of the transaction.[126] While the argument has some appeal, it is unlikely to carry the day. The mere fact that a payment is attributable to a future period is not an adequate reason to defer it, at least in the case of a pure income item. For example, prepaid rents or interest (not representing OID) are included in income when received.[127]

---

124 For a recent discussion of this point, see *Comm'r v. Indianapolis Power & Light Co.*, 493 U.S. 203 (1990).

125 It could be argued that an assumption payment is not a pure income item because of the tax payments required to be made by the transferee (which may not be fully recovered). However, the need to make federal income tax payments should not affect the character of an assumption payment as an income item, because those tax payments would not be deductible. The fact that a transferee may incur a deductible cost by paying someone else to acquire the residual interest before the phantom income has been fully realized does not warrant a different conclusion. A future sale to a new party that may or may not happen should not be taken into account unless and until it occurs.

126 The NYSBA 1993 REMIC report at 5–7 makes this argument. One way to state the argument is that the assumption payment is akin to discount on the required loan to the government, which would be included in income over the term of the loan. Treasury Regulation § 1.1273-2(g)(4) provides that if, as part of a lending transaction, a third party makes a payment to the lender, that payment is treated "in appropriate circumstances" as a payment made by the third party to the borrower and by the borrower to the lender as discount on the loan. This regulation in fact would not apply to an assumption payment because the making of tax payments on income is not considered a loan for tax purposes even if those payments are expected to be recovered through losses in later years.

   Nonperiodic payments under notional principal contracts are not included in the payee's income immediately, but instead are allocated over the life of the contract and included in income in the periods to which they relate. See Treasury Regulation § 1.446-3(f)(2). This rule might be cited for the view that an income payment relating to a particular future period of time should be included in income over that period. On the other hand, the nonperiodic payment is made only because the counterparty has agreed to make other (deductible) payments of equal value in exchange, although not necessarily in the same amount. Thus, a nonperiodic payment can be considered analogous to an advance, or can be said to relate to a transaction in which the payee's income cannot be determined in advance. Accordingly, the treatment of nonperiodic payments can be explained by the principles outlined in the last paragraph in the text. The taxation of notional principal contracts is discussed in Chapter 4 in footnotes 293–296 and the accompanying text.

127 A series of cases involving services and sales of goods require upfront payments to be included in

Taxing a transferee upon receipt of an assumption payment would not increase significantly the present value of its tax obligations by comparison with what they would be if it received no such payment but earned a market rate of return on the money it advances to the government.[128] Although perhaps not directly relevant, it is worth noting that if a REMIC sponsor, in lieu of making an assumption payment, contributed the same amount to the REMIC which then distributed it after a short period to a transferee of the residual interest, then the transferee clearly would have current income in the amount of the distribution.[129]

(iii) Negative basis or issue price. Where a residual interest has a negative value, a question arises as to whether its issue price or tax basis can be negative. Subject to a limited exception for securities dealers described below, the answer should be "no". It is generally understood that the basis of property cannot be negative.[130] The preamble to the proposed REMIC regulations states explicitly, in discussing negative value residuals, that "existing tax rules do not accommodate" the concepts of negative bases or issue prices.[131]

The ban on negative issue prices means that the negative value of a residual interest in a REMIC is not subtracted from the positive issue prices of the regular interests in calculating the REMIC's basis in its assets.[132] For example, if a sponsor transfers mortgages with a basis and value of 100 to a REMIC in exchange for regular interests worth 102 and a residual interest valued at minus 2, the REMIC's basis in its assets would be 102. The sponsor would have a basis of 100 in the regular interests and 0 in the residual interest.[133] If the sponsor sells the regular

---

income currently. See *Schlude v. Comm'r*, 372 U.S. 128 (1963) (services) and *Hagen Advertising Displays, Inc. v. Comm'r*, 407 F.2d 1105 (6th Cir. 1969) (inventory). These cases do not involve pure income payments in that expenses had to be incurred to earn the income. The result was influenced in part by uncertainty as to the amount or timing of those expenses. In *Artnell Co. v. Comm'r*, 400 F.2d 981 (7th Cir. 1968), the court allowed a taxpayer to show that deferring revenues from purchases of season tickets for baseball games to the dates when the games were scheduled to be played clearly would reflect income. By contrast with these cases, an assumption payment comes closer to representing a pure income item (see footnote 125, above) so that the timing of incurrence of expenses may not be very relevant in deciding when to include it in income. Further, the period of deferral that would be involved if assumption payments could be spread over the term of the loan would be far longer than the one year at issue in *Artnell*. Finally, the period of time over which the required interest-free loan to the government will be outstanding is uncertain, because it will depend, among other factors, on mortgage prepayments (although the use of a prepayment assumption could alleviate this concern).

128   If the assumption payment equals the present value of the foregone interest, then (assuming constant tax rates) the tax on that amount would equal the present value of the tax that would have been imposed on the foregone interest.

129   The holder's basis would be initially zero (assuming the residual interest has an initial fair market value of zero). The distribution would exceed the basis and therefore be treated as gain (generally capital gain) from sale of the residual interest under section 860C(c)(2).

130   See Cooper, "Negative Basis," 75 *Harvard Law Review* 1352 (1962).

131   See footnote 119, above. While the same language was not included in the preamble to the final regulations, the Service also did not signal a change in its views.

132   As discussed in footnote 31, above, and accompanying text, a REMIC's initial basis in its assets equals the sum of the issue prices of all REMIC interests.

interests for 102 and pays a third party 2 to acquire the residual interest, then the sponsor would recognize 2 of income upon sale of the regular interests and a loss of 2 on sale of the residual. The third party would recognize income of 2. The REMIC's basis of 102 can be justified by the additional income of 2 reported by the sponsor or its successors as compared with the income that would have been realized by the sponsor had it continued to hold the mortgages directly.[134]

A residual interest held by a securities dealer generally may be marked to market under section 475, unless the interest is considered to have negative value (determined under a formula) at the time when it is acquired by the dealer. Where section 475 applies, the dealer should be allowed to measure income or loss based on the actual market value of the residual interest, even if that value is negative.[135]

---

133   As discussed in Chapter 12, text accompanying footnote 34, the sponsor would allocate its basis in the mortgages between the regular and residual interests in proportion to their (positive) fair market values.

134   For further discussion of this point, see the NYSBA 1992 REMIC report at 8–14.

135   See Chapter 9, Part E.

Chapter 8

Taxation of TMPs and Holders of Equity Interests in TMPs

A. Introduction

As discussed in earlier chapters, effective generally for entities that issue debt on or after January 1, 1992, any entity that meets the definition of a TMP is classified for tax purposes as a separate corporation.[1] The goal of this special classification rule generally is to ensure that income allocable to the equity interests in non-REMIC issuers of multiple-class mortgage-backed securities is subject to at least one layer of tax (the corporate income tax).

Section 7701(i) classifies a TMP as a corporation, but, with limited exceptions, does not alter the way in which a TMP, as a corporation, is taxed. Thus, it is necessary to look to the tax rules governing corporations and shareholders to determine the proper treatment of TMPs and their owners. A comprehensive discussion of corporate taxation is beyond the reach of this book. This chapter will concentrate instead on issues that are unique, or of particular concern, to TMPs. Parts B, C, and D address, respectively, the taxes imposed on TMPs, the treatment of equity owners, and special rules for REITs that are TMPs *(REIT/TMPs)*.

B. Taxes Imposed on TMPs

The tax treatment of a TMP departs from that of a conventional corporation in three ways: (1) a TMP may not file a consolidated return with any other corporation (so that losses of other corporations cannot offset income of a TMP),[2] (2) shareholders

---

1   Chapter 2, Part A, discusses the reasons for the TMP rules. The definition of a TMP is discussed in Chapter 3, Part D. Some care should be taken to investigate the state and local tax treatment of TMPs. Although many states automatically treat as corporations unincorporated entities that are classified as corporations for federal tax purposes, that rule may not hold true in all jurisdictions.

2   Section 7701(i)(1) states that a TMP may not be treated as an "includible corporation with any other corporation for purposes of section 1501." Section 1501 authorizes an affiliated group of corporations to file a consolidated return. An affiliated group is defined in section 1504 as one or more chains of "includible corporations" (as defined generally in section 1504(b)). As discussed further in footnote 11, below, the statute plainly excludes a TMP from membership in an affiliated group only for purposes of section 1501.

of a REIT that is a TMP are required to treat part of their income as an excess inclusion (REIT/TMPs are addressed in Part D below), and (3) under proposed regulations, a TMP may not elect to be an S corporation.[3]

Section 7701(i) classifies a TMP as a corporation, but does not say whether the corporation is domestic or foreign. Accordingly, following the usual Code definitions,[4] a TMP organized under U.S. domestic law would be a domestic corporation and any other TMP would be foreign. A domestic TMP would be subject to U.S. federal corporate income tax on its worldwide income. A foreign TMP would be subject to U.S. tax only on certain passive income from U.S. sources and on income effectively connected with a U.S. trade or business which it conducts. As explained in Chapter 11, a foreign corporation that has no contacts with the U.S. except that it holds a portfolio of U.S. mortgage-backed securities would not itself be subject to any U.S. tax.[5]

The tax imposed on a domestic TMP is based on its taxable income. The taxable income of a TMP would be computed in generally the same way as it is for conduit issuers (as discussed in Chapter 7).[6] Thus, a mismatch between the maturity structure of mortgage assets and pay-through bonds would produce the pattern of phantom income followed by phantom losses discussed in Part E of Chapter 7. Under section 172, losses can be carried forward fifteen years to offset taxable

---

3   Proposed Regulation § 301.7701(i)-4(c)(1). The TRA 1986 legislative history does not anticipate the special rule barring S elections, and it is not clear that it serves any significant policy goal. The opportunities to avoid tax by having a TMP make an S election are limited because, with narrow exceptions for certain trusts and estates, all shareholders of an S corporation must be individuals who are residents or citizens of the U.S. and hence subject to U.S. tax on all their income. Section 1361(b)(1)(B). Individuals are less likely than corporations to have losses that can be used to shelter income of an S corporation. Notwithstanding the prohibition against TMPs electing to be S corporations, a portion of an S corporation can be a TMP. In that event, the S corporation is not considered part of an affiliated group of corporations for purposes of the rule in section 1361(b)(2)(A) prohibiting affiliated group membership by an S corporation. Proposed Regulation § 301.7701(i)-4(c)(2).

4   See sections 7701(a)(4) and (5).

5   Any of its shareholders that are U.S. persons would, of course, be subject to U.S. tax on their shares of the income of the corporation, either upon distribution, or in some cases as earned. Such a shareholder may be subject to one or more of the various regimes that aim to prevent the use of passive foreign corporations to avoid or defer U.S. tax. These include the rules governing foreign personal holding companies (sections 551 through 558), controlled foreign corporations (sections 951 through 964) and passive foreign investment companies (sections 1291s through 1297).

6   One difference is that a TMP is subject to the special rules in section 163(e)(5) that may defer or deny deductions for interest on certain high-yield debt obligations issued by a corporation at a substantial discount with a term exceeding five years. Also, the initial tax basis a TMP may have in collateral received from a shareholder/sponsor will depend on whether the transfer of collateral is a taxable event for the sponsor. As discussed in Chapter 12, Part B, the tax treatment of sponsors differs depending on whether the issuer is a corporation, partnership, or trust. Further, the tax treatment of a corporation is generally unaffected by transfers of its stock, but as discussed in Chapter 7, Part C, transfers of partnership interests can affect the basis used in calculating taxable income of a partnership. If a TMP experiences an ownership change (generally a greater-than-50% change in ownership by 5-percent shareholders over a three-year period), then under section 382, the future use of net unrealized built-in losses at the time of the change would be limited. The possible effect of this rule should be considered if stock of a TMP is transferred when it is on the verge of realizing phantom losses.

income in future years, but can be carried back (e.g., to offset prior phantom income) only three years.[7] Although a TMP may not file a consolidated return, it may be considered part of a group of controlled corporations where that is relevant in computing tax liability.[8] If as a state law matter a TMP is part of a larger legal entity, then it seems likely that the larger entity would be liable for taxes imposed on the TMP if it is generally liable under state law for claims arising from the TMP's activities.[9]

C. Taxation of Equity Owners

Except in the case of a REIT/TMP (see Part D below), there are no special rules governing the tax treatment of the equity owners of a TMP, which are considered to be its stockholders for tax purposes. (The remainder of this Part C assumes that a TMP is not a REIT.) Thus, following the practice for conventional corporations, distributions by a TMP to its equity owners (excluding certain non-pro rata distributions made in redemption of equity interests, and certain liquidating distributions) are included in income by the recipients as dividends to the extent they do not exceed the "earnings and profits" (generally, after-tax earnings) of the TMP, either accumulated through the date of the distribution or earned before or after that date during the TMP's taxable year in which the distribution is made. Phantom income and losses are taken into account in calculating earnings and profits. As a result, earnings and profits of a TMP may be artificially high during the early years following the issuance of multiple classes of debt.

Although TMP dividends must be included in gross income by equity owners, the tax burden on that income may be reduced or eliminated in some circumstances. Dividends received by a domestic corporation may qualify under section 243 for a deduction equal to a percentage of the dividend income. The deduction is available only if the TMP equity is considered to have been held for a minimum period, and may be reduced if the equity is debt financed.[10] In general terms, the deduction would equal 80 percent of the dividend income in the case of a 20 percent or greater equity owner (measured by vote and value), 100 percent in the case of an 80 percent or greater equity owner (again measured by vote and value), and 70 percent in all other cases.[11] Dividends received by a pension plan or other tax-exempt entity

---

7 Corporations are subject to an alternative minimum tax on AMTI to the extent the tax exceeds the regular tax. Section 55(b). For purposes of calculating AMTI, loss carryovers or carrybacks can be used to offset only 90% of AMTI. See section 56(d)(1)(A).

8 See, e.g., section 267(f) (deferral of losses on sales between certain corporations) and section 1561 (limitation on multiple use of tax brackets and certain other threshold amounts).

9 Cf. Treasury Regulation § 1.338-2(d)(4)(i) (continuing state law corporation remains liable for pre-acquisition taxes following a purchase of its stock even though stock purchase is treated under section 338 as a sale of assets by the old corporation and a purchase by a new corporation for substantive tax purposes).

10 See sections 246(c) (holding period) and 246A (debt financing). The deduction also may be reduced under section 246(b) if the recipient's taxable income is less than the amount of dividend income.

generally are subject to tax only if the TMP stock is debt financed.[12] Losses can be offset against dividends received from a TMP to the same extent as if the TMP were a conventional corporation. Dividends paid to a foreign investor are generally subject to a 30 percent withholding tax (subject to reduction under any applicable tax treaty).

The rule in section 582(c) automatically treating gains or losses realized by a bank or thrift from the sale of debt instruments and REMIC securities as ordinary income or loss does not apply to equity in a TMP.

D. REITs

1. Taxation of REITs

A few words on the taxation of REITs will help set the stage for a discussion of REIT/TMPs. A REIT is subject to tax, as a domestic corporation, on its real estate investment trust taxable income *(REIT-TI)*, which is taxable income, less a deduction for dividends paid to shareholders and certain other adjustments. The dividends paid deduction eliminates the corporate tax on currently distributed earnings. A REIT cannot join in a consolidated tax return with other corporations. However, under section 856(i), a corporation that has been at all times 100 percent owned by a REIT (a *qualified REIT subsidiary*) is treated as a division of the REIT and not as a separate corporation. In very general terms, a REIT must invest primarily in (and not hold as a dealer) real estate or real property mortgages, have at least 100 stockholders, meet an ownership diversification test, and distribute substantially all of its income annually.

A number of special rules apply to a REIT that owns a REMIC residual interest and earns excess inclusion income thereon.[13] First, under section 860E(a)(1), the taxable income of the REIT (which is determined before reduction by the dividends paid deduction) cannot be less than the amount of excess inclusion income. Second, although a REIT can reduce its REIT-TI below the amount of its excess inclusion income by making deductible dividend payments, to the extent the excess inclusion income of a REIT exceeds its REIT-TI, under section 860E(d), that excess is allocated among REIT stockholders and treated as excess inclusion income in their

---

11   In the case of a state law corporation, the voting power of stock is measured by the right to vote for directors. Where a TMP is not a state law corporation, it may not be obvious how the voting power test is applied. Certain nonvoting, "straight" preferred stock described in section 1504(a)(4) is disregarded in applying the 20% and 80% ownership tests. The 100% dividends-received deduction applies only if the 80% stock ownership test is met both when the dividend is paid and also during the entire year in which the income that is distributed was earned. See sections 243(b) and (c). Although the 80% ownership test is based on the same definition of "affiliated group" that is used in determining which corporations can join in a consolidated return, the rule preventing a TMP from being an affiliated group member for purposes of filing a consolidated return does not prevent a TMP from being an affiliated group member for other purposes. See footnote 2, above.

12   See Chapter 7, footnote 16, and Chapter 9, Part B.

13   These rules are discussed in detail in Chapter 7, Part E.4.

hands. Finally, section 860E(e)(6) imposes a tax (at the highest marginal income tax rate for corporations) on REITs and other pass-thru entities that are owned by disqualified organizations (generally, nontaxable governmental organizations) based on the amount of excess inclusion income allocable to those owners. The entity level tax is in lieu of the tax that otherwise would apply at the owner level to such income.

2. REIT/TMPs as Quasi-REMICs

A REIT can issue debt and meet the definition of a TMP. However, the basic rule of section 7701(i)(1) treating a TMP as a separate corporation that cannot join in a consolidated return would have no effect on a REIT, because a REIT already is such a corporation. Thus, the issue posed by the REIT regime is how to reconcile the pass-through nature of a REIT with the policy goal of collecting at least one tax on the income of non-REMIC issuers of multiple-class mortgage-backed securities. The TMP rules address the point by treating a REIT/TMP as a quasi-REMIC: the relief from corporate taxation on the distributed earnings of the REIT is preserved, but dividends paid by the REIT are treated, in whole or in part, as if they were excess inclusion income from a REMIC residual interest.

These results are accomplished, somewhat obliquely, by section 7701(i)(3). It states that if a REIT is a TMP,[14] then, under regulations prescribed by the Service, "adjustments similar to the adjustments provided in section 860E(d)" shall apply to the REIT's stockholders. No such regulations have been issued.[15] As described in Part D.1 above, section 860E(d) provides for a pass-through of excess inclusion income to REIT stockholders. Although not entirely clear, it appears that a REIT that is required to allocate excess inclusion income to a stockholder under the TMP rules would itself be subject to tax on any excess inclusions allocable to stockholders that are disqualified organizations.[16]

The "similar adjustments" language in section 7701(i)(3) clearly is intended to require some amount of income of a REIT/TMP shareholder to be treated as an excess inclusion, but the statute does not say how that amount is computed. Excess inclusion income from a REMIC residual interest for any period is defined in section 860E(c), broadly as the excess of the taxable income of the REMIC allocated to the residual interest during the period over the "daily accruals" for the days during the period (generally, the income that would have been earned during the

---

14   Special considerations that arise when a portion of a REIT is a TMP are discussed below in the text accompanying footnote 23.

15   See Proposed Regulation § 301.7701(i)-4(b) (reserves REIT regulations).

16   Section 7701(i)(3) does not refer to section 860E(e)(6), which imposes the tax on REITs referred to in the text. Nevertheless, the language of section 860E(e)(6) easily can be read to apply to any type of excess inclusion income allocable to a REIT shareholder, including any such income that arises because of the "adjustments" required under section 7701(i)(3). The tax imposed by section 860E(e)(1) on transfers of residual interests in REMICs to disqualified organizations does not seem to apply to stock in a REIT/TMP, because there is no rule equating such stock to a REMIC residual interest. This tax is discussed in Chapter 7, Part E.4.e.(i).

period from an investment made at the time of formation of the REMIC in an amount equal to the issue price of the residual interest, if the investment had earned a rate of return over its life equal to 120 percent of the Federal long-term rate at the time of formation of the REMIC).[17] Two key questions that must be answered in applying the excess inclusion definition to a REIT/TMP are (1) whether the daily accruals are based on the original issue prices of the REIT stock or on its value at the time when the REIT became a TMP, and (2) whether the taxable income allocated to REIT stockholders is based on the taxable income of the REIT determined without regard to the TMP rules, or instead on the hypothetical taxable income that would be reported by a REMIC that held the assets of the REIT and was formed at the time when the REIT became a TMP.[18]

The legislative history of TRA 1986 provides a clear answer to the first of these questions and hints at an answer to the second. Daily accruals are based on the value of REIT stock when the REIT becomes a TMP.[19] Although the second question is not squarely addressed, the legislative history describes the amount treated as an excess inclusion as the amount by which "dividends from the REIT" exceed the daily accruals.[20] The reference to dividends, without further embellishment, is most likely a reference to the dividends that would be paid in the absence of the TMP rules.[21] While it may trouble a purist to base part of the measure of excess inclusions on current values and the other part on historical costs, the result can be defended on practical grounds. Regarding daily accruals, the original issue prices of REIT stock may have little to do with the current income potential of a REIT, and it should be feasible in most cases to measure with reasonable accuracy the market value of equity in a REIT/TMP. As to taxable income, a hypothetical calculation of REIT income based on market values and applying REMIC principles could be enormously complex.[22]

---

17   For a more detailed explanation, see Chapter 7, Part E.4.b.

18   To illustrate some of the differences, REMICs take an initial basis in their assets equal to fair market value, are required to include market discount on debt instruments in income as it accrues, and must report all income or loss as ordinary. See, generally, Chapter 7, Part D.

19   See Conference Report at II-240; Blue Book at 428.

20   Id. Query whether the dividends taken into account include capital gains dividends paid under section 857(b)(3).

21   The Conference Report at II-240 includes the following: ". . . the conferees intend that the regulations would provide that to the extent that dividends from the REIT exceed the daily accruals for the REIT (determined in the same manner as if the REIT were a REMIC)" then the dividends would be treated as excess inclusions. The parenthetical seems to modify only "daily accruals" and not "dividends." This view is bolstered by an earlier statement on the same page: "The conferees intend that [the excess inclusion calculation] is to be made as if the equity interests in the REIT were the residual interest in a REMIC and such interests were issued (i.e., the issue price of interests is determined) as of the time that the REIT becomes a TMP." The issue price of REMIC residual interests is the starting point for calculating daily accruals. There is no similar statement referring expressly to the calculation of REIT-TI or dividends.

22   For example, if a REIT/TMP were to take an initial fair market value basis in its assets, what adjustments would be made to account for unrealized built-in gains or losses existing at that time? Another troublesome issue would be how to coordinate the hypothetical income calculation used in measuring excess inclusions with the calculations required under the REIT rules. For example,

The discussion above assumes that a REIT qualifies as a TMP in its entirety. A portion of a REIT also can meet the TMP definition. In that case, the TMP rules are applied first to treat the TMP as a separate corporation, but that corporation is then "disincorporated" and treated as a REIT division under the qualified REIT subsidiary rules in section 856(i).[23] The combined effect of the two sections is to return the REIT to its starting position. However, section 7701(i)(3) upholds the policy of the TMP rules by applying the quasi-REMIC approach outlined above not only to a REIT that is a TMP, but also to a qualified REIT subsidiary that is a TMP.

The legislative history of TRA 1986 states that where a REIT has a qualified REIT subsidiary that is a TMP, "the portion of the REIT's income that is subject to the special [excess inclusion] rules is determined based on calculations made at the level of the REIT subsidiary."[24] Consistent with the approach followed where a REIT as a whole is a TMP, and the principles of section 860E(d), it would seem that a REIT should, in calculating excess inclusion income attributable to a qualified REIT subsidiary, compute taxable income of the subsidiary in the same manner as if the TMP rules did not apply, and base the daily accruals on the fair market value of the equity in the subsidiary at the time it becomes a TMP. The REIT should then treat such excess inclusion income in the same manner as if it were earned from a REMIC residual interest.[25]

Given the uncertainties surrounding these rules, one may wonder how an innocent shareholder would ever determine the portion of its income that is an excess inclusion. The TRA 1986 legislative history expresses the intention that regulations will require a REIT/TMP to report the amount of such excess inclusions to its shareholders.[26]

---

would a REIT/TMP continue to account separately for capital gains and losses even though all income of a REMIC is ordinary? Would the special REIT taxes on income from foreclosure property and dealer transactions (see sections 857(b)(4) and (6)) and the REIT income qualification tests in section 856(c) be based on actual or hypothetical income?

23   Conference Report at II-240, footnote 26; Blue Book at 428, footnote 97 (a portion of a REIT that is a TMP may be a qualified REIT subsidiary).

24   Conference Report at II-241, footnote 27; Blue Book at 428, footnote 99.

25   See the discussion in Part D.1 above and Chapter 7, Part E.4.d.

26   Conference Report at II-241; Blue Book at 428.

Chapter 9

Special Rules for Certain Institutional Investors

This chapter discusses special tax rules that apply to certain categories of institutions investing in mortgage-backed securities (or debt instruments generally). These institutions are thrifts, banks, REITs, pension plans and other tax-exempt organizations, life insurance companies, and securities dealers. The chapter does not attempt to address comprehensively the complex tax rules governing these types of organizations.[1]

A. Thrift Assets and REIT Assets and Income Tests

Thrifts are subject to a tax-related assets test. In particular, a thrift is allowed deductions for additions to bad debt reserves calculated under the percentage-of-taxable-income method, and qualifies for certain other tax benefits available to the thrift industry, only if at least 60 percent of its assets are assets listed in section 7701(a)(19)(C).[2] The list includes, among other assets, loans "secured by an interest in [residential] real property" (but generally not loans secured by commercial real property),[3] cash[4] and taxable obligations of the United States or a state or political

---

1   For a more thorough discussion, see Peat, Marwick, Mitchell & Co., *Taxation of Financial Institutions* (Matthew Bender, looseleaf); L. Rook, *Federal Income Taxation of Banks and Financial Institutions* (Warren, Gorham & Lamont, looseleaf); Ernst & Young, *Federal Income Taxation of Life Insurance Companies* (2d ed., Matthew Bender, looseleaf).

2   Section 7701(a)(19)(C) is reproduced in Appendix C. Section 593 allows a thrift that meets the 60% test (see section 593(a)(2)) to deduct, as an addition to its bad debt reserves, a percentage of its taxable income, with certain adjustments. TRA 1986 reduced the maximum deductible percentage from 32 (40 reduced by 20% under section 291) to 8. Although the percentage-of-taxable-income method is now of diminished importance, there are other significant thrift tax benefits that depend on compliance with the 60% test. A thrift that fails the test (1) is not permitted to use *any* reserve method for calculating bad debt deductions, unless it is a "bank" that is not a "large bank" (generally, more than $500 million of assets) and thus can take advantage of section 585, and further must recapture the portion of its past bad debt deductions that would not have been allowed if it had never met the 60% test (see Proposed Regulation §§ 1.593-12 *et seq*; cf. Revenue Ruling 85-171, 1985-2 C.B. 148), and (2) does not qualify for the thrift exception (described in Chapter 7, Part E.4.c) to the rule prohibiting losses from being offset against excess inclusions. In Revenue Ruling 90-54, 1990-2 C.B. 270, the Service held that a former savings and loan association that was reorganized as a bank is not considered a thrift for federal income tax purposes, notwithstanding that it continued to meet the 60% test and its business did not change.

subdivision thereof,[5] or of a corporation that is an instrumentality of any of the foregoing (including FNMA and FHLMC).[6] In addition, more favorable bad debt reserve rules may apply to loans held by thrifts[7] if those loans are "qualifying real property loans" within the meaning of section 593(d).[8] The treatment of pay-through bonds, pass-through certificates, and REMIC interests under these provisions is discussed below.

An assets test also applies to REITs. An entity qualifies as a REIT only if at least 75 percent of its assets are *real estate assets* (including interests in mortgages

---

3   A loan secured by stock in a cooperative housing corporation is generally considered "secured by an interest in [residential] real property". See Revenue Ruling 89-59, 1989-1 C.B. 317. Certain loans secured by manufactured housing also qualify. See Treasury Regulation § 301.7701-13A(e)(12)(ii). An installment land sales contract qualifies as a loan secured by real property even though the contract is not technically a debt instrument under local law. See P.L.R. 8849033 (September 12, 1988); P.L.R. 8832017 (May 13, 1988). Treasury Regulation § 301.7701-13(k) (which applies to pre-1970 years) discusses the amount of collateral necessary for a loan to qualify as a real property loan in its entirety and the times when the adequacy of collateral is tested.

4   Treasury Regulation § 301.7701-13A(e)(1) defines the term *cash* to mean "cash on hand, and time or demand deposits with, or withdrawable accounts in, other financial institutions." The Service has read this language narrowly. See, e.g., Revenue Ruling 66-318, 1966-2 C.B. 522 (bankers' acceptances are not cash for purposes of section 7701(a)(19)(C)). See also the rulings cited in footnote 9, below.

5   The existence of a guarantee of the United States or a U.S.-sponsored agency does not transform a preexisting obligation into a government obligation for this purpose. See the rulings referred to in footnote 12, below. See also P.L.R. 9006015 (November 8, 1989) in which the Service declined to rule that certain agricultural mortgage-backed securities guaranteed by the Federal Agricultural Mortgage Corporation were government securities. Certain obligations originated under a government guarantee program have been treated as government obligations. See Revenue Ruling 76-426, 1976-2 C.B. 17 (Small Business Administration); G.C.M. 36764 (June 22, 1976); Revenue Ruling 74-440, 1974-2 C.B. 19 (Commodity Credit Corporation).

6   See P.L.R. 9110046 (December 11, 1990) (FHLMC is an instrumentality of the United States). The authors understand that FNMA has received an IRS private letter ruling to the same effect that is not publicly available.

7   The amount of qualifying real property loans held by a thrift will not necessarily affect its bad debt deductions. Under section 593, bad debt reserves are calculated separately for qualifying real property loans and for other loans (nonqualifying loans). Although the percentage-of-taxable-income method (see footnote 2 above) may be used only to compute additions to the reserve for qualifying real property loans, additions under that method depend on taxable income and not (except as indicated below) on the amount of qualifying real property loans. Moreover, the addition to reserves determined under that method is reduced dollar-for-dollar by the addition to the separate reserve for nonqualifying loans (see section 593(b)(2)(B)). One way in which bad debt deductions are tied to the amount of qualifying real property loans is that the addition to the reserve for such loans computed under the percentage-of-taxable-income method may not increase the reserve to more than 6% of the amount of such loans (see section 593(b)(2)(C)).

8   A loan secured by stock in a cooperative housing corporation may be a qualifying real property loan within the meaning of section 593(d). Revenue Ruling 89-59, 1989-1 C.B. 317. Certain loans secured by manufactured housing also qualify. See Treasury Regulation § 1.593-11(e)(2)(i). An installment land sales contract can be a qualifying real property loan even though the contract is not a debt instrument under local law. See P.L.R. 8849033 (September 12, 1988); P.L.R. 8832017 (May 13, 1988). Section 593(d)(1) excludes certain categories of loans from the definition of qualifying real property loan, including corporate obligations in registered form, loans of which the primary obligor is a bank or government, or a member of the same affiliated group, and loans held by a thrift to the extent secured by a deposit in or share of the thrift. Note that qualifying real property loans are *not* limited to residential loans.

on real property), U.S. Government securities, cash items, or cash.[9] In addition, a REIT must derive at least 75 percent of its gross income from real estate related sources, including "interest on obligations secured by mortgages on real property or on interests in real property," and gain from the sale or other disposition of those obligations (assuming they are not held in a dealer capacity).[10]

In general, pay-through bonds do not qualify as real property loans for purposes of the thrift and REIT tests, because they are not directly secured by real property (but only by debt instruments that are so secured).[11] With the possible exception of IO Strips, discussed below, pass-through certificates are considered qualifying thrift and REIT assets to the extent the issuing trust holds such assets, because the holders of such certificates are treated for tax purposes as the owners of the trust's assets under the grantor trust rules.[12]

---

9   See sections 856(c)(5) and (c)(6)(B). *Cash items* include certificates of deposit maturing within one year of issuance (Revenue Ruling 77-199, 1977-1 C.B. 195; G.C.M. 36782 (July 6, 1976)) but do not include sale-repurchase agreements (Revenue Ruling 77-59, 1977-1 C.B. 196; G.C.M. 35876 (June 27, 1974)), or bankers' acceptances (Revenue Ruling 72-171, 1972-1 C.B. 208). See also G.C.M. 39531 (February 5, 1986) ("'overnight loans' of federal funds are not 'cash or cash items' for purposes of section 851(b)(4) [diversification rule that applies to RICs]"). See also footnote 4, above.

10   See section 856(c)(3). A separate 95% passive income test applies under section 856(c)(2). Loans secured by stock in a cooperative housing corporation, by certain manufactured housing, by certain time-share interests, by leaseholds, or by options to acquire leases or land or improvements thereon, qualify as real property mortgages for purposes of the REIT tests. See Treasury Regulation §§ 1.856-3(b)(2)(ii)(A) and -3(c); Revenue Ruling 76-101, 1976-1 C.B. 186 (co-op shares). An installment land sales contract is also considered a real property mortgage even though it is not a debt instrument under local law. See P.L.R. 8849033 (September 12, 1988); P.L.R. 8832017 (May 13, 1988). Treasury Regulation § 1.856-5(c) discusses the amount of collateral necessary for a loan to be considered to be secured by real property in its entirety and the times when the adequacy of collateral is tested.

11   See Conference Report at II-224; Blue Book at 410. But see Revenue Ruling 80-280, 1980-2 C.B. 207 (certain "hypothecation loans" secured by mortgage loans are qualifying loans for REITs); G.C.M. 38364 (May 5, 1980) (same); G.C.M. 38238 (January 9, 1980) (same).

12   See the rulings cited in Chapter 2, footnotes 11-14. These rulings treat the entire pass-through certificate as a qualifying asset if the underlying loans are qualifying assets, notwithstanding that the issuing trust will hold, in addition to the actual loans, loan payments (or rights to receive those payments from servicers) for short periods pending distribution to certificate holders. Compare the rule discussed in footnote 21, below, treating cash flow investments held by REMICs as qualifying loans. The Service has also ruled that pass-through certificates may be qualifying assets even though some portion of the underlying loans are secured by small amounts of personal property in addition to real property assets. See Revenue Ruling 81-203, 1981-2 C.B. 137 (pledged account mortgages). For the effect of "buy-down funds," see P.L.R. 8942001 (April 28, 1989), P.L.R. 8452021 (September 20, 1984), and P.L.R. 8430112 (April 27, 1984), and Chapter 6, footnote 75. See also Treasury Regulation § 301.7701-13(k)(1) (loan treated as secured by residential real property if the "loan value" of the property (the maximum loan that can be made against the property under applicable regulatory rules) exceeds 85% of the amount of the loan). Credit support arrangements generally are considered to be incidental to mortgages rather than separate assets for purposes of the thrift and REIT assets tests. See the rulings cited at the beginning of this footnote, most of which involved some form of credit support. See also P.L.R. 8918045 (February 6, 1989). A similar rule applies in the REMIC area. See Chapter 4, Part C.1.b.(ii). It is possible that a REIT holding a subordinated pass-through certificate would be considered to earn a guarantee fee, which would not be qualifying income for purposes of the REIT income tests. See Chapter 2, footnote 34.

A REIT that owns an equity interest in an owner trust is considered to own qualifying assets to the extent that the trust holds such assets, provided the trust is classified as a trust or partnership for tax purposes. The same would hold true for a thrift investor if the owner trust is a grantor trust. The result is less certain for thrift investors, however, if the owner trust is classified as a partnership for tax purposes.[13]

As indicated above, a pass-through certificate generally is a qualifying loan for thrifts under sections 7701(a)(19)(C) and 593(d) (qualifying thrift loan) if the underlying trust assets are qualifying thrift loans. It is not entirely clear that this principle applies to IO Strips (or generally, any certificate that represents a right to a disproportionately high amount of interest).[14] The reason is that a qualifying thrift loan must be a "loan" within the meaning of these sections, and the relevant definition refers to a "valid and enforceable obligation to pay a fixed or determinable sum of money."[15] Arguably, an IO Strip does not fit within this definition because the payments thereon cease if the underlying loans prepay.

A partial ownership interest in a qualifying thrift loan should itself be considered a qualifying thrift loan without regard to the economic characteristics of the ownership interest. The REMIC and stripped bond rules support this view. An IO Strip is a "qualified mortgage" for purposes of the REMIC assets test if the underlying debt instrument is a qualified mortgage.[16] Furthermore, under section 1286, an IO Strip is taxable under the rules governing debt instruments, even though an IO Strip, if viewed in isolation, might not be characterized as debt.[17]

If the REMIC and section 1286 analogies were not considered controlling, and an IO Strip was tested as a stand-alone security, there still would be at least two

---

13   As discussed in Chapter 3, Part C.2.c.(i), an owner trust that is not a TMP may be classified as a grantor trust or as a partnership. If an owner trust is classified as a grantor trust, thrift and REIT investors in the equity of the trust would be treated as if they owned the underlying mortgage loans directly. The same would be true for a REIT if the owner trust is classified as a partnership because, under Treasury Regulation § 1.856-3(g), a REIT is considered to own directly its proportionate share of the assets of a partnership of which it is a partner. No similar regulation applies to thrifts. Thus, it is uncertain whether an investment by a thrift in an owner trust would be treated as an investment in the underlying assets if the trust is classified as a partnership. Treasury Regulation § 1.856-3(g) appears to permit a REIT to treat its share of the gross assets of an owner trust as real property assets and does not limit such treatment to the fair market value of the equity interest held by the REIT.

14   The same problem does not arise in applying the REIT definition of real estate assets because that definition includes "interests in" mortgages on real property. See section 856(c)(6)(B).

15   Sections 593(d)(1) and 7701(a)(19)(C)(v) both refer to "loans." Section 593(d)(3) and Treasury Regulation § 301.7701-13(j)(1) define a "loan" as "debt," as the term is used in section 166. The language quoted in the text is from the definition of "bona fide debt" in Treasury Regulation § 1.166-1(c). The full quotation is as follows: "A bona fide debt is a debt which arises from a debtor-creditor relationship based upon a valid and enforceable obligation to pay a fixed or determinable sum of money." The "based upon" language provides some (admittedly weak) support for the position advanced in the next paragraph in the text that the character of an IO Strip should depend only on the character of the underlying loans.

16   See Chapter 4, footnote 76 and accompanying text.

17   See Chapter 6, Part D.1.b.

arguments supporting the conclusion that the IO Strip is a "loan." First, a regulation under section 7701(a)(19)(C) states that unamortized premium on a loan shall be taken into account in measuring the amount of the loan for purposes of the section, even though such premium would disappear if the loan were prepaid.[18] Indeed, if an IO Strip had some small principal component, it would fall literally within the regulation. One may speculate, however, that the drafters of the regulation had in mind conventional premiums that serve as an adjustment to future interest income. A second argument for treating an IO Strip as a loan is that the payments on an IO Strip are "determinable" if the rate of mortgage prepayments is known. At least for purposes of calculating taxable income on an IO Strip, future prepayments necessarily will be "determined" using some prepayment assumption.[19]

In evaluating the arguments above, it is important to recognize that treating an IO Strip as a qualifying thrift loan would not result in double counting of such loans. The related PO Strip generally would be accounted for by a purchaser based on its cost, not face amount, and that cost would exclude the value of the IO Strip.[20]

In any calendar quarter, both regular interests and residual interests in REMICs are qualifying assets for thrifts and REITs, and the income on such interests qualifies for the REIT 75 percent income test, in the same proportion that the assets and income of the REMIC are qualifying assets and income.[21] However, if 95 percent or

---

18   Treasury Regulation § 301.7701-13(l)(2)(v).

19   See Chapter 6, Part D.1.b.

20   See Treasury Regulation § 301.7701-13(l)(1) (amount of an asset is its adjusted basis or an amount determined by "such other method as is in accordance with sound accounting principles, provided such method is used in valuing all the assets in a taxable year").

21   See sections 593(d)(4), 856(c)(6)(E), and 7701(a)(19)(C)(xi); Treasury Regulation §§ 1.593-11(e)(1), 1.856-3(b)(2), and 301.7701-13A(e)(12). As described in Chapter 4, Part A.2, the assets of a REMIC may include, in addition to qualified mortgages, cash flow investments, qualified reserve assets and foreclosure property. Cash flow investments and qualified reserve assets could be qualifying assets under the general rule of section 856(c)(5)(A) or 7701(a)(19)(C) (see text accompanying footnotes 4, 5, and 9), but would not ordinarily be qualifying real property loans within the meaning of section 593(d). However, under a special REMIC rule, cash flow investments are always treated as qualifying real property loans for purposes of section 593(d) and real estate assets for purposes of section 856(c)(5)(A). See Treasury Regulation §§ 1.593-11(e)(2)(ii) and 1.856-3(b)(2)(ii)(B). There is no corresponding rule under section 7701(a)(19)(C) (see Treasury Regulation § 301.7701-13A(e)(12)) or for qualified reserve assets. As to foreclosure property, in cases where less than 95% of a REMIC's assets in any quarter are real estate assets (the 95% threshold is discussed below in the text), income from foreclosure property held by a REMIC (as defined in section 860G(a)(8), presumably disregarding, as inapplicable, the last sentence thereof) is reported separately and treated as income from foreclosure property for purposes of the REIT 75 percent income test. See Treasury Regulation §§ 1.860F-4(e)(1)(ii)(B)(3) and 1.6049-7(f)(3)(ii)(C). It is not clear what purpose is served by reporting this item separately. Real property acquired in connection with the default of a mortgage generally would be a qualifying asset under section 7701(a)(19)(C) if the mortgage was such an asset (see Treasury Regulation § 301.7701-13(l)(2)(viii)). The existence of credit support should not affect the status of loans as qualifying assets for REITs or thrifts. See footnote 12, above.

Under section 856(c)(2), an entity qualifies as a REIT only if at least 95% of its gross income (with some adjustments) is interest or is derived from certain other passive sources (whether or not related to real estate). Treasury Regulation §§ 1.860F-4(e)(1)(ii)(B)(3) and 1.6049-7(f)(3)(ii)(C) indicate that all income from the holding of both residual interests and regular interests will count favorably for this test.

more of the assets of the REMIC are qualifying assets during a calendar quarter, then the regular and residual interests will be considered qualifying assets, and the income on such interests will qualify for the REIT 75 percent income test, in their entirety for that quarter.[22] The percentage of assets of any type held by a REMIC in any calendar quarter is based on an average of the assets held at different times during the quarter.[23] If one REMIC owns regular interests in a second REMIC, then the 95 percent test generally is applied separately to each. However, if the REMICs are part of a "tiered structure," the 95 percent test is applied only once to both REMICs, treating them as if they were a single REMIC.[24] Two REMICs are considered "tiered" if it was contemplated when both REMICs were formed that some or all of the regular interests of one REMIC would be held by the other REMIC.[25] The amount of a residual interest that may be counted as a qualifying asset is either the adjusted basis or value of the interest, not the adjusted basis or value of the underlying assets of the REMIC.[26]

B. Tax-Exempt Organizations

Qualified pension plans, charitable institutions, individual retirement accounts, and certain other entities that are otherwise exempt from federal income taxation are nonetheless subject to tax on their unrelated business taxable income. UBTI generally does not include interest or dividend income or gain from the sale of investment property, unless such income is derived from property that is debt-financed. Thus, income from pass-through certificates, pay-through bonds, REMIC regular interests, and equity interest in TMPs would not be considered UBTI, unless the security is itself debt-financed.[27] On the other hand, all or substantially all of the income

---

22   See sections 593(d)(4), 856(c)(6)(E), and 7701(a)(19)(C)(xi). If a REIT holds a residual interest for a principal purpose of avoiding the limitations of section 856(f) or (j) (interest based on mortgagor net profits, shared appreciation mortgages), then, even if the 95% test is met, the REIT is treated as receiving directly its share of the REMIC's income for purposes of section 856. Treasury Regulation § 1.856-3(b)(2)(iii).

23   The average may be computed on a monthly, weekly, or daily basis, but the same computation period must be used for all types of assets. Once a period is adopted it may not be changed in subsequent quarters without the consent of the Service. Treasury Regulation § 1.860F-4(e)(1)(iii).

24   See sections 593(d)(4), 856(c)(6)(E), and 7701(a)(19)(C) (last sentence). While not entirely clear, it appears that the 95% test would be considered to be met in a tiered structure with respect to a category of assets only if 95% of all assets held by both REMICs (disregarding regular interests of one REMIC held by another) are qualifying assets.

25   TAMRA House Report at 85.

26   See Conference Report at II-237 (refers to value); Blue Book at 425 (refers to basis).

27   The debt-financed property rules apply under section 514 only to property with "acquisition indebtedness," and the statement in the text assumes that a trust issuing pass-through certificates does not incur any such debt. However, such a trust may accept servicer or other third party "advances," which the trust is obligated to repay, to replace defaulted or delinquent mortgage payments or to pay expenses. There are at least three possible grounds for concluding that such advances are not acquisition indebtedness: (1) advances could be viewed as incidental to the mortgages and not as true loans (compare the discussion in Chapter 4, Part C.1.b.(i), of the treatment of REMIC credit support arrangements prior to adoption of the REMIC regulations); (2)

from an equity interest in an owner trust that is classified as a grantor trust or partnership would be UBTI even if the equity interest itself is not debt-financed.[28] In the case of a REMIC residual interest, any amount of income that is an "excess inclusion" is deemed to be UBTI in the hands of an investor that is subject to tax on UBTI. Other income from a residual interest should not be UBTI unless the interest is itself debt financed.[29] Special considerations apply to pass-through debt certificates (or more generally to securities that resemble debt but may be considered partnership interests for tax purposes).[30]

C. Life Insurance Companies

The general Code rules pertaining to the accrual of discount on debt securities do not apply to life insurance companies. Under section 811(b), life insurance companies generally are required to take original issue discount into account under the method they regularly employ in maintaining their books, if such a method is reasonable.[31] A life insurance company that realizes excess inclusion income from a REMIC residual interest may not offset such income through an increased deduction for variable contract reserves.[32]

D. Debt Instruments Held by Banks and Thrifts

Under section 582(c), certain banks and thrift institutions are required to report gain or loss from the sale of an "evidence of indebtedness" as ordinary income or loss. Pass-through certificates, pay-through bonds, and both regular and residual interests in REMICs are considered evidences of indebtedness for this purpose.[33]

---

advances could benefit from rulings holding that temporary borrowings that are incidental to an investment and not incurred to finance new investments are not the type of debt to which section 514 was intended to apply (see Revenue Ruling 78-88, 1978-1 C.B. 163; P.L.R. 8721104 (February 27, 1987); P.L.R. 8721107 (February 27, 1987)); and (3) a post-acquisition advance that was not "reasonably forseeable" at the time of the acquisition does not meet the statutory definition of acquisition indebtedness (see section 514(c)(1)(C)).

28 See Chapter 7, footnote 16 and accompanying text.

29 Excess inclusions are discussed in Chapter 7, Part E.4. See Chapter 7, footnote 47 and accompanying text.

30 See Chapter 2, text following footnote 76.

31 Section 811(b) provides for an adjustment to income on debt held by a life insurance company to reflect the appropriate accrual of discount in accordance with the method regularly employed by the company, if such method is reasonable, or in all other cases in accordance with the method prescribed in regulations. Regulations, promulgated in 1961, under the predecessor of section 811(b) provide that the default method of amortizing discount is a straight line method (and not a constant yield method). See Treasury Regulation § 1.818-3(b)(3)(ii). The requirement to include discount in income as it accrues under a book method is limited, in the case of taxable bonds, to original issue discount. See section 811(b)(3)(B); Revenue Ruling 73-60, 1973-1 C.B. 332; see also Revenue Ruling 78-150, 1978-1 C.B. 214. Section 811(b) also provides special rules for amortizing premium but the effect of those rules is in essence to force an election under section 171.

32 See Chapter 7, footnote 73 and accompanying text.

Revenue rulings and Treasury regulations authorize mutual savings banks, building and loan associations, and cooperative banks to amortize mortgage premiums and discounts on a composite basis (that is, ratably over an assumed average life of the loans). It is not clear to what extent the TRA 1984 and TRA 1986 amendments in this area (discussed in Chapter 6) supersede these earlier authorities.[34]

A bank may be considered a dealer in securities and, thus, may be subject to the rules described in Part E.

E. Securities Dealers

Special rules apply to dealers in securities. As described below, the law in this area was changed significantly in 1993 by the enactment of section 475, which expands the definition of dealer and requires dealers to account for income from securities under a mark to market method.

Traditionally, a dealer has been defined as a merchant in securities who, in the ordinary course of business, buys securities for resale to customer with an expectation of earning a profit that is attributable to merchandising efforts.[35] A dealer is distinguished from a trader who seeks to profit from a short-term rise in value not attributable to such marketing efforts, or an investor holding property for the production of income. A bank or thrift that originates mortgages for resale may be a dealer under the traditional definition.[36] For purposes of applying the rules governing securities dealers, a "security" would include most of the conventional types of mortgage-backed securities.[37]

The consequences of being a securities dealer include the following: (1) gain or loss with respect to a security held in a dealer capacity is ordinary income (unless,

---

33 As to REMIC interests, see the last sentence of section 582(c)(1). For a discussion of the application of section 582(c) to equity interests in owner trusts, see Chapter 7, text following footnote 9, and footnote 15 and accompanying text. Section 582(c) applies to thrifts regardless of whether they meet the 60% test described in footnote 2, above, and accompanying text. See section 582(c)(2)(A).

34 See Revenue Ruling 54-367, 1954-2 C.B. 109; Revenue Ruling 216, 1953-2 C.B. 38; Treasury Regulation § 1.1016-9(c). The preamble to the OID regulations (see Chapter 6, footnote 13) states that it may be appropriate to allow financial institutions to account for *de minimis* OID on an aggregate basis, and that the Service is reviewing its published position with respect to the loan liquidation method and plans to issue updated guidance that permits financial institutions to use some form of aggregate accounting.

35 Treasury Regulation § 1.471-5; *Kemon v. Comm'r*, 16 T.C. 1026 (1951), *acq.*, 1951-2 C.B. 3.

36 See Revenue Ruling 72-523, 1972-2 C.B. 242; G.C.M. 34965 (July 28, 1972); see also footnote 45, below, and accompanying text.

37 See sections 1236(c) (security includes an evidence of indebtedness and any evidence of an interest therein) and 475(c)(2) (term includes a partnership or beneficial ownership interest in a widely held or publicly traded partnership or trust, evidence of indebtedness, or evidence of an interest in, or a derivative financial instrument in, any of the foregoing, including short positions). Subject to the special exception for negative value residual interests discussed in the text following footnote 45, below, REMIC residual interest should be considered securities on the ground that they evidence interests in debt instruments.

in the case of loss, the security was identified as held for investment), and gain from the sale of a security held for investment is ordinary unless the security was identified as held for investment,[38] (2) the wash sale rules do not apply to sales of securities by a dealer in the ordinary course of its business,[39] and (3) under section 475, gain or loss is accounted for by marking securities to market (unless, generally, the securities are held for investment, are debt instruments acquired or originated in the ordinary course of business and not held for sale, or are hedges of assets or liabilities not subject to the mark to market regime, and are timely identified as such).[40]

Section 475 was added to the Code by RRA 1993.[41] Before the advent of this section, a dealer could, for tax purposes, inventory securities held in a dealer capacity and value unsold inventory at cost, market value, or the lower of cost or market.[42] In addition to eliminating methods of inventory valuation based to any extent on cost, section 475 extends the mark to market requirement to securities that are not held in a traditional dealer capacity.[43] Thus, acting as a dealer with respect to any securities can have consequences for the treatment of securities held in a non-dealer capacity. Section 475 also adopts an expanded definition of "dealer". A dealer is defined as any person who (1) regularly purchases securities from, or sells securities to, customers in the ordinary course of business, or (2) regularly offers to enter into swaps or other derivative transactions with customers in the ordinary course of business.[44] The first part of this definition may treat as a dealer any person who regularly buys or originates loans and sells them, even if, in effecting the sales, that person is not acting as a traditional merchant.[45]

---

38   See sections 1221(1) (definition of capital asset excludes inventory and property held primarily for sale to customers in the orginary course of business) and 1236 (investments by dealers). In addition, section 475(d)(3) treats gains or losses with respect to noninventory securities that are subject to the mark to market rules of section 475 as ordinary, with exceptions for, among other things, securities not held "in connection with" dealer activities. In the case of a bank, consider also section 582(c) discussed in Part D.

39   Sections 1091(a) and 475(d)(1). The wash sale rules are discussed in Chapter 7, footnote 55 and accompanying text.

40   Treasury Regulation § 1.475(b)-1T(b) requires a taxpayer to treat as "held for investment" (and thus outside of the mark to market rules) equity interests in corporations, or widely held or publicly traded partnerships or trusts, in which the taxpayer owns a 50% or greater interest. The purpose of this regulation is to prevent the mark to market regime from applying to interests in subsidiaries or joint ventures. Hopefully, it will not be read to apply to pass-through certificates, or other evidences of interests in debt instruments, that qualify as securities without regard to their status as partnership or trust equity. See footnote 37, above.

41   Section 475 generally is effective for taxable years ending on or after December 31, 1993, and thus applies starting in 1993 for calendar year taxpayers. Certain transition rules apply. See section 13223(c) of RRA 1993.

42   Treasury Regulation § 1.471-5.

43   See section 475(a)(2). This section requires mark to market accounting for certain securities held by dealers but not in inventory. By contrast, the part of section 475 that treats gains and losses as ordinary applies only to securities held in connection with dealer activities. See footnote 38, above.

44   Section 475(c)(1).

The mark to market rules of section 475 do not apply to REMIC residual interests that, *when acquired*, have "negative value". Specifically, under regulations, a residual interest is not considered to be a "security" for purposes of this section in the hands of any taxpayer if, as of the date the taxpayer acquires the interest, it has negative value, measured under a formula. A residual interest has negative value if the present value of the anticipated tax liabilities associated with holding the interest exceeds the sum of (1) the present value of the expected future distributions on the interest and (2) the present value of the anticipated tax savings associated with holding the interest as the REMIC generates losses.[46] Once it is determined that a residual interest is a security, its value for purposes of applying section 475 should be its actual market value (whether positive or negative).[47]

---

45   Treasury Regulation § 1.475(c)-1T excludes from the definition of "dealer" taxpayers who provide trade credit and factor trade receivables as part of a business of selling or providing nonfinancial goods and services, and taxpayers who regularly buy securities (including by originating loans) but do not regularly sell more than a negligible portion of those securities. The narrow scope of these exclusions serves to confirm the sweeping nature of the definition of dealer in section 475.

46   Treasury Regulation § 1.475(c)-2T. Anticipated tax liabilities, expected future distributions and anticipated tax savings are determined under the rules of Treasury Regulation § 1.860E-2(a)(3), without regard to the operation of section 475 (i.e., disregarding the effect of the mark to market rules on tax liabilities and tax savings). Present values are determined under Treasury Regulation § 1.860E-2(a)(4). This regulation uses the applicable Federal rate as the discount rate. It is not clear if one rate based on the term of the residual interest, or separate rates based on the terms of the cash flows being discounted, are used in the three present value calculations, although it would make more sense to use one rate. The cited regulations are concerned with the tax on transfers of residual interests to disqualified organizations, and are discussed in Chapter 7, Part E.4.e.(i). Treasury Regulation § 1.475(c)-2T also excludes from the definition of "security" any other interest or arrangement that is determined by the Service to have the same economic effect as a negative value residual interest (for example, a widely-held partnership that holds noneconomic residual interests). The preamble to the regulation requests comments regarding whether additional rules are needed to carry out the purposes of section 475 for taxpayers that hold economic residual interests. See T.D. 8505, I.R.B. 1994-4, 4.

47   Section 475 clearly applies to securities that have or may have negative value, such as short positions, options written by the taxpayer, or notional principal contracts.

Chapter 10

Special Rules for Foreign Investors

A principal tax objective of non-U.S. investors purchasing mortgage-backed securities issued in the United States is to avoid the U.S. 30 percent withholding tax on interest income. A second goal may be to hold such securities in bearer (as distinguished from registered) form. Part A of this chapter discusses the *TEFRA registration requirements* that limit the issuance of debt instruments in bearer form. The withholding tax is the subject of Part B. The chapter concludes with a brief comment in Part C on the implications for mortgage-backed securities of the Foreign Investment in Real Property Tax Act of 1980 (FIRPTA).

A. TEFRA Registration Requirements

This part first surveys the debt registration requirements introduced by the Tax Equity and Fiscal Responsibility Act of 1982 (TEFRA). It then discusses how they apply to the different categories of mortgage-backed securities.

1. Overview

With a view to increasing taxpayer compliance, TEFRA amended the Code to prohibit, with limited exceptions, the issuance or holding of debt obligations in the United States in bearer form. More particularly, the TEFRA rules require all *registration-required obligations* (as defined below) to be in *registered form*.[1] An obligation is in registered form for these purposes if (1) it is registered as to both principal and interest with the issuer or its agent, and can be transferred only by the surrender of the old obligation to the registrar and either its reissuance, or the issuance of a new obligation, to the new owner; (2) principal and interest may be transferred only through a book entry system maintained by the issuer or its agent; or (3) the obligation can be transferred only through either of the methods described in (1) or

---

[1] The TEFRA registration requirements are tax related and distinct from any need to register securities with the Securities and Exchange Commission or state agencies under U.S. securities laws.

(2).[2] Any obligation that is not in registered form is considered to be in *bearer form*.[3]

The issuance of a registration-required obligation in bearer form can result in severe issuer sanctions.[4] Any U.S. taxpayer who holds such an obligation in bearer form in violation of the TEFRA rules is also subject to certain tax penalties.[5]

A registration-required obligation is generally defined in section 163(f)(2) as any obligation other than an obligation that (1) is issued by an individual, (2) is not of a type offered to the public,[6] or (3) has a maturity at issue of not more than one year. Thus, the TEFRA registration requirements do not apply directly to home mortgages and other consumer loans that are obligations of individuals. In fact, such obligations are almost never issued or held in registered form.[7] Although most tax practitioners have concluded that conventional commercial mortgages are not of a type offered to the public, the emergence of a market for single class pass-through certificates backed by a single conventional commercial mortgage may, over time, cause a rethinking of that conclusion.

In addition, for purposes of applying the issuer sanctions only, an obligation is not registration required if it is issued under the so-called *Eurobond exception*,

---

2   Treasury Regulation § 5f.103-1(c)(1).

3   Treasury Regulation § 5f.103-1(e)(1). An obligation is considered to be in bearer form if it is currently in bearer form, or if there is a right to convert it into bearer form at any time during the remaining period that it is outstanding.

4   The issuer of a registration-required obligation in bearer form is liable for an excise tax equal to the product of 1% of the principal amount of the obligation and the number of years (or portions thereof) from its issue date to its maturity date (section 4701). Also, the issuer is not permitted to deduct interest paid on the obligation in computing taxable income or earnings and profits (sections 163(f) and 312(m)). The latter sanctions generally affect only U.S. issuers or issuers that are owned by U.S. persons, but the excise tax is potentially applicable to all issuers. For purposes of section 4701 (1% excise tax), the sponsor of a pass-through certificate or REMIC is considered the issuer and is thus liable for the excise tax. Treasury Regulation §§ 1.163-5T(d)(3) and (e)(3).

5   In general, the holder of a registration-required obligation in bearer form is denied deductions for any loss from the obligation (section 165(j)), and any gain from the obligation that otherwise would be capital gain is converted into ordinary income (section 1287). The holder sanctions apply to an obligation only if the issuer was not subject to the section 4701 excise tax (see footnote 4), and thus are generally a concern only for debt obligations that were issued under the Eurobond exception described later in the text. Furthermore, the holder sanctions do not apply if one of the four exceptions set forth in Treasury Regulation § 1.165-12(c) applies. These exceptions relate to obligations (1) held by certain financial institutions in connection with a trade or business, (2) held by certain financial institutions for their own investment account, (3) held through a financial institution which reports information with respect to the obligations to the Service, or (4) that are promptly converted to registered form.

6   An obligation is considered to be "of a type" offered to the public if similar obligations are in fact publicly offered or traded, whether or not the obligation itself is publicly offered or privately placed. See Treasury Regulation §§ 5f.103-1(b)(1) and (f), Example (3). Proposed Regulation § 5f.163-1(b)(2)(i) provides that an obligation also will be considered of a type offered to the public if it is in a form designed to render the obligation "readily tradeable in an established securities market" within the meaning of section 453(f)(5)(B) and the regulations thereunder (with certain adjustments).

7   Such obligations also typically would not be of a type offered to the public. See footnote 6. A note that can be assigned by the holder merely by endorsement, without notifying the issuer or its agent, is not in registered form. Most consumer loans are assignable in this manner.

which allows bearer paper to be offered outside of the United States to non-U.S. investors.[8] In general, an obligation qualifies for the Eurobond exception if (1) the obligation is "targeted" to non-U.S. investors upon its original issuance,[9] (2) the obligation provides for interest to be payable only outside the United States, and (3) for any period during which the obligation is held other than in temporary global form, the obligation and each coupon contains a *TEFRA legend*.[10] However, the Eurobond exception never applies to U.S. Government, or U.S. Government-backed, securities.[11] For this purpose, a U.S. Government security is any security issued or guaranteed by the U.S. or any U.S. owned or sponsored agency, including, for example, GNMA, FNMA and FHLMC. A security is U.S. Government-backed if more than 50 percent of the income or collateral supporting it (whether as an asset underlying a pass-through certificate or as collateral for a debt obligation) consists of income, or principal, of a U.S. Government security. Thus, any pass-through certificates guaranteed by the U.S. or a U.S. sponsored agency, and pay-through bonds more than 50 percent collateralized by such certificates, are ineligible for the Eurobond exception.

Although an obligation issued or backed by the U.S. Government may not be held in bearer form, it can be held in *targeted registered* form if it was targeted to foreign investors upon its original issuance.[12] Targeted registered obligations are considered to be in registered form for purposes of the TEFRA requirements and accordingly may be resold freely to U.S. investors. As discussed in Part B, the

---

8   The Eurobond exception is set forth in section 163(f)(2)(B) and described in detail in Treasury Regulation § 1.163-5(c). Tax sanctions apply to certain U.S. taxpayers that hold in bearer form obligations issued under the Eurobond exception. See footnote 5.

9   In the language of the statute, there must be "arrangements reasonably designed to ensure" that the obligation "will be sold (or resold in connection with the original issue) only to a person who is not a United States person." See section 163(f)(2)(B)(i). To satisfy this arrangements test, generally it is necessary to meet detailed restrictions on offers, sales, and deliveries of obligations during an initial "seasoning" period and to obtain certifications as to the non-U.S. status of investors. See Treasury Regulation § 1.163-5(c)(2)(i)(D). Special rules apply for issuers that have limited U.S. contacts with respect to an issuance. Treasury Regulation § 1.163-5(c)(2)(i)(C). For obligations issued on or before September 7, 1990, the arrangements test could be met by following the procedures necessary to establish that the obligations are exempt from registration under the Securities Act of 1933 because they are targeted to non-U.S. persons. See Treasury Regulation § 1.163-5(c)(2)(i)(A).

10   The TEFRA legend is a statement to the effect that any United States person who holds the obligation will be subject to the TEFRA holder sanctions. See Treasury Regulation § 1.163-5(c)(1)(ii)(B).

11   Treasury Regulation § 1.163-5(c)(1) states that the Eurobond exception does not apply to U.S. Government securities. While the existing regulations do not preclude use of the exception for U.S. Government-*backed* securities, the Treasury has announced that regulations will be issued prohibiting the issuance, after September 7, 1984, of such securities in bearer form. See Treasury Department News Releases R-2835, September 10, 1984, and R-2847, September 14, 1984. The definition of U.S. Government-backed securities given in the text below is taken from these releases.

12   The "targeting" requirements that must be met in order for an obligation to qualify to be held in targeted registered form are described in Treasury Regulation § 35a.9999-5(b), Q&A-13. A targeted registered obligation generally must comply with the regulations implementing the Eurobond exception.

certification requirements that must be met by a foreign investor to receive interest on a registered obligation free of U.S. withholding tax under the portfolio interest exemption are more lenient for a targeted than a nontargeted obligation.

2. Mortgage-Backed Securities

The TEFRA rules apply in a straightforward way to pay-through bonds and REMIC regular interests.[13] They are registration-required obligations[14] and must be issued in registered form unless the Eurobond exception applies. Although REMIC residual interests are probably not "obligations" for TEFRA purposes, they cannot be issued in bearer form without jeopardizing the issuer's status as a REMIC.[15]

The treatment of pass-through certificates under the TEFRA rules is more complex. As described in Chapter 2, Part B, for substantive tax purposes pass-through certificates are not recognized to be debt of the issuing trust; instead, they merely evidence ownership of trust assets by certificate holders. If this analysis were followed in applying the TEFRA rules, then pass-through certificates would not themselves be "obligations" that could be "registration-required." Further, registration of the certificates could not be mandated on the ground that they represent ownership interests in registration-required obligations if the underlying obligations are obligations of individuals or loans not of a type offered to the public. However, it would make little sense to exclude pass-through certificates from the reach of the TEFRA rules. They are generally liquid securities similar to traded debt instruments. In addition, if the status of a pass-through certificate under the TEFRA rules depended solely on the status of the underlying obligations, it would not be possible to issue bearer certificates under the Eurobond exception if the trust assets included any registration-required obligations.

These unsettling results are avoided under regulations issued in 1985 that effectively treat *pass-through certificates* as defined in the regulations as obligations of the issuing trust for TEFRA purposes.[16] Thus, the nature of the underlying obliga-

---

13   Treasury Regulation § 1.163-5T(e) applies the TEFRA registration rules to REMIC regular interests. It effectively treats regular interests as "obligations" of the REMIC for TEFRA purposes, without regard to whether they are in the form of debt instruments. An anti-abuse rule, similar to the one for pass-through certificates described in footnote 21, below, allows the Service to impose issuer sanctions where the issuer of a mortgage in registered form seeks to use a REMIC to convert the mortgage into a bearer obligation that is not issued under the Eurobond exception. Treasury Regulation § 1.163-5T(e)(4).

14   The statement in the text assumes that the pay-through bonds and regular interests in question are publicly offered (or obligations of a type that is publicly offered) and have an original term to maturity of greater than one year.

15   See Treasury Regulation § 1.860D-1(b)(5)(i)(A) discussed in Chapter 4 at footnote 149. A REMIC residual interest would not be treated as an obligation of the REMIC under the 1985 regulations dealing with pass-through certificates described below in the text, because a REMIC is not a grantor trust.

16   Treasury Regulation § 1.163-5T(d) (rules applying definition of registration-required obligation to pass-through certificates); Treasury Regulation § 35a.9999-5(e) (application of portfolio interest exemption, described in Part B, to pass-through certificates). These regulations were anticipated by the Joint Committee on Taxation staff, *General Explanation of the Revenue Provisions of the*

tions is irrelevant in applying the TEFRA rules to such certificates.[17] The certificates must be in registered form unless the Eurobond exception applies based on an offering of the certificates (as distinguished from the obligations held by the trust) outside of the United States.[18]

The regulations define a "pass-through certificate" as a "pass-through or participation certificate evidencing an interest in a *pool* of mortgage loans" (emphasis added) to which the grantor trust rules apply, or a "similar evidence of interest in a similar pooled fund or pooled trust treated as a grantor trust."[19] An example in the regulations concludes that certificates of interest in a trust that holds 1,000 residential mortgages that are obligations of unrelated individuals are "pass-through certificates."[20] Thus, the 1,000 mortgages are considered a "pool."

The regulations also grant the Service broad authority to characterize pass-through securities "in accordance with the substance of the arrangement they represent" and to impose issuer sanctions accordingly.[21] The regulations indicate that this authority might be used to prevent a domestically offered bond from being issued indirectly in bearer form by issuing the bond in registered form to a trust that issues bearer pass-through securities that are not within the Eurobond exception.

Apart from the example of a trust holding 1,000 residential mortgages, the regulations offer no guidance on the distinction between an interest in a "pool" of loans and pass-through securities that are subject to characterization "in accordance with the substance of the arrangement they represent." Nonetheless, applying the regulations to pass-through securities representing interests in residential mortgages should be straightforward. The regulations were apparently written with these securities in mind, and any group of home mortgages large enough to be grouped and used to support a pass-through security should qualify as a pool, even if the number of loans is significantly below 1,000. On the other hand, suppose that a trust holds five commercial mortgage loans, each of which has a principal balance in excess of $5 million. It is much less obvious that those loans would be considered a pool.

Some guidance about the factors that may be relevant in determining whether a pool exists can be gleaned from an examination of typical residential mortgage

---

Deficit Reduction Act of 1984 (JCS-41-84), December 31, 1984, at 396, footnote 19 and accompanying text. Treasury Regulation § 1.163-5T(d) was accidentally repealed by T.D. 8110, 1987-1 C.B. 81, but was then retroactively reinstated by T.D. 8202, 1988-1 C.B. 78.

17   In addition, if the assets of the trust include registration-required obligations in registered form, those obligations will not be considered to be improperly converted into bearer form because the trust issues bearer pass-through certificates under the Eurobond exception. Treasury Regulation § 1.163-5T(d)(1).

18   This statement assumes, as would normally be the case, that the certificates, viewed as trust obligations, are registration-required because they are of a type offered to the public and have an original term to maturity of more than one year. For purposes of applying the section 4701 excise tax on issuers that violate the TEFRA registration requirements, the "issuer" of a pass-through certificate is considered to be the recipient of the proceeds from issuance of the certificate. Treasury Regulation § 1.163-5T(d)(3).

19   Treasury Regulation § 1.163-5T(d)(1).

20   Treasury Regulation § 1.163-5T(d)(6).

21   Treasury Regulation § 1.163-5T(d)(4).

pass-through securities, if they are taken as the clearest example of a pass-through certificate within the meaning of the regulations. Home mortgages have a number of characteristics that make them unattractive as direct investments. First, the credit-worthiness of individual borrowers is unknown. Second, because of the possibility of prepayment, the cash flow from a single loan is unpredictable. Finally, any one loan is too small to make it divisible into units suitable for public trading. A pass-through arrangement addresses these problems by combining many home mortgages in a trust, adding insurance, a guarantee or other credit support, and creating trust interests in relatively small denominations. The aggregation of many mortgages evens out cash flows and credit risk from the perspective of any one investor; the credit support further simplifies the credit analysis; and the size of the pool enables the pass-through securities to trade actively in public markets. Thus, an analysis of these securities suggests that a group of loans held by a trust should be considered a pool (and interests in the trust should be treated as pass-through certificates within the meaning of the regulations) if individual interests in the trust are qualitatively different from the underlying loans by virtue of differences in predictability of payments, credit risk, and liquidity.

B. Withholding Tax

1. Overview

In general, a non-U.S. investor[22] who receives from U.S. sources "fixed or deter-minable annual or periodical income" (FDAP income) is subject to a 30 percent tax on the gross amount of such income, unless a statutory exemption applies, or the tax is reduced or eliminated under an income tax treaty between the U.S. and the country of residence of the investor.[23] The tax is required to be collected and paid over to the Service by any withholding agent in the chain of payment (generally, any person who pays the income to a non-U.S. person), but is due whether or not it is collected by withholding.[24] A withholding agent may not withhold, or may with-

---

22   It is assumed in Part B that the non-U.S. investor has no connection with the United States other than the holding of the mortgage-backed security under discussion, and in particular does not hold the security in connection with a U.S. trade or business conducted directly by the investor. It is further assumed that if the investor is an individual, the investor is not present in the United States for 183 days or more during the year the security is sold. For discussion of whether owner trusts are engaged in a trade or business, see footnote 46, below. It is generally assumed that the holders of pass-through certificates are not engaged in a trade or business because of the activities of the servicer of the underlying mortgages. The 1985 regulations applying the portfolio interest exemp-tion to pass-through certificates (see footnote 53, below) would be nonsensical if this assumption were not true.

23   The tax is imposed by sections 871(a) (individuals) and 881(a) (corporations).

24   The obligation of a withholding agent to withhold tax is imposed by section 1441 (noncorporate payees) or 1442 (corporate payees), as applicable. Section 1461 makes the withholding agent liable for the tax required to be withheld and indemnifies the withholding agent against the claims and demands of any payee for the amount withheld. If a withholding agent fails to withhold a tax it is required to withhold, and the tax is later paid by the investor or is not due (e.g., because it is not income to the investor), the withholding agent is relieved of liability for the tax, but may still

hold at a reduced rate, in reliance on a treaty only if the agent receives an IRS Form 1001 from the foreign investor stating that the investor is eligible for the treaty benefit.[25]

The two types of income that are likely to be earned by an investor in mortgage-backed securities are interest and gain from the sale or exchange of the securities. Interest is FDAP income, and gain from the sale or exchange of securities is not.[26] Thus, the discussion herein of the withholding tax concentrates on interest

---

be liable for penalties and interest. Section 1463. Although any person in the chain of payment may be a withholding agent (see Treasury Regulation § 1.1441-7(a)(1)), a payor that does not know or have reason to know that its payee is a foreign person may escape liability for failing to withhold. See P.L.R. 9237004 (April 8, 1992). But cf. IRS Publication 515 (Revised November 1993) at 5 ("The 30% rate also applies if you are unable to determine whether the alien is a nonresident or a resident of the United States.") and Treasury Regulation § 1.1441-3(c)(4) (requiring withholding on interest on all bonds or securities the owners of which are not known to the withholding agent). A withholding agent can rely on the written statement of a payee that it is a U.S. person. Treasury Regulation § 1.1441-5.

25 Treasury Regulation § 1.1441-6. Form 1001 is generally effective for three calendar years. Although a Form 1001 is typically provided by the foreign investor prior to receipt of the related payment, a form filed afterward is nonetheless sufficient to eliminate (or reduce the rate of) the withholding tax. See *Casanova Co. v. Comm'r.*, 87 T.C. 214 (1988), *acq.*, 1990-2 C.B. 1; see also T.A.M. 8709003 (November 4, 1986). This favorable rule does not apply to all withholding tax exemptions. See *Casa De La Jolla Park, Inc. v. Comm'r*, 94 T.C. 384 (1990) (Form 4224 providing an exemption from withholding for income effectively connected with a U.S trade or business must be given before payment is made). A withholding agent may not rely on a Form 1001 if it knows, or has reason to know, that the statements therein are false. See IRS Publication 515 (revised November 1993) at 5. See also Revenue Ruling 76-224, 1976-1 C.B. 268. A withholding agent is not required, however, to make substantial inquiries in determining whether a non-U.S. payee is entitled to a claimed reduction in the withholding tax rate. See *The Int'l Lotto Fund v. Virginia State Lottery Dep't,* 800 F. Supp. 337 (E.D. Va. 1992). See also P.L.R. 9237004 (April 18, 1992).

26 See Treasury Regulation § 1.1441-2(a). However, as described in footnote 27, below, the tax on accrued original issue discount is imposed at the time of a sale or exchange to the extent not previously imposed. Gain that is treated as interest for most tax purposes under the market discount rules introduced by TRA 1984 is not treated as interest for purposes of the withholding tax. Section 1276(a)(4). See Chapter 6, footnote 91. Treasury Regulation § 1.1441-2(a)(3) excludes from FDAP income "[i]ncome derived from the sale in the United States of property . . ." FDAP income excludes gain from exchanges as well as from sales for money; it would make no sense to treat gain differently based on the consideration received. Income from the retirement of a residential mortgage that is an obligation of an individual should also be excluded from FDAP income even though such a retirement is not treated as an exchange of the retired obligation under section 1271(a). (For discussion of this point, see Chapter 6, footnote 15.) Gain from such a retirement is computed in the same manner as if it were an exchange, taking account of the holder's tax basis, so that imposing a withholding tax on gross proceeds would be inappropriate. Moreover, the legislative history of the portion of TRA 1984 which overhauled the tax treatment of market discount (including market discount on obligations of individuals) indicates that market discount income was not intended to be subject to withholding tax. See Joint Committee on Taxation staff, *General Explanation of the Revenue Provisions of the Deficit Reduction Act of 1984* (JCS-41-84), December 31, 1984, at 94. In any event, even if gain realized by a non-U.S. investor from the retirement of a debt instrument were FDAP income, it would be taxed only if it is sourced in the United States. Under section 865, gain from the "sale" of personal property (which for this purpose includes any "disposition" of personal property, see section 865(i)(2)) is generally sourced based on the residence of the taxpayer.

income. Certain other types of income that may be earned from mortgage-backed securities are discussed at the end of this Part B.

In general, interest income is subject to the withholding tax if it is derived from U.S. sources, unless the exemption for *portfolio interest* described below applies, or the rate is reduced or eliminated under a treaty. Certain special rules apply to original issue discount.[27] In some cases, tax may be required to be withheld from payments of interest even if those payments are not includible in full in the income of the payee. The investor, however, would be entitled to a refund of any excess tax withheld.[28]

The source of interest income depends on the status of the borrower. Interest is generally U.S. source if the borrower is organized or resident in the U.S.[29] Thus, interest on pass-through certificates representing an ownership interest in home mortgages that are obligations of U.S. resident individuals, and interest on pay-through bonds issued by a U.S. corporation or owner trust, typically would be sourced in the United States.[30] Although there is no explicit source rule for REMIC interests, it is highly likely that income from both regular and residual interests would be sourced in the United States if the issuing REMIC is organized and operated in the U.S. and the underlying mortgages are obligations of U.S. borrowers.[31] Apart from the source question, the withholding tax applies to REMIC regular interests in the same way that it applies to conventional debt obligations.[32]

---

27 With an exception for obligations with an original term of 183 days or less, accrued OID earned by a non-U.S. investor is generally subject to the 30% tax in the same manner as other interest income. However, the tax is imposed on the OID on an obligation only when (1) a payment on the obligation is made, in an amount not exceeding the lesser of (a) the total amount of tax on the accrued portion of such discount not previously taken into account and (b) the amount of the payment (net of any withholding tax otherwise imposed on the payment) or (2) the obligation is sold or exchanged, in an amount equal to the total amount of tax on the accrued portion of such discount not previously taken into account. For this purpose, accruals of OID are calculated in the same manner as for domestic taxpayers (see Chapter 6) with an exception for short-term obligations. See sections 871(a)(1)(C) and (g) and 881(a)(3). Until regulations are adopted, only the issuer of an obligation and its agents are required to withhold the tax on accrued OID from the proceeds of a sale or exchange of the obligation under section 1441 or 1442 (described in footnote 24, above, and accompanying text). See Revenue Ruling 68-333, 1968-1 C.B. 390. Regulations imposing a broader withholding requirement have been proposed but not adopted (Proposed Regulation § 1.1441-3(c)(6)).

28 This problem would arise where an investor buys a bond with accrued interest, or possibly with amortizable bond premium (which arguably can be offset against interest income for withholding tax purposes under section 171(e)). See Treasury Regulation § 1.1441-3(c)(3). Withholding is not required, however, by purchasers of bonds between interest dates with respect to amounts treated as accrued interest to the seller. Treasury Regulation § 1.1441-4(h). See also IRS Publication 515 (revised November 1993) at 9.

29 See section 861(a)(1). In addition, certain interest paid by a U.S. branch of a foreign corporation is treated as U.S. source interest. Section 884(f).

30 However, the source of interest paid by an owner trust that is classified as a grantor trust may depend on the residence or place of organization of the trust beneficiaries. Technically, an owner trust that is classified as a partnership would be considered a U.S. resident (so that interest it pays is U.S. source) only if it is engaged in a U.S. trade or business. See Treasury Regulation § 301.7701-5.

31 Conversely, such income should be sourced outside the U.S. if the REMIC is organized and

Income on a REMIC residual interest representing a share of the REMIC's taxable income is treated as interest for withholding tax purposes.[33] No exemption from such tax or reduction in rate applies to the portion of the income from a residual interest that is an excess inclusion.[34] In the unusual case where income from a REMIC residual interest is considered to be derived from sources outside of the U.S., however, such income should not be subject to U.S. withholding tax, even if it is an excess inclusion.[35] The withholding tax generally is imposed on income from a residual interest when such income is paid or distributed (or when the interest is disposed of).[36] Such income may have to be taken into account earlier,

---

operated outside of the U.S. and the underlying mortgages are obligations of non-U.S. borrowers. Different considerations apply in determining the source of income from regular interests and residual interests. Under section 860B(a), a regular interest is treated as debt of the REMIC for purposes of determining the tax treatment of the holder under chapter 1 of subtitle A of the Code, which includes the sections imposing tax on non-U.S. investors. (Although the statute does not say expressly that a regular interest is an obligation "of the REMIC", Treasury Regulation § 1.860G-1(b)(6) does so state.) The treatment of regular interests as REMIC debt suggests that the source of interest on a regular interest would be determined (as it is under section 861(a)(1) for other noncorporate borrowers) based on the "residence" of a REMIC. A REMIC is not treated as a corporation, partnership or trust under the Code (see section 860A(a)) and there are no special residency tests for REMICs. It is not clear, then, whether residence would be based on the law under which the REMIC is organized (the test for corporations), on whether the REMIC is engaged in a U.S. trade or business (the test for partnerships), or on a combination of factors (the test for trusts). See Treasury Regulation § 301.7701-5. For a discussion of the residence of a trust, see *B. W. Jones Trust v. Comm'r*, 46 B.T.A. 531 (1942), *aff'd*, 132 F.2d 914 (4th Cir. 1943); Revenue Ruling 60-181, 1960-1 C.B. 257; Revenue Ruling 70-242, 1970-1 C.B. 89. At least in the absence of other guidance, the trust approach seems most likely, assuming a residence-based source test is adopted. Alternatively, the source of interest on regular interests might be determined by the source of the REMIC's income, based on the fact that REMIC regular interests are treated as ownership interests in REMIC assets for various purposes. See Chapter 2, Part E. It is not clear whether the source of income on a REMIC residual interest would be determined by reference to the source of income earned by the REMIC, the residence or place of organization of the REMIC, or some other factor. The first of these approaches seems by far the most likely. There is no counterpart for residual interests to the debt rule in section 860B(a). Further, the 30% withholding tax applies only to U.S. source income, and it would be odd to adopt a look-through approach for purposes of applying certain aspects of the withholding tax (treating income on a residual interest as interest income and applying the portfolio interest exemption as discussed in footnotes 33 and 58), but not for purposes of determining the source of income. Apart from the withholding tax, the source of income earned on REMIC interests may be relevant to U.S. taxpayers in calculating the foreign tax credit limitation under section 904.

32   Section 860B(c) treats gain from the disposition of a regular interest as ordinary income to the extent needed to produce a yield of 110% of the applicable Federal rate. This section, which is discussed further in Chapter 6, footnote 10, should not cause the gain to become FDAP income. See footnote 26, above.

33   Conference Report at II-237 - II-238; Blue Book at 425; see also Treasury Regulation § 35a.9999-5(e), Q&A-21(ii).

34   See section 860G(b)(2). Excess inclusions are described in Chapter 7, Part E.4.

35   Section 860G(b)(2) provides that no "exemption" from withholding taxes will apply to any excess inclusion. However, the 30% withholding tax is imposed only on income from U.S. sources, and thus no "exemption" is needed to avoid a tax on foreign source income. Furthermore, it is not necessary, in order to protect U.S. tax revenues, to ensure taxation of excess inclusion income attributable to interest paid by non-U.S. mortgagors, because they would not claim U.S. income tax deductions for the interest they pay.

36   See section 860G(b)(1). The Conference Report at II-236, footnote 18, and the Blue Book at 423,

under regulations, if the residual interest does not have significant value, but to date no such regulations have been issued.[37] Instead, the REMIC regulations address the issue by providing that a purported transfer of a residual interest to a foreign investor is ignored for tax purposes—with the hapless transferor retaining owner-ship of the interest for tax purposes—unless the residual interest is reasonably expected to produce cash distributions sufficient to pay withholding tax liabilities no later than the close of the calendar year following the year in which the related income accrues.[38]

The treatment of income earned on a pass-through debt certificate will depend on whether it is characterized as debt for tax purposes or as a partnership interest and, if classified as a partnership interest, whether the partnership is considered to be engaged in a trade or business[39] and whether the amounts paid are treated as guaranteed payments.[40]

For withholding tax purposes, the holder of an equity interest in a non-TMP owner trust, whether taxable as a grantor trust or as a partnership, is treated essen-tially as if it owned directly the underlying mortgages and other trust assets.[41] Thus, the 30 percent tax, to the extent it applies, is based on the *gross* amount of interest received by the trust (that is, without a deduction for interest payments made on the related bonds). For that reason, it is unlikely that a foreign investor would purchase an equity interest in such a trust unless the investor is certain that all interest received by the trust will be exempt from withholding tax, either as portfolio inter-est or under a tax treaty.[42]

---

footnote 85, state that withholding upon the disposition of residual interests is to be similar to withholding upon the disposition of instruments having OID. See footnote 27, above. Curiously, section 860G(b) applies by its terms only to holders of residual interests that are nonresident alien individuals or foreign corporations (and thus, for example, would not literally apply to a holder that is a foreign partnership). Compare section 1441.

37   Section 860G(b), last sentence, states that regulations may accelerate the time when income is taken into account "where necessary or appropriate to prevent the avoidance of tax imposed by this chapter." The Conference Report at II-235 - II-236 and the Blue Book at 423 indicate that this test may be met where a residual interest does not have significant value, and that a residual interest will be considered to have significant value if the value of the residual interest is at least 2% of the combined value of all interests in the REMIC. For further discussion of the significant value test, see Chapter 7, Part E.4.c.

38   See Treasury Regulation § 1.860G-3(a), discussed in Chapter 7, Part E.4.f.

39   See footnote 46, below.

40   See Chapter 2, Part G.2.c.

41   See Treasury Regulation § 1.1443-3(f). See also Revenue Ruling 89-33, 1989-1 C.B. 269 (under Treasury Regulation § 1.1441-3(f), domestic partnerships are required to withhold tax on a foreign partner's distributive share of the partnership's FDAP income that is not effectively connected with a U.S. trade or business, whether or not distributed, although the tax is not withheld a second time upon distribution); Revenue Ruling 70-251, 1970-1 C.B. 183 (amounts credited to an account of a foreign subsidiary but not actually paid are subject to withholding); T.A.M. 9252004 (September 17, 1992) (same).

42   Even if the investor is entitled to such an exemption, there would still be a withholding obligation if the investor failed to supply the withholding agent with any necessary certifications. See foot-notes 25 and 49. If tax is required to be withheld from gross income allocable to a foreign investor's equity interest, distributions to that investor might not be sufficient to pay the tax.

The discussion above assumes that interest income is not effectively connected with a U.S. trade or business engaged in by the investor. Effectively connected income is not subject to the 30 percent withholding tax. Instead such income, net of deductions for expenses and other items, is subject to tax at the regular rates applicable to U.S. taxpayers.[43] A foreign investor owning equity in a partnership (including an owner trust classified as a partnership) that is engaged in a U.S. trade or business must treat its share of the partnership's business income as effectively connected income.[44] Moreover, the partnership would be required to pay estimated taxes on the investor's behalf.[45]

It is unlikely that a typical partnership or owner trust that holds a fixed portfolio consisting largely of performing loans and borrows funds would be considered to be engaged in a trade or business.[46] The risk of finding business activity would be greater for an entity formed to work out financially distressed mortgage loans, particularly if it acquires and manages a number of properties securing the loans.[47]

Because any shortfall might be collected from distributions to other equity owners, they would have a substantial interest in ensuring that there are adequate safeguards to prevent the tax from being withheld.

43   See sections 871(b) and 882.

44   See section 875. Further, a U.S. permanent establishment of the partnership would be attributed to a foreign equity holder for purposes of any income tax treaty between the United States and the holder's country of residence. See *Unger v. Comm'r*, 58 T.C.M. (CCH) 1157 (1990), *aff'd*, 936 F.2d 1316 (D.C. Cir. 1991).

45   Section 1446. Revenue Procedure 89-31, 1989-1 C.B. 895, as modified by Revenue Procedure 92-66, 1992-2 C.B. 428, provides detailed rules for applying section 1446.

46   See *Higgins v Comm'r*, 312 U.S. 212 (1941) (management of investments not a trade or business), recently reaffirmed in *Comm'r v. Groetzinger*, 480 U.S. 23 (1987); *Continental Trading, Inc. v. Comm'r*, 265 F.2d 40 (9th Cir. 1959), *cert. denied*, 361 U.S. 827 (1959) (foreign corporation that borrowed in connection with U.S. stocks and securities was not engaged in a U.S. trade or business). Consider also the possible application of section 864(b)(2) (statutory exception from the definition of a U.S. trade or business for certain securities trading activities). But see Revenue Ruling 73-227, 1973-1 C.B. 338 (borrowing and lending to affiliates assumed to be a trade or business), revoked by Revenue Ruling 88-3, 1988-1 C.B. 268, on the ground that it does not adequately discuss how the trade or business test in section 864(b) applies to the facts of the ruling. In the context of applying the tax on UBTI to tax-exempt organizations, G.C.M. 37513 (April 25, 1978) takes the position that *Higgins* applies only to individuals, but it is not clear that this view would be followed even by the Internal Revenue Service outside of the tax-exempt area. *Higgins* was applied to a corporation in the *Continental Trading* case referred to above. If an owner trust is considered not to have a "business objective" for purposes of determining its tax classification (see Chapter 3, Part C.1), it almost certainly would not be considered to engage in a trade or business. On the other hand, the presence of a business objective does not imply the existence of a trade or business. See *Howell v. Comm'r*, 57 T.C. 546 (1972), *acq.*, 1974-2 C.B. 3 (a corporation which by definition has a business objective need not be engaged in any trade or business); Revenue Ruling 75-188, 1975-1 C.B. 276 (same); Revenue Ruling 75-523, 1975-2 C.B. 257 (investment "partnership" is not engaged in a trade or business). For a discussion of the significance of borrowing in evaluating whether an activity amounts to a business, see Chapter 3, Part C.1.c.(x).

47   Compare the discussion in Chapter 3, Part C.1.b, of the classification of a trust engaging in such activities as a business trust. Even if the trust or partnership were not in fact engaged in a trade or business, gain from the disposition of real property it holds could be subject to tax as income effectively connected with a U.S. trade or business under FIRPTA. See sections 897 and 1445 and Part C of this chapter.

The treatment of non-U.S. holders of equity in a TMP is discussed in Chapter 8, Part C.

2. Portfolio Interest Exemption

Under sections 871(h) and 881(c), enacted by TRA 1984, interest on obligations issued after July 18, 1984 (the date of enactment of TRA 1984) is exempt from withholding tax if such interest qualifies as portfolio interest. With limited exceptions, most significantly for payments to related parties,[48] interest on an obligation (including OID) is portfolio interest if (1) the obligation is in bearer form, and was issued in compliance with the Eurobond exception to the TEFRA registration requirements described in Part A, or (2) the obligation is in registered form, and the beneficial owner provides the withholding agent with a statement, signed under penalties of perjury, giving the owner's name and address and certifying that the owner is not a United States person.[49] In the case of an obligation issued in "targeted registered" form, a more lenient certification procedure applies if the obligation is held through an appropriate foreign financial institution. In such a case, the financial institution need only certify that the beneficial owner of the obligation is not a United States person, without disclosing the beneficial owner's identity.[50]

The portfolio interest exemption applies in different ways to pass-through certificates, pay-through bonds and REMIC regular interests, equity interests in owner trusts, and REMIC residual interests.

Prior to the issuance in 1985 of regulations applying the TEFRA registration requirements to pass-through certificates,[51] it was unclear whether interest paid to non-U.S. investors on residential mortgage pass-through certificates could qualify as portfolio interest. Home mortgages are typically held in bearer form.[52] Interest on

---

48   Portfolio interest does not include (1) any interest paid by a corporation to a 10% shareholder (measured by voting power) or by a partnership to a 10% partner (measured by the higher of the capital or profits interest), or interest paid to a controlled foreign corporation related to the payor, or (2) except in the case of interest paid on an obligation of the United States, interest paid to a bank on an extension of credit pursuant to a loan agreement entered into in the ordinary course of its trade or business. See sections 871(h)(3) and 881(c)(3). For the application of the exception for 10% owners to pass-through certificates and to pay-through bonds and REMIC regular interests, see footnotes 53 and 55, respectively.

49   Such statements are typically made on IRS Form W-8 but use of a substitute form is permitted. See Treasury Regulation § 35a.9999-5(b), Q&A-9.

50   The more lenient certification requirements are described in Treasury Regulation § 35a.9999-5(b), Q&A-14. Foreign financial institutions that are eligible to provide the more limited certifications include banks and other financial institutions that hold customers' securities in the ordinary course of their trade or business. The reduced certification requirements apply for any period during which an obligation originally issued in targeted registered form is held by a qualifying foreign financial institution, whether or not the obligation has been held continuously since issuance by such an institution.

51   See text accompanying footnote 16, above.

52   See text accompanying footnote 7, above. Moreover, Treasury Regulation § 35a.9999-5(b), Q&A-8, adopted by T.D. 7967, 1984-2 C.B. 329, took the position that interest on an obligation in registered form could not qualify as portfolio interest unless the obligation was a registration-required obligation. This position was abandoned in an amended version of Q&A-8 adopted by T.D.

a bearer obligation can qualify as portfolio interest only if the obligation was issued under the Eurobond exception, which would not be true for such mortgages. Thus, interest on residential mortgages, and apparently therefore interest on pass-through certificates representing ownership interests in those mortgages, could not be portfolio interest.

The 1985 regulations solved this problem by treating pass-through certificates as separate obligations of the issuing trust for purposes of the TEFRA rules. Under the regulations, interest on a pass-through certificate can qualify as portfolio interest if (1) the certificate itself is in bearer form and was issued under the Eurobond exception, or (2) the certificate is in registered form and the appropriate investor certification is received, in each case without regard to the status of the underlying obligations.[53] However, a pass-through certificate continues to be treated as an ownership interest in trust assets for other tax purposes, including application of the effective date of the portfolio interest rules. Accordingly, interest on a pass-through certificate can be exempt from withholding tax as portfolio interest only to the extent that the mortgages backing the certificate were originated after July 18, 1984.[54]

Pay-through bonds and REMIC regular interests are considered debt instruments in their own right and thus can qualify for the portfolio interest exemption (assuming, in the case of pay-through bonds, an issue date after July 18, 1984) regardless of the date of origination of the underlying mortgages or mortgage-backed securities.[55]

8111, 1987-1 C.B. 69.

53   Treasury Regulation §§ 35a.9999-5(e), Q&A-21, and 1.163-5T(d)(1). Because neither the issuing trust nor the obligors on the underlying residential mortgages would be corporations or partnerships, the exception to the portfolio interest exemption for 10% owners (see footnote 48) would not pose a problem.

54   Treasury Regulation § 35a.9999-5(e), Q&A-21, Q&A-22. Although Q&A-22 can be read to require interest on a pass-through certificate always to be traced to each of the underlying mortgage loans to determine the percentage of the interest that is portfolio interest, hopefully, the Service will permit simplifying assumptions to be made (such as an assumption that the portion by principal amount of all mortgages backing a certificate that were originated after July 18, 1984 does not change after the issuance of the certificates).

55   For the treatment of REMIC regular interests, see section 860B(a); Treasury Regulation § 35a.9999-5(e), Q&A-21(ii); Conference Report at II-237 – II-238; Blue Book at 425. As described in footnote 48, above, the portfolio interest exemption does not apply to interest paid by a corporation or partnership to a 10% owner. Thus, the exemption would not apply to interest on a pay-through bond issued by a corporation or by an owner trust classified as a partnership if the payee is a 10% owner of the issuer. Further, if an owner trust is classified as a grantor trust, the exemption may not apply to interest paid by the trust that is allocable (as an expense) to any corporate or partnership beneficiary of the trust if the payee is a 10% owner of the beneficiary. It is not clear how the 10% owner limitation would be applied to a REMIC regular interest. Because a REMIC is not treated as a corporation or partnership for tax purposes (section 860A(a)), the limitation should not be based on ownership of a 10% or greater interest in the REMIC. If the rule is applicable at all, it would seem to make sense to apply it based on the relationship between the holder of the regular interest, on the one hand, and the obligors on the loans held by the REMIC, or possibly the holders of residual interests, on the other hand.

In the case of an owner trust which is taxed as a partnership or trust, interest earned by the trust that is allocable to an equity interest held by a foreign investor should be eligible for the portfolio interest exemption to the same extent as if such interest were received directly by the foreign investor.[56] Thus, assuming that the investor provides appropriate certifications to the owner trustee or possibly other withholding agents, such interest should be tax free to the extent it is earned on mortgages or other obligations issued after July 18, 1984 (with the possible exception of interest on certain short-term obligations in bearer form).[57] A similar look-through approach applies to REMIC residual interests.[58] However, income that is an excess inclusion can never benefit from the portfolio interest exemption.[59]

---

56   The portfolio interest exemption applies under sections 871(h) and 881(c) only to interest "received" by a foreign investor, and perhaps it could be argued that the exemption does not apply to interest paid to an owner trust in which an equity interest is owned by a foreign investor on the ground that the interest is not "received" by the investor. However, if the owner trust is classified as a grantor trust, payments received by the trust clearly would be considered to be received by its equity owners. If the trust is classified as a partnership, the argument would still fail. Sections 871(a) and 881(a), which impose the 30% tax, also apply to interest "received" by a foreign investor; thus, the portfolio interest exemption is coterminous with the tax. See Treasury Regulation § 1.1441-3(f) discussed in footnote 41, above, which treats income paid to a U.S. partnership or trust as received by the partner or beneficiaries for withholding tax purposes even if such income is not actually distributed. See also Revenue Ruling 81-244, 1981-2 C.B. 151, *amplified,* Revenue Ruling 86-76, 1986-1 C.B. 284 (interest on bank deposits held by a trust is received by trust beneficiaries for purposes of applying the withholding tax exemption for bank deposits; the conduit theory of taxation of trusts referred to in the ruling applies equally to partnerships).

57   Typically, the mortgage-backed securities owned by an owner trust and the equity interests in the trust are held in registered form. Thus, in determining whether interest earned on those securities is portfolio interest, problems raised by the existence of bearer obligations do not arise. However, an owner trust may also earn interest on short-term obligations that is not portfolio interest because the obligations are held in bearer form and were not issued under the Eurobond exception. (As indicated in the text following footnote 6, short-term obligations are not registration-required. Although the bearer or registered status of the obligations held by an owner trust would be irrelevant if the trust were classified as a grantor trust and the equity interests in the trust were treated as pass-through certificates within the meaning of the 1985 TEFRA regulations (see the text accompanying footnote 16), neither result can be assumed.) Interest on short-term obligations may be exempt from withholding tax on other grounds. For example, there is an exemption for original issue discount on obligations with an original maturity of 183 days or less (section 871(g)(1)(B)(i)) and for interest on bank deposits (sections 871(i)(2)(A) and 881(d)).

58   Treasury Regulation § 35a.9999-5(e), Q&A-21. See also Conference Report at II-237-II-238; Blue Book at 425. Under the look-through approach, interest earned on a residual interest in a REMIC that holds whole mortgages in bearer form would not appear to qualify for the portfolio interest exemption, for the reasons explained above in the text accompanying footnote 52. There is no rule comparable to the one applicable to pass-through certificates and REMIC regular interests (see footnotes 53 and 55, above) that treats interest earned with respect to a REMIC residual interest as interest on a registered obligation because the residual interest is itself in registered form. This gap in the TEFRA rules appears to be an oversight. In many cases, mortgages held by a REMIC that would not otherwise qualify for the portfolio interest exemption (because they are in bearer form or were originated on or before July 18, 1984) can be transformed into qualifying assets through the use of a two-tier REMIC structure. The non-U.S. investors would hold residual interests in the upper-tier REMIC. The qualified mortgages held by the upper-tier REMIC would be regular interests in the lower-tier REMIC, which would be in registered form and issued after July 18, 1984. Two-tier REMICs are discussed in detail in Chapter 4, Part C.7.a.

59   See section 860G(b)(2). Excess inclusions are discussed in Chapter 7, Part E.4.

Recent amendments to the Code exclude from the definition of portfolio interest any interest that, with certain exceptions, is contingent on the profits or cash flow of the debtor (including related parties), the value of its property, or distributions on its equity.[60] Thus, such interest will generally be subject to the 30 percent withholding tax unless a treaty exemption or reduction applies.[61]

This change in law is unlikely to have much significance for mortgage-backed securities. Interest on pay-through bonds and REMIC regular interests might be thought to be contingent in that it is generally payable only out of (and to the extent of) the issuer's cash flow or interest income. Also, any such instrument that is issued at a discount or premium would have a value that depends significantly on the timing of prepayments on the underlying mortgages. Nonetheless, the legislation was not aimed at securities that merely carve up cash flows on mortgages that do not themselves pay contingent interest. The statutory exceptions to the definition of contingent interest cover the features of typical mortgage-backed securities that are likely to raise questions.[62]

Section 2105(b)(3) effectively exempts debt obligations from the U.S. estate tax applicable to nonresident alien individuals if interest thereon would be eligible for the portfolio interest exemption if received by the decedent at the time of his death (without regard to any certification requirement).[63] This exemption should

---

60 Sections 871(h)(4) and 881(c)(4), as added by RRA 1993. The amendments apply to interest received on or after January 1, 1994, with an exception for interest on fixed term debt issued on or before (or under a binding contract in existence on or before) April 7, 1993. The new rules do not apply to interest on a debt solely on account of (1) a contingency as to the timing of any interest or principal payment, (2) the debt being nonrecourse or limited recourse, (3) the interest being determined by reference to interest that itself is not contingent (or by reference to the principal amount of debt that does not bear contingent interest), (4) the debtor entering into a hedging transaction to reduce interest rate or currency risk, or (5) the interest being determined with reference to (a) changes in the value of publicly traded property, including stock, but not including U.S. real property interests, (b) changes in the yield of such property (other than contingent interest debt, or stock or other property that represents a beneficial interest in the debtor), or (c) changes in an index of such value or yield. In the case of a debt instrument that pays both contingent and noncontingent interest, only the contingent interest fails to qualify as portfolio interest. H.R. Rep. No 111, 103d Cong., 1st Sess. (RRA 1993 House Report) at 288. If a debt instrument provides for a minimum rate of noncontingent interest, the minimum interest is treated as noncontingent, notwithstanding any overlap with interest computed under a contingent interest formula. H.R. Rep. No. 312, 103d Cong., 1st Sess., 183-184 (RRA 1993 Conference Report).

61 The legislation would not override treaties. See RRA 1993 House Report at 286, 290. Contingent interest that is not treated as interest under general U.S. tax principles would, of course, generally not be considered to be interest for treaty purposes.

62 See footnote 60, above. The RRA 1993 House Report at 288-289 states that the new rules will not apply to REMIC regular interests merely because, for example, (1) the period they remain outstanding is contingent on mortgage prepayments, earnings on REMIC assets, or expenses, (2) interest equals a percentage of noncontingent interest on qualified mortgages, or (3) interest varies inversely with interest on qualified mortgages.

63 In the case of the estate of a decedent dying on or after January 1, 1994, the estate tax exemption will not apply to the extent interest would fail to be portfolio interest because it is contingent under the rules described above in the text at footnote 60 and accompanying text. Section 2105(b)(3) provides that in the case of a debt instrument that pays both contingent and noncontingent interest "an appropriate portion," determined under regulations, of the value of the debt instrument will be subject to the estate tax. RRA 1993 Conference Report, at 184 states that, until such regulations

apply to any mortgage-backed security to the extent income thereon is portfolio interest, although admittedly the question is a much closer one for equity interests in owner trusts that are classified as partnerships and REMIC residual interests than for pay-through bonds, REMIC regular interests,[64] or interests in grantor trusts.

3. Income from Swaps and Rents

Two other categories of FDAP income that may be realized by holders of mortgage-backed securities are income from swaps and income from the rental of real property. These types of income are discussed in the next two sections.

a. Swaps. Recently, securities have been issued that represent ownership interests in a trust holding both (1) a REMIC regular interest or pass-through certificate and (2) a notional principal contract, such as an interest rate swap, cap or floor agreement. (For further discussion of these securities, see Chapter 3, Part C.1.c.(xi) and Chapter 4, Part C.7.c.) The trust may be classified for tax purposes as a grantor trust or partnership. The withholding tax treatment of regular interests and pass-through certificates is discussed above and would not change because the securities are held through a trust.

The income from payments received on the notional principal contract would generally be FDAP income. Thus, the income would be subject to U.S. withholding tax unless the tax is eliminated or reduced under a tax treaty, or the source of the income is outside of the U.S. (The portfolio interest exemption would not apply, because swap income is not interest.) In fact, the withholding tax rarely applies to income from a notional principal contract, because such income is sourced based on the residence of the taxpayer receiving the payments, not the residence of the payor.[65] A non-U.S. investor that owns an interest in a notional principal contract through a grantor trust would clearly benefit from this source rule. The trust would be ignored. On the other hand, if the owning trust is classified as a partnership, and is organized under U.S. law, the taxpayer receiving the payments would arguably be the domestic partnership, raising the specter of a withholding tax where a treaty exemption does not apply.[66]

---

are promulgated, a taxpayer may use any reasonable method to determine the appropriate portion.

64   Although the rule treating regular interests as debt instruments for purposes of taxing holders (see Treasury Regulation § 1.860G-1(b)(6)) applies by its terms only for purposes of the income tax, it should be relevant in applying section 2105(b)(3) because the estate tax exemption under that section depends on how income from a security is taxed.

65   Treasury Regulation § 1.863-7. Under this regulation, income properly reflected on the books of a qualified business unit is sometimes sourced based on the residence of the unit. Also, income arising from a U.S. trade or business is sourced in the United States.

66   The tax classification of trusts entering into notional principal contracts is discussed in Chapter 3, Part C.1.c.(xi). Under Treasury Regulation § 1.863-7(b)(1), the source of income from a notional principal contract is determined with reference to the residence of "the taxpayer" determined under section 988(a)(3)(B)(i). Under section 988(a)(3)(B)(i), the residence of a partnership which is a U.S. person is the United States. A partnership is a U.S. person if it is a domestic partnership, which is one organized under U.S. law. See sections 7701(a)(4) and (30). Section 988(a)(3)(B)(iii),

b. Rental Income. Rental income from real property located in the U.S. is considered U.S. source FDAP income.[67] There is no withholding tax exemption for such income comparable to the one for portfolio interest. Thus, where a non-U.S. investor holds pass-through certificates, or equity interests in owner trusts that are taxed as a trust or partnership, and the issuer acquires U.S. real property in connection with a default or anticipated default on a mortgage, the withholding tax generally would apply to the investor's share of any rents received on the property.[68] Interesting allocation issues arise where pass-through certificates are divided into junior and senior classes.[69] On the other hand, income earned on an instrument that is taxed as debt of the issuer, such as a pay-through bond or REMIC regular interest, continues to be interest even if it is derived from rental income. Although uncertain, it appears that all income on a REMIC residual interest would be treated as interest income for withholding tax purposes regardless of the REMIC's sources of income.[70]

---

level in the case of partners in a partnership "that are not engaged in a U.S. trade or business by reason of section 864(b)(2)." Subject to various conditions, this section permits non-U.S. persons to trade in securities or commodities in the U.S. without being considered to engage in a trade or business. An investor in a trust holding a notional principal contract and some other type of mortgage-backed security would ordinarily not rely on the trading exemption to establish that it is not engaged in a U.S. trade or business but would instead base the conclusion on the passivity of the trust. It would be very odd, however, to look through a partnership to the partners where the partnership is an active trading vehicle and not look through where it is passive.

67   The source rule is in section 861(a)(4). An election can be made to treat income from real property as income effectively connected with a U.S. trade or business. If such an election is made, the withholding tax would not apply, and tax would be imposed on taxable income from the property (which is net of deductions for depreciation and other expenses). See sections 871(d) and 882(d).

68   There generally is no reduction in the withholding tax on rental income under U.S. tax treaties. As discussed in Part C below, a tax also may apply under FIRPTA to a non-U.S. investor's share of any gain from a disposition of the real property. A mortgagee is not generally treated for tax purposes as owning real property merely because it is operating the property. Cf. Treasury Regulation §§ 1.856-6(b) (a REIT will not be considered to acquire foreclosure property until it acquires ownership for federal income tax purposes and will not be considered to have acquired such ownership when it acts as mortgagee-in-possession where it "cannot receive any profit or sustain any loss except as a creditor of the mortgagor") and 1.897-1(d)(2)(ii)(C) (a creditor acting as mortgagee-in-possession is not for that reason alone treated as holding a noncreditor interest in U.S. real property).

69   As discussed in Chapter 2, Part B.3, senior and subordinated certificates can be viewed, alternatively, as classes with different allocations of trust income based on what they actually receive, or as classes entitled to pro rata shares of trust income, coupled with a guarantee written by the junior class holders in favor of the senior class. Under a direct allocation approach, it would seem that rental income should be allocated to the junior class at least to the extent that, because of the subordination features, variations in the rent affect only the junior class. The same conclusion could be reached under the guarantee approach by viewing the junior class holders as acquiring the senior class holders' interest in the real estate in exchange for payments under the guarantee.

70   See footnote 33, above. It is not clear, however, how the portfolio interest exemption would be applied to "interest" paid out of rental income since that exemption is generally applied by treating interest on a residual interest as being paid on the obligations held by the REMIC. See footnote 58, above.

C. FIRPTA

FIRPTA enacted section 897, which subjects non-U.S. investors to U.S. tax on gain from sales of certain U.S. real property interests (including equity interests in "United States real property holding corporations") in the same manner as if such gain were effectively connected with a U.S. trade or business. Section 1445 imposes a related requirement to withhold tax from the proceeds of sales. The FIRPTA rules do not apply to interests in real property that are solely creditor interests with no participation in the income, revenues, or appreciation of the property.[71] Thus, a foreign investor holding a mortgage-backed security will not be affected by this legislation if the mortgages underlying the security lack such participation features and the issuer does not acquire the underlying real property.

Where a non-U.S. investor holds a pass-through certificate, or an equity interest in an owner trust that is taxed as a grantor trust or partnership, and the issuer acquires a real property interest in connection with a mortgage default, the investor will generally be treated for purposes of FIRPTA as owning a noncreditor interest in such property.[72] Any gain attributable to such property that is allocable to the investor will potentially be taxed under FIRPTA either when the owning entity disposes of the real property, or when the investor disposes of its interest in the entity. A creditor acquiring real property collateral generally would have a basis in the acquired real property equal to its fair market value at the time of acquisition, so that any gain would be limited to increases in the property's value during the period it is held by the entity.[73]

If any class of interests in the entity are regularly traded on an established securities market (including certain over-the-counter markets), then gain from disposition of interests in the entity (whether or not of the traded class) generally would not be subject to tax.[74] This rule does not affect the taxation of gain realized

---

71   Treasury Regulation § 1.897-1(d). A security interest in real property (and ancillary rights, including rights as a mortagee in possession) is considered a creditor interest in real property. See Treasury Regulation § 1.897-1(d)(2)(ii)(C).

72   See Treasury Regulation §§ 1.897-1(c)(1) (U.S. real property interest includes any interest other than solely as a creditor in U.S. real property) and 1.897-1(d)(3) (noncreditor interests include a partnership interest and beneficial interest in a trust).

73   See Treasury Regulation § 1.166-6(c) (basis of acquired property is fair market value when acquired). This rule is tempered somewhat by Treasury Regulation § 1.166-6(b)(2) (fair market value of property acquired by creditor presumed to be bid price in absence of clear and convincing proof to the contrary).

74   Treasury Regulation § 1.897-1(c)(2)(iv). This regulation states that if any class of interests in a partnership or trust is regularly traded on an established securities market ("regularly traded"), then interests in the entity are taxed as if the partnership or trust were a corporation. As a result, gain on disposition of interests in the entity by an investor would be taxed only if (1) the entity cannot establish that at all times during a five year period the U.S. real property it owned was less than 50% of its holdings of real property and other trade or business assets (this parallels the definition of United States real property holding corporation), *and* (2) the investor owned interests exceeding a 5% threshhold (see Treasury Regulation §§ 1.897-1(c)(2)(iii)(A) and 1.897-9T(b)). The rule counting personal property only if it is a trade or business asset is intended to prevent the "stuffing" of an operating company with passive assets. A trust or partnership issuing mortgage-backed securities that is not engaged in any trade or business nonetheless should be able to treat

upon a disposition of real property by the entity. The definition of "regularly traded on an established securities market" is highly technical. For example, under current regulations, a class of interests is not "regularly traded" if 100 or fewer persons own 50 percent or more of the class, or if the market is outside the U.S. and the interests are not in registered form.[75]

The section 1445 withholding tax does not currently apply to dispositions of interests in partnerships or trusts, unless, among other requirements, at least 50 percent of the gross assets of the entity consist of U.S. real property interests.[76] A domestic trust or partnership that disposes of interests in real property is, however, required to withhold tax on a non-U.S. investor's share of any gain.[77]

A REMIC regular interest should be treated as a creditor interest that is not subject to the FIRPTA tax without regard to any holdings of real property by the issuing REMIC.[78]

---

mortgages as "trade or business assets" for purposes of the 50% assets test, with the result that the test rarely would be met by a trust holding a pool of mortgages because of real property acquired in connection with defaults. See Treasury Regulation § 1.897-1(f)(3)(ii).

75   See Treasury Regulation §§ 1.897-1(m) and 1.897-9T(d).

76   See section 1445(e)(5); Treasury Regulation § 1445-11T(d) (withholding applies where 50% or more of the value of gross assets of a partnership or trust consist of U.S. real property interests, and 90% or more of the value of its gross assets consist of U.S. real property interests plus any cash or cash equivalents).

77   Section 1445(e)(1); Treasury Regulation § 1.1445-5(c).

78   To the extent the issuing REMIC holds real property, the regular interests would represent a creditor interest in the REMIC that is secured by the real property (in substitution for the defaulted mortgage). See section 860B(a) (regular interests treated as debt for purposes of determining taxation of holder). The tax treatment of residual interests is less clear. At any rate, the special FIRPTA rules for trusts or partnerships would not apply (see section 860A(a)).

Chapter 11

Legending and Information Reporting

The Code requires issuers of mortgage-backed securities and certain payors of interest on those securities to provide tax information to investors and the Service. This information is disseminated by attaching tax legends to physical securities, and, more importantly, sending or filing tax returns or reports and responding to specific requests for information. Some of the reporting obligations apply to debt instruments generally; others have been tailored to fit the unusual characteristics of mortgage-backed securities.

Information reporting is intended both to prevent tax evasion and to assist investors in determining their tax liability. The second of these objectives is particularly important for mortgage-backed securities. Computing the income on those securities is complex by any standard, and, perhaps more to the point, may require detailed information regarding future payments on the underlying mortgages and their allocation among different classes of securities that is available in the first instance only to issuers. Further, because income on residual interests is based on the taxable income of the issuing REMIC, tax reporting by REMICs to residual interest holders is unavoidable.

The discussion of legending and information reporting in this chapter is divided into six parts. Part A describes the legending and information reporting obligations that must be satisfied by REMICs and issuers of pay-through bonds at the time the instruments are issued. Ongoing reporting for pay-through bonds and REMIC regular interests, pass-through certificates, and equity interests in owner trusts is the subject of Part B. Part C describes REMIC tax returns, which serve primarily as a mechanism for reporting income allocable to holders of residual interests. Although information reporting is generally the same for pay-through bonds and REMIC regular interests, certain additional reporting obligations, also covered in Part C, apply to regular interests. Information reporting relies on taxpayer identification numbers. If a payment is subject to information reporting, and the payee fails to supply his identification number (or certain other conditions are met), then the payor may be required to withhold tax to "back up" the reporting system. A brief description of backup withholding may be found in Part D. Part E comments on reporting to issuers of certain securities by nominee owners of the identities of beneficial owners. The reporting of beneficial ownership by nominees may be required for equity interests in owner trusts, pass-through certificates, or REMIC residual interests. Finally, Part F describes briefly three other information reporting schemes that do not relate directly to mortgage-backed securities but are still of concern to participants in the mortgage markets. Except where otherwise indicated, references in this chapter to debt instruments include REMIC regular interests.

A. Legending and Information Reporting at Time of Issuance by REMICs and Issuers of Pay-Through Bonds

1. Overview

Accruals of OID on a debt instrument cannot be calculated without knowing at a minimum the instrument's issue price and issue date. To make these items and certain other related information more readily available, TRA 1984 authorized the Service to adopt regulations requiring that (1) an OID legend be set forth on the face of any debt instrument having such discount (section 1275(c)(1)) and (2) the issuer of any such instrument that is publicly offered report information relating to the instrument to the Service (section 1275(c)(2)). At present, regulations under section 1275(c)(1) require OID legends only for securities in physical (i.e., not book entry) form that are not publicly offered.[1] Regulations under section 1275(c)(2) require issuers of publicly offered debt instruments to file OID information returns (on Form 8281).[2] Some of the information compiled from these forms is made available to the public in IRS Publication 1212.[3]

None of the regulations just mentioned applies to mortgage-backed securities (REMIC regular interests, pay-through bonds, or pass-through certificates),[4] but this

---

[1]   See Treasury Regulation § 1.1275-3(b). Where a legend is required for a debt instrument it must state that the instrument was issued with OID, and also give *either* (1) the issue price, amount of OID, issue date, and yield to maturity, or (2) the name and either the address or telephone number of a representative of the issuer who, beginning no later than 10 days after the issue date, will make such information available upon request. Following section 1275(c)(1)(B), the legend need not be attached before the instrument is disposed of by the first holder.

[2]   Treasury Regulation § 1.1275-3(c) Under this regulation, a Form 8281 must be filed with the Service within 30 days after the issue date. The form calls for a detailed description of the issue, including the issue price, the amount of OID, the issue date, the maturity date, and the yield to maturity.

[3]   Payors of interest on an obligation (other than issuers) may rely on Publication 1212 to determine whether a publicly traded debt instrument has OID and the amount thereof in complying with their obligations to report interest payments under section 6049 (described in Part B.1). See Treasury Regulation §§ 1.6049-4(d)(2) and -5(c).

[4]   The exceptions for regular interests and pay-through bonds are in Treasury Regulation §§ 1.1275-3(b)(4) and -3(c)(3). Trusts issuing pass-through certificates, and sponsors of those trusts, are not subject to the legending or issuer reporting requirement because they are not "issuers" of new debt instruments. Although such certificates may in some cases be stripped bonds or coupons subject to section 1286 that are considered, for substantive tax purposes, to be reissued each time they change hands (see Chapter 6, Part D.1), the legending and information reporting requirements do not at present apply to stripped bonds or coupons. Id. Section 1275(c)(2) states that any person who makes a public offering of stripped bonds or coupons will be treated, for purposes of the

is not cause for rejoicing. The exclusion of REMIC regular interests and pay-through bonds exists because they are subject to a separate legending and information reporting regime that is more onerous and applies to them alone.[5] These rules are described in the next two sections.

2. OID Legends

Under regulations,[6] the issuer of a REMIC regular interest or pay-through bond with OID must set forth the following information relating to the instrument on its face: (1) the aggregate amount of OID; (2) the issue date;[7] (3) the initial interest rate;[8] (4) the Prepayment Assumption used in accruing OID under the PAC method; (5) the yield to maturity;[9] and (6) if the instrument has a "short accrual period" (generally a short period until the first interest payment date), the method used to determine the yield to maturity and the amount of OID allocable to that short period.[10] A sample form of OID legend may be found in Appendix E.

If any portion of the stated interest on a pay-through bond or regular interest is includable in its stated redemption price at maturity, the aggregate amount of OID on the instrument, and the portion thereof allocable to any short accrual period, will depend on (1) the assumed rate of principal prepayments, and (2) in the case of an instrument that pays interest at a rate based on an interest rate index, the assumed

---

issuer information reporting requirement, as an "issuer" of publicly offered debt instruments having OID. Treasury Regulation § 1.1275-3(c)(3) states, however, that the filing of Form 8281 is not required for stripped bonds and coupons unless the Service otherwise provides in a revenue ruling or revenue procedure. No ruling or procedure imposing the requirement has been issued.

5   See Treasury Regulation § 1.6049-7. This regulation was adopted by T.D. 8366, 1991-2 C.B. 18, which cites sections 860G(e) and 6049(d)(7)(D) (and not section 1275(c)) as specific authority for the regulation. The regulation uses the term "collateralized debt obligation" to refer to a pay-through bond but, to avoid confusion, the latter term will be used in this chapter. Treasury Regulation § 1.6049-7(d)(2) defines a collateralized debt obligation as any debt instrument (other than a tax-exempt obligation) "described" in section 1272(a)(6)(C)(ii) (i.e., any debt instrument, other than a REMIC regular interest, if payments thereunder may be accelerated by reason of prepayments of other obligations securing such debt instrument (or, to the extent provided in regulations, by reason of other events)). Although this definition is used in determining whether OID is accounted for under the PAC method (see Chapter 6, footnote 32), apparently an obligation need not have OID in order to be a collateralized debt obligation under the regulation.

6   See Treasury Regulation § 1.6049-7(g).

7   The issue date of a debt instrument issued for cash is the first settlement date or closing date on which a substantial amount of the debt instruments in the issue is sold, disregarding sales to underwriters, placement agents, or wholesalers. See Treasury Regulation §§ 1.1273-2(a)(2) and (e). This definition is discussed in Chapter 6, footnote 27.

8   Treasury Regulation § 1.6049-7(g)(1)(iii) describes this rate as the "rate at which interest is payable (if any) as of the issue date." Apparently, the legend must include the initial interest rate even if interest is always payable at the same fixed rate.

9   Under Treasury Regulation § 1.1272-1(b)(1)(i), the yield to maturity of a debt instrument, when expressed as a percentage, must be calculated to at least two decimal places. For a general discussion of the yield to maturity, see Chapter 6, Part C.2.

10   The methods for calculating the yield to maturity in the case of a debt instrument that has a short accrual period are discussed in Chapter 6, footnote 41.

value of the index. It would make sense to calculate these amounts for legending purposes using the same assumptions that will be used in figuring accruals of OID.[11]

The legend generally must be set forth on the face of an instrument on its issue date. However, if that is not possible, the issuer may instead deliver to the holder of the instrument a sticker containing the required information within 10 days of the issue date. All instruments issued thereafter (such as upon registration of an instrument in the name of a new owner) should include the legend or have the sticker attached.[12]

An issuer that fails to meet the legending requirement, and does not show that such failure is due to reasonable cause and not willful neglect, is subject, under section 6706(a), to a penalty of $50 for each debt instrument for which the failure exists.[13] Arguably, this penalty would apply separately to each physical debt instrument (so that, for example, a further penalty would apply if a new unlegended security was issued in connection with the registration of an instrument in the name of a transferee).

The legending requirement for REMIC regular interests and pay-through bonds is both superfluous and ineffective. The same information (and more) is made available through the ongoing information reporting system that applies to these securities (described in Part B.1). Also, information on physical securities (which, when they exist, are typically held by custodians) is not readily available to tax return preparers. Hopefully, in the fullness of time, the Service will reassess whether any legending is warranted for regular interests and pay-through bonds.

To avoid misunderstanding, many issuers of REMIC interests set forth on their face a legend stating that the security is a regular interest or a residual interest, as the case may be. There is no specific tax requirement that there be such legends. As discussed in Chapter 4, Part A.3, a residual interest may include a statement de-

---

11   For a discussion of the situations in which stated interest is included in a debt instrument's stated redemption price at maturity, see Chapter 6, Part C.1. Methods of accruing OID on variable rate debt instruments are discussed in Chapter 6, Part C.4.

12   The regulations do not say how the legending requirement can be satisfied in the case of securities issued only in book-entry form, although presumably it would suffice, if legending is required, to deliver one physical certificate with the legend attached to the party maintaining the book-entry system. The more limited legending requirement applicable to debt instruments generally applies only to instruments in physical form. See text accompanying footnote 1, above. The rule in section 1275(c)(1)(B) that allows an issuer to delay legending a privately placed debt instrument until the disposition of the instrument by the first holder is not found in Treasury Regulation § 1.6049-7(g). Apparently, the Service believes that its authority to impose a legending requirement is broader under section 6049(d)(7)(D) than under section 1275(c)(1). See footnote 5, above.

13   Treasury Regulation § 1.6049-7(g)(1) includes a cross-reference to section 6706(a). Although section 6706(a) applies to legends required under section 1275(c)(1), which was not cited by the Service as the source of authority for the legending requirement for REMIC regular interests and pay-through bonds (see footnote 5, above), there is considerable overlap between the two legending rules. There is no rule treating a sponsor of a REMIC as the "issuer" for purposes of section 6706(a), so it appears that any penalties would be imposed on the REMIC itself. Compare the special rule treating sponsors of REMICs and pass-through certificates as issuers for purposes of the section 4701 excise tax (see Chapter 10, footnotes 4 and 18).

scribing restrictions on transfers to disqualified organizations to ensure compliance with the REMIC arrangements test.

3. Information Reporting at Time of Issuance

REMICs and issuers of pay-through bonds are required to file an information return on Form 8811 with the Service relating to the securities they issue within 30 days of the issue date (the startup day in the case of a REMIC).[14] The requirement applies to *all* securities (both privately placed and publicly offered, and with or without OID). The information called for by the form includes: the name, address, and employer identification number of the issuer; the name, title, address and (at the issuer's option) telephone number of a representative of the issuer who will provide tax information to certain investors and middlemen (as described in Part B.1); the issue date (startup day for a REMIC); and the CUSIP number or other identifying information for each class of securities. The form does not require any special information relating to the calculation of OID. The Service publishes a directory of REMICs and issuers of pay-through bonds based on the Form 8811 filings.[15] It is not clear what penalties, if any, apply to the failure to file Form 8811.[16]

B. Ongoing Information Reporting for REMIC Regular Interests and Pay-Through Bonds, Pass-Through Certificates and Equity Interests in Owner Trusts

1. REMIC Regular Interests and Pay-Through Bonds

The principal, ongoing reporting obligations for REMIC regular interests and pay-through bonds arise under section 6049. This section applies to debt instruments generally. With some exceptions, it requires any person who pays interest in a calendar year to file with the Service an information return identifying the payees and showing the amount of interest paid to each during the year. Information for each payee is reported on Form 1099, and a statement containing certain information from the form (or a copy) must be sent to the payee.[17] OID that is includable in

---

14   Treasury Regulation § 1.6049-7(b). A Form 8811 need not be filed by a lower-tier REMIC in a tiered REMIC structure (or more technically, by a REMIC all of whose regular interests are held by one other REMIC). There is no exception to the information reporting requirement for instruments targeted to non-U.S. investors. Filing a Form 8811 does *not* have the effect of making a REMIC election.

15   The directory is Publication 938, *Real Estate Mortgage Investment Conduit (REMIC) and Collateralized Debt Obligation Reporting Information.*

16   Section 6706(b) imposes a penalty for failing to file an issuer OID information return required under section 1275(c)(2), but the requirement to file Form 8811 is not based on section 1275(c)(2) (which is limited to public offerings of securities with OID). See footnote 5, above. While Treasury Regulation § 1.6049-7(g) (the legending requirement) contains a cross-reference to the penalty for failing to legend under section 6706(a) (see footnote 13, above), there is no comparable cross-reference to section 6706(b) in Treasury Regulation § 1.6049-7(b).

17   No reporting is required unless aggregate payments of interest to a payee in a calendar year exceed $10. Section 6049(a). The statement to the payee for any year must be mailed no later than January

income as it accrues under section 1272 is treated for this purpose as if it were paid as it accrues (determined as if all holders were original holders).[18] Certain additional information reporting is required under the OID regulations.[19]

In the case of conventional debt instruments, no information reporting is required for interest paid to corporations, securities dealers, governments, and certain other categories of institutional payees.[20] The practical effect of this exception is to confine information reporting primarily to payments to individuals, and to impose the reporting burden on the person in the chain of payment that makes a direct payment to an individual. For example, if a bond is held by a bank as a nominee for an individual, payments to the bank are not subject to information reporting, but payments by the bank to the individual are. This scheme makes sense if, as is generally the case for conventional debt instruments, investors can calculate income without information from the issuer and the principal function of the reporting system is to prevent tax evasion. (Two items of information that are needed from the issuer to calculate income on a conventional debt instrument if the instrument has OID are the issue date and issue price; however, as described in Part A.1, this information is made available to the public directly, through issuer reporting on Form 8281 and Publication 1212 in the case of publicly offered obligations, and OID legends in the case of privately placed instruments.)

In the case of REMIC regular interests and pay-through bonds, holders may be unable to calculate income—in particular accruals of discount and premium—without obtaining period-by-period information from the issuer regarding actual mortgage prepayments and their effect on future payments on different classes of securities. To address this problem, TRA 1986 amended section 6049 to provide that, in the case of REMIC regular interests and other debt instruments to which the PAC method applies, information reporting applies, except as otherwise provided in regulations, to payments made to all categories of payees, excepting only govern-

---

31 of the following year, and the information return must be filed with the Service no later than February 28 of the following year. See Treasury Regulation §§ 1.6049-4(g) and -6(c). Holders of debt instruments generally may choose different accrual periods in computing accruals of OID. See Chapter 6, footnote 38. The preamble to the OID regulations (see Chapter 6, footnote 13) indicates that until further guidance is issued, an issuer should use the same accrual periods for information reporting purposes as it uses in calculating its own OID deductions.

18   See section 6049(d)(6). Treasury Regulation § 1.6049-5(c). For calendar years prior to 1992, the amount of OID on a debt instrument reported for a holder for a calendar year could be calculated by treating each holder as holding the instrument on each day it was outstanding during the year. Treasury Regulation § 1.6049-4(b)(2).

19   Under the OID regulations, certain determinations made by the issuer of a debt instrument are binding on each holder unless it discloses the use of an inconsistent method on its tax returns. For two examples, see Chapter 6, footnote 40, and Chapter 7, footnote 8. Treasury Regulation § 1.1275-2(e) requires the issuer to provide to holders the information necessary to comply with these provisions in a reasonable manner (for example, by providing the name or title and either the address or telephone number of a representative who will make the information available to holders upon request).

20   See sections 6049(b)(2) and (b)(4); Treasury Regulation § 1.6049-4(c)(1)(ii) (definition of "exempt recipient").

ments and certain tax-exempt entities.[21] This amendment generally has the effect, in the absence of overriding regulations, of imposing a reporting obligation on the issuer (or its paying agent) and each other person in the chain of payment from the issuer to the ultimate holder.[22] Also, where the broader reporting system applies to a debt instrument, except as provided in regulations, Form 1099s must include, in addition to the information normally required, the adjusted issue price of the instrument at the beginning of each accrual period and information necessary to compute accruals of market discount.[23] Further, the Service has the authority to require more frequent or detailed reporting.[24]

An information reporting system based on the chain principle was in effect for reporting periods through the end of 1988.[25] It did not work properly in many cases because of the delays involved in passing information through many hands. Further, a requirement to prepare information returns for payments to corporations was unnecessary because the Service did not match information reported on Form 1099s with information reported on corporate returns.

To address these concerns, in 1989, regulations were adopted under section 6049(d)(7) that reinstated, for regular interests and pay-through bonds, the reporting exemptions for payments to institutional payees that apply to conventional obligations.[26] At the same time, to make tax information available to those who need it to fulfill their own reporting obligations, issuers were required to provide tax information on request to nominees or middlemen and certain categories of investors. This aspect of the information reporting system is discussed below.

Under the regulations, a Form 1099 prepared for a REMIC regular interest or pay-through bond must include the usual accruals of OID and, in the case of pay-through bonds, payments of interest.[27] Interest on a REMIC regular interest is al-

---

21 See section 6049(b)(4), as modified by section 6049(d)(7); Conference Report at II-237; Blue Book at 424-425.

22 Exemptions from information reporting also apply, under section 6049(b)(5), to payments to non-U.S. investors. Those exemptions continue to apply to REMIC regular interests and pay-through bonds.

23 See section 6049(d)(7)(C). Although this section does not refer to information necessary to compute premium amortization, it is mentioned in the Conference Report at II-237 and the Blue Book at 424-425.

24 See section 6049(d)(7)(D).

25 See Treasury Regulation §§ 1.6049-7T(a) through (f), adopted by T.D. 8186, 1988-1 C.B. 37, prior to amendment by T.D. 8259, 1989-2 C.B. 234.

26 Treasury Regulation §§ 1.6049-7T(a) through (g), adopted by T.D. 8259, 1989-2 C.B. 234. These temporary regulations were replaced with final regulations in 1991, which were further amended in 1992. See T.D. 8366, 1991-2 C.B. 18, and T.D. 8431, 1992-2 C.B. 39.

27 See Treasury Regulation §§ 1.6049-7(a)(1) and (b)(2)(iii). In calculating accruals of OID, the special rules in Treasury Regulation § 6049-5(c) do not apply (see Treasury Regulation § 1.6049-7(d)(1)). The -5(c) regulation allows a person filing Form 1099s to rely on IRS Publication 1212 to determine the existence or amount of OID with respect to an obligation, but the publication does not include information on REMIC regular interests or pay-through bonds. The -5(c) regulation also allows OID to be calculated based on the issue price, without any adjustment for the holder's actual cost. This result can be reached directly under the statute, however, without a regulation. See section 6049(d)(6)(A)(i).

ways included in income under an accrual method, and therefore is reported, like OID, as it accrues.[28] A Form 1099 filed for each "pass-through interest holder"[29] in a "single-class REMIC" also must include certain information necessary for that person to take account of its allocable share of the REMIC's investment expenses.[30] The forms for any year must be filed with the Service by February 28 of the following year, the same date that applies to conventional obligations. The copies sent to payees (or statements with the same information) need not be mailed until March 15 (instead of January 31, the deadline for conventional obligations).[31]

One reason for the delay is that payees must be given not only the information reported on Form 1099 but also a supplemental statement.[32] The statement for any year must include information necessary to compute accruals of market discount.[33] In the case of instruments with OID, there must be given for each accrual period included in whole or in part in that year, the adjusted issue price at the beginning of the accrual period, the length of the period, and the amount of OID per $1,000 of original principal amount allocated to each day in the period. The statement for a REMIC regular interest must report information regarding the status of the interest as a qualifying asset for a thrift or REIT.[34]

Holders of REMIC regular interests and pay-through bonds that are exempt, as payees, from information reporting may nonetheless need the tax information in order to calculate their own income tax liability or, in the case of certain middlemen, to comply with their own information reporting obligations. To address this problem, exempt payees (with exceptions for certain tax-exempt entities), and any noncalendar year taxpayers, may request from the issuer, for any calendar quarter,

---

28   Accrual method reporting of interest for regular interests is required under section 860B(b).

29   Whether a regular interest is held by a "pass-through interest holder" depends on the status of the beneficial rather than record holder. Treasury Regulation § 1.67-3T(a)(2)(i)(B), Example (1) (applying same rule to residual interest). The REMIC is permitted, however, to provide the required information to a nominee. In that event, the nominee must include such information in any Form 1099s it files with the Service and in related statements it gives to payees (or if Form 1099s are not required, must give the information to the payees within 30 days after receipt). Treasury Regulation §§ 1.67-3(f)(4) and (f)(5). It is uncertain how a REMIC is supposed to know whether the beneficial owner of a regular interest is a pass-through interest holder; thus, a single-class REMIC may be required, as a practical matter, to report allocations of investment expenses to all holders.

30   See Treasury Regulation § 1.6049-7(b)(2)(iii)(C) (cross-reference to regulations under section 67(c)). The substantive treatment of a single-class REMIC's investment expenses is discussed in Chapter 7, Part D.

31   Treasury Regulation §§ 1.6049-7(f)(1), (f)(5), and (f)(6).

32   Treasury Regulation §§ 1.6049-7(f)(2) and (f)(3) lists the information that must be included in the statement. The information need not be filed with the Service.

33   The information consists of a fraction, for each accrual period, representing the portion accruing during the period of all interest remaining to be accrued on the instrument over its term (or the same portion of OID if the instrument has OID). At the issuer's option, the calculation can be based on OID even if the OID is considered de minimis. The issuer must use a consistent method for all calendar years after 1991. See Treasury Regulation §§ 1.6049-7(f)(2)(i)(G)(2) and (f)(2)(ii)(K). The information used to accrue market discount may also be used in amortizing premium, as described in Chapter 6, Part F.

34   Treasury Regulation §§ 1.6049-7(f)(1) and (3). For further discussion, see Chapter 9, Part A.

information similar to that which is included for the year in Form 1099 and the supplemental statement described above.[35] Holders can locate issuers by consulting IRS Publication 938.[36] The request must be in writing (or, at the election of the issuer, in writing or by telephone).[37] The issuer must reply within two weeks after receipt of the request or, if later, 30 days after the end of the quarter to which the request relates.[38] The issuer may reply by telephone, in writing, or by including the information in a publication generally available to requesting parties and informing those parties, by telephone or in writing, where the published information may be found. Investors may prefer to contact their brokers rather than an issuer for tax information, and to accommodate this group, the regulations impose an independent obligation on brokers and middlemen to provide such information (again on a quarterly basis) to their customers.[39] There are no express penalties for failing to comply with requests for tax information, although the general penalties for faulty information reporting might apply.[40]

2. Pass-Through Certificates

Although section 6049 does not apply to interest on obligations of individuals such as home mortgages,[41] this exception does not extend to interest on pass-through certificates backed by a pool of such mortgages. Such interest must be reported at the pass-through rate (rather than at the gross rate, including mortgage servicing).[42]

---

35 See Treasury Regulation § 1.6049-7(e). Under the PAC method (described in Chapter 6, Part C.2), it is not generally possible to calculate the OID that accrues during any part of an accrual period without knowing the prepayments during the entire period. For that reason, an issuer may not be able to provide the requested information for an accrual period that straddles the end of a calendar quarter within the time required by the regulations (see text below). A similar problem may apply with respect to year-end reporting, although the earliest deadline for filing annual reports is two months after the end of the year. The regulations provide no guidance on how to resolve this problem. One approach might be to make the appropriate calculations (1) by treating the last day of the quarter (year) as the end of an accrual period, using the prepayment experience through that date and (2) accounting for the difference in prepayments in the following quarter (year). Compare Treasury Regulation § 1.446-3(e)(2)(ii) (adopting a similar rule for periodic payments set in arrears on notional principal contracts).

36 As described in footnote 15, above, this publication is compiled from information provided by issuers on Form 8811. An issuer may provide in the form either an address and telephone number or only an address. If only an address is listed in Publication 938, then requests for tax information must be made in writing to that address. Further, the request must specify the calendar quarters and classes of instruments for which information is needed. Treasury Regulation § 1.6049-7(e)(5).

37 See footnote 36, above.

38 Treasury Regulation § 1.6049-7(e)(3). There is a proposal to increase the period to 41 days after the end of the quarter. Proposed Regulation § 1.6049-7(e)(3)(ii)(A).

39 Treasury Regulation § 1.6049-7(f)(7). The information must be provided on or before the later of (1) the 45th day (55th day under proposed regulations) after the close of the calendar quarter for which the information was requested (or, if the request was made for the last calendar quarter in a year, the following March 15) or (2) the 45th day after receipt of the request. Because an issuer must provide quarterly information to brokers within 30 days after the end of the quarter, these time periods allow a broker time (although not much time) to respond to requests.

40 See sections 6722 and 6724(d)(2)(H).

41 Section 6049(b)(2)(A).

Although REMICs are required to report investment expenses (including mortgage servicing costs) separately to holders of interests in the REMIC (see Part C), as yet, no similar requirement applies to grantor trusts.[43] Furthermore, the broader system of information reporting for REMIC regular interests and pay-through bonds, described in the last section, does not currently apply to pass-through certificates.

A grantor trust is required to file an annual trust information return (essentially, an income statement and list of beneficiaries attached to a blank income tax return on Form 1041) and to send summaries of the information on the return to holders of pass-through certificates.[44] Payments made to holders of pass-through certificates that are so reported on the trust return and to such holders are not required to be reported again under section 6049.[45]

3. Owner Trusts

An owner trust that is not taxed as a corporation must file an annual trust information return (essentially, an income statement and list of beneficiaries attached to a blank trust income tax return on Form 1041), or a partnership information return on Form 1065, depending on whether it is classified as a grantor trust or partnership. In either case, summaries of the information on the return must be sent to holders of equity interests.[46]

C. REMIC Tax Returns

REMICs are required to file an annual tax return on Form 1066.[47] The form is based on the partnership information return, but has been modified to reflect some of the

---

42   Treasury Regulation § 1.6049-5(a)(6).

43   The Treasury has authority to require investment expenses to be reported by grantor trusts. See section 67(c) and Conference Report at II-34. Treasury Regulation § 1.67-2T sets out substantive rules regarding the treatment by beneficiaries of a grantor trust of the trust's investment expenses, but does not impose any reporting requirement on such trusts. For a description of the substantive rules, see Chapter 2, footnote 9 and accompanying text.

44   Treasury Regulation § 1.671-4(a); section 6034A(a). It seems, however, that the fiduciary of a state law trust that is considered an agency relationship for federal income tax purposes (see Chapter 3, footnote 10) is not required to file a return. Treasury Regulation § 301.7701-7, in distinguishing an agent from a fiduciary, states that "[i]n cases where no legal trust has been created in the estate controlled by the agent and attorney, the liability to make a return rests with the principal." Although not entirely clear, this last rule seems to apply to trust arrangements that are treated as "agencies" for tax purposes. See G.C.M. 2185, VI-2 C.B. 75 (1927) (trustee that was deemed the agent of a corporation was not required to file a return as trustee). P.L.R. 8533003 (May 7, 1985) holds that a U.S. trust established by, and treated as an agent of, a foreign government must file the same return that would be required of the government (Form 1120F), and not a trust return. Under section 882(f), a return is required to be filed by the U.S. agent of a foreign corporation (or government) if it has no U.S. office or place of business. Revenue Ruling 92-105, 1992-2 C.B. 204, involves an Illinois land trust that was treated as an agent of the beneficiary. The ruling states that the trust beneficiary had agreed to file all the returns with respect to the trust property, but does not discuss what returns were required.

45   Treasury Regulation § 1.6049-4(c)(2).

46   Treasury Regulation § 1.671-4(a) and section 6034A(a) (trusts); section 6031 (partnerships).

peculiar tax characteristics of REMICs.[48] The REMIC return for any year is due by April 15 of the following year, although extensions can be obtained.[49] The Service has issued regulations governing the completion, signing, and filing of the form.[50]

Form 1066 consists of sections for identifying information (the REMIC's own employer identification number, and its startup day and total assets at year end), and for computing taxable income or net loss and the tax on net income from prohibited transactions. There is also space for designating a tax matters person.[51] Further, the form requires information regarding the type of legal entity the REMIC is, the number of residual holders, and the daily accruals for the year (which are used in calculating excess inclusions). If the REMIC has more than one class of regular interests, a schedule identifying the classes, and stating the principal amount of each class outstanding at the end of the year, must be attached. Moreover, if the regular interests have OID, the Prepayment Assumption used in computing accruals of OID under the PAC method (together with documentation supporting the choice) must be attached to the first return filed. Information concerning the terms and conditions of all interests in the REMIC, or a copy of the offering circular or prospectus containing such information, also must be provided with the initial return.[52]

The most important schedule to the return is Schedule Q, which is used to report tax information quarterly to holders of residual interests. In addition, there are schedules requiring a separate accounting for capital gains and losses,[53] a REMIC balance sheet (listing separately qualified mortgages and each category of permitted investments), and a reconciliation of residual interest holders' capital accounts, which seems more appropriate for a partnership than a REMIC.

The REMIC election is made on the Form 1066 filed by the REMIC for its first taxable year.[54] The form does not provide space for making the election. Instead, it

---

47   The form and instructions are reproduced in Appendix D.

48   The primary obligation to file the return and to report to residual interest holders (see below in the text) appears to arise under section 6031, which requires partnerships to file an annual information return and to report certain information to partners. In general, REMICs are considered partnerships, and holders of residual interests are considered partners, for purposes of subtitle F of the Code, which includes section 6031. See section 860F(e); Treasury Regulation § 1.860F-4(a). However, Treasury Regulation § 1.860F-4(b)(2) states that, because a REMIC, unlike a partnership, may be liable for taxes (see Chapter 4, Part B), it must make a tax return (not simply an information return) as required by section 6011(a) on Form 1066. It should make little difference whether Form 1066 is required by section 6031 or 6011. Other procedural rules in subtitle F that affect REMICs are described in Chapter 4, Part D.2.

49   See Treasury Regulation §§ 1.860D-1(d)(1), 1.860F-4(b)(1); section 6072(a). Partnerships, and therefore REMICs, can obtain an automatic three-month extension by filing an application by the original due date on Form 8736. See Treasury Regulation § 1.6081-2T. Requests for additional extensions for reasonable cause are made on Form 8800.

50   Treasury Regulation § 1.860F-4.

51   The tax matters person is discussed in Chapter 4, footnote 317 and accompanying text.

52   For the requirement to describe REMIC interests and to describe and justify the Prepayment Assumption, see Treasury Regulation §§ 1.860D-1(d)(2) and (3).

53   This requirement makes no sense since all income or loss of a REMIC is ordinary. See Chapter 7, text accompanying footnote 27.

54   See section 860D(b). The REMIC election is discussed further in Chapter 4, Part D.1.

is made by filing the form in a timely manner signed by a person authorized to sign.[55] Presumably, only substantial compliance with the requirements of the form will be needed to make a valid election.

Although REMICs generally are considered partnerships for purposes of tax administration, the determination of who can sign a REMIC's tax returns is made as if no REMIC election was in effect.[56] Thus, for example, the return of a REMIC organized as a trust or corporation should be signed by the trustee or a corporate officer, respectively. In the case of a REMIC that is a segregated pool of assets, the return should be signed by a person who could sign the return of the entity that is the state law owner of the REMIC's assets.[57] Properly signing Form 1066 is important because a REMIC election made on a return that is not properly signed may be invalid.

As already noted, each REMIC must report certain tax information quarterly to holders of its residual interest on Schedule Q to Form 1066.[58] The information required to be reported on Schedule Q includes the type of entity the residual holder is (for example, corporation, partnership, or trust), the holder's taxpayer identification number, and the holder's share of the REMIC's (1) taxable income or net loss, (2) excess inclusions and (3) if the holder is a pass-through interest holder, investment expenses.[59]

---

55 See Treasury Regulation § 1.860D-1(d)(1). The availability of extensions is discussed in Chapter 4, Part D.1.

56 Section 860F(e); Treasury Regulation § 1.860F-4(c)(1). Alternatively, for REMICs the startup day of which is before November 10, 1988, Form 1066 may be signed by either (1) any holder of a residual interest in the REMIC during the taxable year covered by the form, or (2) a fiduciary acting for the REMIC (including the trustee, in the case of a REMIC organized as a trust under state law) if such fiduciary has notified the Service of its fiduciary relationship under section 6903 and Treasury Regulation § 301.6903-1(b). See Treasury Regulation § 1.860F-4(c)(2).

57 Treasury Regulation § 1.860F-4(c)(1).

58 Schedule Qs for any calendar quarter must be mailed or otherwise delivered to the residual interest holders by the end of the month following the quarter to which they relate. Nominees that hold residual interests on behalf of others must provide them with the information on Schedule Q within 30 days after the nominee receives such information. Copies of all Schedule Qs for each year must be attached to the Form 1066 for the year but quarterly reporting to the Service is not required. See Treasury Regulation § 1.860F-4(e)(2) through (4).

59 As discussed in Chapter 7, footnotes 42–46 and accompanying text, a REMIC's investment expenses are allocated among holders of REMIC interests and, in the case of a pass-through interest holder, the allocated amount is included in gross income and treated as an investment expense. The only allocations of investment expenses that must be reported to holders and the Service are allocations to pass-through interest holders. Whether a REMIC interest is considered to be held by a pass-through interest holder depends on the status of the interest's beneficial owner, not its registered owner. Treasury Regulation § 1.67-3T(a)(2)(i)(B), Example (1). The REMIC is permitted, however, to provide the required information to a nominee, in which case the nominee is required to provide such information to the beneficial owner no later than 30 days after it receives the information. Treasury Regulation §§ 1.67-3(f)(4) and (f)(5). It is uncertain how a REMIC is supposed to determine whether the beneficial owner of a residual interest is a pass-through interest holder; thus, a REMIC may be required, as a practical matter, to report allocations of investment expenses to all holders. One approach used by some REMICs is to provide in the REMIC's constituent documents that residual interest holders are considered to have represented to the REMIC that they are not pass-through interest holders unless they notify the REMIC to the

A REMIC also must state on the Schedule Q for any quarter whether the percentage of the REMIC's assets for that quarter (computed on the basis of the average adjusted basis of the assets held during that quarter)[60] that are qualifying assets for a thrift or qualifying real estate assets for a REIT is in each case at least 95 percent, or, if the percentage for any category of qualifying assets is less than 95, the actual percentage. Further, if in any quarter less than 95 percent of the REMIC's assets are qualifying real estate assets for a REIT, the REMIC must provide to any REIT that holds a residual interest the percentage of assets that are qualifying assets under section 856(c)(5)(A) (real estate assets, cash, cash items, and government securities) and the percentage of the REMIC's gross income that qualifies for purposes of the 75 percent income test in section 856(c)(3).[61] The categories of qualifying assets for thrifts and REITs, and the status of REMIC interests as such assets, are discussed in Chapter 9, Part A.

D. Backup Withholding

Each person filing a Form 1099 (and certain other information reports) must include on the form the payee's taxpayer identification number or "TIN" (either an employer identification number or social security number). Each payee in turn is required to provide his TIN to the person filing the return upon request.[62] Under section 3406, if any person fails to furnish a TIN to a payor with respect to any "reportable payment," then the payor must withhold 31 percent of the payment.[63] The withheld amount is not an additional tax but is credited against taxes otherwise due by the payee. The definition of "reportable payment" includes interest payments that must be reported on Form 1099.[64]

Backup withholding does not apply to payments to corporations.[65] In addition, backup withholding does not apply to interest payments to foreign investors for

---

contrary. The problem may one day be alleviated by the nominee reporting requirements described in Part E.

60 The REMIC must make the appropriate computation as of the close of each month, week, or day, at its option, during the quarter and then average the percentages. The monthly, weekly, or daily computation period must be applied uniformly during the calendar quarter to all categories of assets and gross income, and may not be changed in succeeding calendar quarters without the consent of the Service. See Treasury Regulation § 1.860F-4(e)(1).

61 Treasury Regulation § 1.860F-4(e)(1)(ii)(B). Income from foreclosure property is listed separately.

62 See section 6109(a)(2); Treasury Regulation § 301.6109-1(b).

63 For payments made prior to 1993, the backup withholding tax rate was 20%. Backup withholding is also required for reportable interest payments if (1) the Service notifies the payor that the TIN supplied by the payee is incorrect, (2) the Service notifies the payor that backup withholding is required because the payee has failed properly to reflect reportable payments in his tax return, or (3) in certain cases, the payee fails to certify that backup withholding is not required on account of (2) above.

64 See section 3406(b)(2)(A)(i).

65 To establish the exemption, the payor may require the payee to supply a certificate, signed under penalties of perjury, stating that the payee is a corporation. However, even if such a certificate is

which withholding otherwise is required or would be required in the absence of a treaty or statutory exemption.[66]

E. Nominee Reporting to Issuers

TRA 1986 authorizes the adoption of regulations requiring any person who holds an interest in a partnership or trust as a nominee for another person to report to the partnership or trust the identity of that other person.[67] This reporting requirement could potentially apply to equity interests in owner trusts, pass-through certificates, or REMIC residual interests.[68] A reporting requirement currently is in effect for entities classified as partnerships, but not for interests in entities classified as trusts or REMICs.[69]

F. Other Mortgage-Related Reporting Obligations

The information reporting requirements described above are aimed at improving tax compliance by holders of mortgage-backed securities. Mortgagors also pay taxes, and the Code has two information gathering schemes aimed at them. One is intended to ensure accuracy in the reporting of interest deductions by individual mortgagors. The other reports on income from the discharge of debt. There is also a general obligation to report miscellaneous items of income paid by persons engaged in a business, including certain issuers of mortgage-backed securities. This section provides a brief overview of these three regimes.

Section 6050H requires any person who, in the course of a trade or business, receives more than $600 of interest in any calendar year from an individual on a mortgage[70] to report to the Service (on Form 1098) the amount of interest received.

---

not forthcoming, the payor may treat the payee as an exempt corporation if the payee's name contains an unambiguous expression of corporate status. See section 3406(g)(1)(B); Treasury Regulation § 35a.9999-1, Q&A-29 (cross-reference to Treasury Regulation § 31.3452(c)-1). A similar exemption from backup withholding applies to governmental agencies, tax-exempt organizations and certain other entities. See section 3406(g)(1)(A).

66   Backup withholding does not apply to payments that are exempt from information reporting and section 6049(b)(5) exempts the payments to foreign investors described in the text from information reporting. See also Treasury Regulation §§ 35a.9999-5(a), Q&A-2, and 35a.9999-5(b), Q&A-11 and Q&A-16 (exemption from backup withholding for payments of portfolio interest). The withholding tax on payments to foreign investors is discussed in Chapter 10, Part B.

67   Sections 6031(c) and 6034A(b).

68   REMICs are treated as partnerships for purposes of subtitle F of the Code, which includes section 6031. See section 860F(e) and Treasury Regulation § 1.860F-4(a).

69   Treasury Regulation § 1.6031(c)-1T. A comparable regulation for REMIC residual interests is reserved. See Treasury Regulation §§ 1.6031(c)-1T(i) and -2T. There are no regulations under section 6034A(b) (dealing with trusts).

70   A mortgage is broadly defined as any obligation secured to any extent by real estate (even if the security interest is not recorded). See Treasury Regulation § 6050H-1(b)(2). Interest paid by a cooperative housing corporation and allocated to tenant-stockholders is considered to be paid by the tenant-stockholders to the corporation and thus is subject to reporting by the corporation. See section 6050H(g).

Where a mortgage servicer receives mortgage payments directly from the mortgagor and has the information needed to file the form, the reporting obligation falls on it and not on the beneficial owner of the loan.[71] The form for any year must be filed no later than the following February 28. A copy of the form, or its equivalent, for a year must be furnished to the mortgagor by January 31 of the following year. For reporting years after 1991, information supplied on the form must include the amount of certain points received with respect to the mortgage and an indication whether they were paid directly by the borrower.[72] The information that must be reported was further expanded for reporting years after 1992 to include taxable reimbursements of overpayments of interest.[73] Probably the most common cause of such overpayments is errors made by mortgage servicers in calculating payments on adjustable rate mortgage loans.

A borrower may realize income in connection with the discharge of debt. A borrower may retire an obligation for an amount less than its adjusted issue price (in which case the borrower has discharge of indebtedness income in the amount of the difference), or may transfer property, voluntarily or not, in satisfaction of debt where the tax basis of the property is less than the amount realized in the transaction (in which case there is gain from disposition of the property in that amount).[74] In order to encourage the correct reporting of income arising from the discharge of debt, section 6050J requires any person who in connection with a trade or business lends money secured by real or personal property and who either acquires any property securing the loan, or has reason to know that such property has been abandoned by the borrower, to file an information return describing the property and the debt. Certain consumer loans secured by personal property are exempt from the reporting obligation,[75] but otherwise it applies to all types of secured loans. A sale to a third party in a foreclosure proceeding is treated as an abandonment for this purpose.[76] Where a loan is owned by multiple owners through a trust or participation arrangement, the reporting obligation falls on the trust or legal owner.[77] A

---

71   Treasury Regulation § 1.6050H-1(c)(2).

72   See Revenue Procedure 92-11, 1992-1 C.B 662. The points to be reported are generally those that are deductible by the borrower under section 461(g)(2). See Chapter 6, footnote 72. Points received, directly or indirectly, by a mortgage broker are reportable to the same extent as if paid to and retained by the lender. Revenue Ruling 92-2, 1992-1 C.B. 360. For a safe harbor for determining whether points are paid by the borrower, see Revenue Procedure 92-12, 1992-1 C.B. 663, clarified by Revenue Procedure 92-12A, 1992-1 C.B. 664.

73   Treasury Regulation § 1.6050H-2(a)(2)(iv).

74   Where property that is security for a recourse loan is transferred in discharge of the obligation, the transaction is treated as if the property was sold for cash equal to its fair market value and the cash was used to retire the obligation. By contrast, where property that secures a nonrecourse loan is transferred in discharge of the loan, the property is considered to be sold for an amount equal to the discharged debt. See Treasury Regulation § 1.1001-2.

75   Section 6050J(b).

76   Section 6050J(f).

77   Treasury Regulation § 1.6050J-1T, Q & A-3.

statement containing the information reported to the Service must be given to the borrower.

RRA 1993 extended the reporting rules for discharge of indebtedness income to unsecured loans by enacting section 6050P.[78] It requires any "applicable financial entity" to file an information return reporting the discharge of any indebtedness if the amount of discharged debt is at least $600. An applicable financial entity includes banks, thrifts, and credit unions and their regulated subsidiaries, and the Resolution Trust Corporation, Federal Deposit Insurance Corporation, and certain other federal agencies. Reports are required for discharges after 1993 (or, in the case of federal agencies, August 6, 1993). Where debt is discharged in connection with the acquisition or abandonment of secured property, information reporting may be required under both sections 6050J and 6050P.[79]

Finally, to encourage the reporting of miscellaneous items of income, under section 6041 any person who in the course of a trade or business makes payments (that are not otherwise reportable) of certain types of income to another person (other than, in general, a corporation) of $600 or more in a taxable year is required to file an information return with respect to such income. The income subject to reporting includes compensation for services and rents. A REMIC is considered to be in a trade or business for this purpose.[80]

---

78   The Service has issued temporary regulations implementing the section. See Treasury Regulation § 1.6050P-1T.

79   Treasury Regulation § 1.6050P-1T(d).

80   Treasury Regulation § 1.6041-1(b)(2).

Chapter 12

Taxation of Sponsors

Previous chapters concentrated on the taxation of issuers and investors. This chapter looks at sponsors. For any issue of securities backed by a pool of mortgages, the term *sponsor* is used here broadly to refer to any person who (1) owned an interest in those mortgages before the securities were issued and (2) immediately after issuance of the securities, holds (at least temporarily) some or all of the securities or another interest in the securities' issuer. The tax treatment of a sponsor may be affected by many factors. Therefore, the discussion in this chapter is intended only as a general summary of the most likely tax results in a number of common situations.

The tax consequences to a sponsor of the issuance and sale of mortgage-backed securities depend primarily on (1) whether the transaction is treated for tax purposes as a financing or sale, and (2) if it is a sale, the proportion of the property held by the sponsor that is considered to be sold.[1] Pledging an asset as security for a loan is not ordinarily considered a taxable disposition of the asset. On the other hand, if the asset (or an interest therein) is sold, the seller recognizes gain or loss equal to the difference between the amount realized in the sale and its adjusted basis in the property sold.

As the discussion below explains, these basic tax principles apply in different ways to sponsors of pass-through certificates, pay-through bonds, and REMIC interests.

Before turning to the different types of mortgage-backed securities, it is worth taking note of special considerations that apply to a sponsor that is also a servicer and receives *excess servicing* (a servicing fee in excess of reasonable compensation for the services performed). In 1991, the Service issued a ruling holding that excess

---

1   The sale-versus-financing distinction is also important for issuers and investors. See Chapter 2, Part D.1 (discussion of whether pay-through bonds are recognized as debt); Chapter 2, Part E (automatic treatment of REMIC regular interests as debt); and Chapter 4, footnote 254 and accompanying text (discussion of whether guaranteed mortgages held by a REMIC are qualified mortgages or instead a loan to the guarantor). See also Chapter 2, Part G (discussion of pass-through debt certificates, which take the form of ownership certificates but are intended to be taxed as debt). In addition, the treatment of pass-through certificates as qualifying assets for thrifts and REITs (see Chapter 9, Part A) assumes that the holders of those certificates are treated as the owners of the assets of the issuing trust rather than as creditors of the sponsor. More generally, if pass-through certificates were characterized as loans to the sponsor, they would be taxed in the same manner as pay-through bonds.

servicing must be treated as an ownership interest in the related mortgages (or, more technically, as a stripped coupon within the meaning of section 1286).[2] As a result, such a sponsor must allocate some part of its basis in the mortgages it sells to excess servicing, thereby increasing its gain (or reducing its loss) from the sale.[3] The ruling was accompanied by two revenue procedures. They provide a schedule of safe harbor reasonable fee rates for typical servicing contracts for one- to four-family residential mortgages,[4] and a procedure for a taxpayer to request automatic consent to a change in its method of accounting for excess servicing from an impermissible method to the method required by the ruling.[5] References in this chapter to owner-ship interests in mortgages, or pass-through certificates evidencing such ownership interests, should be understood to include excess servicing.

A. Pass-Through Certificates

The tax treatment of sponsors of pass-through certificates is for the most part straightforward. The exchange of mortgages for *all* of the pass-through certificates issued by a grantor trust is not a taxable event.[6] When the sponsor sells some or all

---

2   See Revenue Ruling 91-46, 1991-2 C.B. 358, which is discussed in detail in Chapter 3, footnote 101 and accompanying text. One potential difference between excess servicing and a conventional ownership interest is that the payment of excess servicing may be conditioned on the ongoing performance of services. That Revenue Ruling 91-46 was aimed primarily at sponsors is indicated by the fact that the Service took special pains to limit its effect on issuers and investors. See Chapter 3, footnote 101 and accompanying text; Chapter 4, Part A.1.a.(ii) (issuers); Chapter 6, Part D.1.a (exceptions to stripping rules for investors).

      Revenue Ruling 91-46 "obsoleted" Revenue Ruling 66-314, 1966-2 C.B. 296, which held that the right of a seller to service a pool of mortgages was not an amount realized that was taken into account in determining gain or loss on sale of the mortgages. Although Revenue Ruling 66-314 did not discuss the terms of the servicing contract, it was interpreted by many mortgage servicers as permitting all servicing fees (including excess servicing) to be disregarded in measuring gain or loss from the sale of mortgages.

3   See text at footnote 17, below.

4   Revenue Procedure 91-50, 1991-2 C.B. 778. An election to apply the safe harbors is made annu-ally and applies to all servicing contracts with respect to mortgages sold during the year. If the safe harbors apply, then all mortgage interest the servicer is entitled to receive in excess of the safe harbor rates is treated as stripped coupons in the servicer's hands. The safe harbor rates are generally (1) 25 basis points for conventional, fixed rate mortgages, (2) 44 basis points for an FHA or VA insured mortgage that is less than one year old (i.e., the mortgages that are eligible to be included in GNMA guaranteed pass-through certificates), or (3) 37.5 basis points for any other conventional mortgage. The safe harbor rate for a mortgage with an original principal balance less than $50,000 is 44 basis points. There are no safe harbor rates for commercial loans.

5   Revenue Procedure 91-51, 1991-2 C.B. 779. The taxpayer must request consent by filing a Form 3115 with the Service. To encourage voluntary changes in accounting methods under the revenue procedure, mortgage servicers that properly request such consent are not required to change their accounting methods for loans sold in prior years. Further, the revenue procedure does not apply if the accounting method issue is raised on audit before such consent is requested.

6   This result follows from the treatment of holders of pass-through certificates as owners of the underlying assets for tax purposes (see Chapter 2, footnotes 6 and 7 and accompanying text). Where a sponsor receives all of the certificates issued by a trust and those certificates are divided into classes, it would seem to be appropriate to, in effect, disregard the separate classes until they are owned in different proportions, although this result is not clear. If a sponsor wishes to have the

of those certificates, however, it is treated as selling an interest in the underlying mortgages and recognizes gain or loss accordingly. The gain or loss equals the difference between the amount realized in the sale and the portion of its aggregate adjusted basis in the mortgages that is allocated to the certificates sold (which would be a pro rata portion if there is only one class of ownership interests in the trust).

While this brief description will suffice for most pass-through arrangements, a more complete discussion is warranted of two topics: the possible recharacterization of a sale of pass-through certificates as a loan to the sponsor, and the consequences for the sponsor of a sale of pass-through certificates to investors (assuming the sale is not recharacterized as a financing).

1. Possible Recharacterization of a Sale as a Loan

Under general tax principles, a purported sale of pass-through certificates will be recognized to be a sale unless the seller retains, by contract or some other arrangement, the principal economic benefits and burdens of ownership of the underlying mortgages.[7] Sponsors of pass-through certificates often retain a continuing interest in the underlying mortgages consisting of (1) some or all of the risk of mortgage defaults and delinquencies (through a guarantee, a reserve fund, the holding of subordinated certificates, or other means), and (2) loan servicing responsibilities and rights (including a right to end the servicing contract by repurchasing the mortgages pursuant to a clean-up call).[8] Even so, it is well established that the retention of credit risk and servicing will not cause a sale of pass-through certificates to be recharacterized as a loan for tax purposes, at least if the certificates represent interests in residential mortgages of a quality not significantly below the norm and the servicing arrangements are similar to those entered into by third party servicers.[9] This result is appropriate. Both credit support and servicing are regularly

---

class structure recognized from the start (e.g., to establish separate bases in the classes based on their initial values), then consideration should be given to owning the different classes through separate entities. For a discussion of the tax consequences of the transfer of mortgages by two or more sponsors to a single grantor trust, see the discussion of owner trusts classified as grantor trusts in the text accompanying footnote 25, below.

7   See the authorities discussed in footnote 9, below.

8   In the context of pass-through certificates, a clean-up call is a right to repurchase the mortgages from the pass-through trust, generally at par plus accrued interest, when their aggregate principal balance drops below a small percentage (generally 5% or 10%) of their balance when transferred to the trust. The call would be exercised when servicing income, which is usually based on the outstanding principal balance of the mortgages, no longer covers servicing costs. Clean-up calls are viewed as adjuncts of servicing arrangements and not as devices to shift material upside benefits to the servicer.

9   The rulings issued for pass-through certificates guaranteed by GNMA, FNMA, and FHLMC (see Chapter 2, footnotes 11–13) all treat the certificate holders as owners of the underlying mortgages rather than as creditors of the sponsors, even though under all three agency programs, the sponsors typically act as servicers and either must, in the case of GNMA, or may, in the case of FNMA and FHLMC, retain the ultimate risk of credit losses. In addition, the Service has ruled privately that mortgage pass-through transactions constituted sales of the mortgages where the seller arranged

provided for residential mortgages by vendors having no ownership interest in the loans.

It is somewhat more surprising that the sponsor of an issue of pass-through certificates can retain a disproportionately large share of the risk of loss or potential for profit from variations in the rate of prepayment of the underlying mortgages without jeopardizing sale treatment. Such is the case, however, so long as the sponsor achieves the desired allocation of risks and rewards by dividing the certificates into classes of stripped certificates and selling those with less prepayment sensitivity.[10] Each stripped bond or coupon is considered a distinct property item for tax purposes, and can be sold separately from the other stripped interests in the same debt instrument or mortgage pool. On the other hand, the tax status of a purported sale of a pass-through certificate may be seriously questioned if the sponsor guarantees that the underlying mortgages will prepay at a minimum or maximum rate, at least if the guarantee has material economic value and is combined with other factors supporting financing treatment.[11]

---

for mortgage insurance (P.L.R. 7750018 (September 7, 1977) and P.L.R. 7749020 (September 7, 1977)), or the seller established a limited reserve out of which certain deficiencies in interest or principal payments on mortgages could be paid (P.L.R. 8110142 (December 12, 1980)). These authorities deal principally with pass-through certificates backed by residential mortgages. Similar principles should apply to pass-through certificates backed by commercial loans. Because the issue of tax ownership is inherently factual, care must always be taken in relying on any ruling or other authority in analyzing a particular transaction to ensure that there are not material differences in the underlying facts.

The example in the Sears regulations dealing with senior and subordinated pass-through certificates is obviously premised on the treatment of the sale of senior certificates by the sponsor as a sale and not a financing. See Treasury Regulation § 301.7701-4(c)(2), Example (2), and Revenue Ruling 92-32 1992-1 C.B. 434, discussed in Chapter 3 in the text following footnote 71 and accompanying footnote 75. In senior/subordinated structures, the differences in credit quality of the senior and subordinated classes can be explained as incidents of the ownership interests in the trust assets and on that ground may be given less weight as a factor supporting loan treatment. Compare the discussion of stripping transactions in the text accompanying footnote 10, below.

At one time, the Service took the position that the retention of credit risk in connection with the transfer of a pool of receivables was inconsistent with sale treatment. See G.C.M. 34602 (September 9, 1971). The Service has revised its position, however, to permit sale treatment notwithstanding the retention by the transferor of the risk of loss if the total purchase price is fixed when the transfer is made and the purchaser obtains the benefit of any profit that may arise through appreciation of the receivables due to a decline in interest rates. See G.C.M. 39584 (October 10, 1986); G.C.M. 37848 (February 5, 1979). These memoranda list a number of other factors that may be useful in determining whether a transaction should be characterized as a sale or loan for tax purposes. For a general discussion, see W. Cliff & P. Levine, "Reflections on Ownership—Sales and Pledges of Installment Obligations," 39 *Tax Lawyer* 37 (1985).

10   The use of stripped pass-through certificates to allocate prepayment risk is discussed in Chapter 2, Part A.2.

11   See, for example, P.L.R. 7725066 (March 24, 1977) (sale of certificates of beneficial interest in a fixed pool of residential mortgages treated as a financing where the seller guaranteed a minimum prepayment rate, interest and principal on the certificates were passed through semiannually and annually, respectively, and the holders had a right to put the certificates to the seller on a fixed date at par plus accrued interest). This ruling was revoked by P.L.R. 8337016 (May 23, 1983), on the ground that "[t]he rulings were issued on the basis of accepting the guarantees and risk shifting provisions at face value, without evaluating their economic significance or legal effect, as such." As discussed in Chapter 2, Part G, pass-through debt certificates take the form of ownership

2. Consequences of Certificate Sales

Assuming that a sale of pass-through certificates by the sponsor is not recharacterized as a loan, the sponsor generally will recognize gain or loss from the sale equal to the difference between the amount realized in the sale and its tax basis in the certificates that are sold. With limited exceptions, the gain or loss would be capital gain or loss unless the sponsor is considered a dealer in the certificates or is a thrift or bank.[12] Any loss might be deferred or disallowed if the seller is related to the buyer.[13] A loss might also be deferred if the seller purchases an interest in the same mortgage pool within 30 days before or after the sale date.[14] At one time the Service maintained that an exchange of two pools of mortgages was not a taxable event where the pools were sufficiently similar so that the exchange did not produce a book loss and the exchange was undertaken primarily to generate a tax loss. The Supreme Court's 1991 *Cottage Savings* decision squelched this view.[15] Under a special Code provision, for purposes of computing its liability for alternative minimum tax, a corporation generally is allowed to deduct only 25 percent of a loss recognized on the exchange of two mortgage pools having substantially the same effective interest rates and maturities.[16]

---

interests in trusts but are intended to be treated for tax purposes as indebtedness of the trust. These certificates are usually backed by short-term consumer loans and have economic features supporting debt characterization that depart markedly from the terms of typical pass-through certificates.

12 For a summary of special rules applicable to sponsors that are dealers in securities, see Chapter 9, Part E. Ordinary income or loss treatment for certain thrifts and banks is provided by section 582(c). See Chapter 9, Part D. Gain may also be ordinary income to the extent of the accrued market discount that has not previously been taxed. See Chapter 6, Part E. See also Chapter 6, footnote 7, for another possible ground for ordinary income treatment by mortgage originators.

13 Losses may be deferred or disallowed on sales to related persons under section 267 (which applies to sales between persons related in a number of different ways, including sales between members of a controlled group of corporations), section 707(b) (sales between partners and partnerships) or Treasury Regulation § 1.1502-13 (sales between members of a group of corporations filing consolidated returns).

14 Under the wash sale rules of section 1091, a sponsor that is not a securities dealer may be required to defer any loss realized on the sale of a pass-through certificate if the certificate is considered a "security" and the sponsor acquires (or enters into a contract or option to acquire) a "substantially identical" security within the period beginning 30 days before and ending 30 days after the sale of the certificate. G.C.M. 39551 (June 30, 1986) holds that a GNMA guaranteed certificate is a "security" for this purpose because "[p]articipation certificates are readily tradeable assets with a readily ascertainable fair market value." The Tax Court in *Federal National Mortgage Ass'n v. Comm'r*, 90 T.C. 405, 424 (1988) held that two mortgage pools with different mortgagors and collateral are not "substantially identical" within the meaning of section 1091. This conclusion is consistent with the *Cottage Savings* decision discussed in footnote 15, below, although that decision does not specifically consider section 1091.

15 For the Service's earlier position, see Revenue Ruling 81-204, 1981-2 C.B. 157, amplified by Revenue Ruling 85-125, 1985-2 C.B. 180. The ruling held, among other things, that the exchange was not a "realization event" under section 1001 because the mortgage pools did not differ "materially either in kind or in extent." Following a spate of litigation in the lower courts, the U.S. Supreme Court held, in *Cottage Savings Ass'n v. Comm'r*, 499 U.S. 554 (1991), that exchanges of the type dealt with in the ruling are realization events. According to the decision, the pools are materially different because they represent different "legal entitlements" (namely, claims against different mortgagors).

The sponsor's aggregate initial tax basis in the pass-through certificates generally would equal its aggregate basis in the mortgages for which they were exchanged immediately prior to the exchange. Such aggregate basis would be allocated ratably among all certificates if they consist of a single class. On the other hand, if the certificates are stripped pass-through certificates, the sponsor must allocate such aggregate basis, determined at the time when the first certificate is sold, among the different classes in proportion to their respective fair market values at that time (not in proportion to their rights to mortgage principal).[17]

It is not entirely clear how a sponsor who sells a senior class of certificates and retains a subordinated class should account for the subordination feature in a case where the stripped bond rules do not apply. If the subordination feature is analyzed as an incident of the two classes, then basis should be allocated in proportion to fair market value.[18] Alternatively, and less likely, the subordination feature could be accounted for by treating some portion of the amount realized in the sale of senior certificates as a credit support fee (which would be ordinary income) and ignoring the credit quality of the certificates in allocating basis. This approach is suggested by the analysis of junior and senior interests in the Sears regulations as parity interests, coupled with a limited recourse guarantee written by the holder of the junior interest in favor of the senior interest.[19]

---

16   In general, a corporation is subject to a federal alternative minimum tax of 20% of alternative minimum taxable income (AMTI) to the extent such tax exceeds its regular federal income tax liability. Under section 56(g), AMTI includes 75% of the excess of (1) adjusted current earnings (a measure of income based on earnings and profits) over (2) AMTI before such adjustment. The losses described in the text are disallowed in calculating adjusted current earnings. See section 56(g)(4)(E).

17   See section 1286(b)(3). For a general discussion of the bond stripping rules, see Chapter 6, Part D.1. Differences in credit quality would be taken into account in allocating basis. In a number of private letter rulings involving sales of senior certificates that were subject to the bond stripping rules, the Service allowed the sponsor to increase the basis allocated to the senior certificates to reflect their higher credit quality. See, for example, P.L.R. 8640012 (June 30, 1986), amended by P.L.R. 8711011 (December 8, 1986); P.L.R. 8625049 (March 24, 1986); P.L.R. 8619036 (February 7, 1986), reinstating P.L.R. 8546040 (August 19, 1985), which had been suspended by P.L.R. 8603087 (October 24, 1985). P.L.R. 8619036 was amended by P.L.R. 8704019 (October 23, 1986).

18   Under general tax principles, a taxpayer that owns an item of property and sells a partial ownership interest that was not identified when the property was purchased is required to allocate basis in proportion to the values of the different interests at the time of sale. See, e.g., Revenue Ruling 84-53, 1984-1 C.B. 159 (sale of a portion of a partnership interest), and *Eileen M. Hunter v. Comm'r*, 44 T.C. 109 (1965) (allocation between remainder and life estates in land). A fair market value allocation is also required under the REMIC rules. See footnote 34, below, and accompanying text. For further analogies, see Treasury Regulation §§ 1.358-2(a) (fair market value allocation between different classes of stock or securities received in a reorganization) and 1.307-1 (generally the same for stock or stock rights received as tax-free dividend on stock).

19   For further discussion of the alternative approach, see Chapter 2, text following footnote 30. The effect of ignoring credit quality in allocating basis would be to reduce the basis allocated to the senior certificates that are sold. On the other hand, the sales proceeds would be reduced to the extent they are recharacterized as a credit support fee. A credit support fee would be included in income by the sponsor, either upon receipt or, if it continues to hold the subordinated certificates, arguably over the life of the senior certificates. For authorities requiring service fees to be included in income upon receipt, see *American Automobile Ass'n v. United States*, 367 U.S. 687 (1961)

If the pass-through certificates are stripped certificates, then the sponsor may be required to recognize as ordinary income when the first certificate is sold the full amount of market discount and interest on *all* of the underlying mortgages that has accrued since they were acquired by the sponsor but not previously been included in income. In that event, the sponsor's adjusted basis in the certificates immediately prior to such first sale would be increased by the amount so included in income.[20] In addition, at the time of that first certificate sale, the sponsor would be treated, for purposes of applying the bond stripping rules, as if it had purchased the certificates it retains; the deemed purchase price would equal the adjusted basis of the retained certificates in the sponsor's hands. As a result, the difference between that price and the gross amount of payments to be received on the retained certificates would be treated as OID and taxed to the sponsor as it accrues.[21]

B. Pay-Through Bonds

Two steps may be involved in issuing pay-through bonds: (1) the issuance of the bonds for cash and (2) the transfer of all or a portion of the mortgage collateral by a sponsor to the issuer in exchange for cash and/or other consideration.[22] The issuance of the bonds is not considered a sale of the collateral and is not otherwise a taxable event.[23] The tax treatment of the transfer of the mortgages to the issuer is quite complex and would depend on at least three factors, the first two of which are

---

(membership dues) and *Schlude v. Comm'r*, 372 U.S. 128 (1963) (fees for future dance lessons). But see *Artnell Co. v. Comm'r*, 400 F.2d 981 (7th Cir. 1968) (income from advance ticket sales for baseball games at predictable future times can be deferred). A sponsor faced with the guarantee analysis could argue that the imputed guarantee fee should be considered to be paid not up front but instead over time out of additional interest allocated to the senior class. Under that view, the imputed guarantee fee could cause the bond stripping rules to apply (because a portion of the interest paid to the junior class would be considered to be owned by the senior class and paid to the juniors as a fee), which in turn would allow basis to be allocated in proportion to values rather than principal amounts. For further discussion of the treatment of an imputed guarantee fee, see Chapter 2, footnote 34.

20 See section 1286(b)(1). The basis adjustment is provided by section 1286(b)(2). The rules governing market discount generally are described in Chapter 6, Part E.

21 See section 1286(b)(4); Chapter 6, Part D.1. Where a sponsor retains more than one class of ownership interests in a trust (including any excess servicing that is treated as an ownership interest), then an issue will arise as to whether the classes should be treated as a single debt instrument or as separate instruments. See Chapter 6, footnote 64 and accompanying text. If they are treated as a single instrument, then it would seem to be appropriate to apply the bond stripping rules a second time if and when interests in that integrated instrument are separated in subsequent transactions.

22 If a legal entity issues pay-through bonds and the taxable mortgage pool rules apply to treat a portion of the entity as a separate corporation (see Chapter 3, Part D.2.d), then that separate corporation (and not the entity) would be considered for tax purposes to be the issuer of the bonds.

23 The statement in the text assumes that the issuance of the bonds is not recharacterized as a sale of the collateral. The transaction ordinarily would be structured to ensure this result. See Chapter 2, Part D.1. In some circumstances, a pledge of installment obligations received upon a sale of real property can accelerate gain that is being deferred under the installment sales rules. See section 453A(d)(1).

related: (1) whether for tax purposes the transfer is treated as a sale, or is instead viewed as an exchange of mortgages for an equity interest in the issuer,[24] (2) the extent to which equity interests in the issuer are owned by the sponsor rather than unrelated investors, and (3) whether the issuer is, for tax purposes, a grantor trust, partnership, or corporation.

In very general terms, if the issuer is an owner trust that is classified as a grantor trust, then the sponsor would recognize gain or loss as a result of the transfer of mortgages to the issuer only if equity interests in the issuer are owned by persons other than the sponsor, and then only to the extent that the sponsor would recognize gain or loss if it transferred directly to those other persons an interest in the mortgages corresponding to the equity interest they own.[25]

If the issuer is classified as a partnership, gain from a sale of the mortgages to the partnership would be recognized, but loss would not be recognized if the sponsor owns more than 50 percent of the equity interests in the issuer.[26] No gain or loss would be recognized upon an exchange of mortgages for an equity interest.[27]

---

24   A complete discussion of the circumstances under which a purported sale will be recharacterized for tax purposes as an equity contribution, or an equity contribution will be recharacterized as a sale, is beyond the scope of this chapter. The likelihood of recharacterization of a purported sale clearly would be high if the seller owned a substantial equity stake in the issuer and the stated consideration paid in the sale had a value less than the fair market value of the mortgages. A contribution of mortgages to an issuer that is a corporation solely in exchange for stock in a transaction subject to section 351 (see footnote 30, below), and a subsequent related distribution of cash may be integrated and treated as an exchange of the mortgages for stock and cash (and thus at least partially as a sale for purposes of gain recognition).

An exchange of mortgages for an equity interest in an entity that is classified as a partnership, combined with a related distribution of cash by the partnership, may be recharacterized as a sale under section 707(a)(2)(B) if the two events "when viewed together, are properly characterized as a sale or exchange of property." The Service has issued extensive regulations under this section. They provide that a transfer of property by a partner to a partnership in exchange for the proceeds of a partnership borrowing generally will be treated as a sale of the property only to the extent those proceeds exceed the partner's share (as determined under the regulations) of the liability to repay the borrowing. See Treasury Regulation § 1.707-5(b).

The discussion below of the tax consequences of a sale to, or an exchange of mortgages for equity interests in, an owner trust or corporation assumes that it has first been determined that the transaction in question will be characterized for tax purposes as a sale or such an exchange, respectively.

25   See footnote 6, above. If two or more persons transfer interests in different mortgages to a grantor trust, then each would be considered to exchange a partial interest in the mortgages it contributes (corresponding to the equity interest in the trust held by the others) in exchange for an interest in the mortgages contributed by the other parties. An exchange of interests in different mortgages is treated as a taxable exchange even though the mortgages are economically similar. See the *Cottage Savings* case discussed above in footnote 15.

26   If the sponsor is considered to own a greater than 50% interest in the capital or profits of the partnership, then loss would be disallowed under section 707(b). Certain attribution rules apply in determining whether the greater than 50% ownership test is met. If the sale of mortgages to the partnership occurs as part of a larger transaction in which equity interests in the partnership are sold to investors, consideration should be given to the possible characterization of the transaction as (1) a sale by the sponsor to those investors of a partial ownership interest in the mortgages corresponding to their equity interest in the partnership, followed by (2) the contribution by the sponsor and those investors of their respective interests in the mortgages to the partnership in exchange for equity interests. Under that characterization, the sponsor would generally recognize

Finally, if the issuer is a corporation, gain or loss from a sale of mortgages to the issuer by the sponsor generally would be recognized. However, if the sponsor is a corporation that files a consolidated federal income tax return with the issuer, then any such gain or loss would be deferred.[28] Moreover, even if the sponsor and the issuer do not file a consolidated return, loss would be deferred, or in some cases shifted to the issuer, if the sponsor and the issuer are part of the same "controlled group" (a group of corporations tied together through more than 50 percent stock ownership links).[29] If the mortgages are exchanged for stock (or stock and cash) upon formation of the issuer, loss would not be recognized in the exchange. Gain may be recognized, in an amount not exceeding the amount of cash received, but any such gain would be deferred to the same extent as gain from a sale.[30] The transferor may also recognize interest income up to the amount of accrued market discount on the mortgages not previously included in income.[31]

Regardless of the tax status of the issuer or whether gain or loss was recognized upon transfer of the mortgages to the issuer, if the sponsor sells some or all of its equity interest in the issuer to unrelated investors, it will recognize gain or loss in that sale equal to the difference between the amount realized and its adjusted basis in the portion of the equity interest that is sold.[32]

---

gain or loss only upon the initial sale of a partial interest in the mortgages to those investors, which is the same result that the sponsor would obtain if the issuer were classified as a grantor trust.

27   Section 721. Gain (but not loss) would be recognized under section 721(b), however, if the partnership would be considered an "investment company" within the meaning of Treasury Regulation § 1.351-1(c) if it were a corporation. A partnership would not meet this test unless, in general, it held some readily marketable equity securities.

28   Treasury Regulation § 1.1502-13. Any deferred gain or loss would be recognized by the sponsor as the issuer recovers its basis in the mortgages, or when the issuer disposes of the mortgages outside of the group filing consolidated returns, or the sponsor or issuer leaves the group. Under section 7701(i)(1), a corporation that is a taxable mortgage pool cannot join in a consolidated return. For further discussion of the tax treatment of TMPs, see Chapter 8.

29   Sections 267(b)(3) and (f); Treasury Regulation §§ 1.267(f)-1T and -2T. These rules apply equally to a corporation that is a taxable mortgage pool. The seller's losses would not be deferred, but instead would be shifted to the purchasing corporation, if the seller ceased to be a member of the same controlled group as the purchaser. See Treasury Regulation §§ 1.267(f)-1T(c)(6) and (c)(7)(i).

30   Under section 351, gain or loss is not recognized upon a transfer of property to a corporation solely in exchange for stock if the transferors as a group control the corporation (generally, own at least 80% of its voting stock and 80% of each class of nonvoting stock) immediately following the transfer. However, if a transferor receives cash or other property (including debt) in addition to stock, it will recognize gain (but not loss) in the same manner as if the property had been sold, except that the amount of gain recognized will be limited to the amount of cash or other property received.

31   See Chapter 6, footnote 92 and accompanying text.

32   If the issuer is a corporation, such a sale may also trigger the recognition of gains or losses from sales of mortgages to the issuer that were previously deferred, as described in footnotes 28 and 29, above.

C. REMICs

With a limited exception, a sponsor that transfers mortgages to a REMIC in exchange for regular or residual interests, either directly or through intermediaries, does not recognize gain or loss in the exchange.[33] The aggregate adjusted basis of the property transferred (increased by the REMIC's organizational expenses) is allocated among the REMIC interests received in proportion to their respective fair market values on the pricing date or, if none, the startup day.[34] Each time the sponsor sells an interest in the REMIC (whether a regular interest or a residual interest), it recognizes gain or loss[35] equal to the excess of the amount realized (net of syndication expenses) over its basis in that interest.[36] The tax consequences to the sponsor would be the same if the REMIC, instead of issuing regular and residual interests to the sponsor in exchange for mortgages, issued those interests to the

---

33 See section 860F(b)(1)(A); Treasury Regulation § 1.860F-2(b)(2). The bankruptcy court in *In re: Imperial Corp. of America*, 91-2 U.S.T.C. ¶ 50, 342 (Bank. S.D. Cal. 1991), held to the contrary, apparently solely on procedural grounds. The regulations provide that no gain or loss shall be recognized on the "direct or indirect" transfer of property to a REMIC in exchange for REMIC interests. A sponsor is considered to effect such an exchange indirectly if it transfers property to another person that acquires a transitory ownership interest in that property before exchanging it for REMIC interests, after which the transitory owner transfers some or all of those interests to the sponsor. See Treasury Regulation § 1.860F-2(b)(1). Although not entirely clear, it is possible that accrued market discount on any mortgage that has not yet been included in income would be recognized upon transfer of the mortgage to a REMIC. The rule requiring recognition in section 1276(a)(1) applies except as otherwise provided in the section "notwithstanding any other provision of this subtitle," and there is no exception for transfers to REMICs. See Chapter 6, footnote 92 and accompanying text.

34 Treasury Regulation § 1.860F-2(b)(3)(i). Issues raised by the existence of negative value residual interests are discussed in Chapter 7, Part E.4.h. Organizational expenses are expenses incurred by the sponsor (or the REMIC) that are directly related to the creation of the REMIC. They include legal fees for preparation of the REMIC's constituent documents and accounting fees and other administrative expenses related to the formation of the REMIC. Treasury Regulation § 1.860F-2(b)(3)(ii)(A). Syndication expenses (see footnote 36, below) are not organizational expenses. The "pricing date" is the date on which the terms of the regular and residual interests are fixed and the prices at which a substantial portion of the regular interests will be sold are fixed. Treasury Regulation § 1.860F-2(b)(3)(iii).

35 The limitations on the recognition of losses from sales of pass-through certificates described in footnote 13, above, also are relevant for REMIC interests. Special wash sale rules apply to REMIC residual interests. See Chapter 7, footnotes 54–56 and accompanying text.

36 Syndication expenses are expenses incurred by the sponsor or other persons to market interests in the REMIC. They include brokerage fees, registration fees, underwriter or placement agent fees, and the cost of printing sales materials. Treasury Regulation § 1.860F-2(b)(3)(ii)(B). Where all REMIC interests are sold to investors, the distinction between syndication expenses and organizational expenses is inconsequential. Thus, the distinction should not matter to a securities dealer that is acting as a REMIC sponsor and either sells all REMIC interests or is treated as selling them under the mark-to-market rules for securities dealers in section 475 (described in Chapter 9, Part E). In the case of a sponsor that is not a securities dealer, it would seem appropriate to allow a deduction (probably as a capital loss) for syndication expenses allocable to REMIC interests that are not sold at the time when those interests are retired, by equating the retirement to a sale. The regulations do not address the point. Syndication expenses are included in a REMIC's basis in its assets (and in determining the amount of its liabilities), because that basis, and the issue price of regular interests, are determined by reference to the prices paid by investors to purchase REMIC interests (which include syndication costs). See Chapter 7, footnote 31 and accompanying text.

sponsor or unrelated investors for cash and used that cash to purchase the mortgages from the sponsor. The alternative transaction would be characterized for tax purposes as a contribution of the mortgages by the sponsor to the REMIC in exchange for all interests in the REMIC, followed by a sale by the sponsor for cash of those interests which it does not retain.[37]

A REMIC generally is allowed to exchange mortgages that it holds for other mortgages (referred to as qualified replacement mortgages) even if the mortgages given up by the REMIC are not defective, provided the exchange occurs within three months after the startup day.[38] The Service has authority to prevent sponsors from using this rule to achieve a tax advantage. In particular, the Service may adopt regulations (1) providing appropriate rules for the treatment of transfers of qualified replacement mortgages to a REMIC where the transferor holds any interest in the REMIC, or (2) providing that a mortgage will be treated as a qualified replacement mortgage only if it is part of a "bona fide replacement (and not part of a swap of mortgages)."[39] No such regulations have been proposed or issued to date.

To illustrate some of the evils at which the regulation authority is aimed, suppose that a sponsor owns mortgages A, B, and C with bases, respectively, of $80, $100, and $120. Assume that each of the three mortgages has a fair market value of $100. In the absence of special rules, the sponsor might attempt to sell mortgage A without currently recognizing the $20 of built-in gain by contributing the mortgage to a REMIC and having the REMIC swap it for mortgage B. The exchange would result in no gain to the REMIC, and hence no gain to residual interest holders, because the REMIC would have a basis of $100 in mortgage A, and no gain to the sponsor as the transferor of mortgage B, because the sponsor's basis in that mortgage is also $100. Following its sojourn in the REMIC, mortgage A would have a basis of $100 in the sponsor's hands, and therefore could be sold by the sponsor without gain. Alternatively, suppose that the sponsor transferred mortgage B to a REMIC which exchanged it for mortgage C. In the absence of these special rules, the sponsor might claim currently 100 percent of the $20 built-in loss on the exchange of mortgage C, even though the portion of the built-in loss allocable to the interests in the REMIC retained by the sponsor would be deferred (as discussed below) if the sponsor had transferred mortgage C directly to the REMIC.[40]

---

37   See Treasury Regulation § 1.860F-2(a)(1).

38   See Chapter 4, Part A.2.a.(iv).

39   See sections 860G(e)(4) and (5). If a mortgage received by a REMIC in exchange for another mortgage is not treated as a qualified replacement mortgage because the exchange was a "swap" of mortgages rather than a "bona fide replacement," income from the mortgage would be subject to a 100% prohibited transactions tax, provided the mortgage and any other nonqualifying assets are *de minimis*. If they are not *de minimis*, the REMIC election would terminate. See Chapter 4, Parts A.2 and B. Although the statutory language is oblique, any exchange of mortgages that is effected primarily for tax avoidance reasons is likely to be vulnerable under the "swap" rule.

40   The regulation authority referred to above was added to the Code by TAMRA. In explaining the reasons for the new "swap" regulation authority, the TAMRA House Report at 85 refers to the possible avoidance of gain, but not the acceleration of losses. The Code itself does not limit the

As this discussion suggests, the major difference in tax consequences for a sponsor of pay-through bonds of making or not making a REMIC election relates to the portion of the sponsor's overall economic gain or loss (represented by the difference between the sum of the fair market values of the bonds and equity interests in the issuer and the sponsor's basis in the mortgages) that is recognized at the time of the bond offering and upon sale of equity interests in the issuer. If no election is made, the sponsor would not recognize any portion of such gain or loss at the time of the bond sale, but would recognize a portion of such gain or loss each time an equity interest is sold, corresponding to the portion of the equity interest that is sold.[41] By contrast, if a REMIC election is made, the sponsor would recognize a portion of such gain or loss equal to the portion of *all* interests in the issuer (equity and bonds) that is sold, as those interests are sold. Thus, for example, if the bonds represent 95 percent of the value of all REMIC interests, 95 percent of such gain or loss would be recognized when the bonds are sold. Of course, the recognition of gain or loss is only one of a number of factors influencing the decision whether to make a REMIC election.[42]

The tax consequences for a sponsor of the creation and sale of pass-through certificates would be substantially the same whether or not a REMIC election is made.[43]

A REMIC interest that is issued in exchange for mortgages or other property generally is taxed as if it had been issued at a price equal to its initial fair market value.[44] Under section 860F(b)(1), the income of the sponsor from holding any REMIC interest is adjusted to take account of any difference between its issue price and initial basis in the hands of the sponsor.[45] In particular, that difference is re-

---

regulation authority to situations involving built-in gain. The only guidance in the legislative history as to the likely content of regulations dealing with transfers of qualified replacement mortgages to a REMIC in which the transferor holds an interest is the statement that they "may provide rules for determining the basis of mortgages transferred to, or received from, a REMIC as part of a replacement of qualified mortgages, and also may provide rules for determining or adjusting the basis of qualified mortgages held by the REMIC before or after the replacement." TAMRA House Report at 85.

41   The statement in the text contrasts the effect of selling pay-through bonds with the effect of selling REMIC interests. Gain also could be recognized in connection with an issuance of pay-through bonds as a result of the transfer of mortgage collateral to the issuer, particularly if the issuer is a corporation that does not file a consolidated return with the sponsor. See Part B.

42   The principal differences between REMICs and issuers of pay-through bonds are outlined in Chapter 2.

43   This statement assumes, in the case of a sponsor of senior and subordinated pass-through certificates to which the stripped bond rules do not apply, that the sponsor would allocate its basis between the two classes in proportion to their fair market values at the time of sale. See text following footnote 17, above.

44   Treasury Regulation § 1.860G-1(d). Such fair market value is determined on the pricing date, if any (see footnote 34, above), or otherwise on the startup day. For a general discussion of the issue price of REMIC interests, see Chapter 7, footnote 31.

45   This rule also applies to any person whose basis in a REMIC interest is determined by reference to its basis in the hands of the sponsor. Treasury Regulation § 1.860F-2(b)(6). For a discussion of possible adjustments to the income of purchasers of REMIC residual interests to account for differences between "inside" and "outside" basis, see Chapter 7, text accompanying footnote 36.

quired to be included in income if the issue price is higher, or is allowed as a deduction if the issue price is lower, (1) in the case of a regular interest, as if that difference were original issue discount or bond premium, respectively, or (2) in the case of a residual interest, ratably over the anticipated weighted average life of the REMIC.[46]

---

46 See section 860F(b)(1); Treasury Regulation § 1.860F-2(b)(4). The sponsor's basis in a REMIC interest is increased or decreased by the amount of any such income or deductions. Treasury Regulation § 1.860F-2(b)(5). The weighted average life of a REMIC is determined under Treasury Regulation § 1.860E-1(a)(1)(iv), taking account of the prepayment assumption used in applying the PAC method to regular interests, any required or permitted clean-up calls, and any required qualified liquidations. For further discussion of a REMIC's weighted average life, see Chapter 7, footnote 86.

Glossary

References in this glossary to bonds or debt instruments include REMIC regular interests. For references to further discussion in the text of the terms defined herein, consult the index.

Accretion Directed (or *Stated Maturity*) *Class*: A class of bonds that receive principal payments funded by accretions on specified *accrual* (or compound interest or Z) classes. These classes also may receive principal payments from other sources.

Accrual Class: See *Compound Interest Class*.

Accrual Period: A period used in calculating accruals of original issue discount on a debt instrument. Interest (including original issue discount) is compounded at the end of each accrual period.

Acquisition Premium: The excess of the price paid by a purchaser of a debt instrument issued with original issue discount over the adjusted issue price of that instrument on the date of purchase. The term applies only when the instrument is purchased at a price no greater than the instrument's remaining stated redemption price at maturity. The daily portions of original issue discount on a debt instrument acquired with acquisition premium are reduced proportionately by the amount of such premium.

Adjusted Basis or *Adjusted Tax Basis*: The holder's aggregate unrecovered investment in a security as measured for tax purposes. Upon sale of the security, the adjusted basis is compared with the amount realized to determine the seller's gain or loss. In general, a holder's adjusted basis in a security equals the cost of the security to the holder, increased by the income from the security and decreased (but not below zero) by (1) the payments received thereon, and (2) deductions allowed to the holder for losses from holding the security or amortized premium.

Adjusted Issue Price: For a *debt instrument*, an amount used in calculating accruals of original issue discount, which equals the adjusted basis the instrument would have in the hands of an original holder who purchased the instrument at the issue price on the issue date. For a *REMIC residual interest*, an amount calculated at the beginning of each calendar quarter that is used in determining the excess inclusions on the residual interest. It generally equals the amount that would be the adjusted issue price of the residual interest if (1) it were a debt instrument that had a yield to maturity equal to 120 percent of the Federal long-term rate for the month in which the interest was issued, (2) all income on the debt instrument increased, and all distributions on the instrument reduced, the adjusted issue price, and (3) each accrual period ended on the last day of a calendar quarter.

Amortizable Bond Premium: In general, in the case of a debt instrument to which an election under section 171 to amortize bond premium applies, the amount by which the adjusted basis of the instrument exceeds the amount payable on maturity.

Applicable Federal Rate: An average of current yields of U.S. Treasury securities for different ranges of maturities that is computed and published monthly by the Internal Revenue Service for use in various tax calculations. The applicable Federal rate for the longest range of maturities (more than 9 years) is referred to as the *Federal long-term rate.*

Arrangements Test: As used in this book, a requirement (imposed by section 860D(a)(6)) that a REMIC adopt reasonable arrangements designed to ensure that its residual interests are not held by disqualified organizations and that the REMIC will make available information necessary to calculate the tax on transfers of residual interests to such organizations.

Asset(s) Test: See *REMIC Assets Test* and *TMP Asset Test.*

Association Taxable as a Corporation: An entity that is classified as a corporation for tax purposes even though it is not organized as a corporation under state law.

B Class: A term commonly used to refer to a subordinated class of pass-through certificates or bonds.

Backup Withholding: Generally, a 31 percent tax withheld from certain interest and dividend payments, and payments by a broker of the proceeds of a sale of property, usually because of a failure of the payee to furnish a proper taxpayer identification number to the payor. This tax is imposed as a collection device and is fully creditable by the taxpayer.

Basis: See *Adjusted Basis.*

Basis Risk: As used in this book, the risk that there will be a shortfall in funds available to make a payment on a REMIC regular interest arising from a difference between the interest earned on the REMIC's regular interests and interest earned on the REMIC's assets (disregarding mortgage defaults).

Bearer Form: A security is in bearer form if it is not in registered form. These terms are used in applying the TEFRA registration requirements. See also *Registered Form.*

Blue Book: As used in this book, the *General Explanation of the Tax Reform Act of*

1986 (JCS-10-87), May 4, 1987, published (with a blue cover) by the staff of the Joint Committee on Taxation. Blue books are not official legislative history but are helpful in interpreting the related legislation.

Bond Premium: See *Amortizable Bond Premium*.

Call Premium: A premium, in excess of the principal balance and accrued but unpaid interest, paid by the issuer of a debt instrument to exercise an optional right to prepay the instrument.

Cash Flow Investments: One of the three types of permitted investments for a REMIC. Cash flow investments are passive investments of the cash flow received on qualified mortgages for a temporary period before distribution to holders of interests in the REMIC.

Clean-up Call: As applied to pass-through certificates, a right of the servicer to purchase the underlying mortgages when their aggregate principal balance drops below a small percentage (generally 5% or 10%) of their aggregate principal amount when transferred to the trust. As applied to REMICs, the prepayment in full of a class of regular interests when, because of prior payments with respect to those interests, the administrative cost associated with servicing those interests outweighs the benefits of keeping them outstanding. It does not include the prepayment of a class of regular interests undertaken in order to profit from a change in interest rates. Sales of qualified mortgages made to facilitate a clean-up call are not prohibited transactions and cash contributions to a REMIC to facilitate a clean-up call are not subject to the 100 percent tax on contributions to a REMIC after its startup day.

Code: As used in this book, the Internal Revenue Code of 1986.

Collateralized Mortgage Obligation or CMO: A pay-through bond or REMIC regular interest that is part of an issue divided into classes, typically having different maturities and payment priorities.

Component Class: A single class of bonds that provide for payments equal to the sum of the principal and interest payments on defined "components."

Compound Interest Class: A class of bonds that provides for payments of principal and interest at regular intervals except that no payments of principal or interest are made during an initial period (or other specified period) until specified other classes of bonds have been paid. Interest that accrues but is not paid currently is added to principal.

Conduit Issuer: As used in this book, either a REMIC, or an owner trust classified as a grantor trust or partnership that issues pay-through bonds.

Conference Report: As used in this book, the conference committee report on TRA 1986, H.R. Rep. No. 841, 99th Cong., 2d Sess. (September 18, 1986).

Constant Yield Method: A method of calculating accruals of discount (or premium) on a debt instrument under which the discount (premium) that accrues in any period equals the increase (decrease) during the period in the value of the instrument, calculated assuming that the instrument has at all times a constant yield to maturity.

Contingent Payment Debt Instrument: As used in this book, a bond other than a variable rate debt instrument that provides for payments that are contingent in amount.

Contributions Tax: As used in this book, a 100 percent tax imposed on a REMIC by section 860G(d) on certain contributions to the REMIC after the startup day.

Credit Enhancement Contract: A term used in the REMIC regulations. A credit enhancement contract is any arrangement whereby a person agrees to guarantee full or partial payment of the amounts payable on one or more qualified mortgages, or on one or more interests in the REMIC, in the event of defaults or delinquencies on qualified mortgages, unanticipated losses or expenses incurred by the REMIC, or lower than expected returns on cash flow investments. Credit enhancement contracts are not treated as separate assets of (or interests in) a REMIC, but instead are considered part of the REMIC's qualified mortgages. A similar definition and rule apply under the proposed TMP regulations.

Daily Accruals: For a REMIC residual interest, the measure of daily "economic income" that is used in calculating excess inclusions. Income is an excess inclusion to the extent it exceeds the daily accruals.

Daily Portion: The amount of original issue discount on a debt instrument that a holder is required to include in income for any day.

Debt-Financed Income: See *Unrelated Debt-Financed Income*.

De Minimis Rule: A rule under which original issue discount and market discount are considered to be zero if the amounts of such discount are less than a *de minimis* amount (generally, one quarter of one percent of the stated redemption price at maturity times the number of whole years to maturity). A special *de minimis* rule applies to teaser rates and interest holidays.

Disqualified Organization: In general, a governmental entity or other organization that is not subject to federal income tax on excess inclusions. The arrangements test requires a REMIC to adopt reasonable arrangements designed to ensure that residual interests are not held by disqualified organizations. In addition, a tax is imposed on transfers of residual interests to a disqualified organization, and on any pass-thru entity if a disqualified organization owns a residual interest indirectly through such entity.

Entity Classification Regulation: Treasury Regulations §§ 301.7701-2 through 301.7701-4. These regulations determine whether an organization will be classified for federal income tax purposes as a trust, partnership or corporation based on the functional characteristics of the organization. See also *Sears Regulations*.

Eurobond Exception: An exception to the TEFRA registration requirements which allows debt instruments to be issued in bearer form if they are targeted to non-U.S. investors, interest is payable outside the United States, and the instrument bears the TEFRA legend.

Excess Inclusion: A portion, calculated under a formula, of the income from the holding of a REMIC residual interest that cannot be offset with losses, with a limited exception for excess inclusions realized by thrift institutions, or benefit from any tax exemption or reduction in tax rates.

Excess Interest Class: A class of bonds that receive any interest paid on underlying mortgages in excess of the interest required to be paid on all other classes of bonds. Excess interest classes may be interest only classes or may have a specified principal amount.

Excess Servicing Fee: The portion of the fee charged by the servicer of a pool of mortgages that is in excess of a fair market value charge for the services rendered. Excess servicing fees are recharacterized for tax purposes as an ownership interest in the mortgages that are being serviced.

Federal Long-Term Rate: See *Applicable Federal Rate*.

FHLMC: The Federal Home Loan Mortgage Corporation, also known as "Freddie Mac."

FIRPTA: The Foreign Investment in Real Property Tax Act of 1980, Public Law 96-499. FIRPTA enacted section 897, which subjects certain non-U.S. investors to U.S. income tax on gains from the disposition of interests in U.S. real property.

FNMA: The Federal National Mortgage Association, also known as "Fannie Mae."

Foreclosure Property: One of the three types of permitted investments for a REMIC. Foreclosure property is generally real property that was acquired by a REMIC in connection with the default of a qualified mortgage and has been held not longer than a specified grace period.

Form 1066: The annual federal REMIC tax return.

GAAP: U.S. generally accepted accounting principles.

G.C.M.: A General Counsel's Memorandum issued by the Office of Chief Counsel in the Internal Revenue Service.

GNMA: The Government National Mortgage Association, also known as "Ginnie Mae."

Grantor Trust: A state law trust that is essentially ignored for federal income tax purposes because the trust beneficiaries are treated as the direct owners of all of the trust's assets. An investment trust will generally be a grantor trust if the trustee has no power to vary the investment of the beneficiaries and (with limited exceptions) there is only one class of ownership interests in the trust.

Index Allocation Class: Classes of bonds whose principal payment allocations are based on the value of an index.

Installment Obligation: A debt instrument on which principal (or other amounts included in the stated redemption price at maturity) is paid in more than one install-ment.

Intention-to-Call Rule: A rule that treats as ordinary income gain on the sale or exchange of a debt instrument (limited to the amount of unaccrued original issue discount on the instrument) if the issuer is determined to have had, as of the instrument's issue date, an intention to call the instrument prior to maturity. This rule does not apply to bonds to which the PAC method applies.

Interest Accrual Class: See *Compound Interest Class*.

Interest Only Class: A class of bonds that receives only interest payments, or interest payments and a nominal amount of principal. Interest payments may be calculated by reference to a notional or actual principal amount or may be defined as a right to specified interest payments on underlying mortgages or REMIC regular interests.

Interests Test: As used in this book, a requirement (imposed by sections 860D(a)(2) and (3)) that all interests in a REMIC be regular interests or residual interests and that there be one and only one class of residual interests.

Inverse Floating Rate: Interest on a debt instrument that varies inversely with an index of market interest rates.

IO Interests: A class of REMIC regular interests that is an interest only class.

IO Strips: Interest only strips, which are pass-through certificates that entitle the holder solely to a portion of the interest payments made on the mortgages held by the issuing trust. See also *PO Strips*.

Issue Date: For a debt instrument, the settlement date for the sale of the instrument by the issuer to the first holder (apparently, excluding middlemen).

Issue Price: For a debt instrument, the price used to determine the amount of original issue discount, if any, with which the instrument is issued. For a debt instrument that is part of a class of debt instruments issued for cash, the issue price is the initial cash offering price to the public (excluding middlemen) at which a substantial amount of the debt instruments of that class was sold. Special rules apply to debt instruments issued for non-cash property. For REMIC interests, the issue price is determined in the same manner, except that the issue price of an interest issued in exchange for mortgages or other non-cash property is the initial fair market value of such interest.

Kitchen Sink Securities: Bonds or other mortgage-backed securities backed by a portfolio of other mortgage-backed securities (generally including combinations of interest only and principal only securities). The name refers to the fact that the collateral consists of "everything but the kitchen sink."

Legending Requirement: As used in this book, a requirement that a legend setting out certain information regarding original issue discount appear on the face of certain debt instruments (including REMIC regular interests and pay-through bonds) issued with original issue discount. See also *TEFRA Legend*.

Liquid Asset Class: Bonds intended to qualify as "liquid assets" for certain savings institutions. Liquid Asset Classes have final payment dates not later than five years from their issue dates.

Liquidation Period: For a REMIC, the period beginning on the date of adoption of a plan of liquidation in connection with a qualified liquidation and ending at the close of the 90th day after such date. During the liquidation period, the REMIC assets test is suspended and the sale of qualified mortgages is not a prohibited transaction.

Long First Period Bond: A debt instrument for which the period between the issue date and first payment date is greater than the regular interval between payment dates. Subject to a special *de minimis* rule for interest holidays, all or a portion of the stated interest on a long first period bond may be included in the bond's stated redemption price at maturity.

Lower-Tier REMIC: A tiered REMIC that issues regular interests to another tiered REMIC.

Market Discount: In common parlance, any discount at which a debt instrument is purchased below its principal amount that is not original issue discount. There is also a special tax definition, which is the excess of the stated redemption price at maturity of a debt instrument (or its adjusted issue price in the case of a debt instrument having original issue discount) over its basis immediately after its acquisition by the taxpayer, except that market discount is considered to be zero if that difference is less than a *de minimis* amount. See also *De Minimis Rule*.

Mark to Market Rules: As used in this book, refers to the rules in section 475 that require securities dealers to calculate gain or loss from positions in securities by treating the securities as if they were sold for fair market value at the end of each taxable year.

Maturities Test: As used in this book, one element of the definition of a TMP. An entity meets the maturities test if it is the obligor under "debt obligations with 2 or more maturities."

Miscellaneous Itemized Deductions: Certain itemized deductions (including deductions for investment expenses) that are allowed to an individual only to the extent that the aggregate amount of such deductions exceeds 2 percent of the individual's adjusted gross income.

Multiple Class Trust Regulations: See *Sears Regulations*.

Negative Value Residual: See *Noneconomic Residual*.

No Payment Residual: A REMIC residual interest that is entitled to no payments of principal or interest.

Noneconomic Residual: Used colloquially to refer to any REMIC residual interest that has a negative fair value, because the net tax cost of holding the residual interest exceeds the value of any distributions expected thereon. Transfers of certain noneconomic residual interests are disregarded for federal income tax purposes if a significant purpose of the transfer is to impede the assessment or collection of tax. For this purpose, a "noneconomic residual interest" is defined in Treasury Regulation § 1.860E-1(c)(2) using a test that compares cash distributions with the taxes imposed on excess inclusions. Certain negative value residual interests are not treated as "securities" for purposes of the mark-to-market rules.

Non-Sticky Jump Class: A class of bonds whose principal payment priorities change temporarily upon the occurrence of one or more "trigger" events. A Non-Sticky Jump Class "jumps" to its new priority on each payment date when the trigger condition is met and reverts to its original priority (does not "stick" to the new priority) on each payment date when the trigger condition is not met.

Notional Class: A class of bonds having only a notional principal amount. A notional principal amount is used as a reference to calculate interest payments.

Notional Principal Contract: The tax term for interest rate or currency swaps, and cap or floor contracts. More broadly, a notional principal contract, as defined in Treasury Regulation § 1.446-3(c), is a financial instrument that provides for the payment of amounts by one party to another at specified intervals calculated by reference to a specified index upon a notional principal amount in exchange for specified consideration or a promise to pay similar amounts.

NYSBA 1984 Report: As used in this book, the New York State Bar Association, Tax Section, Ad Hoc Committee on Original Issue Discount and Coupon Stripping, "Preliminary Report on Issues to be Addressed in Regulations and Corrective Legislation," reprinted in *Tax Notes*, March 5, 1984 at 993.

NYSBA 1987 Report: As used in this book, the New York State Bar Association, Tax Section, "Report of Ad Hoc Committee on Proposed Original Issue Discount Regulations," reprinted in *Tax Notes*, January 26, 1987 at 363.

NYSBA 1992 REMIC Report: As used in this book, the New York State Bar Association, Tax Section, "Report on the Proposed Real Estate Mortgage Investment Conduit Regulations," March 19, 1992.

OID: see *Original Issue Discount*.

OID Regulations: As used in this book, Treasury regulations, principally under sections 1271 through 1275, dealing with original issue discount.

Original Issue Discount or OID: The excess of the stated redemption price at maturity of a debt instrument over its issue price, except that original issue discount is considered to be zero if it is less than a *de minimis* amount. See also *De Minimis Rule*.

Owner Trust: As used in this book, a non-REMIC trust that holds mortgages or interests therein and issues pay-through bonds. The term is used to distinguish the trust from the indenture trust established for the bonds.

PAC Class (or *Planned Amortization Class*): A class of bonds that are designed to receive principal payments using a predetermined schedule derived by assuming two constant prepayment rates for the underlying qualified mortgages. These two rates are the endpoints for the "structuring range" for the PAC classes.

PAC Method: See *Prepayment Assumption Catch-up Method*.

Pass-Through Certificates: As used in this book, certificates that evidence beneficial ownership interests in a grantor trust that holds mortgages and distributes payments thereon currently to certificate holders. See also *Grantor Trust*.

Pass-Through Debt Certificates: As used in this book, certificates that take the form of ownership interests in a non-REMIC trust but that are intended to be treated as debt of the trust for federal income tax purposes.

Pass-Through Entity or Pass-Thru Entity: A RIC, REIT, bank common trust fund, partnership, trust or estate and certain cooperative corporations. In addition, except as may be provided in Treasury regulations, any person holding an interest in a pass-thru entity as a nominee for another will, with respect to such interest, be treated as a pass-thru entity. A pass-thru entity is taxable on any excess inclusions that it realizes from REMIC residual interests to the extent those excess inclusions are allocable to interests in the entity registered in the name of a disqualified organization.

Pass-Through Interest Holder: An individual, excluding non-resident alien investors, a person (including a trust or estate) that computes its taxable income in the same manner as an individual, and certain pass-through entities, including S corporations but not including REITs. A holder of REMIC interests who is a pass-through interest holder must include in income, and is allowed (subject to limitations on the deductibility of miscellaneous itemized deductions) a deduction for, such holder's allocable share of the REMIC's investment expenses. See also *Single-Class REMIC*.

Payment Lag Bond: A debt instrument that provides for a lag between the end of the period over which interest accrues and the date on which such interest is paid. See also *Long First Period Bond*.

Pay-Through Bond: As used in this book, a debt instrument issued by a non-REMIC issuer (typically an owner trust or a corporation) that is collateralized by mortgages and whose terms provide that principal prepayments on the mortgages are "paid through" to holders.

Permitted Investments: In general, the only assets that a REMIC can hold other than qualified mortgages. There are three types of permitted investments: cash flow investments, qualified reserve assets and foreclosure property.

Phantom Income: As used in this book, that portion of the taxable income realized by holders of residual interests in a REMIC, or by an issuer (or the owners of an issuer) of pay-through bonds, that is not economic income because it necessarily will be offset in future periods with an equal amount of taxable loss. Phantom income in any period may or may not be greater than current cash distributions.

P.L.R. or T.A.M.: A private letter ruling or technical advice memorandum issued by the Internal Revenue Service. Under section 6110(j), P.L.R.s and T.A.M.s may not be used or cited as legal precedent. They do, however, provide guidance as to the position the Internal Revenue Service is likely to take in resolving the issues addressed in the rulings and may represent "substantial authority" for purposes of avoiding penalties imposed on a taxpayer that takes a position on a tax return for which there is no substantial authority.

PO Strips: Principal only strips, which are pass-through certificates that entitle the holders solely to a portion of the principal payments made on the mortgages held by the issuing trust. See also *IO Strips*.

Portfolio Interest: Interest on debt instruments issued after July 18, 1984 that benefits from the limited repeal by TRA 1984 of the 30 percent withholding tax that otherwise applies to U.S. source interest paid to non-U.S. investors.

Premium: See *Acquisition Premium, Amortizable Bond Premium*, and *Call Premium*.

Prepayment Assumption: As used in this book, an assumption used in calculating accruals of discount on a debt instrument under the PAC method about the rate at which the mortgages underlying the debt instrument will be prepaid, and if earnings on temporary investments may affect the timing of payments on the debt instrument, the rate of those earnings.

Prepayment Assumption Catch-Up Method or *PAC Method*: As used in the book, a constant yield method of accruing discount (described in section 1272(a)(6)) that takes account of the Prepayment Assumption and makes "catch-up" adjustments in each accrual period for differences between actual prior experience and the Prepayment Assumption.

Prohibited Transactions: Transactions engaged in by a REMIC that are described in section 860F(a)(2). They include certain dispositions of REMIC assets, and the receipt by the REMIC of income for providing services, or from any asset other than a qualified mortgage or permitted investment. Prohibited transactions are not in fact prohibited but the net income from a prohibited transaction is subject to a 100 percent tax.

Proposed TMP Regulations: As used in this book, proposed Treasury regulations, issued in December 1992 under section 7701(i), relating to the characterization of an entity as a TMP.

Pro Rata Prepayment: An prepayment of a debt instrument that results in a substantially pro rata reduction in each payment remaining to be made on the instrument. Under the OID regulations, a pro rata prepayment is treated as a payment in full retirement of a portion of the instrument.

PSA: A commonly used standard prepayment assumption proposed by the Public Securities Association under which it is assumed that (1) each mortgage loan in a pool prepays in the first month after issuance at an annual rate of 0.2 percent of its outstanding principal balance, (2) this prepayment rate increases each month thereafter at an annual rate of 0.2 percent through the thirtieth month after origination and (3) the prepayment rate remains constant in each month thereafter at an annual rate of 6.0 percent.

Qualified Liquidation: A liquidation of a REMIC that is completed within 90 days after adoption of a plan of liquidation. See also *Liquidation Period*.

Qualified Mortgage: The type of mortgage loan (or interest in a mortgage loan) that may be held by a REMIC. Qualified mortgages include qualified replacement mortgages and certain REMIC regular interests.

Qualified Replacement Mortgage: A type of qualified mortgage that is received by a REMIC in exchange for another qualified mortgage, most often to replace a defective mortgage.

Qualified Reserve Asset: Any intangible property held for investment by a REMIC as part of a qualified reserve fund. Qualified reserve assets are one of the three types of permitted investments for a REMIC.

Qualified Reserve Fund: A reasonably required reserve fund to provide for full payment of expenses of the REMIC, amounts due on REMIC interests in the event of defaults on qualified mortgages or lower than expected returns on cash flow investments and certain other items. A qualified reserve fund must be promptly and appropriately reduced as payments of qualified mortgages are received, and the gross income from the sale of fund assets in any year generally cannot exceed 30 percent of the gross income from all such assets.

Qualified Stated Interest Payments: Payments of stated interest on a debt instrument that, in general, are made at the same rate over the entire life of the instrument and are not included in the instrument's stated redemption price at maturity. Thus, those payments are recognized as interest payments for tax purposes and are not included in original issue discount.

Qualified Subsidiary: A corporation (1) all of the stock of which and substantially all of the debt of which is owned by a thrift and (2) which is organized and operated exclusively in connection with the organization and operation of one or more REMICs. If a thrift has losses and files a consolidated return with a subsidiary that owns a REMIC residual interest, the thrift can offset its losses against excess inclusions realized by the subsidiary only if the subsidiary is a qualified subsidiary.

Qualifying Real Property Loans: Certain real property loans (described in section 593(d)) that are treated favorably in computing deductions of thrift institutions for additions to bad debt reserves.

RA 1987: The Revenue Act of 1987, Public Law 100-203.

Real Estate Assets: A type of asset (defined in section 856(c)(6)(B)) that counts favorably for purposes of the REIT assets test. The term includes real property and interests in mortgages on real property.

Real Estate Investment Trust or REIT: An entity that invests primarily in real estate assets, that elects to be taxed as a REIT, and that meets certain requirements of the Code relating to its organization, assets, sources of income and distributions. Although a REIT must be a corporation or other entity that is classified as a corporation for federal income tax purposes, a REIT generally is not subject to corporate income tax to the extent it distributes its earnings currently to its shareholders.

Real Estate Mortgage Investment Conduit: See *REMIC*.

Registered Form: A debt instrument is considered to be in registered form for purposes of the TEFRA registration requirements if it may be transferred only (1) by surrendering the instrument to the issuer (or its agent) for reissuance and/or (2) through a book entry system maintained by the issuer (or its agent). With some exceptions, the Code requires all debt instruments to be issued in registered form. See also *Eurobond Exception* and *TEFRA Registration Requirements*.

Registration-Required Obligation: An obligation that must be issued or held in registered form to comply with the TEFRA registration requirements.

Regular Interest: One of the two types of permitted interests in a REMIC (the other being a residual interest). A regular interest must unconditionally entitle the holder to receive a specified principal amount (or, if the interest is not in the form of debt, a similar amount), and provide that interest payments (or other similar amounts), if any, at or before maturity are payable based on a fixed rate (or, to the extent permitted in regulations, at a variable rate), or consist of a specified portion of the interest payments on qualified mortgages which does not vary during the period the regular interest is outstanding.

Regulated Investment Company or *RIC*: A corporation registered under the Investment Company Act of 1940 that invests primarily in securities, elects to be a RIC, and meets certain requirements under the Code relating to its assets, sources of income and distributions. A RIC is not subject to corporate income tax to the extent it distributes its earnings currently to shareholders.

REIT: See *Real Estate Investment Trust.*

REIT Assets Test: As used in this book, a requirement (imposed by section 856(c)(5)(A)) that at least 75 percent of the assets of a REIT consist of real estate assets, cash, cash items and Government securities.

Relationship Test: As used in this book, one element of the definition of a TMP. Under the proposed TMP regulations, an entity meets the relationship test if the timing and amount of payments on the debt obligations issued by the entity are in large part determined by the timing and amount of payments on the debt obligations held by the entity.

REMIC or *Real Estate Mortgage Investment Conduit*: A pool of mortgages and related assets that elects under the Code to be a REMIC and that meets the arrangements test, the REMIC assets test and the interests test.

REMIC Assets Test: As used in this book, a requirement (imposed by section 860D(a)(4)) that, as of the close of the third month beginning after the startup day and at all times thereafter, all but a *de minimis* amount of the assets of a REMIC consist of qualified mortgages and permitted investments.

REMIC Regulations: Regulations adopted under section 860A through 860G of the Code.

Residual Interest: One of the two types of permitted interests in a REMIC (the other being a regular interest). A REMIC must have one (and only one) class of residual interest and distributions thereon, if any, must be made pro rata.

Retail Class: A class of bonds designed for sale to retail investors. Retail classes frequently are sold in small "units" or other increments and may receive principal payments in accordance with special priorities and allocation procedures.

Retirement Premium: See *Call Premium.*

Revised Issue Price: With respect to a debt instrument, has the same meaning as the adjusted issue price.

RIC: See *Regulated Investment Company.*

RRA 1993: The Revenue Reconciliation Act of 1993 (within the Omnibus Budget Reconciliation Act of 1993), Public Law 103-66.

Schedule Q: Schedule Q to Form 1066 (the annual federal REMIC tax return). Schedule Q is used by REMICs to report tax information quarterly to residual interest holders.

Scheduled Class: A class of bonds that have a right to receive principal payments according to a predetermined schedule but are not PAC or TAC Classes.

Sears Regulations: The name commonly given to Treasury Regulation § 301.7701-4(c) which provides, with a limited exception, that a trust having more than one class of ownership interests will not be classified as a trust but instead will be classified either as a partnership or as an association taxable as a corporation.

Senior/Subordinated Pass-Through Certificates: Pass-through certificates divided into classes having different priorities to receive payments in the event of a default on a mortgage held by the issuing trust. Senior/subordinated pass-through certificates may also be stripped pass-through certificates.

Sequential Pay Class: A class of bonds that receive principal payments in a prescribed sequence, that do not have predetermined schedules, and that under all circumstances receive payments of principal continuously from the first payment date on which they receive principal until they are retired. Sequential pay classes may receive principal payments concurrently with one or more other sequential pay classes.

Service: As used in this book, the Internal Revenue Service.

Single-Class-REMIC: A REMIC (1) that would be classified as a grantor trust in the absence of a REMIC election, including certain REMICs with multiple classes of interests, or (2) that is substantially similar to such a trust and is structured with the principal purpose of avoiding the requirement of allocating investment expenses to holders of regular interests who are pass-through interest holders. In general, a REMIC's investment expenses are allocated only among holders of the residual interest. However, in the case of a single-class REMIC, investment expenses are allocated among holders of *all* of the interests in the REMICs. See *Pass-Through Interest Holder*.

Sixty Percent Assets Test: See *Thrift Assets Test*.

SPA: Standard prepayment assumption. See *PSA*.

Startup Day: The day on which a REMIC issues all of its regular and residual interests.

Stated or *Coupon Interest*: Those payments on a debt instrument that, under the terms of the instrument, are denominated as interest. Payments of stated interest are treated as interest payments for tax purposes (and thus are not includible in original issue discount) only if they are qualified stated interest payments.

Stated Redemption Price at Maturity: The sum of all payments on a debt instrument other than qualified stated interest payments. Original issue discount is generally defined as the excess of a debt instrument's stated redemption price at maturity over its issue price.

Sticky Jump Class: A class of bonds whose principal payment priorities change permanently upon the occurrence of one or more "trigger" events. A sticky jump class "jumps" to its new priority on the first payment date when the trigger condition is met and retains ("sticks" to) that priority until retired.

Straight-Line Method: A method of amortizing an item of income or expense under which a ratable portion of the income or expense is allocated to each period.

Strip Class: A class of bonds that receives a constant proportion, or "strip," of the principal payments on the underlying mortgages.

Stripped Bond; Stripped Coupon: A stripped bond is a right to a principal payment on any debt instrument if (1) the instrument was issued with interest coupons and (2) there is a separation in ownership between the right to principal and the right to any coupon that has not yet become payable. A stripped coupon is a coupon relating to a stripped bond. For these purposes, the term *coupon* includes any right to interest whether or not represented by an interest coupon. Stripped bonds and coupons are subject to the bond stripping rules of section 1286.

Stripped Pass-Through Certificates: Pass-through certificates representing a right to one fixed percentage of the principal payments on the mortgages held by the issuing trust and a different fixed percentage of the interest payments on those mortgages. See also *IO Strips* and *PO Strips*.

Support (or *Companion*) *Class*: A class of bonds that receives principal payments on any payment date only if scheduled payments have been made on specified PAC, TAC and/or Scheduled Classes.

Swap Rule: A rule to be adopted under Treasury regulations that will prevent a mortgage received by a REMIC in exchange for another mortgage from being a qualified replacement mortgage if the exchange is part of a "swap" of mortgages and not part of a "bona fide replacement."

TAC (or *Targeted Amortization Class*): A class of bonds that are entitled to receive principal payments using a predetermined schedule derived by assuming a single constant prepayment rate for the underlying mortgages.

T.A.M.: See *P.L.R.* or *T.A.M.*

TAMRA: The Technical and Miscellaneous Revenue Act of 1988, Public Law 100-647. TAMRA included a number of amendments to the REMIC provisions of the Code.

TAMRA House Report: The report of the House Ways and Means Committee on TAMRA, H.R. Rep. No. 795, 100th Cong., 2d Sess. (July 26, 1988).

Targeted Registered Form: A debt instrument in registered form that has been targeted to foreign investors. Interest on such an instrument can be paid to a foreign financial institution (including a foreign branch of a U.S. bank) holding the instrument on behalf of a non-U.S. investor without requiring that the identity of the investor be reported to the Internal Revenue Service.

Targeted to Foreign Investors: A debt instrument for which there are arrangements reasonably designed to ensure that the instrument will be sold (or resold in connection with its original issuance) only to non-U.S. persons. The definition is relevant in applying the TEFRA registration requirements.

Tax Basis: See *Adjusted Basis*.

Taxable Mortgage Pool: In general, an entity that holds mortgages and issues pay-through bonds, or similar equity interests, divided into classes with different maturities. A taxable mortgage pool that issues securities after 1991 generally is subject to an entity level tax on its taxable income (after deductions for interest) unless it qualifies as a REMIC or REIT or is organized outside of the United States.

T.D.: A Treasury Decision.

TEFRA: The Tax Equity and Fiscal Responsibility Act of 1982, Public Law 97-248.

TEFRA Legend: A legend that must be placed on each definitive bearer bond and coupon issued under the Eurobond exception to the effect that any U.S. person who holds the obligation will be subject to limitations under U.S. income tax laws.

TEFRA Registration Requirements: Code provisions enacted by TEFRA that generally require debt instruments to be issued and held in registered form. See also *Eurobond Exception*.

Thrift Assets Test: As used in this book, a requirement that 60 percent of the assets of a thrift consist of residential real property loans and other assets described in section 7701(a)(19)(C). A thrift must satisfy this test in order to calculate bad debt deductions under a percentage of taxable income method and to qualify for certain other tax benefits.

Tiered REMIC: A REMIC that is part of a tiered structure with other REMICs. Two REMICs are part of a tiered structure if it was contemplated when both REMICs were formed that some or all of the regular interests of one REMIC would be held by the other.

TMP: See *Taxable Mortgage Pool*.

TMP Asset Test: As used in this book, one element of the definition of a TMP. An entity meets the TMP asset test if substantially all of its assets consist of debt obligations (or interests therein) and more than 50 percent of those debt obligations consist of real property mortgages (or interests therein).

TRA 1984: The Tax Reform Act of 1984, Public Law 98-369. TRA 1984 enacted sections 1271-1288, which set forth the current tax rules governing original issue discount, market discount and stripped bonds and coupons. It also created the exemption from the 30 percent withholding tax for portfolio interest paid to non-U.S. investors.

TRA 1986: The Tax Reform Act of 1986, Public Law 99-514. TRA 1986 enacted sections 860A–860G (REMIC rules) and section 1272(a)(6) (PAC method) and also revised the tax rules governing market discount on installment obligations and bond premium.

Transfer Tax: As used in this book, the tax imposed on transfers of REMIC residual interests to disqualified organizations.

Transferee Affidavit: As used in this book, an affidavit (which includes any statement signed under penalties of perjury) received from a transferee of a residual interest which establishes that the transferee is not a disqualified organization. A transferor of a residual interest will not be subject to the tax imposed on transfers of such interests to disqualified organizations if a transferee affidavit is received (and the transferor does not have actual knowledge that it is false).

Trusts for Investment in Mortgages or *TIMs*: A vehicle for the investment in mortgages by a trust that could have multiple classes of ownership interest without losing its status as a pass-through entity. The Report of the President's Commission on Housing, dated April, 1982, proposed legislation, which was introduced in the Senate in 1983 (S. 1822), to allow the creation of TIMs. The TIMs proposal eventually developed into the REMIC legislation.

Unrelated Business Taxable Income or *UBTI*: Income that is taxable in the hands of certain organizations that are generally treated as tax-exempt organizations under the Code, including qualified pension plans, charitable institutions and individual retirement accounts.

Unrelated Debt-Financed Income: A portion of the income from property held for profit corresponding to the portion of the property that is financed with debt. Such income is included in the UBTI of organizations that are subject to tax on UBTI.

Upper-Tier REMIC: A tiered REMIC that holds regular interests in another tiered REMIC.

Variable Rate Debt Instrument or *VRDI*: A term used in the OID regulations to refer to floating or other variable rate debt instruments that meet certain requirements. OID on such instruments generally is taxed by creating a hypothetical equivalent fixed rate debt instrument, applying the OID rules to that instrument, and then adjusting interest or OID in each period to account for differences between the actual rate and the hypothetical fixed rate.

WAC (or *Weighted Average Coupon*) *Class*: A class of bonds bearing interest at a rate that may change from period to period based on the weighted average rate of interest on the underlying mortgages, or in the case of bonds that are regular interests in an upper-tier REMIC, a weighted average rate of interest on regular interests in a lower-tier REMIC.

Wash Sale: In general, a sale of a security by an investor at a loss that results in no current loss deduction because the seller acquires (or enters into an option or contract to acquire) a substantially identical security within a 30-day period before or after the sale. In the case of sales of REMIC residual interests, the 30-day period is extended to 6 months and a broad category of similar securities is substituted for "substantially identical securities."

Withholding Tax: Generally, a 30 percent withholding tax on interest and other passive income from U.S. sources paid to non-U.S. investors. Except in the case of excess inclusions, the tax may be reduced or eliminated by treaty and is eliminated if the portfolio interest exemption applies.

Yield to Maturity: The discount rate, expressed as an annual rate but calculated assuming compounding at the end of each accrual period, that causes the present value of all payments on a debt instrument (determined, if the PAC method applies, assuming that the instrument will be prepaid in accordance with the Prepayment Assumption) to equal its issue price on the issue date. The yield to maturity is used in calculating accruals of original issue discount.

Appendix A

Phantom Income

Thomas B. Lupo, Ph.D.

A. Introduction

Holders of equity interests in owner trusts and residual interests in REMICs are required to report taxable income calculated as the difference between the gross income from the assets of the issuer and the deductions allowed with respect to its liabilities (including, in the case of a REMIC, regular interests which are treated for tax purposes as if they were liabilities of the REMIC). This method of taxation can result in some periods in the recognition of taxable income that exceeds economic income. That excess is referred to herein as *phantom income.*

Our study will examine the sources of phantom income and different ways of measuring its effect on investors. We will show that the primary cause of phantom income is the deferral of interest expense that arises when liabilities are divided into multiple classes or tranches with different maturities and yields. This deferral of expense is then magnified by leverage and manifests itself as a front loading of taxable income for the residual investment. Such a front loading of taxable income with its consequent front loading of tax payments can have a significant adverse effect on after-tax yield.

During the course of the discussion, it will become clear that the phantom income problem is one of timing. Excess taxable income in the initial periods is offset by reductions in taxable income (or a loss) in the later periods. As a consequence, a sale before maturity may have the effect of moving the tax benefits inherent in the reduced future taxable income (or loss) up to the point of sale. Thus, such a sale can mitigate the phantom income problem.

Finally, we will illustrate our conclusions with examples representative of the types of transactions done over the past two years.

Except where otherwise indicated, the discussion below applies equally to investments in equity interests in CMO owner trusts and REMIC residual interests.* References to CMOs, bonds or liabilities include regular interests in a REMIC even if they do not take the form of debt

---

*   This study assumes that all taxable income is subject to tax and thus does not take account of the possibility that certain holders of REMIC residual interests will be subject to tax only on "excess inclusion" income. See the discussion of excess inclusions in Chapter 7, Part E.4.

obligations of the REMIC. All tax calculations assume a tax rate of 34%. For simplicity, non-interest expenses of the issuer such as administrative costs are ignored.

B. Illustration of Phantom Income

Phantom income arises when the distribution of taxable income differs from the distribution of economic income. Consider the example in Figure 1: *

Figure 1. Simple Example of Phantom Income

Year	Cash Flow	Taxable Income	Economic Income	Phantom Income	Tax on Phantom Income
0	$(100.00)				
1	36.00	$11.00	$9.17	$ 1.83	$ 0.62
2	31.75	6.75	6.71	0.04	0.01
3	28.50	3.50	4.41	(0.91)	(0.31)
4	26.25	1.25	2.21	(0.96)	(0.33)
	22.50	22.50	22.50	0.00	0.00

Present value @ 6% discount rate of tax on phantom income—$.08
Future value @ 6% reinvestment rate of tax on phantom income—$.10

In the example shown in Figure 1, $100 is invested in an asset which has a total cash flow of $122.50. All accounting methods must recognize income of $22.50 over the life of the investment. In the example, however, taxable income is recognized faster than economic income. The difference between economic income and taxable income is what we call phantom income.

---

*   The derivation of this example and in particular the rationale for the income distributions will become clear in the next section. In all examples, columns may not total due to rounding.

Since tax liability is based on taxable income, an investor that purchased the investment described in Figure 1 would pay more taxes in the initial periods and less in the later periods than if taxed according to an economic distribution of income. If the investor had an after-tax rate of return of 6% on reinvested cash flows, this front loading of taxes would result in a $.10 reduction in the value of his portfolio (after paying all taxes due) at the four year horizon as compared with the same investment taxed on an economic basis. Alternatively, an additional $.08 would have to be invested now at a 6% after-tax rate of return in order to counter the $.10 reduction in value at the horizon.

In summary, phantom income is the difference between taxable income and economic income. If taxable income is front loaded relative to economic income, taxes will be commensurately front loaded, resulting in a decrease in portfolio value at an appropriate investment horizon.

C. Phantom Income and the Yield Curve

In this part, we give a simple example which illustrates the main source of phantom income. We will also define what we mean by an economic distribution of income and show why taxable income can differ from economic income.

The transaction we will consider is the leveraged purchase of a fixed income instrument outlined in Figures 2 and 3. The example serves as a model for the purchase of an equity interest in an owner trust and, subject to the discussion in Part H below of secondary market purchases, of residual interests in REMICs.

In the example shown in Figures 2 and 3, an investor raises $400 by incurring $400 of debt, divided into four classes, A through D, having equal amounts of principal payable at maturity. The maturities range from one to four years. He combines this amount with $100 of his own money and purchases for $500 a $500 principal amount debt security bearing interest at a rate of 9%. The asset provides for four equal annual principal payments of $125. In effect, he has purchased the residual cash flow for $100. It is this investment in the residual that we now will examine in detail.

As shown in Figure 3, the elements of the residual are determined as the difference between the corresponding elements of the asset and combined liabilities. For instance, the cash flow to the residual is the difference between the cash flow of the asset and the cash flow of the liabilities. The

Figure 2. Leveraged Purchase of Fixed Income Asset

Asset	Principal Amount $500	Coupon 9%	Price (% of Principal) 100	Yield 9%	Principal Payments $125/yr	Maturity 4 yrs
Liability						
A	100	7	100	7	100	1
B	100	8	100	8	100	2
C	100	9	100	9	100	3
D	100	10	100	10	100	4
ALL	400			8.958		
Equity	100			9.171	25/yr	4

taxable income of the residual is the difference between the income from the asset and the deductions allowed with respect to the liabilities. In Figure 3, the amount given as the "tax basis" of the liabilities is the amount at which they are carried for tax purposes (i.e., the amount which could be paid to retire the liabilities without resulting in any income or loss to the residual investor), and equals their issue price, increased by the deductions allowed for interest expense, reduced by payments of principal and interest, and adjusted for amortization of discount or premium (of which there is none in the example). The tax basis of the residual is the amount that would be used in calculating gain or loss from sale of the residual and equals the equity investment made in the residual, plus taxable income allocated to the residual, less distributions on the residual and any losses. The same terminology is used in the balance of this study.*

---

* Strictly speaking, the basis of an equity interest in an owner trust would include a share of the trust's liabilities but that share is ignored here because such basis would be reduced by repayments of the liabilities and the balance would be included in the amount realized from a sale, thus offsetting the original increase in basis.

Figure 3. Taxable Income and Cash Flow Analysis of Leveraged Purchase

	Assets					Combined Liabilities					Residual				
Year	Tax Basis	Return of Capital	Taxable Income	Taxable Dynamic Yield	Cash Flow	Tax Basis	Return of Capital	Tax Deductions	Taxable Dynamic Yield	Cash Flow	Tax Basis	Return of Capital	Taxable Income	Taxable Dynamic Yield	Cash Flow
0	$500					$400					$100				
1	375	$125	$45.00	9%	$170.00	300	$100	$34	8.5%	$134	75	$25	$11.00	11%	$36.00
2	250	125	33.75	9	158.75	200	100	27	9.0	127	50	25	6.75	9	31.75
3	125	125	22.50	9	147.50	100	100	19	9.5	119	25	25	3.50	7	28.50
4	0	125	11.25	9	136.25	0	100	10	10.0	110	0	25	1.25	5	26.25
													22.50		

Let us focus for a moment on taxable income. Since there is no discount or premium involved, income from the asset and deductions with respect to the liabilities are calculated each year as the interest rate times the outstanding principal balance. In the case of the asset, this product is a constant 9% times a declining balance. In the case of the liabilities, the calculation must be done separately for each tranche and the results summed. Thus, in year 1, the total expense is $7 + $8 + $9 + $10 = $34. In year 2, since the first tranche has matured, the expense is $8 + $9 + $10 = $27.

1. Dynamic Yield

Our primary concern is with the distribution of taxable income over time. Merely listing the income from assets and deductions with respect to liabilities for each period does not lead readily to a determination of whether these amounts are front loaded or back loaded. The amortization of assets and liabilities means that income and deductions naturally decrease with time. The absolute decrease in income therefore is not an indication that it is front loaded. In order to facilitate inter-period comparisons of income and deductions, we introduce the concept of dynamic yield. The dynamic yield pattern will serve as an easily read indication of the extent to which income or deductions are skewed.

The dynamic yield of an asset (or liability) for any period is defined as the income (deductions) for that period with respect to the asset (liability) expressed as a percentage of its tax basis at the beginning of the period, adjusted to be an annual figure if the period is other than a year. In the example set out in Figures 2 and 3, the dynamic yield of the asset is a constant 9%. This is not surprising. When we are dealing with a single asset, the dynamic yield calculation is just the reverse of the income calculation; e.g., with reference to year 1 for the asset:

Income Calculation $500 × 9% = $45
Dynamic Yield Calculation $45 / $500 = 9%

The calculation for the liabilities is more complicated. Again with reference to year 1:

Deduction Calculation
   $100×7% + $100×8% + $100×9% + $100×10% = $34

Dynamic Yield Calculation

$$\frac{\$100\times7\% + \$100\times8\% + \$100\times9\% + \$100\times10\%}{\$400} = 8.5\%$$

From this last equation, we see that, in the case of a multi-tranche liability, the dynamic yield is a weighted average of the cash flow yields of the outstanding tranches.

The dynamic yield of the residual is calculated in the same manner as for the asset, by comparing the taxable income from the residual in each period with its tax basis at the beginning of the period.

An examination of the dynamic yield patterns shown in Figure 3 prompts the following assertions. The constant 9% dynamic yield of the asset implies that income from the asset is evenly distributed. The increasing dynamic yield of the liabilities indicates that interest expense is back loaded. Finally, the decreasing dynamic yield of the residual indicates that residual income is front loaded.

2. Economic Income

Next, let us use the concept of dynamic yield to define what we mean by an economic distribution of income or deductions. We will say that income or deductions are economically distributed when the dynamic yield does not change from period to period. Thus, in Figure 3 the income from the asset is economically distributed while the deductions with respect to the liabilities and the income from the residual are not. The rationale for this definition is that when dynamic yield is constant it equals the internal rate of return. Thus, our definition of economically distributed income amounts

Figure 4. Economic Deductions for Combined Liabilities

Year	Tax Basis	Return of Capital	Economic Deductions	Dynamic Yield	Cash Flow
0	$400.00				
1	301.83	$98.17	$35.83	8.958%	$134
2	201.87	99.96	27.04	8.958	127
3	100.95	100.92	18.08	8.958	119
4	0.00	100.96	9.04	8.958	110

to a requirement that the income reported in each period be determined by the true economic yield of the investment.

Let us apply this definition to calculate the economically distributed deductions with respect to the liabilities. We first calculate the internal rate of return on the combined liabilities to be 8.958%. We then use this rate and the level yield method* of income calculation to arrive at the table shown in Figure 4. Also, let us calculate the economic distribution of income for the residual. The internal rate of return on the residual investment is 9.171%. Applying the level yield method gives us the table shown in Figure 5.

Figure 5. Economic Income of Residual

Year	Tax Basis	Return of Capital	Economic Income	Dynamic Yield	Cash Flow
0	$100.00				
1	73.17	$26.83	$9.17	9.171%	$36.00
2	48.13	25.04	6.71	9.171	31.75
3	24.04	24.09	4.41	9.171	28.50
4	0.00	24.04	2.21	9.171	26.25

3. Phantom Income

We are now in a position to calculate the phantom income on the residual and show its connection to the distribution of expenses on the liabilities.

Figure 6 shows clearly that the deferral of interest deductions is the source of the phantom income on the residual. The pattern of dynamic yields for the liabilities evidences the deferral of interest deductions.

---

* The level yield method calculates income for each period by multiplying the beginning of period carrying value by the internal rate of return of the investment. The carrying value is then increased by income and reduced by cash flow to get the next period's carrying value.

Figure 6. Phantom Income of Liabilities and Residual

	Combined Liabilities				Residual			
Year	Economic Deductions	Taxable Deductions	Dynamic Yield	Contribution to Phantom Income	Economic Income	Taxable Income	Dynamic Yield	Phantom Income
1	$35.83	$34.00	8.5%	$1.83	$9.17	$11.00	11.0%	$1.83
2	27.04	27.00	9.0	.04	6.71	6.75	9.0	.04
3	18.08	19.00	9.5	(.91)	4.41	3.50	7.0	(.91)
4	9.04	10.00	10.0	(.96)	2.21	1.25	5.0	(.96)

The dynamic yield starts at 8.5% and rises to 10%. An economic distribution of expense would allocate a constant percentage, 8.958%, to each year. The increase in dynamic yields is a consequence of the rate/maturity pattern of the liabilities (see Figure 7): low yields coupled with short maturities, high yields coupled with long maturities. In each period, the dynamic yield of the liabilities is a weighted average of the yields of the remaining tranches. As the lower-yield/shorter-maturity tranches are retired, the average must increase.

This deferral of expense on the liabilities results in a front loading of income on the residual. This front loading is evidenced by the pattern of dynamic yields. The dynamic yield changes over time from 11% to 5%. An economic allocation of income would result in a constant dynamic yield, 9.171%, for each year.

Note that the decrease in the dynamic yield of the residual, from 11% to 5%, is much more pronounced than the increase in the dynamic yield of the liability, from 8.5% to 10%. The difference is brought about by leverage. The phantom income is the same in dollar terms for both the liability and the residual. In percentage terms, though, it is greater for the smaller residual.

In summary, then, the above example illustrates that phantom income arises in a leveraged purchase of assets when the liabilities are divided into tranches that exhibit a positive correlation between maturity and rate. The structure of the liabilities gives rise to a back loading of interest deductions and a consequent front loading of income for the residual.

Figure 7. Rate/Maturity Pattern of Liabilities

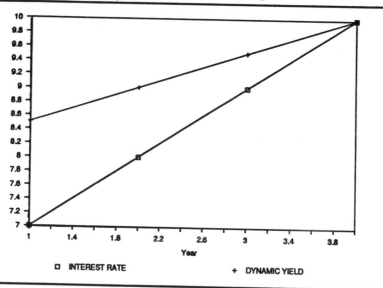

D. Quantifying the Phantom Income Problem

The phantom income problem can be quantified in terms of yield or present value/future value. Recall the analysis done in Part B. In Figure 1, the excess tax on the phantom income was present valued and future valued at 6%, an after-tax opportunity rate. The future value represents the decrease in portfolio value resulting from paying taxes sooner than they would be paid if income was calculated on an economic basis. The present value represents the additional amount of money needed now for investment to counter the decrease in portfolio value stemming from phantom income.

The phantom income problem can also be quantified in terms of its effect on after-tax yield.

Consider the following simple example:

Income Distribution	Pre-Tax Yield	Tax Rate	After-Tax Yield	Yield Lost to Taxes	Effective Tax Rate
Economic	10%	34%	6.6%	3.4%	3.4%/10% = 34%
Taxable	10%	34%	6.0%	4.0%	4.0%/10% = 40%

When income is economically distributed (i.e., dynamic yield is constant for all periods), the fraction of yield lost to taxes always equals the tax rate. In the presence of phantom income, the yield lost to taxes will be greater. The effective tax rate, which is defined as the ratio of yield lost to taxes to pre-tax yield, serves as an indicator of the magnitude of the phantom income problem. In this example. the comparison of a 40% effective tax rate with a statutory 34% tax rate indicates that 6 percent of the pre-tax yield has been lost due to phantom income.

Consider now what happens to the effective tax rate as the size of the residual varies while the liabilities are kept constant. The example in part C above is modified to give the results shown in Figure 8. The example is modified by assuming that the equity investment is reduced first to $50, then to $25. The liabilities are kept constant at a total initial amount of $400. Thus, in the successive cases, the total principal amount purchased shrinks to $450 and $425, respectively. The size of the debt portion of the financing relative to the equity portion increases and leverage increases correspondingly.

Figure 8. Effect of Leverage on Phantom Income

Equity Investment	Leverage	Residual Pre-Tax Yield	Residual After-Tax Yield	Effective Tax Rate	Percent of Pre-Tax Yield Lost Due to Phantom Income	Present Value at 6% of Tax on Phantom Income
$100	4:1	9.171%	6.016%	34.403%	.403%	$.081
50	8:1	9.348	6.093	34.814	.814	.081
25	16:1	9.721	6.254	35.660	1.660	.080

Several results shown in Figure 8 should be noted:

(1) The pre-tax yield increases with leverage, as expected.

(2) The percent of yield lost due to phantom income is almost directly proportional to the leverage.

(3) The cost of the phantom income remains fairly constant in present value terms.

These last two results can be traced to the fact that the phantom income problem is caused by the yield/maturity pattern of the liabilities. Since the liabilities are not changing, the phantom income in all three cases is essentially the same. As the residual cash flow becomes smaller, the yield effects of the phantom income problem become proportionately larger.

From Part C and the results above, we conclude that the phantom income effect on after-tax yield will be most pronounced if (1) the tranched liabilities exhibit an upward sloping yield/maturity pattern and (2) the equity investment is highly leveraged.

E. Horizon Analysis

The economic effect of phantom income may be greatly reduced when the residual is sold before maturity. This result is best understood by comparing the tax basis of the residual to its economic basis. The economic basis is defined in a manner completely analogous to the tax basis; that is, the initial cost is increased by economic income (as opposed to taxable income) and reduced by cash distributions. The economic basis represents the carrying value of the residual. A sale realizing such an amount would not result in an economic gain or loss.

At all times the tax basis exceeds the economic basis by precisely the cumulative net amount of phantom income to that point. Thus, a sale which realizes the economic carrying value as proceeds would result in a loss for tax purposes equal to the cumulative net amount of phantom income. Or, in general, the taxable gain will be reduced (or loss increased) in comparison with the economic gain by the cumulative net amount of phantom income. Figure 9 illustrates this point using the facts of the example used in Part B and assuming a sale of the residual interest at a price of $55 after two years.

The tax savings consequent upon a sale of a residual interest depend on the ability of a seller to benefit from the greater tax basis attributable to phantom income. If the sale results in a taxable loss rather than a reduction in gain, the ability of the seller to recognize such a loss may be limited

Figure 9. Taxable Gain Compared to Economic Gain

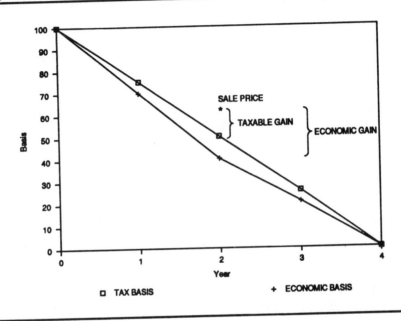

(either because such a loss is a capital loss that can be offset only against capital gain,* or because the "wash sale" rules apply).**

In Figure 10, we split income into two components: periodic income from holding the residual, and gain realized upon sale. We calculate the two components for both taxable and economic income and then, in the usual fashion, compute phantom income as the difference.

---

*   Gain or loss on the sale of a residual investment will be ordinary income for a bank or thrift institution except possibly in the case of an equity interest in an owner trust that is classified as a partnership. See Chapter 9, Part D.

**   The "wash sale" rules are discussed in Chapter 7, footnote 55 and accompanying text. In addition, although the tax rates applicable to ordinary income and capital gain are now the same for corporations, and the same rates are assumed in the examples below, the horizon analysis would be affected by any restoration in the future of the preferential treatment of capital gains (as well as by any change in tax rates generally).

Figure 10. Horizon Analysis

		Tax			Economic			Phantom Income	
Year	Basis	Income	Gain On Sale	Basis	Income	Gain On Sale	Periodic	Sale	Total
0	$100			$100.00					
1	75	$11.00		73.17	$9.17		$1.83		$ 1.83
2	50	6.75	$5	48.13	6.71	$6.87	0.04	$(1.87)	(1.83)
		$17.75			$15.88		$1.87	$(1.87)	0

Note that the cumulative amount of periodic phantom income, $1.87, is exactly equal to the difference between the tax basis and economic basis after two years. Thus, upon sale, the economic gain will exceed the taxable gain by precisely this amount. In effect, accumulated phantom income of earlier periods is reversed through a reduction in the taxable gain recognized from the sale as compared with the economic gain.

An important point, which is not evident in this simple example but which will become clear when we look at more realistic examples, is that phantom income is a problem primarily in those cases where the economic value of the residual is received in the early years. Recall that it is the positively sloped yield curve that is responsible for phantom income. In the case of a standard multiple class CMO that is structured to take advantage of the upward sloping yield curve, cash distributions on the residual will be attributable primarily to the difference between the rate of interest on the mortgages and the lower rate of interest on the earlier-maturing classes of CMOs. As a result, most of the cash distributions on the residual will be made, and most of the economic investment will be recovered, in the early years. See Figure 11 which shows the tax and economic bases for a typical fixed rate CMO. (See also Figure 16.) For this reason, the economic effect of a sale is likely to become small after a few years. If a residual is sold after its economic value has been reduced to a small amount, any phantom income that has been recognized by the holder is more likely to result in a tax loss on the sale rather than a reduction in taxable gain. As noted above, the ability of a holder to take advantage of such a tax loss may be limited. On the other hand, if the seller has realized an economic loss with respect to the residual, concern over the recognition of such a loss as a result of a

Figure 11. Tax Basis Compared to Economic Basis

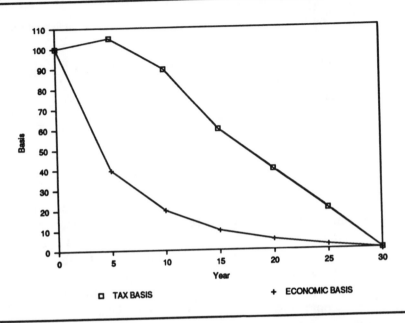

sale should be reduced once the economic value of the investment has been reduced to a small amount.

F. Examples

We now illustrate the concepts developed in the previous parts with some representative examples. We will examine a fixed rate CMO, a floating rate CMO, and an interest only/principal only issue. In each case, the underlying mortgages bear interest at a fixed rate.

1. Fixed Rate CMO

In the first example, shown in Figure 12, $500,000,000 par amount of 30-year maturity, level-pay residential mortgages are used to collateralize a quarterly-pay CMO which has three regular coupon tranches (A-C) and one "compound interest" or "accrual" tranche (Z). The residual is sold for $7,100,000 to yield 10.658%.

Figure 12. Asset and Liabilities for Fixed Rate CMO

	Initial Principal Amount	*Coupon*	*Avg.** Life (years)*	*Price (% of Principal)*	*Price*	*Yield***
Asset	$500*	8.5%	8.7	99.465	$497.3	8.664%

CMOs						
A	274.5	8.000	3.4	100.000	274.5	8.000
B	77.0	8.500	7.8	99.450	76.6	8.598
C	107.8	8.400	11.0	98.200	105.9	8.656
Z	39.3	8.350	19.0	84.667	33.3	9.341
ALL	498.6	8.286	8.7	98.317	490.2	8.604

Residual						
					7.1	10.658***

* 000,000's omitted.

** Assumes that mortgages prepay at 167% of PSA. Yields are calculated assuming quarterly compounding.

*** Assumes that monthly cash flows are reinvested at 6.25% until bond payment date.

a. Yield/Maturity Pattern. The pattern of yields and weighted average maturities of the liabilities is set out in Figure 13.

The positive correlation between yield and maturity suggests that the residual will have phantom income. The following table confirms this.

Pre-tax Yield	10.658%*
After-tax Yield	4.865%*
Statutory Tax Rate	34.000%**
Effective Tax Rate	54.354%

* Assumes quarterly compounding.

** The highest marginal tax rate for corporations for taxable years beginning on or after January 1, 1993 is 35%. For taxable years beginning on or after July 1, 1987 and before January 1, 1993 the rate was 34%.

Figure 13.Yield/Maturity: Fixed Rate CMO

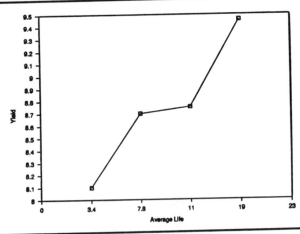

In accordance with our previous discussion, the phantom income of the residual can be traced to the distribution of deductions with respect to the liabilities. Figure 14 shows that income on the asset is essentially economically distributed while interest expense is back loaded. Figure 15 depicts the consequences of this pattern for the taxable income of the residual. During the first seven years, there is phantom income. The phantom income is offset by reduced income or losses in the later years.

Figure 14. Part 1. Dynamic Yields for Fixed Rate CMO

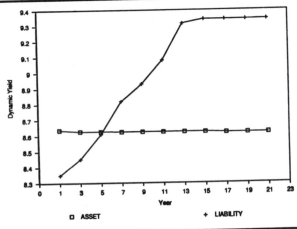

Figure 14. Part 2. Dynamic Yields for Fixed Rate CMO

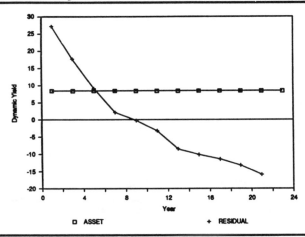

b. Horizon Analysis. Figure 16 shows the relationship between the tax basis and the economic basis of the residual. Note that even as early as the fifth year more than 60% of the economic value has been amortized, while, in the same period, the tax basis has actually increased. The consequences of selling the residual at different times at a price equal to its economic basis are shown in Figure 17 assuming a 34% tax benefit from the resulting tax loss.

Figure 15. Taxable and Economic Income of Residual

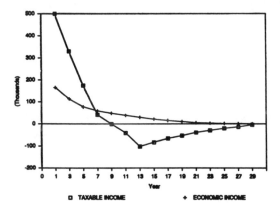

Figure 16. Tax and Economic Basis of Residual

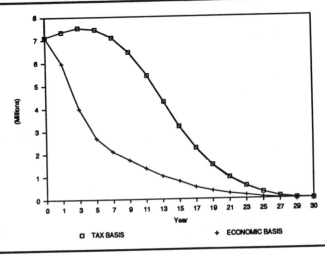

□ TAX BASIS   + ECONOMIC BASIS

Note that in present value terms, the cost of the phantom income is reduced by more than 70% when the residual is sold at the five-year horizon instead of being held to maturity. Note also that by the fifth year, the economic basis has been largely amortized. Only 38% of the original economic basis remains. At this point, the balance sheet impact of a gain or loss upon sale would be small and, presumably, not an impediment to realizing the consequent tax benefits.

Figure 17. Effect of Sale on Phantom Income

	Holding Period			
	5 Years	10 Years	15 Years	30 Years
Present Value of Tax on Phantom Income at 6% Discount Rate	$228*	$545	$722	$799
Effective Tax Rate	44.26%	50.73%	53.35%	54.35%
% of Original Economic Value Remaining	38%	21%	11%	0%

* 000's omitted.

c. Leverage and Effective Tax Rate. Figure 18 outlines the relationship between leverage and effective tax rates. The rows of Figure 18 are obtained by combining successively smaller equity investments with a fixed amount of debt. Thus, successively smaller amounts of collateral are purchased and the ratio of debt to equity increases. It is assumed that the residual is not sold. Note that the yield lost to phantom income is almost directly proportional to the leverage.

Figure 18. Leverage and Effective Tax Rates

Initial Tax Basis of Liability	Initial Tax Basis of Residual	Initial Leverage	Residual Pre-Tax Yield	Residual After-Tax Yield	Effective Tax Rate	Percentage of Pre-Tax Yield Lost to Phantom Income
$497.3*	$28.4	17:1	9.03%	5.49%	39.22%	5.22%
497.3	14.2	34:1	9.49	5.28	44.36	10.36
497.3	7.1	69:1	10.658	4.865	54.35	20.35

* 000,000's omitted.

2. Floating Rate CMO

Let us next consider a CMO having as its major component a tranche (F) that bears interest at a floating rate equal to 40 basis points over LIBOR. For purposes of examining phantom income, we will assume that LIBOR remains constant over the life of the issue.* In addition to the F tranche, the CMOs include a zero coupon support tranche. Principal is paid on the two classes of bonds ratably in proportion to their principal balances. Because the underlying mortgages bear interest at a fixed rate, the residual is an inverse floating rate instrument (i.e., its value increases as LIBOR declines). The terms of the mortgages and CMOs are summarized in Figure 19.

---

* Although interest deductions may, of course, increase or decrease over time in step with the interest index, with the result that the residual holder would recognize correspondingly lesser or greater amounts of taxable income, such changes in taxable income would accurately reflect the holder's economic income.

Figure 19. Asset and Liabilities for Floating Rate CMO

	Initial Principal Amount	Coupon	Avg.** Life (years)	Price (% of Principal)	Price	Yield**
Asset	$350*	10.456%	3.6	106.734***	$373.6	8.119%

CMOs

	Initial Principal Amount	Coupon	Avg.** Life (years)	Price (% of Principal)	Price	Yield**
F	319.2	6.900	3.6	100.000	319.2	6.900****
A	30.8	0.000	3.6	79.500	24.5	7.079
ALL	350.0	6.293	3.6	98.196	343.7	6.913

Residual					29.9	21.426

*   000,000's omitted.

**   Assumes that the mortgages prepay at a constant annual rate of 24%. Yields are calculated assuming quarterly compounding.

*** The collateral for the transaction shown had a value in excess of par but similar results would be realized if par or discount collateral were used.

**** Assumes LIBOR remains constant.

Since the two tranches of CMOs amortize in parallel, there is no positive correlation between yield and maturity. This suggests there will be little or no phantom income for the residual. The following table confirms this result.

Pre-tax Yield	21.426%*
After-tax Yield	14.158%*
Statutory Tax Rate	34.000%
Effective Tax Rate	33.921%

*   Assumes quarterly compounding.

Figure 20. Dynamic Yields for Floating Rate CMO

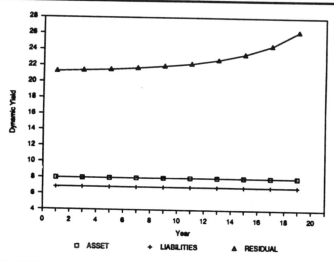

Figure 20 shows the dynamic yields for the asset and liabilities. Both income from the mortgages and interest expense are essentially economically distributed. Figure 21 depicts the taxable income of the residual. It too is essentially economically distributed.

Figure 21. Taxable and Economic Income of Residual

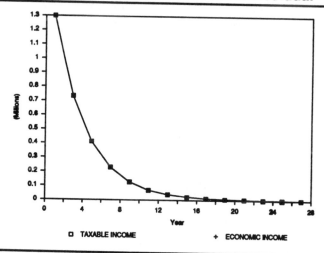

3. REMIC IO/PO Interests

The final example, shown in Figure 22, involves IO (interest only) and PO (principal only) interests in a REMIC. The IO and PO interests are assumed to be residual and regular interests, respectively.

Again, the lack of multiple tranches with a rising yield structutre implies phantom income will not be a problem for an IO interest. The following confirms this result:

Pre-tax Yield	11.711%
After-tax Yield	7.730%
Statutory Tax Rate	34.000%
Effective Tax Rate	33.988%

As shown in Figure 23, the dynamic yields exhibit the expected pattern: both income and interest deductions are economically distributed. It follows that residual income is also economically distributed and this result is shown in Figure 24.

Figure 22. Asset and Liability for REMIC IO/PO Interests

	Initial Principal Amount *	Coupon	Avg. ** Life (years)	Price (% of Principal)	Price	Yield **
Asset	$500	11.50%	2.58	106.018	$530.1	8.591%
Liability (PO)	498.7	0	2.58	83.200	414.9	7.809
Residual (IO)					115.2	11.711

* 000,000's omitted.
** Assumes that the mortgages prepay at a constant annual rate of 32%. Yields are calculated assuming monthly compounding.

Figure 23. Dynamic Yields for REMIC IO/PO Interests

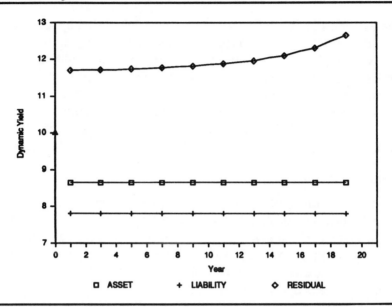

Figure 24. Taxable and Economic Income of REMIC IO Interests

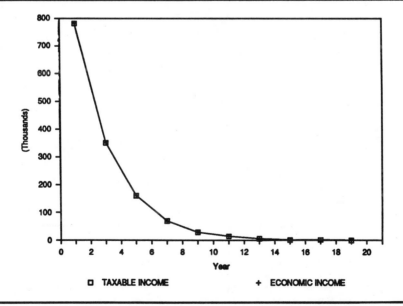

G. Other Sources of Phantom Income

In the examples in Part F, we examined the roles played by leverage and the yield curve in creating phantom income and magnifying its effect on yield. We complete the analysis now by examining two additional sources of phantom income: dynamic leverage, and the reinvestment effect. We will show that the phantom income of the residual has three sources: the phantom income from the liabilities, caused by the yield/maturity pattern of the tranches as discussed above; the phantom income of the asset, caused by the reinvestment effect; and the changing degree of leverage.

1. Dynamic Leverage

An exact description of the relationships between the dynamic yields of the asset, liabilities and residual involves the notion of dynamic leverage. The dynamic leverage for a given period is defined to be the ratio of the tax basis of the liabilities to the tax basis of the residual. The heuristic example in Figure 25 illustrates the relationship that always holds amongst the dynamic yields and dynamic leverage.*

Figure 25. Dynamic Leverage and Dynamic Yields

	Beginning of Period Tax Basis	
Liabilities	$100.00	Dynamic Leverage = 5
Residual	$ 20.00	
	Dynamic Yield for Period	
Residual	15%	
		Spread = 5%
Asset	10%	Ratio = 5
		Spread = 1%
Liabilities	9%	

---

*   See Addendum.

In words, the raito of residual-asset yield spread to asset-liability yield spread equals the dynamic leverage. Or, stated another way, the residual dynamic yield equals the asset dynamic yield plus the product of the dynamic leverage and asset-liability yield spread. This relationship is apparent in Figures 14, 20, and 23. The residual dynamic yields and liability dynamic yields are, roughly speaking, symetric about the asset dynamic yields. The symmetry would be exact, though scaled for leverage, if the leverage were constant. The fact that the leverage changes with time distorts the symmetry somewhat.

Figure 26. Dynamic Leverage and Dynamic Spread for IO/PO

	Year				
	0	5	10	15	20
Tax Basis					
Asset	$530,089*	$174,149	$10,009	$1,252	$128
Liability	414,960	58,253	7,920	1,006	107
Residual	115,129	15,896	2,089	245	21
Dynamic Leverage	3.60	3.66	3.79	4.10	5.09
Dynamic Yield Spread					
Asset–Liability	.84	.84	.84	.84	.84
Residual–Asset	3.03	3.09	3.19	3.46	4.29
Residual Dynamic Yield	11.68%	11.74%	11.84%	12.11%	12.94%

* 000's omitted.

Increasing leveiage explains why the residuals in the floating rate CMO and IO/PO examples above are slightly tax advantaged.* The spread between the dynamic yields of assets and liabilities is essentially constant while the dynamic leverage is increasing. This implies that the product of the two is increasing. It follows that the residual dynamic yield is increasing and taxable income is back loaded. Figure 26 shows the dynamic leverage, dynamic yield spreads and residual dyanmic yield at five year intervals for the IO and PO interests described above.

2. Reinvestment Effect

A close inspection of Figure 14 (which relates to the multiple tranch CMO example described above) shows that the dynamic yield of the asset decreases gradually with time even though the asset provides for a constant interest rate. This is caused by the reinvestment effect. The CMOs provide for quarterly payments, so that mortgage cash flows must be reinvested at a low short term interest rate until the end of each quarter. As the mortgages pay down, the importance of the reinvestment income becomes greater relative to the mortgage income.** Thus, the dynamic yield, which is an average of the yields from all sources, must decrease over time as the ratio of income from the higher yielding mortgages to the income on the lower yielding reinvestments declines. This pattern of decreasing dynamic yields indicates that the income of the asset, and therefore of the residual, is slightly front loaded. The effect this has on phantom income will be quantified below.

---

*   The increase in leverage comes about because the cash flow of the IO interest is front loaded in comparison with the PO interest. This is the natural pattern exhibited by mortgage cash flows: interest payments decrease with time while principal payments increase. In the case of the floating rate CMO the same principle applies, since the residual is just a fraction of the total interest payment. As a consequence of this relative front loading of residual cash flow, the tax basis of the residual portion decreases in comparison to that of the liabilities. Thus, the ratio of liability basis to residual basis increases with time.

**   This is true because the income from a mortgage is a function of its principal balance which declines over time, while reinvestment income is a function of total debt service which remains constant.

3. Quantifying the Components of Phantom Income

Phantom income attributable to changes in the dynamic yields of each of the asset and liabilities can be easily determined since in each case both taxable and economic income or deductions are readily calculated. Moreover, it can be shown that when dynamic leverage is constant, the phantom income of the residual is the sum of the phantom income attributable to the liability and the phantom income of the asset.* This makes it reasonable then to attribute any divergence between the actual phantom income of the residual and that sum to dynamic leverage. If we do this, we can attribute the total phantom income of the residual for each example in Part F to three sources: the yield curve effect, connected with the liabilities; the reinvestment effect, connected with the asset; and dynamic leverage. The results are shown in Figure 27.

Figure 27. The Components of Phantom Income

	Present Value of Phantom Income @ 6% Discount Rate					
	Yield Curve Effect (Liabilities)	+	Reinvestment Effect (Asset)	+	Dynamic Leverage	=	Total Phantom Income
Fixed Rate CMO						
	$2,335* 99.4%	+	$18.8 .8%	+	$(4.8) (.2%)	=	$2,349 100%
Floating Rate CMO						
	0 0%	+	.6 2.4%	+	(25.3) (102.4%)	=	(24.7) 100%
IO/PO						
	0 0%	+	0 0%	+	(8.8) 100%	=	(8.8) 100%

*000's omitted

Two points are noteworthy here. First, the yield curve effect is clearly the dominant source of phantom income. Second, dynamic leverage in all

* See Addendum.

three cases works to mitigate phantom income. This will generally be the case. Most residuals have their cash flow concentrated in the early years. As a result, the dynamic leverage increases with time since the value of the residual decreases relative to the value of the liability. The increase in leverage results in an increasing residual-to-asset dynamic yield spread (see Figure 26) and therefore an increasing residual dynamic yield. An increasing dynamic yield implies a back loading of income with a consequent mitigating effect on phantom income.

H. Phantom Income and Secondary Market Purchases of CMO Residuals

The effect of phantom income on equity in a CMO owner trust purchased in the secondary market depends on whether or not a REMIC election is made with respect to the trust. We examine the two cases separately below, beginning with non-REMIC transactions.

1. Non-REMIC Transactions

In a non-REMIC transaction, following a secondary market purchase of a residual, the tax basis of the asset is generally recalculated to be the sum of the current tax basis of the outstanding liabilities and the purchase price of the residual.* The taxable income on the asset is then calculated taking account of this new basis. The deductions allowed with respect to the liabilities are generally unaffected by the change in owner.**

The adjustment in the tax basis of the asset to reflect the purchase price places the new investor in a tax position that is similar to that of the original purchaser. However, the positions of the new and original purchaser are different in three respects:

---

*   For a discussion of the effect of a secondary market purchase on the basis used in calculating taxable income, see Chapter 7, Part C. Basis is often, but not always, recalculated if an owner trust is classified for federal income tax purposes as a partnership rather than a grantor trust.

**   See Chapter 7, footnote 36 and accompanying text.

1. The yield/maturity pattern of the remaining liabilities.

2. The remaining maturity of the investment.

3. The market value of the investment compared with the amount of remaining liabilities.

The first two of these items reduce phantom income in present value and absolute terms.* However, in terms of effective tax rate, the new purchaser's situation is not much different from that of the original purchaser because of the third item.

Recall that it is the positive correlation between yield and maturity on the liabilities that is the principal cause of phantom income. For a secondary market purchaser, this correlation will be less pronounced to the extent that the earlier-maturing/lower-yielding tranches of liabilities have already been retired at the time of the purchase. Thus, the pattern of dynamic yields on the remaining liabilities is less steep, indicating that expense is less back loaded for the new investor. Also recall that phantom income is a timing problem. Excess taxable income in the early years is offset by reduced taxable income in the later years. Thus, the shortened investment horizon reduces the cost of phantom income in present value terms.

These two positive elements are offset by the fact that the phantom income must be borne by a considerably smaller investment. The net effect of combining these offsetting factors for the fixed rate CMO discussed earlier is examined in Figure 28.

Figure 28 shows that the effective tax rate to the secondary market purchaser is not much reduced until the sale date is at the tenth year or beyond. At that point, the differential between the initial dynamic yield of the liabilities and the final dynamic yield has been reduced to 33 basis points as compared with an initial differential of 102 basis points.

---

*   For the balance of this study we will assume that the CMOs are issued in multiple classes structured to take advantage of the yield curve and will thus generate phantom income in the early years.

Figure 28. Secondary Market Purchase of CMO Equity and Phantom Income:Non-REMIC Transactions

Purchase Date (Years Since Issuance)	Dynamic Yield of Liabilities		Market Value of Residual	Present Value at 6% of Tax on Phantom Income	Effective Tax Rate
	Quarter When Purchased	Final Quarter			
0	8.326%	9.341%	$7,113*	$799	54.4%
5	8.631	9.341	2,689	289	50.1
10	9.014	9.341	1,520	54	41.5
15	9.341	9.341	743	2	34.9

* 000's omitted. The example assumes that the residual is always priced to yield 10.658% based on quarterly compounding.

Figure 29 tests the sensitivity of effective tax rates to changes in purchase yields. It shows that effective tax rates are stable over a wide range of yields.

Figure 29. The Effect of Purchase Yield on Phantom Income: Non-REMIC Transactions

Years Since Issuance	Purchase Yield	Market Value of Residual	Present Value at 6% of Tax on Phantom Income	Effective Tax Rate
5	6.658%	$3,236*	$291	49.6%
5	8.658	2,939	290	50.3
5	10.658	2,689	289	50.1
5	12.658	2,475	288	51.7
5	14.658	2,293	288	52.4

* 000's omitted.

2. REMIC Transactions

In the case of a REMIC transaction, we must distinguish between the net basis of the REMIC in its assets and the tax basis of the residual interest to the new purchaser—respectively referred to as the inside basis and the outside basis.* Under current law, the inside or REMIC basis would be unchanged by the sale of the residual. Thus, the taxable income or losses of the REMIC that is allocated to the purchaser might be the same as for the initial purchaser. The legislative history of the REMIC provisions contemplates that some adjustment to inside basis would be made, but at present there is no mechanism for making such an adjustment.** The new purchaser increases his purchase price or outside basis by the amount of taxable income that is allocated to him and decreases such basis (but not below zero) by the amount of distributions and allocations of net losses. Thus, the purchaser inherits the taxable income schedule of the former owner up to the point where his basis is completely recovered through distributions or losses. Once the outside basis has been amortized, no deductions for losses are allowed and all further distributions are accounted for as gain from the sale of the residual interest. Since the inside basis is generally greater than the outside basis (see the discussion in Part E, above, and Figure 16), the new purchaser, in early periods, gets the benefit of smaller taxable income stemming from the amortization of a relatively large basis. This means that, in many cases, the residual purchased in the secondary market is tax advantaged.

Another way of thinking about this is in terms of the crossover point for taxable income relative to economic income. Recall that phantom income arises because taxable income is greater than economic income in early periods and less in later periods. The point in time where taxable income first becomes less than economic income may be referred to as the *crossover point*. Someone who purchases the residual in the secondary market is closer to, and in some cases beyond, this crossover point. Thus, the present value benefit of the phantom losses can be greater than the present value cost of phantom income. In such a case, the residual is tax advantaged.

---

*   Strictly speaking, a REMIC's inside basis refers to the bases of all of its assets. For our purposes, though, inside basis will refer to the total asset basis net of the tax basis of the liabilities represented by the regular interests.

**   See Chapter 7, footnote 36 and accompanying text.

Figure 30 shows that this is the case even as early as the fifth year for the standard CMO residual we have been discussing.

Figure 30. Secondary Market Purchase of CMO Equity and Phantom Income: REMIC Transactions

Years Since Issuance	Inherited Tax Basis of Residual	Market Value of Residual**	Years to Crossover Point	Present Value at 6% of Tax on Phantom Income	Effective Tax Rate
0	$7,113*	$7,113	6.75	$799	54.4%
5	7,456	2,689	1.75	(71)	28.6
10	6,025	1,520	(3.25)	(96)	15.6
15	3,192	743	(8.25)	(45)	11.0

* 000's omitted.
** The example assumes that the residual is priced to yield 10.658% based on quarterly compounding.

Figure 31 shows that the tax advantaged quality of the residual is present under a wide range of purchase yields. Note than even when the residual is priced at 6.658%—a low yield and high price—the inherited tax basis, $7,456, is still much greater than the market value, $3,236. Thus, the tax benefit of amortizing a relatively large basis is still available.

Figure 31. The Effect of Purchase Yield on Phantom Income: REMIC Transactions

Years Since Issuance	Purchase Yield	Market Value of Residual	Inherited Tax Basis of Residual	Present Value at 6% of Tax on Phantom Income	Effective Tax Rate
5	6.658%	$3,236*	$7,456	$(53)	29.8%
5	8.658	2,939	7,456	(64)	29.1
5	10.658	2,689	7,456	(71)	28.6
5	12.658	2,475	7,456	(75)	28.2
5	14.658	2,293	7,456	(78)	27.9

* 000's omitted.

Addendum

The relationship between the dynamic yield of the residual and the dynamic yields of the asset and liability is given by the following formula:

$$Y_R = Y_A + D \times S$$

where

Y_R	=	dynamic yield of residual
Y_A	=	dynamic yield of asset
Y_L	=	dynamic yield of liability
S	=	the spread between the asset and liability dynamic yields $(Y_A - Y_L)$
D	=	dynamic leverage (L/R)
A	=	asset tax basis
L	=	liability tax basis
R	=	residual tax basis $(A - L)$

The proof is as follows:

$$Y_R = \text{residual income/residual basis}$$

$$
\begin{aligned}
&= (A \times Y_A - L \times Y_L)/R \\
&= (A \times Y_A - L \times Y_A + L \times Y_A - L \times Y_L)/R \\
&= [(A - L) \times Y_A + L \times (Y_A - Y_L)]/R \\
&= [(A - L)/R] \times Y_A + L/R \times (Y_A - Y_L) \\
&= Y_A + D \times S
\end{aligned}
$$

We next show that the residual phantom income can be divided into three components: the asset phantom income, the liability phantom income, and a component attributable to dynamic leverage. We arrive at this point by demonstrating that when dynamic leverage is constant, then residual phantom income is the sum of asset phantom income and liability phantom income. Thus, any divergence of phantom income from the sum must stem from the changing dynamic leverage. For convenience we establish the following notation:

E_A	=	asset economic income
E_L	=	liability economic income
E_R	=	residual economic income

T_A = asset taxable income
T_L = liability taxable income
T_R = residual taxable income
P_A = asset phantom income
P_L = liability phantom income
P_R = residual phantom income

Consider the following chain of equations:

1. $P_R = T_R - E_R$
2. $= (T_A - T_L) - (E_A - E_L)$
3. $= (T_A - E_A) - (T_L - E_L)$
4. $= P_A - P_L$

If each equality in the chain were true the proposition would be proven. The first and fourth equalities are just definitions and therefore true. The third equality is true since the formula in 3 is just a rearrangement of the formula in 2. The first part of equality 2 is true since the taxable income of the residual is by definition the difference between the taxable income of the asset and taxable expense of the liability. The second part, though, is not, in general, true. The economic income of a residual does not always equal the difference between the economic income of the asset and the economic expense of the liability. However, a sufficient condition for this final equality to hold is that the dynamic leverage be constant.

To see this, we approach the problem from the other side. What we show is that when the dynamic leverage is constant, then $(E_A - E_L)$ produces a constant dynamic yield and thus by definition equals the economic income of the residual.

The formula $Y_R = Y_A + D \times S$ was derived above with reference to taxable dynamic yields and bases. The same derivation holds true when economic yields and bases are considered; that is, when Y_A and Y_L correspond, respectively, to E_A and E_L instead of T_A and T_L, and Y_R corresponds to $(E_A - E_L)$ instead of $(T_A - T_L)$.

In the context of economic yields, though, Y_A and Y_L, and thus S, are constant. If L is also constant, it follows that Y_R is constant and thus $(E_A - E_L)$ is economically distributed. Therefore $(E_A - E_L) = E_R$.

Appendix B

State Tax Exemptions for REMICs

STATE	COMMENTS	AUTHORITY
Arizona	Not subject to tax.	Income Tax Ruling No. ITR 91-2, April 2, 1991.
California	Subject to minimum franchise tax. No tax on prohibited transactions.	Cal. Rev. + Tax Code §§ 24873, 24874.
Delaware	Not subject to tax.	33 Del. Rev. Code § 1133(c).
Florida	No federal income tax base, so no Florida starting tax base.	Fla. TAA 88(M)-003, March 10, 1988.
Illinois	Not subject to tax, except to the extent of income from prohibited transactions.	Ill. Priv. Ltr. Rul. IT 90-0082, March 29, 1990; Instructions to Form IL-1120, Corporate Tax Return.
Maryland	Subject to tax on net income from foreclosure property.	MD. Tax Gen. Code § 10-101(a-1), (e-1), 10-104, 10-304.
Massachusetts	Corporate Trust REMIC not subject to tax.	Mass. Law Gen. Ch. 62 § 8(b).
Michigan	Depends on nature of REMIC.	Mich. Rev. Admin. Bulletin 1989-54, June 9, 1989.
Minnesota	Not subject to tax.	Minn. Stat. § 290.9741-2.
New York	Not subject to tax.	NY Tax Law § 8.

STATE	COMMENTS	AUTHORITY
New York City	Not subject to tax.	N.Y.C. Admin. Code § 11-122.
Ohio	Not subject to tax.	Ohio Rev. Code § 5733.09.
Oregon	Not subject to tax, except to the extent of net income from prohibited transactions.	Oregon Rev. Stat. § 314.260.
Virginia	Follows federal law.	P.D. 87-237, October 23, 1987.
Wisconsin	Not subject to tax.	Wisc. Stat. § 71.26(f).

---

1. This chart is accurate as of January 1, 1994 and is subject to change.

2. In certain states in which REMICs are exempt, a REMIC may be required to file information returns as a prequisite for its exemption from tax. The exemptions described herein are often more complex than described, and readers should consult the authorities listed above rather than relying on this chart.

Appendix C

Primary Source Materials

INTERNAL REVENUE CODE SECTIONS

Section 171.

AMORTIZABLE BOND PREMIUM

(a) General rule.—In the case of any bond, as defined in subsection (d), the following rules shall apply to the amortizable bond premium (determined under subsection (b)) on the bond:

(1) Taxable bonds.—In the case of a bond (other than a bond the interest on which is excludable from gross income), the amount of the amortizable bond premium for the taxable year shall be allowed as a deduction.

(2) Tax-exempt bonds.—In the case of any bond the interest on which is excludable from gross income, no deduction shall be allowed for the amortizable bond premium for the taxable year.

(3) Cross reference.—

For adjustment to basis on account of amortizable bond premium, see section 1016(a)(5).

(b) Amortizable bond premium.—

(1) Amount of bond premium.—For purposes of paragraph (2), the amount of bond premium, in the case of the holder of any bond, shall be determined—

(A) with reference to the amount of the basis (for determining loss on sale or exchange) of such bond,

(B)(i) with reference to the amount payable on maturity or on earlier call date, in the case of any bond other than a bond to which clause (ii) applies, or

(ii) with reference to the amount payable on maturity (or if it results in a smaller amortizable bond premium attributable to the period to earlier call date, with reference to the amount payable on earlier call date), in the case of any bond described in subsection (a)(1) which is acquired after December 31, 1957, and

(C) with adjustments proper to reflect unamortized bond premium, with respect to the bond, for the period before the date as of which subsection (a) becomes applicable with respect to the taxpayer with respect to such bond.

In no case shall the amount of bond premium on a convertible bond include any amount attributable to the conversion features of the bond.

(2) Amount amortizable.—The amortizable bond premium of the taxable year shall be the amount of the bond premium attributable to such year. In the case of a bond to which paragraph (1)(B)(ii) applies and which has a call date, the amount of bond premium attributable to the taxable year in which the bond is called shall include an amount equal to the excess of the amount of the adjusted basis (for determining loss on sale or exchange) of such bond as of the beginning of the taxable year over the amount received on redemption of the bond or (if greater) the amount payable on maturity.

(3) Method of determination.—

(A) In general.—Except as provided in regulations prescribed by the Secretary, the determinations required under paragraphs (1) and (2) shall be made on the basis of the taxpayer's yield to maturity determined by—

(i) using the taxpayer's basis (for purposes of determining loss on sale or exchange) of the obligation, and

(ii) compounding at the close of each accrual period (as defined in section 1272(a)(5)).

(B) Special rule where earlier call date is used.—For purposes of subparagraph (A), if the amount payable on an earlier call date is used under paragraph (1)(B)(ii) in determining the amortizable bond premium attributable to the period before the earlier call date, such bond shall be treated as maturing on such date for the amount so payable and then reissued on such date for the amount so payable.

(4) Treatment of certain bonds acquired in exchange for other property.—

(A) In general.—If—

(i) a bond is acquired by any person in exchange for other property, and

(ii) the basis of such bond is determined (in whole or in part) by reference to the basis of such other property, for purposes of applying this subsection to such bond while held by such person, the basis of such bond shall not exceed its fair market value immediately after the exchange. A similar rule shall apply in the case of such bond while held by any other person whose basis is determined (in whole or in part) by reference to the basis in the hands of the person referred to in clause (i).

(B) Special rule where bond exchanged in reorganization.—Subparagraph (A) shall not apply to an exchange by the taxpayer of a bond for another bond if such exchange is a part of a reorganization (as defined in section 368). If any portion of the basis of the taxpayer in a bond transferred in such an exchange is not taken into account in determining bond premium by reason of this paragraph, such portion shall not be taken into account in determining the amount of bond premium on any bond received in the exchange.

(c) Election as to taxable bonds.—

(1) Eligibility to elect; bonds with respect to which election permitted.—In the case of bonds the interest on which is not excludable from gross income, this section shall apply only if the taxpayer has so elected.

(2) Manner and effect of election.—The election authorized under this subsection shall be made in accordance with such regulations as the Secretary shall prescribe. If such election is made with respect to any bond (described in paragraph (1)) of the taxpayer, it shall also apply to all such bonds held by the taxpayer at the beginning of the first taxable year to which the election applies and to all such bonds thereafter acquired by him and shall be binding for all subsequent taxable years with respect to all such bonds of the taxpayer, unless, on application by the taxpayer, the Secretary permits him, subject to such conditions as the Secretary deems necessary, to revoke such election. In the case of bonds held by a common trust fund, as defined in section 584(a), or by a foreign personal holding company, as defined in section 552, the election authorized under this subsection shall be exercisable with respect to such bonds only by the common trust fund or foreign personal holding company. In case of bonds held by an estate or trust, the election authorized under this subsection shall be exercisable with respect to such bonds only by the fiduciary.

(d) Bond defined.—For purposes of this section, the term "bond" means any bond, debenture, note, or certificate or other evidence of indebtedness, but does not include any such obligation which constitutes stock in trade of the taxpayer or any such obligation of a kind which would properly be included in the inventory of the taxpayer if on hand at the close of the taxable year, or any such obligation held by the taxpayer primarily for sale to customers in the ordinary course of his trade or business.

(e) Treatment as offset to interest payments.—Except as provided in regulations, in the case of any taxable bond—

(1) the amount of any bond premium shall be allocated among the interest payments on the bond under rules similar to the rules of subsection (b)(3), and

(2) in lieu of any deduction under subsection (a), the amount of any premium so allocated to any interest payment shall be applied against (and operate to reduce) the amount of such interest payment.

For purposes of the preceding sentence, the term "taxable bond" means any bond the interest of which is not excludable from gross income.

(f) Dealers in tax-exempt securities.—For special rules applicable, in the case of dealers in securities, with respect to premium attributable to certain wholly tax-exempt securities, see section 75.

Section 593(d)

(d) Loans defined.—For purposes of this section—

(1) Qualifying real property loans.—The term "qualifying real property loan" means any loan secured by an interest in improved real property or secured by an interest in real property which is to be improved out of the proceeds of the loan, but such term does not include—

(A) any loan evidenced by a security (as defined in section 165(g)(2)(C));

(B) any loan, whether or not evidenced by a security (as defined in section 165(g)(2)(C)), the primary obligor in which is —

(i) a government or political subdivision or instrumentality thereof;

(ii) a bank (as defined in section 581); or

(iii) another member of the same affiliated group;

(C) any loan, to the extent secured by a deposit in or share of the taxpayer; or

(D) any loan which, within a 60-day period beginning in one taxable year of the creditor and ending in its next taxable year, is made or acquired and then repaid or disposed of, unless the transactions by which such loan was made or acquired and then repaid or disposed of are established to be for bona fide business purposes.

For purposes of subparagraph (B)(iii), the term "affiliated group" has the meaning assigned to such term by section 1504(a); except that (i) the phrase "more than 50 percent" shall be substituted for the phrase "at least 80 percent" each place it appears in section 1504(a), and (ii) all corporations shall be treated as includible corporations (without any exclusion under section 1504(b)).

(2) Nonqualifying loans.—The term "nonqualifying loan" means any loan which is not a qualifying real property loan.

(3) Loan.—The term "loan" means debt, as the term "debt" is used in section 166.

(4) Treatment of interests in REMIC's.—A regular or residual interest in a REMIC shall be treated as a qualifying real property loan; except that, if less than 95 percent of the assets of such REMIC are qualifying real property loans (determined as if the taxpayer held the assets of the REMIC), such interest shall be so treated only in the proportion which the assets of such REMIC consist of such loans. For purposes of determining whether any interest in a REMIC qualifies under the preceding sentence, any interest in another REMIC held by such REMIC shall be treated as a qualifying real property loan under principles similar to the principles of the preceding sentence, except that if such REMIC's are part of a tiered structure, they shall be treated as 1 REMIC for purposes of this paragraph.

Section 856(c)

(c) Limitations.—A corporation, trust, or association shall not be considered a real estate investment trust for any taxable year unless—

(1) it files with its return for the taxable year an election to be a real estate investment trust or has made such election for a previous taxable year, and such election has not been terminated or revoked under subsection (g);

(2) at least 95 percent (90 percent for taxable years beginning before January 1, 1980) of its gross income (excluding gross income from prohibited transactions) is derived from—

(A) dividends;

(B) interest;

(C) rents from real property;

(D) gain from the sale or other disposition of stock, securities, and real property (including interests in real property and interests in mortgages on real property) which is not property described in section 1221(1);

(E) abatements and refunds of taxes on real property;

(F) income and gain derived from foreclosure property (as defined in subsection (e));

(G) amounts (other than amounts the determination of which depends in whole or in part on the income or profits of any person) received or accrued as consideration for entering into agreements (i) to make loans secured by mortgages on real property or on interests in real property or (ii) to purchase or lease real property (including interests in real property and interests in mortgages on real property); and

(H) gain from the sale or other disposition of a real estate asset which is not a prohibited transaction solely by reason of section 857(b)(6);

(3) at least 75 percent of its gross income (excluding gross income from prohibited transactions) is derived from—

(A) rents from real property;

(B) interest on obligations secured by mortgages on real property or on interests in real property;

(C) gain from the sale or other disposition of real property (including interests in real property and interests in mortgages on real property) which is not property described in section 1221(1);

(D) dividends or other distributions on, and gain (other than gain from prohibited transactions) from the sale or other disposition of, transferable shares (or transferable certificates of beneficial interest) in other real estate investment trusts which meet the requirements of this part;

(E) abatements and refunds of taxes on real property;

(F) income and gain derived from foreclosure property (as defined in subsection (e));

(G) amounts (other than amounts the determination of which depends in whole or in part on the income or profits of any person) received or accrued as consideration for entering into agreements (i) to make loans secured by mortgages on real property or on interests in real property or (ii) to purchase or lease real property (including interests in real property and interests in mortgages on real property);

(H) gain from the sale or other disposition of a real estate asset which is not a prohibited transaction solely by reason of section 857(b)(6); and

(I) qualified temporary investment income;

(4) less than 30 percent of its gross income is derived from the sale or other disposition of—

(A) stock or securities held for less than 6 months;

(B) property in a transaction which is a prohibited transaction; and

(C) real property (including interests in real property and interests in mortgages on real property) held for less than 4 years other than—

(i) property compulsorily or involuntarily converted within the meaning of section 1033, and

(ii) property which is foreclosure property within the definition of section 856(e); and

(5) at the close of each quarter of the taxable year—

(A) at least 75 percent of the value of its total assets is represented by real estate assets, cash and cash items (including receivables), and Government securities; and

(B) not more than 25 percent of the value of its total assets is represented by securities (other than those includible under subparagraph (A)) for purposes of this calculation limited in respect of any one issuer to an amount not greater in value than 5 percent of the value of the total assets of the trust and to not more than 10 percent of the outstanding voting securities of such issuer. A real estate investment trust which meets the requirements of this paragraph at the close of any quarter shall not lose its status as a real estate investment trust because of a discrepancy during a subsequent quarter between the value of its various investments and such requirements unless such discrepancy exists immediately after the acquisition of any security or other property and is wholly or partly the result of such acquisition. A real estate investment trust which does not meet such requirements at the close of any quarter by reason of a discrepancy existing immediately after the acquisition of any security or other property which is wholly or partly the result of such acquisition during such quarter shall not lose its status for such quarter as a real estate investment trust if such discrepancy is eliminated within 30 days after the close of such quarter and in such cases it shall be considered to have met such requirements at the close of such quarter for purposes of applying the preceding sentence.

(6) For purposes of this part—

(A) The term "value" means, with respect to securities for which market quotations are readily available, the market value of such securities; and with respect to other securities and assets, fair value as determined in good faith by the trustees, except that in the case of securities of real estate investment trusts such fair value shall not exceed market value or asset value, whichever is higher.

(B) The term "real estate assets" means real property (including interests in real property and interests in mortgages on real property) and shares (or transferable certificates of beneficial interest) in other real estate investment trusts which meet the requirements of this part. Such term also includes any property (not otherwise a real estate asset) attributable to the temporary investment of new capital, but only if such property is stock or a debt instrument, and only for the 1-year period beginning on the date the real estate trust receives such capital.

(C) The term "interests in real property" includes fee ownership and co-ownership of land or improvements thereon, leaseholds of land or improvements thereon, options to acquire land or improvements thereon, and options to acquire leaseholds of land or improvements thereon, but does not include mineral, oil, or gas royalty interests.

(D) **Qualified temporary investment income.—**

(i) **In general.**—The term "qualified temporary investment income" means any income which—

(I) is attributable to stock or a debt instrument (within the meaning of section 1275(a)(1)),

(II) is attributable to the temporary investment of new capital, and

(III) is received or accrued during the 1-year period beginning on the date on which the real estate investment trust receives such capital.

(ii) **New capital.**—The term "new capital" means any amount received by the real estate investment trust—

(I) in exchange for stock (or certificates of beneficial interest) in such trust (other than amounts received pursuant to a dividend reinvestment plan), or

(II) in a public offering of debt obligations of such trust which have maturities of at least 5 years.

(E) A regular or residual interest in a REMIC shall be treated as a real estate asset, and any amount includible in gross income with respect to such an interest shall be treated as interest on an obligation secured by a mortgage on real property; except that, if less than 95 percent of the assets of such REMIC are real estate assets (determined as if the real estate investment trust held such assets), such real estate investment trust shall be treated as holding directly (and as receiving directly) its proportionate share of the assets and income of the REMIC. For purposes of determining whether any interest in a REMIC qualifies under the preceding sentence, any interest held by such REMIC in another REMIC shall be treated as a real estate asset under principles similar to the principles of the preceding sentence, except that, if such REMIC's are part of a tiered structure, they shall be treated as one REMIC for purposes of this subparagraph.

(F) All other terms shall have the same meaning as when used in the Investment Company Act of 1940, as amended (15 U.S.C. 80a-1 and following).

(G) **Treatment of certain interest rate agreements.**—Except to the extent provided by regulations, any—

(i) payment to a real estate investment trust under a bona fide interest rate swap or cap agreement entered into by the real estate investment trust to hedge any variable rate indebtedness of such trust incurred or to be incurred to acquire or carry real estate assets, and

(ii) any gain from the sale or other disposition of such agreement, shall be treated as income qualifying under paragraph (2) and such agreement shall be treated as a security for purposes of paragraph (4)(A).

(7) A corporation, trust, or association which fails to meet the requirements of paragraph (2) or (3), or of both such paragraphs, for any taxable year shall nevertheless be considered to have satisfied the re-

quirements of such paragraphs for such taxable year if—

(A) the nature and amount of each item of its gross income described in such paragraphs is set forth in a schedule attached to its income tax return for such taxable year;

(B) the inclusion of any incorrect information in the schedule referred to in subparagraph (A) is not due to fraud with intent to evade tax; and

(C) the failure to meet the requirements of paragraph (2) or (3), or of both such paragraphs, is due to reasonable cause and not due to willful neglect.

(8) **Treatment of liquidating gains.**— In the case of the taxable year in which a real estate investment trust is completely liquidated, there shall not be taken into account under paragraph (4) any gain from the sale, exchange, or distribution of any property after the adoption of the plan of complete liquidation.

Sections 860A–860G

PART IV—REAL ESTATE MORTGAGE INVESTMENT CONDUITS

SEC. 860A. TAXATION OF REMICs.

(a) **General rule.**—Except as otherwise provided in this part, a REMIC shall not be subject to taxation under this subtitle (and shall not be treated as a corporation, partnership, or trust for purposes of this subtitle).

(b) **Income taxable to holders.**—The income of any REMIC shall be taxable to the holders of interests in such REMIC as provided in this part.

SEC. 860B. TAXATION OF HOLDERS OF REGULAR INTERESTS.

(a) **General rule.**—In determining the tax under this chapter of any holder of a regular interest in a REMIC, such interest (if not otherwise a debt instrument) shall be treated as a debt instrument.

(b) **Holders must use accrual method.**—The amounts includible in gross income with respect to any regular interest in a REMIC shall be determined under the accrual method of accounting.

(c) **Portion of gain treated as ordinary income.**—Gain on the disposition of a regular interest shall be treated as ordinary income to the extent such gain does not exceed the excess (if any) of—

(1) the amount which would have been includible in the gross income of the taxpayer with respect to such interest if the yield on such interest were 110 percent of the applicable Federal rate (as defined in section 1274(d) without regard to paragraph (2) thereof) as of the beginning of the taxpayer's holding period, over

(2) the amount actually includible in gross income with respect to such interest by the taxpayer.

(d) **Cross reference.**—For special rules in determining inclusion of original issue discount on regular interests, see section 1272(a)(6).

SEC. 860C. TAXATION OF RESIDUAL INTERESTS.

(a) **Pass-thru of income or loss.**—

(1) **In general.**—In determining the tax under this chapter of any holder of a residual interest in a REMIC, such holder shall take into account his daily portion of the taxable income or net loss of such REMIC for each day during the taxable year on which such holder held such interest.

(2) **Daily portion.**—The daily portion referred to in paragraph (1) shall be determined—

(A) by allocating to each day in any calendar quarter its ratable portion of the taxable income (or net loss) for such quarter, and

(B) by allocating the amounts so allocated to any day among the holders (on such day) of residual interests in proportion to their respective holdings on such day.

(b) Determination of taxable income or net loss.— For purposes of this section—

(1) Taxable income.—The taxable income of a REMIC shall be determined under an accrual method of accounting and, except as provided in regulations, in the same manner as in the case of an individual, except that—

(A) regular interests in such REMIC (if not otherwise debt instruments) shall be treated as indebtedness of such REMIC,

(B) market discount on any market discount bond shall be included in gross income for the taxable years to which it is attributable as determined under the rules of section 1276(b)(2) (and sections 1276(a) and 1277 shall not apply),

(C) there shall not be taken into account any item of income, gain, loss, or deduction allocable to a prohibited transaction,

(D) the deductions referred to in section 703(a)(2) (other than any deduction under section 212) shall not be allowed, and

(E) the amount of the net income from foreclosure property (if any) shall be reduced by the amount of the tax imposed by section 860G(c).

(2) Net loss.—The net loss of any REMIC is the excess of—

(A) the deductions allowable in computing the taxable income of such REMIC, over

(B) its gross income.
Such amount shall be determined with the modifications set forth in paragraph (1).

(c) Distributions.—Any distribution by a REMIC—

(1) shall not be included in gross income to the extent it does not exceed the adjusted basis of the interest, and

(2) to the extent it exceeds the adjusted basis of the interest, shall be treated

as gain from the sale or exchange of such interest.

(d) Basis rules.—

(1) Increase in basis.—The basis of any person's residual interest in a REMIC shall be increased by the amount of the taxable income of such REMIC taken into account under subsection (a) by such person with respect to such interest.

(2) Decreases in basis.—The basis of any person's residual interest in a REMIC shall be decreased (but not below zero) by the sum of the following amounts:

(A) any distributions to such person with respect to such interest, and

(B) any net loss of such REMIC taken into account under subsection (a) by such person with respect to such interest.

(e) Special rules.—

(1) Amounts treated as ordinary.— Any amount taken into account under subsection (a) by any holder of a residual interest in a REMIC shall be treated as ordinary income or loss, as the case may be.

(2) Limitation on losses.—

(A) In general.—The amount of the net loss of any REMIC taken into account by a holder under subsection (a) with respect to any calendar quarter shall not exceed the adjusted basis of such holder's residual interest in such REMIC as of the close of such calendar quarter (determined without regard to the adjustment under subsection (d)(2)(B) for such calendar quarter).

(B) Indefinite carryforward.— Any loss disallowed by reason of subparagraph (A) shall be treated as incurred by the REMIC in the succeeding calendar quarter with respect to such holder.

(3) Cross reference.—For special treatment of income in excess of daily accruals, see section 860E.

SEC. 860D. REMIC DEFINED.

(a) General rule.—For purposes of this title, the terms "real estate mortgage investment conduit" and "REMIC" mean any entity—

(1) to which an election to be treated as a REMIC applies for the taxable year and all prior taxable years,

(2) all of the interests in which are regular interests or residual interests,

(3) which has 1 (and only 1) class of residual interests (and all distributions, if any, with respect to such interests are pro rata),

(4) as of the close of the 3rd month beginning after the startup day and at all times thereafter, substantially all of the assets of which consist of qualified mortgages and permitted investments,

(5) which has a taxable year which is a calendar year, and

(6) with respect to which there are reasonable arrangements designed to ensure that—

(A) residual interests in such entity are not held by disqualified organizations (as defined in section 860E(e)(5)), and

(B) information necessary for the application of section 860E(e) will be made available by the entity. In the case of a qualified liquidation (as defined in section 860F(a)(4)(A)), paragraph (4) shall not apply during the liquidation period (as defined in section 860F(a)(4)(B)).

(b) Election.—

(1) In general.—An entity (otherwise meeting the requirements of subsection (a)) may elect to be treated as REMIC for its 1st taxable year. Such an election shall be made on its return for such 1st taxable year. Except as provided in paragraph (2), such an election shall apply to the taxable year for which made and all subsequent taxable years.

(2) Termination.—

(A) In general.—If any entity ceases to be a REMIC at any time during the taxable year, such entity shall not be treated as a REMIC for such taxable year or any succeeding taxable year.

(B) Inadvertent terminations.— If—

(i) an entity ceases to be a REMIC,

(ii) the Secretary determines that such cessation was inadvertent,

(iii) no later than a reasonable time after the discovery of the event resulting in such cessation, steps are taken so that such entity is once more a REMIC, and

(iv) such entity, and each person holding an interest in such entity at any time during the period specified pursuant to this subsection, agrees to make such adjustments (consistent with the treatment of such entity as a REMIC or a C corporation) as may be required by the Secretary with respect to such period,

then, notwithstanding such terminating event, such entity shall be treated as continuing to be a REMIC (or such cessation shall be disregarded for purposes of subparagraph (A)) whichever the Secretary determines to be appropriate.

SEC. 860E. TREATMENT OF INCOME IN EXCESS OF DAILY ACCRUALS ON RESIDUAL INTERESTS.

(a) Excess inclusions may not be offset by net operating losses.—

(1) In general.—Except as provided in paragraph (2), the taxable income of any holder of a residual interest in a REMIC for any taxable year shall in no event be less than the excess inclusion for such taxable year.

(2) Exceptions for certain financial institutions.—Paragraph (1) shall not apply to any organization to which section 593 applies. The Secretary may by regulations provide that the preceding sentence shall not apply where necessary or appropriate to prevent avoidance of tax imposed by this chapter.

(3) Special rule for affiliated groups.—All members of an affiliated group filing a consolidated return shall be treated as 1 taxpayer for purposes of this subsection, except that paragraph (2) shall be applied separately with respect to each corporation which is a member of such group and to which section 593 applies.

(4) Treatment of certain subsidiaries.—

(A) In general.—For purposes of this subsection, a corporation to which section 593 applies and each qualified subsidiary of such corporation shall be treated as a single corporation to which section 593 applies.

(B) Qualified subsidiary.—For purposes of this subsection, the term "qualified subsidiary" means any corporation—

(i) all the stock of which, and substantially all the indebtedness of which, is held directly by the corporation to which section 593 applies, and

(ii) which is organized and operated exclusively in connection with the organization and operation of 1 or more REMIC's.

(5) Coordination with section 172.—Any excess inclusion for any taxable year shall not be taken into account—

(A) in determining under section 172 the amount of any net operating loss for such taxable year, and

(B) in determining taxable income for such taxable year for purposes of the 2nd sentence of section 172(b)(2).

(b) Organizations subject to unrelated business tax.—If the holder of any residual interest in a REMIC is an organization subject to the tax imposed by section 511, the excess inclusion of such holder for any taxable year shall be treated as unrelated business taxable income of such holder for purposes of section 511.

(c) Excess inclusion.—For purposes of this section—

(1) In general.—The term "excess inclusion" means, with respect to any residual interest in a REMIC for any calendar quarter, the excess (if any) of—

(A) the amount taken into account with respect to such interest by the holder under section 860C(a), over

(B) the sum of the daily accruals with respect to such interest for days during such calendar quarter while held by such holder.

To the extent provided in regulations, if residual interests in a REMIC do not have significant value, the excess inclusions with respect to such interests shall be the amount determined under subparagraph (A) without regard to subparagraph (B).

(2) Determination of daily accruals.—

(A) **In general.**—For purposes of this subsection, the daily accrual with respect to any residual interest for any day in any calendar quarter shall be determined by allocating to each day in such quarter its ratable portion of the product of—

(i) the adjusted issue price of such interest at the beginning of such quarter, and

(ii) 120 percent of the long-term Federal rate [sic] (determined on the basis of compounding at the close of each calendar quarter and properly adjusted for the length of such quarter).

(B) **Adjusted issue price.**—For purposes of this paragraph, the adjusted issue price of any residual interest at the beginning of any calendar quarter is the issue price of the residual interest (adjusted for contributions)—

(i) increased by the amount of daily accruals for prior quarters, and

(ii) decreased (but not below zero) by any distribution made with respect to such interest before the beginning of such quarter.

(C) **Federal long-term rate.**—For purposes of this paragraph, the term "Federal long-term rate" means the Federal long-term rate which would have applied to the residual interest under section 1274(d) (determined without regard to paragraph (2) thereof) if it were a debt instrument.

(d) Treatment of residual interests held by real estate investment trusts.—If a residual interest in a REMIC is held by a real estate investment trust, under regulations prescribed by the Secretary—

(1) any excess of—

(A) the aggregate excess inclusions determined with respect to such interests, over

(B) the real estate investment trust taxable income (within the meaning of section 857(b)(2), excluding any net capital gain),

shall be allocated among the shareholders of such trust in proportion to the dividends received by such shareholders from such trust, and

(2) any amount allocated to a shareholder under paragraph (1) shall be treated as an excess inclusion with respect to a residual interest held by such shareholder.

Rules similar to the rules of the preceding

sentence shall apply also in the case of regulated investment companies, common trust funds, and organizations to which part I of subchapter T applies.

(e) **Tax on transfers of residual interests to certain organizations, etc.—**

(1) **In general.**—A tax is hereby imposed on any transfer of a residual interest in a REMIC to a disqualified organization.

(2) **Amount of tax.**—The amount of the tax imposed by paragraph (1) on any transfer of a residual interest shall be equal to the product of—

(A) the amount (determined under regulations) equal to the present value of the total anticipated excess inclusions with respect to such interest for periods after such transfer, multiplied by

(B) the highest rate of tax specified in section 11(b)(1).

(3) **Liability.**—The tax imposed by paragraph (1) on any transfer shall be paid by the transferor; except that, where such transfer is through an agent for a disqualified organization, such tax shall be paid by such agent.

(4) **Transferee furnishes affidavit.**—The person (otherwise liable for any tax imposed by paragraph (1)) shall be relieved of liability for the tax imposed by paragraph (1) with respect to any transfer if—

(A) the transferee furnishes to such person an affidavit that the transferee is not a disqualified organization, and

(B) as of the time of the transfer, such person does not have actual knowledge that such affidavit is false.

(5) **Disqualified organization.**—For purposes of this section, the term "disqualified organization" means—

(A) the United States, any State or political subdivision thereof, any foreign government, any international organization, or any agency or instrumentality or any of the foregoing,

(B) any organization (other than a cooperative described in section 521) which is exempt from tax imposed by this chapter unless such organization is subject to the tax imposed by section 511, and

(C) any organization described in section 1381(a)(2)(C).

For purposes of subparagraph (A), the rules of section 168(h)(2)(D) (relating to treatment of certain taxable instrumentalities) shall apply; except that, in the case of the Federal Home Loan Mortgage Corporation, clause (ii) of such section shall not apply.

(6) **Treatment of pass-thru entities.—**

(A) **Imposition of tax.**—If, at any time during any taxable year of a pass-thru entity, a disqualified organization is the record holder of an interest in such entity, there is hereby imposed on such entity for such taxable year a tax equal to the product of—

(i) the amount of excess inclusions for such taxable year allocable to the interest held by such disqualified organization, multiplied by

(ii) the highest rate of tax specified in section 11(b)(1).

(B) **Pass-thru entity.**—For purposes of this paragraph, the term "pass-thru entity" means—

(i) any regulated investment company, real estate investment trust, or common trust fund.

(ii) any partnership, trust, or estate, and

(iii) any organization to which part I of subchapter T applies.

Except as provided in regulations, a person holding an interest in a pass-thru entity as a nominee for another person shall, with respect to such interest, be treated as a pass-thru entity.

(C) **Tax to be deductible.**—Any tax imposed by this paragraph with respect to any excess inclusion of any pass-thru entity for any taxable year shall, for purposes of this title (other than this subsection), be applied against (and operate to reduce) the amount included in gross income with respect to the residual interest involved.

(D) **Exception where holder furnishes affidavit.**—No tax shall be imposed by subparagraph (A) with respect to any interest in a pass-thru entity for any period if—

(i) the record holder of such interest furnishes to such pass-thru entity an affidavit that such record holder is not a disqualified organization, and

(ii) during such period, the pass-thru entity does not have actual knowledge that such affidavit is false.

(7) **Waiver.**—The Secretary may waive the tax imposed by paragraph (1) on any transfer if—

(A) within a reasonable time after discovery that the transfer was subject to tax under paragraph (1), steps are taken so that the interest is no longer held by the disqualified organization, and

(B) there is paid to the Secretary such amounts as the Secretary may require.

(8) **Administrative provisions.**—For purposes of subtitle F, the taxes imposed by this subsection shall be treated as excise taxes with respect to which the deficiency procedures of such subtitle F apply.

(f) **Treatment of variable insurance contracts.**—Except as provided in regulations, with respect to any variable contract (as defined in section 817), there shall be no adjustment in the reserve to the extent of any excess inclusion.

SEC. 860F. OTHER RULES.

(a) **100 Percent tax on prohibited transactions.**—

(1) **Tax imposed.**—There is hereby imposed for each taxable year of a REMIC a tax equal to 100 percent of the net income derived from prohibited transactions.

(2) **Prohibited transaction.**—For purposes of this part, the term "prohibited transaction" means—

(A) **Disposition of qualified mortgage.**—The disposition of any qualified mortgage transferred to the REMIC other than a disposition pursuant to—

(i) the substitution of a qualified replacement mortgage for a qualified mortgage (or the repurchase in lieu of substitution of a defective obligation),

(ii) a disposition incident to the foreclosure, default, or imminent default of the mortgage,

(iii) the bankruptcy or insolvency of the REMIC, or

(iv) a qualified liquidation.

(B) **Income from nonpermitted assets.**—The receipt of any income attributable to any asset which is neither a qualified mortgage nor a permitted investment.

(C) **Compensation for services.**—The receipt by the REMIC of any amount representing a fee or other compensation for services.

(D) **Gain from disposition of cash flow investments.**—Gain from the disposition of any cash flow investment other than pursuant to any qualified liquidation.

(3) **Determination of net income.**—For purposes of paragraph (1), the term "net income derived from prohibited transactions" means the excess of the gross income from prohibited transactions over the deductions allowed by this chapter which are directly connected with such transactions; except that there shall not be taken into account any item attributable to any prohibited transaction for which there was a loss.

(4) **Qualified liquidation.**—For purposes of this part—

(A) **In general.**—The term "qualified liquidation" means a transaction in which—

(i) the REMIC adopts a plan of complete liquidation,

(ii) such REMIC sells all its assets (other than cash) within the liquidation period, and

(iii) all proceeds of the liquidation (plus the cash), less assets retained to meet claims, are credited or distributed to holders of regular or residual interests on or before the last day of the liquidation period.

(B) **Liquidation period.**—The term "liquidation period" means the period—

(i) beginning on the date of the adoption of the plan of liquidation, and

(ii) ending at the close of the 90th day after such date.

(5) **Exceptions.**— Notwithstanding subparagraphs (A) and (D) of paragraph (1), the term "prohibited transaction" shall not include any disposition—

(A) required to prevent default on a regular interest where the threatened default resulted from a default on 1 or more qualified mortgages, or

(B) to facilitate a clean-up call (as defined in regulations).

(b) Treatment of transfers to the REMIC.—

(1) Treatment of transferor.—

(A) **Nonrecognition gain or loss.**—No gain or loss shall be recognized to the transferor on the transfer of any property to a REMIC in exchange for regular or residual interests in such REMIC.

(B) **Adjusted bases of interests.**—The adjusted bases of the regular and residual interests received in a transfer described in subparagraph (A) shall be equal to the aggregate adjusted bases of the property transferred in such transfer. Such amount shall be allocated among such interests in proportion to their respective fair market values.

(C) **Treatment of nonrecognized gain.**—If the issue price of any regular or residual interest exceeds its adjusted basis as determined under subparagraph (B), for periods during which such interest is held by the transferor (or by any other person whose basis is determined in whole or in part by reference to the basis of such interest in the hand of the transferor)—

(i) in the case of a regular interest, such excess shall be included in gross income (as determined under rules similar to rules of section 1276(b)), and

(ii) in the case of a residual interest, such excess shall be included in gross income ratably over the anticipated period during which the REMIC will be in existence.

(D) **Treatment of nonrecognized loss.**—If the adjusted basis of any regular or residual interest received in a transfer described in subparagraph (A) exceeds its issue price, for periods during which such interest is held by the transferor (or by any other person whose basis is determined in whole or in part by reference to the basis of such interest in the hand of the transferor)—

(i) in the case of a regular interest, such excess shall be allowable as a

deduction under rules similar to the rules of section 171, and

(ii) in the case of a residual interest, such excess shall be allowable as a deduction ratably over the anticipated period during which the REMIC will be in existence.

(2) **Basis to REMIC.**—The basis of any property received by a REMIC in a transfer described in paragraph (1)(A) shall be its fair market value immediately after such transfer.

(c) Distributions of property.—If a REMIC makes a distribution of property with respect to any regular or residual interest—

(1) notwithstanding any other provision of this subtitle, gain shall be recognized to such REMIC on the distribution in the same manner as if it had sold such property to the distributee at its fair market value, and

(2) the basis of the distributee in such property shall be its fair market value.

(d) Coordination with wash sale rules.—For purposes of section 1091—

(1) any residual interest in a REMIC shall be treated as a security, and

(2) in applying such section to any loss claimed to have been sustained on the sale or other disposition of a residual interest in a REMIC—

(A) except as provided in regulations, any residual interest in any REMIC and any interest in a taxable mortgage pool (as defined in section 7701(i)) comparable to a residual interest in a REMIC shall be treated as substantially identical stock or securities, and

(B) subsection[s] (a) and (e) of such section shall be applied by substituting "6 months" for "30 days" each place it appears.

(e) Treatment under subtitle F.—For purposes of subtitle F, a REMIC shall be treated as a partnership (and holders of residual interests in such REMIC shall be treated as partners). Any return required by reason of the preceding sentence shall include the amount of the daily accruals determined under section 860E(c). Such return shall be filed by the REMIC. The determination of who may sign such return shall be made without regard to the first sentence of this subsection.

SEC. 860G. OTHER DEFINITIONS AND SPECIAL RULES.

(a) **Definitions.**—For purposes of this part—

(1) **Regular interest.**—The term "regular interest" means any interest in a REMIC which is issued on the startup day with fixed terms and which is designated as a regular interest if—

(A) such interest unconditionally entitles the holder to receive a specified principal amount (or other similar amount), and

(B) interest payments (or other similar amount), if any, with respect to such interest at or before maturity —

(i) are payable based on a fixed rate (or to the extent provided in regulations, at a variable rate), or

(ii) consist of a specified portion of the interest payments on qualified mortgages and such portion does not vary during the period such interest is outstanding.

The interest shall not fail to meet the requirements of subparagraph (A) merely because the timing (but not the amount) of the principal payments (or other similar amounts) may be contingent on the extent of prepayments on qualified mortgages and the amount of income from permitted investments.

(2) **Residual interest.**—The term "residual interest" means an interest in a REMIC which is issued on the startup day, which is not a regular interest, and which is designated as a residual interest.

(3) **Qualified mortgage.**—The term "qualified mortgage" means—

(A) any obligation (including any participation or certificate of beneficial ownership therein) which is principally secured by an interest in real property and which—

(i) is transferred to the REMIC on the startup day in exchange for regular or residual interests in the REMIC, or

(ii) is purchased by the

REMIC within the 3-month period beginning on the startup day if, except as provided in regulations, such purchase is pursuant to a fixed-price contract in effect on the startup day,

(B) any qualified replacement mortgage, and

(C) any regular interest in another REMIC transferred to the REMIC on the startup day in exchange for regular or residual interests in the REMIC.

For purposes of subparagraph (A), any obligation secured by stock held by a person as a tenant-stockholder (as defined in section 216) in a cooperative housing corporation (as so defined) shall be treated as secured by an interest in real property.

(4) **Qualified replacement mortgage.**—The term "qualified replacement mortgage" means any obligation—

(A) which would be a qualified mortgage if transferred on the startup day in exchange for regular or residual interests in the REMIC, and

(B) which is received for—

(i) another obligation within the 3-month period beginning on the startup day, or

(ii) a defective obligation within the 2-year period beginning on the startup day.

(5) **Permitted investments.**—The term "permitted investments" means any—

(A) cash flow investment,

(B) qualified reserve asset, or

(C) foreclosure property.

(6) **Cash flow investment.**—The term "cash flow investment" means any investment of amounts received under qualified mortgages for a temporary period before distribution to holders of interests in the REMIC.

(7) **Qualified reserve asset.**—

(A) **In general.**—The term "qualified reserve asset" means any intangible property which is held for investment and as part of a qualified reserve fund.

(B) **Qualified reserve fund.**—For purposes of subparagraph (A), the term "qualified reserve fund" means any reasonably required reserve to provide for full payment of expenses of the REMIC or amounts due on regular interests in the event of defaults on qualified mortgages or lower than expected returns on cash flow investments. The amount of any such reserve shall be promptly and appropriately reduced as payments of qualified mortgages are received.

(C) **Special rule.**—A reserve shall not be treated as a qualified reserve for any taxable year (and all subsequent taxable years) if more than 30 percent of the gross income from the assets in such fund for the taxable year is derived from the sale or other disposition of property held for less than 3 months. For purposes of the preceding sentence, gain on the disposition of a qualified reserve asset shall not be taken into account if the disposition giving rise to such gain is required to prevent default on a regular interest where the threatened default resulted from a default on 1 or more qualified mortgages.

(8) **Foreclosure property.**—The term "foreclosure property" means property—

(A) which would be foreclosure property under section 856(e) (without regard to paragraph (5) thereof) if acquired by a real estate investment trust, and

(B) which is acquired in connection with the default or imminent default of a qualified mortgage held by the REMIC.

Solely for purposes of section 860D(a), the determination of whether any property is foreclosure property shall be made without regard to section 856(e)(4).

(9) **Startup day.**—The term "startup day" means the day on which the REMIC issues all of its regular and residual interests. To the extent provided in regulations, all interests issued (and all transfers to the REMIC) during any period (not exceeding 10 days) permitted in such regulations shall be treated as occurring on the day during such period selected by the REMIC for purposes of this paragraph.

(10) **Issue price.**—The issue price of any regular or residual interest in a REMIC shall be determined under section 1273(b) in the same manner as if such interest were a debt instrument; except that if the interest is issued for property, paragraph (3) of sec-

tion 1273(b) shall apply whether or not the requirements of such paragraph are met.

(b) **Treatment of nonresident aliens and foreign corporations.**—If the holder of a residual interest in a REMIC is a nonresident alien individual or a foreign corporation, for purposes of sections 871(a), 881, 1441, and 1442—

(1) amount includible in the gross income of such holder under this part shall be taken into account when paid or distributed (or when the interest is disposed of), and

(2) no exemption from the taxes imposed by such sections (and no reduction in the rates of such taxes) shall apply to any excess inclusion.

The Secretary may by regulations provide that such amounts shall be taken into account earlier than as provided in paragraph (1) where necessary or appropriate to prevent the avoidance of tax imposed by this chapter.

(c) **Tax on income from foreclosure property.**—

(1) **In general.**—A tax is hereby imposed for each taxable year on the net income from foreclosure property of each REMIC. Such tax shall be computed by multiplying the net income from foreclosure property by the highest rate of tax specified in section 11(b).

(2) **Net income from foreclosure property.**—For purposes of this part, the term "net income from foreclosure property" means the amount which would be the REMIC's net income from foreclosure property under section 857(b)(4)(B) if the REMIC were a real estate investment trust.

(d) **Tax on contributions after startup date.**—

(1) **In general.**—Except as provided in paragraph (2), if any amount is contributed to a REMIC after the startup day, there is hereby imposed a tax for the taxable year of the REMIC in which the contribution is received equal to 100 percent of the amount of such contribution.

(2) **Exceptions.**—Paragraph (1) shall not apply to any contribution which is made in cash and is described in any of the following subparagraphs:

(A) Any contribution to facilitate

a clean-up call (as defined in regulations) or a qualified liquidation.

(B) Any payment in the nature of a guarantee.

(C) Any contribution during the 3-month period beginning on the startup day.

(D) Any contribution to a qualified reserve fund by any holder of a residual interest in the REMIC.

(E) Any other contribution permitted in regulations.

(e) **Regulations.**—The Secretary shall prescribe such regulations as may be necessary or appropriate to carry out the purposes of this part, including regulations—

(1) To prevent unreasonable accumulations of assets in a REMIC,

(2) permitting determinations of the fair market value of property transferred to a REMIC and issue price of interests in a REMIC to be made earlier than otherwise provided,

(3) requiring reporting to holders of residual interests of such information as frequently as is necessary or appropriate to permit such holders to compute their taxable income accurately,

(4) providing appropriate rules for treatment of transfers of qualified replacement mortgages to the REMIC where the transferor holds any interest in the REMIC, and

(5) providing that a mortgage will be treated as a qualified replacement mortgage only if it is part of a bona fide replacement (and not part of a swap of mortgages).

(b) **Treatment of nonresident aliens and foreign corporations.**—If the holder of a residual interest in a REMIC is a nonresident alien individual or a foreign corporation, for purposes of sections 871(a), 881, 1441, and 1442—

(1) amounts includible in the gross income of such holder under this part shall be taken into account when paid or distributed (or when the interest is disposed of), and

(2) no exemption from the taxes imposed by such sections (and no reduction in the rates of such taxes) shall apply to any excess inclusion.

The Secretary may by regulations provide that such amounts shall be taken into account earlier than as provided in paragraph (1) where necessary or appropriate to prevent the avoidance of tax imposed by this chapter.

(c) **Tax on income from foreclosure property.**—

(1) **In general.**—A tax is hereby imposed for each taxable year on the net income from foreclosure property of each REMIC. Such tax shall be computed by multiplying the net income from foreclosure property by the highest rate of tax specified in section 11(b).

(2) **Net income from foreclosure property.**—For purposes of this part, the term "net income from foreclosure property" means the amount which would be the REMIC's net income from foreclosure property under section 857(b)(4)(B) if the REMIC were a real estate investment trust.

(d) **Tax on contributions after startup date.**—

(1) **In general.**—Except as provided in paragraph (2), if any amount is contributed to a REMIC after the startup day, there is hereby imposed a tax for the taxable year of the REMIC in which the contribution is received equal to 100 percent of the amount of such contribution.

(2) **Exceptions.**—Paragraph (1) shall not apply to any contribution which is made in cash and is described in any of the following subparagraphs:

(A) Any contribution to facilitate a clean-up call (as defined in regulations) or a qualified liquidation.

(B) Any payment in the nature of a guarantee.

(C) Any contribution during the 3-month period beginning on the startup day.

(D) Any contribution to a qualified reserve fund by any holder of a residual interest in the REMIC.

(E) Any other contribution permitted in regulations.

(e) **Regulations.**—The Secretary shall prescribe such regulations as may be necessary or appropriate to carry out the purposes of this part, including regulations—

(1) to prevent unreasonable accumulations of assets in a REMIC,

(2) permitting determinations of the fair market value of property transferred to a REMIC and issue price of interests in a REMIC to be made earlier than otherwise provided,

(3) requiring reporting to holders of residual interests of such information as frequently as is necessary or appropriate to permit such holders to compute their taxable income accurately,

(4) providing appropriate rules for treatment of transfers of qualified replacement mortgages to the REMIC where the transferor holds any interest in the REMIC, and

(5) providing that a mortgage will be treated as a qualified replacement mortgage only if it is part of a bona fide replacement (and not part of a swap of mortgages).

Sections 1271–1273

SEC. 1271. TREATMENT OF AMOUNTS RECEIVED ON RETIREMENT OR SALE OR EXCHANGE OF DEBT INSTRUMENTS.

(a) General rule.—For purposes of this title—

(1) Retirement.—Amounts received by the holder on retirement of any debt instrument shall be considered as amounts received in exchange therefor.

(2) Ordinary income on sale or exchange where intention to call before maturity.—

(A) In general.—If at the time of original issue there was an intention to call a debt instrument before maturity, any gain realized on the sale or exchange thereof which does not exceed an amount equal to—

(i) the original issue discount, reduced by

(ii) the portion of original issue discount previously includible in the gross income of any holder (without regard

to subsection (a)(7) or (b)(4) of section 1272 (or the corresponding provisions of prior law)),

shall be treated as ordinary income.

(B) Exceptions.—This paragraph (and paragraph (2) of subsection (c)) shall not apply to—

(i) any tax-exempt obligation, or

(ii) any holder who has purchased the debt instrument at a premium.

(3) Certain short-term Government obligations.—

(A) In general.—On the sale or exchange of any short-term Government obligation, any gain realized which does not exceed an amount equal to the ratable share of the acquisition discount shall be treated as ordinary income.

(B) Short-term Government obligation.—For purposes of this paragraph, the term "short-term Government obligation" means any obligation of the United States or any of its possessions, or of a State or any political subdivision thereof, or of the District of Columbia, which has a fixed maturity date not more than 1 year from the date of issue. Such term does not include any tax-exempt obligation.

(C) Acquisition discount.—For purposes of this paragraph, the term "acquisition discount" means the excess of the stated redemption price at maturity over the taxpayer's basis for the obligation.

(D) Ratable share.—For purposes of this paragraph, except as provided in subparagraph (E), the ratable share of the acquisition discount is an amount which bears the same ratio to such discount as—

(i) the number of days which the taxpayer held the obligation, bears to

(ii) the number of days after the date the taxpayer acquired the obligation and up to (and including) the date of its maturity.

(E) Election of accrual on basis of constant interest rate.—At the election of the taxpayer with respect to any obligation, the ratable share of the acquisition discount is the portion of the acquisition discount accruing while the taxpayer held the obligation determined (under regulations prescribed by the Secretary) on the basis of—

(i) the taxpayer's yield to maturity based on the taxpayer's cost of acquiring the obligation, and

(ii) compounding daily.

An election under this subparagraph, once made with respect to any obligation, shall be irrevocable.

(4) Certain short-term nongovernment obligations.—

(A) In general.—On the sale or exchange of any short-term nongovernment obligation, any gain realized which does not exceed an amount equal to the ratable share of the original issue discount shall be treated as ordinary income.

(B) Short-term nongovernment obligation.— For purposes of this paragraph, the term "short-term nongovernment obligation" means any obligation which—

(i) has a fixed maturity date not more than 1 year from the date of the issue, and

(ii) is not a short-term Government obligation (as defined in paragraph (3)(B) without regard to the last sentence thereof).

(C) Ratable share.—For purposes of this paragraph, except as provided in subparagraph (D), the ratable share of the original issue discount is an amount which bears the same ratio to such discount as—

(i) the number of days which the taxpayer held the obligation, bears to

(ii) the number of days after the date of original issue and up to (and including) the date of its maturity.

(D) Election of accrual on basis of constant interest rate.—At the election of the taxpayer with respect to any obligation, the ratable share of the original issue discount is the portion of the original issue discount accruing while the taxpayer held the obligation determined (under regulations prescribed by the Secretary) on the basis of—

(i) the yield to maturity based on the issue price of the obligation, and

(ii) compounding daily.

Any election under this subparagraph,

once made with respect to any obligation, shall be irrevocable.

(b) Exceptions.—This section shall not apply to—

(1) Natural persons.—Any obligation issued by a natural person.

(2) Obligations issued before July 2, 1982, by certain issuers.—Any obligation issued before July 2, 1982, by an issuer which—

(A) is not a corporation, and

(B) is not a government or political subdivision thereof.

(c) Transition rules.—

(1) Special rule for certain obligations issued before January 1, 1955.— Paragraph (1) of subsection (a) shall apply to a debt instrument issued before January 1, 1955, only if such instrument was issued with interest coupons or in registered form, or was in such form on March 1, 1954.

(2) Special rule for certain obligations with respect to which original issue discount not currently includible.—

(A) In general.—On the sale or exchange of debt instruments issued by a government or political subdivision thereof after December 31, 1954, and before July 2, 1982, or by a corporation after December 31, 1954, and on or before May 27, 1969, any gain realized which does not exceed—

(i) an amount equal to the original issue discount, or

(ii) if at the time of original issue there was no intention to call the debt instrument before maturity, an amount which bears the same ratio to the original issue discount as the number of complete months that the debt instrument was held by the taxpayer bears to the number of complete months from the date of original issue to the date of maturity,

shall be considered as ordinary income.

(B) Subsection (a)(2)(A) not to apply.— Subsection (a)(2)(A) shall not apply to any debt instrument referred to in subparagraph (A) of this paragraph.

(C) Cross reference.—For current inclusion of original issue discount, see section 1272.

(d) Double inclusion in income not required.—This section and sections 1272 and 1286 shall not require the inclusion of any amount previously includible in gross income.

SEC. 1272. CURRENT INCLUSION IN INCOME OF ORIGINAL ISSUE DISCOUNT.

(a) Original issue discount on debt instruments issued after July 1, 1982, included in income on basis of constant interest rate.—

(1) General rule.—For purposes of this title, there shall be included in the gross income of the holder of any debt instrument having original issue discount issued after July 1, 1982, an amount equal to the sum of the daily portions of the original issue discount for each day during the taxable year on which such holder held such debt instrument.

(2) Exceptions.—Paragraph (1) shall not apply to—

(A) Tax-exempt obligations.—Any tax-exempt obligation.

(B) United States savings bonds.—Any United States savings bond.

(C) Short-term obligations.—Any debt instrument which has a fixed maturity date not more than 1 year from the date of issue.

(D) Obligations issued by natural persons before March 2, 1984.—Any obligation issued by a natural person before March 2, 1984.

(E) Loans between natural persons.—

(i) In general.—Any loan made by a natural person to another natural person if—

(I) such loan is not made in the course of a trade or business of the lender, and

(II) the amount of such loan (when increased by the outstanding amount of prior loans by such natural person to such other natural person) does not exceed $10,000.

(ii) Clause (i) not to apply where tax avoidance a principal purpose.—Clause (i) shall not apply if the loan has as 1 of its principal purposes the avoidance of any Federal tax.

(iii) Treatment of husband and wife.—For purposes of this subparagraph, a husband and wife shall be treated as 1 person. The preceding sentence shall not apply where the spouses lived apart at all times during the taxable year in which the loan is made.

(3) Determination of daily portions.—For purposes of paragraph (1), the daily portion of the original issue discount on any debt instrument shall be determined by allocating to each day in any accrual period its ratable portion of the increase during such accrual period in the adjusted issue price of the debt instrument. For purposes of the preceding sentence, the increase in the adjusted issue price for any accrual period shall be an amount equal to the excess (if any) of—

(A) the product of—

(i) the adjusted issue price of the debt instrument at the beginning of such accrual period, and

(ii) the yield to maturity (determined on the basis of compounding at the close of each accrual period and properly adjusted for the length of the accrual period), over

(B) the sum of the amounts payable as interest on such debt instrument during such accrual period.

(4) Adjusted issue price.—For purposes of this subsection, the adjusted issue price of any debt instrument at the beginning of any accrual period is the sum of—

(A) the issue price of such debt instrument, plus

(B) the adjustments under this subsection to such issue price for all periods before the first day of such accrual period.

(5) Accrual period.—Except as otherwise provided in regulations prescribed by the Secretary, the term "accrual period" means a 6-month period (or shorter period from the date of original issue of the debt instrument) which ends on a day in the calendar year corresponding to the maturity date of the debt instrument or the date 6 months before such maturity date.

(6) Determination of daily portions where principal subject to acceleration.—

(A) In general.—In the case of any debt instrument to which this paragraph applies, the daily portion of the original issue discount shall be determined by allocating to each day in any accrual period its ratable portion of the excess (if any) of—

(i) the sum of (I) the present value determined under subparagraph (B) of all remaining payments under the debt instrument as of the close of such period, and (II) the payments during the accrual period of amounts included in the stated redemption price of the debt instrument, over

(ii) the adjusted issue price of such debt instrument at the beginning of such period.

(B) Determination of present value.—For purposes of subparagraph (A), the present value shall be determined on the basis of—

(i) the original yield to maturity (determined on the basis of compounding at the close of each accrual period and properly adjusted for the length of the accrual period),

(ii) events which have occurred before the close of the accrual period, and

(iii) a prepayment assumption determined in the manner prescribed by regulations.

(C) Debt instruments to which paragraph applies.—This paragraph applies to—

(i) any regular interest in a REMIC or qualified mortgage held by a REMIC, or

(ii) any other debt instrument if payments under such debt instrument may be accelerated by reason of prepayments of other obligations securing such debt instrument (or, to the extent provided in regulations, by reason of other events).

(7) Reduction where subsequent holder pays acquisition premium.—

(A) Reduction.—For purposes of this subsection, in the case of any purchase after its original issue of a debt instrument to which this subsection applies, the daily portion for any day shall be reduced by an amount equal to the amount which would be the daily portion for such day (without regard to this paragraph) multiplied by the fraction determined under subparagraph (B).

(B) Determination of fraction.—For purposes of subparagraph (A), the fraction determined under this subparagraph is a fraction—

(i) the numerator of which is the excess (if any) of—

(I) the cost of such debt instrument incurred by the purchaser, over

(II) the issue price of such debt instrument, increased by the portion of original issue discount previously includible in the gross income of any holder (computed without regard to this paragraph), and

(ii) the denominator of which is the sum of the daily portions for such debt instrument for all days after the date of such purchase and ending on the stated maturity date (computed without regard to this paragraph).

(b) Ratable inclusion retained for corporate debt instruments issued before July 2, 1982.—

(1) General rule.—There shall be included in the gross income of the holder of any debt instrument issued by a corporation after May 27, 1969, and before July 2, 1982—

(A) the ratable monthly portion of original issue discount, multiplied by

(B) the number of complete months (plus any fractional part of a month determined under paragraph (3)) such holder held such debt instrument during the taxable year.

(2) Determination of ratable monthly portion.—Except as provided in paragraph (4), the ratable monthly portion of original issue discount shall equal—

(A) the original issue discount, divided by

(B) the number of complete months from the date of original issue to the stated maturity date of the debt instruments.

(3) Month defined.—For purposes of this subsection—

(A) Complete month.—A complete month commences with the date of original issue and the corresponding day of each succeeding calendar month (or the last day of a calendar month in which there is no corresponding day).

(B) Transfers during month.— In any case where a debt instrument is acquired on any day other than a day determined under subparagraph (A), the ratable monthly portion of original issue discount for the complete month (or partial month) in which such acquisition occurs shall be allocated between the transferor and the transferee in accordance with the number of days in such complete (or partial) month each held the debt instrument.

(4) Reduction where subsequent holder pays acquisition premium.—

(A) Reduction.— For purposes of this subsection, the ratable monthly portion of original issue discount shall not include its share of the acquisition premium.

(B) Share of acquisition premium.— For purposes of subparagraph (A), any month's share of the acquisition premium is an amount (determined at the time of the purchase) equal to—

(i) the excess of—

(I) the cost of such debt instrument incurred by the holder, over

(II) the issue price of such debt instrument, increased by the portion of original issue discount previously includible in the gross income of any holder (computed without regard to this paragraph),

(ii) divided by the number of complete months (plus any fractional part of a month) from the date of such purchase to the stated maturity date of such debt instrument.

(c) Exceptions.— This section shall not apply to any holder—

(1) who has purchased the debt instrument at a premium, or

(2) which is a life insurance company to which section 811(b) applies.

(d) Definition and special rule.—

(1) Purchase defined.— For purposes of this section, the term "purchase" means—

(A) any acquisition of a debt instrument, where

(B) the basis of the debt instrument is not determined in whole or in part

by reference to the adjusted basis of such debt instrument in the hands of the person from whom acquired.

(2) Basis adjustment.— The basis of any debt instrument in the hands of the holder thereof shall be increased by the amount included in his gross income pursuant to this section.

SEC. 1273. DETERMINATION OF AMOUNT OF ORIGINAL ISSUE DISCOUNT.

(a) General rule.— For purposes of this subpart—

(1) In general.— The term "original issue discount" means the excess (if any) of—

(A) the stated redemption price at maturity, over

(B) the issue price.

(2) Stated redemption price at maturity.— The term "stated redemption price at maturity" means the amount fixed by the last modification of the purchase agreement and includes interest and other amounts payable at that time (other than any interest based on a fixed rate, and payable unconditionally at fixed periodic intervals of 1 year or less during the entire term of the debt instrument).

(3) 1/4 of 1 percent de minimis rule.— If the original issue discount determined under paragraph (1) is less than—

(A) 1/4 of 1 percent of the stated redemption price at maturity, multiplied by

(B) the number of complete years to maturity,

then the original issue discount shall be treated as zero.

(b) Issue price.— For purposes of this subpart—

(1) Publicly offered debt instruments not issued for property.— In the case of any issue of debt instruments—

(A) publicly offered, and

(B) not issued for property,

the issue price is the initial offering price to the public (excluding bond houses and brokers) at which price a substantial amount of such debt instruments was sold.

(2) Other debt instruments not is-

sued for property.—In the case of any issue of debt instruments not issued for property and not publicly offered, the issue price of each such instrument is the price paid by the first buyer of such debt instrument.

(3) Debt instruments issued for property where there is public trading.— In the case of a debt instrument which is issued for property and which—

(A) is part of an issue a portion of which is traded on an established securities market, or

(B)(i) is issued for stock or securities which are traded on an established securities market, or

(ii) to the extent provided in regulations, is issued for property (other than stock or securities) of a kind regularly traded on an established market,

the issue price of such debt instrument shall be the fair market value of such property.

(4) Other cases.—Except in any case—

(A) to which paragraph (1), (2), or (3) of this subsection applies, or

(B) to which section 1274 applies,

the issue price of a debt instrument which is issued for property shall be the stated redemption price at maturity.

(5) Property.—In applying this subsection, the term "property" includes services and the right to use property, but such term does not include money.

(c) Special rules for applying subsection (b).—For purposes of subsection (b)—

(1) Initial offering price; price paid by the first buyer.—The terms "initial offering price" and "price paid by the first buyer" include the aggregate payments made by the purchaser under the purchase agreement, including modifications thereof.

(2) Treatment of investment units.—In the case of any debt instrument and an option, security, or other property issued together as an investment unit—

(A) the issue price for such unit shall be determined in accordance with the rules of this subsection and subsection (b) as if it were a debt instrument,

(B) the issue price determined for such unit shall be allocated to each element of such unit on the basis of the relationship of the fair market value of such element to the fair market value of all elements in such unit, and

(C) the issue price of any debt instrument included in such unit shall be the portion of the issue price of the unit allocated to the debt instrument under subparagraph (B).

Sections 1275–1278

SEC. 1275. OTHER DEFINITIONS AND SPECIAL RULES.

(a) Definitions.—For purposes of this subpart—

(1) Debt instrument.—

(A) **In general.**—Except as provided in subparagraph (B), the term "debt instrument" means a bond, debenture, note, or certificate or other evidence of indebtedness.

(B) **Exception for certain annuity contracts.**—The term "debt instrument" shall not include any annuity contract to which section 72 applies and which—

(i) depends (in whole or in substantial part) on the life expectancy of 1 or more individuals, or

(ii) is issued by an insurance company subject to tax under subchapter L—

(I) in a transaction in which there is no consideration other than cash or another annuity contract meeting the requirements of this clause,

(II) pursuant to the exercise of an election under an insurance contract by a beneficiary thereof on the death of the insured party under such contract, or

(III) in a transaction involving a qualified pension or employee benefit plan.

(2) Issue date.—

(A) **Publicly offered debt instruments.**—In the case of any debt instrument which is publicly offered, the term "date of original issue" means the date on which the issue was first issued to the public.

(B) **Issues not publicly offered**

and not issued for property.—In the case of any debt instrument to which section 1273(b)(2) applies, the term "date of original issue" means the date on which the debt instrument was sold by the issuer.

    (C) Other debt instruments.—In the case of any debt instrument not described in subparagraph (A) or (B), the term "date of original issue" means the date on which the debt instrument was issued in a sale or exchange.

    (3) Tax-exempt obligation.—The term "tax-exempt obligation" means any obligation if—

    (A) the interest on such obligation is not includible in gross income under section 103, or

    (B) the interest on such obligation is exempt from tax (without regard to the identity of the holder) under any other provision of law.

    (4) Treatment of obligations distributed by corporations.—Any debt obligation of a corporation distributed by such corporation with respect to its stock shall be treated as if it had been issued by such corporation for property.

    (b) Treatment of borrower in the case of certain loans for personal use.—

    (1) Sections 1274 and 483 not to apply.—In the case of the obligor under any debt instrument given in consideration for the sale or exchange of property, sections 1274 and 483 shall not apply if such property is personal use property.

    (2) Original issue discount deducted on cash basis in certain cases.—In the case of any debt instrument, if—

    (A) such instrument—

    (i) is incurred in connection with the acquisition or carrying of personal use property, and

    (ii) has original issue discount (determined after the application of paragraph (1)), and

    (B) the obligor under such instrument uses the cash receipts and disbursements method of accounting,

notwithstanding section 163(e), the original issue discount on such instrument shall be deductible only when paid.

    (3) Personal use property.—For purposes of this subsection, the term "personal use property" means any property substantially all of the use of which by the taxpayer is not in connection with a trade or business of the taxpayer or an activity described in section 212. The determination of whether property is described in the preceding sentence shall be made as of the time of issuance of the debt instrument.

    (c) Information requirements.—

    (1) Information required to be set forth on instrument.—

    (A) In general.—In the case of any debt instrument having original issue discount, the Secretary may by regulations require that—

    (i) the amount of the original issue discount, and

    (ii) the issue date,

be set forth on such instrument.

    (B) Special rule for instruments not publicly offered.—In the case of any issue of debt instruments not publicly offered, the regulations prescribed under subparagraph (A) shall not require the information to be set forth on the debt instrument before any disposition of such instrument by the first buyer.

    (2) Information required to be submitted to Secretary.—In the case of any issue of publicly offered debt instruments having original issue discount, the issuer shall (at such time and in such manner as the Secretary shall by regulation prescribe) furnish the Secretary the following information:

    (A) The amount of the original issue discount.

    (B) The issue date.

    (C) Such other information with respect to the issue as the Secretary may by regulations require.

For purposes of the preceding sentence, any person who makes a public offering of stripped bonds (or stripped coupons) shall be treated as the issuer of a publicly offered debt instrument having original issue discount.

    (3) Exceptions.—This subsection shall not apply to any obligation referred to in section 1272(a)(2) (relating to exceptions from current inclusion of original issue discount).

(4) Cross reference.—For civil penalty for failure to meet requirements of this subsection, see section 6706.

(d) Regulation authority.—The Secretary may prescribe regulations providing that where, by reason of varying rates of interest, put or call options, indefinite maturities, contingent payments, assumptions of debt instruments, or other circumstances, the tax treatment under this subpart (or section 163(e)) does not carry out the purposes of this subpart (or section 163(e)), such treatment shall be modified to the extent appropriate to carry out the purposes of this subpart (or section 163(e)).

SEC. 1276. DISPOSITION GAIN REPRESENTING ACCRUED MARKET DISCOUNT TREATED AS ORDINARY INCOME.

(a) Ordinary income.—

(1) In general.—Except as otherwise provided in this section, gain on the disposition of any market discount bond shall be treated as ordinary income to the extent it does not exceed the accrued market discount on such bond. Such gain shall be recognized notwithstanding any other provision of this subtitle.

(2) Dispositions other than sales, etc.—For purposes of paragraph (1), a person disposing of any market discount bond in any transaction other than a sale, exchange, or involuntary conversion shall be treated as realizing an amount equal to the fair market value of the bond.

(3) Treatment of partial principal payments.—

(A) In general.—Any partial principal payment on a market discount bond shall be included in gross income as ordinary income to the extent such payment does not exceed the accrued market discount on such bond.

(B) Adjustment.—If subparagraph (A) applies to any partial principal payment on any market discount bond, for purposes of applying this section to any disposition of (or subsequent partial principal payment on) such bond, the amount of ac-

crued market discount shall be reduced by the amount of such partial principal payment included in gross income under subparagraph (A).

(4) Gain treated as interest for certain purposes.—Except for purposes of sections 103, 871(a), 881, 1441, 1442, and 6049 (and such other provisions as may be specified in regulations), any amount treated as ordinary income under paragraph (1) or (3) shall be treated as interest for purposes of this title.

(b) Accrued market discount.—For purposes of this section—

(1) Ratable accrual.—Except as otherwise provided in this subsection or subsection (c), the accrued market discount on any bond shall be an amount which bears the same ratio to the market discount on such bond as—

(A) the number of days which the taxpayer held the bond, bears to

(B) the number of days after the date the taxpayer acquired the bond and up to (and including) the date of its maturity.

(2) Election of accrual on basis of constant interest rate (in lieu of ratable accrual).—

(A) In general.—At the election of the taxpayer with respect to any bond, the accrued market discount on such bond shall be the aggregate amount which would have been includible in the gross income of the taxpayer under section 1272(a) (determined without regard to paragraph (2) thereof) with respect to such bond for all periods during which the bond was held by the taxpayer if such bond had been—

(i) originally issued on the date on which such bond was acquired by the taxpayer,

(ii) for an issue price equal to the basis of the taxpayer in such bond immediately after its acquisition.

(B) Coordination where bond has original issue discount.—In the case of any bond having original issue discount, for purposes of applying subparagraph (A)—

(i) the stated redemption price at maturity of such bond shall be treated as equal to its revised issue price, and

(ii) the determination of the

portion of the original issue discount which would have been includible in the gross income of the taxpayer under section 1272(a) shall be made under regulations prescribed by the Secretary.

(C) **Election irrevocable.**—An election under subparagraph (A), once made with respect to any bond, shall be irrevocable.

(3) **Special rule where partial principal payments.**— In the case of a bond the principal of which may be paid in 2 or more payments, the amount of accrued market discount shall be determined under regulations prescribed by the Secretary.

(c) **Treatment of nonrecognition transactions.**—Under regulations prescribed by the Secretary—

(1) **Transferred basis property.**—If a market discount bond is transferred in a nonrecognition transaction and such bond is transferred basis property in the hands of the transferee, for purposes of determining the amount of the accrued market discount with respect to the transferee—

(A) the transferee shall be treated as having acquired the bond on the date on which it was acquired by the transferor for an amount equal to the basis of the transferor, and

(B) proper adjustments shall be made for gain recognized by the transferor on such transfer (and for any original issue discount or market discount included in the gross income of the transferor).

(2) **Exchanged basis property.**—If any market discount bond is disposed of by the taxpayer in a nonrecognition transaction and paragraph (1) does not apply to such transaction, any accrued market discount determined with respect to the property disposed of to the extent not theretofore treated as ordinary income under subsection (a)— ·

(A) shall be treated as accrued market discount with respect to the exchanged basis property received by the taxpayer in such transaction if such property is a market discount bond, and

(B) shall be treated as ordinary income on the disposition of the exchanged basis property received by the taxpayer in

such exchange if such property is not a market discount bond.

(3) **Paragraph (1) to apply to certain distributions by corporations or partnerships.**—For purposes of paragraph (1), if the basis of any market discount bond in the hands of a transferee is determined under section 732(a), or 732(b), such property shall be treated as transferred basis property in the hands of such transferee.

(d) **Special rules.**—Under regulations prescribed by the Secretary—

(1) rules similar to the rules of subsection (b) of section 1245 shall apply for purposes of this section; except that—

(A) paragraph (1) of such subsection shall not apply,

(B) an exchange qualifying under section 354(a), 355(a), or 356(a) (determined without regard to subsection (a) of this section) shall be treated as an exchange described in paragraph (3) of such subsection, and

(C) paragraph (3) of section 1245(b) shall be applied as if it did not contain a reference to section 351, and

(2) appropriate adjustments shall be made to the basis of any property to reflect gain recognized under subsection (a).

(e) **[Repealed.]**

SEC. 1277. DEFERRAL OF INTEREST DEDUCTION ALLOCABLE TO ACCRUED MARKET DISCOUNT.

(a) **General rule.**—Except as otherwise provided in this section, the net direct interest expense with respect to any market discount bond shall be allowed as a deduction for the taxable year only to the extent that such expense exceeds the portion of the market discount allocable to the days during the taxable year on which such bond was held by the taxpayer (as determined under the rules of section 1276(b)).

(b) **Disallowed deduction allowed for later years.—**

(1) **Election to take into account in later year where net interest income from bond.—**

(A) In general.—If—

(i) there is net interest income for any taxable year with respect to any market discount bond, and

(ii) the taxpayer makes an election under this subparagraph with respect to such bond,

any disallowed interest expense with respect to such bond shall be treated as interest paid or accrued by the taxpayer during such taxable year to the extent such disallowed interest expense does not exceed the net interest income with respect to such bond.

(B) Determination of disallowed interest expense.—For purposes of subparagraph (A), the amount of the disallowed interest expense—

(i) shall be determined as of the close of the preceding taxable year, and

(ii) shall not include any amount previously taken into account under subparagraph (A).

(C) Net interest income.—For purposes of this paragraph, the term "net interest income" means the excess of the amount determined under paragraph (2) of subsection (c) over the amount determined under paragraph (1) of subsection (c).

(2) Remainder of disallowed interest expense allowed for year of disposition.—

(A) In general.—Except as otherwise provided in this paragraph, the amount of the disallowed interest expense with respect to any market discount bond shall be treated as interest paid or accrued by the taxpayer in the taxable year in which such bond is disposed of.

(B) Nonrecognition transactions.—If any market discount bond is disposed of in a nonrecognition transaction—

(i) the disallowed interest expense with respect to such bond shall be treated as interest paid or accrued in the year of disposition only to the extent of the amount of gain recognized on such disposition, and

(ii) the disallowed interest expense with respect to such property (to the extent not so treated) shall be treated as disallowed interest expense—

(I) in the case of a transaction described in section 1276(c)(1), of the transferee with respect to the transferred basis property, or

(II) in the case of a transaction described in section 1276(c)(2), with respect to the exchanged basis property.

(C) Disallowed interest expense reduced for amounts previously taken into account under paragraph (1).—For purposes of this paragraph, the amount of the disallowed interest expense shall not include any amount previously taken into account under paragraph (1).

(3) Disallowed interest expense.— For purposes of this subsection, the term "disallowed interest expense" means the aggregate amount disallowed under subsection (a) with respect to the market discount bond.

(c) Net direct interest expense.—For purposes of this section, the term "net direct interest expense" means, with respect to any market discount bond, the excess (if any) of—

(1) the amount of interest paid or accrued during the taxable year on indebtedness which is incurred or continued to purchase or carry such bond, over

(2) the aggregate amount of interest (including original issue discount) includible in gross income for the taxable year with respect to such bond.

In the case of any financial institution which is a bank (as defined in section 585(a)(2)) or to which section 593 applies, the determination of whether interest is described in paragraph (1) shall be made under principles similar to the principles of section 291(e)(1)(B)(ii). Under rules similar to the rules of section 265(a)(5), short sale expenses shall be treated as interest for purposes of determining net direct interest expense.

(d) [Repealed.]

SEC. 1278. DEFINITIONS AND SPECIAL RULES.

(a) In general.—For purposes of this part—

(1) Market discount bond.—

(A) In general.—Except as provided in subparagraph (B), the term "market discount bond" means any bond having market discount.

(B) Exceptions.—The term "market discount bond" shall not include—

(i) Short-term obligations.—Any obligation with a fixed maturity date not exceeding 1 year from the date of issue.

(ii) Tax-exempt obligations.—Any tax-exempt obligation (as defined in section 1275(a)(3)).

(iii) United States savings bonds.—Any United States savings bond.

(iv) Installment obligations.—Any installment obligation to which section 453B applies.

(C) Treatment of bonds acquired at original issue.—

(i) In general.—Except as otherwise provided in this subparagraph or in regulations, the term "market discount bond" shall not include any bond acquired by the taxpayer at its original issue.

(ii) Treatment of bonds acquired for less than issue price.—Clause (i) shall not apply to any bond if—

(I) the basis of the taxpayer in such bond is determined under section 1012, and

(II) such basis is less than the issue price of such bond determined under subpart A of this part.

(iii) Bonds acquired in certain reorganizations.—Clause (i) shall not apply to any bond issued pursuant to a plan of reorganization (within the meaning of section 368(a)(1)) in exchange for another bond having market discount. Solely for purposes of section 1276, the preceding sentence shall not apply if such other bond was issued on or before July 18, 1984 (the date of the enactment of section 1276) and if the bond issued pursuant to such plan of reorganization has the same term and the same interest rate as such other bond had.

(iv) Treatment of certain transferred basis property.—For purposes of clause (i), if the adjusted basis of any bond in the hands of the taxpayer is determined by reference to the adjusted basis of such bond in the hands of a person who acquired such bond at its original issue, such bond shall be treated as acquired by the taxpayer at its original issue.

(2) Market discount.—

(A) In general.—The term "market discount" means the excess (if any) of—

(i) the stated redemption price of the bond at maturity, over

(ii) the basis of such bond immediately after its acquisition by the taxpayer.

(B) Coordination where bond has original issue discount.—In the case of any bond having original issue discount, for purposes of subparagraph (A), the stated redemption price of such bond at maturity shall be treated as equal to its revised issue price.

(C) De minimis rule.—If the market discount is less than 1/4 of 1 percent of the stated redemption price of the bond at maturity multiplied by the number of complete years to maturity (after the taxpayer acquired the bond), then the market discount shall be considered to be zero.

(3) Bond.—The term "bond" means any bond, debenture, note, certificate, or other evidence of indebtedness.

(4) Revised issue price.—The term "revised issue price" means the sum of—

(A) the issue price of the bond, and

(B) the aggregate amount of the original issue discount includible in the gross income of all holders for periods before the acquisition of the bond by the taxpayer (determined without regard to section 1272(a)(7) or (b)(4)) or, in the case of a tax-exempt obligation, the aggregate amount of the original issue discount which accrued in the manner provided by section 1272(a) (determined without regard to paragraph (7) hereof) during periods before the acquisition of the bond by the taxpayer.

(5) Original issue discount, etc.—The terms "original issue discount," "stated redemption price at maturity," and "issue price" have the respective meanings given such terms by subpart A of this part.

(b) Election to include market discount currently.—

(1) In general.—If the taxpayer makes an election under this subsection—

(A) sections 1276 and 1277 shall not apply, and

(B) market discount on any market discount bond shall be included in the gross income of the taxpayer for the taxable years to which it is attributable (as determined under the rules of subsection (b) of section 1276).

Except for purposes of sections 103, 871(a), 881, 1441, 1442, and 6049 (and such other provisions as may be specified in regulations), any amount included in gross income under subparagraph (B) shall be treated as interest for purposes of this title.

(2) Scope of election.—An election under this subsection shall apply to all market discount bonds acquired by the taxpayer on or after the 1st day of the 1st taxable year to which such election applies.

(3) Period to which election applies.—An election under this subsection shall apply to the taxable year for which it is made and for all subsequent taxable years, unless the taxpayer secures the consent of the Secretary to the revocation of such election.

(4) Basis adjustment.—The basis of any bond in the hands of the taxpayer shall be increased by the amount included in gross income pursuant to this subsection.

(c) Regulations.—The Secretary shall prescribe such regulations as may be necessary to carry out the purposes of this subpart.

Section 1286

TAX TREATMENT OF STRIPPED BONDS

(a) Inclusion in income as if bond and coupons were original issue discount bonds.—If any person purchases after July 1, 1982, a stripped bond or a stripped coupon, then such bond or coupon while held by such purchaser (or by any other person whose basis is determined by reference to the basis in the hands of such purchaser)

shall be treated for purposes of this part as a bond originally issued on the purchase date and having an original issue discount equal to the excess (if any) of—

(1) the stated redemption price at maturity (or, in the case of coupon, the amount payable on the due date of such coupon), over

(2) such bond's or coupon's ratable share of the purchase price.

For purposes of paragraph (2), ratable shares shall be determined on the basis of their respective fair market values on the date of purchase.

(b) Tax treatment of person stripping bond.— For purposes of this subtitle, if any person strips 1 or more coupons from a bond and after July 1, 1982, disposes of the bond or such coupon—

(1) such person shall include in gross income an amount equal to the sum of—

(A) the interest accrued on such bond while held by such person and before the time such coupon or bond was disposed of (to the extent such interest has not theretofore been included in such person's gross income), and

(B) the accrued market discount on such bond determined as of the time such coupon or bond was disposed of (to the extent such discount has not theretofore been included in such person's gross income),

(2) the basis of the bond and coupons shall be increased by the amount included in gross income under paragraph (1).

(3) the basis of the bond and coupons immediately before the disposition (as adjusted pursuant to paragraph (2)) shall be allocated among the items retained by such person and the items disposed of by such person on the basis of their respective fair market values, and

(4) for purposes of subsection (a), such person shall be treated as having purchased on the date of such disposition each such item which he retains for an amount equal to the basis allocated to such item under paragraph (3).

A rule similar to the rule of paragraph (4) shall apply in the case of any person whose basis in any bond or coupon is determined by reference to the basis of the person described in the preceding sentence.

(c) Retention of existing law for stripped bonds purchased before July 2, 1982.—If a bond issued at any time with interest coupons—

(1) is purchased after August 16, 1954, and before January 1, 1958, and the purchaser does not receive all the coupons which first become payable more than 12 months after the date of the purchase, or

(2) is purchased after December 31, 1957, and before July 2, 1982, and the purchaser does not receive all the coupons which first become payable after the date of the purchase,

then the gain or the sale or other disposition of such bond by such purchaser (or by a person whose basis is determined by reference to the basis in the hands of such purchaser) shall be considered as ordinary income to the extent that the fair market value (determined as of the time of the purchase) of the bond with coupons attached exceeds the purchase price. If this subsection and section 1271(a) (2)(A) apply with respect to gain realized on the sale or exchange of any evidence of indebtedness, then section 1271(a)(2)(A) shall apply with respect to that part of the gain to which this subsection does not apply.

(d) Special rules for tax-exempt obligations.—

(1) **In general.**—In the case of any tax-exempt obligation (as defined in section 1275(a)(3)) from which 1 or more coupons have been stripped—

(A) the amount of the original issue discount determined under subsection (a) with respect to any stripped bond or stripped coupon—

(i) shall be treated as original issue discount on a tax-exempt obligation to the extent such discount does not exceed the tax-exempt portion of such discount, and

(ii) shall be treated as original issue discount on an obligation which is not a tax-exempt obligation to the extent such discount exceeds the tax-exempt portion of such discount,

(B) subsection (b)(1)(A) shall not apply, and

(C) subsection (b)(2) shall be applied by increasing the basis of the bond or coupon by the sum of—

(i) the interest accrued but not paid before such bond or coupon was disposed of (and not previously reflected in basis), plus

(ii) the amount included in gross income under subsection (b)(1)(B).

(2) **Tax-exempt portion.**—For purposes of paragraph (1), the tax-exempt portion of the original issue discount determined under subsection (a) is the excess of—

(A) the amount referred to in subsection (a)(1), over

(B) an issue price which would produce a yield to maturity as of the purchase date equal to the lower of—

(i) the coupon rate of interest on the obligation from which the coupons were separated, or

(ii) the yield to maturity (on the basis of the purchase price) of the stripped obligation or coupon.

The purchaser of any stripped obligation or coupon may elect to apply clause (i) by substituting "original yield to maturity of" for "coupon rate of interest on."

(e) Definitions and special rules.—For purposes of this section—

(1) **Bond.**—The term "bond" means a bond, debenture, note, or certificate or other evidence of indebtedness.

(2) **Stripped bond.**—The term "stripped bond" means a bond issued at any time with interest coupons where there is a separation in ownership between the bond and any coupon which has not yet become payable.

(3) **Stripped coupon.**—The term "stripped coupon" means any coupon relating to a stripped bond.

(4) **Stated redemption price at maturity.**—The term "stated redemption price at maturity" has the meaning given such term by section 1273(a)(2).

(5) **Coupon.**—The term "coupon" includes any right to receive interest on a bond (whether or not evidenced by a coupon). This paragraph shall apply for purposes of subsection (c) only in the case of purchases after July 1, 1982.

(6) Purchase.—The term "purchase" has the meaning given such term by section 1272(d)(1).

(f) Regulation authority.—The Secretary may prescribe regulations providing that where, by reason of varying rates of interest, put or call options, or other circumstances, the tax treatment under this section does not accurately reflect the income of the holder of a stripped coupon or stripped bond, or of the person disposing of such bond or coupon, as the case may be, for any period, such treatment shall be modified to require that the proper amount of income be included for such period.

Section 7701(a)(19)(C)

(19) Domestic building and loan association.—The term "domestic building and loan association" means a domestic building and loan association, a domestic savings and loan association, and a Federal savings and loan association—

****

(C) at least 60 percent of the amount of the total assets of which (at the close of the taxable year) consists of—

(i) cash,

(ii) obligations of the United States or of a State or political subdivision thereof, and stock or obligations of a corporation which is an instrumentality of the United States or of a State or political subdivision thereof, but not including obligations the interest on which is excludable from gross income under section 103,

(iii) certificates of deposit in, or obligations of, a corporation organized under a State law which specifically authorizes such corporation to insure the deposits or share accounts of member associations,

(iv) loans secured by a deposit or share of a member,

(v) loans (including redeemable ground rents, as defined in section 1055) secured by an interest in real property which is (or, from the proceeds of the loan, will become) residential real property or real property used primarily for church purposes, loans made for the improvement of residential real property or real property used primarily for church purposes, provided that for purposes of this clause, residential real property shall include single or multifamily dwellings, facilities in residential developments dedicated to public use or property used on a nonprofit basis for residents, and mobile homes not used on a transient basis,

(vi) loans secured by an interest in real property located within an urban renewal area to be developed for predominately residential use under an urban renewal plan approved by the Secretary of Housing and Urban Development under part A or part B of the title I of the Housing Act of 1949, as amended, or located within any area eligible for assistance under section 103 of the Demonstration Cities and Metropolitan Development Act of 1966, as amended, and loans made for the improvement of any such real property,

(vii) loans secured by an interest in educational, health, or welfare institutions or facilities, including structures designed or used primarily for residential purposes for students, residents, and persons under care, employees, or members of the staff of such institutions or facilities,

(viii) property acquired through the liquidation of defaulted loans described in clause (v), (vi) or (vii),

(ix) loans made to the payment of expenses of college or university education or vocational training, in accordance with such regulations as may be prescribed by the Secretary,

(x) property used by the association in the conduct of the business described in subparagraph (B) and,

(xi) any regular or residual interest in a REMIC, but only in the proportion which the assets of such REMIC consist of property described in any of the preceding clauses of this subparagraph; except that if 95 percent or more of the assets of such REMIC are assets described in clauses (i) through (x), the entire interest in the REMIC shall qualify.

At the election of the taxpayer, the percentage specified in this subparagraph shall be applied on the basis of the average assets outstanding during the taxable year, in lieu of the close of the taxable year, computed under regulation prescribed by the Secretary. For purposes of clause (v), if a multifamily structure securing a loan is used in part for nonresidential purposes, the entire loan is deemed a residential real property loan if the planned residential use exceeds 80 percent of the property's planned use (determined as of the time the loan is made). For purposes of clause (v), loans made to finance the acquisition or development of land shall be deemed to be loans secured by an interest in residential real property, if under regulations prescribed by the Secretary, there is reasonable assurance that the property will become residential real property within a period of 3 years from the date of acquisition of such land; but this sentence shall not apply for any taxable year unless, within such 3-year period, such land becomes residential real property. For purposes of determining whether any interest in a REMIC qualifies under clause (xi), any regular interest in another REMIC held by such REMIC shall be treated as a loan described in a preceding clause under principles similar to the principles of clause (xi); except that, if such REMIC's are part of a tiered structure, they shall be treated as 1 REMIC for purposes of clause (xi).

Section 7701(i)

(i) Taxable mortgage pools.—

(1) Treated as separate corporations.—A taxable mortgage pool shall be treated as a separate corporation which may not be treated as an includible corporation with any other corporation for purposes of section 1501.

(2) Taxable mortgage pool defined.—For purposes of this title—

(A) In general.—Except as otherwise provided in this paragraph, a taxable mortgage pool is any entity (other than a REMIC) if—

(i) substantially all of the assets of such entity consists of debt obligations (or interests therein) and more than 50 percent of such debt obligations (or interests) consists of real estate mortgages (or interests therein),

(ii) such entity is the obligor under debt obligations with 2 or more maturities, and

(iii) under the terms of the debt obligations referred to in clause (ii) (or underlying arrangement), payments on such debt obligations bear a relationship to payments on the debt obligations (or interests) referred to in clause (i).

(B) Portion of entities treated as pools.—Any portion of an entity which meets the definition of subparagraph (A) shall be treated as a taxable mortgage pool.

(C) Exception for domestic building and loan.—Nothing in this subsection shall be construed to treat any domestic building and loan association (or portion thereof) as a taxable mortgage pool.

(D) Treatment of certain equity interests.—To the extent provided in regulations, equity interest of varying classes which correspond to maturity classes of debt shall be treated as debt for purposes of this subsection.

(3) Treatment of certain REIT's.—If—

(A) a real estate investment trust is a taxable mortgage pool, or

(B) a qualified REIT subsidiary (as defined in section 856(i)(2)) of a real estate investment trust is a taxable mortgage pool,

under regulations prescribed by the Secretary, adjustments similar to the adjustments provided in section 860E(d) shall apply to the shareholders of such real estate investment trust.

BLUE BOOK

General Explanation of the Tax Reform Act of 1986

(H.R. 3838, 99th Congress; Public Law 99-514)
Prepared by the Staff of the Joint Committee on Taxation
May 4, 1987

[402]

P. Mortgage-Backed Securities (Secs. 671–675 of the Act and secs. 1272, 6049, 7701, and new secs. 860A–860G of the Code)[39]

Prior Law

Taxation of alternative methods of owning income producing assets

Overview

Under prior and present law, income-producing assets (such as mortgages on residential property or other debt instruments) can be owned directly, or they can be owned indirectly by means of an equity interest in an intermediary entity. Income generated by property that is owned directly generally is taxed to the owner of the property. Thus, in the case of property owned directly by an individual, income from such property is subject to only one level of taxation. Income from property owned indirectly may be subject to more than one level of taxation, i.e., tax may be imposed both at the level of the intermediary holder and the indirect owner.

Whether more than one level of tax is imposed where income producing property is held indirectly generally depends on whether the intermediary entity is treated for tax purposes (1) as a separate taxable entity (such as a corporation or an association taxable as a corporation), (2) as a complete conduit entity (such as a partnership or S corporation), or (3) as a partial conduit entity (such as a trust or real estate investment trust) under which income is not taxed to the entity to the extent it is currently distributed to the entity's owners.

Direct ownership of income producing assets

Individual ownership

The most basic form of direct ownership of income producing assets is the holding of such assets by an individual. Where an individual owns income producing assets directly, the individual generally includes all income generated by the property, and deducts all items of expense related to the property. When the individual disposes of the property in a taxable transaction, the individual recognizes gain or loss, which may be capital gain or loss.

Grantor trusts

A grantor trust is an arrangement under which legal title to property is transferred to a trustee, but the transferor retains certain powers over, or interests in, the trust so that the transferors [402/403] are treated as retaining direct ownership of such property for Federal income tax purposes (secs. 671-679). Thus, income, deductions, and credits of the grantor trust are attributed directly to the grantors.[40]

---

39 For legislative background of the provision, see: H.R. 3838, as reported by the Senate Committee on Finance on May 29, 1986, secs. 1441–1445; S. Rep. 99-313, pp. 783–801; and H. Rep. 99-841, Vol. II (September 18, 1986), pp. 222–241 (Conference Report).

40 In some cases, persons other than the transferors are treated as owners of the trust's assets.

Indirect ownership of income producing assets

Separate taxable entities— corporations

One form of indirect ownership of income producing property is the ownership of stock in a corporation that owns such property. Corporations can be used to hold investment property or to engage in the active conduct of a trade or business.

Corporations generally are treated for tax purposes as separate taxable entities, apart from their shareholders.[41] Thus, income earned by a corporation is taxed to the corporation. In addition, when the after-tax earnings of a corporation are distributed to the corporation's stockholders as dividends, generally such earnings also are taxed to the stockholders.[42]

Interest on debt incurred by a corporation to finance the acquisition of income-producing assets generally is deductible to the corporation incurring the debt. To the extent that income from debt-financed property is paid to the debtholders in the form of interest, the interest deduction offsets any corporate-level tax on such income, resulting in the imposition of only a single tax on the income, which tax is borne by the debtholder.

Complete conduit entities

Partnerships.—Another form of indirect ownership of income producing assets is ownership of an interest in a partnership holding such assets. A partnership generally is treated as a complete conduit for Federal income tax purposes.[43] Each partner accounts for his "distributive share" of the partnership's income, loss, deduction, and credit.

The liability for income tax is that of the partner, and not of the partnership, without regard to whether the income of the partnership is actually distributed to the partners. Partnership losses, deductions, and credits pass through to the partners and can be used to offset other income. In general, an entity is treated as a partnership if it is an unincorporated organization through, or by means of which, any business, financial operation or venture is carried on, and it is not treated as a corporation, a trust, or an estate.[44]

S corporations.—Income producing property also may be owned indirectly through ownership of stock in an S corporation. Although [403/404] S corporations are corporate entities, if a corporation so elects, its shareholders generally may account for a proportionate amount of the corporation's items of income, loss, deduction, and credit under subchapter S of the Code (secs. 1361 *et seq.*). The S corporation itself generally has no tax liability for as long as the election is in effect.[45]

In general, a domestic corporation may elect to be treated under subchapter S if it has 35 or fewer shareholders (none of whom are corporations or nonresident aliens), has not more than one class of stock, and is not a financial institution, a life insurance company, or one of several other types of corporations.

Partial conduit entities

Real estate investment trusts.—Another form of indirect ownership is the ownership of shares or interests in a real estate investment trust ("REIT"). Under the provisions of the Code applicable to REITs (secs. 856 *et seq.*), REITs generally are treated as conduits for Federal income tax purposes to the extent of

---

41   Certain corporations may be treated as complete or partial conduit entities, however. *See* discussion of S corporations and real estate investment trusts, below.

42   Under prior law, an individual generally was allowed to exclude from taxable income up to $100 of dividends per year ($200 for a joint return) (sec. 116), and corporations were entitled to a dividends received deduction for 85 or 100 percent of dividends received (secs. 243–245). Section 612 of the Act repeals the limited dividend exclusion for individuals, and section 611 of the Act reduces the 85 percent dividends received deduction for corporations to 80 percent.

43   A partnership is treated as an entity separate from its partners for purposes of calculating items of taxable income, deduction, and credit. It also is treated as an entity for purposes of reporting information to the Internal Revenue Service.

44   *See* discussion of entity classification, below.

45   An S corporation may be subject to tax at the entity level under certain limited circumstances.

the amount of its earnings that are distributed currently to shareholders. Conduit treatment is achieved by allowing the REIT a deduction for earnings distributed on a current basis. Thus, income that is currently distributed to shareholders is not taxed at the REIT level; income that is not currently distributed to shareholders is taxed at the REIT level, as in the case of ordinary corporations.

In general, an entity may qualify as a REIT if it is a trust or corporation with at least 100 different freely transferable interests, which trust or corporation would be taxable as an ordinary domestic corporation but for its meeting certain specified requirements. These requirements relate to the entity's assets being comprised substantially of real estate assets and the entity's income being in substantial part realized from certain real estate and real estate related sources.

The ability of a REIT to engage in regular business activities is limited by the requirement that income from the sale or other disposition of stock or securities held for less than 1 year, or real property held less than 4 years, must account for less than 30 percent of the REIT's income. Further, a 100 percent tax is imposed on gains from the sale of property held for sale to customers in the ordinary course of trade or business (other than foreclosure property).

If a corporation meets these requirements and elects to be treated as a REIT, it generally is subject to the regular corporate tax, but receives a deduction for dividends paid provided that the amount of its dividends paid is not less than an amount generally equal to 95 percent of its ordinary income. These dividends must be paid within a short period following the close of the REIT's taxable year and are generally includible as ordinary income to the shareholders.[46] [404/405]

A REIT that realizes capital gain income may be subject to tax at the corporate level at capital gains rates. If, however, the REIT pays dividends out of such capital gains, the dividends are deductible by the REIT in computing its capital gains tax and are taxable as capital gains to the recipient shareholders.

RICs.—Conduit treatment similar to that granted to REITs also is provided to regulated investment companies ("RICs"). In general, a RIC is an electing domestic corporation that either meets or is excepted from certain registration requirements under the Investment Company Act of 1940 (15 U.S.C. 80), that derives at least 90 percent of its ordinary income from specified sources commonly considered passive investment income, that has a portfolio of investments that meet certain diversification requirements, that distributes at least 90 percent of its income to its shareholders annually, and that also meets certain other requirements.

The ability of a RIC to engage in an active business is limited by a requirement that less than 30 percent of the gross income of the RIC may be derived from gain on the sale or other disposition of stock or securities held for less than three months.

A RIC, like a REIT, generally is subject to the regular corporate tax, but receives a deduction for dividends paid to its shareholders. Rules similar to those applicable for REITs apply to distributions of capital gain dividends, and distributions of deficiency dividends.[47]

Trusts.—Another form of indirect ownership of property is ownership of the beneficial interest of property that is held in a trust. A trust is an arrangement whereby trustees take title to property and become responsible for the protection and conservation of such property on behalf of the persons holding the beneficial interest in the property. A trust generally is treated as a partial conduit for Federal income tax purposes since the trust, although in form a

---

46 A deficiency dividend procedure was added to the REIT provisions as part of the Tax Reform Act of 1976 so that a REIT, acting in good faith but failing to satisfy the distribution requirement, could avoid disqualification. In addition, section 668 of the Act imposes an excise tax that is intended to ensure that a REIT distributes most of the income earned in a calendar year during that year.

47 In addition, section 651 of the Act imposes an excise tax that is intended to ensure that a RIC distributes most of the income earned in a calendar year during that year.

separate taxable entity, is allowed a deduction for amounts distributed to its beneficiaries, which amounts generally are includible in the beneficiaries' income.

A fixed investment trust is a trust used to hold a diversified portfolio of investments for its beneficiaries. Generally, such a trust is treated as a trust for tax purposes (and not as an association) if the trustee does not have the power to vary the investments of the trust.[48]

Rules for classifying entities

Corporation or partnership

Under prior and present law, Treasury regulations provide that whether a particular entity is classified as an association taxable as a corporation or as a partnership, trust, or some other entity not taxable as a corporation is determined by taking into account the presence or absence of certain characteristics associated with corporations. These characteristics are (1) associates, (2) an objective to carry on business and divide the gains therefrom, (3) continuity of life, (4) centralization of management, (5) liability for entity debts [405/406] limited to entity property, and (6) free transferability of interests.[49] These regulations generally are based on the principle stated in *Morrissey v. Commissioner*, 296 U.S. 344 (1935), in which the Supreme Court held that whether an entity is treated as a corporation depends not on the form of its organization, but on whether it more closely resembles a corporate than a noncorporate entity.

Of the characteristics mentioned above, the first two are common to both corporate and partnership enterprises. Consequently, the remaining four factors are determinative of whether the entity is treated as a corporation or as a partnership. Treasury regulations state that the corporate characteristics

of an entity must make it more nearly resemble a corporation than a partnership or a trust for the entity to be treated as a corporation.[50] Under this test, the Treasury regulations provide that most limited partnerships formed under the Uniform Limited Partnership Act are not treated as corporations since these entities generally do not possess continuity of life and also may lack limited liability.

Trust or association

Since both corporations and trusts generally possess centralization of management, continuity of life, free transferability of interests, and limited liability, the Treasury regulations provide that the determination of whether a particular unincorporated entity is treated as a trust or as an association taxable as a corporation depends on whether there are associates and an objective to carry on business and divide the gains therefrom.[51] Generally, if the purpose of an arrangement is to grant to trustees exclusive responsibility for the protection and conservation of trust property, and the persons with the beneficial interest in the property cannot share in the discharge of that responsibility, there are no associates or an objective to carry on business. Such an arrangement generally will be treated as a trust.[52] On the other hand, if a trust is used for carrying on a profit-making business that ordinarily would be carried on through a business organization such as a corporation or partnership, it will not be treated as a trust.[53] However, a trust that is used to hold income-producing assets may be treated as a trust if there is no power under the trust agreement to vary the investment.[54]

In May, 1984, the Treasury Department issued proposed regulations addressing the treatment of trusts that have more than one class of ownership interest. Final regulations were issued by the Treasury Depart-

---

48 *See* discussion of entity classification, below.

49 Treas. Reg. sec. 301.7701-2(a).

50 *Id.*

51 Treas. Reg. sec. 301.7701-2(a)(2).

52 Treas. Reg. sec. 301.7701-4(a).

53 Treas. Reg. sec. 301.7701-4(b).

54 Treas. Reg. sec. 301.7701-4(c).

ment in March, 1985 (Treas. Reg. sec. 301.7701-4(c)(1)). Under these regulations, a trust is treated as having one class of ownership if all of the beneficiaries of the trust have undivided interests in all of the trust property. More than one class of ownership may exist where, for example, some beneficiaries are entitled to receive more than their pro rata share of trust distributions [406/407] in early years and other beneficiaries are entitled to more than their pro rata share in later years.

Under the Treasury regulations, an arrangement having more than one class of ownership interest generally may not be treated as a trust, but is treated as a corporation. Thus, if a trust held a portfolio of mortgages, and interests in the trust assets were divided so that one class of beneficiaries were to receive all principal collected by the trust and a specified rate of interest thereon, until the trust had collected a specified amount of principal on the mortgages, and another class of beneficiaries were to receive all remaining amounts collected by the trust, then such trust would be treated as an association taxable as a corporation under these regulations. The Treasury regulations provide a limited exception for certain trusts with multiple classes, where the existence of multiple classes is incidental to the purpose of facilitating direct investment in the assets of the trust. The Treasury regulations apply to interests issued after April 27, 1984.

Taxation of income from debt obligations

The original issue discount rules

Treatment of original issue discount as interest

Under prior and present law, if the borrower receives less in a lending transaction than the amount to be repaid at the loan's maturity, then the difference represents "discount." Discount performs the same function as stated interest, i.e., compensation of the lender for the use of the lender's money.[55] Code sections 1272 through 1275 and section 163(e) (the "OID rules") generally require the holder of a debt instrument issued at a discount to include annually in income a portion of the original issue discount ("OID") on the instrument, and allow the issuer of such an instrument to deduct a corresponding amount, irrespective of the methods of accounting that the holder and the issuer otherwise use.[56]

Definitions

"Original issue discount" is defined as the excess of a debt instrument's "stated redemption price at maturity" over its "issue price" (provided such excess is not less than a certain de minimis amount).

"Issue price" generally is (1) in the case of a cash loan, the amount borrowed, (2) in the case of a debt instrument that is issued for property where either the debt instrument or the property is publicly traded,[57] the fair market value of the property, or (3) if neither the debt instrument nor the property exchanged for it is [407/408] publicly traded, an amount determined using an adequate interest rate.

"Stated redemption price at maturity" includes all amounts payable at maturity excluding any interest based on a fixed rate and payable unconditionally over the life of the debt instrument at fixed intervals no longer than one year.

Operation of the OID rules

The amount of the OID in a debt instrument, if any, is allocated over the life of the instrument through a series of adjustments to the issue price for each "accrual period." The accrual period generally is each six-month or shorter period ending on the calendar day

---

55 *United States v. Midland-Ross Corp.*, 381 U.S. 54 (1965); *see also Commissioner v. National Alfafa Dehydrating & Milling Co.*, 417 U.S. 134 (1974).

56 Prior to 1982, the OID rules applied only to a limited class of obligations. The Tax Equity and Fiscal Responsibility Act of 1982 and the Tax Reform Act of 1984 greatly expanded the number and types of obligations to which the OID rules apply.

57 Presently, only stock or securities traded on an established securities market are treated as publicly traded. However, section 1803(a)(10) of the Act grants the Treasury Department authority to issue regulations treating as publicly traded other property "of a kind regularly traded on an established market."

corresponding to the date of the debt instrument's maturity and the date six months prior to the date of maturity.[58] The adjustment to the issue price for each accrual period is determined by multiplying the "adjusted issue price" (i.e., the issue price increased by adjustments prior to the beginning of the accrual period) by the instrument's yield to maturity, and then subtracting the interest payable during the accrual period.

The adjustment to the issue price for any accrual period is the amount of OID allocated to that accrual period. These adjustments reflect the amount of the accrued but unpaid interest on the debt instrument in each period. The holder is required to include this amount as interest income and the issuer is permitted a corresponding interest deduction. The holder's basis in the obligation is increased by the amount of OID includible in the holder's income.[59] Under prior law, there was uncertainty about the application of the rules where the maturity of such payments may be accelerated (e.g., based on prepayments on home mortgages that collateralize the obligation).

Gain or loss on disposition or prepayment

In general, the sale or exchange of a debt obligation that is a capital asset results in the realization of a capital gain or loss to the seller. Under section 1271, amounts received by a holder of a debt obligation, other than one issued by an individual, on retirement of such debt obligation is treated as an amount received in exchange for the debt obligation. Thus, subject to certain exceptions discussed below, if a debt obligation not issued by an individual is a capital asset, its satisfaction, either at or in advance of its maturity, generally results in the realization of a capital gain or loss measured by the difference between the amount realized and the basis of the obligation. Since section 1271 does not apply to obligations issued by individuals, repayment of a debt obligation by an [408/409] individual (including prepayment) is not treated as a sale or exchange, and thus may not give rise to capital gain or loss.[60]

Capital gain treatment also is unavailable if an obligation has original issue discount and, at the time of original issue, there was an intention to call the obligation before maturity. In general, in such a case, any gain realized on the sale or exchange (including retirement by the issuer) of the obligation is treated as ordinary income to the extent that the gain does not exceed the amount of unamortized original issue discount (sec. 1271(a)(2)). There is no authority that directly addresses the application of this provision to corporate debt obligations that are issued with original issue discount and that are called prior to maturity upon the prepayment of mortgages in a pool that collateralizes the debt obligation.

The market discount rules

The availability of capital gain treatment on the sale or exchange of a debt obligation also may be limited pursuant to the so-called "market discount" rules. In general, under the market discount rules (secs. 1276-1278), gain on the disposition of a debt obligation that was issued after July 18, 1984, generally is treated as interest income to the extent of accrued market discount. Market discount is de-

---

58 Under proposed Treasury regulations, different accrual periods may be required. *See* Prop. Treas. Reg. sec 1.1272-1(d).

59 The premise of the OID rules is that, for Federal income tax purposes, an obligation issued at a discount should be treated like an obligation issued at par requiring current payments of interest. Accordingly, the effect of the OID rules is to treat the borrower as having paid semiannually to the leader the interest accruing on the outstanding principal balance of the loan, thereby permitting the borrower to deduct as interest expense and requiring the leader to include in income such interest which has accrued but is unpaid. The lender than is deemed to have lent the accrued but unpaid interest back to the borrower, who in subsequent periods is deemed to pay interest on this amount as well as on the principal balance. This concept of accruing interest on unpaid interest is commonly referred to as the "economic accrual" of interest, or interest "compounding."

60 *See* sec. 1271(b)(1). In addition, obligations issued before July 2, 1982, by an issuer other than a corporation or a government (or political subdivision thereof) do not qualify for capital gains treatment. *See* sec. 1271(b)(2).

fined as the excess of the stated redemption price of an obligation over its basis immediately after acquisition (provided that such excess is not less than a certain *de minimis* amount). In the case of a bond that has original issue discount, for purposes of the market discount rules, its stated redemption price is treated as the sum of its issue price and the amount of original issue discount that would have been includible in the income of an original holder.

Accrued market discount on an obligation generally is the amount that bears the same ratio to the market discount on such obligation as the number of days the taxpayer holds the obligation bears to the number of days after the taxpayer acquired the obligation until its maturity (sec. 1276(b) (1)). However, the holder may elect to accrue the market discount on an obligation using a constant interest rate.[61] A holder also may elect to include accrued market discount in income annually (sec. 1278(b)). Under prior law, the method of allocating market discount among principal payments on an obligation where such principal is paid in multiple installments was uncertain.

If indebtedness is incurred to purchase or carry obligations that have market discount, interest on such indebtedness in excess of the amount of interest includible in income with respect to such obligation is deductible only to the extent that such interest exceeds the market discount allocable to the taxable year (sec. 1277). Any interest expense disallowed under this provision is allowable as a deduction in the year that the obligation is disposed of. This limitation on interest deductions is not imposed if the holder elects to include market discount in income currently. [409/410]

The coupon stripping rules

The separation of ownership of the right to receive any payment of principal or interest on a debt obligation generally results in the application of the "coupon stripping" rules (sec. 1286). Under these rules, the holder of a debt obligation who disposes of the right to receive certain payments on the obligation (other than a pro rata share of all payments), must allocate (on the basis of fair market value), his basis in the obligation between the portion of the debt obligation that is disposed of and the portion retained, for purposes of recognizing gain or loss.

Following such a disposition, for purposes of the treatment of the holder, the retained portion is treated as a debt obligation having original issue discount equal to the excess of the amount that will be received upon payment of amounts due at maturity of such retained portion over the amount of basis allocated thereto. Similarly, a purchaser of the disposed of portion of the debt obligation is treated as having purchased a debt obligation having original issue discount equal to the excess of the amount payable upon maturity of such portion over the amount paid therefor. The original issue discount rules then govern the amount that the respective holders must include in income annually.

Withholding on interest paid to foreign taxpayers

In general, a 30-percent withholding tax is imposed on portfolio interest paid to foreign taxpayers (secs. 871, 881, 1441 and 1442).[62] However, the withholding tax is not imposed on interest paid on certain obligations issued after July 18, 1984 (secs. 871(h) and 882(c)). Although obligations issued by individuals generally are not eligible for the exception,[63] most mortgage-backed securities issued after July 18, 1985, are eligible for the exception.[64] This is true even if the mortgage-backed security is in the form of a participation certificate in a grantor trust, in which case, the holder is for all other purposes treated as holding a proportionate share of the underlying mortgages. In such a case, how-

---

61 The constant interest rate method results in small amounts being treated as accrued market discount in the earlier years.

62 A lower rate of tax may be imposed pursuant to a treaty.

63 Temp. Treas. Reg. sec. 35a.9999-5(a) (Q & A 1).

64 Temp. Treas. Reg. sec. 35a.9999-5(d) (Q & A 20).

ever, the withholding tax is applied to the extent that the underlying mortgages were issued on or before July 18, 1984.[65]

Other

Certain thrift institutions are permitted to deduct a percentage of their taxable income as a bad debt deduction provided that a specified portion of the institution's assets are "qualifying assets," including "qualifying real property loans" (secs. 593, 7701(a)(19)). Debt obligations that are secured by real property mortgage loans are not treated as qualifying real property loans.

Issuers of debt instruments that have original issue discount are required to report to certain holders, the amount of interest payments and the annual accrual of OID (sec. 6049). [410/411]

Reasons for Change

The Congress recognized the increasing extent to which real estate mortgages are traded on secondary markets and the increasing extent to which multiple-class arrangements are used in the "packaging" of mortgages. Further, the Congress understood that considerable uncertainty exists concerning several aspects of the Federal income tax treatment of these types of securities. Accordingly, the Congress wished to provide rules to clarify the treatment of such securities. The Congress believed that the best method for doing so is to provide a new type of vehicle for the issuance of such multiple class securities, and to provide rules that are as comprehensive as possible for the taxation of all transactions relating to the use of such vehicles.

The Congress believed that this vehicle should be the exclusive vehicle (accompanied by exclusive tax consequences) relating to the issuance of multiple class mortgage-backed securities, and that availability of other vehicles should be limited to the extent possible. Nevertheless, the Congress believed that the vehicle provided should be the exclusive vehicle only after a reasonable

transition period. The purpose of this transition period is to enable Congress to ascertain whether the vehicle provided is an appropriate and serviceable one.

The Congress believed that there should be some relief from two levels of taxation (i.e., at the entity level and at the shareholder level) where an entity with multiple classes of interests holds only a pool of real estate mortgages and related assets, has no powers to vary the composition of its mortgage assets, and has other powers generally consistent with the preservation of trust status, provided that satisfactory rules are prescribed for the taxation of the multiple interests.[66]

The Congress believed that the new vehicle provided by the Act, since it is intended to be the exclusive one for the issuance of multiple class securities backed by real property mortgages, should be flexible enough to accommodate most legitimate business concerns while preserving the desired certainty of income tax treatment. Accordingly, the Congress believed that the provisions of the Act should apply to any multiple class entity used for packaging interests in mortgages, regardless of the legal form used, provided that the interests satisfy the specified substantive requirements.

Although the Congress believed that no separate corporate level tax should be imposed on a fixed pool of mortgages with multiple classes of interests, the Congress was nevertheless concerned that the provision of a flexible vehicle without the imposition of a separate corporate level tax could lead to certain systematic opportunities to avoid taxation on a portion of income derived from the pool of mortgages through the use of tax-exempt entities, foreign persons, and taxpayers with net operating loss carryovers. Accordingly, the Congress believed that to prevent such opportunities, a portion of the income from the pool of mortgages should be treated as [411/412] unrelated business income for tax-exempt

---

65 *Id.*

66 In the absence of the provision of adequate rules for the taxation of the various interests, the Congress believed that the treatment of multiple class trusts provided by Treas. Reg. sec. 301.7701-4(c) is an appropriate treatment of such entities.

entities, as subject to the full statutory withholding rate for foreign persons, and should not be eligible to be offset by net operating losses. The Congress believed, however, that because of the hardship being experienced by the thrift industry, an exception should be made for net operating losses of thrift institutions.

The Congress recognized that, in order to measure income as accurately as possible, an essential feature of providing satisfactory rules for the taxation of the multiple classes of interests is the clarification of the application of the OID rules and related issues as applied to mortgages and mortgage-backed securities. Given the uncertainty created by the unknown timing of prepayments on mortgages, the Congress believed that the OID rules adopted by the Act provide a reasonable approximation of the economic accrual of income, recognizing that the amount of OID accrued in a particular accrual period under the Act, may be either greater or less than the amount that would be accrued if there were perfect advance knowledge of the timing of prepayments.

Explanation of Provisions

Overview

In general, the Act provides rules relating to "real estate mortgage investment conduits" or "REMICs." In general, a REMIC is a fixed pool of mortgages with multiple classes of interests held by investors. The Act provides rules prescribing (1) the Federal income tax treatment of the REMIC, (2) the treatment of taxpayers who exchange mortgages for interests in the REMIC, (3) the treatment of taxpayers holding interests in the REMIC, and (4) the treatment of disposition of interests in the REMIC.

In general, if the specified requirements are met, the REMIC is not treated as a separate taxable entity. Rather, the income of the REMIC is allocated to, and taken into account by, the holders of the interests therein, under specified rules. Holders of "regular interests" generally take into income that portion of the income of the REMIC that would be recognized by an accrual method holder of a debt instrument that had the same terms as the particular regular interest;

holders of "residual interests" take into account all of the net income of the REMIC that is not taken into account by the holders of the regular interests. Rules are provided that (1) treat a portion of the income of the residual holder derived from the REMIC as unrelated business income for tax-exempt entities or as subject to withholding at the statutory rate when paid to foreign persons, and (2) prevent such portion from being offset by net operating losses, other than net operating losses of certain thrift institutions.

The Act also contains provisions relating to the application of the OID rules to certain debt instruments the timing of whose maturities is contingent upon the timing of payments on other debt instruments. In addition, the Act imposes certain new information reporting requirements.

Further, the Act treats as a corporation any entity or other arrangement, referred to as a "taxable mortgage pool," that is used primarily to hold mortgages, where maturities of debt instruments [412/413] that are issued by the entity in multiple classes, are tied to the timing of payments on the mortgages.

Requirements for qualification as a REMIC

Under the Act, any entity, including a corporation, partnership, or trust, that meets specified requirements would be permitted to elect to be treated as a REMIC. In addition, a segregated pool of assets also may qualify as a REMIC as if it were an entity meeting the requirements. To elect REMIC status, requirements relating to the composition of assets and the nature of the investors' interests must be satisfied, and an election to be treated as a REMIC must be in effect for the taxable year, and if applicable, all prior taxable years.

The asset test

Under the Act, in order to qualify as a REMIC, substantially all of the assets of the entity or segregated pool, as of the close of the third calendar month beginning after the startup day and as of the close of every quarter of each calendar year thereafter, must consist of "qualified mortgages" and "permitted investments." The Congress intended that the term substantially all should be interpreted to allow the REMIC to hold only de minimis amounts of other assets.

A "qualified mortgage" is any obligation (including any participation or certificate of beneficial ownership interest therein) that is principally secured by an interest in real property, and that either (1) is transferred to the REMIC on or before the "startup day," or (2) is purchased by the REMIC within the three-month period beginning on the startup day.[67] A qualified mortgage also includes a "qualified replacement mortgage." A qualified replacement mortgage is any property that would have been treated as a qualified mortgage if it were transferred to the REMIC on or before the startup day, and that is received either (1) in exchange for a defective qualified mortgage[68] within a two year period beginning on the startup day, or (2) in exchange for any other qualified mortgage within a three month period beginning on the startup day. In addition, any regular interest in another REMIC that is transferred to the REMIC on or before the startup day is treated as a qualified mortgage. The startup day is any day selected by the REMIC that is [413/414] on or before the first day on which interests in the REMIC are issued.

"Permitted investments" are "cash flow investments," "qualified reserve assets," and "foreclosure property."

"Cash flow investments" are any investment of amounts received under qualified mortgages for a temporary period before distribution to holders of interests in the REMIC. The Congress intended that these are assets that are received periodically by the REMIC, invested temporarily in passive-type assets, and paid out to the investors at the next succeeding regular payment date. The Congress intended that these temporary investments are to be limited to those types of investments that produce passive income in the nature of interest. For example, the Congress intended that an arrangement commonly known as a "guaranteed investment contract," whereby the REMIC agrees to turn over payments on qualified mortgages to a third party who agrees to return such amounts together with a specified return thereon at times coinciding with the times that payments are to be made to holders of regular or residual interests, may qualify as a permitted investment.

"Qualified reserve assets" are any intangible property held for investment that is part of a "qualified reserve fund." A qualified reserve fund is any reasonably required reserve that is maintained by the REMIC to provide for payments of certain expenses and to provide additional security for the payments due on regular interests in the REMIC that otherwise may be delayed or defaulted upon because of defaults (including late payments) on the qualified mortgages.[69] In determining whether the amount of the reserve is reasonable, the Congress

---

67 The Congress intended that stripped coupons and stripped bonds (within the meaning of sec. 1286) may be treated as qualifying mortgages if the bonds (within the meaning of sec. 1286) from which such stripped coupons or stripped bonds arose would have been qualified mortgages. The Congress also intended that interests in grantor trusts would be treated as qualified mortgages, to the extent that the assets of the trusts that holders of the beneficial interest therein are treated as owning, would be treated as qualifying mortgages. In addition, the Congress intended that interests in qualifying mortgages in the nature of the interests described in Treas. Reg. sec. 301.7701-4(c)(2) (Example 2), and loans principally secured by stock of a tenant-stockholder of a cooperative housing corporation would be treated as qualifying mortgages. Nevertheless, except for regular interests in a REMIC, Congress did not intend that debt obligations that are secured primarily by other debt obligations would be treated as qualified mortgages even where such other debt obligations are secured primarily by interests in real property. A technical correction may be necessary to reflect this intention.

68 For this purpose, Congress intended that a defective qualified mortgage generally would have the same meaning as that used for purposes of determining the ability of a grantor trust that holds mortgages to substitute those mortgages without losing its status as a grantor trust for Federal income tax purposes. Thus, for example, a defective qualified mortgage is a qualified mortgage with respect to which there is a default or threatened default by the obligor.

69 Congress intended that property would not fail to be considered to be held for investment, solely because the REMIC holds the property for these reasons.

believed that it is appropriate to take into account the creditworthiness of the qualified mortgages and the extent and nature of any guarantees relating to the qualified mortgages. Further, amounts in the reserve fund must be reduced promptly and appropriately as regular interests in the REMIC are retired.

Under the Act, a reserve is not treated as a qualified reserve unless for any taxable year (and all subsequent taxable years) not more than 30 percent of the gross income from the assets in such fund for the taxable year is derived from the sale or other disposition of property held for less than three months. For this purpose, gain on the disposition of a reserve fund asset is not taken into account if the disposition of such asset is required to prevent default on a regular interest where the threatened default resulted from a default on one or more qualified mortgages.

"Foreclosure property" is property that would be foreclosure property under section 856(e) if acquired by a real estate investment trust, and which is acquired by the REMIC in connection with the default or imminent default of a qualified mortgage. Property so acquired ceases to be foreclosure property one year after its acquisition by the REMIC. [414/415]

Investors' interests

In order to qualify as a REMIC under the Act, all of the interests in the REMIC must consist of one or more classes of "regular interests" and a single class of "residual interests."

Regular interests.—A regular interest in a REMIC is an interest in a REMIC whose terms are fixed on the startup day, which terms (1) unconditionally entitle the holder to receive a specified principal (or similar) amount, and (2) provide that interest (or similar) payments, if any, at or before maturity are based on a fixed rate (or to the extent provided in Treasury regulations, a variable rate). An interest in the REMIC may qualify as a regular interest where the timing (but not the amount) of the principal

(or similar) payments are contingent on the extent of prepayments on qualified mortgages and the amount of income from permitted investments.

The Congress intended that regular interests in REMICs may be issued in the form of debt, stock, partnership interests, interests in a trust, or any other form permitted by state law. Thus, if an interest in a REMIC is not in the form of debt, the Congress understood that the interest would not have a specified principal amount, but that the interest would qualify as a regular interest if there is a specified amount that could be identified as the principal amount if the interest were in the form of debt. For example, an interest in a partnership could qualify as a regular interest if the holder of the partnership interest were to receive a specified amount in redemption of the partnership interest, and that the amount of income allocated to such partnership interest were based on a fixed percentage of the specified outstanding redemption amount.

The Congress intended that an interest in a REMIC would not fail to be treated as a regular interest if the payments of principal or interest (or similar) amounts with respect to such interest are subordinated to payments on other regular interests in the REMIC in the event of defaults on qualified mortgages. Thus, the Congress intended that regular interests in a REMIC may resemble the types of interests described in Treas. Reg. sec. 301.7701-4(c)(2)(Example 2).[70]

The Congress intended that an interest in a REMIC may not qualify as a regular interest if the amount of interest (or similar payments) is disproportionately high relative to the specified principal amount. For example, if an interest is issued in the form of debt with a coupon rate of interest that is substantially in excess of prevailing market interest rates (adjusted for risk), the Congress intended that the interest would not qualify as a regular interest. Instead, the Congress intended that such an interest may be treated either as a residual interest, or as a combination of a regular interest and a re-

---

70 The status of an interest as a regular interest in this case does not depend on whether the subordinated regular interest is sold or retained.

sidual interest. Congress intended that interests issued at a discount may qualify as a regular interests [sic].

Residual interests.—In general, a residual interest in a REMIC is any interest in the REMIC other than a regular interest, and which is so designated by the REMIC, provided that there is only one class of such interest, and that all distributions (if any) with [415/416] respect to such interests are pro rata. For example, the residual interest in a mortgage pool that otherwise qualifies as a REMIC is held by two taxpayers, one of whom has a 25 percent interest in the residual and the other of whom has a 75 percent interest. Except for their relative size, the interests of the two taxpayers are identical. Provided that all distributions to the residual interest holders are pro rata, the mortgage pool would qualify as a REMIC because there is only one class of residual interest. If, however, the holder of the 25 percent interest is entitled to receive all distributions to which residual holders combined are entitled for a specified period (or up to a specified amount) in return for the surrender of his interest, then the mortgage pool would be considered to have two classes of residual interests and would not qualify as a REMIC.

The Congress intended that an interest in a REMIC could qualify as a residual interest regardless of its value. Thus, for example, an interest need not entitle the holder to any distributions in order to qualify as a residual interest. Nevertheless, the treatment of a holder of a residual interest may depend on the value of the residual interest relative to all of the interests in a REMIC.[71]

Where the REMIC's qualified mortgages are stripped coupons or stripped bonds (within the meaning of section 1286), Congress did not intend that any other stripped coupons or stripped bonds arising from the same debt instruments as the qualified mortgages would be treated as a second class of residual interest in the REMIC. In addition, the Congress intended that the right to receive payment from the REMIC for goods or services rendered in the ordinary operation of the REMIC would not be considered to be an interest in the REMIC for these purposes.

Inadvertent terminations

The Act provides regulatory authority to the Treasury Department to issue regulations that address situations where failure to meet one or more of the requirements for REMIC status occurs inadvertently, and disqualification of the REMIC would occur absent regulatory relief. The Congress anticipated that the Treasury regulations would provide relief only where the failure to meet any of the requirements occurred inadvertently and in good faith. The Congress also intended that the relief may be accompanied by appropriate sanctions, such as the imposition of a corporate tax on all or a portion of the REMIC's income for the period of time in which the requirements are not met.

Formation of the REMIC

Under the Act, no gain or loss is recognized to the transferor upon the transfer of property to a REMIC in exchange for regular or residual interests in the REMIC. Upon such a transfer, the adjusted bases of the regular or residual interests received in the transaction are to be equal in the aggregate to the aggregate of the adjusted bases of the property transferred. The aggregate basis of the interests received is allocated among the regular or residual interests [416/417] received in proportion to their fair market values.[72] The basis of any property received by a REMIC in exchange for regular or residual interests in the REMIC is equal to the aggregate fair market value of the regular or residual interests at the time of transfer (or earlier time provided by Treasury regulations).[73]

---

71 *See* text accompanying nn. 84-87, *infra.*

72 The Congress intended that a holder of a mortgage should not be permitted to recognize loss where mortgages are indirectly transferred to a REMIC. Thus, the Congress intended that no gain or loss would be recognized, for example, if pursuant to a plan, mortgages are sold by one taxpayer to another, and the buyer transfers the purchased mortgages to a REMIC in which interests are purchased by the initial seller of the mortgages.

73 The Congress intended that the Treasury regulations may provide that the basis of qualified mortgages

The Congress intended that any properly allocable costs of acquiring the regular or residual interests would be capitalized and added to the basis of the regular or residual interest. Upon a subsequent sale or exchange of any regular or residual interest, gain or loss is recognized.

The Congress intended that the Federal income tax consequences of forming a REMIC should be the same regardless of whether regular and or residual interests were issued in exchange for qualified mortgages and followed by a sale of some or all of the interests issued, or whether such interests were issued for cash or other property and followed by a purchase of qualified mortgages. The Congress expected that the step transaction doctrine would be applied so that the formation of a REMIC in the latter fashion would be recharacterized as a contribution of mortgages to the REMIC in exchange for regular and residual interests followed by a sale of all or a portion of those interests by the transferor of the mortgages.[74]

In the case of a REMIC that is not formed as a separate entity, but rather as a segregated pool of assets, the Congress intended that the transfer is deemed to occur and the REMIC is deemed to be formed only upon the issuance of regular and residual interests therein.

Federal income tax treatment of the REMIC

Pass-through status

In general, the Act provides that a REMIC is not a taxable entity for Federal income tax purposes. The income of the REMIC generally is taken into account by holders of regular and residual interests in the REMIC as described below. Nevertheless, the REMIC is subject to tax on prohibited transactions, and may be required to withhold on amounts paid to foreign holders of regular or residual interests.[75]

The pass-through status of the REMIC provided by the Act applies regardless of whether the REMIC otherwise would be treated [417/418] as a corporation, partnership, trust, or any other entity. The Congress intended that where the requirements for REMIC status are met, that the exclusive set of rules for the treatment of all transactions relating to the REMIC and of holders of interests therein are to be those set forth in the provisions of the Act. Thus, for example, in the case of a REMIC that would be treated as a partnership if it were not otherwise a REMIC, the provisions of subchapter K of the Code would not be applicable to any transactions involving the REMIC or any of the holders of regular or residual interests.[76]

Prohibited transactions

Under the Act, a REMIC is required to pay a tax equal to 100 percent of the REMIC's net income from prohibited transactions. For this purpose, net income from prohibited transactions is computed without taking into account any losses from prohibited transactions or any deductions relating to prohibited transactions that result in a loss. Prohibited transac-

---

held by the REMIC in certain circumstances may be determined based on the fair market value of such mortgages at a reasonable time prior to transfer to the REMIC where such mortgages were purchased by the transferor solely for the purpose of transfer to the REMIC.

74 Thus, for example, if a REMIC is formed by issuing regular and residual interests for cash and the REMIC subsequently purchases qualified mortgages from a holder of a residual interest, such holder would be treated as transferring the qualified mortgages to the REMIC in exchange for regular and residual interests and then having sold all the interests other than those held at the time of the sale. Moreover, the allocation of basis between the regular and residual interests should reflect the relative fair market values of such interests as if the formation had actually taken place by transferring mortgages in exchange for the regular and residual interests.

75 Withholding also may be required with respect to certain amounts without actual payment to foreign holders, however. *See* text accompanying nn. 86-87, *infra*.

76 For purposes of subtitle F of the Code (relating to certain administrative matters) the REMIC is treated as a partnership in which residual interests are the partnership interests, however. The Congress intended that the initial election of REMIC status is to be made on the first partnership information return that the REMIC is required to file.

tions for the REMIC include the disposition of any qualified mortgage other than pursuant to (1) the substitution of a qualified replacement mortgage for a defective qualified mortgage, (2) the bankruptcy or insolvency of the REMIC, (3) a disposition incident to the foreclosure, default, or imminent default of the mortgage, or (4) a qualified liquidation (described below). In addition, the disposition of a qualified mortgage is not a prohibited transaction if such disposition is required to prevent default on a regular interest where such default on the regular interest is threatened on account of a default on one or more qualified mortgages. Other prohibited transactions include the disposition of any cash flow investment other than pursuant to a qualified liquidation, the receipt of any income from assets other than assets permitted to be held by the REMIC, and the receipt of any compensation for services.[77]

Taxation of the holders of regular interests

In general

Under the Act, holders of regular interests generally are taxed as if their regular interest were a debt instrument to which the rules of taxation generally applicable to debt instruments apply, except that the holder of a regular interest is required to account for income relating to such interest on the accrual method of accounting regardless of the method of accounting otherwise used by the holder.[78] In the case of regular interests that are not debt instruments, the amount of the fixed unconditional payment is treated as the stated principal amount of the instrument, and the periodic payments (i.e., the amounts that are based on the amount of the fixed unconditional payment), if any, are treated as stated interest payments. In other words, generally consistent with the pass-through [418/419] nature of the REMIC, the holders of regular interests generally take into ac-

count that portion of the REMIC's income that would be taken into account by an accrual method holder of a debt instrument with terms equivalent to the terms of the regular interest.[79]

The Congress intended that regular interests are to be treated as if they were debt instruments for all other purposes of the Internal Revenue Code. Thus, for example, regular interests would be treated as market discount bonds, where the revised issue price (within the meaning of section 1278) of the regular interest exceeds the holder's basis in the interest. Moreover, the Congress intended that the REMIC is subject to the reporting requirements of section 1275 with respect to the regular interests. In addition, the Congress intended that regular interests are to be treated as evidences of indebtedness under section 582(c)(1), so that gain or loss from the sale or exchange of regular interests by certain financial institutions would not be treated as gain or loss from the sale or exchange of a capital asset. In addition, any market premium on a regular interest could be amortized currently under section 171.

The issue price of regular interests in the REMIC are determined under the rules of section 1273(b). In the case of regular interests issued in exchange for property, however, the issue price of the regular interest is equal to the fair market value of the property,[80] regardless of whether the requirements of section 1273(b)(3) are met. A holder's basis in the regular interest generally is equal to the holder's cost therefor, but in the case of holders who received their interests in exchange for property, then as discussed above, the holder's basis is equal to the basis of the property exchanged for the REMIC interest. Where property is transferred in exchange for more than one class of regular or residual interest, the basis

---

77 The Congress intended that payment by the obligor on a debt instrument is not to be considered to be a disposition of such debt instrument for these purposes.

78 The Congress intended that the periodic payments of interest (or similar amounts) are to be treated as accruing pro rata between the dates that such interest (or similar amounts) is paid.

79 In the event that the amount so determined exceeds the income of the REMIC, however, there is no diminution of the required inclusions for such holders.

80 For this purpose, the Congress intended that the fair market value of the property is to be determined by reference to the fair market value of the regular interests received in exchange.

of the property transferred is allocated in proportion to the fair market value of the interests received.

Regular interests received in exchange for property

Under the Act, where an exchange of property for regular interests in a REMIC has taken place, any excess of the issue price of the regular interest over the basis of the interest in the hands of the transferor immediately after the transfer is, for periods during which such interest is held by the transferor (or any other person whose basis is determined in whole or in part by reference to the basis of such interest in the hands of the transferor), includible currently in the gross income of the holder under rules similar to the rules of section 1276(b) (i.e., the holder of such an interest is treated like the holder of a market discount bond for which an election under section 1278(b) is in effect). Conversely, the excess of the basis of the regular interest in the hands of the transferor immediately after the transfer over the issue price of the interest is treated for such holders as market premium that is allowable as a deduction under rules similar to the rules of section 171. The Congress [419/420] intended that the holder's basis in the regular interest would be properly adjusted to reflect such current inclusions or deductions.

Disposition of regular interests

The Act treats gain on the disposition of a regular interest as ordinary income to the extent of a portion of unaccrued OID with respect to the interest. Such portion generally is the amount of unaccrued OID equal to the excess, if any, of the amount that would have been includible in the gross income of the taxpayer with respect to such interest if the yield on such interest were 110 percent of the applicable Federal rate (as defined in sec. 1274(d) without regard to paragraph (2) thereof) determined as of the time that the interest is acquired by the taxpayer, over the total amount of ordinary income includible by the taxpayer with respect to such regular interest prior to disposition. In selecting the applicable Federal rate, the Congress intended that the same prepayment assumptions that are used in calculating OID are to be used in determining the maturity of the regular interest.

Taxation of the holders of residual interests

In general

In general, the Act provides that at the end of each calendar quarter, the holder of a residual interest in a REMIC takes into account his daily portion of the taxable income or net loss of the REMIC for each day during the holder's taxable year in which such holder held such interest. The amount so taken into account is treated as ordinary income or loss. The daily portion for this purpose is determined by allocating to each day in any calendar quarter a ratable portion of the taxable income or net loss of the REMIC for such quarter, and by allocating the amounts so allocated to any day among the holders (on such day) of residual interests in proportion to their respective holdings on such day.

For example, a REMIC's taxable income for a calendar quarter (determined as described below) is $1,000. There are two holders of residual interests in the REMIC. One holder of 60 percent of the residual holds such interest for the entire calendar quarter. Another holder has a 40 percent interest, and transfers the interest after exactly one half of the calendar quarter to another taxpayer. As of the end of the calendar quarter, the holder of the sixty percent interest would be treated as receiving $600 ratably over the quarter. Each holder of the 40 percent interest would be treated as receiving $200 ratably over the portion of the quarter in which the interest was held.

Distributions from the REMIC are not included in the gross income of the residual holder to the extent that such distributions do not exceed the adjusted basis of the interest. To the extent that distributions exceed the adjusted basis of the interest, the excess is treated as gain from the sale of the residual interest. Residual interests are treated as evidences of indebtedness for purposes of section 582(c).

The amount of any net loss of the REMIC that may be taken into account by the holder of a residual interest is limited to the adjusted [420/421] basis of the interest as of the close of the quarter (or time of disposition of the interest if earlier), determined without taking into account the net loss for the quarter. Any loss that is disallowed on account of this limitation may be carried over indefinitely by the holder of the interest for whom such loss was disallowed and may be used by such holder only to offset any income generated by the same REMIC.

Except for adjustments arising from the nonrecognition of gain or loss on the transfer of mortgages to the REMIC (discussed below), the holders of residual interests take no amounts into account other than those allocated from the REMIC.[81]

Determination of REMIC taxable income or net loss

In general, under the Act, the taxable income or net loss of the REMIC for purposes of determining the amounts taken into account by holders of residual interests, is determined in the same manner as for an individual having the calendar year as his taxable year and using the accrual method of accounting, with certain modifications. The first modification is that a deduction is allowed with respect to those amounts that would be deductible as interest if the regular interests in the REMIC were treated as indebtedness of the REMIC. Second, in computing the gross income of the REMIC, market discount with respect to any market discount bond (within the meaning of sec. 1278) held by the REMIC is includible for the year in which such discount accrues, as determined under the rules of section 1276(b)(2), and sections 1276(a) and 1277 do not apply. Third, no item of income, gain, loss, or deduction allocable to a prohibited transaction is taken into account. Fourth, deductions under section 703(a)(2) (other than

deductions allowable under section 212) are not allowed.[82]

If a REMIC distributes property with respect to any regular or residual interest, the REMIC recognizes gain in the same manner as if the REMIC had sold the property to such distributee at its fair market value. The Congress intended that the distribution is to be treated as an actual sale by the REMIC for purposes of applying the prohibited transaction rules and the rules relating to qualified reserve funds. The basis of the distributed property in the hands of the distributee is then the fair market value of the property.

Adjusted basis of residual interests

Under the Act, a holder's basis in a residual interest in a REMIC is increased by the amount of the taxable income of the REMIC [421/422] that is taken into account by the holder. The basis of such an interest is decreased (but not below zero) by the amount of any distributions received from the REMIC and by the amount of any net loss of the REMIC that is taken into account by the holder. In the case of a holder who disposes of a residual interest, the basis adjustment on account of the holder's daily portions of the REMIC's taxable income or net loss is deemed to occur immediately before the disposition.

Special treatment of a portion of residual income

Under the Act, a portion of the net income of the REMIC taken into account by the holders of the residual interests may not be offset by any net operating losses of the holder. The Act provides a special exception from this rule in the case of certain thrift institutions,

---

81 The Congress understood that the taxable income allocated to holders of residual interests in a REMIC who purchased such interests from a prior holder after a significant change in value of the interest could be substantially accelerated or deferred on account of any premium or discount in the price paid by such purchaser. Accordingly, the Congress recognized that certain modifications of the rules governing taxation of holders of residual interests may be appropriate where the method of taxation of residual interests prescribed by the Act has such consequences.

82 The Congress intended that no gain or loss is recognized to the REMIC on the exchange of regular or residual interests in the REMIC for property. In addition, the Congress understood that the treatment of deductions allowable under section 212 will be addressed in Treasury regulations. In this regard, the Congress intended that such deductions would be allocated to all holders of interests in REMICs that are similar to single-class grantor trusts under present law. However, the Congress intended that such deductions would be allocated to the holders of the residual interests in the case of other REMICs.

on account of the difficulties currently being experienced by the thrift industry.

In addition, the Act provides that the same portion of the net income of the REMIC that may not be offset by net operating losses is treated as unrelated business income for any organization subject to the unrelated business income tax under section 511, and is not eligible for any reduction in the rate of withholding tax (by treaty or otherwise) in the case of a nonresident alien holder.

The portion of the income of the residual holder that is subject to these rules is the excess, if any, of the amount of the net income of the REMIC that the holder takes into account for any calendar quarter, over the sum of the daily accruals with respect to such interest while held by such holder. The daily accrual for any residual interest for any day in any calendar quarter is determined by allocating to each day in such calendar quarter a ratable portion of the product of the adjusted issue price of the residual interest at the beginning of such accrual period, and 120 percent of the long-term Federal rate. The long-term Federal rate used for this purpose is the Federal long-term rate that would have applied to the residual interest under section 1274(d) (without regard to section 1274(d)(2)) if it were a debt instrument, determined at the time that the residual interest is issued. The rate is adjusted appropriately in order to be applied on the basis of compounding at the end of each quarter.

For this purpose (and for purposes of the treatment of gain or loss that is not recognized upon the transfer of property to a REMIC in exchange for a residual interest, as discussed below), the residual interest is treated as having an issue price that is equal to the amount of money paid for the interest at the time it is issued, or in the case of a residual interest that is issued in exchange for property, the fair market value of the interest at the time it is issued. The adjusted issue price of the residual interest is equal to the issue price of the interest increased by the amount of daily accruals for prior calendar quarters, and decreased (but not below zero) by the amount of any distributions with respect to the residual interest prior to the end of the calendar quarter.

In addition, the Act provides that under Treasury regulations, if a REIT owns a residual interest in a REMIC, a portion of dividends paid by the REIT would be treated as excess inclusions for REIT shareholders. Thus, such income generally could not be offset by net operating losses, would constitute unrelated business taxable [422/423] income for tax-exempt holders, and would not be eligible for and reduction in the rate of withholding tax in the case of a nonresident alien holder.

The Act provides that to the extent provided in Treasury regulations, in the case of a residual interest that does not have significant value, the entire amount of income that is taken into account by the holder of the residual interest is treated as unrelated business income and is subject to withholding at the statutory rate. In addition, in the case of such a residual, income allocated to the holder thereof may not be offset by any net operating losses, regardless of who holds the interest.[83] The Congress intended that the Treasury regulations would take into account the value of the residual interest in relation to the regular interests, and that Treasury regulations would not apply in cases where the value of the residual interest is at least two percent of the combined value of the regular and residual interests.[84]

The Act provides that the partnership information return filed by the REMIC is to supply information relating to the daily accruals of the REMIC.

Treatment of foreign residual holders

The Act provides that in the case of a holder of a residual interest of a REMIC who is a nonresident alien individual or foreign corpo-

---

83 *I.e.,* the exception provided for thrift institutions in section 860E(a)(2) would not be available in these circumstances.

84 The Congress intended that these regulations may apply in appropriate cases to residual interests issued before regulations are issued.

ration, then for purposes of sections 871(a), 881, 1441, and 1442, amounts includible in the gross income of such holder with respect to the residual interest are taken into account only when paid or otherwise distributed (or when the interest is disposed of).[85] The Act also provides that under Treasury regulations, the amounts includible may be taken into account earlier than otherwise provided where necessary to prevent avoidance of tax. The Congress intended that this regulatory authority may be exercised where the residual interest in the REMIC does not have significant value (as described above).[86]

Residual interests received in exchange for property

In the case of a residual interest that is received in exchange for a contribution of property to the REMIC, any excess of the issue price of the residual interest over the basis of the interest in the hands of the transferor of the property immediately after the transfer, is amortized and is included in the residual holder's income on a straight line basis over the expected life of the REMIC. Similarly, any excess of the transferor's basis in the residual interest over the issue price of the interest is deductible by the holder of the interest on a straight line basis over the expected life of the REMIC. In determining the expected life of the REMIC for this purpose, the Congress intended that the assumptions used in [423/424] calculating original issue discount and any binding agreement regarding liquidation of the REMIC are to be taken into account. The Congress intended that the holder's basis in the residual interest would be properly adjusted to reflect such current inclusions or deductions.

Dispositions of residual interests

The Act provides that, except as provided in Treasury regulations, the wash sale rules of section 1091 apply to dispositions of residual interests in a REMIC where the seller of the interest, during the period beginning six months before the sale or disposition of residual interest and ending six months after such sale or disposition, acquires (or enters into any other transaction that results in the application of section 1091) any residual interest in any REMIC or any interest in a "taxable mortgage pool" (discussed below) that is comparable to a residual interest.

Qualified liquidation

Under the Act, a qualified liquidation is a transaction in which the REMIC adopts a plan of complete liquidation, and sells all of its assets (other than cash) within the 90-day period beginning immediately after the date of the adoption of the plan of liquidation, provided that the REMIC distributes or otherwise credits in liquidation all of the sale proceeds plus its cash (other than amounts retained to meet claims) to holders of regular and residual interests within the 90-day period.[87] A holder of a regular or residual interest recognizes gain or loss on the liquidation of the REMIC. Sales of the REMICs assets pursuant to a qualified liquidation are not treated as prohibited transactions.[88]

Other provisions

Compliance provisions

The application of the OID rules contemplated by the Act requires calculations that are based on information that would not necessarily be known by any holder, and is more readily available to the issuer than any other person. Accordingly, the Act requires broader reporting of interest payments and OID accrual by the REMIC, or any issuer of debt that is subject to the OID rules of the Act. The Act specifies that the amounts includible in gross income of the holder of a regular interest in a REMIC are treated as interest for purposes of the reporting requirements of the

---

85 The Congress intended that withholding upon disposition of such interests is to be similar to withholding upon disposition of debt instruments that have original issue discount.

86 The Congress intended that these regulations may apply in appropriate cases to residual interests issued before regulations are issued.

87 The Congress intended that the treatment of a holder to whom amounts merely are credited would be the same as if amounts actually were distributed.

88 *See* discussion of prohibited transactions, *supra.*

Code (sec. 6049), and that the REMIC or similar issuer is required to report interest and OID to a broader group of holders than required under prior law. The holders to whom such broader reporting is required include corporations, certain dealers in commodities or securities, real estate investment trusts, common trust funds, and certain other trusts. In addition to reporting interest and OID, the REMIC or similar issuer is required to report sufficient information to allow holders to compute the accrual of any market discount or [424/425] amortization of any premium in accordance with provisions of the Act.[89]

Treatment of REMIC interests for certain financial institutions and real estate investment trusts

Under the Act, regular and residual interests are treated as qualifying assets for purposes of section 593(d)(1) and section 7701(a)(19), in the same proportion that the assets of the REMIC would be treated as qualifying under those sections.[90] In the case of residual interests, the Congress intended that the amount treated as a qualifying asset not exceed the adjusted basis of the residual interest in the hands of the holder. Both regular and residual interests are treated as real estate assets under section 856(c)(6), and the income from such interests are treated as interest qualifying under section 856(c)(3)(C),[91] in the same proportion that the assets of the REMIC would be treated as real estate assets for purposes of determining eligibility for real estate investment trust status.[92]

Foreign withholding

The Congress intended that for purposes of withholding on interest paid to foreign persons, regular interests in REMICs should be considered to be debt instruments that are issued after July 18, 1984, regardless of the time that any debt instruments held by the REMIC were issued. The Congress intended

that amounts paid to foreign persons with respect to residual interests should be considered to be interest for purposes of applying the withholding rules.

OID rules

The Act provides rules relating to the application of the OID rules to debt instruments that, as is generally the case with regular interests in a REMIC, have a maturity that is initially fixed, but that is accelerated based on prepayments on other debt obligations securing the debt instrument (or, to the extent provided in Treasury regulations, by reason of other events). The OID rules provided by the Act also apply to OID on qualified mortgages held by a REMIC.

In general, the OID rules provided by the Act require OID for an accrual period to be calculated and included in the holder's income based on the increase in the present value of remaining payments on the debt instrument, taking into account payments includible in the instrument's stated redemption price at maturity received on the regular interest during the period. For this purpose, the present value calculation is made at the beginning of each accrual period (1) using the yield to maturity determined for the instrument at the time of its issuance (determined on the basis of compounding [425/426] at the close of each accrual period and properly adjusted for the length of the accrual period), calculated on the assumption that, as prescribed by Treasury regulations, certain prepayments will occur, and (2) taking into account any prepayments that have occurred before the close of the accrual period.

The Congress intended that the Treasury regulations will provide that the prepayment assumption to be used in calculating present values as of the close of each accrual period, and in computing the yield to maturity

---

89   *See* sec. 1803(a)(13) of the Act.

90   If 95% of the assets of the REMIC would be treated as qualifying assets at all times during a calendar year then the entire regular or residual interest is so treated for the calendar year.

91   A technical correction may be necessary to clarify the treatment of income from a REMIC taken into account by a REIT.

92   If 95% of the assets of the REMIC would be treated as real estate assets at all times during a calendar year, then the entire regular or residual is so treated for the calendar year.

used in the calculation of such present values, will be that used by the parties in pricing the particular transaction. The Congress intended that such prepayment assumption will be determined by the assumed rate of prepayments on qualified mortgages held by the REMIC and also the assumed rate of earnings on the temporary investment of payments on such mortgages insofar as such rate of earnings would affect the timing of payments on regular interests.[93]

The Congress intended that the Treasury regulations will require these pricing assumptions to be specified in the first partnership return filed by the REMIC. In addition, the Congress intended that appropriate supporting documentation relating to the selection of the prepayment assumption must be supplied to the Internal Revenue Service with such return. Further, the Congress intended that the prepayment assumptions used must not be unreasonable based on comparable transactions, if comparable transactions exist.[94]

The Congress intended that unless otherwise provided by Treasury regulations, the use of a prepayment assumption based on a recognized industry standard would be permitted. For example, the Congress understood that prepayment assumptions based on a Public Securities Association standard currently is such an industry-recognized standard.

The Congress intended that in no circumstances would the method of accruing OID prescribed by the Act allow for negative amounts of OID to be attributed to any accrual period. If the use of the present value computations prescribed by the Act produce such a result for an accrual period, the Congress intended that the amount of OID attributable to such accrual period

would be treated as zero, and the computation of OID for the following accrual period would be made as if such following accrual period and the preceding accrual period were a single accrual period.

Regulatory authority

The Act grants the Treasury Department authority to prescribe such regulations as are necessary or appropriate to implement the provisions relating to REMICs. The Congress expected that, among [426/427] other things, such regulations will prevent unreasonable accumulations of assets in the REMIC, and require the REMIC to report information adequate to allow residual holders to compute taxable income accurately (including reporting more frequently than annually). Further, such regulations may require reporting of OID accrual more frequently than otherwise required by the Act.

Treasury study

The Congress was concerned about the impact of the REMIC provisions upon the thrift industry. Accordingly, the Act requests that the Treasury Department conduct a study of the effectiveness of the REMIC provisions in enhancing the efficiency of the secondary market in mortgages, and the impact of these provisions upon thrift institutions.

Taxable mortgage pools

The Congress intended that REMICs are to be the exclusive means of issuing multiple class real estate mortgage-backed securities without the imposition of two levels of taxation. Thus, the Act provides that a "taxable mortgage pool" ("TMP") is treated as a taxable corporation that is not an includible corporation for purposes of filing consolidated returns.

Under the Act, a TMP is any entity other

---

93 In computing the accrual of OID (or market discount) on qualified mortgages held by the REMIC, only assumptions about the rate of prepayments on such mortgages would be taken into account.

94 The Congress intended that in the case of publicly offered instruments, a prepayment assumption will be treated as unreasonable only in the presence of clear and convincing evidence. In addition, the Congress intended that in determining whether a prepayment assumption is reasonable, the nature of the debt instruments on which prepayments are being assumed, and the availability of information about prepayments thereon, will be taken into account. Thus, for example, under currently prevailing conditions, the Congress understood that there should be less tolerance in the evaluation of prepayment assumptions relating to pools of home mortgages than prepayment assumptions relating to pools of commercial mortgages.

than a REMIC if (1) substantially all of the assets of the entity consist of debt obligations (or interests in debt obligations) and more than 50 percent of such obligations (or interests) consist of real estate mortgages, (2) such entity is the obligor under debt obligations with two or more maturities,[95] and (3) under the terms of such debt obligations on which the entity is the obligor, payment on such debt obligations bear a relationship to payments on the debt obligations (or interests therein) held by the entity.[96]

Under the Act, any portion of an entity that meets the definition of a TMP is treated as a TMP. For example, if an entity segregates mortgages in some fashion and issues debt obligations in two or more maturities, which maturities depend upon the timing of payments on the mortgages, then the mortgages and the debt would be treated as a TMP, and hence as a separate corporation. The TMP provisions are intended to apply to any arrangement under which mortgages are segregated from a debtor's business activities (if any) for the benefit of creditors whose loans are of varying maturities.

The Act provides that no domestic building and loan association (or portion thereof) is to be treated as a TMP.

Special rule for REITs

The Congress intended that an entity that otherwise would be treated as a TMP may, if it otherwise meets applicable requirements, elect to be treated as a REIT. If so, the Act provides that [427/428] under Treasury regulations, a portion of the REIT's income would

be treated in the same manner as income subject to the special rules provided for a portion of the income of a residual interest in a RE-MIC. The Congress intended that this calculation is to be made as if the equity interests in the REIT were the residual interest in a REMIC and such interests were issued (i.e., the issue price of interests is determined) as of the time that the REIT becomes a TMP.[97]

The Congress intended that the Treasury regulations would provide that dividends paid to the shareholders of a REIT would be subject to the same rules provided for a portion of the income of holders of residual interests in a REMIC. Thus, for example, the Congress intended that the Treasury regulations would provide that to the extent that dividends from the REIT exceed the daily accruals for the REIT (determined in the same manner as if the REIT were a RE-MIC) such dividends (1) may not be offset by net operating losses (except those of certain thrift institutions),[98] (2) are treated as unrelated business income for certain tax-exempt institutions, and (3) are not eligible for any reduction in the rate of withholding when paid to foreign persons. The Congress also intended that the Treasury regulations would require a REIT to report such amounts to its shareholders.[99]

Effective Date

The provisions of the Act are effective with respect to taxable years beginning after December 31, 1986.[100] The amendments made by the Act to the OID rules apply to debt in-

---

95   For this purpose, the Congress intended that debt instruments that may have the same stated maturity but different rights relating to acceleration of that maturity are to be treated as having different maturities. In addition, the Act provides that to the extent provided in Treasury regulations, equity interests of varying classes that correspond to differing maturity classes of debt are to be treated as debt for these purposes.

96   For example, certain arrangements that are commonly known as "Owners' Trusts" would be treated as TMPs under the Act.

97   If a portion of a REIT is treated as a TMP, such portion may qualify as a REIT subsidiary (see sec. 662 of the Act).

98   *But see* section 860E(a)(2).

99   If the REIT has a REIT subsidiary that is a TMP, then the Congress intended that the portion of the REIT's income that is subject to the special rules is determined based on calculations made at the level of the REIT subsidiary.

100 The Congress intended that in the case of REMICs issued after December 31, 1986, such REMICs and the holders of interest therein would be governed by the provisions of the Act regardless of the taxable years of the holders.

struments issued after December 31, 1986. The provisions relating to taxable mortgage pools do not apply to any entity in existence on December 31, 1991, unless there is a substantial transfer of cash or property to such entity (other than in payment of obligations held by the entity) after such date. For purposes of applying the wash sale rules provided by the Act, however, the definition of a TMP is applicable to any interest in any entity in existence on or after January 1, 1987.

Revenue Effect

The provisions are estimated to decrease fiscal budget receipts by $5 million in 1987, $17 million in 1988, $36 million in 1989, $59 million in 1990, and $79 million in 1991.

TAMRA HOUSE REPORT

House of Representatives, H. Rep. 100-795, 100th Cong., 2d Sess,
TECHNICAL AND MISCELLANEOUS REVENUE ACT OF 1988
(July 26, 1988)

[78]

L.Real Estate Mortgage Investment Conduits (secs. 106(t)-106(v) of the bill, secs. 671-675 of the Reform Act, and secs. 860A-860G and 856 of the Code)

Present Law

Requirements for qualification as a REMIC

To qualify as a real estate mortgage investment conduit ("REMIC"), substantially all of an entity's assets must consist of "qualified mortgages" and "permitted investments" as of the close of the fourth month ending after the "startup day" and each calendar quarter ending thereafter (the "asset test").

A qualified mortgage is an obligation principally secured directly or indirectly by an interest in real property. It is unclear whether loans secured by stock in a cooperative housing corporation and debt instruments that are secured by other debt instruments, which other debt instruments are secured principally by interests in real property, may be treated as qualified mortgages. In general, a qualified mortgage must be transferred to a REMIC on or before the startup day, or purchased by the REMIC within three months of the startup day.

Permitted investments consist of cash flow investments, qualified reserve assets, and foreclosure property. A qualified reserve asset is intangible property which is held for investment and is part of a qualified reserve fund. A qualified reserve fund is any reasonably required reserve to provide for full payment of expenses of the REMIC or amounts due on regular interests in the event of defaults on qualified mortgages.

Foreclosure property is property that would be foreclosure property if acquired by a real estate investment trust ("REIT") and which is acquired in connection with the default of a qualified mortgage. Property ceases to be foreclosure property on the date which is one year after the date the REMIC acquired such property. No tax is imposed on the REMIC with respect to income from foreclosure property.

All interests in the REMIC must be "regular interests" or "residual interests." A regular interest is an interest the terms of which are fixed on the startup day, which unconditionally entitles the holder to receive a specified principal amount, and which provides that interest amounts are payable based on a fixed rate (or a variable rate to the extent provided in Treasury regulations). A residual interest is any interest that is so designated and that is not a regular interest in a REMIC. The startup day is any day selected by the REMIC that is on or before the first day on which regular interests in the REMIC are issued.

[79]

Taxes on the REMIC

A REMIC is required to pay a tax equal to 100 percent of its net income from prohibited transactions. With certain exceptions, a disposition of a qualified mortgage is a prohibited transaction. No exception is provided for the repurchase of a defective mortgage in lieu of its substitution. In addition, any disposition of a cash flow asset is treated as a prohibited transaction.

Taxation of holders of residual interests

Generally, the holder of a residual interest in a REMIC takes into account his daily portion of the taxable income or net loss of such REMIC for each day during which he held such interest. With certain exceptions, the taxable income of a REMIC is determined in the same manner as in the case of an individual.

The taxable income of any holder of a residual interest in a REMIC for any taxable year shall not be less than the excess inclusion for that year. Thrift institutions are excepted from this requirement and therefore may offset excess inclusions with net operating losses. The effect of these rules on affiliated groups is unclear.

If a tax-exempt organization subject to the tax on unrelated business income holds a residual interest, its excess inclusion is treated as unrelated business taxable income. The tax consequences of the holding of a residual interest by a tax-exempt organization which is not subject to the tax on unrelated business taxable income are uncertain.

If a residual interest in a REMIC is held by a REIT, the excess of aggregate excess inclusions over REIT taxable income is allocated to the REIT shareholders in proportion to the dividends received by such shareholders and the amount so allocated is treated as an excess inclusion with respect to each such shareholder.

Signing of return

For procedural purposes, a REMIC is treated as a partnership, and holders of a residual interest are treated as partners. As such, the REMIC is required to file certain returns, which must be signed by a holder of a residual interest.

Other provisions

An interest in a REMIC is treated as a qualifying asset for purposes under sections 593 (d)(4), 856(c)(6)(E) and 7701(a)(19)(C) (xi) in the same proportion that the assets of the REMIC would be treated as qualifying for those purposes. In addition, an entire interest in a REMIC is treated as a qualifying asset under these provisions if 95 percent of the as-

sets in the REMIC would so qualify (the "95-percent test"). The application of the 95-percent test to tiered REMICs is unclear. [80]

Explanation of Provisions

Requirements for qualification as a REMIC

Residual interests held by disqualified organizations

To qualify an entity as a REMIC, the bill provides that there must be reasonable arrangements designed to ensure that residual interests in it are not held by disqualified organizations.[63] Such arrangements include restrictions in the governing instruments of the entity prohibiting disqualified organizations from owning a residual interest in the REMIC and notice to residual interest holders of the existence of such restrictions. Such arrangements would not be deemed to have been made if it is contemplated when the REMIC is formed that disqualified organizations will own residual interests in it. For these purposes, a disqualified organization will not be treated as owning a REMIC residual interest if it has a binding contract to sell the interest on the day it receives the interest and such sale occurs within seven days.

In addition, to qualify as a REMIC, the entity must make available information necessary for the application of the tax on certain transfers of residual interests.[64] Such information would include a computation of the present value of the excess inclusions of a residual interest transferred to a disqualified organization. The REMIC would not fail to satisfy the qualification requirement simply because it charged the person liable for the tax a reasonable fee for providing such information. The failure of such a person to pay such fee will not, however, affect the obligation of the REMIC to provide such information to the Internal Revenue Service.

Application of asset test

The bill makes the asset test continuous after

---

63 For the definition of a disqualified organization, see discussion of tax on certain transfers of residual interests, below.

64 See "Tax on certain transfers of residual interests," below.

the third month. Thus, after the third month, substantially all of a REMIC's assets must, at all times, consist only of qualified mortgages and permitted assets. The asset test, however, does not apply during the qualified liquidation period.

Qualified mortgage

The bill clarifies the definition of a qualified mortgage by requiring that the mortgage be principally secured directly by an interest in real property. Thus, under the bill, debt instruments that are secured by other debt instruments, which other debt instruments are secured principally by interests in real property, may not be treated as qualified mortgages.[65] The bill provides, however, that loans secured principally by stock in a cooperative housing corporation may be treated as qualified mortgages. The bill also provides that, to be treated as a qualified mortgage, an obligation must be transferred to a REMIC on the startup day in exchange for regular or residual interests in the REMIC or purchased by the REMIC [81] within three months of the startup day pursuant to a fixed-price contract in effect on the startup day.[66]

Qualified reserve fund

Under the bill, the definition of a qualified reserve fund is broadened to include reasonably required reserves to provide for full payment of amounts due on regular interests in the event of lower than expected returns on cash flow investments.

Regular interest

Under the bill, the definition of regular interest is broadened to encompass interests which entitle the holder to interest payments consisting of a specified portion of the interest payments on qualified mortgages if such portion does not vary during the period the regular interest is outstanding. The broadening of the definition is intended to permit such interests in a REMIC to qualify as regular interests even if the amount of interest is disproportionate to the specified principal amount.

The bill also provides that a regular interest in a REMIC must be issued on the startup day with fixed terms and must be designated as a regular interest. Under the bill, a residual interest also must be issued on the startup day. Under the bill, the startup day is any day in which the REMIC issues all of its regular and residual interests. In addition, to the extent provided in Treasury regulations, all interests issued and all transfers to the REMIC during any period (not exceeding 10 days) permitted in such regulations may be treated as occurring on the startup day.

Taxes on the REMIC

The bill provides that the repurchase of a defective mortgage in lieu of substitution is not treated as a prohibited transaction even if it occurs more than two years after the startup day. It also provides that the sale of cash flow investments required to prevent defaults on a regular interest where the threatened defaults result from a default on one or more qualified mortgages, or to facilitate a "clean-up call" is not treated as a prohibited transaction.

In addition, if any property is contributed to the REMIC after the startup day, the bill imposes a tax on the REMIC for the taxable year in which the contribution is received equal to 100 percent of the amount (by value) of such contribution. Exceptions to this tax are made for cash contributions made to facilitate a clean-up call or a qualified liquidation, made during the three months following the startup day, or made to a qualified reserve fund by a holder of a residual interest. Also excepted are cash payments in the nature of a guarantee and cash contributions as permitted in Treasury regulations.

A clean-up call is the prepayment of the remaining principal balance of a class of

---

65   A regular interest in a REMIC, which is treated as a debt instrument for Federal income tax purposes, may be treated as a qualified mortgage, however.

66   For this purpose, mortgages may be considered to be purchased pursuant to a fixed-price contract despite the fact that the purchase price may be adjusted where the mortgages are not delivered by the seller on the startup day, provided that the adjustment is in the nature of damages for failure to deliver the mortgages rather than as a result of fluctuations in market price between the startup day and the date of delivery.

regular interests when, by reason of prior payments with respect to those interests, the administrative costs asso[82]ciated with servicing that class outweigh the benefits of maintaining the class. It typically occurs when there is no more than a small percentage of the particular class of interests outstanding. It does not include the retirement of a class undertaken in order to profit from a change in interest rates.

Under the bill, a REMIC is subject to tax at the highest rate applicable to corporations on its "net income from foreclosure property." Net income from foreclosure property is the amount that would be the REMIC's net income for foreclosure property under section 857(b)(4)(B) if the REMIC were a REIT. Thus, if a REMIC acquires foreclosure property and receives amounts with respect to such property that would not be treated as certain types of qualifying income if received by a REIT, then the REMIC would be subject to tax on such amounts. Property eligible for treatment as foreclosure property would be so treated for a period of two years, with possible extensions. The amount of the REMIC's taxable income is reduced by any tax paid with respect to income from foreclosure property.

Taxation of holders of residual interests

Under the bill, the Secretary of the Treasury is granted regulatory authority to determine the taxable income of a REMIC in a manner other than as in the case of an individual. It is intended that this authority be used to permit the REMIC generally to treat bad debts as other than nonbusiness bad debts and, as appropriate, to permit a deduction for capital losses without limitation, but not to take the dividends received deduction. It is also intended that the Secretary of the Treasury use its authority to prevent individuals from using the REMIC election to circumvent their limitations on bad debt and capital loss deductions.[67]

The bill clarifies that all members of an affiliated group are treated as one taxpayer for purposes of the rule requiring that tax-able income be no less than excess inclusions. Thus, net operating losses of the group cannot be used to offset excess inclusions. The bill also clarifies that, except as provided below, the exception for thrift institutions is available only if the institution itself, and not any affiliate of the institution, holds the residual interest. Thus, net operating losses of a thrift institution may offset excess inclusions only in the case of residual interests held by the thrift institution.

Notwithstanding the above, a thrift and a qualified subsidiary will be treated as a single corporation under the excess inclusion rule. Consequently, losses of the thrift institution may offset excess inclusions of the subsidiary. A qualified subsidiary of a thrift institution is any corporation all the stock and substantially all of the debt of which is directly owned by the thrift institution and which is organized and operated exclusively for the purpose of organizing and operating one or more REMICs.

Excess inclusions attributable to residual interests held by regulated investment companies ("RICs"), common trust funds, and subchapter T cooperatives will be allocated to shareholders of such en[83]tities using rules similar to those applied to a REIT and its shareholders.

The bill also clarifies that, with respect to a variable contract (within the meaning of sec. 817), there is no adjustment in the reserve of an insurance company taxable under subchapter L of the Code to the extent of any excess inclusion. Thus, the insurance company would be taxed currently on the excess inclusion.

Tax on certain transfers of residual interests

The bill imposes a tax on any transfer of a residual interest in a REMIC to a disqualified organization. The amount of the tax is equal to the top corporate rate times an amount (determined under Treasury regulations) equal to the present value of the total anticipated excess inclusions with respect to such interests for periods after such transfer. It is expected that such Treasury regulations will provide

---

67   It also is intended that the income from residual interests be treated as portfolio income for purposes of the passive loss rules.

that the amount of the anticipated excess inclusions will be determined based on events which have occurred up to the time of the transfer and the prepayment assumption used to determine the accrual of original issue discount under section 1272(a)(6). It is anticipated that the present value of such amount will be determined on the basis of the applicable Federal rate.

The bill defines a disqualified organization as the United States, any State or political subdivision thereof, any foreign government, any international organization or agency or instrumentality of the foregoing; any tax-exempt entity (other than a section 521 cooperative) not subject to the tax on unrelated business income; and any rural electrical and telephone cooperative. A corporation will not be treated as an instrumentality of the United States or of any State or political subdivision thereof if all of its activities are subject to tax, and, with the exception of the Federal Home Loan Mortgage Corporation, a majority of its board of directors is not selected by such governmental unit.

The tax shall be paid by the transferor or, where the transfer is through an agent of the disqualified organization, such agent. The term "agent" includes a broker, nominee, or other middleman. The transferor, or agent as the case may be, will be relieved of liability for this tax if the trustee furnishes an affidavit that it is not a disqualified organization and the person does not have actual knowledge that the affidavit is false.[68]

In addition, the bill provides that the Secretary of the Treasury has the authority to waive the tax in appropriate circumstances where the disqualified organization no longer holds the residual and the transferor (or agent) pays such amount as the Secretary of the Treasury may require. It is expected that such amount will be based on the amount of excess inclusions which accrued with respect to the residual interest while such interest was held by the disqualified organization.

[84]

Tax on pass-through entities and nominees

If a disqualified organization is a record holder of an interest in a pass-through entity in any taxable year, a tax is imposed on the pass-through entity equal to the amount of excess inclusions allocable to the disqualified organization for such taxable year multiplied by the highest corporate tax rate. The tax is not imposed for any period with respect to which the record holder furnishes to the pass-through entity an affidavit that it is not a disqualified organization, and the entity does not have actual knowledge that the affidavit is false. A pass-through entity is any RIC, REIT, common trust fund, partnership, trust, estate, or subchapter T cooperative. Except as provided in Treasury regulations, a person holding an interest in a pass-through entity as a nominee for another person will be treated as a pass-through entity and the holder of the residual interest in the first pass-through entity will be treated as the record holder in the deemed pass-through entity.

Any tax imposed on a pass-through entity by this provision shall be deductible against the gross amount of ordinary income of the entity. Thus, for example, in the case of a REIT, the tax shall be deductible both in determining real estate investment trust taxable income under section 857 and in determining the REIT's ordinary income under section 4981.

It is contemplated that a pass-through entity seeking to assure holders of its interests that it will not incur this tax will adopt measures preventing it from acquiring residual interests. It is also contemplated that a pass-through entity seeking to invest in residual interests without incurring this tax will adopt measures prohibiting ownership of its interests by disqualified organizations (or, where possible, allocating the tax to such entities). The bill provides delayed effective dates to allow certain large pass-through entities time for the adoption of such amendments.

---

68   It is intended that the provision of a social security number under penalties of perjury would satisfy this requirement since disqualified organizations do not have such numbers. In addition, the provision of an employer identification number belonging to an entity other than a disqualified organization might satisfy this requirement.

Signing of return

The bill clarifies that the REMIC has the obligation to file the REMIC return.[69] Although a REMIC is generally treated as a partnership for procedural purposes, the bill provides that the REMIC return would be required to be signed by any person who could sign the return of the entity in the absence of the REMIC election. Thus, the return of a REMIC which is a corporation or trust would be required to be signed by a corporate officer or a trustee, respectively. For REMICs which consist of segregated pools of assets, the return would be required to be signed by any person who could sign the return of the entity which owns the assets of the REMIC under applicable State law.

Other provisions

The bill clarifies that an interest in a REMIC shall be treated as a real estate asset, and that income from the interest shall be treated as interest on an obligation secured by a mortgage on real property, for REIT qualification purposes under section 856. If less [85] than 95 percent of the assets of the REMIC are real estate assets, the REIT is treated as holding directly its proportionate share of the assets of the REMIC and receiving its proportionate share of the income of the REMIC.

The bill clarifies that, where one REMIC owns interests in a second REMIC, the character of the second REMIC's assets flow through for purposes of determining whether interests in the first REMIC constitute qualifying assets to a building and loan association under section 7701(a)(19).

The bill clarifies that the 95-percent test under sections 593(d)(4), 856(c)(6)(E) and 7701(a)(19)(C)(xi) is applied only once with respect to a REMIC which is part of a tiered structure. Thus, for example, if a REIT owns an interest in a REMIC which owns an interest in a second REMIC, the 95-percent test is applied to the REIT's interest in the first REMIC, but not with respect to the REMIC's interest in the second REMIC. Two REMICs are part of a tiered structure if it was contemplated when both REMICs were formed that some or all of the regular interests of one REMIC would be held by the other.

The bill clarifies that certain provisions relating to REMICs are effective as of January 1, 1987. Thus, for example, interests in a REMIC are eligible to be treated as qualifying assets for a thrift institution, regardless of the institution's taxable year. In addition, the bill makes certain clerical and technical amendments to the statute.

Regulatory authority

The bill also grants authority to the Secretary of the Treasury to provide appropriate rules for the treatment of transfers of qualified replacement mortgages to a REMIC where the transferor holds any interest in the REMIC. It is intended that these regulations may provide rules for determining the basis of mortgages transferred to, or received from, a REMIC as part of a replacement of qualified mortgages, and also may provide rules for determining or adjusting the basis of qualified mortgages held by the REMIC before or after the replacement. In addition, the bill grants authority to the Secretary of the Treasury to provide that a mortgage will be treated as a qualified replacement mortgage only if it is part of a bona fide replacement and is not part of a swap of mortgages. Thus, the Secretary of the Treasury is authorized to issue regulations which prevent a taxpayer from avoiding recognition on the exchange of appreciated mortgages by contributing such mortgages to a REMIC, and then having the REMIC (which will have a fair market value basis in the mortgages), exchange the mortgages for other mortgages.

Effective Dates

In general, the provisions of the bill are effective as of January 1, 1987. The provision relating to the definition of the startup day, the definitions of regular and residual interests, the requirement that qualified mortgages be transferred to the REMIC in exchange for regular or residual interests on the startup day or purchased pursuant to a fixed price contract, and the 100-percent tax on contributions of property to REMICs after the startup

---

69   It is expected that the Internal Revenue Service will issue employer identification numbers to REMICS.

day do not [86] apply to any REMIC whose startup day (as defined under present law) is before July 1, 1987. The provision relating to the asset test for REMICs is effective as of January 1, 1988.

The provision requiring REMICs to adopt reasonable arrangements designed to ensure that residual interests in such entities not be held by disqualified organizations is effective for REMICs formed after March 31, 1988, except for REMICs formed pursuant to a binding written contract (i.e., priced) before that date. The tax on transfers of residual interests generally applies to transfers after March 31, 1988. The tax on pass-through entities would generally apply to excess inclusions after March 31, 1988, except for interests in pass-through entities (and residual interests) acquired before that date. In addition, the tax on pass-through entities would not apply to REITs, RICs, common trust funds and publicly traded partnerships for taxable years beginning before January 1, 1989. Binding contract exceptions are provided to the transfer and pass-through entity taxes. Unless otherwise elected, the provision relating to the filing of returns is effective for REMICs with a startup day after the date of enactment of the bill.

STRIPPED BOND REGULATIONS

§ 1.1286-1 Tax treatment of certain stripped bonds and stripped coupons.

(a) **De minimis OID.**—If the original issue discount determined under section 1286(a) with respect to the purchase of a stripped bond or stripped coupon is less than the amount computed under subparagraphs (A) and (B) of section 1273(a)(3) and the regulations thereunder, then the amount of original issue discount with respect to that purchase (other than any tax-exempt portion thereof, determined under section 1286(d)(2)) shall be considered to be zero. For purposes of this computation, the number of complete years to maturity is measured from the date the stripped bond or stripped coupon is purchased.

(b) **Treatment of certain stripped bonds as market discount bonds.**—(1) In general. By publication in the Internal Revenue Bulletin (see § 601.601(d)(2)(ii)(b) of the Statement of Procedural Rules), the Internal Revenue Service may (subject to the limitation of paragraph (b)(2) of this section) provide that certain mortgage loans that are stripped bonds are to be treated as market discount bonds under section 1278. Thus, any purchaser of such a bond is to account for any discount on the bond as market discount rather than original issue discount.

(2) **Limitation.**—This treatment may be provided for a stripped bond only if, immediately after the most recent disposition referred to in section 1286(b)—(i) the amount of original issue discount with respect to the stripped bond is determined under paragraph (a) of this section (concerning de minimis OID); or (ii) the annual stated rate of interest payable on the stripped bond is no more than 100 basis points lower than the annual stated rate of interest payable on the original bond from which it and any other stripped bond or bonds and any stripped coupon or coupons were stripped.

(c) **Effective date.**—This section is effective on and after August 8, 1991.

TREASURY ENTITY CLASSIFICATION REGULATIONS §§ 301.7701-2–301.7701-4

§ 301.7701-2 Associations.

(a) Characteristics of corporations. (1) The term "association" refers to an organization whose characteristics require it to be classified for purposes of taxation as a corporation rather than as another type of organization such as a partnership or a trust. There are a number of major characteristics ordinarily found in a pure corporation which, taken together, distinguish it from other organizations. These are: (i) Associates, (ii) an objective to carry on business and divided the gains therefrom, (iii) continuity of life, (iv) centralization of management, (v) liability for corporate debts limited to corporate property, and (vi) free transferability of interests. Whether a particular organization is to be classified as an association must be determined by taking into account the presence or absence of each of these corporate characteristics. The presence or absence of these characteristics will depend upon the facts in each individual case. In addition to the major characteristics set forth in this subparagraph, other factors may be found in some cases which may be significant in classifying an organization as an association, a partnership, or a trust. An organization will be treated as an association if the corporate characteristics are such that the organization more nearly resembles a corporation than a partnership or trust. See *Morrissey et al. v. Commissioner* (1935), 296 U.S. 344.

(2) Since associates and an objective to carry on business for joint profit are essential characteristics of all organizations engaged in business for profit (other than the so-called one-man corporation and the sole proprietorship), the absence of either of these essential characteristics will cause an arrangement among co-owners of property for the development of such property for the separate profit of each not to be classified as an association. Some of the major characteristics of a corporation are common to trusts and corporations, and others are common to partnerships and corporations. Characteristics common to trusts and corporations are not material in attempting to distinguish between a trust and an association, and characteristics common to partnerships and corporations are not material in attempting to distinguish between an association and a partnership. For example, since centralization of management, continuity of life, free transferability of interests, and limited liability are generally common to trusts and corporations, the determination of whether a trust which has such characteristics is to be treated for tax purposes as a trust or as an association depends on whether there are associates and an objective to carry on business and divide the gains therefrom. On the other hand, since associates and an objective to carry on business and divide the gains therefrom are generally common to both corporations and partnerships, the determination of whether an organization which has such characteristics is to be treated for tax purposes as a partnership or as an association depends on whether there exists centralization of management, continuity of life, free transferability of interests, and limited liability.

(3) An unincorporated organization shall not be classified as an association unless such organization has more corporate characteristics than noncorporate characteristics. In determining whether an organization has more corporate characteristics than noncorporate characteristics, all characteristics common to both types of organizations shall not be considered. For example, if a limited partnership has centralized management and free transferability of interests but lacks continuity of life and limited liability, and if the limited partnership has no other characteristics which are significant in determining its classification, such limited partnership is not classified as an association. Although the limited partnership also has associates and an objective to carry on

497

business and divide the gains therefrom, these characteristics are not considered because they are common to both corporations and partnerships.

(4) The rules of this section and §§ 301.7701-3 and 301.7701-4 are applicable only to taxable years beginning after December 31, 1960. However, for any taxable year beginning after December 31, 1960, but before October 1, 1961, any amendment of the agreement establishing the organization will, in the case of an organization in existence on November 17, 1960, be treated for purposes of determining the classification of the organization as being in effect as of the beginning of such taxable year (i) if the amendment of the agreement is made before October 1, 1961, and (ii) if the amendment results in the classification of the organization under the rules of this section and §§ 301.7701-1, 301.7701-3, and 301.7701-4 in the same manner as the organization was classified for tax purposes on November 17, 1960. The third sentence of paragraph (b)(1) of this section is applicable to taxable years beginning on or after June 14, 1993. However, a taxpayer may apply the third sentence of paragraph (b)(1) of this section for taxable years beginning before June 14, 1993.

(5) All references in this section to the Uniform Limited Partnership Act shall be deemed to refer both to the original Uniform Limited Partnership Act (adopted in 1916) and to the revised Uniform Limited Partnership Act (adopted by the National Conference of Commissioners on Uniform State Laws in 1976).

(b) Continuity of life. (1) An organization has continuity of life if the death, insanity, bankruptcy, retirement, resignation, or expulsion of any member will not cause a dissolution of the organization. On the other hand, if the death, insanity, bankruptcy, retirement, resignation, or expulsion of any member will cause a dissolution of the organization, continuity of life does not exist. If the death, insanity, bankruptcy, retirement, resignation, expulsion, or other event of withdrawal of a general partner of a limited partnership causes a dissolution of the

partnership, continuity of life does not exist; furthermore, continuity of life does not exist notwithstanding the fact that a dissolution of the limited partnership may be avoided, upon such an event of withdrawal of a general partner, by the remaining general partners agreeing to continue the partnership or by at least a majority in interest of the remaining partners agreeing to continue the partnership. See *Glensder Textile Co.* v. *Commissioner,* 46 B.T.A. 176 (1942) (acq., 1942-1 C.B. 8).

(2) For purposes of this paragraph, dissolution of an organization means an alteration of the identity of an organization by reason of a change in the relationship between its members as determined under local law. For example, since the resignation of a partner from a general partnership destroys the mutual agency which exists between such partner and his copartners and thereby alters the personal relation between the partners which constitutes the identity of the partnership itself, the resignation of a partner dissolves the partnership. A corporation, however, has a continuing identity which is detached from the relationship between its stockholders. The death, insanity, or bankruptcy of a shareholder or the sale of a shareholder's interest has no effect upon the identity of the corporation and, therefore, does not work a dissolution of the organization. An agreement by which an organization is established may provide that the business will be continued by the remaining members in the event of the death or withdrawal of any member, but such agreement does not establish continuity of life if under local law the death or withdrawal of any member causes a dissolution of the organization. Thus, there may be a dissolution of the organization and no continuity of life although the business is continued by the remaining members.

(3) An agreement establishing an organization may provide that the organization is to continue for a stated period or until the completion of a stated undertaking or such agreement may provide for the termination of the organization at will or otherwise. In determining whether any member has the power of dissolution, it will be nec-

essary to examine the agreement and to ascertain the effect of such agreement under local law. For example, if the agreement expressly provides that the organization can be terminated by the will of any member, it is clear that the organization lacks continuity of life. However, if the agreement provides that the organization is to continue for a stated period or until the completion of a stated transaction, the organization has continuity of life if the effect of the agreement is that no member has the power to dissolve the organization in contravention of the agreement. Nevertheless, if, notwithstanding such agreement, any member has the power under local law to dissolve the organization, the organization lacks continuity of life. Accordingly, a general partnership subject to a statute corresponding to the Uniform Partnership Act and a limited partnership subject to a statute corresponding to the Uniform Limited Partnership Act both lack continuity of life.

(c) Centralization of management. (1) An organization has centralized management if any person (or any group of persons which does not include all the members) has continuing exclusive authority to make the management decisions necessary to the conduct of the business for which the organization was formed. Thus, the persons who are vested with such management authority resemble in powers and functions the directors of a statutory corporation. The effective operation of a business organization composed of many members generally depends upon the centralization in the hands of a few of exclusive authority to make management decisions for the organization, and therefore, centralized management is more likely to be found in such an organization than in a smaller organization.

(2) The persons who have such authority may, or may not, be members of the organization and may hold office as a result of a selection by the members from time to time, or may be self-perpetuating in office. See *Morrissey et al. v. Commissioner* (1935), 296 U.S. 344. Centralized management can be accomplished by election to office, by proxy appointment, or by any other means which has the effect of concentrating

in a management group continuing exclusive authority to make management decisions.

(3) Centralized management means a concentration of continuing exclusive authority to make independent business decisions on behalf of the organization which do not require ratification by members of such organization. Thus, there is not centralized management when the centralized authority is merely to perform ministerial acts as an agent at the direction of a principal.

(4) There is no centralization of continuing exclusive authority to make management decisions, unless the managers have sole authority to make such decisions. For example, in the case of a corporation or a trust, the concentration of management powers in a board of directors or trustees effectively prevents a stockholder or a trust beneficiary, simply because he is a stockholder or beneficiary, from binding the corporation or the trust by his acts. However, because of the mutual agency relationship between members of a general partnership subject to a statute corresponding to the Uniform Partnership Act, such a general partnership cannot achieve effective concentration of management powers and, therefore, centralized management. Usually, the act of any partner within the scope of the partnership business binds all the partners; and even if the partners agree among themselves that the powers of management shall be exclusively in a selected few, this agreement will be ineffective as against an outsider who had no notice of it. In addition, limited partnerships subject to a statute corresponding to the Uniform Limited Partnership Act generally do not have centralized management, but centralized management ordinarily does exist in such a limited partnership if substantially all the interests in the partnership are owned by the limited partners. Furthermore, if all or a specified group of the limited partners may remove a general partner, all the facts and circumstances must be taken into account in determining whether the partnership possesses centralized management. A substantially restricted right of the limited partners to remove the general partner (*e.g.*, in the event

of the general partner's gross negligence, self-dealing, or embezzlement) will not itself cause the partnership to possess centralized management.

(d) **Limited liability.** (1) An organization has the corporate characteristic of limited liability if under local law there is no member who is personally liable for the debts of or claims against the organization. Personal liability means that a creditor of an organization may seek personal satisfaction from a member of the organization to the extent that the assets of such organization are insufficient to satisfy the creditor's claim. A member of the organization who is personally liable for the obligations of the organization may make an agreement under which another person, whether or not a member of the organization, assumes such liability or agrees to indemnify such member for any such liability. However, if under local law the member remains liable to such creditors notwithstanding such agreement, there exists personal liability with respect to such member. In the case of a general partnership subject to a statute corresponding to the Uniform Partnership Act, personal liability exists with respect to each general partner. Similarly, in the case of a limited partnership subject to a statute corresponding to the Uniform Limited Partnership Act, personal liability exists with respect to each general partner, except as provided in subparagraph (2) of this paragraph.

(2) In the case of an organization formed as a limited partnership, personal liability does not exist, for purposes of this paragraph, with respect to a general partner when he has no substantial assets (other than his interest in the partnership) which could be reached by a creditor of the organization and when he is merely a "dummy" acting as the agent of the limited partners. Notwithstanding the formation of the organization as a limited partnership, when the limited partners act as the principals of such general partner, personal liability will exist with respect to such limited partners. Also, if a corporation is a general partner, personal liability exists with respect to such general partner when the corporation has substantial assets (other than its in-

terest in the partnership) which could be reached by a creditor of the limited partnership. A general partner may contribute his services, but no capital, to the organization, but if such general partner has substantial assets (other than his interest in the partnership), there exists personal liability. Furthermore, if the organization is engaged in financial transactions which involve large sums of money, and if the general partners have substantial assets (other than their interests in the partnership), there exists personal liability although the assets of such general partners would be insufficient to satisfy any substantial portion of the obligations of the organization. In addition, although the general partner has no substantial assets (other than his interest in the partnership), personal liability exists with respect to such general partner when he is not merely a "dummy" acting as the agent of the limited partners. If the limited partnership agreement provides that a general partner is not personally liable to creditors for the debts of the partnership (other than debts for which another general partner is personally liable), it shall be presumed that personal liability does not exist with respect to that partner unless it is established that the provision is ineffective under local law.

(e) **Free transferability of interests.** (1) An organization has the corporate characteristic of free transferability of interests if each of its members or those members owning substantially all of the interests in the organization have the power, without the consent of other members, to substitute for themselves in the same organization a person who is not a member of the organization. In order for this power of substitution to exist in the corporate sense, the member must be able, without the consent of other members, to confer upon his substitute all the attributes of his interest in the organization. Thus, the characteristic of free transferability of interests does not exist in a case in which each member can, without the consent of other members, assign only his right to share in profits but cannot so assign his rights to participate in the management of the organization. Furthermore, although the agreement provides for the transfer of a member's interest, there is no power of substitution and no free transferability of interest if under local law a transfer of a member's interest results in the dissolution of the old organization and the formation of a new organization.

(2) If each member of an organization can transfer his interest to a person who is not a member of the organization only after having offered such interest to the other members at its fair market value, it will be recognized that a modified form of free transferability of interests exists. In determining the classification of an organization, the presence of this modified corporate characteristic will be accorded less significance than if such characteristic were present in an unmodified form.

(f) **Cross reference.** See paragraph (b) of § 301.7701-3 for the application to limited partnerships of the rules relating to corporate characteristics.

(g) **Examples.** The application of the rules described in this section may be illustrated by the following examples:

Example (1). [Reserved]

Example (2). A group of seven doctors forms a clinic for the purpose of furnishing, for profit, medical and surgical services to the public. They each transfer assets to the clinic, and their agreement provides that except upon complete liquidation of the organization on the vote of three-fourths of its members, no member has any individual interest in its assets. Their agreement also provides that neither the death, insanity, bankruptcy, retirement, resignation, nor expulsion of a member shall cause the dissolution of the organization. However, under the applicable local law, a member who withdraws does have the power to dissolve the organization. While the agreement provides that the management of the clinic is to be vested exclusively in an executive committee of four members elected by all the members, this provision is ineffective as against outsiders who had no notice of it; and, therefore, the act of any member within the scope of the organization's business binds the organization insofar as such outsiders are concerned. While the agreement declares that each individual doctor

alone is liable for acts of malpractice, members of the clinic are, nevertheless, personally liable for all debts of the clinic including claims based on malpractice. No member has the right, without the consent of all the other members, to transfer his interest to a doctor who is not a member of the clinic. The organization has associates and an objective to carry on business and divide the gains therefrom. However, it does not have the corporate characteristics of continuity of life, centralized management, limited liability. and free transferability of interests. The organization will be classified as a partnership for all purposes of the Internal Revenue Code.

Example (3). A group of 25 lawyers forms an organization for the purpose of furnishing, for profit, legal services to the public. Their agreement provides that the organization will dissolve upon the death, insanity, bankruptcy, retirement, or expulsion of a member. While their agreement provides that the management of the organization is to be vested exclusively in an executive committee of five members elected by all the members, this provision is ineffective as against outsiders who had no notice of it; and, therefore, the act of any member within the scope of the organization's business binds the organization insofar as such outsiders are concerned. Members of the organization are personally liable for all debts, or claims against, the organization. No member has the right, without the consent of all the other members, to transfer his interest to a lawyer who is not a member of the organization. The organization has associates and an objective to carry on business and divide the gains therefrom. However, the four corporate characteristics of limited liability, centralized management, free transferability of interests, and continuity of life are absent in this case. The organization will be classified as a partnership for all purposes of the Internal Revenue Code.

Example (4). A group of 25 persons forms an organization for the purpose of engaging in real estate investment activities. Each member has the power to dissolve the organization at any time. The management of the organization is vested exclusively in an executive committee of five members elected by all the members, and under the applicable local law, no one acting without the authority of this committee has the power to bind the organization by his acts. Under the applicable local law, each member is personally liable for the obligations of the organization. Every member has the right to transfer his interest to a person who is not a member of the organization, but he must first advise the organization of the proposed transfer and give it the opportunity on a vote of the majority to purchase the interest at its fair market value. The organization has associates and an objective to carry on business and divide the gains therefrom. While the organization does have the characteristics of centralized management and a modified form of free transferability of interests, it does not have the corporate characteristics of continuity of life and limited liability. Under the circumstances presented, the organization will be classified as a partnership for all purposes of the Internal Revenue Code.

Example (5). A group of 25 persons forms an organization for the purpose of engaging in real estate investment activities. Under their agreement, the organization is to have a life of 20 years, and under the applicable local law, no member has the power to dissolve the organization prior to the expiration of that period. The management of the organization is vested exclusively in an executive committee of five members elected by all the members, and under the applicable local law, no one acting without the authority of this committee has the power to bind the organization by his acts. Under the applicable local law, each member is personally liable for the obligations of the organization. Every member has the right to transfer his interest to a person who is not a member of the organization, but he must first advise the organization of the proposed transfer and give it the opportunity on a vote of the majority to purchase the interest at its fair market value. The organization has associates and an objective to carry on business and divide the gains therefrom. While the organization

does not have the corporate characteristics of limited liability, it does have continuity of life, centralized management, and a modified form of free transferability of interests. The organization will be classified as an association for all purposes of the Internal Revenue Code.

Example (6). A group of 25 persons forms an organization for purposes of engaging in real estate investment activities. Each member has the power to dissolve the organization at any time. The management of the organization is vested exclusively in an executive committee of five members elected by all the members, and under the applicable local law, no one acting without the authority of this committee has the power to bind the organization by his acts. Under the applicable local law, the liability of each member for the obligations of the organization is limited to paid and subscribed capital. Every member has the right to transfer his interest to a person who is not a member of the organization, but he must first advise the organization of the proposed transfer and give it the opportunity on a vote of the majority to purchase the interest at its fair market value. The organization has associates and an objective to carry on business and divide the gains therefrom. While the organization does not have the characteristic of continuity of life, it does have limited liability, centralized management, and a modified form of free transferability of interests. The organization will be classified as an association for all purposes of the Internal Revenue Code.

Example (7). A group of 25 persons forms an organization for the purpose of investing in securities so as to educate the members in principles and techniques of investment practices and to share the income from such investments. While the agreement states that the organization will operate until terminated by a three-fourths vote of the total membership and will not terminate upon the withdrawal or death of any member, under the applicable local law, a member has the power to dissolve the organization at any time. The business of the organization is carried on by the members at regular monthly meetings and buy or sell action may be taken only when voted by a majority of the organization's membership present. Elected officers perform only ministerial functions such as presiding at meetings and carrying out the directions of the members. Members of the organization are personally liable for all debts of, or claims against, the organization. No member may transfer his membership. The organization has associates and an objective to carry on business and divide the gains therefrom. However, the organization does not have the corporate characteristics of limited liability, free transferability of interests, continuity of life, and centralized management. The organization will be treated as a partnership for all purposes of the Internal Revenue Code.

§ 301.7701-3 Partnerships.

(a) In general. The term "partnership" is broader in scope than the common law meaning of partnership and may include groups not commonly called partnerships. Thus, the term "partnership" includes a syndicate, group, pool, joint venture, or other unincorporated organization through or by means of which any business, financial operation, or venture is carried on, and which is not a corporation or a trust or estate within the meaning of the Internal Revenue Code of 1954. A joint undertaking merely to share expenses is not a partnership. For example, if two or more persons jointly construct a ditch merely to drain surface water from their properties, they are not partners. Mere co-ownership of property which is maintained, kept in repair, and rented or leased does not constitute a partnership. For example, if an individual owner, or tenants in common, of farm property lease it to a farmer for a cash rental or a share of the crops, they do not necessarily create a partnership thereby. Tenants in common, however, may be partners if they actively carry on a trade, business, financial operation, or venture and divide the profits thereof. For example, a partnership exists if co-owners of an apartment building lease space and in addition provide services to the occupants either directly or through an agent.

(b) Limited partnerships. (1) In general. An organization which qualifies as a limited partnership under State law may be classified for purposes of the Internal Revenue Code as an ordinary partnership or as an association. Such a limited partnership will be treated as an association if, applying the principles set forth in § 301.7701-2, the organization more nearly resembles a corporation than an ordinary partnership or other business entity.

(2) Examples. The principles of this paragraph may be illustrated by the following examples:

Example (1). Three individuals form an organization which qualifies as a limited partnership under the laws of the State in which the organization was formed. The purpose of the organization is to acquire and operate various pieces of commercial and other investment property for profit. Each of the three individuals who are general partners invests $100,000 in the enterprise. Five million dollars of additional capital is raised through contributions of $100,000 or more by each of 30 limited partners. The three general partners are personally capable of assuming a substantial part of the obligations to be incurred by the organization. While a limited partner may assign his right to receive a share of the profits and a return of his contribution, his assignee does not become a substituted limited partner except with the unanimous consent of the general partners. The life of the organization as stated in the certificate is 20 years, but the death, insanity, or retirement of a general partner prior to the expiration of the 20-year period will dissolve the organization. The general partners have exclusive authority to manage the affairs of the organization but can act only upon the unanimous consent of all of them. The organization has associates and an objective to carry on business and divide the gains therefrom, which characterize both partnerships and corporations. While the organization has the corporate characteristic of centralized management, since substantially all of the interests in the organization are owned by the limited partners, it does not have the characteristics of continuity of life, free transferability of interests, or limited liability. The organization will be classified as a partnership for all purposes of the Internal Revenue Code.

Example (2). Three individuals form an organization which qualifies as a limited partnership under the laws of the State in which the organization was formed. The purpose of the organization is to acquire and operate various pieces of commercial and other investment property for profit. The certificate provides that the life of the organization is to be 40 years, unless a general partner dies, becomes insane, or retires during such period. On the occurrence of such death, insanity, or retirement, the remaining general partners may continue the business of the partnership for the balance of the 40-year period under a right so to do stated in the certificate. Each of the three individuals who is a general partner invests $50,000 in the enterprise and has means to satisfy the business obligations of the organization to a substantial extent. Five million dollars of additional capital is raised through the sale of freely transferable interests in amounts of $10,000 or less to limited partners. Nine hundred such interests are sold. The interests of the 900 limited partners are fully transferable, that is, a transferee acquires all the attributes of the transferor's interest in the organization. The general partners have exclusive control over management of the business, their interests are not transferable, and their liability for debts of the organization is not limited to their capital contributions. The organization has associates and an objective to carry on business and divide the gains therefrom. It does not have the corporate characteristics of limited liability and continuity of life. It has centralized management, however, since the three general partners exercise exclusive control over the management of the business, and since substantially all of the interests in the organization are owned by the limited partners. While the interests of the general partners are not transferable, the transferability test of an association is met since substantially all of the interests in the organization are represented by transferable interests. The organization will be classified as a partnership for all purposes of the Internal Revenue Code.

(c) Partnership associations. The laws of a number of States provide for the formation of organizations commonly known as partnership associations. Such a partnership association will be treated as an association if, applying the principles set forth in § 301.7701-2, the organization more nearly resembles a corporation than the other types of business entities.

(d) Partner. The term "partner" means a member of a partnership.

§ 301.7701-4 Trusts.

(a) Ordinary trusts. In general, the term "trust" as used in the Internal Revenue Code refers to an arrangement created either by a will or by an inter vivos declaration whereby trustees take title to property for the purpose of protecting or conserving it for the beneficiaries under the ordinary rules applied in chancery or probate courts. Usually the beneficiaries of such a trust do no more than accept the benefits thereof and are not the voluntary planners or creators of the trust arrangement. However, the beneficiaries of such a trust may be the persons who create it and it will be recognized as a trust under the Internal Revenue Code if it was created for the purpose of protecting or ...serving the trust property for beneficiaries who stand in the same relation to the trust as they would if the trust had been created by others for them. Generally speaking, an arrangement will be treated as a trust under the Internal Revenue Code if it can be shown that the purpose of the arrangement is to vest in trustees responsibility for the protection and conservation of property for beneficiaries who cannot share in the discharge of this responsibility and, therefore, are not associates in a joint enterprise for the conduct of business for profit.

(b) Business trusts. There are other arrangements which are known as trusts because the legal title to property is conveyed to trustees for the benefit of beneficiaries, but which are not classified as trusts for purposes of the Internal Revenue Code because they are not simply arrangements to protect or conserve the property for the beneficiaries. These trusts, which are often known as business or commercial trusts, generally are created by the beneficiaries simply as a device to carry on a profit-making business which normally would have been carried on through business organizations that are classified as corporations or partnerships under the Internal Revenue Code. However, the fact that the corpus of the trust is not supplied by the beneficiaries is not sufficient reason in itself for classifying the arrangement as an ordinary trust rather than as an association or partnership. The fact that any organization is technically cast in the trust form, by conveying title to property to trustees for the benefit of persons designated as beneficiaries, will not change the real character of the organization if, applying the principles set forth in §§ 301.7701-2 and 301.7701-3, the organization more nearly resembles an association or a partnership than a trust.

(c) **Certain investment trusts.** (1) An "investment" trust will not be classified as a trust if there is a power under the trust agreement to vary the investment of the certificate holders. *See Commissioner v. North American Bond Trust*, 122 F.2d 545 (2d Cir. 1941), *cert. denied*, 314 U.S. 701 (1942). An investment trust with a single class of ownership interests, representing undivided beneficial interests in the assets of the trust, will be classified as a trust if there is no power under the trust agreement to vary the investment of the certificate holders. An investment trust with multiple classes of ownership interests will ordinarily be classified as an association or a partnership under § 301.7701-2; however, an investment trust with multiple classes of ownership interests, in which there is no power under the trust agreement to vary the investment of the certificate holders, will be classified as a trust if the trust is formed to facilitate direct investment in the assets of the trust and the existence of multiple classes of ownership interests is incidental to that purpose.

(2) The provisions of paragraph (c)(1) of this section may be illustrated by the following examples:

Example (1). A corporation purchases a portfolio of residential mortgages and transfers the mortgages to a bank under a trust agreement. At the same time, the bank as trustee delivers to the corporation certificates evidencing rights to payments from the pooled mortgages; the corporation sells the certificates to the public. The trustee holds legal title to the mortgages in the pool for the benefit of the certificate holders but has no power to reinvest proceeds attributable to the mortgages in the pool or to vary investments in the pool in any other manner. There are two classes of certificates. Holders of class A certificates are entitled to all payments of mortgage principal, both scheduled and prepaid, until their certificates are retired; holders of class B certificates receive payments of principal only after all class A certificates have been retired. The different rights of the class A and class B certificates serve to shift to the holders of the class A certificates, in addition to the earlier scheduled payments of principal, the risk that mortgages in the pool will be prepaid so that the holders of the class B certificates will have "call protection" (freedom from premature termination of their interests on account of prepayments). The trust thus serves to create investment interests with respect to the mortgages held by the trust that differ significantly from direct investment in the mortgages. As a consequence, the existence of multiple classes of trust ownership is not incidental to any purpose of the trust to facilitate direct investment, and accordingly, the trust is classified as an association or a partnership under § 301.7701-2.

Example (2). Corporation M is the originator of a portfolio of residential mortgages and transfers the mortgages to a bank under a trust agreement. At the same time, the bank as trustee delivers to M certificates evidencing rights to payments from the pooled mortgages. The trustee holds legal title to the mortgages in the pool for the benefit of the certificate holders, but has no power to reinvest proceeds attributable to the mortgages in the pool or to vary investments in the pool in any other manner. There are two classes of certificates. Holders of class C certificates are entitled to receive 90 percent of the payments of principal and interest on the mortgages; class D certificate holders are entitled to receive the other ten percent. The two classes of certificates are identical except that, in the event of a default on the underlying mortgages, the payment rights of class D certificate holders are subordinated to the rights of class C certificate holders. M sells the class C certificates to investors and retains the class D certificates. The trust has multiple classes of ownership interests, given the greater security provided to holders of class C certificates. The interests of certificate holders, however, are substantially equivalent to undivided interests in the pool of mortgages, coupled with a limited recourse guarantee running from M to the holders of class C certificates. In such circumstances, the existence of multiple classes of ownership interests is incidental to the trust's purpose of facilitating direct investment in the assets of the trust. Accordingly, the trust is classified as a trust.

Example (3). A promoter forms a trust in which shareholders of a publicly traded corporation can deposit their stock. For each share of stock deposited with the trust, the participant receives two certificates that are initially attached, but may be separated and traded independently of each other. One certificate represents the right to dividends and the value of the underlying stock up to a specified amount; the other certificate represents the right to appreciation in the stock's value above the specified amount. The separate certificates represent two different classes of ownership interest in the trust, which effectively separate dividend rights on the stock held by the trust from a portion of the right to appreciation in the value of such stock. The multiple classes of ownership interests are designed to permit investors, by transferring one of the certificates and retaining the other, to fulfill their varying investment objectives of seeking primarily either dividend income or capital appreciation from the stock held by the trust. Given that the trust serves to create investment interests with respect to the stock held by the trust that differ significantly from direct investment in such stock,

the trust is not formed to facilitate direct investment in the assets of the trust. Accordingly, the trust is classified as an association or a partnership under § 301.7701-2.

Example (4). Corporation N purchases a portfolio of bonds and transfers the bonds to a bank under a trust agreement. At the same time, the trustee delivers to N certificates evidencing interests in the bonds. These certificates are sold to public investors. Each certificate represents the right to receive a particular payment with respect to a specific bond. Under section 1286, stripped coupons and stripped bonds are treated as separate bonds for federal income tax purposes. Although the interest of each certificate holder is different from that of each other certificate holder, and the trust thus has multiple classes of ownership. the multiple classes simply provide each certificate holder with a direct interest in what is treated under section 1286 as a separate bond. Given the similarity of the interests acquired by the certificate holders to the interests that could be acquired by direct investment, the multiple classes of trust interests merely facilitate direct investment in the assets held by the trust. Accordingly, the trust is classified as a trust.

(d) Liquidating trusts. Certain organizations which are commonly known as liquidating trusts are treated as trusts for purposes of the Internal Revenue Code. An organization will be considered a liquidating trust if it is organized for the primary purpose of liquidating and distributing the assets transferred to it, and if its activities are all reasonably necessary to, and consistent with, the accomplishment of that purpose. A liquidating trust is treated as a trust for purposes of the Internal Revenue Code because it is formed with the objective of liquidating particular assets and not as an organization having as its purpose the carrying on of a profit-making business which normally would be conducted through business organizations classified as corporations or partnerships. However, if the liquidation is unreasonably prolonged or if the liquidation purpose becomes so obscured by business activities that the declared purpose of liquidation can be said to be lost or abandoned, the status of the organization will no longer be that of a liquidating trust. Bondholders' protective committees, voting trusts, and other agencies formed to protect the interests of security holders during insolvency, bankruptcy, or corporate reorganization proceedings are analogous to liquidating trusts but if subsequently utilized to further the control or profitable operation of a going business on a permanent continuing basis, they will lose their classification as trusts for purposes of the Internal Revenue Code.

PREAMBLE TO FINAL SEARS REGULATIONS (T.D. 8080)

Classification of Investment Trusts with Multiple Classes of Ownership

EXPLANATION OF PROVISIONS

Section 301.7701-4(c) of the Regulations on Procedure and Administration provides guidance as to the classification for federal tax purposes of certain "investment" trusts. Before its amendment by this Treasury decision, those regulations (the "prior regulations") classified an entity of the type known as a "fixed investment trust" as a trust or as an association (taxable as a corporation), depending upon whether the governing instrument created a power to vary the investment of the certificate holders. The prior regulations did not address whether an investment trust that permitted investors to choose among different classes of ownership interests with varying investment attributes would be classified as a trust for federal tax purposes.

In general, a trust for federal tax purposes is limited to a trust created simply to conserve or protect property for the trust beneficiaries. Ordinarily, the beneficiaries of the trust do no more than accept its benefits and are not its creators or voluntary planners. Certain "investment" trusts, however, are recognized as serving the traditional custodial purposes of an ordinary trust even though interests therein are voluntarily acquired by the beneficiaries. Thus, investment trusts have been treated as trusts for federal tax purposes where employed simply to hold investment assets, albeit for the benefit of voluntary investors. *Commissioner v. Chase National Bank*, 122 F.2d 450 (2d Cir. 1941).

Historically, the issue of whether an investment trust serves the mere custodial purpose of holding investment assets has focused on whether the beneficiaries' investment was fixed or could instead be varied under the terms of the trust agreement. The existence of a power to vary the beneficiaries' investment, even though only contingent in form, is sufficient to "turn the venture into a 'business.'" *Commissioner v. North American Bond Trust*, 122 F.2d 545, 546 (2d Cir. 1941), *cert. denied*, 314 U.S. 701 (1942). Thus, the prior regulations limited trust classification to "fixed investment trusts" where there was no power under the trust agreement to vary the investment of the certificate holders.

Recently, new forms of investment trusts have been created that involve not only voluntary acquisition of interest by investors but also different classes of beneficial interests with varying investment attributes. These so called "multiple class trusts" vest no discretionary power in the trustee over investment of the trust assets and thus assertedly satisfy the fixed investment requirement of the prior regulations. At the time the prior regulations were first promulgated, however, the entities commonly known as fixed investment trusts had only one class of investment certificates. The certificates represented undivided interests in the trust property, and were, in form, receipts for the securities held by the trust.[*] Thus, where the trustee had no power to vary investment, a fixed investment trust was little more than a depository arrangement, formed to hold a pool of specific investment assets. Although the trust device permitted individual investors to diversify investment risk, the arrangement in substance provided a form of direct, if common, ownership of the trust assets. This use of a trust to hold investment assets and thereby facilitate direct investment by a pool of investors is consistent with the custodial purposes that have traditionally limited trust classification.

---

[*] "The investor [in a fixed trust] . . . has a beneficial undivided interest in specific deposited securities or property. . . . In the fixed trust . . . only one class of security is issued—the certificate of beneficial interest which is, in form, a receipt issued by the trustee for the deposited property." Investment Trusts and Investment Companies, H.R. Doc. 567, 76th Cong., 3d Sess. 8-9 (1940) (footnote omitted).

Multiple class trusts depart from the traditional form of fixed investment trust in that the interests of the beneficiaries are not undivided, but diverse. The existence of varied beneficial interests may indicate that the trust is not employed simply to hold investment assets, but serves a significant additional purpose of providing investors with economic and legal interests that could not be acquired through direct investment in the trust assets. Such use of an investment trust introduces the potential for complex allocations of trust income among investors, with correspondingly difficult issues of how such income is to be allocated for tax purposes. These issues are properly foreign to the taxation of trust income, where rules have not developed to accommodate the varied forms of commercial investment, and no comprehensive economic substance requirement governs the allocation of income for tax purposes.

Based on the above considerations, proposed amendments to prior § 301.7701-4 would have denied trust classification to investment trusts with multiple classes of ownership. Generally, the final regulations retain this rule. However, in response to public comment, the proposed regulations have been modified to provide that trust classification may be appropriate for a multiple class trust if the trust is formed to serve the traditional custodial purposes of a fixed investment trust and the existence of multiple classes of beneficial interests is incidental to such purposes.

Thus, under the standard contained in the final regulations, the classification of multiple class trusts depends on the purposes for which the trust is formed, and the significance of multiple classes of ownership interests in relation to those purposes. A fixed investment trust with multiple classes of ownership interests, that otherwise possesses the characteristics of a trust, would be classified as a trust if the trust is employed to facilitate direct investment in the assets of the trust, and the existence of multiple classes of ownership interests is incidental to such purpose. Whether the exist-

ence of multiple classes of ownership interests is incidental to the use of an investment trust as a vehicle to facilitate direct investment, or instead reflects a purpose to provide investors with diverse interests in the trust assets, generally depends on the extent to which the investment attributes of interests in the trust diverge from direct ownership of the trust assets. The extent of such divergence may, in turn, be reflected by the extent to which the interests of the investors in a multiple class trust could be reproduced without resort to multiple classes of ownership. For example, the creation of a subordinated and preferred class of interests in a trust holding real estate mortgages may be incidental to the purpose of the trust to facilitate direct investment in the mortgages, where the subordinated interest is retained as a security device by the originator of the mortgages, and is in lieu of a direct guarantee to investors. The final regulations provide additional examples of the classification of investment trusts with multiple classes of ownership interests. Further guidance as to the application of the new standard will be provided through the administrative rulings process.

The final regulations apply only to investment trusts, and hence have no applicability to trusts that would be classified as "ordinary trusts" under existing § 301.7701-4(a) or "business trusts" under existing § 301.7701-4(b). Moreover, the final regulations are not intended to affect existing standards for classification of fixed investment trusts with a single class of ownership interests.

On May 17, 1984, the Internal Revenue Service announced that the final regulations would not apply to certain state and local government financing arrangements the substance of which is the issuance of a series of separate debt obligations directly by the governmental unit (Announcement 84-62, 1984-24 I.R.B. 29). The Internal Revenue Service will treat those financing arrangements in accordance with that announcement.

PROPOSED TAXABLE MORTGAGE POOL REGULATIONS

(1) In general.
(2) Governmental purpose.
(3) Determinations by the Commissioner.
(b) REITs. (Reserved)
(c) Subchapter S corporations.
(1) In general.
(2) Portion of an S corporation treated as a separate corporation.

§ 301.7701(i)-1 Definition of a taxable mortgage pool.

(a) **Purpose.** This section provides rules for applying section 7701(i), which defines taxable mortgage pools. The purpose of section 7701(i) is to prevent income generated by a pool of real estate mortgages from escaping Federal income taxation when the pool is used to issue multiple class mortgage-backed securities. The regulations in this section and in §§ 301.7701(i)-2 through 301.7701(i)-4 are to be applied in accordance with this purpose. The taxable mortgage pool provisions apply to entities that qualify for REMIC status but do not elect to be taxed as REMICs as well as to certain entities or portions of entities that do not qualify for REMIC status.

(b) **In general—**

(1) A taxable mortgage pool is any entity or portion of an entity (as defined in § 301.7701(i)-2) that satisfies the requirements of section 7701(i)(2)(A) and this section as of any testing day, as defined in § 301.7701(i)-3(c)(1). An entity or portion of an entity satisfies the requirements of section 7701(i)(2)(A) and this section if substantially all of its assets are debt obligations, more than 50 percent of those debt obligations are real estate mortgages, the entity is the obligor under debt obligations with two or more maturities, and payments on the debt obligations under which the entity is obligor bear a relationship to payments on the debt obligations the entity holds as assets.

(2) Paragraph (c) of this section provides the tests for determining whether substantially all of an entity's assets are debt obligations and for determining whether

more than 50 percent of its debt obligations are real estate mortgages. Paragraph (d) of this section defines real estate mortgages for purposes of the 50 percent test. Paragraph (e) of this section defines "two or more maturities" and paragraph (f) of this section provides rules for determining when debt obligations "bear a relationship" to the assets held by an entity. Paragraph (g) of this section provides anti-avoidance rules. Section 301.7701(i)-2 provides rules for applying section 7701(i) to portions of entities and § 301.7701(i)-3 provides effective dates. Section 301.7701(i)-4 provides special rules for certain entities. For purposes of the regulations under section 7701(i), any reference to "entity" includes a reference to "portion of an entity" within the meaning of section 7701(i)(2)(B), unless the context clearly indicates otherwise.

(c) **Asset composition tests—**

(1) **Determination of amount of assets.** An entity must use the Federal income tax basis of an asset for purposes of determining whether substantially all of its assets consist of debt obligations (or interests therein) and whether more than 50 percent of those debt obligations (or interests) consist of real estate mortgages (or interests therein).

(2) **Substantially all—**

(i) **In general.** Whether substantially all of the assets of an entity consist of debt obligations (or interests therein) is based on all the facts and circumstances.

(ii) **Safe harbor.** Notwithstanding paragraph (c)(2)(i) of this section, if less than 80 percent of the assets of an entity consist of debt obligations (or interests therein), then less than substantially all of the assets of the entity consist of debt obligations (or interests therein).

(3) **Equity interests in pass-through arrangements.** The equity interest of an entity in a partnership, S corporation, trust, REIT, or other pass-through arrangement is deemed to have the same composition as the entity's share of the assets of the pass-through arrangement. For example, if an entity's stock interest in a REIT has an ad-

justed basis of $20,000, and the assets of the REIT consist of equal portions of real estate mortgages and other real estate assets, then the entity is treated as holding $10,000 of real estate mortgages and $10,000 of other real estate assets.

(4) Treatment of certain credit enhancement contracts—

(i) In general. A credit enhancement contract (as defined in paragraph (c)(4)(ii) of this section) is not treated as a separate asset of an entity for purposes of the asset composition tests set forth in section 7701(i)(2)(A)(i), but instead is treated as part of the asset to which it relates. Furthermore, any collateral supporting a credit enhancement contract is not treated as an asset of an entity solely because it supports the guarantee represented by that contract.

(ii) Credit enhancement contract defined. For purposes of this section, a credit enhancement contract is any arrangement whereby a person agrees to guarantee full or partial payment of the principal or interest payable on a debt obligation (or interest therein) or on a pool of such obligations (or interests), or full or partial payment on one or more classes of debt obligations under which an entity is the obligor, in the event of defaults or delinquencies on debt obligations, unanticipated losses or expenses incurred by the entity, or lower than expected returns on investments. Types of credit enhancement contracts may include, but are not limited to, pool insurance contracts, certificate guarantee insurance contracts, letters of credit, guarantees, or agreements whereby an entity, a mortgage servicer, or other third party agrees to make advances (regardless of whether, under the terms of the agreement, the payor is obligated, or merely permitted, to make those advances). An agreement by a debt servicer to advance to an entity out of its own funds an amount to make up for delinquent payments on debt obligations is a credit enhancement contract. An agreement by a debt servicer to pay taxes and hazard insurance premiums on property securing a debt obligation, or other expenses incurred to protect an entity's security interests in the collateral in the event that the debtor fails to pay such taxes, insurance premium, or other expenses, is a credit enhancement contract.

(5) Certain assets not treated as debt obligations—

(i) In general. For purposes of section 7701(i)(2)(A), real estate mortgages that are seriously impaired are not treated as debt obligations. Whether a mortgage is seriously impaired is based on all the facts and circumstances.

(ii) Safe harbors. Single family residential real estate mortgages are seriously impaired if payments on the mortgages are more than 89 days delinquent. Multi-family residential and commercial real estate mortgages are seriously impaired if payments on the mortgages are more than 59 days delinquent. However, this paragraph (c)(5)(ii) does not apply if an entity is receiving, or anticipates receiving—

(A) Any payments on the obligation as defined in paragraph (f)(2)(i) of this section if those payments are substantial and relatively certain as to amount; or

(B) Any payments on the obligation as defined in paragraph (f)(2) (ii) or (iii) of this section.

(d) Real estate mortgages or interests therein defined—

(1) In general. For purposes of section 7701(i)(2)(A)(i), the term "real estate mortgages (or interests therein)" includes all—

(i) Obligations (including participations or certificates of beneficial ownership therein) that are principally secured by an interest in real property (as defined in paragraph (d)(3) of this section);

(ii) Regular and residual interests in a REMIC; and

(iii) Stripped bonds and stripped coupons (as defined in section 1286(e)(2) and (3)) if the bonds (as defined in section 1286(e)(1)) from which such stripped bonds or stripped coupons arose would have qualified as real estate mortgages or interests therein.

(2) Interests in real property and real property defined—

(i) In general. The definition of

"interests in real property" set forth in § 1.856-3(c) and the definition of "real property" set forth in § 1.856-3(d) apply to define those terms for purposes of paragraph (d) of this section.

(ii) **Manufactured housing.** For purposes of this section, the definition of "real property" includes manufactured housing, provided the properties qualify as single family residences under section 25(e)(10) and without regard to the treatment of the properties under state law.

(3) **Principally secured by an interest in real property—**

(i) **Tests for determining whether an obligation is principally secured.** For purposes of paragraph (d)(1) of this section, an obligation is principally secured by an interest in real property only if it satisfies either the test set in paragraph (d)(3)(i)(A) of this section or the test set out in paragraph (d)(3)(i)(B) of this section.

(A) **The 80 percent test.** An obligation is principally secured by an interest in real property if the fair market value of the interest in real property (as defined in paragraph (d)(2) of this section) securing the obligation was at least equal to 80 percent of the adjusted issue price of the obligation at the time the obligation was originated. For purposes of this test, the fair market value of the real property interest is first reduced by the amount of any lien on the real property interest that is senior to the obligation being tested, and is reduced further by a proportionate amount of any lien that is in parity with the obligation being tested.

(B) **Alternative test.** An obligation is principally secured by an interest in real property if substantially all of the proceeds of the obligation were used to acquire, improve, or protect an interest in real property that, at the origination date, is the only security for the obligation. For purposes of this test, loan guarantees made by Federal, state, local governments or agencies, or other third party credit enhancement, are not viewed as additional security for a loan. An obligation is not considered to be secured by property other than real

property solely because the obligor is personally liable on the obligation.

(ii) **Obligations secured by other obligations.** Obligations secured by other obligations are treated as principally secured by interests in real property if the underlying obligations are principally secured by interests in real property. Thus, for example, a collateralized mortgage obligation may be an obligation principally secured by an interest in real property. This section is applicable only to obligations issued after December 31, 1991.

(e) **Two or more maturities—**

(1) **In general.** For purposes of section 7701(i)(2)(A)(ii), debt obligations have two or more maturities if they have different stated maturities or if the holders of the obligations possess different rights concerning the acceleration of or delay in the maturities of the obligations.

(2) **Obligations that are allocated credit risk unequally.** Debt obligations that are allocated credit risk unequally do not have, by that reason alone, two or more maturities. Credit risk is the risk that payments of principal or interest will be reduced or delayed because of a default on an asset that supports the debt obligations.

(3) **Examples.** The following examples illustrate the principles of this paragraph (e).

Example 1

(i) Corporation M transfers a pool of real estate mortgages to a trustee in exchange for Class A bonds and a certificate representing the residual beneficial ownership of the pool. All Class A bonds have a stated maturity of March 1, 2002, but if cash flows from the real estate mortgages and investments are sufficient, the trustee may select one or more bonds at random and redeem them earlier.

(ii) The Class A bonds do not have different maturities. Each outstanding Class A bond has an equal chance of being redeemed because the selection process is random. The holders of the Class A bonds, therefore, have identical rights concerning the maturities of their obligations.

Example 2

(i) Corporation N transfers a pool of real estate mortgages to a trustee in exchange for Class C bonds, Class D bonds, and a certificate representing the residual beneficial ownership of the pool. The Class D bonds are subordinate to the Class C bonds so that cash flow shortfalls due to defaults or delinquencies on the real estate mortgages are borne first by the Class D bond holders. The terms of the bonds are otherwise identical in all relevant aspects except that the Class D bonds carry a higher coupon rate because of the subordination feature.

(ii) The Class C bonds and the Class D bonds share credit risk unequally because of the subordination feature. However, neither this difference, nor the difference in interest rates, causes the bonds to have different maturities. The result is the same if, in addition to the other terms described in paragraph (i) of this Example 1, the Class C bonds are accelerated as a result of the issuer becoming unable to make payments on the Class C bonds as they become due.

(f) Relationship test—

(1) In general. For purposes of section 7701(i)(2)(A)(iii), payments on debt obligations under which an entity is the obligor (liability obligations) "bear a relationship" to payments (as defined in paragraph (f)(2) of this section) on debt obligations an entity holds as assets (asset obligations) if under the terms of the liability obligations (or underlying arrangement) the timing and amount of payments on the liability obligations are in large part determined by the timing and amount of payments or projected payments on the asset obligations. For purposes of the relationship test, any payment arrangement that achieves a substantially similar result is treated as satisfying the test. For example, any arrangement where the timing and amount of payments on liability obligations are determined by reference to a group of assets (or an index or other type of model) that has an expected payment experience similar to that of the asset obligations is treated as satisfying the relationship test.

(2) Payments on asset obligations defined. For purposes of section 7701(i)(2)(A)(iii) and this section, payments on asset obligations include—

(i) Payments of principal and interest on asset obligations, including prepayments of principal and payments under credit enhancement contracts (as defined in § 301.7701(i)-1(c)(4)(ii)), but excluding settlements at a substantial discount;

(ii) Payments from settlements at a substantial discount and foreclosures on asset obligations if the settlement or foreclosure was arranged, whether in writing or otherwise, prior to the issuance of the liability obligations; and

(iii) Proceeds from sales of asset obligations, if the sales were arranged, whether in writing or otherwise, prior to the issuance of the liability obligations.

(3) Safe harbor for entities formed to liquidate assets. Payments on liability obligations of an entity do not bear a relationship to payments on asset obligations of the entity if—

(i) The entity's organizational documents manifest clearly that the entity is formed for the primary purpose of liquidating its assets and distributing proceeds of liquidation;

(ii) The entity's activities are all reasonably necessary to and consistent with the accomplishment of liquidating assets;

(iii) The entity plans to satisfy at least 50 percent of the total issue price of each of its liability obligations having a different maturity with proceeds from liquidation and not with scheduled payments on its asset obligations; and

(iv) The terms of the entity's liability obligations or other arrangement provide that either the entity liquidates within three years of the time it first acquires assets to be liquidated or, if the entity does not liquidate within that time, the payments the entity receives on its asset obligations after that time are paid through to the holders of its liability obligations in proportion to their adjusted issue prices.

(g) Anti-avoidance rules—

(1) In general. For purposes of determining whether an entity meets the definition of a taxable mortgage pool, the Commissioner may disregard or make other adjustments to a transaction (or series of transactions) if the transaction (or series) is entered into with a view to achieving the same economic effect as that of an arrangement subject to section 7701(i) while avoiding the application of that section. The Commissioner's authority includes treating equity interests issued by a non-REMIC as debt if the entity issues equity interests that correspond to maturity classes of debt.

(2) **Certain investment trusts.** Notwithstanding paragraph (g)(1) of this section, an ownership interest in an entity that is classified as a trust under § 301.7701-4(c) will not be treated as a debt obligation of the trust.

(3) **Examples.** The following examples illustrate the principles of this paragraph (g).

Example 1.

(i) Partnership P, in addition to its other investments, owns $10,000,000 of mortgage pass-through certificates guaranteed by FNMA (FNMA Certificates). On May 15, 1997, Partnership P transfers the FNMA Certificates to Trust 1 in exchange for 100 Class A bonds and Certificate 1. The Class A bonds, under which Trust 1 is the obligor, have a stated principal amount of $5,000,000 and bear a relationship to the FNMA Certificates (within the meaning of § 301.7701(i)-1(f)). Certificate 1 represents the residual beneficial ownership of the FNMA Certificates.

(ii) On July 5, 1997, with a view to avoiding the application of section 7701(i), Partnership P transfers Certificate 1 to Trust 2 in exchange for 100 Class B bonds and Certificate 2. The Class B bonds, under which Trust 2 is the obligor, have a stated principal amount of $5,000,000, bear a relationship to the FNMA Certificates (within the meaning of § 301.7701(i)-1(f)), and have a different maturity than the Class A bonds (within the meaning of § 301.7701(i)-1(e)). Certificate 2 represents the residual beneficial ownership of Certificate 1.

(iii) For purposes of determining whether Trust 1 is classified as a taxable mortgage pool, the Commissioner may disregard the separate existence of Trust 2 and treat Trust 1 and Trust 2 as a single trust.

Example 2.

(ii) Corporation Q files a consolidated return with its two wholly-owned subsidiaries, Corporation R and Corporation S. Corporation R is in the business of building and selling single family homes. Corporation S is in the business of financing sales of those homes.

(ii) On August 10, 1998, Corporation S transfers a pool of its real estate mortgages to Trust 3, taking back Certificate 3 which represents beneficial ownership of the pool. On September 25, 1998, with a view to avoiding the application of section 7701(i), Corporation R issues bonds that have different maturities (within the meaning of § 301.7701(i)-1(e)) and that bear a relationship (within the meaning of § 301.7701(i)-1(f)) to the real estate mortgages in Trust 3. The holders of the bonds have an interest in a credit enhancement contract that is written by Corporation S and collateralized with Certificate 3.

(iii) For purposes of determining whether Trust 3 is classified as a taxable mortgage pool, the Commissioner may treat Trust 3 as the obligor of the bonds issued by Corporation R.

Example 3

(i) Corporation X, in addition to its other assets, owns $110,000,000 in Treasury securities. From time to time, Corporation X acquires pools of real estate mortgages, which it immediately uses to issue multiple-class debt obligations.

(ii) On October 1, 1996, Corporation X transfers $11,000,000 in Treasury securities to Trust 4 in exchange for Class C bonds, Class D bonds, Class E bonds, and Certificate 4. Trust 4 is the obligor of the bonds. The different classes of bonds have the same stated maturity date, but if cash flows from the Trust 4 assets exceed the amounts needed to make interest payments, the trustee uses the excess to retire the classes of bonds in alphabetical order.

Certificate 4 represents the residual beneficial ownership of the Treasury securities.

(iii) With a view to avoiding the application of section 7701(i), Corporation X reserves the right to replace any Trust 4 asset with real estate mortgages or guaranteed mortgage pass-through certificates. In the event the right is exercised, cash flows on the real estate mortgages and guaranteed pass-through certificates will be used in the same manner as cash flows on the Treasury securities. Corporation X exercises this right of replacement on February 1, 1997.

(iv) For purposes of determining whether Trust 4 is classified as a taxable mortgage pool, the Commissioner may treat February 1, 1997, as a testing day (within the meaning of § 301.7701(i)-3(c)(1)). The result is the same if Corporation X has an obligation, rather than a right, to replace the Trust 4 assets with real estate mortgages and guaranteed pass-through certificates.

§ 301.7701(i)-2 Special rules for portions of entities.

(a) **Portion defined.** Except as provided in paragraph (b) of this section and § 301.7701(i)-1, a portion of an entity includes all assets that support one or more of the same issues of debt obligations. For this purpose, an asset supports a debt obligation if, under the terms of the debt obligation (or underlying arrangement), the timing and amount of payments on the debt obligation are in large part determined, either directly or indirectly, by the timing and amount of payments or projected payments on the asset or a group of assets that includes the asset. Indirect payment arrangements include, for example, arrangements where the timing and amount of payments on the debt obligations are determined by reference to an index that has an expected payment experience similar to that of the assets. For purposes of this paragraph, the term "payments" includes all proceeds and receipts from an asset.

(b) **Certain assets and rights to assets disregarded—**

(1) **Credit enhancement assets.** A portion does not include assets that primarily serve the same function as credit enhancement contracts.

(2) **Assets unlikely to service obligations.** A portion does not include assets that are unlikely to produce any significant cash flows for the holders of the debt obligations. This paragraph applies even if the holders of the debt obligations are legally entitled to cash flows from the assets. Thus, for example, even if the sale of a building causes a series of debt obligations to be redeemed, the building is not included in a portion if it is not likely to be sold.

(3) **Recourse.** An asset is not included in a portion solely because the holders of the debt obligations have recourse to the holder of that asset.

(c) **Portion as obligor.** For purposes of section 7701(i)(2)(A)(ii), a portion of an entity is treated as the obligor of all debt obligations supported by the assets in that portion.

(d) **Example.** The following example illustrates the principles of this section.

Example

(i) Corporation Z owns $1,000,000,000 in assets including an office complex and $90,000,000 of real estate mortgages.

(ii) On November 30, 1998, Corporation Z issues eight classes of bonds, Class A through Class H. Each class is secured by a separate letter of credit and by a lien on the office complex. One group of the real estate mortgages supports Class A through Class D, another group supports Class E through Class G, and a third group supports Class H. It is anticipated that the cash flows from each group of mortgages will service its related bonds.

(iii) Each of the following constitutes a separate portion of Corporation Z: the group of mortgages supporting Class A through Class D; the group of mortgages supporting Class E through Class G; and the group of mortgages supporting Class H. No other asset is included in any of the three portions notwithstanding the lien of the bonds on the office complex and the fact that Corporation Z is the issuer of the bonds. The letters of credit are treated as incidents of the mortgages to which they relate.

(iv) For purposes of section 7701(i)(2)(A)(ii), each portion described above is treated as the obligor of the bonds of that portion, notwithstanding the fact that Corporation Z is the legal obligor with respect to the bonds.

§ 301.7701(i)-3 Effective dates and duration of taxable mortgage pool classification.

(a) **Effective dates.** Except as otherwise provided, the regulations under section 7701(i) are effective and applicable (insert date that is thirty days after this regulation is published as a Final Regulation).

(b) **Entities in existence on December 31, 1991—**

(1) **In general.** For transitional rules concerning the application of section 7701(i) to entities in existence on December 31, 1991, see section 675(c) of the Tax Reform Act of 1986.

(2) **Special rule for certain transfers.** A transfer made to an entity on or after (insert date that is thirty days after this regulation is published as a Final Regulation) is a substantial transfer for purposes of section 675(c)(2) of the Tax Reform Act of 1986 only if— (i) The transfer is significant in amount; and (ii) The transfer is connected to the entity's issuance of related debt obligations (as defined in paragraph (b)(3) of this section) that have different maturities (within the meaning of § 301.7701-1(e)).

(3) **Related debt obligation.** A related debt obligation is one whose payments bear a relationship (within the meaning of § 301.7701-1(f)) to payments on debt obligations that the entity holds as assets.

(4) **Example.** The following example illustrates the principles of this paragraph (b).

Example. On December 31, 1991, Partnership Q holds a pool of real estate mortgages that it acquired through retail sales of single family homes.

Partnership Q raises $10,000,000 on Oc-

tober 25, 1996, by using this pool to issue related debt obligations with multiple maturities. The transfer of the $10,000,000 to Partnership Q is a substantial transfer within the meaning of § 301.7701(i)-3(b)(2).

(c) **Duration of taxable mortgage pool classification—**

(1) **Commencement.** An entity is classified as a taxable mortgage pool on the first testing day that it meets the definition of a taxable mortgage pool. A "testing day" is any day on or after (insert date that is thirty days after this regulation is published as a Final Regulation), on which an entity issues a related debt obligation (as defined in paragraph (b)(3) of this section) that is significant in amount.

(2) **Termination.** Once an entity is classified as a taxable mortgage pool, that classification continues through the day the entity retires its last related debt obligation.

(d) **Section 708(b)(1)(B) terminations.** An entity is not treated as issuing a related debt obligation solely because the entity is terminated pursuant to section 708(b)(1)(B).

§ 301.7701(i)-4 Special rules for certain entities.

(a) **States and Municipalities—**

(1) **In general.** Regardless of whether an entity satisfies any of the requirements of section 7701(i)(2)(A), an entity is not classified as a taxable mortgage pool if—

(i) The entity is a State, the District of Columbia, or a political subdivision within the meaning of § 1.103-1(b), or is empowered to issue obligations on behalf of one of the foregoing;

(ii) The entity issues the debt obligations in the performance of a governmental purpose; and

(iii) Until the debt obligations issued by the entity are satisfied, the entity holds the remaining interest in any asset that supports those debt obligations.

(2) **Governmental purpose.** The term "governmental purpose" means an essential governmental function within the meaning of section 115. A governmental

purpose does not include the mere packaging of debt obligations for re-sale on the secondary market even if any profits from the sale are used in the performance of an essential governmental function.

(3) **Determinations by the Commissioner.** If an entity is not described in paragraph (a)(1) of this section, but has a similar purpose, then the Commissioner may determine that the entity is not classified as a taxable mortgage pool.

(b) **REITs. (Reserved)**

(c) **Subchapter S corporations—**

(1) **In general.** An entity that is classified as a taxable mortgage pool may not elect to be an S corporation under section 1362(a) or maintain S corporation status.

(2) **Portion of an S corporation treated as a separate corporation.** An S corporation is not treated as a member of an affiliated group under section 1361(b)(2)(A) solely because a portion of the S corporation is treated as a separate corporation under section 7701(i).

REMIC REGULATIONS

(1) In general.
(2) Income tax return.
(c) Signing of REMIC return.
   (1) In general.
   (2) REMIC whose startup day is before November 10, 1988.
      (i) In general.
      (ii) Startup day.
      (iii) Exception.
(d) Designation of tax matters person.
(e) Notice to holders of residual interests.
   (1) Information required.
      (i) In general.
      (ii) Information with respect to REMIC assets.
         (A) 95 percent asset test.
         (B) Additional information required if the 95 percent test not met.
         (C) For calendar quarters in 1987.
         (D) For calendar quarters in 1988 and 1989.
      (iii) Special provisions.
   (2) Quarterly notice required.
      (i) In general.
      (ii) Special rule for 1987.
   (3) Nominee reporting.
      (i) In general.
      (ii) Time for furnishing statement.
   (4) Reports to the Internal Revenue Service.
(f) Information returns for persons engaged in a trade or business.

§ 1.860G-1 Definition of regular and residual interests.

(a) Regular interest.
   (1) Designation as a regular interest.
   (2) Specified portion of the interest payments on qualified mortgages.
      (i) In general.
      (ii) Specified portion cannot vary.
      (iii) Defaulted or delinquent mortgages.
      (iv) No minimum specified principal amount is required.
      (v) Examples.
   (3) Variable rate.
      (i) Rate based on index.

      (ii) Weighted average rate.
         (A) In general.
         (B) Reduction in underlying rate.
      (iii) Additions, subtractions, and multiplications.
      (iv) Caps and floors.
      (v) Funds-available caps.
         (A) In general.
         (B) Facts and circumstances test.
         (C) Examples.
      (vi) Combination of rates.
   (4) Fixed terms on the startup day.
   (5) Contingencies prohibited.
(b) Special rules for regular interests.
   (1) Call premium.
   (2) Customary prepayment penalties received with respect to qualified mortgages.
   (3) Certain contingencies disregarded.
      (i) Prepayments, income, and expenses.
      (ii) Credit losses.
      (iii) Subordinated interests.
      (iv) Deferral of interest.
      (v) Prepayment interest shortfalls.
      (vi) Remote and incidental contingencies.
   (4) Form of regular interest.
   (5) Interest disproportionate to principal.
      (i) In general.
      (ii) Exception.
   (6) Regular interest treated as a debt instrument for all Federal income tax purposes.
(c) Residual interest.
(d) Issue price of regular and residual interests.
   (1) In general.
   (2) The public.

§ 1.860G-2 Other rules.

(a) Obligations principally secured by an interest in real property.
   (1) Tests for determining whether an obligation is principally secured.
      (i) The 80-percent test.

§ 1.860G-3 Treatment of foreign persons.

§ 1.860A-1 Effective dates and transition rules.

(a) In general. Except as otherwise provided in paragraph (b) of this section, the regulations under sections 860A through 860G are effective only for a qualified entity (as defined in § 1.860D-1(c)(3)) whose startup day (as defined in section 860G(a)(9) and § 1.860G-2(k)) is on or after November 12, 1991.

(b) Exceptions—(1) Reporting regulations—(i) Sections 1.860D-1(c)(1) and (3), and § 1.860D-1(d)(1) through (3) are effective after December 31, 1986.

(ii) Sections 1.860F-4(a) through (e) are effective after December 31, 1986 and are applicable after that date except as follows:

(A) Section 1.860F-4(c)(1) is effective for REMICs with a startup day on or after November 10, 1988.

(B) Sections 1.860F-4(e)(1)(ii)(A) and (B) are effective for calendar quarters and calendar years beginning after December 31, 1988.

(C) Section 1.860F-4(e)(1)(ii)(C) is effective for calendar quarters and calendar years beginning after December 31, 1986 and ending before January 1, 1988.

(D) Section 1.860F-4(e)(1)(ii)(D) is effective for calendar quarters and calendar years beginning after December 31, 1987 and ending before January 1, 1990.

(2) Tax avoidance rules—(i) Transfers of certain residual interests. Section 1.860E-1(c) (concerning transfers of noneconomic residual interests) and § 1.860G-3(a)(4) (concerning transfers by a foreign holder to a United States person) are effective for transfers of residual interests on or after September 27, 1991.

(ii) Transfers to foreign holders. Generally, § 1.860G-3(a) (concerning transfers of residual interests to foreign holders) is effective for transfers of residual interests after April 20, 1992. However, § 1.860G-3(a) does not apply to a transfer of a residual interest in a REMIC by the REMIC's sponsor (or by another transferor contemporaneously with formation of the REMIC) on or before June 30, 1992, if—

(A) The terms of the regular interests and the prices at which regular interests were offered had been fixed on or before April 20, 1992;

(B) On or before June 30,

1992, a substantial portion of the regular interests in the REMIC were transferred, with the terms and at the prices that were fixed on or before April 20, 1992, to investors who were unrelated to the REMIC's sponsor at the time of the transfer; and

(C) At the time of the transfer of the residual interest, the expected future distributions on the residual interest were equal to at least 30 percent of the anticipated excess inclusions (as defined in § 1.860E-2(a)(3)), and the transferor reasonably expected that the transferee would receive sufficient distributions from the REMIC at or after the time at which the excess inclusions accrue in an amount sufficient to satisfy the taxes on the excess inclusions.

(iii) Residual interests that lack significant value. The significant value requirement in § 1.860E-1(a)(1) and (3) (concerning excess inclusions accruing to organizations to which section 593 applies) generally is effective for residual interests acquired on or after September 27, 1991. The significant value requirement in § 1.860E-1(a)(1) and (3) does not apply, however, to residual interests acquired by an organization to which section 593 applies as a sponsor at formation of a REMIC in a transaction described in § 1.860F-2(a)(1) if more than 50 percent of the interests in the REMIC (determined by reference to issue price) were sold to unrelated investors before November 12, 1991. The exception from the significant value requirement provided by the preceding sentence applies only so long as the sponsor owns the residual interests.

(3) Excise taxes. Section 1.860E-2(a)(1) is effective for transfers of residual interests to disqualified organizations after March 31, 1988. Section 1.860E-2(b)(1) is effective for excess inclusions accruing to pass-thru entities after March 31, 1988.

§ 1.860C-1 Taxation of holders of residual interests.

(a) Pass-thru of income or loss. Any holder of a residual interest in a REMIC must take into account the holder's daily portion of the taxable income or net loss of the REMIC for each day during the taxable year on which the holder owned the residual interest.

(b) Adjustments to basis of residual interests—

(1) Increase in basis. A holder's basis in a residual interest is increased by—

(i) The daily portions of taxable income taken into account by that holder under section 860C(a) with respect to that interest; and

(ii) The amount of any contribution described in section 860G(d)(2) made by that holder.

(2) Decrease in basis. A holder's basis in a residual interest is reduced (but not below zero) by—

(i) First, the amount of any cash or the fair market value of any property distributed to that holder with respect to that interest; and

(ii) Second, the daily portions of net loss of the REMIC taken into account under section 860C(a) by that holder with respect to that interest.

(3) Adjustments made before disposition. If any person disposes of a residual interest, the adjustments to basis prescribed in paragraph (b)(1) and (2) of this section are deemed to occur immediately before the disposition.

(c) Counting conventions. For purposes of determining the daily portion of REMIC taxable income or net loss under section 860C(a)(2), any reasonable convention may be used. An example of a reasonable convention is "30 days per month/90 days per quarter/360 days per year."

§ 1.860C-2 Determination of REMIC taxable income or net loss.

(a) Treatment of gain or loss. For purposes of determining the taxable income or net loss of a REMIC under section 860C(b), any gain or loss from the disposition of any asset, including a qualified mortgage (as defined in section 860G(a)(3)) or a permitted investment (as defined in section 860G(a)(5) and § 1.860G-2(g)), is treated as gain or loss from the sale or exchange of property that is not a capital asset.

(b) Deductions allowable to a REMIC—

(1) In general. Except as otherwise provided in section 860C(b) and in paragraph (b)(2) through (5) of this section, the deductions allowable to a REMIC for purposes of determining its taxable income or net loss are those deductions that would be allowable to an individual, determined by taking into account the same limitations that apply to an individual.

(2) Deduction allowable under section 163. A REMIC is allowed a deduction, determined without regard to section 163(d), for any interest expense accrued during the taxable year.

(3) Deduction allowable under section 166. For purposes of determining a REMIC's bad debt deduction under section 166, debt owed to the REMIC is not treated as nonbusiness debt under section 166(d).

(4) Deduction allowable under section 212. A REMIC is not treated as carrying on a trade or business for purposes of section 162. Ordinary and necessary operating expenses paid or incurred by the REMIC during the taxable year are deductible under section 212, without regard to section 67. Any expenses that are incurred in connection with the formation of the REMIC and that relate to the organization of the REMIC and the issuance of regular and residual interests are not treated as expenses of the REMIC for which a deduction is allowable under section 212. See § 1.860F-2(b)(3)(ii) for treatment of those expenses.

(5) Expenses and interest relating to tax-exempt income. Pursuant to section 265(a), a REMIC is not allowed a deduction for expenses and interest allocable to tax-exempt income. The portion of a REMIC's interest expense that is allocable to tax-exempt interest is determined in the manner prescribed in section 265(b)(2), without regard to section 265(b)(3).

§ 1.860D-1 Definition of a REMIC.

(a) In general. A real estate mortgage investment conduit (or REMIC) is a qualified entity, as defined in paragraph (c)(3) of this section, that satisfies the requirements of section 860D(a). See paragraph (d)(1) of this section for the manner of electing REMIC status.

(b) Specific requirements—

(1) Interests in a REMIC—

(i) **In general.** A REMIC must have one class, and only one class, of residual interests. Except as provided in paragraph (b)(1)(ii) of this section, every interest in a REMIC must be either a regular interest (as defined in section 860G(a)(1) and § 1.860G-1(a)) or a residual interest (as defined in section 860G(a)(2) and § 1.860G-1(c)).

(ii) **De minimis interests.** If, to facilitate the creation of an entity that elects REMIC status, an interest in the entity is created and, as of the startup day (as defined in section 860G(a)(9) and § 1.860G-2(k)), the fair market value of that interest is less than the lesser of $1,000 or 1/1,000 of one percent of the aggregate fair market value of all the regular and residual interests in the REMIC, then, unless that interest is specifically designated as an interest in the REMIC, the interest is not treated as an interest in the REMIC for purposes of section 860D(a)(2) and (3) and paragraph (B)(1)(i) of this section.

(2) Certain rights not treated as interests. Certain rights are not treated as interests in a REMIC. Although not an exclusive list, the following rights are not interests in a REMIC.

(i) **Payments for services.** The right to receive from the REMIC payments that represent reasonable compensation for services provided to the REMIC in the ordinary course of its operation is not an interest in the REMIC. Payments made by the REMIC in exchange for services may be expressed as a specified percentage of interest payments due on qualified mortgages or as a specified percentage of earnings from permitted investments. For example, a mortgage servicer's right to receive reasonable compensation for servicing the mortgages owned by the REMIC is not an interest in the REMIC.

(ii) **Stripped interests.** Stripped bonds or stripped coupons not held by the REMIC are not interests in the REMIC even if, in a transaction preceding or contemporaneous with the formation of the REMIC, they and the REMIC's qualified mortgages were created from the same mortgage obligation. For example, the right of a mortgage servicer to receive a servicing fee in excess of reasonable compensation from payments it receives on mortgages held by a REMIC is not an interest in the REMIC. Further, if an obligation with a fixed principal amount provides for interest at a fixed or variable rate and for certain contingent payment rights (e.g., a shared appreciation provision or a percentage of mortgagor profits provision), and the owner of the obligation contributes the fixed payment rights to a REMIC and retains the contingent payment rights, the retained contingent payment rights are not an interest in the REMIC.

(iii) **Reimbursement rights under credit enhancement contracts.** A credit enhancer's right to be reimbursed for amounts advanced to a REMIC pursuant to the terms of a credit enhancement contract (as defined in § 1.860G-2 (c)(2)) is not an interest in the REMIC even if the credit enhancer is entitled to receive interest on the amounts advanced.

(iv) **Rights to acquire mortgages.** The right to acquire or the obligation to purchase mortgages and other assets from a REMIC pursuant to a clean-up call (as defined in § 1.860G-2(j)) or a qualified liquidation (as defined in section 860F(a)(4)), or on conversion of a convertible mortgage (as defined in § 1.860G-2(d)(5)), is not an interest in the REMIC.

(3) Asset test.

(i) **In general.** For purposes of the asset test of section 860D(a)(4), substantially all of a qualified entity's assets are qualified mortgages and permitted investments if the qualified entity owns no more than a de minimis amount of other assets.

(ii) **Safe harbor.** The amount of assets other than qualified mortgages and permitted investments is de minimis if the aggregate of the adjusted bases of those assets is less than one percent of the aggregate of the adjusted bases of all of the REMIC's assets. Nonetheless, a qualified entity that does not meet this safe harbor may demonstrate that it owns no more than a de minimis amount of other assets.

(4) Arrangements test. Generally, a qualified entity must adopt reasonable arrangements designed to ensure that —

(i) Disqualified organizations (as defined in section 860E(e)(5)) do not hold residual interests in the qualified entity; and

(ii) If a residual interest is acquired by a disqualified organization, the qualified entity will provide to the Internal Revenue Service, and to the persons specified in section 860E(e)(3), information needed to compute the tax imposed under section 860E(e) on transfers of residual interests to disqualified organizations.

(5) Reasonable arrangements—

(i) Arrangements to prevent disqualified organizations from holding residual interests. A qualified entity is considered to have adopted reasonable arrangements to ensure that a disqualified organization (as defined in section 860E(e)(5)) will not hold a residual interest if—

(A) The residual interest is in registered form (as defined in § 5f.103-1(c) of this chapter); and

(B) The qualified entity's organizational documents clearly and expressly prohibit a disqualified organization from acquiring beneficial ownership of a residual interest, and notice of the prohibition is provided through a legend on the document that evidences ownership of the residual interest or through a conspicuous statement in a prospectus or private offering document used to offer the residual interest for sale.

(ii) **Arrangements to ensure that information will be provided.** A qualified entity is considered to have made reasonable arrangements to ensure that the Internal Revenue Service and persons specified in section 860E(e)(3) as liable for the tax imposed under section 860E(e) receive the information needed to compute the tax if the qualified entity's organizational documents require that it provide to the Internal Revenue Service and those persons a computa-

tion showing the present value of the total anticipated excess inclusions with respect to the residual interest for periods after the transfer. See § 1.860E-2(a)(5) for the obligation to furnish information on request.

(6) Calendar year requirement. A REMIC's taxable year is the calendar year. The first taxable year of a REMIC begins on the startup day and ends on December 31 of the same year. If the startup day is other than January 1, the REMIC has a short first taxable year.

(c) Segregated pool of assets —

(1) Formation of REMIC. A REMIC may be formed as a segregated pool of assets rather than as a separate entity. To constitute a REMIC, the assets identified as part of the segregated pool must be treated for all Federal income tax purposes as assets of the REMIC and interests in the REMIC must be based solely on assets of the REMIC.

(2) Identification of assets. Formation of the REMIC does not occur until —

(i) The sponsor identifies the assets of the REMIC, such as through execution of an indenture with respect to the assets; and

(ii) The REMIC issues the regular and residual interests in the REMIC.

(3) Qualified entity defined. For purposes of this section, the term "qualified entity" includes an entity or a segregated pool of assets within an entity.

(d) Election to be treated as a real estate mortgage investment conduit —

(1) In general. A qualified entity, as defined in paragraph (c)(3) of this section, elects to be treated as a REMIC by timely filing, for the first taxable year of its existence, a Form 1066, U.S. Real Estate Mortgage Investment Conduit Income Tax Return, signed by a person authorized to sign that return under § 1.860F-4(c). See § 1.9100-1 for rules regarding extensions of time for making elections. Once made, this election is irrevocable for that taxable year and all succeeding taxable years.

(2) Information required to be reported in the REMIC's first taxable year. For the first taxable year of the REMIC's existence, the qualified entity, as defined in paragraph (c)(3) of this section, must provide either on its return or in a separate statement attached to its return.

(i) The REMIC's employer identification number, which must not be the same as the identification number of any other entity.

(ii) Information concerning the terms and conditions of the regular interests and the residual interest of the REMIC, or a copy of the offering circular or prospectus containing such information.

(iii) A description of the prepayment and reinvestment assumptions that are made pursuant to section 1272(a)(6) and the regulations thereunder, including a statement supporting the selection of the prepayment assumption.

(iv) The form of the electing qualified entity under State law or, if an election is being made with respect to a segregated pool of assets within an entity, the form of the entity that holds the segregated pool of assets, and

(v) Any other information required by the form.

(3) **Requirement to keep sufficient records.** A qualified entity, as defined in paragraph (c)(3) of this section, that elects to be a REMIC must keep sufficient records concerning its investments to show that it has complied with the provisions of sections 860A through 860G and the regulations thereunder.

§ 1.860E-1 Treatment of taxable income of a residual interest holder in excess of daily accruals.

(a) **Excess inclusion cannot be offset by otherwise allowable deductions—**

(1) **In general.** Except as provided in paragraph (a)(3) of this section, the taxable income of any holder of a residual interest for any taxable year is in no event less than the sum of the excess inclusions attributable to that holder's residual interests for that taxable year. In computing the amount of a net operating loss (as defined in section 172(c)) or the amount of any net operating loss carryover (as defined in section 172(b)(2)), the amount of any excess inclu-

sion is not included in gross income or taxable income. Thus, for example, if a residual interest holder has $100 of gross income, $25 of which is an excess inclusion, and $90 of business deductions, the holder has taxable income of $25, the amount of the excess inclusion, and a net operating loss of $15 ($75 of other income - $90 of business deductions).

(2) **Affiliated groups.** If a holder of a REMIC residual interest is a member of an affiliated group filing a consolidated income tax return, the taxable income of the affiliated group cannot be less than the sum of the excess inclusions attributable to all residual interests held by members of the affiliated group.

(3) **Special rule for certain financial institutions—**

(i) **In general.** If an organization to which section 593 applies holds a residual interest that has significant value (as defined in paragraph (a)(3)(iii) of this section), section 860E(a)(1) and paragraph (a)(1) of this section do not apply to that organization with respect to that interest. Consequently, an organization to which section 593 applies may use its allowable deductions to offset an excess inclusion attributable to a residual interest that has significant value, but, except as provided in section 860E(a)(4)(A), may not use its allowable deductions to offset an excess inclusion attributable to a residual interest held by any other member of an affiliated group, if any, of which the organization is a member. Further, a net operating loss of any other member of an affiliated group of which the organization is a member may not be used to offset an excess inclusion attributable to a residual interest held by that organization.

(ii) **Ordering rule—**

(A) **In general.** In computing taxable income for any year, an organization to which section 593 applies is treated as having applied its allowable deductions for the year first to offset that portion of its gross income that is not an excess inclusion and then to offset that portion of its income that is an excess inclusion.

(B) **Example.** The following example illustrates the provisions of paragraph (a)(3)(ii) of this section: Example. Corp. X, a corporation to which section 593 applies, is a member of an affiliated group that files a consolidated return. For a particular taxable year, Corp. X has gross income of $1,000, and of this amount, $150 is an excess inclusion attributable to a residual interest that has significant value. Corp. X has $975 of allowable deductions for the taxable year. Corp. X must apply its allowable deductions first to offset the $850 of gross income that is not an excess inclusion, and then to offset the portion of its gross income that is an excess inclusion. Thus, Corp. X has $25 of taxable income ($1,000-$975), and that $25 is an excess inclusion that may not be offset by losses sustained by other members of the affiliated group.

(iii) **Significant value.** A residual interest has significant value if—

(A) The aggregate of the issue prices of the residual interests in the REMIC is at least 2 percent of the aggregate of the issue prices of all residual and regular interests in the REMIC; and

(B) The anticipated weighted average life of the residual interests is at least 20 percent of the anticipated weighted average life of the REMIC.

(iv) **Determining anticipated weighted average life—**

(A) **Anticipated weighted average life of the REMIC.** The anticipated weighted average life of a REMIC is the weighted average of the anticipated weighted average lives of all classes of interests in the REMIC. This weighted average is determined under the formula in paragraph (a)(3)(iv)(B) of this section, applied by treating all payments taken into account in computing the anticipated weighted average lives of regular and residual interests in the REMIC as principal payments on a single regular interest.

(B) **Regular interests that have a specified principal amount.** Generally, the anticipated weighted average life of a regular interest is determined by multiplying the amount of each anticipated principal payment to be made on the interest by the number of years (including fractions thereof) from the startup day (as defined in

section 860G(a)(9) and § 1.860G-2(k)) to the related principal payment date; adding the results; and dividing the sum by the total principal paid on the regular interest.

(C) **Regular interests that have no specified principal amount or that have only a nominal principal amount, and all residual interests.** If a regular interest has no specified principal amount, or if the interest payments to be made on a regular interest are disproportionately high relative to its specified principal amount (as determined by reference to § 1.860G-1(b)(5)(i)), then, for purposes of computing the anticipated weighted average life of the interest, all anticipated payments on that interest, regardless of their designation as principal or interest, must be taken into account in applying the formula set out in paragraph (a)(3)(iv)(B) of this section. Moreover, for purposes of computing the weighted average life of a residual interest, all anticipated payments on that interest, regardless of their designation as principal or interest, must be taken into account in applying the formula set out in paragraph (a)(3)(iv)(B) of this section.

(D) **Anticipated payments.** The anticipated principal payments to be made on a regular interest subject to paragraph (a)(3)(iv)(B) of this section, and the anticipated payments to be made on a regular interest subject to paragraph (a)(3)(iv)(C) of this section or on a residual interest, must be determined based on the prepayment and reinvestment assumptions adopted under § 1272(a)(6), or that would have been adopted had the REMIC's regular interests been issued with original issue discount; and any required or permitted clean up calls or any required qualified liquidation provided for in the REMIC's organizational documents.

(b) **Treatment of residual interests held by REITs, RICs, common trust funds, and subchapter T cooperatives.** [Reserved]

(c) **Transfers of noneconomic residual interests—**

(1) **In general.** A transfer of a noneconomic residual interest is disregarded for all Federal tax purposes if a significant purpose of the transfer was to enable the trans-

feror to impede the assessment or collection of tax. A significant purpose to impede the assessment or collection of tax exists if the transferor, at the time of the transfer, either knew or should have known (had "improper knowledge") that the transferee would be unwilling or unable to pay taxes due on its share of the taxable income of the REMIC.

(2) **Noneconomic residual interest.** A residual interest is a noneconomic residual interest unless, at the time of the transfer—

(i) The present value of the expected future distributions on the residual interest at least equals the product of the present value of the anticipated excess inclusions and the highest rate of tax specified in section 11(b)(1) for the year in which the transfer occurs; and

(ii) The transferor reasonably expects that, for each anticipated excess inclusion, the transferee will receive distributions from the REMIC at or after the time at which the taxes accrue on the anticipated excess inclusion in an amount sufficient to satisfy the accrued taxes.

(3) **Computations.** The present value of the expected future distributions and the present value of the anticipated excess inclusions must be computed under the procedure specified in § 1.860E-2(a)(4) for determining the present value of anticipated excess inclusions in connection with the transfer of a residual interest to a disqualified organization.

(4) **Safe harbor for establishing lack of improper knowledge.** A transferor is presumed not to have improper knowledge if—

(i) The transferor conducted, at the time of the transfer, a reasonable investigation of the financial condition of the transferee and, as a result of the investigation, the transferor found that the transferee had historically paid its debts as they came due and found no significant evidence to indicate that the transferee will not continue to pay its debts as they come due in the future; and

(ii) The transferee represents to the transferor that it understands that, as the holder of the noneconomic residual interest, the transferee may incur tax liabilities in excess of any cash flows generated by the interest and that the transferee intends to pay taxes associated with holding the residual interest as they become due.

(d) **Transfers to foreign persons.** Paragraph (c) of this section does not apply to transfers of residual interests to which § 1.860G-3(a)(1), concerning transfers to certain foreign persons, applies.

§ 1.860E-2 Tax on transfers of residual interests to certain organizations.

(a) **Transfers to disqualified organizations —**

(1) **Payment of tax.** Any excise tax due under section 860E(e)(1) must be paid by the later of March 24, 1993, or April 15th of the year following the calendar year in which the residual interest is transferred to a disqualified organization. The Commissioner may prescribe rules for the manner and method of collecting the tax.

(2) **Transitory ownership.** For purposes of section 860E (e) and this section, a transfer of a residual interest to a disqualified organization in connection with the formation of a REMIC is disregarded if the disqualified organization has a binding contract to sell the interest and the sale occurs within 7 days of the startup day (as defined in section 860G(a)(9) and § 1.860G-2(k)).

(3) **Anticipated excess inclusions.** The anticipated excess inclusions are the excess inclusions that are expected to accrue in each calendar quarter (or portion thereof) following the transfer of the residual interest. The anticipated excess inclusions must be determined as of the date the residual interest is transferred and must be based on—

(i) Events that have occurred up to the time of the transfer;

(ii) The prepayment and reinvestment assumptions adopted under section 1272(a)(6), or that would have been adopted had the REMIC's regular interests been issued with original issue discount; and

(iii) Any required or permitted clean-up calls, or required qualified liquidation provided for in the REMIC's organizational documents.

(4) Present value computation. The present value of the anticipated excess inclusions is determined by discounting the anticipated excess inclusions from the end of each remaining calendar quarter in which those excess inclusions are expected to accrue to the date the disqualified organization acquires the residual interest. The discount rate to be used for this present value computation is the applicable Federal rate (as specified in section 1274(d)(1)) that would apply to a debt instrument that was issued on the date the disqualified organization acquired the residual interest and whose term ended on the close of the last quarter in which excess inclusions were expected to accrue with respect to the residual interest.

(5) Obligation of REMIC to furnish information. A REMIC is not obligated to determine if its residual interests have been transferred to a disqualified organization. However, upon request of a person designated in section 860E(e)(3), the REMIC must furnish information sufficient to compute the present value of the anticipated excess inclusions. The information must be furnished to the requesting party and to the Internal Revenue Service within 60 days of the request. A reasonable fee charged to the requestor is not income derived from a prohibited transaction within the meaning of section 860F(a).

(6) Agent. For purposes of section 860E(e)(3), the term "agent" includes a broker (as defined in § 6045(c) and § 1.6045-1(a)(1)), nominee, or other middleman.

(7) Relief from liability—

(i) Transferee furnishes information under penalties of perjury. For purposes of section 860E(e)(4), a transferee is treated as having furnished an affidavit if the transferee furnishes—

(A) A social security number, and states under penalties of perjury that the social security number is that of the transferee; or

(B) A statement under penalties of perjury that it is not a disqualified organization.

(ii) Amount required to be paid. The amount required to be paid under sec-

tion 860E(e)(7)(B) is equal to the product of the highest rate specified in section 11(b)(1) for the taxable year in which the transfer described in section 860E(e)(1) occurs and the amount of excess inclusions that accrued and were allocable to the residual interest during the period that the disqualified organization held the interest.

(b) Tax on pass-thru entities —

(1) Tax on excess inclusions. Any tax due under section 860E(e)(6) must be paid by the later of March 24, 1993, or by the fifteenth day of the fourth month following the close of the taxable year of the pass-thru entity in which the disqualified person is a record holder. The Commissioner may prescribe rules for the manner and method of collecting the tax.

(2) Record holder furnishes information under penalties of perjury. For purposes of section 860E(e)(6)(D), a record holder is treated as having furnished an affidavit if the record holder furnishes—

(i) A social security number and states, under penalties of perjury, that the social security number is that of the record holder; or

(ii) A statement under penalties of perjury that it is not a disqualified organization.

(3) Deductibility of tax. Any tax imposed on a pass-thru entity pursuant to section 860E(e)(6)(A) is deductible against the gross amount of ordinary income of the pass-thru entity. For example, in the case of a REIT, the tax is deductible in determining real estate investment trust taxable income under section 857(b)(2).

(4) Allocation of tax. Dividends paid by a RIC or by a REIT are not preferential dividends within the meaning of section 562(c) solely because the tax expense incurred by the RIC or REIT under section 860E(e)(6) is allocated solely to the shares held by disqualified organizations.

§ 1.860F-1 Qualified liquidations.

A plan of liquidation need not be in any special form. If a REMIC specifies the first day in the 90-day liquidation period in a statement attached to its final return, then the REMIC will be considered to have adopted a plan of liquidation on the specified date.

§ 1.860F-2 Transfers to a REMIC.

(a) Formation of a REMIC—

(1) In general. For Federal income tax purposes, a REMIC formation is characterized as the contribution of assets by a sponsor (as defined in paragraph (b)(1) of this section) to a REMIC in exchange for REMIC regular and residual interests. If, instead of exchanging its interest in mortgages and related assets for regular and residual interests, the sponsor arranges to have the REMIC issue some or all of the regular and residual interests for cash, after which the sponsor sells its interests in mortgages and related assets to the REMIC, the transaction is, nevertheless, viewed for Federal income tax purposes as the sponsor's exchange of mortgages and related assets for regular and residual interests, followed by a sale of some or all of those interests. The purpose of this rule is to ensure that the tax consequences associated with the formation of a REMIC are not affected by the actual sequence of steps taken by the sponsor.

(2) Tiered arrangements—

(i) Two or more REMICs formed pursuant to a single set of organizational documents. Two or more REMICs can be created pursuant to a single set of organizational documents even if for state law purposes or for Federal securities law purposes those documents create only one organization. The organizational documents must, however, clearly and expressly identify the assets of, and the interests in, each REMIC, and each REMIC must satisfy all of the requirements of section 860D and the related regulations.

(ii) A REMIC and one or more investment trusts formed pursuant to a single set of documents. A REMIC (or two or more REMICs) and one or more investment trusts can be created pursuant to a single set of organizational documents and the separate existence of the REMIC(s) and the investment trust(s) will be respected for

Federal income tax purposes even if for state law purposes or for Federal securities law purposes those documents create only one organization. The organizational documents for the REMIC(s) and the investment trust(s) must, however, require both the REMIC(s) and the investment trust(s) to account for items of income and ownership of assets for Federal tax purposes in a manner that respects the separate existence of the multiple entities. See § 1.860G-2(i) concerning issuance of regular interests coupled with other contractual rights for an illustration of the provisions of this paragraph.

(b) Treatment of sponsor—

(1) Sponsor defined. A sponsor is a person who directly or indirectly exchanges qualified mortgages and related assets for regular and residual interests in a REMIC. A person indirectly exchanges interests in qualified mortgages and related assets for regular and residual interests in a REMIC if the person transfers, other than in a nonrecognition transaction, the mortgages and related assets to another person who acquires a transitory ownership interest in those assets before exchanging them for interests in the REMIC, after which the transitory owner then transfers some or all of the interests in the REMIC to the first person.

(2) Nonrecognition of gain or loss. The sponsor does not recognize gain or loss on the direct or indirect transfer of any property to a REMIC in exchange for regular or residual interests in the REMIC. However, the sponsor, upon a subsequent sale of the REMIC regular or residual interests, may recognize gain or loss with respect to those interests.

(3) Basis of contributed assets allocated among interests—

(i) In general. The aggregate of the adjusted bases of the regular and residual interests received by the sponsor in the exchange described in paragraph (a) of this section is equal to the aggregate of the adjusted bases of the property transferred by the sponsor in the exchange, increased by the amount of organizational expenses (as described in paragraph (b)(3)(ii) of this section). That total is allocated among all the interests received in proportion to their fair market values on the pricing date (as defined in paragraph (b)(3)(iii) of this section) if any, or, if none, the startup day (as defined in section 860G(a)(9) and § 1.860G-2(k)).

(ii) Organizational expenses—
(A) Organizational expense defined. An organizational expense is an expense that is incurred by the sponsor or by the REMIC and that is directly related to the creation of the REMIC. Further, the organizational expense must be incurred during a period beginning a reasonable time before the startup day and ending before the date prescribed by law for filing the first REMIC tax return (determined without regard to any extensions of time to file). The following are examples of organizational expenses: legal fees for services related to the formation of the REMIC, such as preparation of a pooling and servicing agreement and trust indenture; accounting fees related to the formation of the REMIC; and other administrative costs related to the formation of the REMIC.

(B) Syndication expenses. Syndication expenses are not organizational expenses. Syndication expenses are those expenses incurred by the sponsor or other person to market the interests in a REMIC, and, thus, are applied to reduce the amount realized on the sale of the interests. Examples of syndication expenses are brokerage fees, registration fees, fees of an underwriter or placement agent, and printing costs of the prospectus or placement memorandum and other selling or promotional material.

(iii) Pricing date. The term "pricing date" means the date on which the terms of the regular and residual interests are fixed and the prices at which a substantial portion of the regular interests will be sold are fixed.

(4) Treatment of unrecognized gain or loss—
(i) Unrecognized gain on regular interests. For purposes of section 860F(b)(1)(C)(i), the sponsor must include in gross income the excess of the issue price of a regular interest over the sponsor's basis in the interest as if the excess were market dis-

count (as defined in section 1278(a)(2)) on a bond and the sponsor had made an election under section 1278(b) to include this market discount currently in gross income. The sponsor is not, however, by reason of this paragraph (b)(4)(i), deemed to have made an election under section 1278(b) with respect to any other bonds.

(ii) Unrecognized loss on regular interests. For purposes of section 860F(b)(1)(D)(i), the sponsor treats the excess of the sponsor's basis in a regular interest over the issue price of the interest as if that excess were amortizable bond premium (as defined in section 171(b)) on a taxable bond and the sponsor had made an election under section 171(c). The sponsor is not, however, by reason of this paragraph (b)(4)(ii), deemed to have made an election under section 171(c) with respect to any other bonds.

(iii) Unrecognized gain on residual interests. For purposes of section 860F(b)(1)(C)(ii), the sponsor must include in gross income the excess of the issue price of a residual interest over the sponsor's basis in the interest ratably over the anticipated weighted average life of the REMIC (as defined in § 1.860E-1(a)(3)(iv)).

(iv) Unrecognized loss on residual interests. For purposes of section 860F(b)(1)(D)(ii), the sponsor deducts the excess of the sponsor's basis in a residual interest over the issue price of the interest ratably over the anticipated weighted average life of the REMIC.

(5) Additions to or reductions of the sponsor's basis. The sponsor's basis in a regular or residual interest is increased by any amount included in the sponsor's gross income under paragraph (b)(4) of this section. The sponsor's basis in a regular or residual interest is decreased by any amount allowed as a deduction and by any amount applied to reduce interest payments to the sponsor under paragraph (b)(4)(ii) of this section.

(6) Transferred basis property. For purposes of paragraph (b)(4) of this section, a transferee of a regular or residual interest is treated in the same manner as the sponsor to the extent that the basis of the transferee in the interest is determined in whole or in part by reference to the basis of the interest in the hands of the sponsor.

(C) REMIC's basis in contributed assets. For purposes of section 860F(b)(2), the aggregate of the REMIC's bases in the assets contributed by the sponsor to the REMIC in a transaction described in paragraph (a) of this section is equal to the aggregate of the issue prices (determined under section 860G(a)(10) and § 1.860G-1(d)) of all regular and residual interests in the REMIC.

§ 1.860F-4 REMIC reporting requirements and other administrative rules.

(a) In general. Except as provided in paragraph (c) of this section, for purposes of subtitle F of the Internal Revenue Code, a REMIC is treated as a partnership and any holder of a residual interest in the REMIC is treated as a partner. A REMIC is not subject, however, to the rules of subchapter C of chapter 63 of the Internal Revenue Code, relating to the treatment of partnership items, for a taxable year if there is at no time during the taxable year more than one holder of a residual interest in the REMIC.

(b) REMIC tax return—

(1) In general. To satisfy the requirement under section 6031 to make a return of income for each taxable year, a REMIC must file the return required by paragraph (b)(2) of this section. The due date and any extensions for filing the REMIC's annual return are determined as if the REMIC were a partnership.

(2) Income tax return. The REMIC must make a return, as required by section 6011(a), for each taxable year on Form 1066, U.S. Real Estate Mortgage Investment Conduit Income Tax Return. The return must include—

(i) The amount of principal outstanding on each class of regular interests as of the close of the taxable year,

(ii) The amount of the daily accruals determined under section 860E(c), and

(iii) The information specified in § 1.860D-1(d)(2) (i), (iv), and (v).

(c) Signing of REMIC return—

(1) In general. Although a REMIC is generally treated as a partnership for purposes of subtitle F, for purposes of determining who is authorized to sign a REMIC's income tax return for any taxable year, the REMIC is not treated as a partnership and the holders of residual interests in the REMIC are not treated as partners. Rather, the REMIC return must be signed by a person who could sign the return of the entity absent the REMIC election. Thus, the return of a REMIC that is a corporation or trust under applicable State law must be signed by a corporate officer or a trustee, respectively. The return of a REMIC that consists of a segregated pool of assets must be signed by a person who could sign the return of the entity that owns the assets of the REMIC under applicable State law.

(2) REMIC whose startup day is before November 10, 1988—

(i) In general. The income tax return of a REMIC whose startup day is before November 10, 1988, may be signed by any person who held a residual interest during the taxable year to which the return relates, or, as provided in section 6903, by a fiduciary, as defined in section 7701(a)(6), who is acting for the REMIC and who has furnished adequate notice in the manner prescribed in § 301.6903-1(b) of this chapter.

(ii) Startup day. For purposes of paragraph (c)(2) of this section, startup day means any day selected by a REMIC that is on or before the first day on which interests in such REMIC are issued.

(iii) Exception. A REMIC whose startup day is before November 10, 1988, may elect to have paragraph (c)(1) of this section apply, instead of paragraph (c)(2) of this section, in determining who is authorized to sign the REMIC return. See section 1006(t)(18)(B) of the Technical and Miscellaneous Revenue Act of 1988 (102 Stat. 3426) and § 5h.6(a)(1) of this chapter for the time and manner for making this election.

(d) Designation of tax matters person. A REMIC may designate a tax matters person in the same manner in which a partnership may designate a tax matters partner under § 301.6231(a)(7)-1T of this chapter. For purposes of applying that section, all holders of residual interests in the REMIC are treated as general partners.

(e) Notice to holders of residual interests—

(1) Information required. As of the close of each calendar quarter, a REMIC must provide to each person who held a residual interest in the REMIC during that quarter notice on Schedule Q (Form 1066) of information specified in paragraphs (e)(1)(i) and (ii) of this section.

(i) In general. Each REMIC must provide to each of its residual interest holders the following information—

(A) That person's share of the taxable income or net loss of the REMIC for the calendar quarter;

(B) The amount of the excess inclusion (as defined in section 860E and the regulations thereunder), if any, with respect to that person's residual interest for the calendar quarter;

(C) If the holder of a residual interest is also a pass-through interest holder (as defined in § 1.67-3T(a)(2)), the allocable investment expenses (as defined in § 1.67-3T(a)(4)) for the calendar quarter, and

(D) Any other information required by Schedule Q (Form 1066).

(ii) Information with respect to REMIC assets—

(A) 95 percent asset test. For calendar quarters after 1988, each REMIC must provide to each of its residual interest holders the following information: the percentage of REMIC assets that are qualifying real property loans under section 593, the percentage of REMIC assets that are assets described in section 7701(a)(19), and the percentage of REMIC assets that are real estate assets defined in section 856(c)(6)(B), computed by reference to the average adjusted basis (as defined in section 1011) of the REMIC assets during the calendar quarter (as described in paragraph (e)(1)(iii) of this section). If the percentage of REMIC assets represented by a category is at least 95 percent, then the REMIC need only specify that the percentage for that category was at least 95 percent.

(B) Additional information required if the 95 percent test not met. If, for any calendar quarter after 1988, less than 95 percent of the assets of the REMIC are real estate assets defined in section 856(c)(6)(B), then, for that calendar quarter, the REMIC must also provide to any real estate investment trust (REIT) that holds a residual interest the following information: the percentage of REMIC assets described in section 856(c)(5)(A), computed by reference to the average adjusted basis of the REMIC assets during the calendar quarter (as described in paragraph (e)(1)(iii) of this section), the percentage of REMIC gross income (other than gross income from prohibited transactions defined in section 860F (a)(2)) described in section 856(c)(3)(A) through (E), computed as of the close of the calendar quarter, and the percentage of REMIC gross income (other than gross income from prohibited transactions defined in section 860F(a)(2)) described in section 856(c)(3)(F), computed as of the close of the calendar quarter. For purposes of this paragraph (e)(1)(ii)(B), the term "foreclosure property" contained in section 856(c) (3)(F) has the meaning specified in section 860G(a)(8). In determining whether a REIT satisfies the limitations of section 856(c)(2), all REMIC gross income is deemed to be derived from a source specified in section 856(c)(2).

(C) For calendar quarters in 1987. For calendar quarters in 1987, the percentages of assets required in paragraphs (e)(1)(ii)(A) and (B) of this section may be computed by reference to the fair market value of the assets of the REMIC as of the close of the calendar quarter (as described in paragraph (e)(1)(iii) of this section), instead of by reference to the average adjusted basis during the calendar quarter.

(D) For calendar quarters in 1988 and 1989. For calendar quarters in 1988 and 1989, the percentages of assets required in paragraphs (e)(1)(ii)(A) and (B) of this section may be computed by reference to the average fair market value of the assets of the REMIC during the calendar quarter (as described in paragraph (e)(1)(iii) of this section), instead of by reference to the average adjusted basis of the assets of the REMIC during the calendar quarter.

(iii) **Special provisions.** For purposes of paragraph (e)(1)(ii) of this section, the percentage of REMIC assets represented by a specified category computed by reference to average adjusted basis (or fair market value) of the assets during a calendar quarter is determined by dividing the average adjusted bases (or for calendar quarters before 1990, fair market value) of the assets in the specified category by the average adjusted basis (or, for calendar quarters before 1990, fair market value) of all the assets of the REMIC as of the close of each month, week, or day during that calendar quarter. The monthly, weekly, or daily computation period must be applied uniformly during the calendar quarter to all categories of assets and may not be changed in succeeding calendar quarters without the consent of the Commissioner.

(2) **Quarterly notice required—**

(i) **In general.** Schedule Q must be mailed (or otherwise delivered) to each holder of a residual interest during a calendar quarter no later than the last day of the month following the close of the calendar quarter.

(ii) **Special rule for 1987.** Notice to any holder of a REMIC residual interest of the information required in paragraph (e)(1) of this section for any of the four calendar quarters of 1987 must be mailed (or otherwise delivered) to each holder no later than March 28, 1988.

(3) **Nominee reporting—**

(i) **In general.** If a REMIC is required under paragraphs (e)(1) and (2) of this section to provide notice to an interest holder who is a nominee of another person with respect to an interest in the REMIC, the nominee must furnish that notice to the person for whom it is a nominee.

(ii) **Time for furnishing statement.** The nominee must furnish the notice required under paragraph (e)(3)(i) of this section to the person for whom it is a nominee no later than 30 days after receiving this information.

(4) **Reports to the Internal Revenue Service.** For each person who was a resid-

ual interest holder at any time during a REMIC's taxable year, the REMIC must attach a copy of Schedule Q to its income tax return for that year for each quarter in which that person was a residual interest holder. Quarterly notice to the Internal Revenue Service is not required.

(f) **Information returns for persons engaged in a trade or business.** See § 1.6041-1(b)(2) for the treatment of a REMIC under sections 6041 and 6041A.

§ 1.860G-1 Definition of regular and residual interests.

(a) **Regular interest—**

(1) **Designation as a regular interest.** For purposes of section 860G(a)(1), a REMIC designates an interest as a regular interest by providing to the Internal Revenue Service the information specified in § 1.860D-1(d)(2)(ii) in the time and manner specified in § 1.860D-1(d)(2).

(2) **Specified portion of the interest payments on qualified mortgages—**

(i) **In general.** For purposes of section 860G(a)(1)(B)(ii), a specified portion of the interest payments on qualified mortgages means a portion of the interest payable on qualified mortgages, but only if the portion can be expressed as—

(A) A fixed percentage of the interest that is payable at either a fixed rate or at a variable rate described in paragraph (a)(3) of this section on some or all of the qualified mortgages;

(B) A fixed number of basis points of the interest payable on some or all of the qualified mortgages; or

(C) The interest payable at either a fixed rate or at a variable rate described in paragraph (a)(3) of this section on some or all of the qualified mortgages in excess of a fixed number of basis points or in excess of a variable rate described in paragraph (a)(3) of this section.

(ii) **Specified portion cannot vary.** The portion must be established as of the startup day (as defined in section 860G(a)(9) and § 1.860G-2(k)) and, except as provided in paragraph (a)(2)(iii) of this section, it cannot vary over the period that begins on the startup day and ends on the day that the interest holder is no longer entitled to receive payments.

(iii) Defaulted or delinquent mortgages. A portion is not treated as varying over time if an interest holder's entitlement to a portion of the interest on some or all of the qualified mortgages is dependent on the absence of defaults or delinquencies on those mortgages.

(iv) No minimum specified principal amount is required. If an interest in a REMIC consists of a specified portion of the interest payments on the REMIC's qualified mortgages, no minimum specified principal amount need be assigned to that interest. The specified principal amount can be zero.

(v) Examples. The following examples, each of which describes a pass-thru trust that is intended to qualify as a REMIC, illustrate the provisions of this paragraph (a)(2).

Example 1.

(i) A sponsor transferred a pool of fixed rate mortgages to a trustee in exchange for two classes of certificates. The Class A certificate holders are entitled to all principal payments on the mortgages and to interest on outstanding principal at a variable rate based on the current value of One-Month LIBOR, subject to a lifetime cap equal to the weighted average rate payable on the mortgages. The Class B certificate holders are entitled to all interest payable on the mortgages in excess of the interest paid on the Class A certificates. The Class B certificates are subordinate to the Class A certificates so that cash flow shortfalls due to defaults or delinquencies on the mortgages will be borne first by the Class B certificate holders.

(ii) The Class B certificate holders are entitled to all interest payable on the pooled mortgages in excess of a variable rate described in paragraph (a)(3)(vi) of this section. Moreover, the portion of the interest payable to the Class B certificate holders is not treated as varying over time solely because payments on the Class B certifi-

cates may be reduced as a result of defaults or delinquencies on the pooled mortgages. Thus, the Class B certificates provide for interest payments that consist of a specified portion of the interest payable on the pooled mortgages under paragraph (a)(2)(i)(C) of this section.

Example 2.

(i) A sponsor transferred a pool of variable rate mortgages to a trustee in exchange for two classes of certificates. The mortgages call for interest payments at a variable rate based on the current value of the One-Year Constant Maturity Treasury Index (hereinafter "CMTI") plus 200 basis points, subject to a lifetime cap of 12 percent. Class C certificate holders are entitled to all principal payments on the mortgages and interest on the outstanding principal at a variable rate based on the One-Year CMTI plus 100 basis points, subject to a lifetime cap of 12 percent. The interest rate on the Class C certificates is reset at the same time the rate is reset on the pooled mortgages.

(ii) The Class D certificate holders are entitled to all interest payments on the mortgages in excess of the interest paid on the Class C certificates. So long as the One-Year CMTI is at 10 percent or lower, the Class D certificate holders are entitled to 100 basis points of interest on the pooled mortgages. If, however, the index exceeds 10 percent on a reset date, the Class D certificate holders' entitlement shrinks, and it disappears if the index is at 11 percent or higher.

(iii) The Class D certificate holders are entitled to all interest payable on the pooled mortgages in excess of a qualified variable rate described in paragraph (a)(3) of this section. Thus, the Class D certificates provide for interest payments that consist of a specified portion of the interest payable on the qualified mortgages under paragraph (a)(2)(i)(C) of this section.

Example 3.

(i) A sponsor transferred a pool of fixed rate mortgages to a trustee in exchange for two classes of certificates. The fixed interest rate payable on the mortgages varies from mortgage to mortgage, but all rates are between 8 and 10 percent. The Class E certificate holders are entitled to receive all principal payments on the mortgages and interest on outstanding principal at 7 percent. The Class F certificate holders are entitled to receive all interest on the mortgages in excess of the interest paid on the Class E certificates.

(ii) The Class F certificates provide for interest payments that consist of a specified portion of the interest payable on the mortgages under paragraph (a)(2)(i) of this section. Although the portion of the interest payable to the Class F certificate holders varies from mortgage to mortgage, the interest payable can be expressed as a fixed percentage of the interest payable on each particular mortgage.

(3) **Variable rate.** A regular interest may bear interest at a variable rate. For purposes of section 860G(a)(1)(B)(i), a variable rate of interest is a rate described in this paragraph (a)(3).

(i) **Rate based on index.** A rate that is a qualifying variable rate for purposes of sections 1271 through 1275 and the related regulations is a variable rate. For example, a rate based on the average cost of funds of one or more financial institutions is a variable rate. Further, a rate equal to the highest, lowest, or average of two or more objective interest indices is a variable rate for purposes of this section.

(ii) **Weighted average rate—**
(A) **In general.** A rate based on a weighted average of the interest rates on some or all of the qualified mortgages held by a REMIC is a variable rate. The qualified mortgages taken into account must, however, bear interest at a fixed rate or at a rate described in this paragraph (a)(3). Generally, a weighted average interest rate is a rate that, if applied to the aggregate outstanding principal balance of a pool of mortgage loans for an accrual period, produces an amount of interest that equals the sum of the interest payable on the pooled loans for that accrual period. Thus, for an accrual period in which a pool of

mortgage loans comprises $300,000 of loans bearing a 7 percent interest rate and $700,000 of loans bearing a 9.5 percent interest rate, the weighted average rate for the pool of loans is 8.75 percent.

(B) **Reduction in underlying rate.** For purposes of paragraph (a)(3)(ii)(A) of this section, an interest rate is considered to be based on a weighted average rate even if, in determining that rate, the interest rate on some or all of the qualified mortgages is first subject to a cap or a floor, or is first reduced by a number of basis points or a fixed percentage. A rate determined by taking a weighted average of the interest rates on the qualified mortgage loans net of any servicing spread, credit enhancement fees, or other expenses of the REMIC is a rate based on a weighted average rate for the qualified mortgages. Further, the amount of any rate reduction described above may vary from mortgage to mortgage.

(iii) **Additions, subtractions, and multiplications.** A rate is a variable rate if it is—

(A) Expressed as the product of a rate described in paragraph (a)(3)(i) or (ii) of this section and a fixed multiplier;

(B) Expressed as a constant number of basis points more or less than a rate described in paragraph (a)(3)(i) or (ii) of this section; or

(C) Expressed as the product, plus or minus a constant number of basis points, of a rate described in paragraph (a)(3)(i) or (ii) of this section and a fixed multiplier (which may be either a positive or a negative number).

(iv) **Caps and floors.** A rate is a variable rate if it is a rate that would be described in paragraph (a)(3)(i) through (iii) of this section except that it is—

(A) Limited by a cap or ceiling that establishes either a maximum rate or a maximum number of basis points by which the rate may increase from one accrual or payment period to another or over the term of the interest; or

(B) Limited by a floor that establishes either a minimum rate or a maximum number of basis points by which the rate may decrease from one accrual or payment period to another or over the term of the interest.

(v) **Funds-available caps—**

(A) **In general.** A rate is a variable rate if it is a rate that would be described in paragraph (a)(3)(i) through (iv) of this section except that it is subject to a "funds-available" cap. A funds-available cap is a limit on the amount of interest to be paid on an instrument in any accrual or payment period that is based on the total amount available for the distribution, including both principal and interest received by an issuing entity on some or all of its qualified mortgages as well as amounts held in a reserve fund. The term "funds-available cap" does not, however, include any cap or limit on interest payments used as a device to avoid the standards of paragraph (a)(3)(i) through (iv) of this section.

(B) **Facts and circumstances test.** In determining whether a cap or limit on interest payments is a funds-available cap within the meaning of this section and not a device used to avoid the standards of paragraph (a)(3)(i) through (iv) of this section, one must consider all of the facts and circumstances. Facts and circumstances that must be taken into consideration are: whether the rate of the interest payable to the regular interest holders is below the rate payable on the REMIC's qualified mortgages on the startup day; and whether, historically, the rate of interest payable to the regular interest holders has been consistently below that payable on the qualified mortgages.

(C) **Examples.** The following examples, both of which describe a pass-thru trust that is intended to qualify as a REMIC, illustrate the provisions of this paragraph (a)(3)(v).

Example 1.

(i) A sponsor transferred a pool of mortgages to a trustee in exchange for two classes of certificates. The pool of mortgages has an aggregate principal balance of $100x. Each mortgage in the pool provides for interest payments based on the eleventh

district cost of funds index (hereinafter COFI) plus a margin. The initial weighted average rate for the pool is COFI plus 200 basis points. The trust issued a Class X certificate that has a principal amount of $100x and that provides for interest payments at a rate equal to One-Year LIBOR plus 100 basis points, subject to a cap described below. The Class R certificate, which the sponsor designated as the residual interest, entitles its holder to all funds left in the trust after the Class X certificates have been retired. The Class R certificate holder is not entitled to current distributions.

(ii) At the time the certificates were issued, COFI equalled 4.874 percent and One-Year LIBOR equalled 3.375 percent. Thus, the initial weighted average pool rate was 6.874 percent and the Class X certificate rate was 4.375 percent. Based on historical data, the sponsor does not expect the rate paid on the Class X certificate to exceed the weighted average rate on the pool.

(iii) Initially, under the terms of the trust instrument, the excess of COFI plus 200 over One-Year LIBOR plus 100 (excess interest) will be applied to pay expenses of the trust, to fund any required reserves, and then to reduce the principal balance on the Class X certificate. Consequently, although the aggregate principal balance of the mortgages initially matched the principal balance of the Class X certificate, the principal balance on the Class X certificate will pay down faster than the principal balance on the mortgages as long as the weighted average rate on the mortgages is greater than One-Year LIBOR plus 100. If, however, the rate on the Class X certificate (One-Year LIBOR plus 100) ever exceeds the weighted average rate on the mortgages, then the Class X certificate holders will receive One-Year LIBOR plus 100 subject to a cap based on the current funds that are available for distribution.

(iv) The funds available cap here is not a device used to avoid the standards of paragraph (a)(3)(i) through (iv) of this section. First, on the date the Class X certificates were issued, a significant spread existed between the weighted average rate payable on the mortgages and the rate payable on the Class X certificate. Second, historical data suggest that the weighted average rate payable on the mortgages will continue to exceed the rate payable on the Class X certificate. Finally, because the excess interest will be applied to reduce the outstanding principal balance of the Class X certificate more rapidly than the outstanding principal balance on the mortgages is reduced, One-Year LIBOR plus 100 basis points would have to exceed the weighted average rate on the mortgages by an increasingly larger amount before the funds available cap would be triggered. Accordingly, the rate paid on the Class X certificates is a variable rate.

Example 2.

(i) The facts are the same as those in Example 1, except that the pooled mortgages are commercial mortgages that provide for interest payments based on the gross profits of the mortgagors, and the rate on the Class X certificates is 400 percent on One-Year LIBOR (a variable rate under paragraph (a)(3)(iii) of this section), subject to a cap equal to current funds available to the trustee for distribution.

(ii) Initially, 400 percent of One-Year LIBOR exceeds the weighted average rate payable on the mortgages. Furthermore, historical data suggest that there is a significant possibility that, in the future, 400 percent of One-Year LIBOR will exceed the weighted average rate on the mortgages.

(iii) The facts and circumstances here indicate that the use of 400 percent of One-Year LIBOR with the above-described cap is a device to pass through to the Class X certificate holder contingent interest based on mortgagor profits. Consequently, the rate paid on the Class X certificate here is not a variable rate.

(iv) Combination of rates. A rate is a variable rate if it is based on—

(A) One fixed rate during one or more accrual or payment periods and a different fixed rate or rates, or a rate or rates described in paragraph (a)(3)(i) through (v) of this section, during other accrual or payment periods; or

(B) A rate described in paragraph (a)(3)(i) through (v) of this section during one or more accrual or payment periods and a fixed rate or rates, or a different rate or rates described in paragraph (a)(3)(i) through (v) of this section in other periods.

(4) **Fixed terms on the startup day.** For purposes of section 860G(a)(1), a regular interest in a REMIC has fixed terms on the startup day if, on the startup day, the REMIC's organizational documents irrevocably specify—

(i) The principal amount (or other similar amount) of the regular interest;

(ii) The interest rate or rates used to compute any interest payments (or other similar amounts) on the regular interest; and

(iii) The latest possible maturity date of the interest.

(5) **Contingencies prohibited.** Except for the contingencies specified in paragraph (b)(3) of this section, the principal amount (or other similar amount) and the latest possible maturity date of the interest must not be contingent.

(b) **Special rules for regular interests—**

(1) **Call premium.** An interest in a REMIC does not qualify as a regular interest if the terms of the interest entitle the holder of that interest to the payment of any premium that is determined with reference to the length of time that the regular interest is outstanding and is not described in paragraph (b)(2) of this section.

(2) **Customary prepayment penalties received with respect to qualified mortgages.** An interest in a REMIC does not fail to qualify as a regular interest solely because the REMIC's organizational documents provide that the REMIC must allocate among and pay to its regular interest holders any customary prepayment penalties that the REMIC receives with respect to its qualified mortgages. Moreover, a REMIC may allocate prepayment penalties among its classes of interests in any manner specified in the REMIC's organizational documents. For example, a REMIC could allocate all or substantially all of a prepayment penalty that it receives to holders of an interest-only class of interests because that

class would be most significantly affected by prepayments.

(3) Certain contingencies disregarded. An interest in a REMIC does not fail to qualify as a regular interest solely because it is issued subject to some or all of the contingencies described in paragraph (b)(3)(i) through (vi) of this section.

(i) Prepayments, income, and expenses. An interest does not fail to qualify as a regular interest solely because—

(A) The timing of (but not the right to or amount of) principal payments (or other similar amounts) is affected by the extent of prepayments on some or all of the qualified mortgages held by the REMIC or the amount of income from permitted investments (as defined in § 1.860G-2(g)); or

(B) The timing of interest and principal payments is affected by the payment of expenses incurred by the REMIC.

(ii) Credit losses. An interest does not fail to qualify as a regular interest solely because the amount or the timing of payments of principal or interest (or other similar amounts) with respect to a regular interest is affected by defaults on qualified mortgages and permitted investments, unanticipated expenses incurred by the REMIC, or lower than expected returns on permitted investments.

(iii) Subordinated interests. An interest does not fail to qualify as a regular interest solely because that interest bears all, or a disproportionate share, of the losses stemming from cash flow shortfalls due to defaults or delinquencies on qualified mortgages or permitted investments, unanticipated expenses incurred by the REMIC, lower than expected returns on permitted investments, or prepayment interest shortfalls before other regular interests or the residual interest bear losses occasioned by those shortfalls.

(iv) Deferral of interest. An interest does not fail to qualify as a regular interest solely because that interest, by its terms, provides for deferral of interest payments.

(v) Prepayment interest shortfalls. An interest does not fail to qualify as a regular interest solely because the amount of interest payments is affected by prepayments of the underlying mortgages.

(vi) Remote and incidental contingencies. An interest does not fail to qualify as a regular interest solely because the amount or timing of payments of principal or interest (or other similar amounts) with respect to the interest is subject to a contingency if there is only a remote likelihood that the contingency will occur. For example, an interest could qualify as a regular interest even though full payment of principal and interest on that interest is contingent upon the absence of significant cash flow shortfalls due to the operation of the Soldiers and Sailors Civil Relief Act, 50 U.S.C.A. 526 (1988).

(4) Form of regular interest. A regular interest in a REMIC may be issued in the form of debt, stock, an interest in a partnership or trust, or any other form permitted by state law. If a regular interest in a REMIC is not in the form of debt, it must, except as provided in paragraph (a)(2)(iv) of this section, entitle the holder to a specified amount that would, were the interest issued in debt form, be identified as the principal amount of the debt.

(5) Interest disproportionate to principal—

(i) In general. An interest in a REMIC does not qualify as a regular interest if the amount of interest (or other similar amount) payable to the holder is disproportionately high relative to the principal amount or other specified amount described in paragraph (b)(4) of this section (specified principal amount). Interest payments (or other similar amounts) are considered disproportionately high if the issue price (as determined under paragraph (d) of this section) of the interest in the REMIC exceeds 125 percent of its specified principal amount.

(ii) Exception. A regular interest in a REMIC that entitles the holder to interest payments consisting of a specified portion of interest payments on qualified mortgages qualifies as a regular interest even if the amount of interest is disproportionately high relative to the specified principal amount.

(6) Regular interest treated as a debt instrument for all Federal income tax purposes. In determining the tax under chapter 1 of the Internal Revenue Code, a REMIC regular interest (as defined in section 860G(a)(1)) is treated as a debt instrument that is an obligation of the REMIC. Thus, sections 1271 through 1288, relating to bonds and other debt instruments, apply to a regular interest. For special rules relating to the accrual of original issue discount on regular interests, see section 1272(a)(6).

(c) Residual interest. A residual interest is an interest in a REMIC that is issued on the startup day and that is designated as a residual interest by providing the information specified in § 1.860D-1(d)(2)(ii) at the time and in the manner provided in § 1.860D-1(d)(2). A residual interest need not entitle the holder to any distributions from the REMIC.

(d) Issue price of regular and residual interests—
(1) In general. The issue price of any REMIC regular or residual interest is determined under section 1273(b) as if the interest were a debt instrument and, if issued for property, as if the requirements of section 1273(b)(3) were met. Thus, if a class of interests is publicly offered, then the issue price of an interest in that class is the initial offering price to the public at which a substantial amount of the class is sold. If the interest is in a class that is not publicly offered, the issue price is the price paid by the first buyer of that interest regardless of the price paid for the remainder of the class. If the interest is in a class that is retained by the sponsor, the issue price is its fair market value on the pricing date (as defined in § 1.860F-2(b)(3)(iii)), if any, or, if none, the startup day, regardless of whether the property exchanged therefor is publicly traded.
(2) The public. The term "the public" for purposes of this section does not include brokers or other middlemen, nor does it include the sponsor who acquires all of the regular and residual interests from the REMIC on the startup day in a transaction described in § 1.860G-2(a).

§ 1.860G-2 Other rules.

(a) Obligations principally secured by an interest in real property—
(1) Tests for determining whether an obligation is principally secured. For purposes of section 860G(a)(3)(A), an obligation is principally secured by an interest in real property only if it satisfies either the test set out in paragraph (a)(1)(i) or the test set out in paragraph (a)(1)(ii) of this section.
(i) The 80-percent test. An obligation is principally secured by an interest in real property if the fair market value of the interest in real property securing the obligation—
(A) Was at least equal to 80 percent of the adjusted issue price of the obligation at the time the obligation was originated (see paragraph (b)(1) of this section concerning the origination date for obligations that have been significantly modified); or
(B) Is at least equal to 80 percent of the adjusted issue price of the obligation at the time the sponsor contributes the obligation to the REMIC.
(ii) Alternative test. For purposes of section 860G(a)(3)(A), an obligation is principally secured by an interest in real property if substantially all of the proceeds of the obligation were used to acquire or to improve or protect an interest in real property that, at the origination date, is the only security for the obligation. For purposes of this test, loan guarantees made by the United States or any state (or any political subdivision, agency, or instrumentality of the United States or of any state), or other third party credit enhancement are not viewed as additional security for a loan. An obligation is not considered to be secured by property other than real property solely because the obligor is personally liable on the obligation.
(2) Treatment of liens. For purposes of paragraph (a)(1)(i) of this section, the fair market value of the real property interest must be first reduced by the amount of any lien on the real property interest that is sen-

ior to the obligation being tested, and must be further reduced by a proportionate amount of any lien that is in parity with the obligation being tested.

(3) Safe harbor—

(i) **Reasonable belief that an obligation is principally secured.** If, at the time the sponsor contributes an obligation to a REMIC, the sponsor reasonably believes that the obligation is principally secured by an interest in real property within the meaning of paragraph (a)(1) of this section, then the obligation is deemed to be so secured for purposes of section 860G(a)(3). A sponsor cannot avail itself of this safe harbor with respect to an obligation if the sponsor actually knows or has reason to know that the obligation fails both of the tests set out in paragraph (a)(1) of this section.

(ii) **Basis for reasonable belief.** For purposes of paragraph (a)(3)(i) of this section, a sponsor may base a reasonable belief concerning any obligation on—

(A) Representations and warranties made by the originator of the obligation; or

(B) Evidence indicating that the originator of the obligation typically made mortgage loans in accordance with an established set of parameters, and that any mortgage loan originated in accordance with those parameters would satisfy at least one of the tests set out in paragraph (a)(1) of this section.

(iii) **Later discovery that an obligation is not principally secured.** If, despite the sponsor's reasonable belief concerning an obligation at the time it contributed the obligation to the REMIC, the REMIC later discovers that the obligation is not principally secured by an interest in real property, the obligation is a defective obligation and loses its status as a qualified mortgage 90 days after the date of discovery. See paragraph (f) of this section, relating to defective obligations.

(4) **Interests in real property; real property.** The definition of "interests in real property" set out in § 1.856-3(c), and the definition of "real property" set out in § 1.856-3(d), apply to define those terms for

purposes of section 860G(a)(3) and paragraph (a) of this section.

(5) **Obligations secured by an interest in real property.** Obligations secured by interests in real property include the following: mortgages, deeds of trust, and installment land contracts; mortgage pass-thru certificates guaranteed by GNMA, FNMA, FHLMC, or CMHC (Canada Mortgage and Housing Corporation); other investment trust interests that represent undivided beneficial ownership in a pool of obligations principally secured by interests in real property and related assets that would be considered to be permitted investments if the investment trust were a REMIC, and provided the investment trust is classified as a trust under § 301.7701-4(c) of this chapter; and obligations secured by manufactured housing treated as single family residences under section 25(e)(10) (without regard to the treatment of the obligations or the properties under state law).

(6) **Obligations secured by other obligations; residual interests.** Obligations (other than regular interests in a REMIC) that are secured by other obligations are not principally secured by interests in real property even if the underlying obligations are secured by interests in real property. Thus, for example, a collateralized mortgage obligation issued by an issuer that is not a REMIC is not an obligation principally secured by an interest in real property. A residual interest (as defined in section 860G(a)(2)) is not an obligation principally secured by an interest in real property.

(7) **Certain instruments that call for contingent payments are obligations.** For purposes of section 860G(a)(3) and (4), the term "obligation" includes any instrument that provides for total noncontingent principal payments that at least equal the instrument's issue price even if that instrument also provides for contingent payments. Thus, for example, an instrument that was issued for $100x and that provides for noncontingent principal payments of $100x, interest payments at a fixed rate, and contingent payments based on a percentage of the mortgagor's gross receipts, is an obligation.

(8) Defeasance. If a REMIC releases its lien on real property that secures a qualified mortgage, that mortgage ceases to be a qualified mortgage on the date the lien is released unless—

(i) The mortgagor pledges substitute collateral that consists solely of government securities (as defined in section 2(a)(16) of the Investment Company Act of 1940 as amended (15 U.S.C. 80a-1));

(ii) The mortgage documents allow such a substitution;

(iii) The lien is released to facilitate the disposition of the property or any other customary commercial transaction, and not as part of an arrangement to collateralize a REMIC offering with obligations that are not real estate mortgages; and

(iv) The release is not within 2 years of the startup day.

(9) Stripped bonds and coupons. The term "qualified mortgage" includes stripped bonds and stripped coupons (as defined in section 1286(e) (2) and (3)) if the bonds (as defined in section 1286(e)(1)) from which such stripped bonds or stripped coupons arose would have been qualified mortgages.

(b) Assumptions and modifications— (1) Significant modifications are treated as exchanges of obligations. If an obligation is significantly modified in a manner or under circumstances other than those described in paragraph (b)(3) of this section, then the modified obligation is treated as one that was newly issued in exchange for the unmodified obligation that it replaced. Consequently—

(i) If such a significant modification occurs after the obligation has been contributed to the REMIC and the modified obligation is not a qualified replacement mortgage, the modified obligation will not be a qualified mortgage and the deemed disposition of the unmodified obligation will be a prohibited transaction under section 860F(a)(2); and

(ii) If such a significant modification occurs before the obligation is contributed to the REMIC, the modified obligation will be viewed as having been originated on

the date the modification occurs for purposes of the tests set out in paragraph (a)(1) of this section.

(2) Significant modification defined. For purposes of paragraph (b)(1) of this section, a "significant modification" is any change in the terms of an obligation that would be treated as an exchange of obligations under section 1001 and the related regulations.

(3) Exceptions. For purposes of paragraph (b)(1) of this section, the following changes in the terms of an obligation are not significant modifications regardless of whether they would be significant modifications under paragraph (b)(2) of this section—

(i) Changes in the terms of the obligation occasioned by default or a reasonably foreseeable default;

(ii) Assumption of the obligation;

(iii) Waiver of a due-on-sale clause or a due on encumbrance clause; and

(iv) Conversion of an interest rate by a mortgagor pursuant to the terms of a convertible mortgage.

(4) Modifications that are not significant modifications. If an obligation is modified and the modification is not a significant modification for purposes of paragraph (b)(1) of this section, then the modified obligation is not treated as one that was newly originated on the date of modification.

(5) Assumption defined. For purposes of paragraph (b)(3) of this section, a mortgage has been assumed if—

(i) The buyer of the mortgaged property acquires the property subject to the mortgage, without assuming any personal liability;

(ii) The buyer becomes liable for the debt but the seller also remains liable; or

(iii) The buyer becomes liable for the debt and the seller is released by the lender.

(6) Pass-thru certificates. If a REMIC holds as a qualified mortgage a pass-thru certificate or other investment trust interest of the type described in paragraph (a)(5) of this section, the modification of a mortgage loan that backs the pass-thru certificate or other interest is not a modification of the pass-thru certificate or other interest unless the investment trust structure was created to avoid the prohibited transaction rules of section 860F(a).

(c) **Treatment of certain credit enhancement contracts—**

(1) **In general.** A credit enhancement contract (as defined in paragraph (c)(2) and (3) of this section) is not treated as a separate asset of the REMIC for purposes of the asset test set out in section 860D(a)(4) and § 1.860D-1(b)(3), but instead is treated as part of the mortgage or pool of mortgages to which it relates. Furthermore, any collateral supporting a credit enhancement contract is not treated as an asset of the REMIC solely because it supports the guarantee represented by that contract. See paragraph (g)(1)(ii) of this section for the treatment of payments made pursuant to credit enhancement contracts as payments received under a qualified mortgage.

(2) **Credit enhancement contracts.** For purposes of this section, a credit enhancement contract is any arrangement whereby a person agrees to guarantee full or partial payment of the principal or interest payable on a qualified mortgage or on a pool of such mortgages, or full or partial payment on one or more classes of regular interests or on the class of residual interests, in the event of defaults or delinquencies on qualified mortgages, unanticipated losses or expenses incurred by the REMIC, or lower than expected returns on cash flow investments. Types of credit enhancement contracts may include, but are not limited to, pool insurance contracts, certificate guarantee insurance contracts, letters of credit, guarantees, or agreements whereby the REMIC sponsor, a mortgage servicer, or other third party agrees to make advances described in paragraph (c)(3) of this section.

(3) **Arrangements to make certain advances.** The arrangements described in this paragraph (c)(3) are credit enhancement contracts regardless of whether, under the terms of the arrangement, the payor is obligated, or merely permitted, to advance funds to the REMIC.

(i) **Advances of delinquent principal and interest.** An arrangement by a REMIC sponsor, mortgage servicer, or other third party to advance to the REMIC out of its own funds an amount to make up for delinquent payments on qualified mortgages is a credit enhancement contract.

(ii) **Advances of taxes, insurance payments, and expenses.** An arrangement by a REMIC sponsor, mortgage servicer, or other third party to pay taxes and hazard insurance premiums on, or other expenses incurred to protect the REMIC's security interest in, property securing a qualified mortgage in the event that the mortgagor fails to pay such taxes, insurance premiums, or other expenses is a credit enhancement contract.

(iii) **Advances to ease REMIC administration.** An agreement by a REMIC sponsor, mortgage servicer, or other third party to advance temporarily to a REMIC amounts payable on qualified mortgages before such amounts are actually due to level out the stream of cash flows to the REMIC or to provide for orderly administration of the REMIC is a credit enhancement contract. For example, if two mortgages in a pool have payment due dates on the twentieth of the month, and all the other mortgages have payment due dates on the first of each month, an agreement by the mortgage servicer to advance to the REMIC on the fifteenth of each month the payments not yet received on the two mortgages together with the amounts received on the other mortgages is a credit enhancement contract.

(4) **Deferred payment under a guarantee arrangement.** A guarantee arrangement does not fail to qualify as a credit enhancement contract solely because the guarantor, in the event of a default on a qualified mortgage, has the option of immediately paying to the REMIC the full amount of mortgage principal due on acceleration of the defaulted mortgage, or paying principal and interest to the REMIC according to the original payment schedule for the defaulted mortgage, or according to some other deferred payment schedule. Any deferred payments are payments pursuant to a

credit enhancement contract even if the mortgage is foreclosed upon and the guarantor, pursuant to subrogation rights set out in the guarantee arrangement, is entitled to receive immediately the proceeds of foreclosure.

(d) Treatment of certain purchase agreements with respect to convertible mortgages—

(1) In general. For purposes of sections 860D(a)(4) and 860G(a)(3), a purchase agreement (as described in paragraph (d)(3) of this section) with respect to a convertible mortgage (as described in paragraph (d)(5) of this section) is treated as incidental to the convertible mortgage to which it relates. Consequently, the purchase agreement is part of the mortgage or pool of mortgages and is not a separate asset of the REMIC.

(2) Treatment of amounts received under purchase agreements. For purposes of sections 860A through 860G and for purposes of determining the accrual of original issue discount and market discount under sections 1272(a)(6) and 1276, respectively, a payment under a purchase agreement described in paragraph (d)(3) of this section is treated as a prepayment in full of the mortgage to which it relates. Thus, for example, a payment under a purchase agreement with respect to a qualified mortgage is considered a payment received under a qualified mortgage within the meaning of section 860G(a)(6) and the transfer of the mortgage is not a disposition of the mortgage within the meaning of section 860F(a)(2)(A).

(3) Purchase agreement. A purchase agreement is a contract between the holder of a convertible mortgage and a third party under which the holder agrees to sell and the third party agrees to buy the mortgage for an amount equal to its current principal balance plus accrued but unpaid interest if and when the mortgagor elects to convert the terms of the mortgage.

(4) Default by the person obligated to purchase a convertible mortgage. If the person required to purchase a convertible mortgage defaults on its obligation to purchase the mortgage upon conversion, the REMIC may sell the mortgage in a market transaction and the proceeds of the sale will be treated as amounts paid pursuant to a purchase agreement.

(5) Convertible mortgage. A convertible mortgage is a mortgage that gives the obligor the right at one or more times during the term of the mortgage to elect to convert from one interest rate to another. The new rate of interest must be determined pursuant to the terms of the instrument and must be intended to approximate a market rate of interest for newly originated mortgages at the time of the conversion.

(e) Prepayment interest shortfalls. An agreement by a mortgage servicer or other third party to make payments to the REMIC to make up prepayment interest shortfalls is not treated as a separate asset of the REMIC and payments made pursuant to such an agreement are treated as payments on the qualified mortgages. With respect to any mortgage that prepays, the prepayment interest shortfall for the accrual period in which the mortgage prepays is an amount equal to the excess of the interest that would have accrued on the mortgage during that accrual period had it not prepaid, over the interest that accrued from the beginning of that accrual period up to the date of the prepayment.

(f) Defective obligations—

(1) Defective obligation defined. For purposes of sections 860G(a)(4)(B)(ii) and 860F(a)(2), a defective obligation is a mortgage subject to any of the following defects.

(i) The mortgage is in default, or a default with respect to the mortgage is reasonably foreseeable.

(ii) The mortgage was fraudulently procured by the mortgagor.

(iii) The mortgage was not in fact principally secured by an interest in real property within the meaning of paragraph (a)(1) of this section.

(iv) The mortgage does not conform to a customary representation or warranty given by the sponsor or prior owner of the mortgage regarding the characteristics of the mortgage, or the characteristics of the pool of mortgages of which the mortgage is a part. A representation that payments on a qualified mortgage will be received at a rate no less than a specified minimum or no greater than a specified maximum is not customary for this purpose.

(2) Effect of discovery of defect. If a REMIC discovers that an obligation is a defective obligation, and if the defect is one that, had it been discovered before the startup day, would have prevented the obligation from being a qualified mortgage, then, unless the REMIC either causes the defect to be cured or disposes of the defective obligation within 90 days of discovering the defect, the obligation ceases to be a qualified mortgage at the end of that 90 day period. Even if the defect is not cured, the defective obligation is, nevertheless, a qualified mortgage from the startup day through the end of the 90 day period. Moreover, even if the REMIC holds the defective obligation beyond the 90 day period, the REMIC may, nevertheless, exchange the defective obligation for a qualified replacement mortgage so long as the requirements of section 860G(a)(4)(B) are satisfied. If the defect is one that does not affect the status of an obligation as a qualified mortgage, then the obligation is always a qualified mortgage regardless of whether the defect is or can be cured. For example, if a sponsor represented that all mortgages transferred to a REMIC had a 10 percent interest rate, but it was later discovered that one mortgage had a 9 percent interest rate, the 9 percent mortgage is defective, but the defect does not affect the status of that obligation as a qualified mortgage.

(g) Permitted investments—

(1) Cash flow investment—

(i) In general. For purposes of section 860G(a)(6) and this section, a cash flow investment is an investment of payments received on qualified mortgages for a temporary period between receipt of those payments and the regularly scheduled date for distribution of those payments to REMIC interest holders. Cash flow investments must be passive investments earning a return in the nature of interest.

(ii) Payments received on qualified mortgages. For purposes of paragraph (g)(1) of this section, the term "payments received on qualified mortgages" includes—

(A) Payments of interest and principal on qualified mortgages, including prepayments of principal and payments under credit enhancement contracts described in paragraph (c)(2) of this section;

(B) Proceeds from the disposition of qualified mortgages;

(C) Cash flows from foreclosure property and proceeds from the disposition of such property;

(D) A payment by a sponsor or prior owner in lieu of the sponsor's or prior owner's repurchase of a defective obligation, as defined in paragraph (f) of this section, that was transferred to the REMIC in breach of a customary warranty; and

(E) Prepayment penalties required to be paid under the terms of a qualified mortgage when the mortgagor prepays the obligation.

(iii) Temporary period. For purposes of section 860G(a)(6) and this paragraph (g)(1), a temporary period generally is that period from the time a REMIC receives payments on qualified mortgages and permitted investments to the time the REMIC distributes the payments to interest holders. A temporary period may not exceed 13 months. Thus, an investment held by a REMIC for more than 13 months is not a cash flow investment. In determining the length of time that a REMIC has held an investment that is part of a commingled fund or account, the REMIC may employ any reasonable method of accounting. For example, if a REMIC holds mortgage cash flows in a commingled account pending distribution, the first-in, first-out method of accounting is a reasonable method for determining whether all or part of the account satisfies the 13 month limitation.

(2) Qualified reserve funds. The term qualified reserve fund means any reasonably required reserve to provide for full payment of expenses of the REMIC or amounts due on regular or residual interests in the event of defaults on qualified mortgages, prepayment interest shortfalls (as defined in paragraph (e) of this section), lower than expected returns on cash flow investments, or any other contingency that could be provided for under a credit enhancement contract (as defined in paragraph (c)(2) and (3) of this section).

(3) Qualified reserve asset—

(i) In general. The term "qualified reserve asset" means any intangible property (other than a REMIC residual interest) that is held both for investment and as part of a qualified reserve fund. An asset need not generate any income to be a qualified reserve asset.

(ii) Reasonably required reserve—

(A) In general. In determining whether the amount of a reserve is reasonable, it is appropriate to consider the credit quality of the qualified mortgages, the extent and nature of any guarantees relating to either the qualified mortgages or the regular and residual interests, the expected amount of expenses of the REMIC, and the expected availability of proceeds from qualified mortgages to pay the expenses. To the extent that a reserve exceeds a reasonably required amount, the amount of the reserve must be promptly and appropriately reduced. If at any time, however, the amount of the reserve fund is less than is reasonably required, the amount of the reserve fund may be increased by the addition of payments received on qualified mortgages or by contributions from holders of residual interests.

(B) Presumption that a reserve is reasonably required. The amount of a reserve fund is presumed to be reasonable (and an excessive reserve is presumed to have been promptly and appropriately reduced) if it does not exceed—

(1) The amount required by a nationally recognized independent rating agency as a condition of providing the rating for REMIC interests desired by the sponsor; or

(2) The amount required by a third party insurer or guarantor, who does not own directly or indirectly (within the meaning of section 267(c)) an interest in the REMIC (as defined in § 1.860D-1(b)(1)), as a condition of providing credit enhancement.

(C) Presumption may be rebutted. The presumption in paragraph (g) (3)(ii)(B) of this section may be rebutted if the amounts required by the rating agency

or by the third party insurer are not commercially reasonable considering the factors described in paragraph (g)(3)(ii)(A) of this section.

(h) Outside reserve funds. A reserve fund that is maintained to pay expenses of the REMIC, or to make payments to REMIC interest holders is an outside reserve fund and not an asset of the REMIC only if the REMIC's organizational documents clearly and expressly—

(1) Provide that the reserve fund is an outside reserve fund and not an asset of the REMIC;

(2) Identify the owner(s) of the reserve fund, either by name, or by description of the class (e.g., subordinated regular interest holders) whose membership comprises the owners of the fund; and

(3) Provide that, for all Federal tax purposes, amounts transferred by the REMIC to the fund are treated as amounts distributed by the REMIC to the designated owner(s) or transferees of the designated owner(s).

(i) Contractual rights coupled with regular interests in tiered arrangements—

(1) In general. If a REMIC issues a regular interest to a trustee of an investment trust for the benefit of the trust certificate holders and the trustee also holds for the benefit of those certificate holders certain other contractual rights, those other rights are not treated as assets of the REMIC even if the investment trust and the REMIC were created contemporaneously pursuant to a single set of organizational documents. The organizational documents must, however, require that the trustee account for the contractual rights as property that the trustee holds separate and apart from the regular interest.

(2) Example. The following example, which describes a tiered arrangement involving a pass-thru trust that is intended to qualify as a REMIC and a pass-thru trust that is intended to be classified as a trust under § 301.7701-4(c) of this chapter, illustrates the provisions of paragraph (i)(1) of this section.

Example.

(i) A sponsor transferred a pool of

mortgages to a trustee in exchange for two classes of certificates. The pool of mortgages has an aggregate principal balance of $100x. Each mortgage in the pool provides for interest payments based on the eleventh district cost of funds index (hereinafter COFI) plus a margin. The trust (hereinafter REMIC trust) issued a Class N bond, which the sponsor designates as a regular interest, that has a principal amount of $100x and that provides for interest payments at a rate equal to One-Year LIBOR plus 100 basis points, subject to a cap equal to the weighted average pool rate. The Class R interest, which the sponsor designated as the residual interest, entitles its holder to all funds left in the trust after the Class N bond has been retired. The Class R interest holder is not entitled to current distributions.

(ii) On the same day, and under the same set of documents, the sponsor also created an investment trust. The sponsor contributed to the investment trust the Class N bond together with an interest rate cap contract. Under the interest rate cap contract, the issuer of the cap contract agrees to pay to the trustee for the benefit of the investment trust certificate holders the excess of One-Year LIBOR plus 100 basis points over the weighted average pool rate (COFI plus a margin) times the outstanding principal balance of the Class N bond in the event One-Year LIBOR plus 100 basis points ever exceeds the weighted average pool rate. The trustee (the same institution that serves as REMIC trust trustee), in exchange for the contributed assets, gave the sponsor certificates representing undivided beneficial ownership interests in the Class N bond and the interest rate cap contract. The organizational documents require the trustee to account for the regular interest and the cap contract as discrete property rights.

(iii) The separate existence of the REMIC trust and the investment trust are respected for all Federal income tax purposes. Thus, the interest rate cap contract is an asset beneficially owned by the several certificate holders and is not an asset of the REMIC trust. Consequently, each certificate

holder must allocate its purchase price for the certificate between its undivided interest in the Class N bond and its undivided interest in the interest rate cap contract in accordance with the relative fair market values of those two property rights.

(j) **Clean-up call—**

(1) **In general.** For purposes of section 860F(a)(5)(B), a clean-up call is the redemption of a class of regular interests when, by reason of prior payments with respect to those interests, the administrative costs associated with servicing that class outweigh the benefits of maintaining the class. Factors to consider in making this determination include—

(i) The number of holders of that class of regular interests;

(ii) The frequency of payments to holders of that class;

(iii) The effect the redemption will have on the yield of that class of regular interests;

(iv) The outstanding principal balance of that class; and

(v) The percentage of the original principal balance of that class still outstanding.

(2) **Interest rate changes.** The redemption of a class of regular interests undertaken to profit from a change in interest rates is not a clean-up call.

(3) **Safe harbor.** Although the outstanding principal balance is only one factor to consider, the redemption of a class of regular interests with an outstanding principal balance of no more than 10 percent of its original principal balance is always a clean-up call.

(k) **Startup day.** The term "startup day" means the day on which the REMIC issues all of its regular and residual interests. A sponsor may, however, contribute property to a REMIC in exchange for regular and residual interests over any period of 10 consecutive days and the REMIC may designate any one of those 10 days as its startup day. The day so designated is then the startup day, and all interests are treated as issued on that day.

§ 1.860G-3 Treatment of foreign persons.

(a) Transfer of a residual interest with tax avoidance potential—

(1) In general. A transfer of a residual interest that has tax avoidance potential is disregarded for all Federal tax purposes if the transferee is a foreign person. Thus, if a residual interest with tax avoidance potential is transferred to a foreign holder at formation of the REMIC, the sponsor is liable for the tax on any excess inclusion that accrues with respect to that residual interest.

(2) Tax avoidance potential—

(i) Defined. A residual interest has tax avoidance potential for purposes of this section unless, at the time of the transfer, the transferor reasonably expects that, for each excess inclusion, the REMIC will distribute to the transferee residual interest holder an amount that will equal at least 30 percent of the excess inclusion, and that each such amount will be distributed at or after the time at which the excess inclusion accrues and not later than the close of the calendar year following the calendar year of accrual.

(ii) Safe harbor. For purposes of paragraph (a)(2)(i) of this section, a transferor has a reasonable expectation if the 30-percent test would be satisfied were the REMIC's qualified mortgages to prepay at each rate within a range of rates from 50 percent to 200 percent of the rate assumed under section 1272(a)(6) with respect to the qualified mortgages (or the rate that would have been assumed had the mortgages been issued with original issue discount).

(3) Effectively connected income. Paragraph (a)(1) of this section will not apply if the transferee's income from the residual interest is subject to tax under section 871(b) or section 882.

(4) Transfer by a foreign holder. If a foreign person transfers a residual interest to a United States person or a foreign holder in whose hands the income from a residual interest would be effectively connected income, and if the transfer has the effect of allowing the transferor to avoid tax on ac-

crued excess inclusions, then the transfer is disregarded and the transferor continues to be treated as the owner of the residual interest for purposes of section 871(a), 881, 1441, or 1442.

(b) [Reserved]

Treasury Regulation § 1.67-3— Allocation of expenses by real estate mortgage investment conduits

(a) Allocation of allocable investment expenses. [Reserved]

(b) Treatment of allocable investment expenses. [Reserved]

(c) Computation of proportionate share. [Reserved]

(d) Example. [Reserved]

(e) Allocable investment expenses not subject to backup withholding. [Reserved]

(f) Notice to pass-through interest holders—(1) Information required. A REMIC must provide to each pass-through interest holder to which an allocation of allocable investment expense is required to be made under § 1.67-3T(a)(1) notice of the following—

(i) If, pursuant to paragraph (f)(2) (i) or (ii) of this section, notice is provided for a calendar quarter, the aggregate amount of expenses paid or accrued during the calendar quarter for which the REMIC is allowed a deduction under section 212;

(ii) If, pursuant to paragraph (f)(2)(ii) of this section, notice is provided to a regular interest holder for a calendar year, the aggregate amount of expenses paid or accrued during the calendar quarter that the regular interest holder held the regular interest in the calendar year and for which the REMIC is allowed a deduction under section 212; and

(iii) The proportionate share of these expenses allocated to that pass-through interest holder, as determined under § 1.67-3T(c).

(2) Statement to be furnished—(i) To residual interest holder. For each calendar quarter, a REMIC must provide to each pass-through interest holder who holds a residual interest during the calendar quarter the notice required under paragraph (f)(1) of this section on Schedule Q (Form 1066), as required in § 1.860F-4(e).

(ii) **To regular interest holder.** For each calendar year, a single-class REMIC (as described in § 1.67-3T(a)(2)(ii)(B)) must provide to each pass-through interest holder who held a regular interest during the calendar year the notice required under paragraph (f)(1) of this section. Quarterly reporting is not required. The information required to be included in the notice may be separately stated on the statement described in § 1.6049-7(f) instead of on a separate statement provided in a separate mailing. See § 1.6049-7(f)(4). The separate statement provided in a separate mailing must be furnished to each pass-through interest holder no later than the last day of the month following the close of the calendar year.

(3) **Returns to the Internal Revenue Service—(i) With respect to residual interest holders.** Any REMIC required under paragraphs (f)(1) and (2)(i) of this section to furnish information to any pass-through interest holder who holds a residual interest must also furnish such information to the Internal Revenue Service as required in § 1.860F-4(e)(4).

(ii) **With respect to regular interest holders.** A single-class REMIC (as described in § 1.67-3T(a)(2)(ii)(B)) must make an information return on Form 1099 for each calendar year, with respect to each pass-through interest holder who holds a regular interest to which an allocation of allocable investment expenses is required to be made pursuant to § 1.67-3T(a)(1) and 2(ii). The preceding sentence applies with respect to a holder for a calendar year only if the REMIC is required to make an information return to the Internal Revenue Service with respect to that holder for that year pursuant to section 6049 and § 1.6049-7(b)(2)(i) (or would be required to make an information return but for the $10 threshold described in section 6049(a)(1) and § 1.6049-7(b)(2)(i)). The REMIC must state on the information return—

(A) **The sum of—**

(1) The aggregate amounts includible in gross income as interest (as defined in § 1.6049-7(a)(1)(i) and (ii)), for the calendar year; and

(2) The sum of the amount of allocable investment expenses required to be allocated to the pass-through interest holder for each calendar quarter during the calendar year pursuant to § 1.67-3T(a); and

(B) Any other information specified by the form or its instructions.

(4) **Interest held by nominees and other specified persons—(i) Pass-through interest holder's interest held by a nominee.** If a pass-through interest holder's interest in a REMIC is held in the name of a nominee, the REMIC may make the information return described in paragraphs (f)(3)(i) and (ii) of this section with respect to the nominee in lieu of the pass-through interest holder and may provide the written statement described in paragraphs (f)(2)(i) and (ii) of this section to that nominee in lieu of the pass-through interest holder.

(ii) **Regular interests in a single-class REMIC held by certain persons.** If a person specified in § 1.6049-7(e)(4) holds a regular interest in a single-class REMIC (as described in § 1.67-3T(a)(2)(ii)(B)), then the single-class REMIC must provide the information described in paragraphs (f)(1) and (f)(3)(ii)(A) and (B) of this section to that person with the information specified in § 1.6049-7(e)(2) as required in § 1.6049-7(e).

(5) **Nominee reporting—(i) In general.** In any case in which a REMIC provides information pursuant to paragraph (f)(4) of this section to a nominee of a pass-through interest holder for a calendar quarter or, as provided in paragraph (f)(2)(ii) of this section, for a calendar year—

(A) The nominee must furnish each pass-through interest holder with a written statement described in paragraph (f)(2)(i) or (ii) of this section, whichever is applicable, showing the information described in paragraph (f)(1) of this section; and

(B) The nominee must make an information return on Form 1099 for each calendar year, with respect to the pass-through interest holder and state on this information return the information described in paragraphs (f)(3)(ii)(A) and (B) of this section, if—

(1) The nominee is a nominee for a pass-through interest holder who holds a regular interest in a single-class REMIC (as described in § 1.67.3T(a)(2)(ii)(B)); and

(2) The nominee is required to make an information return pursuant to section 6049 and § 1.6049-7(b)(2)(i) and (b)(2)(ii)(B) (or would be required to make an information return but for the $10 threshold described in section 6049(a)(2) and § 1.6049.7(b)(2)(i)) with respect to the pass-through interest holder.

(ii) Time for furnishing statement. The statement required by paragraph (f)(5)(i)(A) of this section to be furnished by a nominee to a pass-through interest holder for a calendar quarter or calendar year must be furnished to this holder no later than 30 days after receiving the written statement described in paragraph (f)(2)(i) or (ii) of this section from the REMIC. If, however, pursuant to paragraph (f)(2)(ii) of this section, the information is separately stated on the statement described in § 1.6049-7(f), then the information must be furnished to the pass-through interest holder in the time specified in § 1.6049-7(f)(5).

(6) Special rules—(i) Time and place for furnishing returns. The returns required by paragraphs (f)(3)(ii) and (f)(5)(i)(B) of this section for any calendar year must be filed at the time and place that a return required under section 6049 and § 1.6049-7(b)(2) is required to be filed. See § 1.6049-4(g) and § 1.6049-7(b)(2)(iv).

(ii) Duplicative returns not required. The requirements of paragraphs (f)(3)(ii) and (f)(5)(i)(B) of this section for the making of an information return are satisfied by the timely filing of an information return pursuant to section 6049 and § 1.6049-7(b)(2) that contains the information required by paragraph (f)(3)(ii) of this section.

Temporary Treasury Regulation 1.67-3T—Allocation of expenses by real estate mortgage investment conduits (temporary)

(a) Allocation of allocable investment expenses—(1) In general. A real estate mortgage investment conduit or REMIC (as defined in section 860D) shall allocate to each of its pass-through interest holders that holds an interest at any time during the calendar quarter the holder's proportionate share (as determined under paragraph (c) of this section) of the aggregate amount of allocable investment expenses of the REMIC for the calendar quarter.

(2) Pass-through interest holder—(i) In General—(A) Meaning of term. Except as provided in paragraph (a)(2)(ii) of this section, the term "pass-through interest holder" means any holder of a REMIC residual interest (as defined in section 860G(a)(2)) that is—

(1) An individual (other than a nonresident alien whose income with respect to his or her interest in the REMIC is not effectively connected with the conduct of a trade or business within the United States),

(2) A person, including a trust or estate, that computes its taxable income in the same manner as in the case of an individual, or

(3) A pass-through entity (as defined in paragraph (a)(3) of this section) if one or more of its partners, shareholders, beneficiaries, participants, or other interest holders is (i) a pass-through entity, or (ii) a person described in paragraph (a)(2)(i)(A)*(1)* or *(2)* of this section.

(B) Examples. The provisions of this paragraph (a)(2)(i) may be illustrated by the following examples:
Example 1.
Corporation X holds a residual interest in REMIC R in its capacity as a nominee or custodian for individual A, the beneficial

owner of the interest. Because the owner of the interest for Federal income tax purposes is an individual, the interest is owned by a pass-through interest holder.

Example 2.

Individual retirement account I holds a residual interest in a REMIC. Because an individual retirement account is not a person described in paragraph (a)(2)(i)(A) of this section, the interest is not held by a pass-through interest holder.

(ii) **Single-class REMIC—(A) In general.** In the case of a single-class REMIC, the term "pass-through interest holder" means any holder of either—

(1) A REMIC regular interest (as defined in section 860G(a)(1)), or

(2) A REMIC residual interest, that is described in paragraph (a)(2)-(i)(A)*(1)*,*(2)*, or *(3)* of this section.

(B) **Single-class REMIC.** For purposes of paragraph (a)(2)(ii)(A) of this section, a single-class REMIC is either—

(1) A REMIC that would be classified as an investment trust under § 301.7701-4(c)(1) but for its qualification as a REMIC under section 860D and § 1.860D-1T, or

(2) A REMIC that—

(i) Is substantially similar to an investment trust under § 301.77014 (c)-(1), and

(ii) Is structured with the principal purposes of avoiding the requirement of paragraph (a)(1) and (2)(ii)(A) of this section to allocate allocable investment expenses to pass-through interest holders that hold regular interests in the REMIC. For purposes of this paragraph (a)(2)(ii)(B), in determining whether a REMIC would be classified as an investment trust or is substantially similar to an investment trust, all interests in the REMIC shall be treated as ownership interests in the REMIC without regard to whether or not they would be classified as debt for Federal income tax purposes in the absence of a REMIC election.

(C) **Examples.** The provisions of paragraph (a)(2)(ii) of this section may be illustrated by the following examples:

Example 1.

Corporation M transfers mortgages to a bank under a trust agreement as described in Example (2) of § 301.7701-4(c)(2). There are two classes of certificates. Holders of class C certificates are entitled to receive 90 percent of the payments of principal and interest on the mortgages; holders of class D certificates are entitled to receive the remaining 10 percent. The two classes of certificates are identical except that, in the event of a default on the underlying mortgages, the payment rights of class D certificate holders are subordinated to the rights of class C certificate holders. M sells the class C certificates to investors and retains the class D certificates. The trust would be classified as an investment trust under § 301.7701-4(c)(1) but for its qualification as a REMIC under section 860D. The class C certificates represent regular interests in the REMIC and the class D certificates represent residual interests in the REMIC. The REMIC is a single-class REMIC within the meaning of paragraph (a)(2)(ii)(B)*(1)* of this section and, accordingly, holders of both the class C and class D certificates who are described in paragraph (a)(2)(i)(A)*(1)*, *(2)*, or *(3)* of this section are treated as pass-through interest holders.

Example 2.

Assume that the facts are the same as in Example (1) except that M structures the REMIC to include a second regular interest presented by class E certificates. The principal purpose of M in structuring the REMIC to include class E certificates is to avoid allocating allocable investment expenses to class C certificate holders. The class E certificate holders are entitled to receive the payments otherwise due the class D certificate holders until they have been paid a stated amount of principal plus interest. The fair market value of the class E certificate is ten percent of the fair market value of the class D certificate and, therefore, less than one percent of the fair market value of the REMIC. The REMIC would not be classified as an investment trust under § 301.7701-4(c)(1) because the existence of the class E certificates is not incidental to the trust's purpose of facilitating direct investment in the assets of the trust. Nevertheless, because the fair market value of the class E certificates is de minimis, the REMIC is substantially similar to an investment trust under § 301.7701-4(c)(1). In addition, avoidance of the requirement to allocate allocable investment expenses to regular interest holders is the principal purpose of M in structuring the REMIC to include class E certificates. Therefore, the REMIC is a single-class REMIC within the meaning of paragraph (a)(2)(ii)(B)*(2)* of this section, and, accordingly, holders of both residual and regular interests who are described in paragraph (a)(2)(i)(A)*(1)*, *(2)*, or *(3)* of this section are treated as pass-through interest holders.

(3) **Pass-through entity—(i) In general.** Except as provided in paragraph (a)(3)(ii) of this section, for purposes of this section, a pass-through entity is—

(A) A trust (or any portion thereof) to which subpart E, part 1, subchapter J, chapter 1 of the Code applies,

(B) A partnership,

(C) An S corporation,

(D) A common trust fund described in section 584,

(E) A nonpublicly offered regulated investment company (as defined in paragraph (a)(5)(i) of this section),

(F) A REMIC, and

(G) Any other person—

(1) Which is not subject to income tax imposed by subtitle A, chapter 1, or which is allowed a deduction in computing such tax for distributions to owners or beneficiaries, and

(2) The character of the income of which may affect the character of the income recognized with respect to that person by its owners or beneficiaries.

Entities that do not meet the requirements of paragraph (a)(3)(i)(G)*(1)* and *(2)*, such as qualified pension plans, individual retirement accounts, and insurance companies holding assets in separate asset accounts to fund variable contracts defined in section 817(d), are not described in this paragraph (a)(3)(i).

(ii) **Exception.** For purposes of

this section, a pass-through entity does not include—

(A) An estate,

(B) A trust (or any portion thereof) not described in paragraph (a)(3)(i)-(A) of this section,

(C) A cooperative described in section 1381(a)(2), determined without regard to subparagraphs (A) and (C) thereof, or

(D) A real estate investment trust.

(4) **Allocable investment expenses.** The term "allocable investment expenses" means the aggregate amount of the expenses paid or accrued in the calendar quarter for which a deduction is allowable under section 212 in determining the taxable income of the REMIC for the calendar quarter.

(5) **Nonpublicly offered regulated investment company—(i) In general.** For purposes of this section the term "nonpublicly offered regulated investment company" means a regulated investment company to which part I of subchapter M of the Code applies that is not a publicly offered regulated investment company.

(ii) **Publicly offered regulated investment company.** For purposes of this section, the term "publicly offered regulated investment company" means a regulated investment company to which part I of subchapter M of the Code applies, the shares of which are—

(A) Continuously offered pursuant to a public offering (within the meaning of section 4 of the Securities Act of 1933, as amended (15 U.S.C. 77a to 77aa)),

(B) Regularly traded on an established securities market, or

(C) Held by or for no fewer than 500 persons at all times during the taxable year.

(b) **Treatment of allocable investment expenses—(1) By pass-through interest holders—(i) Taxable year ending with calendar quarter.** A pass-through interest holder whose taxable year is the calendar year or ends with a calendar quarter shall be treated as having—

(A) Received or accrued income, and

(B) Paid or incurred an expense described in section 212 (or section 162 in the case of a pass-through interest holder that is a regulated investment company), in an amount equal to the pass-through interest holder's proportionate share of the allocable investment expenses of the REMIC for those calendar quarters that fall within the holder's taxable year.

(ii) Taxable year not ending with calendar quarter. A pass-through interest holder whose taxable year does not end with a calendar quarter shall be treated as having—

(A) Received or accrued income, and

(B) Paid or incurred an expense described in section 212 (or section 162 in the case of a pass-through interest holder that is a regulated investment company),

in an amount equal to the sum of—

(C) The pass-through interest holder's proportionate share of the allocable investment expenses of the REMIC for those calendar quarters that fall within the holder's taxable year, and

(D) For each calendar quarter that overlaps the beginning or end of the taxable year, the sum of the daily amounts of the allocable investment expenses allocated to the holder pursuant to paragraph (c)(1)(ii) of this section for the days in the quarter that fall within the holder's taxable year.

(2) Proportionate share of allocable investment expenses. For purposes of paragraph (b) of this section, a pass-through interest holder's proportionate share of the allocable investment expenses is the amount allocated to the pass-through interest holder pursuant to paragraph (a)(1) of this section.

(3) Cross-reference. See § 1.67.1T with respect to limitations on deductions for expenses described in section 212 (including amounts treated as such expenses under this section).

(4) Interest income to holders of regular interests in certain REMICs. Any amount allocated under this section to the holder of a regular interest in a single-class REMIC (as described in paragraph

(a)(2)(ii)(B) of this section) shall be treated as interest income.

(5) No adjustment to basis. The basis of any holder's interest in a REMIC shall not be increased or decreased by the amount of the holder's proportionate share of allocable investment expenses.

(6) Interest holders other than pass-through interest holders. An interest holder of a REMIC that is not a pass-through interest holder shall not take into account in computing its taxable income any amount of income or expense with respect to its proportionate share of allocable investment expenses.

(c) Computation of proportionate share—(1) In general. For purposes of paragraph (a)(1) of this section, a REMIC shall compute a pass-through interest holder's proportionate share of the REMIC's allocable investment expenses by—

(i) Determining the daily amount of the allocable investment expenses for the calendar quarter by dividing the total amount of such expenses by the number of days in that calendar quarter,

(ii) Allocating the daily amount of the allocable investment expenses to the pass-through interest holder in proportion to its respective holdings on that day, and

(iii) Totaling the interest holder's daily amount of allocable investment expenses for the calendar quarter.

(2) Other holders taken into account. For purposes of paragraph (c)(1)(ii) of this section, a pass-through interest holder's proportionate share of the daily amount of the allocable investment expenses is determined by taking into account all holders of residual interests in the REMIC, whether or not pass-through interest holders.

(3) Single-class REMIC—(i) Daily allocation. In lieu of the allocation specified in paragraph (c)(1)(ii) of this section, a single-class REMIC (as described in paragraph (a)(2)(ii)(B) of this section) shall allocate the daily amount of the allocable investment expenses to each pass-through interest holder in proportion to the amount of income accruing to the holder with respect to its interest in the REMIC on that day.

(ii) **Other holders taken into account.** For purposes of paragraph (c)(3)(i) of this section, the amount of the allocable investment expenses that is allocated on any day to each pass-through interest holder shall be determined by multiplying the daily amount of allocable investment expenses (determined pursuant to paragraph (c)(1)(i) of this section) by a fraction, the numerator of which is equal to the amount of income that accrues (but not less than zero) to the pass-through interest holder on that day and the denominator of which is the total amount of income (as determined under paragraph (c)(3)(iii) of this section) that accrues to all regular and residual interest holders, whether or not pass-through interest holders, on that day.

(iii) **Total income accruing.** The total amount of income that accrues to all regular and residual interest holders is the sum of—

(A) The amount includible under section 860B in the gross income (but not less than zero) of the regular interest holders, and

(B) The amount of REMIC taxable income (but not less than zero) taken into account under section 860C by the residual interest holders.

(4) **Dates of purchase and disposition.** For purposes of this section, a pass-through interest holder holds an interest on the date of its purchase but not on the date of its disposition.

(d) **Example.** The provisions of this section may be illustrated by the following example:

Example.

(i) During the calendar quarter ending March 31, 1989, REMIC X, which is not a single-class REMIC, incurs $900 of allocable investment expenses. At the beginning of the calendar quarter, X has 4 residual interest holders, who hold equal proportionate shares, and 10 regular interest holders. The residual interest holders, all of whom have calendar-year taxable years, are as follows:

A, an individual,

C, a C corporation that is a nominee for individual I,

S, an S corporation, and

M, a C corporation that is not a nominee.

(ii) Except for A, all of the residual interest holders hold their interests in X for the entire calendar quarter. On January 31, 1989, A sells his interest to S. Thus, for the first month of the calendar quarter, each residual interest holder holds a 25 percent interest (100%/4 interest holders) in X. For the last two months, S's holding is increased to 50 percent and A's holding is decreased to zero. The daily amount of allocable investment expenses for the calendar quarter is $10 ($900/90 days).

(iii) The amount of allocable investment expenses apportioned to the residual interest holders is as follows:

(A) $75 ($10 x 25% x 30 days) is allocated to A for the 30 days that A holds an interest in X during the calendar quarter. A includes $75 in gross income in calendar year 1989. The amount of A's expenses described in section 212 is increased by $75 in calendar year 1989. A's deduction under section 212 (including the $75 amount of the allocation) is subject to the limitations contained in section 67.

(B) $225 ($10 x 25% x 90 days) is allocated to C. Because C is a nominee for I, C does not include $225 in gross income or increase its deductible expenses by $225. Instead, I includes $225 in gross income in calendar year 1989, her taxable year. The amount of I's expenses described in section 212 is increased by $225. I's deduction under section 212 (including the $225 amount of the allocation) is subject to the limitations contained in section 67.

(C) $375 (($10 x 25% x 30 days) + ($10 x 50% x 60 days)) is allocated to S. S includes in gross income $375 of allocable investment expenses in calendar year 1989. The amount of S's expenses described in section 212 for that taxable year is increased by $375. S allocates the $375 to its shareholders in accordance with the rules described in sections 1366 and 1377 in calendar year 1989. Thus, each shareholder of S includes its pro rata share of the $375 in gross income in its taxable year in which or with which calendar year 1989 ends. The amount of each shareholder's expenses described in section 212 is increased by the amount of the shareholder's allocation for the shareholder's taxable year in which or with which calendar year 1989 ends. The shareholder's deduction under section 212 (including the allocation under this section) is subject to the limitations contained in section 67.

(D) No amount is allocated to M. However, M's interest is taken into account for purposes of determining the proportionate share of those residual interest holders to whom an allocation is required to be made.

(iv) No allocation is made to the 10 regular interest holders pursuant to paragraph (a) of this section. In addition, the interests held by these interest holders are not taken into account for purposes of determining the proportionate share of the residual interest holders to whom an allocation is required to be made.

(e) **Allocable investment expenses not subject to backup withholding.** The amount of allocable investment expenses required to be allocated to a pass-through interest holder pursuant to paragraph (a)(1) of this section is not subject to backup withholding under section 3406.

(f) **Notice to pass-through interest holders—(1) Information required.** A REMIC must provide to each pass-through interest holder to which an allocation of allocable investment expense is required to be made under paragraph (a)(1) of this section notice of the following—

(i) If, pursuant to paragraph (f)(2) (i) or (ii) of this section, notice is provided for a calendar quarter, the aggregate amount of expenses paid or accrued during the calendar quarter for which the REMIC is allowed a deduction under section 212;

(ii) If, pursuant to paragraph (f)(2) (ii) of this section, notice is provided to a regular interest holder for a calendar year, the aggregate amount of expenses paid or accrued during each calendar quarter that the regular interest holder held the regular interest in the calendar year and for which

the REMIC is allowed a deduction under section 212; and

(iii) The proportionate share of these expenses allocated to that pass-through interest holder, as determined under paragraph (c) of this section.

(2) **Statement to be furnished—(i) To residual interest holder.** For each calendar quarter, a REMIC shall provide to each pass-through interest holder who holds a residual interest during the calendar quarter the notice required under paragraph (f)(1) of this section on Schedule Q (Form 1066), as required in § 1.860F-4(e).

(ii) **To regular interest holder— (A) In general.** For each calendar year, a single-class REMIC (as described in paragraph (a)(2)(ii)(B) of this section) must provide to each pass-through interest holder who held a regular interest during the calendar year the notice required under paragraph (f)(1) of this section. Quarterly reporting is not required. The information required to be included in the notice may be separately stated on the statement described in § 1.6049-7(f) instead of on a separate statement provided in a separate mailing. See § 1.6049-7(f)(4). The separate statement provided in a separate mailing must be furnished to each pass-through interest holder no later than the last day of the month following the close of the calendar year.

(B) **Special rule for 1987.** The information required under paragraph (f)(2)(ii)(A) of this section for any calendar quarter of 1987 shall be mailed (or otherwise delivered) to each pass-through interest holder who holds a regular interest during that calendar quarter no later than March 28, 1988.

(3) **Returns to the Internal Revenue Service—(i) With respect to residual interest holders.** Any REMIC required under paragraphs (f)(1) and (2)(i) of this section to furnish information to any pass-through interest holder who holds a residual interest shall also furnish such information to the Internal Revenue Service as required in § 1.860F-4(e)(4).

(ii) **With respect to regular interest holders.** A single-class REMIC (as described in paragraph (a)(2)(ii)(B) of this section) shall make an information return on Form 1099 for each calendar year beginning after December 31, 1987, with respect to each pass-through interest holder who holds a regular interest to which an allocation of allocable investment expenses is required to be made pursuant to paragraphs (a)(1) and (2)(ii) of this section. The preceding sentence applies with respect to a holder for a calendar year only if the REMIC is required to make an information return to the Internal Revenue Service with respect to that holder for that year pursuant to section 6049 and § 1.6049-7(b)(2)(i) (or would be required to make an information return but for the $10 threshold described in section 6049 (a)(1) and § 1.6047(b)(2)(i)). The REMIC shall state on the information return—

(A) The sum of—

(1) The aggregate amounts includible in gross income as interest (as defined in § 1.6049-7(a)(1)(i) and (ii)), for the calendar year, and

(2) The sum of the amount of allocable investment expenses required to be allocated to the pass-through interest holder for each calendar quarter during the calendar year pursuant to paragraph (a) of this section, and

(B) Any other information specified by the form or its instructions.

(4) Interest held by nominees and other specified persons—(i) Pass-through interest holder's interest held by a nominee. If a pass-through interest holder's interest in a REMIC is held in the name of a nominee, the REMIC may make the information return described in paragraphs (f)(3)(i) and (ii) of this section with respect to the nominee in lieu of the pass-through interest holder and may provide the written statement described in paragraphs (f)(2)(i) and (ii) of this section to that nominee in lieu of the pass-through interest holder.

(ii) Regular interests in a single-class REMIC held by certain persons. For calendar quarters and calendar years after December 31, 1991, if a person specified in § 1.6049-7(e)(4) holds a regular interest in a single-class REMIC (as described in paragraph (a)(2)(ii)(B) of this section), then the single-class REMIC must provide the infor-

mation described in paragraphs (f)(1) and (f)(3)(ii)(A) and (B) of this section to that person with the information specified in § 1.6049-7(e)(2) as required in § 1.6049-7(e).

(5) Nominee reporting—(i) In general. In any case in which a REMIC provides information pursuant to paragraph (f)(4) of this section to a nominee of a pass-through interest holder for a calendar quarter or, as provided in paragraph (f)(2)(ii) of this section, for a calendar year—

(A) The nominee shall furnish each pass-through interest holder with a written statement described in paragraph (f)-(2)(i) or (ii) of this section, whichever is applicable, showing the information described in paragraph (f)(1) of this section, and

(B) If—

(1) The nominee is a nominee for a pass-through interest holder who holds a regular interest in a single-class REMIC (as described in paragraph (a)(2(ii)-(B) of this section), and

(2) The nominee is required to make an information return pursuant to section 6049 and § 1.6049-7(b)(2)(i) and (b)(2)(ii)(B) (or would be required to make an information return but for the $10 threshold described in section 6049(a)(2) and § 1.6049-7(b)(2)(i) with respect to the pass-through interest holder,

the nominee shall make an information return on Form 1099 for each calendar year beginning after December 31, 1987, with respect to the pass-through interest holder and state on this information return the information described in paragraph (f)(3)(ii)(A) and (B) of this section.

(ii) Time for furnishing statement. The statement required by paragraph (f)(5)(i)(A) of this section to be furnished by a nominee to a pass-through interest holder for a calendar quarter or calendar year shall be furnished to this holder no later than 30 days after receiving the written statement described in paragraph (f)(2)(i) or (ii) of this section from the REMIC. If, however, pursuant to paragraph (f)(2)(ii) of this section, the information is separately stated on the statement described in § 1.6049-7(f), then the information must be furnished to the pass-through interest holder in the time specified in § 1.6049-7(f)(5).

(6) Special rules—(i) Time and place for furnishing returns. The returns required by paragraphs (f)(3)(ii) and (f)(5)(i)(B) of this section for any calendar year shall be filed at the time and place that a return required under section 6049 and § 1.6049-7(b)(2) is required to be filed. See § 1.6049-4(g) and § 1.6049-7(b)(2)(iv).

(ii) Duplicative returns not required. The requirements of paragraphs (f)(3)(ii) and (f)(5)(i)(B) of this section for the making of an information return shall be met by the timely filing of an information return pursuant to section 6049 and § 1.6049-7(b)(2) that contains the information required by paragraph (f)(3)(ii) of this section.

Treasury Regulation § 1.856-3

Definitions.—For purposes of the regulations under part II, subchapter M, chapter 1 of the Code, the following definitions shall apply.

***

(a) Real estate assets.—(1) In general. The term "real estate assets" means real property, interests in mortgages on real property (including interests in mortgages on leaseholds of land or improvements thereon), and shares in other qualified real estate investment trusts. The term "mortgages on real property" includes deeds of trust on real property.

(2) Treatment of REMIC interests as real estate assets— (i) In general. If, for any calendar quarter, at least 95 percent of a REMIC's assets (as determined in accordance with § 1.860F-4(e)(1)(ii) or § 1.6049-7(f)(3)) are real estate assets (as defined in paragraph (b)(1) of this section), then, for that calendar quarter, all the regular and residual interests in that REMIC are treated as real estate assets and, except as provided in paragraph (b)(2)(iii) of this section, any amount includible in gross income with respect to those interests is treated as interest on obligations secured by mortgages on real property. If less than 95 percent of a REMIC's assets are real estate assets, then

the real estate investment trust is treated as holding directly its proportionate share of the assets and as receiving directly its proportionate share of the income of the REMIC. See §§ 1.860F-4(e)(1)(ii)(B) and 1.6049-7-(f)(3) for information required to be provided to regular and residual interest holders if the 95-percent test is not met.

(ii) Treatment of REMIC assets for section 856 purposes —(A) Manufactured housing treated as real estate asset. For purposes of paragraphs (b)(1) and (2) of this section, the term "real estate asset" includes manufactured housing treated as a single family residence under section 25(e)-(10).

(B) Status of cash flow investments. For purposes of this paragraph (b)(2), cash flow investments (as defined in section 860G(a)(6) and § 1.860G-2(g)(1)) are real estate assets.

(iii) Certain contingent interest payment obligations held by a REIT. If a REIT holds a residual interest in a REMIC for a principal purpose of avoiding the limitation set out in section 856(f) (concerning interest based on mortgagor net profits) or section 856(j) (concerning shared appreciation provisions), then, even if the REMIC satisfies the 95-percent test of paragraph (b)(i) of this section, the REIT is treated as receiving directly the REMIC's items of income for purposes of section 856.

(b) Interests in real property. The term "interest in real property" includes fee ownership and co-ownership of land or improvements thereon, leaseholds of land or improvements thereon, options to acquire land or improvements thereon, and options to acquire leaseholds of land or improvements thereon. The term also includes timeshare interests that represent an undivided fractional fee interest, or undivided leasehold interest, in real property, and that entitle the holders of the interests to the use and enjoyment of the property for a specified period of time each year. The term also includes stock held by a person as a tenant-stockholder in a cooperative housing corporation (as those terms are defined in section 216). Such term does not, however, include mineral, oil, or gas royalty interests, such as a retained economic interest in coal or iron ore with respect to which the special provisions of section 631(c) apply.

§ 1.6049-7 Returns of information with respect to REMIC regular interests and collateralized debt obligations.

(a) **Definition of interest—**

(1) **In general.** For purposes of section 6049(a), for taxable years beginning after December 31, 1986, the term interest includes:

(i) Interest actually paid with respect to a collateralized debt obligation (as defined in paragraph (d)(2) of this section);

(ii) Interest accrued with respect to a REMIC regular interest (as defined in section 860G(a)(1)); or

(iii) Original issue discount accrued with respect to a REMIC regular interest or a collateralized debt obligation.

(2) **Interest deemed paid.** For purposes of this section and in determining who must make an information return under section 6049(a), interest as defined in paragraphs (a)(1)(ii) and (iii) of this section is deemed paid when includible in gross income under section 860B(b) or section 1272.

(b) **Information required to be reported to the Internal Revenue Service—**

(1) **Requirement of filing Form 8811 by REMICs and other issuers—**

(i) **In general.** Except in the case of a REMIC all of whose regular interests are owned by one other REMIC, every REMIC and every issuer of a collateralized debt obligation (as defined in paragraph (d)(2) of this section) must make an information return on Form 8811, Information Return for Real Estate Mortgage Investment Conduits (REMICs) and Issuers of Collateralized Debt Obligations. Form 8811 must be filed in the time and manner prescribed in paragraph (b)(1)(iii) of this section. The submission of Form 8811 to the Internal Revenue Service does not satisfy the election requirement specified in § 1.860D-1T(d) and does not require election of REMIC status.

(ii) **Information required to be reported.** The following information must be reported to the Internal Revenue Service on Form 8811—

(A) The name, address, and employer identification number of the REMIC or the issuer of a collateralized debt obligation (as defined in paragraph (d)(2) of this section);

(B) The name, title, and either the address or the address and telephone number of the official or representative of the REMIC or the issuer of a collateralized debt obligation who will provide to any person specified in paragraph (e)(4) of this section the interest and original issue discount information specified in paragraph (e)(2) of this section;

(C) The startup day (as defined in section 860G(a)(9)) of the REMIC or the issue date (as defined in section 1275(a)(2)) of the collateralized debt obligation;

(D) The Committee on Uniform Security Identification Procedure (CUSIP) number, account number, serial number, or other identifying number or information, of each class of REMIC regular interest or collateralized debt obligation;

(E) The name, title, address, and telephone number of the official or representative of the REMIC or the issuer of a collateralized debt obligation whom the Internal Revenue Service may contact; and

(F) Any other information required by Form 8811.

(iii) **Time and manner of filing of information return—**

(A) **Manner of filing.** Form 8811 must be filed with the Internal Revenue Service at the address specified on the form. The information specified in paragraph (b)(1)(ii) of this section must be provided on Form 8811 regardless of whether other information returns are filed by use of electronic media.

(B) **Time for filing.** Form 8811 must be filed by each REMIC or issuer of a collateralized debt obligation on or before the later of July 31, 1989, or the 30th day after—

(1) the startup day (as defined in section 860G(a)(9)) in the case of a REMIC, or

(2) the issue date (as defined in section 1275(a)(2)) in the case of a collateralized debt obligation. Further, each REMIC or issuer of a collateralized debt obligation must file a new Form 8811 on or before the 30th day after any change in the information previously provided on Form 8811.

(3) Requirement of reporting by REMICs, issuers, and nominees—

(i) In general. Every person described in paragraph (b)(2)(ii) of this section who pays to another person $10 or more of interest (as defined in paragraph (a) of this section) during any calendar year must file an information return on Form 1099, unless the interest is paid to a person specified in paragraph (c) of this section.

(ii) Person required to make reports. The persons required to make an information return under section 6049(a) and this section are—

(A) REMICs or issuers of collateralized debt obligations (as defined in paragraph (d)(2) of this section), and

(B) Any broker who holds as a nominee or middleman who holds as a nominee any REMIC regular interest or any collateralized debt obligation.

(iii) Information to be reported—

(A) REMIC regular interests and collateralized debt obligations not issued with original issue discount. An information return on Form 1099 must be made for each holder of a REMIC regular interest or collateralized debt obligation not issued with original issue discount, but only if the holder has been paid interest (as defined in paragraph (a) of this section) of $10 or more for the calendar year. The information return must show—

(1) The name, address, and taxpayer identification number of the record holder,

(2) The CUSIP number, account number, serial number, or other identifying number or information, of each REMIC regular interest or collateralized debt obligation, with respect to which a return is being made,

(3) The aggregate amount of interest paid or deemed paid to the record holder for the period during the calendar year for which the return is made,

(4) The name, address, and taxpayer identification number of the person required to file this return, and

(5) Any other information required by the form.

(B) REMIC regular interests and collateralized debt obligations issued with original issue discount. An information return on Form 1099 must be made for each holder of a REMIC regular interest or a collateralized debt obligation issued with original issue discount, but only if the holder has been paid interest (as defined in paragraph (a) of this section) of $10 or more for the calendar year. The information return must show—

(1) The name, address, and taxpayer identification number of the record holder,

(2) The CUSIP number, account number, serial number, or other identifying number or information, of each REMIC regular interest or collateralized debt obligation, with respect to which a return is being made,

(3) The aggregate amount of original issue discount deemed paid to the record holder for the period during the calendar year for which the return is made,

(4) The aggregate amount of interest, other than original issue discount, paid or deemed paid to the record holder for the period during the calendar year for which the return is made,

(5) The name, address, and taxpayer identification number of the person required to file this return, and

(6) Any other information required by the form.

(C) Cross-reference. See § 1.67-3T(f)(3)(ii) for additional information required to be included on an information return on Form 1099 with respect to certain holders of regular interests in REMICs described in § 1.67-3T(a)(2)(ii).

(iv) Time and place for filing a return with respect to amounts includible as interest. The returns required under paragraph (b)(2) of this section for any calendar year must be filed after September 30 of that year, but not before the payor's final payment to the payee for the year, and on or before February 28 of the following year. These returns must be filed with the appropriate Internal Revenue Service Center, the address of which is listed in the instructions for Form 1099. For extensions of time for filing returns under this section, see § 1.6081-1. For magnetic media filing requirements, see § 301.6011-2 of this chapter.

(c) **Information returns not required.** An information return is not required under section 6049(a) and this section with respect to payments of interest on a REMIC regular interest or collateralized debt obligation, if the holder of the REMIC regular interest or the collateralized debt obligation is—

(1) An organization exempt from taxation under section 501(a) or an individual retirement plan;

(2) The United States or a State, the District of Columbia, a possession of the United States, or a political subdivision or a wholly-owned agency or instrumentality of any one or more of the foregoing;

(3) A foreign government, a political subdivision thereof, or an international organization;

(4) A foreign central bank of issue (as defined in § 1.895-1(b)(1) to be a bank which is by law or government sanction the principal authority, other than the government itself, issuing instruments intended to circulate as currency);

(5) A trust described in section 4947(a)(1) (relating to certain charitable trusts);

(6) For calendar quarters and calendar years after 1988, a broker (as defined in section 6045(c) and § 1.6045-1(a)(1));

(7) For calendar quarters and calendar years after 1988, a person who holds the REMIC regular interest or collateralized debt obligation as a middleman (as defined in § 1.6049-4(f)(4));

(8) For calendar quarters and calendar years after 1988, a corporation (as defined in section 7701(a)(3)), whether domestic or foreign;

(9) For calendar quarters and calendar years after 1988, a dealer in securities or commodities required to register as such under the laws of the United States or a State;

(10) For calendar quarters and calendar years after 1988, a real estate investment trust (as defined in section 856);

(11) For calendar quarters and calendar years after 1988, an entity registered at all times during the taxable year under the Investment Company Act of 1940;

(12) For calendar quarters and calendar years after 1988, a common trust fund (as defined in section 584(a));

(13) For calendar quarters and calendar years after 1988, a financial institution such as a mutual savings bank, savings and loan association, building and loan association, cooperative bank, homestead association, credit union, industrial loan association or bank, or other similar organization;

(14) For calendar quarters and calendar years after 1988, any trust which is exempt from tax under section 664(c) (i.e., a charitable remainder annuity trust or a charitable remainder unitrust); and

(15) For calendar quarters and calendar years after 1988, a REMIC.

(d) **Special provisions and definitions—**

(1) **Incorporation of referenced rules.** The special rules of § 1.6049-4(d) are incorporated in this section, as applicable, except that § 1.6049-4(d)(2) does not apply to any REMIC regular interest or any other debt instrument to which section 1272(a)(6) applies. Further, § 1.6049-5(c) does not apply to any REMIC regular interest or any other debt instrument to which section 1272(a)(6) applies.

(2) **Collateralized debt obligation.** For purposes of this section, the term "collateralized debt obligation" means any debt instrument (except a tax-exempt obligation) described in section 1272(a)(6)(C)(ii) that is issued after December 31, 1986.

(e) **Requirement of furnishing information to certain nominees, corporations, and other specified persons—**

(1) **In general.** For calendar quarters and calendar years after 1988, each REMIC or issuer of a collateralized debt obligation (as defined in paragraph (d)(2) of this section) must provide the information specified in paragraph (e)(2) of this section in the time and manner prescribed in paragraph (e)(3) of this section to any persons speci-

fied in paragraph (e)(4) of this section who request the information.

(2) Information required to be reported. For each class of REMIC regular interest or collateralized debt obligation and for each calendar quarter specified by the person requesting the information, the REMIC or issuer of a collateralized debt obligation must provide the following information—

(i) The name, address and Employer Identification Number of the REMIC or issuer of a collateralized debt obligation;

(ii) The CUSIP number, account number, serial number, or other identifying number or information, of each specified class of REMIC regular interest or collateralized debt obligation and, for calendar quarters and calendar years after 1991, whether the information being reported is with respect to a REMIC regular interest or a collateralized debt obligation;

(iii) Interest paid on a collateralized debt obligation in the specified class for each calendar quarter, and the aggregate amount for the calendar year if the request is made for the last quarter of the calendar year;

(iv) Interest accrued on a REMIC regular interest in the specified class for each accrual period any day of which is in the specified calendar quarter, and the aggregate amount for the calendar year if the request is made for the last quarter of the calendar year;

(v) Original issue discount accrued on a collateralized debt obligation or REMIC regular interest in the specified class for each accrual period any day of which is in that calendar quarter, and the aggregate amount for the calendar year if the request is made for the last quarter of the calendar year;

(vi) The daily portion of original issue discount per $1,000 of original principal amount (or for calendar quarters prior to 1992, per other specified unit) as determined under section 1272(a)(6) and the regulations thereunder for each accrual period any day of which is in the specified calendar quarter;

(vii) The length of the accrual period;

(viii) The adjusted issue price (as defined in section 1275(a)(4)(B)(ii)) of the REMIC regular interest or the collateralized debt obligation at the beginning of each accrual period any day of which is in the specified calendar quarter;

(ix) The information required by paragraph (f)(3) of this section;

(x) Information required to compute the accrual of market discount including, for calendar years after 1989, the information required by paragraphs (f)(2)(i)(G) or (f)(2)(ii)(K) of this section; and

(xi) For calendar quarters and calendar years after 1991, if the REMIC is a single class REMIC (as described in § 1.67-3T(a)(2)(ii)(B)), the information described in § 1.67-3T(f)(1) and (f)(3)(ii)(A) and (B).

(3) Time and manner for providing information—

(i) Manner of providing information. The information specified in paragraph (e)(2) of this section may be provided as follows—

(A) By telephone;

(B) By written statement sent by first class mail to the address provided by the requesting party;

(C) By causing it to be printed in a publication generally read by and available to persons specified in paragraph (e)(4) and by notifying the requesting persons in writing or by telephone of the publication in which it will appear, the date of its appearance, and, if possible, the page upon which it appears; or

(D) By any other method agreed to by the parties. If the information is published, then the publication should also specify the date and, if possible, the page on which corrections, if any, will be printed.

(ii) Time for furnishing the information. Each REMIC or issuer of a collateralized debt obligation must furnish the information specified in paragraph (e)(2) of this section on or before the later of—

(A) The 30th day after the close of the calendar quarter for which the information was requested, or

(B) The day that is two weeks after the receipt of the request.

(4) Persons entitled to request information. The following persons may request the information specified in paragraph (e)(2) of this section with respect to a specified class of REMIC regular interests or collateralized debt obligations from a REMIC or issuer of a collateralized debt obligation in the manner prescribed in paragraph (e)(5) of this section—

(i) Any broker who holds on its own behalf or as a nominee any REMIC regular interest or collateralized debt obligation in the specified class,

(ii) Any middleman who is required to make an information return under section 6049(a) and paragraph (b)(2) of this section and who holds as a nominee any REMIC regular interest or collateralized debt obligation in the specified class,

(iii) Any corporation or non-calendar year taxpayer who holds a REMIC regular interest or collateralized debt obligation in the specified class directly, rather than through a nominee,

(iv) Any other person specified in paragraphs (c)(9) through (15) of this section who holds a REMIC regular interest or collateralized debt obligation in the specified class directly, rather than through a nominee, or

(v) A representative or agent for a person specified in paragraphs (e)(4)(i), (ii), (iii) or (iv) of this section.

(5) Manner of requesting information from the REMIC. A requesting person specified in paragraph (e)(4) of this section should obtain Internal Revenue Service Publication 938, Real Estate Mortgage Investment Conduit (REMIC) and Collateralized Debt Obligation Reporting Information (or other guidance published by the Internal Revenue Service). This publication contains a directory of REMICs and issuers of collateralized debt obligations. The requesting person can locate the REMIC or issuer from whom information is needed and request the information from the official or representative of the REMIC or issuer in the manner specified in the publication. The publication will specify either an address or

an address and telephone number. If the publication provides only an address, the request must be made in writing and mailed to the specified address. Further, the request must specify the calendar quarters (e.g., all calendar quarters in 1989) and the classes of REMIC regular interests or collateralized debt obligations for which information is needed.

(f) Requirement of furnishing statement to recipient—

(1) In general. Every person filing a Form 1099 under section 6049(a) and this section must furnish to the holder (the person whose identifying number is required to be shown on the form) a written statement showing the information required by paragraph (f)(2) of this section. The written statement provided by a REMIC must also contain the information specified in paragraph (f)(3) of this section.

(2) Form of statement—

(i) REMIC regular interests and collateralized debt obligations not issued with original issue discount. For a REMIC regular interest or collateralized debt obligation issued without original issue discount, the written statement must specify for the calendar year the following information—

(A) The aggregate amount shown on Form 1099 to be included in income by that person for the calendar year;

(B) The name, address, and taxpayer identification number of the person required to furnish this statement;

(C) The name, address, and taxpayer identification number of the person who must include the amount of interest in gross income;

(D) A legend, including a statement that the amount is being reported to the Internal Revenue Service, that conforms to the legend on Form 1099, Copy B, For Recipient;

(E) The CUSIP number, account number, serial number, or other identifying number or information, of each REMIC regular interest or collateralized debt obligation, with respect to which a return is being made;

(F) All other items shown on Form 1099 for the calendar year; and

(G) Information necessary to compute accrual of market discount. For calendar years after 1989, this requirement is satisfied by furnishing to the holder for each accrual period during the year a fraction computed in the manner described in either paragraph (f)(2)(i)(G)(*1*) or (f)(2)(i)-(G)(*2*) of this section. For calendar years after December 31, 1991, the REMIC or the issuer of the collateralized debt obligation must be consistent in the method used to compute this fraction.

(*1*) The numerator of the fraction equals the interest, other than original issue discount, allocable to the accrual period. The denominator of the fraction equals the interest, other than original issue discount, allocable to the accrual period plus the remaining interest, other than original issue discount, as of the end of that accrual period. The interest allocable to each accrual period and the remaining interest are calculated by taking into account events which have occurred before the close of the accrual period and the prepayment assumption, if any, determined as of the startup day (as defined in section 860G(a)(9)) of the REMIC or the issue date (as defined in section 1275(a)(2)) of the collateralized debt obligation that would be made in computing original issue discount if the debt instrument had been issued with original issue discount.

(*2*) If the REMIC regular interest or the collateralized debt obligation has de minimis original issue discount (as defined in section 1273(a)(3) and any regulations thereunder), then, at the option of the REMIC or the issuer of the collateralized debt obligation, the fraction may be computed in the manner specified in paragraph (f)(2)(ii)(K) of this section taking into account the de minimis original issue discount. The interest allocable to each accrual period and the remaining interest are calculated by taking into account events which have occurred before the close of the accrual period and the prepayment assumption, if any, determined as of the startup day (as defined in section 860G(a)(9)) of the REMIC or the issue date (as defined in section 1275(a)(2)) of the collateralized debt obligation that would be made in computing original issue discount if the debt instrument had been issued with original issue discount.

(ii) REMIC regular interests and collateralized debt obligations issued with original issue discount. For a REMIC regular interest or collateralized debt obligation issued with original issue discount, the written statement must specify for the calendar year the following information—

(A) The aggregate amount of original issue discount includible in the gross income of the holder for the calendar year with respect to the REMIC regular interest or the collateralized debt obligation;

(B) The aggregate amount of interest, other than original issue discount, includible in the gross income of the holder for the calendar year with respect to the REMIC regular interest or the collateralized debt obligation;

(C) The name, address, and taxpayer identification number of the person required to file this form;

(D) The name, address, and taxpayer identification number of the person who must include the amount of interest specified in paragraphs (f)(2)(ii)(A) and (B) of this section in gross income;

(E) For calendar years after 1987, the daily portion of original issue discount per $1,000 of original principal amount (or for calendar years prior to 1992, per other specified unit) as determined under section 1272(a)(6) and the regulations thereunder for each accrual period any day of which is in that calendar year;

(F) For calendar years after 1987, the length of the accrual period;

(G) All other items shown on Form 1099 for the calendar year;

(H) A legend, including a statement that the information required under paragraphs (f)(2)(ii) (A), (B), (C), (D) and (G) of this section is being reported to the Internal Revenue Service, that conforms to the legend on Form 1099, Copy B, For Recipient;

(I) For calendar years after 1987, the adjusted issue price (as defined in section 1275(a)(4)(B)(ii)) of the REMIC regular interest or the collateralized debt obligation at the beginning of each accrual period with respect to which interest income is required to be reported on Form 1099 for the calendar year;

(J) The CUSIP number, account number, serial number, or other identifying number or information, of each class of REMIC regular interest or collateralized debt obligation, with respect to which a return is being made; and

(K) Information necessary to compute accrual of market discount. For calendar years after 1989, this information includes:

(1) For each accrual period in the calendar year, a fraction, the numerator of which equals the original issue discount allocable to that accrual period, and the denominator of which equals the original issue discount allocable to that accrual period plus the remaining original issue discount as of the end of that accrual period; and

(2) [Reserved]

The original issue discount allocable to each accrual period and the remaining original issue discount are calculated by taking into account events which have occurred before the close of the accrual period and the prepayment assumption determined as of the startup day (as defined in section 860G(a)(9)) of the REMIC or the issue date (as defined in section 1275(a)(2)) of the collateralized debt obligation.

(3) **Information with respect to REMIC assets—**

(i) **95 percent asset test.** For calendar years after 1988, the written statement provided by a REMIC must also contain the following information for each calendar quarter—

(A) The percentage of REMIC assets that are qualifying real property loans under section 593,

(B) The percentage of REMIC assets that are assets described in section 7701(a)(19), and

(C) The percentage of REMIC assets that are real estate assets defined in section 856(c)(6)(B), computed by reference to the average adjusted basis (as defined in

section 1011) of the REMIC assets during the calendar quarter (as described in § 1.860F-4(e)(1)(iii)). If for any calendar quarter the percentage of REMIC assets represented by a category is at least 95 percent, then the statement need only specify that the percentage for that category, for that calendar quarter, was at least 95 percent.

(ii) **Additional information required if the 95 percent test not met.** If, for any calendar quarter after 1988, less than 95 percent of the assets of the REMIC are real estate assets defined in section 856(c)(6)(B), then, for that calendar quarter, the REMIC's written statement must also provide to any real estate investment trust (REIT) that holds a regular interest the following information—

(A) The percentage of REMIC assets described in section 856(c)(5)(A), computed by reference to the average adjusted basis of the REMIC assets during the calendar quarter (as described in § 1.860F-4(e)(1)(iii)),

(B) The percentage of REMIC gross income (other than gross income from prohibited transactions defined in section 860F(a)(2)) described in section 856(c)(3)-(A) through (E), computed as of the close of the calendar quarter, and

(C) The percentage of REMIC gross income (other than gross income from prohibited transactions defined in section 860F(a)(2)) described in section 856(c)(3)-(F), computed as of the close of the calendar quarter. For purposes of this paragraph (f)(3)(ii)(C), the term "foreclosure property" contained in section 856(c)(3)(F) shall have the meaning specified in section 860G(a)(8). In determining whether a REIT satisfies the limitations of section 856(c)(2), all REMIC gross income is deemed to be derived from a source specified in section 856(c)(2).

(iii) **Calendar years 1988 and 1989.** For calendar years 1988 and 1989, the percentage of assets required in paragraphs (f)(3)(i) and (ii) of this section may be computed by reference to the average fair market value of the assets of the REMIC during the calendar quarter (as described in § 1.860F-4(e)(1)(iii)), instead of by reference to the average adjusted basis of the assets of the REMIC during the calendar quarter.

(4) Cross-reference. See § 1.67-3T-(f)(2)(ii) for additional information that may be separately stated on the statement required by this paragraph (f) with respect to certain holders of regular interests in REMICs described in § 1.67-3T(a)(2)(ii).

(5) Time for furnishing statements—

(i) For calendar quarters and calendar years after 1988. For calendar quarters and calendar years after 1988, each statement required under this paragraph (f) to be furnished to any person for a calendar year with respect to amounts includible as interest must be furnished to that person after April 30 of that year and on or before March 15 of the following year, but not before the final interest payment (if any) for the calendar year.

(ii) For calendar quarters and calendar years prior to 1989—

(A) In general. For calendar quarters and calendar years prior to 1989, each statement required under this paragraph (f) to be furnished to any person for a calendar year with respect to amounts includible as interest must be furnished to that person after April 30 of that year and on or before January 31 of the following year, but not before the final interest payment (if any) for the calendar year.

(B) Nominee reporting. For calendar quarters and calendar years prior to 1989, each statement required under this paragraph (f) to be furnished by a nominee must be furnished to the actual owner of a REMIC regular interest or a collateralized debt obligation to which section 1272(a)(6) applies on or before the later of—

• The 30th day after the nominee receives such information, or

• January 31 of the year following the calendar year to which the statement relates.

(6) Special rules—

(i) Copy of Form 1099 permissible. The requirements of this paragraph (f) for the furnishing of a statement to any person, including the legend requirement of paragraphs (f)(2)(i)(D) and (f)(2)(ii)(H) of this section, may be met by furnishing to that person—

(A) A copy of the Form 1099 filed pursuant to paragraph (b)(2) of this section in respect of that person, plus a separate statement (mailed with the Form 1099) that contains the information described in paragraphs (f)(2)(i)(E) and (G), (f)(2)(ii)(E), (F), (I), and (K), (f)(3), and (f)(4) of this section, if applicable, or

(B) A substitute form that contains all the information required under this paragraph (f) and that complies with any current revenue procedure concerning the reproduction of paper substitutes of Form 1099 and the furnishing of substitute statements to forms recipients. The inclusion on the substitute form of the information specified in this paragraph (f) that is not required by the official Form 1099 will not cause the substitute form to fail to meet any requirements that limit the information that may be provided with a substitute form.

(ii) Statement furnished by mail. A statement mailed to the last known address of any person shall be considered to be furnished to that person within the meaning of this section.

(7) Requirement that nominees furnish information to corporations and certain other specified persons—

(i) In general. For calendar quarters and calendar years after 1988, every broker or middleman must provide in writing or by telephone the information specified in paragraph (e)(2) of this section to—

(A) A corporation,

(B) A non-calendar year taxpayer, or

(C) Any other person specified in paragraphs (c)(9) through (15) of this section who requests the information and for whom the broker or middleman holds as a nominee a REMIC regular interest or a collateralized debt obligation. A corporation, non-calendar year taxpayer, or any other person specified in paragraphs (c)(9) through (15) of this section may request the information in writing or by telephone for any REMIC regular interest or collateralized debt obligation for calendar quarters any day of which the person held the interest or obligation.

(ii) Time for furnishing information. The statement required in paragraph (f)(7)(i) of this section must be furnished on or before the later of—

(A) The 45th day after receipt of the request,

(B) The 45th day after the close of the calendar quarter for which the information was requested, or

(C) If the request is made for the last calendar quarter in a year, March 15 of the year following the calendar quarter for which the information was requested.

(g) Information required to be set forth on face of debt instrument—

(1) In general. In the case of any REMIC regular interest or collateralized debt obligation that is issued after April 8, 1988, and that has original issue discount, the issuer must set forth on the face of the REMIC regular interest or collateralized debt obligation—

(i) The amount of the original issue discount,

(ii) The issue date,

(iii) The rate at which interest is payable (if any) as of the issue date,

(iv) The yield to maturity, including a statement as to the assumption made under section 1272 (a)(6)(B)(iii),

(v) The method used to determine yield where there is a short accrual period, and

(vi) The amount of the original issue discount allowable to the short accrual period based on the prepayment assumption determined on the startup day (as defined in section 860G(a)(9)) or the issue date (as defined in section 1275(a)(2)). In cases where it is not possible to set forth the information required by this paragraph (g) on the face of the REMIC regular interest or collateralized debt obligation by the issue date, the issuer must deliver to the holder a sticker containing this information within 10 days after the issue date. For rules relating to the penalty imposed for failure to show the information required by this paragraph (g) on the regular interest or collateralized debt obligation, see

section 6706(a) and the regulations thereuder.

(2) Issuer. For purposes of this paragraph (g), the term "issuer" includes not only domestic issuers but also any foreign issuer who is otherwise subject to United States income tax law, unless the issue is neither listed on an established securities market (as defined in § 1.453-3 (d)(4)) in the United States nor offered for sale or resale in the United States in connection with its original issuance.

§ 301.7701-13A Post-1969 domestic building and loan association.

(e) Assets defined. The assets defined in this paragraph are—

(12) Regular or residual interest in a REMIC—

(a) In general. If for any calendar quarter at least 95 percent of a REMIC's assets (as determined in accordance with § 1.860F-4(e)(1)(ii) or § 1.6049-7(f)(3) of this chapter) are assets defined in paragraph (e)(1) through (e)(11) of this section, then for that calendar quarter all the regular and residual interests in that REMIC are treated as assets defined in this paragraph (e). If less than 95 percent of a REMIC's assets are assets defined in paragraph (e)(1) through (e)(11) of this section, the percentage of each REMIC regular or residual interest treated as an asset defined in this paragraph (e) is equal to the percentage of the REMIC's assets that are assets defined in paragraph (e)(1) through (e)(11) of this section. See §§ 1.860F-4(e)(1)(ii)(B) and 1.6049-7(f)(3) of this chapter for information required to be provided to regular and residual interest holders if the 95 percent test is not met.

(ii) Loans secured by manufactured housing. For purposes of paragraph (e)(12)(i) of this section, a loan secured by manufactured housing treated as a single family residence under section 25(e)(10) is an asset defined in paragraph (e)(1) through (e)(11) of this section.

(b) Special rules. [Reserved]

INTERNAL REVENUE SERVICE NOTICE

Notice 93-11
Real Estate Mortgage Investment Conduits—Variable Rate of Interest

February 8, 1993

This notice provides guidance with respect to certain provisions of the Income Tax Regulations issued under section 860G of the Internal Revenue Code concerning real estate mortgage investment conduits, or REMICs. Taxpayers may rely on this notice until final regulations issued under sections 1271 through 1275 of the Code relating to variable rate debt instruments become effective. At that time, § 1.860G-1(a)(3) of the Income Tax Regulations will be amended to conform to the language of the final regulations.

Section 860G(a)(1) of the Code defines the term "regular interest" to mean an interest that, among other things, "provides that interest payments (or other similar amounts), if any, at or before maturity are payable based on a fixed rate (or to the extent provided in regulations, at a variable rate)."

Section 1.860G-1(a)(3)(i) of the regulations provides that a rate that is a "qualifying variable rate" for purposes of sections 1271 through 1275 of the Code and the related regulations is a variable rate.

Proposed section 1.1275-5, as published in the Federal Register for December 22, 1992, (57 F.R. 60750, 60775), provides rules under sections 1271 through 1275 of the Code for variable rate debt instruments. These rules are proposed to be effective for debt instruments issued on or after the date that is 60 days after the date the regulations are finalized.

Solely for purpose of section 860G(a)(1) of the Code, a qualified floating rate as defined in proposed § 1.1275-5(b)(1) set at a current value, as defined in proposed § 1.1275-5(a)(4), is a "qualifying variable rate" within the meaning of § 1.860G-1(a)(3)(i) of the regulations.

The principal author of this notice is Carol Schwartz of the Office of Assistant Chief Counsel (Financial Institutions & Products). For further information regarding this notice contact Carol Schwartz on (202) 622-3920 (not a toll-free call).

REVENUE RULINGS

Revenue Ruling 70-359

In June 1966, a domestic corporation (the taxpayer) floated a bond issue at an expense of 20x dollars. The bonds matured serially and were to be retired at the rate of 25x dollars a year over a period of 10 years. In June 1968, the taxpayer anticipated payments on the bonds and retired the bond series due in 1968, 1969, 1970, and 1971 by paying 100x dollars to the bond holders.

Held, since there were ten distinct series of bonds floated for the aggregate expense of 20x dollars, one-tenth of the 20x or 2x dollars is the proportionate expense of each series. This amount of 2x dollars expense of issuance of each series should be prorated over the life of each series, that is, in the case of one-year bonds the entire amount should be deducted in the first year; in the case of the two-year bonds one-half should be deducted in the first year and one-half deducted in the second year, and so on with the three, four, five, six, seven, eight, nine, and ten year bonds. See Rev. Rul. 70-353, page 39, this Bulletin.

Since the series 1968, 1969, 1970, and 1971 were retired in 1968, the remaining fractional part of the expense of the 1968 series should be charged off in that year plus (1) the fractional part of the expense of the 1969 series for the years 1968 and 1969, (2) the fractional part of the expense of the 1970 series for the year 1968, 1969, and 1970, (3) the fractional part of the expense of the 1971 series for the years 1968, 1969, 1970, and 1971.

I.T. 1412, C.B. 1-2, 91 (1922), is hereby superseded, since the position stated therein set forth under the current statute and regulations in this Revenue Ruling.

Revenue Ruling 70-544

Advice has been requested as to certain of the Federal income tax consequences associated with "straight pass-through" mortgage-backed certificates to various parties under the facts and circumstances set forth below.

N, a savings and loan association engaged in the financing of residential mortgages, established a "pool" of mortgages, all of which are insured by the Federal Housing Administration, the Farmers Home Administration, or are insured or guaranteed by the Veterans Administration.

Some of the mortgages were originated by *N* and some were acquired by it. The amount of the "pool" was for $2 million, which represented the unpaid balances on the mortgages. The average cost of the mortgages in the "pool" was 94 percent of par or $1,880,000 for the entire "pool". All of the mortgages in the "pool" bear interest at the rate of $8\frac{1}{2}$ percent per annum and were issued during the month prior to the establishment of the "pool". Once the "pool" is established, no additional mortgages may be added to the "pool".

N after application to the Government National Mortgage Association (GNMA), received a commitment from GNMA to guarantee an issue of "straight pass-through" mortgage-backed certificates (certificates). The certificates represent a proportionate interest in each of the mortgages in the above-described "pool." After obtaining the GNMA commitment, *N*, pursuant to a separate agreement, delivered the mortgages to a custodian (a commercial bank). The custodian's sole function is to hold the mortgages, and it has no power of reinvestment.

In addition neither *N* nor GNMA will ever have the power to reinvest any of the proceeds attributable to the mortgages in the "pool". Within four months after GNMA issues its guarantee, GNMA may require *N* to replace defective mortgages included in the "pool". Thereafter, no substitution of mortgages may be required by GNMA. At no time will *N* have the power to substitute mortgages for the initial mortgages in the "pool" on its own initiative.

After the custodian verified to GNMA that it had the mortgages in its custody, N arranged for the sale of the entire issue of mortgage-backed certificates to various investors for 94.75 percent of par or a total of $1,895,000.

The certificate holders included other savings and loan associations, real estate investment trusts, individuals, and exempt employees' pension and profit-sharing trusts. The certificates called for payments by N to the certificate holders of specified monthly installments. These installments were based on the amortization schedules of each of the mortgages in the "pool". If a default or late payment on any mortgage occurs, N may advance funds to keep up the payments to the certificate holders until the deficiency is corrected by the mortgagor or foreclosure occurs. In addition, the certificates provide for payment of each of the certificate holders of its proportionate share of prepayments or other early recoveries of principal including foreclosure proceeds. An amount equal to $1/24$ of one percent of the outstanding principal amount on the mortgages is withheld by N each month, which amount is used by N to discharge the certificate holders' obligations to pay N's servicing fee, the custodian's fee, and the GNMA guarantee fee.

When N notified GNMA of the sales agreement, GNMA prepared the certificates in the total amount of $2 million. GNMA guaranteed to the certificate holders only the proper performance of the mortgage servicing by N, with the certificate holders entitled only to interest and principal actually collected or collectable through due diligence. The sale of the certificates was consummated by delivery of the certificates to the certificate holders. The certificates were issued in minimum denominations of $50,000. The GNMA regulations provide, in part, that the certificates are transferable, but the share of the proceeds collected on account of the "pool" of mortgages may not be payable to more than one holder with respect to any certificate.

When all the mortgages in the "pool" are paid, and the final payments on the certifi-cates are made to the certificate holders, the "pool" will be terminated.

Based solely on the foregoing facts, certain of the Federal income tax consequences are as follows:

(1) The "pool" will not be considered an association taxable as a corporation, but is classified as a trust of which the certificate holders are the owners under Subpart E of Subchapter J of the Internal Revenue Code of 1954.

(2) N is a fiduciary and will be required to file Form 1041. See section 1.671-4 of the Income Tax Regulations.

(3) Each certificate holder is treated as the owner of an undivided interest in the entire trust (corpus as well as ordinary income). See section 1.671-3(a)(1) of the regulations.

(4) The sale of the mortgage-backed certificates transfers to the certificate holders the equitable ownership in each of the mortgages in the "pool". Thereafter, N has only a contractual right to service the mortgages for a specified fee.

(5) N will recognize ordinary income or loss upon the sale of its interest in each of the mortgages in the "pool" measured by the differences between the proportionate amount of the proceeds realized with respect to the sale of each of the mortgages and its adjusted basis in each of such mortgages.

(6) The certificate holders must report their ratable share of the entire interest income on each of the mortgages as ordinary income consistent with their method of accounting, and may deduct the servicing, custodian, and guarantee fees under section 162 or section 212 of the Code.

(7) The certificate holders must also report their ratable share of the discount income realized on the purchase of each of the mortgages as ordinary income, consistent with their methods of accounting. The special rules of section 1232 of the Code will be applicable to the certificate holders' proportionate shares of the discount on any mortgages in the "pool" which are obligations of corporations, or of governments or their political subdivisions if, and to the ex-

tent that, the other conditions for the application of that section are met.

(8) The interest income is considered "interest on obligations secured by mortgages on real property" as that phrase is used in section 856(c)(3)(B) of the Code.

(9) A real estate investment trust which owns a certificate is considered as owning "real estate assets" as that phrase is used in section 856(c)(5)(A) of the Code.

(10) A certificate owned by a savings and loan association is considered as representing "loans secured by an interest in real property" within the meaning of section 7701(a)(19)(C)(v) of the Code, provided the real property is (or from the proceeds of the loan will become) the type of real property described in that section of the Code.

(11) The exempt status of an employees' pension and profit-sharing trust under section 501(a) of the Code is not adversely affected by the purchase of certificates.

Revenue Ruling 70-545

Advice has been requested as to certain of the Federal income tax consequences associated with "fully-modified pass-through" mortgage-backed certificates to various parties under the facts and circumstances set forth below.

M, a savings and loan association engaged in the financing of residential mortgages, established a "pool" of mortgages which are insured by the Federal Housing Administration, the Farmers Home Administration, or are insured or guaranteed by the Veterans Administration and which were originated by *M* at par.

The amount of the "pool" was $2 million, which represented the sum of the unpaid balances on the mortgages. Each of the mortgages in the "pool" bears interest at the rate of $8\frac{1}{2}$ percent per annum. Once the "pool" is established no additional mortgages may be added to the "pool."

M, after application to the Government National Mortgage Association (GNMA), received a commitment from GNMA to guarantee an issue of "fully-modified pass-through" mortgage-backed certificates (cer-

tificates). Each of the certificates represents a proportionate interest in each of the mortgages in the above described "pool" of mortgages. After obtaining the GNMA commitment, pursuant to a separate agreement, *M* delivered the mortgages to a custodian (a commercial bank). The custodian's sole function is to hold the mortgages and it has no power of reinvestment.

In addition neither *M* nor GNMA will ever have the power to reinvest any of the proceeds attributable to the mortgages in the "pool." Within four months after GNMA issues its guarantee, GNMA may require *M* to replace defective mortgages included in the "pool." Thereafter, no substitution of mortgages may be required by GNMA. At no time will *M* have the power to substitute mortgages for the initial mortgages in the "pool" on its own initiative.

After the custodian verified to GNMA that it had the mortgages in its custody, *M* arranged for the sale of the entire issue of certificates to various certificate holders at par or $2 million.

The certificate holders included savings and loan associations, real estate investment trusts, individuals, and exempt employees' pension and profit-sharing trusts. The certificates called for payment by *M* to the certificate holders of specified monthly installments. These installments were based on the amortization schedules of each of the mortgages in the "pool," but were to be made by *M* irrespective of whether the mortgagors actually make the payments due on their loans.

In addition, the certificates provided for payment to each of the certificate holders of its proportionate share of prepayments or other early recoveries of principal including foreclosure proceeds. An amount equal to $\frac{1}{24}$ of one percent of the outstanding principal amount on the mortgages was to be withheld by *M* each month, which amount is to be used by *M* to discharge the certificate holders' obligations to pay *M*'s servicing fee, the custodian's fee, and the GNMA guarantee fee.

When *M* notified GNMA of the sales agreement, GNMA prepared the certificates in the total amount of $2 million with the full guarantee of GNMA to the certificate holders as to payment of principal and interest. The sale was consummated by delivery of the certificates to the certificate holders. The certificates were issued in minimum denominations of $50,000. The GNMA regulations provide, in part, that the certificates are transferable, but the share of the proceeds collected on account of the "pool" of mortgages may not be payable to more than one holder with respect to any certificate. Each certificate contains a statement that the full faith and credit of the United States is pledged to the payment of all amounts required by the certificates. When all the mortgages in the "pool" are paid, and the final payments on the certificates are made to the certificate holders, the "pool" will be terminated.

Based solely on the foregoing facts certain of the Federal income tax consequences are as follows:

1. The "pool" will not be considered an association taxable as a corporation, but is classified as a trust of which the certificate holders are the owners under Subpart E of Subchapter J of the Internal Revenue Code of 1954.

2. M is a fiduciary and will be required to file Form 1041. See section 1.671-4 of the Income Tax Regulations.

3. Each certificate holder is treated as the owner of an undivided interest in the entire trust (corpus as well as ordinary income). See section 1.671-3(a)(1) of the regulations.

4. The sale of the mortgage-backed certificates transfers to the certificate holders the equitable ownership in each of the mortgages in the pool. Thereafter, M has only a contractual right to service the mortgages for a specified fee.

5. The certificate holders must report their ratable share of the entire interest income on the mortgages, including those amounts advanced by M, as ordinary income consistent with their method of accounting and may deduct the servicing, custodian, and guarantee fees under section 162 or section 212 of the Code.

6. The interest income is considered "in-

terest on obligations secured by mortgages on real property" as that phrase is used in section 856(c) (3) (B) of the Code.

7. A real estate investment trust which owns a certificate is considered as owning "real estate assets" as that phrase is used in section 856(c)(5)(A) of the Code.

8. A certificate owned by a savings and loan association is considered as representing "loans secured by an interest in real property" within the meaning of section 7701(a)(19)(C)(v) of the Code, provided the real property is (or from the proceeds of the loan will become) the type of real property described in that section of the Code.

9. The exempt status of an employees' pension and profit-sharing trust under section 501(a) of the Code is not adversely affected by the purchase of certificates.

Revenue Ruling 71-399

Advice has been requested as to certain of the Federal income tax consequences associated with mortgage participations under the facts and circumstances set forth below.

The Federal Home Loan Mortgage Corporation (FHLMC) purchased from N, an insured savings and loan association, five mortgage participation certificates. The mortgage participation certificates represent fractional undivided interests aggregating 85 percent in each mortgage contained on a list of mortgages ("List"). All of the mortgages on the List are loans within the meaning of section 7701(a)(19)(C)(v) of the Internal Revenue Code of 1954 and are qualifying real property loans as defined in section 593(e) of the Code. The mortgage participation certificates are in denominations of approximately $100,000 and are purchased by FHLMC at face value.

FHLMC issues a certificate corresponding to each mortgage participation certificate it purchases from N, endorses thereon its guarantee of principal and interest payment by the mortgagor, and sells these certificates at face value to other savings and loan associations and exempt employees' pension and profit sharing trusts (certificate holders). The FHLMC guarantee to the certificate holders is a guarantee of timely payment of interest and collection of principal by N.

The mortgage participation certificates acquired by FHLMC from N and those certificates sold to certificate holders are transferable only upon the books of FHLMC.

FHLMC has the power within two years after it purchases mortgage participation certificates to require N to repurchase any mortgage on the List. In lieu of repurchase, N may, with FHLMC's consent, substitute other mortgages in substantially similar amounts and of a quality acceptable to FHLMC. FHLMC's replacement power is only applicable with respect to defective mortgages, i.e., mortgages which are not of the quality established for the particular List prior to the date of sale of the mortgage participation certificates by N to FHLMC. The two year period provides FHLMC sufficient time to ascertain whether the quality of the mortgages conforms to representations made by N at the time the mortgage participation certificates are sold to FHLMC. After the expiration of the two year period, no substitution of mortgage loans may be required by FHLMC. At no time will N have the power to substitute mortgage loans for the original mortgage on the List on its own initiative. There will be no change in the criteria applied to a particular List of mortgages after the sale of mortgage participation certificates to FHLMC.

N is permitted by FHLMC to make "open-end" advances to the mortgagor on any given mortgage up to the original amount of the loan. Such advances will be subordinated to the rights of the certificate holders in the event of default by the mortgagor(s) on the loan or loans with respect to which open-end advances were made. In other words, neither FHLMC nor the certificate holders will have any interest, right, or obligation in the open-end advances or any income earned thereon.

N is required to service the mortgages on the List and pass through to FHLMC payments of principal and interest thereon to the extent necessary to produce the yield specified on each certificate (certificate yield). To the extent that the certificate

yield rate exceeds any specific mortgage interest rate, N makes up the difference to FHLMC from the interest it (N) receives on its 15 percent participation in such mortgage.

The use of a certificate yield computation amounts to a sale of each individual mortgage at a premium or discount depending upon the relationship of the certificate yield to the mortgage interest rate. For example, if the certificate yield is $7^{1}/_{2}$ percent, mortgages on the List with an interest rate of exactly $7^{1}/_{2}$ percent are sold at par. Mortgages on the List with an interest rate of less than $7^{1}/_{2}$ percent are sold at a discount, and mortgages on the List with an interest rate of more than $7^{1}/_{2}$ percent are sold at a premium. The amount of the interest payable (at the mortgage interest rate) on any specific mortgage on the List will never be less than the amount of the interest payable (at the certificate yield rate) on the certificate holders' participations in that mortgage.

In the month following the month of receipt by FHLMC from N, FHLMC passes through to the certificate holders the principal and interest payments received by FHLMC from N after deducting a specified amount therefrom to discharge the certificate holders' obligations to pay FHLMC's guarantee and management fees.

With the exception of any late charges collected by N, all receipts of principal and interest, prepayment premiums, net proceeds from the sale of foreclosed properties, income from property management, and any costs incident to protection and preservation of the real property security for the mortgage loans will be shared by each certificate holder in direct proportion to each certificate holders' pro rata interest in the mortgage loans.

Based solely on the foregoing facts, certain of the Federal income tax consequences are as follows:

1. The arrangement described does not create an association taxable as a corporation, but constitutes a trust.

2. The certificate holders are owners of the trust under Subpart E of Subchapter J of the Code. Each certificate holder is treated as the owner of an undivided interest in the

entire trust (corpus as well as ordinary income). See Section 1.671-3(a)(1) of the Income Tax Regulations.

3. FHLMC is a fiduciary and will be required to file Form 1041. See section 1.671-4 of the regulations.

4. *N* will recognize ordinary income or loss upon the sale of the 85 percent undivided interest in each of the mortgages on the List measured by the differences between the proportionate proceeds realized with respect to the sale of the 85 percent undivided interest in each of the mortgages on the List and the appropriate portion of its adjusted basis in those mortgages.

5. The sale of certificates by FHLMC to the certificate holders transfers to the certificate holders 85 percent equitable ownership in each of the mortgages on the List.

6. Each certificate holder using the cash receipts and disbursements method of accounting shall take into account its pro rata share of the mortgage interest and other items of income as and when they are collected by FHLMC.

7. Each certificate holder using an accrual method of accounting shall take into account its pro rata share of the entire interest on each mortgage and other items of income as they become due to FHLMC.

8. The special rules of section 1232 of the Code will be applicable to the certificate holders' proportionate shares of any mortgages which are obligations of corporations, or of governments or their political subdivisions if, and to the extent that, the other conditions for the application of the section are met. With respect to any interest in a mortgage purchased at a discount, and not subject to section 1232, the excess of the ratable portion of the certificate yield over the ratable portion of the entire interest income on the mortgages constitutes ordinary income to the certificate holders.

9. With respect to any undivided interest in a mortgage purchased at a premium, the certificate holder may be entitled to a deduction for amortization in accordance with applicable rules.

10. The certificate holders may deduct FHLMC's guarantee and management fees under section 162 of the Code consistent with their method of accounting.

11. A certificate held by a savings and loan association (certificate holder) is considered as representing "loans secured by an interest in real property" within the meaning of section 7701(a) (19) (C) (v) of the Code.

12. A certificate held by a domestic building and loan association (certificate holder) within the meaning of section 7701(a)(19) of the Code is considered as representing "qualifying real property loans" within the meaning of section 593(e) of the Code.

13. The qualification of an employees' pension or profit-sharing trust (certificate holder) under section 401 of the Code and its exemption under section 501(a) will not be adversely affected by the purchase of certificates, provided that the purchase meets the applicable investment requisites set forth in Revenue Ruling 69-494, C.B. 1969-2, 88.

Revenue Ruling 72-376

Advice has been requested whether the conclusions of Revenue Ruling 71-399, C.B. 1971-2, 433, are applicable to the purchase and sale of mortgage participation certificates by the Federal Home Loan Mortgage Corporation (FHLMC) under the circumstances set forth below.

In order to reduce the complexity of purchasing mortgage participation interests in groups of mortgages owned by *N*, an insured savings and loan association, FHLMC adopted the procedure of purchasing a single mortgage participation certificate from *N* representing an undivided interest of at least 50 percent in each of the mortgage loans in a group of mortgage loans which *N* offered for sale. FHLMC then sold mortgage participation certificates in denominations of approximately $100,000 at face value to other savings and loan associations and exempt employees' pension and profit sharing trusts (certificate holders), with each such certificate representing a smaller percentage of participation in the mortgage loans than that represented by the certificate purchased by *N*. The result of this procedure is that FHLMC consolidated the purchase of mortgage participation interests from *N* into a single certificate and then broke the single certificate down into smaller certificates of its own which it sold in denominations of approximately $100,000 to other savings and loan associations and other qualified purchasers.

Under the facts and circumstances contemplated by Revenue Ruling 71-399, FHLMC purchased mortgage participation certificates from *N* having a face amount of approximately $100,000, with each such certificate representing an undivided interest in mortgage loans. FHLMC then issued a certificate corresponding to each mortgage participation certificate purchased from *N* and sold them at face value to qualified purchasers.

In the instant case, the only difference in the procedure used by FHLMC from that contemplated by Revenue Ruling 71-399 is that FHLMC consolidates into a single certificate the mortgage participation interests which it purchases from *N*. Thus, for example, FHLMC may purchase a single mortgage participation certificate in a denomination of $500,000 and then sell mortgage participation certificates in denominations of approximately $100,000 representing approximately five such certificates based on the single certificate purchased from *N*.

Based on the foregoing facts, it is held that the modification in procedures used by FHLMC from that contemplated by Revenue Ruling 71-399, as described herein, will not alter the Federal income tax consequences to FHLMC, purchasers, and sellers described in Revenue Ruling 71-399, provided that the $100,000 certificates sold by FHLMC bear sufficient identification so as to permit tracing them to the $500,000 certificates purchased by FHLMC from *N* to which they relate and to the underlying mortgages represented by the $500,000 certificates.

Revenue Ruling 71-399 is hereby amplified.

Revenue Ruling 73-160

The purpose of this Revenue Ruling is to update and restate, under the current statute and regulations, the position set forth in G.C.M. 22056, 1940-2 C.B. 189.

The question presented is whether, under the circumstances described below, the extension by the issuer of the maturity date of its notes was a taxable transaction resulting in gain or loss for Federal income tax purposes.

M Company had outstanding notes in the face amount of 4*x* dollars. *M* extended the maturity date of the notes under the terms of an agreement that provided that if the noteholders deposited their notes with certain depositaries, the notes would be returned to the noteholders with an agreement extending the maturity to a certain date and with interest coupons providing for payment of the same rate of interest as in the original notes. The agreement further provided that the notes were to continue to be secured by the trust indenture under which mortgage bonds of *M* were held as security and were to be guaranteed by the original guarantor, *O* Company. *O* which owned 2*x* dollars of the 4*x* dollars of the outstanding notes, agreed that it would not have any of the notes owned by it redeemed by *M* until all notes other than those owned by *O* were retired or their retirement provided for. *O* also agreed that the lien of the notes owned by it upon the collateral security would be subordinated to the lien of the other notes until such other notes were retired or provision made for their retirement.

The income tax liability resulting from a particular transaction involving a change in the terms of outstanding securities is not controlled entirely by the mechanical means used for the accomplishment of the change. Where the changes are so material as to amount virtually to the issuance of a new security, the same income tax consequences should follow as if the new security were actually issued. Each case of this nature must be governed by its own facts.

In the instant case there was not an actual exchange of one security for another. All that occurred was that the maturity date of an existing series of notes was extended and the holder of a part thereof agreed that none of the notes owned by it would be redeemed during the period of extension until all the other notes were retired or their retirement provided for and the lien of the notes owned by it upon the collateral security should be subordinated to the lien of the other notes.

Accordingly, in the instant case, the mere extension of the maturity of the notes, accompanied by the agreement of some of the noteholders not to resort to the underlying security until other noteholders have been paid does not constitute in substance the exchange of the outstanding note for a new and materially different note or a closed and completed transaction upon which gain or loss may be determined. Therefore, neither gain or loss to any of the noteholders resulted from the above-described transactions.

G.C.M. 22056 is hereby superseded, since the position stated therein is restated under current law in this Revenue Ruling.

Revenue Ruling 73-460

Advice has been requested whether, under the circumstances described below, a fixed investment trust qualifies as a trust or as an association which is taxable as a corporation.

A corporate stockbrokerage firm (depositor) executed a trust agreement with a bank (trustee) which provided for the establishment of a fixed investment trust. The depositor deposited with the trustee certain interest-bearing municipal obligations, contracts for the purchase of such obligations, and the cash required for such purchases. The trustee delivered to the depositor a registered certificate for 20,000 units which represented the entire ownership of the fixed investment trust. The depositor, who

was the sole underwriter of the units, subsequently sold such units to investor clients.

The certificates may be transferred by the owners upon proper endorsement and surrender to the trustee, and a certificate holder may tender his certificates to the trustee for redemption at any time and, thus, terminate the trust as to himself. The trustee is authorized to sell certain bonds if insufficient cash is available to redeem certificates tendered for redemption. The certificates shall remain outstanding until redeemed by any certificate holder, which may include the depositor, or until the termination of the trust agreement. Neither the death nor incapacity of any certificate holder shall operate to terminate the fixed investment trust.

The fixed investment trust shall terminate upon the maturity, redemption, sale or other disposition of the last obligation held unless sooner terminated as provided in the trust agreement. In no event shall the fixed investment trust continue beyond January 1, 2010.

In order to preserve the sound investment character of the fixed investment trust, the depositor may direct the trustee to sell obligations, provided the depositor has determined the existence of certain conditions specifically set out in the trust agreement such as, for example, defaults in the payment of principal or interest on obligations or a substantial decline in the market value of the obligations.

The trust agreement further provides that the trustee will collect interest income on the obligations and all moneys other than interest income and credit such amounts to the interest account and the principal account respectively. The trustee is authorized under the trust agreement to withdraw from the cash on deposit in the interest account or the principal account such amounts as it deems necessary to establish a reserve for any applicable taxes or other governmental charges that may be payable out of the funds of the fixed investment trust.

On each semiannual distribution date, each certificate holder of record on the preceding record date will receive his pro rata share of the balance of the interest account, computed as of the next preceding computation date, plus such certificate holder's pro rata share of the cash balance of the principal account, computed as of the next preceding record date.

In the event that an offer is made by an obligor of any of the obligations to issue new obligations in exchange and substitution for any issue of obligations pursuant to a plan for the refunding or refinancing of such obligations the depositor shall instruct the trustee in writing to reject such offer and either to hold or sell such obligations, except that if (1) the issuer is in default with respect to such obligations or (2) in the opinion of the depositor, the issuer will probably default with respect to such bonds in the reasonably foreseeable future, the depositor shall instruct the trustee in writing to accept or reject such offer or take any other action with respect thereto as the depositor may deem proper.

Section 301.7701-4(c) of the Procedure and Administration Regulations provides as follows:

(c) Certain investment trusts. An "investment" trust of the type commonly known as a management trust is an association, and a trust of the type commonly known as a fixed investment trust is an association if there is power under the trust agreement to vary the investment of the certificate holders. See *Commissioner v. North American Bond Trust* (C.C.A. 2d 1941) 122 F.2d 545, *cert. denied,* 314 U.S. 701. However, if there is no power under the trust agreement to vary the investment of the certificate holders, such fixed investment trust shall be classified as a trust.

Under the terms of the trust agreement, the depositor and the trustee do not have the power to reinvest moneys in additional obligations or to vary the investment of the certificate holders. Furthermore, since the trust agreement requires that the moneys in the interest account and the principal account must be distributed to the certificate holders, no reinvestment of such moneys is possible.

Accordingly, it is held, in the instant case, that the fixed investment trust qualifies as a trust under section 301.7701-4(c) of the regulations.

Revenue Ruling 74-169

Rev. Rul. 70-544, 1970-2 C.B. 6, and Rev. Rul. 70-545, 1970-2 C.B. 7, concerned the tax consequences of transactions involving certain certificates guaranteed by the Government National Mortgage Association ("GNMA") that represent a proportionate interest in mortgages on real property maintained in a "pool" by a savings and loan association.

The above Revenue Rulings held, in part, that a certificate owned by a savings and loan association is considered as representing "loans secured by an interest in real property" within the meaning of section 7701(a)(19)(C)(v) of the Internal Revenue Code of 1954, provided the real property is (or, from the proceeds of the loan, will become) the type of real property described in the section of the Code.

Held, a certificate issued in accordance with the terms of Rev. Rul. 70-544 and Rev. Rul. 70-545 which is held by a domestic building and loan association (or other eligible mortgage institutions) within the meaning of section 7701(a)(19) of the Code is considered as representing "qualifying real property loans" within the meaning of section 593(e) provided the real property underlying the mortgages is (or, from the proceeds of the loan, will become) the type of real property described in that section.

Rev. Rul. 70-544 and Rev. Rul. 70-545 are hereby modified.

Revenue Ruling 74-221

Advice has been requested whether the conclusions of Rev. Rul. 71-399, 1971-2 C.B. 433, as amplified by Rev. Rul. 72-376, 1972-2 C.B. 647, relating to the purchase and sale of mortgage participation certificates by the Federal Home Loan Mortgage Corporation (FHLMC) are applicable under modified procedures now being used by FHLMC.

FHLMC purchases mortgage participation certificates (participation certificates) and sells participation sales certificates (sales certificates). In order to attract a broader range of investors, FHLMC recently adopted the procedure of combining participation certificates it purchased, and whole loans (or interests therein) owned by it, and issuing sales certificates representing undivided interests in each of the whole loans and in each of the mortgage loans represented by the participation certificates. The certificate yields at which such sales certificates are sold may differ from the certificate yields at which the underlying certificates were purchased by FHLMC and may differ from the mortgage interest rate on the whole loans owned by FHLMC. The sales certificates are guaranteed as to principal and interest in the same manner as the certificates described in Rev. Rul. 71-399.

Rev. Rul. 71-399, as amplified by Rev. Rul. 72-376, contemplates that FHLMC will sell sales certificates corresponding to, and representing undivided interests in, each of the mortgage loans covered by participation certificates which FHLMC purchased from a seller. FHLMC may sell one sales certificate representing the identical undivided interests covered by the participation certificate(s) which it purchased, or it may sell several sales certificates corresponding to one participation certificate which it purchased.

Rev. Rul. 71-399 holds that the use of a certificate yield computation amounts to a sale of each individual mortgage interest at a premium or discount depending upon the relationship of the certificate yield to the mortgage interest rate.

Under the procedures recently adopted by FHLMC, sales to the certificate holders are at certificate yields that may vary from the yields of the particular participation certificates purchased by FHLMC and from yields of the underlying individual mortgages. Thus, the certificate holder's premium or discount will be measured by the relationship between his certificate yield and the individual mortgage interest rates.

Based on the foregoing facts, it is held that the modification in procedures used by FHLMC from that contemplated by Rev. Rul. 71-399, amplified by Rev. Rul. 72-376, as described herein, will not alter the Federal income tax consequences to FHLMC, the purchasers, and the sellers described in Rev. Rul. 71-399, provided that the sales certificates sold by FHLMC bear sufficient identification so as to permit tracing them to the participation certificates purchased by FHLMC and to the whole loans owned by FHLMC to which they relate and to the underlying mortgages represented by the purchased certificates and the whole loans.

Rev. Rul. 71-399 as amplified by Rev. Rul. 72-376 is further amplified.

Revenue Ruling 74-300

Advice has been requested whether the conclusions of Rev. Rul. 70-544, 1970-2 C.B. 6, and Rev. Rul. 70-545, 1970-2 C.B. 7, concerning mortgage-backed certificates guaranteed by the Government National Mortgage Association (GNMA) that are purchased by a real estate investment trust are also applicable to the participation certificates issued by the Federal Home Loan Mortgage Corporation (FHLMC) that are purchased by a real estate investment trust.

Rev. Rul. 70-544 and Rev. Rul. 70-545 hold, in part, that interest income from mortgage participation certificates guaranteed by the GNMA is interest on obligations secured by mortgages on real property under section 856(c)(3)(B) of the Internal Revenue Code of 1954, and that such certificates qualify as "real estate assets" within the meaning of section 856(c)(5)(A).

Rev. Rul. 71-399, 1971-2 C.B. 433, as amplified by Rev. Rul. 72-376, 1972-2 C.B. 647, and Rev. Rul. 74-221, page 365, sets forth the tax consequences of the purchase of mortgage participation certificates by the FHLMC and the sale of corresponding certificates to other savings and loan associations and exempt employees' trusts. Rev. Rul. 71-399 holds, in part, that FHLMC is a fiduciary and the sale of a certificate transfers equitable ownership in the underlying mortgages to the purchaser of the certificate. However, neither Rev. Rul. 71-399, Rev. Rul. 72-376, nor Rev. Rul. 74-221, set forth the tax consequences where a real estate investment trust owns such certificates.

In the case of both the FHLMC and the GNMA participating certificates, processing is commenced by an insured savings and loan association which assembles a "list" or "pool" of mortgages which are both "loans secured by an interest in real property" within the meaning of section 7701(a)(19)(C)(v) of the Code and "qualifying real property loans" within the meaning of section 593(e).

FHLMC purchases mortgage participation certificates representing fractional undivided interests aggregating 85 percent in each mortgage contained on the list of residential real estate mortgages prepared by the originating savings and loan association. For each such mortgage participation certificate purchased from the originating savings and loan association, FHLMC issues a corresponding certificate bearing its guarantee of principal and interest payment by the mortgagor and sells these corresponding certificates at par to other savings and loan associations, exempt employees' pension and profit sharing trusts, and real estate investment trusts.

GNMA does not purchase participations but instead issues to the originating savings and loan association, or other eligible mortgage institution a commitment to guarantee certificates representing an undivided interest in the pool of mortgages to be established by the originating savings and loan association. Based on this commitment the originating savings and loan association places the pool of mortgages with a commercial bank acting as custodian and then arranges for the sale of "pass-through" certificates backed by the mortgage pool in minimum denominations of $25,000 to other savings and loan associations, real estate investment trusts, exempt employees' pension and profit sharing trusts, and individuals. In the case of "straight pass-through" certificates, GNMA guarantees to the certificate holders only the proper performance of the mortgage servicing and the payment only of that interest and principal actually collected or collectable through due diligence by the originating association. In

the case of "modified pass-through" certificates, GNMA guarantees the timely payment of principal and interest, whether or not collected by the originating association.

Based on the foregoing facts the conclusions of Rev. Rul. 70-544 and Rev. Rul. 70-545, as applied to the GNMA certificates owned by a real estate investment trust, also apply to FHLMC certificates owned by a real estate investment trust. Accordingly, the interest income on such certificates is considered "interest on obligations secured by mortgages on real property or on interests in real property" within the meaning of section 856(c)(3)(B) of the Code, and a real estate investment trust which owns participation certificates is considered as owning "real estate assets" within the meaning of section 856(c)(5)(A).

Rev. Rul. 71-399, as amplified by Rev. Rul. 72-376 and Rev. Rul. 74-221, is further amplified.

Revenue Ruling 75-192

Advice has been requested concerning the classification, for Federal income tax purposes, of an arrangement entered into by a number of persons to make a large-scale investment in individual homeowner mortgages insured or guaranteed by the Federal Housing Administration (FHA) or the Veterans Administration (VA).

Under the proposed arrangement, an investment bank will locate investors and form investment groups. These investors may include banks, trust companies, insurance companies, ordinary corporations, and individuals each willing to commit itself to invest at least 50x dollars. Investor commitments may be satisfied only by payments in cash. When the investment bank has assembled aggregate commitments of 1,000x dollars, it will close a group. Any number of groups may be assembled. Each group will choose a trust company to act as trustee and the invested funds will be turned over to the trustee. M company, a corporation specializing in the administration of mortgages, will be retained by the trustee, under a separate agreement, to service the mortgages.

Under the agreement between M and the

trustee, *M* will arrange to purchase existing FHA and VA mortgages of a specified quality on behalf of the trustee. *M* will collect the principal and interest payments on the mortgages and turn over the proceeds, less fees, to the trustee.

Under the trust agreement, the trustee will make quarterly distributions of all principal and interest payments received to each investor in proportion to his interest therein. During the period between quarterly distribution dates, the trustee is required to invest cash on hand in short-term obligations (or guaranteed by) the United States, or any agency or instrumentality thereof, and in certificates of deposit of any bank or trust company having a minimum stated surplus and capital. The trustee is permitted to invest only in obligations maturing prior to the next distribution date and is required to hold such obligations until maturity. All the proceeds received from the mortgage payments along with the interest earned on these short-term investments and deposits will be distributed to the investors quarterly. The trustee has no authority under the trust agreement to purchase new securities or mortgages, or to make any other new investments.

Section 7701(a)(3) of the Internal Revenue Code of 1954 provides, in part, that, as used in the Code, the term "corporation" includes associations.

Section 301.7701-4(c) of the Regulations on Procedure and Administration includes in the term "association" an investment trust of the type commonly known as a fixed investment trust if there is a power under the trust agreement to vary the investment of the certificate holders. However, if there is no power under the trust agreement to vary the investment, such fixed investment trust will be classified as a trust, rather than as an association taxable as a corporation.

A power to vary the investment of the certificate holders, within the meaning of section 301.7701-4(c) of the regulations, means one whereby the trustee, or some other person, has some kind of managerial power over the trusteed funds that enables

him to take advantage of variations in the market to improve the investment of all the beneficiaries. See *Commissioner v. North American Bond Trust,* 122 F. 2d 545, 546 (2d Cir. 1941), *cert. denied,* 314 U.S. 701 (1942).

Although a trustee may not actually exercise all the powers and discretion granted him under the trust agreement, the parties are not at liberty to say that their purpose was other or narrower than that which they formally set forth in the instrument under which their activities were conducted. *Helvering v. Coleman-Gilbert Associates,* 296 U.S. 369, 374 (1935), XV-1 C.B. 261 (1936).

The short-term obligations in which the trustee may invest are subject to daily market fluctuations. In the instant case, however, the trustee is permitted to invest only in obligations that mature prior to the next distribution date and is required to hold such obligations until maturity. These requirements limit the trustee to a fixed return similar to that earned on a bank account and eliminate any opportunity to profit from market fluctuations.

Accordingly, since once *M* purchases the FHA and VA mortgages on behalf of the trustee neither *M* nor the trustee has the power under the trust agreement to vary the trust's investment after the initial purchase of the mortgages, the arrangement in question will be classified as a trust for Federal income tax purposes and not as an association taxable as a corporation.

The interests in the income from the trust have been reserved to the various investor-grantors in proportion to their respective contributions. Therefore, each investor-grantor will be treated, by reason of section 677(a) of the Code, as the owner of an aliquot portion of the trust, and all income, deductions, and credits attributable to that portion are to be treated as those of the investor-grantor under section 671.

Any income taxable to the investor-grantors under section 671 of the Code should not be reported on Form 1041, but should be shown in a separate statement to be attached to the Form 1041. See section 1.671-4 of the Income Tax Regulations.

Revenue Ruling 77-349

Advice has been requested as to certain of the Federal income tax consequences associated with "straight pass-through" mortgage-backed certificates to various parties under the circumstances described below.

X, a commercial bank, pursuant to a pooling and servicing agreement (the "Agreement"), formed a "pool" of residential mortgage loans by assigning such loans to Y, an unrelated commercial bank, serving as trustee of the "pool." The assignment of mortgage loans included all principal and interest received by X with respect to the mortgage loans after the day of assignment, other than principal and interest due on the day of assignment. X's assignment is without recourse and X's obligations with respect to the mortgage loans is limited to the representations and warranties made by it as well as its servicing obligations, described below, under the Agreement.

The pool consists of 3x mortgage notes representing an aggregate principal amount of mortgage loans of 1,000x dollars each having a loan-to-value ratio at origination of 80 percent or less. The stated fixed interest rate on each mortgage note is 8.75 percent simple annual interest.

Concurrent with assignment of mortgage loans, Y delivered to X certificates in exchange for the mortgage loans. The certificates, issued in registered form, represent fractional undivided interests in the "pool" and bear a pass-through rate of interest which represents the 8.75 percent simple annual interest rate on all of the mortgage loans in the pool less X's regular monthly servicing compensation which is reasonable. Interest and principal are payable to certificate holders in monthly installments corresponding to collections by X on the mortgage loans. X immediately sold the certificates to a group of underwriters in a firm commitment underwriting whereby the certificates were resold to investors. The

certificate holders included domestic building and loan associations, real estate investment trusts, and individuals. X used the net proceeds from such sale to originate new conventional residential mortgage loans.

Under the Agreement, Y holds and X services the mortgage loans in the "pool." In addition to the compensation for its monthly services, X is entitled to retain as additional servicing compensation prepayment penalties, late payment charges, and assumption fees. X is required to pay the expenses of its servicing activities, including trustee fees to Y and mortgage insurance premiums. X is obligated under the Agreement to collect payments on the mortgage loans and to follow such collection procedures as are customary with respect to its comparable mortgage loans.

The aforementioned mortgage insurance premiums refer to an insurance contract with Z, a domestically incorporated mortgage insurer that is not related to X or Y and is not affiliated with any federal, state, or local government. Z issued a mortgage guaranty insurance policy in an amount equal to 5 percent of the initial aggregate principal balance of the mortgage loans in the "pool," with X designated as beneficiary of the policy as servicer of the mortgage loans on behalf of the certificate holders. The original amount of coverage under the insurance policy will be reduced over the life of the certificates by the aggregate dollar amount of claims paid.

For the duration of the "pool," neither X, Y, nor Z is empowered to reinvest proceeds attributable to the mortgages in the "pool." Similarly, neither X, Y, nor Z is empowered to substitute new mortgages for the original mortgages in the "pool." Y, however, may require X to repurchase mortgages included in the "pool" that do not meet the representations and warranties given by X in its assignment to the "pool."

Based solely on the foregoing facts, certain of the Federal income tax consequences are as follows:

1. The "pool" will not be considered an association taxable as a corporation, but is

classified as a trust of which the certificate holders are the owners under Subpart E of Subchapter J of the Internal Revenue Code of 1954. See Rev. Rul. 61-175, 1961-2 C.B. 128.

2. Y is the trustee of a grantor trust and will be required to file Form 1041. See section 1.671-4 of the Income Tax Regulations.

3. Each certificate holder is treated as the owner of an undivided interest in the entire trust (corpus as well as ordinary income). See section 1.671-3(a)(1) of the regulations.

4. The sale of the mortgage-backed certificates transfers to the certificate holders the pro rata share of their equitable ownership in each of the mortgages in the "pool."

5. X will recognize ordinary income or loss upon the sale of its interest in each of the mortgages in the "pool" measured by the differences between the proportionate amount of the proceeds realized with respect to the sale of each of the mortgages and its adjusted basis in each of such mortgages.

6. Each certificate holder using the cash receipts and disbursements method of accounting shall take into account its pro rata share of the mortgage interest and other items of income as and when they are collected by X, including prepayment penalties, assumption fees, and late payment charges.

7. Each certificate holder using an accrual method of accounting shall take into account the pro rata share of the mortgage interest and other items of income as they become due to X, including prepayment penalties, assumption fees and late payment charges.

8. The certificate holders must also report their ratable share of the discount income realized on the purchase of each of the mortgages as ordinary income, consistent with their method of accounting. The special rules of section 1232 of the Code will be applicable to the certificate holders' proportionate shares of the discount on any mortgages in the "pool" that are obligations of corporations, or of governments or their political subdivisions, if and to the extent that the other conditions for the application of that section are met.

9. Certificate holders may deduct their pro rata shares of X's servicing fees including prepayment penalties, late payment charges, and assumption fees collected by X under section 162 or section 212 of the Code consistent with their methods of accounting.

10. A real estate investment trust that owns a certificate is considered as owning "real estate assets" within the meaning of section 856(c)(5)(A) of the Code, and interest income will be considered "interest on obligations secured by mortgages on real property" within the meaning of section 856(c)(3)(B).

11. A certificate owned by a domestic building and loan association is considered as representing "loans secured by an interest in real property" within the meaning of section 7701(a)(19)(C)(v) of the Code, provided the real property is (or from the proceeds of the loan will become) the type of real property described in that section of the Code.

12. A certificate owned by a domestic building and loan association within the meaning of section 7701(a)(19) of the Code, is considered as representing "qualifying real property loans" within the meaning of section 593(d) provided the real property underlying the mortgages is (or, from the proceeds of the loan, will become) the type of real property described in that section.

Revenue Ruling 78-149

Advice has been requested whether, under the circumstances described below, a fixed investment trust possessing certain limited powers to reinvest is classified for federal income tax purposes as a trust or as an association taxable as a corporation.

The trust, whose corpus consists of a portfolio of municipal obligations, was formed to provide its investors with continuing tax-free income over a reasonable period of time. It will terminate upon the maturity, redemption, sale, or other disposition of the last obligation held thereunder, but in no event will the trust extend beyond December 31, 2023. The trust can be terminated under certain circumstances if the value of the trust decreases to less than $2,000,000, and must be terminated if the value of the trust decreases to less than $1,000,000.

In order to protect its investors from early termination of the trust due to bond issuers exercising the privilege of redeeming outstanding high-interest rate bonds from the proceeds of newly issued lower interest rate bonds, the trust agreement permits limited reinvestment of certain funds under specified limited conditions during the first 20 years of the trust's existence. Reinvestment is permitted only of funds derived from the redemption by the issuing municipality of municipal obligations prior to maturity, and is limited to municipal obligations maturing no later than the last maturity date of the municipal obligations originally deposited in the trust. The original corpus consisted solely of bonds rated at least "medium grade" by specified bond rating organizations, and reinvestment is further limited to new offerings of municipal obligations that are similarly rated. Funds derived from early redemption are distributed to certificate holders, unless within 20 days of receiving such funds, the trustee makes a commitment to reinvest them.

Section 301.7701-2(a)(2) of the Procedure and Administration Regulations provides, in part, that since centralization of management, continuity of life, free transferability of interests, and limited liability are generally common to trusts and corporations, the determination whether a trust that has such characteristics is to be treated for tax purposes as a trust or as an association depends on whether there are associates and an objective to carry on business and divide the gains therefrom. Section 301.7701-4(b) of the regulations states, in part, that there are other arrangements that are known as trusts because the legal title to property is conveyed to trustees for the benefit of beneficiaries, but are not classified as trusts for purposes of the Code, because they are not simply arrangements to protect or conserve the property for the beneficiaries. These trusts, which are often known as business or commercial trusts, generally are created by the beneficiaries simply as a device to carry on a profit-making business that normally would have been carried on through business organizations that are classified as corporations or partnerships under the Code.

Section 301.7701-4(c) of the regulations provides that an investment trust of the type commonly known as a management trust is an association, and a trust of the type commonly known as a fixed investment trust is an association if there is power under the trust agreement to vary the investment of the certificate holders. See *Commissioner v. North American Bond Trust*, 122 F.2d 545 (2d Cir. 1941), *cert. denied*, 314 U.S. 701 (1942). However, if there is no power under the trust agreement to vary the investment of the certificate holders, such fixed investment trust shall be classified as a trust.

The existence of a power to sell trust assets does not give rise to a power to vary the investment. Rather, it is the ability to substitute new investments, the power to reinvest, that requires an investment trust to be classified as an association. See *Pennsylvania Co. for Insurances on Lives and Granting Annuities v. United States*, 146 F.2d 392 (3rd Cir. 1944).

A power to vary the investment of the certificate holders exists where there is a managerial power, under the trust instrument, that enables a trust to take advantage of variations in the market to improve the investment of the investors. See *Commissioner v. North American Bond Trust*, 122 F.2d at 546; Rev. Rul. 75-192, 1975-1 C.B. 384.

In the instant case, the power in the trust agreement permitting reinvestment of the proceeds of obligations redeemed prior to maturity, even though limited to reinvestment of the proceeds of redemptions over which the trust has no control, is a managerial power that enables the trust to take advantage of variations in the market to improve the investment of the investors. It therefore is a power to vary the investment of the certificate holders within the meaning of section 301.7701-4(c) of the regulations.

Accordingly, the trust, in the instant case, will be classified as an association taxable as a corporation for federal income tax purposes.

In Rev. Rul. 73-460, 1973-2 C.B. 424, the trustee had the power to accept an issuer's offer to exchange new obligations for existing obligations of that issuer. This power was limited to offers made by issuers who were attempting to refinance the existing obligations and who already had or probably would default with respect to those obligations. This power did not give the trustee the power to take advantage of variations in the market. Rev. Rul. 73-460 is therefore distinguished.

Revenue Ruling 79-106

Advice has been requested whether the factors described below will be considered "other factors" that are significant in determining the classification of arrangements formed as limited partnerships for purposes of the regulations under section 7701 of the Internal Revenue Code of 1954.

The term "association" refers to an organization whose characteristics require it to be classified for purposes of taxation as a corporation rather than as another type of organization such as a partnership or a trust.

Section 301.7701-2(a)(1) of the Procedure and Administration Regulations lists six major characteristics ordinarily found in a pure corporation which, taken together, distinguish it from other organizations. These are (i) associates, (ii) an objective to carry on business and divide the gains therefrom, (iii) continuity of life, (iv) centralization of management, (v) liability for corporate debts limited to corporate property, and (vi) free transferability of interests. Whether a particular organization is to be classified as an association must be determined by taking into account the presence or absence of each of these corporate characteristics.

In addition to the major characteristics, section 301.7701-2(a)(1) of the regulations provides, in part, that "other factors" may be found in some cases which may be significant in classifying an organization as an association, a partnership or a trust.

The Internal Revenue Service will follow, in classifying organizations under section 7701 of the Code, the decision of the United States Tax Court in *Larson v. Commissioner*, 66 T.C. 159 (1976), acq., page 1, this Bulletin, in which the court held that two real estate syndicates organized under the California Uniform Limited Partnership Act were partnerships for federal income tax purposes. In *Larson*, the court, while not concluding that additional "factors" are never relevant, found that some of the following "factors" were elements of the major characteristics and that the other "factors" were not of critical importance for purposes of classifying the partnership.

(1) the division of limited partnership interests into units or shares and the promotion and marketing of such interests into units or shares and the promotion and marketing of such interests in a manner similar to corporate securities,

(2) the managing partner's right or lack of the discretionary right to retain or distribute profits according to the needs of the business,

(3) the limited partner's right or lack of the right to vote on the removal and election of general partners and the right or lack of the right to vote on the sale of all, or substantially all, of the assets of the partnership,

(4) the limited partnership interests being represented or not being represented by certificates,

(5) the limited partnership's observance or lack of observance of corporate formalities and procedures,

(6) the limited partners being required or not being required to sign the partnership agreement, and

(7) the limited partnership providing a means of pooling investments while limiting the liability of some of the participants.

Accordingly, as a result of the *Larson* case, the Service will not consider the factors enumerated above as "other factors" that have significance (independent of their bearing on the six major corporate characteristics) in determining the classification of arrangements formed as limited partnerships.

Revenue Ruling 80-96

ISSUE

Do the holdings of Rev. Rul. 71-399, 1971-2 C.B. 433, as amplified by Rev. Rul. 72-376, 1972-2 C.B. 647; Rev. Rul. 74-221, 1974-1 C.B. 365; and Rev. Rul. 74-300, 1974-1 C.B. 169, involving the purchase by the Federal Home Loan Mortgage Corporation (FHLMC) of mortgage loans and interests therein from savings and loan associations and other eligible sellers and the sale of participation sales certificates to investors including other savings and loan associations, remain applicable under the circumstances described below?

FACTS

Rev. Rul. 71-399, as amplified by Rev. Rul. 72-376 and Rev. Rul. 74-221, set forth the tax consequences of the purchase of mortgage participation certificates and whole mortgage loans by FHLMC from savings and loan associations and the issuance by FHLMC of sales certificates to other savings and loan associations and exempt employees trusts. Rev. Rul. 74-300 holds that a real estate investment trust owning certificates issued by the FHLMC is considered as owning "real estate assets" within the meaning of section 856(c)(5)(A) of the Internal Revenue Code and its interest income from such certificates is "interest on obligations secured by mortgages on real property" under section 856(c)(3)(B).

Rev. Rul. 71-399, as amplified, states in part, that the arrangement whereby FHLMC purchases mortgage participation certificates and whole mortgage loans from savings and loan associations followed by FHLMC's sale of its own sales certificates to certain other organizations does not create an association taxable as a corporation, but constitutes a trust; the holders of FHLMC certificates discussed in Rev. Rul. 71-399, as amplified, are owners of the trust under Subpart E of Subchapter J of the Code and each certificate holder is treated as the owner of an undivided interest in the entire trust (corpus as well as ordinary income), and that the sale of the FHLMC certificates to the holders transfers equitable ownership in the underlying mortgages to the holders of the certificates.

As described in the above-mentioned rulings, FHLMC combines participation certificates and whole mortgage loans (or interests therein) purchased by it into a "pool" and sells its own participation sales certificates (PCs) representing undivided interests in each of the mortgage loans represented by the participation certificates purchased by FHLMC and undivided interests in each of the whole loans owned by FHLMC. The savings and loan associations and other mortgage originators ("seller/servicers") from whom FHLMC purchases either participation certificates or whole loans generally continue to service such loans.

Rev. Rul. 72-376 and Rev. Rul. 74-221 require that the PCs sold by FHLMC must bear sufficient identification so as to permit tracing them to the participation certificates purchased by FHLMC and to the whole loans owned by FHLMC to which PCs relate and to the underlying mortgages represented by the participation certificates in FHLMC's hands. FHLMC uses a number of internal accounting systems between itself and the seller/servicers, including a fiscal reporting month by the seller/servicers, to insure not only the presence of an ability to trace required by those revenue rulings, but also the ability for FHLMC to verify that the payments received by FHLMC from the seller/servicers are correct.

Under FHLMC procedures PCs are sold by FHLMC representing undivided interests in a pool of mortgages and interests therein as constituted at that time. The ultimate size of a pool formed by FHLMC is adjusted to meet increased or decreased market demands of the purchasers of PCs, as well as to take into account information regarding specific mortgages that is not furnished to FHLMC by the seller/servicer until after the month the pool is formed, or to the extent furnished, has not yet been processed by FHLMC. The adjustments to the pool size by FHLMC are made no later than the date of the first remittance check to holders of its PCs in such pool.

FHLMC is obligated under an agreement with the PC holders to remit to each PC holder the PC holder's pro rata share of principal received by FHLMC and interest to the extent of the certificate rate. The agreement permits FHLMC to make regular monthly payments of principal and interest to PC holders on an estimated basis before actual mortgage loan payment data is processed by FHLMC. In arriving at the amount to be paid to a PC holder, FHLMC makes a calculation based in part on its own experience as to how much principal is due for the normal calendar month to its PC holders. Any minor variances in making this calculation of principal are adjusted by FHLMC in the payment for the following month to its PC holders. This process is repeated for the life of the PC and upon the final payment with respect to the PC all the principal acquired by the PC holder will have been remitted by FHLMC.

In making the calculation discussed in the preceding paragraph, FHLMC follows a set procedure to handle mortgage loans that are prepaid. FHLMC retains any interest remitted by the seller/servicer for the period from the first day of the calendar month to the date of prepayment if the mortgage loan is paid in full or in part on or before the 20th day of the month. FHLMC remits a full 30 days' interest to its PC holders with respect to mortgage loans which are prepaid after the 20th of the month. This FHLMC procedure is fully disclosed to prospective PC holders in FHLMC's PC Offering Circular, as an adjustment to FHLMC's guarantee and management fee.

Upon the sale of a PC, FHLMC retains the right to repurchase such PC from its holder for an amount equal to the then unpaid principal balance of the undivided interest in each mortgage loan represented by each PC. The right to repurchase can be exercised when the dollar size of the pool, and of each PC holder's interest therein, is 10 percent or less of the initial unpaid principal balance of the pool.

While PC holders may sell their PCs to third parties (when the certificates are transferable on the books of FHLMC), the agreement with PC holders does not authorize PC holders to use PCs as a basis for forming any more pools.

HOLDING

The holdings of Rev. Rul. 71-399, as amplified by Rev. Rul. 72-376, Rev. Rul. 74-221, and Rev. Rul. 74-300, are not altered by the above-described procedures under which FHLMC purchases and sells mortgage loans provided the PCs sold by FHLMC continue to bear sufficient identification so as to permit tracing them to the participation certificates purchased by FHLMC and to whole loans owned by FHLMC to which they relate and to the underlying mortgages.

EFFECT ON OTHER DOCUMENTS

Rev. Rul. 71-399, as amplified by Rev. Rul. 72-376, Rev. Rul. 74-221, and Rev. Rul. 74-300, is further amplified.

Revenue Ruling 81-203

ISSUES

1. Does a pledged account mortgage loan (PAM) or an undivided interest in a PAM included in a mortgage pool constitute a loan secured by an interest in real property within the meaning of section 7701(a)(19)(C)(v) of the Internal Revenue Code under the circumstances described below?

2. Will the Internal Revenue Service treat the full face amount of participation certificates (PCs) in a mortgage pool containing PAMs as a qualifying real property loan within the meaning of section 593(d)(1) of the Code under the circumstances described below?

FACTS

The federal income tax consequences of the issuance and sale of PCs by the Federal Home Loan Mortgage Corporation (FHLMC) are the subject of Rev. Rul. 71-399, 1971-2 C.B. 433, as amplified by Rev. Rul. 72-376, 1972-2 C.B. 647; Rev. Rul. 74-221, 1974-1 C.B. 365, Rev. Rul. 74-300, 1974-1 C.B. 169, and Rev. Rul. 80-96, 1980-1 C.B. 317.

FHLMC purchases whole conventional residential mortgage loans and undivided interests in such loans from savings and loan associations and other mortgage loan originators. FHLMC combines the whole loans and the undivided interests in such loans in mortgage pools and issues PCs representing undivided interests in such mortgage pools.

FHLMC will include in certain of its mortgage pools whole PAMs and undivided interests in PAMs that it has purchased from savings and loan associations and other mortgage loan originators. These PCs are sold by FHLMC as described in the Revenue Rulings cited above.

A PAM is a type of residential mortgage loan secured by an interest in real property. At the origination of a PAM, all or a portion of the borrower's cash otherwise available for downpayment is placed in a savings account which is pledged as additional collateral for the mortgage loan. The principal amount of the loan may be increased by the amount of the pledged account. The depository for such account may, but need not, be the lender. In accordance with an established schedule, monthly withdrawals are made from the savings account for a fixed period at the beginning of the loan term in order to supplement the out-of-pocket mortgage payments made by the borrower.

When the savings and loan associations or other mortgage loan originators sell PAMs to FHLMC, these lenders must also assign their security interests in the pledged savings accounts to FHLMC. In the case of the sale of an undivided fractional interest in a PAM, such sale must convey a proportionate security interest in the pledged account.

PCs sold by FHLMC represent an undivided interest in mortgage pools that may include PAMs. Under the standards prescribed by FHLMC, the gross mortgage amount of a PAM can never exceed the fair market value of the property securing such loan. However, the percentage of PAMs included in the mortgage pool is limited to no more than 5 percent of the total value of the pool. In addition, none of the pledged accounts may exceed 20 percent of the total principal amount of the loan. Thus, with respect to any PC whose underlying mortgage pool includes PAMs, the maximum portion of the face value of such PC that can be attributed to pledge accounts is 1 percent.

LAW

Section 7701(a)(19)(C)(v) of the Code defines a domestic building and loan association as an institution at least 60 percent of the amount of the total assets of which (at the close of the taxable year) consists of loans secured by an interest in real property which is (or, from the proceeds of the loan, will become) residential real property.

Section 593(d)(1) of the Code provides that the term "qualifying real property loan" means any loan secured by an interest in improved real property or secured by an interest in real property which is to be improved out of the proceeds of the loan.

Section 593(d)(1) of the Code and section 1.593-11(b)(5) of the Income Tax Regulations state that the term "qualifying real property loan" does not include any loan to the extent such loan is secured by a deposit in or share of the taxpayer.

HOLDINGS

1. A PAM included in a FHLMC mortgage pool constitutes a loan secured by an interest in residential real property within the meaning of section 7701(a)(19)(C)(v) of the Code.

2. Based on the circumstances set forth above, the Service will permit the full face amounts of the PAMs that are included in mortgage pools underlying PCs purchased by a savings and loan association to be treated as qualifying real property loans for purposes of section 593(d)(1) of the Code provided the PAMs included in the mortgage pool constitute no more than 5 percent of the total value of the pool and none of the pledged accounts exceed 20 percent of the total principal amount of the loan.

EFFECT ON OTHER DOCUMENTS

Rev. Rul. 71-399, as amplified by Rev. Rul. 72-376, Rev. Rul. 74-221, Rev. Rul. 74-300, and Rev. Rul. 80-96, is further amplified.

Revenue Ruling 81-238

ISSUE

Is the classification of a fixed investment

trust as a trust for federal income tax purposes terminated by the adoption of an automatic reinvestment plan in the circumstances described below?

FACTS

Under the terms of a fixed investment trust instrument, units of beneficial interest (trust units) in the trust property are represented by certificates issued to each investor. The minimum initial investment amount is $1,000 per investor. Neither the trustee nor anyone else holds power to vary the investments of the trust.

The sponsor of this fixed investment trust and several similar trusts has adopted what is described as an "automatic reinvestment plan," which allows certificate holders to make further investments of income and principal distributions from the trusts. Shortly before each semiannual distribution date the sponsor will cause the creation of a new fixed investment trust in which the certificate holders in the existing trusts may invest their distributions. A bank is designated to receive trust distributions on behalf of those certificate holders who elect to participate. The bank combines the distributions and purchases certificates of beneficial interest in the new trust.

Each participant's account is charged with a pro rata share of the total cost of the certificates and is credited with its share of the certificates, including fractional interests.

A certificate holder electing to participate in the plan must give the bank an authorization form that authorizes the bank to act as the agent for the participating certificate holder and authorizes the trustee to pay trust distributions to the bank. The bank accounts to each participant with respect to the amounts received and the certificates of beneficial interest in the new trust that it purchases.

Certificate holders in the original trust may choose to participate in the automatic reinvestment plan at any time, and they may terminate their participation in the plan at any time by delivering written instructions to the bank. Holders of trust units may also withdraw from the plan with respect to particular distributions and directly receive current distributions, or they may withdraw with respect to only some of the certificates they own.

Prior to the adoption of the automatic reinvestment plan, the fixed investment trust was classified as a trust rather than an association taxable as a corporation, and it was a grantor trust of which the holders of 1981-2 C.B. 248; 1981 IRB LEXIS 218, the trust units were considered pro rata owners for federal income tax purposes.

LAW AND ANALYSIS

Section 301.7701-2(a)(2) of the Regulations on Procedure and Administration provides that the determination of whether a trust is to be treated as an association taxable as a corporation rather than as a trust depends on whether there are (1) associates and (2) an objective to carry on a business and divide the gains therefrom.

Section 301.7701-4(c) of the regulations provides that a fixed investment trust is classified as an association if there is power under the trust agreement to vary the investment of the certificate holders.

In Rev. Rul. 70-627, 1970-2 C.B. 159, a bank, which was the agent of a corporation for purposes of paying out dividends on the corporation's securities, created an automatic dividend reinvestment plan under which shareholders of the corporation could have the bank use their dividends to purchase, on their behalf, additional shares of the corporation. Rev. Rul. 70-627 concludes, among other things, that the dividend reinvestment arrangement is neither a trust, a partnership, nor an association taxable as a corporation.

Under the automatic reinvestment plan in this case, certificate holders in the trust are electing to use distributions to purchase certificates in new fixed investment trusts. The plan does not involve reinvestment in the original trust and there is no change in, or addition to, the assets of the original trust. The investment of each certificate holder in the original trust remains fixed as does the beneficial interest of each certificate holder in the assets of the trust. Thus, the reinvestment plan does not result in the power to vary the investment of the certificate holders within the meaning of section 301.7701-4(c) of the regulations.

Further, the automatic reinvestment plan in this case is not a trust, partnership, association taxable as a corporation, or any other separate entity. The bank in this case, like the bank in Rev. Rul. 70-627, is an agent of the certificate holders who elect to participate in the reinvestment plan. The bank has no discretion with respect to investments and merely accepts distributions and purchases certificates in the new fixed investment trusts pursuant to the prearranged plan.

HOLDING

The classification of the fixed investment trust as a trust for federal income tax purposes is not terminated by the adoption of the automatic reinvestment plan.

Revenue Ruling 84-10

ISSUE

What are the federal income tax consequences associated with the mortgage pool trusts described below?

FACTS

The Federal National Mortgage Association (FNMA) is a publicly held corporation established to provide assistance to the secondary market for home mortgage loans. FNMA has initiated a guaranteed mortgage pass-through securities program under Federal National Mortgage Association Charter Act § 304(d), 12 U.S.C.A. § 1719(d) (West 1980). Pursuant to a trust agreement, FNMA creates home mortgage pools and serves as trustee of each pool. Each pool consists of residential mortgages transferred to it by a single mortgage lender, X, in exchange for trust certificates. The trust certificates generally will be sold by X to investors. FNMA charges X a processing fee when it pools mortgages acquired from X.

In the capacity of pool trustee, FNMA collects principal and interest payments on each mortgage and makes monthly distributions to the certificate holders. FNMA receives a fee for its services as trustee consisting of a monthly service charge retained from the interest collected on the mortgages

and other compensation including all late payment charges, assumption fees and prepayment penalties collected by FNMA. Pool proceeds are held in noninterest bearing accounts and cannot be reinvested. Neither the trustee nor X has the power to substitute a new mortgage for an original mortgage in the pool, except that within 120 days of the date the pool is established FNMA may require X to replace defective mortgages in the pool. Each of the pools will terminate when all mortgages are liquidated and all proceeds are distributed. FNMA may terminate a pool by purchasing all trust certificates with respect to the pool when the aggregate outstanding principal amount of mortgages in the pool is 10 percent or less of the initial pool principal balance.

FNMA guarantees that the certificate holders will receive timely payment of interest and collection of principal. If a mortgage is in default or if there is a foreclosure on mortgaged property, FNMA has the right to withdraw the mortgage from the pool and deem the mortgage prepaid.

The trust certificates, which are in registered form, state that they represent fractional undivided interests in the mortgage loans, pool proceeds, mortgaged property acquired by foreclosure that has not been withdrawn from the pool, and FNMA's obligation to supplement the pool proceeds to the extent necessary to make distributions.

LAW

The Service has discussed the federal income tax consequences of similar pooling arrangements in Rev. Rul. 71-399, 1971-2 C.B. 433, amplified by Rev. Rul. 81-203, 1981-2 C.B. 137, Rev. Rul. 80-96, 1980-1 C.B. 317, Rev. Rul. 74-300, 1974-1 C.B. 169, Rev. Rul. 74-221, 1974-1 C.B. 365, and Rev. Rul. 72-376, 1972-2 C.B. 647 (concerning mortgage pools established by the Federal Home Loan Mortgage Corporation); Rev. Rul. 70-544, 1970-2 C.B. 6, and Rev. Rul. 70-545, 1970-2 C.B. 7, both modified by Rev. Rul. 74-169, 1974-1 C.B. 147 (concerning mortgage pools guaranteed by the Government National Mortgage Association); and Rev. Rul. 77-349, 1977-2 C.B. 20 (concerning a mortgage pool created by a commercial bank).

HOLDINGS

1. Each pool will not be considered an association taxable as a corporation, but is classified as a trust of which the certificate holders are the owners under Subpart E of Subchapter J of the Internal Revenue Code.

2. FNMA is the trustee of each trust and will be required to file Form 1041. See section 1.671-4 of the Income Tax Regulations.

3. FNMA will recognize ordinary income in the amount of the processing fees charged X for pooling mortgages.

4. Each certificate holder is treated as the owner of an undivided interest in the entire trust (corpus as well as ordinary income). See section 1.671-3(a)(1) of the regulations.

5. The sale of a trust certificate transfers to the certificate holder a proportionate share of equitable ownership in each of the mortgages in the pool.

6. X will recognize ordinary income or loss on the sale of its interest in each of the mortgages in the pool (evidenced by the trust certificates) measured by the difference between the proportionate amount of the proceeds realized with respect to the sale of each of the mortgages and its adjusted basis in each of such mortgages.

7. Certificate holders shall take into account their proportionate share of the mortgage interest and other items of income, including prepayment penalties, assumption fees, and late payment charges, consistent with their methods of accounting.

8. The certificate holders must also report their proportionate share of the discount income realized on the purchase of each of the mortgages as ordinary income, consistent with their methods of accounting. The special rules of section 1232 of the Code will be applicable to the certificate holders' proportionate shares of the discount on any mortgages in the pool that are obligations of corporations, or of governments or their political subdivisions, if and to the extent that the other conditions for the application of that section are met. Similarly, the rules of section 1232A(a)(1) will apply to the certificate holders' proportionate shares of obligations in the pool that are not obligations described in section 1232A (a)(2)(A) of the Code (relating to any obligation issued by a natural person).

9. Certificate holders may amortize their proportionate shares of any premium paid to acquire mortgages to the extent allowed by section 171 of the Code. The provisions of section 171 will be applicable to the premium on mortgages in the pool that are issued by a corporation as described in section 171(d) of the Code.

10. Certificate holders may deduct their proportionate share of FNMA's fee for servicing the mortgages comprised of the monthly service charge, late payment charges, assumption fees, and prepayment penalties under section 162 or section 212 of the Code, consistent with their method of accounting.

11. A certificate owned by a real estate investment trust is considered as representing "real estate assets" within the meaning of section 856(c)(5)(A) of the Code, and the interest income is considered "interest on obligations secured by mortgages on real property" within the meaning of section 856(c)(3)(B).

12. A certificate owned by a domestic building and loan association is considered as representing "loans secured by an interest in real property" within the meaning of section 7701(a)(19)(C)(v) of the Code, provided the real property is (or from the proceeds of the loan will become) the type of real property described in that section of the Code.

13. A certificate owned by a domestic building and loan association, within the meaning of section 7701(a)(19) of the Code, is considered as representing "qualifying real property loans" within the meaning of section 593(d) provided the real property underlying the mortgages is (or, from the proceeds of the loan, will become) the type of real property described in that section.

EFFECT ON OTHER REVENUE RULINGS

Rev. Rul. 70-544, 1970-2 C.B. 6, and Rev. Rul. 70-545, 1970-2 C.B. 7, are clarified with respect to the reporting of service fees, assumption fees, prepayment penalties and late charges by the certificate holders.

Revenue Ruling 85-42

ISSUE

Whether a corporation that transfers assets to a trust that it has established for the sole purpose of making payments of principal and interest on its outstanding bond issue will be considered to have transferred the assets to its bondholders in satisfaction of the outstanding bonds, or, will the corporation continue to be regarded as the owner of the assets held in trust.

FACTS

Corporation X bought $300x of United States Government securities and contributed these securities to an irrevocable trust. The trust instrument directs the trustee, a commercial bank, to apply the trust corpus and the interest thereon solely to satisfy the scheduled payments of principal and interest on a $500x outstanding bond issue of Corporation X. The trust instrument further provides that neither Corporation X nor its creditors can rescind or revoke the trust or otherwise obtain access to the trust assets. Any amount remaining in the trust when the Corporation X bonds are retired will revert to Corporation X.

Because the government securities yield 14 percent and the outstanding Corporation X bonds yield only 6 percent, the $300x of government securities, coupled with the earnings thereon, will generate sufficient funds to service the $500x outstanding debt. Further, the government securities will provide cash flows (from interest and maturity of those securities) that approximately coincide, as to timing and amount, with the scheduled interest and principal payments on the outstanding Corporation X bonds. Moreover, because the assets of the trust are essentially risk free as to timing and amount of payments of principal and interest, the possibility that Corporation X will be required to make future payments on the outstanding bonds is remote. However, Corporation X is not legally released from being the primary obligor on the outstanding bonds.

The Financial Accounting Standards Board has announced, in FASB statement No. 76, *Extinguishment of Debt,* Nov. 1983, that in trust arrangements such as the one described above, sometimes referred to as "in-substance defeasances," the debtor corporation shall consider the debt to be extinguished for financial accounting purposes.

LAW AND ANALYSIS

Section 1.61-13(b) of the Income Tax Regulations provides that if a corporation, for the sole purpose of securing the payment of its bonds or other indebtedness, places property in trust or sets aside certain amounts in a sinking fund under the control of a trustee who may be authorized to invest and reinvest such sums from time to time, the property or fund thus set aside by the corporation and held by the trustee is an asset of the corporation, and any gain arising therefrom is income of the corporation and shall be included as such in its gross income.

For financial accounting purposes, in accordance with FASB Statement No. 76, Corporation X will be considered to have extinguished the debt owed to its bondholders upon the transfer of assets to the trust because the assets are essentially risk free and the likelihood that Corporation X will be required to make future payments to the bondholders is remote. However, Corporation X is not legally released from being the primary obligor on the bonds. Consequently, for federal income tax purposes, Corporation X cannot be considered to have discharged the debt owed to its bondholders upon the transfer of assets to the trust. *See* section 1.61-13(b) of the regulations.

HOLDINGS

Corporation X will continue to be regarded as the owner of the assets held in trust and any income generated by the trust assets will be includible in the gross income of Corporation X.

Revenue Ruling 86-92

ISSUE

If contracts to purchase certain bonds are deposited in an investment trust and, in the event the specified bonds cannot be obtained, the trust agreement permits the sponsor of the trust to provide instead different bonds of the same character and quality as those specified in the contracts or to provide no bonds at all, then for purposes of section 301.7701-4(c) of the Regulations on Procedure and Administration, does the sponsor possess a power to vary the investment of the certificate holders?

FACTS

A securities broker, as sponsor, formed an investment trust with a bank as trustee. The sponsor deposited in the trust certain tax-exempt bonds and contracts to purchase tax-exempt bonds (contracts to purchase). In exchange for these contributions, the sponsor received certificates representing a single class of undivided beneficial ownership in the assets of the trust. The sponsor then sold all of the certificates to investors.

The contracts to purchase permit the trust to purchase bonds on a "when, as, and if issued" basis. The contracts to purchase provide that all bonds subject to the contracts must be transferred to the trust within 90 days of the creation of the trust. If bonds subject to the contracts to purchase are not transferred to the trust within the 90-day period and if this failure is due to reasons beyond the control of the sponsor or the trustee, the sponsor has 20 days within which to transfer to the trust different bonds of substantially the same character and quality as those covered by the "failed" contracts to purchase. If the sponsor does not do so, the trustee must refund to the certificate holders on the next payment date that portion of the sales charge, principal, and accrued interest attributable to the failed contracts to purchase.

Any bond acquired to replace a bond in a "failed" contract to purchase (1) must be tax-exempt, (2) must have a fixed maturity date no later than the date of maturity of the bond it replaces, (3) must have a fixed interest rate not less than that of the bond it replaces and a yield to maturity at least equal to that of the bond it replaces, (4) must have a rating at least equal to the bond it replaces, (5) must have a purchase price no greater than the principal attributable to the bond it replaces, and (6) must not be a "when, as, and if issued" bond.

LAW AND ANALYSIS

Section 301.7701-4(c) of the regulations provides that an investment trust will not be classified as a trust if there is a power under the trust agreement to vary the investment of the certificate holders. See Commissioner v. North American Bond Trust, 122 F.2d 545 (2d Cir. 1941), cert. denied, 314 U.S. 701 (1942). An investment trust with a single class of ownership interests, representing undivided beneficial interests in the assets of the trust, will be classified as a trust and not as an association taxable as a corporation if there is no power under the trust agreement to vary the investment of the certificate holders.

A power to vary the investment of the certificate holders exists if there is a managerial power under the trust instrument that enables a trust to take advantage of market variations to improve the investment of the investors. See North American Bond Trust, 122 F.2d at 546; Rev. Rul 75-192, 1975-1 C.B. 384; and Rev. Rul. 78-149, 1978-1 C.B. 448.

Under the trust agreement in the present revenue ruling, neither the trustee nor the sponsor has the power to take advantage of market variations to improve the investment of the certificate holders. The trustee may only accept bonds specified in the contracts to purchase or bonds of substantially the same character and quality selected by the sponsor, and even the latter may be done only if bonds are not furnished under one of the contracts to purchase. Should a contract to purchase fail, the sponsor has only the power to provide bonds of the same character and quality as those specified in the failed contract to purchase, or simply to fail to provide some bonds. In the latter case, the trustee must refund to the certificate holders that portion of the sales charge, principal, and accrued interest that is attributable to the failed contract. The powers at issue here are unlike those in Rev. Rul. 78-149, where reinvestment was used to take advantage of variations in the market over a twenty-year period. The powers in the present case are merely incidental to the organization of the trust during its first 110 days and do not constitute a power to vary the investment of the certificate holders. Once the bonds are placed in the trust, there is no change in the make-up of the trust corpus and no additional investment.

HOLDING

For purposes of section 301.7701-4(c) of the regulations, an investment trust agreement does not contain a power to vary the investment of the certificate holders solely because the governing instrument of an investment trust provides that, in the event of a contract failure, the sponsor may provide bonds of substantially the same character and quality as those bonds specified in the contracts to purchase that were deposited in the trust. Accordingly, under the facts set forth above, the trust is classified for federal income tax purposes as a trust and not as an association taxable as a corporation.

Revenue Ruling 87-19

ISSUES

1. If a financial institution holds an issue of bonds the interest on which is tax-exempt under section 103 of the Internal Revenue Code and waives its right under an interest adjustment clause to receive a higher rate of interest, does the waiver result in a deemed exchange under section 1001 of the old bonds for new bonds?

2. If so, and if the interest on the new bonds is exempt from tax, is the financial institution subject to the interest expenses disallowance rule of section 265(b) of the Code?

FACTS

FI, a financial institution described in section 265(b)(5) of the Code, is the holder of $1,000,000 of bonds with a base interest rate of 7 percent issued by city CI in 1981. CI issued the bonds in connection with a conduit financing in which CI loaned the proceeds to

X, a business corporation, and X issued a note to CI that was assigned to FI as the security for CI's obligation on the bonds. X used the proceeds of the loan to acquire a newly constructed manufacturing facility that it owns and operates. The bonds were issued as an exempt small issue of bonds described in section 103(b)(6) of the Code, the interest on which is exempt from federal income tax under section 103(a).

Interest on the bonds is payable each January 1 and July 1 until maturity. The terms of the bonds provide that in the event there is a change in the maximum marginal federal corporation income tax rate, the interest rate on the bonds will be equal to the base interest rate multiplied by the quotient of (1 minus the new maximum marginal federal corporation income tax rate) divided by (1 minus the original maximum marginal federal corporation income tax rate). For example, a reduction in the maximum marginal federal corporation income tax rate from 46 to 34 percent would result in an interest rate on the bonds of 8.56 percent computed as follows:

$$7 \times \frac{1-0.34}{1-0.46} = 8.56$$

An amendment of section 11 of the Code by section 601 of the Tax Reform Act of 1986, 1986-3 (Vol. 1) C.B. 166, decreases the maximum marginal federal corporation income tax rate. This reduction will trigger the interest adjustment clause for CI's bonds.

On January 15, 1987, FI waived its right to receive the higher rate of interest under the interest adjustment clause with the result that interest will continue to be paid at the base rate of 7 percent after the change in the maximum tax rate becomes effective. In connection with FI's waiver, CI and X satisfied all applicable requirements for interest on a refunding bond to be tax-exempt under section 103 of the Code. These requirements include the registration requirement, the information reporting requirement, the maturity limitation requirement, and other applicable requirements imposed by the enactment of the Tax Equity and Fiscal Responsibility Act of 1982, 1982-2 C.B. 462, the Tax Reform Act of 1984, 1984-3 (Vol. 1) C.B. 1, and the Tax Reform Act of 1986.

LAW AND ANALYSIS

Section 1001 of the Code provides that gain or loss from the sale of other disposition of property will be determined by reference to the amount realized and the adjusted basis of such property. The entire amount of the gain or loss will be recognized unless otherwise provided.

Section 1.1001-1(a) of the Income Tax Regulations provides that the gain or loss from the exchange of property for other property differing materially either in kind or in extent it treated as income or as loss sustained.

Rev. Rul. 81-169, 1981-1 C.B. 429, concludes that an exchange of bonds that contain materially different terms is a taxable event under section 1001 of the Code. In Rev. Rul. 81-169, the taxpayer exchanged a municipal bond bearing interest at 9 percent, maturing February 1, 1996, and subject to sinking fund payments calculated to provide for level debt service, for a bond of equal face amount bearing interest at 8 1/2 percent, maturing February 1, 2006, and not subject to a sinking fund provision.

Section 265(b)(1) of the Code provides that in the case of a financial institution no deduction shall be allowed for that portion of the taxpayer's interest expense that is allocable to tax-exempt interest.

Section 265(b)(2) of the Code provides that the portion of the taxpayer's interest expense that is allocable to tax-exempt interest is an amount that bears the same ratio to such interest expense as (A) the taxpayer's average adjusted bases of tax-exempt obligations acquired after August 7, 1986, bears to (B) such average adjusted bases for all assets of the taxpayer. For purposes of the disallowance of interest rule of section 265(b), the acquisition date of an obligation is the date on which the holding period begins with respect to the obligation in the hands of the acquiring financial institution. See 2 H.R. Rep. No. 99-841 (Conf. Rep.) 99th Cong., 2d Sess. II-333 (1986).

Generally, the holding period of an obligation begins on the day after it is acquired. See Rev. Rul. 70-598, 1970-2 C.B. 168.

An adjustment to the interest rate on an issue of bonds pursuant to an interest adjustment clause does not result in an exchange under section 1001 of the Code. Although the interest payable on the bonds changes as the result of the adjustment, the adjustment is fixed by the terms of the bonds upon issuance and does not change.

In this case, however, *FI* has waived its right under the interest adjustment clause and will receive interest at the rate of 7 percent rather than at the higher rate to which it would have been entitled under the terms of the bonds issued in 1981. This represents a material change in the terms of the bonds and results in a taxable exchange under section 1001 of the Code and a deemed issuance of new bonds. See Rev. Rul. 81-169.

The date that the new bonds will be deemed to have been issued is January 15, 1987, the date of the waiver. Even though this date is prior to the date that the interest adjustment is triggered and the date on which interest at the new rate is due, it is the waiver of the interest adjustment clause that changed the terms of the bonds and resulted in a reissuance.

Because *FI*'s waiver on January 15, 1987, resulted in a deemed acquisition by *FI* of new bonds on that date, and because the new bonds satisfied all the requirements for interest on a refunding bond to be tax-exempt, *FI* is deemed to hold tax-exempt obligations acquired after August 7, 1986.

HOLDINGS

1. *FI*'s waiver of its right under the interest adjustment clause to receive a higher rate of interest results in a material change in the terms of the bonds and, therefore, is a deemed exchange under section 1001 of the Code of the old bonds for new bonds.

2. Because *FI* is deemed to have acquired on January 15, 1987, new bonds the interest on which is tax-exempt and the acquisition occurred after August 7, 1986, *FI* is precluded from deducting the portion of

its interest expense that is allocable to tax-exempt interest on the new bonds under section 265(b) of the Code.

Revenue Ruling 89-124

ISSUE

If, under the terms of a trust agreement, (1) a financial services corporation conveys securities to a trustee in exchange for certificates that the corporation sells to investors, (2) for a period of 90 days following the creation of the trust, the corporation can convey to the trustee additional securities that are substantially similar to those initially deposited in exchange for additional certificates that it can sell to new investors, and (3) each certificate represents an identical undivided ownership interest in each asset of the trust, does the corporation have a power to vary the investment of the certificate holders within the meaning of section 301.7701-4(c) of the Procedure and Administration Regulations?

FACTS

X, a financial services corporation, created an investment trust by executing a trust instrument and by conveying to a bank, as trustee, certain debt securities in exchange for certificates of beneficial ownership in the trust. The certificates each represent an identical undivided ownership interest in the assets held in trust ("Trust Certificates"). X immediately sold the Trust Certificates to investors.

The trust instrument provides that, during the 90-day period immediately following the inception of the trust, X may deposit additional securities in the trust in exchange for additional Trust Certificates. The trust instrument requires that the additional securities be substantially similar to the securities initially deposited in the trust. After the 90-day period expires, neither X nor the trustee may deposit additional securities in the trust.

X retained the above-described power to deposit additional debt securities in order to facilitate the organization of the trust by adjusting its size in order to accommodate market demand for Trust Certificates.

LAW AND ANALYSIS

Section 301.7701-4(c) of the regulations provides that an investment trust will not be classified as a trust if there is a power under the trust agreement to vary the investment of the certificate holders. An investment trust with a single class of ownership interests representing undivided beneficial interests in the assets of the trust is classified as a trust if there is no power under the trust agreement to vary the investment of the certificate holders.

A power to vary the investment of the certificate holders is one that enables the trustee or some other person to take advantage of variations in the market to improve the investment of all the beneficiaries. The existence of such a power is sufficient to turn the venture into a business, thereby precluding classification of the entity as a trust for federal income tax purposes. See *Commissioner v. North American Bond Trust,* 122 F.2d 545 (2d Cir. 1941), *cert. denied,* 314 U.S. 701 (1942).

The term 'power to vary' has been further defined in revenue rulings. For example, Rev. Rul. 78-149, 1978-1 C.B. 448, holds that a trustee's restricted power to reinvest funds received upon the redemption of municipal obligations exercisable at any time during the first 20 years of the trust's inception is a power to vary the beneficiaries' investments within the meaning of the regulations. Rev. Rul. 75-192, 1975-1 C.B. 384, holds that a limited power to invest income between distribution dates is not a power to vary the investment within the meaning of the regulations.

Rev. Rul. 86-92, 1986-2 C.B. 214, considers whether an investment trust initially funded with bonds and contracts to purchase bonds was properly classified as a trust for federal income tax purposes. The trust agreement provided that, if a contract failed, the depositor could deposit additional bonds different from those that were the subject of the failed contracts. The power was limited to a reasonable time at the inception of the trust and was limited to bonds substantially similar to those subject to the failed contracts. The ruling concludes that the investment trust was classified as a trust because the power was "merely incidental to the organization of the trust." Moreover, the power was not one that could be used throughout the term of the trust to take advantage of market fluctuations, thereby improving the investment of the beneficiaries.

In the present case, the trust has a single class of ownership interests representing undivided beneficial interests in the assets of the trust. Although the trust instrument permits the depositor to introduce new investors and new securities to the investment trust, that power, like the power in Rev. Rul. 86-92, is intended solely to facilitate the organization of the trust and is limited to a short period at the inception of the trust. It is neither intended nor available for use throughout the term of the trust to vary the beneficiaries' investment. Thus, the power is merely incidental to the organization of the trust. Even though the additional securities to be deposited are not required to be identical to those initially deposited, the limited time in which the power may be exercised restricts the ability of the depositor to take advantage of market fluctuations and thereby conduct a business for profit using the trust corpus.

HOLDING

The power to deposit in the trust additional securities that are substantially similar to those initially deposited and to issue additional certificates (which, like the certificates issued initially, represent undivided beneficial interests in the trust assets), if exercisable only for a period of 90 days following the creation of the trust, is not a power to vary the beneficiaries' investment within the meaning of section 301.7701-4(c) of the regulations.

Revenue Ruling 90-7

ISSUE

If a taxpayer holds certificates in an investment arrangement classified as a trust for federal tax purposes under section 301.7701-4(c) of the Procedure and Administration Regulations, does the taxpayer realize gain or loss upon exchanging the certificates for a proportionate share of each of the trust's assets?

FACTS

TR is an arrangement created under a trust instrument and classified as a trust under section 301.7701-4(c) of the Procedure and Administration Regulations. TR holds a fixed portfolio consisting of common stock in 15 different corporations. Interests in TR are represented by certificates.

Under the terms of the trust instrument, the trustee collects dividends paid on the common stock being held by TR and distributes the entire amount (less an amount deposited in a reserve for administrative expenses) to the various certificate holders. Certificate holders have an undivided interest in the trust assets and share equally in any income or loss realized with respect to such assets. Certificate holders also have the right to exchange their certificates for proportionate amounts of the stocks held by TR.

In 1982, A, an individual, paid 200x dollars to TR in exchange for 100 certificates issued by TR. A exercised the exchange right in 1987, when the value of A's share of TR's assets was 300x dollars. In return for surrendering all 100 trust certificates, A received a proportionate amount of the stock held by TR in each of the 15 corporations, 1x dollars of cash as A's proportionate share of the reserve for administrative expenses, and 4x dollars of cash in lieu of fractional shares of stock. The 4x dollars of cash that A received in lieu of fractional shares was funded from the other certificate holders' shares of the reserve for administrative expenses. The total value of the stock and cash A received was 300x dollars.

LAW AND ANALYSIS

Section 1001(a) of the Internal Revenue Code provides that the gain from the sale or other disposition of property shall be the excess of the amount realized over the adjusted basis provided in section 1011 for determining gain, and the loss shall be the excess of the adjusted basis provided in section 1011 for determining loss over the amount realized.

Section 1001(b) of the Code provides that the amount realized from the sale or other disposition of property shall be the sum of any money received plus the fair market value of the property (other than money) received.

Section 1001(c) of the Code provides that, except as otherwise provided in subtitle A, the entire amount of the gain or loss, determined under section 1001(a), on the sale or exchange of property shall be recognized.

Section 1.1001-1(a) of the Income Tax Regulations provides that gain or loss realized from the conversion of property into cash, or from the exchange of property for other property differing materially either in kind or extent, is treated as income or as loss sustained.

Rev. Rul. 56-437, 1956-2 C.B. 507, concludes that there is no sale or exchange when a joint tenancy in the stock of a corporation is severed in a partition action. A division of stock among parties having undivided ownership interests in the stock is a nontaxable transaction for federal income tax purposes.

Sections 673 through 679 of the Code set forth the rules for determining when a grantor or other taxpayer is treated as the owner of an entire trust, section 671 and the regulations thereunder require the grantor to take into account in computing the grantor's tax liability, all of the trust's items of income, deduction, and credit as though the trust had not been in existence during the period the grantor is treated as the owner. Section 1.671-3(a)(1) of the regulations.

Rev. Rul. 84-10, 1984-1 C.B. 155, considers mortgage pools created by the Federal National Mortgage Association (FNMA) pursuant to a trust agreement. Each pool consists of residential mortgages transferred to FNMA by a single mortgage lender in exchange for trust certificates. The trust certificates represent fractional undivided interests in the mortgage loans, pool proceeds, mortgaged property acquired by foreclosure that has not been withdrawn from the pool, and FNMA's obligation to supplement the pool proceeds in certain events. Rev. Rul. 84-10 concludes that each pool is classified as a trust and that each certificate holder is treated as the owner of an undivided interest in the entire trust under section 671 of the Code.

When a grantor is treated as the owner of an entire trust, the grantor is considered to be the owner of the trust assets for federal income tax purposes. Rev. Rul. 85-13, 1985-1 C.B. 184.

Under the terms of TR's trust instrument, A's certificates represented an undivided interest in TR's assets and any income or loss realized on them. Therefore, like a certificate holder in the mortgage pool described in Rev. Rul. 84-10, A was an TR owner of an undivided interest in all of TR under section 671 of the Code. As an owner of an undivided interest in all of TR under section 671, A was considered an owner of an undivided interest in all of TR's assets for federal income tax purposes. Rev. Rul. 85-13. Thus, when A exchanged the certificates, A went from being a co-owner of all TR's stock to being sole owner of a proportionate share of that stock. A realized no gain or loss because like a partition of stock among co-owners, the exchange effected no material difference in A's position. Rev. Rul. 56-437.

A also received 4x dollars of cash in lieu of fractional shares of the stock held by TR. A realized and must recognize gain or loss measured by the difference between the amount of cash received and the adjusted basis in the fractional shares as determined under section 1011 of the Code. A recognized no gain or loss on the receipt of A's 1x dollar share of the reserve for administrative expenses.

Rev. Rul. 68-633, 1968-2 C.B. 329, considers the conversion of shares in an investment trust into the underlying stock held by the trust. That transaction does not materially differ from the one between A and TR. Rev. Rul. 68-633 concludes that the transaction results in the recognition of gain or loss. Rev. Rul. 68-633 is inconsistent with the position of the Internal Revenue Service that the holder of the undivided interest in the investment trust owns an undivided interest in the trust assets for federal income tax purposes so that after the exchange the holder is in essentially the same position as before the exchange. Accordingly, Rev. Rul. 68-633 is revoked.

HOLDING

A does not realize gain or loss upon exchanging certificates in TR for a proportionate share of the stock held by TR. However, gain or loss is realized and recognized to the extent cash received in lieu of fractional shares exceeds (or falls short of) A's adjusted basis in the fractional shares.

EFFECT ON OTHER DOCUMENTS

Rev. Rul. 68-633 is revoked.

PROSPECTIVE APPLICATION

Pursuant to the authority granted by section 7805(b) of the Code, the holding of this ruling will not be applied adversely to a taxpayer if the exchange of trust certificates for trust assets occurred before January 29, 1990. Any gain or loss reported pursuant to Rev. Rul. 68-633 must be reflected in corresponding adjustments to the basis of the trust assets received, pursuant to section 1.1016-6 of the Income Tax Regulations.

Revenue Ruling 90-55

ISSUE

If a trust is treated as wholly-owned by a grantor under the rules of subpart E, part I, of subchapter J, chapter 1, subtitle A of the Internal Revenue Code (sections 671-679), is the taxable year of the trust required to be the calendar year under section 645(a) of the Code?

FACTS

Pursuant to a trust agreement, corporation X established a trust and transferred money to bank Y, as trustee. The trust agreement provides that X may revoke the trust at any time. Corporation X is an accrual basis taxpayer and has a fiscal year accounting period, ending January 31.

LAW AND ANALYSIS

Section 645(a) of the Code provides that for purposes of subtitle A, the taxable year of any trust shall be the calendar year. Section 645(b) provides that subsection (a) shall not apply to a trust exempt from taxation under section 501(a) or a trust described in section 4947(a)(1).

Section 676(a) of the Code provides, in part, that the grantor shall be treated as the owner of any portion of a trust, where at any time the power to revest in the grantor title to such portion is exercisable by the grantor of a nonadverse party, or both.

Section 671 of the Code provides that subparts A through D, part I, subchapter J, chapter 1, subtitle A of the Code apply only to the portion of a trust that is not treated as owned by the grantor under the rules of subpart E, part I, subchapter J, chapter 1, subtitle A of the Code. Similarly, section 1.641-0(b) of the Income Tax Regulations provides that subpart A does not apply to the portion of corpus or income that is treated as owned by the grantor under the rules of subpart E. Section 645 of the Code is in subpart A, part I, subchapter J, chapter 1, subtitle A of the Code. Thus, although section 645 does not explicitly exclude grantor trusts from the reach of its provisions, the Code and regulations contemplate that the provisions generally applicable to trusts do not apply to grantor trusts.

The legislative history of section 645 of the Code indicates that the purpose of the provision was to limit the ability to defer income tax through selection of a taxable year for a trust that is different from the taxable year of the trust beneficiaries. This concern is not present in the case of a trust that is treated as wholly-owned by the grantor under subpart E, part I, subchapter J, chapter 1, subtitle A of the Code because the taxable year of the trust is disregarded and the grantor must report the gross income from the trust property as if the trust does not exist. See S. Rep. No. 313, 99th Cong., 2d Sess. 872 (1986), 1986-3 (Vol. 3) C.B. 872; section 1.671-3(a)(1) of the regulations; Rev. Rul. 57-390, 1957-2 C.B. 326.

Corporation X, as the grantor of the trust, is treated as the owner of the entire corpus and income of the trust under section 676(a) of the Code. Accordingly, section 645 does not apply to the trust because the entire trust is subject to the rules of subpart

E, part I, subchapter J, chapter 1, subtitle A of the Code.

HOLDING

The taxable year of a trust that is treated as wholly owned by a grantor under the rules of subpart E, part I, subchapter J, chapter 1, subtitle A of the Code is not required to be the calendar year under section 645(a).

Revenue Ruling 90-63

ISSUE

If the trustee of an investment trust has a power to consent to changes in the credit support of debt obligations that is exercisable only to the extent the trustee reasonably believes the change is advisable to maintain the value of trust property by preserving the credit rating of the obligations, is such power a "power to vary the investment" within the meaning of section 301.7701- 4(c) of the Procedure and Administration Regulations?

FACTS

S, a financial services corporation, created an investment trust funded with a fixed portfolio that included a certain issue of tax-exempt debt obligations.

The tax-exempt debt obligations are exempt facility bonds issued by C, a municipal corporation, to provide a solid waste disposal facility described in section 142(a)(6) of the Internal Revenue Code. The bonds are payable only from the revenues derived from the facility and are nonrecourse as to C.

C and D, a corporation, entered into a loan agreement pursuant to which C loaned the proceeds from the issuance of the bonds to D for the development of the facility. Under the terms of the loan agreement, D is required to provide credit support in the form of a letter of credit from a financial institution specified in the agreement.

Under the terms of the trust agreement, the trustee, at C's request, may consent to a change in the credit support if the trustee reasonably believes that the change is advisable to maintain the value of trust assets by preserving the credit rating of the bonds.

LAW AND ANALYSIS

Section 301.7701-4(c) of the regulations provides that an investment trust with a single class of ownership interests, representing undivided beneficial interests in the assets of the trust, is properly classified as a trust if there is no power under the trust agreement to vary the investment of the beneficiaries.

A power to vary the investment of the certificate holders is one that enables the trustee or another person to take advantage of market variations to improve the investment of all the beneficiaries. The existence of such a power is sufficient to turn the venture into a business, thereby precluding classification of the entity as a trust for federal tax purposes. See *Commissioner v. North American Bond Trust*, 122 F.2d 545 (2d Cir. 1941), *cert. denied*, 314 U.S. 701 (1942).

In the present case, the power to consent to changes in the credit support provided under the loan agreement does not permit the trustee to alter any of the other terms of the bond issue held by the trust. Furthermore, the trustee is permitted to accept changes in the credit support only when the trustee reasonably believes the change is advisable to maintain the value of trust property by preserving the credit rating of the bonds. Although it is possible that a proposed change would result in an increase in the value of the bonds held by the trust, any such increase would be incidental to maintaining the value of trust property. Thus, the increase would not be the result of trading in securities and thereby profiting from market fluctuations. Accordingly, the power is not a power to vary the investment as that term is used in section 301.7701-4(c) of the regulations.

HOLDING

The power to consent to changes in the credit support for debt obligations held in an investment trust is not a "power to vary the investment" within the meaning of section 301.7701-4(c) of the Procedure and Administration Regulations if it is exercisable only to the extent the trustee reasonably believes the change is advisable to maintain the value of trust property by preserving the credit rating of the bonds.

Revenue Ruling 91-46

ISSUES

(1) If a taxpayer sells mortgage loans (mortgages) and at the same time enters into a contract to service the mortgages for amounts received from interest payments on the mortgages, under what circumstances are the mortgages "stripped bonds" and the taxpayer's rights to receive interest "stripped coupons" within the meaning of section 1286 of the Internal Revenue Code?

(2) How are the respective fair market values of the stripped bonds and stripped coupons determined?

FACTS

Mortgage company M is in the business of originating and servicing residential mortgages. Agency A is in the business of purchasing residential mortgages and selling interests in those mortgages to investors. M originated a pool of mortgages with a total principal amount of $100,000,000 and an annual interest rate equal to the then-current market interest rate. Later, when the market interest rate had declined, M transferred the $100,000,000 pool of mortgages to A in exchange for $100,000,000.

At the time of the transfer, M and A entered into a contract for M to service the mortgages transferred. Under this contract, M is obligated to perform various services. For example, M is required to collect the monthly mortgage payments from the mortgagors and remit these payments to A. M also is required to accumulate escrows for the payment of insurance and taxes, to disburse these funds as the payments come due, to maintain records relating to the mortgages, and to handle delinquency problems.

The mortgage servicing contract provides that M is entitled to receive amounts from interest payments collected on the mortgages. The annual amount to be received is equal to 1.25 percent of the outstanding principal balance of the mortgages. In addition, M is entitled to retain certain income that it receives in the course of servicing the mortgages. This other income includes the income earned on principal and interest payments between the time they are collected and the time they are remitted to A, income from sources such as fees for late payments, bad checks, insurance, and assumptions with respect to the mortgages, and income earned through the maintenance of escrow accounts.

The minimum annual amount allowed by A for servicing mortgages of the type sold by M is equal to 0.25 percent of the outstanding principal balance of the mortgages. This amount is commonly referred to as "normal" servicing. Thus, of the annual amount that M is entitled to receive from interest payments collected on the mortgages, the portion that exceeds the normal servicing is equal to 1 percent of the outstanding principal balance of the mortgages. This portion is commonly referred to as "excess" servicing.

With the estimated prepayment rate on the mortgages taken into account, the present value of amounts that represent reasonable compensation for performing services under the contract is less than the sum of the present value of the amounts that M is entitled to receive as normal servicing and the present value of the income from other sources. M does not elect to use the safe harbor provided by Rev. Proc. 91-50 [reproduced at page 608] for determining the extent to which amounts that a taxpayer is entitled to receive under a mortgage servicing contract represent reasonable compensation for the services provided.

LAW AND ANALYSIS

ISSUE 1

Section 1286(e)(1) of the Code defines the term "bond" to include a certificate or other evidence of indebtedness. In the present situation, the mortgages sold by M to A are evidences of indebtedness and, therefore, are "bonds" within the meaning of section 1286(e)(1).

Section 1286(e)(5) of the Code defines the term "coupon" to include any right to receive interest on a bond (whether or not evidenced by a coupon). To some extent,

M's rights to receive amounts under the mortgage servicing contract are rights to receive reasonable compensation for the services that the contract requires M to perform. Because of the nature of these services, it is traditional in the mortgage servicing industry to compensate servicers with amounts of interest collected on the mortgages serviced. Therefore, to the extent that M's rights to receive amounts under the mortgage servicing contract represent rights to receive reasonable compensation for services to be performed under the contract, they will be treated as rights to receive compensation from A. However, to the extent that the contract entitles M to receive amounts in excess of reasonable compensation for services, M's rights to receive amounts from interest payments collected on the mortgages will be treated as "coupons" under section 1286(e)(5).

Section 1286(e)(2) of the Code defines the term "stripped bond" as a bond issued with interest coupons where there is a separation in ownership between the bond and any coupon that has not yet become payable. Section 1286(e)(3) defines a "stripped coupon" as any coupon relating to a stripped bond. When M sells the mortgages to A and enters into the mortgage servicing contract, the transaction results in a separation in ownership between the mortgages (bonds) and rights to receive some of the interest payable in the future (coupons) on those mortgages. Thus, the transaction causes the mortgages purchased by A to become "stripped bonds" and the coupons held by M to become "stripped coupons" within the meaning of section 1286(e)(2) and (3).

ISSUE 2

Section 1286(b) of the Code provides that, for purposes of subtitle A of the Internal Revenue Code, if any person strips one or more coupons from a bond and, after July 1, 1982, disposes of the bond or the coupon, the basis of the bond and coupons immediately before the disposition is allocated among the items retained and the items disposed of on the basis of their respective fair market values.

Since the transaction between M and A results in stripped bonds and stripped coupons, section 1286(b) requires M to allocate its total basis in the mortgages immediately before their sale to A between (1) the items sold (i.e., the stripped bonds) and (2) the items retained (i.e., the stripped coupons). This allocation must be made on the basis of the respective fair market values of the stripped bonds and stripped coupons at the time of the transaction between M and A.

The fair market value of the stripped bonds, which are the mortgages held by A, is the purchase price that A paid for the mortgages. This amount is \$100,000,000.

The fair market value of the stripped coupons, which are M's rights to receive interest other than as compensation for services, is determined on the basis of all of the relevant facts and circumstances. Facts to be considered in determining this amount include, but are not necessarily limited to, recent sale prices of comparable rights.

In the present situation, no portion of the excess servicing is reasonable compensation for services. Therefore, the full value of M's right to receive the excess servicing is included in the fair market value of the stripped coupons.

A portion of the value of M's right to receive the normal servicing of 0.25 percent also is included in the fair market value of the stripped coupons. This portion is the excess of (1) the value of M's right to receive the normal servicing, over (2) the excess, if any, of (i) the value of amounts that represent reasonable compensation for providing services under the mortgage servicing contract, over (ii) the value of the other income that M is expected to receive.

HOLDINGS

(1) If a taxpayer sells mortgages and at the same time enters into a contract to service the mortgages for amounts received from interest payments on the mortgages, and if the contract entitles the taxpayer to receive amounts that exceed reasonable compensation for the services to be performed, the mortgages are "stripped bonds" within the meaning of section 1286(e)(2). The taxpayer's rights to receive amounts

under the contract are "stripped coupons" within the meaning of section 1286(e)(3) to the extent that they are rights to receive mortgage interest other than as reasonable compensation for the services to be performed.

(2) The fair market value of the stripped bonds is their sale price in the transaction. The fair market value of the stripped coupons is determined on the basis of all of the relevant facts and circumstances.

APPLICATION

As a consequence of these holdings:

(1) To the extent that the amounts received by M from interest payments are treated as compensation for services, they are treated as received by A from mortgagors and paid by A to M as compensation. To the extent that the amounts received by M are treated as payments with respect to stripped coupons held by M, they are treated as received directly by M from the mortgagors.

(2) M's ownership of the mortgage servicing rights is not an interest in either an entity that owns the related stripped bonds or the assets of such an entity. Thus, if the holder of these stripped bonds otherwise qualified as a REMIC within the meaning of section 860D of the Code, the fact that M stripped coupons from the bonds would not cause the stripped coupons to be treated as interests in the REMIC for purposes of sections 860A through 860G. Similarly, if the holder of these stripped bonds otherwise qualified as a trust for federal income tax purposes, the fact that M stripped coupons from the bonds would not cause the stripped coupons to be treated as a separate class of ownership interest in the assets of the trust within the meaning of section 301.7701-4(c) of the Regulations on Procedure and Administration.

Three revenue procedures accompany this revenue ruling. Rev. Proc. 91-51, page 779, this Bulletin, provides expeditious consent for a taxpayer to change its method of accounting for sales of mortgages to comply with section 1286 of the Code. Rev. Proc. 91-50 [reproduced at page 608] provides an elective safe harbor for determining the ex-

tent to which amounts that a taxpayer is entitled to receive under a mortgage servicing contract represent reasonable compensation for the services provided. Rev. Proc. 91-49 [reproduced at page 606] provides simplified tax treatment for certain mortgages that are stripped bonds.

EFFECT ON OTHER REVENUE RULINGS

Rev. Rul. 66-314, 1966-2 C.B., 296 is obsoleted.

Revenue Ruling 92-32

ISSUE

A sponsor formed an investment trust by transferring a pool of debt securities to a trustee in exchange for two classes of pass-through certificates, senior certificates and subordinated certificates. The sponsor sold both classes of certificates to investors. Does the sponsor's sale of the subordinated certificates affect the classification of the investment trust as a trust for Federal income tax purposes?

FACTS

Sponsor owns a pool of automobile installment sale contracts (hereinafter, "contracts"). Each contract in the pool is secured by an automobile, is fully self-amortizing, has a fixed interest rate, and provides for level monthly payments over its term.

Under the terms of a trust agreement, Sponsor created an investment trust by transferring the pool of contracts to a trustee in exchange for two classes of pass-through certificates: Senior Certificates and Subordinated Certificates. The certificates represent undivided beneficial ownership interests in the pooled contracts. The trustee holds legal title to the contracts for the benefit of the certificate holders but has no power to vary the investment of the certificate holders.

Holders of the Senior Certificates are, in the aggregate, entitled to receive monthly distributions consisting of 90 percent of all scheduled payments of principal and interest on the pooled contracts and 90 percent of all prepayments on those contracts. Holders of the Subordinated Certificates are, in the aggregate, entitled to receive monthly distributions consisting of the remaining 10 percent of the payments on the pooled contracts.

The terms of the Senior Certificates are identical to the terms of the Subordinated Certificates except that, if there is in any month a shortfall in payments on the pooled contracts due to defaults or delinquencies, the amount of that shortfall will first reduce the monthly distribution on the Subordinated Certificates. The monthly distribution on the Senior Certificates will be reduced only after the monthly distribution on the Subordinated Certificates has been reduced to zero by shortfalls.

Sponsor sold both the Senior Certificates and the Subordinated Certificates to investors.

LAW AND ANALYSIS

Section 301.7701-4(c)(1) of the Procedure and Administration Regulations provides, in part, that an investment trust that has multiple classes of ownership interests is ordinarily classified as an association or a partnership under section 301.7701-2. However, an investment trust that has multiple classes of ownership interests is classified as a trust for tax purposes if (1) there is no power under the trust agreement to vary the investment of the certificate holders, and (2) the trust is formed to facilitate direct investment in the assets of the trust and the existence of multiple classes of ownership interests is incidental to that purpose.

Section 301.7701-4(c)(2) of the regulations, Example (2), describes a typical senior/subordinated mortgage pool arrangement. In that example, Corporation M originated mortgages secured by residential real estate and, under the terms of a trust agreement, transferred those mortgages to a trustee in exchange for Class C certificates and Class D certificates. The trustee held legal title to the mortgages for the benefit of the certificate holders but had no power to vary the investments in the pool. Class C certificate holders were entitled to receive 90 percent of the payments of principal and interest on the mortgages, and the Class D

certificate holders were entitled to receive the other 10 percent. The two classes of certificates were identical except that, in the event of a default on the underlying mortgages, the payment rights of the Class D certificate holders were subordinated to the rights of the Class C certificate holders. Corporation M sold the Class C certificates to investors and retained the Class D certificates.

Example (2) states that the trust has multiple classes of ownership interests because of the greater security provided the Class C certificate holders. The example goes on to state, however, that the interests of the certificate holders are substantially equivalent to undivided interests in the pool of mortgages, coupled with a limited recourse guarantee running from Corporation M to the holders of the Class C certificates. Example (2) concludes that the existence of multiple classes of ownership interests is incidental to the trust's purpose of facilitating direct investment in the assets of the trust, and the trust is therefore classified as a trust for Federal income tax purposes.

The transaction described in this ruling is substantially identical in all material respects to the one described in Example (2), except that, here, Sponsor sold the Subordinated Certificates to investors, whereas the sponsor in Example (2) retained the subordinated certificates. Despite this difference, the analysis in Example (2) is applicable. Sponsor's sale of the Subordinated Certificates to third party investors is equivalent to Sponsor's sale of an undivided interest in the pool of contracts encumbered by the limited recourse guarantee made by Sponsor to the Senior Certificate holders. Sponsor's transfer of the Subordinated Certificates to investors transfers the burden of the limited recourse guarantee to those investors but does not alter the trust's purpose of facilitating direct investment in the trust's assets.

HOLDING

If a sponsor creates an investment trust otherwise meeting the requirements of section 301.7701-4(c)(1) of the regulations by transferring a pool of debt securities to a trustee in exchange for two classes of pass-through certificates, senior certificates and subordinated certificates, the sponsor's sale of the subordinated certificates to investors does not affect the classification of the investment trust as a trust for Federal income tax purposes.

Revenue Ruling 92-105

ISSUE

Does a taxpayer's interest in an Illinois land trust constitute real property which may be exchanged for other real property without recognition of gain or loss under section 1031 of the Internal Revenue Code?

FACTS

A, an individual, created an Illinois land trust, described in section 8.31 of chapter 29 of the Illinois Annotated Statutes (Smith-Hurd 1990), under which A was the beneficiary. The purpose of the Illinois land trust was to hold title to Blackacre, which is Illinois real property that A has held for investment purposes. Under Illinois state law, a beneficiary's interest in an Illinois land trust is characterized as personal property, the beneficiary or any person designated by the beneficiary has the exclusive power to direct or control the trustee in dealing with the title to the property in the land trust, and the beneficiary has the exclusive control of the management of the property and the exclusive right to the earnings and proceeds from the property.

To create the Illinois land trust, A executed two instruments: (1) a deed in trust; and (2) a land trust agreement. These instruments named T, a domestic corporation, as trustee.

Under the deed in trust, A transferred legal and equitable title in Blackacre to T, subject to the provisions of the accompanying land trust agreement. Pursuant to the deed in trust, any person dealing with T would take any interest in Blackacre free and clear of the claims of A.

The land trust agreement entered into between A and T authorized T, in return for an annual fee, to execute deeds, mortgages, or otherwise deal with the legal title of Blackacre at the direction of A. Under the land trust agreement, A retained the exclusive control of the management, operation,

renting, and selling of Blackacre, together with the exclusive right to the earnings and proceeds from Blackacre. A also retained the right to assign A's interest in the Illinois land trust. Under the land trust agreement, A was required to file all tax returns, pay all taxes, and satisfy any other liabilities with respect to Blackacre. The land trust agreement precluded T from disclosing that A was the trust beneficiary unless directed to do so by A in writing. No other agreement regarding Blackacre existed between A and T.

A subsequently entered into a written agreement with X, a domestic corporation, for an exchange of properties. Under the agreement, A agreed to transfer A's interest in the Illinois land trust to X, and X agreed to transfer Whiteacre to A. Whiteacre is real property owned by X and is of a like kind to Blackacre. Pursuant to the agreement, A exchanged A's interest in the Illinois land trust for Whiteacre. Thereafter, A held Whiteacre for investment purposes.

LAW AND ANALYSIS

Section 1031(a)(1) of the Code provides that no gain or loss is recognized on the exchange of property held for productive use in a trade or business or for investment if such property is exchanged solely for property of like kind that is to be held either for productive use in a trade or business or for investment.

Section 1031(a)(2) of the Code provides that section 1031(a)(1) does not apply to any exchange of specified types of property. In particular, section 1031(a)(2)(E) provides that section 1031(a)(1) does not apply to any exchange of certificates of trust or beneficial interests.

Section 301.7701-4(a) of the Procedure and Administration Regulations provides that the term "trust" as used in the Code refers to an arrangement created by a will or by an inter vivos declaration whereby trustees take title to property for the purpose of protecting or conserving it for the beneficiaries under the ordinary rules applied in chancery or probate courts. Generally, an arrangement is treated as a trust under the Code if it can be shown that the purpose of the arrangement is to vest in trustees responsibility for the protection and conservation of property for beneficiaries who cannot share in the discharge of this responsibility.

The purpose of the Illinois land trust created by A was to vest legal and equitable title in a "trustee." However, under applicable Illinois law, the deed in trust, and the land trust agreement, A retained sole authority and responsibility for dealing directly with Blackacre for all purposes other than the transfer of title. A retained the direct right to manage and control Blackacre, the direct right to collect any rent or sales proceeds from Blackacre, and the direct obligation to pay any taxes and liabilities relating to Blackacre.

Because T's only responsibility was to hold and transfer title at the direction of A, a trust (as defined in section 301.7701-4(a) of the regulations) was not established. Moreover, there were no other agreements between A and T (or between A and any other person) that would cause the overall arrangement to be classified as a partnership (or any other type of entity) for federal income tax purposes. Cf. Rev. Rul. 64-220, 1964-2 C.B. 335. Instead, T was a mere agent for the holding and transfer of title to Blackacre, and A has retained direct ownership of Blackacre for federal income tax purposes.

Accordingly, A's transfer of A's interest in the Illinois land trust holding title to Blackacre in exchange for Whiteacre was an exchange of the underlying real property, not an exchange of a certificate of trust or beneficial interest (under section 1031(a)(2)

(E) of the Code) for Whiteacre. Blackacre is like-kind property to Whiteacre, and provided the requirements of section 1031 are otherwise satisfied, this exchange will qualify for nonrecognition of gain or loss under section 1031.

HOLDING

A taxpayer's interest in an Illinois land trust constitutes real property which may be exchanged for other real property without recognition of gain or loss under section 1031 of the Code, provided the requirements of that section are otherwise satisfied. This holding is not applicable if an arrangement involving an Illinois land trust creates an entity (such as a partnership).

Several states in addition to Illinois, including, for example, California, Florida, Hawaii, Indiana, North Dakota, and Virginia, have laws that statutorily or judicially sanction arrangements that are similar to the Illinois land trust arrangement described herein. The holding in this revenue ruling also applies to an interest in a similar arrangement created under the laws of any state, pursuant to which (1) the trustee has title to real property, (2) the beneficiary (or a designee of the beneficiary) has the exclusive right to direct or control the trustee in dealing with the title to the property, and (3) the beneficiary has the exclusive control of the management of the property, the exclusive right to the earnings and proceeds from the property, and the obligation to pay any taxes and liabilities relating to the property.

REVENUE PROCEDURES

Revenue Procedure 91-49

SECTION 1. PURPOSE

This revenue procedure provides simplified tax treatment, pursuant to section 1.1286-1T of the temporary Income Tax Regulations, for certain mortgage loans (mortgages) that are stripped bonds under section 1286 of the Internal Revenue Code. See Rev. Rul. 91-46, page 5, this Bulletin.

SEC. 2. BACKGROUND

.01 Section 1286(a) of the Code provides that a stripped bond or stripped coupon purchased after July 1, 1982, is treated by the purchaser (or by any person whose basis is determined by reference to the purchaser's basis) as a bond originally issued on the purchase date and having an original issue discount (OID) equal to the excess of (1) the stated redemption price at maturity (or, in the case of a coupon, the amount payable on the due date of the coupon), over (2) the bond's or coupon's ratable share of the purchase price. Sections 1271 through 1275 provide rules for bonds having OID.

.02 Section 1286(b)(4) of the Code provides that, for purposes of section 1286(a), a person that strips one or more coupons from a bond and disposes of the bond or coupon is treated as having purchased on the date of the disposition each item retained, for an amount equal to the basis allocated to the item under section 1286(b)(3). Section 1286(b)(3) provides that the basis of the bond and coupons immediately before the disposition is allocated among the items retained and the items disposed of on the basis of their respective fair market values.

.03 Under section 1273(a)(3) of the Code, if the OID on a bond is less than one-fourth of 1 percent of the stated redemption price of the bond at maturity, multiplied by the number of complete years to maturity, then the OID is considered to be zero. In

appropriate cases, the number of complete years to maturity means the weighted average maturity of the remaining principal payments under the bond.

.04 Section 1278(a)(1) of the Code defines the term "market discount bond" as any bond having market discount. Subject to a de minimis rule, section 1278(a)(2) defines "market discount" as the excess of the stated redemption price of the bond at maturity, over the basis of the bond immediately after its acquisition by the taxpayer. Sections 1276 through 1278 provide rules for market discount bonds.

.05 Under section 1278(a)(2)(C) of the Code, if the market discount on a bond is less than one-fourth of 1 percent of the stated redemption price of the bond at maturity, multiplied by the number of complete years to maturity (after the taxpayer acquired the bond), then the market discount is considered to be zero. In appropriate cases, the number of complete years to maturity means the weighted average maturity of the remaining principal payments under the bond.

.06 Section 1.1286-1T(a) of the temporary regulations provides that, if the OID determined under section 1286(a) with respect to the purchase of a stripped bond or stripped coupon is less than the amount computed under the OID de minimis rule of section 1273(a)(3), then the amount of OID with respect to that purchase is considered to be zero. Section 1.1286-1T(b) authorizes the Internal Revenue Service to provide, by publication in the Internal Revenue Bulletin, that certain mortgage loans that are stripped bonds are to be treated as market discount bonds under section 1278. This treatment may be provided for a stripped bond only if, immediately after the most recent disposition referred to in section 1286(b), either (1) the amount of OID is considered to be zero under section 1.1286-1T(a), or (2) the annual stated rate of interest payable on the stripped bond is no more than 100 basis points lower than the annual stated rate of interest on the original bond (before any stripping occurred).

.07 In Rev. Rul. 91-46, page 5, this Bulletin, a taxpayer sold mortgages and at the same time entered into a contract to service the mortgages for amounts received from interest payments collected on the mortgages. The ruling holds that the mortgages are "stripped bonds" within the meaning of section 1286(e)(2) of the Code if the contract entitles the taxpayer to receive amounts that exceed reasonable compensation for the services to be performed under the contract. The ruling also holds that the taxpayer's rights to receive amounts under the contract are "stripped coupons" within the meaning of section 1286(e)(3) to the extent that they are rights to receive mortgage interest other than as reasonable compensation for the services to be performed.

SEC. 3. SCOPE

.01 This revenue procedure applies to a mortgage that is a stripped bond if —

(1) The mortgage is secured by real property;

(2) But for this revenue procedure, the tax treatment of the stripped bond would be governed by section 1286(a) of the Code; and

(3) The stripped bond satisfies the criterion set forth in subsection .02.

.02 A stripped bond satisfies the criterion of this subsection if, immediately after the most recent disposition referred to in section 1286(b) —

(1) The amount of OID with respect to the stripped bond is considered to be zero under section 1.1286-1T(a) of the temporary regulations; or

(2) The annual stated rate of interest payable on the stripped bond is no more than 100 basis points lower than the annual stated rate of interest payable on the original bond from which it and any other stripped bond or bonds and any stripped coupon or coupons were stripped. (For this purpose, the annual stated rate of interest payable on the stripped bond includes amounts treated as reasonable compensation for purposes of Rev. Rul. 91-46.)

SEC. 4. PROCEDURE

Any purchaser of a stripped bond to which this revenue procedure applies must —

.01 Treat the stripped bond as a "market discount bond" described in section 1278(a)(1) of the Code if the bond has market discount within the meaning of section 1278(a)(2) (including the de minimis rule in section 1278(a)(2)(C)); and

.02 Treat the stripped bond as having zero OID under section 1286(a).

SEC. 5. APPLICATION

As a consequence of section 4 —

.01 If the stripped bond is not subject to an election made under section 1278(b), gain on the disposition of the stripped bond and on any partial principal payment on the stripped bond must be treated under the rules of section 1276.

.02 If the stripped bond is not subject to a constant interest rate election made under section 1276(b)(2), accrued market discount on the stripped bond must be determined as otherwise provided in section 1276(b). See also 2 H.R. Conf. Rep. No. 841, 99th Cong., 2d Sess. II-842, 1986-3 (Vol. 4) C.B. 842 (describing a method of computing accrued market discount on market discount bonds the principal of which may be paid in two or more installments).

.03 The tax treatment of any stripped coupon that was separated from the mortgage to produce the stripped bond remains unchanged. For example, under sections 1286(b)(4) and 1286(a) of the Code, the stripped coupon is treated as having OID.

SEC. 6. METHOD OF ACCOUNTING

.01 In general. The tax treatment provided in this revenue procedure is a method of accounting. Thus, if a taxpayer has an existing method of accounting for stripped bonds that are described in section 3 of this revenue procedure and if that method is consistent with the treatment provided in section 4, the taxpayer must continue to use that method.

.02 Change in method. If a taxpayer has an existing method of accounting for stripped bonds that are described in section 3 of this revenue procedure and if that method is not consistent with the treatment provided in section 4, the taxpayer must change its method of accounting in accordance with section 446 and the regulations thereunder. If the taxpayer's existing method is otherwise permissible under section 1286(a), then, in accordance with section 1.446-1(e)(3)(ii) of the regulations, the Commissioner hereby waives the 180-day rule and, in accordance with section 1.446-1(e)(2)(i), the Commissioner hereby grants consent to a taxpayer that requests to change its method of accounting for those bonds to the method provided in this revenue procedure. This consent must be requested on a statement attached to the timely filed return for the first tax year (year of change) ending on or after August 8, 1991.

.03 Cut-off basis. The consent is granted for stripped bonds purchased on or after the first day of the year of change. Because this change is implemented on a "cut-off" basis, no adjustment under section 481(a) is required to prevent amounts from being duplicated or omitted.

.04 Protection for years prior to the year of change. If a taxpayer changes its method of accounting under the consent granted in subsection .02, an examining agent may not propose that the taxpayer change the same method of accounting for a year prior to the year of change.

SEC. 7. EFFECTIVE DATE

This revenue procedure is effective August 8, 1991.

Revenue Procedure 91-50

SECTION 1. PURPOSE

This revenue procedure provides a safe harbor that taxpayers may elect to use in applying section 1286 of the Internal Revenue Code to certain mortgage servicing contracts. When elected, this safe harbor determines the extent to which amounts that a taxpayer is entitled to receive under a mortgage servicing contract represent reasonable compensation for the services provided.

SEC. 2. BACKGROUND

.01 In Rev. Rul. 91-46, page 5, this Bulletin, a taxpayer sold mortgage loans (mortgages) and at the same time entered into a contract to service the mortgages for amounts received from interest payments collected on the mortgages. The ruling holds that the mortgages are "stripped bonds" within the meaning of section 1286(e)(2) of the Code if the contract entitles the taxpayer to receive amounts that exceed reasonable compensation for the services to be performed under the contract. The ruling also holds that the taxpayer's rights to receive amounts under the contract are "stripped coupons" within the meaning of section 1286(e)(3) to the extent that they are rights to receive mortgage interest other than as reasonable compensation for the services to be performed.

.02 A mortgage servicing contract generally requires the servicer to perform various services. For example, a contract generally requires the servicer to collect the periodic mortgage payments from the mortgagors and remit these payments to the owner of the mortgages. In addition, a contract generally requires the servicer to accumulate escrows, if any, for the payment of insurance and taxes and disburse these funds as the payments come due, to maintain records relating to the mortgages, and to handle delinquency problems.

.03 A mortgage servicing contract generally states the servicer's entitlement to receive amounts from interest payments collected on the mortgages as an annual percentage of the outstanding principal balance of the mortgages to be serviced.

.04 In addition, a mortgage servicing contract generally entitles the servicer to retain certain other income that it receives in the course of servicing the mortgages, including income earned on principal and interest payments between the time they are collected and the time they are remitted to the owner of the mortgages, income from sources such as fees for late payments, bad checks, insurance, and assumptions with respect to the mortgages, and income earned through the maintenance of escrow accounts.

SEC. 3. SCOPE

This revenue procedure applies only to contracts to service one- to four-unit residential mortgages. This revenue procedure does not apply to contracts to perform services that do not include substantially all of the services described in section 2.02 of this revenue procedure.

SEC. 4. SAFE HARBOR

.01 If the safe harbor applies to a mortgage servicing contract, then for purposes of applying section 1286 of the Code and Rev. Rul. 91-46, reasonable compensation for providing services under the contract is deemed to be the sum of: (1) the amounts that the taxpayer is entitled to receive from mortgage interest collections, up to the applicable safe harbor rate set forth in section 4.02 as applied to the outstanding principal balance of the mortgages to be serviced; and (2) the other income described in section 2.04 that the taxpayer is entitled to receive in the course of servicing the mortgages. Any mortgage interest that the taxpayer is entitled to receive in excess of the safe harbor rate is a payment with respect to stripped coupons held by the taxpayer.

.02 For purposes of section 4.01, the following annual rates are the safe harbor rates for servicing one- to four-unit residential mortgages: (1) for a conventional, fixed rate mortgage, 0.25 percent; (2) for a mortgage less than one year old that is insured or guaranteed by the Federal Housing Administration, Veterans Administration, or Farmers Home Administration, 0.44 percent; and (3) for any other one- to four-unit residential mortgage, 0.375 percent. However, if the original principal balance of any mortgage was $50,000 or less, the safe harbor rate for servicing that mortgage is 0.44 percent.

.03 If all of the mortgages to be serviced under a contract do not qualify for the same safe harbor rate under section 4.02 of this revenue procedure, the safe harbor rate for servicing these mortgages is a weighted average of the safe harbor rates for the individual mortgages. This average is weighted on the basis of the outstanding principal balances of the mortgages at the time the taxpayer enters into the servicing contract.

.04 A taxpayer may elect to use the safe harbor for any taxable year and may revoke this election for any later taxable year. An election to use the safe harbor is effective for all taxable years until a taxable year for which it is revoked. If the safe harbor is elected for a taxable year, the safe harbor applies to all contracts, to which this revenue procedure applies (as described in section 3), to service mortgages that the taxpayer sells during the year.

SEC. 5. METHOD OF ELECTION OR REVOCATION

To elect or revoke the safe harbor, a taxpayer must attach a statement to its timely filed federal income tax return for the first taxable year for which the safe harbor is elected (or revoked). This attachment must state that the taxpayer is electing (or revoking) the safe harbor for mortgage servicing contracts that is provided by Revenue Procedure 91-50.

SEC. 6. EFFECTIVE DATE

This revenue procedure is effective for tax years ending on or after August 8, 1991.

TECHNICAL ADVICE MEMORANDUM

T.A.M. 8533003

May 7, 1985

ISSUE

(1) Whether as a result of a "Trust Instrument", the Government of Country X created an association taxable as a corporation or a trust for federal income tax purposes.

(2) Whether the exemption under section 892 of the Internal Revenue Code is restricted to income from investments within the United States, or does the exemption apply to all income from U.S. sources received by a foreign government (including income from commercial activities).

(3) If Country X is subject to U.S. tax, is the foreign government required to file a Form 1120 F?

FACTS

Country X, a non-treaty country, appointed Bank A by letter dated January 19, 1966, to act as Trustee for the investment of funds. The letter stated that the funds and other property of Country X, which from time to time would be transferred to Bank A, were to be held and administered as a trust estate for the benefit of Country X on terms and conditions specified in the letter. The relevant terms and conditions specified in the letter are as follows. Articles 1 and 2 provide that until the Trust is terminated the Trustee shall hold, manage, invest and reinvest the trust estate, shall collect and receive the income thereof, and shall add the net income thereof to Principal. The Trustee shall pay over to Country X, or upon its order, out of the trust estate, such sum or sums, including the whole thereof, as Country X, at any time or from time to time, shall direct by an instrument in writing directed to the Trustee.

Article 3 provides, in part, that the Trustee shall have the following powers and authority in the administration of the trust estate to be exercised in its uncontrolled discretion:

A. To purchase or otherwise acquire any property for cash or on credit, either alone or jointly with others, and to retain such property, whether originally a part of the trust estate or subsequently acquired ... G. To manage, administer, operate, lease for any number of years, regardless of any restrictions on leases made by fiduciaries, develop, improve, repair, alter, demolish, mortgage, pledge, grant options with respect to, sell for cash or on credit, or exchange for other property, or otherwise deal with any real property or interest therein at any time held by the Trustee, and to hold any such real property of record or otherwise in the Trustee's name or in the name of a nominee, with or without the addition of words indicating that such property is held in a fiduciary capacity.

Article 4 provides, in part, that the word "property" shall be deemed to refer to any property, real or personal or part interest therein, situated in the United States of America (or with respect to intangible property, the evidence of ownership thereof being issued by the government of the United States of America or any political subdivision thereof or by a citizen thereof or by an organization existing under its laws or the laws of any political subdivision thereof).

Articles 3A and 4 were subsequently amended to modify certain definitional terms and the limitations on the amount of the trust estate invested in certain types of property.

Article 6 provides, in part, that the Trustee shall render accounts of its transactions to Country X quarter-annually (on a fiscal year basis) and Country X may approve such accounts by an instrument in writing delivered to the Trustee. In the absence of the filing in writing with the Trustee by Country X of exceptions or objections to any such account ... Country X shall be deemed to have approved such account; and in such case or upon the written approval of Country X of any such account, the Trustee shall be released, relieved and discharged with respect to all matters and things set forth in such account as though such account had been settled by the decree of a court of competent jurisdiction.

Article 8 provides, in part, that Country X expressly reserves the right to revoke the trust in whole or in part.

Article 10 provides, in part, that the terms of the January 19, 1966, letter and the trust thereby created shall be construed, regulated and administered under the laws of State B and the Trustee shall be liable to account only in the courts of that State.

Article 11 provides, in part, that should it be determined at any time that the duration of the term of this trust is limited by the application of the Rule against Perpetuities or any other rule of law, then, and in that event, this trust shall terminate not later than twenty-one years after the date of death of the last to die of the employees of the Trustee who are living on the date of the January 19, 1966, letter.

Since its creation the trust corpus has been invested in common stocks, bonds, mortgages, short-term debt instruments (including bank deposits, foreign bank deposits and U.S. obligations). Country X, through the trust, has also owned various U.S. real estate interests through several different forms of ownership (e.g., sole owner or partner). Many of the real estate interests have been properties subject to net leases. For example, for the fiscal year ending 3/31/80, which is representative of the tax years involved in this technical advice request, the trust had interest income of $1 X from (1) Eurodollars received from foreign branches, (2) commercial paper issued by U.S. obligors, and (3) loans and mortgages. The trust also derived income from 2 X partnerships in which it participated in the amount of $3 X. Generally, these partnerships are involved in real estate activities.

In some instances, the trust's ownership of real estate is evidenced by either a general or limited position in a partnership. In each instance but two where the trust and its affiliates had all interests, the general partner is a real estate professional who has invested significant amounts in the partnership, is engaged generally in a local real estate business and is familiar with local real estate conditions. In every instance where the property was not net leased, the partnership retained a local real estate management company to provide all necessary real estate management services. The trust's involvement consists of reviewing periodic financial reports and annual budgets, conferring periodically with its partners about the property and participating in the major decisions concerning the property, such as possible refinancing or sale of the property.

The day-to-day managing of the partnerships is done by managing agents who are in that trade or business.

In addition, the trust derived income directly from net leases of 4 X real properties in the amount of $5 X for this period.

Bank A maintains that pursuant to the terms of the "Trust Instrument", all income was to be distributed or distributable to Country X and the trust was revocable. Therefore, the trust was deemed to be a grantor trust under section 671 of the Code.

Bank A contends that a grantor trust is not required to file a return of its income for the reason that all of its income is treated as the income of the grantor. It is argued that since the grantor of the trust is Country X, a foreign government, and since all of its income is exempt from taxation under section 892 of the Code, no return was required to be filed by Country X. An audit by the Service of the "trust" revealed that the "trust" was involved in real estate activities in the United States through various partnerships and received various types of income. The Service considered those activities to be commercial activities, the income from which is not exempt under section 892. The Bank was advised by the Service that under section 674(a) and a Special Ruling dated March 9, 1966, annual returns on Form 1041 are required to be filed with respect to trusts the income from which is taxable to the grantor. No tax returns were filed prior to the fiscal year ending March 31, 1981, at which time Bank A filed a Form 1120 F pursuant to the regulations under section 892.

Despite the fact that Bank A reported taxable income, a statement was attached to each return stating that:

Counsel advises that it remains of the opinion that the exemption is complete and that the amended [section 892] regulation may be applied to the income and expense received before its effective date only if the foreign government so elects.

The Internal Revenue Service examiners maintain that the exemption from tax under section 892 of the Code only applies to income derived from investments in the United States and not to all income derived from sources within the United States (whether from investments or commercial activities). It is the position of the examiners that the income derived from the partnerships is from commercial activities which are considered to be the conduct of a trade or business in the United States and is not exempt under section 892. Any income effectively connected with the conduct of the trade or business in the United States is also not exempt under section 892. Further, the examiners consider the trust estate to be a controlled entity of Country X by virtue of the trust agreement, with the result that the trust estate is taxable on its income from commercial activities.

APPLICABLE LAW AND RATIONALE

Section 301.7701-1(b) of the Procedure and Administration Regulations provides, in part, that the Code prescribes certain categories, or classes, into which various organizations fall for purposes of taxation. These categories, or classes, include associations (which are taxable as corporations), partnerships, and trusts. The tests, or standards, which are to be applied in determining the classification which an organization belongs (whether it is an association, a partnership, a trust, or other taxable entity) are determined under the Code.

Section 301.7701-1(c) provides, in part, that the term "corporation" is not limited to an artificial entity usually known as a corporation, but includes also an association, a trust classified as an association because of its nature or its activities, a joint-stock company, and an insurance company. Although it is the Code rather than local law which establishes the tests or standards in which an organization belongs, local law governs in determining whether legal relationships which have been established in the formation of an organization are such that the standards are met.

Section 301.7701-2(a)(1) provides, in part, that the term "association" refers to an organization whose characteristics require it to be classified for purposes of taxation as a corporation rather than as another type of organization such as a partnership or trust. There are a number of major characteristics ordinarily found in a pure corporation which, taken together, distinguish it from other organizations. These are: (i) associates, (ii) an objective to carry on business and divide the gains therefrom, (iii) continuity of life, (iv) centralization of management, (v) liability for corporate debts limited to corporate property, and (vi) free transferability of interests. Whether a particular organization is to be classified as an association must be determined by taking into account the presence or absence of each of these corporate characteristics. The presence or absence of these corporate characteristics will depend upon the facts in each individual case. Section 301.7701-2 (a)(2) provides, in part, that some of the major characteristics of a corporation are common to trusts and corporations, and others are common to partnerships and corporations. Characteristics common to trusts and corporations are not material in attempting to distinguish between a trust and an association. For example, since centralization of management, continuity of life, free transferability of interests, and limited liability are generally common to trusts and corporations, the determination of whether a trust which has such characteristics is to be treated for tax purposes as a trust or as an association depends on whether there are associates and an objective to carry on business and divide the gains therefrom. Section 301.7701-2(a)(3) provides, in part, that an unincorporated organization shall not be classified as an association unless such organization has more corporate characteristics than noncorporate characteristics. Section 892 of the Code generally excludes from gross income and exempts from taxation the income of foreign governments received from investments in securities in the United States and from interest on United States bank deposits, and certain income from any other source within the United States.

RATIONALE

With regard to issue Number 1:

In the present case, a determination must be made whether the organization created possesses associates and an objective to carry on business and divide the gains therefrom. In regard to the characteristics of an objective to carry on business and divide the gains therefrom, the Supreme Court in *Helvering v. Coleman-Gilbert Associates,* 296 U.S. 369 (1935); XV-1 C.B. 261 (1936), emphasized the paramount status which is to be accorded the terms of the creating document by stating

The parties are not at liberty to say that their purpose was other or narrower than that which they formally set forth in the instrument under which their activities were conducted. Undoubtedly they wished to avoid partition of the property of which they had been co-owners, but their purpose as declared in their agreement was much broader than that.

See also, *Elm Street Realty Trust v. Commissioner,* 76 T.C. 803 (1981); *acq.* 1981-2 C.B. 1.

In the instant case, the creating document provides the Trustee with broad powers to be exercised in its uncontrolled discretion. For example, the Trustee had the power to purchase any real or personal property situated in the United States for cash or on credit, either alone or jointly with others, and to retain such property, whether originally a part of the trust estate or subsequently acquired. The Trustee is authorized to manage, administer, operate, develop, improve, alter, demolish, or otherwise deal with any real property or interest therein at any time held. In accordance with *Helvering v. Coleman-Gilbert Associates* and *Elm Street Realty Trust,* supra, we conclude that the powers granted the Trustee go beyond protecting and conserving. Accord-

ingly, the organization possesses an objective to carry on business and divide the gains therefrom within the meaning of section 301.7701-2(a). The next determination is whether the organization possesses associates. In *Elm Street,* 76 T.C. at 815, the court stated:

We believe that the above-mentioned factors, particularly the role of beneficiaries in a trust's creation and the extent of their participation in its affairs, provide a helpful framework for ascertaining whether a trust's beneficiaries should be deemed associates.

In fact, this framework is suggested by various cases which have considered the issue. In *Hynes v. Commissioner,* 74 T.C. 1266 (1980), the court held that the trust had associates where the grantor was the sole beneficiary. In 74 T.C. at 1280, the court stated:

Although the trust stood to realize, in the first instance, any profits from the business, such profits were under the control of the petitioner, and he could demand their distribution to him at any time. An associate is like a shareholder of a corporation who provides the capital for the business carried on by the corporation and who has a right to receive the profits of the business.

In applying the principles established in Elm Street Realty Trust and Hynes to the present case, the terms of the creating document disclose that Country X is the sole beneficiary of the trust. The beneficiary, like a shareholder of a corporation who provides the capital for the business carried on by the corporation and who has a right to receive the profits, may order the Trustee to pay out of the trust estate any sum including the whole thereof at any time. The beneficiary's influence over the trust's activities is further illustrated by the beneficiary's right to amend the trust's terms in any respect whatsoever or to revoke the trust. Further, although no certificates evidencing ownership interests are issued, the trust instrument does not prohibit the transfer on any portion of the beneficiary's interest. Accordingly, we conclude that the organization possesses associates within the meaning of section 301.7701-2(a) for purposes of determining if it is an association.

Because the organization has both associates and an objective to carry on business and divide the gains therefrom, it cannot be classified as a trust for federal income tax purposes. Section 301.7701-4(a) and 4(b). Despite the fact that under *Hynes* a single member organization can be treated as having associates for purposes of determining if it is an association, no single member organization possesses associates in the partnership sense and an organization with only a single member cannot be a partnership. Thus, although the organization in this case possesses associates for purposes of determining if it is an association and has a business objective, an unincorporated organization shall not be classified as an association unless such organization has more corporate characteristics than noncorporate characteristics. Section 301.7701-2(a)(3). Therefore, if the organization lacks more than one of the following corporate characteristics of free transferability of interests, centralization of management, continuity of life and limited liability, it will be treated as an agency relationship between Country X and the Trustee, and not as an association or a partnership.

In regard to free transferability of interests, section 301.7701-2(e)(1) provides, in part, that an organization has the corporate characteristic of free transferability of interests if each of its members or those members owning substantially all of the interests in the organization have the power, without the consent of the other members, to substitute for themselves in the same organization a person who is not a member of the organization. Although the terms of the creating document are silent on transferability of interests, under the local law of New York, the interest of the beneficiary in the trust is transferable without the consent of anyone. See *N.Y., Est., Powers & Trusts Law* (Mckinney, Section 7-1.5).

Accordingly, the organization possesses the corporate characteristic of free transferability of interests.

In regard to centralization of management, section 301.7701-2(c)(1) provides, in part, that an organization has centralized management if any person (or any group of persons which does not include all the

members) has continuing exclusive authority to make the management decisions necessary to the conduct of the business for which the organization was formed. Centralized management means a concentration of continuing exclusive authority to make independent business decisions on behalf of the organization which do not require ratification by members of such organization. Section 301.7701-2(c)(3). Under Article 3 of the creating document, the Trustee is provided with broad powers and authority to make management decisions to be exercised in its "uncontrolled discretion." This uncontrolled discretion is not affected by Article 6 which essentially provides that if Country X either approves of a transaction that has been consummated either by an instrument in writing or failure to respond within a certain time period, the Trustee is discharged with respect to all matters and things set forth in such account as though such account had been settled by the decree of a court of competent jurisdiction. Accordingly, the organization possesses the corporate characteristic of centralization of management.

In regard to continuity of life, section 301.7701-2(b)(1) provides, in part, that an organization has continuity of life if the death, insanity, bankruptcy, retirement, resignation, or expulsion of any member will not cause a dissolution of the organization.

Section 301.7701-2(b)(3) provides, in part, that an agreement establishing an organization may provide that the organization is to continue for a stated period or until the completion of a stated undertaking or such agreement may provide for the termination of the organization at will or otherwise. In determining whether any member has the power of dissolution, it will be necessary to examine the agreement and to ascertain the effect of such agreement under local law. For example, if the agreement expressly provides that the organization can be terminated by the will of any member, it is clear that the organization lacks continuity of life. However, if the agreement provides that the organization is to continue for a stated period or until the completion of a stated transaction, the organization has continuity of life if the effect of the agreement is that no member has the power to dissolve the organization in contravention of the agreement.

Under Article 8 of the creating document, Country X/beneficiary reserved the right to revoke the entity at any time. Accordingly, the organization lacks the corporate characteristic of continuity of life.

The final corporate characteristic that must be examined is limited liability. Section 301.7701-2(d)(1) provides, in part, that an organization has the corporate characteristic of limited liability if under local law there is no member who is personally liable for the debts of or claims against the organization. Personal liability means that a creditor of any organization may seek personal satisfaction from a member of the organization to the extent that the assets of such organization are insufficient to satisfy the creditor's claim.

Based on the condition that under local law Country X/beneficiary is personally liable for the debts of or claims against the organization in the present case, the organization lacks the corporate characteristic of limited liability.

Therefore, because the organization lacks continuity of life and limited liability, it does not have more corporate than non-corporate characteristics. Section 301.7701-2. Further, because the organization does not possess associates in the partnership sense, it cannot be a partnership for federal income tax purposes. Thus, we conclude that the organization is classified as an agency relationship in which Country X conducts business through an agent, the Trustee.

With respect to issue number 2:

(a) For income earned after July 22, 1980 Section 1.892-1(a)(2) of the Income Tax Regulations provides that the income derived by an integral part of a foreign sovereign from investments in the United States in stocks, bonds, or other securities, owned by such integral part, or from interest on deposits in banks of moneys belonging to such integral part, or from any other investment source within the United States, is generally treated as income of a foreign government,

which is not included in gross income and is exempt from taxation.

Section 1.892-1(a)(3) of the regulations provides that income derived by an integral part of a foreign sovereign from commercial activities in the United States is not income of a foreign government for purposes of the exemption from taxation provided in section 892 of the Code. These amounts are included in income and taxed under appropriate Internal Revenue Code provisions. Section 1.892-1(c)(1) provides that all activities conducted in the United States which are ordinarily conducted with a view towards the current or future production of income are commercial activities. For example, leases on real property, other than holding leases described in section 1.892-1(c)(2)(i), is a commercial activity, rather than an investment.

Section 1.892-1(c)(2)(i) of the regulations provides that investments in the United States in stocks, bonds or other securities, loans, net leases on real property, land which is not producing income or the holding of deposits in banks are not commercial activities. However, this section further states that consideration of all of the facts and circumstances will determine whether an activity with respect to property described in section 1.892-1(c)(2)(i) constitutes an investment. Section 1.892-1(c)(2)(i)(a) provides that an activity undertaken as a dealer will not be an investment for purposes of section 1.892-1(c)(2)(i). Section 1.892-1(c)(2)(i)(b) provides that an activity will not cease to be an investment solely because of the volume of transactions of that activity or because of other unrelated activities. Under section 1.892-1(c)(2)(i)(e), the rules for net leases on real property are reserved.

Section 1.892-1(h) states that this section applies to income derived by a foreign government after July 22, 1980, unless the sovereign elects to have it apply to income derived before that date.

In the present case, it has been determined that the organization is an agency relationship in which Country X conducts business through an agent, the Trustee. Thus, for items of income derived by Country X from the activities of its agent in the United States, it is necessary to determine whether the activities with respect to each of the various properties of Country X are investments that are described in section 1.892-1(c)(2)(i), for the period after July 22, 1980.

Rev. Rul. 73-522, 1973-2 C.B. 226, provides guidance concerning making a determination whether real estate activities, including property subject to net leases, amount to the conduct of a trade or business in the United States. Rev. Rul. 73-522 states that activities in connection with domestic real estate that are beyond the mere receipt of income from rented property and the payment of expenses incidental to the collection thereof would indicate the conduct of a trade or business within the United States, provided that such activity is considerable, continuous and regular. Even though the rules for net leases on real property are reserved in the regulations, it is our view that, with respect to each real property involved, activities performed which amount to the conduct of a U.S. trade or business should be treated as commercial activities within the meaning of section 1.892-1(c)(1) of the regulations. Thus, with respect to each real property involved, if Country X's agent performs activities beyond the mere receipt of income which are considerable, continuous and regular, those activities constitute a trade or business under the principles expressed in Rev. Rul. 73-522 and Country X would be engaged in commercial activities within the United States with respect to that real property for the purposes of section 892 of the Code.

Because the National Office does not have all the facts concerning all the properties under examination, a determination must be made by the District Office with respect to each item of income derived by Country X from sources within the United States as to whether the income is from an investment or a commercial activity in the United States. For example, income from real property subject to a net lease would be exempt from U.S. tax under section 892 if the real estate activities conducted with respect to that property do not amount to the conduct of a trade or business in the United States under Rev. Rul. 73-522.

(b) For income earned on or before July 22, 1980

On August 15, 1978, the Service published proposed regulations under section 892 of the Code that would have taxed the income of an integral part of a foreign sovereign from commercial activities in the United States retroactively. The provisions of the proposed section 892 regulations relating to controlled entities were given prospective application only, but the Service had previously clarified the taxability of such entities. See Rev. Rul. 66-73, 1966-1 C.B. 174 and Rev. Rul. 75-298, 1975-2 C.B. 290.

The final section 892 regulations published on July 22, 1980 contain an effective date that is completely prospective unless the foreign government elects retroactive application. The technical memorandum to the final section 892 regulations states that the prospective date is appropriate since section 1.892-1 represents the first time the Service published a position with respect to the income of the foreign government itself as opposed to its controlled entities.

Since the section 892 regulations are prospective in application, the Service will not exercise its taxing authority with respect to the income of Country X for the period beginning on or before July 22, 1980, the effective date of the section 892 regulations.

With respect to issue number 3:

Section 1.892-1(e) of the regulations provides that a return with respect to income taxes under subtitle A shall be made by a foreign sovereign, controlled entity, political subdivision, or a transnational entity with respect to certain amounts included in gross income. See section 6012. Section 1.892-1(a)(3) of the regulations provides that income derived by an integral part of a foreign sovereign from commercial activities in the United States is not income of a foreign government for purposes of the exemption from taxation provided in section 892 of the Code. These amounts are included in income and taxed under appropriate Internal Revenue Code provisions. See also section 1.892-1(g), example 1. In that example, an integral part of a foreign government purchased a hotel in the United States which is operated by its U.S. agent. Income derived from the operation of the hotel is subject to tax since the integral part of the foreign government is engaged in a commercial activity in the United States by reason of its hotel operations. In the example, the income is not income of a foreign government under section 1.892-1(a)(3), and pursuant to section 864(c)(3) and section 1.864-4(b), is effectively connected with the conduct of a trade or business within the United States by the integral part of the foreign government. The example concludes that the income is taxed under section 882. Also in the example, the integral part of the foreign sovereign made investments of funds from the foreign sovereign's treasury in property described in section 1.892-1(c)(2)(i) of the regulations, such as publicly traded stocks and bonds. Income from the investments is exempt from U.S. tax under section 1.892-1(a)(2).

Section 882 of the Code provides that a foreign corporation engaged in a trade or business within the United States during the taxable year shall be taxable as provided in section 11 or 1201(a) on its taxable income which is effectively connected with the conduct of a trade or business within the United States. Thus, for filing purposes Country X should be deemed to be a foreign corporation. Under section 6012, a foreign corporation is required to file a return. Section 882(f) of the Code provides that if any foreign corporation has no office or place of business in the United States but has an agent in the United States, the return required under section 6012 shall be made by the agent.

In the present case, should the District Office conclude that Country X derives income for the period beginning after July 22, 1980 which is not exempt from tax under section 892 of the Code, and is subject to tax under section 882 of the Code, Country X, or its agent, would be required to file a return using Form 1120 F.

CONCLUSIONS

(1) The organization is classified as an agency relationship in which Country X conducts business through an agent, the Trustee.

(2) a. For the period beginning after July 22, 1980, any income which is derived by Country X from commercial activities in the United States is not exempt from federal tax pursuant to section 892 of the Code and is subject to tax under section 882. Section 1.892-1 of the regulations.

b. For the period beginning on or before July 22, 1980, the income of Country X is exempt from federal tax pursuant to section 892.

(3) If Country X derives income for the period beginning after July 22, 1980 which is not exempt from tax under section 892 of the Code and is subject to tax under section 882 of the Code, Country X, or its agent, would be required to file a return using Form 1120 F.

PRIVATE LETTER RULINGS

P.L.R. 8632025

May 12, 1986

* * *

Dear * * *

This is in further reply to a letter dated May 19, 1983, and subsequent correspondence, submitted on behalf of Company by its authorized representatives, in which rulings are requested concerning certain federal income tax consequences of the organization and operation of the Trust and the Partnership. This letter affects two ruling letters previously issued to you by the Internal Revenue Service dated December 7, 1983 (CC:C: E:E:4 - 3E4462) and September 6, 1984 (CC: IND:S:1:1-3L3921).

Based on all the information submitted, we understand certain facts to be substantially as follows:

Company is engaged, directly and through its subsidiaries, in the exploration for and production of oil and gas and other minerals. Company files its federal income tax returns on a consolidated basis, utilizing a fiscal year ending December 31 and the accrual method of accounting. The outstanding stock of Company is traded on the New York Stock Exchange and is widely held.

When the transaction described herein was proposed, Company held interests in certain developed and exploratory oil and gas properties located in the United States. Company desired to distribute to its stockholders certain royalty interests in such properties; however, it was impractical for Company to distribute undivided interests in such royalties to a large number of stockholders. Therefore, Company accomplished its objective through the creation of the Trust to indirectly hold such royalties for the Company's stockholders. Title to the royalty interests is held by the Partnership of which the Trust is a general partner. The primary reasons for the interposition of the Partnership between the royalties and the Trust was to avoid potential probate problems for Unit holders and to solve certain accounting problems.

The Trust was created pursuant to a trust agreement ("Trust Agreement") between Company, acting on behalf of its stockholders as Trustor, and Bank, as trustee ("Trustee"), for the purpose of distributing (i) overriding royalty interests from selected producing properties ("Overriding Royalties") and (ii) royalty interests from selected unleased and undeveloped properties ("Fee Lands Royalties") to the holders of Company's common stock as a dividend. The Overriding Royalties and the Fee Lands Royalties are hereinafter collectively referred to as the 'Royalties.' Properties of the Company burdened by the Royalties are referred as to the 'Properties.' Simultaneously with the conveyance of the Royalties to the Trust and the formation of the Partnership, Company distributed to its stockholders one unit ("Unit") of beneficial interest in the Trust for every two shares of stock held by each stockholder. Company made cash payment to any stockholder who would hold a fractional interest in a Unit under the above computation. As more fully described below, the Trust and the Trustee are prohibited from engaging in any business or investment activities.

The Partnership was created pursuant to a partnership agreement ("Partnership Agreement") between Company and the Trust. The Trustee contributed the Royalties to the Partnership in exchange for a 99 percent Partnership interest which became the sole asset of the Trust, and Company contributed additional royalties in the Properties to the Partnership in exchange for a one percent Partnership interest. Company's conveyance was equivalent to 1/99 of the Royalties conveyed to the Partnership by the Trustee and occurred at the same time the Trustee conveyed the Royalties to the Partnership. Except for the amount, the royalties contributed to the Partnership by Company in exchange for its Partnership interest were identical to the Royalties conveyed by the Trustee.

The Overriding Royalties consist of overriding royalty interests (equivalent to net profits interests) equal to various percentages of the Net Proceeds, as defined, from production of oil, gas and other hydrocarbons on certain Properties. The Fee Lands Royalties constitute royalty interests equal to three percent of the future gross oil and gas production free of the expense of drilling, completion, development, operating and other costs incident to the production of such oil and gas. Only Company, and not the Trust, has the power to enter into lease agreements, endorse all lease provisions, and is entitled to receive any applicable bonuses or delay rentals with respect to the Properties subject to the Fee Lands Royalties. The conveyances of the various Royalties provide for the monthly computation and payment of each Royalty. The Company is required to operate the Properties in accordance with reasonable and prudent business judgment and good oil and gas field practices. Company will market the production, whether under existing sales contracts or under agreements entered into in the future, on terms and conditions deemed by it to be the best reasonably obtainable under the circumstances.

The distribution of the Units to the holders of the Company's common stock was the subject of the registration statement filed with the Securities and Exchange Commission. The Units distributed represent fractional undivided interests in the Trust. The owners of the Units have the right to participate, indirectly through the Partnership, in the revenues produced by the Royalties. The Units represent no interest in, or obligation of, the Company.

The Trust Agreement sets out the governing provisions of the Trust. In general, the Trust Agreement gives the Trustee only such rights and powers as are necessary and proper for the conservation and protection of the assets of the Trust. Section 2.02 of the Trust Agreement provides that the purposes of the Trust are (a) to protect and conserve, for the benefit of the owners of Units, the assets held in the Trust, (b) to receive any income accruing to such assets, and (c) to pay or provide for the payment of any liabilities incurred in carrying out the

purposes of the Trust, and thereafter to distribute the remaining amounts received by the Trust pro rata to the owners of the Units. It is the stated intent of the parties to the Trust Agreement to create an express trust under the law of State B, for the benefit of the owners of Units, and a grantor trust for federal income tax purposes of which the owners of Units are the grantors. In summary, the Trust is intended to be a passive entity whose activities are limited to the receipt of revenues attributable to the assets it holds and the distribution of such revenues, after payment of or provision for Trust expenses and liabilities, to the owners of Units.

Section 2.03 of the Trust Agreement requires that the Trustee accept the conveyance of the Royalties from the Company to the Trust and immediately thereafter execute and deliver on behalf of the Trust the Partnership Agreement with Company and assign the Royalties to the Partnership in exchange for a 99 percent interest in the Partnership.

Section 3.01 of the Trust Agreement provides for the creation of the Units.

Section 3.03 describes the rights of owners of the Units. Units will be freely transferable. Section 3.04 provides that the sole interest of each owner of a Unit with respect to the Trust shall be his pro rata portion of the beneficial interest and the obligations of the Trustee expressly created under the Trust Agreement.

Section 4 of the Trust Agreement provides that the Trustee shall make 12 distributions in each year no later than ten days after each 'Monthly Record Date'. The amount distributed will be the 'Monthly Distribution Amount'. The term 'Monthly Distribution Amount' for any calendar month means the sum of the cash received during the month less the amount of cash used during the month to pay liabilities or to fund reserves for the payment of such liabilities.

Section 6 of the Trust Agreement concerns the administration of the Trust and the powers of the Trustee. Section 6.01 provides that the Trustee, subject to the limitations set forth in the Trust Agreement, is authorized to take such actions as in its judgment are necessary, desirable or advisable best to achieve the purposes of the Trust. The Trustee does not possess the authority to dispose of the Partnership interest held by the Trust. Disposition of the Partnership interest held by the Trust is permitted only if the provisions of section 6.04 of the Trust Agreement are satisfied. In general, such provisions require the approval of a majority of the Unit owners. Section 6.06 of the Trust Agreement provides that the Trustee shall not, in its capacity as Trustee under the Trust, acquire any oil and gas lease, royalty or other mineral interest or any other asset other than the Royalties, including such portion thereof as may be held indirectly through ownership of the Partnership interest or directly upon a distribution from the Partnership, nor engage in any business or investment activity of any kind whatsoever. Section 6.07 of the Trust Agreement provides the Trustee with the authority to use trust funds to pay any and all expenses. Section 6.10 empowers the Trustee to establish reserves for contingent liabilities. Such power, however, is extremely restricted. Section 6.10 also establishes the types of investments in which the Trustees may invest the cash of the Trust which is being held between distribution dates or in a reserve for contingencies. In general, such investments may include only non-interest bearing demand accounts with specifically defined commercial banks. However, the Trustee has the power to place such cash funds in bank certificates of deposit or United States Government securities maturing on the next 'Monthly Record Date' (this limitation restricts the maximum maturity to 31 days) if the Trustee has received an opinion of counsel to the effect that such investment will not jeopardize the federal income tax treatment of the Trust as a trust.

The Trust Agreement provides that the Trust is irrevocable. Section 10.01 of the Trust Agreement. Section 10.02 of the Trust Agreement provides, in part, that in no event may an amendment be made which would (a) alter the rights to the owners of

Units as against each other, (b) provide the Trustee with the power to engage in business or investment activities other than as specifically provided in the Trust Agreement, and (c) adversely affect the characterization of the Trust as an express trust under State B law and as a grantor trust for federal income tax purposes.

The Partnership Agreement provides that the Partnership is a general partnership formed by Company and the Trust pursuant to and governed by the State B Uniform Partnership Act, a statute that materially corresponds to the Uniform Partnership Act. The Partnership, according to section 2.01 of the Partnership Agreement, was effective as of the time immediately prior to the distribution of the Units.

The purposes of the Partnership as stated in section 4.01 of the Partnership Agreement are:

(a) to receive and hold the Royalties for profit;

(b) to receive the proceeds (and the profits, if any, inherent in such proceeds) of production payable with respect to the Royalties; and

(c) to pay, or, in accordance with the terms hereof, to provide for the payment of, any liabilities of the Partnership, and, subject to section 5.02 hereof (dealing with the establishment of a cash reserve), to distribute the net proceeds from the Royalties and any other Partnership income to the partners in accordance with their sharing ratios.

Section 4.01 of the Partnership Agreement goes on to provide that except as set forth in items (a) through (c) above and section 5.02 of the Partnership Agreement, neither the Partnership nor the Managing General Partner (Company), in its capacity as Managing General Partner, shall acquire any oil and gas lease, royalty or other mineral interest or other asset or right or engage in any business or investment activity of any kind whatsoever. The sharing ratios of Company and the Trust are one percent and 99 percent, respectively.

Section 6.01 of the Partnership Agreement provides that Company and the Trust shall assign the interests in the burdened

Properties to the Partnership, such assignments to be in proportion to the respective sharing ratios of the partners.

Based on the information submitted our conclusions and rationale are as follows:

Sections 761(a) and 7701(a)(2) of the Internal Revenue Code provide that the term 'partnership' includes a syndicate, group, pool, joint venture or other unincorporated organization through or by means of which any business, financial operation or venture is carried on and which is not, within the meaning of Subtitle A of the Code, a corporation or a trust or estate.

In order not to be classified as an association taxable as a corporation, an unincorporated organization that possesses the corporate characteristics of associates and an objective to carry on business and divide the gains therefrom must not have a preponderance of the following corporate characteristics: continuity of life, centralization of management, limited liability and free transferability of interests. See sections 301.7701-2 and 3 of the Procedure and Administration Regulations. Section 301.7701-2(b)(3) of the regulations provides that a general partnership subject to a statute corresponding to the Uniform Partnership Act lacks continuity of life. Section 301.7701-2(c)(4) of the regulations provides that a general partnership subject to a statute corresponding to the Uniform Partnership Act lacks centralization of management. Accordingly, the Partnership will be classified and treated as a partnership for federal income tax purposes and not as an association taxable as a corporation.

Section 301.7701-4(c) of the regulations provides that an investment trust of the type commonly known as a fixed investment trust is an association if there is power under the trust agreement to vary the investment of the certificate holders. However, if there is no power under the trust agreement to vary the investment of the certificate holders, such fixed investment trust shall be classified as a trust.

A fixed investment trust is an organization in which a trustee holds the legal title to investment assets for the benefit of multiple beneficiaries. The trust is not actively engaged in a trade or business, but is merely a conduit for passing through the investment income to the beneficiaries. There must be no power to vary the trust's initial investments, because such power would allow the certificate holders to profit from the buying and selling of the investment assets rather than from the investments themselves. See Commissioner v. Chase National Bank, 122 F.2d 540 (2d Cir. 1941), and Commissioner v. North American Bond Trust, 122 F.2d 545 (2d Cir. 1941); cert. denied 314 U.S. 701 (1942).

In the instant case, the Royalties received by the Trust were required to be and were immediately assigned to the Partnership in exchange for a 99 percent Partnership interest. Thus, the sole asset of the Trust was such Partnership interest. The Trust Agreement prohibits the Trustee from engaging in any business activity. The Trustee may not sell the Partnership interest without the approval of the Unit holders. In general, the sole function of the Trustee is to receive the funds generated by the Royalties held by the Partnership and to distribute such funds to the Unit holders. Only under very limited circumstances, as described hereinabove and in the Trust Agreement, can cash be temporarily invested in certain accounts and certificates of deposit. These temporary investments do not constitute the carrying on of a business. See Rev. Rul. 75-192, 1975- 1 C.B. 384.

It is also well established that non-working mineral interests such as oil royalties or net-profits interests can be placed into a fixed investment trust without the loss of trust status if the trustee does not have the power to change the trust corpus. Royalty Participation Trust v. Commissioner, 20 T.C. 466 (1953) acq., 1953-2 C.B. 6. Similarly, mineral fee interests may be placed in a fixed investment trust if the trustee merely holds the fee and is required to lease the working interest. Rev. Rul. 57-112, 1957-1 C.B. 494. Although the Trust holds an interest in the Partnership, which holds the Royalties, under the facts of the instant case, the Partnership Agreement sufficiently limits the activities of the Partnership so that even if all the activities and powers of the Partnership were attributed to its partners, including the Trust, such activities would not cause the Trust to possess an objective to carry on business or the power to vary the Trust's investment. Accordingly, based on the facts of the instant case, the Trust will be classified as a trust and not as an association taxable as a corporation for federal income tax purposes.

Section 677 of the Code provides that a grantor shall be treated as the owner of any portion of a trust whose income is or may be distributed to him. In general, if a grantor is treated as the owner of a portion of a trust, such grantor includes in computing its taxable income and credits those items of income, deductions, and credits against tax of the trust which are attributable to that portion of the trust. See section 671 of the Code. Each Unit holder is entitled to an undivided, pro rata interest in the entire Trust (corpus as well as ordinary income) based on the number of Units owned. Accordingly, pursuant to Subpart E of Subchapter J of the Code, each Unit holder will be treated as the owner of an undivided interest in the entire Trust (corpus as well as ordinary income) as represented by the Unit or Units owned. See section 1.671- 3 (a)(l) of the regulations.

The owner of an undivided interest in the entire Trust (Unit holder) is treated as the owner of an undivided interest in the assets of the Trust for federal income tax purposes. See Rev. Rul. 85-13, 1985-1 C.B. 184. Therefore, the transfer of a Unit of the Trust will be considered for federal income tax purposes to include the transfer of the proportionate part of the Partnership interest attributable to such Unit.

While the term 'partnership' is broader in scope than the common law meaning of partnership and may include groups not commonly called partnerships, a partnership must have associates to be treated as a partnership for federal income tax purposes. See section 1.761-1 of the Income Tax Regulations and sections 301.7701-2 and 3 of the regulations. According to the information submitted, Company chose to accomplish

the distribution of the Royalties in the manner described hereinabove. Namely, Company first transferred the Royalties to the Trust and became the holder of all the Units. Second, immediately after this step, Trust contributed the Royalties to the Partnership in exchange for a 99 percent Partnership interest and Company contributed additional identical royalties in the Properties to the Partnership in exchange for a one percent Partnership interest. Third, Company distributed the Units to its stockholders.

As concluded above, pursuant to Subpart E of Subchapter J of the Code, the Trust is a grantor trust and the owner of each Unit is treated as the owner of an undivided interest in the entire Trust. Further, the owner of an undivided interest in the entire Trust is treated as the owner of an undivided interest in the assets of the Trust. Therefore, after the transfer of the Royalties to the Trust and prior to the distribution of the Units to its stockholders, Company held all of the Units. Accordingly, Company still owned the Royalties at such time for federal income tax purposes.

This result raises a technical issue regarding the classification of the Partnership. Because Company would be treated as owner of the assets of the Trust (the Royalties) under the rationale contained in Rev. Rul. 85-13, Company would be treated as the owner of the Partnership interest (99 percent) the Trust received in exchange for the Royalties. But, Company also is the owner of the other one percent of the Partnership. In order for there to be a partnership for federal income tax purposes, there must be associates (two or more parties). Under this analysis, the Partnership could not be created or exist for federal income tax purposes unless and until there were associates. Therefore, the absence of the Partnership due to a lack of associates would cause Company to be treated as owner of the Royalties until an associate (other than Company) is treated as being a partner in the Partnership. This we believe occurred when the stockholders of Company actually received their Units from Company. Accordingly, based on the foregoing, we conclude that the distribution described herein will be treated for federal income tax purposes as a distribution of the Royalties by Company to its stockholders, followed by the contribution of the Royalties by the stockholders to the Partnership in exchange for interests therein, which in turn was followed by the contribution by the stockholders of the interests in the Partnership to the Trust in exchange for the Units.

P.L.R. 8931056

May 10, 1989

* * *

Dear * * *

This is in reply to a letter dated November 21, 1988, and subsequent correspondence, submitted on behalf of Sponsor in which a ruling is requested concerning section 301.7701-4(c)(1) of the Income Tax Regulations. Specifically, the Sponsor requests that its power to deposit certain securities with the trustee of an investment trust during the 90 day period following the initial deposit of securities with the trustee is not a power under the trust agreement to vary the investment of the trust's certificate holders.

The Sponsor proposes to establish a trust the terms of which are set forth in the Indenture which incorporates by reference all the provisions of the Agreement. The Sponsor will create the trust by making an initial deposit of certain securities with the trustee. In exchange for this initial deposit, the trustee will deliver certificates to the Sponsor representing the entire beneficial ownership of the trust. In turn, the Sponsor will sell the certificates to the public. Each certificate will represent the ownership of a unit of the trust. A unit will be a fractional undivided interest in and ownership of the corpus and income of the trust.

Section 2.06(a) of the Indenture provides that the Sponsor, at any time during the 90 day period following the date of the initial deposit of securities with the trustee, may deposit with the trustee additional securities and the trustee shall execute and deliver to

or on the order of the Sponsor in exchange therefor a specified number of units. Additional securities deposited under section 2.06 shall maintain to the extent practicable the original proportionate relationship among the face amounts of each security in the trust established on the date of the initial deposit of securities.

Section 2.06(b) of the Indenture provides that if securities of an issue of securities initially deposited ("original issue") are unavailable at the time of a subsequent deposit under section 2.06(a) of the Indenture, in lieu of the portion of the deposit which would otherwise be represented by the unavailable securities, the Sponsor may (1) deposit (or instruct the trustee to purchase) (i) securities of other original issues or (ii) replacement securities complying with the conditions of sections 2.06(c) and (d), or (2) deposit cash or a letter of credit with instructions to acquire the securities of the original issue when they become available. Any cash or letter of credit deposited under section 2.06(b) to acquire securities of an original issue or replacement securities which at the end of the 90 day period has not been used to purchase securities shall be used to purchase other securities in accordance with clause (1) of section 2.06(b), provided that if an instruction to purchase a security has not been given and such cash or letter of credit remain in the trust fund after 110 days from the date of the initial deposit, the amount thereof shall be distributed, together with the attributable sales charge, to certificate holders.

Among the conditions prescribed by section 2.06(c) of the Indenture is that the replacement securities shall (1) be bonds, notes, debentures or other straight debt obligations (whether secured or unsecured and whether senior or subordinated to other indebtedness) of the same type as the securities of the original issue, without equity or conversion features, (2) not have warrants or subscription privileges attached, and (3) be payable in the same currency as the securities of the original issue.

Section 2.06(d) of the Indenture provides that a replacement security must: (i) have a fixed maturity or disposition date substantially the same as that of the security of the original issue it replaces; (ii) be deposited with the trustee at a price that results in a yield to maturity and a current return, in each case as of the date the replacement security is deposited with or purchased by the trustee, which are equivalent (taking into consideration current market conditions and the relative credit worthiness of the underlying obligation) to the yield to maturity and the current return of the security of the original issue it replaces; (iii) bear fixed interest (not contingent upon income or other factors); (iv) have a rating at least equal to that of the security of the original issue it replaces (or have, in the opinion of the Sponsor, comparable credit characteristics, if not actually rated); and (v) not be "when, as, and if issued" obligations.

Section 301.7701-4(c)(1) of the Income Tax Regulations provides that an "investment" trust will not be classified as a trust if there is a power under the trust agreement to vary the investment of the certificate holders. See *Commissioner v. North American Bond Trust,* 122 F.2d 545 (2d Cir. 1941), *cert. denied,* 314 U.S. 701 (1942).

A power to vary the investment of the certificate holders exists if there is a managerial power under the trust instrument that enables a trust to take advantage of market variations to improve the investment of the investors. See *North American Bond Trust,* 122 F.2d at 546; Rev. Rul. 86-92, 1986-2 C.B. 214. Powers incidental to the organization of a trust during its first 110 days do not constitute a power to vary the investment of the certificate holders. Rev. Rul. 86-92; see also, Rev. Rul. 80-96, 1980-1 C.B. 317 (an arrangement wherein the organizer of an investment pool has the power to adjust the size of the pool during a short-term initial sales period to meet the increased or decreased demand of investors is classified as a trust not an association taxable as a corporation).

Based solely on the information submitted, we conclude that the power of the Sponsor to deposit additional securities, which do not maintain the exact original proportionate relationship of the securities deposited with the trustee on the initial de-

posit date, with the trustee and receive additional certificates in exchange therefor during the 90 day period following the initial deposit date does not constitute a power under the trust agreement to vary the investment of the certificate holders under section 301.7701-4(c) of the regulations.

P.L.R. 9018053

February 6, 1990

* * *

Dear * * *

This is in reply to your request for rulings that you submitted on behalf of Depositor. You have asked about the consequences of using a method of credit enhancement for a mortgage pass-through certificate issued under an arrangement structured as a trust.

The Depositor proposes to form an investment trust (Trust) under the terms of a trust agreement among the Depositor, the trustee, and the master servicer. The Depositor will simultaneously acquire a portfolio of mortgage loans from the prior owner of the loans and transfer the portfolio to the Trust in exchange for a single class of pass-through certificates. The certificates will represent 100 percent of the beneficial ownership interests in the Trust.

The certificates will entitle the certificate holders to receive payments of principal and interest at the pass-through rate from the portfolio of mortgage loans held by the Trust. The certificate holders will receive payments on each distribution date out of available funds in the certificate account. In general, the certificate account is an account into which receipts from the mortgages are deposited. It will be maintained by the trustee or, if the master servicer has a sufficient credit rating, by the master servicer. The principal balance of the certificates will be reduced over time as principal payments are received by the Trust on the mortgages. Certificate holders will receive payments styled as interest at a specified pass-through rate. Interest received by the Trust in excess of the pass-through rate will be used to pay expenses of the Trust.

The Depositor will cause the Surety to issue the Financial Guaranty Insurance Policy (Policy) to assure that the certificates will be assigned the rating that the Depositor considers necessary to consummate the transaction. The Surety, an insurance company licensed to engage in the financial guaranty insurance business, will receive a premium for issuing the Policy. The premium will be an expense of the Trust and will either be paid up-front or in a series of annual payments.

The Policy will guarantee receipt by the certificate holders of an amount equal to a minimum principal distribution amount, plus interest at the pass-through rate on the outstanding principal balance of the senior certificates. The minimum principal distribution amount for any distribution date is equal to the amount needed to reduce the principal balance of the certificates to an amount for that distribution date set forth on a payment schedule. If the trustee has insufficient funds on any regular distribution date for distribution of the minimum principal distribution amount, plus the interest at the pass-through rate on the outstanding principal balance of the certificates, then the trustee will make a claim on the Policy in the amount of the shortfall and request the Surety to pay that amount. If a claim is made, the Surety will be entitled to elect under the Policy to make its payments relating to the defaulted mortgage loan in any of the following ways: (1) on an accelerated basis, reducing the principal balance of the certificates faster than required by the payment schedule, (2) in accordance with the payment schedule, or (3) in a lump sum at some deferred date not later than the Trust's final maturity based on the original terms of the mortgage loans.

If the Surety pays under the Policy, it will acquire the right to be reimbursed by the trustee. On each distribution date, funds in the certificate account will be used first for scheduled distributions to the certificate holders and then for reimbursement to the Surety. Thus, the Surety will be reimbursed under its rights of subrogation, whether from late collections or prepayments, to the extent that the Trust's actual cash flows after a claim is made under the Policy exceed expected cash flows under the payment schedule. The Surety may also have a direct right of reimbursement against the Trust, which is not structured as a subrogation right.

The Surety may require additional credit enhancement, including mortgage pool insurance or a letter of credit in an amount equal to a specified percentage of the aggregate principal balance of the mortgage collateral. A provider of additional credit enhancement may require certain reimbursement rights, similar to those of the Surety, either against the Trust or directly against the prior owner of the mortgage collateral.

Section 301.7701-4(c) of the regulations states that an "investment trust" with a single class of ownership interests, representing undivided beneficial interests in the assets of the trust will be classified as a trust if there is no power under the trust agreement to vary the investment of the certificate holders.

In Rev. Rul. 70-544, 1970-2 C.B. 6, and in Rev. Rul. 70-545, 1970-2 C.B. 7, the Government National Mortgage Association guaranteed, through a separate agreement, certificates in mortgage pools that were classified as trusts. In the present case, the Policy is a separate agreement that will be held for the benefit of all the certificate holders. The Policy will not change during the term of the Trust, and the trust agreement does not allow the trustee to take advantage of fluctuations in any market. If a claim is made against the Policy, the Surety will be reimbursed with funds from the Trust but will not receive an interest in the Trust.

Based upon the facts and documents submitted, we rule that the proposed arrangement will be classified as a trust under section 301.7701-4(c) of the regulations.

No opinion is expressed on whether the servicing fee retained by the master servicer and the premium paid to the Surety for issuing the Policy are reasonable.

GENERAL COUNSEL'S MEMORANDA

G.C.M. 34347

In re: Government National Mortgage
Association
September 14, 1970

* * *

Two proposed revenue rulings in the instant
case were concurred in by this office on July
31, 1970. Since that date the proposed rulings
have been considered in detail by the office of
the Assistant Secretary for Tax Policy and a
considerable amount of additional information has been received with respect to the
mortgage backed certificates which are considered by the proposed revenue rulings. At a
conference on September 1, 1970, representatives of the Income Tax Division requested that we reconsider the proposed
revenue rulings in the light of the additional
information.

The proposed revenue rulings consider
various aspects of the Federal income tax
treatment of issuers and purchasers of
"straight pass-through" and "fully modified
pass-through" mortgage backed certificates.
In the situations considered in the proposed
revenue rulings, the certificates are issued
by savings and loan associations with respect to pools of mortgages which are insured by the Federal Housing Administration or the Farmers' Home Administration,
or insured or guaranteed by the Veterans
Administration. We note at this point that
the term "issuer" as applied to the savings
and loan is misleading to the extent that it
suggests that the savings and loan or other
issuer incurs a debt in connection with the
issuance of the certificates. Both the
"straight pass-through" and the "fully modified pass-through" certificate forms provide
explicitly that the certificates do not constitute a liability of, nor evidence any recourse
against, the issuer. The function of the issuer after the certificates have been sold is
to service the mortgages in the pool. Legal

title to the mortgages is in the Government
National Mortgage Association (GNMA)
and the actual mortgage documents are held
by an independent custodian.

The "straight pass-through" certificates
call for payments by the issuer of specified
monthly installments based upon the amortization schedules of each of the mortgages in
the underlying pool. If a default or late payment on any mortgage occurs, the issuer
will normally advance funds to keep up the
payments until the deficiency is corrected
by the mortgagor or foreclosure occurs. The
issuer will make such advances because the
servicing arrangement is an important
source of income. In addition, the issuer is
allowed to retain any late charges which are
collected from the mortgagors.

In addition to the scheduled payments,
the certificates provide for payment to each
of the certificate holders of its proportionate
share of any prepayments or other early recoveries of principal including foreclosure
proceeds. An amount equal to $1/24$ of one
percent of the outstanding principal amount
on the mortgages is withheld by the issuer
each month, which amount is used by the
issuer to discharge the certificate holders'
obligations to pay a servicing fee to the issuer, a custodian fee, and a GNMA guarantee fee. With respect to the "straight pass-
through" certificates GNMA guarantees that
the issuer will faithfully perform its obligations as a servicing agent.

The "fully modified pass-through" certificates differ from the "straight pass-
through" type in that the GNMA guarantee
is expanded to encompass the scheduled
payments of principal and interest. Accordingly, if default on any of the underlying
mortgages occurs, GNMA guarantees that
the certificate holders will receive the
scheduled payments even if the issuer is unable or unwilling to make the necessary advances.

The proposed revenue rulings each contain a number of holdings with respect to the tax effect of the sale and ownership of the certificates. We have reexamined the holdings of the two proposed revenue rulings and it remains our opinion that the conclusions of the proposed rulings are legally sound. Because of the additional information which has been obtained, we believe it is appropriate to set forth the basis for our concurrence in certain of the holdings of the proposed revenue rulings. In addition, this memorandum suggests certain additions to the proposed revenue rulings which we now consider appropriate.

Both of the proposed revenue rulings conclude that the mortgage pooling arrangement does not constitute an association taxable as a corporation. The proposed rulings do not specifically classify the pool arrangement. We concur in the conclusion of the proposed revenue ruling on the ground that the pooling arrangement is analogous to a grantor trust under Subpart E of Subchapter J, section 671 et seq. of the Internal Revenue Code of 1954 and that the pool arrangement thus does not create an association. In addition, we believe that specific reference to Subpart E should be made in the proposed revenue rulings. The purchasers of the mortgage backed certificates have rights in the pool which are within the scope of section 671 because they are entitled to receive all distributions of income and corpus. See section 677(a). The purchasers of the certificates should also be considered grantors because the nominal creator of the pool, the issuer, was motivated by the expectation of the sale of the certificates. Thus the function of the issuer is essentially that of a broker acting on behalf of the original purchasers who are providing the corpus of the pool held for their benefit.

It was suggested in conference with representatives of your office that the mortgage pool might not be considered an entity at all for Federal tax purposes and that the certificate holders might be considered tenants in common of the mortgages. See e.g., Regs. § 1.761-1(a)(1). We have considered this possibility and it is our opinion that the pool must be considered a person and classified for Federal tax purposes. See Regs. § 301.7701-1(a). The certificate holders may not be considered simply tenants in common because they lack the power to control the mortgages in the pool. The separation of control from beneficial ownership which is present in the instant case makes characterization of the mortgage pool as a mere coownership by the certificate holders untenable.

The instant case is similar to that considered in G.C.M. 31451, in re. *** (A-619 421) dated November 27, 1959.* G.C.M. 31451 considered a proposed municipal bond trust fund. *** a securities broker proposed to acquire a portfolio of state and municipal obligations, the interest on which was exempt from tax under section 103 of the Code, to transfer these securities to a trustee *** in exchange for certificates of ownership in the trust fund and to sell the certificates to investors. The trustee agreed to hold all of the securities, collect the interest due on them and to disburse all collections semiannually. Under modifications agreed to by the taxpayer, the trustee's only power to reinvest was an authorization to receive new municipal obligations of an issuer in exchange for other obligations of the same issuer pursuant to a refunding or refinancing of obligations which were part of the original corpus if the issuer of such obligations was in default or if the trustee was advised by *** that the issuer would probably default with respect to such obligations in the reasonably foreseeable future.

The situation considered in G.C.M. 31451 differs from the instant case in that a formal trust instrument was present there. It is our opinion that whether it is concluded that the pool is a trust or a quasi-trust is not critical. The same result should be reached so long as the issuer and GNMA are under fiduciary obligations to the certificate holders. See e.g., G.C.M. 33708, in re:

---

* A proposed revenue ruling based on the ruling letter considered by G.C.M. 31451 is now with our Legislation and Regulations Division for coordination with a pending regulations project under section 7701. See memorandum dated September 18, 1968, in re: *** (I-2077) addressed to the Assistant Commissioner (Technical), Attention: Director, Income Tax Division.

*** (I-2567) which concluded that a gift of a legal life estate in corporate stock was nonetheless a gift "for the use of" rather than "to" a charity and therefore was not eligible for the broader limitation on contribution deductions provided by section 170(b)(1)(A) of the Internal Revenue Code of 1954.

Although the proposed revenue rulings do not address themselves to the problem of return filing requirements, it is our opinion that Form 1041, U.S. Fiduciary Income Tax Return should be filed by the issuer. See Rev. Rul. 61-102, C.B. 1961-1, 245, G.C.M. 31690, in re: *** (A-633160) dated June 20, 1960 holding that a taxpayer who has the power to sell property in which he has a life estate, but who is required to reinvest and conserve the sale proceeds for future distribution to remaindermen, must report the gain from the sale on Form 1041 and pay the tax due on such gain. In the instant case Form 1041 would be filed only as an information return. See Reg. § 1.671-4. Accordingly, you may wish to add references to these requirements in the proposed revenue rulings.

A further problem arising from the characterization of the pool is the status of transferees of the original investors in the pool. We note that in G.C.M. 32554, in re: *** (I-558) and *** (I-556) dated April, 1963, this office suggested that transferees of the grantors of a Subpart E trust would not themselves be grantors of the trust. The proposed revenue rulings in the instant case do not consider the problem of transferees.

The remaining issues considered by the proposed revenue rulings concern the tax consequences of the sale of the mortgage backed certificates, and the characterization of the interests which the certificate holders acquire, and of the income which they receive. The proposed revenue rulings conclude that the sale of the mortgage backed certificates effects a transfer of the equitable ownership of the mortgages in the pool to the certificate holders and that the issuer will recognize ordinary income or loss upon its sale of each of the mortgages in the pool.

Under the proposed revenue rulings the certificate holders are required to report the entire interest income attributable to their pro rata share of the mortgages and may deduct their ratable portion of the servicing, custodian and guarantee fees. The proposed revenue rulings also note that section 1232 of the Code may be applicable to the discount (if any) on the underlying mortgages. They further indicate that for purposes of the real estate investment trust provisions, section 856 et seq., and the definition of a domestic building and loan association under section 7701(a)(19), a certificate holder will be considered to receive its proportionate share of the income of the pool and will be considered to own its proportionate share of the assets of the pool. Finally, the proposed revenue rulings conclude that purchase of a mortgage backed certificate by an exempt employees' pension and profit-sharing trust will not affect adversely the exemption of such a trust under section 501(a).

We have reexamined the holdings of the proposed revenue rulings in the light of the additional information and it is still our opinion that these holdings are correct and that they are not inconsistent with the conclusion that the pool constitutes a Subpart E trust. The powers and obligations retained by the issuer with respect to the mortgage pools do not, in our opinion, derogate from the conclusion that the issuer has sold the mortgages. The issuer's function as a servicing agent appears to be essentially the same as that of any other mortgage servicer. The limited obligation of the issuer to replace or repurchase defective mortgages is essentially a warranty of its title to the pooled mortgages. As to the characterization of the gain or loss on the sale of the mortgages see Rev. Rul. 60-346, C.B. 1960-2, 217. As to mortgages originated by the issuer see also *Burbank Liquidating Corp.*, 39 T.C. 999, 1009 (1963) *Acq.* C.B. 1965-1, 5 (sub nom. *United Associates, Inc.*).

The conclusions with respect to the reporting of income and deductions and the income and ownership tests for real estate investment trusts and domestic building and loans are, in our opinion, consistent with the established rules with respect to Subpart E trusts. Regs. § 1.671-3(a)(1) provides that:

> If a grantor or another person is treated as the owner of an entire trust (corpus as well as ordinary income), he takes into account in computing his income tax liability all items of income, deduction, and credit (including capital gains and losses) to which he would have been entitled had the trust not been in existence during the period he is treated as owner.

Similar conclusions were reached where the taxpayer owned a fractional share of an entire trust. See Rev. Rul. 61-175, C.B. 1961-2, 128 and Rev. Rul. 63-228, C.B. 1963-2, 229.

With respect to the ownership tests of the real estate investment trust and the domestic building and loan provisions, we believe it is appropriate to consider that a taxpayer who is treated under Subpart E as the owner of an entire trust or of an undivided interest in an entire trust should be considered the owner of his proportionate share of the assets of the trust.

The provisions of Subpart E are largely derived from the decision of the Supreme Court in *Helvering v. Clifford,* 309 U.S. 331 (1940) Ct. D. 1444, C.B. 1940-1, 105. Much of the discussion of the Court in Clifford is in terms of the taxpayer's continued ownership of the corpus of the trust, e.g.

> In this case we cannot conclude as a matter of law that respondent ceased to be the owner of the corpus after the trust was created. Rather, the short duration of the trust, the fact that the wife was the beneficiary, and the retention of control over the corpus by the [taxpayer] all lead irresistibly to the conclusion that [the taxpayer] continued to be the owner for purposes of section [61].

The principles of the Clifford decision were subsequently embodied in detailed regulations. See Regulations 118, § 39.22(a)-21.

Prior to the 1954 Code certain trusts which provided for distribution of income to the grantor were not considered "Clifford" trusts but were instead governed by section 167 of the 1939 Code which provided inter alia that such income was to be included in the income of the grantor. In 1954, Congress codified the "Clifford" rules in Subpart E of the 1954 Code and also included therein the provisions of section 167 of the 1939 Code. See S. Rept. 1622, 83d Cong., 2d Sess. (1954) at 86 and 371.

Under the provisions of the 1954 Code we believe it is appropriate to consider the taxpayers in the instant case to be owners of their proportionate shares of the assets of the trust. Similar conclusions were reached in Rev. Rul. 70-376, I.R.B. 1970-29, 15, G.C.M. 34048, in re: *** (I-3267) dated March 7, 1969 which held that the grantor of a trust who was considered the owner of a reversionary interest under section 677 (a)(2) was the "taxpayer" entitled to make the election under section 1033 to replace property which had been involuntarily converted. See also Rev. Rul. 66-159, C.B. 1966-1, 162 which concluded that where a taxpayer was considered the owner of the entire trust under section 676(a), where the assets of the trust included property used as the personal residence of the grantor, and where the trustee sold the property at a gain and used the entire proceeds to purchase other property which the taxpayer and his family occupied as their personal residence, the nonrecognition provisions of section 1034 operated to defer recognition of the gain realized on the sale. Cf., Rev. Rul. 63-228, supra.

Although we have concluded that the certificate holders should be treated as owners of their proportionate shares of the assets and income of the pool, the pool is a reporting entity and must, in our opinion, file Form 1041 as an information return in accordance with the provisions of section 1.671-4 of the regulations. In addition, a trust of which the grantor is treated as the owner under Subpart E is nonetheless a trust for purposes of section 1491 of the Code which imposes an excise tax upon certain transfers of stock or securities to foreign corporations, trusts and partnerships. See G.C.M. 33867, in re: *** (I-2643) dated July 1, 1969.

Upon reconsideration of the proposed revenue rulings, it remains our opinion that their conclusions are legally correct. Accordingly, subject to the modifications suggested herein, we concur in their publication.

* * *

G.C.M. 35893

July 3, 1974

* * *

ISSUES

(1) Whether a certificate of beneficial interest in a mortgage pool issued by an intervening mortgagee and secured by the mortgages in the pool represents a "qualifying real property loan" for purposes of Int. Rev. Code of 1954, § 593(b) [hereinafter cited as Code] and a "loan secured by an interest in real property" under Code § 7701(a)(19)(C)?

(2) Whether a nonrecourse note issued by an intervening mortgagee and secured by mortgages in a pool represents a "qualifying real property loan" for purposes of Code § 593(b) and a "loan secured by an interest in real property" under Code § 7701(a)-(19) (C)?

CONCLUSIONS

We concur in the holding of the proposed ruling that both the note and the certificate of beneficial interest represent "qualifying real property loans" for purposes of computing additions to the bad debt reserve of a savings institution under Code § 593(b). They also represent loans secured by interests in real property under Code § 7701(a)(19)(C). However we think the rationale of the proposed ruling should be clarified and expanded. Furthermore, we believe the ruling should deal with the question of whether the note is a "security" under Code § 165(g)(2)(C) and, therefore, not a "qualifying real property loan" under Code § 593(e).

FACTS

In 1971, a mutual savings bank organized without capital stock represented by shares, within the meaning of Code § 593(a), purchased two separate interests in certain real property mortgage loans. The purchases were made under financing arrangements in which proportionate interests in "pools" of mortgages are issued and sold by an intervening mortgagee corporation, X, to financial institutions. All the mortgage loans in the pools are "qualifying real property loans" under Code § 593(e) and "loans secured by an interest in real property" under Code § 7701(a) (19)(C). Under the terms of the financing arrangements, X services and enforces all the mortgages in the pools for the benefit of the interest holders.

The first real property mortgage interest purchased by the bank was a certificate of beneficial interest. In return for the certificate, the bank places mortgage loan funds at risk equal to the face amount of the certificate purchased and is entitled to receive all payments of principal and interest collected by X, less specified service fees. Losses arising from defaults on the mortgages in the pool are passed through by X to the bank, X having no liability to the bank other than to service and enforce the mortgage loans. The financing arrangement between the bank and X terminates when all mortgages in the pool have been liquidated or upon thirty days notice by the bank to X and payment of and servicing fees due X.

The second interest in real property loans purchased by the bank was a note issued by X. X issued the notes in series, each series being secured by specifically identified mortgages in a pool. No interest rate was specified in the note. However, principal and interest payments are payable on the note in amounts equal to the principal and interest payments (less expenses) received by X from the mortgages in the pool. X has no liability to the bank other than to service and enforce the mortgage loans. In general, the note creates the same rights and liabilities as the certificate. Although the proposed ruling does not so state, the request for a ruling letter in the underlying case states that the note was in registered form, i.e., it was transferable only on the books of X corporation.

ANALYSIS

Code § 593(b) provides that certain types of savings institutions shall be entitled to an addition to their bad debt reserves equal to the sum of (1) the amount determined to be a reasonable addition for losses on "nonqualifying loans" and (2) an amount determined to be a reasonable addition for losses on "qualifying real property loans," but not to exceed certain limitations. One limitation on the latter addition is that the amount shall not exceed the largest amount determined under three alternative methods of computation: (1) the percentage of taxable income method, (2) the percentage method, and (3) the experience method. The percentage of taxable income method may not be used unless the percentage of the taxpayer's assets that are assets under Code § 7701(a)(19)(C) is at least 60 percent. Furthermore, the percentage of taxable income considered as an addition to the reserve for losses on "qualifying loans" may vary according to the percentage of the taxpayer's assets represented by Code § 7701(a)(19)(C) assets.

Code § 593(e)(1) defines "qualifying real property loans" as—

> ... any loan secured by an interest in improved real property or secured by an interest in real property which is to be improved out of the proceeds of the loan, but such term does not include—
> (A) any loan evidenced by a security (as defined in section 165(g)(2)(C));

Code § 165(g)(2)(C) defines a security. One definition is—

> (c) a bond, debenture, note, or certificate, or other evidence of indebtedness, issued by a corporation or by a government or political subdivision thereof, with interest coupons or in registered form.

Code § 7701(a)(19)(C) defines a "domestic building and loan association" as one which has at least 60 percent of its assets in, among other things, "loans secured by an interest in [specified types of] real property." A loan may meet the definition of Code § 7701(a)(19)(C) but not Code § 593(e). Rev. Rul. 66-238, 1966-2 C.B. 521.

The Service has previously ruled that certificates representing proportionate interests in mortgages in a pool can meet the definitions of Code §§ 593(e) and 7701(a)(19)(C). In Rev. Rul. 70-544, 1970-2 C.B. 6, a savings and loan association established

a "pool" of mortgages. The association received a commitment from the *** to guarantee an issue of "straight pass-through" mortgage-backed certificates. The certificates represented a proportionate interest in each of the mortgages in the pool. The certificates called for payments by the savings and loan association to the certificate holders of specified monthly installments. The installments were based on the amortization schedules of each of the mortgages in the pool. *** guaranteed to the certificate holders only the proper performance of the mortgage servicing by the savings and loan association, with the certificate holders entitled only to interest and principal actually collected or collectible through due diligence. The ruling held that the sale of the mortgage-backed certificate transferred to the certificate holders an equitable ownership in each of the mortgages in the pool. Any certificate owned by a savings and loan association were held to be "loans secured by an interest in real property" within the meaning of Code § 7701(a)(19)(C)(v), provided the real property was of the type specified in that section. See Rev. Rul. 70-545, 1970-2 C.B. 8, a similar ruling; G.C.M. 34347, *** I-3821 (Sept. 14, 1970). In Rev. Rul. 74-169, 197415 I.R.B. 13, it was held that the certificates in Rev. Ruls. 70-544 and 70-545 constituted "qualifying real property loans" within the meaning of Code § 593(e).

Rev. Rul. 66-263, 1966-2 C.B. 237 also concerned the question of whether a participating interest in a real property loan was a "qualifying real property loan" as defined in Code § 593(e). X and Y were both organizations to which Code § 593 applies. X advanced money to M, an organization to which Code § 593 did not apply. The advance met the definition of qualifying real property loan under Code § 593(e). X subsequently sold a participating interest in the M loan to Y without recourse. Thus X was a mere assignor of the participating interest. Because the only security for Y's participating interest in the loan was the real property of M, the participating interest was held to be a "qualifying real property loan."

In Rev. Rul. 71-399, 1971-2 C.B. 433,

mortgage participation certificates were purchased by the *** then issued its own certificate corresponding to each mortgage participation certificate it purchased. *** guaranteed to the purchasers of its own certificates the timely payment of interest and collection of principle. Both the mortgage participation certificates acquired by *** and those sold to certificate holders were transferable only on the books of *** The ruling held that the certificates sold by *** represented "qualifying real property loans" within the meaning of Code § 593(e) and "loans secured by an interest in real property" under Code § 7701(a)(19)(C). See I-4115 (Jan. 31, 1974), relating to Rev. Rul. 71-399. But see Rev. Rul. 66-238, 1966-2 C.B. 521 in which participating certificates sold by the *** were not *** "qualifying real property loans," because the certificates were either stock or a "security" as defined in Code § 165(g)(2)(C). Although the published ruling gives no explanation for the holding that the certificate was possibly a security, the ruling file indicates that it was because the certificates were in registered form.

In our opinion, both the note and the certificate are documents evidencing the bank's beneficial interest in its aliquot share of its underlying mortgages in the pools. It is the underlying mortgages that provide the security for the payment of the note and the certificate. Therefore, under the authorities cited above, the certificate and the note are "qualifying real property loans" under Code § 593(e). For the same reasons we think the certificate and the note represent "loans secured by an interest in real property" within the meaning of Code § 7701(a)(19)(C). The fact that the note is in registered form does not make it a "security" under Code § 165(g)-(2)(C) and therefore, disqualify it under Code § 593(e). Although the note was issued by X, a corporation, it did not evidence the indebtedness of the corporation to pay a fixed or determinable sum of money as required by Treas. Reg. § 1.165-5(a)(3), but evidenced a portion of the underlying mortgages, none of which were in registered form.

We think that the proposed ruling should be expanded to state the rationale for the ruling, i.e., that the certificate and note represent no more than proportionate interests in the mortgages in the pools. Since the underlying mortgages qualify under the two pertinent Code provisions, the certificate and the note should qualify too.

We also believe the proposed ruling contains an incorrect statement of law. The ruling states:

> Section 593(b) of the Code prescribes the method by which certain mutual savings banks shall compute a reasonable addition to the reserve for bad debts and in effect requires qualifying assets under section 7701(a)(19)(C) of the Code to be taken into account for this purpose.

An analysis of Code § 593(b) shows that loans qualifying under Code § 7701(a)(19)(C) do not automatically qualify under Code § 593(b). First, Code § 593(e) refers to "any loan secured by an interest in improved real property." Code § 7701(a)(19)(C) refers only to loans secured by specified types of improved realty. Second, only if the percentage of taxable income method is used in determining the "reasonable addition" does Code § 7701(a)(19)(C) have anything to do with the computation. See Rev. Rul. 66-238, 1966-2 C.B. 521 where participation certificates were held to meet the definition of Code § 7701(a)(19)(C) but not Code § 593(e).

Finally, we think that there is a possible conflict between Rev. Rul. 71-399, 1971-2 C.B. 433 and Rev. Rul. 66-238, 1966-2 C.B. 521, with respect to whether an instrument of indebtedness otherwise meeting the definition of Code § 593(e), fails to do so because it is in registered form. In both rulings the instruments were in registered form. Rev. Rul. 71-399 holds that the certificate meets the definition of Code § 593(e). The "registered" certificate in Rev. Rul. 66-238 did not. The rulings may be distinguishable on the ground that the certificate did not represent the indebtedness of *** the issuer, and the *** certificate did represent the indebtedness of the issuer. If that is correct, then Rev. Rul. 66-238 may be inconsistent with Rev. Rul. 70-545, 1970-2 C.B. 8. In the latter ruling *** certificates were held to represent equitable ownership of mortgages in the underlying pool, not the indebtedness of *** even though guaranteed payment of principal and interest. Compare Rev. Rul. 71-399, 1971-2 C.B. 433. We are not stating here that these inconsistencies in fact exist. We are merely suggesting their possibility so that you may review the rulings if you deem it necessary.

We have drafted a revised revenue ruling consistent with the views expressed in this memorandum.

* * *

REV. RUL.

Advice has been requested whether, under the circumstances described below, a certificate of beneficial interest and a nonrecourse note evidence "qualifying real property loans" for purposes of computing additions to bad debt reserves under section 593(b)(1)(B) of the Internal Revenue Code of 1954.

In 1971, a mutual savings bank organized without capital stock represented by shares, within the meaning of section 593(a) of the Code, purchased two separate interests in certain real property mortgage loans. The purchases were made under financing arrangements in which proportionate interests in "pools" of mortgages were issued and sold by an intervening mortgagee corporation, X, to several financial institutions. All the mortgage loans in the pools would be "loans secured by interests in real property" under section 7701(a)(19)(C) if held directly by the bank. Under the terms of the financing agreements, X services and enforces all the mortgages in the pools for the benefit of the interest holders.

The first real property mortgage interest purchased by the bank was a certificate of beneficial interest, in exchange for which the bank places mortgage loan funds at risk equal to the face amount of the certificate purchased. The bank is entitled to receive all payments of principal and interest collected by X, less specified service fees. Losses arising from defaults on the mortgages in the pool are passed through by X to the bank, X having no liability to the bank other than to service and enforce the mortgage loans. The financing arrangement

between the bank and X terminates when all mortgages in the pool have been liquidated or upon thirty days notice by the bank to X and payment of any servicing fees due X.

The second interest in real property loans purchased by the bank was a note issued by X. X issued the notes in series, each series being secured by specifically identified mortgages in a pool. No interest rate was specified in the note. However, principal and interest are payable on the note in amounts equal to the principal and interest payments (less expenses) received by X from the mortgages in the pool. X has no liability to the bank other than to service and enforce the mortgage loans. In general, the note creates the same rights and liabilities as the certificate. The note is transferable only on the books of X.

Section 593(b)(1) of the Code provides that a reasonable addition for the taxable year to the reserve for bad debts of a mutual savings bank includes the "amount determined" by the taxpayer to be a reasonable addition to the reserve for losses on "qualifying real property loans." One of the methods under which the "amount determined" may be computed is the percentage of taxable income method described in section 593(b)(2). However, this method may not be used if the percentage of the assets of the taxpayer that are assets described in section 7701(a)(19)(C) is less than 60 percent.

Section 593(e) defines a "qualifying real property loan" as any loan secured by an interest in improved real property or secured by an interest in real property which is to be improved out of the proceeds of the loan. Section 593(e)(1)(A) provides that the term does not include a loan evidenced by a "security" as defined in section 165(g)(2)(C). Under section 165(g)(2)(C) and Treas. Reg. § 1.165-5(a)(3) a note, certificate, or other evidence of indebtedness to pay a fixed or determinable sum of money issued by a corporation in registered form is a "security".

Held, the certificate of beneficial interest and the note are "qualifying real property loans" for purposes of computing the bad debt reserve under section 593(b) of the Code. Both the note and the certificate are documents evidencing the bank's beneficial interest in its aliquot shares of the underlying mortgages in the pools. The underlying mortgages provide the security for the payment of the note and certificate. See Rev. Rul. 66-263, 1966-2 C.B. 237. Even though the note was in registered form, it was not a loan evidenced by a security within the meaning of section 165(g)(2)(C). Although the note was issued by X, a corporation, it did not evidence the indebtedness of the corporation to pay a fixed or determinable sum of money, but only evidenced ownership in a portion of the underlying mortgage indebtedness. See Rev. Rul. 71-399, 1971-2 C.B. 433. Accordingly, the note is not a security for purposes of a loss deduction under section 165(g).

The certificate and note in the hands of the mutual savings bank also represented "loans secured by an interest in real property" within the meaning of section 7701(a)(19)(C) provided the real property is the type described in that section. See Rev. Rul. 70-544, 1970-2 C.B. 6, modified by Rev. Rul. 74-169, 1974-15 I.R.B. 13.

G.C.M 36132

January 8, 1975

* * *

ISSUE

When a trustee is required to make quarterly income distributions and also to distribute at such times funds received upon liquidation of trust assets, and is also required to invest cash on hand between distributions in obligations issued or guaranteed by the United States Government or in certain certificates of deposit, should the trust be classified as an association taxable as a corporation?

CONCLUSIONS

The proposed revenue ruling concludes that the arrangement should be classified as a trust because the investment power of the trustee does not permit taking advantage of variations in the market to improve the trust portfolio and, therefore, is not a power to vary the investment of the certificate holders.

Although we agree that a trustee should be permitted to make interim purchases of government securities, we are concerned that such securities are subject to market fluctuations and are freely transferable so that they may be acquired to improve the investments of the certificate holders and need not be acquired merely as incidents to the protection and conservation of trust property. In order to insure that the trustee's activities in the proposed revenue ruling are not speculative and that the return earned on these securities is fixed, we recommend that the trustee be required to purchase government securities maturing prior to distribution dates and to hold such securities until maturity.

FACTS

Under a proposed arrangement, an investment bank locates investors and forms investment groups. These investors may include banks, trust companies, insurance companies, ordinary corporations, and individuals, each willing to commit itself to invest a substantial amount of money. Investor commitments may be satisfied only by payments in cash. When the investment bank has assembled aggregate commitments of 1,000x dollars, it closes a group. Any number of groups may be assembled. Each group chooses a trust company to act as trustee, and the invested funds are turned over to the trustee. Under a separate agreement, a corporation specializing in the administration of mortgages is retained by the trustee to service the mortgages.

Under the agreement between the servicer and the trustee, the servicer arranges to purchase existing FHA and VA mortgages of a specified quality on behalf of the trustee. The servicer will collect the principal and interest payments on the mortgages and turn over the proceeds, less fees, to the trustee.

Under the trust agreement, the trustee makes quarterly distributions of all principal and interest payments to each investor in proportion to his interest. The trustee must also distribute proceeds from the liquidation of trust assets as the result of foreclosure, condemnation, etc. During the period between quarterly distribution dates, the trustee is required to invest cash on hand in short-term obligations of, or guaranteed by, the United States, or any agency or instrumentality thereof, and in certificates of deposit of any bank or trust company having a specified minimum stated surplus and capital. Interest earned on these short-term deposits and investments is distributed quarterly to the investors along with all the proceeds received from the mortgage payments. The trustee has no authority under the trust agreement to purchase new securities or mortgages, or to make any other new investments other than the short-term investments described above.

ANALYSIS

Treas. Reg. § 301.7701-2(a)(2) provides in part that since centralization of management, continuity of life, free transferability of interests, and limited liability are generally common to trusts and corporations, the determination whether a trust that has such characteristics is to be treated for tax purposes as a trust or as an association depends on whether there are associates and an objective to carry on business and divide the gains therefrom. See also, Treas. Reg. § 301.7701-4(b). In the case of investment trusts created by or for associates, an objective to carry on business and divide the gains therefrom is in effect deemed to exist if there is power under the trust agreement to vary the investment of the certificate holders. Treas. Reg. § 301.7701-4(c). In determining the full amount of permitted managerial activity and its object, the powers and duties of the trustee should be added to those of the settlor. *Commissioner v. Chase National Bank,* 122 F.2d 540, 543 (1941). If there is no power under the trust agreement to vary the investment of the certificate holders, a fixed investment trust shall be classified as a trust. Treas. Reg. § 301.7701-4(c).

The existence of a power to sell trust assets does not give rise to a power to vary the investment. Rather, it is the ability to substitute new investments, the power to reinvest, that requires an investment trust to be classified as an association. *Pennsylvania Co. for Ins. on Lives & Granting Annuities v. United States,* 146 F.2d 392 (3rd Cir. 1944); *Commissioner v. Buckley,* 128 F.2d 125 (9th Cir. 1942); *American Participa-*

tions-Trust, 14 T.C. 1457 (1950), *acq.,* 1950-2 C.B. 1. Similarly, a power to vary the investment has been explained as a power to take advantage of market variations to improve the investments of the certificate holders. *Commissioner v. North American Bond Trust,* 120 F.2d 545 (2d Cir. 1941).

Although a trustee may not actually exercise all the powers and discretion granted him under the trust agreement, the parties are not at liberty to say that their purpose was other or narrower than that which they formally set forth in the instrument under which their activities were conducted. *Helvering v. Coleman-Gilbert Associates,* 296 U.S. 369, 374 (1935).

Although investments cannot be varied if association status is to be avoided, historically the Service has never taken the position that the proceeds from the sale of securities in a fixed portfolio had to be maintained in a non-productive state pending distribution. It was not thought that a variation of the investment would occur if such proceeds were placed in interest-bearing bank accounts or in certain custodial instruments such as governmental obligations that are traditionally regarded as vehicles for the conservation and preservation of capital rather than as "investment securities". Indeed, in G.C.M. 29356, *** A-219510 (June 22, 1956), this Office stated that a power to invest in government securities is not a power to vary the investment. See also, 12 U.S.C. § 24 (1974 Supp.) in which the limitations and restrictions imposed on national banks with respect to dealing in, underwriting or purchasing investment securities do not apply to these types of instruments.

Nonetheless, although government securities are frequently acquired without any intention on the part of the purchaser to engage in investment activities, many of these securities are freely transferable and are subject to daily market fluctuations. It is thus possible that the trustee in the instant case could purchase such securities with a view toward taking advantage of market fluctuations. Were the trustee in the proposed revenue ruling empowered to purchase government securities for this purpose, we would have no choice but to conclude that there is a power to vary the investment.

Consequently, we think that limitations should be placed on the purchase of government securities in the proposed revenue ruling to insure that such purchases are merely to prevent funds from becoming non-productive and not for purposes of taking advantage of market fluctuations. For this reason we recommend adding to the proposed revenue ruling a statement of fact indicating that the trustee is permitted to purchase only securities issued or guaranteed by the United States Government or any agency or instrumentality thereof that mature prior to the quarterly distribution dates and that the trustee is required to hold such securities until maturity. These requirements limit the trustee to a fixed return similar to that earned on a bank account and bar any attempts to profit on market fluctuations.

A draft of the proposed revenue ruling incorporating this recommendation is attached for your consideration.

* * *

REV. RUL.

Advice has been requested concerning the classification, for Federal income tax purposes, of an arrangement entered into by a number of persons to make a large-scale investment in individual homeowner mortgages insured or guaranteed by the Federal Housing Administration or the Veterans Administration. Under the proposed arrangement, an investment bank will locate investors and form investment groups. These investors may include banks, trust companies, insurance companies, ordinary corporations, and individuals, each willing to commit itself to invest at least 50x dollars. Investor commitments may be satisfied only by payments in cash. When the investment bank has assembled aggregate commitments of 1,000x dollars, it will close a group. Any number of groups may be assembled. Each group will choose a trust company to act as trustee and the invested funds will be turned over to the trustee. M company, a corporation specializing in the administration of mortgages, will be retained by the trustee, under a separate agreement, to service the mortgages.

Under the agreement between M and the trustee, M will arrange to purchase existing FHA and VA mortgages of a specified quality on behalf of the trustee. M will collect the principal and interest payments on the mortgages and turn over the proceeds, less fees, to the trustee.

Under the trust agreement, the trustee will make quarterly distributions of all principal and interest payments received to each investor in proportion to his interest therein. During the period between quarterly distribution dates, the trustee is required to invest cash on hand in short-term obligations of (or guaranteed by) the United States, or any agency or instrumentality thereof, and in certificates of deposit of any bank or trust company having a minimum stated surplus and capital. The trustee is permitted to invest only in obligations maturing prior to the next distribution date and is required to hold such obligations until maturity. All the proceeds received from the mortgage payments along with the interest earned on these short-term investments and deposits will be distributed to the investors quarterly. The trustee has no authority under the trust agreement to purchase new securities or mortgages, or to make any other new investments.

Section 7701(a)(3) of the Internal Revenue Code of 1954 provides, in part, that, as used in the Code, the term "corporation" includes association.

Section 301.7701-4(c) of the Regulations on Procedure and Administration includes in the term "association" an investment trust of the type commonly known as a fixed investment trust if there is a power under the trust agreement to vary the investment of the certificate holders. However, if there is no power under the trust agreement to vary the investment, such fixed investment trust will be classified as a trust, rather than as an association taxable as a corporation.

A power to vary the investment of the certificate holders, within the meaning of section 301.7701-4(c) of the regulations, means one whereby the trustee, or some other person, has some kind of managerial power over the trusteed funds that enables him to take advantage of variations in the market to improve the investment of all the beneficiaries. See *Commissioner v. North American Bond Trust,* 122 F.2d 545, 546 (2d Cir. 1941), *cert. denied,* 314 U.S. 701 (1942).

Although a trustee may not actually exercise all the powers and discretion granted him under the trust agreement, the parties are not at liberty to say that their purpose was other or narrower than that which they formally set forth in the instrument under which their activities were conducted. *Helvering v. Coleman-Gilbert Associates,* 296 U.S. 369, 374 (1935).

Short-term obligations issued or guaranteed by the United States Government or any agency or instrumentality thereof may be subject to daily market fluctuations. In the instant case, however, the trustee is permitted to invest only in obligations issued or guaranteed by the United States Government or any agency or instrumentality thereof that mature prior to the next distribution date and is required to hold such obligations until maturity. These requirements limit the trustee to a fixed return similar to that earned on a bank account and eliminate any opportunity to profit from market fluctuations.

Accordingly, the trustee does not have a power to vary the investment of the certificate holders and the arrangement in question will be classified as a trust for Federal income tax purposes and not as an association taxable as a corporation.

The interests in the income from the trust have been reserved to the various investor-grantors in proportion to their respective contributions. Therefore, each investor-grantor will be treated, by reason of section 677(a) of the Code, as the owner of an aliquot portion of the trust, and all income, deductions and credits attributable to that portion are to be treated as those of the investor-grantor under section 671 of the Code.

Any income taxable to the investor-grantors under section 671 of the Code should not be reported on Form 1041, but should be shown in a separate statement to be attached to the Form 1041. See section 1.671-4 of the Income Tax Regulations.

G.C.M. 36292
May 29, 1975

* * *

ISSUES

Whether a purported limited partnership in which the general partner holds a 20 percent interest will be deemed to lack the corporate characteristic of centralization of management within the meaning of Treas. Reg. § 301.7701-2(c) because the limited partners do not hold substantially all of the interests in such partnership?

Whether a purported limited partnership will be deemed to have the corporate characteristic of continuity of life if the partnership agreement states that the organization is to exist for 40 years and that notwithstanding the retirement, bankruptcy, or dissolution of the general partner (a corporation), the partnership shall not dissolve but shall be continued by the successor of the general partner?

CONCLUSIONS

The Income Tax Division took the position in the proposed revenue ruling that if a general partner owns a 20 percent interest in a limited partnership, the limited partners will not be considered to own substantially all of the interests therein within the meaning of Treas. Reg. § 301.7701-2(c)(4). Thus, the organization will lack the corporate characteristic of centralization of management. Although we agree with the conclusion reached based on the facts of the instant case, our agreement should not be interpreted to mean that a 20 percent interest is necessary in all cases. Whether substantially all of the interests are held by the limited partners is a question of fact.

In addition, the Individual Tax Division took the position that in the event of an inconsistency between the provisions of the organizational agreement and the Uniform Limited Partnership Act, as in the facts of the instant case, the statute will govern. Thus, the conclusion is reached that the organization lacks the corporate characteristic of continuity of life.

In view of the inconsistency in the provisions of the organizational agreement and the Uniform Limited Partnership Act and the uncertainty as to the legal effect that would be given to such provisions under local law, we deem it inadvisable to conclude that the organization does not have continuity of life.

FACTS

The facts of the proposed revenue ruling present a hypothetical situation. Under the facts, an organization was formed pursuant to a state statute corresponding to the Uniform Limited Partnership Act. The sole general partner is a corporation which has exclusive control of the business and which has a substantial net worth in excess of its partnership interest. The limited partners are individuals who have no interest in the general partner or any of its affiliates. The sole general partner holds a 20 percent interest in the partnership and the limited partners hold, in the aggregate, an 80 percent interest in the partnership. The partnership agreement provides that the life of the partnership is to be 40 years, that the retirement, bankruptcy, or dissolution of the general partner will not dissolve the partnership, and that the business of the partnership will be continued by the successor of the general partner.

ANALYSIS

The proposed revenue ruling concludes that the organization lacks the corporate characteristics of centralization of management and continuity of life, and, therefore holds that the organization will be classified as a partnership for federal income tax purposes. Each of the conclusions is discussed separately below.

I. Centralization of Management.

Treas. Reg. § 301.7701-2(c)(4) provides that limited partnerships subject to a statute corresponding to the Uniform Limited Partnership Act generally do not have centralized management, but centralized management ordinarily does exist in such a limited partnership if substantially all the interests in the partnership are owned by the limited partners. This regulation is seemingly based on the rationale that when the limited partners own substantially all the interests in the partnership, the general partners can be said to be acting in a representative capacity for a body of persons having a limited investment and limited liability rather than acting for their own interests. However, if the limited partners do not own substantially all the interests in the partnership, the general partners can be said to be acting on their own behalf rather than in a representative capacity, and therefore, centralization of management does not exist. See Glensder Textile Company, 46 B.T.A. 172 (1942), Acq. 1941-1 C.B. 8. Where the facts indicate that the sole general partner owns a 20 percent interest in the capital and profits of the partnership, we agree that the limited partners will not own "substantially all" of the interests in the partnership. See, G.C.M. 29332, *** A-619043 (Feb. 29, 1956), indicating that in such instance the general partners will be acting in their own interests and will not be acting merely as agents of the limited partners.

However, our concurrence in the foregoing does not mean we concur in a strict rule which would treat limited partners as owning substantially all the interests in those partnerships where the general partners did not own at least a 20 percent interest. In the last analysis, whether or not the limited partners will be considered to own substantially all the interests in the partnership when the general partner owns less than 20 percent interest will depend on the surrounding facts and circumstances.

In G.C.M. 29600, *** A-618623 (Aug. 3, 1956) we took the position that a limited partnership did not have the characteristic of centralization of management when the general partners had contributed only .83 percent of the total capital of the partnership and had only a potential 40 percent interest in profits (i.e., it was to arise only when the limited partners had recovered their initial capital investment in the venture). The general partners had substantial assets that were at the risk of the business. A memorandum in the file seems to indicate that the position was adopted because of the potential 40 percent interest in profits, and the potential liability of the general partners, i.e., the point was made that general partners need not contribute capital to put it at the risk of the business so long as they possess substantial assets that are at risk because of their unlimited liability. See Memorandum to Mr. Barnes dated July 29, 1956, *** A-618623 (Dec. 3, 1953). Due to the potential profits interest and the general partners having substantial personal assets at risk, it was thought the general partners were acting on their own behalf and not in a purely representative capacity under the rationale of *Glensder Textile Co.,* supra.*

Subsequently, however, Treas. Reg. § 301.7701-2(c)(4) was promulgated providing that

...limited partnerships subject to a statute corresponding to the Uniform Limited Partnership Act, generally do not have centralized management, but centralized management ordinarily does exist in such a limited partnership if substantially all the interests in the partnership are owned by the limited partners.

Treas. Reg. § 301.7701-3(b)(2) sets forth two examples in which the issue is also considered. The examples consider general partners who contribute a maximum of six percent of the capital of the partnership and have the means to satisfy the obligations of the partnership to a substantial extent. The

conclusion is reached that the limited partners own substantially all of the interests and, therefore, that the organization possesses the corporate characteristic of centralization of management.

The regulation indicates that the word "interests" used in Treas. Reg. § 301.7701-2(c)(4) does not include the uncontributed assets of a general partner that are at the risk of the business (as noted in the memorandum written in connection with G.C.M. 29600, supra). This is based on the fact that in Treas. Reg. § 301.7701-3(b)(2) Examples (1) and (2) organizations are found to have centralization of management based on the fact that the general partners hold less than a six percent interest in the partnership, notwithstanding the fact that the general partners have uncontributed assets sufficient to satisfy the obligations of the partnership to a substantial extent. If the general partner's assets which are at the risk of the business were considered relevant the regulation could not have concluded that the organization had centralization of management.

Although the meaning of the term "substantially all" as used in other places in the Int. Rev. Code of 1954 has varied,** we believe that the Service would be justified in adopting the position that if the general partners hold a 20 percent interest in the capital and profits of the partnership the

---

* Under the rationale of the memorandum written in connection with G.C.M. 29600 *** A-618623 (Aug. 3, 1956), a general partner who has a substantial net worth and a one percent interest in income in an investment partnership which is highly leveraged could, conceivably, argue that the organization lacked the corporate characteristic of centralization of management.

** The Service has adopted various positions concerning the meaning of "substantially all" when used in other contexts, sometimes based on the facts of the particular case, see, e.g., Rev. Rul. 57-518, 1957-2 C.B. 253 (in which the Service took the position that a transfer by one corporation of 70 percent of its assets to another corporation solely in exchange for voting stock satisfied the 'substantially all' requirement of Code § 368(a)(1)(C) if the retained assets were used to pay off the transferor corporation's liabilities and consisted only of cash, accounts receivable and three percent of total inventory); Rev. Proc. 66-34, 1966-2 C.B. 1232 (in which the Service took the position that for ruling purposes the 'substantially all' tests of Code §§ 354(b)(1)(A), 368(a)(1)(C) and 368(a)(2)(B)(i) are met if there is a transfer of assets representing at least 90 percent of the fair market value of the net assets and 70 percent of the fair market value of the gross assets held by the corporation immediately before the transfer); G.C.M. 34060, *** I-2919 (Mar. 3, 1969) (in which the position was taken that the 'substantially all' requirement of Code § 521(b)(2) was met by producers holding 85 percent of outstanding stock because 85 percent was a figure used commonly in the Code and regulations). See also, Treas. Reg. § 1.279-3(a)(4) (imposing a 66.67 percent requirement); and Treas. Reg. § 1.514(b)-1(b) (1)(ii) (imposing an 85 percent requirement).

limited partners do not hold substantially all of the interests. Thus we agree with the position taken in the proposed revenue ruling.

II. *Continuity of Life.*

Treas. Reg. § 301.7701-2(b) provides that if the agreement provides that the organization is to continue for a stated period or until the completion of a stated transaction, the organization has continuity of life if the effect of the agreement is that no member has the power to dissolve the organization in contravention of the agreement. Nevertheless, if, notwithstanding such agreement, any member has the power under local law to dissolve the organization, the organization lacks continuity of life. Accordingly, a general partnership subject to a statute corresponding to the Uniform Partnership Act and a limited partnership subject to a statute corresponding to the Uniform Limited Partnership Act both lack continuity of life.

Being subject to a statute corresponding to the Uniform Limited Partnership Act [hereinafter referred to as ULPA] so as to trigger the automatic application of this latter sentence of the regulations contemplates that the organization be both organized and operated in substantial compliance with the ULPA.

Section 1 of the ULPA defines a limited partnership as a partnership having as members one or more general partners and one or more limited partners.

Section 9(1) of the ULPA provides that without the written consent or ratification of the specific act by all limited partners, a general partner or all of the general partners have no authority to continue the business with partnership property on the death, retirement or insanity of a general partner, unless the right to do so is given in the certificate.

Section 20 of the ULPA provides that the retirement, death or insanity of a general partner dissolves the partnership, unless the business is continued by the remaining general partners (a) under a right to do so stated in the certificate, or (b) with the consent of all members.

Section 24(2)(a) of the ULPA provides a

certificate shall be amended when a general partner retires, dies or becomes insane and the business is continued under section 20.

The foregoing provisions of the ULPA indicate the need for having a consenting general partner at all times in order for the organization to operate in a manner consistent with the ULPA. The ULPA does not contemplate continuation of the partnership after the retirement, death or dissolution of the only general partner.

The partnership agreement in the instant case provides that the organization is to exist for 40 years and that in no event shall the retirement, bankruptcy or dissolution of a general partner dissolve the partnership, it being agreed that the business of the partnership shall be continued by the successor of the general partner. Such provision is inconsistent with an organization purporting to operate in conformity with the ULPA since it permits the organization to continue operation without an existing general partner. That is, such provision permits the business of the organization to be carried on by a successor to the general partner, there being no requirement that such successor be an existing general partner.

Just what effect would be given to such provision under local law is unsettled. That is, it is not clear whether a local court would find that (1) the ULPA governed the operation of the organization and, therefore, contrary provisions of the agreement would not be given effect, or that (2) notwithstanding the partners' ostensible formation as a limited partnership, the ULPA was not applicable because the agreement manifested an intent on the part of the members to bypass the normal legal course of events attributable to organizations formed as limited partnerships. See *Lanier v. Bowdoin,* 282 N.Y. 32, 24 N.E.2d 732 (1939) *rearg. denied,* 282 N.Y. 611, 25 N.E.2d 391 (1940); *Mist Properties, Inc. v. Fitzsimmons Realty Co.,* 228 N.Y.S.2d 406 (1962). In this latter instance the court, in all probability, would give effect to the instrument in accordance with its tenor. If this occurred, the last sentence of Treas. Reg. § 301.7701-2(b) would not become operative and the organization would, in accordance with the provisions of the agreement, have continuity of life.

Since the effect which a state court would give such provisions is unsettled, publication of a ruling on this issue is inadvisable.

* * *

G.C.M. 37067

March 28, 1977

* * *

The proposed ruling concludes that the trustee's power of reinvestment is a power to vary the investment of the certificate holders and that under Treas. Reg. § 301.7701-4(c) the trust will be classified as an association taxable as a corporation. We agree with this conclusion.

Treas. Reg. § 301.7701-4(c) states, "[A] trust of the type commonly known as a fixed investment trust is an association if there is power under the trust agreement to vary the investment of the certificate holders. See *Commissioner v. North American Bond Trust* (C.C.A. 2d 1941), 122 F.2d 545, 27 AFTR 892, *cert. den.* 314 U.S. 701." The trust in North American Bond Trust was held to be an association taxable as a corporation because the "Depositor" had the power to take advantage of market variations to improve the investment of the certificate holders. 122 F.2d at 546. Relying on this case, the Service takes the position that a power to vary the investment of the certificate holders within the meaning of Treas. Reg. § 301.7701-4(c) means a power whereby the trustee has some kind of managerial power over the trusteed funds that enables him to take advantage of variations in the market to improve the investment of all the beneficiaries. Rev. Rul. 75-192, 1975-1 C.B. 384-85, considered in G.C.M. 36132, *** I-270-73 (January 8, 1975), at 4.

The trustee's power to reinvest redemption proceeds falls within this definition. It gives the trustee the opportunity to take ad-

vantage of variations in price among bonds that are of a caliber equal to the ones redeemed and thereby to increase the income of the portfolio without sacrificing quality. Additionally, it gives the trustee the opportunity to take advantage of variations in quality among bonds which produce the same yield as the ones redeemed and thereby to upgrade the quality of the portfolio without sacrificing income. Finally, the trustee may invest in any obligations that are rated at least "medium grade" by specified bond-rating organizations.* Variations in market conditions since the inception of the trust may change the attractiveness of low-yield, high-quality obligations as compared to high-yield, low-quality obligations. The power of reinvestment therefore gives the trustee the opportunity to take advantage of these variations by changing the "mix" of the portfolio so that an increased portion will consist of the more desirable type of obligation.

We do not believe that Rev. Rul. 73-460, 1973-2 C.B. 424, is inconsistent with this position. The trustee in that Ruling had the power to accept an issuer's offer to exchange new obligations for existing obligations of that issuer. This power of acceptance was limited to offers made by an issuer who is attempting to refinance the existing obligations and who already has defaulted or probably will default with respect to them. The administrative file underlying this Ruling indicates that new obligations received by the trustee in this manner were to "be subject to the terms and conditions of [the trust indenture] to the same extent as the [obligations] originally deposited" with the trustee. In a broad sense this power of acceptance enabled the trustee to vary the investment of the certificate holders. However, as a result of the limitations placed upon it, this power did not give the trustee the power to take advantage of variations in the market, and hence it was not a power to vary the investment of the certificate holders within the meaning of Treas. Reg. § 301.7701-4(c). Rather, this power

---

*   This fact is not contained in the proposed ruling but is evident from the administrative file.

was more in the nature of a vehicle for the conservation and preservation of capital. See G.C.M. 36132, supra, at 4-5.

Accordingly, on page 5 of the proposed ruling we have suggested a modification that sets forth the rationale for holding that the power in the present case is a power to vary the investment of the certificate holders. Additionally, on page 6 we have suggested a modification that reflects the above-discussed position with respect to Rev. Rul. 73-460. A copy of the proposed ruling with these suggested modifications is attached for your consideration.

* * *

REV. RUL.

Advice has been requested whether, under the circumstances described below, a fixed investment trust possessing certain limited [powers to reinvest] is classified for Federal income tax purposes as a trust or as an association taxable as a corporation.

The trust, whose corpus consists of a portfolio of municipal obligations, was formed to provide its investors with continuing tax-free [interest] over a reasonable period of time. It would terminate upon the maturity, redemption, sale, or other disposition of the last obligation held thereunder, but in no event would the trust extend beyond December 31, 2023. The trust can be terminated under certain circumstances if the value of the trust decreases to less than $2,000,000, and must be terminated if the value of the trust decreases to less than $1,000,000.

In order to protect its investors from early termination of the trust due to bond issuers exercising the privilege of redeeming outstanding high-interest rate bonds from the proceeds of newly issued lower interest rate bonds, the trust agreement permits limited reinvestment of certain funds under specified limited conditions during the first 20 years of the tenant's existence. Reinvestment is permitted only of funds derived from the redemption by the issuing municipality of municipal obligations prior to maturity, is limited to municipal obliga-

tions maturing no later than the last maturity date of the municipal obligations originally deposited in the trust. The original corpus consisted solely of bonds rated at least "investment grade" by specified bond rating organizations, and reinvestment is further limited to new offerings of municipal obligations that are similarly rated. Funds derived from early redemptions are distributed to certificate holders, unless within 20 days of receiving such funds, the trustee makes a commitment to reinvest them, and, within 60 days of such receipt, he reinvests them.

Section 301.7701-2(a)(2) of the Procedure and Administration Regulations provides, in part, that since centralization of management, continuity of life, free transferability of interests, and limited liability are generally common to trusts and corporations, the determination whether a trust that has such characteristics is to be treated for tax purposes as a trust or as an association depends on whether there are associates and an objective to carry on business and divide the gains therefrom. Section 301.7701-4(b) of the regulation states, in part, that there are other arrangements that are known as trusts because the legal title to property is conveyed to trustees for the benefit of beneficiaries, but are not classified as trusts for purposes of the Code because they are not simply arrangements to protect or conserve [the assets of the trust] for the beneficiaries. These trusts, which are often known as business or commercial trusts, generally are created by the beneficiaries simply, as a device to carry on a profit-making business that normally would have been carried on through business organizations that are classified as corporations or partnerships under the Code.

Section 301.7701.4(c) of the regulations provides that an investment trust of the type commonly known as a management trust is an association and a trust of the type commonly known as a fixed investment trust is an association if there is power under the trust agreement to vary the investment of the certificate holders. See *Commissioner v. North American Bond Trust* 122 F.2d 545

(2d Cir. 1941), *cert. denied,* 314 U.S. 701 (1942). However, if there is no power under the trust agreement to vary the investment of the certificate holders, such fixed investment trust shall be classified as a trust.

The existence of a power to sell trust assets does not give rise to a power to vary the investment. Rather, it is the ability to [make new] investments, the power to reinvest, that requires an investment trust to be classified as an association. See *Pennsylvania Co. for Insurances on Lives and Granting Annuities v. United States,* 146 F.2d 392 (3rd Cir. 1944).

In the instant case the power in the trust agreement of reinvestment of the proceeds of obligations redeemed prior to maturity, even though limited to reinvestment of the proceeds of redemptions over which the trust has no control, is a managerial power that enables the trust to take advantage of variations in the market to improve the investment of the investors. It therefore is a power to vary the investment of the certificate holders within the meaning of section 301.7701-4(c) of the regulations. See *Commissioner v. North American Bond Trust,* 122 F.2d at 546; Rev. Rul. 75-192, 1975-1 C.B. 384.

Accordingly, the trust, in the instant case, will be classified as an association taxable as a corporation for Federal income tax purposes.

Compare Rev. Rul. 75-192, supra, which holds that a provision in a trust agreement requiring a trustee, during the period between quarterly distribution dates, to invest cash on hand in short-term obligations issued (or guaranteed by) the United States, or any agency or instrumentality thereof, or in certificates of deposit maturing prior to the next distribution date, is not a power to vary the investment of the certificate holders within the meaning of section 301.7701-4(c) of the regulations.

Compare also Rev. Rul. 73-460, 1973-2 C.B. 424, which holds that a power to vary the investment of the certificate holders does not exist where a depositor has the power under certain limited circumstances to accept an offer of new obligations in exchange and substitution for obligations that were part of the original trust corpus.

G.C.M. 38201
December 14, 1979

* * *

ISSUE

Whether a fixed investment trust that holds a ten percent interest in a limited partnership that is engaged in a business enterprise is in the trade or business of the partnership and thus is an association taxable as a corporation.

CONCLUSION

The proposed revenue ruling concludes that in both Situation 1 and Situation 2 the trustees, as limited partners in the partnerships, are engaged in the trade or business of the partnerships and that, since the beneficiaries of the trusts are associates in the trusts' businesses, the trusts should be classified as associations taxable as corporations for federal income tax purposes. We agree that a limited partner may, under certain circumstances, be considered to be engaged in the trade or business of the partnership. We do not agree, however, that as a matter of law all trusts holding limited partnership interests in partnerships are engaged in the trades or businesses of the partnerships. We think many partnership interests merely represent investments in partnership businesses and are held by trusts solely for purposes of protection and conservation. We see no basis for attributing the businesses of the partnerships to those trusts for purposes of the classification regulations.

FACTS

Situation 1. A, an individual, executed a trust agreement with a bank, as trustee, that provided for the establishment of a fixed investment trust. A deposited with the trustee a ten percent limited partnership interest in M, a partnership engaged in commercial farming operations. Certificates evidencing the beneficial ownership of units of interest in the trust were issued by the trustee of A who sold them to the public. The certificates are in registered form and are freely transferable.

The trust agreement provides that the trust fund shall consist of the limited partnership interest in M and any undistributed cash realized from the sale or other disposition thereof.

The agreement further provides that neither the death nor incapacity of any certificate holder will operate to terminate the trust. The trust will terminate upon the sale or other disposition of the limited partnership interest, but in no event will the trust continue beyond January 1, 2000.

The agreement also provides that during the term of the trust the trustee will have sole authority with respect to the management of the trust estate. Under the agreement the trustee does not have any power to vary the investment of the certificate holders.

Situation 2. The facts in Situation 2 are identical to those in Situation 1 except that A deposited with the trustee a 10 percent limited partnership interest in P, a partnership engaged in investing in commodity futures.

ANALYSIS

Treas. Reg. § 301.7701-4(a) states that a trust is: [a]n arrangement created either by a will or by an inter vivos declaration whereby trustees take title to property for the purpose of protecting or conserving it for the beneficiaries under the ordinary rules applied in chancery or probate courts. . . . Generally speaking, an arrangement will be treated as a trust under the Internal Revenue Code if it can be shown that the purpose of the arrangement is to vest in trustees responsibility for the protection and conservation of property for beneficiaries who cannot share in the discharge of this responsibility and, therefore, are not associates in a joint enterprise for the conduct of business for profit.

Treas. Reg. § 301.7701-4(b) recognizes that certain business trusts more closely resemble associations and are to be treated as associations for tax purposes. These entities are trusts because the legal title to property is conveyed to trustees for the benefit of beneficiaries, but are not classified as trusts for purposes of the Internal Revenue Code because they are not simply arrangements to protect or conserve property for the beneficiaries. Business or commercial trusts generally are created by the beneficiaries simply as a device to carry on a profit-making business which normally would have been carried on through business organizations that are classified as corporations or partnerships under the Internal Revenue Code. The fact that any organization is technically cast in the trust form, by conveying title to property to trustees for the benefit of persons designated as beneficiaries, will not change the real character of the organization if, applying the principles set forth in Treas. Reg. §§ 301.7701-2 and 301.7701-3, the organization more nearly resembles an association or a partnership than a trust.

Treas. Reg. § 301.7701-2(a)(2) states, in part, that characteristics common to trusts and corporations are not material in attempting to distinguish between a trust and an association. For example, continuity of life, free transferability of interests, and limited liability are generally common to trusts and corporations. The determination of whether a trust which has such characteristics is to be treated for tax purposes as a trust or as an association depends on whether there are associates and an objective to carry on business and divide the gains therefrom.

Treas. Reg. § 301.7701-4(c) states that an investment trust of the type commonly known as a management trust is an association, and a trust of the type commonly known as a fixed investment trust is an association if there is power under the trust agreement to vary the investment of the certificate holders. However, if there is no power under the trust agreement to vary the investment of the certificate holders, such fixed investment trust shall be classified as a trust.

The proposed revenue ruling states that the trusts in both situations are fixed investment trusts. Thus, the trusts in this case would ordinarily be classified as trusts for federal income tax purposes. The proposed revenue ruling concludes, however, that because the trusts hold ten percent limited partnership interests in partnerships engaged in trade or business, the trusts should be classified as associations taxable as corporations for federal income tax purposes even though there is no indication that the trustees of the trusts are active participants in the partnerships' businesses.

As authority for the conclusion that the trusts in this case are engaged in the trade or business of their partnerships, the proposed revenue ruling cites *Butler v. Commissioner,* 36 T.C. 1097 (1961), acq., 1962-1 C.B. 3, and *Donroy v. United States,* 301 F.2d 200 (9th Cir. 1962).

In Butler, the taxpayer, whose primary business was the practice of law, was a limited partner in a partnership that manufactured and sold prefabricated houses. During 1951 and 1952, the taxpayer loaned the partnership the aggregate amount of $51,655.87. In 1952, $50,000 loaned by the taxpayer to the partnership became worthless and the taxpayer deducted the loss as a business bad debt. The Service argued that the debt was not incurred in the taxpayer's trade or business and, therefore, was a nonbusiness debt to be treated as a short-term capital loss. The court found that the loans of $50,000 were made by the taxpayer in furtherance of the business of which he was a limited partner and were proximately related to the business activities of the partnership. Thus, the court held that the debt was a business bad debt.*

Although not specifically stated, implicit in the court's decision is the fact that a limited partner is individually engaged in the trade or business of the partnership. The court, at page 1106, citing *Ward v. Commissioner,* 20 T.C. 332 (1953), *aff'd,* 224 F.2d 547 (9th Cir. 1955), stated that "[b]y reason of being a partner in a business petitioner was individually engaged in business."

In *Donroy v. United States,* 301 F.2d 200 (9th Cir. 1962), the question before the court was whether a Canadian limited partner in a California limited partnership had a "permanent establishment" in the United States. The court reasoned that a partnership is an aggregate of individuals rather than an entity and that the general partners are the general agents of the partnership and have the power to act for and bind the partnership, including the limited partners. Thus, the court held that the California limited partnership was the permanent establishment of the Canadian limited partners for purposes of conducting business in the United States.

There are, of course, many other situations in which it is necessary to consider whether a partner is in the trade or business of his partnership. In at least two areas, the question is resolved by the Code itself. Section 875(1) provides that a nonresident alien individual or a foreign corporation is considered as being in the trade or business of the partnership in which the individual or corporation is a partner. Section 1402(a) defines the term "net earnings from self-employment" as including an individual's distributive share of income or loss from the trade or business of a partnership of which he is a member.

Although both section 875(1) and section 1402(a) result in a partner being treated the same as if he were directly engaged in the trade or business of his partnership, neither section lends significant support to the general premise that, as a matter of law, a partner is engaged in the trade or business of his partnership. As an initial matter, if the general premise is accepted, the specific provisions in both sections would presumably be unnecessary. We think it likely that Congress recognized that there might be a question of whether a partner is always considered to be engaged in the trade or business of his partnership and provided a specific rule in each section that was certain to effect the policy of that section. In one case

---

* Although it is beyond the scope of this memorandum, it should be noted that one commentator has suggested that, despite the Service's acquiescence, the Butler decision may not be good law. 1 McKee, Nelson and Whitmire, Federal Taxation of Partnerships and Partners § 13.02[1] (1977). The argument is that the years at issue in Butler predated subchapter K and that the decision does not reflect the entity concept now embodied in section 707(a). The McKee treatise also suggests that the decision is internally inconsistent in employing an entity rule to recognize the partnership as a debtor but an aggregate concept to say that the partner is in the trade or business of the partnership.

arising under section 1402, the taxpayer argued that the partnership should be viewed as an entity and that, as a limited partner, his distributive share of partnership income should not be considered income from a trade or business. The court reasoned, however, that the taxpayer's distributive share was clearly "net earnings from self-employment" under the statute and that it was unnecessary to consider the taxpayer's argument that he was not in the trade or business of the partnership. *Estate of Ellsasser v. Commissioner,* 61 T.C. 241 (1973).

There have been a number of prior memoranda issued by this office in which we have said that a partner is deemed to be individually engaged in the trade or business of his partnership. In most instances, however, we have made this statement in memoranda concluding that certain determinations with respect to a partnership's trade or business are made at the partnership level. For example, in G.C.M. 37532, *** I-436-77 (May 12, 1978), we concluded that previous activities of the partners were not relevant to the question of when a partnership commenced a trade or business. Similarly, in O.M. 18426, *** I-273-75 (Feb. 2, 1976), which later was made a part of G.C.M. 36577, Abusive Tax Shelters, I-196-75 (Feb. 26, 1976), we concluded that the determination of whether an activity is engaged in for profit for purposes of section 183 must be made at the partnership level. See also Rev. Rul. 78-22, 1978-1 C.B. 72. Finally, in G.C.M. 33157 *** I-1813 (Dec. 20, 1965 and Feb. 27, 1967) we concluded that the status of a general partner as a dealer in real estate would not preclude partnership real estate from being treated as section 1231 property.

Our statements in these memoranda that a partner is engaged in the trade or business of his partnership reflect the fact that the character of items of partnership income, after being determined at the partnership level, passes through to the partners under section 702(a). The partner is taxed as if he earned the income in his individual trade or business. Although it is the partnership that carries on the trade or business, it does so

on behalf of the partners. See G.C.M. 33157, supra.

Although we continue to believe that a partner is engaged in the trade or business of his partnership in the sense described above, we believe that this fact has little bearing on the classification of an entity that holds a partnership interest. Subchapter K employs an aggregate theory in taxing the partners, but in other situations treats the partnership as an entity and the partnership interests as investments in the entity. See, e.g., sections 741 et seq. Moreover, as a practical matter, many partnership interests are held solely as investments with the partners taking no part in the management of the partnership's trade or business. The question presented by the instant case is whether it is inconsistent with the status of a trust to hold a partnership interest.

The regulations describe trusts as arrangements whereby "trustees take title to property for the purpose of protecting or conserving it for the beneficiaries." The regulations describe business trusts as entities which are created not to protect or conserve property but "simply as a device to carry on a profit-making business which normally would have been carried on through business organizations that are classified as corporations or partnerships." Treas. Reg. § 301.7701-4. As the Supreme Court said in *Morrissey v. Commissioner,* 296 U.S. 344 (1935): "[t]he nature and purpose of the cooperative undertaking will differentiate it from an ordinary trust. In what are called 'business trusts' the object is not to hold and conserve particular property, with incidental powers, as in the traditional type of trusts, but to provide a medium for the conduct of a business and sharing its gains."

We think that a trust cannot be considered a device or medium for carrying on a trade or business merely because the trust holds an interest in a partnership that engages in trade or business. We see no reason why a partnership interest could not be held by trustees for protection and conservation, and when a partnership interest is held for this purpose, we see no basis for classifying the trust as an association for tax purposes. Neither Morrissey nor the regulations require this result.

We think that the proposed revenue ruling is in error in not allowing consideration of the purpose for which a partnership interest is held in trust. By employing the analysis that a partner is engaged in the trade or business of his partnership, the ruling would mandate association classification in all cases. Thus, a trust holding a very small limited partnership interest in a very large syndicated partnership would be an association even though the trust's investment was really no different than if it held corporate stock. Although the proposed ruling describes a fixed investment trust, its rationale would apply to any trust holding a partnership interest. The trust would be in the trade or business of the partnership, and would be classified as an association.

Publication of the proposed revenue ruling would undoubtedly affect the status of thousands of trusts now holding partnership interests. To our knowledge, the Service has never used the rationale of the proposed ruling to challenge such trusts. Moreover, the regulations concerning family partnerships envision a partnership interest being held in trust without suggesting that the status of the trust is subject to question. Treas. Reg. 1.704-1(e)(2)(vi). In view of its impact on existing trusts, we would recommend that the Service take the position of the proposed ruling only if there were a clear legal basis for such a position. We think that the authorities cited in the proposed ruling fail to provide such a basis.

ADDENDUM

At a reconciliation conference attended by representatives of this Office and the Individual Tax Division, it was agreed that, for the reasons set forth above, the proposed revenue ruling should not be published. The representatives of the Individual Tax Division expressed the view, however, that there should be an alternative basis for classifying fixed investment trusts that hold partnership interests as associations. Although we are not prepared to advance a rationale that would support this conclusion, we understand that

you may want to pursue the question further as new cases arise. It was agreed therefore that this memorandum should not be read as foreclosing further consideration of the issue. Our comments in this memorandum are limited to rejection of the rationale of the ruling that was submitted for our review, and recommendation is limited to nonpublication of the proposed ruling.

G.C.M. 38311 (Revoked by G.C.M. 39040)
March 18, 1980

* * *

ISSUES

(1) Whether a "pool" of mortgages evidenced by "straight pass-through" certificates will be considered an association taxable as a corporation or a grantor trust under the facts described below.

(2) Assuming that such a "pool" of mortgages is considered a grantor trust, what is the proper tax treatment of trust distributions under a subordination agreement in the trust as described below.

CONCLUSIONS

(1) The proposed ruling letter prepared by the Individual Income Tax Branch (T:I:I:2:2) holds that the pool arrangement described below will be considered a fixed investment trust and not an association taxable as a corporation. We agree. The reserve fund element in the trust agreement will not destroy the fixed investment character of the pool and will not render the pool an association provided that withheld funds are not speculatively invested.

(2) The proposed ruling letter concludes that distributions which under the subordination agreement are to be distributed to the other investors in the trust rather than to the subordinated parties are nevertheless taxable to the subordinated parties under the grantor trust rules of Subpart E of Subchapter J of the Code. We disagree. In our opinion payments under the subordination agreement are taxable only to the recipients. Payments into the reserve fund, however, are treated as taxable income to the subordinated par-

ties. Payments from the reserve fund are deductible by the subordinated parties as provided in Treas. Reg. 1.166-9(e)(2).

FACTS

The Bank, ***, pursuant to a pooling and servicing agreement ("the Agreement"), will form a pool of residential mortgage loans by assigning such loans to Y, an independent party, as trustee. Concurrent with the assignment of the mortgage loans, Y will deliver to the Bank certificates in registered form representing undivided interests in the pool. Sales of certificates in the pool may be made through private placements to institutional investors, although if the pool is large, sales certificates may be registered with the Securities and Exchange Commission under the Securities Act of 1933 and sold through underwriters.

The pool will consist of mortgages selected by the Bank from those originated by the Bank in the ordinary course of its real estate lending practices. Once the pool has been established, the Bank will not exchange or substitute mortgages in its portfolio for mortgages in the pool, and except in the limited situations described below, will not have any repurchase obligation with respect to the mortgage and mortgage notes in the pool.

The assignment to Y will be without recourse and the Bank's obligations with respect to the mortgages will be limited to its servicing obligations under the Agreement and to the obligation to repurchase mortgages in the following two situations. Within 45 days of assignment of the mortgages to the trustee, Y will examine certain documents related to each mortgage, including the mortgage itself, an assignment of the trustee of the mortgage in recordable form, and a mortgage note endorsed without recourse. If Y finds any of such documents to be defective in any material respect and the Bank cannot cure the defect, the Bank must repurchase the mortgage and mortgage note to which the defective document relates. In addition to its repurchase obligation with respect to defective documents, the Bank will make representations and warranties upon assignment of the mortgage loans to the trustee. If such representations and warranties are breached and the Bank cannot cure the breach, the Bank must repurchase the mortgage and the mortgage note to which the breach relates. The repurchase price in either of the above-described situations is the sum of unpaid principal on the mortgage loan and interest at the pass-through rate to the first day of the month next succeeding the month of repurchase.

The certificates representing interests in the pool will be of two classes, Class A and Class B, and will be freely transferable. They will indicate prominently that they are not obligations of the Bank or insured by the Federal Deposit Insurance Corporation. The holders of the Class A certificates will possess a 93.5 percent interest in the pool and the holders of the Class B certificates will possess the remainder. The Class A certificates will be sold to institutional investors, such as domestic building and loan associations, real estate investment trusts, pension funds, and insurance companies, and to individuals. The Bank will generally retain the Class B certificates, although there will be no restriction on the right of the Bank to sell at any time all or any of the Class B certificates. The proceeds from the sale of the certificates will be added to the Bank's general funds and will be used to originate new conventional residential mortgage loans.

The certificates will be of a "pass-through" type and bear a pass-through rate of interest equal to the aggregate simple annual interest rate on all the mortgage loans in the pool, less the Bank's service fee. As additional compensation for its services, the Bank will be entitled to all late payment charges, prepayment charges, and assumption fees paid in connection with mortgage loans in the pool. After payment of the servicing fee to the Bank, mortgagor payments of principal and interest (to the extent of the pass-through rate) and prepayment of principal will be passed through to certificate holders monthly. The rights of Class A and Class B certificate holders will be substantially identical except that, as described in the following paragraph, rights of the holders of Class B certificates to pass-through payments of principal and interest will be subordinated to such rights of the holders of Class A certificates. In addition, a reserve fund will be established which will be used to make distributions to Class A certificate holders in the event the subordination feature does not provide sufficient funds to make full distributions to Class A certificate holders. Distributions otherwise payable to Class B certificate holders will be withheld as necessary to attain and maintain such reserve fund in an amount equal to the greater of (i) 1 percent of the aggregate outstanding principal balance of all mortgage loans in the pool or (ii) the aggregate outstanding principal balance of the two largest mortgage loans in the pool. The amount required to be maintained in the reserve fund will decline as the outstanding principal amounts of all the mortgage loans and the two largest mortgage loans then held in the pool decline.

Generally speaking, the Class B certificate holders will not receive distributions of principal and interest in a particular month, other than their share of proceeds of mortgage loans repurchased by the Bank by reason of defective documentation or the Bank's breach of warranty pursuant to the Agreement, unless the Class A certificate holders have received their full distributions in accordance with the Agreement and the reserve fund has been fully funded. The remainder, if any, will be paid pro rata to the Class B certificate holders. In other words, if there is a shortfall in the mortgage pool because of a default or delinquency by a mortgagor, the Class A beneficiaries will still receive 93.5% of funds which Y was entitled to receive (with a ceiling of amounts actually received by Y available for distribution). Class B certificate holders will not be required to refund any amounts previously distributed to them, regardless of whether there are sufficient funds on any monthly distribution date to pay the Class A certificate holders the amounts to which they are otherwise entitled.

The Bank, as servicing agent, will not make payments of principal and interest to certificate holders if such payments are not received from the mortgagors. In the event of default, recourse of certificate holders will be limited to the mortgages comprising the pool. The Bank will not repurchase defaulted mortgages, except as provided above.

For the duration of the pool, neither the Bank nor Y will be empowered to reinvest proceeds attributable to the mortgages in the pool. Similarly, neither the Bank nor Y is empowered to substitute new mortgages for the original mortgages in the pool. However, as described previously, Y may require the Bank to repurchase mortgages included in the pool that do not meet the representations and warranties given by the Bank in the Agreement. Neither the Bank nor Y shall have the right to purchase any mortgage originally included in the pool, except that the Bank has the option to repurchase all of the mortgages in the pool once the pool has amortized down to 10 percent of its original amount.

ANALYSIS

(1) Treas. Reg. § 301.7701-4(c) provides as follows:

> (c) Certain investment trusts. An "investment" trust of the type commonly known as a management trust is an association if there is power under the trust agreement to vary the investment of the certificate holders. See *Commissioner v. North American Bond Trust* (C.C.A. 2d 1941) 122 F.2d 545, *cert. denied* 314 U.S. 701. However, if there is no power under the trust agreement to vary the investment of the certificate holders, such fixed investment trust shall be classified as a trust.

The Service has ruled on several occasions that mortgage pools similar to the one described in the facts above are to be classified as fixed investment trusts taxable as trusts. See Rev. Rul. 77-349, 1977-2 C.B. 20; Rev. Rul. 71-399, 1971-2 C.B. 433, modified by Rev. Rul. 72-376, 1972-2 C.B. 647, Rev. Rul. 74-221, 1974-1 C.B. 365, and Rev. Rul. 74-300, 1974-1 C.B. 169. See also Rev. Rul. 70-545, 1970-2 C.B. 7 and Rev. Rul. 70-544, 1970-2 C.B. 6, considered by this office in G.C.M. 34347, *** I-3821 (Sept. 14, 1970).

The major difference in the present mortgage pool from the pool described in Rev. Rul. 77-349 is the existence of a reserve fund equal to the greater of (a) 1% of the outstanding aggregate principal balance of the mortgage loans in the pool or (b) the aggregate outstanding principal balance of the two largest mortgage loans in the pool. The issue, therefore, is whether the use of such a reserve fund can be considered to constitute a power to vary the investment such that the pool will be considered an association taxable as a corporation.

The proposed ruling letter states that there is no power to reinvest under the trust agreement. The taxpayer at conference stated that the reserve fund was a mere bookkeeping entry and would not be invested. A careful reading of the "Pooling and Servicing Agreement" in the file, however, does not indicate what is to be done with the money in the reserve fund pending such money's distribution.

The issue of the tax consequences associated with the use of a reserve fund in a fixed investment trust has arisen in only one court case. In *Royalty Participation Trust v. Commissioner,* 20 T.C. 466 (1953), *acq.* 1953-2 C.B. 6, certain investment trusts involving oil and gas royalty interests contained provisions requiring the trustee to establish a reserve fund for purposes of acquiring additional properties for the trust. Under these provisions, five percent of the income of each trust was set aside in the reserve fund. The Tax Court did not find these provisions to be so expansive as to destroy the fixed investment character of the trust. It noted:

> [T]his power existed because of the wasting quality of the assets involved, that is, oil and gas properties subject to natural depletion. We do not think the existence of this limited power in the indicated trusts sufficient to taint them with the business character necessary to render them taxable as associations....Id. at 474.

The Tax Court apparently felt that the fact that the reserve funds served a valid purpose and were limited in scope justified their use and did not alter the fixed investment character of the trusts. Surprisingly, the Tax Court did not seem concerned about

the use of moneys in the reserve funds prior to the purchase of additional properties.

In the present case, the amount of money placed in the reserve fund cannot exceed the greater of (a) 1% of the aggregate outstanding principal balance of all mortgage loans in the pool or (b) the aggregate outstanding principal balance of the two largest mortgages in the pool. While comparisons with the size of the reserve fund in the Royalty Participation Trust case are difficult in that any contribution to the fund in that case was measured in terms of trust income while here the amounts deposited in the fund are dependent upon the size of the trust corpus, it is obvious that the size of the reserve fund in the mortgage pool arrangement here will be relatively small in most cases. Further, as in the Royalty Participation Trust case, the fund serves a legitimate investment purpose. The reserve fund and subordination agreements have become economically necessary because the price of mortgage insurance for the pool has become prohibitive.

We therefore conclude that the presence of the reserve fund in the mortgage pool arrangement will not necessarily destroy the fixed investment character of the trust. We feel, however, that the trust agreement must specifically prohibit the trustee from reinvesting the money in such a fund in a speculative manner. As previously noted, the "Pooling and Servicing Agreement" does not state how the money in the reserve fund is to be invested prior to its distribution. Taxpayer's counsel has stated that the funds will not be reinvested, but it is the power given by the trust instrument which determines the investment discretion given to the trustee for tax purposes. *Helvering v. Coleman-Gilbert Associates,* 296 U.S. 369, 374 (1935).

In this regard we note Rev. Rul. 75-192, 1975-1 C.B. 384, considered in G.C.M. 36132, *** I-270-73 (Jan. 8, 1975). This ruling held that where proceeds from a fixed investment trust's holdings were distributable only quarterly, the trustee's power to invest such proceeds prior to distribution must be extremely limited in order to prevent the trustee from having a power to vary the investment which would render the trust an association taxable as a corporation. Under the trust agreement in the ruling, the trustee had the responsibility to invest cash on hand in short-term obligations of the United States or bank certificates of deposit which matured prior to the next distribution date. The trustee was required to hold these obligations until maturity and to distribute all interest received on such short-term investments. The trustee could not under any circumstances invest in new securities or mortgages. The ruling stated:

> The short-term obligations in which the trustee may invest are subject to daily market fluctuations. In the instant case, however, the trustee is permitted to invest only in obligations that mature prior to the next distribution date and is required to hold such obligations until maturity.
>
> These requirements limit the trustee to a fixed return similar to that earned on a bank account and eliminate any opportunity to profit from market fluctuations.

Since in the instant case the money in the reserve fund may be required to be distributed in any month where the subordination feature is insufficient to satisfy the payout requirements of the Class A certificate holders, any of the short-term investment uses of the money should have a short-term maturity date prior to a monthly distribution date. Since in the instant case mortgage pool distributions are made monthly (unlike Rev. Rul. 75-192), since it is unlikely that distributions from the reserve will be made monthly, and since we are not aware of any thirty day government obligations, we are not suggesting that invested securities must mature in thirty days. We think it is reasonable to require that any fixed investments be short-term, maturing just prior to a distribution date. Certainly the placement of such funds into a bank account would be an acceptable investment. We emphasize again that these restrictions on investment must be in the trust agreement itself in order to conclude that the trustee has no power to vary the investment of the certificate holders.

Therefore, we agree with your conclusion that the pool arrangement in this case qualifies as a fixed investment trust provided that the trust agreement specifically restricts the trustee's ability to invest the funds comprising the reserve fund as discussed above.

With respect to the second issue, the income tax treatment of the beneficiaries, we generally agree with your result, although we differ as to the reasoning. You have concluded that the Class A and Class B beneficiaries are always taxable on their pro rata share of trust income (93.5% or 6.5%). Under the subordination agreement, in the event of a shortfall in the mortgage pool, additional income sufficient to make up the Class A beneficiaries' 93.5% share is paid to the Class A beneficiaries. Your conclusion is that this income is taxed to the Class B beneficiaries, and a deduction is allowed to the Class B beneficiaries. The same income is also taxed to the Class A beneficiaries. Income paid into the reserve fund is taxed to the Class B beneficiaries, and a deduction is allowed them if and when amounts are paid from the reserve fund to the Class A beneficiaries. The nature of the deduction is not described in your proposed ruling letter. Apparently, your rationale is that under section 671, the Class A beneficiaries will be taxed on 93.5% of the income received by Y, and the Class B beneficiaries will be taxed on 6.5%. If there is a shortfall, the Class B beneficiaries are regarded as making a payment to the Class A beneficiaries in an amount necessary to give the Class A beneficiaries 93.5% of the amount that should have been received by Y. If the shortfall is reimbursed from the reserve, a deduction is given the Class B beneficiaries.

We reach similar ultimate tax treatment by a slightly different route. Section 671 treats the "grantors" as though they had individually received or paid each item of income or deduction "to the extent that such items would be taken into account under this chapter in computing taxable income or credits against the tax of an individual". We interpret this language as in effect disregarding the existence of the trust. It is true that Treas. Reg. § 1.671-3(a)(3) states that if the portion of a trust treated as owned by a grantor or another person consists of an undivided fractional interest in the trust, or of an interest represented by a dollar amount, a pro rata share of each item of income, deduction and credit is normally allocated to the portion. This seems to suggest that if there is a shortfall, the Class A beneficiaries, under section 671, will only be taxed on 93.5% of what Y actually receives, even though the Class A beneficiaries receive more.

We do not read section 671 and the statements regarding the subordination agreement so rigidly. We view the arrangement as one in which the proportionate share of the Class A beneficiaries in the mortgage pool varies depending on whether there is a shortfall. If there is a shortfall, additional amounts paid to the Class A beneficiaries to make up the necessary 93.5% are derived from the mortgage pool and not from the Class B beneficiaries.* The term "subordination" suggests that the Class B beneficiaries are not entitled to any payment from the mortgage pool until the Class A beneficiaries are made whole. Section 671 generally taxes the beneficiaries as individuals, as though no trust existed. It is not unusual for a partnership, joint venture or other arrangement to provide for varying amounts or percentages of income to be paid to different taxpayers under different circumstances. We do not read section 671 or the regulations as taxing beneficiaries on a fixed percentage of trust income notwithstanding these variations. We have found no case which interprets the section so inflexibly. Accordingly, we believe that the Class A beneficiaries should be taxed on the amounts they receive. Class B beneficiaries should not be taxed on amounts they do not receive because of the subordination agreement.

With respect to the amounts placed in the reserve, we agree with your conclusion that such amounts are taxed to the Class B beneficiaries. In effect the Class B beneficiaries have assigned their right to income to the reserve to serve the purpose of a guaranty fund in the event of a shortfall. The Class B beneficiaries are the grantors of the reserve and are taxed on any income earned by the reserve. The reserve is not a separate entity but is part of trust, and, according to the taxpayer, a mere "bookkeeping" entry. The Class B beneficiaries are the grantors of this reserve and are charged with items of income and deductions. When and if payments are made from the reserve to the Class A beneficiaries, the Class A beneficiaries will take such payments into income except to the extent such payments represent a guaranty of principal, and the Class B beneficiaries will be entitled to a deduction, as guarantors or indemnitors, as provided in Treasury Reg. § 1.166-9(e)(2). Since the Class B beneficiaries are subrogated to the rights of the Class A beneficiaries to mortgage income or principal, there will be a bad debt deduction in the year in which the right of subrogation becomes totally worthless. *Putnam v. Commissioner,* 352 U.S. 82 (1956).

* * *

G.C.M. 38456

July 25, 1980

* * *

ISSUE

Whether a trust is an association taxable as a corporation where the sales proceeds from trust certificates are placed in second mortgage loans.

CONCLUSION

The proposed revenue ruling concludes that a trust established as a fixed investment trust is an association taxable as a corporation because it is considered actively engaged in the business of lending funds for second mortgages, even though there is no power to reinvest the corpus once the trustee has acquired the second mortgages. On the facts presented in the proposed ruling, we disagree.

---

*   The prospectus at 19 states that "if there are not sufficient eligible funds in the Certificate Account to make the full distribution to which Class A Certificateholders are entitled on any Class A Distribution Date, the Bank will distribute the funds eligible for distribution to the Class A Certificateholders, and the Class B Certificateholders will not receive any diustributions. . . ."

FACTS

X, a corporation, is the trustee of a trust that sold to the public certificates representing fractional individual beneficial interests in the trust property. The certificates entitle the owners to receive monthly distributions of principal and interest received by the trust on second mortgage loans made by the trust. The certificates are freely transferable. The prospectus describes the trust as a "fixed investment trust."

The proceeds from the sale of the certificates are temporarily deposited in savings accounts and are then withdrawn to make interest bearing loans secured by second mortgages on real property. The mortgage loans placed by X are subject to criteria established under the agreement.

X makes the decisions with regard to these criteria; that is, X decides to whom it will make the loans, the terms thereof, and the type of security for the loan. After the trust has been fully funded and all of its monies invested, no more certificates will be sold and no mortgage loans will be placed. At this point, the principal and interest payments on the mortgage loans will be distributed periodically to the certificate holders until all such principal and interest have been distributed.

ANALYSIS

Section 7701(a)(3) provides that, as used in the Code, the term "corporation" includes associations.

Under Treas. Reg. § 301.7701-2 the term "association" refers to an organization whose characteristics require it to be classified, for purposes of taxation, as a corporation rather than as another type of organization such as a partnership or a trust. Six characteristics are described. These are associates, an objective to carry on a business and divide the gains therefrom, continuity of life, centralization of management, liability for corporate debts limited to corporate property, and free transferability of interests.

Treas. Reg. § 301.7701-2(a)(2) provides that because centralization of management, continuity of life, free transferability of interests, and limited liability are generally common to trusts and corporations, the determination whether a trust that has such characteristics is to be treated for tax purposes as a trust or as an association depends on whether there are associates and an objective to carry on business and divide the gains thereof.

Treas. Reg. § 301.7701-4(b) states that there are other arrangements that are known as trusts because the legal title to property is conveyed to trustees for the benefit of beneficiaries, but are not classified as trusts for purposes of the Code, because they are not simply arrangements to protect or conserve the property for the beneficiaries. These trusts, which are often known as business or commercial trusts, generally are created by the beneficiaries simply as a device to carry on a profit making business that normally would have been carried on through organizations that are classified as corporations or partnerships under the Code.

Treas. Reg. § 301.7701-4(c) includes in the term "association" an investment trust of the type commonly known as a "fixed investment trust" if there is a power under the trust agreement to vary the investment of the certificate holders. However, if there is no power under the trust agreement to vary the investment, such fixed investment trust will be classified as a trust, rather than as an association taxable as a corporation.

The Service has often considered whether arrangements similar to the one considered in the present case should be classified as trusts or associations for federal income tax purposes. See, e.g., Rev. Rul. 75-192, 1975-1 C.B. 384; Rev. Rul. 70-544, 1970-2 C.B. 6; Rev. Rul. 70-545, 1970-2 C.B. 6; and Rev. Rul. 77-349, 1977-2 C.B. 20.

Rev. Rul. 75-192 is the ruling most closely resembling the present case. In that ruling, an investment bank formed investment groups with each group choosing a trust company to act as trustee. The investment bank retained a corporation specializing in the administration of mortgages to purchase existing FHA and VA mortgages of a specified quality on behalf of the trustee and to collect the principal and interest payments on those mortgages.

Under the trust agreement, the trustee

made quarterly distributions of all principal and interest payments received to each investor in proportion to his interest therein. During the period between quarterly distribution dates, the trustee was required to invest cash on hand in certain short-term obligations, maturing prior to the next distribution date. The trustee was required, moreover, to hold all such obligations until maturity. The trust agreement did not authorize the trustee to purchase new securities or mortgages, or to make any other new investments.

The issue presented was the classification of this arrangement for Federal income tax purposes. The revenue ruling concludes that the arrangement is a trust and not an association taxable as a corporation. Because the short-term obligations in which the trustee invested had to mature prior to the next distribution date, the trustee was limited to a fixed return, and, thus, had no opportunity to profit from fluctuations in the market. Moreover, after the initial purchase of the mortgages, there was no power under the trust agreement to vary the trust's investment.

The only real difference between the trust described in Rev. Rul. 75-192 and the trust described in the proposed ruling in the instant case is that the former purchased existing mortgages while the latter actually made mortgage loans. The proposed ruling does not specify the number of loans that were made, the length of time over which loans were made, or the activity involved in making loans. The rationale of the ruling, however, is that "the circumstances surrounding the making of the loans are such that the activity and operation of the trust is similar to the activity and operation of a business that lends money." Because the ruling does not focus on the extent of the activity, it would apparently stand for the proposition that direct placement of mortgage loans will automatically cause a fixed investment trust to be classified as an association.

Although we agree that when a fixed investment trust makes mortgage loans either directly or through a broker there is the possibility that the trust is the equivalent of a commercial lender, we think that it is incorrect to assume that this will always be the case. The making of loans is not necessarily different from other types of investments typically made by trustees. Moreover, we see no basis for imposing an absolute limit on the amount of activity that the trustee of a fixed investment trust may undertake in initially placing the funds held in trust. The regulations and the case law restrict the ability of the trustee to vary the investments of the trust, but do not focus on the initial investment activity. See, e.g., *Commissioner v. North American Bond Trust,* 122 F.2d 545 (2d Cir. 1941); *Commissioner v. Chase National Bank,* 122 F.2d 540 (2d Cir. 1941); and *Pennsylvania Company for Insurance on Lives and Granting Annuities v. United States,* 146 F.2d 392 (3d Cir. 1944).

Whether a fixed investment trust, or even a traditional trust formed to protect and conserve property for its beneficiaries, is engaged in the mortgage loan business and therefore should be classified as an association is a factual question. If the trustee elects to invest in mortgage loans, it should make no difference whether he buys existing mortgages or makes new loans. Typically the placement of new loans would be done by a mortgage broker who could readily find borrowers and handle the mechanics of making the loans. Even if the broker is considered as acting as an agent of the trustee, the total activity involved in making the one-time loans of the trust corpus would not suggest the conduct of a trade or business. Under the standards of *Morrissey v. Commissioner,* 296 U.S. 344 (1935) and the regulations, it would be difficult to conclude that the trust was, to a greater extent than any fixed investment trust, a vehicle for the conduct of a business and the sharing of its gains.

Although we disagree with the conclusion of the proposed revenue ruling and think that making mortgage loans may be acceptable for a fixed investment trust, we agree with your decision in the underlying case to refuse to give a favorable ruling. The case file indicates a number of facts that are not entirely consistent with a mere investment of the trust corpus. Such facts as the relatively large number of loans to be made, and the reinvestment of the proceeds of loans that were prepaid suggest the possibility of a mortgage loan business. This case file also raises questions as to whether the trustee had the power to vary the investments of the trust. The return to the trust remained fixed at 10 percent, but the actual investment began as a loan to the trustee, shifted to mortgage loans, and in the case of loans that were prepaid, shifted again to new mortgage loans. Although this issue was not the subject of the proposed ruling and we need not resolve it here, there is a question of whether this type of change in investments is permissible under *North American Bond Trust* and the regulations.

Although it would be possible to redraft the proposed revenue ruling to describe a fixed investment trust that is engaged in the mortgage loan business, it would be necessary to make certain assumptions about the operation of the trust in the underlying case. We question, however, whether this would be worthwhile. We would expect that most fixed investment trusts are merely investing in existing mortgages rather than placing new loans. The transaction in the underlying case was structured to allow compliance with the California usury statute, and the recent repeal of that statute and those of most other states makes the transaction unnecessary. Thus, we doubt that the ruling would be helpful to either taxpayers or Service personnel.

For the above reasons, we are returning this case with the recommendation that the proposed ruling not be published.

G.C.M. 38707

May 1, 1981

***

The purpose of this memorandum is to advise you of a change in our position concerning the classification for federal income tax purposes of business trusts with one beneficiary.

In G.C.M. 36596, *** I-112-74 (February 26, 1976), we considered whether a business trust with only one beneficiary can be an association taxable as a corporation within the meaning of I.R.C. § 7701(a)(3) and the Regulations under that section. We concluded that the Regulations require a trust to have multiple beneficiaries for it to possess the corporate characteristic of associates, and that an unincorporated organization cannot be an association taxable as a corporation without that characteristic.

More recently, the Tax Court has spoken on the issue in *Hynes v. Commissioner,* 74 T.C. No. 93 (September 15, 1980). Mr. Hynes had formed a trust to develop and sell real estate. He was one of three trustees, but he held all the shares of beneficial interest in the trust. The trustees had broad powers to conduct the trust business. Hynes argued that the trust was a grantor trust and not an association for federal income tax purposes. He relied principally on the fact that there was but one beneficiary and, therefore, there were no associates and no sharing of profits.

The Tax Court rejected Hynes' argument concerning the necessity of associates. Citing the parenthetical reference to the "one-man corporation" in Treas. Reg. section 301.7701-2(a)(2), the court found it "clear that when there is a single owner, the regulations are not intended to require multiple associates or a sharing of profits among them." The court also cited with approval *Lombard Trustees v. Commissioner,* 136 F.2d 22 (9th Cir. 1943), in which a trust with one beneficiary was held taxable as an association. The Tax Court went on to apply the remaining criteria of Treas. Reg. section 301.7701-2 and classified the Hynes' trust as an association.

Our position to G.C.M. 36596 was based in large part on our reading of the Regulations as precluding a finding of a one-member association. The Tax Court, however, has shown a willingness to interpret the Regulations more broadly and to allow a business trust with one beneficiary to be classified as an association. We certainly have no objection to the result reached in *Hynes* and we believe that the *Hynes* decision should be defended if the taxpayer appeals.

Accordingly, we revoke G.C.M. 36596. We also modify the following memoranda to the extent they conclude that an association must have more than one associate: G.C.M. 34259, *** A-630256 (Jan. 1970), and G.C.M. 31735 dated July 11, 1960, regarding the same case; G.C.M. 29685, *** A-618353 (Sept. 28, 1956); and G.C.M. 25547, Oil and Gas Operators—Taxable Status of Leases of, A-311834 (Jan. 9, 1948).

Our action in revoking and modifying these G.C.M.s is designed to make possible a defense of the *Hynes* decision on appeal and is not intended to set forth any standard with respect to when a trust with a single beneficiary should be considered an association for federal tax purposes. In the typical business trust under Treas. Reg. section 301.7701-4(b), the trust is the vehicle through which two or more persons pool their resources for investment or the conduct of a trade or business. We recognize that there may be only limited situations in which one person would use a trust as a vehicle for conducting a trade or business. Thus, although we favor defense of *Hynes* on appeal, we believe that a one beneficiary trust should be classified as an association only when the facts of a case clearly warrant such treatment. We will, of course, be happy to work with you on such cases as they arise.

* * *

G.C.M. 39395

In re: Characterization of a New York business trust for federal tax purposes.

June 24, 1983

* * *

ISSUE

Whether an organization created by, and maintained by a trustee for the sole benefit of, the * * *, is an association taxable as a corporation for federal income tax purposes.

CONCLUSION

The organization was formed to conduct business for profit. Thus, it has associates and a joint profit objective, and is not a trust. To be an association, the organization must possess a preponderance of the four remaining corporate characteristics. It has centralization of management and free transferability of interests; it lacks continuity of life and limited liability. Therefore, we conclude that the organization is not an association, but should be treated as the *** making investments through an agent (the trustee).

FACTS

In a letter dated ***, appointed *** to act as trustee for the investment of its funds. The trust agreement embodied in the letter accords the trustee broad management powers over the trust corpus, including the power to reinvest the principal, to sell trust assets and purchase other assets, and to manage, operate, lease, develop, improve, or otherwise deal with any real property in the trust. The ***, the grantor and sole beneficiary of the trust, has reserved the rights to amend the trust, to revoke it in whole or part and to request payments from income or principal at any time. The trust agreement does not purport to limit *** liability for trust debts or to restrict *** ability to transfer its beneficial interest in the trust. The trust is to be regulated and administered, and the terms of the trust instrument are to be construed, under the laws of New York State.

ANALYSIS

Treas. Reg. section 301.7701-2(a)(1) sets forth six corporate characteristics to be considered in determining whether an organization is to be classified as an association: associates; an objective to carry on business and divide the gains therefrom; continuity of life; centralization of management; limited liability; and free transferability of interests. Treas. Reg. sections 301.7701-2(a)(2) and (3) provide that an unincorporated organization shall not be classified as an association unless it has more corporate than non-corporate characteristics and, in making that determination, all corporate characteristics common to an alternative classification category shall not be considered.

For example, since centralization of management, continuity of life, free transferability of interests, and limited liability are generally common to trusts and corporations, the determination of whether a trust which has such characteristics is to be treated for tax purposes as a trust or as an association depends on whether there are associates and an objective to carry on business and divide the gains therefrom. Treas. Reg. section 301.7701-2(a)(2) (emphasis added).

The first step in classifying the organization in question is to determine whether it more nearly resembles a trust or a corporation. For this purpose only the two characteristics not common to corporations and trusts—associates and a joint profit objective—should be considered. The fact that the organization has a single member does not prevent it from having these two characteristics. *Lombard Trustees, Ltd. v. Commissioner,* 136 F.2d 22 (9th Cir., 1943); *Hynes v. Commissioner,* 74 T.C. 1266, 1279-81 (1980); *** G.C.M. 38707, I-112-74 (May 1, 1981). Under *Lombard Trustees* and *Hynes,* the organization is in effect deemed to possess associates and a joint profit objective if it is formed to conduct business. The organization was formed to conduct a business for profit and not for the limited purpose of protecting or conserving property, because the trustee has broad discretion in dealing with the trust property, including the power to sell property and reinvest the proceeds, and virtually unrestricted authority to choose property in which to invest. *See* Treas. Reg. sections 301.7701-4(a) and (b). Thus, the organization has both associates and a joint profit objective, and is not a trust.

However, it does not follow from the above analysis that the organization in question is necessarily an association. In determining that the organization more nearly resembles a corporation than a trust, we did not consider the four characteristics common to trusts and corporations. Thus, we assumed for purposes of that comparison that the organization has those four characteristics. *See* above underscored language from Treas. Reg. section 301.7701-2(a)(2). We believe the organization actually must possess at least three of those characteristics to be an association. For example, an or-

ganization with associates, a joint profit objective, centralization of management and free transferability, but lacking continuity of life and limited liability is not an association. Such an organization would normally be classified as a partnership. Treas. Reg. section 301.7701-2(a)(3). Despite the fact that under *Lombard Trustees* and *Hynes* a single-member organization can be treated as having associates for purposes of determining if it is an association, we believe that no single-member organization possesses associates in the partnership sense and that an organization with only a single member cannot be a partnership. Thus, if the organization in this case lacks more than one of the four characteristics common to trusts and corporations, it is neither an association nor a partnership. Assuming that the organization lacks two or more of these characteristics (and, thus, is not an association), we would classify it as an arrangement along the lines of a sole proprietorship that conducts business through an agent (the trustee). You conclude that the organization has centralization of management and free transferability, and we agree these characteristics are present. For the reasons discussed below, we believe the organization lacks continuity of life and limited liability. Therefore, we conclude that the organization is not an association.

I. CONTINUITY OF LIFE

Treas. Reg. section 301.7701-2(b)(3) (emphasis added) states, "if the agreement (establishing an organization) expressly provides that the organization can be terminated at the will of any member, it is clear that the organization lacks continuity of life." A literal application of this regulation leads to the conclusion that the organization in this case lacks continuity, since the beneficiary reserved the right to revoke it at will. However, you have suggested that the quoted language must be read in context; that because the rest of Treas. Reg. section 301.7701-2(b) concerns the technical dissolution of an organization under local law, the ability to terminate at will does not preclude continuity unless the termination also causes a technical dissolution; and that a technical dissolution is impossible in the case of a single-member organization, since it has no personal relationships to be altered. Thus, you conclude that the organization in this case has continuity of life.

We do not agree with this conclusion for several reasons. First, the quoted regulation uses the term "terminated" rather than "dissolved." This is a conspicuous departure from the rest of Treas. Reg. section 301.7701-2(b), which consistently refers to dissolution. Although the regulation defines the term "dissolution," the word "terminate" is not defined and, thus, should be accorded its customary meaning. To terminate usually means to bring to an end, and we believe the drafters of the regulation would have assigned the word a different meaning or used another word if they had intended something else.

We believe that continuity in the corporate sense requires a greater degree of permanence of an organization than would allow a single individual to withdraw that individual's investment by terminating the enterprise at will. *Estate of Smith v. Commissioner,* 313 F.2d 724, 735–36 (8th Cir. 1963), suggesting, in dictum, that the ability to unilaterally withdraw one's investment, even if the withdrawal does not cause the organization to terminate or dissolve, might prevent the organization from having continuity of life; *Hynes,* 74 T.C. at 1282, implying that the organization in that case would have lacked continuity had the sole beneficiary been able to "dissolve" it at will; cf. Rev. Rul. 57-341, 1957-2 C.B. 884, 886, considered in ***, G.C.M. 29455, A-619355 (May 2, 1956), concluding that a syndicate formed for the limited purpose of buying a single issue of tax-exempt bonds lacks continuity of life.

Finally, we believe that making technical dissolution the litmus for whether the ability to terminate at will precludes continuity would unduly extend the result in *Hynes.* Having won the point that a single-member organization can be an association, the Service would appear to be overreaching in adopting the stance that there is no way such an organization could be formed so as to avoid having the corporate characteristic of continuity. In concluding that the ability

of a single member to terminate an organization at will is enough to prevent the organization from having continuity, we are mindful that authorities sometimes refer to technical dissolution as the test for continuity. *See,* e.g., *Larson v. Commissioner,* 66 T.C. 159, 205 (1976) (Quealy, J., dissenting), *acq.,* 1979-1 C.B. 1, which states, "respondent's regulations adopt 'dissolution' as the sole test in determining whether there is the requisite continuity"; 1 W. McKee, W. Nelson and R. Whitmire, *Federal Taxation of Partnerships and Partners,* Para. 3.06(4)(a), at 3-45 (1977), stating, "(t)he event negating continuity of life is the 'dissolution' of the organization, not the termination and liquidation of the organization's business and property." However, these comments were made in the context of discussions distinguishing between partnerships and associations and reflect the tacit assumption that ordinarily continuity of life is used in differentiating those two types of organizations. We believe that the preoccupation of Treas. Reg. section 301.7701-2(b) with technical dissolution betrays a similar bias. Further, as suggested by the above-quoted language from McKee, it is generally assumed that a technical dissolution is something less drastic than a termination. We find nothing in the above authorities to suggest that it might be easier for an organization to terminate than to technically dissolve. We are also aware that sole-shareholder corporations normally can be terminated at the will of the shareholder and, thus, would lack continuity of life as we have described it. However, we do not view this as a problem because such organizations are classified as corporations "per se" and not based on the corporate resemblance tests in Treas. Reg. section 301.7701-2. *See* generally ***, G.C.M. 37127, I-110-77 (May 18, 1977), modified by G.C.M. 37953 (same case) (May 14, 1979), discussing "per se" corporations.

II. LIMITED LIABILITY

Treas. Reg. section 301.7701-2(d)(1) states that an organization has the corporate characteristic of limited liability if under local law there is no member who is personally liable for the debts of or claims against the organization.

Under New York common law, business trusts are recognized and members (that is, beneficiaries) of such trusts may exempt themselves from personal liability for trust debts. *Brown v. Bedell*, 263 N.Y. 177, 179, 188 N.E. 641, 643, *reh'g denied*, 264 N.Y. 453, 191 N.E. 510, *motion denied*, 264 N.Y. 513, 191 N.E. 541 (1934). This is in accord with the generally accepted view that a business trust may possess limited liability if its members so desire. *See* G. Bogert, *The Law of Trusts and Trustees*, section 247, at 163 and n.60 (rev. 2d ed. 1977); 4A R. Powell, *The Law of Real Property*, Para. 573A(8), at 456 (1981); Annot., 156 A.L.R. 22, 104–13 (1945). However, in most states even if the trust instrument purports to limit a member's liability, the member will be liable for trust debts if the member has the express power to control the management of the trust. Bogert at 167; Powell Para. 573A(11), at 461; 156 A.L.R. at 112–13. There appears to be a split of authority regarding what other powers held by a member amount to practical control so as to deprive the member of limited liability. Compare Bogert at 169 (footnotes omitted) (emphasis added) (stating, '(w)here the (members) are given the power at any time to remove and replace the trustees and to modify the terms of the trust agreement, liability is usually imposed, and either of these powers alone would seem to give sufficient practical control') with Powell at 461-64 (to the effect that reservation of the power to remove trustees, or to amend or revoke the trust instrument is not enough to impose liability, but the reservation of two or more of these powers might be) (and) 156 A.L.R. at 116-19 (stating that the power to amend or revoke the trust instru-

ment, or to replace trustees will not, of itself, render a member liable, but the reservation of any of these powers with certain other powers has caused liability to be imposed). We have found no New York law bearing directly on the question of what powers are sufficient to deprive a trust member of limited liability.

Although the matter is not entirely free from doubt, we believe that the organization in this case lacks limited liability. Nothing in the trust instrument purports to limit the beneficiary's liability and since New York business trusts are creatures of common law, no statute accords such trusts limited liability. Thus, there does not appear to be any reason why the beneficiary should expect to be exempt from personal liability.* Moreover, despite the uncertainty of New York law on this question, there is a reasonable basis for concluding that the beneficiary could be held personally liable because of the powers reserved to it, irrespective of whether the trust instrument purports to limit its liability. The beneficiary has the powers to amend and revoke the trust, although it does not have the express power to control management of the trust or to replace the trustee.** Based on the authorities discussed above, we believe that the reservation of the powers to amend and revoke would be enough to render the beneficiary personally liable.

***

G.C.M. 39040

September 27, 1983

***

In ***, G.C.M. 38311, I-322-79 (March 18, 1980), we considered a proposed revenue rul-

---

* We presume that the *** would not be entitled to sovereign immunity with respect to claims arising from trust activities because such activities are commercial in nature and, thus, are excepted from the protection against lawsuits generally accorded foreign governments. *See* Foreign Sovereign Immunities Act of 1976, 28 U.S.C.A. section 1605(a)(2) (West Cum. Ann. Pocket Part 1982) (commercial activities exception). In addition, the * * * does not have a treaty with the United States that would exempt it from liability for such claims.

** A memorandum, at 21, attached to a January 7, 1983 letter from the taxpayer's attorney states that the beneficiary has retained the power to remove the trustee. However, the trust instrument does not reserve this power explicitly to the beneficiary. (See administrative file.)

ing concerning the tax treatment of a mortgage "pool" in which interests were evidenced by two classes of certificates and in which there was a reserve fund. The primary issue was the classification of the pool and the G.C.M. concluded that it was a fixed investment trust and not an association taxable as a corporation.

At this time Congress is actively considering the status of mortgage pools. Furthermore, there have been considerable developments in this area and the Service is reconsidering whether a fixed investment trust can ever have classes of equitable ownership. See Rev. Proc. 83-52, 1983-29 I.R.B. 62. It follows, therefore, that the conclusions of G.C.M. 38311 must also be reconsidered at this time.

G.C.M. 38311 is revoked.

* * *

G.C.M. 39113

January 12, 1984

* * *

The proposed ruling concludes that a trust created by the Federal National Mortgage Association (FNMA) to pool home mortgage loans for the secondary mortgage market should be classified as a grantor trust, and that the trust certificate holders are the grantors and owners of proportionate, undivided interests in each mortgage in the pool. Numerous other conclusions in the proposed ruling are based on this classification.

We asked to see the proposed ruling formally because of a possible conflict between the proposed ruling and Rev. Rul. 66-238, 1966-2 C.B. 521, which concludes that participation certificates sold by FNMA under the Participation Sales Act of 1966, Pub. L. No. 89-429, 80 Stat. 164, are stock or obligations of an instrumentality of the United States for purposes of I.R.C.

§ 7701(a)(19)(c)(ii) and are not qualifying real property loans under former § 593(e) (now 593(d)). Thus, unlike the certificate holders in the proposed ruling, the participation certificate holders in Rev. Rul. 66-238 were not treated as the owners of the underlying loans.

The trust certificates in this case are not issued under the Participation Sales Act of 1966, the relevant section of which (§ 2(b)) is codified as amended as Federal National Mortgage Association Charter Act (FNMA Charter Act) § 302(c)(2), 12 U.S.C.A. § 1717(c)(2) (West 1980),* but under FNMA Charter Act § 304(d), 12 U.S.C.A. § 1719(d) (West 1980). This distinguishes the proposed revenue ruling from Rev. Rul. 66-238. As revealed in a May 19, 1966, file memorandum and a June 2, 1966, addendum to the file memorandum (see administrative file for Rev. Rul. 66-238), the 1966 ruling was based on the conclusion that trusts created under the Participation Sales Act of 1966 are associations taxable as corporations. That conclusion, in turn, was grounded on two considerations not present in this case. First, the trustee had the power to substitute new obligations for those forming the trust corpus and, thus, could vary the trust investments. Second, the Participation Sales Act of 1966 contains a statement indicating that trusts created thereunder should be classified as associations for federal tax purposes. The Act itself states, "the trust or trusts shall be exempt from all taxation." Participation Sales Act of 1966, § 2(b), codified as amended as FNMA Charter Act section 302(c)(2). And the legislative history of that provision makes explicit what its language implies. Participation Sales Act of 1966: Hearings on H.R. 14544 Before the Comm. on Banking and Currency, 89th Cong., 2d Sess. 14 (1966) (attachment to letter of transmittal from the President), states:

New paragraph (2) of FNMA Charter Act section 302(c) would also specifically

---

* It should be noted that although the Federal National Mortgage Association was authorized to issue the participation certificates in 1966, that authority subsequently was transferred to, and is now vested in, the Government National Mortgage Association. See Federal National Mortgage Assocation Charter Act sections 302(a)(2)(A) and (c)(2), 12 U.S.C.A. §§ 1717(a)(2)(A) and (c)(2) (West 1980).

exempt any such trusts from all taxation. This, in effect, would categorize the trust as a corporation and exempt its income from tax. Since the trust is a corporation, the income received by the participation holders would be taxable dividends, even if part of the income earned by the corporation would have been tax exempt if owned directly by an investor.

Accord, H.R. Rep. No. 1448, 89th Cong., 2d Sess. 5 (1966).

In contrast with the situation in Rev. Rul. 66-238, in this case the trustee has only a limited power of substitution during the first 120 days after the trust is created, and the certificates are issued under a section of the FNMA Charter Act that is silent concerning the classification of the trust. Accordingly, this case is distinguishable from Rev. Rul. 66-238. We would identify in the facts of the proposed ruling FNMA's statutory authority for creating the mortgage pools in this case to make taxpayers aware that this case does not involve the Participation Sales Act of 1966.

On other matters, we suggest that the facts of the proposed ruling be expanded to more completely describe the FNMA trust arrangement. We also suggest that the proposed ruling cite a series of revenue rulings the Service has published classifying Government National Mortgage Association and Federal Home Loan Mortgage Corporation mortgage pools as grantor trusts. We suggest other, minor changes.

A proposed revenue ruling incorporating our suggested changes is attached.

* * *

PROPOSED REVENUE RULING
ISSUE

What are the federal tax consequences associated with the mortgage pool trusts described below?

FACTS

The Federal National Mortgage Association (FNMA) is a publicly held corporation established to provide assistance to the secondary market for home mortgage loans. FNMA has initiated a guaranteed mortgage pass-through securities program under Federal National Mortgage Association Charter Act § 304(d), 12 U.S.C.A. § 1719(d) (West 1980). Pursuant to a trust agreement, FNMA creates home mortgage pools and serves as trustee of each pool. FNMA either acquires mortgages for the pools from mortgage sellers in exchange for trust certificates, or sets aside mortgagee from FNMA's own portfolio in exchange for trust certificates. The trust certificates may be sold by the sellers or FNMA to investors. FNMA charges the sellers a processing fee when it pools mortgages acquired from them.

In the capacity of pool trustee, FNMA collects principal and interest payments on each mortgage and makes monthly distributions to the certificate holders. FNMA receives a fee for its services as trustee consisting of a monthly service charge retained from the interest collected on the mortgages and other compensation including all late payment charges, assumption fees and prepayment penalties collected by FNMA. Pool proceeds are held in noninterest bearing accounts and cannot be reinvested. Neither the trustee nor any seller has the power to substitute a new mortgage for an original mortgage in the pool, except that within 120 days of the date the pool is established FNMA may replace defective mortgages in the pool. Each of the pools will terminate when all mortgages are liquidated and all proceeds are distributed. FNMA may terminate a pool by repurchasing all trust certificates with respect to the pool when the aggregate outstanding principal amount of mortgages in the pool is 10 percent or less of the initial pool principal balance.

FNMA guarantees that the certificate holders will receive timely payment of interest and collection of principal. If a mortgage is in default or if there is a foreclosure on mortgaged property, FNMA has the right to withdraw the mortgage from the pool and deem the mortgage prepaid.

The trust certificates, which are in registered form, state that they represent fractional undivided interests in the mortgage loans, pool proceeds, mortgaged property acquired by foreclosure that has not been withdrawn from the pool, and FNMA's obligation to supplement the pool proceeds to the extent necessary to make distributions.

LAW

The Service has discussed the federal income tax consequences of similar pooling arrangements in Rev. Rul. 71-399, 1971-2 C.B. 433, amplified by Rev. Rul. 81-203, 1981-2 C.B. 137, Rev. Rul. 80-96, 1980-1 C.B. 317, Rev. Rul. 74-300, 1974-1 C.B. 169, Rev. Rul. 74-221, 1974-1 C.B. 365, and Rev. Rul. 72-376, 1972-2 C.B. 647 (concerning mortgage pools established by the Federal Home Loan Mortgage Corporation); Rev. Rul. 70-544, 1970-2 C.B. 6, and Rev. Rul. 70-545, 1970-2 C.B. 7, both modified by Rev. Rul. 74-169, 1974-1 C.B. 147 (concerning mortgage pools guaranteed by the Government National Mortgage Association); and Rev. Rul. 77-349, 1977-2 C.B. 20 (concerning a mortgage pool created by a commercial bank).

HOLDINGS

(1) Each pool will not be considered an association taxable as a corporation, but is classified as a trust of which the certificate holders are the owners under Subpart E of Subchapter J of the Internal Revenue Code.

(2) FNMA is the trustee of each trust and will be required to file Form 1041. See section 1.671-4 of the Income Tax Regulations.

(3) Each certificate holder is treated as the owner of an undivided interest in the entire trust (corpus as well as ordinary income). See section 1.671-3(a)(1) of the regulations.

(4) The sale of the trust certificates transfers to the certificate holders a proportionate share of equitable ownership in each of the mortgages in the pool.

(5) FNMA will recognize ordinary income or loss on the sale of its interest in each of the mortgages in the pool from its portfolio measured by the difference between the proportionate amount of the proceeds realized with respect to the sale of each of the mortgages and its adjusted basis in each of such mortgages. FNMA will recognize ordinary income in the amount of the processing fees charged mortgage sellers for pooling mortgages acquired from them.

(6) Each certificate holder using the cash receipts and disbursements method of accounting shall take into account its proportionate share of the mortgage interest and other items of income, including prepayment penalties, assumption fees, and late payment charges, as and when they are collected by the trust. Each certificate holder using an accrual method of accounting shall take into account its proportionate share of the income items as they become due to the trust.

(7) The certificate holders also must report their proportionate shares of any discount income realized with respect to the mortgages as ordinary income to the extent required by section 1232A of the Internal Revenue Code or section 1232, consistently with their methods of accounting.

(8) Certificate holders may amortize their proportionate shares of any premium paid to acquire mortgages to the extent allowed by section 171 of the Code.

(9) Certificate holders may deduct their proportionate shares of FNMA's fee for servicing the mortgages comprised of the monthly service charge, late payment charges, assumption fees, and prepayment penalties under section 162 or section 212 of the Code, consistently with their methods of accounting.

(10) A certificate owned by a real estate investment trust is considered as representing "real estate assets" within the meaning of section 856(c)(5)(A) of the Code, and the interest income is considered "interest on obligations secured by mortgages on real property" within the meaning of section 856(c)(3)(B).

(11) A certificate owned by a domestic building and loan association is considered as representing "loans secured by an interest in real property" within the meaning of section 7701(a)(19)(C)(v) of the Code, provided the real property is (or from the proceeds of the loan will become) the type of real property described in that section of the Code.

(12) A certificate owned by a domestic building and loan association, within the meaning of section 7701(a)(19) of the Code, is considered as representing "qualifying real property loans" within the meaning of section 593(d) provided the real

property underlying the mortgages is (or, from the proceeds of the loan, will become) the type of real property described in that section.

G.C.M. 39309

May 31, 1984

* * *

ISSUE

Whether a "call premium" received by a holder on the early redemption of a bond or debenture should be treated as interest or capital gain income?

CONCLUSION

The proposed ruling holds that a "call premium" received by a holder on the early redemption of a bond or debenture should be treated as interest income. We disagree for the reasons herein expressed.

FACTS

In 1974, A, who is not an insurance company, broker, trader, or dealer in securities, acquired a $10,000 face value bond for $10,000. The bond provided for an 8 percent interest rate and was due in 1984. The bond further provided that the issuer of the bond could call it for early redemption provided the issuer paid a "call" premium with respect to the bond.

In 1980, the issuer of the bond notified A that it was calling its bond for early redemption. The issuer paid A, in addition to accrued interest and principal, the "call" premium provided for in the bond in the event of early redemption.

ANALYSIS

Section 61(a) of the Internal Revenue Code provides that except as otherwise provided gross income means all income from whatever source derived including interest income.

Section 1232(a)(1) of the Code provides that amounts received by the holder on retirement of bonds or other evidences of indebtedness shall be considered as amounts received in exchange therefor.

Section 1232(a)(2)(A) of the Code provides that on the sale, exchange or redemption before maturity of bonds issued after May 27, 1969 and held by the taxpayer more than 1 year, any gain realized shall (except as provided in the following sentence) be considered gain from the sale or exchange of a capital asset held for more than 1 year. If at the time of original issue there was an intention to call the bond or other evidence of indebtedness before maturity, any gain realized on the sale or exchange thereof shall be considered as ordinary income to the extent that such gain does not exceed an amount equal to the original issue discount reduced by the portion of original issue discount previously includible in the gross income (i.e., the earned OID that was ratably includible).*

Section 1232(a)(2)(B)(ii) of the Code provides, that on the sale, exchange or redemption before maturity of bonds issued after December 31, 1954 and on or before May 29, 1969, and held by the taxpayer more than 1 year; any gain realized that does not exceed an amount that bears the same ratio to the original issue discount as the number of complete months that the bond was held by the taxpayer bears to the number of complete months from the date of original issue to the date of maturity (i.e., the earned discount amount that was not ratably includible)** shall be considered ordinary income if at the time of issuance there

---

* Section 1232(a)(3) of the Code provides that when a corporation issues at a discount after May 27, 1969 bonds or other evidences of indebtedness, the amount of the original issue discount shall be included as interest in the holder's gross income on a ratable basis over the life of the indebtedness. The term "original issue discount" means the difference between issue price and the stock redemption price at maturity. I.R.C. § 1232(b)(1).

** Originally, under section 1232, taxation of the original issue discount was deferred until the year the indebtedness was retired, sold, or exchanged. In 1969, however, Congress amended section 1232 and added section 1232(a)(3) to provide parallel treatment between corporations issuing indebtedness with original issue discount who amortized the discount over the life of the bond and the persons acquiring the indebtedness. H.R. Rep. No. 413, 91st Cong. 1st Sess. 109 (1969).

was no intention to call the bonds before maturity. Gain in excess of such amount shall be considered gain from the sale or exchange of a capital asset held for more than a year.

Congress' intent in enacting section 1232(a)(2) as originally drafted to require the earned portion of OID to be included in income as ordinary income on the sale or retirement of a bond was to distinguish between the portion of proceeds received upon the sale, exchange or retirement of an obligation which represented interest income and the portion which represented capital gain. See H. Rep. No. 1337, 83d Cong., 2d Sess. 83, 276 (1954); S. Rep. No. 1622, 83d Cong., 2d Sess. 112, 434 (1954). Under the predecessor of section 1232(a)(1) (section 117(f)), when bonds in registered form were retired the transaction was treated as a sale or exchange and there was some uncertainty as to the status of the proceeds—i.e., whether the amounts received should be treated as capital gain or as interest income when the bond or other evidence of indebtedness was issued at a discount. (Compare *Commissioner v. Caulkins*, 144 F.2d 482 (6th Cir. 1944), *aff'g*, 1 T.C. 656 (1943) (where the court held that the capital gain statute section 117(f) required the amount received on the retirement of the bond issued at a discount to be treated as capital gain income although it found the discount amount presented no true aspect of capital gain) with *Commissioner v. Morgan*, 272 F.2d 936 (9th Cir. 1956) and *Rosen v. United States*, 288 F.2d 658 (1961) (where the amount received on retirement of an evidence of indebtedness issued at a discount was broken down into interest and capital gain on the indebtedness' early retirement, and section 117(f) was not considered an overriding statute converting what otherwise should be ordinary income into capital gain.)

The proposed ruling states that Congress when enacting section 1232(a)(2) to provide that the earned discount portion of the amounts received on the retirement of a bond or other evidence of indebtedness is to be considered ordinary interest income obviously codified the case law which holds that section 1232(a) is not an overriding statute, converting what would otherwise be ordinary income into capital gain. Thus, because section 1232(a) of the Code does not convert what would otherwise be ordinary income into capital gain, the true character of a call premium received on the early redemption of a bond must be determined for income tax purposes.

Citing for authority *Pattiz v. United States*, 311 F.2d 947 (Ct. Cl. 1975) (where the court said that prepayment charges are an additional fee for the use of money for a shorter period of time) and *Union Pacific Railroad Co. v. United States*, 524 F.2d 1343 (Ct. Cl. 1975), *cert. den.*, 429 U.S. 827 (1976) (where the court said that unamortized bond discounts and call premiums paid on the early redemption of bonds are no different than amortized discounts), the ruling determines that the amount paid for the privilege of redeeming bonds and other evidence of indebtedness early represents an additional fee for the use of money. Consequently, because interest is defined as the "amount which one has contracted to pay for the use of borrowed money," *Old Colony Railroad Co. v. Commissioner*, 284 U.S. 552, (1932), the ruling reasons that call premiums should be considered interest. We disagree.

While Congress in enacting section 1232(a) may not have necessarily intended for that section to be overriding, converting what would otherwise be ordinary income into capital gain, we believe that Congress did intend for call premiums, as well as unearned OID,* received by bond holders on the early redemption of the bonds to be considered as capital gains income when providing in section 1232(a)(2) as initially enacted that amounts in excess of earned OID received on redemption shall be considered gain from the sale or exchange of a capital asset** The legislative history to the 1958 amendment to section 1232(a)(2) confirms

---

* Unearned OID is considered to be capital gain income under section 1232(a)(2). *See Bolnick v. Commissioner*, T.C. 245 (1965).

this view. That amendment changed section 1232(a)(2) to require that unearned, as well as earned, OID be included in gross income as ordinary income on the early redemption of a bond issued at a discount, if at the time of original issue there was an intention to call the bond.

The history to that amendment provides:

A practice has developed in some areas of issuing bonds with an artificially large discount and then redeeming them at par or at a special call price before their maturity date. Where such bonds are sold or retired before maturity at a price above the issue price plus the discount attributable to the period the bond has been held, a portion of the original issue discount receives capital gains treatment rather than ordinary income treatment. As a result, although the entire difference between the issue price and the redemption price is claimed by the corporation as a deduction against ordinary income, the bondholder obtains capital gains treatment with respect to his gain in excess of the discount attributable to the period up to redemption. To eliminate this abuse the House bill provided that any gain realized on the sale or exchange of a bond or other evidence of indebtedness containing an original issue discount is to be considered as ordinary income to the extent of the original issue discount. S. Rept. 1983, 85th Cong. 2d Sess. 76 (1958). Thus, this report indicates that the unearned original issue discount and call premiums would continue to be taxed at capital gains rates if there was no intention to call before maturity. 1958-3 C.B. 928.

An example in the legislative history to the 1969 amendment to section 1232(a) which changed 1232 to require the ratable inclusion of OID also provides support for our position that Congress, as well as the Treasury, intended for call premiums to be considered capital gains income when pro-

viding in section 1232(a)(2) as initially enacted that amounts in excess of earned OID received on the redemption of a bond issued at a discount shall be treated as capital gains income. The Technical Explanation of Treasury Tax Reform Proposal on ratable reporting of OID provides:

The proposal may be illustrated by the following example:

On January 1, 1970, A, an individual, purchases at original issue for $80, X corporation's 10-year 3 percent coupon bond which has a stated redemption price of $100. The ratable amount of original issue discount to be included in A's gross income in each taxable year (until the bond is sold, exchanged or redeemed) is $2 ($\frac{1}{10}$ of $100 stated redemption price less $80 issue price). In addition, A would include in gross income each year the $3 of interest income received. Each year that A holds the bond he would also increase his basis by the reported $2 of original issue discount. *If X corporation purchases the bond on January 1, 1975, for $105 A will have a gain of $15 ($105 amount realized $90 adjusted basis) all of which will be capital gain.* If A holds the bond to maturity, he reports no gain or loss on retirement ($100 stated redemption price less $100 adjusted basis)...[Emphasis added.] Committee on Ways and Means on Tax Reform Proposals, 91st. Cong., 1st Sess. 187 (Comm. Print 1969).

In view of the above legislative history, we believe Congress, when enacting section 1232(a)(2), intended to characterize call premiums as capital gain income, and we find this intent consistent with the capital gain concept of not taxing the realization of appreciation in value accrued over a period of time at ordinary income tax rates, but at the lesser capital gain rates. See *United States v. Midland Ross,* 381 U.S. 54 (1964). As indicated from the following discussion,

***Note that although we refer to Congress's intent when originally enacting section 1232(a)(2), that section has not been significantly changed and thus there is no indication that an intent different than that which existed when the statute was originally enacted now exists under section 1232(a)(2). As noted earlier, section 1232(a)(2)(B)(ii) provides, in pertinent part, that for bonds issued before 1969 gain in excess of earned OID received on the sale or retirement of a bond shall be treated as capital gain income. Section 1232(a)(2)(A) now provides that, for bonds issued after 1969, any gain received on the sale or retirement of a bond shall be treated as capital gain income. This minor change does not show a change in Congressional intent with respect to the gain received on the sale or retirement of a bond issued at a discount.

the early redemption of a bond at a premium usually is directly related to the appreciation of the bond over some period of time due to a downward fluctuation in the interest rate and thus the premium should be logically taxed at the lesser capital gain rates.

Call options on bonds are usually exercised in order to retire high yielding bonds to engage in other more feasible means of corporate financing. Because the provision is usually antagonistic to the investor since the investor loses income if he either accepts the new bond issue or reinvests the payment received on redemption in an issue of the same quality at current market yields; callable bonds are usually made redeemable at a price above issue price (i.e., at a premium) to add to the bonds' market-ability. This premium is a penalty fee paid to the holder by the corporation for calling the holder's appreciated asset early and serves as partial compensation to the holder for giving up his appreciated investment. Despite this premium, however, when the going rate on bonds is lower than the corporation's similarly situated bonds, the corporation will usually redeem because the corporation will save funds by virtue of retiring the high yielding bonds even after payment of the premium.*

Assume, for instance, that X corp wants to raise funds by issuing a 20 year 1,000x bond at the prevailing rate of 10 percent and wants to make the bond callable after 5 years. X will ordinarily never call the bond after five years if the bond depreciates in value due to a rise in the cost of borrowing, for example, to 13 percent. However, if the bond appreciates in value because the cost of borrowing goes down, for example, to 7 percent, X will ordinarily always call the bond and raise funds at a lower rate; and the purchaser of the bond will be put in a losing situation since the purchaser loses income if he either accepts the new bond issue or reinvests the proceeds received on redemption at the lesser market rate. Recog-

nizing that the bondholder will be put in this losing situation, X will usually make the bond callable at a premium for the privilege of calling the holders appreciated asset early to increase the bonds' marketability.

We believe it would be reasonable to say that call premiums represent the amount above issue price that corporations will pay to retire a bondholder's appreciated asset. Because a callable bond will be redeemed and the call premium thereon will be received by the holder only if the bond appreciates in value, it also would be reasonable to say that the receipt of the call premium by the holder on redemption of the bond is a realization of appreciation on the bond accrued over a period of time and should be taxed at the lesser capital gains rates just as though the call premium were the amount above issue price (i.e., gain) received on sale of the bond resulting from its appreciation. Section 1232(a)(1), which equates the retirement and sale of a bond, would seem to require this parallel treatment of call premiums and gain on the sale of a bond because they are so substantially similar.

In *United States v. Midland-Ross,* supra, the taxpayer purchased noninterest bearing notes issued by corporations at an original issue discount. Prior to maturity but after holding the notes for longer than 6 months, the taxpayer sold the notes for less than their face amounts but at a price in excess of the issue price. The taxpayer thus realized gains on the sales. The issue was whether these gains were taxable as long-term capital gains or ordinary income. It was conceded that the gain was the economic equivalent of interest for the use of the money to the date of the sale. The Court held that the earned original issue discount which was involved in that case, being the equivalent of interest, or compensation for the use or forbearance of money, see *Deputy v. DuPont,* 308 U.S. 488 (1940), should be taxed as ordinary income.

The Court noted that:

> Unlike the typical case of capital ap-

---

* See generally H. Ballantine, *Ballantine on Corporations* 509 (1946); H. Guthmon and H. Dugell, *Corporate Financial Policy,* 90 (3rd ed., 1955), and D. Belkmore, S.J. Ritchie, Jr., *Investment Principles, Practices, Analysis* (3rd ed. 1969).

preciation the earning of discount to maturity is predictable and measurable, and is "essentially a substitute for . . . interest payments which § 22(a) expressly characterize as gross income."

381 U.S. at 57. However, the Court specifically refused to pass on the tax treatment under the 1939 Code of the unearned portion of the original issue discount which, like call premiums, might properly be attributable to fluctuations in the interest rate and market price of obligations. *Ted Bolnick v. Commissioner,* 44 T.C. 245, 252 (1965).

In *Bolnick,* supra, however, the court did pass on the tax treatment under the 1939 Code of unearned OID received on the early redemption of a bond issued at a discount which might properly be attributable to the fluctuation in the interest rate.* The court said it did not believe that the unearned portion of the OID received on redemption served the same function as interest under *Midland Ross,* supra. The court found that it was difficult to say just what the amount representing the unearned portion of discount is paid for, but was confident that it was not intended for the entire amount of the discount to be compensation for the use of money. The court noted that the unearned discount paid on redemption, like call premiums paid on early redemption, could be said to have been paid for the privilege of retiring a bond before maturity. But absent some compelling reason to treat unearned OID as ordinary income, the court found no need to characterize unearned OID specifically because section 1232(a)(1) does characterize it as amounts received in exchange for the bonds, and hence capital gain.   44 T.C. at 256.

We, like the *Bolnick* court, believe that it would be reasonable to say that both unearned OID and call premiums are paid for the privilege of retiring bonds early; and under section 1232(a)(2) call premiums, as well as unearned OID, are not ordinary, but capital gain income. Unearned OID and call premiums usually are only paid if the bonds

are redeemed prior to maturity, because of a downward fluctuation in the interest rate and thus may be said to be amounts paid for the privilege of redeeming the holder's appreciated asset before maturity; and they both do not accrue over time in a "predictable and measurable fashion" as, according to the *Midland Ross* Court, interest does, but rather diminishes over time and is not paid at all if the bonds remain outstanding. See Proposed Modification of Rev. Rul. 72-587 (Republication of G.C.M. 21890), G.C.M. 38171, I-4693 (Nov. 16, 1979). We reemphasize, however, that because section 1232(a)(2) treats the amounts in excess of earned OID received on exchange or retirement of a bond as capital gains income, call premiums, like unearned OID, need not be characterized. Section 1232(a)(2) simply requires both OID and call premiums to be treated as capital gains income.

In G.C.M. 21890, 1940-1 C.B. 85 and Rev. Rul. 72-587, 1972-2 C.B. 74, which superseded G.C.M. 21890, the Service concluded that call premiums are not interest because they are paid for the privilege of redeeming the bonds before maturity rather than for the use of borrowed money. Similarly, in *District Bond Co. v. Commissioner,* 1 T.C. 837 (1943), the Tax Court held that six months "advance" interest paid to the bondholders upon redemption of the bonds before maturity was a premium rather than additional interest. The court reasoned that such was not compensation for the use of borrowed money, but was in effect a bonus or premium for the premature relinquishment of the obligation in order that the debtor might be relieved of the obligation to pay interest in the future. 1 T.C. at 840. Accord, *Bryant v. Commissioner,* 2 T.C. 789 (1943); *Bolnick,* supra; G.C.M. 24886, *** (Feb. 28, 1946); Rev. Rul. 60-37, 1960-1 C.B. 309.

Rev. Rul. 72-587 was further modified in Rev. Rul. 80-143, 1980-1 C.B. 19, considered in G.C.M. 38171, supra, to hold that the unearned portion of original issue dis-

---

*   The court pointed out that unearned OID is capital gain income under sec. 1232(a)(2) of the 1954 Code, but that provision applies only to bonds or other evidences of indebtedness issued after Dec. 31, 1954, and the bonds in issue were not issued after such time. See S. Rept. No. 1622, to accompany H.R. 8300 (Pub. L. 591), 83d Cong., 2d Sess., p. 436 (1954).

count, received upon redemption of tax-exempt bonds before maturity, is capital gains income. Both Rev. Rul. 80-143 and G.C.M. 38171 reiterate arguments for our conclusion here based on the legislative history of section 1232 and some of the court decisions discussed in this memorandum.

Since the Service and Tax Court initially stated its position with respect to call premiums in 1940 and 1943 respectively, Congress has amended section 1232(a)(2) in which case it was specifically concerned with whether amounts received on redemption should be treated as capital gain or ordinary income. See S. Rept. 7983, supra. This action must be assumed was taken with the knowledge of the construction placed upon that section by the Service and the Tax Court in view of the legislative history, supra, which adopts the Service's and Tax Court's current view of treating call premiums as capital gains income.* Surely, if the legislative body had considered these interpretations of section 1232 by the Service and Tax Court to be erroneous, it would have amended the section to indicate that call premiums should not be characterized as capital gains income, but as ordinary income. The ruling, as well as Tax Court opinions, therefore should be deemed to have Congressional approval. See *Cammarano v. United States,* 358 U.S. 498 (1959); *Helvering v. Winmill,* 305 U.S. 79 (1938); *Sperapani v. Commissioner,* 42 T.C. 308 (1964). Accordingly, we do not find persuasive the two fairly recent Court of Claims opinions, *Pattiz* and *Union Pacific Railroad Co.,* supra, you cite for the proposition that call premiums should be treated like interest.

Moreover, both of these cases you cite for this proposition were concerned with evidences of indebtedness issued before 1954; and thus section 1232(a)(2) did not apply. Consequently, we do not find these cases precedential in interpreting section 1232(a)(2), since as indicated earlier Congress in enacting section 1232(a)(2) specifically intended to clarify what characterization should be given to gain received

on the redemption of bonds when providing that amounts in excess of earned OID received on redemption shall be considered capital gain income. In addition, your argument that call premiums are compensation for use of borrowed money for a shorter period of time and thus should be treated as interest income since section 1232(a)(2) is not an overriding statute converting what otherwise would be ordinary income into capital gains income would equally apply to unearned discount. For example, the Union pacific case that you cite for your proposition states that call premiums, as well as unearned OID, should be treated as amortized discount. Consequently, we find your theory of carving out the call premium portion of the gain in excess of earned OID received on the redemption of a bond issued at a discount and treating such portion as interest income somewhat inconsistent when your argument equally applies to unearned OID which you do not carve out as ordinary income. See Rev. Rul. 80-143, supra.

We recognize, that we have previously questioned the correctness of treating call premiums as capital gain income in view of the fact that penalties paid to life insurance companies for prepayment of mortgages are considered to be interest income under section 804. See G.C.M. 37670, *** I-118-78 (Sept. 8, 1978). However, as indicated in G.C.M. 38171, supra, after further consideration of this issue we believe that:

It may be reasonably argued that section 1232(a)(1) requires that call premiums on obligations falling within the scope of that section be treated as capital gain whether or not they are economically indistinguishable from interest.

Section 804(b)(1) provides that the gross investment income of a life insurance company includes amounts received in termination of a mortgage. See Treas. Reg. § 1.804-3. Section 201(c)(1) of the 1939 Code provided only that the gross income of a life insurance company included interest, dividends, and rents. However, even under the provisions of the 1939 Code courts have held

---

* See 1 Mertens, Law of Federal Income Taxation, § 3.22 (rev. perm. ed. 1981).

that prepayment penalties are gross income to life insurance companies since they fall within the definition of interest. See *General American Life Insurance Company v. Commissioner*, 25 T.C. 1265 (1956), *acq.* 1956-1 C.B. 5; *Equitable Life Assurance Society of the United States v. United States*, 181 F. Supp. 241 (Ct. Cl. 1960), *cert. denied*, 364 U.S. 829; *Prudential Insurance Company of America v. United States*, 319 F.2d 161 (Ct. Cl. 1963); G.C.M. 34767, *Prudential Ins. Co. of America*, I-3901 (Feb. 7, 1971).

Presumably the prepayment of a mortgage and accompanying cancellation of the mortgage bond may fall within the literal language of section 1232(a)(1) assuming the other requirements of that section are met. See Rev. Rul. 73-141, 1973-1 C.B. 331; G.C.M. 34767. Since call premiums and prepayment penalties serve the same economic function it could be argued that the cases cited above are inconsistent with the position that call premiums must be treated as capital gain under 1232(a)(1). However, one possible explanation of the holdings in these cases is that where both sections 1232(a)(1) and 804(b) are applicable, section 804(b) as the more specific section controls. See 2A Sutherland Statutory Construction § 51.05 (4th ed. 1973).

G.C.M. 38171 at 9.

We note that Rev. Rul. 57-198, 1957-1 C.B. 94, holds that penalty payments for the privilege of prepaying a mortgage which are substantially similar to call premiums are deductible as interest under the provisions of section 163. See also, *Union Pacific*, supra, and *12701 Shaker Boulevard Co. v. Commissioner*, 36 T.C. 255 (1961), *aff'd*, 312 F.2d 749 (6th Cir. 1963). However, we do not find that this possible inconsistency with our characterization of call premiums as capital gains income under section 1232(a)(2) necessitates a change in our position. Unearned OID which is treated under section 1232(a)(2) as capital gain income on the early redemption of a bond is also deductible as interest under section 163. In

fact, the regulations under section 163 imply that both unearned OID and call premiums are deductible as interest. See Treas. Reg. § 1.163-3(a)(1) and (c)(1), and § 1.163-4(c). We find the fact that corporations deduct unearned OID and call premiums as interest under section 163 while bondholders receive capital gain income on such amounts under section 1232(a)(2) merely illustrative of the fact that Congress in enacting section 1232(a)(2) intended for the amount in excess of earned OID received on the early redemption of a bond to be treated as capital gain income whatever the amount's true characterization may be.

* * *

G.C.M. 39543
August 4, 1986

* * *

ISSUE

Is a call premium received by a holder on the early redemption of a debt instrument, subject to IRC 1271, interest income or capital gain?

CONCLUSION

A call premium received by a holder on the early redemption of a debt instrument subject to IRC 1271 is capital gain income. In ***** GCM 39309, I-113-83 (May 31, 1984), we concluded that a call premium was capital gain under former section 1232(a)(2). We have reconsidered that result in view of the repeal of section 1232 and its functional replacement by section 1271 in the Tax Reform Act of 1984. In our opinion, the result of GCM 39309 remains correct under present law even though current section 1271 does not explicitly provide, as did its predecessor, former section 1232, that amounts in excess of earned original issue discount (OID) received on redemption of a bond or other evidence of indebtedness shall be considered gain from the sale or exchange of a capital asset.

We agree with you that Congress did not specifically intend the elimination of that statutory language to change the holder's treatment of call premiums. Furthermore, in our opinion, the background of former section 1232 and the judicial and administrative interpretations of that statute, as well as the legislative history of the new OID and market discount provisions (sections 1271-78), indicate the holder can continue to treat a call premium as capital gain income.

FACTS

In *** GCM 39309, I-113-83 (May 31, 1984), this office concluded that under former section 1232, a call premium received by a holder on the early redemption of a bond or debenture should be treated as capital gain income. In doing so, we found that Congress specifically intended that result in enacting section 1232(a)(2). By enactment of the Tax Reform Act of 1984, Congress replaced section 1232 with newly enacted section 1271, whose structure is dissimilar. Section 1271 does not explicitly provide, as did former section 1232(a), that amounts in excess of earned original issue discount received on redemption of a debt instrument shall be considered gain from the sale or exchange of a capital asset. The Joint Committee on Taxation has asked whether the result of GCM 39309 remains correct after this change.

ANALYSIS

Section 1271(a)(1) of the Code provides that amounts received by the holder on retirement of any debt instrument shall be considered as amounts received in exchange therefor.*•

Section 1271(a)(2)(A) provides that generally, if at the time of original issue there was an intention to call a debt instrument before maturity, any gain realized on the sale or exchange thereof which does not exceed an amount equal to—

(i) the original issue discount, reduced by

(ii) the portion of original issue discount previously includible in the gross income of any holder (without regard to subsection (a)(6) or (b)(4) of section 1272 (or the corresponding provision of prior law)),

shall be treated as ordinary income.

Former section 1232(a)(2), as enacted in 1954, provided that gain in excess of earned original issue discount received by a holder on the redemption of bonds or other evidences of indebtedness is considered gain from the sale or exchange of a capital asset. In GCM 39309, we determined that the original Congressional intent in enacting this provision was that call premiums as well as unearned OID, be considered gain from the sale or exchange of a capital asset. Id. at 4, 7. Our determination relied on the legislative histories of the 1958 and 1969 amendments to section 1232(a) as confirming this characterization of Congressional intent. Id. at 4-6. Because there had been no change in the requirement of capital gain treatment subsequent to 1954, we concluded that amounts received as call premiums were capital gains. Id. at 10-11.

You indicate that the omission in section 1271 of an express provision that gain in excess of earned original issue discount received on redemption of a debt instrument shall be considered gain from the sale or exchange of a capital asset does not mean that call premiums should now be treated as interest income. You suggest that the omission can be explained by the simultaneous enactment of the market discount rules of section 1276(a)(1), with that of the new OID rules. Had the specific provision for capital gain treatment been retained, it would have conflicted with the ordinary income treatment of market discount required by new section 1276. You indicate that the omission was not intended to change the treatment on redemption of a call premium. You further indicate that absent a specific Congressional intent to alter the administrative and judicial treatment of call premiums by enactment of the Tax Reform Act of 1984, section 1271 (a)(1) requires their treatment as capital gain income.

The legislative history of the new OID and market discount rules (sections 1271-78 of the Code) accords with your explanation

---

* Section 1271(b)(1) excepts from its coverage any obligation issued by a natural person. Section 1271(b)(2) generally excepts any obligation issued before July 2, 1982, by an issuer which is not a corporation and is not a government or political subdivision thereof.

of the omission in section 1271 of a provision that gain in excess of earned OID be considered gain from the sale or exchange of a capital asset. It indicates that a major impetus for including provisions relating to bonds and other debt instruments in the Tax Reform Act of 1984 was the tax reform component of the President's 1985 budget. *See* 130 Cong. Rec. H2597 (daily ed. Apr. 11, 1984) (statement of Rep. Conable).* We have found no evidence that in its budget proposals, the Administration recommended a change in the treatment of call premiums received on the early redemption of debt instruments. The sole Administration proposal reflected in sections 1271-78 was the taxation at the time of sale or exchange of bonds and other debt instruments of accrued market discount. *See* Staff of the Joint Committee on Taxation, Summary of Administration's Revenue Proposals in the Fiscal Year 1985 Budget Proposals 26 (Comm. Print 1984).

The language of section 1271(a) was derived from HR 4170 as passed by the House of Representatives. *See* HR Rep. No. 98-861, 98th Cong., 2d Sess. 804 (1984) (conference report). In the Ways and Means Committee Report on HR 4170, section 1271's immediate predecessor, former section 1232, was identified as an obstacle to the treatment of market discount as ordinary income. It was observed that under the language of section 1232, capital gain treatment was accorded to the appreciation in value attributable to market discount on an obligation held for more than one year. *See* HR Rep. No. 432, pt. 2, 98th Cong., 2d Sess. 1170 (1984); *see also* S. Rep. No.

169, vol. 1, 98th Cong., 2d Sess. 155 (1984).

Nevertheless, when the market discount rules were added to HR 4170 in the House, the accompanying OID provisions included the capital gain requirement. Proposed section 1276(a)(1), contained in section 41 of HR 4170 as reported by the Committee on Ways and Means on March 5, 1984, provided for the ordinary income treatment of gain realized on the disposition of any market discount bond, to the extent of accrued market discount. *See* 130 Cong. Rec. H2629, H2638 (daily ed. Apr. 11, 1984). The version of section 1271(a) then contained in HR 4170 included an explicit provision for the treatment of amounts received on the sale, exchange, or retirement of a debt instrument as capital gain with an exception for unearned OID if there was an intent at the time of original issue to call the debt instrument before maturity.**

Deletion of this explicit requirement for capital gain treatment on the redemption of a debt instrument was recommended as part of a comprehensive amendment to the reported bill offered on the floor of the House on April 11, 1984, by the Committee on Ways and Means. The amendment was offered as a purely technical one and of no substantive effect.*** 130 Cong. Rec. H 2740 (daily ed. Apr. 11, 1984). The proposed alternative language, identical to current section 1271(a)(2)(A) of the Code, *see* 130 Cong. Rec. H2734-35 (daily ed. Apr. 11, 1984), was agreed to by the House. *Id.* at H2740.

We would conclude on the basis of this sequence of events that in deleting the lan-

---

* No comparable provisions were included in a version of the bill underlying the Tax Reform Act of 1984, HR 4170, reported on October 21, 1983. *See* HR Rep. No. 432, pt. 2, 98th Cong., 2d Sess. 872-73 (1983).

** Proposed section 1271(a)(2)(A)(i) provided that on the sale or exchange of debt instruments held by the taxpayer more than one year, any gain realized shall generally be considered gain from the sale or exchange of a capital asset held for more than one year. *See* 130 Cong. Rec. H2629, H2635 (daily ed. Apr. 11, 1984). It further provided for the treatment of amounts received on retirement of a debt instrument as amounts received in exchange therefor. *Id.* at H2635. (HR 4170 as reported by the Committee on Ways and Means on March 5, 1984 is reprinted in HR Rep. No. 432, pt. 2. 98th Cong., 2d Sess. (supplemental report) (1984).)

***The Chairman of the Committee on Ways and Means emphasized that "there is no substantive effect to the amendment. Rather, the amendment perfects the bill in order to insure that the committee's intent, the explanation in the committee report and the actual statutory language are consistent. It also contains corrections of printing errors, miscites, language usage, cross-references and similar clarification." 130 Cong. Rec. H2740 (daily ed. Apr. 11, 1984).

guage relating to capital gain treatment from proposed section 1271(a), the House acted to conform proposed section 1271 with proposed section 1276, and in doing so did not affirmatively intend to change the income tax treatment of call premiums by a holder. Furthermore, the recognition in the Senate report on HR 4170 of the effect of the language of former section 1232 on the income tax treatment of market discount, *see* S. Rep. No. 169, vol. 1, 98th Cong., 2d Sess. 155 (1984), and the lack in the report of any expressed intent to change the treatment of call premiums, convinces us that the Congress as a whole did not affirmatively intend to change the income tax treatment of call premiums by a holder of a debt instrument in including section 41 in the Tax Reform Act of 1984.

On the basis of this evident lack of affirmative intent to change the income tax treatment of call premiums, you would further conclude that section 1271(a)(1) requires that a call premium be considered as received in exchange for the bond or other debt instrument retired, and be treated as capital gain income. We agree with the result of capital gain treatment for call premiums under section 1271, for the following reasons.

Section 1271(a)(1) provides that amounts received by the holder on retirement of any debt instrument shall be considered as amounts received in exchange therefor. The courts have construed similar language in the 1939 Code predecessor of former section 1232 as permitting the division of amounts received into separate increments representing interest income and capital gain. *See,* e.g., *United States v. Midland-Ross Corp.,* 381 US 54, 65-66 (1954). Fur-

thermore, under section 1271(a)(1), the retirement of a debt instrument is treated as a sale or exchange without regard to whether the instrument is a capital asset. *See* HR Rep. No. 861, 98th Cong., 2d Sess. 804-05 (1984). Therefore, we would not construe the bare language of section 1271(a)(1) as mandating the capital gain treatment of call premiums.

However, we believe that section 1271 (a)(1), read in the context of the original issue discount and market discount provisions and in light of the consistent treatment of call premiums as capital gain income under the 1954 Code, requires that call premiums should be treated as capital gain income. In this connection, we note that in the new original issue discount and market discount provisions, Congress fixed the stated redemption price at maturity as the ceiling for both original issue discount and market discount. See section 1273(a)(2); 1278(a)(2). Stated redemption price at maturity was also the ceiling on original issue discount under former section 1232(b). A call premium is an amount in addition to the stated redemption price at maturity.* Cf. S. Rep. No. 1622, 83d Cong., 2d Sess. 435 (1954) (stated redemption price, under former section 1232, does not include call premiums); accord HR Rep. No. 1337, 83d Cong., 2d Sess. A277 (1954).

We also believe that the fact of express statutory provision for the treatment of earned original issue discount and market discount as ordinary income, coupled with the historical treatment of call premiums as capital gain income, supports the treatment of call premiums as capital gain under section 1271(a)(1).** This rationale is similar to the one relied on by the Tax Court when

---

* By definition, a call premium is an amount received in excess of face value. *See* D M. Stigum, *The Money Market* 55 (rev. ed. 1980). For example, the holder described in GCM 39309 purchased a bond without OID and received an amount in excess of the face amount on early redemption. Had the bond been an OID bond, and the holder received on early call an amount in excess of earned OID, but not in excess of the face amount of the bond, there would have been no call premium in issue, but instead only unearned OID. *See* Rev. Rul. 80-143, 1980-1 CB 19. Because OID, but not a call premium, was specifically referred to in former section 1232, the analysis of their proper tax treatment is not identical.

** Although the scope of sections 1271-78 is broad, the provisions may contain gaps required to be filled by common law concepts of "interest," as enunciated in *Midland Ross* and similar cases. For example, the cited sections do not appear to deal adequately with bankers' acceptances in payment of goods when the draft is subsequently accepted by a bank and then sold to an investor at a discount. If the investor holds the banker's acceptance until maturity, the discount arguably would be interest income.

it held that only the earned portion of OID on corporate debentures redeemed before maturity was interest income, and the remainder was capital gain. *See Bolnick v. Commissioner,* 44 T.C. 245 (1965), *acq. on this issue,* 1980 C.B. 1, *withdrawing nonacq.,* 1967-1 C.B. 3. Under former section 1232 (a)(2), as under current section 1271(a)(2), unearned original issue discount was taxable as ordinary income if there was an intent to redeem before maturity. The *Bolnick* court reasoned that former section 1232(a)(2) implied that unearned original issue discount was not taxable as ordinary income, but as capital gain. Although section 1232(a)(2) could not have applied to the bonds considered in the case because of their date of issue, the court viewed section 1232(a)(2) as evidence of a Congressional recognition about what amounts should be treated as ordinary income on the retirement of a debt instrument. *Bolnick* at 256. In *Proposed Modification of Rev. Rul. 72-587 (Republication of G.C.M. 21890),* G.C.M. 38171, I-4693 (Nov. 16, 1979), we adopted the *Bolnick* court's rationale to conclude that the unearned portion of OID received upon redemption of tax exempt bonds before maturity is capital gain not excludable from the gross income of the bondholder under section 103. This position was published as Rev. Rul. 80-143, 1980-1 C.B. 19.

Current section 1271(a)(2) requires ordinary income treatment of unearned original issue discount on the redemption of a debt instrument subject to section 1271 if there was an intention to call the debt instrument before maturity. This similarly suggests that a holder is not required to treat unearned original issue discount as ordinary income in the absence of that intent. In G.C.M. 38171, we remarked on the economic similarity between call premiums and unearned OID. *Id.* at 7-8. This similarity between unearned OID and call premiums, and the capital gain treatment generally accorded unearned original issue discount, indicates that our conclusion is not at odds with legislative intent.

The lack of an affirmative provision in section 1271 that call premiums be treated as interest income, given their treatment under section 1232 as capital gain, likewise suggests that Congress did not intend to change their treatment by a holder. Therefore, absent an intention at original issue to call a debt instrument before maturity, we conclude that a call premium received on the early retirement of a debt instrument subject to section 1271 should receive capital gain treatment.

In reaching this conclusion, we acknowledge that the contrary arguments raised in G.C.M. 38171 and G.C.M. 39309 remain applicable. For example, Rev. Rul. 57-198, 1957-1 C.B. 94, holds that penalty payments made on prepayment of a mortgage, which are similar to call premiums, are deductible as interest under section 163. We also recognize that the result in G.C.M. 39309 that we here reaffirm relied expressly on the language that was deleted from the Code by the 1984 changes. However, we think it a sufficient rejoinder to the contrary arguments to state that the result in this case is not based on an original determination by us that a call premium is not compensation for the use of money, and thus not interest. Instead, it turns on our judgment, made in light of the historical income tax treatment of call premiums, about the Congressional intent evidenced by the legislative history of the Tax Reform Act of 1984 and expressed in the current statutory scheme of sections 1271–78.

* * *

G.C.M. 39551
June 30, 1986

* * *

ISSUE

Is the loss purportedly suffered by taxpayer with respect to the sale of Government National Mortgage Association mortgage-backed certificates ("GNMA certificates") described below allowable?

CONCLUSION

The taxpayer's loss is disallowed by IRC § 1091 because the taxpayer acquired substantially similar GNMA certificates within

30 days of selling GNMA certificates at a loss. In addition, because the transactions in question were entered into by the taxpayer solely to generate a tax loss, and possessed no business or economic utility apart from anticipated tax consequences, the deduction is not allowed under section 165(a).

FACTS

The taxpayer is a cooperative bank. In the fiscal year ending April 30, 1982, the taxpayer owned an 8 percent GNMA certificate (No. 10286), which had a cost basis of $186,952, and an 8.5 percent GNMA certificate (No. 05531), which had a cost basis of $127,498. On March 26, the taxpayer bought a second 8 percent GNMA certificate (No. 19239) for $122,085. On April 1, 1982, the taxpayer bought a second 8.5 percent GNMA certificate (No. 08077) for $85,718 and sold the first 8 percent GNMA certificate (No. 10286) for $116,845. On April 6, 1982, the taxpayer sold the first 8.5 percent GNMA certificate for $82,555. For the tax year ending April 30, 1982, the taxpayer claimed an ordinary loss from the sale of securities of $115,050, which resulted from the sales of GNMA certificates Nos. 10286 and 05631. For financial accounting purposes, taxpayer treated the purchases and subsequent sales of GNMA certificates as wash sales.

The District Director disallowed the claimed loss, arguing that taken as a whole the transactions were a sham and entered into solely for their tax benefits. The District Director concluded that taxpayer had not realized a loss within the meaning of Treas. Reg. 1.1001-1(a) because the taxpayer had exchanged mortgage pools that did not differ materially either in kind or extent. In addition, the District Director disallowed the loss under section 165 because taxpayer's true economic position was unchanged since its investment portfolio was basically the same after April 6, 1982 as it had been before March 26, 1982.

BACKGROUND

This case is the latest variation of a transaction that has been dubbed a mortgage swap. The purpose of a mortgage swap is to create a tax loss that can be used to reduce a savings and loan association's current taxable income to zero and produce a loss carryback that will generate a refund for prior taxable years. The rapid rise in the use of mortgage swaps can be traced to the soaring interest rates of the late seventies and the early eighties.

As interest rates soared, many savings and loans found themselves in precarious financial condition. Although mortgages are essentially a savings and loan association's inventory, savings and loan associations have traditionally not been permitted to write down devalued loans for tax purposes because they have been presumed to hold such loans, not for sale in the ordinary course of business, but for long term investment. When a loan is underwater, the interest income paid to the association with respect to that loan represents a losing investment. If the savings and loan associations could get a higher rate of return with respect to that money, the association would have more money to invest at a higher rate of return.

Although the savings and loans were eager to gain capital through refunds generated by carried back losses, most of them could not afford to recognize the losses for regulatory or financial purposes. The Federal Home Loan Bank Board (FHLBB), the agency that regulates federally insured savings and loan associations, therefore decided to assist the troubled savings and loan associations by providing that, in certain limited circumstances, an exchange of devalued mortgages need not be treated as a loss for regulatory accounting purposes (RAP).

FHLBB-R-Memo 49 announced: "a loss resulting from a difference between market value and book value in connection with reciprocal sales of substantially identical mortgage loans need not be recorded."

Memorandum R-49 set forth ten criteria that had to be met before the exchanged mortgages would be considered substantially identical. Those criteria were intended to maintain the savings and loan's position with respect to three types of risks in a loan portfolio. Those risks relate to credit (collectibility), rate (future earnings potential), and repayment (extent of principal repayments and prepayments). The FHLBB believed that a change in any of those risks would change the economic factors underlying a savings and loan's loan portfolio and would, therefore, require that the resulting gain or loss be recorded.

Transactions which met the criteria of R-49 were also treated as nonrecognition events under generally accepted accounting principles (GAAP). Accounting principles Board Opinion No. 29, para. 21 provides that no gain or loss will be recognized if a nonmonetary exchange does not culminate an earnings process. An example of a nonmonetary exchange that does not culminate an earnings process is "an exchange of a productive asset not held for sale in the ordinary course of business for a similar productive asset or an equivalent interest in the same or a similar productive asset." The continuation of the earning process necessary to justify nonrecognition is not merely a continuation of the income stream, but also a lack of interruption of the level and nature of the risks associated with the assets. Opinion No. 29 appears to be the accounting profession's equivalent of the section 1001 requirement that a realization be an exchange of assets materially different in kind and extent.

The original mortgage swap case considered by the Service was easily attacked as a sham transaction. That case involved a swap of mortgage pools by three savings and loan associations located in the same locality. The interest rates of the pooled mortgages were identical, as was nearly everything else about the mortgages. The pooled mortgages were exchanged simultaneously. The Service examined this transaction in Rev. Rul. 81-204, 1981-2 C.B. 157, considered in *** G.C.M. 38838, I-49-81 (April 19, 1982). The ruling concluded that the pooled mortgages were, in the hands of the savings and loan associations, "mass, indivisible assets that averaged out the unique characteristics and risks inherent in each constituent mortgage." Since the mortgages had the same contract interest rates and the same stated terms to maturity, the ruling concluded that the exchanged pools did not differ materially either in kind or in extent and

therefore that transaction was not a realization event within the meaning of section 1001 and the regulations thereunder. In addition, the ruling concluded that the exchange of mortgage pools was a sham that had no significant economic or business purpose or utility apart from its anticipated tax consequences, and hence could not result in a bona fide loss for which a deduction was allowable under section 165(a).

In the next generation of cases, the savings and loan associations sought to overcome the Service's 1001 argument by "buying" and "selling" the mortgage pools rather than exchanging them. The associations' theory was that if cash were received for a mortgage pool, the Service could not argue that the transactions were exchanges, but rather would be compelled to treat them as dispositions which resulted in the recognition of loss.

A transaction in which mortgage pools were purportedly "bought" and "sold" was considered in Rev. Rul. 85-125, 1985-32 I.R.B. 10, considered in *** G.C.M. 39149, I-166-82 (March 1, 1984). In that ruling, X, Y and Z, three unrelated savings and loan associations, entered into a series of concurrent transactions in which each party "sold" and "purchased," on a round-robin basis, mortgage pools among themselves. The revenue ruling discounts the purported purchases and sales of the mortgage pools and again refuses to recognize the losses. In analyzing the proposed ruling that was eventually published as Rev. Rul. 85-125, G.C.M. 39149 states:

> In the instant case, the transfers do not have independent adequacy; each part of the transaction is dependent on every other part. In substance, the round-robin transfer of participation interests in packages of mortgages for cash and other mortgages constitutes one integrated transaction in which each bank ends up with the same amount of cash and essentially the same kind of property with which it started. In each bank's case, the transfer is so hedged, in terms of economic reality, that it cannot be considered to be the closing out of a losing venture, whether or not there is a business purpose for the transaction. Hence, we do not believe that the dispositions here can be considered to be

sales; they are exchanges of property for other property not materially different either in kind or extent and, therefore, are subject to Rev. Rul. 81-204, both as to the nature of the disposition as well as to the lack of economic purpose or utility apart from the tax consequences. [G.C.M. 39149 at pp. 5-6.]

In many ways, the early cases addressed in the two revenue rulings are much easier to analyze than the later cases, because banking regulations then in effect required the mortgages swapped be nearly identical in order to qualify for nonrecognition under regulatory accounting principles. In the intervening period two things have happened which make the later generation of mortgage swap cases more difficult to deal with.

First, in 1981, the FHLBB revised their regulations to permit savings and loan associations to amortize the gains or losses with respect to the sale or other disposition of mortgages. See 12 C.F.R. 563c.14. This new regulation does not require that the exchanged mortgages be substantially identical. As a result, the savings and loan associations have attempted to structure their transactions so that the exchanged pools will be considered substantially different in extent or kind so that they will be able to claim a loss for tax purposes.

Second, the secondary market in mortgages and mortgage backed securities has become much more organized so that the parties no longer need to arrange swaps among themselves. Broker-dealers now provide a relatively formal market in which pools of mortgages as well as mortgage backed securities can be bought and sold much the way stock and bonds are sold. Accordingly, the buyer and the seller of a mortgage pool may not know of each other's existence, let alone have arranged the exchange of their mortgage backed certificates.

Although this case arose under the new FHLBB regulations, it is still like the early cases in that taxpayer recorded no loss for financial or regulatory purposes. This nonrecognition treatment is possible because since the revision of the FHLBB regulations relating to the sale or exchanges of mortgages, the FHLBB has also announced that for regulatory purposes, savings and loan associations may use either RAP or GAAP accounting, so long as they use the elected method of accounting consistently. The FHLBB also permits savings and loan associations to change their election annually. Such flexibility is in line with the FHLBB's desire to keep the savings and loan associations afloat through any means possible.

Accordingly, savings and loan associations now have the option of amortizing losses under RAP or simply not recognizing them, if the exchanged assets are sufficiently similar, under GAAP. The financial health of the particular savings and loan presumably determines which method of accounting the savings and loan takes. If the savings and loan can afford to amortize the loss, it will presumably choose RAP accounting, and since the new RAP rules do not require near identity of assets, the assets sold or exchanged will be as different as taxpayer can make them. If the savings and loan cannot afford to recognize the loss, even amortized over the life of the mortgages, it will presumably seek to fall into the nonrecognition provision for financial accounting purposes where substantial identity of assets is still required.

ANALYSIS

In Rev. Rul. 81-204 and Rev. Rul. 85-125, purported losses created by the early mortgage swap transactions were disallowed under section 1001. In the first ruling, identical pools of mortgages were exchanged. In the second ruling, cash changed hands, but the parties had all agreed before the transaction took place to exchange substantially identical mortgages. In both cases the transactions were viewed by the Service as exchanges of mortgage pools that did not differ materially either in kind or in extent within the meaning of Treas. Reg. § 1.1001-1(a), and hence did not result in the realization of gain or loss under section 1001(a).

The instant case represents a departure from these patterns in that participation certificates were purchased and sold through a broker-dealer. Taxpayer's disposition of two GNMA certificates and acquisition of substantially identical certificates through a broker-dealer is similar to an investor's sale and repurchase of substantially identical stock in a "wash-sale." Service personnel involved in this case have suggested that the section 1001 argument relied upon in the earlier rulings should also be applied in this case. We believe it is unnecessary to consider the application of the section 1001 argument to this case, however, because we believe that a more appropriate theory for disallowing the taxpayer's loss on the taxpayer's sale of GNMA certificates is that this sale is a "wash sale" subject to the provisions of section 1091.

Section 1091 disallows a loss sustained from the sale or other disposition of shares of stock or other securities when it appears that, within a period beginning thirty days before the date of such sale and ending thirty days after the date of such sale, the taxpayer has acquired substantially identical stock or securities.

Neither section 1091 nor the regulations thereunder define the term "securities". Other sections of the Code define the terms "security" or "securities" but those definitions are not identical.

Section 165(g)(2) defines the term "security" for purposes of section 165(g), which deals with losses from worthless securities, as (A) a share of stock in a corporation, (B) a right to subscribe for, or to receive, a share of stock in a corporation, or (C) a bond, debenture, note or certificate or other evidence of indebtedness, issued by a corporation or by a government or political subdivision thereof, with interest coupons or in registered form.

Section 593(d)(1)(A), which defines "qualifying real property loans" for purposes of calculating the bad debt reserves for mutual savings banks, excludes from that definition any loan evidenced by a security as defined in section 165(g)(2)(C). A qualifying real property loan is generally defined as any loan secured by an interest in improved real property or secured by an interest in real property which is to be improved out of the proceeds of the loan.

The issue of whether a certificate of beneficial interest in a mortgage pool secured by the mortgages in the pool repre-

sents a "qualifying real property loan" for purposes of section 593(b) was considered in *** G.C.M. 35893, I-5012 (July 3, 1984). That G.C.M. concluded that since the certificate represented no more than a proportionate interest in the mortgages in the pool and since the mortgages in the pools qualified as qualifying real property loans, the certificate should be treated as a qualifying real property loan as well [G.C.M. 35893 at page 7]. Although G.C.M. 35893 does not specifically address the question, it would seem to follow that neither the underlying mortgage nor a participation certificate secured by a pool of mortgages would qualify as a security within the meaning of section 165(g)(2).

Section 1236(c), which relates to transactions by dealers in securities, is more expansive. It defines the term security to mean any share in the stock of a corporation, certificate of stock or interest in any corporation, note, bond, debenture, or evidence of indebtedness, or any evidence of an interest in or right to subscribe to or purchase any of the foregoing. This definition is also used in section 1083(f) for purposes of certain exchanges or distributions of stock or securities in obedience of orders of the Securities and Exchange Commission.

Section 402(a)(3) defines "securities" for purposes of section 402(a), which deals with the taxability of a beneficiary of an employees' trust, to mean only shares of stock and bonds or debentures issued by a corporation with interest coupons or in registered form.

Section 6323(h)(4) defines the term "security" for purposes of section 6323 and 6324, which deal with the validity of certain tax liens, to mean any bond, debenture, note or certificate, or evidence of indebtedness, issued by a corporation or a government or a political subdivision thereof, with interest coupons or in registered form, share of stock, voting trust certificate, or any certificate of interest or participation in, certificate of deposit or receipt for, temporary or interim certificate for, or warrant or right to subscribe to or purchase, any of the foregoing, negotiable instrument, or money.

When the issue of whether an instrument

should be deemed to be a security for purposes of section 1091 has been considered previously, this division has concluded that other definitions of "security" used in the Code should not be relied upon but rather that general Congressional intent that can be gleaned from the Code generally and section 1091 in particular should determine whether an instrument is a security within the meaning of section 1091.* See Treasury Bill Future Buy Contracts, G.C.M. 38369, I-100-79 (May 9, 1980) at page 4. That G.C.M. states that the purpose of the wash sale provision is to prevent tax manipulation by a taxpayer who attempts to recognize a loss on the sale of "securities" while maintaining an identical or nearly identical investment position. See J. Krane, Losses from Wash Sales of Stock or Securities, 4 J. Corp. Tax 226 (1978).

In general, the term "security" has been expansively defined for purposes of section 1091. The major exception to an expansive definition has been the exclusion of traditional commodity futures which have been determined by the Service not to be securities within the meaning of section 1091 or any other Code provision largely because they have always been separately dealt with whenever Congress has intended to include them. See *** G.C.M. 34630, I-4245 (Oct. 4, 1971), published as Rev. Rul. 71-568, 1971-2 C.B. 312. Thus the exclusion of traditional commodity futures has no bearing on the issue of whether GNMA certificates should be treated as securities since GNMA certificates were not in existence when the wash sale provisions were first adopted and they have not been a separately treated category in other Code sections.

The only argument raised by the taxpayer in the subject case against treating participation certificates as securities for purposes of section 1091 is the position,

noted above, that the certificates are qualifying real property loans for purposes of mutual savings bank reserves and therefore not securities for purposes of the worthless securities provisions of section 165(g). We do not believe, however, that the classification of participation certificates for purposes of section 165(g) should have any bearing on whether those certificates are securities for purposes of the wash sale rules. Logically any loan that is a qualifying loan for purposes of calculating a savings and loan association's reserves should not also be treated as a security for which a deduction for worthlessness should be allowed. By including the loan in the calculation of reserves, the potential worthlessness of the loan has been taken into account. Allowance of a deduction when the loan actually goes bad would in effect allow a double deduction.

The policy considerations of treating participation certificates as securities for purposes of the wash sale provisions are entirely different. Participation certificates are readily tradable assets with a readily ascertainable fair market value. Although GNMA certificates are not yet traded on an established securities market, trading in participation certificates secured by mortgages is highly organized, and prices are quoted daily.

The purpose of the wash sale provisions is to prevent taxpayers from claiming tax losses on artificial transactions, that is, claiming a tax loss while they maintained essentially the same economic position which they had had before they entered into the transaction. Given the essential fungibility of participation certificates, allowing a loss when one participation certificate is traded for a substantially identical certificate would permit taxpayers to claim such artificial losses. If GNMA certificates had been

---

*   This position has arguably been obsoleted by Temp. Reg. 1.1092(b)-5T(q) which defines "securities" for purposes of section 1092 by referencing to the definition of securities in section 1236(c). Section 1092 provides rules for accounting for gains and losses with respect to straddles. Those rules often must operate in tandem with the wash-sale rules. We believe that the definition of securities for section 1092 should be identical to the definition of securities in section 1091. Accordingly, we view Temp. Reg. 1.1092(b)-5T(g) as defining the term "securities" in section 1091 with reference to the definition of "securities" in section 1236(c). We note that this change would not affect the outcome of this case since GNMA certificates would also be considered "securities" within the 1236 definition.

in existence when Congress adopted the wash sale rules, our opinion might be otherwise. But given the relative newness of participation certificates and the relative infancy of the secondary mortgage markets, we cannot say that Congress would have intended to exclude participation certificates from the scope of the wash sale provisions.

The argument can also be raised that GNMA participation certificates cannot be considered securities because the Service has concluded that participation certificates are no more than an instrument representing a beneficial interest in the underlying mortgages and that the underlying mortgages cannot be considered securities. See Rev. Rul. 70-544, 1970-2 C.B. 6; Rev. Rul. 70-545, 1970-2 C.B. 7, both considered in ***, G.C.M. 34347, I-3821 (September 14, 1970). We believe it unnecessary to consider whether the underlying mortgages could be considered securities when marketed in a pool, because we believe that the existence of a federal guarantee makes participation certificates more marketable instruments than the underlying mortgages which have no such guarantee. Accordingly, we conclude that GNMA certificates are securities within the meaning of section 1091 even if the underlying mortgages, when pooled, are not.

We also believe that for purposes of section 1091 the GNMA certificates purchased by the taxpayer were "substantially identical" to the GNMA certificates with the same interest rate sold by the taxpayer. Participation certificates represent beneficial interests in pools of mortgages. The individual risks inherent in the individual mortgages which make up the pool are irrelevant to both the buyer and the seller of those beneficial interests. Savings and loan associations deal with large pools of mortgages essentially as interchangeable, fungible assets. The concern in the purchase or sale of a mortgage pool, or of participation certificates secured by a pool or mortgages, is the risk inherent to the pool as a whole, not to the individual mortgages included in the pool. No examination is made of the individual mortgages included in the pool, either by the purchaser or the seller. The as-

sumption is that a certain portion of the mortgages will default or prepay, and the percentage probability, not the actual experience of any one mortgage, is the relevant factor for the savings and loan association. The risks are averaged and the pool as a whole is treated as the investment vehicle. Accordingly, one 8% GNMA certificate is essentially equivalent to an other 8% GNMA certificate with the same maturity date.

Taxpayer has argued that the replacement certificates cannot be considered substantially identical because the geographic locations of the securing property is different, the borrowers are different, the principal amounts of the mortgages are different and the maturity dates of the mortgages are different. We cannot agree. As noted above, taxpayers who exchange mortgage pools have no interest in the underlying assets or the underlying borrowers. Whatever place the uniqueness of real property has in the case of a taxpayer who holds a single mortgage, it has none in the context of mortgage pools which are considered mass undivided assets in the hands of savings and loan associations. What matters to the savings and loan association is that the yield from the newly acquired mortgage pool matches the yield from the relinquished pool. In this case, taxpayer represented that the exchanged certificates were substantially identical for financial and regulatory accounting purposes. Accordingly, we believe that the taxpayer considered certificates bearing the same interest rate as identical, interchangeable assets, and it was a matter of economic indifference to the taxpayer which of those two certificates it held. Therefore, the certificates were substantially identical for purposes of section 1091. See *Hanlin v. Commissioner,* 108 F.2d 429, 430 (3rd Cir. 1939); GCM 38838, at 24, 25.

Since the taxpayer bought the replacement GNMA certificates within seven days of selling substantially identical GNMA certificates, we conclude that the wash sale provisions of section 1091 preclude the taxpayer from recognizing the losses attributable to the sale of the certificates originally held by the taxpayer.

An additional grounds for denying the taxpayer's loss deduction is based upon Treas. Reg. § 1.165-1(b), which provides:

> To be allowable as a deduction under section 165(a), a loss must be evidenced by closed and completed transactions, fixed by identifiable events, and ... actually sustained during the taxable year. Only a bona fide loss is allowable. Substance and not mere form shall govern in determining a deductible loss.

In GCM 38838, supra, we reasoned that because the mortgage pool swap transaction involved in that GCM was entered into by the taxpayer solely to generate a tax loss, and the transaction possessed no business or economic utility apart from its anticipated tax consequences, the transaction lacked substance and the claimed loss was not within the the the intent of section 165(a) and Treas. Reg. § 1.165-1(b). See GCM 38388, at 18-23. The facts of the subject case, like those in GCM 38388 and Rev. Rul. 81-204, indicate that the transactions here did not result in any material change in the taxpayer's economic position, and therefore possessed no economic or business utility apart from their anticipated tax consequences. We have concluded above that the GNMA certificates sold by the taxpayer were substantially identical to those that had been purchased a few days earlier, because it was a matter of economic indifference to the taxpayer whether it owned the GNMA certificates sold or those purchased. It is true that in the course of these transactions, there were brief periods during which there was a temporary increase in the taxpayer's holdings in the certificates. The purchase and sale transactions involved a five day period (March 26 to April 1, 1982) during which the taxpayer owned both 8% GNMA certificates, and a second five day period (April 1 to April 6, 1982) during which the taxpayer owned both 8½% GNMA certificates. It is apparent from the facts, however, that the temporary "doubling up" of the taxpayer certificate holdings was in each case merely an intermediate step in the process by which the taxpayer substituted one GNMA certificate for a different GNMA certificate bearing the same interest rate. The only economic purpose served by the

taxpayer's temporary ownership of two GNMA certificates with the same interest rate was that this enabled the taxpayer to sell the devalued certificate at a loss while nevertheless remaining in the same economic position as before the transaction took place. Accordingly, we do not believe that the taxpayer's temporary increased ownership of GNMA certificates should be viewed as representing any substantive change in the taxpayer ownership position.

In this regard the fact situation here closely parallels that of *Horne v. Commissioner*, 5 TC 250 (1945). In that case the taxpayer, a commodities broker who owned a membership certificate in a commodities exchange bought a second membership certificate then sold the first certificate at a loss a few days later. The taxpayer claimed a loss deduction on the sale of the first certificate. The Tax Court, however, disallowed the deduction, reasoning that no loss had been recognized by the taxpayer because he stood in exactly the same position before the purchase and sale transaction as after. The court stated:

> Petitioner here concedes, as set out in the stipulation, not only that the purchase of the new certificate and the sale of the old one were for the purpose of establishing a tax loss, but also that both of those transactions were component parts of a unified plan to carry out that purpose. It is no aid to the petitioner, of course, that the new certificate was purchased before rather than after or at the same time of the sale of the old one. That was done to assure petitioner uninterrupted membership in the exchange and in the use of the exchange's facilities. The numerical identification of the certificates meant nothing to the petitioner and the temporary ownership of two certificates was of no business advantage to him.

5 TC at 255.

The taxpayer has argued that the fact that it sold GNMA certificates for the purpose of recognizing a tax loss is not reason in itself to disallow the loss, citing *Widener Trust v. Commissioner*, 80 TC 304 (1983), *acq.* 1984-1 C.B. 2. See the taxpayer's memorandum dated August 23, 1983 in protest of the proposed deficiency.

In *Widener Trust*, two trusts that had the

same trustee and income beneficiary exchanged devalued stock in different corporations. The court held that the exchange resulted in the recognition of losses by both trusts, despite its finding that the transaction were solely tax motivated. We believe that the fact situation in Widener Trust is distinguishable from the subject case. Since the shares of stock exchanged by the trust in that case were materially different, each trust was in a different economic position after the exchange from that before. Thus the transfers had a significant economic effect apart from their tax impact. In the subject case, by contrast, the sales transactions of GNMA certificates had no economic or business impact upon the taxpayer that was independent of their tax consequences.

In accordance with the above, we believe the loss deduction on the taxpayers sales of devalued GNMA certificates should be disallowed.

* * *

G.C.M. 39626

April 29, 1987.

* * *

ISSUES

I. Are obligations issued by, or fully guaranteed as to principal and interest by, the Federal National Mortgage Association (FNMA), the Government National Mortgage Association (GNMA), the Student Loan Marketing Association (SLMA), a Federal Home Loan Bank (FHLB), and the Federal Home Loan Mortgage Corporation (FHLMC) "securities" under IRC section 851(b)?*

II. Are they "Government securities" under section 851(b)(4)?

CONCLUSIONS

I. We conclude that notes and bonds issued by FNMA, GNMA, SLMA, a FHLB, and FHLMC, and certain pass-through mortgage-backed certificates** guaranteed as to principal and interest by FNMA, GNMA, and FHLMC (the so-called fully-modified pass-through mortgage-backed FNMA and GNMA certificates*** and FHLMC mortgage participation certificate****) are "securities" under section 851(b).

II. These instruments are also "Government securities" under section 851(b)(4).

FACTS

***** (the Trust) is registered with the Securities and Exchange Commission (the SEC) as an investment company under the Investment Company Act of 1940 (the 1940 Act), 15 USC 80-a-1 et seq. and files its return as a regulated investment company (RIC) as de-

---

* FNMA, GNMA, SLMA, and FHLMC are also referred to as Fannie Mae, Ginnie Mae, Sallie Mae, and Freddie Mac, respectively.

** The mortgage-backed certificate is called such because it is an obligation that is secured by or represents an interest in mortgages which have been assembled in a pool to represent or secure payment of such obligations. Lore, *Securities Law Series: Mortgage-Backed Securities* 3-1 (1985). In the case of pass-through mortgage-backed certificates, "the holders of the certificates receive a 'pass through' of all of the principal and interest paid for mortgages in the pool in accordance with their respective, undivided interests in the pool." *Id.* at 3-6. The sponsor of the pool generally retains only servicing fees. *Id.* at 3-6.

*** A pass-through mortgage-backed FNMA or GNMA certificate represents an undivided interest in a pool of mortgages. The fully-modified pass-through mortgage-backed certificates are to be distinguished from the straight pass-through mortgage-backed certificates in respect of FNMA or GNMA. With respect to the latter class of certificates, the guarantee is that the entity establishing the mortgage pool or trust underlying the certificates could properly perform mortgage servicing. The certificate holders generally are only entitled to interest and principal actually collected or collectible through due dilligence. On the other hand, where the certificates are fully-modified pass-through mortgage-backed FNMA or GNMA certificates, FNMA or GNMA, respectively, itself guarantees that the principal and interest will be paid.

**** The FHLMC mortgage participation certificate represents an undivided interest in groups of residential mortgages acquired by FHLMC from eligible seller/servicers. 1 *Moody's Municipal & Government Manual* 42-43 (1986). Some recently issued FHLMC mortgage participation certificates are described in Rev. Rul. 81-203, 1981-2 C.B. 137.

fined in section 851. The trust provides a pooled investment vehicle for its participants. It invests principally in federally insured or guaranteed mortgages and construction loan certificates, fully-modified pass-through mortgage-backed GNMA certificates, certificates of deposit, and other short-term obligations. *****.

The fund (the Fund) in ***** is a diversified, open-end investment company that is registered under the 1940 Act and that has elected to be treated as a RIC pursuant to subchapter M of the Code. The authorized capital stock of the Fund currently consists of four portfolios. The Fund's ruling request is limited to the portfolio (Portfolio) that is designed to give savings institutions for which this portfolio is an eligible investment* the ability to invest conveniently in investment grade corporate bonds.

The "United States Government securities" in which the Fund intends to invest include obligations issued by, or fully guaranteed as to principal and interest by, the United States, FNMA, GNMA, SLMA, a FHLB, and FHLMC.

ANALYSIS

Section 851(b) provides that a corporation shall not be considered a RIC for any year unless—

. . .

(2) at least 90 percent of its gross income is derived from dividends, interest, payments with respect to securities loans (as defined in section 512(a)(5)), and gains from the sale or other disposition of stock or securities (as defined in section 2(a)(36) of the Investment Company Act of 1940, as amended) or foreign currencies, or other income (including but not limited to gains from options, futures, or forward contracts) derived with respect to its business of investing in such stock, securities, or currencies;

(3) less than 30 percent of its gross income is derived from the sale or other disposition of stock or securities held for less than 3 months; and

(4) at the close of each quarter of the taxable year—

(A) at least 50 percent of the value of its total assets is represented by—

(i) cash and cash items (including receivables), Government securities and securities of other RICs, and

(ii) other securities for purposes of this calculation limited, except and to the extent provided in subsection (e), in respect to any one issuer to an amount not greater in value than 5 percent of the value of the total assets of the taxpayer and to not more than 10 percent of the outstanding voting securities of such issuer, and

(B) not more than 25 percent of the value of its total assets is invested in the securities (other than Government securities or the securities of other RICs) of any one issuer, or of two or more issuers which the taxpayer controls and which are determined, under regulations pre-

---

* Eligible investments for federal savings and loan associations include shares or certificates in any open-end management investment company which is registered with the Securities and Exchange Commission under the 1940 Act and the portfolio of which is restricted by such management company's investment policy, changeable only if authorized by shareholder vote, solely to any such investments as an association by law or regulation may, *without limitation as to percentage of assets,* invest in, sell, redeem, hold, or otherwise deal with. 12 USCA 1464(c)(1)(Q) (West 1980). Without limitation as to percentage of assets, a savings and loan association may invest in investments in several types of obligations *including obligations issued or fully guaranteed as to principal and interest by, FNMA, SLMA, or GNMA or any other agency of the United States.* 12 USCA 1464(c)(1)(F) West 1980). Under the Federal Home Loan Bank board's regulations, the association may also invest in financial futures transactions using financial futures contracts designated by the Commodity Futures Trading Commission and based upon a financial instrument in which the association has authority to invest. 12 CFR 545.136 and 563.17-4(c) (1986). The association may invest in financial options contracts entered into with a primary dealer in government securities, and based upon a financial instrument in which the association has authority to invest, or based upon a financial futures contract. 12 CFR 545.137 and 563.17-(c) (1986).

scribed by the Secretary, to be engaged in the same or similar trades or business or related trades or businesses.

We are considering two cases here, one arising from a ruling request and the other from a proposed revenue ruling: ***** and *****, respectively.

The issue under consideration in our ***** case is whether, for purposes of section 851(b), obligations issued or fully guaranteed as to principal and interest by FNMA, GNMA, SLMA, or FHLB, and FHLMC are "securities" under section 851(b) and "Government securities" under section 851(b)(4). Though this was not a specific issue in the ***** ruling request, we are being asked to address the question in relation to that case because in making its ruling request, the Fund has assumed they were. We will consider specific instruments: notes and bonds issued by FNMA, GNMA, SLMA, a FHLB, and FHLMC, and certain mortgage-backed certificates guaranteed as to principal and interest by FNMA, GNMA, and FHLMC (the so-called FNMA and GNMA fully-modified pass-through mortgage-backed certificates and FHLMC mortgage participation certificates).

The issue in our second case, ***** is, are mortgage-backed certificates guaranteed as to principal and interest by GNMA "Government securities" for purposes of section 851(b)(4) of the Code? The GNMA certificates described in the proposed ruling are fully modified pass-through mortgage-backed certificates. Because the classification of these GNMA certificates pursuant to section 851(b)-(4) is also at issue in ***** we have combined the two cases into a single one here.

The first issue is, are notes and bonds issued by FNMA, GNMA, SLMA, a FHLB, and FHLMC, fully modified pass-through mortgage-backed FNMA and GNMA certificates and FHLMC mortgage participation certificates "securities" under section 851(b)?

This office has consistently looked to the definition of "securities" in section 2(a)(36) of the 1940 Act for guidance in defining the term under section 851(b). *See, e.g.,* *****, G.C.M. 36782, I-179-76 (July 6, 1976); *****, G.C.M. 37233, I-106-77 (Aug. 25,

1977); *****, G.C.M. 38994, I-316-82 (Jan. 21, 1983); *****, G.C.M. 39295, I-316-82 (March 30, 1984); *****, G.C.M. 39316, I-360-83 (July 31, 1984); *****, G.C.M. 38447, I-226-84 (Dec. 5, 1984); *****, G.C.M. 39531, I-212-85 (Feb. 5, 1986); and *****, G.C.M. 39526, I-228-85 (Feb. 24, 1986). Moreover, recent legislation specifically directs us to look to section 2(a)(36) of the 1940 Act when defining the term under section 851(b)(2). *See* section 851(b)(2) as amended by section 653 of the Tax Reform Act of 1986, Pub. L. No. 99-514, 100 Stat. 2085, 2297.

Section 2(a)(36) of the 1940 Act lists notes and bonds as categories of securities. Any such instrument whether directly issued by, or guaranteed by, FNMA, GNMA, SLMA, a FHLB, or FHLMC is a security under section 2(a)(36) of the 1940 Act and thus under section 851(b) of the Code.

We believe that the FHLMC mortgage participation certificates and fully modified pass-through mortgage-backed FNMA and GNMA certificates could be described as *certificates of interest or participation in notes, bonds, debentures, and evidences of indebtedness,* and also as investment contracts. The underlined instruments are listed as "securities" under section 2(a)(36) of the 1940 Act although we could find no cases or administrative decisions addressing the issue whether mortgage-backed certificates were in fact to be treated as securities under the section. It is generally assumed without discussion that the certificates are. *See* the comments on mortgage-backed securities generally at Lore, *Securities Law Series: Mortgage-Backed Securities* 4-9 (1985). *See also* the comments on GNMA certificates at *Clarifying the Jurisdiction of the Securities and Exchange Commission and the Definition of Security,* H.R. Rep. No. 626, Part 1, 97th Cong., 2d Sess. 3 (1982), and A. Bromberg, *Securities Law—Relationship to Commodities Law,* Business Lawyer 787, 791 (1980). And *Federal Home Loan Mortgage Corp.,* SEC No-Action letter (July 24, 1971) (LEXIS, Fedsec Library, Noact file), concluding that the FHLMC mortgage participation certificates discussed therein are securities under section 2(a)(16) of the 1940

Act and thus implying that they are securities under section 2(a)(36) of the Act.

The Seventh Circuit opinion in *Abrams v. Oppenheimer Government Securities, Inc.,* 737 F.2d 582 (7th Cir. 1984), discusses fully modified pass-through mortgage-backed GNMA certificates in a context that is relevant. In *Abrams,* the Seventh Circuit considered whether these GNMA certificates were "securities" under the Securities Act of 1933 (the 1933 Act), 15 U.S.C. 77a et seq. and the Securities Exchange Act of 1934 (the 1934 Act), 15 USC 78a et seq. The court determined that the GNMA certificates were "securities" under the 1933 Act and the 1934 Act because they were notes, bonds, or debentures having a maturity at the time of issuance not exceeding nine months, exclusive of days of grace, or any renewal thereof the maturity of which is likewise limited. *See* section 2(1) of the 1933 Act and section 3(a)(10) of the 1934 Act, each of which defines "security" for purposes of the respective securities act. While the definition of securities under these two acts may differ in some respects from that of "securities" under the 1940 Act, we see no basis for defining notes, bonds, and debentures differently under the three acts. Therefore, in effect the seventh Circuit's classification of the GNMA certificates as securities under the 1933 and 1934 Acts amounts to a categorization of these certificates as such under section 2(a)(36) of the 1940 Act and thus under section 851(b) of the Code. *See also Board of Trade of the City of Chicago v. Securities and Exchange Commission,* 677 F.2d 1137 (7th Cir. 1982), the holding of which was changed for other reasons by Congress* when it enacted the Futures Trading Act of 1982, Pub. L. No. 97-444, 96 Stat. 2294 (1983).**

The second issue is, are notes and bonds issued by FNMA, GNMA, SLMA, a FHLB, and FHLMC, fully modified pass-through mortgage-backed FNMA and GNMA certificates, and FHLMC mortgage participa-

tion certificates "*Government* securities" under section 851(b)(4) of the Code?

Section 851(c) contains definitions applicable to section 851(b)(4). Since section 851(c) does not specifically define "Government securities" for purposes of section 851(b)(4), that term has the same meaning as when used in the 1940 Act. Section 851(c)(5). The 1940 Act's definition of Government security is in section 2(a)(16) of the act. It is that section which the Service has looked to in defining Government securities under section 851(b)(4) of the Code. *See, e.g.,* *****, G.C.M. 36522, I-515-75 (Dec. 17, 1975), and *****, G.C.M. 36764, I-560-73 (June 22, 1976), published as Rev. Rul. 77-342, 1977-2 C.B. 238, and Rev. Rul. 76-426, 1976-2 C.B. 17, respectively, explaining why the instruments under consideration were classified as Government securities under section 851(b)(4). *Compare* Briefing Note, re: *****, dated Jan. 28, 1964 in the administrative file for Rev. Rul. 64-85, 1964-1 C.B. 230, no CC:I consideration, discussing why in the published ruling certain securities were Government securities pursuant to a section in the real estate investment trust rules corresponding to section 851(b)(4).

There are two ways for securities to qualify as *Government* securities under section 2(a)(16) of the 1940 Act and thus section 851(b)(4) of the Code: one, if they are issued or guaranteed as to principal or interest by the United States, and two, if they are issued or guaranteed as to principal or interest by a person controlled or supervised by and acting as an instrumentality of the Government of the United States pursuant to authority granted by the Congress of the United States.

We believe the securities here all meet either one or both of these requirements and are thus "Government securities" under section 851(b)(4).

Each of the GNMA securities satisfies at least one of these criteria. Under 12 U.S.C.A.

---

* *See* the discussion at H.R. Rep. No. 626, Part 2, (97th Cong., 2d Sess. 2 (1982) and H.R. Rep. No. 565, Part 1, 97th Cong., 2d Sess. 40 (1982).

** Note that the *Board of Trade* court states that GNMA certificate is *also* a commodity.

1717(a)(2)(A) (West 1980), GNMA is in the Department of Housing and Urban Development (HUD), an agency of the Government of the United States pursuant to authority granted by the Congress of the United States. Consequently any securities issued or guaranteed as to principal or interest by GNMA are also issued or guaranteed by a person controlled or supervised by and acting as an instrumentality of the Government of the United States pursuant to authority granted by the Congress of the United States. Moreover, pursuant to 12 U.S.C.A. 1721(g) (West Supp. 1986), the mortgage-backed GNMA certificates are backed by the full faith and credit of the United States. The GNMA securities are thus "Government securities" under section 851(b)(4). *See also* *****, G.C.M. 38447, I-226-84 (Dec. 5, 1984) at p. 7 stating that GNMA certificates were classifiable as such.

FHLB obligations were previously considered in Rev. Rul. 64-85, 1964-1 C.B. 230, no CC:I consideration. That ruling held that securities issued or guaranteed as to principal or interest by FHLB were Government securities under section 856(c)(5), the real estate investment trust (REIT) diversification provision. As under the RIC diversification provision, the definition of "Government securities" pursuant to the REIT diversification provision is to be found in the 1940 Act. Section 856(c)(6)(D). Consistent with this, the administrative file for the ruling indicates that the pivotal issue in Rev. Rul. 64-85 was, are securities issued or guaranteed as to principal or interest by FHLB Government securities under section 2(a)(16) of the 1940 Act? The administration file notes that this query was answered in the affirmative based on the taxpayer's rationale in his incoming letter in the case, dated November 23, 1962: namely, since the FHLB are supervised by the Home Loan Bank Board, an instrumentality of the United States Government pursuant to authority granted by the Congress of the United States, their obligations should be deemed to be Government securities. There also is a buckslip dated January 2, 1963 in the file indicating that at the time the ruling

was issued the SEC was treating the securities of a FHLB as "Government securities" pursuant to the 1940 Act.

The FHLB are still supervised by the Home Loan Bank Board. 12 U.S.C.A. 1437(a) (West Supp. 1984). In addition, it is our understanding that the SEC still treats securities issued by a FHLB or guaranteed as to principal or interest by a FHLB as "Government securities" under the 1940 Act. Rev. Rul. 64-85 thus would require us to continue to deem such instruments as securities for purposes of section 851(b)(4) of the Code. Thus the securities here in respect of a FHLB are, under section 851(b)(4), "Government securities."

Rev. Rul. 64-85 in addition involved securities issued or guaranteed as to principal or interest by FNMA. As with the FHLB obligations, the ruling concluded that these obligations were Government securities within the meaning of section 856(c)(5). Like the conclusion in respect of the FHLB obligations, the holding in respect of FNMA obligations was based on the fact that the obligations satisfied the test for treatment as a Government security under section 2(a)(16) of the 1940 Act. They were issued or guaranteed as to principal or interest by an entity supervised by the Housing and Home Finance Agency which in turn was an instrumentality of the Government of the United States pursuant to authority granted by the Congress of the United States. Moreover, the SEC was treating these obligations as Government securities under the 1940 Act. *See* the administrative file underlying the ruling.

FNMA obligations were also the subject of a later ruling: Rev. Rul. 66-238, 1966-2 C.B. 521. In Rev. Rul. 66-238, the Service held that, for purposes of section 7701(a)(19)(C)(ii), participation certificates sold by FNMA pursuant to the Participation Sales Act of 1966, Pub. L. No. 89-429, 80 Stat. 164, to a domestic building and loan association were stock or obligations of an instrumentality of the United States.

Seemingly Rev. Rul. 64-85 and Rev. Rul. 66-238 would provide precedent for us to conclude that the FNMA obligations are Government securities under section

851(b)(4). However, since the publication of Rev. Rul. 64-85 and Rev. Rul. 66-238, FNMA has changed significantly in structure. What used to be a single corporation was, in 1968, split into two corporations: a GNMA corporation and a new FNMA corporation. This new FNMA was created as a Government sponsored private corporation and is not supervised by the Housing and Home Finance Agency. In light of this restructuring, the holdings in Rev. Rul. 64-85 and Rev. Rul. 68-238 in respect of FNMA obligations must be re-examined.

As under pre-Rev. Rul. 64-85 and pre-Rev. Rul. 66-238 law, the obligations of FNMA are not issued or guaranteed as to principal or interest by the United States. 12 U.S.C.A. 1719 (West 1980 and Supp. 1986). Thus, as before, they can only be Government securities if they are deemed issued or guaranteed as to principal or interest by a person controlled or supervised by and acting as an instrumentality of the Government of the United States pursuant to authority granted by the Congress of the United States.

This is not a simple assessment to make, as FNMA is a hybrid. It has characteristics of both a public corporation and a private one.

On the one hand, in 1968, FNMA was created as a private corporation, the obligations of which are not guaranteed by the United States or by any agency or instrumentality thereof. Like private corporations, it is taxable under federal tax laws. 12 U.S.C.A. 1723a(c)(2) (West 1980). FNMA can sue and be sued as a corporate entity. 12 U.S.C.A. 1723a(a) (West 1980). It is subject to attachment, injunction and similar processes against its property or against itself in respect of its property. 12 U.S.C.A. 1723a(a) (West 1980). It selects and appoints or employs its own officers, attorneys, employees, and agents, and must compensate them from its own funds. 12 U.S.C.A. 1723a(d)(2) (West 1980).

On the other hand, FNMA is Government sponsored (12 U.S.C.A. 1716b (West 1980)) and is to some extent supervised and controlled by the Government. Approximately one third of its board is selected by

the President of the United States who may remove any member of the board for good cause. 12 U.S.C.A. 1723(b) (West Supp. 1986). Its personalty is exempt from state and local taxation: only realty of FNMA is subject to such taxation. 12 U.S.C.A. 1723a(c) (2) (West 1980). The Secretary of Housing and Urban Development has general regulatory power over FNMA and may make such rules and regulations as are necessary and proper to insure that the purposes of FNMA's enabling legislation are accomplished. 12 U.S.C.A. 1723a(h) (West Supp. 1986). The Secretary may examine and audit the books and financial transactions of FNMA and require FNMA to make reports. 12 U.S.C.A. 1723a(h) (West Supp. 1986). The Secretary may require that a reasonable portion of FNMA's mortgage purchases be related to the national goal of providing adequate housing for low and moderate income families, but with reasonable economic return to FNMA. 12 U.S.C.A. 1723a(h) (West Supp. 1986). The corporation's obligations are, to the same extent as securities that are direct obligations of or obligations guaranteed as to principal or interest by the United States, deemed exempt securities within the meaning of laws administered by the SEC. 12 U.S.C.A. 1723c (West Supp. 1986). FNMA was intended to have a status analogous to Federal Home Loan Banks. H.R. Rep. No. 1585, 90th Cong., 2d Sess. 69 (1968).

Notwithstanding the basic structural changes in FNMA, we believe that FNMA is still a person controlled or supervised by and acting as an instrumentality of the United States pursuant to an Act of Congress. The SEC has concluded this and in so doing has classified securities issued or guaranteed as to principal or interest by FNMA as "Government securities" under section 2(a)(16) of the 1940 Act. *Federal National Mortgage Association,* SEC No-Action Letter (May 6, 1971) (LEXIS, Fedsec library, Noact file). Since we are interpreting a statutory provision under the jurisdiction of the SEC, the SEC's interpretation is persuasive.

In Rev. Rul. 77-342, 1977-2 C.B. 238, considered by this office in ***** G.C.M.

36522, I-515-75 (December 17, 1975), the issue was, are certain participation certificates issued by the General Services Administration (GSA) to finance the construction of public buildings "Government securities" within the meaning of section 851(b)(4)? Because GSA had received an opinion of the Chief Counsel, Division of Investment Company Regulation, Securities and Exchange Commission, that the participation certificates were Government securities, the Service held that the certificates were such under section 851(b)(4) of the Code. According to G.C.M. 36522, such an opinion is an important, if not a controlling, consideration in the interpretation of section 851. *See also* *****, G.C.M. 36764, I-560-73 (June 22, 1976) published as Rev. Rul. 76-426, 1976-2 C.B. 17; and Rev. Rul. 74-177, 1974-1 C.B. 165.

We consequently conclude that notes and bonds issued by FNMA, and fully modified pass-through mortgage-backed FNMA certificates are section 851(b)(4) "Government securities."

As with FNMA, the SEC has indicated that securities issued or guaranteed as to principal or interest by FHLMC and SLMA* are Government securities. SEC No-Action letters, *Federal Home Loan Mortgage Corp.* (July 24, 1971) and *Student Loan Marketing Association* (Nov. 17, 1983) (LEXIS, Fedsec library, Noact file). For the same reasons as stated in respect of FNMA securities, we conclude that the securities here in respect to FHLMC and SLMA are section 851(b)(4) "Government securities."

Though it would seem that there is no question but that fully modified pass-through mortgage-backed FNMA and GNMA certificates and FHLMC mortgage participation certificates are securities under section 851(b) and Government securities under section 851(b)(4), several published revenue rulings raise the query whether these certificates can be classifiable as Government securities under any Code section. These rulings all considered certain federal income tax consequences associated with pass-through mortgage-backed certificates. *See* Rev. Rul. 70-545, 1970-2 C.B. 7 (fully modified pass-through mortgage-backed GNMA certificates) and Rev. Rul. 70-544, 1970-2 C.B. 6 (straight pass-through mortgage-backed GNMA certificates) both considered by this office in *****, G.C.M. 34347, I-3821 (Sept., 14, 1970) and both modified by Rev. Rul. 74-169, 1974-1 C.B. 147. *See also* Rev. Rul. 84-10, 1984-1 C.B. 155 (fully modified pass-through mortgage-backed FNMA certificates) considered by CC:I in *****, G.C.M. 39113, I-229-83 (Oct. 7, 1983) and clarifying Rev. Rul. 70-545 and 70-544, *supra*. *See also* Rev. Rul. 71-399, 1971-2 C.B. 433 (FHLMC mortgage participation certificates) amplified by Rev. Rul. 81-203, 1981-2 C.B. 137, Rev. Rul. 80-96, 1980-1 C.B. 317, Rev. Rul. 74-300, 1974-1 C.B. 169, Rev. Rul. 74-221, 1974-1 C.B. 365, and Rev. Rul. 72-376, 1972-2 C.B. 647. In addition, *see* Rev. Rul. 77-349, 1977-2 C.B. 20 (straight pass-through mortgage-backed certificates). In some cases, the certificates were fully modified pass-through mortgage-backed certificates or mortgage participation certificates as we have here. In others, the certificates were straight pass-through mortgage-backed certificates. In each case the result was the same. In effect, any trust or pool underlying the respective certificates was a conduit. The arrangement did not create an association classifiable as a corporation under section 7701 but was a grantor trust under subpart E of subchapter J. Each certificate holder was the owner of an undivided interest in the entire trust (corpus as well as ordinary income). Each was deemed to hold an ownership interest in the mortgages in the trust. Adding to the complexity is the holding in the rulings that the certificates were "real estate assets" as that term is defined in section 856(c)(5), the REIT diversification provision corresponding to section 851(b)(4).

Memoranda underlying the rulings indicate that the conclusions in the rulings were

---

* Like FNMA, SLMA is a Government sponsored private corporation. 20 U.S.C.A. 1087-2(a)(1) (West Supp. 1986).

at least in part based on the fact that the certificates considered in the rulings were in the nature of *pass-through* certificates and the custodian or trustee of the pool or trust had no power to vary the obligations. Since the principal and interest paid on the mortgages in the pool passed through to the holders as though they actually held the mortgages, the holders were treated as though they held the mortgages themselves.

The holdings in and the rationale underlying the rulings raise two concerns. If the pool or trust is looked through, and the holders are holding interests in the mortgages (residential mortgages to be exact), *arguably* what they are holding

(1) are not securities since they are "merely" interests in residential mortgages, and

(2) are not Government securities except to the extent the United States Government, or a person controlled or supervised by an instrumentality of the United States Government pursuant to the authority of an Act of Congress, has *directly* guaranteed any of the mortgages.

Although there are admittedly logical inconsistencies in concluding that the certificates backed by the mortgage pools are both interests in real estate based on a conduit principle and "securities" under section 851(b) that qualify as "Government securities" for purposes of section 851(b)(4), we believe that the latter classification is mandated. Under section 851(b)(2), we are specifically directed to use the definition of "security" found in section 2(a)(36) of the 1940 Act when defining "security" under section 851(b)(2). Similarly, section 851(c)(5) requires us to look to the definition of "Government securities" under the 1940 Act when defining the term under section 851(b)(4). The Code generally does not cross reference to the 1940 Act for definitions of terms. Other Code sections thus may view the certificates differently from section 851(b)(4).

The apparent inconsistency on the question whether the instruments are "Government securities" under section 851(b)(4) can also be explained in another way. The cer-

tificates in question really consist of multiple obligors: the mortgagors who are liable on the separate mortgages, and GNMA, FNMA or other entity that guarantees payment on the certificates. In determining whether the obligations are "Government securities" under section 851(b)(4), we focus on the guarantee by the Government instrumentality because that is the thrust of the 1940 Act. The Code sections involved in the cited rulings focus on the obligations of the underlying mortgagors. At page 10 of *****, G.C.M. 39551, I-087-84 (June 30, 1986), this office recently noted that the existence of the federal guarantee makes GNMA certificates more marketable than the underlying mortgages that have no such guarantee. Thus the GNMA certificates were determined to be securities under the wash sale rules of section 1091 whether or not the underlying mortgages when pooled would have been. Similarly we believe that the guarantee of the mortgage-backed certificates by the respective entity secures those instruments and ensures their status as securities under section 851(b) and as *Government* securities under section 851(b)(4) regardless of whether the mortgages underlying the certificates could be said to be such.

Moreover, even if certificate holders are considered as holding a direct interest in the underlying mortgages themselves, we believe that the answer is the same. The certificates are section 851(b) "securities" and section 851(b)(4) "Government securities."

A holder of a FHLMC mortgage participation certificate or fully modified pass-through mortgage-backed FNMA or GNMA certificate would, in effect, own a participation interest in the mortgages in the trust. This interest comes within the "investment contract" and the "certificate of interest or participation in a note" portions of the 1940 Act's section 2(a)(36) "securities" definition. It is thus a "security" under section 851(b). This security, which is guaranteed by the United States Government or by a person controlled or supervised by and acting as an instrumentality of the United States under an Act of Congress, is a "Government security" under the 1940 Act and thus under section 851(b)(4). That the mortgages are on residential property is not detrimental. *Compare Commercial Discount Corp. v. Lincoln First Commercial Corp.,* 445 F. Supp. 1263, 1265 (S.D.N.Y. 1978); and *NBI Mortgage Investment Corp. v. Central Nat'l Bank of Jacksonville,* 409 F.2d 989, 992 (5th Cir. 1969), noting that a participation in a loan may be an investment contract or a certificate of interest or participation in a note and therefore a security under the 1933 and 1934 Acts though the underlying loan may not be. *Compare also Mortgage Associates, Inc.,* SEC NoAction Letter [1972–1973 Transfer Binder] Fed. Sec. L. Rep. (CCH) paragraph 79,288 at 82,817 (Dec. 11, 1972), in which a proposed sale of participations in privately insured conventional home mortgages to professional lending institutions was classified as a security for purposes of section 15(a)(1) of the 1934 Act.

There is one aspect of the published rulings which deserves further discussion: the holding in the respective rulings that a REIT holding a mortgage-backed certificate under the circumstances described therein actually owns "real estate assets" as that phrase is used in section 856(c)(5)(A).

Section 856(c)(5)(A) is the REIT provision requiring that, at the end of each quarter of the taxable year, at least 75 percent of the value of a REIT's total assets must be represented by *real estate assets, cash, and Government securities.* As under the corresponding RIC section (section 851(b)(4)—the subsection under which we are defining "Government security" here), "Government security" is to have the same meaning as in the 1940 Act. Section 856(c)(6)(D). The definition of a "real estate asset," which is not a relevant concept under section 851(b), is specifically delineated in section 856(c)(6)(B) as real property, interests in mortgages on real property, shares in other qualified REITs and deeds of trust on real property. Its scope is not controlled by the 1940 Act, which should be noted, as section 851(b), has no corresponding concept anyway.

Treas. Reg. 1.856-3(e) caveats the definition of "securities" under section 856: "the term 'security' does not include…'real estate assets' as [that term is] defined in section 856." Treas. Reg. 1.856-3(e) arguably implies that an instrument can at the same time meet the definition of both a "real estate asset" under section 856 and a "security" under the 1940 Act, but that where such does occur the "real estate asset" characterization will supersede a "security" one. It could be construed to preclude an instrument meeting the definition of a "real estate asset" from being classifiable as a "security," including a "Government security," for any purpose.

However, since there is no provision corresponding to Treas. Reg. 1.856-3(e) under the RIC provisions, presumably a certificate in a mortgage pool or trust that comes within the definition of Government security under the 1940 Act would be deemed a Government security under the RIC rules. *See* *****, G.C.M. 36737, I-336-75 (May 21, 1976), in which this office recognized that fully modified pass-through mortgage-backed *GNMA* certificates would be securities under other Code sections and left open the question whether they could be securities under other subsections of section 856; and *****, G.C.M. 39551, I-087-84 (June 30, 1986), in which this office concluded that "GNMA participation certificates" were securities under section 1091 despite the holdings in Rev. Rul. 70-544 and Rev. Rul. 70-545 that those certificates represented interests in real estate assets.

This brings us to our final point. If an investment company having multiple classes of stock is allowed to count mortgage-backed certificates as "securities" under section 851(b) in determining whether it qualifies as a RIC, then we may have RICs that do not meet the REMIC (the real estate mortgage investment conduit) rules offering alternative modes for owning multiple-class mortgage-backed certificates. This would seem to be contrary to legislation enacted by section 671 of the Tax Reform Act of 1986 creating the REMIC as the exclusive vehicle for the issuance of multiple-class mortgage-backed certificates. *See* the new sections 860A to 860F. The REMIC rules do not seem to be a problem where the RIC has only one class of stock as we assume the RIC here has. We defer, until an actual case is presented, the issue whether a RIC having multiple classes of stock may class-ify mortgage-backed certificates as "securities" under the RIC rules.

We generally approve the revenue ruling proposed in ***** for publication and recommend that the ruling letter issued in ***** conform with the discussion herein.

* * *

Appendix D

Internal Revenue Service Forms

Form **1066**	**U.S. Real Estate Mortgage Investment Conduit**	OMB No. 1545-1014
Department of the Treasury Internal Revenue Service	**Income Tax Return** For calendar year 1993 ▶ **See separate instructions.**	19**93**

	Name	**A** Employer identification number
Please Type or Print	Number, street, and room or suite no. (If a P.O. box, see page 3 of the instructions.)	**B** Date REMIC started
	City or town, state, and ZIP code	**C** Enter total assets at end of tax year $

D Check applicable boxes: (1) ☐ Final return   (2) ☐ Change in address   (3) ☐ Amended return

Section I—Computation of Taxable Income or Net Loss

Income (excluding amounts from prohibited transactions)

1	Taxable interest	**1**	
2	Accrued market discount under section 860C(b)(1)(B)	**2**	
3	Capital gain (loss) (Schedule D)	**3**	
4	Ordinary gain (loss) (attach Form 4797)	**4**	
5	Other income (attach schedule)	**5**	
6	**Total** income (loss). Add lines 1 through 5	**6**	

Deductions (excluding amounts allocable to prohibited transactions)

7	Salaries and wages	**7**	
8	Rent	**8**	
9	Amount accrued to regular interest holders in the REMIC that is deductible as interest	**9**	
10	Other interest	**10**	
11	Taxes	**11**	
12	Depreciation (see instructions)	**12**	
13	Other deductions (attach schedule)	**13**	
14	**Total** deductions. Add lines 7 through 13	**14**	
15	Taxable income (net loss). Subtract line 14 from line 6	**15**	

Section II—Tax and Payments

1	**Total tax.** Schedule J, line 13	**1**	
2	Tax paid with: ☐ Form 8736 ☐ Form 8800	**2**	
3	**Tax Due.** Enter excess of line 1 over line 2. (See instructions for **Payment of Tax Due.**) .	**3**	
4	**Overpayment.** Enter excess of line 2 over line 1	**4**	

Please Sign Here	Under penalties of perjury, I declare that I have examined this return, including accompanying schedules and statements, and to the best of my knowledge and belief, it is true, correct, and complete. Declaration of preparer (other than taxpayer) is based on all information of which preparer has any knowledge.		
	▶ _____ Signature		▶ _____ Date

Paid Preparer's Use Only	Preparer's ▶ signature		Date	Check if self- employed ☐	Preparer's social security number
	Firm's name (or yours if self-employed) and address	▶		E.I. No. ▶ ZIP code ▶	

For Paperwork Reduction Act Notice, see page 1 of the instructions.   Cat. No. 64383U   Form **1066** (1993)

Form 1066 (1993)   Page **2**

Schedule D	Capital Gains and Losses

(Caution: Use Form 4797 instead of Schedule D if the startup day was after November 11, 1991. See instructions.)

Part I—Short-Term Capital Gains and Losses—Assets Held One Year or Less

(a) Description of property (Example: 100 shares 7% preferred of "Z" Co.)	(b) Date acquired (mo., day, yr.)	(c) Date sold (mo., day, yr.)	(d) Sales price (see instructions)	(e) Cost or other basis (see instructions)	(f) Gain (loss) (col. (d) less (e))
1					

2	Short-term capital gain from installment sales from Form 6252	**2**	
3	Short-term capital loss carryover	**3**	
4	**Net short-term capital gain (loss).** Combine lines 1 through 3	**4**	

Part II—Long-Term Capital Gains and Losses—Assets Held More Than One Year

5					

6	Long-term capital gain from installment sales from Form 6252	**6**	
7	Capital gain distributions	**7**	
8	Enter gain, if applicable, from Form 4797	**8**	
9	Long-term capital loss carryover	**9**	
10	**Net long-term capital gain (loss).** Combine lines 5 through 9	**10**	

Part III—Summary of Parts I and II

11	Combine lines 4 and 10 and enter the net gain (loss) here	**11**		
12	If line 11 is a gain, enter here and also on line 3, Section I (page 1)	**12**		
13	If line 11 is a loss, enter here and as a loss on line 3, Section I (page 1), the **smaller** of:			
a	The amount on line 11; or			
b	$3,000	**13**	(	)

Part IV—Computation of Capital Loss Carryovers From 1993 to 1994
(Complete this part if the loss on line 11 is more than the loss on line 13.)

14	Enter loss shown on line 4. If none, enter -0- and skip lines 15 through 18	**14**	
15	Enter gain shown on line 10. If that line is blank or shows a loss, enter -0-	**15**	
16	Subtract line 15 from line 14	**16**	
17	Enter the smaller of line 13 or 16	**17**	
18	Subtract line 17 from line 16. This is your **short-term capital loss carryover from 1993 to 1994**	**18**	
19	Enter loss from line 10. If none, enter -0- and skip lines 20 through 23	**19**	
20	Enter gain shown on line 4. If line 4 is blank or shows a loss, enter -0-	**20**	
21	Subtract line 20 from line 19	**21**	
22	Subtract line 17 from line 13. (**Note:** *If you skipped lines 15 through 18, enter the amount from line 13.*)	**22**	
23	Subtract line 22 from line 21. This is your **long-term capital loss carryover from 1993 to 1994.**	**23**	

Schedule J   Tax Computation

Part I—Tax on Net Income From Prohibited Transactions

1 Income—See instructions.		
a Gain from certain dispositions of qualified mortgages	1a	
b Income from nonpermitted assets	1b	
c Compensation for services	1c	
d Gain from the disposition of cash flow investments (except pursuant to a qualified liquidation) .	1d	
2 **Total** income. Add lines 1a through 1d	2	
3 Deductions directly connected with the production of income shown on line 2 (excluding amounts attributable to prohibited transactions resulting in a loss)	3	
4 Net income from prohibited transactions. Subtract line 3 from line 2	4	
5 Tax on net income from prohibited transactions. Enter 100% of line 4	5	

Part II—Tax on Net Income From Foreclosure Property (as defined in section 860G(a)(8)) (Caution: *See instructions before completing this part.*)

6 Net gain (loss) from the sale or other disposition of foreclosure property described in section 1221(1) (attach schedule)	6	
7 Gross income from foreclosure property (attach schedule)	7	
8 Total income from foreclosure property. Add lines 6 and 7	8	
9 Deductions directly connected with the production of income shown on line 8 (attach schedule)	9	
10 Net income from foreclosure property. Subtract line 9 from line 8	10	
11 Tax on net income from foreclosure property. Enter 35% of line 10	11	

Part III—Tax on Contributions After the Startup Day (*Do not* complete this part if the startup day was before July 1, 1987. See instructions.)

12 Amount of taxable contributions received during the calendar year after the startup day. See instructions (attach schedule)	12	

Part IV—Total Tax

13 **Total tax.** Add lines 5, 11, and 12. Enter here and on page 1, Section II, line 1	13	

Designation of Tax Matters Person

Enter below the residual interest holder designated as the tax matters person (TMP) for the calendar year of this return.

Name of
designated TMP ▶ _____

Identifying
number of TMP ▶ _____

Address of
designated TMP ▶ _____

Additional Information

		Yes	No
E	What type of entity is this REMIC? Check box ▶ ☐ Corporation ☐ Partnership ☐ Trust ☐ Segregated Pool of Assets		
	If you checked "Segregated Pool of Assets," state name and type of entity that owns the assets: Name _____ . Type _____ .		
F	Number of residual interest holders in this REMIC ▶		
G	Check this box if this REMIC is subject to the consolidated entity-level audit procedures of sections 6221 through 6231 . . . . ▶ ☐		
H	At any time during calendar year 1993, did the REMIC have an interest in or a signature or other authority over a financial account in a foreign country (such as a bank account, securities account, or other financial account)? (See the instructions for exceptions and filing requirements for Form TD F 90-22.1.)		
	If "Yes," enter name of foreign country ▶		
I	Was the REMIC the grantor of, or transferor to, a foreign trust that existed during the current tax year, whether or not the REMIC has any beneficial interest in it? If "Yes," you may have to file Forms 3520, 3520-A, or 926		
J	Enter the amount of tax-exempt interest accrued during the year ▶........................... .		
K	Check this box if the REMIC had more than one class of regular interests . . . . ▶ ☐ If so, attach a schedule identifying the classes and principal amounts outstanding for each at the end of the year.		
L	Enter the sum of the daily accruals determined under section 860E(c) for the calendar year ▶		

Schedule L **Balance Sheets**	**(a)** Beginning of year		**(b)** End of year	
Assets				
1 Permitted investments (see instructions):				
a Cash flow investments				
b Qualified reserve assets				
c Foreclosure property				
2 Qualified mortgages				
3 Other assets (attach schedule)				
4 **Total** assets				
Liabilities and Capital				
5 Current liabilities (attach schedule)				
6 Other liabilities (attach schedule)				
7 Regular interests in REMIC				
8 Residual interest holders' capital accounts . . .				
9 **Total** liabilities and capital				

Schedule M **Reconciliation of Residual Interest Holders' Capital Accounts**
(Show reconciliation of each residual interest holder's capital account quarterly on Schedule Q (Form 1066), Item E.)

(a) Residual interest holders' capital accounts at beginning of year	**(b)** Capital contributed during year	**(c)** Taxable income (net loss) from Section I, line 15	**(d)** Nontaxable income	**(e)** Unallowable deductions	**(f)** Withdrawals and distributions	**(g)** Residual interest holders' capital accounts at end of year (combine cols. (a) through (f))
			( )	( )		

1993

 **Department of the Treasury
Internal Revenue Service**

Instructions for Form 1066

U.S. Real Estate Mortgage Investment Conduit Income Tax Return

Section references are to the Internal Revenue Code unless otherwise noted.

Paperwork Reduction Act Notice

We ask for the information on this form to carry out the Internal Revenue laws of the United States. You are required to give us the information. We need it to ensure that you are complying with these laws and to allow us to figure and collect the right amount of tax.

The time needed to complete and file this form and related schedule will vary depending on individual circumstances. The estimated average times are:

	Form 1066	Schedule Q (Form 1066)
Recordkeeping	28 hr., 28 min.	6 hr., 13 min.
Learning about the law or the form	6 hr., 36 min.	1 hr., 16 min.
Preparing the form	9 hr., 13 min.	2 hr., 21 min.
Copying, assembling, and sending the form to the IRS	32 min.	16 min.

If you have comments concerning the accuracy of these time estimates or suggestions for making these forms more simple, we would be happy to hear from you. You can write to both the **Internal Revenue Service**, Attention: Reports Clearance Officer, PC:FP, Washington, DC 20224; and the **Office of Management and Budget**, Paperwork Reduction Project (1545–1014), Washington, DC 20503. **DO NOT** send the tax form to either of these offices. Instead, see **Where To File** on page 2.

General Instructions

Purpose of Form

Form 1066 is used to report the income, deductions, and gains and losses from the operation of a real estate mortgage investment conduit (REMIC). In addition, the form is used by the REMIC to report and pay the taxes on net income from prohibited transactions, net income from foreclosure property, and contributions after the startup day.

Who Must File

An entity that elects to be treated as a REMIC for its first tax year (and for which the election is still in effect) **and** that meets the requirements of section 860D(a) must file Form 1066.

A REMIC is any entity:

1. To which an election to be treated as a REMIC applies for the tax year and all prior tax years,

2. All of the interests in which are regular interests or residual interests,

3. That has one (and only one) class of residual interests (and all distributions, if any, with respect to such interests are pro rata),

4. Substantially all of the assets of which consist of qualified mortgages

and permitted investments (as of the close of the 3rd month beginning after the startup day and at all times thereafter),

5. That has a tax year that is a calendar year, and

6. For which reasonable arrangements have been designed to ensure that **(a)** residual interests are not held by disqualified organizations (as defined in section 860E(e)(5)), and **(b)** information needed to apply section 860E(e) will be made available by the entity.

Note: *Paragraph 6 does not apply to REMICs with a startup day before April 1, 1988 (or those formed under a binding contract in effect on March 31, 1988).*

See section 860G for definitions and special rules. See section 860D(a) regarding qualification as a REMIC during a qualified liquidation.

Making the Election

The election to be treated as a REMIC is made by timely filing, for the first tax year of its existence, a Form 1066 signed by an authorized person. Once the election is made, it stays in effect for all years until it is terminated.

First Tax Year

For the first tax year of a REMIC's existence, the REMIC must furnish the following in a separate statement attached to the REMIC's initial return:

1. Information concerning the terms of the regular interests and the designated residual interest of the REMIC, or a copy of the offering circular or prospectus containing such information, and

2. A description of the prepayment and reinvestment assumptions made in accordance with section 1272(a)(6) and its regulations, including documentation supporting the selection of the prepayment assumption.

Termination of Election

If any entity ceases to be a REMIC at any time during the tax year, the election to be a REMIC terminates for that year and all future years. An entity is considered to cease being a REMIC when it no longer meets the requirements of section 860D(a).

When To File

A REMIC must file Form 1066 by the 15th day of the 4th month following the close of its tax year. If the regular due date falls on a Saturday, Sunday, or legal holiday, file on the next business day. A business day is any day that is not a Saturday, Sunday, or legal holiday.

If you need more time to file a REMIC return, get **Form 8736,** Application for Automatic Extension of Time To File U.S. Return for a Partnership, REMIC, or for Certain Trusts, to request an automatic 3-month extension of time to file. You must file Form 8736 by the regular due date of the REMIC return.

If, after you have filed Form 8736, you still need more time to file the REMIC return, get **Form 8800,** Application for Additional Extension of Time To File U.S. Return for a Partnership, REMIC, or for Certain Trusts, to request an additional extension of up to 3 months. To obtain this additional extension of time to file, you must show reasonable cause for the additional time you are requesting. Ask for the additional extension early so that if it is denied, the return can still be filed on time.

Cat. No. 64231R

Where To File

File Form 1066 with the Internal Revenue Service Center listed below.

If the REMIC's principal place of business or principal office or agency is located in	Use the following address
New Jersey, New York (New York City and counties of Nassau, Rockland, Suffolk, and Westchester)	Holtsville, NY 00501
New York (all other counties), Connecticut, Maine, Massachusetts, New Hampshire, Rhode Island, Vermont	Andover, MA 05501
Florida, Georgia, South Carolina	Atlanta, GA 39901
Indiana, Kentucky, Michigan, Ohio, West Virginia	Cincinnati, OH 45999
Kansas, New Mexico, Oklahoma, Texas	Austin, TX 73301
Alaska, Arizona, California (counties of Alpine, Amador, Butte, Calaveras, Colusa, Contra Costa, Del Norte, El Dorado, Glenn, Humboldt, Lake, Lassen, Marin, Mendocino, Modoc, Napa, Nevada, Placer, Plumas, Sacramento, San Joaquin, Shasta, Sierra, Siskiyou, Solano, Sonoma, Sutter, Tehama, Trinity, Yolo, and Yuba), Colorado, Idaho, Montana, Nebraska, Nevada, North Dakota, Oregon, South Dakota, Utah, Washington, Wyoming	Ogden, UT 84201
California (all other counties), Hawaii	Fresno, CA 93888
Illinois, Iowa, Minnesota, Missouri, Wisconsin	Kansas City, MO 64999
Alabama, Arkansas, Louisiana, Mississippi, North Carolina, Tennessee	Memphis, TN 37501
Delaware, District of Columbia, Maryland, Pennsylvania, Virginia	Philadelphia, PA 19255

Accounting Method

A REMIC must compute its taxable income (or net loss) using the accrual method of accounting. See section 860C(b).

Under the accrual method, an amount is includible in income when all the events have occurred that fix the right to receive the income and the amount can be determined with reasonable accuracy.

Generally, an accrual basis taxpayer can deduct accrued expenses in the tax year that all events occurred that determine the liability and the amount of the liability can be determined with reasonable accuracy. However, all the events that establish liability for the amount are treated as occurring only

Page 2

when economic performance takes place. There are exceptions for recurring items. See section 461(h).

Rounding Off to Whole Dollars

You may round off cents to the nearest whole dollar on the return and accompanying schedules. To do so, drop any amount less than 50 cents and increase any amount from 50 cents through 99 cents to the next higher dollar.

Recordkeeping

The REMIC records must be kept as long as their contents may be material in the administration of any Internal Revenue law. Copies of the filed tax returns should also be kept as part of the REMIC's records. See **Pub. 583,** Taxpayers Starting a Business, for more information.

Final Return

If the REMIC ceases to exist during the year, check the box at Item D(1), page 1, Form 1066.

Amended Return

If after the REMIC files its return it later becomes aware of any changes it must make to income, deductions, etc., the REMIC should file an amended Form 1066 and amended Schedule Q (Form 1066), Quarterly Notice to Residual Interest Holder of REMIC Taxable Income or Net Loss Allocation, for each residual interest holder to correct the forms already filed. Check the box at Item D(3), page 1, Form 1066. Give corrected Schedules Q (Form 1066) labeled "Amended" to each residual interest holder.

Note: *If a REMIC does not meet the small REMIC exception under sections 860F(e) and 6231, and the regulations thereunder, or if a REMIC makes the election described in section 6231(a)(1)(B)(ii) not to be treated as a small REMIC, the amended return will be a request for administrative adjustment, and* **Form 8082,** *Notice of Inconsistent Treatment or Amended Return (Administrative Adjustment Request (AAR)), must be filed by the Tax Matters Person. See sections 860F(e) and 6227 for more information.*

If the REMIC's Federal return is changed for any reason, it may affect its state return. This would include changes made as a result of an examination of the REMIC return by the IRS. Contact the state tax agency where the state return is filed for more information.

Attachments

If you need more space on the forms or schedules, attach separate sheets. Use

the same size and format as on the printed forms. **But show the totals on the printed forms.** Be sure to put the REMIC's name and employer identification number on each sheet. Also, each separate sheet should clearly indicate the line or section on the printed form to which the information relates.

Please complete every applicable entry space on Form 1066. If you attach statements, do not write "See Attached" instead of completing the entry spaces on this form.

Other Forms and Returns That May Be Required

Form 1096, Annual Summary and Transmittal of U.S. Information Returns. Use this form to summarize and send information returns to the Internal Revenue Service Center.

Form 1098, Mortgage Interest Statement. This form is used to report the receipt from any individual of $600 or more of mortgage interest and points in the course of the REMIC's trade or business.

Forms 1099-A, B, INT, MISC, OID, R and S. You may have to file these information returns to report abandonments and acquisitions through foreclosure, proceeds from broker and barter exchange transactions, real estate transactions, interest payments, medical and dental health care payments, miscellaneous income, original issue discount, distributions from pensions, annuities, retirement or profit-sharing plans, IRAs, insurance contracts, etc., and proceeds from real estate transactions. Also, use these returns to report amounts that were received as a nominee on behalf of another person.

For more information, see the **Instructions for Forms 1099, 1098, 5498, and W-2G.**

Note: *Generally, a REMIC must file Forms 1099-INT and 1099-OID, as appropriate, to report accrued income of $10 or more of regular interest holders. See Regulations section 1.6049-7. Also, every REMIC must file Forms 1099-MISC if, in the course of its trade or business during the calendar year, it makes payments of rents, commissions, or other fixed or determinable income (see section 6041) totaling $600 or more to any one person.*

Form 8300, Report of Cash Payments Over $10,000 Received in a Trade or Business. Generally, this form is used to report the receipt of more than $10,000 in cash or foreign currency in one transaction (or a series of related transactions).

Form 8811, Information Return for Real Estate Mortgage Investment Conduits (REMICs) and Issuers of Collateralized Debt Obligations. A REMIC uses this form to provide the information required by Regulations section 1.6049-7(b)(1)(ii). The information will be published in **Pub. 938,** Real Estate Mortgage Investment Conduits (REMICs) Reporting Information. This publication contains a directory of REMICs.

Form 8822, Change of Address, may be used to inform the IRS of a new REMIC address if the change is made after filing Form 1066.

Payment of Tax Due

The REMIC must pay the tax due (line 3, Section II, page 1) in full by the 15th day of the 4th month following the end of the tax year. Attach to Form 1066 a check or money order for the amount due payable to "Internal Revenue Service."

Interest and Penalties

Interest and penalty charges are described below. If a REMIC files late or fails to pay the tax when due, it may be liable for penalties unless it can show that failure to file or pay was due to reasonable cause and not willful neglect.

Interest.—Interest is charged on taxes not paid by the due date, even if an extension of time to file is granted. Interest is also charged on penalties imposed for failure to file, negligence, fraud, gross valuation overstatement, and substantial understatement of tax from the due date (including extensions) to the date of payment. The interest charge is figured at a rate determined under section 6621.

Late filing penalty.—A penalty may be charged if **(a)** the return is filed after the due date (including extensions), or **(b)** the return does not show all the information required. However, the penalty will not be charged if you can show reasonable cause for the late filing or for the failure to include the required information on the return.

If no tax is due, the amount of the penalty is $50 for each month or part of a month (up to 5 months) the failure continues, multiplied by the total number of persons who were residual interest holders in the REMIC during any part of the REMIC's tax year for which the return is due. If tax is due, the penalty is the amount stated above plus 5% of the unpaid tax for each month or part of a month the return is late, up to a maximum of 25% of the unpaid tax. If the return is more than 60 days late, the minimum penalty is $100 or the balance of the tax due on the return, whichever is smaller.

Late payment penalty.—The penalty for not paying the tax when due is usually ½ of 1% of the unpaid tax for each month or part of a month the tax is unpaid. The penalty cannot exceed 25% of the unpaid tax. The penalty will not

be charged if you can show reasonable cause for not paying on time.

Other penalties.—Penalties can also be imposed for negligence, substantial understatement of tax, and fraud. See sections 6662 and 6663.

Contributions to the REMIC

Generally, no gain or loss is recognized by the REMIC or any of the regular or residual interest holders when property is transferred to the REMIC in exchange for an interest in the REMIC. The adjusted basis of the interest received equals the adjusted basis of the property transferred to the REMIC.

The basis to the REMIC of property transferred by a regular or residual interest holder is its fair market value immediately after its transfer.

If the issue price of a regular interest exceeds its adjusted basis, the excess is included in income by the regular interest holder as accrued market discount for the tax years to which it is attributable under the rules of section 1276(b). If the issue price of a residual interest exceeds its adjusted basis, the excess is amortized and included in the residual interest holder's income ratably over the anticipated life of the REMIC.

If the adjusted basis of a regular interest exceeds its issue price, the regular interest holder treats the excess as amortizable bond premium subject to the rules of section 171. If the adjusted basis of a residual interest exceeds its issue price, the excess is deductible ratably over the life of the REMIC.

Payments Subject to Withholding at Source

If there are any nonresident alien individuals, foreign partnerships, or foreign corporations as regular interest holders or residual interest holders, and the REMIC has items which constitute gross income from sources within the United States (see sections 861 through 865), see **Form 1042,** Annual Withholding Tax Return for U.S. Source Income of Foreign Persons.

Who Must Sign

REMIC with a startup day after November 9, 1988.—For a REMIC with a startup day after November 9, 1988, Form 1066 may be signed by any person who could sign the return of the entity in the absence of the REMIC election. Thus, the return of a REMIC which is a corporation or trust would need to be signed by a corporate officer or a trustee, respectively. For REMICs that consist of segregated pools of assets, the return would be required to be signed by any person who could sign the return of the entity which owns the assets of the REMIC under applicable state law.

REMIC with a startup day before November 10, 1988.—A REMIC with a startup day before November 10, 1988, may elect to apply the rules applicable to REMICs with a startup day after November 9, 1988. In the absence of such an election, Form 1066 must be signed by a residual interest holder or, as provided in section 6903, by a fiduciary as defined in section 7701(a)(6) who is acting for the REMIC and who has furnished adequate notice in the manner prescribed in Regulations section 301.6903-1(b).

Paid preparer's information.—If someone prepares the return and does not charge the REMIC, that person should not sign the REMIC return.

Generally, anyone who is paid to prepare the REMIC return must sign the return and fill in the **Paid Preparer's Use Only** area of the return.

The preparer required to sign the REMIC's return **must** complete the required preparer information and:

● Sign it, by hand, in the space provided for the preparer's signature. (Signature stamps or labels are not acceptable.)

● Give the REMIC a copy of the return in addition to the copy to be filed with the IRS.

Specific Instructions

General Information

Name, address, and employer identification number.—Print or type the REMIC's legal name and address on the appropriate lines. Include the suite, room, or other unit number after the street address. If the Post Office does not deliver mail to the street address and the REMIC has a P.O. box, show the box number instead of the street address.

Note: *Each REMIC must have its own employer identification number.*

Show the correct employer identification number (EIN) in Item A on page 1 of Form 1066. If the REMIC does not have an EIN, get **Form SS-4,** Application for Employer Identification Number, for details on how to obtain an EIN immediately by telephone. If the REMIC has previously applied for an EIN, but has not received it by the time the return is due, write "Applied for" in the space for the EIN. **Do not** apply for an EIN more than once. See Pub. 583 for details.

Item B—Date REMIC started.—Enter the "startup day" selected by the REMIC as defined in section 860G(a)(9).

Item C—Total assets at end of tax year.—Enter the total assets of the REMIC. If there are no assets at the end of the tax year, enter the total assets as of the beginning of the tax year.

Section I

Income—(Lines 1–6).—Do not include on lines 1–6 any income that is tax-exempt or any income from prohibited transactions.

Line 1—Taxable interest.—Enter the total taxable interest. "Taxable interest" is interest that is included in ordinary income from all sources except interest exempt from tax and interest on tax-free covenant bonds. If you so elect, reduce the amount of interest accrued on taxable bonds acquired after 1987 (or after 1986 if you so elect) by the amount of amortizable bond premium on those bonds attributable to the current tax year under section 171(e).

Line 2—Accrued market discount under section 860C(b)(1)(B).—Enter the amount of market discount attributable to the current tax year determined on the basis of a constant interest rate under the rules of section 1276(b)(2).

Line 3—Capital gain (loss).—Enter the amount shown on line 12 or 13 (as applicable), Schedule D, page 2.

Line 4—Ordinary gain (loss).—Enter the net gain (loss) from line 20, Part II, **Form 4797,** Sales of Business Property.

Line 5—Other income.—Enter any other taxable income not listed above and explain its nature on an attached schedule. If the REMIC issued regular interests at a premium, the net amount of such premium is income that must be prorated over the term of such interests. Include such income on this line.

Deductions—(Lines 7–14).—Do not include any nondeductible amounts on lines 7–14. A REMIC is not allowed any of the following deductions in computing its taxable income:

- The net operating loss deduction;
- The deduction for taxes paid or accrued to foreign countries and U.S. possessions;
- The deduction for charitable contributions;
- The deduction for depletion under section 611 for oil and gas wells; and,
- Losses or deductions allocable to prohibited transactions.

Line 9—Amount accrued to regular interest holders in the REMIC that is deductible as interest.—Regular interests in the REMIC are treated as indebtedness for Federal income tax purposes. Enter the amount of interest, including original issue discount, paid or accrued to regular interest holders for the tax year. Do not deduct any amounts paid or accrued with respect to residual interests in the REMIC.

Line 10—Other interest.—Do not include interest deducted on line 9 or interest on indebtedness incurred or continued to purchase or carry obligations on which the interest is wholly exempt from income tax. If you

so elect, include amortization of bond premium on taxable bonds acquired before 1988, unless you elected to offset amortizable bond premium against the interest accrued on the bond (see the Section I, line 1, instructions on this page). Do not include any amount attributable to a tax-exempt bond.

Line 11—Taxes.—Enter taxes paid or accrued during the tax year but do not include the following:

- Federal income taxes (except the tax on net income from foreclosure property);
- Foreign or U.S. possession income taxes;
- Taxes not imposed on the REMIC; or
- Taxes, including state or local sales taxes, that are paid or incurred in connection with an acquisition or disposition of property (such taxes must be treated as a part of the cost of the acquired property or, in the case of a disposition, as a reduction in the amount realized on the disposition).

Note: *If you have to pay tax on net income from foreclosure property, you should include this tax (from line 11 of Schedule J) here on line 11.*

See section 164(d) for apportionment of taxes on real property between the seller and purchaser.

Line 12—Depreciation.—See the Instructions for Form 4562 or **Pub. 534,** Depreciation, to figure the amount of depreciation to enter on this line. You must complete and attach **Form 4562,** Depreciation and Amortization, if the REMIC placed property in service during 1993, claims a section 179 expense deduction, or claims depreciation on any car or other listed property.

Line 13—Other deductions.—Enter any other allowable deductions for which no line is provided on Form 1066.

Schedule D—General Instructions

Purpose of schedule.—For a REMIC with a startup day before November 12, 1991, use Schedule D to report the sale or exchange of capital assets. To report sales or exchanges of property other than capital assets, see Form 4797 and its instructions.

A REMIC with a startup day after November 11, 1991, must use Form 4797 instead of Schedule D because all of its gains and losses from the sale or exchange of any property are treated as ordinary gains and losses.

For amounts received from an installment sale, the holding period rule in effect in the year of sale will determine the treatment of amounts received as long-term or short-term capital gain.

Report every sale or exchange of property in detail, even though there is no gain or loss.

For details, see **Pub. 544,** Sales and Other Dispositions of Assets.

Capital gain distributions.—On line 7, report as long-term capital gain distributions: **(a)** a capital gain dividend, and **(b)** the REMIC's share of the undistributed capital gain from a mutual fund or other regulated investment company.

For details, see **Pub. 564,** Mutual Fund Distributions.

Losses on worthless securities.—If any securities that are capital assets become worthless during the tax year, the loss is a loss from the sale or exchange of capital assets as of the last day of the tax year.

Losses from wash sales.—The REMIC cannot deduct losses from a wash sale of stock or securities. A wash sale occurs if the REMIC acquires (by purchase or exchange), or has a contract or option to acquire, substantially identical stock or securities within 30 days before or after the date of the sale or exchange. See section 1091 for details.

Installment sales.—If the REMIC sold property (except publicly traded stock or securities) at a gain, and will receive any payment in a tax year after the year of sale, it must use the installment method and **Form 6252,** Installment Sale Income, unless it elects not to use the installment method.

If the REMIC wants to elect out of the installment method, it must report the full amount of the gain on a timely filed return (including extensions).

Schedule D—Specific Instructions

Column (d)—Sales price.—Enter in this column either the gross sales price or the net sales price from the sale. On sales of stocks and bonds, report the gross amount as reported to the REMIC by the REMIC's broker on **Form 1099-B,** Proceeds From Broker and Barter Exchange Transactions, or similar statement. However, if the broker advised the REMIC that gross proceeds (gross sales price) minus commissions and option premiums were reported to the IRS, enter that net amount in column (d).

Column (e)—Cost or other basis.—In general, the cost or other basis is the cost of the property plus purchase commissions and improvements, minus depreciation. If the REMIC got the property in a tax-free exchange, involuntary conversion, or wash sale of stock, it may not be able to use the actual cash cost as the basis. If the REMIC uses a basis other than cash cost, attach an explanation.

When selling stock, adjust the basis by subtracting all the nontaxable distributions received before the sale. This includes nontaxable dividends from utility company stock and mutual funds. Also, adjust the basis for any stock splits.

See section 852(f) for the treatment of certain load charges incurred in acquiring stock in a mutual fund with a reinvestment right.

Increase the cost or other basis by any expense of sale, such as broker's fee, commission, and option premium before making an entry in column (e), unless the REMIC reported net sales price in column (d).

For details, see **Pub. 551,** Basis of Assets.

Schedule J

Part I—Tax on Net Income from Prohibited Transactions

Income—(Lines 1a–1d).—Do not net losses from prohibited transactions against income or gains from prohibited transactions in determining the amounts to enter on lines 1a through 1d. These losses are not deductible in computing net income from prohibited transactions.

Note: *For purposes of lines 1a and 1d below, the term "prohibited transactions" does not include any disposition that is required to prevent default on a regular interest where the threatened default resulted from a default on one or more qualified mortgages, or to facilitate a clean-up call. A clean-up call is the redemption of a class of regular interests when, by reason of prior payments with respect to those interests, the administrative costs associated with servicing that class outweigh the benefits of maintaining the class. It does not include the redemption of a class undertaken in order to profit from a change in interest rates.*

Line 1a—Gain from certain dispositions of qualified mortgages.— Enter the amount of gain from the disposition of any qualified mortgage transferred to the REMIC other than a disposition resulting from:

1. The substitution of a qualified replacement mortgage for a qualified mortgage (or the repurchase in lieu of substitution of a defective obligation).

2. The foreclosure, default, or imminent default of the mortgage.

3. The bankruptcy or insolvency of the REMIC.

4. A qualified liquidation.

See section 860F(a) for details and exceptions.

Line 1b—Income from nonpermitted assets.—Enter the amount of any income received or accrued during the year which is attributable to any asset other than a qualified mortgage or

permitted investment. See section 860G(a) for definitions.

Line 1c—Compensation for services.— Enter the amount of fees or other compensation for services received or accrued during the year.

Line 1d—Gain from the disposition of cash flow investments (except pursuant to a qualified liquidation).— Enter the amount of gain from the disposition of any "cash flow investment" except pursuant to a qualified liquidation. A cash flow investment is any investment of amounts received under qualified mortgages for a temporary period (not to exceed 13 months) before distribution to holders of interests in the REMIC. See section 860F(a)(4) for the definition of a qualified liquidation.

Line 3—Deductions directly connected with the production of income shown on line 2.—Enter the total amount of allowable deductions directly connected with the production of the income shown on lines 1a through 1d except for those deductions connected with prohibited transactions resulting in a loss.

Part II—Tax on Net Income From Foreclosure Property

Note: *The Revenue Reconciliation Act of 1993 increased the tax rate on net income from foreclosure property from 34% to 35%.*

For a definition of foreclosure property, see instructions on page 6 for Schedule L, line 1c. Net income from foreclosure property must also be included in the computation of taxable income (or net loss) shown in Section I, page 1, Form 1066.

Line 7—Gross income from foreclosure property.—Do not include on line 7 amounts described in section 856(c)(3)(A), (B), (C), (D), (E) or (G).

Line 9—Deductions.—Only those expenses which are proximately related to earning the income shown on line 8 may be deducted to arrive at net income from foreclosure property. Allowable deductions include depreciation on foreclosure property, interest paid or accrued on debt of the REMIC that is attributable to the carrying of foreclosure property, real estate taxes, and fees charged by an independent contractor to manage foreclosure property. **Do not** deduct general overhead and administrative expenses.

Line 11—Tax on net income from foreclosure property.—The REMIC is allowed a deduction for the amount of tax shown on this line. Include this amount in computing the deduction for taxes to be entered on line 11, Section I, page 1, Form 1066.

Part III—Tax on Contributions After the Startup Day

Do not complete this part if the startup day (as defined in section 860G(a)(9) as in effect **before** the enactment of the Technical and Miscellaneous Revenue Act of 1988) was before July 1, 1987.

The tax imposed by section 860G(d) is 100% of the amount shown on line 12.

Line 12—Amount of taxable contributions.—Enter the amount of contributions received during the calendar year after the startup day (as defined in section 860G(a)(9)), excluding cash contributions described below:

1. Any contribution to facilitate a clean-up call or a qualified liquidation.

2. Any payment in the nature of a guarantee.

3. Any contribution during the 3-month period beginning on the startup day.

4. Any contribution to a qualified reserve fund by any holder of a residual interest in the REMIC.

Attach a schedule showing your computation.

Designation of Tax Matters Person (TMP)

A REMIC may designate a tax matters person in the same manner that a partnership may designate a tax matters partner under Temporary Regulations section 301.6231(a)(7)-1T. For purposes of applying that section, all holders of a residual interest in the REMIC are treated as general partners. The designation may be made by completing the **Designation of Tax Matters Person** section on page 4 of Form 1066.

Additional Information

Be sure to answer the questions and provide other information in items E through L.

Item E—Type of entity.—Check the box for the entity type of the REMIC recognized under state or local law. If the REMIC is not a separate entity under state or local law, check the box for "Segregated Pool of Assets," and state the name and type of entity which owns the assets in the spaces provided.

Item F—Number of residual interest holders.—Enter the number of persons who were residual interest holders at any time during the tax year.

Item G—Consolidated REMIC proceedings.—Generally, the tax treatment of REMIC items is determined at the REMIC level in a consolidated REMIC proceeding, rather than in separate proceedings with individual residual interest holders.

Check the box for Item G if any of the following applies:

Page 5

- The REMIC had more than 10 residual interest holders at any time during the tax year.
- Any residual interest holder was a nonresident alien or was other than a natural person or estate, **unless** there was at no time during the tax year more than **one** holder of the residual interest.
- The REMIC has elected to be subject to the rules for consolidated REMIC proceedings.

"Small REMICs," as defined in sections 860F(e), 6231(a)(1)(B), and the regulations thereunder, are not subject to the rules for consolidated REMIC proceedings but may make an irrevocable election to be covered by them.

For details on the consolidated entity-level audit procedures, see "Examination of Partnerships and S Corporations" in **Pub. 556,** Examination of Returns, Appeal Rights, and Claims for Refund, and sections 860F(e) and 6231.

Item H—Foreign accounts.—Check "Yes" if either **1** OR **2** below applies:

1. At any time during calendar year 1993, the REMIC had an interest in or signature or other authority over a bank account, securities account, or other financial account in a foreign country, AND

- The combined value of the accounts was more than $10,000 at any time during the calendar year, AND
- The accounts were NOT with a U.S. military banking facility operated by a U.S. financial institution.

2. The REMIC owns more than 50% of the stock in any corporation that would answer the question "Yes" based on item **1** above.

Get Form **TD F 90-22.1,** Report of Foreign Bank and Financial Accounts, to see if the REMIC is considered to have an interest in or signature or other authority over a bank account, securities account, or other financial account in a foreign country.

If you checked "Yes" for Item H, file Form TD F 90-22.1 by June 30, 1994, with the Department of the Treasury at the address shown on the form. Form TD F 90-22.1 is not a tax return. **Do not file it with Form 1066.**

Item I—Foreign trusts.—Check "Yes" if the REMIC was a grantor of, or a transferor to, a foreign trust that existed during the tax year.

A U.S. REMIC that has (at any time) transferred property to a foreign trust may have to include the income from that property in the REMIC's taxable income if the trust had a U.S. beneficiary during 1993. (See section 679.)

If the REMIC transfers property to a foreign corporation as paid-in surplus or

as a contribution to capital, or to a foreign estate or trust, or to a foreign partnership, an excise tax is imposed under section 1491 (see **Form 926,** Return by a U.S. Transferor of Property to a Foreign Corporation, Foreign Estate or Trust, or Foreign Partnership). To avoid this excise tax, the REMIC may choose to treat the transfer as a taxable sale or exchange as specified in section 1057.

Item L—Sum of the daily accruals.— Enter the sum of the daily accruals for all residual interests for the calendar year. See section 860E(c)(2) for details.

Schedule L—Balance Sheets

The amounts shown should agree with the REMIC's books and records. Attach a statement explaining any differences.

Line 1a.—Cash flow investments are any investments of amounts received under qualified mortgages for a temporary period (not to exceed 13 months) before distribution to holders of interests in the REMIC.

Line 1b.—Qualified reserve assets include any intangible property that is held for investment and as part of any reasonably required reserve to provide for full payment of expenses of the REMIC or amounts due on regular interests in the event of defaults on qualified mortgages or lower than expected returns on cash flow investments. No more than 30% of the gross income from such assets may be derived from the sale or disposition of property held for less than 3 months. See section 860G(a)(7)(C) for details and exceptions.

Line 1c.—Foreclosure property is any real property (including interests in real property), and any personal property incident to such real property, acquired by the REMIC as a result of the REMIC's having bid in such property at foreclosure, or having otherwise reduced such property to ownership or possession by agreement or process of law, after there was a default or imminent default on a qualified mortgage held by the REMIC. Generally, such property ceases to be foreclosure property on the date that is 2 years after the date that the REMIC acquired the property. See sections 860G(a)(8), 856(e), and Regulations section 1.856-6 for more details.

Note: Solely for purposes of section 860D(a), the determination of whether any property is foreclosure property shall be made without regard to section 856(e)(4).

Line 7.—Regular interests are interests in the REMIC that are issued on the startup day with fixed terms and that are designated as regular interests, if:

1. Such interest unconditionally entitles the holder to receive a specified principal amount or other similar amounts; and

2. Interest payments (or other similar amounts), if any, with respect to such interest at or before maturity are payable based on a fixed rate (or at a variable rate described in Regulations section 1.860G-1(a)(3)), or consist of a specified portion of the interest payments on qualified mortgages and this portion does not vary during the period that the interest is outstanding.

The interest will not fail to meet the requirements of subparagraph **1** merely because the timing (but not the amount) of the principal payments (or other similar amounts) may be contingent on the extent of prepayments on qualified mortgages and the amount of income from permitted investments.

Schedule M—Reconciliation of Residual Interest Holders' Capital Accounts

Show what caused the changes in the residual interest holders' capital accounts during the tax year.

The amounts shown should agree with the REMIC's books and records and the balance sheet amounts. Attach a statement explaining any differences.

Include in column (d) tax-exempt interest income, other tax-exempt income, income from prohibited transactions, income recorded on the REMIC's books but not included on this return, and allowable deductions not charged against book income this year.

Include in column (e) capital losses in excess of the $3,000 limitation (for a REMIC with a startup day before November 12, 1991), other nondeductible amounts (such as losses from prohibited transactions and expenses connected with the production of tax-exempt income), deductions allocable to prohibited transactions, expenses recorded on books not deducted on this return, and taxable income not recorded on books this year.

Schedule Q—Quarterly Notice to Residual Interest Holder of REMIC Taxable Income or Net Loss Allocation

Attach a separate Copy A, Schedule Q (Form 1066), to Form 1066 for each person who was a residual interest holder at any time during the tax year and for each quarter in which such person was a residual interest holder.

Page 6

*U.S. Government Printing Office: 1993 — 301-628/80243

SCHEDULE Q	**Quarterly Notice to Residual Interest Holder of**	OMB No. 1545-1014
(Form 1066)	**REMIC Taxable Income or Net Loss Allocation**	Expires 10-31-95
(Rev. October 1992)	For calendar quarter ended .... , 19	**Copy B—For**
Department of the Treasury		**Residual**
Internal Revenue Service	(Complete for each residual interest holder—See instructions on back of Copy C.)	**Interest Holder**

Residual interest holder's identifying number	REMIC's identifying number

Residual interest holder's name, address, and ZIP code	REMIC's name, address, and ZIP code

A What type of entity is this residual interest holder? ▶ ....

B Enter residual interest holder's percentage of ownership of all residual interests:

   1 Before change ▶ .... %

   2 End of quarter ▶............... %

C Enter the percentage of the REMIC's assets for the quarter represented by each of the following:

   1 Qualifying real property loans under section 593(d)(1) ▶ .... %

   2 Real estate assets under section 856(c)(6)(B) ▶ .... %

   3 Assets described in section 7701(a)(19)(C) (relating to the
definition of a domestic building and loan association) ▶ .... %

D IRS Center where REMIC files return ▶

E Reconciliation of residual interest holder's capital account

(a) Capital account at beginning of quarter	(b) Capital contributed during quarter	(c) Taxable income (net loss) from line 1b below	(d) Nontaxable income	(e) Unallowable deductions	(f) Withdrawals and distributions	(g) Capital account at end of quarter (combine cols. (a) through (f))
				( )	( )	

Caution: *See the Instructions for Residual Interest Holder on back of Copy B before entering information from this schedule on your tax return.*

1a Taxable income (net loss) of the REMIC for the calendar quarter . . . .

  b Your share of the taxable income (net loss) for the calendar quarter . . . .

2a Sum of the daily accruals under section 860E for all residual interests for the
calendar quarter . . . .

  b Sum of the daily accruals under section 860E for your interest for the calendar quarter . . . . .

  c Excess inclusion for the calendar quarter for your residual interest (subtract line 2b from line 1b, but
do not enter less than zero) . . . .

3 **Residual interest holders who are individuals or other pass-through interest holders. (See
instructions.) Not required to be completed for other entities.**

  a Section 212 expenses of the REMIC for the calendar quarter . . . .

  b Your share of section 212 expenses for the calendar quarter. (If you are an individual, this amount must
be included in gross income in addition to the amount shown on line 1b. See instructions for treatment
of this amount as a miscellaneous itemized deduction.) . . . .

For Paperwork Reduction Act Notice, see Form 1066 instructions.   **Schedule Q (Form 1066)** (Rev. 10-92)

Instructions for Residual Interest Holder

(Section references are to the Internal Revenue Code unless otherwise noted.)

Purpose of Form

The real estate mortgage investment conduit (REMIC) uses Schedule Q to notify you of your share of the REMIC's quarterly taxable income (or net loss), the excess inclusion with respect to your interest, and your share of the REMIC's section 212 expenses for the quarter.

Keep your copy of this schedule for your records. Do not file it with your tax return.

General Instructions

Tax treatment of REMIC items.—Although the REMIC is not subject to income tax (except on net income from prohibited transactions, net income from foreclosure property, and contributions made after the startup date), you are liable for tax on your share of the REMIC's taxable income, whether or not distributed, and you must include your share on your tax return. Generally, you must report REMIC items shown on your Schedule Q (and any attached schedules) or similar statement consistent with the way the REMIC treated the items on the return it filed. This rule does not apply if your REMIC falls within the "small REMIC" exception and does not elect to be subject to the consolidated entity-level audit procedures.

If your treatment on your original or amended return is (or may be) inconsistent with the REMIC's treatment, or if the REMIC was required to file but has not filed a return, you must file **Form 8082**, Notice of Inconsistent Treatment or Amended Return (Administrative Adjustment Request (AAR)), with your original or amended return to identify and explain the inconsistency (or to note that a REMIC return has not been filed). See sections 860F(e) and 6222 for the inconsistent treatment rules.

Errors.—If you believe the REMIC has made an error on your Schedule Q, notify the REMIC and ask for a corrected Schedule Q. Do not change any items on your copy. Be sure that the REMIC sends a copy of the corrected Schedule Q to the IRS. If you are unable to reach an agreement with the REMIC about the inconsistency, you must file Form 8082 as explained in the previous paragraph.

Limitation on losses.—Generally, you may not claim your share of the quarterly net loss from a REMIC that is greater than the adjusted basis of your residual interest in the REMIC at the end of the calendar quarter (determined without regard to your share of the net loss of the REMIC for that quarter). Any loss disallowed because it exceeds your adjusted basis is treated as incurred by the REMIC in the following quarter, but only for the purpose of offsetting your share of REMIC taxable income for that quarter.

Items that increase your basis are:

1. Money and your adjusted basis in property contributed to the REMIC.

2. Your share of the REMIC's taxable income.

3. Any income reported under section 860F(b)(1)(C)(ii).

Items that decrease your basis are:

1. Money and the fair market value of property distributed to you.

2. Your share of the REMIC's losses.

3. Any deduction claimed under section 860F(b)(1)(D)(ii).

Passive activity limitations under section 469.—Amounts includible in income (or deductible as a loss) by a residual interest holder are treated as portfolio income (loss). Such income (or loss) is not taken into account in determining the loss from a passive activity under section 469.

Specific Instructions

Item C—REMIC assets.—This information is provided only for the use of a residual interest holder that qualifies as a domestic building and loan association, mutual savings bank, cooperative bank subject to section 593, or real estate investment trust.

Line 1b—Your share of the taxable income (net loss) for the calendar quarter.—

Calendar year taxpayers and fiscal year taxpayers whose tax years end with a calendar quarter: If you are an individual, you must report, as ordinary income or loss, the total of the amounts shown on line 1b of Schedule Q for each quarter included in your tax year, after applying any basis limitations, on Schedule E (Form 1040), Part IV, column (d). If you are not an individual, report the amounts as instructed on your tax return.

Fiscal year taxpayers whose tax years do not end with a calendar quarter: You must figure the amount to report based on your tax year. For each calendar quarter that overlaps the beginning or end of your tax year, divide the amount shown on line 1a by the number of days in that quarter. Multiply the result by your percentage of ownership of all residual interests for each day of your tax year included in that quarter. Total the daily amounts of taxable income (net loss) for the overlapping quarters. Add these amounts to the amounts shown on line 1b for the full quarters included in your tax year. Report the resulting income or loss in the same manner as explained above for calendar year taxpayers.

Line 2c. Excess inclusion for the calendar quarter for your residual interest.—

Calendar year taxpayers and fiscal year taxpayers whose tax years end with a calendar quarter: The total of the amounts shown on line 2c for all quarters included in your tax year is the smallest amount of taxable income you may report for that year. The preceding sentence does not apply to a financial institution to which section 593 applies, except where necessary or appropriate to prevent avoidance of Federal income tax. (Special rules apply to members of affiliated groups filing consolidated returns. See sections 860E(a)(3) and (4).) The line 2c amount is treated as "unrelated business taxable income" if you are an exempt organization subject to the unrelated business tax under section 511. If you are an individual, enter this amount as an item of information on Schedule E (Form 1040), Part IV, column (c). If you must also report this amount as your taxable income, enter the amount shown on line 2c on the taxable income line of your return and write "Sch. Q" on the dotted line to the left of the entry space.

Fiscal year taxpayers whose tax years do not end with a calendar quarter: The same rules explained above for calendar year taxpayers apply, except that you must figure the excess inclusion based on your tax year. For each calendar quarter that overlaps the beginning or end of your tax year, divide the amount shown on line 2a by the number of days in that quarter. Multiply the result by your percentage of ownership of all residual interests for each day of your tax year included in that quarter. Total the daily amounts for the overlapping quarter. Subtract this total from your share of the taxable income for the part of the quarter included in your tax year, as previously figured. Add the resulting amounts for the overlapping quarters to the amounts shown on line 2c for the full quarters included in your tax year and report it in the same manner as explained above for calendar year taxpayers.

Line 3b. Your share of section 212 expenses for the calendar quarter. —

Calendar year taxpayers and fiscal year taxpayers whose tax years end with a calendar quarter: If you are an individual or other pass-through interest holder (as defined in Temporary Regulations section 1.67-3T), you must report as ordinary income the total of the amounts shown on line 3b of Schedule Q for each quarter included in your tax year. This amount must be reported in addition to your share of taxable income (net loss) determined above. If you are an individual, report this total on Schedule E (Form 1040), Part IV, column (e). If you are not an individual, report the amounts as instructed on your tax return.

If you are an individual and itemize your deductions on your return, you may be able to deduct the total as a miscellaneous itemized deduction. It should be included with the other miscellaneous deductions that are subject to the 2% of adjusted gross income limit.

Fiscal year taxpayers whose tax years do not end with a calendar quarter: The same rules explained above for calendar year taxpayers apply, except that you must figure your share of section 212 expenses based on your tax year. For each calendar quarter that overlaps the beginning or end of your tax year, divide the amount shown on line 3a by the number of days in that quarter. Multiply the result by your percentage of ownership of all residual interests for each day of your tax year included in that quarter. Total the daily amounts of section 212 expenses for the overlapping quarters. Add these amounts to the amounts shown on line 3b for the full quarters included in your tax year. Report the resulting amount in the same manner as explained above for calendar year taxpayers.

Instructions for REMIC

(Section references are to the Internal Revenue Code unless otherwise noted.)

Purpose of Form

Schedule Q (Form 1066) shows each residual interest holder's share of the REMIC's quarterly taxable income (net loss), the excess inclusion for the residual interest holder's interest, and the residual interest holder's share of the REMIC's section 212 expenses for the quarter.

Although the REMIC is not subject to income tax (except on net income from prohibited transactions, net income from foreclosure property, and contributions made after the startup day), the residual interest holders are liable for tax on their shares of the REMIC's taxable income, whether or not distributed, and must include their shares on their tax returns.

General Instructions

Complete Schedule Q (Form 1066) for each person who was a residual interest holder at any time during the calendar quarter. File Copy A with Form 1066. Give Copy B to the residual interest holder by the last day of the month following the month in which the calendar quarter ends. Keep Copy C with a copy of Form 1066 as part of the REMIC's records.

Specific Instructions

On each Schedule Q, enter the names, addresses, and identifying numbers of the residual interest holder and REMIC. For each residual interest holder that is an individual, you must enter the residual interest holder's social security number. For all other residual interest holders, you must enter the residual interest holder's employer identification number. However, if a residual interest holder is an individual retirement arrangement (IRA), enter the identifying number of the IRA trust. Do not enter the social security number of the individual for whom the IRA is maintained.

Item A—What type of entity is this residual interest holder?— State on this line whether the residual interest holder is an individual, a corporation, a fiduciary, a partnership, an exempt organization, a nominee (custodian), or another REMIC. If the residual interest holder is a nominee, use the following codes to indicate in parentheses the type of entity the nominee represents.

I – Individual; C – Corporation; F – Fiduciary; P – Partnership; E – Exempt Organization; R – REMIC; or IRA – Individual Retirement Arrangement.

Item B—Residual interest holder's percentage of ownership.— Enter in item B(2) the percentage at the end of the calendar quarter. However, if a residual interest holder's percentage of ownership changed during the quarter, enter in item B(1) the percentage immediately before the change. If there are multiple changes in the percentage of ownership during the quarter, attach a statement giving the date and percentage before each change.

Item C—REMIC assets.—Enter in Item C the percentage of the REMIC's assets during the calendar quarter represented by each of the following three categories of assets:

1. Qualifying real property loans under section 593(d)(1);
2. Real estate assets under section 856(c)(6)(B); and
3. Assets described in section 7701(a)(19)(C) (relating to definition of a domestic building and loan association).

These percentages must be computed using the average adjusted basis of the assets held during the calendar quarter. To do this, the REMIC must make the appropriate computation as of the close of each month, week, or day and then average the monthly, weekly, or daily percentages for the quarter. The monthly, weekly, or daily computation period must be applied uniformly during the calendar quarter to all categories of assets and gross income, and may not be changed in succeeding calendar quarters without IRS consent. If the percentage of the REMIC's assets for any category is at least 95%, the REMIC may show "95 or more" for that category in item C.

Note: *If less than 95% of the assets of the REMIC are real estate assets (as defined in section 856(c)(6)(B)), the REMIC must also report to any real estate investment trust that holds a residual interest the information specified in Regulations section 1.860F-4(e)(1)(ii)(B).*

Item E—Reconciliation of residual interest holder's capital account.— See the instructions for Schedule M of Form 1066.

Line 1a—Taxable income (net loss) of the REMIC for the calendar quarter.—Enter the REMIC's taxable income (net loss) for the calendar quarter. The sum of the totals for the 4 quarters in the calendar year must equal the amount shown on line 15, section I of Form 1066.

Line 1b—Your share of the taxable income (net loss) for the calendar quarter.—Enter the residual interest holder's share of the taxable income (net loss) shown on line 1a (determined by adding the holder's daily portions under section 860C(a)(2) for each day in the quarter the holder held the residual interest). If line 1a is a loss, enter the residual interest holder's full share of the loss, without regard to the adjusted basis of the residual interest holder's interest in the REMIC.

Line 2a—Sum of the daily accruals under section 860E for all residual interests for the calendar quarter.—Enter the product of the sum of the adjusted issue prices of all residual interests at the beginning of the quarter and 120% of the long-term Federal rate (determined on the basis of compounding at the end of each quarter and properly adjusted for the length of such quarter). See section 860E(c) for details.

Line 2b—Sum of the daily accruals under section 860E for your interest.—Enter zero if line 2a is zero. Otherwise, divide the amount shown on line 2a by the number of days in the quarter. Multiply the result by the residual interest holder's percentage of ownership for each day in the quarter that the residual interest holder owned the interest. Total the daily amounts and enter the result.

Line 3—Complete lines 3a and 3b only for residual interest holders who are individuals or other pass-through interest holders (as defined in Temporary Regulations section 1.67-3T).

Line 3a—Section 212 expenses of the REMIC for the calendar quarter.—Enter the REMIC's allocable section 212 expenses for the calendar quarter. The term "allocable section 212 expenses" means the aggregate amount of the expenses paid or accrued in the calendar quarter for which a deduction is allowable under section 212 in determining the taxable income of the REMIC for the calendar quarter.

Section 212 expenses generally include operational expenses such as rent, salaries, legal and accounting fees, the cost of preparing and distributing reports and notices to interest holders, and litigation expenses.

Line 3b—Your share of section 212 expenses for the calendar quarter.—Enter the residual interest holder's share of the amount shown on line 3a.

Form **8811** (Rev. January 1992) Department of the Treasury Internal Revenue Service	**Information Return for Real Estate Mortgage Investment Conduits (REMICs) and Issuers of Collateralized Debt Obligations**	OMB No. 1545-1099 Expires 1-31-95

1 Name of REMIC or issuer of a collateralized debt obligation	**2 Employer identification number**

3 Address (Number, street, and room or suite no., or P.O. box no., city or town, state, and ZIP code)

4 Name and title of the representative to be contacted by the public (see instructions)	5 Telephone number of representative (optional) ( )

6 Address of the representative to be contacted by the public (if different from REMIC's or issuer's)

7 CUSIP number(s) (see instructions)	8 Startup day or issue date
9 Name and title of the representative to be contacted by the IRS (see instructions)	**10** Telephone number of representative ( )

11 Address of the representative to be contacted by the IRS

Under penalties of perjury, I declare that I have examined this return, including accompanying schedules and statements, and to the best of my knowledge and belief, it is true, correct, and complete.

Signature ▶   Title ▶   Date ▶

General Instructions

(Section references are to the Internal Revenue Code.)

Paperwork Reduction Act Notice

We ask for the information on this form to carry out the Internal Revenue laws of the United States. You are required to give us the information. We need it to ensure that you are complying with these laws and to allow us to figure and collect the right amount of tax.

The time needed to complete and file this form will vary depending on individual circumstances. The estimated average time is:

Recordkeeping . . 2 hr., 38 min.

Learning about the law or the form . . . . . . 24 min.

Preparing, copying, assembling, and sending the form to the IRS . . . . . 27 min.

If you have comments concerning the accuracy of these time estimates or suggestions for making this form more simple, we would be happy to hear from you. You can write to both

the **Internal Revenue Service,** Washington, DC 20224, Attention: IRS Reports Clearance Officer, T:FP; and the **Office of Management and Budget,** Paperwork Reduction Project (1545-1099), Washington, DC 20503. **DO NOT** send the tax form to either of these offices. Instead, see **Where To File** below.

Purpose of Form

A REMIC or another issuer of an instrument to which section 1272(a)(6) applies (collateralized debt obligation) uses Form 8811 to provide the information required by Regulations section 1.6049-7(b)(1)(ii). The information in Box 1 and Boxes 3 through 8 will be published in **Pub. 938,** Real Estate Mortgage Investment Conduits (REMICs) Reporting Information. This publication contains a directory of REMICs and issuers of collateralized debt obligations.

Who Must File

Entities that elect to be treated as a REMIC and issuers of a collateralized debt obligation must file Form 8811.

When To File

File Form 8811 no later than 30 days after (a) the startup day of the REMIC or (b) the issue date of the collateralized debt obligation.

The REMIC or issuer of a collateralized debt obligation must file a new Form 8811 within 30 days after the change of any of the information provided on a previously filed Form 8811. If the REMIC or other issuer ceases to have interests outstanding, file Form 8811 with the word "VOID" written across the form. The IRS will delete the information on this REMIC or issuer from Pub. 938.

Where To File

Send Form 8811 to REMIC Publication Project, Internal Revenue Service, 1111 Constitution Avenue, N.W., Room 5607, Washington, DC 20224.

Signatures

REMIC with a startup day after November 9, 1988.—For a REMIC with a startup day after November 9, 1988, Form 8811 must be signed by a person who could sign the return

Cat. No. 10460C   Form **8811** (Rev. 1-92)

of the entity in the absence of the REMIC election. Thus, the return of a REMIC that is a corporation or trust must be signed by a corporate officer or a trustee, respectively. For REMICs that consist of segregated pools of assets, the return must be signed by a person who could sign the return of the entity that owns the assets of the REMIC under applicable state law.

REMIC with a startup day before November 10, 1988.—A REMIC with a startup day before November 10, 1988, may elect to apply the rules applicable to REMICs with a startup day after November 9, 1988. Otherwise, Form 8811 must be signed by a residual interest holder or, as provided in section 6903, by a fiduciary who is acting for the REMIC and who has furnished adequate notice in the manner prescribed in Regulations section 301.6903-1(b). The term "fiduciary"

means a guardian, trustee, executor, administrator, receiver, conservator, or any person acting in any fiduciary capacity for any person.

Issuer of a collateralized debt obligation.—Form 8811 must be signed by a person who could sign the return of the issuer of the collateralized debt obligation.

Specific Instructions

Boxes 4, 5, and 6

Enter the name, title, and either the address or the address and telephone number of the official or representative designated by the REMIC or issuer of the collateralized debt obligation to provide information necessary to calculate the amount of interest and original issue discount (OID) that the holder is required to report on the appropriate tax return.

Box 7

Enter the Committee on Uniform Security Identification Procedure (CUSIP) number assigned to each class of REMIC regular interest or to each collateralized debt obligation.

Box 8

Generally, the "startup day" is the day on which the REMIC issues all of its regular and residual interests. See section 860G(a)(9). For non-REMIC debt obligations, the "issue date" is defined in section 1275(a)(2).

Boxes 9, 10 and 11

Enter the name and title, address and telephone number of the official or representative of the REMIC or issuer of the collateralized debt obligation whom the IRS may contact if questions arise concerning this form. This information will not appear in Pub. 938.

☆U.S. GPO: 1992-312-699/60020

Form **8831**
(March 1993)
Department of the Treasury
Internal Revenue Service

Excise Taxes on Excess Inclusions of REMIC Residual Interests

OMB No. 1545-1379
Expires 3-31-96

Please Type or Print	Name		Identifying number
	Number, street, and room or suite no. (If a P.O. box, see instructions.)		
	City or town, state, and ZIP code		

Part I — Transfers to Disqualified Organizations

Section A—Information on the Transfer

1 Enter the date the residual interest was transferred to a disqualified organization . . . . ▶ ___/___/___

2 Within a reasonable time after discovering this transfer was subject to tax under section 860E(e)(1), were steps taken so that the residual interest you transferred is no longer held by a disqualified organization? . . . . ☐ Yes ☐ No

3 If you answered "Yes" to question 2, enter the date the disqualified organization disposed of the residual interest . . . . ▶ ___/___/___

If you answered "Yes" to question 2, the tax due under section 860E(e)(1) will be waived if you pay the amount due under Regulations section 1.860E-2(a)(7)(ii). Skip Section B and go to Section C to figure the amount due.

If you answered "No" to question 2, use Section B to figure the tax due under section 860E(e)(1). Do not complete Section C.

Section B—Tax Due Under Section 860E(e)(1). Complete this section ONLY if you answered "No" to question 2.

4 Enter the present value of the excess inclusions allocable to the residual interest you transferred that are expected to accrue in each calendar quarter (or part thereof) following the transfer of that interest to the disqualified organization (see instructions) . . . . | 4 |

5 **Tax due.** Multiply line 4 by 34%. . . . . | 5 |

Section C—Amount Due Under Regulations Section 1.860E-2(a)(7)(ii). Complete this section ONLY if you answered "Yes" to question 2.

6 Enter the amount of excess inclusions allocable to the residual interest you transferred that accrued during the period the disqualified organization held that interest . . . . | 6 |

7 **Amount due.** Multiply line 6 by 34% . . . . | 7 |

Part II — Tax on Pass-Through Entities With Interests Held by Disqualified Organizations

8 Enter the ending date of the pass-through entity's tax year for which this return is being filed . . . . ▶ ___/___/___

9 Enter the amount of excess inclusions allocable to interests in the pass-through entity for which the record holder is a disqualified organization . . . . | 9 |

10 **Tax due.** Multiply line 9 by 34%. . . . . | 10 |

Part III — Tax and Payments

11 Enter the amount from line 5, 7, or 10, whichever applies . . . . | 11 |

12 Less: Amount paid with Form 2758 . . . . | 12 |

13 **Amount due.** Enter the excess of line 11 over line 12 . . . . | 13 |

14 **Overpayment.** Enter the excess of line 12 over line 11 . . . . | 14 |

Under penalties of perjury, I declare that I have examined this return, including accompanying schedules and statements, and to the best of my knowledge and belief, it is true, correct, and complete.

▶ _____ ▶ _____ ▶ _____
Signature   Date   Title (if any)

General Instructions

(Section references are to the Internal Revenue Code unless otherwise noted.)

Paperwork Reduction Act Notice

We ask for the information on this form to carry out the Internal Revenue laws of the United States. You are required to give us the information. We need it to ensure that you are complying with these laws and to allow us to figure and collect the right amount of tax.

The time needed to complete and file this form will vary depending on individual circumstances. The estimated average time is:

Recordkeeping . . . . . 4 hr., 32 min.
Learning about the law or the form . . . . . 1 hr., 5 min.
Preparing and sending the form to the IRS . . . 1 hr., 13 min.

If you have comments concerning the accuracy of these time estimates or suggestions for making this form more simple, we would be happy to hear from you. You can write to both the **Internal Revenue Service,** Washington, DC 20224, Attention: IRS Reports Clearance Officer, T:FP; and the **Office of Management and Budget,** Paperwork Reduction Project (1545-1379), Washington, DC 20503. **DO NOT** send this form to either of these offices. Instead, see **Where To File** on page 2.

Purpose of Form

Use Form 8831 to report and pay:

● The excise tax due under section 860E(e)(1) on any transfer of a residual interest in a REMIC to a disqualified organization;

● The amount due under Regulations section 1.860E-2(a)(7)(ii) if the tax under section 860E(e)(1) is to be waived; or

● The excise tax due under section 860E(e)(6) on pass-through entities with interests held by disqualified organizations.

Cat. No. 13377A

Form **8831** (3-93)

Definitions

Disqualified organization.—A "disqualified organization" is:

1. The United States, any state or subdivision thereof, any foreign government, any international organization, or any of their agencies (except for certain taxable instrumentalities described in section 168(h)(2)(D) and the Federal Home Loan Mortgage Corporation);

2. Any tax-exempt organization (other than a farmers' cooperative described in section 521), unless that organization is subject to the unrelated business income tax; and

3. Any cooperative described in section 1381(a)(2)(C).

Pass-through entity.—A "pass-through entity" is a regulated investment company, real estate investment trust, common trust fund, partnership, trust, estate, or a cooperative described in section 1381. A person holding an interest in a pass-through entity as a nominee for another person is also treated as a pass-through entity.

Who Must File

You must file Form 8831 if you are liable for the excise tax due under section 860E(e)(1) (or the amount due under Regulations section 1.860E-2(a)(7)(ii)) because you transferred a residual interest in a REMIC to a disqualified organization after March 31, 1988 (unless the transfer was made under a binding contract in effect on that date).

You will not be treated as having transferred your interest to a disqualified organization if you obtain an affidavit from the transferee signed under penalties of perjury that either furnishes his or her social security number or states that the transferee is not a disqualified organization, provided you do not have actual knowledge at the time of the transfer that the affidavit is false.

A pass-through entity must file Form 8831 if it is liable for the tax due under section 860E(e)(6). The entity may pay this tax if, at any time during the entity's tax year, excess inclusions from a residual interest in a REMIC are allocable to an interest in the entity for which the record holder is a disqualified organization. The tax applies to excess inclusions for periods after March 31, 1988, but only to the extent the inclusions are allocable either to an interest in the pass-through entity acquired after March 31, 1988, OR to a residual interest acquired by the pass-through entity after March 31, 1988. Any interest acquired under a binding contract in effect on March 31, 1988, is treated as acquired before that date. A real estate investment trust, regulated investment company, common trust fund, or publicly traded partnership is subject to the tax due under section 860E(e)(6) ONLY for tax years beginning after 1988.

A pass-through entity is not subject to the excise tax under section 860E(e)(6) if it obtains an affidavit from the record holder signed under penalties of perjury that either furnishes his or her social security number or states that the record holder is not a disqualified organization, provided the pass-through entity does not have actual knowledge at the time of the transfer that the affidavit is false.

A pass-through entity that owes both the excise tax due under section 860E(e)(1) (or

the amount due under Regulations section 1.860E-2(a)(7)(ii)) and the excise tax due under section 860E(e)(6) must file a separate form for each tax.

When To File

For the excise tax due under section 860E(e)(1), file Form 8831 and pay the tax by the later of March 24, 1993, or April 15 of the year following the calendar year in which the residual interest is transferred to a disqualified organization. A pass-through entity must file Form 8831 and pay the tax due under section 860E(e)(6) by the later of March 24, 1993, or the 15th day of the 4th month following the close of its tax year.

If more time is needed, use Form 2758, Application for Extension of Time To File Certain Excise, Income, Information, and Other Returns, to request an extension of time to file Form 8831. However, Form 2758 does not extend the time for payment of tax.

Where To File

File Form 8831 with the Internal Revenue Service Center used for filing your income tax return. If you have no legal residence, principal place of business, or office or agency in the United States, file Form 8831 with the Internal Revenue Service Center, Philadelphia, PA 19255.

Rounding Off to Whole Dollars

Money items may be shown on the return as whole dollars. To do so, drop any amount less than 50 cents and increase any amount from 50 cents through 99 cents to the next higher dollar.

Amended Return

To amend a previously filed Form 8831, file a corrected Form 8831 marked "Amended" at the top of the form.

Signature

See the instructions for the "Signature" section of your Federal income tax return.

Interest and Penalties

Interest.—Interest is charged on taxes not paid by the due date at a rate determined under section 6621.

Late filing of return.—A penalty of 5% a month or part of a month, up to a maximum of 25%, is imposed on the net amount due if the excise tax return is not filed when due.

Late payment of tax.—Generally, the penalty for not paying tax when due is ½ of 1% of the unpaid amount, up to a maximum of 25%, for each month or part of a month the tax remains unpaid. The penalty is imposed on the net amount due.

Specific Instructions

Name and Address

Enter the name shown on your most recently filed Federal income tax return. Include the suite, room, apartment, or other unit number after the street address. If the Post Office does not deliver mail to the street address and you have a P.O. box, show the box number instead of the street address.

Identifying Number

If you are an individual, enter your social security number. Other filers, enter your employer identification number.

Line 4

The excess inclusions expected to accrue must be determined as of the date the residual interest is transferred and must be based on (a) events that have occurred up to the time of the transfer, (b) the prepayment and reinvestment assumptions adopted under section 1272(a)(6) (or that would have been adopted if the REMIC's regular interests had been issued with original issue discount), and (c) any required or permitted clean-up calls, or required qualified liquidation provided under the REMIC's organizational documents.

The present value of the excess inclusions expected to accrue is determined by discounting all remaining excess inclusions expected to accrue on the residual interest from the end of each calendar quarter in which those inclusions are expected to accrue to the date the disqualified organization acquired the residual interest. The discount rate to be used in this computation is the applicable Federal rate under section 1274(d)(1) that would apply to a debt instrument issued on the date the disqualified organization acquired the residual interest and with a term that ends on the last day of the last quarter in which excess inclusions are expected to accrue for the interest.

The REMIC must furnish the information needed to figure the amount on line 4 upon your request. The information must be furnished within 60 days of the request. The REMIC may charge a fee for this information.

Line 6

Enter the amounts reported on Schedule Q (Form 1066), Quarterly Notice to Residual Interest Holder of REMIC Taxable Income or Net Loss Allocation, line 2c, to the disqualified organization for the period it held the residual interest.

Line 9

Enter the amounts reported on Schedule Q (Form 1066), line 2c, for the tax year of the pass-through entity that are allocable to all disqualified organizations that held an interest in the entity.

Line 10

You may deduct the amount on line 10 in figuring the amount of ordinary income of the pass-through entity. For example, the tax is deductible by a real estate investment trust in figuring its real estate investment trust taxable income under section 857(b)(2).

Line 12

If you filed Form 2758, enter the amount paid, if any, when you filed that form.

Line 13

Full payment of the amount due must accompany Form 8831. Make your check or money order payable to the "Internal Revenue Service." Write your name, address, identifying number, and "Form 8831" on the check or money order.

Line 14

The IRS will refund the amount on line 14 if you owe no other taxes.

Appendix E

Model Original Issue Discount and REMIC Legends

Original Issue Discount Legend[1]

The following information is provided solely for purposes of applying the U.S. federal income tax original issue discount ("OID") rules to this Bond.[2] The issue date of this Bond is [CLOSING DATE].[3] The initial per annum rate of interest on this Bond is [INTEREST RATE%].[4] Assuming that principal payments are made on the mortgage collateral underlying the Bonds at [X% of the Standard Prepayment Assumption (as defined in the Indenture)] [[, that interest is earned on temporary investments of payments on the mortgage collateral ("temporary investments") at an annual rate of Y%]] [[[and that interest on the Bonds will be payable in each period in the amount that would be payable under the terms of the Bonds if the value of {LIBOR or other appropriate index} remained constant over the life of the Bonds and equaled its value on the pricing date of the Bonds]]],[5] this Bond has been issued with no more than [$ MAXIMUM TOTAL OID][6] of OID per $1,000 of initial principal amount,

---

1 The original issue discount legending requirement is discussed in Chapter 11, Part A.2. The legend shown should be used for REMIC regular interests and pay-through bonds that have original issue discount, whether or not publicly offered.

2 Throughout the legend, substitute "Certificate" for "Bond," "Pooling and Servicing Agreement" for "Indenture" and "mortgages" for "mortgage collateral," as appropriate.

3 Insert settlement date of the sale of the Bonds to the first purchaser thereof. For discussion of the issue date, see Chapter 6, footnote 27.

4 Insert interest rate for the period that includes the issue date. This information must be supplied for all Bonds, even those that provide for interest to be paid in all periods at the same fixed rate.

5 Insert appropriate prepayment speed where indicated inside the single brackets. If prepayments are based on a constant prepayment rate, the phrase "a constant annual prepayment rate of X%" can be inserted without the need for a definition. "Standard Prepayment Assumption" or another appropriate defined term should be defined in the Indenture.

    Insert double bracketed language only if the rate at which interest is earned on temporary investments will affect the rate at which payments will be made on the Bonds.

    Insert triple bracketed language only if the Bond pays interest based on a variable rate, or based on a weighted average of the rates paid on mortgage collateral that bear interest at a variable rate. Insert "(as defined in the Indenture)" after "LIBOR" or other specified index, if appropriate.

6 Insert maximum amount of original issue discount with which a bond of $1,000 original principal amount is issued. The "no more than" language is designed to permit the issuer, solely for the purpose of the legend, to resolve any uncertainties in applying the definition in favor of increasing the amount of discount without taking a position that the amount shown is necessarily the correct figure.

the yield to maturity is [YIELD TO MATURITY %][7] and the amount of OID attributable to the initial[8] short accrual period is no more than [$ MAXIMUM INITIAL PERIOD OID][9] per $1,000 of initial principal amount, calculated under the [METHOD][10] method. No representation is made as to the rate at which principal payments will be made on the mortgage collateral [[, the rate at which interest (if any) will be earned on temporary investments]] [[[or the value of {LIBOR or other index} over the life of the Bonds]]].[11]

REMIC Legend[12]

Solely for U.S. federal income tax purposes, this Bond[13] is a [regular interest] [residual interest] in a "real estate mortgage investment conduit" ("REMIC") (as those terms are defined in sections 860G and 860D, respectively, of the Internal Revenue Code of 1986).

---

7   Insert yield to maturity, calculated to at least two decimal places.

8   Most Bonds provide for a short *initial* accrual period; substitute "final" for "initial" if appropriate.

9   Insert maximum amount of original issue discount allocable to the short accrual period.

10 Insert method (exact, approximate, or other) of calculating original issue discount for the short accrual period.

11 Insert bracketed language where appropriate. See footnote 5, second and third paragraphs.

12 The REMIC legend is used for REMIC regular and residual interests whether or not, in the case of regular interests, they are issued with original issue discount. The legend is not required by the Code but is often provided for the convenience of holders.
      As discussed in Chapter 4, Part A.3., in order to meet the arrangements test to qualify as a REMIC, an entity must include restrictions in its governing documents prohibiting "disqualified organizations" from holding a residual interest and must notify residual interest holders of the existence of these restrictions. In order to satisfy this notice requirement, as well as to give notice of the restrictions for nontax reasons, a separate legend describing the transfer restrictions is typically placed on the securities evidencing the residual interest.

13 Substitute "Certificate" for "Bond," as appropriate.

Table of Citations

Treasury Regulations

Revenue Rulings

General Counsel's Memoranda

Internal Revenue Service and Treasury Department Administrative Releases

Treasury Department News Releases

Conference Report

Blue Book

Cases

Index

Further references are listed under relevant sections of the Internal Revenue Code and Treasury regulations and other authorities in the Table of Citations. Bold face entries are defined in the Glossary.

REMIC regular interests, 225
stated redemption price at maturity, 229
variable rates, 240-43
  contingent payment debt instruments,
    241-42
  varariable rate debt instruments,
    241-42, 241 n.48
  yield to maturity, 235
Outside reserve funds, 79, 163
Ownership interest, 63-65
Owner trustee, 14
Owner trusts, 4, 14
  banks as equity owners, and gain on sale,
    277
  basis in assets, 277
  grantor trust, effect of being classified
    as a, 275
  information reporting, 358
  section 754 election, 277
  tax-exempt investors, 277-78
  termination of partnership, 277
  that are not TMPs, 76-77
  thrift institutions as equity investors, 277
  TMP as example of, 4

P

PAC **class** of bonds, 15
PAC **method**, 232-40
  see also Original issue discount
  VRDI rules and, 242-43
Partnership item, 175
Partnerships
  defined, 31 n.2
  foreign investors and, 27-28
  investment trusts electing out of, 75
  owner trusts classified as, 4
  publicly traded, 29 n.79, 31 n.1
  issuers of pass-through debt certificates
    classified as, 27-29
  tax-exempt investors owning interests in,
    28-29, 277-78
  transfers to, 372
Passive losses, REMIC residual interests,
  279 n.21
Pass-through certificates, 5-13, 221,
  243-52
  and CMOs compared, 15-16
  considered qualifying thrift and REIT
    assets, 321
  deductibility of expenses, 7
  foreign investors, 332-34, 340-41

information reporting, 357-58
market discount, 255
original issue discount. *See* Original issue
  discount
pass-through rate of interest, 6
residential mortgages and, 8-9
senior/subordinated, 11-13
single class issuance, 6
stripped bonds, 244-48
  defined, 244-46
  treatment of, 246-48
stripped pass-through certificates, 10-11
taxable as debt. *See* Pass-through debt
  certificates
tax rules applied to, 221-22
timing of income, cash and accrual
  method taxpayers, 7
trusts issuing taxed under grantor trust
  rules, 6
Pass-through debt certificates, 5, 24-30
  application to mortgages, 29-30
  classification of issuer, 77-79
Pass-through entities, 297-98
Pass-through interest holder (allocation
  of REMIC investment expenses), 283
Pay-through bonds, 3, 13-16, 57 n.80
  see also CMOs, Owner trusts; REMICs
  CMOs, 14-16
  equity interests in issuers of, 16-21
    economic features, 17-19
    GAAP treatment, 17, 20-22
    tax features, 19-20
  not qualified as real property loans, 321
Phantom income, 20, 23, 57 n, 80,
  287-309, Appendix A
  sales of equity interests, effect of, 293
  technical description, 291-92
  TMP rules and, 94
P.L.R. (IRS private letter ruling). *See*
  Table of Citations
Planned amortization class. *See* PAC bonds
Pledged account mortgage, 8 n.12
PO strips, 11
Points, 249
Portfolio interest exemption, 27, 336,
  340-44
Portion rule, 89-91
Power-to-vary test, for investment trusts,
  38-51
  assets acquired after formation, 40-41
  certificateholder approval, 48-49
  existence of a "power", 39-40